汽车材料的热机械性能 （下）

Automotive Engineering Materials–Thermomechanical Properties

江永瑞　著

重庆大学出版社

图书在版编目(CIP)数据

汽车材料的热机械性能 = Automotive Engineering
Materials-Thermomechanical Properties：上中下：
英文／江永瑞著. -- 重庆：重庆大学出版社，2022.4
（自主品牌汽车实践创新丛书）
ISBN 978-7-5689-3293-6

Ⅰ.①汽… Ⅱ.①江… Ⅲ.①汽车—工程材料—热机
械效应—性能—英文 Ⅳ.①U465

中国版本图书馆 CIP 数据核字(2022)第 080037 号

汽车材料的热机械性能
QICHE CAILIAO DE REJIXIE XINGNENG
（下）
江永瑞 著
策划编辑:杨粮菊 孙英姿 鲁黎
责任编辑:陈 力 苟荟羽 版式设计:杨粮菊
责任校对:姜 凤 责任印制:张 策
＊
重庆大学出版社出版发行
出版人:饶帮华
社址:重庆市沙坪坝区大学城西路 21 号
邮编:401331
电话:(023)88617190 88617185(中小学)
传真:(023)88617186 88617166
网址:http://www.cqup.com.cn
邮箱:fxk@ cqup.com.cn（营销中心）
全国新华书店经销
重庆升光电力印务有限公司印刷
＊
开本:889mm×1194mm 1/16 印张:23.75 字数:774 千
2022 年 4 月第 1 版 2022 年 4 月第 1 次印刷
ISBN 978-7-5689-3293-6 总定价:498.00 元

Ceramics

Carbon

Chapter 121　Diamond

Chapter 122　Graphite and Graphene

Chapter 123　Carbon Fullerenes and Reinforcements

Electromagnetic Materials

Natural Materials

Chapter 133　Cellulosics

Chapter 134　Wood and Bamboo

Chapter 135　Roads

Chapter 136　Human Beings

Automobile Fluids

Chapter 137　Powertrain Lubricants

Chapter 138　Hydraulic Fluids

Chapter 139　Coolants

Chapter 140　Fuels

Chapter 141　*IMDS（International Material Data System）*

Ceramics

Chapter 102

AlN (Aluminum Nitride)

102.1   Introduction

AlN (Aluminum Nitride) is a nitride of aluminum, with a hexagonal crystal structure as a covalently bonded material. Aluminum nitride has good dielectric properties, high thermal conductivity, low thermal expansion, and it is non-reactive with normal semiconductor process chemicals and gases. Mechanical properties of AlN are given in Table 102.1.

102.2   Applications

AlN (Aluminum Nitride) is used in electronic applications similar to those of Al_2O_3 (alumina) and BeO (beryllia; beryllium oxide), such as electronic substrates and chip carriers where high thermal conductivity is critical. AlN is a non-toxic alternative to beryllia.

References

DORNEICH A D, et al, 1998. Quantitative Analysis of Valence Electron Energy-Loss Spectra of Aluminum Nitride[J]. Journal of Microscience, 191(3): 286-296.

SPRIGGS R M, et al, 2006. Mechanical Properties of Pre, Dense Aluminum Oxide as a Function of Temperature and Grain Size[J]. Journal of the American Ceramic Society, 47(7): 323-327.

TANIYASU Y, et al, 2006. An Aluminum Nitride Light-emitting Diode with a Wavelength of 210 Nanometers [J]. Nature, 441(7091): 325-328.

WATARI K, et al, 1996. Densification and Thermal Conductivity of AlN Doped with Y_2O_3, CaO, and Li_2O [J]. Journal of the American Ceramic Society, 79(12): 3103-3108.

YOSHIMURA H N, et al, 2007. Porosity Dependence of Elastic Constants in Aluminum Nitride Ceramics[J]. Materials Research, 10(2): 127-133.

Table 102.1   Mechanical Properties of AlN (Aluminum Nitride)

Material	$T/℃$	E_T	ρ	ν	(σ, ε)	α	k	γ	$\tan\delta$	K_{IC}
AlN (Bulk)	23	330	3.26	0.25	$\sigma_{ucs}=-2068$; $\sigma_R=428$	4.5	30.1	730	—	3
	400	—	—	—	—	—	22.2	950	—	—
	600	—	—	—	—	—	20.1	1003	—	—
	1000	317	—	—	—	—	—	—	—	—
	1400	276	—	—	—	—	—	—	—	—
	1600 (High service temperature)									
	2200 (T_m)	—	—	—	—	—	—	—	—	—
	2500 (Dissociated between Al and N)									
AlN (Crystal)	23	—	—	—	—	—	285	—	—	—

Chapter 103

Al_2O_3 (Aluminum Oxide; Alumina)

103.1　Introduction

Al_2O_3 (Aluminum Oxide), also called alumina, is the most useful ceramic material due to its robust strength properties and flexibility in fabrication-having great sizing and shaping capability. There are several polymorphs including stable α-phase (trigonal) and metastable γ-phase (cubic). Its modulus of elasticity and thermal conductivity increases with its purity, as shown in Table 103.1.

Al_2O_3 (Alumina) is hard and wear-resistant. The disadvantage of alumina ceramic limiting its use in tribological applications is insufficient fracture toughness, which results in increased wear by micro-fracture mechanism. The tetragonal phase can martensitically transform concurrently with crack propagation in the Al_2O_3 (Alumina) if it is stressed enough to fracture. It can be toughened by the incorporation of tetragonal ZrO_2 into it.

Al_2O_3 has excellent dielectric properties for electronic applications ranging from direct current to alternating current with gega-Hz frequencies.

103.2　Applications

Typical automotive uses of Al_2O_3 (Alumina) are high temperature electric insulators, electronic substrates, and ballistic armor. Nanoscale alumina composites reinforced with carbon nanotubes (CNT) combine good fracture toughness and low coefficient of friction due to the lubricating effect of CNT. Such materials present a great potential for tribological applications such as ceramic liners of combustion chambers, pistons, piston rings, cylinder heads, valves and valve guides, rotors, vanes, shrouds, and exhaust components.

References

AGARWAL A, et al, 2003. Net Shape Nanostructured Aluminum Oxide Structures Fabricated by Plasma Spray Forming[J]. Journal of Thermal Spray Technology, 12(3): 350-359.

CANNON R M, et al, 1980. Plastic Deformation of Fine-grained Alumina: 1. Interface Controlled Diffusion Creep[J]. Journal of American Ceramic Society, 63(1-2): 48-53.

FRENCH R, et al, 1998. Optical Properties of Aluminum Oxide: Determined from Vacuum Ultraviolet and Electron Energy-loss Spectroscopies[J]. Journal of American Society of Ceramics, 81(10): 2549-2557.

LEVIN L A, et al, 1997. Cubic to Monoclinic Phase Transformations in Alumina[J]. Acta Materialia, 45(9): 3659-3669.

LI G, JIANG A, ZHANG L, 1996. Mechanical and Fracture Properties of Nano Al$_2$O$_3$[J]. Journal of Material Science Letters, 15(19): 1713-1715.

WOLFENDEN A, 1991. Measurement and Analysis of Elastic and Anelastic Properties of Alumina and Silicon Carbide[J]. Journal of Materials Science, 32(9): 2275-2282.

XIONG Z, et al, 2007. Cyclic Fatigue of Alumina Ceramics as Evaluated by Modified Small Punch Tests[J]. Key Engineering Materials, 336/338: 2426-2428.

ZOK F, LEVI C, 2001. Mechanical Properties of Porous-Matrix Ceramic Composites[J]. Advanced Engineering Materials, 3(1-2): 15-23.

Table 103.1   Mechanical Properties of Al$_2$O$_3$ (Aluminum Oxide; Alumina)

Material	T/°C	E_T	ρ	ν	(σ, ε)	α	k	γ	$\tan \delta$	K_{IC}
Al$_2$O$_3$(94% Purity)	23	300	3.69	0.26	$\sigma_{ucs}=-2000$	7.3	18	775	—	3.5
	2054 (T_m)	—	—	—	—	—	—	—	—	—
Al$_2$O$_3$(96% Purity)	23	315	3.72	0.26	—	7.5	25	800	—	4
	2054 (T_m)	—	—	—	—	—	—	—	—	—
Al$_2$O$_3$(97.5% Purity)	23	330	3.85	0.26	$\sigma_{ucs}=-2070$	7.7	31	860	—	4
	2054 (T_m)	—	—	—	—	—	—	—	—	—
Al$_2$O$_3$(98.4% Purity)	23	360	3.89	0.26	$\sigma_{ucs}=-2340$; $\sigma_{uts}=255$	8.3	34	880	—	4
	2054 (T_m)	—	—	—	—	—	—	—	—	—
Al$_2$O$_3$(99.5% Purity)	23	375	3.9	0.27	$\sigma_{ucs}=-2450$; $\sigma_{uts}=345$	8.4	36	880	—	5
	400	—	—	—	—	—	14	—	—	—
	1000	—	—	—	—	—	7	—	—	—
	1750 (High service temperature)									
	2054 (T_m)	—	—	—	—	—	—	—	—	—
Al$_2$O$_3$-α (Crystal; Sapphire)	23	430	3.98	0.29	$\sigma_{ucs}=-2400$; $\sigma_{uts}=400$	5/6.7*	40	800	—	1.9
Al$_2$O$_3$(Oxide or as Coating)	23	—	—	—	—	—	—	—	—	—
	1000	85	—	—	—	6.8	—	—	—	—
Al$_2$O$_3$/40TiO$_2$ (Coating)	23	—	—	—	—	—	—	—	—	—
	700	77	—	—	—	—	—	—	—	—

continued

Material	$T/^{\circ}C$	E_T	ρ	ν	(σ, ε)	α	k	γ	$\tan \delta$	K_{IC}
$Al_2O_3/10ZrO_2$ (Unstabilized)	23	—	—	—	—	—	—	—	—	5
$Al_2O_3/10ZrO_2$ (Yttria stabilized)	23	—	—	—	—	—	—	—	—	4

Notes: $*\alpha$: 5/6.7 means that 5 $\perp$ c-axis and 6.7 // c-axis, respectively.

Chapter 104

B_4C *(Boron Carbide)*

104.1　Introduction

The hardness of B_4C (Boron Carbide) is just next to diamond (C) and cubic boron nitride (cBN). Another special material property is the high cross-section for absorption of neutrons, i.e. good shielding properties against neutrons. Because of the robust bond of the B_{12} icosahedra in the neighboring layer as a B_{12} structural unit, the chemical formula of "ideal" boron carbide is often written as $B_{12}C_3$ instead of B_4C. Mechanical properties B_4C (Boron Carbide) are listed in Table 104.1.

104.2　Applications

Its high hardness and light weight make it one of the best bullet-proof vests and tank armors.

Reference

KITAMURA J, et al, 2003. Structure and Mechanical Properties of Boron Nitride Coatings Formed by Electromagnetically Accelerated Plasma Spraying[J]. Diamond and Related Materials, 12 (10-11): 1891-1896.

Table 104.1　Mechanical Properties B_4C (Boron Carbide)

Material	$T/℃$	E_T	ρ	ν	(σ, ε)	α	k	γ	$\tan \delta$	K_{IC}
B_4C (Hot pressed; Porosity<5%)	23	445	2.51	0.2	$\sigma_{ucs}=-2900$; $\sigma_{uts}=155$; $\sigma_R=330$	5.5	28	950	—	3.3
	2450 (T_m)	—	—	—	—	—	—	—	—	—

Chapter 105

BN (Boron Nitride)

105.1　Introduction

BN (Boron Nitride) is divided into four groups-aBN, cBN, hBN, and wBN. Their Mechanical properties are listed in Table 105.1.

105.2　aBN (Amorphous Boron Nitride)

aBN (amorphous boron nitride) has some singular properties, such as high optical transmission in the visible and near-UV range, low electrical conductivity, extreme hardness of the cubic phase, corrosion resistance, chemical inertness, high melting point and high thermal conductivity, which are interesting for many optical, electronic, mechanical and tribological applications. A limitation of aBN is its low strength at high temperatures.

aBN (amorphous boron nitride) has been conventionally used as a membrane material in the fabrication of X-ray masks, because of its desirably low linear absorption coefficient at short wavelengths. One interesting application is its ability to absorb neutrons without forming long-lived radio nuclides. Boron nitride is made in the form of shielding, control rods, and shutdown pellets for applications in nuclear power plants.

105.3　hBN (Hexagonal Boron Nitride)

hBN (hexagonal boron nitride) is a good lubricant at both low and high temperatures even in an oxidizing atmosphere, up to 900 ℃. hBN lubricant is particularly useful while the electrical conductivity or chemical reactivity of graphite (alternative lubricant) would be problematic.

hBN mixed with a binder (boron oxide) is used, in the automotive industry, for sealing oxygen sensors, which provide feedback for adjusting fuel flow.

105.4　cBN (Cubic Boron Nitride)

cBN (cubic boron nitride) is made by annealing hBN powder at higher temperatures, under pressures above 5 GPa. cBN (cubic Boron Nitride) has hardness just next to diamond. It is an important material for machine tools-arising from its insolubility in iron, nickel, and related alloys at high temperatures, whereas diamond is soluble in these metals to give carbides.

A combination of high toughness and heat resistance enables high speeds of grinding using cBN tools. The flank wear in tools, initially occurs due to abrasion and as the wear progresses, the temperature increases causing diffusion. Diffusion processes between the chip and the top rake face of the cutting edge result in crater wear, and oxidation reactions with the environment induce scaling of the cutting edge. It is a transfer of chemical elements between the tool and chip.

105.5   wBN (Wurtsite Boron Nitride)

wBN (Wurtsite boron nitride), similar to cBN, is formed by compressing hBN, but the formation of wBN occurs at a lower temperature close to 1700 ℃.

105.6   BN Coatings on Bearing Steels

BN coatings on steels have a two-phase structure, with the presence of soft hBN and hard wBN (or wBN + cBN) phases, which may be advantageous in tribological applications of these coatings.

References

BAI X, WANG E, YU J, et al, 2000. Blue-Violet Photoluminescence from Large-Scale Highly Aligned Boron Carbonitride Nanofibers[J]. Applied Physics Letters, 77(1): 67-69.

BLASE X, RUBIO A, LOUIE S, et al, 1994. Stability and Band Gap Constancy of Boron Nitride Nanotubes [J]. Europhysics Letters, 28(5): 335-340.

BOTANI C, et al, 2002. Structural and Elastic Properties of Cubic Boron Nitride Films[J]. Surface and Coatings Technology, 151/152: 151-154.

DOU Q, MA H, 2008. The Electric Properties and the Current-Controlled Differential Negative Resistance of cBN Crystal[J]. Science in China Series E: Technological Sciences, 51(12): 2305-2310.

FIELD J E, FREEMAN C J, 1981. Strength and Fracture Properties of Diamond[J]. Philosophical Magazine, A, 43(3): 595-618.

GOCMAN K, et al, 2011. Structural and Mechanical Properties of Boron Nitride Thin Films Deposited on Steel Substrates by Pulsed Deposition[J]. Journal of KONES Powertrain and Transport, 18(1): 150-156.

GOLBERG D, et al, 2007. Direct Force Measurements and Kinking under Elastic Deformation of Individual Multiwalled Boron Nitride Nanotubes[J]. Nano Letters, 7(7): 2146-2151.

GOLBERG D, BANDO Y, KURASHIMA K, et al, 2001. Synthesis and Characterization of Ropes Made of BN Multiwalled Nanotubes[J]. Scripta Materialia, 44(8-9): 1561-1565.

HANSEN J O, COPPERTHWAITE R G, DERRY T E, et al, 1989. A Tensiometric Study of Diamond (111) and (110) Faces[J]. Journal of Colloid and Interface Science, 130(2): 347-358.

HUANG Y, et al, 2007. CBN Tool Wear in Hard Turning: a Survey on Research Progress[J]. International Journal of Advanced Manufacturing Technology, 35(5-6): 443-453.

IAKOUBOVSKII K, ADRIAENSSENS G J. 2002. Optical Characterization of Natural Argyle Diamonds[J]. Diamond and Related Materials, 11(1): 125-131.

JIANG X, et al, 2003. Hardness and Young's Modulus of High-Quality Cubic Boron Nitride Films Grown by Chemical Vapor Deposition[J]. Journal of Applied Physics, 93(3): 1515-1519.

LAN J H, et al, 2009. Thermal Transport in Hexagonal Boron Nitride Nanoribbons[J]. Physical Review, B, 79 (11): 115401.

LEE Y C, et al, 2007. Mechanical Properties and Energy Absorption of Ceramic Particulate and Resin-Impregnation[J]. Materials Science Forum, 31: 52-56.

LIU K, 2003. CBN Tool Wear in Ductile Cutting of Tungsten Carbide[J]. Wear, 255(7-12): 1344-1351.

KIM P, SHI L, MAJUMDAR A, et al, 2001. Thermal Transport Measurements of Individual Multiwalled Nanotubes[J]. Physical Review Letters, 87(21): 215502.

PAN Z, SUN H, ZHANG Y, et al, 2009. Harder than Diamond: Superior Indentation Strength of Wurtzite BN and Lonsdaleite[J]. Physical Review Letters, 102(5): 055503.

PASCUAL E, et al, 1996. Spectroscopic Ellipsometric Study of Boron Nitride Thin Films[J]. Diamond and Related Materials, 5(3-5): 539-543.

SHEN Z Q, et al, 2005. Boron Nitride Nanotubes Filled with Zirconium Oxide Nanorods[J]. Journal of Materials Research, 17(11): 2761-2764.

SOMA T, et al, 1974. Characterization of Wurtzite Type Boron Nitride Synthesized by Shock Compression[J]. Materials Research Bulletin, 9 (6): 755.

SURYAVANSHI A, et al, 2004. Elastic Modulus and Resonance Behavior of Boron Nitride Nanotubes[J]. Applied Physics Letters, 84(14): 2527-2529.

TIAN Y, et al, 2013. Ultrahard Nanotwinned Cubic Boron Nitride[J]. Nature, 493 (7432): 385-388.

XIAO Y, et al, 2004. Specific Heat and Quantized Thermal Conductance of Single-Walled Boron Nitride Nanotubes[J]. Physics Review, B, 69(20): 1324-1332.

YU J, AHN J, YOON S, 2000. Semiconducting Boron Carbonitride Nanostructures: Nanotubes and Nanofibers

［J］. Applied Physics Letters, 77(13): 1949-1951.

ZEDLITZ R. 1996. Properties of Amorphous Boron Nitride Thin Films［J］. Journal of Non-Crystalline Solids, 198/200: 403-306.

ZHI C, et al, 2007. Boron Nitride Nanotubes: Nanoparticles Functionalization and Junction Fabrication［J］. Journal of Nanoscience and Nanotechnology, 7(2): 530-534.

Table 105.1   Mechanical Properties of BN (Boron Nitride)

Material	$T/℃$	E_T	ρ	ν	(σ, ε)	α	k	γ	$\tan \delta$	K_{IC}
aBN	23	675	2.28	0.05	$\sigma_R=58$	1.5	20	950	—	3
(Amorphous)	2973 (T_m)	—	—	—	—	—	—	—	—	—
cBN	23	706	3.45	0.16	—	1.2	740	670	—	—
(Cubic)	2973 (T_m)	—	—	—	—	—	—	—	—	—
hBN (Boric oxide binder; Porosity=2.8%)	23	47/74	1.9	—	$\sigma_{ucs}=-143$ (//); $\sigma_{ucs}=-186$ ($\perp$)	3/12	30/33	1610	—	—
	2500 (T_m)	—	—	—	—	—	—	—	—	—
hBN (Calcium borate binder; Porosity=15%)	23	34/75	1.9	—	$\sigma_{ucs}=-30$ (//); $\sigma_{ucs}=-45$ ($\perp$)	3/0.9	27/31	1470	—	—
	2500 (T_m)	—	—	—	—	—	—	—	—	—
hBN (XP grade; Porosity=14%)	23	14	1.9	—	$\sigma_{ucs}=-18$ (//); $\sigma_{ucs}=-23.4$ ($\perp$)	0.6/-0.6	11/21	1460	—	—
wBN (Bulk)	23	400	3.49	—	—	2.7	—	—	—	—
wBN (Coating phase on 52100 bearing steel)	23	92	—	—	—	—	—	—	—	—
hBN (Coating phase on 52100 bearing steel)	23	65	—	—	—	—	—	—	—	—

Notes: // = parallel to pressing direction;
　　　 $\perp$ = perpendicular to pressing direction.

Chapter 106

BaTiO$_3$ (Barium Titanate)

106.1   Introduction

$BaTiO_3$ (Barium Titanate) is the first commercial piezoelectric ceramics, discovered in early 1940s. It has a cubic perovskite structure and a high Curie point (1200 ℃). It is mechanically and chemically stable, and also amenable for different compositional changes-useful for tailoring electric properties for various applications. There are five different kinds of polymorphs:

(a) Hexagonal (Temperature > 1460 ℃);
(b) Cubic (1460 ℃ > Temperature > 130 ℃);
(c) Tetrahedral (130 ℃ > Temperature > 0 ℃);
(d) Rhombohedral (0 ℃ > Temperature > −90 ℃);
(e) Orthorhombic (−90 ℃ > Temperature).

$BaTiO_3$ (Barium Titanate) is a ferroelectric ceramic material, with a photorefractive effect and piezoelectric properties. Mechanical properties of $BaTiO_3$ (Barium Titanate) are given in Table 106.1.

106.2   Applications

Barium Titanate ($BaTiO_3$) is a dielectric ceramic that can be polarized and used as capacitors. It is currently the most widely used dielectric material in ceramic capacitors.

References

ARLT G, et al, 1985. Dielectric Properties of Fined-grained Barium Titanate Ceramics[J]. Journal of Applied Physics, 58(4): 1619-1625.

BALARAMAN D, et al, 2004. $BaTiO_3$ Films by Low-temperature Hydrothermal Techniques for Next generation Packaging Applications[J]. Journal of Electroceramics, 13: 95-100.

BERLINCOURT D A, JAFFE H, 1958. Elastic and Piezoelectric Coefficient of Single-Crystal Barium Titanate [J]. Physics Review, 111(1): 143-148.

BLAMEY J M, PARRY T V, 1993. Strength and Toughness of Barium Titanate Ceramics [J]. Journal of Material Science, 28(18): 4988-4993.

CHAISAN W, et al, 2007. Changes in Ferroelectric Properties of Barium Titanate Ceramic with Compressive Stress[J]. Physica Scripta, 2007: T129.

CHANDRADASS J, BAE D, 2009. Influence of Barium Titanate Nanopowder on the Thermo-Mechanical, Damping and Vibration Characteristics of Epoxy Laminates [J]. Journal of Reinforced Plastics and Composites, 28(10): 1235-1243.

CHENG B L, et al, 1996. Mechanical Loss and Young's Modulus Associated with Phase Transition in Barium Titanate Based Ceramics[J]. Journal of Material Science, 31(18): 4951-4955.

DENT A C, et al, 2007. Effective Elastic Properties for Unpoled Barium Titanate[J]. Journal of the European Ceramic Society, 27: 3739-3743.

DUFFY W, 1995. Anelastic Behavior of Barium-Titanate-Based Ceramic Materials [J]. Metallurgical & Materials Transactions A, 26(7): 1735-1739.

FELTEN F, et al, 2004. Modeling and measurement of Surface Displacements in Bulk Material in Piezoresponse Force Microscopy[J]. Journal of Applied Physics, 96(1): 563-568.

GRETHER M F, et al, 1980. The Mechanical Stability of Barium Titanate (Ceramic) Implants in Vitro[J]. Biomaterials Medical Devices and Artificial Organs, 8(3): 265-272.

HE Y, 2004. Heat Capacity, Thermal Conductivity, and Thermal Expansion of Barium Titanate-Based Ceramics [J]. Thermochimica Acta, 419(1-2): 135-141.

HUYBRECHTS K, et al, 1995. Review the Positive Temperature Coefficient of Resistivity in Barium Titanate [J]. Journal of Materials Science, 30: 2463-2474.

IZUHARA T, et al, 2003. Single-crystal Barium Titanate Thin Film by Ion Slicing [J]. Applied Physics Letters, 82(4): 616-618.

LEE J H, et al, 2000. Characteristics of BaTiO₃ Powders Synthesized by Hydrothermal Process[J]. Journal of Material Science, 35(17): 4271-4274.

LEE B W, AUH K H, 2001. Effect of Internal Stress on the Dielectric Properties of Barium Titanate Ceramics [J]. Journal of Ceramic Processing Research, 2(3): 134-138.

MCNEAL M P, JANG S, NEWNHAM R E, 1998. The Effect of Particle Size on the Microwave Properties of Barium Titanate[J]. Journal of Applied Physics, 83(6): 3288.

MOON, et al, 2009. Nanostructural and Physical Features of BatiO₃ Ceramics Prepared by Two-step Sintering [J]. Journal of the Ceramic Society of Japan, 117(1366): 729-731.

PANTENY S, BROWN C, STEVENS R, 2006. Characteristics of Barium Titanate-silver Composites Part Ⅱ: Electric Properties[J]. Journal of Materials Science, 41(12): 3845-3851.

PARK J B, et al, 1977. Mechanical Property Changes of Barium Titanate (Ceramic) after in-Vivo and in-Vitro Aging[J]. Artificial Cells, Blood Substitutes and Biotechnology, 5(3): 267-276.

SHIEH J, et al, 2009. Hysteretic Behaviors of Barium Titanate Single Crystals Based on the Operation of

Multiple 90° Switching Systems[J]. Material Science and Engineering B, 161: 50-54.

SHUT V N, GARVRILOV A V, 2007. Temperature Stresses in Barium Titanate-Based Semiconductor Ceramics [J]. Journal of Engineering Physics & Thermophysics, 81(3): 627-632.

SUBBARAO E C, et al, 1957. Domain Effects in Polycrystalline Barium Titanate[J]. Journal of Applied Physics, 28: 1194-1200.

STRUKOV B, et al, 2003. Specific Heat and Heat Conductivity of $BaTiO_3$ Polycrystalline Films in the Thickness Range 20-1100 nm[J]. Journal of Physics, 15(25): 4331-4340.

WANG X H, et al, 2006. Two-step Sintering of Ceramics with Constant Grain-size, II: $BaTiO_3$ and Ni-Cu-Zn Ferrite[J]. Journal of American Ceramic Society, 89(2): 438-443.

WU L, et al, 2009. Dielectric Properties of Barium Titanate Ceramics with Different Materials Powder Sizes[J]. Ceramic International, 35(3): 957-960.

YOON S, LEE B, 2002. $BaTiO_3$ Properties and Powder Characteristics for Ceramic Capacitors[J]. Journal of Ceramic Processing Research, 3(2): 41.

ZGONIK M, et al, 1994. Dielectric, Elastic, Piezoelectric, and Elasto-optic Tensors of $BaTiO_3$ Crystals[J]. Physics Reviews B, 50(9): 5941-5948.

ZHONG W, et al, 1994. Size Effect on the Dielectric Properties of $BaTiO_3$[J]. Ferroelectrics, 160(1): 55-59.

Table 106.1　Mechanical Properties of $BaTiO_3$

Material	$T/℃$	E_T	ρ	ν	(σ, ε)	α	k	γ	$\tan\delta$	K_{IC}
	23	67	6	0.34	$\sigma_R = 67$	6	3	406	—	1.36
$BaTiO_3$	122 (T_c)	—	—	—	—	11	—	—	—	—
	1625 (T_m)	—	—	—	—	—	—	—	—	—

Chapter 107

BeO (Beryllium Oxide; Beryllia)

107.1 Introduction

BeO (Beryllium Oxide or Beryllia) is an electrical insulator, with a thermal conductivity higher than any other non-metal except diamond. Its thermal conductivity exceeds some metals'. It is piezoelectric and pyroelectric. BeO (Beryllia) is also a promising optimal ceramic, which transmits light in a wide spectrum, ranging from VUV (0.12 μm) to IR (9 μm). Mechanical properties of BeO are given in Table 107.1.

107.2 Applications

For the past few decades, BeO (Beryllia) has been the main substrate material used for RF resistors and terminations for high-power semiconductor devices.

BeO (Beryllia) is also used in rocket engines.

References

GORBUNAVA M A, et al, 2007. Electronic and Magnetic Properties of Beryllium Oxide with 3D Impurities from First-Principles Calculations[J]. Physica B: Condensed Matter, 400(1-2): 47-52.

IVANOVSKII A L, et al, 2009. Electronic Structure and Properties of Beryllium Oxide [J]. Inorganic Materials, 45(3): 223-234.

Table 107.1 Mechanical Properties of BeO (Beryllium Oxide; Beryllia)

Material	$T/℃$	E_T	ρ	ν	(σ, ε)	α	k	γ	$\tan \delta$	K_{IC}
BeO (Sintered; Porosity = 3.5%)	23	311	3.01	0.34	$\sigma_{uts} = 111;$ $\sigma_R = 210$	6	330	2841	—	—
	200	294	—	0.34	—	6.9	155	—	—	—
	600	286	—	0.34	—	10.6	46	—	—	—
	1000	214	—	0.35	—	10.9	19	—	—	—
	1200	124	—	0.35	—	10.9	15	—	—	—
	2507 (T_m)	—	—	—	—	—	—	—	—	—

Chapter 108

MgO (Magnesia) and MgAl$_2$O$_4$ (Magnesium Aluminum Oxide)

108.1   Introduction

MgO (Magnesia) and $MgAl_2O_4$ (Magnesium Aluminum Oxide) are two commonly used Mg-based ceramics. Their mechanical properties are given in Table 108.1.

108.2   MgO (Magnesia)

MgO (Magnesia) is a natural mineral of magnesium oxide, formed by an ionic bond between one magnesium atom and one oxygen atom. By far, the largest consumer of magnesia worldwide is the refractory industry.

MgO (Magnesia) has been used as an insulator for industrial electric cables. Magnesia-spinel composite ceramics are candidate materials for supporting solid oxide fuel cells. MgO is one of the raw materials for making Portland cement in dry process plants.

108.3 $MgAl_2O_4$ (Spinel; Magnesium Aluminum Oxide)

$MgAl_2O_4$ (Spinel) is a mineral crystallizing in the isometric system, usually as octahedrons. A normal spinel structure is usually cubic close-packed oxide with one octahedral and two tetrahedral sites per oxide. $MgAl_2O_4$ (Spinel) has been a treasured gem.

References

ATKINSON A, BASTID P, LIU Q, 2007. Mechanical Properties of Magnesia-Spinel Composites[J]. Journal of the American Ceramic Society, 90(8): 2489-2496.

HALL D, STEVENS I, EL-JAZAIRI B, 2010. The Effect of Retarders on the Microstructure and Mechanical Properties of Magnesia-Phosphate Cement Mortar[J]. Cement and Concrete Research, 31(2): 455-465.

HULSE C O, PASK J A, 1960. Mechanical Properties of Magnesia Single Crystal Compression[J]. Journal of the American Ceramics Society, 43(7): 373-378.

KOKSAL K S, et al, 2004. Mechanical Properties of Magnesia and Magnesia-Chromite Refractory Materials[J]. Key Engineering Materials, 264/268: 1779-1782.

PLEKHANOVA T A, KERIENE J, GAILIUS A, et al, 2007. Structural, Physical and Mechanical Properties of

Modified Wood-Magnesia Composite[J]. Construction and Building Materials, 21(9): 1833-1838.

SAVOINI B, et al, 2004. Optical and Mechanical Properties of MgO Crystals Implanted with Lithium Ions[J]. Journal of Applied Physics, 95(5): 2371-2378.

BURDETT J, PRICE G, PRICE S, 1982. Role of the Crystal-field Theory in Determining the Structures of Spinels[J]. Journal of American Chemical Society, 104(1): 92-95.

SUZUKI I, OHNO I, ANDERSON L, 2000. Harmony and Anharmonic Properties of Spinel[J]. American Mineralogist, 85(2): 304-311.

TARUTA S, et al, 2005. Preparation and Mechanical Properties of Machinable Spinel/Mica Composites[J]. Journal of Ceramic Society of Japan, 113(1314): 185-187.

Table 108.1 Mechanical Properties of MgO (Magnesia) and MgAl$_2$O$_4$ (Magnesium Aluminum Oxide)

Material	$T/℃$	E_T	ρ	ν	(σ, ε)	α	k	γ	$\tan \delta$	K_{IC}
MgO (Sintered; Low Porosity)	23	330	3.58	0.36	$\sigma_{ucs} = -1667$; $\sigma_{uts} = 167$; $\sigma_R = 200$	12	60	1000	—	2.8
	400	—	—	—	—	—	16	—	—	—
	1000	—	—	—	—	—	7	—	—	—
	2852 (T_m)	—	—	—	—	—	—	—	—	—
MgO (Sintered)	23	270	3.54	0.36	$\sigma_{ucs} = -833$; $\sigma_{uts} = 83$; $\sigma_R = 100$	9	30	880	—	2.7
	2852 (T_m)	—	—	—	—	—	—	—	—	—
MgAl$_2$O$_4$ (Spinel)	23	238	3.6	—	$\sigma_R = 150$	7.6	15	—	—	—
	400	—	—	—	—	—	10	—	—	—
	1000	—	—	—	—	—	6	—	—	—
	2135 (T_m)	—	—	—	—	—	—	—	—	—

Table 108.2 Fatigue ε-N Properties of MgO and MgAl$_2$O$_4$

Material	$T/℃$	$d\varepsilon/dt$	σ_f'	ε_f'	b	c	K'	n'	$\sigma_f @ 2N_f$	R
MgO $(\rho = 3.58)$	23	—	—	—	—	—	—	—	111	—
MgO $(\rho = 3.54)$	23	—	—	—	—	—	—	—	95	—

Chapter 109

PZT (Lead Zirconate Titanate)

109.1 Introduction

PZT (Lead Zirconate Titanate) ceramic elements may be pressed to shape, fired, electroded, and polarized to become a piezoelectric ceramic. Polarization uses a high electric field to align the material domains along a primary axis. Mechanical properties of PZT are given in Table 109.1. PZT can be used as an actuator or sensor.

109.2 Actuators

Being piezoelectric, PZT develops an electric voltage across two of its faces when compressed (useful for sensor applications), or physically changes shape when an external electric field is applied (useful for actuator applications). PZT, i.e. $Pb(Zr_x Ti_{1-x})O_3$, is one of the most promising materials for ferroelectric thin films due to its high remnant polarization, high Curie temperature, high switching speed and resistivity. To be commercialized, the ferroelectric memories are required to have an endurance of more than 10^{15} cycles and retention of more than ten years.

In tensor notation, the electric field-induced strain, ε_{ij}, can be written as a power series in an electric field, E_k, as

$$\varepsilon_{ij} = d_{ijm} E_m + M_{ijkl} E_k E_l + \text{higher-ordered terms} \tag{109.1}$$

where:
ε_{ij}: Electric filed-induced strain;
d_{ijm}: Piezoelectric coefficient;
M_{ijkl}: Electrostrictive coefficient;
E_k, E_l, E_m: Electric fields.

Subscript i ranges from 1 to 3 in the 3-dimensional space, so does subscript j. In the linear range, only the first term on the right-hand side of Eq. (109.1) is considered, and

$$\varepsilon_{ij} = d_{ij} E \tag{109.2}$$

The stress induced can be calculated as the sum of mechanical strain and piezoelectric strain,

$$\sigma_{ij} = D_{ijkl} \varepsilon_{kl} - D_{ij} d_{ij} E \tag{109.3}$$

D_{ijkl} is the stiffness matrix of the material. For comparison, typical coefficient d_{33}'s for different materials are on the order of the following data [Rodel et al.]:

Material	p_{33}(pc/N)	d_{33}(pm/V)	T_c(℃)
SiO_2	—	2	—
$Bi_{1/2}Na_{1/2}TiO_3$(BNT)	—	20	—
$K_xNa_{1-x}NbO_3$(KNN)	120	—	400
$K_xNa_{1-x}NbO_3/6\%$ Li	250	175	450
$K_xNa_{1-x}NbO_3/Cu$	180	225	402
$K_xNa_{1-x}NbO_3/Li,Ta,Sb$	300	400	253
PZT	—	4200×10^{-11}	275
Single crystal of $Pb(Zn_{1/3}Nb_{2/3})O_3$	—	42000	—

PZT-based multilayer actuators are utilized under small compressive stress, less than 20 MPa generally in order to reduce the tendency to crack at electrode edges. Piezo fuel injectors for Diesel engines based on stacked PZT disks can improve fuel efficiency and reduce NO_x emission and noise. Probability design sensitivity analysis based on finite element methods may be used to optimize the design of PZT-multilayered piezo-actuator.

109.3   Piezoelectric Sensor

Piezoelectric sensors are widely used to detect strains (or stresses), i.e. ε_{kl} (or σ_{ij}), by monitoring the dielectric displacement vector q_n. Coefficient d_{nkl}, referred to as just the piezoelectric coefficient, is based on the following equation:

$$q_n = d_{nkl}\,\varepsilon_{kl} + D_{nm}\,E_m \tag{109.4}$$

where:
q_n: Dielectric displacement vector;
D_{nm}: Material's dielectric property.

If only one-dimensional displacement is considered and the dielectric displacement is induced by the applied force without any electric field, then Eq. (109.4) reduces to

$$q = p_{kl}\,\sigma_{kl} \tag{109.5}$$

In accordance to the obtainable strain, $\varepsilon_{kl,\,max}$, the piezoelectric coefficient is a complex function of the magnitude of the mechanical or electric driving field, bias electric field, frequency, temperature, and pressure.

Flexible active fiber composites use piezoelectric ceramic fibers of PZT to create robust, comfortable sensing devices, or even actuators.

References

COLLA E, et al, 2003. Direct Observation of Inversely Polarized Frozen Nanodomains in Fatigued Ferroelectric Memory Capacitors[J]. Applied Physics Letters, 82(10): 1604-1606.

DENG Q, et al, 2012. Evaluation of Fatigue of the Lead Zirconate Titanate Ceramics under Electro-Mechanical Coupling Field[J]. Journal of Inorganic Materials , 27(4): 358-362.

FETT T, et al, 2003. Stress-strain Behavior of a Soft PZT Ceramic under Tensile and Compression Loading and a Transverse Electric Field[J]. Ferroelectrics, 297(1): 83-90.

FETT T, MUNZ D, 2000. Measurement of Young's Moduli for Lead Zirconate Titanate Ceramics[J]. Journal of Testing and Evaluation, 28(1): 27-35.

GERBER P, et al, 2005. Effects of Ferroelectric Fatigue on the Piezoelectric Properties (ε_{33}) of Tetragonal Lead Zirconate Titanate Thin Films[J]. Applied Physics Letters, 86: 112908.

GROSS S J, et al, 2005. Lead-Zirconate-Titanate-based Piezoelectric Micromachined Switch [J]. Applied Physics Letters, 83(1): 174-176.

IMOTO K, NISHIURA M, YAMAMOTO K, et al, 2005. Elasticity Control of Piezoelectric Lead Zirconate Titanate (PZT) Materials Using Negative-Capacitance Circuits[J]. Japan Journal of Applied Physics, 44: 7019-7023.

KITAGAWA K, et al, 2005. Cyclic Fatigue Behavior and Mechanical Properties of PZT Piezoelectric Ceramics [J]. Journal of the Japan Society of Powder and Powder Metallurgy, 52(1): 16-21.

KRURGER H H, 1968. Stress Sensitivity of Piezoelectric Ceramics: Part 3, Sensitivity to Compressive Stress Perpendicular to the Polar Axis[J]. Journal of Acoustic Society, 43(3): 636-645.

KUGEL V D, CROSS L E, 1998. Behavior of Soft Piezoelectric Ceramics under High Sinusoidal Electric Fields [J]. Journal of Applied Physics, 84(5): 2815-2830.

LI G, et al, 1997. Stress-enhanced Displacement in the PLZT Rainbow Actuators[J]. Journal of American Ceramic Society, 80(6): 1382-1388.

LI X, et al, 2002. Effect of a Transverse Tensile Stress on the Electric-field-induced Domain Reorientation in Soft PZT: In Situ XRD Study[J]. Journal of American Ceramic Society, 85(4): 844-850.

LIU W, JIANG B, ZHU W, 2000. Self-Biased Dielectric Bolometer from Epitaxially Grown $Pb(Zr,Ti)O_3$ and Lanthanum-Doped $Pb(Zr,Ti)O_3$ Multilayered Thin Films[J]. Applied Physics Letters, 77(7): 1047-1049.

LOU X J. et al, 2006. Local Phase Decomposition as a Cause of Polarization Fatigue in Ferroelectric Thin Films [J]. Physical Review Letters, 97(17): 177601.

MUELLER V, ZHANG Q M, 1998. Nonlinear and Scaling Behavior in Donor-doped Lead Zirconate Titanate Piezoceramic[J]. Applied Physics Letters, 72(21): 2691-2694.

NIETO, et al, 1996. Multilayer Piezoelectric Devices Based on PZT[J]. Journal of Material Science, 7(1): 55-60.

OKAYASU M, et al, 2010. In Situ Measurement of Material Properties of Lead Zirconate Titanate Piezoelectric Ceramics during Cyclic Mechanical Loading[J]. Journal of European Ceramics Society, 30(6): 1445-1452.

OKAYASU M, et al, 2010. Fatigue Failure Characteristics of Lead Zirconate Titanate Piezoelectric Ceramics [J]. Journal of European Ceramics Society, 30(3): 713-725.

OKAYASU M, et al, 2009. Temperature Dependence of the Fatigue and Mechanical Properties of Lead Zirconate Titanate Piezoelectric Ceramics[J]. International Journal of Fatigue, 31(8-9): 1254-1261.

PAYO I, HALE J, 2011. Sensitivity Analysis of Piezoelectric Paint Sensors Made Up of PZT Ceramic Powder and Water-based Acrylic Polymer[J]. Sensors and Actuators, A: Physical, 168: 77-89.

PINTELIE L, et al, 2006. Polarization Fatigue and Frequency-Dependent Recovery in $Pb(Zr,Ti)O_3$ Epitaxial Thin Films with $SrRuO_3$ Electrodes[J]. Applied Physics Letters, 88: 102908.

RODEL J, et al, 2009. Perspective on the Development of Lead-free Piezoceramics[J]. Journal of American Ceramics Society, 92(6): 1153-1177.

ROUQUETTE J, et al, 2004. Pressure Tuning of the Morphotropic Phase Boundary in Piezoelectric Lead Zirconate Titanate[J]. Physics Review B, 70 (1): 014108.

SHAUFER A B, 1996. Ferroelastic Properties of Lead Zirconate Titanate Ceramics[J]. Journal of American Ceramics Society, 79(10): 2631-2640.

TAKAHARA K, et al, 2006. Basic Study of Application for Elasticity Control of Piezoelectric Lead Zirconate Titanate Materials Using Negative Capacitance Circuit to Sound Shielding Technology[J]. Japan Journal of Applied Physics, 45: 7422-7425.

TSURUMI T, et al, 1997. Domain Reorientation and Electric-Field Induced Strain of Tetragonal Lead Zirconate Titanate Ceramic Part I [J]. Japan Journal of Applied Physics, 36: 5970-5975.

WANG H, et al, 2010. Strength Properties of Poled Lead Zirconate Titanate Subjected to Biaxial Flexural Loading in High Electric Field[J]. Journal of the American Ceramics Society, 93(9): 2843-2849.

WANG Q M, et al, 1999. Nonlinear Piezoelectric Behavior of Ceramic Bending Mode Actuators under Strong Electric Fields[J]. Journal of Applied Physics, 86(6): 3352-3360.

YU S, et al, 2011. The Electric Fatigue and Thermal Effect for Ferroelectric Materials under Cyclic Electric

Loading[J]. Strength, Fracture and Complexity, 7(1): 33-41.

ZHANG Q M, et al, 1994. Direct Evaluation of Domain-Wall and Intrinsic Contributions to Dielectric and Piezoelectric Response and Their Temperature Dependence on the Lead Zirconate Titanate Ceramics[J]. Journal of Applied Physics, 75(1): 454-459.

ZHANG Y, et al, 2005. Heterogeneity of Fatigue in Bulk Lead Zirconate Titanate[J]. Acta Materialia, 53: 2203-2213.

ZHENG X J, ZHOU Y C, LI J Y, 2003. Nano-indentation Fracture Test of Pb ($Zr_{0.52}$-$Ti_{0.48}$)O_3 Ferroelectric Thin Films[J]. Acta Materialia, 51: 3985-3997.

Table 109.1 Mechanical Properties of PZT (Lead Zirconate Titanate) [NUWC-NPT Technical Report 11184]

Material	$T/^\circ\mathrm{C}$	E_T	ρ	ν	(σ, ε)	α	k	γ	$\tan \delta$	K_IC
PZT (Unpoled; (Piezoelectric Material)	23	76	7.8	0.43	$(-1045, -1\%)$ $(-175, -0.4\%)$ $(-145, -0.2\%)$; $(460, 0.5\%)$	4.5	1.8	420	—	1.2
	275 (T_c)	—	—	—	—	—	—	—	—	—
	2300 (T_m)	—	—	—	—	—	—	—	—	—
PZT (Poled ⊥)	23	83	7.8	0.44	$(-945, -0.9\%)$ $(-375, -0.4\%)$ $(-170, -0.2\%)$; $(460, 0.5\%)$	4.5	1.8	420	—	1.4

Chapter 110

SiC (Silicon Carbide)

110.1   Introduction

SiC (Silicon Carbide) exhibits high Mode I fracture toughness (cleavage), yet brittle in Mode III fracture toughness (out-of-plane tearing) at elevated temperatures. The creep rate of SiC is low in comparison to metals and metallic alloys. Mechanical properties of SiC are given in Table 110.1.

110.2   Applications

SiC (Silicon Carbide) is used for power-semiconductors controllers for electric vehicles, car brakes, bullet-proof vests, and high temperature/high voltage semiconductor electronics.

To meet the need for compatible power electronic devices capable of efficient and effective operation at elevated temperatures, power conversion modules of electric vehicles (e.g. inverters) are developed with power MOSFETs that use silicon carbide (SiC) and gallium nitride (GaN) technologies. These devices can offer lower energy loss during power conversion and operational characteristics that surpass traditional silicon counterparts [Davis]. The SiC MOSFET module has 38% lower conduction losses and 60% lower switching losses than its counterpart Si IGBT, when operating at 20 kHz with the junction temperature at 150 ℃ [Davis].

The filtering material shows isotropic distributions of the SiC grains and the pores. It is characterized by marked stability of the mechanical and thermal properties in the explored temperature range (up to 1100 ℃). The grout with higher porosity is prone to important thermal transformations with no further consequences on filtration and durability. Due to the low thermal conductivity compared to the filtering material, its essential function is the isolation of the SiC bars from each other. From experience, it is known that the durability of diesel particulate filters (DPFs) may be limited by the high transient thermomechanical stresses created during severe regeneration rather than by mechanical fatigue.

References

DICARLO J A, 1986. Creep of Chemically Vapor Deposited SiC Fibers[J]. Journal of Materials Science, 21: 217-224.

LARSON D, ADAMS J, JOHNSON L, et al, 1985. Ceramic Materials for Advanced Heat Engines: Technical and Economical Evaluation[J]. Journal of Engineering Materials & Technology, 109(1): 99.

LI X, et al, 2005. Micro/Nanoscale Mechanical and Tribological Characterization of SiC for Orthopedic Applications[J]. Journal of Biomedical Materials Research, Part B: Applied Biomaterials, 72B: 353-361.

REDDY J D. et al, 2000. Mechanical Properties of 3C-SiC Films for MEMS Applications[J]. Mater. Res. Soc. Symp. Proc., 1049-AA03-06.

WERESZCZAK A, LIN H, GILDE G, 2006. The Effect of Grain Growth on Hardness in Hot-pressed Silicon Carbides[J]. Journal of Materials Science, 41: 4996-5000.

WOLFENDEN A, et al, 1995. Measurement of Elastic and Anelastic Properties of Reaction-formed Silicon Carbide Materials[J]. Journal of Materials Science, 30: 5502-5507.

YOSHIMURA H, CRUZ A, ZHOU Y, et al, 2002. Sintering of 6H(α)-SiC and 3C(β)-SiC Powders with B_4C and C additives[J]. Journal of Materials Science, 37(8): 1541-1546.

ZIEGLER G, et al, 1987. Relationships between Processing, Microstructure and Properties of Dense and Reaction-bonded Silicon Carbide[J]. Journal of Materials Science, 22(9): 3041-3086.

Table 110.1 Mechanical Properties of SiC (Silicon Carbide) [Morgan Advanced Materials]

Material	$T/°C$	E_T	ρ	ν	(σ, ε)	α	k	γ	$\tan \delta$	K_{IC}
SiC (Hot Pressed; Porosity<1%)	23	420	3.3	0.19	$\sigma_{ucs}=-2100$; $\sigma_{uts}=500$; $\sigma_R=720$	2	80	670	—	4.2
	600	—	—	—	$\sigma_R=530$	4.2	51	—	—	4.2
	1000	—	—	—	—	—	—	—	—	4.2
	1200	367	—	—	—	5.5	—	—	—	—
	1650 (High service temperature)									
	2300 (T_m)	—	—	—	—	—	—	—	—	—
SiC (Thin Film)	23	428	3.3	0.19	(800, 0.2%) (1200, 0.3%)	2	80	670	—	4.2
SiC (Sintered; Porosity=2%)	23	390	3.2	0.16	$\sigma_{uts}=310$; $\sigma_R=485$	2	71	590	—	3
	600	—	—	—	—	4.2	48	—	—	3
	1500	—	—	—	—	—	—	—	—	3
SiC (Reaction-Bonded)	23	414	3.1	0.24	$\sigma_R=390$	2	120	750	—	4
	600	—	—	—	—	4.2	70	—	—	4

continued

Material	$T/℃$	E_T	ρ	ν	(σ, ε)	α	k	γ	$\tan \delta$	K_{IC}
SiC (CVD; Polycrystalline)	23	450	3.2	0.24	$\sigma_R = 560$	2	250	660	—	3
	500	—	—	—	—	3.9	100	1160	—	3
	1000	—	—	—	—	4.7	55	1280	—	—
	1300	420	—	—	$\sigma_R = 450$	—	—	1360	—	—
	2830 (Decomposition temperature)									
SiC (Crystal; 3C-SiC CVDed on Si(100))	23	433	—	—		—	—	—	—	—

Chapter 111

Si_3N_4 (Silicon Nitride)

111.1　Introduction

Si_3N_4 (Silicon Nitride) exhibits the highest Mode I fracture toughness (cleavage) of all ceramics, yet is also the most brittle. Its Mode Ⅲ fracture toughness (out-of-plane tearing) dominates at elevated temperature even when the homologous temperature is unity. Mechanical properties of Si_3N_4 are given in Table 111.1. The creep rate of Si_3N_4 is low in comparison with metallic alloys. Based on data from [Lason et al.], the following creep equation for Si_3N_4 at 1200 ℃ was derived by [Park and Holmes] as

$$\frac{d \varepsilon_{\text{creep}}}{d t} = 2.833 \times 10^{-13} \sigma^2 \tag{111.1}$$

At 1200 ℃ the $Si_3N_4/30\%SiC$ composite ($V_f = 30\%$) exhibited a linear stress-strain response up to a stress higher than 188 MPa [Holmes].

Orthotropic material properties of Si_3N_4(Silicon Nitride) composites reinforced with well-aligned fibers are listed in Tables 111.1 and 111.2, respectively.

111.2　Applications

Si_3N_4 (Silicon Nitride) has been used for car engine parts, gas turbines, bearings, turbocharger rotors, and cutting tools, due to its high fracture toughness at elevated temperatures as a ceramic. A ceramic bearing set usually consists of ZrO_2 races and Si_3N_4 balls.

References

HOLMES J W, 1991. Influence of Stress Ratio on the Elevated−Temperature Fatigue of a Silicon Carbide Fiber-Reinforced Silicon Nitride Composite[J]. Journal of American Ceramics Society, 74(7): 1639-1945.

KUSUNOSE T, et al, 2002. Fabrication and Microstructure of Silicon Nitride/Boron Nitride Nanocomposites [J]. Journal of the American Ceramic Society, 85: 2678-2688.

LARSON D, ADAMS J, JOHNSON L, et al, 1985. in Ceramic Materials for Advanced Heat Engines: Technical and Economical Evaluation[J]. Journal of Engineering Materials & Technology, 109(1): 99.

PARK Y, HOMES J, 1992. Finite Element Modeling of Creep Deformation in Fiber-Reinforced Ceramic Composites[J]. Journal of Materials Science, 27: 6341-6351.

SREEJITH P , 2005. Machining Force Studies on Ductile Machining of Silicon Nitride[J]. Journal of Materials Processing Technology, 169(3): 414-417.

Table 111.1 Mechanical Properties of Si₃N₄(Silicon Nitride)

Material- DAM	$T/℃$	E_T	ρ	ν	(σ, ε)	α	k	γ	$\tan \delta$	K_{IC}
Si₃N₄ (Hot-Pressed)	23	304	3.29	0.3	$\sigma_{uts}=520$	2.7	30	780	—	6.1
	600	—	—	—	$\sigma_R=805$	—	22	—	—	—
	1200	274	—	0.27	—	3.2	—	—	—	—
	1900 (T_m)	—	—	—	—	—	—	—	—	—
Si₃N₄ (Sintered)	23	275	3.25	0.27	$\sigma_R=700$	3.1	27	711	—	6.0
	600	—	—	—	—	—	18	—	—	—
Si₃N₄ (Sintered)	23	275	3.18	0.24	$\sigma_R=800$	3.1	27	711	—	5.2
	600	—	—	—	$\sigma_R=725$	—	18	—	—	—
Si₃N₄ (Reaction-Bonded)	23	200	2.7	0.23	$\sigma_{ucs}=-690$; $\sigma_{uts}=360$; $\sigma_R=295$	3.2	10	870	—	3
Si₃N₄ [Sharpe et al.]	23	258	3.18	0.22	(2600, 1%) (5830, 1.2%)	—	—	—	—	—

Table 111.2 Mechanical Properties of Si₃N₄ Reinforced by Continuous Fibers [Holmes]

Material-DAM	$T/℃$	ρ	E_{11}	E_{22}	E_{33}	G_{12}	G_{13}	G_{23}	ν_{12}	ν_{13}	ν_{23}
Si₃N₄/30%SiC ($V_f=30\%$; UD)	23	—	—	—	—	—	—	—	—	—	—
	1200	—	284	—	—	—	—	—	—	—	—

Table 111.3 Mechanical Strengths of Si₃N₄ Reinforced by Continuous Fibers [Holmes]

Material	$T/℃$	$(\sigma_{11u}, \varepsilon_{11u})$	$(\sigma_{22u}, \varepsilon_{22u})$	$(\sigma_{33u}, \varepsilon_{33u})$	$(\sigma_{12u}, \varepsilon_{12u})/(\sigma_{23u}, \varepsilon_{23u})/(\sigma_{13u}, \varepsilon_{13u})$
Si₃N₄/30%SiC ($V_f=30\%$; UD)	23	—	—	—	—
	1200	(188, 0.07%) (200, 0.1%) (350, 0.15%) (380, 0.19%)	—	—	—

Chapter 112

SiO$_2$ (Silicon Dioxide)

112.1   Introduction

SiO_2 (Silicon Dioxide), also called silica or silica glass, is amorphous glass. It is a 3-dimensional network formed when each corner oxygen atom in each tetrahedron is shared by adjacent tetrahedral. Mechanical Properties of SiO_2 are given in Table 112.1.

Silica is used primarily in the production of glass for windows, drinking glasses, beverage bottles, and many other uses.

112.2 SiO_2 (Fused Silica)

Fused silica is a noncrystalline form of SiO_2, i.e. amorphous SiO_2 made to have a high degree of atomic randomness embedded in a cross-linked 3-dimensional structure. It is also called vitreous silica. Due to its mechanical resistance, high dielectric strength, and selectivity for chemical modification, fused silica has also become a key material in microelectronics and chromatography.

Fused silica is quintessential for a broad range of applications: chips, optical fibers, and telescope glasses are manufactured on silica. Thin films of silica grown on silicon wafers via thermal oxidation methods can be quite beneficial in microelectronics, where they act as electric insulators with high chemical stability.

112.3   Quartz, Cristobalite, and Tridymite

If the tetrahedral of silica is arranged in an ordered array, it may become one of the following polymorphic crystalline forms: quartz, cristobalite, and tridymite.

Quartz crystals have piezoelectric properties-developing an electric potential upon the application of mechanical stress. The resonant frequency of a quartz crystal oscillator is changed by mechanically loading it, and this principle is used for very accurate measurements of very small mass changes in the quartz crystal microbalance and in thin-film thickness monitors.

The mineral cristobalite and tridymite are high-temperature polymorphs of silica, meaning that they have the same chemical formula, i.e. SiO_2, but individual distinct crystal structures.

References

CHEN Q, et al, 2008. Nanoscale and Effective Mechanical Behavior and Fracture of Silica Nanocomposites[J]. Composites Science and Technology, 68(15-16): 3137-3144.

JANG H, CHO M, PARK D, 2008. Micro Fluidic Channel Machining on Fused Silica Glass Using Powder Platting[J]. Sensors, 8: 700-710.

PABST W, GREGOROVA E, 2013. Elastic Properties of Silica Polymorphs-A Review[J]. Ceramics-Silikáty, 57(3): 167-184.

WU Y, et al, 2008. The Influence of In Situ Modification of Silica on Filler Network and Dynamic Mechanical Properties of Silica-Filled Solution Styrene-Butadiene Rubber[J]. Journal of Applied Polymer Science, 108: 112-118.

XU H H K, et al, 2004. Wear and Mechanical Properties of Nano-silica-fused Whisker Composites[J]. Journal of Dental Research, 83(12): 930-935.

Table 112.1   Mechanical Properties of SiO$_2$

Material-DAM	$T/℃$	E_T	ρ	ν	(σ, ε)	α	k	γ	$\tan \delta$	K_{IC}
SiO$_2$(Silica Glass; Amorphous)	23	72	2.2	0.17	$\sigma_R = 48$	0.5	1.6	740	—	0.8
	400	—	—	—	—	—	—	1100	—	—
	550	79.3	2.199	0.187	—	0.5	—	—	—	—
	1000	84.4	2.197	0.175	—	0.5	—	—	—	—
	1400	—	—	—	—	—	—	1350	—	—
SiO$_2$ (99.99%; Fused)	23	73	2.2	0.17	$(-1150, -1.4\%)$; $(50, 0.2\%)$ $(54, 6\%)$	0.55	1.4	740	—	0.8
	400	—	—	—	—	—	1.9	—	—	—
	1200 (T_g)	—	—	—	—	—	—	—	—	—
	1650 (T_m)	—	—	—	—	—	—	—	—	—
α-Quartz	23	95.4	2.65	0.17	$\sigma_R = 48$	0.5	1.6	740	—	—
	400	—	—	—	—	—	1.9	—	—	—
	1710 (T_m)	—	—	—	—	—	—	—	—	—
Quartz (Fused)	23	73	2.2	0.17	$(-1150, -1.4\%)$; $\sigma_R = 49$	0.5	1.4	1096	—	—
	400	—	—	—	—	—	1.9	—	—	—
	1200 (T_g)	—	—	—	—	—	—	—	—	—

continued

Material-DAM	$T/℃$	E_T	ρ	ν	(σ, ε)	α	k	γ	$\tan\delta$	K_{IC}
Quartz, Low	23	95.6	2.65	0.084	—	12.3	1.6	742	—	—
(Trigonal	550	68.2	2.59	—	—	56.7	—	1239	—	—
Crystal)	1710 (T_m)	—	—	—	—	—	—	—	—	—
Quartz, High (Hexagonal Crystal)	23	99.1	2.53	0.194	—	12.3	1.6	742	—	—
Cristobalite, Low (Monoclinic)	23	65	2.3	0.17	—	10.3	—	748	—	—
Cristobalite, High (Hexagonal Crystal)	23	62.3	2.2	—	—	—	—	—	—	—
Tridymite, Low (Tetragonal)	23	58	2.3	0.17	—	21	—	742	—	—
Tridymite, High (Cubic)	23	53	2.22	—	—	—	—	—	—	—

Chapter 113

TiC (Titanium Carbide)

113.1 Introduction

TiC (Titanium Carbide), having the appearance of black powder with NaCl-type face-centered cubic crystal structure, is an extremely hard (Mohs 9-9.5) refractory ceramic material, similar to tungsten carbide. Mechanical properties of TiC are given in Table 113.1.

113.2 Applications

TiC (Titanium Carbide) is added to tungsten carbide for the better resistance to wear, corrosion, and oxidation of a tungsten carbide-cobalt material. Cermets made of titanium carbide dispersed in nickel-cobalt matrix can be used as a heat shield for space shuttles.

References

BRODKIN D, et al, 2009. Ambient- and High-temperature Properties of Titanium Carbide-Titanium Boron Composites Fabricated by Transient Plastic Phase Processing[J]. Journal of the American Ceramic Society, 82(3): 665-672.

GUO B, KERNS K, CASTLEMAN A, 1992. $Ti_8C_{12}^+$-Metallo-Carbohedrenes: A New Class of Molecular Clusters? [J]. Science, 255 (5050): 1411-1413.

PAULING L, 1992. Molecular Structure of Ti_8C_{12} and Related Complexes[J]. Proc. Natl. Acad. Sci., 89 (17): 8175-8176.

TAYLOR R, MORREALE J, 1964. Thermal Conductivity of Titanium Carbide, Zirconium Carbide, and Titanium Nitride at High Temperatures[J]. Journal of the American Ceramic Society, 47(2): 69-73.

WOLTER S D, et al, 1995. Biased-enhanced Nucleation of Highly Oriented Diamond on Titanium Carbide (111) Substrates[J]. Applied Physics Letters, 66(21): 2810-2812.

Table 113.1　Mechanical Properties of TiC（Titanium Carbide）

Material-DAM	$T/℃$	E_T	ρ	ν	(σ, ε)	α	k	γ	$\tan \delta$	K_{IC}
TiC（Hot pressed; Porosity < 2%）	23	439	4.93	0.188	$\sigma_{uts}=258$; $\sigma_R=363$	9.4	24	700	—	225
	300	—	—	—	—	—	—	741	—	—
	600	—	—	—	—	—	—	821	—	—
	1000	310	—	—	$\sigma_{uts}=110$	—	5.7	878	—	—
	2000	—	4.85	—	$\sigma_{uts}=93.8$	17	—	—	—	—
	3160 (T_m)	—	—	—	—	—	—	—	—	—
TiC（Cermet）	23	439	4.93	—	$\sigma_{uts}=258$; $\sigma_R=363$	9.4	35	—	—	—
	400	—	—	—	—	—	17	—	—	—
	1000	—	—	—	—	17	8.4	—	—	—
	3160 (T_m)	—	—	—	—	—	—	—	—	—
TiC（Crystal）	23	497	4.93	—	$(20000, 0.2\%)$	7.4	330	—	—	—
	3160 (T_m)	—	—	—	—	—	—	—	—	—
TiC-25Ni-5Mo	23	380	—	—	$\sigma_{uts}=800$	—	—	—	—	—

Chapter 114

WC (Tungsten Carbide)

114.1　Introduction

WC (Tungsten Carbide) can be prepared by the reaction of tungsten and carbon at a temperature above 1400 ℃. Oxidation of WC may occur at a temperature above 500 ℃. It is resistant to most acids, but attacked by hydrofluoric acid/nitric acid (HF/HNO$_3$) mixtures at an elevated temperature (above the room temperature). It reacts with fluorine gas at room temperature and chlorine above 400 ℃. Tungsten carbide has a high melting point (2870 ℃) and is extremely hard. Its electrical resistivity (~2×10^{-7} Ohm · m) is comparable with metals.

Mechanical properties of WC and related materials are given in Table 114.1.

WC (Tungsten Carbide) is readily wetted by molten nickel and cobalt. WC (Tungsten Carbide) alloyed with Co (Cobalt) is the most used material for cutting tools. Cobalt is used as a bonding matrix because its wetting or capillary action during liquid phase sintering allows the achievement of high densities and good resistance to wear. For the purpose of extending tool life, a layer of hard material such as diamond may be deposited onto the area of the cutting tool nose. Some empirical predictive equations of the tool life of WC-Co with different coating materials for cutting M42 tool steel were obtained from experiments [Jackson] as follows:

$$V T^{0.3} = 33 \quad \text{for TiN coating} \tag{114.1}$$

$$V T^{0.35} = 38 \quad \text{for Ti-0.46\%Al-0.54\%N coating} \tag{114.2}$$

$$V T^{0.37} = 43 \quad \text{for Ti-0.44\%Al-0.53\%Cr-0.03\%N coating} \tag{114.3}$$

$$V T^{0.37} = 50 \quad \text{for Ti-0.43\%Al-0.52\%Cr-0.03\%Y-0.02\%N coating} \tag{114.4}$$

where V is the cutting speed (meter/minute) and T is the tool life (minutes). The resistance to wear, corrosion, and oxidation of a tungsten carbide-cobalt material can be increased by adding 6%~30% of titanium carbide to tungsten carbide. This forms a solid solution that is more brittle and susceptible to breakage than the original material.

114.2　Applications

WC (Tungsten Carbide) has been conventionally used for cutting steel. It also makes up about 95% of cutting tools with a PCD or CBN tip for the cutting edge. WC-Co coated with diamond-like carbon or brazed with diamond is used for cutting abrasive materials such as aluminum and carbon-fiber-reinforced composites.

References

JACOBS L, et al, 1998. Comparative Study of WC-cermet Coatings Sprayed via the HVOF and the HVAF Process[J]. Journal of Thermal Spray Technology, 7(2): 213-218.

KRAWITZ A, REICHEL D, HITTERMAN R, 1989. Thermal Expansion of Tungsten Carbide at Low Temperature[J]. Journal of the American Ceramic Society, 72: 515.

LACKNER A, FILZWIESER A, 2002. Gas Carburizing of Tungsten Carbide (WC) Powder: US, US6447742 B1[P]. 2002-09-10.

LEVY R B, BOUDART M, 1973. Platinum-Like Behavior of Tungsten Carbide in Surface Catalysis[J]. Science, 181 (4099): 547-549.

NERZ J, KUSHNER B, ROTOLICO A, 1992. Microstructural Evaluation of Tungsten Carbide-Cobalt Coatings [J]. Journal of Thermal Spray Technology, 1(2): 147-152.

SARA R V, 1965. Phase Equilibrium in the System Tungsten-Carbon[J]. Journal of the American Ceramic Society, 48 (5): 251-257.

SICKAFOOSE S, SMITH A, MORSE M, 2002. Optical Spectroscopy of Tungsten Carbide (WC)[J]. Journal of Chemical Physics, 116(3): 993-1002.

SPRINCE N, CHAMBERLIN R, HALES C, et al, 1984. Respiratory Disease in Tungsten Carbide Production Workers[J]. Chest, 86(4): 549-557.

ZENG K, CHIU C, 2001. An Analysis of Load-Penetration Curves from Instrumented Indentation[J]. Acta Materialia, 49: 3539-3551.

ZHANG S, LIU Z, 2008. An Analytical Model for Transient Temperature Distributions in Coated Carbide Cutting Tools[J]. International Communications in Heat and Mass Transfer, 35: 1311-1315.

ZHONG Y, et al, 2011. A study on the Synthesis of Nanostructured WC-10 wt% Co Particles from WO_3, Co_3O_4, and Graphite[J]. Journal of Materials Science, 46(19): 6323-6331.

ZHU Y, et al, 2001. Tribological Properties of Nanostructured and Conventional WC-Co Coating Deposited by Plasma Spraying[J]. Thin Solid Films, 388: 277-282.

Table 114.1　Mechanical Properties of WC（Tungsten Carbide）

Material-DAM	$T/^{\circ}C$	E_T	ρ	ν	(σ, ε)	α	k	γ	$\tan\delta$	K_{IC}
WC	23	550	15.7	0.24	$\sigma_{ucs}=-2683$; $\sigma_{uts}=334$	4	84	880	—	3.6
	400	—	—	—	—	4.3	—	—	—	—
	800	—	—	—	—	4.8	—	—	—	—
	1000	—	—	—	$\sigma_{ucs}=-1400$	7.2	—	—	—	—
	2870 (T_m)	—	—	—	—	—	—	—	—	—
WC-3Co	23	673	15.3	0.23	—	4.3	121	—	—	6
	400	—	—	—	—	4.7	—	—	—	—
	800	—	—	—	—	5.1	—	—	—	—
WC-4Co	23	648	15	0.23	$\sigma_R=1900$	4.4	112	—	—	8
	400	—	—	—	—	4.8	—	—	—	—
	800	—	—	—	—	5.2	—	—	—	—
	1000	—	—	—	—	5.6	—	—	—	—
WC-9Co （Coating）	23	—	—	—	—	—	—	—	—	—
	540	218	—	—	—	8.1	—	—	—	—
WC-10Co	23	580	14.5	0.23	$\sigma_R=2700$	5.2	110	—	—	15
	400	—	—	—	—	5.4	—	—	—	—
	800	—	—	—	—	6.0	—	—	—	—
WC-13Co （Coating）	23	—	—	—	—	—	—	—	—	—
	540	218	—	—	—	8.1	—	—	—	—
WC-15Co	23	510	—	0.23	$\sigma_R=2700$	—	—	—	—	—
WC-20Co	23	490	13.6	0.23	$\sigma_R=3100$	6.4	100	—	—	25
	400	—	—	—	—	6.6	—	—	—	—
	800	—	—	—	—	7.0	—	—	—	—
WC-5Ni （Coating）	23	—	—	—	—	—	—	—	—	—
	760	56	—	—	—	8.3	—	—	—	—
W2C	23	420	14.8	—	—	4.0	—	—	—	—
	2785 (T_m)	—	—	—	—	—	—	—	—	—

Chapter 115

ZnO (Zinc Oxide)

115.1　Introduction

ZnO (Zinc Oxide) has attracted extensive attention for half a century because of its excellent performance in optics, electronics, and photoelectronics. Mechanical properties of ZnO are given in Table 115.1.

Ultrafine ZnO is able to grow with self-organizing ability. Under steady-state conditions, the interaction of molecules is evident- making molecules grow rigorously along with the epitaxial interface of crystal lattice to form a homogenous structure. Ultrafine ZnO has not only a strong ability to absorb electromagnetic waves, but also shield ultraviolet rays, absorb infrared rays, and disinfect them. Mechanical elasticities of nanorods of zinc oxide exhibit orthotropic.

115.2　Applications

It is used in green, blue-ultraviolet, and white light-emitting devices at a low cost, due to its wide band gap (≈ 3.37 eV) and large excitation binding energy (≈ 60 meV) [Yoshimura]. They can also be used as sensors and actuators owing to their strong piezoelectricity.

Due to its lightweight, light-color and strong wave absorption ability, ultrafine ZnO is able to escape detection of radar in a broad frequency range- significant for national defense. The ultrafine ZnO had become the research focus of radar-absorbing materials.

References

CATTI M, et al, 2003. Full Piezoelectric Tensors of Wurtzite and Zinc Blended ZnO and ZnS by First-Principles Calculations[J]. Journal of Physical Chemistry and Solids, 64(11): 2183-2190.

GADZHIEV G G, 2009. The Thermal and Elastic Properties of Zinc Oxide-Based Ceramics at High Temperatures[J]. High Temperature, 41(6): 778-782.

HEO Y W, et al, 2004. ZnO Nanowire Growth and Devices[J]. Materials Science and Engineering, 47(1-2): 1-47.

HOFFMAN S, et al, 2007. Fracture strength and Young's modulus of ZnO nanowires[J]. Nanotechnology, 18 (20): 205503.

INOUE Y, et al, 2005. Thermoelectric Properties of Amorphous Zinc Oxide Thin Films Fabricated by Pulsed Laser Deposition[J]. Materials Transactions, 46(7): 1470-1475.

KOBIAKOV I B, 1980. Elastic, piezoelectric and dielectric properties of ZnO and Cds single crystals in a wide range of temperatures[J]. Solid State Communications, 35(3): 305-310.

LU J G, et al, 2006. Quasi-one-dimensional Metal Oxide Materials-Synthesis, Properties and Applications[J]. Material Science and Engineering: R: Reports, 52(1-3): 49-91.

MAITI U, et al, 2008. Enhanced Optical and Field Emission Properties of CTAB-Assisted Hydrothermal Grown ZnO Nanorods[J]. Applied Surface Science, 254(22): 7266-7271.

MOFOR A, et al, 2005. Magnetic Property Investigations on Mn-doped ZnO Layers on Sapphire[J]. Applied Physics Letters, 87(6): 062501.1-062501.3.

PARK B, et al, 2010. Stretchable, Transparent Zinc Oxide Thin Film Transistors[J]. Advanced Functional Materials, 20: 3577-3582.

SHEN X, et al, 2010. Preparation and Characterization of Ultrafine Zinc Oxide Powder by Hydrothermal Method[J]. Transactions of Nonferrous Metals Society of China, 20(S1): 236-239.

SONG Y, et al, 2010. Anisotropic Growth and Formation Mechanism Investigation of 1D ZnO Nanorods in Spin-Coating Sol-Gel Process[J]. Journal of Nanoscience and Nanotechnology, 10: 426-432.

SUN Y, et al, 2006. Mechanism of ZnO Nanotube Growth by Hydrothermal Methods on ZnO Film-Coated Si Substrates[J]. Journal of Physical Chemistry B, 110(31): 15186-15277.

TU Z C, HU X, 2006. Elasticity and Piezoelectricity of Zinc Oxide Crystals, Single Layers, and Possible Single-Walled Nanotubes[J]. Physical Review B, 74(3): 035434.

VON PREISSIG F J, et al, 1998. Measurement of Piezoelectric Strength of ZnO Thin Films for MEMS Applications[J]. Smart Structures and Materials, 7(3): 396-403.

YOSHIMURA H, et al, 2006. Mechanical Properties and Microstructure of Zinc Oxide Varistor Ceramics[J]. Materials Science Forum, 530: 408-413.

ZNAIDI L, et al, 2003. Oriented ZnO Thin Films Synthesis by Sol-gel Process for Laser Application[J]. Thin Solid Films, 428(1-2): 257-262.

Table 115.1　Mechanical Properties of ZnO（Zinc Oxide）

Material-DAM	$T/°C$	E_T	ρ	ν	(σ, ε)	α	k	γ	$\tan \delta$	K_{IC}
ZnO	23	119	5.66	0.351	—	3	60	643	—	—
（Porosity = 0.5%）	1975（T_m）	—	—	—	—	—	—	—	—	—
ZnO	23	116	5.61	0.348	—	4	—	—	—	—
（Porosity = 1.8%）	1975（T_m）	—	—	—	—	—	—	—	—	—
ZnO	23	105	—	0.337	—	—	—	—	—	—
（Porosity = 5.8%）	1975（T_m）	—	—	—	—	—	—	—	—	—
ZnO	23	79	—	0.299	—	—	—	—	—	—
（Porosity = 14.6%）	1975（T_m）	—	—	—	—	—	—	—	—	—
ZnO	23	32	—	0.233	—	—	—	—	—	—
（Porosity = 33.6%）	1975（T_m）	—	—	—	—	—	—	—	—	—

Chapter 116

ZrO$_2$ (Zirconia) and Other Zr-based Ceramics

116.1   Introduction

ZrO_2 (Zirconia) is a white crystalline oxide of zirconium. Zr-based ceramics are transparent to radio frequencies, allowing transmissions to pass through without being absorbed by the device. Mechanical properties of ZrO_2 and related materials are given in Table 116.1.

The cubic phase of zirconium also has a very low thermal conductivity, which has led to its use as a thermal barrier coating (TBC) in jet and diesel engines to allow operation at higher temperatures. A typical ceramic bearing set consists of ZrO_2 races and Si_3N_4 balls. Zirconia is also an important high-k dielectric material being investigated for potential applications as an insulator in transistors in future nanoelectronic devices.

It has been used to demonstrate that strain-induced martensitic transformations can substantially increase ceramic toughness.

116.2   Transformation-toughened Zirconia Ceramics

Certain alloying elements make ZrO_2 (Zirconia) partially stable in two different phases-cubic and tetragonal allotromorphs. The tetragonal allotromorph transforms martensitically into the monoclinic form at low temperatures as catalyzed by applied stress. Transformation-toughened zirconia ceramics are among the strongest and toughest ceramics made. These materials are of four main types, given as follows:

(a) Mg-PSZ (Zirconia partially stabilized with magnesium oxide);
(b) Y-TZP (Yttria stabilized tetragonal zirconia polycrystals);
(c) ZTA (Zirconia-toughened alumina);
(d) Ce-TZP (Ceria stabilized tetragonal zirconia polycrystals).

Applications of transformation-toughened zirconia ceramics are principally in parts requiring wear and corrosion resistance:

(A) Mg-PSZ: pump and valve parts, seals, bushings, impellers, and knife blades at room or elevated temperatures;

(B) Y-TZP: pump and valve components requiring wear and corrosion resistance at room temperature, also a dental ceramic;

(C) ZTA: for parts that have a density, better thermal shock resistance, though brittle; less costive than Mg-PSZ and Y-TZP.

References

BUSSO E P, QIAN Z Q, 2006. A Mechanistic Study of Microcracking in Transversely Isotropic Ceramic-Metal Systems[J]. Acta Materialia, 52: 325-338.

CHANG J P, LIN Y S, CHU K, 2001. Rapid Thermal Chemical Vapor Deposition of Zirconium Oxide for Metal-oxide-semiconductor Field Effect Transistor Application [J]. Journal of Vacuum Science and Technology B, 19(5): 1782-1787.

CHEN H, DING C X, 2002. Nanostructured Zirconia Coating Prepared by Atmospheric Plasma Spray[J]. Surface Coating Technology, 150: 31-36.

HAYES T, et al, 2012. Steady-State Creep of α-Zirconium at Temperatures up to 850 ℃[J]. Metallurgical and Materials Transactions A, 33A: 337-343.

KOTLYARCHUK B K, 2003. Pulsed Laser Deposition of ZrO$_2$ Thin Films for Application in Microelectronic Devices[J]. Physics and Chemistry of Solid State, 4(3): 434-439.

LECLERCQ B, et al, 2003. Thermal Conductivity of Zirconia-based Thermal Barrier Coating [J]. Materialwissenschaft und Werkstofftechik, 34(4): 406-409.

PAPASPYRIDAKOS P, KUNAL L, 2008. Complete Arch Implant Rehabilitation using Subtractive Rapid Prototyping and Porcelain Fused Zirconia Prosthesis: A Clinical Report[J]. Journal of Prosthetic Dentistry, 100(3): 165-172.

PITTAYACHAWAN P, et al, 2007. The Biaxial Flexural Strength and Fatigue Property of Lava Y-TZP Dental Ceramic[J]. Dental Materials, 23(8): 1018-1029.

QIAO D, et al, 2007. Compression-Compression Fatigue and Fracture Behaviors of Zr$_{50}$Al$_{10}$Cu$_{37}$Pd$_3$ Bulk-Metallic Glass[J]. Materials Transactions, 48(7): 1828-1833.

RAMASWAMY P, et al, 2007. Thermo-mechanical Fatigue Characterization of Zirconia (8% Y$_2$O$_3$-ZrO$_2$) and Mullite Thermal Barrier Coatings on Diesel Engine Components [J]. Proceedings of the Institution of Mechanical Engineers-Part C, Journal of Mechanical Engineering Science, 214 (5): 729-742.

SAYAN S, et al, 2005. Structural, Electronic, and Dielectric Properties, of Ultra-thin Zirconia Films on Silicon[J]. Applied Physics Letters, 86(15): 152920.1-152902.3.

WALLACE J S, ILAVSKY J, 1998. Elastic Modulus Measurements in Plasma Sprayed Deposits[J]. Journal of Thermal Spray Technology, 7(4): 521-526.

YOO J, et al, 2002. Physical and Electrical Characteristics of ZrO$_2$ Thin Films as a Promising Gate Dielectrics [J]. Journal of Electronic Materials, 7(31): X5.

Table 116.1 Mechanical Properties of ZrO$_2$(Zirconia) and Zr-based Ceramics

Material-DAM	$T/℃$	E_T	ρ	ν	(σ, ε)	α	k	γ	$\tan\delta$	K_{IC}
ZrO$_2$	23	200	6.02	0.3	$\sigma_{ucs}=-2500$; $\sigma_{uts}=248$	10.3	2.7	420	—	13
	2715 (T_m)	—	—	—	—	—	—	—	—	—
ZrO$_2$ (Porosity=5%)	23	153	5.6	0.27	$\sigma_{uts}=138$; $\sigma_R=189$	9.5	1.97	420	—	10
	400	—	—	—	—	—	2.05	—	—	—
	1000	—	—	—	—	—	2.30	—	—	—
	2715 (T_m)	—	—	—	—	—	—	—	—	—
ZrO$_2$(Coating; Plasma sprayed Partially Stabilized)	23	—	—	0.27	—	—	0.92	474	—	—
	400	—	—	—	—	—	0.90	591	—	—
	600	—	—	—	—	—	0.87	606	—	—
	800	—	—	—	—	—	0.87	618	—	—
Ce-TZP (Ce-Tetragonal Zirconia Polycrystals)	23	215	6.15	—	$\sigma_R=350$	8	2	—	—	18
Mg-PSZ (Partially Stabilised Zirconia)	23	205	5.6	0.23	$\sigma_{ucs}=-1800$; $\sigma_R=800$	8	2	418	—	8
Y-TZP (Tetragonal Zirconia Polycrystals)	23	210	6	0.3	$\sigma_{ucs}=-2000$; $\sigma_R=1000$	10.3	2	400	—	13
ZTA (Zirconia Toughened Al$_2$O$_3$)	23	380	4.15	0.3	$\sigma_R=500$	8	23	—	—	4.5
3Y20A	23	260	5.51	0.3	$\sigma_R=2400$	9.4	3	—	—	6
Zr-10Al-37Cu-3Pd	23	—	—	—	$\sigma_{ucs}=-3584$; $\sigma_{uts}=2469$	—	—	—	—	—
Zr-10Al-37Cu-3Pd	23	—	—	—	$\sigma_{ucs}=-3584$; $\sigma_{uts}=2469$	—	—	—	—	—

Table 116.2   Mechanical Creep Parameters of Zirconium and Zr-based Ceramics

Material	T/℃	Stress /MPa	Strain Rate /s^{-1}	A /$(MPa^{-n} \cdot s^{m-1})$	Q /$(J \cdot mol^{-1})$	n	m
α-Zirconium	300~850	$\sigma_{th}=0$; Low	—	—	90000	1.1	0
	300~850	$\sigma_{th}=0$; Moderate	—	—	270000	6.4	0

Notes: Creep equation $= \dfrac{d\varepsilon_{creep}}{dt} = A\left(\dfrac{\sigma - \sigma_{th}}{E}\right)^n t^m \exp\left(\dfrac{-Q}{R\,T_k}\right)$, $\sigma > \sigma_{th}$;

σ_{th} = Stress threshold and $\sigma_{th} = 0$, if not specified;

Low & Moderate = Low and moderate stress levels;

E = Young's modulus; If given that $E = 1$, it means E is not specified.

Table 116.3   Orthotropic Elastic Properties of ZrO₂(Zirconia) and Zr-based Ceramics

Material-DAM	T/℃	ρ	E_{11}	E_{22}	E_{33}	G_{12}	G_{13}	G_{23}	ν_{12}	ν_{13}	ν_{23}
YSZ (ZrO₂-8Y₂O₃; Coating; Low Porosity)	23	—	—	—	210	—	—	—	0.18	0.18	—
	400	—	—	—	192	—	—	—	—	—	—
	800	—	—	—	181	—	—	—	—	—	—
	1000	—	—	—	—	—	—	—	—	—	—
	1200	—	—	—	175	—	—	—	—	—	—
YSZ (ZrO₂-8Y₂O₃; Coating; Porosity = 5%)	23	—	—	—	165	—	—	—	—	—	—

Table 116.4   Orthotropic Thermal Properties of ZrO₂(Zirconia) and Zr-based Ceramics

Material-DAM	T/℃	α_1	α_2	α_3	k_1	k_2	k_3	γ	β_1	β_2	β_3
YSZ (ZrO₂-8Y₂O₃; Coating; Low Porosity)	23	9.7	9.7	—	—	—	—	—	—	—	—
	600	9.9	9.9	—	—	—	—	—	—	—	—
	800	10	10	—	—	—	—	—	—	—	—
	1000	10.1	10.1	—	—	—	—	—	—	—	—

Chapter 117

Glass, Glass Ceramics, Glass Reinforcements

117.1　Introduction

Mechanical properties of glasses are dual in nature. Below T_g (glass transition temperature), glass is a rigid, brittle material. Above T_g, glass behaves as a viscous liquid with behavior characterized by continuous deformation at a rate inversely related to viscosity, rather than a fixed elastic strain in response to stress.

117.2　Glass

Glasses produced commercially on a large scale mostly belong to these three main groups: soda-lime (Na-glass), lead (Pb-glass) and borosilicate (B-glass), of which soda-lime is by far the most popular one. Mechanical properties of glasses and the related are given in Table 117.1 and their fatigue properties in Table 117.2.

117.2.1　Soda Lime Glass (Na-glass)

Soda-lime glass (Na-glass) is also known as float glass containing sodium and calcium, usually formed by drawing the glass over molten tin baths. The nominally colorless types transmit a very high percentage of visible light. Flat glass (used for window panes) is similar in composition to container glass (used for containers) except that it contains a higher proportion of magnesium oxide.

Soda-lime glass (Na-glass) is the most prevalent type of glass, used for window panes (called float glass) and glass containers (called container glass). Other products include mirrors, microscopic slides, touch screens, filters, photomasks, glass masters, data storage disks, printed circuit substrates, photographic plates, substrates, wafers and optical windows.

117.2.2　Lead Glass (Pb-glass)

The use of lead oxide instead of calcium oxide, and of potassium oxide instead of all or most of the sodium oxide, gives the type of glass commonly known as lead crystal. Glass containing at least 24% PbO can be legitimately described as lead crystal. The addition of lead oxide to glass raises its refractive index and lowers its working temperature and viscosity.

Pb-glass with higher lead oxide (PbO) contents may be used as radiation shielding glasses because of the well-known ability of lead to absorb gamma rays and other forms of harmful radiation.

117.2.3   Borosilicate Glass (B-glass)

As the name implies, borosilicate glass is composed mainly of boric oxide (7%~13%) and silica (70%~80%) with smaller amounts of the alkalis (sodium and potassium oxides) and aluminum oxide. Borosilicate glass has excellent thermal properties with its low coefficient of expansion and high softening point. It offers a high level of resistance to attack from water, acids, salt solutions, organic solvents and halogens. Resistance to alkaline solutions is moderate, as strong alkaline solutions cause rapid corrosion of the glass, as does hydrofluoric acid and hot concentrated phosphoric acid. Fiberglass wool, formed from resin-bonded borosilicate glass fibers, is a lightweight, flexible, thermal and acoustical insulation material designed to provide the ultimate noise reduction. Its density in a non-pressed state is 5~20 kg · m^{-3}, and its thermal conductivity is 0.03~0.04 W/(m^2 · K) at 10 ℃.

Borosilicate glass is widely used for laboratory glassware in light of its low thermal expansion.

117.3   Glass Reinforcements

Traditional glass fibers are used for reinforcing rubbers and plastics and Alkali resistant for reinforcing cement. Frequently used glass is classified into the following categories:

E-Glass: General purpose fiber, resistant to leaching in water;
C-Glass: Corrosion-resistant applications, not generally used as reinforcing material;
AR-glass: Alkali resistant and used for strengthening cement;
A-Glass: Surfacing veils and mats and typical window glass for comparison purposes;
S-Glass: High strength and stiffness.

The nominal composition of each type of glass fibers are given as follows:

Glass Fiber	SiO_2	Al_2O_3	Fe_2O_3	B_2O_3	MgO	CaO	Na_2O	K_2O	TiO_2	ZrO_2
A-glass	73%	1%	0.1%	—	4%	8%	13%	0.5%	—	—
AR-glass	65%	2.5%	—	4%	—	5%	12.5%	—	6%	10%
C-glass	66%	4%	0.2%	5%	3%	13%	9%	0.5%	—	—
E-glass	54%	14%	0.25%	10.5%	3%	20.5%	—	—	—	—
S2-glass	65%	24%	—	—	10%	—	—	—	—	—

117.4　Glass Ceramics

Glass-ceramics are produced by the controlled crystallization method, in which the crystalline phases are nucleated and grown in a glass by means of heat treatment. Both the microstructure and chemical composition of a glass-ceramic determine the general physical, chemical, and optical properties of the final material.

They are also used for glass-ceramic cooktops. The surface of the glass-ceramic cooktop above the burner heats up, but the adjacent surface remains cool because of the low heat conduction coefficient of the material [Smoke].

117.5　Glass Frit Bonding

As a stable hermetical sealing with high reliability, glass frit bonding is used as glass soldering and seal glass bonding, i.e. a wafer bonding technique with an intermediate glass layer [Knechtel]. It is a widely used encapsulation technology for surface micro-machined structures, e.g. accelerometers and gyroscopes [Dresbach et al.].

References

ALBAKRY M, GUAZZATO M, SWAIN M, 2004. Influence of Hot Pressing on the Microstructure and Fracture Toughness of two Pressable Dental Glass-Ceramics [J]. Journal of Biomedical Materials Research: Part B Applied Biomaterials, 71(1): 99-107.

DELLA-BONA A, MECHOLSKY Jr. J, ANUSAVICE K, 2004. Fracture Behavior of Lithia Disilicate- and Leucite-Based Ceramics[J]. Dental Materials, 20(10): 956-962.

DRESBACH C, KROMBHOLZ A, EBERT M, et al, 2006. Mechanical Properties of Glass Frit Bonded Micro Packages[J]. Microsystem Technologies, 12(5): 473-480.

GONZAGA C C, et al, 2008. Mechanical Properties and Porosity of Dental Glass-Ceramics Hot-Pressed at Different Temperatures[J]. Materials Research, 11(3): 301-306.

GRAZIANO P, 1991. Lead Exposure from Lead Crystal[J]. The Lancet, 337(8734): 550.

HOLAND W, BEALL G, 2002. Glass-Ceramics Technology[M]. Westerville: The American Ceramics Society.

KARAMANOV A, PELINO M, 2010. Induced Crystallization Porosity and Properties of Sintered Diopside and Wollastonite Glass-Ceramics[J]. Journal of the European Ceramic Society, 28: 555-562.

KARAMANOV A, PELINO M, 1999. Evaluation of the Degree of Crystallization in Glass-Ceramics by Density Measurements[J]. Journal of European Ceramic Society, 19(5): 649-654.

KNECHTEL R, WIEMER M, FRÖMEL J, 2006. Wafer level encapsulation of microsystems using glass frit bonding[J]. Microsystem Technologies, 12: 468-472.

KNECHTEL R, 2005, Glass Frit Bonding: an Universal Technology for Wafer Level Encapsulation and Packaging[J]. Microsystem Technologies, 12: 63-68.

REKJSON S M, 1986, Viscoelasticity of Glass[J]. Glass: Science and Technology , 3: 1-117.

SEWARD T P, VASCOTT T, 2005. High Temperature Glass Melt Property Database for Process Modeling[M]. American Ceramic Society, Westerville.

SMOKE E J, 1951. Ceramic Compositions Having Negative Linear Thermal Expansion[J]. Journal or the American Ceramic Society, 34 (3): 87-90.

SUN Z, PAN D, WEI J, et al, 2004. Ceramics Bonding Using Solder Glass Frit[J]. Journal of Electronic Materials, 33(12): 1516-1523.

TITE M S, et al, 1998. Lead Glazes in Antiquity: Methods of Production and Reasons for Use [J]. Archaeometry, 40(2): 241-260.

VENKATREDDY P, et al, 2006, Optical and Thermoluminescence Properties of RO-RF-BO Glass Systems Doped with MnO[J]. Journal of Non-Crystalline Solids, 352(32-35): 3561-3566.

WIEDERHORN S M, 1969. Fracture Stress Energy of Glass[J]. Journal of the American Ceramic Society, 52 (2): 99-105.

Table 117.1　Mechanical Properties of Glasses

Material-DAM	$T/{}^\circ\text{C}$	E_T	ρ	ν	(σ, ε)	α	k	γ	$\tan \delta$	K_IC
B-Glass (Borosilicate;	23	64	2.2	0.21	$\sigma_\text{ucs} = -200$; $\sigma_\text{uts} = 68 \pm 33$	3.3	1.2	785	—	0.7
SiO_2-$13\text{B}_2\text{O}_3$-	100	—	—	—	—	—	—	980	—	—
$4(\text{Na}_2\text{O}+\text{K}_2\text{O})$-	568 (T_g)	—	—	—	—	—	—	—	—	—
$2.3\text{Al}_2\text{O}_3$)	1649 (T_m)	—	—	—	—	—	—	—	—	—

continued

Material-DAM	$T/°C$	E_T	ρ	ν	(σ, ε)	α	k	γ	$\tan \delta$	K_{IC}
Na-Glass (Soda Lime; Container Glass; Annealed)	23	71	2.52	0.23	$\sigma_{ucs} = -330$; $\sigma_{uts} = 19$; $\sigma_{crs,3} = 63$ $\sigma_{crs,28} = 52$ $\sigma_{crs,2778} = 49$	8.6	0.96	800	—	0.7
	400	—	—	—	—	—	1.93	—	—	—
	573 (T_g)	—	—	—	—	—	—	—	—	—
Na-Glass (Soda Lime; Container Glass; Toughened by Tempering)	23	72	2.52	0.23	$\sigma_{ucs} = -330$; $\sigma_{uts} = 175$; $\sigma_{crs,3} = 200$ $\sigma_{crs,28} = 185$ $\sigma_{crs,280} = 179$	9	1.05	720	—	0.8
	400	—	—	—	—	—	1.93	—	—	—
	573 (T_g)	—	—	—	—	—	—	—	—	—
Pb-Glass (Glass-48Pb-15Ba; X-ray protection)	23	62.7	4.8	0.23	—	8.2	—	—	—	—
Glass-Ceramic ($MgO-Al_2O_3-SiO_2$)	23	—	—	0.24	$\sigma_R = 245$	—	—	—	—	—
Silica Glass	23	72.4	—	0.23	—	—	—	—	—	—

Notes: Mechanical strengths profoundly weakened if stressed flaws were exposed to water vapor.

Table 117.2 Fatigue ε-N Parameters of Glasses

Material	$T/°C$	$d\varepsilon/dt$	σ_f'	ε_f'	b	c	K'	n'	$\sigma_f @ 2N_f$	R
B-Glass (Annealed)	23	—	—	—	—	—	—	—	49	—
Na-Glass (Annealed)	23	—	—	—	—	—	—	—	49	—

Chapter 118

Porcelains

118.1　Introduction

Porcelains are ceramic materials made by heating selected and refined materials, often including clay in the form of kaolinite to high temperatures. Mechanical properties of porcelains are given in Table 118.1.

118.2　Steatite (MgO-SiO_2)

Steatite, also known as soapstone or soaprock, is a metamorphic rock, a talc-schist. It is primarily composed of the mineral talc and is rich in magnesium. It has good electrical resistance, strength and temperature resistance; lower cost than alumina.

118.3　Cordierite ($2MgO$-$2Al_2O_3$-$5SiO_2$)

Cordierite is a crystalline magnesium aluminosilicate. It has excellent resistance to thermal shock due to low thermal expansion; similar strength and electrical resistance properties to steatite.

118.4　Mullite ($3Al_2O_3$-SiO_2)

Compared with average porcelain, mullite is a much better insulator with more shock resistance, and less expansion.

118.5　Applications

One special application of porcelain ceramics in the automotive industry is caliper brake pads.

References

DAS R, et al, 2002. Rheological Studies on Cordierite Honeycomb Extrusion [J]. Journal of the European

Ceramic Society, 22(16): 2893-2900.

ROHAN P, et al, 2004. Thermal and Mechanical Properties of Cordierite, Mullite and Steatite Produced by Plasma Spraying[J]. Ceramics International, 30(4): 597-603.

TOMBA M A, et al, 2006. Thermal Stress Analysis of Cordierite Materials Subjected to Thermal Shock[J]. Journal of Materials Science, 43(8): 2731-2738.

TRUMBULOVIC L, 2003. Influence of the Cordietrite Lining on the Lost Form Casting Processes[J]. Journal of Mining and Metallurgy, 39(3-4): 475-487.

URTEKIN L, USLAN I, TUC B, 2012. Investigation of Properties of Powder Injection- Molded Steatites[J]. Journal of Materials Engineering and Performance, 21(3): 358-365.

XIAO X L, SHAW L, 2005. Microstructure of Dental Porcelains in a Laser-Assisted Rapid Prototyping Process [J]. Dental Materials, 21(4): 336-346.

ZHANG Y, et al, 2011. Measuring Residual Stress in Ceramic Zirconia-Porcelain Dental Crowns by Nanoindentation[J]. Journal of the Mechanical Behavior of Biomedical Materials, 6: 120-127.

Table 118.1   Mechanical Properties of Porcelains

Material-DAM	$T/°C$	E_T	ρ	ν	(σ, ε)	α	k	γ	$\tan \delta$	K_{IC}
Cordierite ($2MgO\text{-}2Al_2O_3\text{-}5SiO_2$)	23	70	2.6	0.31	$\sigma_{ucs} = -350$; $\sigma_{uts} = 26$	1.7	3.0	1470	—	—
	500	—	—	—	—	3.5	—	—	—	—
	1050 (T_g)	—	—	—	—	—	—	—	—	—
	1470 (T_m)	—	—	—	—	—	—	—	—	—
Mullite ($3Al_2O_3\text{-}SiO_2$; Porosity<5%)	23	150	2.8	0.25	$\sigma_{ucs} = -551$; $\sigma_{uts} = 104$; $\sigma_R = 175$	5.3	6.1	950	—	2
	400	—	—	—	—	—	4.6	—	—	—
	573 (T_g)	—	—	—	—	4.2	—	—	—	—
	1840 (T_m)	—	—	—	—	3.8	—	—	—	—
Steatite (L-3; $H_2Mg_3(SiO_3)_4$)	23	97	2.7	0.24	$\sigma_R = 70$	7.0	2.9	921	—	—
	500	—	—	—	—	8.3	—	—	—	—
	1050 (High service temperature)									
Steatite (L-5; $H_2Mg_3(SiO_3)_4$)	23	138	2.7	0.24	$\sigma_{ucs} = -621$; $\sigma_{uts} = 62$	7.0	2.9	921	—	—
	500	—	—	—	—	8.3	—	—	—	—
	1050 (High service temperature)									

continued

Material-DAM	$T/℃$	E_T	ρ	ν	(σ, ε)	α	k	γ	$\tan \delta$	K_{IC}
Porcelain, Alumina	23	59	2.45	—	$\sigma_{ucs} = -450$; $\sigma_R = 45$	5.7	1.9	1000	—	—
	400 (High service temperature)									
	1625 (T_m)	—	—	—	—	—	—	—	—	—
Porcelain, Zirconia	23	172	3.65	—	—	4.5	5.23	—	—	—
	1100 (High service temperature)									
Brake Pad, Porcelain-Based	23	220	2.3	0.22	$\sigma_R = 172$	11	1.5	878	—	—

Chapter 119

Friction Materials

119.1 Introduction

Automotive friction materials mainly for brakes and clutches are usually metal-based composites. They can be further classified into the following three categories according to their manufacturing process:

(a) Molded- made of binders, reinforcing fibers, friction modifying additives, and fillers;

(b) Woven-spinning fibers into yarn and twisted onto thermal conductive metals (e.g.Cu);

(c) Sintered-expensive but needed for application at elevated temperatures (> 260 ℃).

The dynamic coefficient of friction of such materials has to be stable over the applicable temperature range as meeting the following selective conditions:

(a) Static coefficient of friction being close to dynamic coefficient of friction in order to avoid slip-and-stick problem;

(b) High resistance to high abrasive and adhesive wear;

(c) Good thermal conductivity to dissipate the heat;

(d) Low thermal coefficient of expansion;

(e) High elastic resilience to have a uniform contact pressure distribution;

(f) Insensitive to moisture, oil, dirt, and/or other foreign debris.

Mechanical properties of isotropic brake disks, rotors, and pads are listed in Table 119. 1. Mechanical elastic constants and strengths of orthotropic frictional materials are given in Tables 119.2 and 119.3, respectively.

119.2 Wheel Brake Disks

Disk brakes and drum brakes, as illustrated in Fig. 119.1, are used respectively for front wheels and rear wheels in an economical passenger car, while all disk brakes for more advanced ones. Lateral runout of the friction surface, i.e. the difference between the maximum and minimum read from the dial tip around a circle at 12.7 mm away from the outer circle, is controlled to be less than 0. 05 mm. Automotive brake disks are commonly manufactured out of metals-based composites:

(a) Iron castings, e.g. gray cast iron;

(b) Ti-alloys, e.g. Ti/7.5WC/7.5TiC;

(c) Aluminum-metal matrix composites, e.g. AA 6061/20SiC and AA6061-Cu/20SiC.

Carbon-reinforced disks and ceramic disks may be used for racing and luxurious vehicles, railway trains, and airplanes. Both moduli of elasticity and damping capacity of cast iron play a significant role in the propensity of the brake rotor to generate noise. The high carbon composite rotor material reduces the squeal noise propensity.

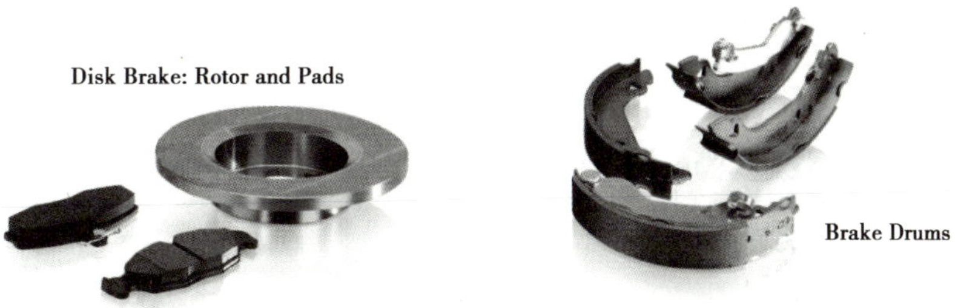

Fig. 119.1   Disk and Drum Brakes of a Passenger Car

Brake discs may be damaged in one of the following four ways: scarring, cracking, warping and excessive rusting. Excessive or heavy and continuous braking may warp brake rotors. It may also cause the rotors to warp when braking hard (heating the rotors a lot) and then to go through water (which quickly cools the hot rotors). If the brake pads or brake rotors are thin, the rotors tend to warp.

119.3   Wheel Disk Brake Pads

A typical friction pad (non-asbestos) consists of polymer/ceramic/metallic fibers (also called fillers), abrasives, binders, and solid lubricants.

Fibers: Fibers are major constituents of non-asbestos organic brake pad materials. It is generally a combination of relatively inexpensive minerals and fibers such as steel wool, potassium titanate, aramid pulp, barytes ($BaSO_4$), calcium carbonate ($CaCO_3$), calcium hydroxide [$Ca(OH)_2$].

Abrasives: Abrasive particulates are added to friction material formulation in order to attain an increased level of dynamic friction. Abrasives include alumina (Al_2O_3), silica (SiO_2), magnesia (MgO), magnetite (Fe_3O_4), chromium (Cr_2O_3), zirconium silicate ($ZrSiO_4$), and silicon carbide-carborundum (SiC-carborundum).

Binders: Straight phenolic resin (SR), cashew nut shell liquid modified resin (CR), epoxy-modified resin (ER) and melamine resin (MR) are binding materials of choice for automotive brakes.

Solid Lubricants: They provide friction stability over the given range of interfacial temperatures. They also reduce the wear of the friction material components and enable the minimization of slip-stick interactions. Antimony trisulfide (Sb_2S_3), copper sulphide (CuS), zinc sulfide (ZnS), and copper sulfide (Cu_2S) are typical solid lubricants.

Ceramic compounds, copper fibers and carbon fibers in place of the semi-metallic pad's steel fibers accommodate higher temperatures with less heat fade and generate less dust and wear on both the pads and rotors.

119.4   Flywheel Clutch Disks

A flywheel clutch consists of friction discs, floater plates, pressure plate donuts and a pressure plate cover, of which each component has a distinct material designation. A clutch provides smooth engagement and dampens engine vibrations. Clutch friction disks are designed for smooth operation as engineered for driver's comfort, less likelihood for the drivetrain to stall, and cushioning between engine and transmission. The flywheel clutch disk is installed between the pressure plate and flywheel. Low- and high-ended materials for flywheel clutch disk are listed, respectively, as follows:

  (a) Organic disk: Phenolic composites, with reinforcing cellulose and heat-resisting stuff (e.g. mineral wool);
  (b) Kevlar disk: Chopped kevlar strands-reinforced phenolic composites.

The splined hub, opening at the center of Fig. 119.2, is mated to a splined transmission shaft when the clutch is engaged.

Fig. 119.2   Clutch Disk Installed between Pressure Plate and Flywheel [Courtesy of MotoIQ]

119.5   Transmission Clutches-Friction Disks and Separator Plates

Most multiple-disk clutches (Fig. 119.3) used in automotive transmissions operate wet. Clutch plates are fixed to the stationary drum, while clutch disks slide freely in the axial direction but rotate with the transmission shaft before they are engaged. When actuated (e.g. axially pushed together by a piston), they are pressed against each other to transmit the torque by friction. The lubricant serves as a promising coolant. More than one set of disks/plates are employed to enhance the torque transmission as

$$T = \frac{2\ F\mu_{\mathrm{D}}(R_{\mathrm{o}}^{3} - R_{\mathrm{i}}^{3})}{3\ (R_{\mathrm{o}}^{2} - R_{\mathrm{i}}^{2})}\ N$$

where:

F: Actuating force;

μ_{D}: Dynamic coefficient of friction;

R_{o}: Outside radius in contact with clutch plate;

R_{i}: Inside radius in contact with clutch plate;

N: Number of frictional interfaces.

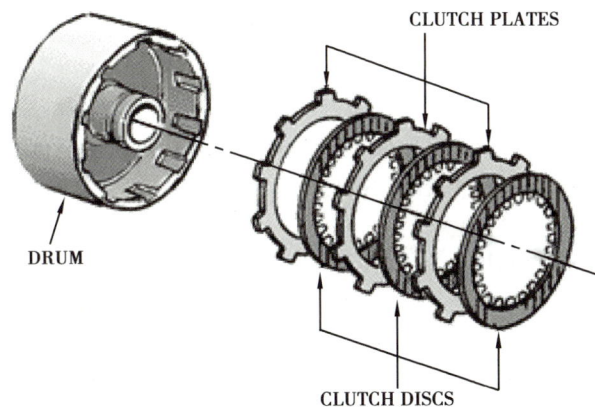

Fig. 119.3   **Exploded View of Clutch Plates and Disks as Packed in a Transmission Drum**

119.6   Accelerator and Brake Pedals

An accelerator pedal is expected to have a steady force-displacement hysteresis loop in one operating cycle, and so is a brake pedal. Inexpensive frictional materials may be used to achieve this goal.

References

ABDULLAH O I, SCHLATTMANN J, 2012. Finite Element Analysis of Temperature Field in Automotive Dry Friction Clutch[J]. Tribology in Industry, 34(4): 206-216.

BERETTA S, et al, 2008. An Investigation of the Effects of Corrosion on the Fatigue Strength of AlN Axle Steel [J]. Journal of Rail and Rapid Transit, 222(2): 129-143.

BIJWE J N, MUJUMDAR N, SATAPATHY B K, 2005. Influence of Modified Phenolic Resin on the Fade and Recovery Behavior of Friction Materials[J]. Wear, 259: 1068-1078.

BLAU P, et al, 2007. Tribological Investigation of Titanium-Based Materials for Brakes[J]. Wear, 263: 1202-1211.

BOZ M, KURT A, 2007. The Effect of Al_2O_3 on the Friction Performance of Automotive Brake Friction Materials[J]. Tribology International, 40: 1161-1169.

BREZOLIN A, SOARES M, 2007. Influence of Friction Material Properties on Thermal Disc Crack Behavior in Brake Systems[J]. SAE 2007-01-2790.

CHO M H, KIM S J, CHO K H, et al, 2007. Complementary Effects of Solid lubricants in the Automotive Brake Lining[J]. Tribology International, 40(1): 15-20.

CHOI Y, LIU R, 2006. Rolling Contact Fatigue Life of Finish Hard Machined Surfaces[J]. Wear, 261 (5-6): 429-499.

CHOON Y L, ILSUP C, YOUNG S C, 2007. Finite Element Analysis of an Automobile Clutch System[J]. Key Engineering Materials, 353/358(4): 2707-2711.

CUEVA G, SINATORA A, GUESSER W, et al, 2003. Wear Resistance of Cast Irons Used in Brake Disc[J]. Wear, 255: 1256-1260.

GAO Y, LONG R, PANG Y, et al, 2010. Fatigue Properties of an Electrical Steel and Design of EV/HEV IPM Motor Rotors for Durability and Efficiency[J]. SAE 2010-01-1308.

GOO B, LIM C, 2012. Thermal Fatigue of Cast Iron Brake Disk Materials[J]. Journal of Mechanical Science and Technology, 26(6): 1719-1724.

HAN L, HUANG L, ZHANG J, et al, 2006. Optimization of Ceramic Friction Materials [J]. Composites Science and Technology, 66: 2895-2906.

HEE K W, FILP P, 2005. Performance of Ceramic Enhanced Phenolic Matrix Brake Lining Materials for Automotive Brake Lining[J]. Wear, 259: 1088-1096.

HO S, CHERN L J, JU C, 2005. Effect of Fiber Addition on Mechanical and Tribological Properties of a Copper/Phenolic Based Friction Material[J]. Wear, 258: 861-869.

HOWELL G J, BALL A, 1995. Dry Sliding Wear of Particulate-Reinforced Aluminum Alloys against Automobile Friction Materials[J]. Wear, 181/183: 379-390.

HWANG P, WU X, 2010. Investigation of Temperature and Thermal Stress in Ventilated Disc Brake Based on 3D Thermomechanical Coupling Model[J]. Journal of Mechanical Science and Technology, 24: 81-84.

IVANOVIÉ V, et al, 2009. Experimental Characterization of Wet Clutch Friction Behaviors Including Thermal Dynamics[J]. SAE International Journal of Engines, 2(1): 1211-1220.

JACOBSSON H, 2003. Aspects of Disc Brake Judder[J]. Journal of Automobile Engineering, Proc. Instn Mech. Engrs, 217: Part D.

KIM J, CHO M, LIM D, et al, 2001. Synergistic Effects of Aramid Pulp and Potassium Titanate Whiskers in the Automotive Friction Material[J]. Wear, 251: 1484-1491.

KIM M G, et al, 1996. Sensitivity Analysis of Chassis System to Improve Shimmy and Brake Judder Vibration on the Steering Wheel[J]. SAE 960734.

KINKAID N M, O'REILLY, 2003. Review: Automotive Discbrake Squeal[J]. Journal of Sound and Vibration, 267: 105-166.

LUCENTE G, et al, 2011. Modeling of an Automated Manual Transmission System[J]. Mechatronics, 17(2-3): 73-91.

MOHANTY S, CHUGH Y, 2007. Development of Fly Ash-Based Automotive Brake Lining[J]. Tribology International, 40: 1217-1224.

OZTURK B, OZTURK S, 2011. Effects of Resin Type and Fiber Length on the Mechanical and Tribological Properties of Brake Friction Materials[J]. Tribology Letters, 42(3): 339-350.

PRUETT J G, 1997. Modeling of Friction Performance in Carbon/Carbon Brake Materials[J]. Proceedings of the Carbon, 2: 578-579.

QI G, ZHANG G, PU X, 2013. The Effect of the Composition and Microstructure of Gray Cast Iron Brake Rotor on Squeal Noise[J]. SAE 2013-01-2031.

RAMOUSSE S, HOJ J W, SORENSEN O T, 2001. Thermal Characterization of Brake Pads[J]. Journal of Thermal Analysis and Calorimetry, 64: 933-943.

RASHID A, STRÖMBERG N, 2013. Sequential simulation of thermal stresses in disc brakes for repeated braking[J]. Proceedings of the Institution of Mechanical Engineers, Part J: Journal of Engineering Tribology, 227(8): 919-929.

SHAHZAMANIAN M M, 2010. Transient and Thermal Contact Analysis for the Elastic Behavior of Functionally Graded Brake Disks due to Mechanical and Thermal Loads[J]. Materials and Design, 31(10): 4655-4665.

SHAW P, RIEHLE M, KUNG S, 2003. Mechanical Properties of Friction Materials and the Effect on Brake System Stability[J]. SAE 2003-01-1619.

SILVA J, PEREIRA C, CASARIL A, et al, 2012. Modeling of the Elastic Modulus of Brake Pad Materials with High Viscoelastic Content[J]. SAE 2012-01-1786.

SLAVIĚ J, BRYANT M, BOLTEŽAR M, 2007. A New Approach to Roughness-Induced Vibrations on a Slider

[J]. Journal of Sound and Vibration, 306(3-5): 732-750.

TALATI F, JALALIFAR S, 2009. Analysis of Heat Conduction in a Disk Brake System[J]. Heat Mass Transfer, 45(8): 1047-1059.

WANG G, FU R, 2013. Impact of Brake Pad Structure on Temperature and Stress Fields of Brake Disc[J]. Advances in Materials Science and Engineering, 2013(1): 1-9.

WANG R M, SURAPPA M K, 1998. Microstructure and Interface Structure Studies of SiCp-Reinforced Al (6061) Metal-Matrix Composites[J]. Materials Science and Engineering A, 254 (1-2): 219-226.

WAWRZONEK L, BIALECKI R, 2008. Temperature in a Disk Brake, Simulation and Experimental Verification[J]. International Journal of Numerical Methods for Heat & Fluid Flow, 18(3-4): 387-400.

YAMABE J, et al, 2002. Development of Disc Brake Rotors for Trucks with High Thermal Fatigue Strength[J]. JSAE Review, 23(1): 105-112.

YOO J S, et al, 1998. Mechanical Characteristics of Carbon/Carbon Composite for Aircraft Brake Disk[J]. Journal of the Korean Society for Composite Materials, 11: 59-73.

YOUSEF M, et al, 2009. Generalized Braking Characteristics of Friction Pad Synthetic Graphite Composites [J]. Tribology International, 43: 838-843.

ZAGRODZKI P, 2009. Thermoelastic Instability in Friction Clutches and Brakes-Transient Modal Analysis Revealing Mechanisms of Excitation of Unstable Modes[J]. International Journal of Solids and Structures, 46: 2463-2476.

ZAGRODZKI P, 1990. Analysis of Thermomechanical Phenomena in Multi－Disk Clutches and Brakes[J]. Wear, 140: 291-308.

ZHANG S, WANG F, 2007. Comparison of Friction and Wear Performances of Brake Material Dry Sliding against Two Aluminum Matrix Composites Reinforced with Different SiC Particles[J]. Journal of Materials Processing Technology, 182: 122-127.

Table 119.1 Mechanical Properties of Isotropic Brake Disks/Rotors/Pads

Material-DAM	$T/^\circ C$	E_T	ρ	ν	(σ, ε)	α	k	γ	$\tan \delta$	μ_d
G6000 (GJL 400)	See Chapter 76									
GJV450	See Chapter 76									
Ti/7.5WC/7.5TiC	23	—	4.68	0.3	$\sigma_{ucs} = -1300$	9	—	510	—	0.31
Al6061/SiC	23	—	2.7	—	$\sigma_{ucs} = -406$	—	—	980	—	0.35
Al6061-Cu/SiC	23	—	2.8	—	$\sigma_{ucs} = -761$	—	—	920	—	0.44

Notes: μ_d = Dynamic coefficient of friction.

Table 119.2   Elastic Constants of Orthotropic Automotive Friction Materials

Specification	$T/\text{°C}$	ρ	E_{11}	E_{22}	E_{33}	G_{12}	G_{13}	G_{23}	ν_{12}	ν_{13}	ν_{23}
C/C Brake Disk	23	2.3	103	20.2	3.5	17	5.5	1.38	0.3	0.2	0.2
SiC/C (Brake Disk)	23	1.8	—	—	—	—	—	—	—	—	—
Pad (Brake; Density-Dependent)	23	2.3	11	11	3	—	—	—	0.25	0.25	0.25
	23	3.2	25	25	7	—	—	—	—	—	—
Disk (Clutch)	23	1.3	70	70	70	—	—	—	—	—	—

Table 119.3   Orthotropic Mechanical Strengths of Automotive Friction Materials

Material	$T/\text{°C}$	$(\sigma_{11u}, \varepsilon_{11u})$	$(\sigma_{22u}, \varepsilon_{22u})$	$(\sigma_{33u}, \varepsilon_{33u})$	$(\sigma_{12u}, \varepsilon_{12u})/(\sigma_{23u}, \varepsilon_{23u})/(\sigma_{13u}, \varepsilon_{13u})$
C/C Brake Disk	23	$\sigma_{11c}=-90$ $\sigma_{11t}=60$	$\sigma_{22c}=-14.1$ $\sigma_{11t}=11.8$	$\sigma_{33c}=-120$ $\sigma_{33t}=3$	$\sigma_{12u}=54/\sigma_{23u}=1.1/\sigma_{13u}=5.7$

Notes: C = Carbon;

σ_{iit} (MPa) & ε_{iit} = Ultimate tensile stresses & strains in the material axes (1, 2, 3);

σ_{iic} (MPa) & ε_{iic} = Ultimate compressive stresses & strains in the material axes (1, 2, 3);

σ_{iju} (MPa) & ε_{iju} = Ultimate shear stresses & strains in primary material axes (1, 2, 3).

Table 119.4   Orthotropic Thermal Properties of Automotive Friction Materials

Specification	$T/\text{°C}$	ρ	α_1	α_2	α_3	k_1	k_2	k_3	γ	μ
SiC/Carbon Fabrics (Brake Disk)	23	1.8	3.9	3.9	4.0	4.5	4.5	3.4	800	—
	100	—	—	—	—	—	—	—	—	0.46
	200	—	—	—	—	—	—	—	—	0.47
	400	—	—	—	—	—	—	—	—	0.55
	600	—	—	—	—	—	—	—	—	0.62
	800	—	—	—	—	—	—	—	1200	—
Pad (Brake)	23	2.5	60	60	60	12	12	12	900	—
Disc (Brake)	23	7.85	—	—	—	43	43	43	445	—
Disc (Clutch)	23	1.3	—	—	—	0.25	0.25	0.25	1274	—

Notes: ρ (g/cm^3) = Density;

α_1, α_2, α_3 (μm/m/°C) = Coefficients of linear thermal expansion of a unidirectional lamina;

k_1, k_2, k_3 (W/m/°C) = Thermal conductivities of a unidirectional lamina;

β_1, β_2, β_3 (μm/m/%) = Swelling coefficients of linear moisture expansion;

γ (J/kg/°C) = Specific heat capacity;

μ = Coefficient of friction.

Chapter 120

Anti-Friction Materials (Bearing Materials)

120.1   Introduction

Bearing is a member designed to permit relative motion between two mechanical elements. The durable operation of a bearing is achieved if its material combines high strength (load capacity, wear resistance, cavitation resistance) with the softness (compatibility, conformability, embeddability). So bearing materials should be both strong and soft. It sounds paradoxical but all existing bearing materials are designed to combine those contradictory properties with a certain compromise. All these, factors of concern are listed as follows:

Fatigue Strength (*Load Capacity*): It is the maximum value of cycling stress a bearing can withstand without developing fatigue cracks after an infinite number of cycles.

Wear resistance: It is the ability of the bearing material to maintain its dimensional stability (oil clearance) under conditions of mixed lubrication regime and in the presence of foreign particles carried by the lubricant.

Compatibility: The shaft and bearing materials in rubbing conditions should resist localized welding and seizing especially during startup and shutdown when thin-film lubrication is expected. A good bearing-shaft metal combination is necessary.

Conformability: It helps accommodate misalignment and increases the pressure bearing area (reduction in the localized force). Relatively soft-bearing alloys are better off in this respect. The bearing material should usually be softer than that of the journal to prevent shaft wear but hard enough to resist adhesive and abrasive wear of its own surface.

Embeddability: It is the ability of a material to hide dirt and foreign particles to prevent scoring and wear. Materials with high hardness are better off.

Low Coefficient of Friction: Sliding surfaces, along with the lubricant, can provide a low friction coefficient for reducing damage at high efficiency.

Low Thermal Expansion: The size should remain nearly constant during periods of temperature change.

High Thermal Conductivity: The ability to quickly dissipate heat due to friction.

Wettability: An affinity for lubricants to adhere to the bearing surface and spread to form a protective film.

Cavitation resistance: It is the ability of the bearing material to withstand impact stresses caused by collapsing cavitation bubbles, which form as a result of sharp and localized drops of pressure in the circulating lubricant.

Elasticity : Material should be elastic enough to allow the bearing to return to its original shape upon relief of stresses that may cause temporary distortion, such as misalignment and overloading, even at elevated temperatures. Its yield strength must be high enough to take care of all load-speed combinations.

Corrosion Resistance : Some protection can be provided by forming a thin layer of anti-corrosion materials on the bearing alloy surface since oxidized products of oils corrode bearing alloys.

Bearings are easier to replace than shafts that require the dismantling of the machine. If one bearing is worn out, only that bearing needs replacement instead of the whole shaft. Automotive bearings in practice are mostly aluminum-, copper-, lead-, tin-, and zinc-based alloys. Their mechanical properties and related overlay/coating materials are listed in the following tables, respectively

 (a) Aluminum-based plain bearings : Table 120.1 ;
 (b) Copper-based plain bearings : Table 120.2 ;
 (c) Lead-based plain bearings : Table 120.3 ;
 (d) Tin-based plain bearings : Table 120.4 ;
 (e) Zinc-based plain bearings : Table 120.5 ;
 (f) Overlay/coating materials : Table 120.6.

Mechanical fatigue parameters for these materials are given in Table 120.7.

120.2   Plain Bearings

A plain bearing structure may be layered with a soft overlay applied over strong linings or a particulate structure, in which small particles of a soft material are distributed in a relatively strong matrix. In general, the load-carrying capacity of the conventional tri-metal bearing with lead-based overlay is about 70 MPa which is higher than that of bi-metal bearings with Al-Sn-Si lining at 55 MPa. The length of bearing should be at least equal to the diameter, but preferable to have it two times the diameter. The three major automotive journal bearings are

 (a) Main bearings between the crankshaft and engine block ;
 (b) Crank bearings between the connecting rod and crankshaft ;
 (c) Cross-head bearings between the piston pin and connecting rod.

When there is one layer of coating material over a backing substrate, it is called a bimetal bearing. In bimetal bearings, the maximum thickness of the overlay is kept within 0.8 mm. The wall thickness of backing material in bimetal bearings is of the order of 30% of the bore diameter with a minimum value of 1.5 μm.

When there is one layer of intermediate material between the overlay and the backing substrate, it is called a trimetal bearing. Fatigue of a tri-metal bearing starts from the fatigue of its overlay. Since the overlay is thin (0.012 ~ 0.020 mm), the fatigue cracks are thin and not deep. The bearing with the fatigued overlay may continue to work for a long but limited time. Gradual development of the fatigue cracks causes the overlay fragments to flake off from the surface and leads to the complete loss of the overlay from a part of the bearing area.

A housing fit for journal bearings should be around 0.0125 mm to 0.050 mm tight (i.e. in interference) for bearings up to 100 mm in diameter. Care must be taken in selecting housing and shaft diameters to assure that there is a loose fit (with clearance) between the bearing bore and the shaft. Eq. (1.71) can be applied to determining the reduction in bore diameter due to a tight housing fit:

$$
\frac{\delta_r}{R_c} = P_c \frac{\dfrac{1 + k_1^{-2}}{1 - k_1^{-2}} - \nu_1}{E_1} + \frac{\dfrac{1 + k_2^{-2}}{1 - k_2^{-2}} + \nu_2}{E_2}
$$

Where:

$k_1 \equiv R_{o,1} / R_{i,1}$;
$k_2 \equiv R_{o,2} / R_{i,2}$;
$R_{o,1}$ & $R_{i,1}$: Outer and inner radii of the bearing (cylinder 1);
$R_{o,2}$ & $R_{i,2}$: Outer and inner radii of the housing (cylinder 2).

Assume that parameter $R_{o,2}$ is relatively larger than parameter $R_{i,2}$ and the journal bearing is thin. One has $k_1^{-2} \approx 1$ and

$$
\frac{\delta_r}{R_c} = P_c \frac{\dfrac{1 + k_1^{-2}}{1 - k_1^{-2}} - \nu_1}{E_1} + \frac{1 + \nu_2}{E_2}
$$

Thus, the reduction in the bearing bore radius due to a tight housing fit as

$$
\frac{\delta_b}{R_c} = \frac{k_1}{(1 + k_1^{-2}) - (1 - k_1^{-2})\left[-\nu_1 + (1 + \nu_2)\dfrac{E_1}{E_2}\right]} \left(\frac{\delta_r}{R_c}\right)
$$

or

$$
\delta_b = \frac{k_1}{(1 + k_1^{-2}) - (1 - k_1^{-2})\left[-\nu_1 + (1 + \nu_2)\dfrac{E_1}{E_2}\right]} \delta_r
$$

Note that the reduction in bearing bore diameter is twice as much, i.e. $2\delta_b$. A simplified formula to determine how much a bearing bore diameter changes in size as a result of temperature change (ΔT) is

$$2\delta_{b,\text{thermal}} = (R_{o,1} + R_{i,1})\ \alpha_1\ \Delta T$$

where:

$\delta_{b,\text{thermal}}$: Bearing bore change in radius due to temperature change;

α_1: Apparent coefficient of linear thermal expansion of bearing material;

ΔT: Temperature change.

120.3　Bi-metal Plain Bearings

120.3.1　Aluminum-based Bimetal Plain Bearings

Aluminum-based bearing alloys commonly contain tin ($6\% \sim 40\%$) as a soft component. Tin remains in the free state to provide a better bearing surface. Aluminum matrix of engine bearing alloys may be strengthened by an addition of copper, nickel, chromium, manganese, magnesium, and/or zinc etc. Aluminum-tin-silicon bearings are much more reliable when a mixed regime of lubrication is realized.

Aluminum bimetal bearings have good fatigue strength, load-bearing capacity, thermal conductivity, and low corrosion resistance. Generally they have no overlay (babbitt materials) and may embed foreign particles of a greater size (greater than 0.0125 mm). Such macro-particles cannot be retained by thin Babbitt overlays of tri-metal bearings and they are actually responsible for damaging journals and bearings and ultimately causing engine failure.

Thermal expansion is relatively high and this restricts their usage at high temperatures.

120.3.2　Cadmium-Based Bi-metal Plain Bearings

Cadmium alloys offer good fatigue resistance and excellent compatibility. However, the material is expensive and its corrosion resistance is poor.

120.3.3　Silver-Based Bi-metal Plain Bearings

Silver may be used as deposited material on steel with an overlay of lead. The addition of lead improves the embeddability, anti-weld and anti-scoring properties. It is expensive, while lead is poisonous.

120.4   Multi-Layered Plain Bearings

A multi-layered plain bearing may be designed to meet the application need, i.e. obtain good embeddability conformability and compatibility.

Trimetal bearings are derived from electroplating, casting, or high-velocity oxyfuel (HVOF) spraying [Sturgeon et al.] a thin layer of soft material (e.g. tin-copper overlay) on a bimetal bearing. In trimetal bearings, the surface layer thickness could be as low as 25 μm. Al-Sn-Cu (e.g. Al-20Sn-1Cu) is the typical overlay material. The thin overlay of bearing metal can be worn away before the end of the normal operating life of the bearing. It is normal to have one or two thicker and harder layers of bearing materials beneath the soft thin top layer, as being bonded to a steel backing strip. In the event of loss of the soft, thin layer, the harder layer can still protect the journal. With an increase in overlay (babbitt) thickness, the overall fatigue strength decreases. The thickness of the overlay can be as low as 0.12 mm for most overlays (babbitts).

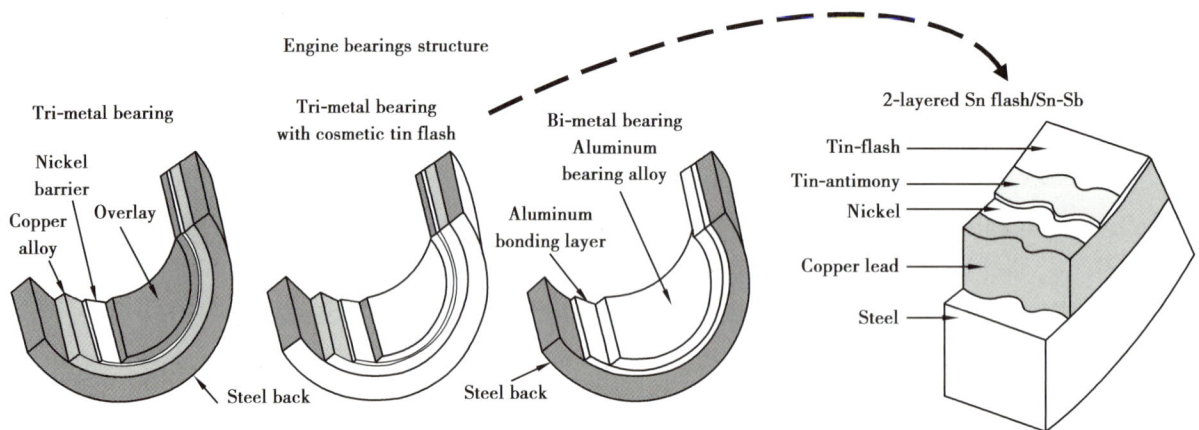

Fig. 120.1   Multi-layered Engine Bearing Structure

In general, the load-carrying capacity of the conventional tri-metal bearing with lead-based overlay is about 70 MPa which is higher than that of bi-metal bearings with Al-Sn-Si lining at 55 MPa. Fatigue of a tri-metal bearing starts from the fatigue of its overlay. Since the overlay is thin (0.012~0.02 mm), the fatigue cracks are thin and not deep. The bearing with the fatigued overlay may continue to work for a long (but limited) time. Gradual development of the fatigue cracks causes the overlay fragments to flake off from the surface and leads to the complete loss of the overlay from a part of the bearing area.

Traditional main journal bearings linking crankshaft to conrod for heavy-duty internal combustion engines are multi-layered as demonstrated in Fig. 120.1. A modern tri-metal bearing in fact has five layers:

(a) Backing substrate: Steel, such as SAE 1008, SAE 1010, or SAE1020, is generally used for the backing substrate material.

(b) Copper layer: It provides mild structural stiffness with excellent heat dissipation.

(c) Nickel barrier plating: It prevents or limits the diffusion of metallic components from the babbitt layer (anti-friction) into the copper supporting layer and vice versa.

(d) Overlay layer or coating of a relatively softer material on barrier plating, e. g. tin-antimony.

(e) Tin flash coating is to protect and provide potential boundary lubrication.

120.5   Rubber Bearings

It is used where quiet operation is desired, large clearances and misalignment are encountered. Found in bearings for propeller and rudder shafts of boats and ships. Found where water acts as a lubricant or is likely to be a contaminant. Even when sand and gravel are present, the resilience of water is an added advantage. Wet rubber is very slippery; hence it is used in such situations to reduce friction.

120.6   Graphite-Based Bearings

It is used for food handling equipment and in the textile industry. Because of the self-lubricating property, no additional lubricant is required, hence limiting lubricant contamination prospects. Since it is resistant to corrosion, it can be used even in water.

120.7   Teflon-Based Bearings

It is a plastic with self-lubricating properties and low friction. However, it has poor strength, low wear resistance and a tendency to deform under load. Being reinforced with fibers improves the strength. A typical Teflon-based is shown in Fig. 120.2. The key to self-lubricating bearings is the rapid transfer of PTFE from the bearing ID to the shaft surface during the initial break-in phase. The film of PTFE on the shaft functions as a dry lubricant, which reduces the friction and wear rate.

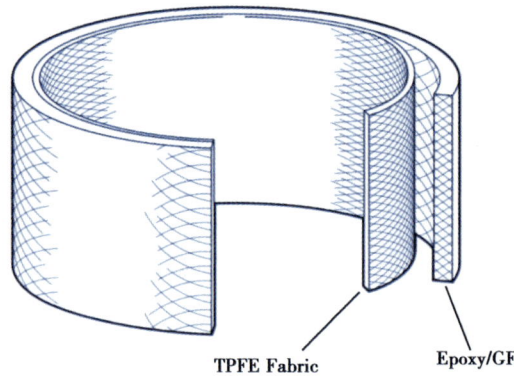

TPFE Fabric   Epoxy/GF

Fig. 120.2   PTFE Fabric-Based Self-Lubricating Journal Bearing

120.8   Phenolic-Based Bearings

Laminated phenolics are formed by treating sheets of either paper or cotton fabric with asbestos or other filler materials bonded using phenolic resin. These are stacked to obtain the desired thickness and subjected to heat and pressure to bond the sheets firmly and later formed into required shapes. It has been used in aircraft landing gears. It is used in several applications where water is a lubricant, such as in rolling mills where water is used for cooling and lubricating; also used in rudder bearings and centrifugal pumps.

120.9   Porous Bearings

Porous bearings are made using powder metallurgy techniques by sintering powdered bronze, iron, brass, graphite etc, and obtaining the requisite bearing housing shape by compressing the powder. This is then impregnated with oil/grease. Most porous-metal bearings consist of either bronze or iron which has interconnecting pores. These voids take up to 10% to 35% of the total volume. The quantity of oil depends on load and speed, for which the bearing is used. Adding from 1% to 3.5% graphite frequently enhances self-lubricating properties, but lowers the strength of the bearings. After sintering, the bearing must be sized to the specified dimensions. Sizing reduces interconnected porosity and produces greater strength, lower ductility, and a smoother finish. High porosity with a maximum amount of lubricating oil is used for high-speed light-load applications, such as fractional-horsepower motor bearings. A low-oil-content low-porosity material with a high content of graphite is more satisfactory for oscillating and reciprocating motions where it is hard to build up an oil film.

The variation of pressure along the circumferential direction and the temperature variation cause oil to flow through the pores due to capillary action into the clearance space between the bearing housing and journal. Any oil, which is forced from the loaded zone of the bearing, is reabsorbed by capillary action. Because these bearings can operate for long periods without additional lubricant, they can be used in inaccessible or inconvenient places where re-lubrication would be difficult.

Powder producers can control powder characteristics such as purity, hydrogen loss, particle size and distribution, and particle shape. Each of these properties affects the bearing performance. Lubricants used in the mix have only a slight influence on dimensional change, but a more pronounced effect on the apparent density and flow rate. Materials used for porous bearings are given as follows:

Bronzes: The most common porous bearing material, consisting of Cu-10Sn (90% copper and 10% tin). These bronze bearings are wear-resistant, ductile, conformable, and corrosion resistant. Their lubricity, embeddability, and low cost give them a wide range of applications from home appliances to farm machinery.

Leaded bronze: It is Cu-8Sn-15Pb, which results in a lower coefficient of friction and good resistance to galling in case the lubricant supply is interrupted in comparison with Cu-10Sn. These alloys also have higher conformability than Cu-10Sn bronze.

Copper iron: The inclusion of iron in the composition boosts compressive strength, although the speed limit drops accordingly. These materials are useful in applications involving shock and heavy loads and should be used with hardened shafts.

Hardenable copper iron: The addition of 1.5% free carbon to copper-iron materials allows them to be heat treated to a particle hardness of Rockwell C65. They provide high impact resistance and should be used with hardened-and-ground shafts.

Iron: This yields a combination of low cost with good bearing qualities, widely used in automotive applications, toys, farm equipment, and machine tools. Powdered iron is frequently blended with up to 10% copper for improved strength. These materials have a relatively low limiting value of PV (on the V side), but have high oil-volume capacity because of high porosity. They have good resistance to wear, but should be used with hardened-and-ground steel shafts.

Leaded iron: Provide improved speed capability, but are still low-cost bearing materials.

Aluminum: They provide cooler operation, greater tolerance for misalignment, lower weight, and longer oil life than porous bronze or iron. The limiting PV value is 50000, which is the same as porous bronze and porous iron. Al-Sn-Si alloy with MoS_2 layer showed about 70% lower friction and about 10% lower wear depth compared to the corresponding Al-Sn-Si alloy [Miyajima et al.].

120.10   Rolled Bearing（Strip Bearing）

As made by rolling a sheet or strip, and due to the nature of the manufacturing process, the bearing housing is split requiring various joining techniques to close this split. Sometimes they are provided with a fiber-lined cloth of PTFE/Graphite fibers on the inside of the housing for friction reduction and improved strength. Among non-metallic bushes, rubber and graphite have been traditionally used. Nylon is a valuable plastic material for bushing because of low friction though it has low strength and is suitable for low speeds due to heating effect. These are used in grinders and mixers because of their resistance to corrosion and quiet operation.

120.11   Lubrication Supply

The lubricating oil must enter the bearing faster than it leaks out. The lubricating oil can be supplied by means of oil rings, oil collars, splash, oil bath, oil grooves/holes, and even oil pump. If the minimum oil film thickness is 1.5 μm（0.0015 mm）or lower, mixed lubrication regime occurs frequently and the multi-layered（tri-metal）bearings with soft thin overlays are less suitable than Al-Si bearings.

A classical lubrication path can be illustrated using a diesel engine lubrication system. Engine oil is stored in the oil pan and pumped through channeled holes into the main journal bearings and cam journal bearings. Grooves are provided in bearing surfaces to enable oil flow into the bearing area and to spread along the surface such as the diesel engine liners and piston wrist pins. Crankshaft journals are case-hardened to the extent where they can abrade foreign particles. The bearing surfaces are kept soft such as tin-based babbitt as this allows the foreign particles to become embedded in the soft bearing material and reduces the probability of wear elsewhere in the engine.

120.12   Coating and Spray

Coatings applied to a bearing have to be taken into consideration when making a bearing selection. A bearing coating is a polymer composite consisting of a polymer matrix（e.g. PAI, PI, Epoxy, and Phenolics）filled with particles of solid lubricants, including MOS_2（molybdenum disulfide）and graphite. Coatings can help eliminate or reduce metal-to-metal contact between the bearing and the journal surfaces during start-up and the initial period of bearing operation. Some coatings and tin flash（100% Sn）materials are given in Table 120.6.

In order to meet the demands of hybrid and other start/stop engines, FDML comes up with IROX [FDML] bearings that have an overlay that is a PAI (PolyAmideImide) polymer resin binder containing a number of additives dispersed throughout the matrix. These additives provide a variety of properties to the finished coating, such as wear resistance, mechanical strength, thermal conductivity and embeddability that is the ability to safely envelop loose abrasive particles. With the Irox overlay [PAI + micro particulates], a combination of the embedded hard particles' polishing effect and the polymer's ductility help reduce wear based one aluminum alloy A-650 substrate (Al-6Sn-4Si-...), as shown in Fig. 120.3 [Adam et al.].

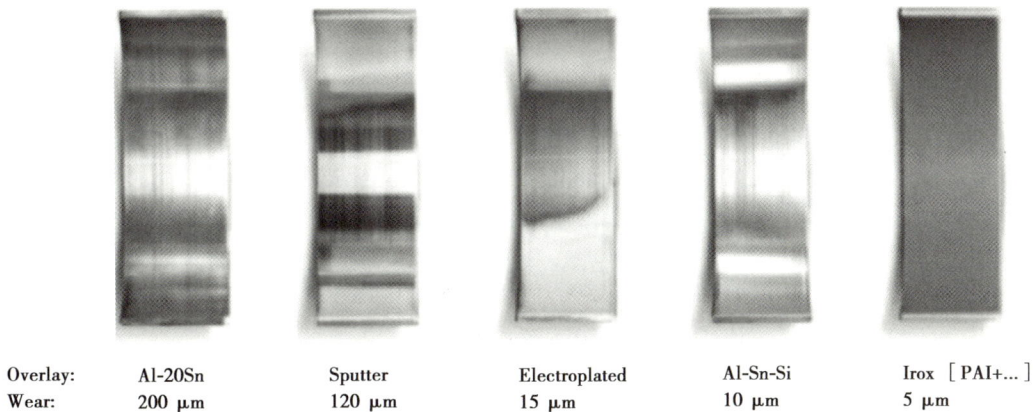

| Overlay: | Al-20Sn | Sputter | Electroplated | Al-Sn-Si | Irox [PAI+...] |
| Wear: | 200 μm | 120 μm | 15 μm | 10 μm | 5 μm |

Fig. 120.3   Wear Patterns under Start-Stop Conditions after 15000 Cycles

However, coatings are often sacrificial layers, and they can wear fast under a high load in mixed lubrication regime metal-to-metal contact. When the coating is removed by friction, the bearing clearance is increased by the value of the coating thickness.

120.13   Failure Modes of Journal Bearings

Multi-layered (tri-metal) bearings are recommended for steel crankshafts, while Al/Si-based bi-metal bearings are more compatible with nodular cast iron crankshafts. Nodular ductile cast iron crankshafts have a rough surface resulting from the cast iron microstructure. Such rough surface causes increased wear of soft overlays (Al-Sn) of multi-layered (tri-metal) bearings. Silicon has high hardness and its inclusions distributed over the aluminum matrix serve as abrasive particles polishing the mating journal surface. There are seven major categories we can put these failures into and we can usually get some idea of what happened by looking at the old bearings. These categories are:

1. Dirt	Foreign particles/dirt in the lubricant and/or in lining
	Foreign particles/dirt on the bearing back
2. Oil Starvation	Malfunction in the lubrication system
	Oil seal failure
3. Misassembly	Bearing reversed
	Reversed conrod or bearing caps
	Locating lugs not nested
	Shifting bearing caps
4. Improper machining	Improper ground housing (faceted or polygonal)
	Fillet ride
	Out of shape journal (hourglass- or barrel-shaped; tapered)
	Misalignment of shaft and housing
	Insufficient or excessive crush
5. Overloading	Surface fatigue- patterned cracks
	Bent or twisting conrod
	Bent crankshaft
	Distorted engine block (crankcase)
6. Corrosion	
7. Cavitation	

Some failures will inevitably result from a combination of more than one cause.

120.13.1 Wear Modes

Typically the normal wear of a multi-layered (trimetal) bearing surface due to operation covers 2/3 of the bearing surface. Wear diminishes near both parting-line ends of the bearing surface. The wear pattern is uniform across the bearing surface in the axial direction.

The following wear patterns are abnormal to a multi-layered (trimetal) bearing: accelerated wear, fatigued (turtle-shelled cracks of overlay), fatigue (other than overlay), fretting, scoring, wiped, hot short, oil starvation, cap shift, dirt embedment, dirt on back, distorted crankcase, and corrosion. Failure modes of trimetal bearings as further addressed hereafter.

(A) Accelerated wear: Shining polished appearance without any blackening at an abnormal wear rate. It is caused by a rough journal surface.

(B) The bearing surface is streaked and smeared with the worst damage at the center. It may end up with hot short. It happens due to oil starvation.

(C) Fretting, scoring, scratched, wiped (partial wear-out/blackening) and even hot short (severe wear, heavy overheating even blackening, torn surface, bearing metal melted and re-solidified/extruded along the edges) are signs of metal-to-metal contacts (generating concentrated loads). Causes are

(a) Insufficient oil conditions (oil starvation) :

-Lubrication system not primed before startup,

-Clogged passages,

-Failed engine oil pump,

-Blocked oil hole;

(b) Breaking the oil film caused by fatigued bearing material;

(c) Misalignment (e.g. distorted connecting rod);

(d) Insufficient clearance;

(e) Poor journal surface finish;

(f) Imperfect journal geometry (tapered, barrel, or hour-glass shapes);

(g) Foreign particles embedded into the bearing surface;

(h) Distorted crankcase due to engine overheating and improper tightening of parts.

Concentrated area of distress of bearing ID with corresponding mark of discontinuity on OD. It happens because of particles trapped between the bearing back and housing. Damage to bearing on back or housing bore (nick, burr, etc.). High spots on bearing back or housing bore are due to fretting.

Misalignment causes localized excessive wear of the bearing surface due to metal-to-metal contact (boundary or mixed lubrication) occurring near the bearing edge.

Wear or fatigue near bearing parting lines on opposite sides and in upper and lower bearing halves occurs due to cap shift. It happens because of poor doweling of the cap to housing, mixed bearing caps, or even reversed bearing caps.

120.13.2 Fatigue

Fatigue of an overlay appears in the form of a network of thin cracks. Thinner overlays form thinner fatigue cracks. Running the bearing with a fatigued overlay for a long time may cause partial flaking of the overlay and lower the oil film thickness. Typical syndromes are bearing surface cracked, lining broken with smooth-bottomed, and sharp-edged craters. Causes are

(a) Overloading

-High load at low speed;

-Over fueling;

-Detonation.

(b) Concentrating loads due to misalignment

-Edge loading;

-Bent rod;

-Tapered bearing profile;

-Hourglass-shaped journal profile;

-Barrel-shaped journal profile.

(c) Insufficient bearing-material strength.

Fatigue limit of an overlay is determined by the strength of the material and the thickness of the overlay. The thinner the overlay, the higher its fatigue strength. The fatigue of a copper-based, as well as aluminum-based, lining starts from fatigue of the overlay. The overlay flakes out from the copper lining resulting in breaking the oil film and changing the lubrication regime from hydrodynamic to boundary. The load localizes in the contact area, causing the information of small cracks on the lining surface. The cracks propagate throughout the lining thickness and then meet the steel back surface and continue to advance along the steel-copper boundary. Consequently, parts of the intermediate layer detach from the steel surface. Fatigue properties of some bearing materials are listed in Table 120.7.

Overloading of an internal combustion engine due to detonation or running under high torque at low rotation speeds may cause distortion of connecting rods, resulting in the non-parallel orientation of the bearing journal surfaces.

120.13.3   Corrosion

Bearing surface is darkened, spongy, or etched by a chemical attack. Causes are

(a) Acids in oil;

(b) Excessive operating temperature;

(c) Excessive blow-by;

(d) Coolant contamination of oil;

(e) Use of high sulfur fuel;

(f) Excessive oil change.

120.13.4   Creep of Bearing Coating

Thermomechanical creep parameters of some thermal barrier coatings are given in Table 120.10.

120.14   Thrust Bearings

If the pressure is parallel to the axis of the shaft, the bearing is called thrust bearing. Journal bearing materials can also be used for thrust bearings. For example, Al-20Sn-Cu is commonly used for Diesel engine crankshafts. A thrust bearing can be further divided into the following two groups:

(a) Pivot Bearing: If the shaft terminates at the bearing, it is called pivot bearing.
(b) Collar Bearing: If the shaft continues beyond the bearing it is called collar bearing.

Thrust washers, long-wearing flat bearings in the shape of washers, transmit and resolve axial forces in rotating mechanisms to keep components aligned along a shaft. Thrust washers are an economical alternative to rolling thrust bearings whenever forces and velocities are mild.

120.15   Ball Bearings

Components of a typical ball bearing are listed in Table 120.8 and the four major components are exhibited in Fig. 120.4. There are essentially two favored choices for the material used in ball bearings- chrome steel (e.g. AISI 52100) or stainless steel (e.g. AISI 400 series) for balls and raceways. A cage, also called a retainer, is to retain each ball in its evenly-distributed position. Typical materials for ball bearings are listed in Table 120.8 and their mechanical properties are given in Table 120.9. A ball bearing joint configuration is given in Fig. 120.5.

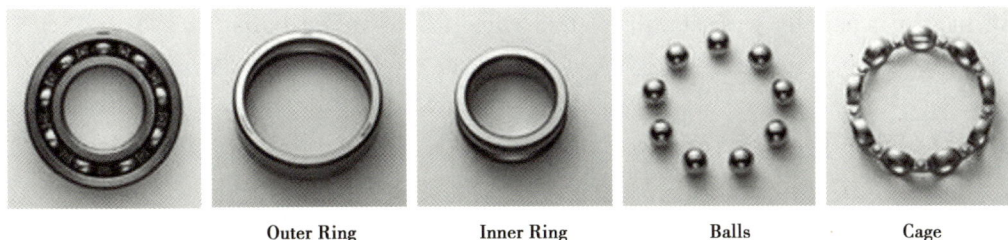

Outer Ring   **Inner Ring**   **Balls**   **Cage**

Fig. 120.4   Ball Bearing with Its four Major Components-(a) Outer Ring, (b) Inner Ring, (c) Balls, and (d) Cage (i.e. Retainer)

Case-hardened steels such as SAE 52100 (X1 02CrMo17 or 1.3543), containing a lower carbon content of about 0.2%, are used in load-carrying components (balls, races, rollers, tapered rollers) for automobiles and railroad equipment. AISI 400 series martensitic stainless steel is the standard material for miniature and instrument ball bearings where corrosion resistance is more important than load capacity, while AISI 440C is the standard material in the area of miniature and small-size ball bearings with higher loadings. ACD34 (X65Cr13) stainless steel is a relatively new martensitic chrome-carbide formulation with excellent machinability that allows raceway finish characteristics (e.g. less noise) approaching those of SAE 52100, combined with a corrosion resistance no less than AISI 440C. SV30, martensitic stainless steel based on chrome- nitride has been proven even superior to ACD34 as a bearing material.

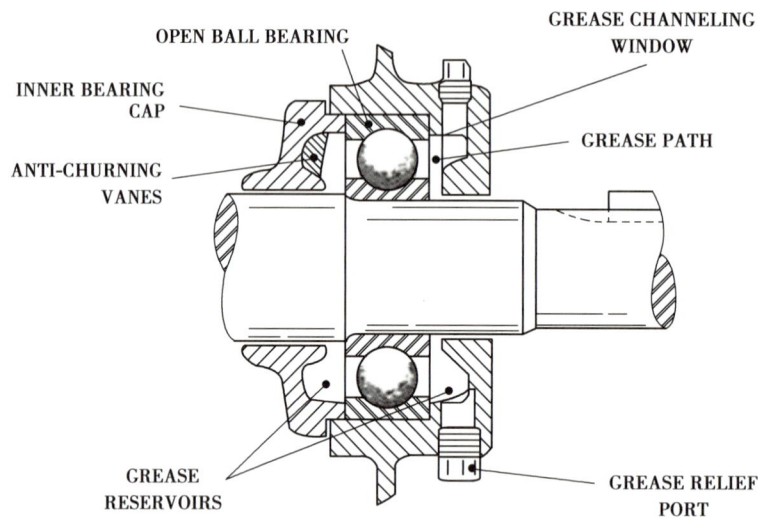

Fig. 120.5   An Example Alternating-Current Motor Bearing

Continually higher temperatures are being encountered by bearings in gas turbines, diesel engines, gas engines, turbochargers, nuclear plant equipment, and rocket engines. High temperature strength often leads to the selection of alloys of nickel, cobalt, and chromium for use from 500 ℃ to 850 ℃. Ceramics find high temperatures used to over 800 ℃. Bearings made with ceramic materials fall into a specialty niche in the bearing industry. The most common arrangement is a hybrid bearing, usually with stainless steel rings and ceramic balls.

120.16   Roller Bearings

The common materials used in rolling-element bearings include 52100 chrome steel, 440C stainless steel, M50/M50 Nil tool steel, and cobalt-based alloys. Cobalt-based alloys are specifically designed for operating at an elevated temperature up to 525 ℃.

References

ADAM A, et al, 2010. Crankshaft Bearings for Engine with Start-Stop Systems[J]. MTZ, 71(12): 22-25.

ALLEY E S, NEU R W, 2010. Microstructure-Sensitive Modeling of Rolling Contact Fatigue[J]. International Journal of Fatigue, 32: 841-850.

ARAKERE N K, et al, 2010. Rolling Contact Fatigue Life and Spall Propagation of AISI M50, M50NiL, and AISI 52100, Part II: Stress Modeling[J]. Tribology Transactions, 53: 42-51.

ASTM B23, 2010. Standard Specification for White Metal Bearing Alloys (Known Commercially as Babbitt Metal)[S].

BOCKSTEDT J, KLAMECKI B E, 2007. Effects of Pulsed Magnetic Field on Thrust Bearing Washer Hardness [J]. Wear, 262: 1086-1096.

BOUYAHIA F, HAJJAM M, EL K M, et al, 2006. Three-Dimensional Non-Newtonian Lubricants Flows in Sector-Shaped, Tilting-pads Thrust Bearings[J]. Proceedings of the Institution of Mechanical Engineers, Part J, 220(4): 375-384.

BRANAGAN L A, 2015. Survey of Damage Investigation of Babbitted Industrial Bearings[J]. Lubricants, 3: 91-112.

BRANCH N A, et al, 2010. Stress Field Evolution in a Ball Bearing Raceway Fatigue Spall[J]. Journal of ASTM International, 7(2): JAI 102529.

BRAUN M J, CHOI F K, HU Y, 1990. Nonlinear Effects in Plain Journal Bearing: 2. Results[J]. Journal of Tribology, LB(3): 555-561.

CANTOR N, 2004. Nanotribology: the Science of Thinking Small[J]. Tribology and Lubrication Technology, STLE, 60(6): 43-49.

CHAKRABORTY J, MANNA I, 2012. Development of Ultrafine Ferritic Sheaves/Plates in SAE 52100 Steel for Enhancement of Strength by Controlled Thermomechanical Processing [J]. Materials Science and Engineering, A, 548: 33-42.

CHENG K, ROWE W B, 1995. A Selection Strategy for the Design of Externally Pressurized Journal Bearings [J]. Tribology International, 28: 465-474.

CHERNENKOFF R, LALL C, HUO S, 2006. Strain-Life Fatigue Characteristics of Powder Metallurgy Aluminum Composites[J]. Advances in Powder Metallurgy and Particulate Materials-2006, MPIF, NJ, USA, 2(9): 123-138.

CHINN R L, 2009. Hardness, Bearings, and Rockwells[J]. Advanced Materials & Processes, 167(10): 29-31.

CHOI F K, BRAUN M J, HU Y, 1990. Nonlinear Effects in Plain Journal Bearing: 1. Analytical Study[J]. Journal of Tribology, 113(3): 555-561.

CHOI Y, LIU C R, 2006. Rolling Contact Fatigue Life of Finish Hard Machined Surfaces Part 2. Experimental Verification[J]. Wear, 261: 492-499.

CLEMONS K, et al, 2007. Effects of heat treatments on steels for bearing applications[J]. Journal of Materials Engineering and Performance, 16: 592-596.

COUSSEAU T, et al, 2011. Friction Torque in Grease Lubricated Thrust Ball Bearings [J]. Tribology International, 44: 523-531.

DAMMAK L, HADJ TAÏEB E, 2008. A Finite Element Analysis of Hydrodynamic Cylindrical Journal Bearing [J]. International Journal of Engineering Simulation, 6(4): 419-429.

DOBRICA M B, FILLON M, 2012. Performance Degradation in Scratched Journal Bearings[J]. Tribology International, 51: 1-10.

DOERNER M F, NIX W D, 1986. A Method for Interpreting the Data From Depth-Sensing Indentation Instruments[J]. Journal of Materials Research, 1: 601-609.

DUBOIS G B, OEVIRK F W, 1955. The Short Bearing Approximation for Plain Journal Bearing[J]. Trans. ASME, 77: 1173-1178.

EBERT F J, 2010. Fundamentals of Design and Technology of Rolling Element Bearings[J]. Chinese Journal of Aeronautics, 23(1): 123-136.

ETTLES C M, SEYLER J, BOTTENSHEIN M, 2006. Calculation of a Safety Margin for Hydro Generator Thrust Bearings[J]. Tribology and Lubrication Technology, 48(4): 450-456.

EL-SHERBINY M, SALEM M, EL-HEFNAWY N, 1984. Optimum Design of Hydrostatic Journal Bearings: I. Maximum Load Capacity[J]. Tribology International, 17(3): 155-161.

EL-SHERBINY M, SALEM M, EL-HEFNAWY N, 1984. Optimum Design of Hydrostatic Journal Bearings: II. Minimum Power[J]. Tribology International, 17(3): 162-166.

FAYOLLE P, CHILDS D W, 1999. Rotor-dynamic Evaluation of a Roughed-land Hybrid Bearing[J]. Journal of Tribology, 121: 133-138.

GABELLI A, LAI L, et al, 2012. The Fatigue Limit of Bearing Steels-Part II: Characterization for Life Rating Standards[J]. International Journal of Fatigue, 38: 169-180.

GARG H C, SHARDA H B, KUMAR V, 2006. On the Design and Development of Hybrid Journal bearings: a Review[J]. Tribotest, 12: 1-9.

GLAVATSKIH S B, PARAMONOV G A, 2009. PTFE-Faced Bearing Technology: Advantages and Practical Examples[J]. Waterpower XVI Conference Proceedings CD-Rom, Pennwell Corporation, Tulsa, OK, USA.

HARRIS T A, et al, 1992. On the Fatigue Life of M50 NiL Rolling Bearings[J]. STLE Tribology Transactions (ISSN 0569-8197), 35(4): 731-737.

HARRIS T A, 1991. Rolling Bearing Analysis[M]. 3rd Edition, John Wiley & Sons, New York, NY.

HARRIS T A, 1991. How to Compute the Effects of Preloaded Bearings[J]. Production Engineering, 36(15): 84-93.

ISO TC123/SC 3 N (2012-06-29), Plain Bearings-Recommendations for Automotive Crankshaft Bearing Environments[S]. ISO/CD 27507.

IVES D, ROWE W B, 1992. The Performance of Hybrid Journal Bearings in Superlaminar Flow Regimes[J]. STLE Tribology Transaction, 35(4): 627-634.

JACOBSON M, GUNNBERG F, 2004. Effects of Hard Turning on the Fatigue Life of Ball Bearings[J]. Proceedings of the Institution of Mechanical Engineers, Part B, Journal of Engineering Manufacture, 218: 855-1859.

KANE N R, SIHLER J, SLOCUM A H, 2003. A Hydrostatic Rotary Bearing with Angled Surface Self-Compensation[J]. Precision Engineering, 27: 125-139.

KERSCHER E, LANG K H, 2010. Influence of Thermal and Thermomechanical Treatments on the Fatigue Limit of a Bainitic High-Strength Bearing Steel[J]. Procedia Engineering, 2: 1731-1739.

KHONSARI M M, BOOSER E R, 2004. An Engineering Guide for Bearing Selection[J]. Tribology and Lubrication Technology, STLE, 60(2): 26-32.

KOLAWOLE F, MOHAMMED R, 2013. The Effect of Silicon Particulate on the Mechanical Properties of Microstructure of Aluminum-Based Bearing Materials (Al-6%Sn-0.25-1.40Si)[J]. International Journal of Scientific & Engineering Research, 4(9): 1124-1127.

KOPELIOVICH D, 2011. The Proper Selection of Engine Bearing Materials[J]. AERA., April-June 2011: 48-62.

KRUS D, CRIBB W, 2004. ToughMet Alloy: Improving Thrust Bearing Performance Enhanced Material Properties[J]. SAE 2004-01-2675.

KUMAR K, DESAI C, FLINN M, 1994. A CFD Study on Squeeze Film[J]. SAE 941083.

KUMAR V, SHARMA S C, JAIN S C, 2004. Stability Margin of Hybrid Journal Bearing: Influence of Thermal and Elastic Effects[J]. Journal of Tribology, ASME, 126: 630-631.

KUNC R, et al, 2007. Verification of Numerical Determination of Carrying Capacity of Large Rolling Bearings with Hardened Raceway[J]. International Journal of Fatigue, 29: 1913-1919.

LAI J, et al, 2012. The Fatigue Limit of Bearing Steels-Part I: A Pragmatic Approach to Predict Very High Cycle Fatigue Strength[J]. International Journal of Fatigue, 37: 155-168.

LI G Z, 2008. Study on High Temperature Mechanical Properties of Bearing Steel GCr_{15}[J]. Materials Science Forum, 575/578: 1101-1105.

LINM F S, STARKE E A, 1979. The Effect of Copper Content and Degree of Recrystallization on the Fatigue Resistance of 7×××-Type Aluminum Alloys-Part I: Low Cycle Corrosion Fatigue[J]. Material Science and Engineering, 39: 27-41.

LIU Y B, et al, 2010. Prediction of the S-N Curves of High-Strength Steels in the Very High Cycle Fatigue Regime[J]. International Journal of Fatigue, 32: 1351-1357.

MARROCCO T, DRIVER L, HARRIS S, et al, 2006. Microstructure and Properties of Thermal Sprayed Al-Sn Based Alloys for Plain Bearing Applications[J]. Journal of Thermal Spray Technology, 15(4): 634-639.

MARTSINKOVSKY V, et al, 2012. Designing Thrust Sliding Bearings of High Bearing Capacity[J]. Procedia Engineering, 39: 148-156.

MAYER H, et al, 2009. Very High Cycle Fatigue Properties of Bainitic High Carbon-Chromium Steel[J]. International Journal of Fatigue, 31: 242-249.

MIHARA K, INADA Y, MASHIKO T, 1991. Anti-Seizure Properties of Bearing in Heavy-Duty Diesel Engines [J]. SAE 910890.

MIYAJIM T, et al, 2013. Friction and Wear Properties of Lead-free Aluminum Alloy Bearing Material with Molybdenum Disulfide Layer by a Reciprocating Test[J]. Tribology International, 59: 17-22.

NIKANOROV S P, et al, 2005. Structural and Mechanical Properties of Al-Si Alloys Obtained by Fast Cooling of a Levitated Melt[J]. Materials Science and Engineering, A, 390: 63-69.

PRATT G C, PERKINS C A, 1981. Aluminum Based Crankshaft Bearings for the High Speed Diesel Engine [J]. SAE 810199.

RAIMONDI A A, BOYD J, 1957. An Analysis of Orifice and Capillary Compensated Hydrostatic Journal Bearings[J]. Lubrication Engineering, 13(1): 28-37.

RAMESHKUMAR T, et al, 2010. Investigation on the Mechanical and Tribological Properties of Aluminum-Tin Based Plain Bearing Material[J]. Tribology in Industry, 32(2): 3-10.

SAKAI T, SATO Y, OGUMA N, 2002. Characteristic S-N Properties of High-carbon- chromium-bearing Steel under Axial Loading in Long-Life Fatigue[J]. Fatigue and Fracture of Engineering Materials and Structures, 25: 765-773.

RIPPLE H C, 1963. Design of Hydrostatic Bearings[J]. Machine Design, (25): 108-117.

ROSALES I, et al, 2014. Bismuth Effect on the Mechanical Properties of Antifriction Al-Sn Alloys [J]. Materials Sciences and Applications, 5: 330-337.

ROWE W B, KOSHAL D, 1977. Investigation of Recessed Hydrostatic and Slot-entry Journal Bearings for Hybrid Hydrodynamic and Hydrostatic Operation[J]. Wear, 43: 55-69.

SAN A L, 1993. The Effect of Journal Misalignment on the Operation of a Turbulent Flow Hydrostatic Bearing [J]. Journal of Tribology, ASME, 115: 355-363.

SATO Y, OGISO S, 1983. Load Capacity and Stiffness of Misaligned Hydrostatic Recessed Journal Bearing[J]. Wear, 92: 231-241.

SCHOUWENAARS R, et al, 2007. Tailoring the Mechanical Properties of Al-Sn-Alloys for Tribological Applications[J]. Materials Science Forum, 317: 539-543.

SERGEI B, et al, 2001. The Significance of Oil Thermal Properties on the Performance of a Tilting-Pad Thrust Bearing[J]. Journal of Tribology, 124(2): 377-385.

SEXTON T N, COOLEY C H, 2009. Polycrystalline Diamond Thrust Bearings for Down-Hole Oil and Gas Drilling Tools[J]. Wear, 267: 1041-1045.

SLAVIC J, et al, 2011. Typical Bearing-Fault Rating Using Force Measurements: Application to Real Data[J]. Journal of Vibration and Control, 17 (14): 2164-2174.

SLINEY H E, 1990. Some Composite Bearing and Seal Materials for Gas Turbine Applications-A Review[J]. Journal of Engineering for Gas Turbines and Power, 112(4): 486-491.

STICKELS C A, 1977. Plastic Deformation of Quenched and Tempered 52100 Bearing Steel in Compression [J]. Metallurgical & Materials Transactions, A, 8: 63-70.

STURGEON A J, et al, 2006. Development of Thermal Sprayed Plain Bearings for Automotive Engine Applications[J]. Paper Presented at Tribology 2006: Surface Engineering & Tribology for Future Engine and Drivelines, IMechE, London, 12-14 July 2006.

SUH C M, KIM J H, 2009. Fatigue Characteristics of Bearing Steel in Very High Cycle Fatigue[J]. Journal of Mechanical Science and Technology, 23: 420-425.

SUNG C, et al, 2013. Effects of Inclusion Size and Stress Ratio on Fatigue Strength for High-Strength Steels with Fish-Eye Mode Failure[J]. International Journal of Fatigue, 48: 19-27.

TANIZAWA K, et al, 2012. Effects of Penetrated Graphite on Tribological Properties of Copper Based Journal Bearing[J]. Key Engineering Materials, 523/524: 805-808.

TAYLOR M, et al, 2006. Creep Properties of Pt-Aluminide Coating[J]. Acta Materialia, 54: 3241-3252.

TSUNEKAWA Y, et al, 2014. Improvement in Mechanical Properties of Hypereutectic Al-Si-Cu Alloys through Sono-solidified Slurry[J]. China Foundry, 11(4): 396-401.

WANG Q Y, et al, 2005. Very Long Life Fatigue Behavior of Bearing Steel AISI 52100[J]. Key Engineering Materials, 297/300: 1846-1851.

WASILCZUK M, 2003. Comparison of an Optimal-Profile Hydrodynamic Thrust Bearing with a Typical Tilting-Pad Thrust Bearing[J]. Lubrication Science, 15(3): 265-273.

XU S, 1994. Experimental Investigation of Hybrid Bearings[J]. STLE Tribology Transaction, 37(2): 285-292.

ZELIN M G, MUKHERJEE A K, 1993. Deformation Strengthening of Grain-Boundary Sliding in Pb-63% Sn Alloy[J]. Philosophical Magazine Letters, 68: 201-206.

Table 120.1   Mechanical Properties of Aluminum-based Journal Bearing Materials

Material-DAM	$T/{}^\circ\text{C}$	E_T	ρ	ν	(σ, ε)	α	k	γ	$\tan\delta$	K_{IC}
Al-3.5Cu-3.5Sn	23	—	—	—	(335, 10%)	—	—	—	—	—
Al-3.8Cu-1.2Mg-0.5Si-0.5Fe-0.3Mn-0.25Zn-0.1Cr	23	—	2.5	—	(205, 0.2%) (340, 23%)	—	—	—	—	—
Al-4Cu-2Mg-0.5Si	23	—	2.55	—	(193, 0.2%) (241, 3%)	—	—	—	—	—
Al-4Cu-0.7Si-0.5Mg	23	—	2.5	—	(152, 0.2%) (192, 2%)	—	—	—	—	—
Al-4Cu-0.7Si-0.5Mg/ 5%Al$_2$O$_3$	23	—	2.5	—	(152, 0.2%) (193, 3%)	—	—	—	—	—
Al-4.4Cu-3.3Sn	23	—	—	—	(350, 8%)	—	—	—	—	—
Al-5Pb-0.5Si-0.3Mn-0.1Cu-0.1Mg	23	—	—	—	—	—	—	—	—	—
Al-8.5Pb-4Si-1.5Sn-1Cu	23	—	—	—	—	—	—	—	—	—
Al-15Pb-8Sn	23	110	8.28	—	(132, 0.2%) (189, 8%)	—	—	—	—	—

continued

Material-DAM	$T/℃$	E_T	ρ	ν	(σ, ε)	α	k	γ	$\tan \delta$	K_{IC}
Al-4Si-0.5Cu-0.5Mg	23	72	2.68	—	—	—	—	—	—	—
Al-4Si-1Cd	23	72	2.68	—	—	22	—	—	—	—
Al-4Si-1Cu	23	72	2.68	—	—	22	—	—	—	—
Al-7Si	23	73	2.67	—	(175, 27%)	—	—	—	—	—
Al-7Si-4Cu	23	73	2.7	—	(220, 1%)	—	—	—	—	—
Al-7Si-4Cu (T6; Rheo DC)	23	73	2.7	—	(260, 10%)	—	—	—	—	—
Al-8.8Si-3.3Cu	23	74	—	—	(200, 1%)	—	—	—	—	—
Al-11Si-2Cu-...	23	75	—	—	(140, 0.2%) (240, 1%)	—	—	—	—	—
	300	65	—	—	—	—	—	—	—	—
Al-11Si-11Mg-1Cu-1Ni	23	75	—	—	—	—	—	—	—	—
	300	65	—	—	—	—	—	—	—	—
Al-11Si-1Cu-0.2Sn-0.1Ni-0.3Fe-0.1Mn-0.1Ti	23	75	—	—	—	—	—	—	—	—
	300	65	—	—	—	—	—	—	—	—
Al-12.7Si-7Sn-1.5Cu-Cr-Zr	23	78	—	—	—	—	—	—	—	—
	300	66	—	—	—	—	—	—	—	—
Al-14Si-2.5Cu-0.7Mg	23	79	2.6	—	(152, 0.2%) (207, 1%)	—	—	—	—	—
Al-17Si-4Cu	23	82	—	—	(210, 1%)	—	—	—	—	—
	300	65	—	—	—	—	—	—	—	—
Al-17Si-4Cu (T6; Rheo DC)	23	82	—	—	(250, 2%)	—	—	—	—	—
	300	65	—	—	—	—	—	—	—	—
Al-17Si-4Cu (T6; Rheo DC; Sono-solidified slurry)	23	82	—	—	(230, 4%)	—	—	—	—	—
	300	65	—	—	—	—	—	—	—	—
Al-20Si-1Cu	23	70	—	—	—	24	—	—	—	—
Al-1Sn-4Bi	23	—	—	—	—	—	—	—	—	32
Al-2Sn-3Bi	23	—	—	—	—	—	—	—	—	35
Al-3.5Sn-1.5Bi	23	—	—	—	—	—	—	—	—	34
Al-4.5Sn-0.5Bi	23	—	—	—	—	—	—	—	—	29

continued

Material-DAM	$T/°C$	E_T	ρ	ν	(σ, ε)	α	k	γ	$\tan\delta$	K_{IC}
Al-5Sn	23	—	—	—	—	—	—	—	—	26
Al-6Sn	23	70	—	—	(130, 30%)	—	—	—	—	—
Al-6Sn-1Cu-1Ni	23	70	—	—	(160, 24%)	24	—	—	—	—
Al-6Sn-0.35Si	23	70	—	—	(135, 24%)	—	—	—	—	—
Al-6Sn-0.7Si	23	70	—	—	(140, 20%)	—	—	—	—	—
Al-6Sn-1.05Si	23	70	—	—	(145, 16%)	—	—	—	—	—
Al-6Sn-1.4Si	23	70	—	—	(160, 13%)	—	—	—	—	—
Al-6Sn-2.5Si-1Cu-0.2V-0.25Mn	23	70	—	—	(75, 0.2%) (180, 21%)	—				
Al-6.25Sn-1Cu 1.3Ni-0.7Si-0.7Fe-0.7Mn-0.2Ti	23	—	—	—	—	24	—	—	—	—
Al-6.5Sn-1Cu-0.5Ni (Solid thrust washer; while trimetal with Pb-18Sn-2Cu and Ni barrier for high-loaded washer)	23	—	—	—		—	—	—	—	—
Al-8Sn-2.5Si-2Pb-0.8Cu-0.2Cr (Low- & medium-loaded)	23	—	—	—		—	—	—	—	—
Al-9Sn-1Cu-0.1Ti	23	—	3.3	—	—	—	—	—	—	—
Al-10Sn-2.5Si-1.5Cu	23	—	—	—	(183, 22%)	—	—	—	—	—
Al-10Sn-4Si-1Cu	23	—	—	—	—	—	—	—	—	—
Al-10Sn-3Si-1.8Pb-0.4Cu-0.2Cr	23	—	—	—		—	—	—	—	—
Al-10Sn-2Ni-1Mn-0.6Cu	23	—	—	—	—	—	—	—	—	—
Al-11Sn-4Si-1.5Cu	23	—	—	—	—	24	—	—	—	—
Al-12Sn-2.5Si-0.7Cu	23	—	—	—	(130, 30%)	—	—	—	—	—
Al-12Sn-4Si-1Cu	23	70	—	0.33	(65, 0.2%) (160, 20%)	24	—	—	—	—

continued

Material-DAM	$T/°C$	E_T	ρ	ν	(σ, ε)	α	k	γ	$\tan\delta$	K_{IC}
Al-12Sn-4Si-2Cu	23	—	—	—	(150, 18%)	—	—	—	—	—
Al-12Sn-4Si-2Cu	23	—	—	—	(150, 18%)	—	—	—	—	—
Al-13Sn-3Si-2Pb-0.3Cu	23	—	—	—	—	—	—	—	—	—
Al-15Sn-3Si-1Cu	23	—	—	—	—	—	—	—	—	—
Al-17Sn-1Cu	23	—	—	—	—	—	—	—	—	—
Al-18Sn-1Cu-0.2Cr	23	—	—	—	—	—	—	—	—	—
Al-20Sn-1Cu-0.1Ni-0.7Si-0.7Fe-0.7Mn-0.2Ti	23	18.7	3.7	—	(130, 0.2%) (300, 1%) (350, 1.5%) (398, 3.3%)	24	—	—	—	—
	232 (High service temperature)									
	280 (T_m)	—	—	—	—	—	—	—	—	—
Al-25Sn-1.4Cu-0.6Mn	23	—	—	—	—	—	—	—	—	—
Al-40Sn-0.4Cu (Low-loaded applications)	23	—	4.7	—	—	—	—	—	—	—
Al-4.5Zn-1Cu-1Pb-0.5Mg (for Trimetal; on top of Al-20Sn & Ni barrier for high-loaded conrod bearing)	23	—	—	—	—	—	—	—	—	—
Al-4.5Zn-1.5Si-1Cu-1Pb-0.5Mg-0.1Ti	23	—	—	—	—	—	—	—	—	—
Al-4.5Zn-1.5Si-1Pb-0.5Mg (ISO 4383)	23	—	2.7	—	—	—	—	—	—	—
Al-5.5Zn-2.5Mg-1.5Cu	23	—	2.7	—	(172, 0.2%) (276, 1%)	—	—	—	—	—
Al-5Zn-1.5Si-1Cu-1Pb-0.6Fe-0.6Mg-0.3Mn-0.2Sn-0.2Ni-0.2Ti	23	—	—	—	(67, 2%)	—	—	—	—	—
Al-41Zn-5Cu	23	—	3.7	—	—	—	—	—	—	—

Table 120.2 Mechanical Properties of Copper-Based Journal Bearing Materials

Material-DAM	$T/°C$	E_T	ρ	ν	(σ, ε)	α	k	γ	$\tan\delta$	K_{IC}
Cu-6Sn-Ag	23	—	—	—	—	—	—	—	—	—
Cu-8Sn-Ni	23	—	8.5	—	(180, 8%)	18	47	—	—	—
Cu-10Sn	23	—	—	—	$\sigma_{ucs}=-1200$; (260, 0.2%) (370, 16%)	—		—	—	—
Cu-18Sn-1P-0.25Fe-0.25Pb	23	—	—	—	(100, 2%) (200, 12%)					
Cu-18Sn-1P-0.25Fe-0.25Pb/8WC	23	—	—	—	(150, 2%) (250, 7%)					
Cu-9Pb-5Sn	23	—	—	—	—	18	—	—	—	—
Cu-10Pb-10Sn-0.7Fe-0.5Zn-0.5Ni-0.2Si-0.1P	23	—	—	—	—	18	—	—	—	—
Cu-12.3Pb-7.6Sn (Cu-15Pb-8Sn)	23	110	8.3	—	(132, 0.2%) (189, 8%)	—	—	—	—	—
Cu-17Pb-5Sn-0.7Fe-0.5Zn-0.5Ni-0.2Si-0.1P	23	—	—	—	—	18	—	—	—	—
Cu-20Pb-5Sn	23	—	—	—	—	18	—	—	—	—
Cu-22Pb-1Sn	23	—	—	—	—	18	—	—	—	—
Cu-24Pb-1Sn-0.7Fe-0.5Zn-0.5Ni-0.2Si-0.1P	23	—	—	—	—	18	—	—	—	—
Cu-24Pb-4Sn-0.7Fe-0.5Zn-0.5Ni-0.2Si-0.1P	23	—	—	—	—	18	—	—	—	—
Cu-30Pb-0.5Sn-0.7Fe-0.5Zn-0.5Ni-0.2Si-0.1P	23	—	—	—	—	16	—	—	—	—
Cu-8Sb-4Cu	23	—	—	—	—	23	—	—	—	—
Cu-8Sb-4Cu-1Cd	23	—	—	—	—	23	—	—	—	—
Cu-4.9Zn-5Al-4.1Sn	23	—	8.3	—	(101, 4.9%)	—	—	—	—	—

continued

Material-DAM	$T/\text{℃}$	E_T	ρ	ν	(σ, ε)	α	k	γ	$\tan \delta$	K_{IC}
Cu-29.6Zn-3.1Al	23	—	8.24	—	(160, 2%)	—	—	—	—	—
Cu-30Zn-4Al (C26000)	See Table 75.1									
Cu-31Zn-1Si	23	—	—	—	(593, 0.2%) (654, 14%)	—	—	—	—	—
Cu-37Zn-3Mn-2Al-.Pb-.Si	23	93	8.1	—	(345, 0.2%) (640, 18%)	20.4	63	—	—	—

Table 120.3   Mechanical Properties of Lead-Based Journal Bearing Materials

Material-DAM	$T/\text{℃}$	E_T	ρ	ν	(σ, ε)	α	k	γ	$\tan \delta$	K_{IC}
Pb	23	16	11.37	0.44	(5.5, 0.2%) $\sigma_{uts} = 12$	29	35	130	1.5	—
	327.5 (T_m)	—	—	—	—	—	—	—	—	—
Pb-10Sn	23	—	—	—	—	—	—	—	—	—
Pb-10Sn-3Cu (Medium pressure)	23	—	—	—	—	—	—	—	—	—
Pb-18Sn-2Cu (Working with Ni barrier for small-end bushing)	23	—	—	—	—	—	—	—	—	—
Pb-15Sb-10Sn-0.7Cu-0.6As (ASTM Grade 7; Heavy Pressure)	23	—	—	—	(−25, −0.13%)	—	—	—	—	—
	100	—	—	—	(−11, −0.13%)	—	—	—	—	—
	240 (T_m)	—	—	—	—	—	—	—	—	—
Pb-15Sb-5Sn-0.45As (ASTM Grade 8)	23	—	—	—	(−23, −0.13%)	—	—	—	—	—
	100	—	—	—	(−12, −0.13%)	—	—	—	—	—
	237 (T_m)	—	—	—	—	—	—	—	—	—
Pb-10Sb-6Sn (ASTM Grade 13)	23	—	—	—	—	28	—	—	—	—
	100	—	—	—	—	—	—	—	—	—
Pb-16Sb-1Sn (ASTM Grade 15)	23	—	—	—	—	—	—	—	—	—
	100	—	—	—	—	—	—	—	—	—

Notes: Pb (Lead) is basically prohibited in the automotive industry, though it once used to be a key element for solders and in lead-acid batteries for electric vehicles released in late 1990s.

Table 120.4 Mechanical Properties of Tin-based Journal Bearing Materials（ASTM B23；Pb ≤0.35%）

Material-DAM	$T/^\circ\text{C}$	E_T	ρ	ν	(σ, ε)	α	k	γ	$\tan\delta$	K_IC
Sn-11Pb-6Cu-3Sb	23	29	—	—	$\sigma_\text{ucs}=-224$； $(70, 0.2\%)$ $(100, 3.5\%)$	—	—	—	—	—
Sn-4.5Sb-4.5Cu （ASTM Grade 1）	23	50	7.34	0.35	$\sigma_\text{ucs}=-89$， $(-30, -0.13\%)$； $(62, 2\%)$	—	—	—	—	—
	100	—	—	—	$(-18, -0.13\%)$	—	—	—	—	—
	223 (T_m)									
Sn-6.75Sb-5.5Cu （Diesel Special）	23	50	—	—	—	—	—	—	—	—
Sn-6.75Sb-5.75Cu （ASTM Grade 11）	23	51	—	—	—	—	—	—	—	—
Sn-7Sb-8Cu （Turbine）	23	51	—	—	—	—	—	—	—	—
Sn-7.5Sb-3.5Cu （ASTM Grade 2； Typical Pb-free bearing lining）	23	51	7.4	—	$\sigma_\text{ucs}=-103$， $(-42, -0.13\%)$； $(77, 18\%)$	23	40.1	297	—	—
	100	—	—	—	$(-21, -0.13\%)$； $\sigma_\text{uts}=45$	—	—	—	—	—
	150	—	—	—	$\sigma_\text{uts}=20.7$	—	—	—	—	—
	241 (T_m)	—	—	—	—	—	—	—	—	—
Sn-8Sb-4Cu-1Cd	23	—	—	—	—	23	—	—	—	—
Nickel Genuine （Similar to ASTM Grade 2）	23	50	7.39	—	$\sigma_\text{uts}=75.2$	—	—	—	—	—
	100	—	—	—	$\sigma_\text{uts}=40.7$	—	—	—	—	—
	150	—	—	—	$\sigma_\text{uts}=25.5$	—	—	—	—	—
	200	—	—	—	$\sigma_\text{uts}=11.7$	—	—	—	—	—
	241 (T_m)	—	—	—	—	—	—	—	—	—
Sn-7.5Sb-6.5Cu （SAE 11）	23	50	—	—	—	—	—	—	—	—

continued

Material-DAM	$T/^\circ C$	E_T	ρ	ν	(σ, ε)	α	k	γ	$\tan\delta$	K_{IC}
Sn-8Sb-8Cu (ASTM Grade 3)	23	52	7.46	—	$\sigma_{ucs}=-121$, $(-46, -0.13\%)$; $(85, 1\%)$	—	—	—	—	—
	100	—	—	—	$(-22, -0.13\%)$; $\sigma_{uts}=45.5$	—	—	—	—	—
	150	—	—	—	$\sigma_{uts}=26.2$	—	—	—	—	—
	240 (T_m)	—	—	—	—	—	—	—	—	—
Sn-12Sb-3Cu-10Pb (ASTM Grade 4)	23	—	—	—	—	—	—	—	—	—

Table 120.5   Mechanical Properties of Zinc-Based Journal Bearing Materials

Material-DAM	$T/^\circ C$	E_T	ρ	ν	(σ, ε)	α	k	γ	$\tan\delta$	K_{IC}
Zn-26.2Al-2.3Cu-0.02Mg	23	138	5	—	$(353, 0.2\%)$ $(451, 16.7\%)$	—	—	—	—	—
Zn-14.4Al-1.3Cu-0.02Mg	23	—	6.1	—	$(210, 0.2\%)$ $(305, 10.2\%)$	—	—	—	—	—

Table 120.6   Mechanical Properties of Overlay/Coatings for Journal Bearing Materials

Material-DAM	$T/^\circ C$	E_T	ρ	ν	(σ, ε)	α	k	γ	$\tan\delta$	K_{IC}
Irox (Overlay=PAI+ additives)	23	—	—	—	—	—	—	—	—	—
PAI/MoS_2(Coating)	23	—	—	—	—	—	—	—	—	—
Sn (Overlay)	23	—	—	—	—	—	—	—	—	—

Note: IROX = overlay made of PAI resin binder + additives dispersed [Federal-Mogul].

Table 120.7   Fatigue ε-N Properties of Bearing Materials

Material	$T/^\circ C$	$d\varepsilon/dt$	σ'_f	ε'_f	b	c	K'	n'	$\sigma_f@2N_f$	R
52100 (Q&T)	23	—	2709	0.243	−0.096	−0.642	—	—	$610@10^6$	—
Al-20Sn-1Cu	23	—	—	—	—	—	—	—	90	—
Al-Sn-Si	23	—	—	—	—	—	—	—	118	—

continued

Material	$T/°C$	$d\varepsilon/dt$	σ_f'	ε_f'	b	c	K'	n'	$\sigma_f @ 2N_f$	R
Al-6Zn-2Mg-2.1Cu (T651)	23	—	—	0.46	—	−0.63	1076	0.114	—	—
Al-6Zn-2Mg-1.6Cu (T651)	23	—	—	1.1	—	−0.77	1080	0.088	—	—
Al-6Zn-2Mg-1Cu (T651)	23	—	—	1.15	—	−0.78	937	0.075	—	—
Al-6Zn-2Mg-1Cu (T7351)	23	—	—	0.71	—	−0.72	616	0.006	—	—
Al-6Zn-2Mg-0.01Cu (T651)	23	—	—	1.25	—	−0.82	824	0.063	—	—
Cu-30Pb	23	—	—	—	—	—	—	—	95	—
Sn-4.5Sb-4.5Cu (Babbitt Metal; ASTM Grade 1)	23	—	—	—	—	—	—	—	26@ $2×10^7$	—
Sn-7.5Sb-3.5Cu (Babbitt Metal; ASTM Grade 21)	23	—	—	—	—	—	—	—	33@ $2×10^7$	—

Table 120.8   Mechanical Properties of Ball Bearing Materials

Component	Material	Reference Materials
Ball	Si_3N_4 and Other Ceramics	
	SV30 (X30CrMoN15-1)	Stainless Steel
	AISI 440D (X65Cr13; ACD34)	Stainless Steel
	SAE 440C (X1 02CrMo 1)	Stainless Steel
	SKH4	
	SAE 52100 (100Cr6)	Alloy Steel
	SAE 51100	Alloy Steel
	SAE 8620 (Low load)	Alloy Steel
	SAE 4320 (Low load)	Alloy Steel
	AISI 316 (Low load)	Stainless Steel
Rings, Outer & Inner	SV30 (X30CrMoN15-1)	Stainless Steel
	AISI 440D (X65Cr13; ACD34)	Stainless Steel
	SAE 52100 (Chrome Steel)	Alloy Steel

continued

Component	Material	Reference Materials
Cage（i.e. Retainer）	JIS G3141-SPCC	Strip Steel
	SAE 1010	Plain Carbon Steel
	SAE 1008	Plain Carbon Steel
	Brass	
	Phenolic	
	PEEK	
	PA6,6	
	PA4,6	
	Acetal（POM）	
Seal	Nitrile Silicone FKM	
Slinger, Lubrication	JIS G3141-SPCC	
Adaptor Washer （e.g. Wavy Washer）	AISI 303	Stainless Steel
	AISI 304	Stainless Steel
Adaptor Nut	SAE 1025; JIS G4051-S25C	Plain Carbon Steel
Adaptor Sleeve	SAE 1025; JIS G4051-S25C	
Rivet	JIS G3507-SWRCH 12A	
Hexagon Wrench Key	JIS G4103-SNCM435	
Hexagon Set Screw	SAE 4135; JIS G4105-SCM435	
Housing	SAE G3500; JIS G5501-FC200	
Grease Nipple	JIS H3250-C3604	

Table 120. 9　Mechanical Properties of Ball Bearing Materials （AISI 52100-Dependent on Heat-Treatment Levels）

Material-DAM	$T/℃$	E_T	ρ	ν	(σ, ε)	α	k	γ	$\tan\delta$	K_{IC}
52100（Annealed） （Fe-1C-1.71Cr- 0.31Mn-0.28Si- 0.21Ni-0.013P- 0.003S）	23	208	7.8	0.29	（903, 0.2%） （1151, 15%）	11.6	16	477	—	—
	1414（T_m）									

continued

Material-DAM	$T/℃$	E_T	ρ	ν	(σ, ε)	α	k	γ	$\tan \delta$	K_{IC}
52100 (Q&T; Bearing)	23	208	7.8	0.29	$(1394, 0.2\%)$ $(1748, 10\%)$	11.6	16	477	—	—
	150	—	—	—	$(-3080, -1\%)$ $(-3500, -7\%)$	—	—	—	—	—
	200	163	—	—	$(-2740, -1\%)$ $(-2950, -4.5\%)$; $(1161, 0.2\%)$ $\sigma_{uts}=2151$	—	—	—	—	—
	260	—	—	—	$(-2720, -1\%)$ $(-2700, -10\%)$	—	—	—	—	—
	400	154	—	—	$(984, 0.2\%)$ $\sigma_{uts}=1551$	—	—	—	—	—
	600	113	—	—	$(414, 0.2\%)$ $\sigma_{uts}=934$	—	—	—	—	—
	800	103	—	—	$(303, 0.2\%)$ $\sigma_{uts}=311$	—	—	—	—	—
52100 (Q&T)	23	208	7.8	0.29	$(2030, 0.2\%)$ $(2240, 5\%)$	11.6	16	477	—	—
52100 (Q&T)	23	208	7.81	0.3	$(2344, 1.2\%)$ $(2827, 3\%)$	11.6	16	477	—	—

Table 120.10   Mechanical Creep Parameters of Thermal Barrier Coating

Material	$T/℃$	Stress /MPa	Strain Rate $/\mathrm{s}^{-1}$	A $/(\mathrm{MPa}^{-n} \cdot \mathrm{s}^{m-1})$	Q $/(\mathrm{J} \cdot \mathrm{mol}^{-1})$	n	m
Ni-38.5Al-8.6Pt 3.7Co-0.2Ti; ($\approx 52~\mu\mathrm{m}$ Coating)	$650\sim$ 1150^*	—	—	6.3×10^{13}	125000	4	0
TGO (Thermally Grown Oxide)							
Bond Coating ($\approx 50~\mu\mathrm{m}$)	—	—	—	—	—	—	
IDZ ($\approx 50~\mu\mathrm{m}$; Inter-diffusion zone)	900	$E=1$	—	—	—	—	—

continued

Material	$T\,/℃$	Stress /MPa	Strain Rate $/\mathrm{s}^{-1}$	A $/(\mathrm{MPa}^{-n}\cdot\mathrm{s}^{m-1})$	Q $/(\mathrm{J}\cdot\mathrm{mol}^{-1})$	n	m
CMSX-4 （Ni-Based substrate）	900	$E=1$; $\varepsilon=3\%$	—	1.03×10^{-13}	125000	4.7	0

Notes：Creep equation $= \dfrac{\mathrm{d}\varepsilon_{\text{creep}}}{\mathrm{d}t} = A\left(\dfrac{\sigma - \sigma_{\text{th}}}{E}\right)^{n} t^{m} \exp\left(\dfrac{-Q}{RT_{\text{k}}}\right)$, $\sigma > \sigma_{\text{th}}$;

$\sigma_{\text{th}} =$ Stress threshold and $\sigma_{\text{th}} = 0$, if not specified；

$E =$ Young's modulus；when $E = 1$ means E is not specified；

$\ast = E\,(\mathrm{GPa}) = 118 - 0.024\,T.$

Carbon

Chapter 121

Diamond

121.1　Introduction

There are three carbon allotropes: diamond, graphite, and carbon fullerenes. Diamond is known for its exceptional strength, wear resistance, and low friction. Diamond doesn't oxidize in the air unless it is heated over 700 ℃ [John et al.].

121.2　Natural Diamonds

Natural diamonds are the hardest natural mineral known to man. They can be divided into the following three groups:

Type Ia: This is the most common type of natural diamond, containing up to 0.3% nitrogen.

Type Ib: Very few natural diamonds are of this type (~0.1%), but nearly all synthetic industrial diamonds are. Type Ib diamonds contain up to 500 ppm nitrogen.

Type IIa: This type is very rare in nature. Type IIa diamonds contain so little nitrogen that it is not readily detected using infrared or ultraviolet absorption methods.

Type IIb: This type is also very rare in nature. Type IIb diamonds contain so little nitrogen (even lower than type IIa) that the crystal is a p-type semiconductor.

121.3　Synthetic Diamonds

Synthetic diamonds are produced via the process of High Pressure High Temperature Synthesis (HPHT). Synthetic diamonds are usually a few millimeters in size and too flawed for use as gemstones, but they are extremely useful in industrial applications such as edges on cutting tools and drill bits. It was found the synthetic diamond with a nitrogen impurity concentration of 0.3 ppm exceeds other diamond types with respect to hardness and wear resistance, and reveals anisotropy of the mechanical properties, different from other diamond types [Blank et al.].

121.4   Thin Film Diamonds

121.4.1   Chemical Vapor Deposition (CVD)

Thin films of the polycrystalline diamond can be formed via Chemical Vapor Deposition (CVD). CVD diamond is an ideal choice for highly demanding applications for machining hard and rough materials such as cutting tools for composites and non-ferrous metals, surgical knives, and wear-resistant coatings.

121.4.2   PCD

121.5   Applications

Applications of diamonds include cutting tools, anti-friction and wear-resistant components, thermal management in substrates, heat spreaders and sinks, semiconductor devices, and optical components.

References

ANTHONY T R, BANHOLZER W F, FLEISCHER J F, et al, 1990. Thermal Conductivity of Isotopically Enriched C_{12} Diamond[J]. Physical Review B, 42(2): 1104-1111.

BARNARD A S, 2004. Structural Properties of Diamond Nanowires: Theoretical Predictions and Experimental Progress[J]. Reviews on Advanced Material Science, 6: 94-119.

BAUSCH C L, 1929. Diamonds as Metal Cutting Tools[J]. Transactions of ASME, 51: 125-128.

BEJAMIN R J, 1978. Diamond Turning at a Large Optical Manufacturer[J]. Optical Engineering, 17(6): 574-577.

BLANK V, et al, 1999. Mechanical Properties of Different Types of Diamond[J]. Diamond and Related Materials, 8(8-9): 1531-1535.

BRUNO L, et al, 2003. Mechanical Characterization of a CVD Diamond Coating by Nanoindentation Test[J].

Journal of Engineering Materials and Technology, 125(3): 309-314.

EKIMOV E, SIDOROV V A, BAUER E D, et al, 2004. Superconductivity in Diamond[J]. Nature, 428 (6982): 542-545.

FIELD J E, FREEMAN C J, 1981. Strength and Fracture Properties of Diamond[J]. Philosophical Magazine, A, Taylor and Francis Ltd., 43(3): 595-618.

JOHN P, POLWART N, TROUPE C E, et al, 2002. The Oxidation of (100) Textured Diamond[J]. Diamond and Related Materials, 11 (3-6): 861.

KARL E S, JOHN P D, 1994. Synthetic Diamond: Emerging CVD Science and Technology[M]. Wiley and Sons, New York, NY, USA.

KOIZUMI S, NEBEL C E, NESLADEK M, 2008. Physics and Applications of CVD Diamond[M]. Wiley VCH, Berlin, DE.

KRŽAN B, et al, 2009. Tribological Behavior of Tungsten-doped DLC Coating under Oil Lubrication[J]. Tribology International, 42(2): 229-235.

LIANG Q, et al, 2009. Enhancing the Mechanical Properties of Single-Crystal CVD Diamond[J]. Journal of Physics: Condensed Matter, 21(36): 364215.

MIYOSHI, 1998. Structures and Mechanical Properties of Natural and Synthetic Diamonds[J]. Diamond Films & Technology, 8(3): 153-172.

NAZARE M, NEVES A, 2001. Properties, Growth and Application of Diamond[M]. Institution of Electric Engineers, London, UK.

ONG T P, CHANG R P H, 1991. Properties of Diamond Composite Films Grown on Iron Surfaces[J]. Applied Physics Letters, 58(4): 358-360.

PACI J T, 2006. Mechanical Properties of Ultrananocrystalline Diamond Prepared in a Nitrogen-Rich Plasma: A Theoretical Study[J]. Physical Review B, 74(18): 184112 · 1-184112 · 9.

PAGEL-THEISEN V, 2001. Diamond Grading ABC: The Manual[M]. 9th edition, Rubin & Son, Antwerp, Belgium.

RICHARDSON A F, et al, 2003. Developing Diamond MMCs to Improve Durability in Aggressive Abrasive Conditions[J]. Wear, 255: 593-605.

ROBERTSON J, 2002. Diamond-like Amorphous Carbon[J]. Materials Science and Engineering R, 37(4-6): 129-281.

SEKARIC L, et al, 2002. Nanomechanical Resonant Structures in Nanocrystalline Diamond [J]. Applied Physics Letters, 81(23): 4455-4457.

SHATSKIY A, et al, 2009. Boron-doped Diamond Heater and its Application to Large-volume, High-pressure, and High-temperature Experiments[J]. Review of Scientific Instruments, 80(2): 023907.

SUMIYA H, IRIFUNE T, 2005. Synthesis of High-purity Nano-Polycrystalline Diamond and Its Characterization [J]. SEI Technical Review, 59: 52-59.

SULLIVAN J P, et al, 2001. Developing a New Materials for MEMS Amorphous Diamond-Like Carbon[J]. Materials Research Society Symposium Proceedings, 657: 71(2000).

TAKANO Y, TAKENOUCHI T, ISHII S, et al, 2007. Superconducting Properties of Homoepitaxial CVD Diamond[J]. Diamond and Related Materials, 16 (4-7): 911-914.

TELLING R H, PICKARD C J, PAYNE M C, et al, 2000. Theoretical Strength and Cleavage of Diamond[J]. Physical Review Letters, 84(22): 5160-5163.

WANG W, et al, 2015. Diamond Based Field-Effect Transistors of Zr Gate with SiN_x Dielectric Layers[J]. Journal of Nanomaterials, 2015: 1-5.

WEI L, et al, 1993. Thermal Conductivity of Isotopically Modified Single Crystal Diamond[J]. Physical Review Letters, 70(24): 3764-3767.

WILKS J, WILKS E, 1991. Properties and Applications of Diamond[M]., Butterworth-Heinemann, Oxford, UK.

Table 121.1 Mechanical Properties of Diamond and Related Alloys

Material	$T/°C$	E_T	ρ	ν	(σ, ε)	α	k	γ	ρ_E	K_{IC}
Diamond (Natural)	−200	—	—	—	—	—	5500	—	—	—
	−150	—	—	—	—	—	3500	—	—	—
	23	1080	3.515	0.07	$\sigma_{uts} = 6000$	0.8	2200	510	—	2
	100	—	—	—	—	—	1500	—	—	—
	300	—	—	—	—	—	1000	—	—	—
	700 (Oxidation in the air)									
	1500 (Decomposition temperature in N_2)									
	3650 (T_m)	—	—	—	—	—	—	—	—	—
Diamond (Synthetic; ^{12}C, 99.9%)	−169	—	—	—	—	—	41000	—	—	—
	23 °C	860	3.2	0.07	$\sigma_{uts} = 3800$	1.7	3320	510	—	5.3
	3650 (T_m)	—	—	—	—	—	—	—	—	—

continued

Material	$T/℃$	E_T	ρ	ν	(σ, ε)	α	k	γ	ρ_E	K_{IC}
Diamond (Crystal)	23	$C_{11} = 1076$ $C_{12} = 125$ $C_{44} = 577$	3.515	0.07	—	1.0	3320	510	—	5.3
Diamond (Ultranano-crystalline; Theory)	23	690	—	—	(61000, 13%)	—	—	—	—	—
Diamond (CVD; 60~170 μm Film)	23	800	3.52	0.07	(1600, 0.2%) (4800, 0.6%)	2.5	2008	502	—	4.5
	100	—	—	—	—	—	1344	—	—	—
	500	—	—	—	—	3.5	306	—	—	—
	1000	—	—	—	—	—	—	93	—	—
	3650 (T_m)	—	—	—	—	—	—	—	—	—
Diamond (PCD; Polycrystalline)	23	843	3.43	0.09	$\sigma_{ucs} = -7250$; $\sigma_{uts} = 1450$	1.3 ~ 3.9	500	543	—	14
	3650 (T_m)	—	—	—	—	—	—	—	—	—

Chapter 122

Graphite and Graphene

122.1   Introduction

Atoms of pristine graphene, a truly 2-dimensional planar material, are bonded covalently, with only three of the four potential bonding sites satisfied. Graphene has fantastic mechanical properties with in-plane $E \approx 1000$ GPa (Young's modulus) and intrinsic $\tau_{us} \approx 130$ GPa (ultimate shear strength) and is among the strongest substances known. However, graphene is relatively brittle with a fracture toughness of about 4 MPa $\cdot$ m$^{\frac{1}{2}}$ [Zhang et al.], which is of the same order as diamond.

122.2   Graphite

Graphite is a planar structure that consists of layered graphene. Bonding between layers relies on van der Waals bonds that allow layers of graphene to be easily separated, or to slide past each other. The fourth electron is free to migrate in the plane, making graphite electrically conductive in the plane while not conductive in the direction perpendicular to the plane. Graphite, Natural and synthetic, are used to make anodes in most battery constructions as applied to electric vehicles.

Natural graphite is also an excellent conductor of heat. It is stable over a wide range of temperatures. Similar to the electric conductivity, thermal and acoustic properties of graphite are highly anisotropic.

122.3   Graphite Fibers

Graphite fibers are fibers of 5~10 μm in diameter and several mm in length. They are composed mostly of carbon atoms. Composites reinforced with graphite/carbon fibers have high stiffness, high tensile strength, low weight, high chemical resistance, high-temperature tolerance and low thermal expansion, as compared with those reinforced with glass fibers. Graphite fibers-reinforced composites are popular in the aerospace industry and their market share in automotive structural parts increases steadily.

References

AKINWANDE D, et al, 2015. Large-Area Graphene Electrodes: Using CVD to Facilitate Applications In commercial Touchscreens, Flexible Nanoelectronics, and Neural Interfaces [J]. IEEE Nanotechnology Magazine, 9(3): 6-14.

BUNCH J S, 2010. Mechanical and Electric Properties of Graphene Sheets, PhD Dissertation, Cornell University, NY, USA.

CLAUSING R E, et al, 1991. Diamond and Diamondlike Films and Coatings[M]. New York: Plenum Press.

DIENWIEBEL M, et al, 2004. Superlubricity of Graphite[J]. Physical Review Letters, 92(12): 126101.1-126101.4.

DIKIN D A, et al, 2007. Preparation and Characterization of Graphene Oxide Paper[J]. Nature, 448: 457-460.

El-Kady M, Strong V, Dubin S, et al, 2012. Laser Scribing of High-Performance and Flexible Graphene-Based Electrochemical Capacitors[J]. Science, 335(6074): 1326-1330.

FRANK I W, TANENBAUM D M, Van Der ZANDE A M, et al, 2007. Mechanical Properties of Suspended Graphene Sheets[J]. J. Vac. Sci. Technol. B, 25(6): 2558-2561.

GRIMA J, et al, 2014. Tailoring Graphene to Achieve Negative Poisson's Ratio Properties[J]. Advanced Materials, 27: 1455-1459.

KAWAGUCHI M, et al, 2008. Electronic Structure and Intercalation Chemistry of Graphite-Like Layered Material with a Composition of BC_6N[J]. Journal of Physics and Chemistry of Solids, 69 (5-6): 1171.

LALWANI G, et al, 2013. Two-dimensional Nanostructure-reinforced Biodegradable Polymeric Nanocomposites for Bone Tissue Engineering[J]. Biomacromolecules, 14(3): 900-909.

LEE C G, et al, 2009. A Study on the Tribology Characteristics of Graphite Nano Lubricant[J]. International Journal of Precision Engineering and Manufacturing, 10(1): 85-90.

LEE C, WEI X, KYSAR J, et al, 2008. Measurement of the Elastic Properties and Intrinsic Strength of Monolayer Graphene[J]. Science, 321: 385-388.

LI Z, et al, 2015. Field and Temperature Dependence of Intrinsic Diamagnetism in Graphene: Theory and experiment[J]. Physical Review B, 91(9): 094429.

LIU J, WRIGHT A R, ZHANG C, et al, 2008. Strong Terahertz Conductance of Graphene Nanoribbons under a Magnetic Field[J]. Applied Physics Letters, 93(4): 41106.

LIU L, et al, 2012. Mechanical Properties of Graphene Oxide[J]. Nanoscale, 4: 5910-5916.

LIU Y, XIE B, XU Z, 2011. Mechanics of Coordinative Crosslinks in Graphene Nanocomposites: A First Principles Study[J]. Journal of Materials Chemistry, 21: 6707-6712.

MEDHEKAR N V, et al, 2010. Hydrogen Bond Networks in Graphene Oxide Composite Paper: Structure and Mechanical properties[J]. ACS Nano, 4: 2300-2306.

NETO A, et al, 2009. The Electronic Properties of Graphene[J]. Rev Mod Phys., 81: 109-162.

OVID'KO I A, 2013. Mechanical Properties of Graphene[J]. Rev. Adv. Mater. Sci., 34: 1-11.

LIPSON H, STOKES A R. 1942. A New Structure of Carbon[J]. Nature, 149(3777): 328.

RAFIEE M A, et al, 2010. Graphene Nanoribbon Composites[J]. ACS Nano, 4: 7415-7420.

ROBINSON A M, et al, 2001. Measurement of Stiffness of Joints in a Graphite Brick Assembly[J]. Journal of Mechanical Engineering Science, 215(2): 167-177.

STANKOVICH S, et al, 2006. Graphene-based Composite Materials[J]. Nature, 442, 282-286.

WANG S, et al, 2000. A New Carbonaceous Material with Large Capacity and High Efficiency for Rechargeable Li-ion Batteries[J]. J. of the Electrochemical Society, 147(7): 2498.

WIMOLKIATISAK A S, BELL J P, 1989. Interfacial Shear Strength and Failure Modes of Interphase-Modified Graphite-Epoxy Composites[J]. Polymer Composites, 10(3): 162-172.

ZHANG P, et al, 2014. Fracture Toughness of Graphene[J]. Nature Communications, 5: 3782(2014).

ZHAO Z, GOU J, 2009. Improved Fire Retardancy of Thermoset Composites Modified with Carbon Nanofibers [J]. Sci. Technol. Adv. Mater., 10: 015005.

ZHENG Q, et al, 2008. Self-Retracting Motion of Graphite Microflakes[J]. Physics Review Letters, 100(6): 067205.

ZHU Y, et al, 2010. Graphene and Graphene Oxide: Synthesis, Properties, and Applications[J]. Advanced Materials, 22: 3906-3924.

Table 122.1 Mechanical Properties of Graphite, Graphene, and Related Materials

Material	T/℃	E_{T}	ρ	ν	(σ, ε)	α	k	γ	ρ_{E}	K_{IC}
Graphite (//)	23	15	1.76	0.126	$\sigma_{\mathrm{ucs}} = -200$	−1.2	470	830	—	0.945
	3650 (T_{m})	—	—	—	—	—	—	—	—	—
Graphite (⊥)	23	8	1.76	0.126	$\sigma_{\mathrm{ucs}} = -20$	25	25	710	—	0.945

Notes: C = Carbon;

      Gr = Graphite.

Table 122.2   Elastic Constants of Graphite, Graphene, and Related Materials

Material-DAM	$T/℃$	ρ	E_{11}	E_{22}	E_{33}	G_{12}	G_{13}	G_{23}	ν_{12}	ν_{13}	ν_{23}
Graphene (Pristine; In-plane; Intrinsic)	23	1.75	1000	—	—	—	—	—	—	—	—
GO (Graphene Oxide)	23	—	250± 150	—	—	—	—	—	—	—	—
Electrographite	23	1.65	7	—	—	—	—	—	—	—	—
Graphite	23	1.76	15	8	—	—	—	—	0.126	—	—
	3650 (T_{m})	—	—	—	—	—	—	—	—	—	—
Graphite Fiber (AS4; $\rho=1.75$; $d_{\mathrm{f}}=0.3$ mm)	23	1.75	224	14	14	27	27	7	0.2	0.2	—
Graphite Fiber (HM; $\rho=1.94$)	23	1.94	385	6.3	6.3	7.7	7.7	—	0.2	0.2	—
Kevlar-29 Fiber	23	1.44	61	4.2	4.2	2.9	2.9	2	0.32	0.32	0.4
	450 (Decomposition temperature)										
Kevlar-29 Yarn	23	1.44	53	2.4	2.4	1.6	1.6	—	0.36	0.36	0.36
Kevlar-49 Fiber	23	1.44	154	7	7	5	5	—	0.32	0.32	0.4
	550 (Decomposition temperature)										
Kevlar-149 Fiber	23	1.47	186	10	10	5	5	—	0.32	0.32	0.4
70C/30Gr (Lamina)	23	1.72	17	—	—	—	—	—	—	—	—
30C/70Gr (Lamina)	23	1.75	14	—	—	—	—	—	—	—	—

Notes: ρ (g/cm^3) = Density;

    d_{f}(mm) = Mean diameter of fibers;

    E_{T} & E_{C}(GPa) = Tensile and compression moduli of elasticity;

    E_{11}, E_{22}, E_{33}(GPa) = Young's moduli in axial, transverse, and out-of-plane directions;

    G_{12}, G_{13}, G_{23}(GPa) = Shear moduli of a unidirectional lamina;

    σ_{uts}(MPa) & $\varepsilon_{\mathrm{uts}}$ = Ultimate tensile strength and strain;

    ν_{12}, ν_{13}, ν_{23} = Poisson's ratios of a unidirectional lamina;

    $\nu_{\mathrm{ij}} E_{\mathrm{jj}} = \nu_{\mathrm{ji}} E_{\mathrm{ii}}$($i = 1, 2, 3; j = 1, 2, 3; i \neq j$);

    AS = As spun;

    HM = High modulus;

    HT = High tensile strength;

    LCP = Liquid crystal polymer.

Table 122.3   Thermal Properties of Graphite, Graphene, and Related Materials

Material-DAM	$T/°C$	α_1	α_2	α_3	k_1	k_3	k_3	γ	β_1	β_2	β_3
Graphene (Pristine; In-plane; Intrinsic)	23	—	—	—	—	—	—	—	—	—	—
Graphite	23	−1.2	25	—	470	25	—	710	—	—	—
Graphite Fiber (AS4; $\rho=1.75$)	23	−0.7	15	15	66	11.6	11.6	712	—	—	—
	80	—	—	—	85	—	—	785	—	—	—
	100	—	—	—	—	—	—	850	—	—	—
	125	—	—	—	120	—	—	900	—	—	—
Graphite Fiber (HM; $\rho=1.94$)	23	−1	10	10	8.6	8.6	8.6	710	—	—	—
Electrographite	23	4	—	—	55	—	—	—	—	—	—
70C/30Gr	23	2	—	—	9	—	—	—	—	—	—
30C/70Gr	23	3	—	—	35	—	—	—	—	—	—

Notes: α_1, α_2, α_3 ($\mu m/m/°C$) = Coefficients of linear thermal expansion of a unidirectional lamina;

k_1, k_2, k_3 ($W/m/°C$) = Thermal conductivities of a unidirectional lamina;

β_1, β_2, β_3 ($\mu m/m/\%$) = Swelling coefficients of linear moisture expansion;

γ ($J/kg/°C$) = Specific heat capacity.

Table 122.4   Orthotropic Mechanical Strengths of Graphite, Graphene, and Related Materials

Material	$T/°C$	$(\sigma_{11}, \varepsilon_{11})$	$(\sigma_{22}, \varepsilon_{22})$	$(\sigma_{33}, \varepsilon_{33})$	$(\sigma_{12}, \varepsilon_{12})/(\sigma_{23}, \varepsilon_{23})/(\sigma_{13}, \varepsilon_{13})$
Graphene (Pristine bulk; In-plane; Intrinsic)	23	$\sigma_{11t}=130000$	—	—	—/—/—
Graphite	23	$\sigma_{11c}=-200$ $K_{IC}=0.945$	$\sigma_{22c}=-20$	—	—/—/—
Electrographite (Bulk)	23	$\sigma_{11t}=14$ $\sigma_{11c}=-65$	—	—	—/—/—
Graphite Fiber (AS4)	23	$\sigma_{11t}=3700$	—	—	—/—/—
Kevlar-29 Fiber	23	$\sigma_{11t}=2900$	—	—	—/—/—
Kevlar-49 Fiber	23	$(-750, -0.63\%)$; $(3700, 2.8\%)$	—	—	—/—/—

continued

Material	$T/℃$	$(\sigma_{11}, \varepsilon_{11})$	$(\sigma_{22}, \varepsilon_{22})$	$(\sigma_{33}, \varepsilon_{33})$	$(\sigma_{12}, \varepsilon_{12})/(\sigma_{23}, \varepsilon_{23})/(\sigma_{13}, \varepsilon_{13})$
70C/30Gr (Lamina)	23	$\sigma_{11t}=23$ $\sigma_{11c}=-208$	—	—	—/—/—
30C/70Gr (Lamina)	23	$\sigma_{11t}=21$ $\sigma_{11c}=-145$	—	—	—/—/—

Table 122.5　Fatigue ε-N Properties of Graphite Fibers in the Longitudinal Direction

Material	$T/℃$	$d\varepsilon/dt$	σ_f'	ε_f'	b	c	K'	n'	$\sigma_f@2N_f$	R
Kevlar-29	23	—	—	—	—	—	—	—	1456@ 7.3×10^5 1820@ 2.6×10^5	— —

Chapter 123

Carbon Fullerenes and Reinforcements

123.1 Introduction

123.1.1 Carbon Black

Carbon black (CB), as ultrafine particles (< 100 nm) is mainly used as a reinforcing filler and/or pigment in tires, belts, hoses and other rubber products in the automotive industry. It enhances the rubber strength and wear resistance increasing tire life, and also helps conduct heat away from the tread and belt area of the tire reducing thermal damage. As used in tires, black carbon particles are primarily spherical and can be characterized as follows:

Carbon Black (Size)	Tensile Strength	Abrasion Resistance
N110 (20~25 nm)	25 MPa	1.25
N220 (24~33 nm)	23 MPa	1.15
N300 (30~35 nm)	21.5 MPa	0.8
N330 (28~36 nm)	22.5 MPa	1.0 (Base)
N550 (39~55 nm)	18 MPa	0.64
N660 (49~73 nm)	16 MPa	0.56
N770 (70~96 nm)	15 MPa	0.48
N880 (180~200 nm)	13 MPa	0.22
N990 (250~350 nm)	10 MPa	0.18

The tensile strength of a generic rubber is around 2.5 MPa. Mechanical properties including the tensile strength of a CB-reinforced rubber composite are enhanced significantly, but may vary according to the extent of interfacial adhesion between the rubber and carbon black. The particle size, surface characteristics/treatment, and structure of carbon black are the main factors having effects on the quality of reinforcement.

123.1.2 Carbon Fibers

In carbon fiber, the sheets of carbon atoms are crumpled together. Haphazard-folded carbon fibers are different from parallel-stacked graphite sheets. Carbon fibers are generally classified into the following two categories:

(a) PAN-based Carbon Fiber: Carbon fibers derived from Polyacrylonitrile (PAN) are turbostratic. Turbostratic carbon fibers tend to have high tensile strength.

(b) Pitch-based Carbon Fiber: Carbon fibers derived from mesophase pitch are graphitic after heat treatment at temperatures exceeding 2200 ℃. Heat-treated mesophase- pitch-derived carbon fibers have higher Young's modulus and higher thermal conductivity, but lower strength whereas compared with PAN-based carbon fibers.

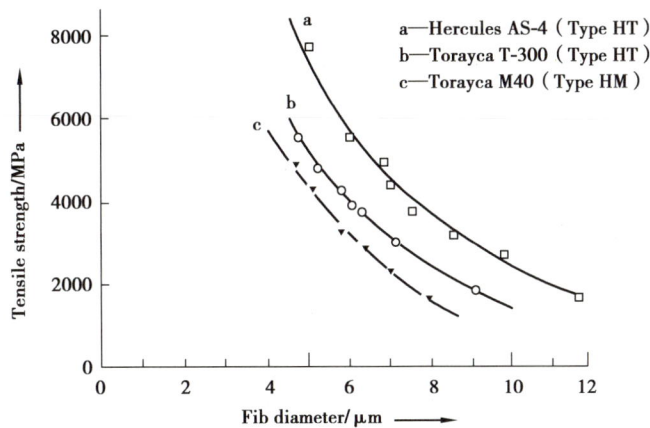

Fig. 123.1   Relation between the tensile strength of fiber diameter

More than 50% of produced carbon/carbon fiber composites are used for aircraft disk brake liners due to their high thermal conductivities, low thermal expansion, and high heat capacity (2.5 times as much as steel brake liners) at high temperatures. Three different patterns of carbon fibers have been developed for aircraft disk brakes: fabrics, semi-randomly chopped, and cross laminates.

123.2   Fullerenes

Fullerenes are a family of carbon allotropes in addition to the other two (i. e. graphite and diamond). Each fullerene consists of molecules, of which carbon atoms are arranged in the 3-dimensional form of hollow tubes, spheres, or ellipsoids, with both pentagonal and hexagonal faces. When one or more carbon atoms in a fullerene molecule are replaced by metal atoms, the resultant compound is called a fulleride.

123.2.1   Buckminsterfullerene

When a substance consists of 60 carbon atoms (C_{60}) taking the shape of a sphere with twenty hexagon and twelve pentagon faces [Kroto et al.], it is called Buckminsterfullerene.

123.2.2　Carbon Nanotubes

Nanotubes are tubular fullerenes, of which carbons are usually shaped like a cylinder with a few nanometers in diameter and up to several millimeters in length. They were discovered in 1991 by Sumio Iijima. Carbon nanotubes are the strongest and stiffest materials yet discovered on Earth, resulting from the covalent sp^2 bonds formed between individual carbon atoms. Nanotubes have extraordinary heat conductivity, mechanical properties, electrical conductivity, and electron field-emitting capacity.

Nanotubes are classified into two groups: (a) SWNT (Singled-Walled Nano Tubes) and (b) MWNT (Multi-Walled Nano Tubes). It was reported that double- walled CNT (DWCT) could increase both tensile strength and fracture toughness [Gojny et al.] as compared with SWNT.

Transistors form the basis for modern integrated circuits functioning as digital switches. A nanotube switch gate (transistor) is about one nanometer in size, i.e. three orders of magnitude smaller than a silicon chip.

Carbon nanotubes can be made into thin, flexible energy storage device working like a battery [Pushparaj].

References

ABRAHAMSON J, WILES P, RHOADES B, 1999. Structure of Carbon Fibers Found on Carbon Arc Anodes [J]. Carbon, 37(11):1873.

AJAYAN P M, TOUR J M, 2007. Materials Science: Nanotube Composites[J]. Nature, 447: 1066-1068.

AJAYAN P, SCHADLER L, GIANNARIS C, et al, 2000. Single-walled Carbon Nanotube-polymer Composites: Strength and Weakness[J]. Advanced Materials, 12(10): 750-753.

ANDREWS R, WEISENBERGER M, 2004. Carbon Nanotube Polymer Composites[J]. Current Opinion in Solid State and Materials Science, 8(1): 31-37.

BARBER A, COHEN S, WAGNER H, 2003. Measurement of Carbon Nanotube-Polymer Interfacial Strength [J]. Applied Physics Letters, 82(23): 4140-4142.

BERBER S, KWON Y, TOMANEK D, 2000. Unusually High Thermal Conductivity of Carbon Nanotubes[J]. Physics Review Letters, 84: 4613.

CHEN Y, GU Y, 2007. Thermal Conductivities of Single-walled Carbon Nanotubes Calculated from Complete Phonon Dispersion Relations[J]. Physics Review, B, 76.

COOPER C A, YOUNG R J, HALSALL M, 2001. Investigation into the Deformation of Carbon Nanotubes and Their Composites Through the Use of Raman Spectroscopy[J]. Composites, Part A, 32(3-4): 401-411.

DALTON A, COLLINS S, MUÑOZ E, 2003. Super-Tough Carbon-Nanotube Fibers[J]. Nature, 423(6941): 703.

DONNET J, BANSAL R, WANG M, 1993. Carbon Black[M]. 2nd Edition, Marcel Dekker, NY.

DONNET J B, BANSAL R C, 1990. International Fiber Science and Technology, 10 (Carbon Fibers)[M]. 2nd Edition, Marcel Dekker, NY.

EITAN A, et al, 2003. Surface Modification of Multiwalled Carbon Nanotubes: toward the Tailoring of the Interface in Polymer Composites[J]. Chemistry of Materials, 15(6): 3198-3201.

GOJNY F, WICHMANN M, KOPKE U, et al, 2004. Carbon nanotube-reinforced epoxy-composite: enhanced stiffness and fracture toughness at low nanotube content[J]. Composites Science and Technol. 64: 2363-2371.

HARRIS P, 2009. Carbon Nanotube Science: Synthesis, Properties and Applications [M]. Cambridge University Press, Cambridge, UK.

HARRIS P, 2004. Carbon Nanotube Composites[J]. International Materials Reviews, 49(1): 31-43.

HERNáNDEZ E, GOZE C, BERNIER P, et al, 1998. Elastic Properties of C and Composite Nanotubes[J]. Physical Review Letters, 80(20): 4502-4505.

HONE J, et al, 2002. Thermal Properties of Carbon Nanotubes and Nanotube-based Materials[J]. Applied Physics A, 74: 339-343.

HOPKINS A, STRAW D, BEKEY I, 2009. Inkjetting Single-Walled Carbon Nanotubes for Net 3-D Structures [J]. Polymer Preprints, 50(1): 459.

HOPKINS A, KRUK N, LIPELES R, 2007. Macroscopic Alignment of Single-Walled Carbon Nanotubes (SWNTs)[J]. Surface & Coatings Technology, 202: 1282-1286.

HOPKINS A, LIPELES R, O'MALLEY M, 2005. Preparation and Characterization of Single Wall Carbon Nanotube-Reinforced Polycyanurate Nanocomposite[J]. Polymer, 46(2): 787.

HU J, RUAN X, CHEN Y, 2009. Thermal Conductivity and Thermal Rectification in Graphene Nanoribbons: A Molecular Dynamics Study[J]. Nano Letters, 9(7): 2730.

IIJIMA S, 1991. Helical Microtubules of Graphitic Carbon[J]. Nature, 354: 56-58.

JEON Y, ALWAY-COOPER R, MORALES M, et al, 2013. Handbook of Advanced Ceramics [M]. 2nd Edition. Elsevier, Amsterdam.

KUMAR S, 1990. in Proc. Znt. SAMPE Symp. and Exhib., 35, Advanced Materials: Challenge Next Decade

[J]. edited by G. Janicki, V. Bailey, and H. Schjelderup, 1990: 2224-2235.

KROTO H W, 1985. C60: Buckminsterfullerene[J]. Nature, 318: 162-163.

LAFITTE M H, BUNSELL A R, 1982. The Fatigue Behavior of Kevlar-29 Fibers[J]. Journal of Materials Science, 17(8): 1300-1308.

LU L, et al, 1999. Linear Specific Heat of Carbon Nanotubes[J]. Physical Review B, 59(14): R9015.

MANOCHA L M, YASUDA E, TANABE Y, et al, 1988. Effect of Carbon Fiber Surface-Treatment on Mechanical Properties of C/C Composites[J]. Carbon, 26(3): 333-337.

MARTEL R, et al, 2001. Ambipolar Electrical Transport in Semiconducting Single-Wall Carbon Nanotubes[J]. Physical Review Letters. 87(25):256805.

KIM P, SHI L, MAJUMDAR A, et al, 2001. Thermal Transport Measurements of Individual Multi-walled Nanotubes[J]. Physical Review Letters, 87: 215502-1.

MINGO N, BROIDO D A, 2005. Carbon Nanotube Ballistic Thermal Conductance and Its Limits[J]. Physical Review Letters, 95(9): 096105.

MORGAN P, 2005. Carbon Fibers and Their Composites[M]. Taylor and Francis, FL.

NAN C, et al, 2004. Interface Effect on Thermal Conductivity of Carbon Nanotube Composites[J]. Applied Physics Letters, 85: 3549.

O'CONNELL, M, 2006. Carbon Nanotubes: Properties and Applications[M]. CRC Press, Boca Raton, FL.

OGALE A, ANDERSON D, LIN C, et al, 2002. Orientation and Dimensional Changes in Mesophase Pitch-based Carbon Fibers[J]. Carbon, 40(8): 1309-1319.

PALACI I, et al, 2005. Radial Elasticity of Multiwalled Carbon Nanotubes[J]. Physics Review Letter, 94: 175502.

PRADERE C, et al, 2013. Thermal Properties of Carbon Fibers at Very High Temperature[J]. Carbon, 47 (3): 737-743.

PUSHPARAJ V L, et al, 2007. Flexible Energy Storage Devices Based on Nanocomposite Paper [J]. Proceedings of the National Academy of Sciences, 104(34): 13574-13577.

QIAN D, DICKEY E, ANDREWS R, et al, 2000. Load Transfer and Deformation Mechanisms in Carbon Nanotube-Polystyrene Composites[J]. Applied Physics Letters, 76(2): 2868-2870.

SALVETAT J, KULIK A, BONARD J, 1999. Elastic Modulus of Ordered and Disordered Multiwalled Carbon Nanotubes[J]. Advanced Materials, 11(2):161-165.

SHENDEROVA O B, ZHIRNOV V V, BRENNER D W, 2002. Carbon Nanostructures[J]. Critical Reviews in Solid State and Materials Sciences, 27(3-4): 227-356.

SU P, et al, 2009. Fabrication of Flexible NO$_2$ Sensors by Layer-by-Layer Self-Assembly of Multi-walled Carbon Nanotubes and Their Gas Sensing Properties[J]. Sensors and Actuators B: Chemical, 139: 488-493.

SUI X, et al, 2010. Effect of Carbon Nanotube Surface Modification on Dispersion and Structural Properties of Electro-spun Fibers[J]. Applied Physics Letters, 95(23): 233113.1-233113.3.

SUN Y, WANG H, XIA M, 2008. Single-walled Carbon Nanotubes Modified with Pd Nanoparticles: Unique Building Blocks for High-Performance, Flexible Hydrogen Sensors[J]. Journal of Physical Chemistry, C, 112: 1250-1259.

THOSTENSON E, CHOU T, 2002. Aligned Multi-Walled Carbon Nanotube-Reinforced Composites: Processing and Mechanical Characterization[J]. Journal of Physics D, 35(16): L77-L80.

UEDA T, et al, 2008. Development of Carbon Nanotube Based Gas Sensors for NO$_x$ Gas Detection Working at Low Temperature[J]. Physica, E, 40: 2272-2277.

VILATELA J J, KHARE R, WINDLE A H, 2011. Multifunctional Carbon Nanotube Fiber Composites: Hierarchical Structure and Properties[J]. Carbon, 50: 1227-1234.

WAGNER H, LOURIE O, FELDMAN Y, et al, 1998. Stress-Induced Fragmentation of Multiwall Carbon Nanotubes in a Polymer Matrix[J]. Applied Physics Letters, 72(2): 188-190.

WAGONER G, BACON R, 1989. Elastic Constants and Thermal Expansion Coefficients of Various Carbon Fibers[C]. Extended Abstracts of 19th Biennial Carbon Conference, 296-297.

WEISENBERGER M, GRULKE E, JACQUES D, et al, 2003. Enhanced Mechanical Properties of Polyacrylonitrile/Multiwall Carbon Nanotube Composite Fibers [J]. Journal of Nanoscience and Nanotechnology, 3(6): 535-539.

XUE W, CUI T, 2008. Electrical and Electromechanical Characteristics of Self-Assembled Carbon Nanotube Thin Films on Flexible Substrates[J]. Sensors and Actuators A: 145(1): 330-335.

YU M, et al, 2000. Tensile Loading of Ropes of Single Wall Carbon Nanotubes and Their Mechanical Properties [J]. Physical Review Letters, 84(24): 5552-5555.

YU M, et al, 2000. Strength and Breaking Mechanism of Multiwalled Carbon Nanotubes under Tensile Load [J]. Science, 287(5453): 637-640.

Zhuang H, Wightman J P, 1996. The Influence of Surface Properties on Carbon Fiber/Epoxy Matrix Interfacial Adhesion[J]. Journal of Adhesion, 62: 213-245.

ZHAO Z, GOU J, 2009. Improved Fire Retardancy of Thermoset Composites Modified with Carbon Nanofibers [J]. Science and Technology of Advanced Materials, 10(1): 015005.

Table 123.1 Elastic Constants of Carbon Fullerenes and Reinforcements

Material-DAM	$T/°C$	ρ	E_{11}	E_{22}	E_{33}	G_{12}	G_{13}	G_{23}	ν_{12}	ν_{13}	ν_{23}
Carbon (Bulk)	23	1.64	124	124	124	—	—	—	0.2	0.2	0.2
	100	—	119	119	119	—	—	—	—	—	—
	200	—	107	107	107	—	—	—	—	—	—
	600	—	45	45	45	—	—	—	—	—	—
Ta-C (Membrane; Hydrogen-Free Tetrahedral Amorphous Carbon)	23	—	800	800	800	—	—	—	—	—	—
Amoco PAN-based Carbon Fibers:											
Thornel 300	23	—	517	—	—	—	—	—	—	—	—
Amoco Pitch-based Carbon Fibers:											
Thornel P25	23	—	140	—	—	—	—	—	—	—	—
Thornel P55	23	—	380	—	—	—	—	—	—	—	—
Thornel P75	23	—	500	—	—	—	—	—	—	—	—
Thornel P100	23	2.2	690	—	—	—	—	—	—	—	—
Thornel P120	23	2.1	827	—	—	—	—	—	0.2	0.2	0.2
Celanese PAN-based Carbon Fibers:											
Celion GY-70	23	—	517	—	—	—	—	—	—	—	—
Celion 1000	23	—	234	—	—	—	—	—	—	—	—
Celion ST	23	—	235	—	—	—	—	—	—	—	—
Hercules PAN-based Carbon Fibers:											
AS-1	23	1.8	228	—	—	—	—	—	—	—	—
AS-4	23	1.8	234	—	—	—	—	—	—	—	—
AS-4 (Ni-coated)	23	2.97	210	—	—	—	—	—	—	—	—
AS-6	23	—	241	—	—	—	—	—	—	—	—
HM-S Magnamite	23	—	345	—	—	—	—	—	—	—	—
IM-6	23	—	276	—	—	—	—	—	—	—	—
IM-7	23	1.74	310	21	21	14	14	—	0.2	0.2	0.2
Toray PAN-based Carbon Fibers:											
M50	23	—	500	—	—	—	—	—	—	—	—

continued

Material-DAM	$T/℃$	ρ	E_{11}	E_{22}	E_{33}	G_{12}	G_{13}	G_{23}	ν_{12}	ν_{13}	ν_{23}
T50	23	1.64	400	—	—	—	—	—	0.2	0.2	0.2
T300	23	1.76	230	15	15	9	9	4	0.2	0.2	—
T400	23	—	226	—	—	—	—	—	—	—	—
T700	23	—	234	—	—	—	—	—	—	—	—
T800	23	—	300	—	—	—	—	—	—	—	—
Carbon Fiber（EC6）	23	1.79	294	—	—	—	—	—	0.2	0.2	0.2
Generic Pitch-based Carbon Fibers：											
E-35	23	—	241	—	—	—	—	—	—	—	—
E-55	23	—	378	—	—	—	—	—	—	—	—
E-75	23	—	516	—	—	—	—	—	—	—	—
E-105	23	—	724	—	—	—	—	—	—	—	—
E-120	23	—	827	—	—	—	—	—	—	—	—
E-130	23	—	894	—	—	—	—	—	—	—	—
Impact of Heat-Treatment on Young's Modulus of Pitch-based Carbon Fibers：											
Carbon Fiber	23	1.75	482	—	—	—	—	—	0.2	0.2	0.2
（Pitch；$d_f=9$ μm；Heat-treated$=2600$ ℃）											
Carbon Fiber	23	1.75	412	—	—	—	—	—	0.2	0.2	0.25
（Pitch；$d_f=9$ μm；Heat-treated$=2100$ ℃）											
Carbon Fiber	23	1.75	206	—	—	—	—	—	0.2	0.2	0.2
（Pitch；$d_f=9$ μm；Heat-treated$=1500$ ℃）											
Carbon Fiber	23	1.75	174	—	—	—	—	—	0.2	0.2	0.2
（Pitch；$d_f=9$ μm；Heat-treated$=1200$ ℃）											
Nanotubes：											
SWNT（Bulk；Measured）	−173	—	—	—	—	—	—	60	—	—	—
	−40	—	—	—	—	—	—	190	—	—	—
	23	1.4	1000	—	—	—	—	210	—	—	—
CNT：MWNT（Single）	23	1.4	850	5	5	—	—	—	—	—	—
CNT：SWNT（Single）	23	1.4	1000	5	5	—	—	—	—	—	—

continued

Material-DAM	$T/℃$	ρ	E_{11}	E_{22}	E_{33}	G_{12}	G_{13}	G_{23}	ν_{12}	ν_{13}	ν_{23}
SWNT (Bulk; Measured)	23	1.4	1000	—	—	—	—	—	—	—	—

Table 123.2   Thermal Properties of Carbon Fullerenes and Reinforcements

Material-DAM	$T/℃$	α_1	α_2	α_3	k_1	k_3	k_3	γ	β_1	β_2	β_3
Amoco PAN-based Carbon Fibers:											
Thornel 300	23	—	—	—	—	—	—	—	—	—	—
Amoco Pitch-based Carbon Fibers:											
K1100X	23	−1.6	—	—	1100	—	—	—	—	—	—
Epoxy/K1100X (V_f=60%)	23	−1.6	—	—	627	—	—	—	—	—	—
C/K1100X (V_f=53%)	23	−1.6	—	—	696	—	—	—	—	—	—
Thornel P25	23	—	—	—	—	—	—	—	—	—	—
Thornel P55	23	—	—	—	—	—	—	—	—	—	—
Thornel P75	23	—	—	—	—	—	—	—	—	—	—
Thornel P100	23	−1.6	—	—	520	—	—	—	—	—	—
Thornel P120	23	−1.4	6.8	6.8	640	—	—	837	—	—	—
Celanese PAN-based Carbon Fibers:											
Celion GY-70	23	—	—	—	—	—	—	—	—	—	—
Celion 1000	23	—	—	—	—	—	—	—	—	—	—
Celion ST	23	—	—	—	—	—	—	—	—	—	—
Hercules PAN-based Carbon Fibers:											
AS-4 (d_f=7 μm)	23	−1.7	—	—	7.2	—	—	—	—	—	—
AS-4 (Ni-coated)	23	−0.8	—	—	10.7	—	—	—	—	—	—
AS-6	23	—	—	—	—	—	—	—	—	—	—
HM-S Magnamite	23	—	—	—	—	—	—	—	—	—	—
IM-6	23	—	—	—	—	—	—	—	—	—	—
IM-7	23	—	—	—	—	—	—	—	—	—	—

continued

Material-DAM	$T/℃$	α_1	α_2	α_3	k_1	k_3	k_3	γ	β_1	β_2	β_3
Toray PAN-based Carbon Fibers:											
T300 ($d_f = 7$ μm)	23	−0.3	9	9	15	0.533	0.533	710	—	—	—
Generic Pitch-based Carbon Fibers:											
Carbon Fiber	23	—	—	—	1200	—	—	837	—	—	—
(Pitch; Vapor-grown)											
Carbon Fiber	23	—	—	—	466	—	—	837	—	—	—
(Pitch; $d_f = 9$ μm; Heat-treated $= 2600$ ℃)											
Carbon Fiber	23	—	—	—	120	—	—	837	—	—	—
(Pitch; $d_f = 9$ μm; Heat-treated $= 2100$ ℃)											
Carbon Fiber	23	—	—	—	66	—	—	837	—	—	—
(Pitch; $d_f = 9$ μm; Heat-treated $= 1500$ ℃)											
Carbon Fiber	23	—	—	—	31	—	—	837	—	—	—
(Pitch; $d_f = 9$ μm; Heat-treated $= 1200$ ℃)											
Nanotubes:											
CNT (Bulk)	23	—	—	—	1000	—	1100	—	—	—	—
CNT (fiber of 8.84 mm×12.9 μm; Measured)	23	—	—	—	456	1.52	1.52	735	—	—	—
CNT: MWNT (Single unit; Measured)	−200	—	—	—	500	—	—	—	—	—	—
	−40	—	—	—	2800	—	—	—	—	—	—
	23	—	—	—	3000	1.52	1.52	735	—	—	—
	50	—	—	—	3200	—	—	750	—	—	—
	100	—	—	—	2500	—	—	775	—	—	—
	125	—	—	—	—	—	—	800	—	—	—
CNT: MWNT (Random; Thin Film)	23	—	—	—	—	—	—	710	—	—	—
	80	—	—	—	—	—	—	790	—	—	—
	100	—	—	—	—	—	—	875	—	—	—
	120	—	—	—	—	—	—	900	—	—	—
CNT: SWNT (Single; theoretical)	−228	—	—	—	31000	—	—	—	—	—	—
	−173	—	—	—	37000	—	—	—	—	—	—
	−73	—	—	—	19000	—	—	—	—	—	—
	23	—	—	—	3000	—	—	—	—	—	—

continued

Material-DAM	$T/^\circ C$	α_1	α_2	α_3	k_1	k_3	k_3	γ	β_1	β_2	β_3
SWNT (Bulk; Random; Thin Film)	−173	—	—	—	60	—	—	—	—	—	—
	−40	—	—	—	190	—	—	—	—	—	—
	23	—	—	—	210	—	—	755	—	—	—
	80	—	—	—	—	—	—	810	—	—	—
	100	—	—	—	—	—	—	900	—	—	—
	125	—	—	—	—	—	—	1030	—	—	—
Kevlar-29 Fiber ($\rho = 1.44$)	23	−4	60	60	2.5	0.5	0.5	1230	—	—	—
Kevlar-49 Fiber ($\rho = 1.44$)	23	−2	54	54	3.5	0.5	0.5	1230	—	—	—
Kevlar-149 Fiber ($\rho = 1.47$)	23	—	—	—	4	0.5	0.5	1230	—	—	—
	550 (Decomposition temperature)										

Table 123.3 Orthotropic Mechanical Strengths of Carbon Fullerenes and Reinforcements

Material	$T/^\circ C$	$(\sigma_{11u}, \varepsilon_{11u})$	$(\sigma_{22u}, \varepsilon_{22u})$	$(\sigma_{33u}, \varepsilon_{33u})$	$(\sigma_{12u}, \varepsilon_{12u})/(\sigma_{23u}, \varepsilon_{23u})/(\sigma_{13u}, \varepsilon_{13u})$
Amoco PAN-based Carbon Fibers:					
Thornel 300	23	(3100, 1.3%)	—	—	—/—/—
Amoco Pitch-based Carbon Fibers:					
Thornel P25	23	(1400, 1.0%)	—	—	—/—/—
Thornel P55	23	(2100, 0.5%)	—	—	—/—/—
Thornel P75	23	(2000, 0.4%)	—	—	—/—/—
Thornel P100	23	(2200, 0.3%)	—	—	—/—/—
Thornel P120	23	$\sigma_{11c} = -500$; (2250, 0.27%)	—	—	—/—/—
Hysol Grafil PAN-based Carbon Fibers:					
Graphil HM	23	(2750, 0.7%)	—	—	—/—/—
Appolo HS 38-750	23	(5000, 1.9%)	—	—	—/—/—
Appolo IM 43-600	23	(4000, 1.3%)	—	—	—/—/—
Appolo HS 38-750	23	(5000, 1.9%)	—	—	—/—/—

continued

Material	$T/°C$	$(\sigma_{11u}, \varepsilon_{11u})$	$(\sigma_{22u}, \varepsilon_{22u})$	$(\sigma_{33u}, \varepsilon_{33u})$	$(\sigma_{12u}, \varepsilon_{12u})/(\sigma_{23u}, \varepsilon_{23u})/$ $(\sigma_{13u}, \varepsilon_{13u})$
Celanese PAN-based Carbon Fibers:					
Celion GY-70	23	$(1860, 0.4\%)$	—	—	—/—/—
Celion 1000	23	$(3240, 1.4\%)$	—	—	—/—/—
Celion ST	23	$(4340, 1.8\%)$	—	—	—/—/—
Hercules PAN-based Carbon Fibers:					
AS-4	23	$(3582, 1.53\%)$	—	—	—/—/—
AS-4 (Ni-coated)	23	$(2582, 1.33\%)$	—	—	—/—/—
AS-6	23	$(4140, 1.7\%)$	—	—	—/—/—
HM-S Magnamite	23	$(2210, 0.6\%)$	—	—	—/—/—
IM-6	23	$(4400, 1.4\%)$	—	—	—/—/—
IM-7	23	$\sigma_{11c} = -1100;$ $(4900, 1.7\%)$	—	—	—/—/—
Toray PAN-based Carbon Fibers:					
T50	23	$\sigma_{11c} = -1600$	—	—	—/—/—
T300	23	$\sigma_{11c} = -2800;$ $(3530, 2.36\%)$	—	—	—/—/—
T800	23	$(5700, 1.9\%)$	—	—	—/—/—
Generic Pitch-based Carbon Fibers:					
E-35	23	$\sigma_{11t} = 2800$	—	—	—/—/—
E-55	23	$\sigma_{11t} = 3200$	—	—	—/—/—
E-75	23	$\sigma_{11t} = 3100$	—	—	—/—/—
E-105	23	$\sigma_{11t} = 3300$	—	—	—/—/—
E-120	23	$\sigma_{11t} = 3400$	—	—	—/—/—
E-130	23	$\sigma_{11t} = 3900$	—	—	—/—/—
Carbon Fiber (EC6)	23	$\sigma_{11t} = 5000$	—	—	—/—/—
Carbon Fiber (M40A)	23	$(2400, 0.6\%)$	—	—	—/—/—

continued

Material	$T/^\circ\text{C}$	$(\sigma_{11u}, \varepsilon_{11u})$	$(\sigma_{22u}, \varepsilon_{22u})$	$(\sigma_{33u}, \varepsilon_{33u})$	$(\sigma_{12u}, \varepsilon_{12u})/(\sigma_{23u}, \varepsilon_{23u})/$ $(\sigma_{13u}, \varepsilon_{13u})$
Carbon Fiber	23	$(1900, 0.42\%)$	—	—	—/—/—
(Pitch; $d_f = 9$ μm; Heat-treated at 2600 ℃)					
Carbon Fiber	23	$(2700, 0.7\%)$	—	—	—/—/—
(Pitch; $d_f = 9$ μm; Heat-treated at 2100 ℃)					
Carbon Fiber	23	$(2300, 1.1\%)$	—	—	—/—/—
(Pitch; $d_f = 9$ μm; Heat-treated at 1500 ℃)					
Carbon Fiber	23	$(2000, 1.1\%)$	—	—	—/—/—
(Pitch; $d_f = 9$ μm; Heat-treated at 1200 ℃)					
Nanotubes:					
CNT: MWNT (Single)	23	$\sigma_{11t} = 63000$	—	—	—/—/—
CNT: SWNT (Single)	23	$(33000, 16\%)$	—	—	—/—/—

Table 123.4   Fatigue ε-N Properties of Carbon Reinforcements in the Longitudinal Direction

Material	$T/^\circ\text{C}$	$d\varepsilon/dt$	σ_f'	ε_f'	b	c	K'	n'	$\sigma_f @ 2N_f$	R
Kevlar-29 Fiber	23	—	—	—	—	—	—	—	1456@ 7.3×10^5	—
									1820@ 2.6×10^5	—

Electromagnetic Materials

Chapter 124

Conductors and Resistors

124.1 Introduction

A resistor is an electric component that resists the flow of electric currents. The voltage across the two terminals of a resistor is proportional to the current passing through it (Ohm's Law), as

$$V = IR \tag{124.1}$$

where:
V (V): Voltage;
I (A): Current;
R (Ω): Resistance.

Mechanical properties of resistive elements of chip resistors are listed in Table 124.1. Most chip resistors are of the "film" construction, where patterns of inks containing glass frit and a mix of metal and oxides are printed onto a ceramic substrate and converted to adherent. Films are stabilized at high temperatures, called co-fired, such as 850 ℃. The following three-layered elements are essential to make a chip resistor:

(a) Substrate (on the bottom): Alumina of high purity is a popular ceramic substrate.
(b) Resistive element (middle layer): TaN, RuO_2, $Bi2Ru_2O_7$, $Bi_2Ir_2O_7$, NiCr, or PbO.
(c) Glass (top layer): Protecting resistive elements.

Besides the three layers of materials given above, there need two electric conductors. They are

(d) Termination (at both ends): Typically AgPd, Ni, and Sn, solderable to the PCB.
(e) Electrode (connecting resistive elements to terminations): Typically Ag and AgPd.

Several resistive elements can be printed onto a single substrate to make a resistor network curtailed for applications. For example, TaN has been chosen for resistor fabrication because of its good resistivity uniformity, low TCR, low VCR, good thermal stability, and the fact that it can be tuned to achieve a wide range of electrical properties by varying the film stoichiometry.

124.2 Applications

TaN resistors are commonly used in RFIC (Radio Frequency Integrated Circuit) applications besides GaAs and are gaining acceptance in traditional CMOS (Complementary Metal-Oxide-Semiconductor) designs. TaN materials, frequently used in the fabrication of copper interconnects, can easily be applied to the fabrication of thin-film resistors.

References

BIROL H, MAEDER T, RYSER P, 2006. Influence of Processing and Conduction Materials on Properties of Co-fired Resistors in LTCC Structures[J]. Journal of the European Ceramic Society, 26: 1937-1941.

BLACKHOUSE C J, et al, 1997. Six Thin Films for Resistors[J]. Thin Solid Films, 311: 299-303.

CHUEH Y, et al, 2007. RuO_2 Nanowires and RuO_2/TiO_2 Core/Shell Nanowires: From Synthesis to Mechanical, Optical, Electrical, and Photoconductive Properties[J]. Advanced Materials, 19(1): 143-149.

FELMETSGERIS V, 2000. Controlled Sputtering Enables Better SiCr Films[J]. Semiconductor International, 23(12): 181-182, 184.

HAN C, SONG B, 2006. Development of Life Prediction Model for Lead-free Solder at Chip Resistor[C]. IEEE Electronics Packaging Technology Conference, 781-786.

HSI C S, LEE M W, 2002. Properties of Ruthenia-based Resistor Embedded in Low-temperature Co-firable Ceramic Substrate[J]. Japanese Journal of Applied Physics, 41(8): 5323-5328.

JONES W K, et al, 2000. Chemical, Structural and Mechanical Properties of LTCC Tapes[J]. International Symposium on Microelectronics, 23(4): 469-473.

KHANNA P K, et al, 2004. Miniature Pressure Sensor and Micromachined Actuator Structure based on Low-temperature Co-fired Ceramics and Piezoelectric Material[J]. Materi. Chem. Phys., 87: 173-178.

MENG L, SANTOS M, 2000. A Study of Residual Stress on RF Reactively Sputtered RuO_2 Thin Films[J]. Thin Solid Films, 375(1-2): 29-32.

PRUDENZIATI M, et al, 1994. Influence of The Preparing Conditions on the Physicochemical Characteristics of Glasses for Thick Film Hybrid Microelectronics[J]. Journal of Materials Research, 9: 2304-2313.

SCANDURRA A, et al, 2007. Tantalum Nitride (TaN) Thin Film Resistors by Low Temperature (100 ℃) Reactive Sputtering for Plastic Electronics[J]. Surface and Interface Analysis, 40(3-4): 758-762.

SUTTERLIN R C, et al, 2000. Thick-Film Resistor/Dielectric Interactions in a LTCC Package[J]. IEEE Transactions on Components, Packaging, and Manufacturing Technology, 18: 346-351.

TING C J, et al, 2000. Interactions between Ruthenia-based Resistors and Cordeite-Glass Substrate in Low-temperature Co-fired Ceramics[J]. Journal of American Ceramic Society, 83(12): 2945-2953.

WAITS R K, 1971. Silicide Resistors for Integrated Circuits[J]. IEEE Proceedings, 59(10): 1425-1429.

WU F Y, 2004. Theory of Resistor Networks: The Two-Point Resistance [J]. Journal of Physics A: Mathematical and General, 37(26): 6653.

WU F, et al, 1998. The Effects of the Process Parameters on the Electrical and Microstructure Characteristics of the CrSi Thin Resistor Films[J]. Thin Solid Films, 332: 418-422.

YANG P, et al, 2002. Processing, Microstructure and Electric Properties of Buried Resistors in Low-temperature Co-fired Ceramics[J]. Journal of Applied Ceramics, 89(7): 4175-4182.

Table 124.1 Mechanical Properties of Resistive Elements of Chip Resistors

Material-DAM	$T/^{\circ}\mathrm{C}$	E_{T}	ρ	ν	(σ, ε)	α	k	γ	ρ_{E}	K_{IC}
AgPd Electrode	23	72	—	0.17	—	16	140	—	—	—
(Dupont 6139)	150	—	—	—	—	—	—	—	—	—
AgPd Termination	−40	—	—	—	—	18	381	—	—	—
	23	72	—	0.17	—	16	140	—	—	—
$Bi_2Ru_2O_7$	23	—	—	—	—	—	—	—	—	—
$Bi_2Ir_2O_7$	23	—	—	—	—	—	—	—	—	—
Ni(Termination)	See Chapter 91									
NiCr	See Chapter 91									
PbO	23	—	9.38	—	—	—	—	—	—	—
	290 (T_{m})									
RuO_2(Ruthenia)	23	—	—	—	—	—	—	—	—	—
Sn(Termination)	23	See Chapter 94								
TaN	23	—	—	—	—	—	—	—	—	—

Chapter 125

Inductors

125.1 Introduction

An inductor, such as a wire or coil, is a passive 2-terminal electrical component that can store energy in a magnetic field created by the electric current passing through it. Energy is stored in a magnetic field in the coil as long as current flows. According to Faraday's law of electromagnetic induction, the time-varying magnetic field induces a voltage in the conductor when the current flowing through inductor changes, The induced voltage is directly proportional to the rate of change of the current across its terminals, as

$$V_{\mathrm{L}} = L \frac{\mathrm{d}i}{\mathrm{d}t} \tag{125.1}$$

where:
$V_{\mathrm{L}}(\mathrm{V})$: Voltage across terminals;
L (H): Inductance; Henry $\equiv$ V · s/A;
i (A): Current;
t (s): Time.

125.2 Applications

An inductor is characterized by its inductance. An inductor is usually made with a coil (conductor) wound on a core as a passive two-terminal element designed to store energy in its magnetic field. There are four different kinds of cores:

(a) Ceramic: A ceramic-cored inductor has a very linear response to changes in current, low distortion, and low hysteresis.
(b) Steel: A steel core offers low resistance and high inductance, but it may have problems with magnetic saturation.
(c) Ferrite: A ferrite core offers the highest resistance, but saturates more quickly than a steel core.
(d) Air: If no hard core is provided, it is called an air inductor. Since air does not possess magnetic properties, there is a little distortion but the coil has to be long to compensate for the low air inductance.

Mechanical properties of inductors are listed in Table 125.1. Inductors can be molded using plastic or ceramic insulation. Often used in circuit boards, they can assume either a cylindrical or bar formation, with windings featuring terminations at each end.

References

AHN C H, ALLEN, MARK, 1998. Micromachined Planar Inductors on Silicon Wafers for MEMS Applications [J]. IEEE Transactions on Industrial Electronics, 45(6): 866-876.

BLASCHKE V, VICTORY J, 2007. Accurate Inductance De-embedding Technique for Scalable Inductor Models[C]. 2007 IEEE International Conference on Microelectronic Test Structures, March 19-22, Tokyo, Japan.

CAO Y, et al, 2003. Frequency-independent Equivalent-circuit Model for On-chip Spiral Inductors[J]. IEEE Journal of Solid State Circuits, 38: 419-425.

DANIEL L, SULLIVAN C R, SANDERS S R, 1999. Design of Microfabricated Inductors [J]. IEEE Transactions on Power Electronics, 14(4): 709-723.

DEZUARI O, et al, 2000. High Inductance Planar Transformers[J]. Sensors and Actuators, A, Physics, 81 (1-3): 355-358.

GARCIA-ARRIBAS A, et al, 2013. Tailoring the Magnetic Anisotropy of Thin Film Permalloy Microstrips by Combined Shape and Induced Anisotropies[J]. European Physical Journal B, 86(4): 1-7.

GARDNER D S, et al, 2009. Review of On-chip Inductor Structures with Magnetic Films[J]. IEEE Trans. Magn., 45: 4760-4766.

GREENHOUSE H M, 1974. Design of Planar Rectangular Microelectronic Inductors[J]. IEEE Transactions on Parts, Hybrids, and Packaging, 10(2): 101-109.

HE X, et al, 1999. Low Temperature Sintering of Ni-Cu-Zn Ferrite for Multilayer-chip Inductor[J]. Journal of Inorganic Materials, 14(1): 71-77.

LI H, BANERJEE, KAUSTAV, 2009. High Frequency Analysis of Carbon Nanotube Interconnects and Implications for On-Chip Inductor Design[J]. IEEE Transactions on Electronic Devices, 56(10): 2202-2214.

HSIANG H I, et al, 2011. Ferrite Load Effects on the Mechanical and Electromagnetic Properties of NiZn Ferrite Powders-Epoxy Resin Coatings [J]. American Journal of Materials Science, 1(1): 40-44.

HURLEY W G, DUFFY M C, 1997. Calculation of Self- and Mutual Impedances in Planar Sandwich Inductors [J]. IEEE Transactions on Magnetics, 33: 2282-2290.

JIANG H, et al, 2000. On-Chip Spiral Inductors Suspended over Deep Copper-Lined Cavities[J]. IEEE Transactions on Microwave Theory Techniques, 48: 2415-2423.

KAISER, KENNETH L, 2004. Electromagnetic Compatibility Handbook[M]. CRC Press, Boca Raton.

KRISHNAVENI T, et al, 2006. Fabrication of Multilayer Chip Inductors Using Ni-Cu-Zn Ferrites[J]. Journal of Alloys and Compounds, 414(1-2): 282-286.

LUDWIG M, et al, 2003. PCB Integrated Inductors for Low Power DC/DC Converter[J]. IEEE Transactions on Power Electronics, 18(4): 937-945.

LUDWIG M, et al, 2003. Design Study for Ultrafast PCB-integrated Inductors for Low-power Conversion Applications[J]. IEEE Transactions on Magnetics, 39(5): 3193-3195.

MURTHY S R, 2013. Thermal Variation of Elastic Modulus on Nanocrystalline NiCuZn Ferrites[J]. Journal of Ceramics, 2013: 451863.

PURCELL E M, MORIN D J, 2013. Electricity and Magnetism[M]. Cambridge University Press, UK.

RYU H J, et al, 1998. 2D and 3D Simulation of Toroidal Type Thin Film Inductors[J]. IEEE Transactions on Magnetics, 34(4): 1360-1362.

SNELLING E C, GILES A D, 1986. Ferrites for Inductors and Transformers[M]. Research Studies Press, England.

TANG S C, et al, 2001. A Low-profile Power Converter Using Printed-Circuit Board (PCB) Power Transformer with Ferrite Polymer Composite[J]. IEEE Transactions on Power Electronics, 16: 493-498.

TIEMEIJER L F, et al, 2005. Comparison of the Pad-Open-Sort and Open-Short-Load De-embedding Techniques for Accurate On-Wafer RF Characterization of High-Quality Passives[J]. IEEE Transactions on MTT, 53(2): 723-729.

XU M, et al, 1998. A Micro-fabricated Transformer for High-Frequency Power or Signal Conversion[J]. IEEE Transactions on Magnetics, 34(4): 1369-1371.

XUE C, et al, 2006. Effect of the Silicon Substrate Structure on Chip Spiral Inductor[J]. Frontier of Electric and Electronic Engineering in China, 3(1): 110-115.

YAMAGUCHI M, et al, 1999. Microfabrication and Characteristics of Magnetic Thin-film Inductors in the High Frequency Region[J]. Journal of Applied Physics, 85: 7919-7922.

YOKOYAMA Y, et al, 2003. On-chip Variable Inductor Using Microelectromechanical Systems Technology[J]. Japanese Journal of Applied Physics, 42: 2190-2182.

YUE C P, WONG S S, 2000. Physical modeling of spiral inductor on silicon[J]. IEEE Transactions on Electronic Devices, 47(3): 560-568.

Table 125.1   Mechanical Properties of Inductors

Material-DAM	$T/℃$	E_T	ρ	ν	(σ, ε)	α	k	γ	ρ_E	K_{IC}
Carbon Fiber (Nano)	23	220	1.78	—	—	21.5	1000	710	—	—
70NiZn/30Ferrite	23	2.7	—	—	—	—	—	—	—	—
50NiZn/50Ferrite	23	1.37	—	—	—	—	—	—	—	—
30NiZn/70Ferrite	23	1.8	—	—	—	—	—	—	—	—
NiCuZn/Ferrite (Sintered)	23	182	5.4	0.24	—	9.7	—	—	—	—
	300	140	—	—	—	13.5	—	—	—	—

Chapter 126

Capacitors

126.1　Introduction

Capacitors are typically a solid dielectric material with high permittivity as the intervening medium between the stored positive and negative charges. Capacitance can be characterized as that property of a circuit element in which energy is able to be stored in an electric field. An electric circuit element showing the property of yielding a current directly proportional to the rate of change of the voltage across its terminal is called a capacitor. Thus, the voltage-current relationship involving a capacitance parameter in an electric circuit is

$$i = C \frac{\mathrm{d}V_{\mathrm{L}}}{\mathrm{d}t} \tag{126.1}$$

A capacitor is a passive electric component mainly made of a couple of conductors separated by a dielectric (insulator). Detailed estimated figures in value for the main capacitor families are:

(a) Ceramic Capacitors;
(b) Electrolytic Capacitors;
(c) Film and Paper Capacitors;
(d) Super Capacitors;
(e) Natural Capacitors.

Ceramic and film capacitors are electrostatic capacitors as they are non-polarized and can be applied to both Ac and DC operations. Aluminum and tantalum capacitors are electrolytic capacitors as they are polarized and only applicable to the DC operation. An electrolytic capacitor can have very high capacitance.

126.2　Ceramic Capacitors

There are almost a thousand electronic components on a cell phone PCB, of which more than 80% are capacitors and most of them (more than 60%) are ceramic capacitors. A perspective view of a capacitor soldered to a PCB for automotive electronics is shown in Fig. 126.1. Dielectric materials used for the construction of ceramic capacitors include: zirconium barium titanate, strontium titanate (ST), calcium titanate (CT), magnesium titanate (MT), calcium magnesium titanate (CMT), zinc titanate (ZT), lanthanum titanate (TLT), and neodymium titanate (TNT), barium zirconate (BZ), calcium zirconate (CZ), lead magnesium niobate (PMN), lead zinc niobate (PZN), lithium niobate (LN), barium stannate (BS), calcium stannate (CS), magnesium aluminum silicate, magnesium silicate, barium tantalate, titanium dioxide, niobium oxide, zirconia, silica, sapphire, beryllium oxide, and zirconium tin titanate.

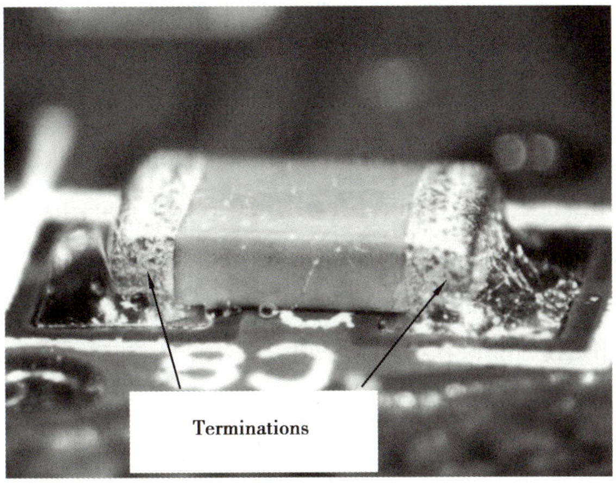

Fig. 126.1   Perspective View of a Capacitor as Soldered to a PCB

126.3   Multilayer Ceramic Capacitors

A multilayer capacitor consists of a monolithic ceramic brick with thin layers of printed electrodes being interleaved, Fig. 126.2. The distance between electrode surfaces is very small. Typical materials for electrodes and terminations of ceramic capacitors are listed as follows:

Classification	Embedded	Termination		
		Inner	Middle	Outer
Noble metal electrode	Ag/Pd	Ag	Ni	Sn
Base metal electrode	Ni/Cu	Cu	Ni	Sn

Fig.126.2   Schematic View of a Multilayered Ceramic Capacitor

Mechanical properties of multilayer ceramic capacitors are given in Table 126. 1. After the electrodes are screen-printed onto sheets of doped ceramic (e.g. barium titanate), the laminate is stacked under pressure, dried, cut to size and sintered at a high temperature (e.g. 1300 ℃), called co-fired. The termination for a chip capacitor is the same as that for a resistor. The electrodes must be of a metal with a melting point that is higher than the sintering temperature.

Typically electrodes are made of Pt (platinum), AgPd (Silver-Palladium), or less expensive substitutes such as Ni/Cu.

One set of electrodes extends to one surface end of the ceramic brick, where an electric contact is made by burnt-in metallic layers. The other set of electrodes goes to the other end. Each burnt-in metallic end is called termination. Generally there are three burnt-in metallic layers at each termination, made of the following materials: Ag (inner layer), Ni (intermediate layer), and Sn (external layer), of which Ag may be replaced by Cu (less costive). The capacitance of a multilayer capacitor is

$$C = \frac{\varepsilon_d (N - 1) A}{d} \qquad (126.2)$$

where $\quad \varepsilon = \varepsilon_{d0} \varepsilon_{dr} \qquad (126.3)$

where:

C (F): Capacitance of capacitor and 1 Farady = 1 A/V;

ε_{d0} (8.854×10^{-12} F/meter): Absolute die constant (permittivity) of vacuum;

ε_{d0} (F/m): Absolute dielectric constant and $\varepsilon_{d0} = 8.85 \times 10^{-12}$ F/m;

ε_{dr} (F/m): Relative dielectric constant (permittivity of material), $\varepsilon_{dr} = 1.0006$ for air;

N: Number of electrodes;

A (m^2): Effective electrode area per electrode;

d: Distance between electrode surfaces, usually very small.

Ceramic capacitors may fail due to manufacturing defects (voids, knitting, ...), flex cracks, thermal shock cracks, and placement cracks. As cracks develop, the capacitance decreases and the leakage current increases, and sometimes shorting of electrode occurs. Flex cracks are induced by bending PCB (printed circuit board) that may occur during depaneling, connector insertion, screwing, stand-off attachment, in-circuit testing, and customer use. A simply-supported bending test using a 1.6 mm PCB with a 90 mm span has been used for studying mechanical reliability of capacitors, Fig. 126.3. The deflection at the center of either 1 mm or 2 mm is used for the standard failure analysis, depending on the application and class of a capacitor. A capacitor with 10% drop in capacitance is considered a failure. Numbers of failures versus deflections such as 1 mm, 2 mm, 3 mm, and so on can be used for Weibull analysis.

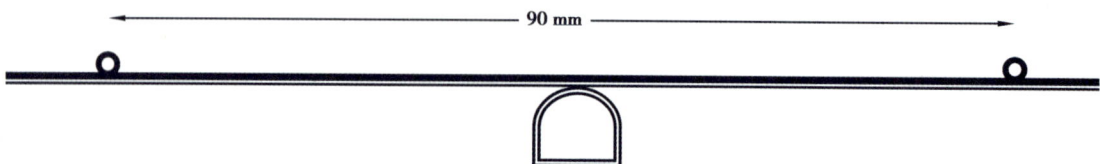

Fig. 126.3　Simple-supported Bending Test of a Capacitor

126.4   Film Capacitors

The dielectric films (mainly plastics) are drawn to a thin layer, provided with metallic electrodes and wound into a cylindrical winding. The electrodes of film capacitors may be metalized aluminum or zinc, applied on one or both sides of the plastic film, resulting in metalized film capacitors or a separate metallic foil overlying the film, called film/foil capacitors. The plastic films can be

(a) PEN (Polyethylene naphthalate): $0.9 \sim 1.4$ μm;
(b) PET (Polyethylene terephthalate): $0.7 \sim 0.9$ μm;
(c) PP (Polypropelene): $2.4 \sim 3.0$ μm;
(d) PPS (Polyphenylene sulfide): 1.2 μm;
(e) PTFE (Polytetrafluoroethylene).

PP and PET are the two most used plastic films. Film capacitors with their different plastic film material do have a small spread in dimension for a given capacitance/voltage value of a film capacitor because the minimum dielectric film thickness differs between the different film materials.

126.5   Electrolytic Capacitors

An electrolytic capacitor is a type of capacitor that uses an electrolyte, an ionic conducting liquid, as one of its plates, to achieve a larger capacitance per unit volume than other types. Mechanical properties of electrolytic capacitors are listed in Table 126.2. There are three different capacitor family members. They are aluminum electrolytic capacitors, tantalum electrolytic capacitors, and niobium electrolytic capacitors.

Aluminum electrolytic capacitors are constructed from two conducting aluminum foils, one of which is coated with an insulating oxide layer, and a paper spacer soaked in electrolyte. The foil insulated by the oxide layer is the anode while the liquid electrolyte and the second foil act as the cathode. This stack is then rolled up, fitted with pin connectors and placed in a cylindrical aluminum casing. The two most popular geometries are axial leads coming from the center of each circular face of the cylinder, or two radial leads or lugs on one of the circular faces.

The major use for tantalum, as tantalum metal powder, is in the production of mainly tantalum electrolytic capacitors, of which the frequently used dielectric material is Ta_2O_5 (Tantalum

Pentoxide). Tantalum (Ta) has the features of ductile, easily fabricated, highly resistant to distortion by high temperature and corrosion by strong acids, and a good conductor of heat and electricity and has a high melting point. Major end uses for tantalum capacitors include portable telephones, pagers, personal computers, and automotive electronics.

Niobium electrolytic capacitors, having Nb_2O_5(Niobium Pentoxide) as dielectric material, form another family of electrolytic capacitors.

126.6 Super Capacitors

Super capacitors have plates filled with two layers of an identical substance, which allows for separating the charge, also known as ultracapacitors, electric double-layer capacitors, super condensers, electrochemical double-layer capacitors, and pseudocapacitors. Without the need for a dielectric used in a conventional capacitor, the plates of a supercapacitor are packed with a larger surface area resulting in high capacitance. A super capacitor contains a positive cathode that uses activated carbon material. Charges are stored in an electric double layer. Development of the layer happens at the interface between the electrolyte and the carbon [Future Electronics]. Super capacitors have a high economic potential to become the main-stream power source for electric vehicles, as illustrated in Fig. 126.4.

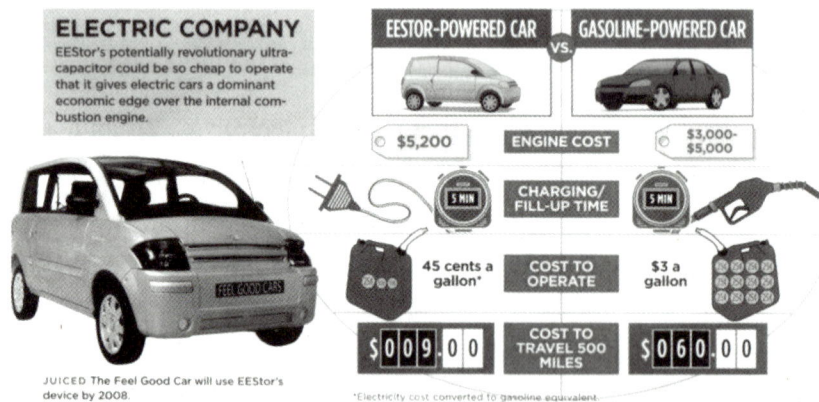

Fig. 126.4   Comparison between Super Capacitors-Powered and Gasoline-Powered Vehicles

Supercapacitors have a much higher power density than batteries, meaning they can provide power far more quickly than existing battery technology. On the other hand, supercapacitors have a very low energy density, meaning they cannot store as much energy per kg of weight as lithium-ion batteries.

126.7 Natural Capacitors

Natural things such as vacuum, air, mica, glass, and some other natural materials can be used for dielectrics to form capacitors.

References

BÉGUIN F, et al, 2009. Carbons for Electrochemical Energy Storage and Conversion Systems [M]. Boca Raton: CRC Press.

BREZESINSKI T, et al, 2010. Ordered Mesoporous α-MoO$_3$ with Iso-oriented Nanocrystalline Walls for Thin-film Pseudocapacitors[J]. Nature Materials, 9: 146-151.

CHAN Y C, YEUNG F, 1996. Electrical Failure of Multilayer Ceramic Capacitors Subjected to Environmental Screening Testing[J]. IEEE Transactions on Components, Packaging, and Manufacturing Technology, C, 19(3): 138-143.

CHEN K Y, et al, 2000. Advanced Characterization of Mechanical Properties of Multilayer Ceramic Capacitors [J]. Journal of Materials Science: Materials in Electronics, 25(2): 627-634.

CHIUO B S, et al, 1991. Temperature Cycling Effect between Sn/Pb Solder and Thick Film Pd/Ag Conductor Metallization[J]. IEEE Transactions on Components, Packaging, and Manufacturing Technology, B, 14 (1): 233-237.

DEN T J, RADEMAKER C, HU C, 2003. Residual Stresses in Multilayer Ceramic Capacitors: Measurement and Computation[J]. Journal of Electronic Packaging, 125(4): 506-511.

EL-HUSSEINI M H, et al, 2002. Thermal Simulation for Geometric Optimization of Metalized Polypropylene Film Capacitors[J]. IEEE Transactions on Industry Applications, 38(3): 713.

FARHAN M S, ZALNEZHAD E, BUSHROA A R, 2013. Properties of Ta$_2$O$_5$ Thin Films Prepared by On-assisted Deposition[J]. Materials Research Bulletin, 48(10): 4206-4209.

FRIEMAN S W, POHANKA R C, 1989. Review of Mechanical Related Failures of Ceramic Capacitors and Capacitor Materials[J]. Journal of the American Ceramic Society, 72(12): 2258-2263.

FU C Y, HUANG R F, 2000. BGA Reliability of Multilayer Ceramic Integrated Circuit Devices [J]. International Journal of Microcircuits and Electronic Packaging, 23(4): 393-399.

HÉCTOR D, ABRUÑA Y, HENDERSON J, 2008. Batteries and Electrochemical Capacitors [J]. (in German), Physics Today, 12: 43-47.

HSUEH C, FERBER M K, 2002. Apparent Coefficient of Thermal Expansion and Residual Stresses in Multilayer Capacitors[J]. Composites, Part A, 33(8): 1115-1121.

ISSHIKI N, et al, 2010. Preparation and Mechanical Properties of Rubber Composites Reinforced with Carbon Nanohorns[J]. Journal of Nanoscience and Nanotechnology, 10(6): 3810-3814.

KEIMASI M, AZARIAN M, PECHT M, 2007. Isothermal Aging Effects on Flex Cracking of Multilayer Ceramic Capacitors with Standard and Flexible Terminations[J]. Microelectronics Reliability, 47: 2215-2225.

KER M D, et al, 2008. On-Chip Transient Detection Circuit for System-Level ESD Protection in CMOS Integrated Circuits to Meet Electromagnetic Compatibility Regulation [J]. IEEE Transactions on Electromagnetic Compatibility, February 2008, 50(1): 13-21.

KORIPELLA C R, 1991. Mechanical Behavior of Ceramic Capacitors[J]. IEEE Transactions on Components, Hybrid, and Manufacturing Technology, 14(4): 718-724.

LEE Y C, et al, 2009. Investigation of Thin Film End Termination on Multilayer Ceramic Capacitors with Base-Metal Electrode[J]. Ceramic International, 35(2): 869-874.

LEITNER K W, WINTER M, BESENHARD J O, 2003. Composite Supercapacitor Electrodes[J]. Journal of Solid State Electrochemistry, 8(1): 15-16.

LI H, ZENG X, 2007. Study on the Structure and Properties of Thick-film Capacitors Fabricated by Laser Micro-cladding and Rapid Prototyping[J]. Journal of Materials Processing Technology, 184(1-3): 184-189.

LIN R, et al, 2011. Capacitive Energy Storage from −50 to 100 ℃ Using an Ionic Liquid Electrolyte[J]. Journal of Physical Chemistry Letters, 2: 2396-2401.

MUTHANA P, et al, 2005. Design Modeling and Characterization of Embedded Capacitors for Mid-frequency Decoupling in Semiconductor System[J]. Electromagnetic Compatibility, 2(1): 638-643.

OH J, NAM S, 2010. Causes of High Leakage Currents in Thin $BaTiO_3$ Films Prepared by Aerosol Deposition Method[J]. Journal of Korean Physics Society, 56(1): 448-452.

OUSTEN Y, XIONG B, 1993. Simulation of Assembly Generated Constraints of Ceramic Capacitors during SMT Processing and Size Optimization of the Capacitors by Design of Experiments [J]. Microelectronics International, 10(3): 26-32.

PARK J, et al, 2007. Thermo-mechanical Stresses and Mechanical Reliability of Multilayer Ceramic Capacitors (MLCC)[J]. Journal of the American Ceramic Society, 90(7): 2151-2158.

PARK J, et al, 2005. Residual Stress Evolution in Multilayer Ceramic Capacitors Corresponding to Layer Increase and Its Correlation to the Dielectric Constant[J]. Journal of Applied Physics, 97(9): 094504.

PARK S, 2005. Properties of Multilayer Ceramic Capacitors with $BaTiO_3$ Thin layers Deposited by E-Beam Evaporation[J]. Integrated Ferroelectrics, 74(1): 87-94.

PRUME K, et al, 1999. 3-Dimensional FEM Simulations of Resonances in the Impedance Characteristics of Ceramic Multilayer Capacitors[J]. Ferroelectrics, 224(1): 185-194.

PRYMAK J D, BERGANTHAL J, 1995. Capacitance Monitoring with Flex Testing[J]. IEEE Transactions on CPMT, 18(1): 180-186.

ROSTAMZADEH C, et al, 2009. Electrostatic Discharge Analysis of Multi-layer Ceramic Capacitors[J]. IEEE 978-1-4244-4267-6/09, 35-40.

SHAH M K, et al, 1989. Analysis of Parameters Influencing Stresses in the Solder Joints of Leadless Chip Capacitors[J]. ASME Paper No. 89-WA/EEP-31.

SHIH S, TUAN W, 2004. Solusability of Silver in $BaTiO_3$[J]. Journal of American Ceramic Society, 87: 401-407.

SMITH L, et al, 1999. Power Distribution System Design Methodology and Capacitor Selection for Modern CSMO Technology[J]. IEEE Transactions on Advanced Packaging, 22(3): 284.

SIMON P, GOGOTSI Y, 2008. Materials for Electrochemical Capacitors[J]. Nature Materials, 7: 845-854.

TIEN C L, et al, 2001. Simultaneous Determination of the Thermal Expansion Coefficient and the Elastic Modulus of Ta_2O_5 Thin Film Using Phase Shifting Interferometry[J]. Journal of Modern Optics, 47(10): 1681-1691.

TORTAI J H, et al, 2001. Self-healing of Capacitors with Metalized Film Technology: Experimental Observations and Theoretical Model[J]. Journal of Electrostatics, 53: 159-169.

VU-QUOC L, et al, 2003. Finite Element Analysis of Advanced Multilayer Capacitors[J]. International Journal for Numerical Methods in Engineering, 58: 397-461.

WANG X H, et al, 2001. Synthesis and Properties of Barium Titanate Based X7R Ceramics by Chemical Method[J]. Ferroelectrics, 262(1-4): 225-230.

WEI Q, et al, 2011. Microstructure and Mechanical Properties at Different Length Scales and Strain Rates of Nanocrystalline Tantalum Produced by High-Pressure Torsion[J]. Acta Materialia, 59: 2423-2436.

WERESZCZAK A A, et al, 1999. In-situ Mechanical Properties Evaluation of Dielectric Ceramics in Multilayer Capacitors[J]. SAE 00FCC-116.

YANG G, et al, 2006. Dielectric Behavior of $BaTiO_3$-based Ceramic Multilayer Capacitors under High DC Biased Field[J]. Journal of Physics, D: Applied Physics, 39(16): 3702.

YOON J, LEE K, LEE S, 2009. Analysis and Reliability of Multilayer Ceramic Capacitor with Inner Ni Electrode under Highly Accelerated Life test Conditions[J]. IEEE Transactions on Electrical and Electronics Materials, 10(1): 5-8.

YU B, WEI W, 2005. Defects of Base Electrode Layers in Multilayer Ceramic Capacitor[J]. Journal of

American Ceramic Society, 88(8): 2328-2331.

ZENNICEK T, et al, 2004. Technology of Niobium Oxide Capacitor[J]. Advancing Microelectronics, 31(3): 6-10.

Table 126.1 Mechanical Properties of Multilayer Ceramic Capacitors

Material-DAM	$T/℃$	E_T	ρ	ν	(σ, ε)	α	k	γ	ρ_E	K_{IC}
BaTiO$_3$	23	110	6.02	0.34	$\sigma_R = 62$	10.2	4.5	—	—	—
(Ceramic)	1625 (T_m)	—	—	—	—	—	—	—	—	—
AgPd (Electrode; DuPont 6139)	23	72	—	0.17	—	16	140	—	—	—
	150	—	—	—	—	—	—	—	—	—
AgPd (Termination)	23	—	—	—	—	18	381	—	—	—

Table 126.2 Mechanical Properties of Electrolytic Capacitors

Material-DAM	$T/℃$	E_T	ρ	ν	(σ, ε)	α	k	γ	ρ_E	K_{IC}
Tantalum (Purity>99.95%)	23	186	16.6	—	(180,0.2%) $\sigma_{uts} = 200$	6.4	54	145	—	—
	600	—	—	—	—	6.85	57	149	—	—
	1000	155	—	—	—	7.1	57	155	—	—
	1400	—	—	—	—	—	—	180	—	—
	2000	128	—	—	—	—	—	—	—	—
	2996 (T_m)	—	—	—	—	—	—	—	—	—
Ta$_2$O$_5$-β (Orthorhombic)	23	—	8.18	—	—	3.6	—	—	—	—
Ta$_2$O$_5$-α (Tetragonal)	23	—	8.37	—	—	3.2	—	—	—	—

Chapter 127

Permanent Magnets

127.1　Introduction

Material that produces a magnetic field is called a magnet. If the material is so magnetized that it has its own persistent magnetic field, it is called a permanent magnet. A permanent magnet is a magnet that is permanent in contrast to an electromagnet, which only behaves like a magnet when an electric current is flowing through it. Each permanent magnet for example the earth, has two poles, named north and south. Engineering specifications of permanent magnets may include the following:

(a) Material type;

(b) Nominal, minimum and/or maximum magnetic properties;

(c) Geometry and tolerances of magnet;

(d) Orientation direction (and tolerance of orientation direction if critical);

(e) Whether to be supplied magnetized or not;

(f) Marking requirements;

(g) Coating requirements;

(h) Acceptance tests or performance requirements;

(i) Inspection sampling plan;

(j) Packaging and identification.

MMPA (Magnet Materials Producers Association) is represented on the United States National Committee of IEC/TC68, IEC (International Electrochemical Commission). IEC was given the responsibility of securing the cooperation of technical societies to consider the question of international electrical standardization including magnets. Magnets are in principle classified into the following four categories:

(a) Rare Earth Magnets (R4 & R5): Permanent magnets such as Nd-Fe-B;

(b) Iron-Chromium-Cobalt Magnets (R2);

(c) Alnico Magnets (R1): Permanent magnets lack ductility, i.e. inherently extremely brittle;

(4) Ferrites, Ceramic (S1): Containing nickel, zinc, and/or manganese compounds.

Mechanical properties of magnets are given in Table 127.1. Most permanent magnet materials lack ductility and are inherently brittle.

127.2　Retentivity and Coercivity

The Curie temperature (T_c) is the temperature, at which a ferromagnetic (magnetic spins are aligned parallel within) or a ferrimagnetic material (magnetic spins are aligned anti-parallel within) becomes paramagnetic (magnetic moments in a completely disordered state) upon heating. The effect is reversible. In other words, a magnet will lose its magnetism if heated above the Curie temperature and regain it once cooled down below Curie temperature.

Principal magnetic parameters, such as B_R(retentivity), H_C(coercivity), H_{CI}(intrinsic coercivity), and $(BH)_{max}$ of a magnetic material, are used to characterize a specific subgrade within a material class. B_R and H_C are defined in Chapter 133. H_{CI} is the demagnetizing force, which reduces the intrinsic induction in the material to zero ($B_I = 0$) after magnetizing to saturation.

BH, the product of H (taken as positive) and B at the point (H, B) on the B-H demagnetization curve, is called the energy product. $(BH)_{max}$ is the maximum value of energy product, of which the init is J/m^3 or kJ/m^3 in the metric unit system. It measures the maximum amount of magnetic flux taken out from the magnet per unit volume. When a magnetic circuit is designed up to the maximum energy product point, the magnet volume can be made the smallest. However, when a magnet operates at $(BH)_{max}$ it may not be generating a large enough magnetic field for a particular application and therefore, a greater volume may be required. Most magnets used in applications are not designed to operate at $(BH)_{max}$.

Note that retentivity is also called residual induction, and coercivity is also called coercive force. Each magnet parameter as a function of the magnet's temperature can be predicted utilizing the following regression parameters:

(a) Reversible temperature coefficient of retentivity, %/℃ ;
(b) Reversible temperature coefficient of coercivity, %/℃ ;
(c) Reversible temperature coefficient of intrinsic coercivity, %/℃ ;
(d) Curie temperature (T_c), ℃ ;
(e) Maximum service temperature T_{max}, ℃.

Magnetic properties of magnets are given in Table 127.2.

127.3   Rare Earth Magnets (R4 & R5)

Bonded Nd-Fe-B magnets are produced by mixing the magnetic Nd-Fe-B powder with polymer resins (e. g. PA, PPS, and LCP) and followed by a molding process-injection molding, compression molding, extrusion, or calendaring. PPS and LCP have higher melting points than PA and can be used for higher operating temperatures. PPS is more brittle than PA (Nylon).

The linear coefficient of thermal expansion of binding polymer is much higher than Nd-Fe-B magnets, especially at a working temperature higher than its corresponding glass transition point (T_g). Debonding in interfacial areas between Nd-Fe-B and polymers is the main cause of failure at a temperature between 100 ℃ and 180 ℃. It is foreseeable via Fig. 127.1. It was found that the coercive force of NdFeB sintered magnets decreases as the increasing grain alignment of $Nd_2Fe_{14}B$.

BLDC electric motors of electric cars work through an interaction between an Nd-Fe-B permanent magnet and an electromagnetic field.

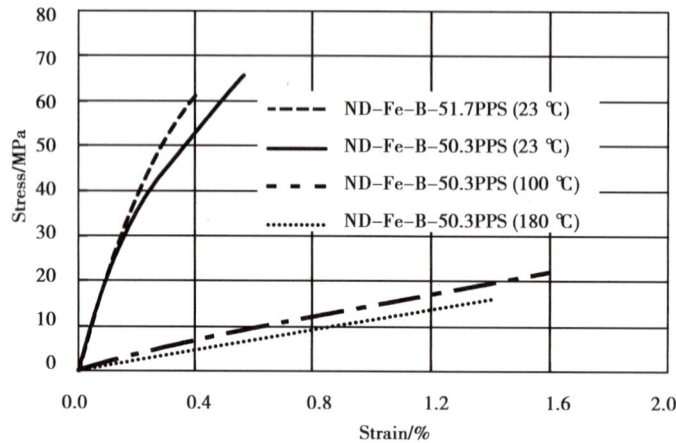

Fig. 127.1   Stress-Strain Curves of Bonded Nd-Fe-B/ %50.3PPS and Nd-Fe-B/ %51.7PPS（50.3% and 51.7% of PPS by Volume, Respectively）

127.4   Iron-Chromium-Cobalt Magnets（R2）

Fe-Cr-Co magnets provide a compromising solution between magnetic and mechanical properties. As a magnet, its performance is similar to Alnico magnet 5, but better magnetic consistency than Alnico 5. Fe-Cr-Co alloys can be shaped into different shapes such as block, rod, tube, strip, and wire of the desired size; and machined by probing, drilling, grinding, punching and so on. An Fe-Cr-Co magnetic wire of 0.05 mm in diameter or a strip of 0.1 mm in thickness is feasible. The working temperature can be as high as 400 ℃.

127.5   Alnico Magnets（R1）

Alnico magnets mainly consist of aluminum, nickel, copper, iron cobalt, and titanium, while cobalt and titanium are optional. Also, an alnico magnet may contain additions of silicon, columbium, zirconium or other elements, which enhance heat treatment response of one of the magnetic characteristics. The magnetic performance of most alnico magnets can be increased in a preferred direction by applying a magnetic field during heat treatment, thus producing magnetic anisotropy. Alnico magnets are hard and extremely brittle and do not lend themselves to conventional machining.

127.6   Ceramic Ferrites (S1)

Ferrites are usually non-conductive ferrimagnetic ceramic compounds derived from iron oxides such as hematite (Fe_2O_3) or magnetite (Fe_3O_4) as well as oxides of other metals. Ceramic ferrites are brittle like most other ceramics.

127.6.1   Flexible Ferrites

Commonly used flexible ferrites are divided into the following two categories [Ullah]:

(a) Manganese-zinc ferrites ($Mn_\delta Zn_{(1-\delta)} Fe_2O_4$), have higher permeability and saturation induction than Ni-Zn ferrites.

(b) Nickel-zinc ferrites ($Ni_\delta Zn_{(1-\delta)} Fe_2O_4$), show higher resistivity than Mn-Zn ferrites, and are therefore more suitable for frequencies above 1 MHz.

$Mn_\delta Zn_{(1-\delta)} Fe_2O_4$ and $Ni_\delta Zn_{(1-\delta)} Fe_2O_4$ are flexible ferrites and usually are used in transformer or electromagnetic cores.

127.6.2   Hard Ferrites

There are three major hard ferrites. They are $BaO\text{-}6Fe_2O_3$, $CoO\text{-}6Fe_2O_3$, and $SrO\text{-}6Fe_2O_3$. They are mainly used in micro-wave devices, recording media, magneto-optic media, subwoofers, telecommunication, and the electronic industry.

127.7   Metglas

Certain metal alloys, however, can be cooled so fast that the atoms do not have time to arrange themselves in a regular fashion but are instead arranged in a "more or less" amorphous manner like the atoms in ordinary glass. They are called Metglas. As a family of magnetic materials made this way, they are an ideal solution for a wide of applications, ranging from distribution transformers, magnetic anti-theft tags, motors, high-frequency inductors, etc. Metglas includes

(a) Metglas 2605SA1 (Fe-based): High permeability and extremely low core loss;

(b) Metglas 2605S3A (Fe-based): High permeability, high service temperature;

(c) Metglas 2705M (Co-based): Near-zero magnetostriction with square BH loop;

(d) Metglas 2714A (Co-based): Ultra permeability; may be annealed for linear BH loop;

(e) Metglas 2826MB (Fe-Ni-based): Medium saturation while good corrosion resistance.

Metglas offers the potential of reducing the core losses of motors and transformers. Core losses of 2605CO and 2605SA1 at 60 Hz and under 1.4 Tesla are 0.22 W/kg and 0.29 W/kg, respectively.

Inductive filters to reduce electromagnetic interference (EMI) are commonly made by winding coils around a magnetic material with high permeability. This permeability should remain high at high frequencies, so that the impedance of the inductor made from it can be large in order to block off any high-frequency EMI signals.

References

CAMPBELL P. 1994. Permanent Magnet Materials and Their Application [M]. Cambridge: Cambridge University Press.

CHEN C, WALMER M, WALMER M, et al, 1999. The Relationship of Thermal Expansion to Magnetocrystalline Anisotropy, Spontaneous Magnetization, and T_c for Permanent Magnets[J]. Journal of Applied Physics, 85(8): 5669-5671.

CHEN M, NIKLES, DAVID E, 2002. Synthesis, Self-assembly, and Magnetic Properties of $Fe_xCo_yPt_{100-x-y}$ Nanoparticles[J]. Nano Letters, 2(3): 211-214.

COCHARDT A W. 1956. High Damping Ferromagnetic Alloys[J]. Journal of Metallurgy, 206: 1295-1298.

CROAT J J, et al, 1984. Pr-Fe and Nd-Fe Based Materials: A New Class of High-Performance Permanent Magnets[J]. Journal of Applied Physics, 55: 2078-2082.

DAIGLE A, et al, 2011. Structure, Morphology and Magnetic Properties of $Mg_{(x)}Zn_{(1-x)}Fe_2O_4$ Ferrites Prepared by Polyol and Aqueous Co-precipitation Methods: a Low-Toxicity Alternative to $Ni_{(x)}Zn_{(1-x)}Fe_2O_4$ Ferrites[J]. Nanotechnology, 22(30): 305708.

DE CAMPOS M F, et al, 1998. Chemical Composition and Coercivity of $SmCo_5$ Magnets[J]. Journal of Applied Physics, 84(1): 368-373.

DEMAREST K, 1997. Engineering Electromagnetics[M]. Prentice Hall, New York, NY, USA.

FURLANI E P, 2001. Permanent Magnet and Electromechanical Devices: Materials, Analysis, and Applications[M]. Sault Lake City: Academic Press.

GARRELL M G, et al, 2003. Mechanical Properties of Nylon Bonded Nd-Fe-B Permanent Magnets[J]. Journal of Magnetism and Magnetic Materials, 257(1): 32-43.

GARRELL M G, et al, 2003. Mechanical Properties of Polyphenylene Sulfide (PPS) Bonded Nd-Fe-B

Permanent Magnets[J]. Materials and Engineering, A, 359: 375-383.

GRIMBERG R, et al, 2000. Magnetic Sensor Used for the Determination of Fatigue State in Ferromagnetic Steels[J]. Sensors and Actuators A: Physical, 81(1-3): 371-373.

HORTON J A, WRIGHT J L, HERCHENROEDER J W, 1996. Fracture Toughness of Commercial Magnets [J]. IEEE Transactions on Magnetism, 32: 4374-4376.

IKUMA K, et al, 1994. High-Energy Extrusion-Molded Nd-Fe-B Magnets[J]. Journal of Magnets Japan, 9: 94-99.

JIANG J, et al, 2000. Influence on Alloying Elements on Mechanical Properties and Microstructures of Sintered Nd-Fe-Co-B Magnets[J]. Journal of Magnetism and Magnetic Materials, 214: 61-68.

KIM T H, et al, 2003. Finite Element Analysis of Brushless DC Motor Considering Freewheeling Diodes and DC Link Voltage Ripple[J]. IEEE Transactions on Magnetics, 39(5): 3274-3276.

LADDHA S, Van AKEN D C, 1995. On the Application of Magnetomechanical Models to Explain Damping in an Antiferromagnetic Copper-Manganese Alloys[J]. Metallurgical and Materials Transactions, 26(4): 957-964.

LUO HONG M, et al, 2005. Magnetic Cobalt Nanowire Thin Films[J]. Journal of Physical Chemistry B, 109 (5): 1919-1922.

MATSUURA Y, et al, 2013. Relation between $Nd_2Fe_{14}B$ Grain Alignment and Coercive Force Decrease Ratio in NdFeB Sintered Magnets[J]. Journal of Magnetism and Magnetic Materials, 336(6): 88-92.

OKAMOTO A, 2009. The Invention of Ferrites and Their Contribution to the Miniaturization of Radios[C]. 2009 IEEE Globecom Workshops, 1-6.

RABINOVICH Y M, et al, 1996. Physical and Mechanical Properties of Sintered Nd-Fe-B Type Permanent Magnets[J]. Intermetallics, 4: 641-645.

SAGAWA M, FUJIMURA S, TOGAWA N, et al, 1984. New Material for Permanent Magnets on a Base of Nd and Fe[J]. Journal of Applied Physics, 55: 2083-2087.

ULLAH Z, ATIQ S, NASEEM S. 2013. Influence of Pb Doping on Structural, Electrical and Magnetic Properties of Sr-Hexaferrites[J]. Journal of Alloys and Compounds, 555: 263-267.

XIAO J, OTAIGBE J, 2000. Polymer Bonded Magnets: II. Effect of Liquid Crystal Polymer and Surface Modification on Magneto-Mechanical Properties[J]. Polymer Composites, 21(2): 332-342.

Table 127.1　Mechanical Properties of Magnets ［ETCO］［MMPA］

Material-DAM	$T/^{\circ}\mathrm{C}$	E_{T}	ρ	ν	(σ, ε)	α	k	γ	ρ_{E}	K_{IC}
Rare Earth Magnets（***R***4 & ***R***5），***Sintered***：										
Fe-1Sm-5Co （1~5 Alloys）	23	160	8.2	—	$\sigma_{\mathrm{uts}}=41$	6/13	2	—	—	—
	300（High service temperature）									
	750（T_{c}）	—	—	—	—	—	—	—	—	—
Fe-2Sm-17Co （2~17 Alloys）	23	118	8.4	—	$\sigma_{\mathrm{uts}}=35$	8/11	2	—	—	—
	350（High service temperature）									
	825（T_{c}）	—	—	—	—	—	—	—	—	—
Nd-Fe-B	23	118	7.4	—	$\sigma_{\mathrm{uts}}=83$	3.4/4.8	2	—	—	—
	100（High service temperature）									
	310（T_{c}）	—	—	—	—	—	—	—	—	—
Nd-Fe-B /50.3PPS （Bonded； $V_{\mathrm{f}}=50.3\%$）	−40	—	—	—	$\sigma_{\mathrm{uts}}=82$	—	—	—	—	—
	23	100	7.5	0.24	(35, 0.2%) (66, 0.57%)	—	10	—	—	—
	100	—	—	—	(4, 0.2%) (22, 1.6%)	—				
	180	—	—	—	(2, 0.2%) (16, 1.4%)	—	—			
	310（T_{c}）	—	—	—	—	—	—	—	—	—
Nd-Fe-B /52PPS （Bonded； $V_{\mathrm{f}}=52\%$）	−40	—	—	—	$\sigma_{\mathrm{uts}}=77$	—	—	—	—	—
	23	100	7.5	0.24	(40, 0.2%) (62, 0.42%)	—	10	—	—	—
	100	—	—	—	$\sigma_{\mathrm{uts}}=22$	—	—	—	—	—
	180	—	—	—	$\sigma_{\mathrm{uts}}=17$	—	—	—	—	—
	310（T_{c}）	—	—	—	—	—	—	—	—	—
Nd-Fe-B /60PPS （Bonded； $V_{\mathrm{f}}=60\%$）	−40	—	—	—	$\sigma_{\mathrm{uts}}=48$	—	—	—	—	—
	23	100	7.5	0.24	(43, 0.2%) (46, 0.23%)	—	10	—	—	—
	100	—	—	—	$\sigma_{\mathrm{uts}}=12$	—	—	—	—	—
	310（T_{c}）	—	—	—	—	—	—	—	—	—
Nd-Fe-B /72PPS （Bonded； $V_{\mathrm{f}}=72\%$）	−40	—	—	—	$\sigma_{\mathrm{uts}}=37$	—	—	—	—	—
	23	100	7.5	0.24	(17, 0.2%) (19, 0.39%)	—	10	—	—	—
	100	—	—	—	$\sigma_{\mathrm{uts}}=2$	—	—	—	—	—
	310（T_{c}）	—	—	—	—	—	—	—	—	—
2Nd-84Fe-14B （Sintered）	23	152	7.5	0.24	$\sigma_{\mathrm{uts}}=83$	—	10	420	—	—
	310（T_{c}）	—	—	—	—	—	—	—	—	—

continued

Material-DAM	$T/^\circ\mathrm{C}$	E_T	ρ	ν	(σ, ε)	α	k	γ	ρ_E	K_IC
15Nd-77Fe-8B	23	—	—	—	$\sigma_\mathrm{uts}=285$	—	10	—	—	—
14.5Nd-1.5Dy-1Nb-76Fe-7B	23	—	—	—	$\sigma_\mathrm{uts}=240$	—	10	—	—	—
Iron-Chromium-Cobalt Magnets (R2):										
Fe-Cr-Co (2)	23	—	7.7	—	—	10	21	—	—	—
Fe-Cr-Co (5)	23	—	7.7	—	—	10	21	—	—	—
Fe-Cr-Co (250)	23	—	7.7	—	—	10	21	—	—	—
	550 (High service temperature)									
	860 (T_c)	—	—	—	—	—	—	—	—	—
Alnico Magnets (R1):										
Alnico (R1-0-1)	23	150	6.9	—	$\sigma_\mathrm{uts}=28$; $\sigma_\mathrm{R}=97$	12.6	—	425	—	—
	540 (High service temperature)									
	860 (T_c)	—	—	—	—	—	—	—	—	—
Alnico (R1-0-2)	23	150	6.9	—	$\sigma_\mathrm{uts}=83$; $\sigma_\mathrm{R}=158$	13	—	425	—	—
	540 (High service temperature)									
	860 (T_c)	—	—	—	—	—	—	—	—	—
Alnico (R1-0-4)	23	150	6.9	—	—	13	—	425	—	—
	450 (High service temperature)									
	810 (T_c)	—	—	—	—	—	—	—	—	—
Alnico (R1-1-1)	23	150	7.3	—	$\sigma_\mathrm{uts}=37$; $\sigma_\mathrm{R}=72$	11.4	—	425	—	—
	525 (High service temperature)									
	860 (T_c)	—	—	—	—	—	—	—	—	—
Alnico (R1-1-2)	23	150	7.3	—	$\sigma_\mathrm{uts}=36$; $\sigma_\mathrm{R}=62$	11	—	425	—	—
Alnico (R1-1-3)	23	150	7.3	—	$\sigma_\mathrm{uts}=34$; $\sigma_\mathrm{R}=55$	11	—	425	—	—
Alnico (R1-1-4)	23	150	7.3	—	$\sigma_\mathrm{uts}=158$; $\sigma_\mathrm{R}=310$	11	—	425	—	—
	525 (High service temperature)									
	860 (T_c)	—	—	—	—	—	—	—	—	—

continued

Material-DAM	$T/°C$	E_T	ρ	ν	$(\sigma,\ \varepsilon)$	α	k	γ	ρ_E	K_{IC}
Alnico (R1-1-5)	23	150	7.3	—	$\sigma_{uts}=69$; $\sigma_R=207$	11	—	425	—	—
	550 (High service temperature)									
	860 (T_c)	—	—	—	—	—	—	—	—	—
Alnico (R1-1-6)	23	150	7.3	—	$\sigma_{uts}=48$; $\sigma_R=55$	11	—	425	—	—
	550 (High service temperature)									
	860 (T_c)	—	—	—	—	—	—	—	—	—
Alnico (R1-1-7)	23	150	7.3	—	$\sigma_{uts}=69$; $\sigma_R=207$	11.0	—	425	—	—
	550 (High service temperature)									
	860 (T_c)	—	—	—	—	—	—	—	—	—
Alnico (R1-1-10)	23	150	6.9	—	$\sigma_{uts}=345$; $\sigma_R=379$	11.4	—	425	—	—
Alnico (R1-1-11)	23	150	6.9	—	$\sigma_{uts}=379$; $\sigma_R=689$	11.4	—	425	—	—
Alnico (R1-1-12)	23	150	7.0	—	$\sigma_{uts}=345$; $\sigma_R=379$	11	—	425	—	—
Ferrites, Ceramic (S1):										
$Mn_\delta Zn_{(1-\delta)}Fe_2O_4$ ($\delta=0.1$; Flexible)	23	180	3.7	0.28	$\sigma_{ucs}=-895$; $\sigma_{uts}=3$	14/10	2.9	750	—	—
	450 (T_c)	—	—	—	—	—	—	—	—	—
$Ni_\delta Zn_{(1-\delta)}Fe_2O_4$ ($\delta=0.1$; Flexible)	23	180	3.7	0.28	$\sigma_{ucs}=-895$; $\sigma_{uts}=3$	7.5	2.9	750	—	—
	450 (T_c)	—	—	—	—	—	—	—	—	—
$BaO\text{-}6Fe_2O_3$ (Barium Ferrite; Hard; Sintered)	23	180	4.9	0.28	$\sigma_{ucs}=-895$; $\sigma_{uts}=35$	10	3	750	—	—
	400 (High service temperature)									
	450 (T_c)	—	—	—	—	—	—	—	—	—
$CoO\text{-}6Fe_2O_3$ (Cobalt Ferrite; Hard; Sintered)	23	180	4.9	0.28	$\sigma_{ucs}=-895$; $\sigma_{uts}=35$	10	3	750	—	—
	400 (High service temperature)									
	450 (T_c)	—	—	—	—	—	—	—	—	—

continued

Material-DAM	$T/℃$	E_T	ρ	ν	(σ, ε)	α	k	γ	ρ_E	K_{IC}
SrO-6Fe$_2$O$_3$ (Strontium Ferrite Hard)	23	180	4.9	0.28	$\sigma_{ucs}=-895$; $\sigma_{uts}=35$	10	3	750	—	—
	400 (High service temperature)									
	460 (T_c)	—	—	—	—	—	—	—	—	—
Metglas (Metallic Glass):										
2605SA1 (Fe-based; Fe$_{32}$Ni$_{36}$Cr$_{14}$P$_{12}$B$_6$)	23	105	7.18	—	$\sigma_{ucs}=-1500$;	7.6	—	—	1.3	—
	150 (High service temperature)									
	399 (T_c)	—	—	—	—	—	—	—	—	—
	508 ($T_{crysta lization}$)									
2605S3A (Fe-based)	23	105	—	—	—	—	—	—	—	—
	399 (T_c)	—	—	—	—	—	—	—	—	—
2705M (Co-based)	23	105	—	—	—	—	—	—	—	—
	— (T_c)	—	—	—	—	—	—	—	—	—
2714A (Co-based)	23	105	7.59	—	$\sigma_{ucs}=-1300$;	12.7	—	—	—	—
	90 (High service temperature)									
	225 (T_c)	—	—	—	—	—	—	—	—	—
2826MB (Fe-Ni-based)	23	105	—	—	—	—	—	—	—	—
	— (T_c)	—	—	—	—	—	—	—	—	—

Notes: Ferrites (ceramic magnets) = Mn$_\delta$Zn$_{(1-\delta)}$Fe$_2$O$_4$, Ni$_\delta$Zn$_{(1-\delta)}$Fe$_2$O$_4$, & Mg$_\delta$Zn$_{(1-\delta)}$Fe$_2$O$_4$;

Alnico magnets = Alloys made of Al, Ni, Co, Cu, Fe, Ti, & others; brittle for structural parts;

Nd-Fe-B = As averaged for Nd-2Fe-14B, while actual data may vary much;

T_c (℃) = Curie temperature;

σ_{uts} (MPa), ε_{uts} = Ultimate tensile strength and strain; $\sigma_{ucs} \gg \sigma_{uts}$ for a magnet;

σ_R (MPa) = Rupture strength, resulting from 3-point bending tests;

α (mm/m/℃) = Coefficient of linear thermal expansion, // & ⊥ to magnetization directions;

ρ_E (mΩ · m) = Electric resistivity.

Table 127.2   Electromagnetic Properties of Magnets [MMPA]

Code (IEC)	$T/℃$	$(BH)_{max}$ /(J · m^{-3})	B_R/T	H_C/(kA · m^{-1})	H_{CI} /(kA · m^{-1})	ρ_E /(Ω · m)
Ferrites, Ceramic (S1):						
S1-0-1	23	8.35×10^3	0.23	$150-0.002(23-T)$	260	0.7×10^{-6}
S1-1-2	23	21.9×10^3	0.34	$260-0.002(23-T)$	320	0.7×10^{-6}
S1-1-5	23	27.8×10^3	0.39	$235-0.002(23-T)$	245	0.7×10^{-6}
S1-1-6	23	27.1×10^3	0.38	$190-0.002(23-T)$	200	0.7×10^{-6}

continued

Code (IEC)	$T/℃$	$(BH)_{max}$ $/(J \cdot m^{-3})$	B_R/T	$H_C/(kA \cdot m^{-1})$	H_{CI} $/(kA \cdot m^{-1})$	ρ_E $/(\Omega \cdot m)$
Alnico Magnets (R1):						
R1-0-1	23	11.1×10^3	0.72	37	38	0.75×10^{-6}
R1-0-2	23	10.7×10^3	0.70	38	40	0.6×10^{-6}
R1-0-4	23	13.5×10^3	0.75	45-0.02(23-T)	46	0.65×10^{-6}
R1-1-1	23	43.8×10^3	1.28	51+0.01(23-T)	51	0.47×10^{-6}
R1-1-2	23	57.7×10^3	1.33	53	53	0.47×10^{-6}
R1-1-3	23	59.7×10^3	1.35	59	59	0.47×10^{-6}
R1-1-4	23	31×10^3	1.05	62	64	0.5×10^{-6}
R1-1-5	23	42.2×10^3	0.82	131	148	0.53×10^{-6}
R1-1-6	23	71.6×10^3	1.06	119+0.01(23-T)	119	0.53×10^{-6}
R1-1-7	23	39.8×10^3	0.72	151	173	0.54×10^{-6}
R1-1-8	23	—	—	—	—	0.54×10^{-6}
R1-1-10	23	—	—	—	—	0.5×10^{-6}
R1-1-11	23	—	—	—	—	0.54×10^{-6}
R1-1-12	23	—	—	—	—	0.54×10^{-6}
R1-1-13	23	—	—	—	—	0.54×10^{-6}
Iron-Chromium-Cobalt Magnets (R2):						
Fe-Cr-Co(1)	23	12.8×10^3	0.89	38	—	0.7×10^{-6}
Fe-Cr-Co(2)	23	12.7×10^3	0.99-0.00036(T-23)	28	—	0.7×10^{-6}
Fe-Cr-Co(5)	23	41.8×10^3	1.35-0.0002(T-23)	48	700	0.7×10^{-6}
Fe-Cr-Co(250)	23	15.9×10^3	1.4-0.0003(T-23)	20	—	0.7×10^{-6}
Fe-Cr-Co(640)	23	35×10^3	1.2	51	—	0.7×10^{-6}
Rare Earth Magnets (R4 & R5), Sintered:						
Fe-1Sm-5Co	23	130×10^3	0.83	600-0.04(T-23)	1510	0.53×10^{-6}
Fe-2Sm-17Co	23	140×10^3	0.87	680-0.035(T-23)	1390	0.86×10^{-6}
$Nd_2Fe_{14}B$	23	300×10^3	1.25 *	950-0.09(T-23)	190	1.6×10^{-6}

continued

Code (IEC)	$T/°C$	$(BH)_{max}$ $/(J \cdot m^{-3})$	B_R/T	$H_C/(kA \cdot m^{-1})$	H_{CI} $/(kA \cdot m^{-1})$	ρ_E $/(\Omega \cdot m)$
Metglas:						
2605SA1	23	—	1.5	—	—	1.3×10^{-6}
2605S3A	23	—	—	—	—	—
2705M	23	—	—	—	—	—
2714A	23	—	0.45	—	—	—
2826MB	23	—	—	—	—	—
Stainless Steels:						
410 (Annealed)	23	—	—	0.48	—	—
410 (Hard)	23	—	—	2.9	—	—
420 (Annealed)	23	—	—	0.8	—	—
420 (Hard)	23	—	—	3.6	—	—
430F (Annealed Solenoid)	23	—	—	0.16	—	—
430FR (Annealed Solenoid)	23	—	—	0.16	—	—
440B (Hard)	23	—	—	5.1	—	—

Notes: $(BH)_{max}(J/m^3)$ = Maximum energy product;

$B_R(T)$ = Coercivity, i.e. coercive force;

$H_C(kA/m)$ = Coercivity, i.e. coercive force;

$H_{CI}(kA/m)$ = Intrinsic coercivity;

$\rho_E(Wm)$ = Resistivity as an electric conductor;

T (°C) = Temperature, with the nominal value taken at the room temperature (23 °C);

* = As averaged, while actual data may vary much.

Chapter 128

Solders

128.1　Introduction

Mechanical properties of solder materials at different temperatures [Siewert et al.] are given in Table 128.1.

Intermetallic layers laid between solder alloys and bonding pads play a crucial role in the structural integrity of solder joints, such as compatibility in thermal expansion. Cu_6Sn_5, Cu_3Sn, and Ni_3Sn_4 are widely used in Cu- and Au-Ni-Cu-based solder systems and their mechanical properties are given in Table 128.2 [Fields et al.] [Yang et al.].

128.2　Sn-based Solder Joints

Sn-Ag-Cu (Tin-Silver-Copper) alloys have emerged as the most beloved lead-free alternatives for electronic solder joints. SAC stands for an Sn-Ag-Cu solder and its composition is sometimes written as

　　SACxyz

where:
Silver (Ag) content in solder by weight as $x.y\%$;
Cu content in solder by weight as $0.z\%$;
Sn content $= 100\% - x.y\% - 0.z\%$ (by weight).

As an example, SAC405 (Sn-4Ag-0.5Cu) means that the solder consists of 95.5% Sn, 4% Ag, and 0.5% Cu by weight. Sn-based solder joints with silver content ranging from 3.4% to 4.1% and copper content ranging from 0.45% to 0.9% have been studied ever since the early 1990s [Kariaya and Otsuka] [Lau and Pao] [Schubert et al.]. Though Sn-3Ag-0.5Cu is the frequently used lead- free solder [Bath et al.], it has been proven by Intel that Sn-4Ag-0.5Cu can outperform SnPb in a working environment ranging between −40 ℃ and 100 ℃.

The stress-strain curves (loops) due to a temperature variation between −25 ℃ and 125 ℃ behave hysteretic with wide scatter [Hall]. The compressive strength is considerably higher than the tensile strength. An increase in Ag content enhances the solder's fatigue life.

Tensile creep at elevated temperatures is of great concern due to its practical application to the estimation of the fatigue life of solders. Few publications on isochronous stress-strain curves of bulk Sn-3.0Ag-0.5Cu (SAC in short) subjected to creep at elevated temperatures are available.

The creep behavior of Sn-based solders may be described by the hyperbolic power law as given by

[Pang & and Xiong]:

$$\frac{d\varepsilon_{creep}}{dt} = A \left[\sinh(B\sigma)\right]^{N} \exp\left(\frac{-Q}{RT}\right) \tag{128.1}$$

The challenge of Sn-based solder joints is their application at elevated temperatures, e.g. temperature > 125 ℃.

Creep behavior of bulk, PCB sample, and flip-chip solder joint samples of Sn-4.0Ag-0.5Cu solder may be classified into two mechanisms for steady-state creep- climb controlled (low stress) and combined glide/climb (high stress) mechanisms. The steady-state creep behavior using a double power law model is shown below [Wiese et al.].

$$(d\varepsilon_{creep}/ dt) = (ds / dt) / E + A_1 D_1(\sigma / \sigma_n)^3 + A_2 D_2(\sigma / \sigma_n)^{12} \tag{128.2}$$

where:
ε_{creep}: Uniaxial equivalent creep strain;
σ (MPa): Equivalent stress (flow stress);
E (MPa) = 59533 − 200 (T − 273) / 3: Young's modulus for solders;
T (℃): Temperature;
$A_1 = 4 \times 10^{-7}\ \text{s}^{-1}$;
$A_2 = 1 \times 10^{-12}\ \text{s}^{-1}$;
$D_1 = \exp(-3223 / (T - 273))$;
$D_2 = \exp(-7348 / (T - 273))$;
$\sigma_n(\text{MPa}) = 1$.

Creep properties of solder materials are given in Table 128.3.

128.3 Bi-based Solder Joints

Bi-based solder joints have gained their momentum in high-temperature applications such as inverters of fuel cell-based electric vehicles. The major drawback of Bi-based solder joints is brittleness at cold temperatures.

128.4 Pb-based Solder Joints

The creep behavior of most solders can also be described by the hyperbolic power law as given by Eq. (6.1) [Darveaux & Banerji]. Pb-based solders are prohibited because they are toxic.

128.5 Fatigue Life

Factors affecting the solder life are listed as follows [Intel]:

(a) Component to board CTE (coefficient of linear thermal expansion) mismatch;

(b) Component type such as BGA vs. Socket;

(c) Pad size (component and board);

(d) Pad size ratio;

(e) Metallurgy (e.g. PbSn vs. SAC405);

(f) Component die size (Range: 8 mm to 12 mm);

(g) Body size (package size ranging from 14 to 42.5 mm sq);

(h) Body (package) thickness/stiffness;

(i) Ball array design;

(j) PCB board thickness/stiffness;

(k) Joint shape;

(l) Load on solder joint;

(m) Bend mode;

(n) Finish compatibility.

The fatigue properties of solders are listed in Table 128.4.

References

AMAGAI M, 1999. Chip Scale package (CSP) Solder Joint Reliability and Modeling[J]. Microelectronics Reliability, 39: 463-477.

BASARAN C, CHANDAROY R, 2002. Thermomechanical Analysis of Solder Joints under Thermal and Vibration Loading[J]. Journal of Electronic Packaging, 124: 60-66.

BATH J, et al, 2000. Research Update: Lead Free Solder Alternatives[J]. Journal of Circuit Assembly, 11 (5): 31-40.

CHROMIC R R, 2003. Measuring the Mechanical Properties of Pb-Free Solder and Sn-Based Intermetallics by Nanoindentation[J]. JOM, 55(6): 66-69.

DARVEAUX R, BANERJI K, 1992. Constitutive Relations for Tin-based Solder Joints[J]. IEEE Transactions on Components, Hybrids and Manufacturing Technology, 15(6): 1013-1024.

EL-DALLY A A, et al, 2008. Influences of Ag and Au Additions on Structure and Tensile Strength of Sn-5Sb Lead Free Solder Alloy[J]. Journal of Materials Science and Technology[J]. 24(6): 921-925.

ERINC M, et al, 2008. Intergranular Thermal Fatigue Damage Evolution in SnAgCu Lead-Free Solder[J]. Mechanics of Materials, 40: 780-791.

GUO X, et al, 2012. Vibration Fatigue Analysis of the Solder Connector[J]. Applied Mechanics and Materials, 105/107: 294-298.

HAMPSHIRE W B, 1992. The Search for Lead-free Solders[J]. Soldering & Surface Mount Technology, 5 (2): 49-52.

KARIAYA Y, OTSUKA, M, 2004. Mechanical Fatigue Characteristics of Sn-3.5Ag-*X* (*X*=Bi, Cu, Zn) Solder Alloys[J]. Journal of Electronic Materials, 27(11): 1229-1235.

KARIAYA Y, OTSUKA M, 2001. Mechanical Properties of Sn-3.0mass% Ag-0.5mass% Cu Alloy [J]. Proceedings of the 7th Symposium on Micro-joining and Assembly Technology in Electronics, 7: 383-388.

KAWASHIMA K, ITO T, SAKRAGI M, 1992. Strain-rate and Temperature-dependent Stress- strain Curves of Sn-Pb Eutectic Alloy[J]. Journal of Material Science, 27(23): 6387-6390.

KIM D, et al, 2005. Effect of Aging Conditions on Interfacial Reaction and Mechanical Joint Strength between Sn-3Ag-0.5Cu solder and Ni-P UBM[J]. Material Science and Engineering B, 121(3): 204-210.

KIM K, et al, 2004. The Observation and Simulation of Sn-Ag-Cu Solder Solidification in Chip-Scale Packaging [J]. JOM, June 2004, 39-43.

KING J A, 1988. Material Handbook for Hybrid Microelectronics[M]. Artec House, Norwood, MA, USA.

LAI Y S, et al, 2007. Evaluation of Solder Joint Strengths under Ball Impact Test[J]. Microelectronics Reliability, 47(1): 111-117.

LALENA J N, et al, 2002. Experimental Investigation of Ge-Doped Bi-11Ag as a New Pb-Free Alloys for Power Die Attachment[J]. Journal of Electronic Materials, 31(11): 1244-1249.

LANG F, et al, 2005. The Effect of Strain Rate and Temperature on the Tensile Properties of Sn-3.5Ag Solder [J]. Materials Characterization, 54(3): 223-229.

LAU J H, PAO Y H, 1997. Solder Joint Reliability of BGA, CSP, Flip Chip, and Fine Pitch SMT Assemblies [M]. McGraw-Hill, New York, NY, USA.

LAU J H, RICKY L S, 2002. Modeling and Analysis of 96.5Sn-3.5Ag Lead free Solder Joint of Wafer Level Chip Scale Package on Buildup Microvia Printed Circuit Board[J]. IEEE Transactions on Electronics Packaging Manufacturing, 25(1): 51-58.

LEE J E, et al, 2005. Interface Properties of Zn-Sn Alloys as High Temperature Lead-free Solder on Cu Substrate[J]. Materials Transactions, 46(11): 2413-2418.

LEE T, LEE J, JUNG I, 1998. Finite Element Analysis for Solder Ball Failures in Chip Scale Package[J]. Microelectronics Reliability, 38: 328-337.

LEE W, et al, 2000. Solder Joint Fatigue Models: Review and Applicability to Chip Scale Package[J]. Microelectronics Reliability, 40: 231-244.

MCCABE R J, FINE M E, 2000. The Creep Properties of Precipitation-Strengthened Tin-Based Alloys[J]. Journal of Materials, 57: 33-35.

MANKO H H, 1992. Solders and Soldering[M]. McGraw-Hill, New York, NY, USA.

MIAO H, et al, 2004. Thermal Cycle Test in Sn-Bi and Sn-Bi-Cu Solder Joints[J]. Journal of Material Science: Materials in Electronics, 11(8): 609-618.

MILLER C M, ANDERSON I E, SMITH J F, 1994. A Viable Tin-Lead Solder Substitute: Sn-Ag-Cu[J]. Journal Electronic Materials, 23(7): 595-601.

OSTERMAN M, DASGUPTA A, 2007. Life Expectancies of Pb-Free SAC Solder Interconnects in Electronic Hardware[J]. Journal of Material Science, 18: 229-236.

PANG H L J, XIONG B S, 2005. Mechanical Properties for 95.5Sn3.8Ag0.7Cu Lead-free Alloys[J]. IEEE Transactions on Components and Packaging Technology, 28: 830-840.

PANG H L J, 2004. Low Cycle Fatigue Models for Lead-Free Solders[J]. Thin Solid Films, 462/463: 408-412.

PANG H L J, 2002. A New Creep Constitutive Model for Eutectic Solder Alloy[J]. Journal of Electronic Packaging, 124: 85-90.

PANG H L J, CHONG D Y R, 2001. Flip Chip on Board Solder Joint Reliability Analysis[J]. IEEE Transactions on Advanced Packaging, 24(4): 499-506.

PAO Y H, et al, 1994. Thermomechanical and Fatigue Behavior of High Temperature Lead and Lead-free Solder Joints[J]. Fatigue of Electronic Materials, 60-81.

REN F, NAH J, TU K, et al, 2006. Electromigration Induced Ductile-to-Brittle Transition in Lead-Free Solder Joints[J]. Applied Physics Letters, 89(14): 141914.1-141914.3.

REN W, et al, 1997. Thermal Mechanical Property Tests of New Lead-free Solder Joints[J]. Soldering and Surface Mounting Technology, 9(3): 37-40.

RETTENMAYR M, et al, 2002. Zn-Al Based Alloys as Pb-free Solders for Die Attach[J]. Journal of Electronic Materials, 31(4): 278-285.

ROELLIG M, et al, 2008. Fatigue Analysis of Miniaturized Lead-free Solder Contacts Based on a Novel Test Concept[J]. Microelectronics Reliability, 47(2-3): 187-195.

SARIHAN V, 1999. Temperature dependent Viscoplastic Simulation of Controlled Collapse Sold Joint under Thermal Cycling[J]. Journal of Electronic Packaging, 115: 16-21.

SASAKI K, et al, 2001. Viscoplastic Deformation of 40Pb/60Sn Solder Alloys-Experiment and Constitutive Modeling[J]. Journal of Electronic Packaging, 123: 379-387.

SCHUBERT A, et al, 2001. Thermo-Mechanical Properties and Creep Deformation of Lead-containing and Lead-free Solders[J]. Proceedings of International Symposium on Advanced Packaging Materials, 129-134.

SEELIG K, SURASKI D, 2000. The Status of Lead-Free Solder Alloys[J]. Circuits Assembly, 11(9): 56, 58, 60-61.

SHI X Q, WANG Z P, YANG Q J, et al, 2003. Creep Behavior and Deformation Mechanism Map of Sn-Pb Eutectic Solder Alloy[J]. Journal of Engineering Materials & Technology, 125(1): 81-88.

SHOHJI I, YOSHIDA T, TAKAHASHI T, et al, 2004. Tensile Properties of Sn-Ag Based Lead-Free Solders and Strain Rate Sensitivity[J]. Material Science and Engineering A, 366(1): 50-55.

SPRAUL M, et al, 2007. Reliability of SnPb and Pb-free Flips under Different Test Conditions [J]. Microelectronics Reliability, 47: 252-258.

SUN P, et al, 2006. Coffin-Manson Constant Determination for a Sn-8Zn-3Bi Lead-free Solder Joint[J]. Soldering and Surface Mounting Technology, 18(2): 4-11.

TAKAO H, et al, 2002. Mechanical Properties and Solder Joint Reliability of Low-Melting Sn-Bi-Cu Lead Free Solder Alloy[J]. R&D Review of Toyota CRDL, 5(2): 152-158.

TANG H, BASARAN C, 2003. A Damage Mechanics-based Fatigue Life Prediction Model for Solder Joints[J]. Journal of Electronic Packaging, 125: 120-125.

VANDEVELDE B, et al, 2007. Thermal Cycling Reliability of SnAgCu and SnPb Solder Joints: A Comparison for Several IC-packages[J]. Microelectronics Reliability, 47: 259-265.

VASUDEVAN V, FAN X, 2008. An Acceleration Model for Lead-Free (SAC) Solder Joint Reliability under Thermal Cycling[J]. IEEE Electronic Components and Technology Conference, 139-145.

VIANCO P T, et al, 2003. The Compression Stress-strain Behavior of Sn-Ag-Cu Solder [J]. Journal of Minerals, Metals and Materials Society, 55(6): 50-55.

WEI Y, CHOW C L, 2006. Isothermal Fatigue Damage Model for Lead-free Solder[J]. International Journal of Damage Mechanics, 15: 109-119.

WIESE S, et al, 2003. Microstructural Dependence of Constitutive Properties of Eutectic SnAg and SnAgCu Solders[J]. 53rd ECTC 2003, 197-206.

XU L, et al, 2010. Intermediate Strain Rate Dependent Mechanical Properties for Lead-Free Solder[C]. 12th IEEE Intersociety Conference on Thermal and Thermomechanical Phenomena in Electronic Systems (ITherm), 1-6.

YAMADA Y, et al, 2006. Novel Bi-based High-temperature Solder for Mounting Power Semiconductor Devices

[J]. R&D Review of Toyota CRDL, 41(2): 43-48.

YAN C, QIN Q, MAI Y, 2001. Nonlinear Analysis of Plastic Ball Grid Array Solder Joints[J]. Journal of Materials Science: Material Electronics, 12: 667-673.

YANG P F, et al, 2007. Mechanical Properties of Cu_6Sn_5, Cu_3Sn, and Ni_3Sn_4 Intermetallic Compounds Measured by Nanoindentation[C]. Electronic Packing Technology, 1-5.

YOON J, et al, 2005. Interfacial Reaction and Mechanical Properties of Eutectic Sn-0.7Cu/Ni BGA Solder Joints during Isothermal Long-term Aging[J]. Journal of Alloys & Compounds, 391(1-2): 82-89.

ZHAI C J, et al, 2003. Board Level Solder Reliability versus Ramp Rate and Dwell Time during Temperature Cycling[J]. IEEE Transactions on Devices and Materials Reliability, 3(4): 207-212.

ZHOU H, ZHANG Z, 2008. Ductile-to-Brittle Transition Induced by Increasing Strain Rate in Sn-3Cu/Cu Joints[J]. Journal of Materials Research, 23(6): 1614-1617.

ZHU F, et al, 2007. The Effect of Temperature and Strain Rate on the Tensile Properties of a Sn99.3-Cu0.7(Ni) Lead-Free Solder Alloy[J]. Microelectronic Engineering, 84(1): 144-150.

Table 128.1 Mechanical Properties of Solders and Intermetallics for Electronic Packaging

Material-DAM	$T/℃$	E_T	ρ	ν	(σ, ε)	α	k	γ	ρ_E	K_{IC}
95Au-3Si-...	23	83	15.7	—	—	—	27	147	—	—
	363 (T_m)	—	—	—	—	—	—	—	—	—
88Au-12Ge	23	69.3	14.7	—	(215, 1%)	13	44	—	—	—
	85	—	—	—	—	—	44	—	—	—
	150	62.7	—	—	—	—	—	—	—	—
	356 (T_m)	—	—	—	—	—	—	—	—	—
80Au-20Sn	23	59.2	14.5	—	(276, 2%)	16	57	388	0.16	—
	85	—	—	—	—	—	57	—	—	—
	150	35.8	—	—	—	—	—	—	—	—
	280 (T_m)	—	—	—	—	—	—	—	—	—
Bi	23	31.7	9.8	0.33	—	13.4	8	122	1.29	—
	85	—	—	—	—	—	8	—	—	—
	271 (T_m)	—		—	—	—	—	—	—	—
Bi/Cu-23Al-2Mn	−40	—	—	—	(21.5, 0.2%)	—	—	—	—	—
	23	—	—	—	(17, 0.5%)	—	—	—	—	—
	105	—	—	—	(19, 3.9%)	—	—	—	—	—
	195	—	—	—	(11, 4.1%)	—	—	—	—	—
	270 (T_m)	—	—	—	—	—	—	—	—	—

continued

Material-DAM	$T/℃$	E_T	ρ	ν	(σ, ε)	α	k	γ	ρ_E	K_{IC}
Bi-42Sn	23	—	8.56	—	(57, 55%)	14.3	19	46	0.383	—
	85	—	—	—	—	—	19	—	—	—
	138 (T_m)	—	—	—	—	—	—	—	—	—
Cr	23	—	7.1	—	—	8.2	91	449	0.2	—
	1860 (T_m)	—	—	—	—	—	—	—	—	—
In	23	—	7.31	—	(8.6, 20%)	32.1	86	239	0.0837	—
	156 (T_m)	—	—	—	—	—	—	—	—	—
In-3Ag	23	—	7.38	—	(7.3, 55%)	—	73	—	0.075	—
	143 (T_m)	—	—	—	—	—	—	—	—	—
In-10Ag	23	—	7.54	—	(6.7, 115%)	—	67	—	0.078	—
	143 (T_m)	—	—	—	—	—	—	—	—	—
Mo	23	324	10.22	0.31	—	4.8	138	245	0.05	—
	2623 (T_m)	—	—	—	—	—	—	—	—	—
Pb (Sand Cast)	23	14	11.32	0.42	(1.5, 0.2%) $\sigma_{uts}=5.5$	29	35	—	—	—
	327 (T_m)	—	—	—	—	—	—	—	—	—
Pb-9Sb	23	—	—	—	$\sigma_{uts}=52$	—	35	—	—	—
Sb (Antimony)	23	55	6.7	0.375	$\sigma_{uts}=11.4$	11	24	209	0.39	—
	631 (T_m)	6.53	—	—	—	—	—	—	—	—
Sn-0.3Ag-0.7Cu	23	52	7.33	—	(30, 22%)	—	—	—	—	—
	228 (T_m)	—	—	—	—	—	—	—	—	—
Sn-0.5Ag-4Cu	23	52	7.4	—	$\sigma_{uts}=29.7$	—	—	—	—	—
	226 (T_m)	—	—	—	—	—	—	—	—	—
Sn-0.8Ag-0.7Cu	23	52	7.33	—	(31, 21%)	—	—	—	0.14	—
	85	—	—	—	—	—	60	—	—	—
	225 (T_m)	—	—	—	—	—	—	—	—	—
Sn-1Ag-0.5Cu	23	52	7.32	—	(40, 13%)	—	—	—	0.133	—
	85	—	—	—	—	—	60	—	—	—
	227 (T_m)	—	—	—	—	—	—	—	—	—
Sn-2.5Ag-0.8Cu-0.5Sb	23	52	7.36	—	(34, 0.2%) (39.5, 50%)	27	57.3	219	0.121	—
	216 (T_m)	—	—	—	—	—	—	—	—	—

continued

Material-DAM	$T/℃$	E_T	ρ	ν	(σ, ε)	α	k	γ	ρ_E	K_{IC}
Sn-2.8Ag-20In	23	39	7.25	0.4	$(47, 47\%)$	28	53.5	—	0.132	—
Sn-3Ag-0.5Cu	−25	57	—	—	$(42, 0.2\%)$ $\sigma_{uts}=66$	19	—	—	—	—
	23	48	7.44	0.39	$(37, 0.2\%)$ $(43, 47\%)$	21	—	—	0.132	—
	75	47	—	—	$(21, 0.2\%)$ $\sigma_{uts}=33$	22	—	—	—	—
	85	—	—	—	—	—	58	—	—	—
	125	46	—	—	$(14, 0.2\%)$ $\sigma_{uts}=22$	23	—	—	—	—
	160	43	—	—	$(10, 0.2\%)$ $\sigma_{uts}=16$	24	—	—	—	—
	200	38	—	—	—	—	—	—	—	—
	221 (T_m)	—	—	—	—	—	—	—	—	—
Sn-3.1Ag-0.5Cu	23	45	7.44	0.39	$(40, 0.2\%)$ $\sigma_{uts}=49$	21	—	—	0.132	—
Sn-3.2Ag-0.8Cu (As Cast)	23	48	7.44	0.39	$(28, 0.2\%)$ $(32, 26\%)$	21	—	—	0.132	—
Sn-3.5Ag (As cast)	−50	62	—	—	—	—	—	—	—	—
	0	53	—	—	—	—	—	—	—	—
	23	50	7.37	0.38	$(24, 0.2\%)$ $(28, 21\%)$; $\sigma_{crs,1000}=14$	20	78	—	0.123	—
	85	—	—	—	—	21.5	55	—	—	—
	100	34	—	—	$\sigma_{crs,1000}=5.5$	—	—	—	—	—
	150	25	—	—	—	23	—	—	—	—
	221 (T_m)	—	—	—	—	—	—	—	—	—
Sn-3.5Ag-0.7Cu	23	46	—	0.38	—	—	—	—	—	—
	100	42	—	—	—	—	—	—	—	—
Sn-3.5Ag-0.5Sb-1Cd	23	—	7.39	0.38	—	20.5	—	64	0.123	—
	221 (T_m)	—	—	—	—	—	—	—	—	—

continued

Material-DAM	$T/°C$	E_T	ρ	ν	(σ, ε)	α	k	γ	ρ_E	K_{IC}
Sn-3.8Ag-0.7Cu	0	50.2	—	—	$(43.2, 0.2\%)$	—	—	—	—	—
	23	46	7.5	0.38	$(35, 0.2\%)$ $(40, 16\%)$	16.7	60	—	0.132	—
	50	44	—	—	$(32.4, 0.2\%)$	17.6	—	—	—	—
	85	—	—	—	—	—	60	—	—	—
	100	35	—	—	—	18.8	60	—	—	—
	150	27.7	—	0.4	$(21.4, 0.2\%)$	—	—	—	—	—
Sn-3.9Ag-0.5Cu	23	49.5	7.44	0.37	$(35, 0.2\%)$ $\sigma_{uts} = 41$	—	60	—	0.132	—
	160	—	—	—	$(10, 0.2\%)$	—	—	—	—	—
Sn-4Ag-0.5Cu	23	40	7.44	0.36	$(32, 0.2\%)$ $(40, 17\%)$	—	62	—	0.132	—
	85	—	—	—	—	—	60	—	—	—
	221 (T_m)	—	—	—	—	—	—	—	—	—
Sn-4.1Ag-0.5Cu	23	43	7.44	0.36	$(33, 0.2\%)$ $\sigma_{uts} = 36$	—	60	—	0.132	—
Sn-4.7Ag-1.7Cu (As Drawn)	−50	56.4	—	—	—	—	—	—	—	—
	−25	—	—	—	$(42, 0.2\%)$	—	—	—	—	—
	23	51	—	0.34	$(32, 0.2\%)$ $\sigma_{uts} = 44$	—	—	—	—	—
	100	44.8	—	—	—	—	—	—	—	—
	160	39.5	—	—	$(11, 0.2\%)$	—	—	—	—	—
	200	36	—	—	—	—	—	—	—	—
Sn-5Ag	23	43	7.4	0.36	$(25, 0.2\%)$ $(57, 30\%)$	—	—	—	0.137	—
	221 (T_m)	—	—	—	—	—	—	—	—	—
Sn-25Ag-10Sb	23	—	7.8	—	$\sigma_{uts} = 118$	—	—	—	—	—
	85	—	—	—	—	—	36	—	—	—
	233 (T_m)	—	—	—	—	—	—	—	—	—
Sn-40Bi-0.1Cu	23	—	8.12	—	$(53, 171\%)$	14	—	—	0.345	—
	80	—	—	—	$(17, 516\%)$	14	30	—	—	—
	170 (T_m)	—	—	—	—	—	—	—	—	—
Sn-58Bi	23	—	—	—	$\sigma_{crs,1000} = 3.3$	—	—	—	—	—
	100	—	—	—	$\sigma_{crs,1000} = 0.9$	—	—	—	—	—

continued

Material-DAM	$T/°C$	E_T	ρ	ν	(σ, ε)	α	k	γ	ρ_E	K_{IC}
Sn-0.7Cu	23	—	7.31	—	(15, 0.2%) (22, 41%)	—	65	—	0.126	—
	85	—	—	—	—	—	66	—	—	—
	227 (T_m)	—	—	—	—	—	—	—	—	—
Sn-1Cu	23	—	7.31	—	$\sigma_{crs,1000} = 7.8$	—	—	—	—	—
	100	—	—	—	$\sigma_{crs,1000} = 2.2$	—	—	—	—	—
Sn-3Cu	23	—	7.32	—	—	—	—	—	0.128	—
	227 (T_m)	—	—	—	—	—	—	—	—	—
Sn-Cu-Ni	23	—	—	—	—	—	64	—	—	—
	85	—	—	—	—	—	—	—	—	—
	227 (T_m)	—	—	—	—	—	—	—	—	—
Sn-50In	23	—	7.3	—	(12, 83%)	—	—	—	0.147	—
	85	—	—	—	—	—	34	—	—	—
	118 (T_m)	—	—	—	—	—	—	—	—	—
Sn-37Pb	−70	38	—	0.35	(35, 0.2%)	—	—	—	—	—
	0	32	—	0.35	—	—	—	—	—	—
	20	30	8.42	0.36	(30, 0.2%) (35, 1%) (35, 2%) (35, 64%)	24	51	180	0.145	—
	80	25	—	0.37	(14, 0.2%) (16, 54%)	26.5	50	—	—	—
	140	20	—	0.37	—	—	—	—	—	—
	183 (T_m)	—	—	—	—	—	—	—	—	—
Sn-40Pb	−40	46.4	—	0.32	—	—	—	—	—	—
	0	43.7	—	0.33	—	—	—	—	—	—
	23	42.2	8.52	0.34	$\sigma_{crs,1000} = 3.5$	21.6	—	—	—	—
	50	40.4	—	0.35	—	—	—	—	—	—
	100	37	—	0.37	$\sigma_{crs,1000} = 1.1$	—	—	—	—	—
	150	33.7	—	0.4	—	—	—	—	—	—
	200	30.3	—	0.43	—	—	—	—	—	—
Sn-5Sb	23	58	7.25	—	(42, 38%); $\sigma_{crs,1000} = 11$	20	31	57	0.145	—
	70	—	—	—	(33, 56%)	—	28	—	—	—
	100	—	—	—	$\sigma_{crs,1000} = 3.6$	—	—	—	—	—
	233 (T_m)	—	—	—	—	—	—	—	—	—

continued

Material-DAM	$T/°C$	E_T	ρ	ν	(σ, ε)	α	k	γ	ρ_E	K_{IC}
Sn-5Sb-3.5Ag	23	—	—	—	—	—	—	—	—	—
	70	—	—	—	(42, 74%)	—	—	—	—	—
	216 (T_m)	—	—	—	—	—	—	—	—	—
Sn-5Sb-1.5Au	23									
	70	—	—	—	(50, 61%)	—	—	—	—	—
	204 (T_m)	—	—	—	—	—	—	—	—	—
Sn-8Zn-3Bi	23	36	—	0.3	(41.2, 0.2%) (66.6, 1%) (78.7, 3%)	—	—	—	—	—
	189 (T_m)	—	—	—	—	—	—	—	—	—
Sn-9Zn	23	39	7.27	0.3	(36, 0.2%) (37.4, 1%) (50, 2%) (56, 33%)	—	—	—	0.115	—
	85	—	—	—	—	—	61	—	—	—
	199 (T_m)	—	—	—	—	—	—	—	—	—

Notes: $\rho_E(\mu\Omega \cdot m)$ = Electric Resistivity; See Table 124.1 for more data.

Table 128.2 Mechanical Properties of Intermetallics for Electronic Packaging

Material-DAM	$T/°C$	E_T	ρ	ν	(σ, ε)	α	k	γ	ρ_E	K_{IC}
Ag_3Sn	23	99	—	—	—	—	—	—	—	—
Cu_6Sn_5	23	118	8.3	0.31	—	16.3	34	286	—	1.4
Cu_3Sn	23	133	8.9	0.3	—	19	70.4	326	—	1.7
Ni_3Sn_4	23	141	8.65	0.33	—	13.7	20	272	—	1.2

Table 128.3 Thermomechanical Creep Parameters of Solder Alloys

Material	$T/°C$	Stress /MPa	Strain Rate /s^{-1}	A /($MPa^{-n} \cdot s^{m-1}$)	Q /($J \cdot mol^{-1}$)	n	B
Sn-2Ag-0.5Cu	23	—	—	0.3	66000	4.0	0.19
Sn-2Ag-1.5Cu	23	—	—	2.1	55000	5.6	0.09
Sn-3.5Ag	23	—	—	—	41570	5.04	0.0509
Sn-3.5Ag-0.8Cu	23	—	—	1.46	60000	4.9	0.09

continued

Material	$T/℃$	Stress /MPa	Strain Rate $/s^{-1}$	A $/(MPa^{-n} \cdot s^{m-1})$	Q $/(J \cdot mol^{-1})$	n	B
Sn-3.8Ag-0.7Cu	$-55 \sim 150$	$2 \sim 100$	$3.8 \times 10^{-9} \sim 10^{-3}$	—	67900	6	0.0356
Sn-4Ag-0.5Cu	23	—	—	0.17	55000	4.2	0.14
Sn-4Ag-1.5Cu	23	—	—	0.48	53000	5.9	0.05
Sn-37Pb	23	—	—	—	67437	3.3	0.087

Notes: Creep equation $= \dfrac{d\varepsilon_{creep}}{dt} = A \left[\sinh(B\sigma) \right]^n \exp\left(\dfrac{-Q}{RT_k} \right)$;

$T =$ Test temperature ($℃$), at which the data are obtained.

Table 128.4 Fatigue ε-N Properties of Solders and Intermetallics

Material	$T/℃$	$d\varepsilon/dt$	σ'_f	ε'_f	b	c	K'	n'	$\sigma_f @ 2N_f$	R
Sn-3.5Ag	23	—	—	—	—	—	—	—	$18.6 @ 10^3$	—
	100	—	—	—	—	—	—	—	$10.5 @ 10^3$	—
Sn-3Ag-0.5Cu	23	—	—	—	—	—	—	—	$19 @ 10^3$	—
	125	—	—	—	—	—	—	—	$10 @ 10^3$	—
Sn-40Bi-0.1Cu	23	—	—	—	—	—	—	—	$16 @ 10^3$	—
	80	—	—	—	—	—	—	—	$8 @ 10^3$	—
Sn-58Bi	23	—	—	—	—	—	—	—	$16 @ 10^3$	—
	100	—	—	—	—	—	—	—	$7.9 @ 10^3$	—
Sn-1Cu	23	—	—	—	—	—	—	—	$14.9 @ 10^3$	—
	100	—	—	—	—	—	—	—	$8.3 @ 10^3$	—
Sn-37Pb	23	—	93.3	10^{-6}	-0.085	-0.6	93.3	0.15	$17 @ 10^3$	—
	140	—	20	—	—	—	—	—	$10 @ 10^3$	—
Sn-5Sb	23	—	—	—	—	—	—	—	$20.9 @ 10^3$	—
	100	—	—	—	—	—	—	—	$14.1 @ 10^3$	—
Sn (Generic)	23	—	Eq. (6.14)	Eq. (6.15)	—	—	$\sigma'_f / (\varepsilon'_f)^{n'}$	b/c	$13.7 @ 10^3$	—
	100	—	—	—	—	—	—	—	$9 @ 10^3$	—

Chapter 129

Packaging of Integrated Electronic Circuits- Adhesives

129.1   Introduction

A variety of metals including Cu (Copper), Ag (Silver), Ni (Nickel), LMP (Low Melting Point) fillers, and LMP-coated Cu have been used to make conductive adhesives. Adhesives are applied onto Cu substrates by printing or coating. Mechanical properties of adhesives for electronic packaging are listed in Table 129.1.

The influence of the dwell time of loading wave on the fatigue life of Epoxy/Ag (conductive adhesive) is more complicated in addition to the temperature effect. There is no effect of the dwell time at 25 ℃ (298 K). The dwell time at 125 ℃ (398 K) reduces the fatigue life, the fatigue crack initiates and propagates at the interface between Ag fillers and epoxy resin for all test cases [Kariya1 et al.].

The low-cycle fatigue life of the conductive adhesive increases when the test temperature is elevated beyond the glass transition point. On the other hand, the dwell time at 125 ℃ (398 K) reduces the fatigue life, while the life is extended if the dwell time is set at 75 ℃ (348 K). The cross-sectional image suggests the embrittlement of epoxy resin during the dwell time at 125 ℃ (398 K), which reduces the fatigue endurance of the conductive adhesive.

129.2   Thermally Conductive Adhesives

Thermal conductive adhesives are generally aluminum metal-filled epoxy. Adoption of thermally conductive epoxy adhesives increases microchip packaging density.

References

CHIN M, et al, 2008. Design Guidelines for Anisotropic Conductive Adhesive Assemblies in Microelectronics Packaging[J]. Journal of Electronic Packaging, 130(2): 44-46.

GAYNES M A, SHAUKATULLAH H, 1993. Evaluation of Thermal Conductive Adhesives for Bonding Heat Sinks to Electronic Packages[C]. 43rd Electronic Components and Technology Conference, Orlando, FL, USA.

GOH C F, YU H, YONG S S, et al, 2006. The Effect of Annealing on the Morphologies and Conductivities of Sub-Micrometer Sized Nickel Particles Used for Electrically Conductive Adhesive[J]. Thin Solid Films, 5044 (1-2): 416-420.

GRUJICIC M, et al, 2007. An Overview of the Polymer-to-Metal Direct-Adhesion Hybrid Technologies for Load-Bearing Automotive Components[J]. Journal of Materials Processing Technology, 197(1-3): 363-373.

HU K X, et al, 1997. Electro-Thermo-Mechanical Responses of Conductive Adhesive Materials[J]. IEEE Transactions of Components and Packaging Technology, 20(4): 470-477.

HUSSEY R, WILSON J, 1996. Structural Adhesives: Directory and Data Book[M]. Chapman and Hall, London, UK.

INOUE M, SUGANUMA K, 2006. Effect of Curing Conditions on the Electric Properties of Isotropic Conductive Adhesives Composed of Epoxy-based Binder[J]. Solder and Mounting Technology, 18: 40-46.

JAN C H, 2002. Carbon Black Filled Conducting Polymers and Polymer Blends[J]. Polymers for Advanced Technologies, 21: 299-313.

JEONG W J, NISHIKAWA H, ITOU D, et al, 2005. Electrical Characteristics of a New Class of Conductive Adhesive[J]. Materials Transactions, 46(10): 2276-2281.

JIANG H J, MOON K S, LU J X, et al, 2005. Conductivity Enhancement of Nano Silver-Filled Conductive Adhesives by Particle Surface Functionalization[J]. Journal of Electronic Materials, 34(11): 1432-1439.

KARIYAL Y, KANDA Y, IGUCHI K, et al, 2010. Influence of Temperature and Dwelling Time on Low-Cycle Fatigue Characteristic of Isotropic Conductive Adhesive Joint[J]. Materials Transactions, 51(10): 1779-1784.

KRISTASEN H, et al, 2009. Development of Low Modulus Conductive Adhesives for MEMS Interconnects[J]. Proceedings of Pan Pacific Microelectronics Symposium, 306-310.

LI Y, LU D, WONG C P, 2010. Electrically Conductive Adhesives with Nanotechnologies[M]. Springer, New York, NY, USA.

LI Y, WONG C P, 2006. Recent Advances of Conductive Adhesives as a Lead-free Alternative in Electronic packaging: Materials, Processing, Reliability, and Applications[J]. Material Sciences and Engineering, 51(1-3): 1-35.

LI Y, MOON K S, WONG C P, 2005. Monolayer-Protected Silver Nano-Particle-Based Anisotropic Conductive Adhesives: Enhancement of Electrical and Thermal Properties[J]. Journal of Electronic Materials, 34(12): 1573-1578.

LIU J, 1999. Conductive Adhesives for Electronics Packaging[M]. Electrochemical Publications, Port Erin.

MIR I, KUMAR D, 2008. Recent Advances in Isotropic Conductive Adhesives for Electronic Packaging Applications[J]. International Journal of Adhesion and Adhesives, 28(7): 362-371.

THURN J, HERMEL D T, 2007. Thermal Stress Hysteresis and Stress Relaxation in an Epoxy Film[J]. Journal of Material Science, 42(14): 5686-5691.

WILLIAMS D J, WHALLEY D C, 1993. The Effects of Conductive Particle Distribution on the Behavior of Anisotropic Conductivity: Non-uniform Conductivity and Shorting between Connections [J]. Journal of Electronic Manufacturing, 3: 85-94.

Table 129.1   Mechanical Properties of Adhesives for Electronic Packaging

Material-DAM	$T/^\circ C$	E_T	ρ	ν	(σ, ε)	α	k	γ	ρ_E	K_{IC}
Ep/Ag (Simmons; Thermally Conductive)	23	10.5	—	—	—	34	1.7	—	—	—
	87	—	—	—	$\sigma_{ucs} = -190$; (85, 0.8%)	70	—	—	—	—
	125 (T_g)	—	—	—	—	—	—	—	—	—
	150	—	—	—	—	140	—	—	—	—
	350 (Thermal decomposition)									
EP/1CB	23	—	—	—	—	—	0.15	—	—	—
EP/5CB	23	—	—	—	—	—	0.214	—	—	—
EP/10CB	23	—	—	—	—	—	0.24	—	—	—
EP1330 (Ellsworth Ep)	23	8.3	1.91	0.33	(31, 0.2%) (48, 1%)	30	1.07	—	—	—
	41	4.0	—	—	—	—	—	—	—	—
	47	2.02	—	—	—	—	—	—	—	—
	92 (T_g)	—	—	—	—	70	—	—	—	—
	150	—	—	—	—	124	—	—	—	—

Chapter 130

Integrated Circuits (IC) Components and Packaging

130.1   Introduction

An integrated circuit (IC) consists of a number of devices manufactured and interconnected on a single semiconductor substrate or wafer. Integrated electronic circuit packaging means that a block of semiconducting materials is encased in a supporting structure that prevents reliability problems. The typical reliability qualification includes the following types of environmental factors: burn-in, temperature cycle, thermal shock, vibration resistance and resonance reduction, solderability, moisture resistance. A three-dimensional integrated circuit package is called a system in package (SIP) or multi-chip module (MCM). A flip-chip ball grid array (FCBGA) package allows the die to be mounted upside-down (flipped) and connects to the package balls via a substrate as a surface interface rather than peripheral wiring.

Integrated circuits are engraved onto a silicon and/or germanium wafer. A typical IC package consists of the following structural parts:

(a) Encapsulation: Fused silica (SiO_2), mixed with epoxy/phenol resin and carbon black;
(b) Chip/die: Silicon (Si), Germanium (Ge), or a combination (SiGe);
(c) Die attach: Epoxy with noble metal (silver) and ionic (Na^+, K^+, Cl^-);
(d) Die paddle: Noble metal (silver);
(e) Wires: Noble metal (gold);
(f) Frame: Copper alloy (copper with nickel, silicon, magnesium);
(g) Finish: Tin.

Realistic mechanical properties of IC components are given in Table 130.1. Ideal tensile strengths of 23 GPa and 14 GPa and ideal shear strengths of 6.5 GPa, and 4.5 GPa, respectively for Si and Ge were identified by [Roundy and Cohen]. Note that the shear calculation is performed on the (1 1 1) slip plane sheared in a {1 1 2} direction and the tensile load is applied in the {1 1 1} direction.

The integrated circuit is implemented onto a substrate called die, chip, or wafer, mostly made of silicon, germanium, or gallium arsenide. Being brittle by nature, A silicon die at a moderate stress level die may result in detrimental failure such as cracking. For example, a die may crack subject to a high molding pressure. The failure stress of silicon substrates varies with respect to their thickness. Before going through manufacturing processes such as photolithography and patterning, the failure stress tested using the 3-point bending method varies with respect to the chip thickness as follows: 540 MPa @ 0.15 mm, 570 MPa @ 0.18 mm, 1000 MPa @ 0.204 mm, 780 MPa @ 0.274 mm, 540 MPa @ 0.3 mm, 410 MPa @ 0.32 mm, and 330 MPa @ 0.394 mm [Chong et al.]. However, the strength of silicon chips reduces significantly after photolithography and patterning such as 425 MPa @ 0.155 mm and 490 MPa @ 0.3 mm [McLellan et al.].

Mismatch of thermal expansions between IC components and its mounting PCB may bend and stretch their joining solders at elevated temperatures. Complicated by the free boundary effect, high normal stress and shear stress along adjacent edges (such as hole edges) may be created between a solder and its connecting IC lead frame. Free boundary effect is induced by dissimilar materials with different stiffness in contact with each other.

130.2   Si (Silicon)

Polysilicon, polycrystalline silicon of several μm in thickness, is the most widely used structural material in current micro-devices manufactured by surface micromachining.

130.3   Ge (Germanium)

Below about 500 ℃, Ge is a brittle solid. Tensile fracture is preceded by no yielding or plastic formation. Its maximum tensile strength is determined by the sizes and distribution of flaws present in the material, of which the flaw distribution is a function of the volume. Smaller samples will have a narrow distribution of smaller flaws and therefore will be inherently stronger. When loaded in compression at a temperature between 500 ℃ and 750 ℃, Ge displays a definite yield point.

130.4   GaAs (Gallium Arsenide)

As Gallium Arsenide (GaAs) has higher carrier mobility and less parasitic issues with resistive devices than silicon, it has been used for circuitry in mobile phones or some other devices operated at high frequencies.

130.5   GaN (Gallium Nitride)

GaN (Gallium Nitride) provides the following five key characteristics: high dielectric strength, high operating temperature, high current density, high-speed switching, and low on-resistance. In speed, temperature and power handling, GaN is set to take over as silicon power devices reach their limits. GaN is the technology that will allow us to implement essential future clean-technology innovations where efficiency is a key requirement.

130.6 Diodes

Diodes are two-terminal electronic components, which conduct electric current in only one direction. Semiconductor diodes are used for most electronic circuits nowadays, while vacuum tube diodes are used for exceptional high-power applications. The unidirectional behavior of a diode is called rectification, and it may be used to convert alternating current to direct current. Germanium and gallium are two major metallic materials for diodes.

A semiconductor diode is a crystalline piece of semiconductor material connected to two electrical terminals (P-N junction). A two-terminal semiconductor diode is used mainly as a rectifier-changing alternating current into direct current. Diodes have more complicated behavior than simple on-off action. This is due to their complex non-linear electrical characteristics, which can be tailored by varying the construction of their P-N junctions.

A vacuum diode is a vacuum tube with two electrodes: a plate (anode) and a cathode. The heated cathode releases excited electrons that flow to the plate (anode) and become the rectified current.

Light-emitting diodes (LEDs) are used in the display of letters, numbers, and other symbols in calculators, watches, clocks, televisions, bulbs, and other electronic units. Currently, there is much research into developing light-emitting diodes to operate in the ultraviolet using the gallium nitride-based semiconductors and, using the alloy aluminum gallium nitride, wavelengths as short as 250 nanometers have been achieved.

130.7 MOSFET

MOSFET (metal-oxide-semiconductor field-effect transistor) is a device used as an electronic switch [Wintrich et al.]. When no gate voltage is applied, there is no inversion electron in the channel and the device is "off". As the gate voltage increases, the inversion electron density in the channel increases, current increases, and the device turns on. It is also in an electronic amplifier.

130.8 IGBT

An insulated-gate bipolar transistor (IGBT) is a power semiconductor device primarily used as an electronic switch with three terminals. It is a semiconductor device with four alternating layers (P-N-P-N) that are controlled by a metal-oxide-semiconductor (MOS) gate structure [Wintrich et al.].

References

BASARAN C, et al, 2005. Failure Modes of Flip Chip Solder Joints Under High Electrical Current Density[J]. Journal of Electronic Packaging, 127(53): 157-163.

BECK M, et al, 2016. Thermal Performance of MR-16 Light Emitting Diode Products [J]. Journal of Electronics Cooling and Thermal Control, 6: 127-138.

BENDER V C, IARONKA O, MARCHESAN T B, 2013. Study on the Thermal Performance of LED Luminaire Using Finite Element Method[J]. IECON 2013: 39 th Annual Conference of the IEEE Industrial Electronics Society, Vienna, November 2013, 6099-6104.

BLAKE P N, SCATTERGOOD R O, 1990. Ductile-Regime Machining of Germanium and Silicon[J]. Journal of American Ceramics Society, 73(4): 949-957.

BURKETT S, et al, 2007. Material Aspect to Consider in the Fabrication of Through-Silicon-Vias [J]. Proceedings of Material Research Society Symposium, 0970-Y06-01.

CHEN Y S, et al, 2008. Combining Vibration Test with Finite Element Analysis for the Fatigue Life Estimation of PBGA Components[J]. Microelectronics Reliability, 48(4): 638-644.

CHENG T, LUO X, HUANG S, et al, 2010. Thermal Analysis and Optimization of Multiple LED Packaging Based on a General Analytical Solution[J]. International Journal of Thermal Sciences, 49: 196-201.

CHI W, CHOU T, HAN C, et al, 2010. Analysis of Thermal and Luminous Performance of MR-16 LED Lighting Module[J]. IEEE Transactions on Components and Packaging Technologies, 33: 713-721.

EDWARDS D R, et al, 1995. Thermal Enhancement of Plastic IC Packages[J]. IEEE Transactions on Components, Packaging, and Manufacturing Technology A, 18(1): 57-67.

GREIG W J, 2007. Integrated Circuit Packaging Assembly and Interconnection[M]. Berlin, D E: Springer Verlag.

HE Y, et al, 2007. Passivation Cracking Analysis of Integrated-Circuit Microstructure under Aeronautical Conditions[J]. Material Science and Engineering A, 483/484: 340-342.

HEY M, HUANG Y, 2008. Thermal Analysis and Optimal Design of Lamp Type Light-emitting Diodes[J]. Journal of Chinese Institute of Engineers, 31(2): 271-278.

HOPCROFT M A, et al, April 2010. What is the Young's Modulus of Silicon? [J]. Journal of Microelectromechanical Systems, 19(2): 229-238.

HU J, YANG L, SHIN M, 2005. Mechanism and Thermal Effect of Delamination in Light-Emitting Diode Packages[J]. Tima Editions/Therminic, 249-254.

HULL R, 1999. Properties of Crystalline Silicon[M]. INSPEC, London, UK.

HUNG N, FU Y, 2000. Effect of Crystalline Orientation in Ductile-Regime Machining Silicon[J]. International Journal of Advanced Manufacturing Technology, 16: 871-876.

IWASHITA R, SASAHARA H, 2008. Study of Micro-cutting Process of Alternative-arranged Resin and Metal [J]. Journal of Advanced Mechanical Design, Systems, and Manufacturing, 2(4): 711-718.

JAIN P, et al, 2002. Flame Retarding Epoxies with Phosphorous[J]. Journal of Molecular Science-Polymer Reviews, 42(2): 139-183.

JASINEVICIUS R G, et al, 2007. Structure Evaluation of Sub-micrometer Silicon Chips Removed by Diamond Turning[J]. Semiconductors Science and Technology, 22: 561-573.

JASINEVICIUS R G, 2006. Influence of Cutting Conditions Scaling in the Machining of Semiconductors Crystals with Single Point Diamond Tool[J]. Journal of Material Processing Technology, 179: 111-116.

KARIM N, et al, 2006. Thermal Analysis of LED Package[J]. Microelectronics International, 23(1): 19-25.

KASPER E, 1995. Properties of Strained and Relaxed Silicon Germanium[M]. INSPEC, London, UK.

KIM D, et al, 2008. Complementary Metal Oxide Silicon Integrated Circuits Incorporating Monolithically Integrated Stretchable Wavy Interconnects[J]. Applied Physics Letters, 93(4): 412-414.

KNICKERBOCKER J U, et al, 2005. Development of Next Generation System-on-Package (SOP) Technology Based on Silicon Carriers with Fine-Pitch Chip Interconnection [J]. IBM Journal of Research and Development, 49(4): 725-753.

KO M, KIM M, 1998. Effect of Post-Mold Curing on Plastic IC Package Reliability[J]. Journal of Applied Polymer Science, 69(11): 2187-2193.

LALL P, et al, 2007. Reliability of BGA and CSP on Metal-Backed Printed Circuit Boards in Harsh Environments[J]. Journal of Electronic Packaging, 129(4): 382-390.

LAU J, 1996. Flip Chip Technologies[M]. McGraw Hill, New York, NY, USA.

LAU J, et al, 2001. Design and Manufacturing of Micro Via-in-pad Substrates for Solder Bumped Flip Chip Applications[J]. Journal of Electronics Manufacturing, 10(1): 79-87.

LEE T H, et al, 2004. Thermal Analysis of GaN-based LEDs Using the Finite element Method and Unit temperature Profile Approach[J]. Physica Status Solidi, 241(12): 2681-2684.

LI X P, et al, 2003. Nano-precision Measurement of Diamond Tool Edge Radius for Wafer Fabrication[J]. Journal of Material Processing Technology, 140: 358-362.

LI X, et al, 2006. A New SPICE Reliability Simulation Method for Deep Sub-micrometer CMOS VLSI Circuits [J]. IEEE Transactions on Devices and Materials Reliability, 6(2): 247-257.

MCLELLAN N, et al, 2003. Effects of Wafer Thinning Condition on the Roughness, Morphology, and Fracture Strength of Silicon Die[J]. Journal of Electronic Packaging, 126(1): 110-114.

NARENDRAN N, et al, 2004. Solid-state Lighting: Failure Analysis of White LEDs[J]. Journal of Crystal Growth, 268(3-4): 449-456.

OSONE Y, 2006. Thermal design of Power Semiconductor Modules for Mobile Communication Systems[J]. Proceeding of International Workshop on Thermal Investigations of ICs, (15): 673-674.

PEI M, QU J, 2008. Creep and Fatigue Behavior of SnAg Solders With Lanthanum Doping[J]. IEEE Transactions on Components and Packaging Technologies, 31(3): 712-718.

PENG B, et al, 2004. IC HTOL Test Stress Condition Optimization[C]. 19th IEEE International Symposium on Defect and Fault Tolerance in VLSI Systems.

ROUNDY D, COHEN M, 2001. Ideal Strength of Diamond, Si, and Ge[J]. Physics Review B, 64(21): 212103.

SCHOLAND M J, DILLON H E, 2012. Life-Cycle Assessment of Energy and Environmental Impacts of LED Lighting Products. Part 2: LED Manufacturing and Performance[J]. Office of Scientific & Technical Information Technical Report, 35(1): 523-527.

SELVANAYAGAM C S, 2008. Nonlinear Thermal Stress/Strain Analyses of Copper Filled TSV (Through Silicon Via) and Their Flip-chip Microbumps[C]. IEEE Electronic Components and Technology Conference, 1073-1081.

SOHN Y, et al, 2010. Mechanical Properties of Silicon Nanowires[J]. Nanoscale Research Letters, 5(1): 211-216.

SZE S M, 1981. Physics of Semiconductor Devices[M]. John Wiley & Sons, New York, NY.

TAKANA N, et al, 2002. Mechanical Effects of Copper Through-via in a 3D Die-stacked Module[C]. IEEE Electronic Components and Technology Conference.

TAO S H, BOLGER P M, 1997. Hazard Assessment of Germanium Supplements[J]. Regulatory Toxicology and Pharmacology, 25(3): 211-219.

TEAL G K, 1976. Single Crystals of Germanium and Silicon-Basic to the Transistor and Integrated Circuit[J]. IEEE Transactions on Electron Devices, ED-23 (7): 621-639.

TURLEY J, 2002. The Essential Guide to Semiconductors[M]. Prentice Hall, NY, USA.

WINTRICH A, et al, 2015. Application Manual Power Semiconductors[M]. 2nd Edition, Germany: ISLE Verlag.

WUNDERLE B, et al, 2007. Thermo-Mechanical Reliability of 3D-Integrated Microstructures in Stacked Silicon[J]. Materials Research Society Symposium Proceedings, 970.

XUN T, et al, 2009. A Compact High Current Vacuum Diode Based on a Ceramic-metal Welding Interface[J]. DACTA Physica Polonica, 115: 1013-1015.

YABLONOVITCH E, MILLER O D, KURTZ S R, 2012. The Optoelectronic Physics That Broke the Efficiency Limit in Solar Cells[C]. 38th IEEE Photovoltaic Specialists Conference.

YAN J, et al, 2006. Ultra-precision Machining Characteristics of Poly-Crystalline Germanium[J]. JSME International Journal, C- Mechanical Systems, 49(1): 63-69.

YU P Y, CARDONA M, 2004. Fundamentals of Semiconductors: Physics and Materials Properties[M]. Springer, NY, USA.

ZARUDI I, et al, 2004. Effect of Temperature and Stress on Plastic Deformation in Non-crystalline Silicon Introduced by Scratching[J]. Applied Physics Letters, 86(1): 011922.1-011922.3.

ZHANG L C, ZARUDI I, 2001. Towards a Deeper Understanding of Plastic Deformation in Mono-crystalline Silicon[J]. International Journal of Mechanical Science, 43: 1985-1996.

ZHANG Q, et al, 2004. Partitioned Viscoplastic-Constitutive Properties of the Pb-Free Sn-3.9Ag-0.6Cu Solder [J]. Journal of Electronic Materials, 33(11): 1338-1349.

ZHANG X R, et al, 2005. Comprehensive Hygro-thermal-mechanical Modeling and Testing of Stacked Die BGA Module with Molded Underfill[C]. Electronic Components and Technology Conference, 196-200.

ZHAO X, BHUSHAN B, 1998. Material Removal Mechanisms of Single-Crystal Silicon on Nano-scale and at Ultra-low Loads[J]. Wear, 223: 66-78.

Table 130.1   Mechanical Properties of IC Components

Material-DAM	$T/^\circ\mathrm{C}$	ρ	E_{11}	E_{22}	E_{33}	G_{23}	G_{31}	G_{12}	ν_{23}	ν_{31}	ν_{12}
$\mathrm{Al}_x\mathrm{Ga}_{1-x}\mathrm{As}$	23	5.32	85.3	—	—	—	—	—	0.31	—	—
[100]		$-1.56x$	$-1.8x$	—	—	—	—	—	$+0.1x$	—	—
GaAs (Gallium Arsenide)	23	5.318	83	83	83	—	—	—	0.31	—	—
	1238 (T_m)	—	—	—	—	—	—	—	—	—	—
GaN	23	6.15	181	181	181	—	—	—	0.35	0.35	0.35
	2500 (T_m)	—	—	—	—	—	—	—	—	—	—
Ge, Bulk	23	5.8	103	103	103	—	—	—	—	—	—
	938 (T_m)	—	—	—	—	—	—	—	—	—	—
Ge (Crystal)	23	5.8	$C_{11}=1260$, $C_{12}=440$, $C_{44}=677$, and other $C_{ij}=0$								
75Ge-25Si, Bulk	23	4.58	—	—	—	—	—	—	—	—	—
	1057 (T_m)	—	—	—	—	—	—	—	—	—	—

continued

Material-DAM	$T/℃$	ρ	E_{11}	E_{22}	E_{33}	G_{23}	G_{31}	G_{12}	ν_{23}	ν_{31}	ν_{12}
50Ge-50Si Bulk	23	3.83	—	—	—	—	—	—	—	—	—
	1176 (T_m)	—	—	—	—	—	—	—	—	—	—
25Ge-75Si Bulk	23	3.08	—	—	—	—	—	—	—	—	—
	1296 (T_m)	—	—	—	—	—	—	—	—	—	—
InGa, Bulk	23	6.85	—	—	—	—	—	—	—	—	—
53In/47Ga-As (InGaAs)	23	—	69	69	69	—	—	—	0.16	0.16	0.16
	1100 (T_m)	—	—	—	—	—	—	—	—	—	—
InGaN, Bulk	23	—	58	58	58	—	—	—	—	—	—
Si, Bulk	23	2.33	160	160	160	—	—	—	0.22	0.22	0.22
	1414 (T_m)	—	—	—	—	—	—	—	—	—	—
Si, Poly Film	23	2.33	160	160	160	65	65	65	0.22	0.22	0.22
Si, Wafer ([1 0 0] [0 1 0] [0 0 1])	23	2.33	130	130	130	79.6	79.6	79.6	0.28	0.28	0.28
	150	2.2	128.4	128.4	128.4	—	—	—	—	—	—
Si, Wafer [1 1 0] [−1 1 0] [0 0 1]	23	2.33	169	169	130	79.6	79.6	50.9	0.36	0.28	0.064

Material-DAM	$T/℃$	E_T	ρ	ν	(σ, ε)	α	k	γ	ρ_E	K_{IC}
Al$_x$Ga$_{1-x}$As	23	85.3	5.32	0.31	—	5.73	55	330	—	—
		$-1.8x$	$-1.56x$	$+0.1x$	—	$-0.53x$	$-212x$ $+248x^2$	$+12x$	—	—
		[1 0 0]	—	[1 0 0]	—	—	—	—	—	—
GaAs (Gallium Arsenide)	23	83	5.318	0.31	$\sigma_R = 138$	5.73	55	330	—	—
	1238 (T_m)	—	—	—	—	—	—	—	—	—
GaN	23	181	6.15	0.352	—	3.17	130	490	—	—
	2500 (T_m)	—	—	—	—	—	—	—	—	—
Ge (Bulk)	23	103	5.8	0.26	(95, <1%)	5.8	60.2	310	—	—
	938 (T_m)	—	—	—	—	—	—	—	—	—

continued

Material-DAM	$T/°C$	E_T	ρ	ν	(σ, ε)	α	k	γ	ρ_E	K_{IC}
Ge (Lattice)	23	$C_{11} =$ 1260 $C_{12} =$ 440 $C_{44} =$ 677	5.323	—	—	5.8	—	310	—	—
75Ge-25Si	23	—	4.58	—	—	5.0	11	408	—	—
	1057 (T_m)	—	—	—	—	—	—	—	—	—
50Ge-50Si	23	—	3.827	—	—	4.2	8.3	505	—	—
	1176 (T_m)	—	—	—	—	—	—	—	—	—
25Ge-75Si	23	—	3.08	—	—	3.4	8.5	602.5	—	—
	1296 (T_m)	—	—	—	—	—	—	—	—	—
InGa	23	—	6.85	—	—	3.4	45	300	—	—
53In/ 47Ga-As (InGaAs)	23	69	—	0.16	—	5.66	5	300	—	—
	1100 (T_m)	—	—	—	—	—	—	—	—	—
InGaN	23	58	—	—	—	—	—	—	—	—
Si (Bulk)	−40	—	—	—	—	1.9	236	—	—	—
	23	129.6	2.33	0.28	—	2.81	156	700	—	0.81
	150	128.4	2.2	—	—	3.11	—	—	—	—
	200	—	—	—	—	3.5	88	—	—	—
	1414 (T_m)	—	—	—	—	4.612	22	—	—	—
Si (Crystal; Averaged)	−173	—	—	—	—	−0.5				
	−73	—	—	—	—	1.1				
	23	190	2.33	0.17	(7000, <1%)	2.33	157	700	—	0.91
	127	—	—	—	—	2.7	—	—	—	—
Si, Poly [Sharpe et al.]	23	169	2.33	0.22	(1200, 0.7%)	4	—	—	—	0.94
	670	—	—	—	(200, 0.2%) (500, 0.5%) (745, 1%) (650, 1.5%)	—	—	—	—	—
	700	—	—	—	(150, 0.2%) (400, 0.5%) (610, 0.9%)	—	—	—	—	—

continued

Material-DAM	$T/°C$	E_T	ρ	ν	(σ, ε)	α	k	γ	ρ_E	K_{IC}
SiO$_2$ (Fused; Film)	23	—	2.15	—	—	0.5	1.4	—	—	—

Notes: Fused = High purity.

Table 130.2   Thermal Properties of IC Components

Material-DAM	$T/°C$	α_1	α_2	α_3	k_1	k_2	k_3	γ	β_1	β_2	β_3
Al$_x$Ga$_{1-x}$As ([100]// 1-axis)	23	5.73	—	—	55	—	—	330	—	—	—
		$-0.53x$	—	—	$-212x$	—	—	$+12x$	—	—	—
		—	—	—	$+248x^2$	—	—	—	—	—	—
GaAs (Gallium Arsenide)	23	5.73	—	—	55	—	—	330	—	—	—
	1238 (T_m)	—	—	—	—	—	—	—	—	—	—
GaN, Bulk	23	3.17	3.17	3.17	130	130	130	490	—	—	—
	2500 (T_m)	—	—	—	—	—	—	—	—	—	—
Ge, Bulk	23	5.8	5.8	5.8	60.2	60.2	60.2	310	—	—	—
75Ge-25Si, Bulk	23	5.0	5.0	5.0	11	11	11	408	—	—	—
	1057 (T_m)	—	—	—	—	—	—	—	—	—	—
50Ge-50Si, Bulk	23	4.2	4.2	4.2	8.3	8.3	8.3	505	—	—	—
	1176 (T_m)	—	—	—	—	—	—	—	—	—	—
25Ge-75Si, Bulk	23	3.4	3.4	3.4	8.5	8.5	8.5	602.5	—	—	—
	1296 (T_m)	—	—	—	—	—	—	—	—	—	—
InGa	23	3.4	3.4	3.4	45	45	45	300	—	—	—
53In/47Ga-As (InGaAs)	23	5.66	5.66	5.66	5	5	5	300	—	—	—
	1100 (T_m)	—	—	—	—	—	—	—	—	—	—
Si, Bulk	−40	1.9	1.9	1.9	236	236	236	—	—	—	—
	23	2.81	2.81	2.81	156	156	156	700	—	—	—
	150	3.11	3.11	3.11	—	—	—	—	—	—	—
	200	3.5	3.5	3.5	88	88	88	—	—	—	—
	1414	4.61	4.61	4.61	22	22	22	—	—	—	—

Table 130.3 Orthotropic Mechanical Strengths of IC Components

Material	$T/℃$	$(\sigma_{11u}, \varepsilon_{11u})$	$(\sigma_{22u}, \varepsilon_{22u})$	$(\sigma_{33u}, \varepsilon_{33u})$	$(\sigma_{12u}, \varepsilon_{12u})/(\sigma_{23u}, \varepsilon_{23u})/(\sigma_{13u}, \varepsilon_{13u})$
Si, Poly [Sharpe et al.]	23	(1200, 0.7%)	—	—	—/—/—
	670	(200, 0.2%) (500, 0.5%) (745, 1%) (650, 1.5%)	—	—	—/—/—
	700	(150, 0.2%) (400, 0.5%) (610, 0.9%)	—	—	—/—/—

Chapter 131

PCB (Printed Circuit Board)

Introduction

The primary function of a PCB (printed circuit board) is to work as an electric inter-connector for electronic components. Structural integrity and a safe working environment are two major challenges to a PCB. FR-4 is a popular PCB (Printed Circuit Board) material, which is epoxy matrix reinforced by woven E-glass fibers, Fig. 131.1. Copper cladding is used for the connector. FR-4 laminates are normally available in thickness ranging from 0.05 mm to 5 mm. It consists of 4 or more layers of glass-fiber-reinforced epoxy, which are thermo-structurally stable. FR-4 offers high mechanical strength and machinability, outstanding electric characteristics, consistent drilling properties, and fire-resistant. Orthogonal mechanical properties, thermal properties, and mechanical strengths of FR-4 and other dielectric materials are listed in Tables 131.1 and 131.2, and 131.3, respectively.

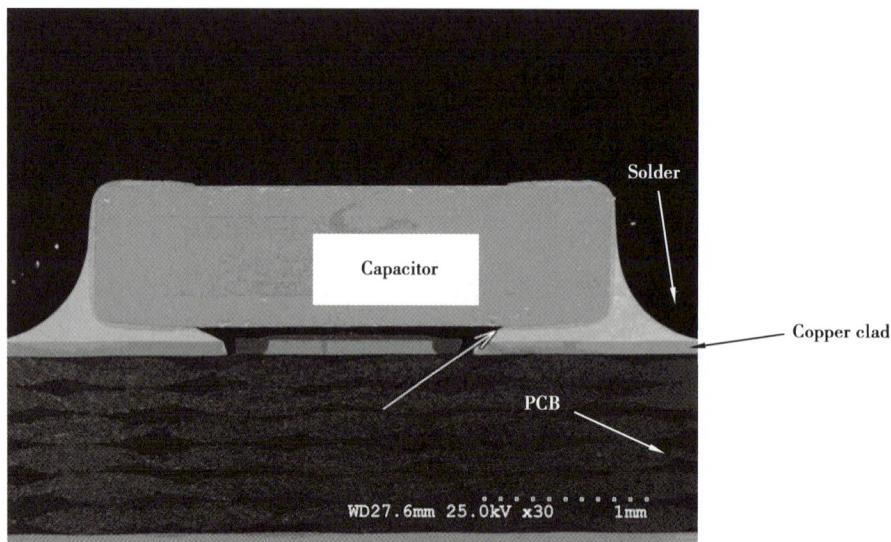

Fig. 131.1   Cross-sectional View of a Capacitor Soldered to a 6-layered PCB

At its T_g (Glass Transition Temperature) the matrix material of an FR-4 PCB (resin here) transforms from a glass-like state to a rubbery state due to reversible breakage of van der Waals bonds between molecular chains. T_g (Glass Transition Temperature) usually occurs at a temperature between 130 ℃ and 180 ℃ for most FR-4 PCBs. Another important index of FR-4 PCB is its T_d (Decomposition Temperature), beyond which the matrix (resin) irreversibly undergoes physical and chemical degradations with thermal destruction of cross-links, resulting in weight loss of the matrix. T_d comes between T_g and T_m (Melting Temperature). One interesting aspect of thermal analysis of a PCB is to measure the time to delamination at a high temperature.

Stress singularities between laminae are expected to as the thermal stress arises. T260 is the time-to-delamination when exposed to an environment of 260 ℃, which is the peak temperature reached in a lead-free soldering process. The material deemed lead-free must be able to survive multiple 260 ℃ reflow cycles without impacting reliability, per iNEMI.

One major concern about a PCB is its thermal expansion in the out-of-plane direction. Coefficients of linear thermal expansion (CTE) on the FR-4 PCB laminate plane, i.e. α_x and α_y, fall between 11 and 16 μm/m/℃(PPM/℃) at room temperature. α_x and α_y decrease but do not vary much as long as the temperature is below the decomposition temperature (lower than melting temperature). The coefficient of linear thermal expansion normal to the FR-4 PCB laminate, α_z, increases mildly when the working temperature is below T_g(Glass Transition Temperature), Fig. 131.2. After the working temperature exceeds T_g, α_z grows much faster. It is recommended not to create stress risers, such as drilling holes for screws and welding, right next to heat-generating elements. The thermal cycle may make the fastened area creepy and consequently fasteners get loosened.

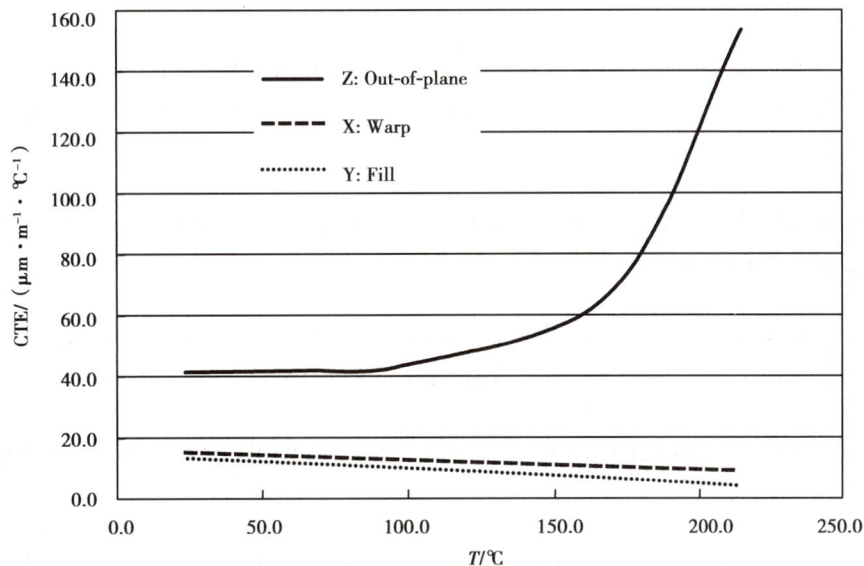

Fig. 131.2   CTE (Coefficient of Linear Thermal Expansion) of a PCB Laminate (T_g = 170 ℃ FR-4)

Carbon fibers are introduced into a PCB to replace glass fibers as requirements for control of thermal expansions and enhancement of structural rigidity. There are two kinds of carbon fibers. The thermal conductivity of low-modulus carbon fibers (700 GPa ⩾ E ⩾ 210 GPa) ranges between 8 and 12 W/m/℃ and the thermal conductivity of high-modulus carbon fibers (E > 700 GPa) can go as high as 300 W/m/℃.

References

AUERSPERG J, 1997. Fracture and Damage Evaluation in Chip Scale Packages and Flip Chip Assemblies by FEA and Microdac[J]. American Society of Mechanical Engineers, 133-138.

ENGEL P A, 1993. Structural Analysis of Printed Circuit Board Systems[M]. Springer-Verlag, New York, NY.

EHRLER S, 2005. The Compatibility of Epoxy-based Printed Circuit Boards with Lead-free Assembly[J]. Circuit World, 31(4): 3-13.

FANG K, 2004. High Performance Epoxy Copper Clad Laminate[J]. Circuit World, 30(4): 16-19.

GLASSBRENNER C J, SLACK G A, 1964. Thermal conductivity of silicon and germanium from ε_k to the melting point[J]. Physics Review, 134: A1058-A1069.

GONON P, et al, 2001. Combined Effects of Humidity and Thermal Stress on the Dielectric Properties of Epoxy-Silica Composites[J]. Material Science and Engineering, B, 83(1-3): 158-164.

HAI H L, et al, 2008. Millimeter Wave Printed Circuit Board Developments-Improvement for Mechanical Packaging and Electric Requirements[J]. Global Symposium on Millimeter Waves, Nanjing, China, April 21-24, 2008.

HSU HSIANG C, et al, 2008. Thermo-Hygro-Mechanical Design and Reliability Analysis for CMOS Image Sensor[J]. Journal of Thermal Stresses, 31(10): 917-934.

IJI M, KIUCHI Y, 2004. Flame Resistant Glass-epoxy Printed Wiring Boards with No Halogen or Phosphorous Compounds[J]. Journal of Material Science: Materials in Electronics, 15: 175-182.

IPC-4121 (2000), Guidelines for Selecting Core Constructions for Multilayer Printed Wiring Board Applications [S]. Bonockburn, IL, USA.

LAU D, et al, 2006. Experimental testing and failure Prediction of PBGA Package Assembles under 3-Point bending Condition through Computational Stress Analysis [C]. IEEE 7th International Conference on Electronic Packaging Technology.

LAU J H, LEE S W, 1995. Fracture Mechanics Analysis of Low Cost Solder Bumped Flip Chip Assemblies with Imperfect Underfills[J]. Journal of Electronic Packaging, 122(4): 306-310.

LEE J W, HARRIS C E, 1988. A Micromechanics Model for the Effective Young's Modulus of a Piecewise-Isotropic Laminate with Wavy Patterns[J]. Journal of Composite Materials, 22(8): 717-741.

LEE M, 1997. Finite Element Modeling of Printed Circuit Board for Structural Analysis[C]. IEEE PEP 1997, 42-51.

LI, et al, 2007. Finite Element Modeling and Simulation for Bending Analysis of Multi-layer Printed Circuit

Boards Using Woven Fiber Composite[J]. Journal of Materials Processing Technology, 201(1-3): 746-750.

MANGROLI A, VASOYA K, 2007. Optimizing Thermal and Mechanical Performance in PCBs[J]. Global SMT and Packaging, 10-12.

PENG Y, QI X, CHRISAFIDES C, 2005. The Influence of Curing Systems on Epoxide-based PCB Laminate Performance[J]. Circuit World, 31(4): 14-20.

READ D T, CHEN Y W, GEISS R, 2004. Morphology, Microstructure, and Mechanical Properties of a Copper Electrodeposit[J]. Microelectronic Engineering, 75: 63-70.

RZEPKA S, et al, 2008. A Multilayer PCB Material Modeling Approach Based on Laminate Theory [C]. Proceedings of the 9th International Conference on Thermal, Mechanical and Multi-physics Simulation and Experiments in Micro-electronics and Micro-systems, Freiburg, Germany, 234-243.

SHROTRIYA P, SOTTOS N R, 1998. Creep and Relaxation of Woven Glass/Epoxy Substrates for Multilayer Circuit Board Applications[J]. Polymer Composites, 19(5): 567-578.

SOTTOS R, et al, 1999. Thermo-elastic Properties of Plain Weave Composites for Multilayer Circuit Board Applications[J]. Journal of Electronic Packaging, 121(1): 37-44.

TANAKA Y, ONODERA M, 1999. Liquid Crystal Polymer Materials for LSI Mounting[J]. Journal of Japanese Society of Electronics Mounting, 2(2): 84-89.

VERICK A M, 2003. Vibration Protection of Critical Components of Electronic Equipment in Harsh Environmental Conditions[J]. Journal of Sound and Vibration, 259(1): 161-175.

VOZKOVA P, 2007. Elastic Properties of Woven Composites[C]. Proceedings of 15th Annual International Conference on Composites/Nano Engineering, Haikou, Hainan, China.

WEIDE Z K, et al, 2005. Moisture Diffusion in Printed Circuit Boards: Measurements and Finite Element Simulations[J]. Microelectronics Reliability, 45: 1662-1667.

WU T, GUO Y, CHEN W, 1993. Thermal-Mechanical Strain Characterization for Printed Wiring Boards[J]. IBM Journal of Research and Development, 37(5): 621-634.

YEH C L, LAI Y S, 2006. Support Excitation Scheme for Transient Analysis of JEDEC Board-level Drop Test [J]. Microelectronics Reliability, 47(8): 626-636.

YUAN J, FALANGA L, 1993. The In-plane Thermal Expansion of Glass Fabric Reinforced Epoxy laminates [J]. Journal of Reinforced Plastics and Composites, 12: 489-496.

ZHAN B A, 2000. Comprehensive Solder fatigue and Thermal Characterization of a Silicon Based Multi-chip Module package Utilization Finite Element Analysis Methodologies[C]. Proceedings of 9th International ANSYS Conference and Exhibition, August 2000.

Table 131.1 Mechanical Properties of Dielectric Materials for PCB (Printed Circuit Boards)

Material	$T/℃$	ρ	E_{11}	E_{22}	E_{33}	G_{12}	G_{13}	G_{23}	ν_{12}	ν_{13}	ν_{23}
FR-4 (T_g = 170 ℃)	−40	—	32.4	27.2	11	0.74	0.28	0.235	0.02	0.16	0.14
	23	1.8	29.9	25.1	10	0.71	0.267	0.224	0.02	0.16	0.14
	95	—	27.6	23.2	9	0.67	0.254	0.213	0.02	0.16	0.14
	150	—	23.9	20.1	8	0.5	0.19	0.159	0.02	0.16	0.14
	170 (T_g)	—	—	—	—	—	—	—	—	—	—
	270	—	21.4	17.9	0.6	0.49	0.186	0.156	0.02	0.16	0.14
FR-4 (T_g = 140 ℃)	−40	—	24.3	24.3	10.5	0.66	0.21	0.21	0.02	0.16	0.14
	23	1.7	22.4	22.4	9.5	0.63	0.2	0.2	0.02	0.16	0.14
	95	—	20.7	20.7	8.5	0.6	0.19	0.19	0.02	0.16	0.14
	140 (T_g)	—	—	—	—	—	—	—	—	—	—
	150	—	17.9	17.9	0.7	0.45	0.142	0.142	0.02	0.16	0.14
	270	—	16.0	16.0	0.6	0.44	0.139	0.139	0.02	0.16	0.14
FR-4 (T_g = 130 ℃)	−40	—	21.7	21.7	10	4	3.2	3.2	0.02	0.16	0.14
	23	—	19.7	19.7	9	3.7	2.9	2.9	0.02	0.16	0.14
	80	—	18	18	8	3.4	2.6	2.6	0.02	0.16	0.14
	130 (T_g)	—	—	—	—	—	—	—	—	—	—
	150	—	15	15	0.6	3	2.4	2.4	0.02	0.16	0.14
	270	—	140	14	0.4	2.6	2.2	2.2	0.02	0.16	0.14
GFRP-weave (FR-4 substrate [Ham & Lee])	0	—	18	18	8	2.5	2.5	2.0	0.11	0.39	0.39
	23	1.8	—	—	—	—	—	—	—	—	—
	100	—	14	14	6.1	2	2	1.6	0.11	0.39	0.39
	170 (T_g)	—	—	—	—	—	—	—	—	—	—
EP/70%GF (V_f = 70%; weave 1008)	23	—	12	12	—	—	—	—	—	—	—
	170 (T_g)	—	—	—	—	—	—	—	—	—	—
EP/66%GF (V_f = 66%; weave 2116)	23	—	14.8	14.8	—	—	—	—	—	—	—
	170 (T_g)	—	—	—	—	—	—	—	—	—	—
EP/GF (Weave 7628)	23	—	12	12	—	—	—	—	—	—	—
	170 (T_g)	—	—	—	—	—	—	—	—	—	—
Phenolic/GF	23	1.814	19.42	19.42	3.42	6.8	1.44	1.44	0.25	0.16	0.16
	100	—	15.14	15.14	0.864	4.6	0.44	0.44	0.27	0.18	0.18
	200	—	14.42	14.42	0.096	4.3	0.133	0.133	0.46	0.48	0.48
	260 (T_g)	—	—	—	—	—	—	—	—	—	—

continued

Material	$T/℃$	ρ	E_{11}	E_{22}	E_{33}	G_{12}	G_{13}	G_{23}	ν_{12}	ν_{13}	ν_{23}
PI/GF	23	1.6	27.6	27.6	2.1	0.7	0.24	0.24	0.16	0.16	0.16
PCB Substrate	23	—	22	22	22	—	—	—	0.28	0.28	0.28
Underfill (Hysol FR4526)	−73	—	9.8	9.8	9.8	—	—	—	0.3	0.3	0.3
	23	—	9.5	9.5	9.5	—	—	—	0.3	0.3	0.3
	102	—	7.7	7.7	7.7	—	—	—	0.3	0.3	0.3
	127	—	5.4	5.4	5.4	—	—	—	0.3	0.3	0.3
Silicon Chip	23	—	131	131	131	—	—	—	0.3	0.3	0.3
Solder Mask	23	—	6.9	6.9	6.9	—	—	—	0.35	0.35	0.35
Si_3Ni_4	23	—	314	314	314	—	—	—	0.33	0.33	0.33
Micro via Filler	23	—	7	7	7	—	—	—	0.3	0.3	0.3
BT (Bismaleimide Triazene)	23	—	26	26	26	—	—	—	0.39	0.39	0.39
Cu (Via in Pad)	23	8.93	76	76	76	—	—	—	0.35	0.35	0.35
Heavy Copper	23	8.93	96.5	96.5	96.5	—	—	—	0.32	0.32	0.32
C11000 (Hard)	23	8.93	117	117	117	—	—	—	0.33	0.33	0.33

Notes: GF = E-glass fibers;

   x = Manufacturing direction in the laminate coordinate system (in-plane);

   y = Perpendicular to manufacturing direction (in-plane);

   z = Out-of-plane direction;

   E_{xx}, E_{yy}, and E_{zz}(GPa) = Tensile moduli in the laminate coordinate system;

   G_{xy}, G_{xz}, and G_{yz}(GPa) = Shear moduli in the laminate coordinate system.

Table 131.2 Thermal Properties of Dielectric Materials for PCB (Printed Circuit Boards)

Material	$T/℃$	α_1	α_2	α_3	k_1	k_2	k_3	γ	β_1	β_2	β_3
EP/Aramids (non-woven)	23	11	11	115	—	—	—	—	—	—	—
FR-4 (T_g = 170 ℃)	23	14.5	12.8	41	0.5	0.5	—	1300	—	—	—
	170	—	—	154	—	—	—	—	—	—	—
	217 (T_m)										

continued

Material	$T/\text{℃}$	α_1	α_2	α_3	k_1	k_2	k_3	γ	β_1	β_2	β_3
FR-4 ($T_g = 140\ \text{℃}$)	−40	14	13	63	—	—	—	—	—	—	—
	23	14	13	63	0.35	0.35	—	1300	—	—	—
	140	—	—	154	—	—	—	—	—	—	—
GFRP (Weave) (FR-4 Substrate [Ham & Lee])	0	—	13	13	45	—	—	—	—	—	—
	23	1.8	13	13	45	—	—	—	—	—	—
	100	—	13	13	45	—	—	—	—	—	—
	170 (T_g)										
Phenolic/GF	23	19.5	19.5	37.7	—	—	—	—	—	—	—
	100	15.5	15.5	50.2	—	—	—	—	—	—	—
	200	12.5	12.5	261	—	—	—	—	—	—	—
PI/E-glass	23	13	13	53	0.3	0.3	—	—	—	—	—
PCB Substrate	23	18.5	18.5	18.5	—	—	—	—	—	—	—
Cu (Via-in-Pad)	23	17	17	17	392	392	392	—	—	—	—
Underfill	23	30	30	30	—	—	—	—	—	—	—
Silicon Chip	−73	1.4	1.4	1.4	—	—	—	—	—	—	—
	23	2.8	2.8	2.8	—	—	—	—	—	—	—
	127	3.23	3.23	3.23	—	—	—	—	—	—	—
Solder Mask	23	19	19	19	—	—	—	—	—	—	—
Si_3Ni_4	23	3	3	3	—	—	—	—	—	—	—
Micro via Filler	23	35	35	35	—	—	—	—	—	—	—
BT (Bismaleimide Triazene)	23	15	15	15	—	—	—	—	—	—	—
Heavy Copper	23	18	18	18	392	392	392	—	—	—	—
C11000 (Hard)	23	16.7	16.7	16.7	392	392	392	—	—	—	—

Notes: x, y, z = Laminate coordinate system;

α_x, α_y, α_z (mm/m/℃) = Coefficients of linear thermal expansion in laminate coordinates;

k_x, k_y, k_z (W/m/℃) = Thermal conductivities in laminate coordinates;

W_A = Water absorption.

Table 131.3 Mechanical Failure Parameters of Dielectric Materials for PCB（Printed Circuit Boards）

Material	$T/℃$	$(\sigma_{11u}, \varepsilon_{11u})$	$(\sigma_{22u}, \varepsilon_{22u})$	$(\sigma_{33u}, \varepsilon_{33u})$	$(\sigma_{12u}, \varepsilon_{12u})/(\sigma_{23u}, \varepsilon_{23u})/(\sigma_{13u}, \varepsilon_{13u})$
FR-4	23	—	—	—	—
	170 (T_g)				
PI/E-Glass	23	—	—	—	—

Notes：FR-4＝Epoxy reinforced with woven E-glass；

PI/E-glass＝Polyimide reinforced with woven E-glass；

σ_{iit}(MPa) & ε_{iit}＝Ultimate tensile stresses/strains along the primary material axes；

σ_{iic}(MPa) & ε_{iic}＝Ultimate compressive stresses/strains along the primary material axes；

σ_{iju}(MPa) & ε_{iju}＝Ultimate shear stresses/strains in the primary material axes（1, 2, 3）.

Chapter 132

Ferroelectrics, Piezoelectrics, and Pyroelectrics

132.1　Introduction

Crystal structures can be divided into 32 crystal classes according to the number of rotational axes and reflection planes. Dielectric crystals can be further divided into two groups according to the positions of atoms: centro-symmetric (11 classes) and non-centro-symmetric (21 classes). 20 of the 21 non-centro-symmetric crystal classes are piezoelectric.

Piezoelectric crystals can be again divided into two groups according to their responses to temperature variation: non-pyroelectric and pyroelectric. 10 out of the 20 piezoelectric classes are able to exhibit a pyroelectric effect when heated or cooled-a spontaneous polarization with a dipole in its unit cell as the temperature varies.

Pyroelectric crystals can be again divided into two groups according to the polarization response to an electromagnetic field: non-ferroelectric and ferroelectric. If this dipole can be reversed by the application of an electric field, the material is said to be ferroelectric.

Thermo-mechanical properties like nonlinear stress-strain relations, bipolar and unipolar electric field strain relations, dynamic response, creep, fatigue, and fracture toughness, are of interest to researchers in the area of mechanics of dielectric materials.

132.2　Ferroelectric Materials

Ferroelectric materials, as a sub-group of dielectrics, exhibit an "almost spontaneous" electric polarization (i.e. electric charge generation) and can be reversed in direction by the application of an appropriate electric field. The separation of the center of positive and negative electric charges in an external electric field, makes one side of the dielectric material positive and the opposite side negative. For example, the crystal unit of barium titanate ($BaTiO_3$) has a typical ferroelectric dipole. Ferroelectricity ceases when the operating temperature is higher than the Curie temperature, at which the agitating thermal energy repeals the polarization.

The time lag between the polarization and the external electric field is called ferroelectric hysteresis.

132.3   Pyroelectric Materials

A pyroelectric material is able to generate a temporary voltage as heated or cooled. For example, the atoms in a GaN (Gallium Nitride) crystal are displaced such that electric polarization varies accordingly and subsequently resulting in electric charge generation. Conversely, when subjected to an electromagnetic field, the piezoelectric material exhibits a change in temperature. The pyroelectric coefficient may be described as the change in the spontaneous polarization vector with temperature [Naranjo]:

$$\partial P_r = c_{pr}\, \partial T \tag{132.1}$$

where:
P_r (C or Charge): Polarization;
c_{pr} (C/m^2/℃): Pyroelectric charge coefficient;
T (℃ or K): Temperature.

The crystal of lithium tantalate (LiTaO$_3$), as a nuclear fusion material, is pyroelectric and piezoelectric.

132.4   Piezoelectric Materials

When mechanical strain is applied, the coupling between mechanical and electrical energy results in an electric polarization in a piezoelectric material. It is called the piezoelectric effect that electric charge generation is due to electric potential. Conversely, when subjected to an electromagnetic field, the piezoelectric material exhibits a change in mechanical strain and dimension. They are used in a broad range of applications that includes ultrasonic devices, fuel injection systems, smart structures, high precision positioning equipment for electronic manufacturing, and advanced scanning probe microscopy. When a relaxor, such as Pb(Mg$_{\frac{1}{3}}$Nb$_{\frac{2}{3}}$)O$_3$ or Pb(Zn$_{\frac{1}{3}}$Nb$_{\frac{2}{3}}$)O$_3$, is exposed to an electric field, the induced strain can be attributed to both piezoelectric effect and electrostrictive effect as

$$\varepsilon_{ij} = d_{(ij)k}\, E_k + Q_{ijkl}\, E_k\, E_l \tag{132.2}$$

where:
ε_{ij}: Mechanical strains;
$d_{(ij)k}$ (m/V): Piezoelectric strain constants;
Q_{ijkl}: Electrostrictive constants and $Q_{ijkl} = 0$ for simple piezoelectric materials;
E_k (V/m): Electric fields with $k = 1, 2,$ or 3.

For simple piezoelectric materials, $Q_{ijkl} = 0$ and the above equation reduces to

$$\varepsilon_{(ij)} = d_{(ij)k} E_k \tag{132.3}$$

Or $\quad \varepsilon_{11} = d_{11} E_1 + d_{12} E_2 + d_{13} E_3 \quad$ (Loading plane $\perp$ 1-axis) $\tag{132.3}_a$

$\quad \varepsilon_{22} = d_{21} E_1 + d_{22} E_2 + d_{23} E_3 \quad$ (Loading plane $\perp$ 2-axis) $\tag{132.3}_b$

$\quad \varepsilon_{33} = d_{31} E_1 + d_{32} E_2 + d_{33} E_3 \quad$ (Loading plane $\perp$ 3-axis) $\tag{132.3}_c$

$\quad \tau_{23} = d_{41} E_1 + d_{42} E_2 + d_{43} E_3 \quad$ (Shear plane $\perp$ 1-axis) $\tag{132.3}_d$

$\quad \tau_{31} = d_{51} E_1 + d_{52} E_2 + d_{53} E_3 \quad$ (Shear plane $\perp$ 2-axis) $\tag{132.3}_e$

$\quad \tau_{12} = d_{61} E_1 + d_{62} E_2 + d_{63} E_3 \quad$ (Shear plane $\perp$ 3-axis) $\tag{132.3}_f$

Single crystal ferroelectrics, such as PMN (lead magnesium niobate) and PZN/PT (solid solution of lead zirconate niobate / barium titanate), have received great attention from research and development due to their ability to provide a high degree of polarization domain well aligned with electric poling, which gives rise to superb piezoelectric characteristics.

Langasite (LGS), $LiNbO_3$(LN), AlN, and YCOB [yttrium calcium oxyborate; $YCa_4O(BO_3)_3$] are the most widely used piezoelectric materials for high-temperature applications (> 600 ℃) due to their stable performance at elevated temperatures. YCOB-based devices in particular, including accelerometers, ultrasound transducers, and acoustic emission sensors give rise to a highly steady and reliable operation even at temperatures over 1000 ℃.

Pb-based Materials -$Pb(Mg, Zr, Ti)O_3$.

Layered perovskites-$SrBi_2Ta_2O_9$, $Bi4Ti_3O_{12}$, $BaTiO_3$-based materials -$(Ba, Sr)TiO_3$.

132.2.1　Pb-based Materials -$Pb(Mg, Zr, Ti)O_3$

$Pb(Mg_{\frac{1}{3}}Nb_{\frac{2}{3}})O_3$

132.2.2　PZN (Lead Zirconium Niobate)

$Pb(Zn_{\frac{1}{3}}Nb_{\frac{2}{3}})O_3$

132.5　Piezoresistive Materials

The piezoresistive effect is defined as a change in the electrical resistivity (not electric voltage potential) of a material (e.g. silicon, germanium, and metal) when mechanical strain is applied [Kinda]. Its applications include pressure sensors and acceleration sensors based on piezoresistive effect. On the other hand, such an effect has to be balanced out in a Hall-effect sensor.

References

DAMIANOVICI D, 1998. Ferroelectric, Dielectric and Piezoelectric Properties of Ferroelectric Thin Films and Ceramics[J]. Reports on Progress in Physics, 61(9): 1267.

FIEBIG M, 2005. Revival of the Magnetoelectric Effect[J]. Journal of Physics, D, 36(8): R123-R152.

HOPCROFT M A, et al, 2010. What is the Young's Modulus of Silicon? [J]. Journal of Microelectronic Systems, 19(2): 229-238.

KEPPENSL V, 2013. Structural transitions: "Ferroelectricity" in a metal[J]. Nature Materials, 12: 952-953.

KANDA Y, 1991. Piezoresistance Effect of Silicon[J]. Sensors and Actuators, A28(2): 83-91.

LUPASCU D C, et al, 2013. Mechanical Properties of Ferro-Piezoceramics[J]. Multifunctional Polycrystalline Ferroelectric Materials, 140, 469-542.

NARANJO B, GIMZEWSKI J, PUTTERMAN S, 2005. Observation of Nuclear Fusion Driven by a Pyroelectric Crystal[J]. Nature, 434 (7037): 1115-1117.

OR Y T, et al, 2003. Modeling of Poling, Piezoelectric and Pyroelectric Properties of Ferroelectric 0-3 Composites[J]. Journal of Applied Physics, 94(5): 3319-3325.

SCOTT J F, 1998. The Physics of Ferroelectric Ceramic Thin Films for Memory Applications[J]. Ferroelectrics Review, 1(1): 1-129.

URSIC H, DAMJANOVIC D, 2013. Anelastic Relaxor Behavior of $Pb(Mg_{\frac{1}{3}}Nb_{\frac{2}{3}})O_3$ [J]. Applied Physics Letters, 103(7): 072904.

ZU H F, et al, 2014. Properties of Single Crystal Piezoelectric $Ca_3TaGa_3Si_2O_{14}$ and $YCa_4O(BO_3)_3$ Resonators at High-temperature and Vacuum Conditions[J]. Sensors and Actuators A, 216: 167-175.

Table 132.1   Mechanical Properties of Ferroelectrics, Pyroelectrics, and Piezoelectrics

Material-DAM	$T/^{\circ}C$	ρ	E_{11}	E_{22}	E_{33}	G_{12}	G_{13}	G_{23}	ν_{12}	ν_{13}	ν_{23}
Pyroelectrics :											
$CsNO_3$	23	—	—	—	—	—	—	—	—	—	—
GaN	23	6.15	181	181	181	—	—	—	0.352	0.352	0.352
	2500 (T_m)										
$LiTaO_3$ (Lithium Tantalate)	23	—	—	—	—	—	—	—	—	—	—
PVDF	−35 (T_g)	—	—	—	—	—	—	—	—	—	—
	23	1.78	—	—	—	—	—	—	—	—	—
	175 (T_m)										
ZnO (hexagonal Crystal)	23	5.606	—	—	—	—	—	—	—	—	—
	1975 (T_m)										
Piezoelectrics :											
$Ba_2NaNb_5O_5$	23	—	—	—	—	—	—	—	—	—	—
$GaPO_4$ (Crystal; Gallium Orthophosphate)	23	—	—	—	—	—	—	—	—	—	—
$KNbO_3$ (Potassium Niobate)	23	—	—	—	—	—	—	—	—	—	—
$La_3Ga_5SiO_{14}$ (Crystal; Langasite)	23	—	—	—	—	—	—	—	—	—	—
$Pb(Mg_{\frac{1}{3}}Nb_{\frac{2}{3}})O_3$ (PMN; Unpoled)	23	7.8	111	—	—	—	—	—	0.46	0.46	—
$PbTiO_3$ (Lead Titanate)	23	—	—	—	—	—	—	—	—	—	—

continued

Material-DAM	$T/°C$	ρ	E_{11}	E_{22}	E_{33}	G_{12}	G_{13}	G_{23}	ν_{12}	ν_{13}	ν_{23}
$Pb(Zn_{\frac{1}{3}} Nb_{\frac{2}{3}})O_3$ (PZN)	23	—	—	—	—	—	—	—	—	—	—
$Pb_2KNb_5O_{15}$	23	—	—	—	—	—	—	—	—	—	—
PT/PEO ($PbTiO_3$/ PEOxide)	23	—	—	—	—	—	—	—	—	—	—
Quartz (Crystal)	23	—	—	—	—	—	—	—	—	—	—
Si [(100) plane Wafer] [Hopcroft]	23	2.33	169	169	130	0.064	0064	0.36	50.9	79.6	79.6
ZnO (zincblende Crystal)	23	5.606	—	—	—	—	—	—	—	—	—
	1975 (T_m)										

Table 132.2   Thermal Properties of Ferroelectrics, Pyroelectrics, and Piezoelectrics

Material	$T/°C$	α_1	α_2	α_3	k_1	k_2	k_3	γ	β_1	β_2	β_3
Pyroelectrics:											
$CsNO_3$	23	—	—	—	—	—	—	—	—	—	—
GaN	23	3.17	5.59	5.59	130	130	130	490	—	—	—
$LiTaO_3$ (Lithium Tantalate)	23	—	—	—	—	—	—	—	—	—	—
PVDF	−35 (T_g)	—	—	—	—	—	—	—	—	—	—
	23	1.78	—	—	—	—	—	—	—	—	—
	175 (T_m)										
ZnO (hexagonal Crystal)	23	5.606	—	—	—	—	—	—	—	—	—
	1975 (T_m)										
Piezoelectrics:											

Table 132.3   Mechanical Failure Parameters of Ferroelectrics, Piezoelectrics, and Pyroelectrics

Material	$T/^\circ C$	$(\sigma_{11u}, \varepsilon_{11u})$	$(\sigma_{22u}, \varepsilon_{22u})$	$(\sigma_{33u}, \varepsilon_{33u})$	$(\sigma_{12u}, \varepsilon_{12u})/(\sigma_{23u}, \varepsilon_{23u})/$ $(\sigma_{13u}, \varepsilon_{13u})$
PMN [Unpoled; $Pb(Mg_{\frac{1}{3}}Nb_{\frac{2}{3}})O_3$]	23	$(-1309, -0.9\%)$ $(-525, -0.4\%)$ $(-270, -0.2\%)$	—	—	—/—/—

Table 132.4   Properties of Ferroelectric, Pyroelectric, and Piezoelectric Effects

Material	$T/^\circ C$	ρ	d_{11}	d_{22}	d_{33}	d_{31}				
Pa-11 (Nylon-11)	23	—	—	—	—	3	—	—	—	—
	168 (T_g)	—	—	—	—	—	—	—	—	—
	107	—	—	—	—	14	—	—	—	—
	195 (T_m)	—	—	—	—	—	—	—	—	—
PAN	23	—	—	—	—	2	—	—	—	—
Polyurea-9	23	—	—	—	—	—	—	—	—	—
	50 (T_g)	—	—	—	—	—	—	—	—	—
	180 (T_m)	—	—	—	—	—	—	—	—	—
PVC	23	—	—	—	—	5	—	—	—	—
PVDF/TrFE (75/25 mol% copolymer; crystal)	23	—	—	—	-38	—	—	—	—	—
PZT	23	7.8	—	—	—	175	—	—	—	—
TrFE (Trifluoroethylene)	23	—	—	—	—	12	—	—	—	—
	32 (T_g)	—	—	—	—	—	—	—	—	—
	150 (T_m)	—	—	—	—	—	—	—	—	—

Note: The unit for d_{ij} is 10^{-9} m/V.

Natural Materials

Chapter 133

Cellulosics

133.1 Introduction

Cellulosics are a family of tough and hard cellulosic materials, including the following thermoplastics: cellulose acetate, cellulose nitrate, propionate, acetate butyrate, and ethyl cellulose. Cellulose is synthesized in plants, algae, tunicate sea animals, and some bacteria. Some of the nano-cellulose fibers are almost as stiff as Kevlar. Nano-cellulose fibers are completely renewable, but Kevlar and other traditional plastics are made from petroleum or natural gas.

Cellulosic nanocrystals (also known as cellulose whiskers) may be derived from several sources such as pineapple, curcuma, banana and coir into thermoplastics matrix composites for automotive applications. Though the family tree of natural fibers for automotive applications mainly consists of plants, natural fibers come from the following three groups:

(a) Plant and Vegetable;
(b) Animal;
(c) Mineral.

133.2 Plant and Vegetable

133.2.1 Wood and Bamboo

Details of wood and bamboo are to be discussed in the next Chapter.

133.2.2 Nonwood Plants and Vegetables

As the structure of a plant or vegetable is, nonwood natural fibers can be divided into the following:

(a) Bast: Flax, Hemp, Jute, Kenaf, and Ramie;
(b) Leaf: Abaca, Banana, Henequen, Pineapple, and Sisal;
(c) Seed: Coir, Cotton, Kapok, Milkweed, Oil Palm, and Rice Husk;
(d) Grass Stalk/Stem: Bagasse, Barley, Canary, Communis, Esparto, Phragmites, Maize, Oat, Reed, Rice, Rye, Sabei, and Wheat.

133.2.3 Animal

Wool and silk are a typical natural fiber from animals.

133.2.4 Mineral

Asbestos is a typical natural fiber from minerals.

133.3 Mechanical Properties of Cellulosic

Mechanical properties of cellulosic plastics derived from natural resources are desirable. They are light, but strong. Because cellulosics may be compounded with many different plasticizers in widely varying concentrations, property ranges are broad, though averaged mechanical and thermal properties are given in Tables 133.1 and 133.2 for reference. Cellulosics is capable of working as a load-bearing constituent. The percentages of material constituents with averaged values by weight of some natural fibers are listed as follows [Mariesidicula et al.] [Mohanty et al.] [Raju et al.] [Higuchi] [Mukhopadhyay et al.] [Stevulova et al.]:

Natural Fiber	Cellulose/%	Hemicellulose/%	Lignin/%	Ash/%
Areca	—	50	19	—
Bagasse	43	27	16	2
Bamboo (Heterocycla)	49.1	27.7	26.1	1.3
Bamboo (Nigra)	42.3	23.8	24.1	2
Bamboo (Reticulata)	25.3	26.5	25.3	1.9
Banana	63.5	19	5	—
Banana Pseudostem	31.3	15	15.1	8.65
Coir	37	0.2	43	—
Groundnut shell	36	19	30	6
Hemp	44.5	33	21.3	1.4
Jute	66	16	13	2
Kenaf	35	21.5	17	—
Maize Stalks	40	22	12	—
Maple (hardwood)	47	28	26	—
Pine (softwood)	42	27	30	—
Pineapple	81	—	13	—
Rice husk	31	24	14	24
Sisal	69	12	12	—

Hemp, also called cannabis sativa, is a commercial source of long natural fibers. It is an annual herbaceous plant native to Asia and widely cultivated in Europe. Flax is another commercial source of long natural fibers. Kenaf bast fibers are used for reinforcing UP (unsaturated polyester) and the tensile strength of the UP/Kenaf fiber composite reaches the maximum with the fiber content at 20% (by weight).

133.4　Moisture Diffusion

Cellulosic fiber composites tend to swell considerably at water uptake and as a consequence mechanical properties, such as stiffness and strength, are negatively influenced. The fiber-matrix adhesion may be improved and the fiber swelling reduced by various modification techniques.

133.5　Applications

Nowadays, door panels, seat backs, headliners, dashboards, interior parts, package trays, furniture, packaging, building and constructions are made from natural fiber-reinforced composites, and so are even some military vehicles and aircraft spare parts.

Cellulose acetate is the material in wide use for eyeglass frames.

An insulation system consisting of natural cellulosics and mineral oil has been used for liquid-immersed power transformers for more than a century [Singh et al.]. Such transformer insulation is subjected to combined stresses resulting from thermal and electrical effects.

References

ANDERSONS J, SPARRNINŠ E, JOFFE R, et al, 2005. Strength Distribution of Elementary Flax Fibers[J]. Composites Science and Technology, 65: 693-702.

ARBELAIZ A, et al, 2005. Mechanical Properties of Flax Fiber/Poly Propylene Composites: Influence of Fiber/Matrix Modification and Glass Fiber Hybridization[J]. Composites, Part A, 36: 1637-1644.

ARIFUZZAMAN K G M, et al, 2009. Surface Modification of Okra Bast Fiber and its Physico-chemical Characteristics[J]. Fibers and Polymers, 1: 65-70.

AZWA Z, YOUSIF B, MANALO A, et al, 2013. A Review on the Degradability of Polymeric Composites Based on Natural Fibers[J]. Materials and Design, 47: 424-442.

BALEY C, 2002. Analysis of Flax Fibers Tensile Behavior and Analysis of the Tensile Stiffness Increase[J]. Composites, Part A, 33: 939-948.

BECKERMANN G W, PICKERING K L, 2008. Engineering and Evaluation of Hemp Fiber Reinforced Poly propylene Composites: Fiber Treatment and Matrix Modification[J]. Composites, Part A, 39: 979-988.

BEHZAD T, SAIN M, 2007. Measurement and Prediction of Thermal Conductivity for Hemp Fiber Reinforced Composites[J]. Polymer Engineering and Science, 47(7): 977-983.

BISMARCK A, et al, 2002. Surface Characterization of Flax, Hemp and Cellulose fibers: Surface Properties and the Water Uptake Behavior[J]. Journal of Polymer Composites, 23, 872-889.

BLEDZKI A, GASSAN J, 1999. Composites Reinforced with Cellulose Based Fibers[J]. Progress of Polymer Science, 24(2): 221-274.

BOS H L, et al, 2002. Tensile and Compressive Properties of Flax Fibers for Natural Fiber Reinforced Composites[J]. Journal of Materials Science, 37: 1683-1692.

CAO Y, et al, 2006. Mechanical Properties of Biodegradable Composites Reinforced with Bagasse Fiber before and after Alkali Treatments[J]. Composites, Part A, 37: 423-429.

CHOW C, XING X, LI R, 2007. Moisture Absorption Studies of Sisal Fiber Reinforced Polypropylene Composites[J]. Composites Science and Technology, 67: 306-313.

CICHOCKI Jr. F R, THOMASON J L, 2002. Thermoelastic Anisotropy of a Natural Fiber[J]. Composites Science and Technology, 62: 669-678.

DAVIES G, BRUCE D, 1998. Effect of Environmental Relative Humidity and Damage on the Tensile Properties of Flax and Nettle Fibers[J]. Textile Research Journal, 68(9): 623-629.

DHAKA H N, et al, 2007. Effect of Water Absorption on the Mechanical Properties of Hemp Fiber Reinforced Unsaturated Polyester Composites[J]. Composites Science and Technology, 67(7/8): 1674-1683.

DU Y, ZHANG J, XUE Y A, 2008. Temperature-duration Effects on Tensile Properties of Kenaf Bast Fiber Bundles (Statistical Table)[J]. Forest Product Journal, 58(9): 59-65.

ELICES M, et al, 2005. Finding Inspiration in Argiope Trifasciata Spider Silk Fibers[J]. JOM, 57(2): 60-66.

FELIX M J, GATENHOLM P, 1993. Formation of Entanglements as Brushlike Interfaces in Cellulose-Polymer Composites[J]. Journal of Applied Polymer Science, 50(4): 699-708.

FERREIRA J, CAPELAL C, COSTA J, 2010. A Study of the Mechanical Properties of Natural Fibre Reinforced Composites[J]. Fibers and Polymers, 11(8): 1181-1186.

GODA K, CAO Y, 2007. Research and Development of Fully Green Composites Reinforced with Natural Fibers [J]. Journal of Solid Mechanics and Materials Engineering, 1: 1073-1084.

GOMES A, et al, 2004. Effects of Alkali Treatment to Reinforcement on Tensile Properties of Curaua Fiber Green Composites[J]. JSME International Journal Series, A, 47: 5416-546.

GORDON S, HSIEH Y, 2007. Cotton: Science and Technology [M]. Woodhead Publishing Limited, Cambridge, UK.

HABIBI Y, et al, 2008. Processing and Characterization of Reinforced Polyethylene Composites Made with Lignocellulosic Fibers from Egyptian Agro-industrial Residues [J]. Journal of Composites Science and Technology, 68: 1877-1885.

HAMID K, et al, 2006. Short Palm Tree Fibers-Thermoset Matrices and Composites[J]. Composites, Part A, 37: 1413-1422.

HARZALLSH O, et al, 2013. Preliminary Examination of the Effects of Relative Humidity on the Fracture Morphology of Cotton Flat Bundles[J]. Textile Research Journal, 83(10): 1044-1054.

HARRIETTE L, et al, 2006. Mechanical Properties of Short-Flax-Fiber Reinforced Compounds [J]. Composites, Part A, 37: 1591-1604.

HENRIKSSON M, BERGLUND L, 2007. Structure and Properties of Cellulose Nanocomposite Films Containing Melamine Formaldehyde[J]. Journal of Applied Polymer Science, 106: 2817-2824.

HERRERA F P, VALADEZ G A, 2005. A Study of the Mechanical Properties of Short Natural-Fiber Reinforced Composites[J]. Composites, B, 36(8): 597-608.

HOLBERY J, HOUSTON D, 2006. Natural-fiber-reinforced Polymer Composites in Automotive Applications [J]. Journal of the Minerals, Metals and Materials Society, 58: 80-86.

HU R, SUN M, LIM J, 2010. Moisture Absorption, Tensile Strength and Microstructure Evolution of Short Jute Fiber[J]. Materials and Design, 31: 3167-3173.

IDICULA M, et al, 2010. Mechanical Performance of Short Banana/Sisal Hybrid Fiber Reinforced Polyester Composites[J]. Journal of Reinforced Plastics and Composites, 29(1): 12-29.

ISHA M R, et al, 2009. Mechanical Properties of Kenaf Bast and Core Fiber Reinforced Unsaturated Polyester Composites[J]. 9th National Symposium on Polymeric Materials, 4(3): 316-320.

ISHAK M R, et al, 2009. The Effect of Sea Water Treatment to Impact and Flexural Strength of Sugar Palm Fiber Reinforced Epoxy Composites[J]. International Journal of Mechanical and Material Engineering, 4, 316-320.

JAWAID M, et al, 2011. Chemical Resistance, Void Content and Tensile Properties of Oil Palm/Jute Fiber Reinforced Polymer Hybrid Composites[J]. Materials and Design, 32(2): 1014-1019.

KAWABATA S, KOTANI T, YAMASHITA Y, 1995. Measurement of the Longitudinal Mechanical Properties of High-performance Fibers[J]. Journal of Textile Institute, 86: 347-359.

KAMATH M G, et al, 2005. Cotton Fiber Nonwovens for Automotive Composites[J]. International Nonwoven Journal, 14: 34-40.

KELLER A, 2003. Compounding and Mechanical Properties of Biodegradable Hemp Fiber Composites[J]. Composites Science and Technology, 63: 1307-1316.

KIM E, KIM B, KIM D, 2007. Physical Properties and Morphology of Polycaprolactone /Starch/Pine-Leaf Composites[J]. Journal of Applied Polymer Science, 103: 928-934.

LEMAN Z, et al, 2008. Moisture Absorption Behavior of Sugar Palm Fiber Reinforced Epoxy Composite[J]. Materials and Design, 29: 1666-1670.

LILHOLT H, LAWTHER J M, 2000. Natural Organic Fibers[M]. Oxford, UK: Pergamon Press.

LUZ S, et al, 2010. Environmental Benefits of Substituting talc by Sugarcane Bagasse Fibers as Reinforcement in Polypropylene Composites: Ecodesign and LCA as Strategy for Automotive Components[J]. Resources, Conservation and Recycling, 54(12): 1135-1144.

MALKAPURAM R, et al, 2008. Recent Development in Natural Fiber Reinforced Polypropylene Composites [J]. Journal of Reinforced Plastics and Composites, 28: 1169-1189.

MARIESIDICULA A B, et al, 2006. Thermophysical Properties of Natural Fiber Reinforced Polyester Composites[J]. Composites Science and Technology, 66(15): 2719-2725.

MOHAMMAD L, et al, 2010. Mechanical, Optical, and Electrical Properties of Cellulosic Semiconductor Nanocomposites[J]. Journal of Applied Polymer Science, 115(5): 2847-2854.

MOHANTY A K, MISRA M, DRZAL L T, 2005. Natural Fibers, Biopolymers, and Their Bio-Composites[M]. Boca Raton: CRC Press.

MOHANTY A K, et al, 2004. Effect of Process Engineering on the Performance of Natural Fiber Reinforced Cellulose Acetate Biocomposites[J]. Composites, Part A, 35: 363-370.

MOHANTY A K, MISRA M, HINRICHSEN G, 2000. Biofibres, Biodegradable Polymers and Biocomposites: an Overview[J]. Journal of Macromolecular Materials and Engineering, 276: 1-24.

MUELLER D H, 2005. Improving the Impact Strength of Natural Fiber Reinforced Composites by Specifically Designed Material and Process Parameters[J]. International Nonwoven Journal, 13: 31-38.

MUKHOPADHYAY S, et al, 2008. Banana Fibers-Variability and Fracture Behavior[J]. Journal of Engineered Fibers and Fabrics, 3(2): 39-45.

NISHITANI T, OGURA H, 1989. Temperature-dependent Mechanical Properties and Constitutive Equation of Cellulose Nitrate[J]. Polymer Engineering & Science, 29(33): 1588-1591.

NISHINO T, HIRAO K, KOTERA M, et al, 2003. Kenaf-Reinforced Biodegradable Composite[J]. Composites Science and Technology, 63: 1281-1286.

OZTURK S, 2010. Effect of Fiber Loading on the Mechanical Properties of Kenaf and Fiberfrax Fiber-Reinforced Phenol-Formaldehyde Composites[J]. Journal of Composite Materials, 44(19): 2265-2288.

PANTHAPULAKKAL S, ZERESHKIAN A, SAIN M, 2006. Preparation and Characterization of Wheat Straw Fibers for Reinforcing Application in Injection Molded Thermoplastic Composites[J]. Biores Technology, 97: 265-272.

PLAZA G R, et al, 2006. Thermo-hygro-mechanical Behavior of Spider Dragline Silk: Glassy and Rubbery States[J]. Journal of Polymer Science, Part B: Polymer Physics, 44 (6): 994-999.

QIN J J, CAO Y M, LI Y, 2005. Effect of Hypochlorite Concentration on Properties of Post Treated Outer-Skin Ultrafiltration Membranes Spun from Cellulose Acetate/Poly (Vinyl Pyrrolidone) Blends [J]. Journal of Applied Polymer Science, 97: 227-231.

RAFEADAH R, et al, 2011. Stress Transfer in Cellulose Nanowhisker Composites-Influence of Whisker Aspect Ratio and Surface Charge[J]. Biomacromolecules, 12(4): 1363-1369.

RAJU G U, et al, 2012. Experimental Study on Optimization of Thermal Properties of Groundnut Shell Particle Reinforced Polymer Composites[J]. International Journal of Emerging Science, 2(3): 433-454.

RAJU G U, KUMARAPPA S, 2011. Experimental Study on Mechanical Properties of Groundnut Shell Particle Reinforced Epoxy Composites[J]. Journal of Reinforced Plastics and Composites, 30(12): 1029-1037.

RATNA P A V, et al, 2007. Flexural Properties of Rice Straw Reinforced Polyester Composites[J]. Indian Journal of Fiber and Textile Research, 32: 399-403.

REN W, et al, 2014. Mechanical and Thermal Properties of Bamboo Pulp Fiber Reinforced Polyethylene Composites[J]. BioResource, 9(3): 4117-4127.

ROBITSCHECK P, 1965. Flammability Characteristics of Cellular Plastics[J]. Journal of Cellular Plastics, 1 (3): 395-399.

ROTRIGUEZ M, et al, 2010. Modeling Corn Fiber Strength[J]. BioResiources, 5(4): 2535-2546.

SHINOJ S, VISVANATHAN R, PANIGRAHI S, et al, 2011. Oil Palm Fiber (OPF) and Its Composites: a Review[J]. Industrial Crops and Products, 33(1): 7-22.

SINGH J, SOOD Y, VERMA P, 2010. Review of Different Prorated Models Which Detects the Effect of Accelerated Stresses on Power Transformer Insulation[J]. International Journal of Computer and Electrical Engineering, 2(3): 569-573.

SOOM R M, et al, 2006. Thermal Properties of Oil Palm Fiber, Cellulose and Its Derivatives[J]. Journal of Oil Palm Resarch, 18: 272-277.

SREEKALA M S, THOMAS S, 2003. Effect of Fiber Surface Modification on Water-sorption Characteristics of Oil Palm Fibers[J]. Composites Science and Technology, 63: 861-869.

SREEKALA M S, et al, 1997. Oil Palm Fibers: Morphology, Chemical Composition, Surface Modification, and Mechanical Properties[J]. Journal of Applied Polym. Science, 66: 821-835.

SREEKUMAR P A, et al, 2008. Mechanical and Water Absorption Studies of Eco-Friendly Banana Fiber Reinforced Polyester Composites Fabricated by RTM[J]. Journal of Applied Polymer Science, 109: 1547-1555.

SRINIVASABAB N, et al, 2008. Experimental Determination of Tensile Properties of Okra, Sisal and Banana Fiber Reinforced Polyester Composites[J]. Indian Journal of Science and Technology, 2(7): 35-38.

STEVULOVA N, et al, 2014. Long-Term Water Absorption Behavior of Hemp Hurds Composites[J]. Chemical Engineering Transactions, 39: 559-564.

TAMRAKAR S, LOPEZ A R, 2011. Water Absorption of Wood Polypropylene Composite Sheet Piles and Its Influence on Mechanical Properties[J]. Construction and Building Materials, 25: 3977-3988.

THOMASON J L, CARRUTHERS L, KELLY J, et al, 2011. Fiber Cross-Section Determination and Variability in Sisal and Flax and Its Effects on Fiber Performance Characterization [J]. Composites Science and Technology, 71(7): 1008-1015.

WANG W, et al, 2006. Study of Moisture Observation in Natural Fiber Plastic Composites[J]. Composites Science and Technology, 66: 379-386.

WONGSRIRAKSA P, et al, 2013. Continuous Natural Fiber Reinforced Thermoplastic Composites by Fiber Surface Modification[J]. Advances in Mechanical Engineering, 2013(1): 143-148.

YOUSIF B F, 2010. Effect of Oil Palm Fibers Volume Fraction on Mechanical Properties of Polyester Composites[J]. International Journal of Modern Physics, B, 24(23): 4459-4470.

Table 133.1   Nominal Mechanical Properties of Cellulosics (Thermoplastics)-Averaged Values

Material-DAM	$T/℃$	E_T	ρ	ν	(σ, ε)	α	k	γ	β	K_{IC}
CA (Cellulose Acetate)	23	1.63	1.28	0.39	$\sigma_{ucs}=-42$; $\sigma_{uts}=43$	130	0.25	1480	—	2
	59 (T_g)	—	—	—	—	—	—	—	—	—
	230 (T_m)	—	—	—	—	—	—	—	—	—
CAB (Cellulose Acetate Butyrate)	23	0.86	1.18	—	(30, 45%)	210	0.22	1500	—	—
Ethyl Cellulose	23	1.62	1.13	—	(35, 22%)	120	0.2	—	—	—
	215 (T_m)	—	—	—	—	—	—	—	—	—
Nitrocellulose (Cellulose Nitrate)	−20 (Low service temperature)									
	23	1.41	1.38	—	(51, 43%)	100	0.23	—	—	—
	75 (T_g)	—	—	—	—	—	—	—	—	—
	165 (T_m)	—	—	—	—	—	—	—	—	—

continued

Material-DAM	$T/℃$	E_T	ρ	ν	(σ, ε)	α	k	γ	β	K_{IC}
CP (Cellulose Propionate)	23	0.95	1.2	—	$\sigma_{uts}=30$	134	0.22	—	—	—

Notes: Cellulosics = Compounded with many different plasticizers in widely varying concentrations, property ranges are broad;

DAM = Dry as Molded;

MFC = Microfibrillated cellulose having a width in the range of 10~100 nm;

$T_g(℃)$ & $T_m(℃)$ = Glass transition point and melting point, respectively.

Table 133.2 Orthotropic Elastic Properties of Natural Fibers

Specification	$T/℃$	ρ	E_{11}	E_{22}	E_{33}	G_{12}	G_{13}	G_{23}	ν_{12}	ν_{13}	ν_{23}
Plants:											
Abaca (蕉麻;20 μm;)	23	1.5	41	—	—	—	—	—	—	—	—
Areca	23	—	1.2	—	—	—	—	—	—	—	—
Bamboo Fiber (200 μm)	23	1.32	5.3	4.52	5.3	—	—	—	—	—	—
Bamboo Pulp Fiber	23	1.32	6.73	—	—	—	—	—	—	—	—
Banana Plant ($d_f=0.19$ mm)	23	1.35	30	—	—	—	—	—	—	—	—
Banana Fiber	23	1.35	3.5	—	—	—	—	—	—	—	—
Barley Straw-top	23	—	0.53	—	—	—	—	—	—	—	—
Barley Straw-mid	23	—	0.44	—	—	—	—	—	—	—	—
Cabuya	23	—	—	—	—	—	—	—	—	—	—
Coconut (椰子)	23	1.15	3.5	—	—	—	—	—	—	—	—
Coir (椰子皮壳; 18 μm)	23	1.25	5	—	—	—	—	—	—	—	—
Corn Stalk ($d_f=17$ μm)	23	—	20	—	—	—	—	—	—	—	—
Cotton	23	1.51	3.5	0.93	0.93	0.11	—	—	—	—	—
Cotton (15 μm)	23	1.51	8	—	—	—	—	—	—	—	—
Cotton (9 μm)	23	1.51	30	—	—	—	—	—	—	—	—

continued

Specification	$T/℃$	ρ	E_{11}	E_{22}	E_{33}	G_{12}	G_{13}	G_{23}	ν_{12}	ν_{13}	ν_{23}
Curaua	23	1.1	27.5	—	—	—	—	—	—	—	—
Flax（亚麻；23 μm）	23	1.4	70	—	—	—	—	—	—	—	—
Hemp（大麻；31 μm）	23	1.48	44	—	—	—	—	—	—	—	—
Jute（黄麻；120 μm）	23	1.4	8.8	—	—	—	—	—	—	—	—
Kapok（25 μm；木棉）	23	0.384	4	—	—	—	—	—	—	—	—
Kenaf（槿麻）	23	1.45	53	—	—	—	—	—	—	—	—
Maize Stalks（L×1.5×0.5 mm）	23	—	8.6	—	—	—	—	—	—	—	—
Nettle，Stinging（20 μm）	23	—	87	—	—	—	—	—	—	—	—
Palm，Fan（L×0.3 mm×0.75 mm）	23	0.75	5.5	—	—	—	—	—	—	—	—
Palm，Oil（Raw）	23	1.45	6.7	—	—	—	—	—	—	—	—
Palm，Oil（Acrylated）	23	1.45	11.1	—	—	—	—	—	—	—	—
Palm，Oil（Silane-treated）	23	1.45	5.3	—	—	—	—	—	—	—	—
Pineapple Leaf	23	1.44	58	—	—	—	—	—	—	—	—
Ponderosa	23	—	4.2	—	—	—	—	—	—	—	—
Ramie（苎麻；50 μm）	23	1.56	23	—	—	—	—	—	—	—	—
Rayon（嫘萦）	23	1.5	6.9	—	—	—	—	—	—	—	—
Rayon（13 μm）	23	1.5	23	—	—	—	—	—	—	—	—
Reed，Canary Grass	23	—	6.3	0.29	0.29	—	—	—	—	—	—
Rice Husk（Bulk）	23	0.75	—	—	—	—	—	—	—	—	—
Sisal（波尔麻；Raw）	23	1.33	13	—	—	—	—	—	—	—	—
Sugar Cane	23	1.25	—	—	—	—	—	—	—	—	—

continued

Specification	$T/{}^\circ\text{C}$	ρ	E_{11}	E_{22}	E_{33}	G_{12}	G_{13}	G_{23}	ν_{12}	ν_{13}	ν_{23}
Viscose（Cord）	23	—	11.4	—	—	—	—	—	—	—	—
Wheat Straw-top	23	—	1.82	—	—	—	—	—	—	—	—
Wheat Straw-mid	23	—	1	—	—	—	—	—	—	—	—
Animals：（*Originated from Protein*）											
Silkworm Silk	23	1.3	5	0.57	0.57	—	—	—	—	—	—
Silkworm Cocoon Inner pelage-45°	23	1.65	—	—	—	—	—	—	—	—	—
Silkworm Cocoon -Inner pelage-0°	23	1.14	—	—	—	—	—	—	—	—	—
Spider Silk Adult （Tetrabychus Urticae）	23	1.31	24	—	—	—	—	—	—	—	—
Spider Silk Larval （Tetrabychus Urticae）	23	1.3	15	—	—	—	—	—	—	—	—
Silk，Spider （Dragline）	23	1.31	—	—	—	—	—	—	—	—	—
Wool（41 μm）	23	1.32	3.4	1.1	1.1	1.47	—	—	—	—	—

Notes：$\nu_{ij} E_{jj} = \nu_{ji} E_{ii}$（$i = 1, 2, 3; j = 1, 2, 3; i \neq j$）.

Table 133.3　Orthotropic Thermal Properties of Natural Fibers

Material-DAM	$T/{}^\circ\text{C}$	α_1	α_2	α_3	k_1	k_2	k_3	γ	β_1	β_2	β_3
Plants：											
Abaca （蕉麻；20 μm）	23	—	—	—	—	—	—	—	—	—	—
Bamboo Fiber （200 μm）	23	—	—	—	—	0.07	0.07	—	—	—	—
Bamboo Pulp Fiber	23	—	—	—	—	—	—	—	—	—	—
Banana Fiber	23	—	—	—	—	—	—	—	—	—	—
Cabuya	23	—	—	—	—	—	—	—	—	—	—

continued

Material-DAM	$T/{}^{\circ}C$	α_1	α_2	α_3	k_1	k_2	k_3	γ	β_1	β_2	β_3
Coconut（椰子）	23	—	—	—	—	—	—	—	—	—	—
Coir（椰子皮壳；18 μm）	23	—	—	—	—	—	—	—	—	—	—
Cotton	23	—	—	—	—	0.06	0.06	1160	—	—	—
Cotton（15 μm）	23	—	—	—	—	0.06	0.06	1160	—	—	—
Curaua	23	—	—	—	—	—	—	—	—	—	—
Flax（亚麻；23 μm）	23	—	—	—	—	—	—	—	—	—	—
Hemp（大麻；31 μm）	23	—	—	—	1.48	0.115	0.115	2200	—	—	—
	100	—	—	—	—	—	—	3400	—	—	—
Jute（黄麻；120 μm）	23	—	—	—	—	—	—	—	—	—	—
Kapok（25 μm；木棉）	23	—	—	—	—	—	—	—	—	—	—
Kenaf（槿麻）	23	—	—	—	—	0.055	0.055	—	—	—	—
Nettle, Stinging（20 μm）	23	—	—	—	—	—	—	—	—	—	—
Palm, Fan（L×0.3 mm×0.75 mm）	23	—	—	—	—	—	—	—	—	—	—
Palm, Oil（Raw）	23	—	—	—	—	—	—	—	—	—	—
Palm, Oil（Acrylated）	23	—	—	—	—	—	—	—	—	—	—
Palm, Oil（Silane-treated）	23	—	—	—	—	—	—	—	—	—	—
Pineapple Leaf	23	—	—	—	—	—	—	—	—	—	—
Ramie（苎麻）	−253	—	—	—	0.8	—	—	—	—	—	—
	−223	—	—	—	1.9	—	—	—	—	—	—
	−123	—	—	—	3.6	—	—	—	—	—	—
	23	—	—	—	—	—	—	—	—	—	—
Rayon（嫘萦）	23	—	—	—	—	—	—	—	—	—	—
Reed, Canary Grass	23	—	—	—	—	0.073	0.073	—	—	—	—
Rice Husk	23	—	—	—	—	—	—	—	—	—	—
Sisal（波尔麻；Raw）	23	—	—	—	—	—	—	—	—	—	—

continued

Material-DAM	$T/°C$	α_1	α_2	α_3	k_1	k_2	k_3	γ	β_1	β_2	β_3
Sugar Cane	23	—	—	—	—	—	—	—	—	—	—
Wheat Straw	23	—	—	—	—	—	—	—	—	—	—
Animals:											
Silkworm Silk	23	—	—	—	—	—	—	—	—	—	—
Spider Silk Adult (Tetrabychus Urticae)	23	—	—	—	—	—	—	—	—	—	—
Spider Silk Larval (Tetrabychus Urticae)	23	—	—	—	—	—	—	—	—	—	—
Wool	23	—	—	—	—	—	—	—	—	—	—

Notes: α_1, α_2, α_3 (μm/m/°C) = Coefficients of linear thermal expansion of a unidirectional lamina;

k_1, k_2, k_3 (W/m/°C) = Thermal conductivities of a unidirectional lamina;

β_1, β_2, β_3 (μm/m/%) = Swelling coefficients of linear moisture expansion;

γ (J/kg/°C) = Specific heat capacity.

Table 133.4　Thermomechanical Strengths of Natural Fibers-Nominal Values

Material	$T/°C$	$(\sigma_{11u}, \varepsilon_{11u})$	$(\sigma_{22u}, \varepsilon_{22u})$	$(\sigma_{33u}, \varepsilon_{33u})$	$(\sigma_{12u}, \varepsilon_{12u})/(\sigma_{23u}, \varepsilon_{23u})/(\sigma_{13u}, \varepsilon_{13u})$
Plants:					
Abaca (蕉麻; 20 μm)	23	(41, 3.4%)	—	—	—/—/—
Areca (D=0.4 mm)	23	(83, 5%) (100, 12%)	—	—	—/—/—
Bamboo Fiber (200 μm)	23	σ_{uts}=600	—	—	—/—/—
Bamboo Pulp Fiber	23	(508, 7.4%)	—	—	—/—/—
Banana Plant	23	(642, 2%)	—	—	—/—/—
Banana Fiber (d_f=0.19 mm)	23	(167, 3%)	—	—	—/—/—
Barley Straw-top	23	—	—	—	σ_{12u}=4.5/—/—
Barley Straw-mid	23	—	—	—	σ_{12u}=3.9/—/—

continued

Material	$T/℃$	$(\sigma_{11u}, \varepsilon_{11u})$	$(\sigma_{22u}, \varepsilon_{22u})$	$(\sigma_{33u}, \varepsilon_{33u})$	$(\sigma_{12u}, \varepsilon_{12u})/(\sigma_{23u}, \varepsilon_{23u})/$ $(\sigma_{13u}, \varepsilon_{13u})$
Cabuya	23	—	—	—	—/—/—
Coconut（椰子）	23	(153, 27%)	—	—	—/—/—
Coir （椰子皮壳;18 μm）	23	(175, 30%)	—	—	—/—/—
Cotton（9 μm）	23	(1066, 5%)	—	—	—/—/—
Curaua	23	(193, 30%)	—	—	—/—/—
Flax（亚麻;23 μm）	23	(1340, 2.6%)	—	—	—/—/—
Hemp （大麻;31 μm）	23	(790, 1.8%)	—	—	—/—/—
Jute （黄麻;120 μm）	23	(580, 7.5%)	—	—	—/—/—
Kapok （木棉;25 μm）	23	(93, 1.2%)	—	—	—/—/—
Kenaf（槿麻）	23	(750, 2.2%)	—	—	—/—/—
Maize Stalks	23	(90, 1%) (150, 2.2%) (60, 12.5%)	—	—	—/—/—
Nettle, Stinging （20 μm）	23	(1594, 2.1%)	—	—	—/—/—
Palm, Fan （L × 0.3 mm × 0.75 mm）	23	(95, 1.8%)	—	—	—/—/—
Palm, Oil（Raw）	23	(230, 14%)	—	—	—/—/—
Palm, Oil（Acrylated）	23	(275, 26%)	—	—	—/—/—
Palm, Oil （Silane-treated）	23	(273, 14%)	—	—	—/—/—
Pineapple Leaf	23	(614, 1.2%)	—	—	—/—/—
Ponderrosa	23	(28.2, 2%)	—	—	—/—/—
Ramie（苎麻; 50 μm）	23	(670, 3%)	—	—	—/—/—
Rayon（13 μm）	23	(545, 12%)	—	—	—/—/—

continued

Material	$T/{}^\circ\mathrm{C}$	$(\sigma_{11u}, \varepsilon_{11u})$	$(\sigma_{22u}, \varepsilon_{22u})$	$(\sigma_{33u}, \varepsilon_{33u})$	$(\sigma_{12u}, \varepsilon_{12u})/(\sigma_{23u}, \varepsilon_{23u})/$ $(\sigma_{13u}, \varepsilon_{13u})$
Reed, Canary Grass	23	$(-52.3, -1.8\%)$ $(-39.2, -0.6\%)$	$(-6, -3\%)$ $(-4.8, -1.7\%)$	$(-6, -3\%)$ $(-4.8, -1.7\%)$	—/—/—
Rice Husk	23	$\sigma_{ucs} = -26;$ $\sigma_{uts} = 22$	—	—	—/—/—
Sisal (波尔麻; Raw)	23	$(550, 5\%)$	—	—	—/—/—
Sugar Cane	23	$\sigma_{uts} = 290$	—	—	—/—/—
Viscose (Cord)	23	$(593, 11.4\%)$	—	—	—/—/—
Wheat Straw-top	23	—	—	—	$\sigma_{12u} = 7.1$
Wheat Straw-mid	23	—	—	—	$\sigma_{12u} = 6.8$
Animals:					
Silkworm Silk	23	$(150, 5\%)$ $(198, 22\%)$	—	—	—/—/—
Silkworm Cocoon -Inner pelage-45°	23	$(62, 12.6\%)$	—	—	—/—/—
Silkworm Cocoon -Inner pelage-0°	23	$(50, 10.5\%)$	—	—	—/—/—
Silk, Spider (Argiope Trifascita; RH = 50%)	23	$(180, 0.2\%)$ $(500, 20\%)$ $(900, 36\%)$	—	—	—/—/—
	90	$(75, 50\%)$ $(450, 80\%)$	—	—	—/—/—
Silk, Spider Larval (Tetrabychus Urticae)	23	$\sigma_{uts} = 200$	—	—	—/—/—
Silk, Spider Adult (Tetrabychus Urticae)	23	$(150, 5\%)$ $(300, 25\%)$ $(350, 40\%)$	—	—	—/—/—
Silk, Spider (Dragline)	23	$(1350, 33\%)$	—	—	—/—/—
Silk, Spider (Darwin's Bark)	23	$(1850, 33\%)$	—	—	—/—/—
Wool (41 μm)	23	$(135, 27\%)$	—	—	—/—/—

Chapter 134

Wood and Bamboo

134.1　Introduction

The material properties of wood and bamboo are orthotropic. The mechanical elasticity and strength are much stronger along the grain direction (growing direction). The compressive strength along the grain direction of wood is of the same order as the tensile strength along the grain direction, and so does the compressive strength perpendicular to the grain direction of wood to its corresponding tensile strength. Material properties vary as the moisture content goes from green condition to dry condition. The (x, y, z) coordinate system corresponding to tree trunk coordinate system (grain, radial, tangential) is shown in Fig. 134.1. Mechanical properties, thermal properties, material strengths of wood listed respectively in Tables 134.1—134.3 are taken at 12% moisture content. Balsa is the softest and lightest commercial wood available.

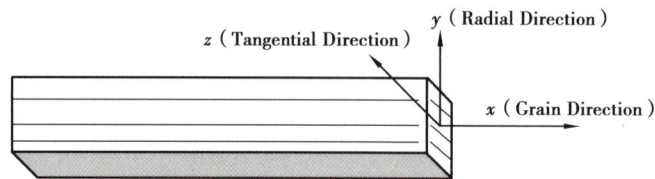

Fig. 134.1　Principal Directions (x, y, z) in Correspondence with Wood/Bamboo Grain Fibers

134.2　Thermal Properties of Wood

134.2.1　Thermal Conductivity

The thermal conductivity along the wood fibers varies from 0.1 W/m/℃ to 0.17 W/m/℃ at 12% moisture content, depending on species. The thermal expansion of wood is significantly smaller than swelling due to moisture absorption. The specific heat capacity of wood is approximately 1500 J/(kg · ℃) at 12% moisture content and 23 ℃.

134.2.2　Specific Heat Capacity

The measurement of the specific heat capacity of wood is complicated by the moisture content, heating temperature, and heating rate. For wood products, a significant increase in the specific heat is expected in the temperature range between 160 ℃ to 230 ℃, when wood polymers pass their glass transition point. Chemical reactions in wood polymers lead to an overall heat release, which (e.g. working above 150 ℃) can affect the evaluation of specific heat capacity, especially at low heating rates. In the work by [Olsson and Back], the specific heat of a dry unbleached kraft liner (wood hardboard) has been estimated as follows:

(a) The heat capacity of wood (hardboard) shows a rapid rise to 3000 J/(kg · ℃) at a high heating rate, within the temperature range of 230 ℃ to 250 ℃.

(b) The heat capacity of wood (hardboard) gave a value for the specific heat of 2800 J/(kg · ℃) at an intermediate heating rate, between 160 ℃ and 170 ℃.

(c) The heat capacity of wood (hardboard) gave a value for the specific heat of 2000 J/(kg · ℃) at a very low heating rate of between 1 ℃/s and 4 ℃/s.

134.3　Hygroscopic Property of Wood

Wood at intermediate moisture levels (about 8% to 20%) expand when first heated, and then gradually shrink to a volume smaller than the initial volume as the wood gradually loses water while in the heated condition [Forest Products Laboratory]. People tend to call a piece of wood dry if its moisture content is at 19% or less (percentage in weight), as the fibrous moisture saturation averages around 28%. Owing to the hygroscopic nature of the cell wall polymers (e.g. amorphous cellulose and hemicelluloses), micropillars swell and shrink upon changes in environmental humidity, Fig. 134.2. The presence of microfibrils in wood cell walls is also likely to induce anisotropy of swelling. The greatest dimensional change due to moisture occurs in the direction tangential to the growth rings, and least in the growing direction (i.e. microfibrils direction): $\beta_3 > \beta_2 > \beta_1$. The swelling coefficients in the fibril direction (β_1) and transverse to the fibril (β_2) can be obtained from [Rosen & Hashin], respectively as

$$\beta_1 = \beta_m \left\{ 1 - \frac{1}{K_f^{-1} - K_m^{-1}} \left[\frac{3(1-2\nu_L)\nu_L}{E_L} - \frac{1}{E_M} \right] \right\} \tag{134.1}$$

And $$\beta_2 = \beta_m \left\{ 1 - \frac{1}{K_f^{-1} - K_m^{-1}} \left[\frac{3}{2K} - \frac{3(1-2\nu_L)\nu_L}{E_L} - \frac{1}{E_M} \right] \right\} \tag{134.2}$$

Where:

β_m: Swelling coefficient of the matrix;

K_f and K_m: Bulk moduli of fiber and matrix;

K, E_L and ν_L: Effective bulk modulus, longitudinal elastic modulus and Poisson's ratio.

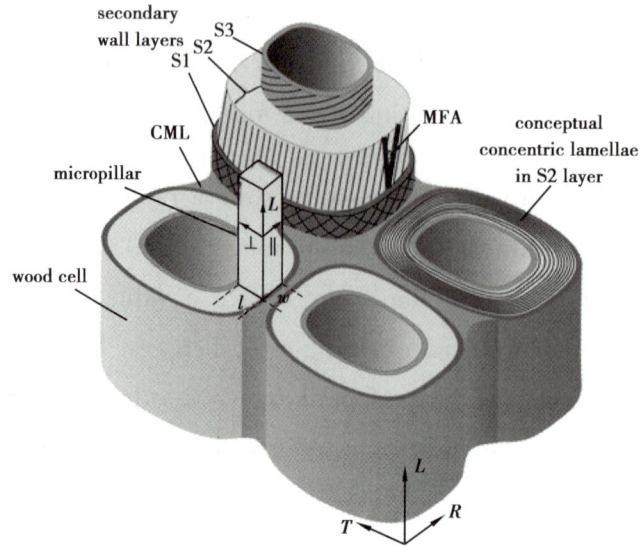

Fig. 134.2   The Secondary Wall of Wood Cells Composed of Three Layers- S1, S2 and S3

134.4   Hydrothermal Effects on Mechanical Properties

Effects of temperature and moisture content on mechanical properties of wood are listed as follows [Gerhards]:

Mechanical Property	Temperature = 20 ℃		Moisture Content (MC) = 12%	
	MC = 6%	MC = 20%	$T = -50$ ℃	$T = 50$ ℃
E_{11}	9%	−13%	17%	−7%
E_{22}	20%	−23%	—	−35%
G_{12}	20%	−20%	—	−25%
σ_{11t}	8%	−15%	—	−4%
σ_{11c}	35%	−35%	50%	−25%
σ_{22t}	12%	−20%	—	−20%
σ_{22c}	30%	−30%	—	−35%
τ_{12}	18%	−18%	—	−25%

The base data for the variational mechanical properties given above are taken at the temperature of 20 ℃ and moisture content of 12%.

134.5   Bamboo

Mechanical properties of bamboo depend on age and its anatomy (inner, middle, and outer parts), Fig. 134.3. Average specific weight increased about 58% from year one to year three, indicating cell wall thickening occurs mostly in the first two years. Its average density can grow from 0.5 (one year old) to 0.8 (5 years old), while its modulus of elasticity grows from 8 GPa to 13 GPa.

Fig. 134.3   Bamboo Cross-section View and Painting by Xu Wei, Ming Dynasty, China

The tensile strength of bamboo fiber-reinforced plastics does not decrease below 140 ℃. It has a tendency to decrease gradually starting from 160 ℃ and it decreases rapidly around 180 ℃ [Ochi].

References

AMADA S, LAKES R S, 1997. Viscoelastic Properties of Bamboo[J]. Journal of Materials Science, 32: 2693-2697.

BAI X, et al, 1999. Finite Element Analysis of Moso Bamboo-Reinforced Southern Pine OSB Composite Beams [J]. Wood Science and Technology, 31(4): 403-415.

CHUNG K F, YU W K, 2002. Mechanical Properties of Structural Bamboo for Bamboo Scaffoldings[J]. Engineering Structures, 24: 429-442.

DELIISKI N, 2012. Transient Heat Conduction in Capillary Porous Bodies[M]. Bulgaria: University of Forestry.

FERABOLI P, 2008. Notched Response of OSB Wood Composites[J]. Composites, Part A, 39(9): 1355-1361.

GREEN D W, EVANS J W, LOGAN J D, et al, 1999. Adjusting Modulus of Elasticity of Lumber for Changes in Temperature[J]. Forest Products Journal, 49(10): 82-94.

GU L B, GARRAHAN P, 1984. The Temperature and Moisture Content in Lumber during Preheating and Drying[J]. Wood Science and Technology, 18, 121-135.

HANAFI I, et al, 2002. Bamboo Fiber Filled Natural Rubber Composites: the Effects of Filler Loading and Bonding Agent[J]. Polymer Testing, 21: 139-144.

HANHIJRVI A, MACKENZIE H P, 2003. Computational Analysis of Quality Reduction during Drying of Lumber due to Irrecoverable Deformation. I: Orthotropic Viscoelasticmechanosorptive-plastic Material Model for the Transverse Plane of Wood[J]. Journal of Engineering Mechanics, 129(9): 996-1005.

JANSSEN J J A, 1995. Building with Bamboo[M]. 2nd Edition, Intermediate Technology Publication Limited, London.

KUMIKO M, YAMAUCHI H, YAMADA M, et al, 2001. Manufacture and Properties of Fiberboard Made from Moso Bamboo[J]. Mokuzai Gakkaishi, 47(2): 111-119.

LAKKAD S C, PATEL J M, 1981. Mechanical Properties of Bamboo, a Natural Composite[J]. Fiber Science and Technology, 14(3): 319-322.

LI H, SHEN S, 2011. The Mechanical Properties of Bamboo and Vascular Bundles[J]. Journal of Materials Research, 14(26): 2749-2756.

LIESE W, 1995. Anatomy and Utilization of Bamboos[J]. European Bamboo Society Journal, 5-12.

MACKENZIE H P, HANHIJRVI A, 2003. Computational Analysis of Quality Reduction during Drying of Lumber due to Irrecoverable Deformation. II: Algorithmic Aspects and Practical Application[J]. Journal of Engineering Mechanics, 129(9): 1006-1016.

MACKERLE J, 2005. Finite Element Analyses in Wood Research: a Bibliography[J]. Wood Science and Technology, 39: 579-600.

NUGROHO N, NAOTO A, 2001. Development of Structural Composite Products Made from Bamboo II: Fundamental Properties of Laminated Bamboo Lumber[J]. Journal of Wood Science, 47: 237-242.

OCHI S, 2011. Mechanical Properties of Press-Molded Products Using Bamboo Fiber of Different Shape[J]. Journal of Materials Science and Engineering with Advanced Technology, 3: 99-113.

OLSSON A, BACK E, 1989. One the Specific heat of Paper and Wood Products between 180~250 ℃ [J].

Nordic Pulp and Paper, 4(4): 258-262.

RAHMAN M U, CHIANG Y J, ROWLANDS R E, 1991. Stress and Failure Analysis of Double-Bolted Joints in Douglas Fir/Sitka Spruce[J]. Wood and Fiber Science, 23(4): 567-589.

RAJULU A V, BAKSH S A, REDDY G R, et al, 1998. Chemical Resistance and Tensile Properties of Short Bamboo Fiber Reinforced Epoxy Composites[J]. Journal of Reinforced Plastics and Composites, 17: 1507-1511.

RAFSANJANI A, et al, 2014. Hygroscopic Swelling and Shrinkage of Latewood Cell Wall Micropillars Reveal Ultrastructural Anisotropy[J]. 11(95), June 2014.

RAFSANJANI A, et al, 2014. Computational Up-scaling of Anisotropic Swelling and Mechanical Behavior of Hierarchical Cellular Materials[J]. Composites Science & Technology, 72(6): 744-751.

ROSEN B W, HASHIN Z, 1970. Effective Thermal Expansion Coefficients and Specific Heats of Composite Materials[J]. International Journal of Engineering Science, 8: 157-173.

ROWLANDS R E, RAHMAN M U, WILKINSON T L, et al, 1982. Single- and Multiple-Bolted Joints in Orthotropic Materials[J]. Composites, 13(3): 273-279.

SAKARAY H, et al, 2012. Investigation on Properties of Bamboo as Reinforcing Material in Concrete[J]. International Journal of Engineering Research and Applications, 2(1): 77-83.

SEEMA J, KUMAR R, 1992. Mechanical Behavior of Bamboo and Bamboo Composite[J]. Journal of Material Science, 27: 4598-4604.

SHI S Q, GARDNER D J, 2001. Dynamic Adhesive Wettability of Wood[J]. Wood and Fiber Science, 33 (1): 58-68.

SIMPSON W T, WANG X, FORSMAN J W, et al, 2005. Heat Sterilization Times of Five Hardwood Species [R]. Research Paper FPL-RP-626, Forest Products Laboratory, Forest Service, United States Department of Agriculture, Wisconsin, USA.

SILVA S P, 2005. Cork: Properties, Capabilities and Applications[J]. International Materials Review, 50 (6): 345-365.

STARK N M, ROWLANDS R E, 2003. Effects of Wood Fiber Characteristics on Mechanical Properties of Wood/Polypropylene Composites[J]. Wood and Fiber Science, 35(2): 167-174.

WEATHERWAX R C, STAMM A J, 1956. The Coefficients of Thermal Expansion of Wood and Wood Products [R]. Forest Products Laboratory Report 1487, Forest Service, DOA, USA.

Table 134.1   Mechanical Properties of Wood at 12% Moisture Content

Specification	$T/℃$	ρ	E_{11}	E_{22}	E_{33}	G_{12}	G_{13}	G_{23}	ν_{12}	ν_{13}	ν_{23}
Ash, White	23	0.67	12	1.5	0.96	1.31	0.91	—	0.371	0.44	0.684
Aspen, Quaking	23	0.38	8.1	—	—	—	—	—	0.489	0.374	—
Balsa (Ochroma pyramidale)	23	0.08	—	—	—	—	—	—	0.229	0.488	0.665
Balsa	23	0.16	1.3	—	—	—	—	—	0.229	0.488	0.665
Balsa	23	0.23	3.4	—	—	—	—	—	0.229	0.488	0.665
Bamboo-Guadua (1 year old)	23	0.5	8.5	—	—	—	—	—	—	—	—
Bamboo-Guadua (5$^+$ years old)	23	0.67	13.3	—	—	—	—	—	—	—	—
Bamboo-Moso (5$^+$ years old)	23	0.61	8.5	—	—	—	—	—	—	—	—
Bamboo/Resin (Fiberboard; 7% resin)	23	0.6	2.5	2.5	—	—	—	—	—	—	—
Basswood	23	0.37	10.1	0.67	0.27	0.57	0.47	—	0.364	0.406	0.912
Beech	23	0.64	11.9	—	—	—	—	—	—	—	—
Birch, Yellow	23	0.62	13.9	1.08	0.67	1.03	0.95	0.24	0.426	0.451	0.697
Cedar, White Northern	23	0.31	5.5	1	0.45	1.16	1.03	0.083	0.337	0.34	0.458
Cedar, Western Red	23	0.32	7.7	0.62	0.42	0.67	0.66	0.04	0.378	0.296	0.484
Cherry, Black	23	0.5	10.3	2.03	0.89	1.51	1.0	—	0.338	0.326	0.411
Chestnut, American	23	0.43	8.5	—	—	—	—	—	—	—	—
Cottonwood	23	0.4	9.4	0.78	0.44	0.71	0.49	—	0.344	0.42	0.875
Cypress, Bald	23	0.5	9.9	0.83	0.39	0.62	0.54	0.07	0.392	0.428	0.695
Elm, American	23	0.5	9.2	—	—	—	—	—	—	—	—
Fir, Douglas	23	0.5	13.4	0.91	0.67	0.86	1.045	0.094	0.292	0.449	0.39
Fir, Subalpine	23	0.32	8.9	0.91	0.35	0.62	0.52	0.053	0.341	0.332	0.437
Gum, Sweet	23	0.52	11.3	1.3	0.57	1.0	0.69	0.24	0.325	0.403	0.682

continued

Specification	$T/°C$	ρ	E_{11}	E_{22}	E_{33}	G_{12}	G_{13}	G_{23}	ν_{12}	ν_{13}	ν_{23}
Helmlock, Western	23	0.4	8.3	0.48	0.26	0.32	0.27	0.025	0.485	0.423	0.442
Hickory, Pecan	23	0.66	11.9	—	—	—	—	—	—	—	—
Iroko	23	0.66	—	—	—	—	—	—	—	—	—
Larch, Western	23	0.52	12.9	1.02	0.84	0.81	0.89	0.09	0.355	0.276	0.389
Mahogany, African	23	0.67	10.8	—	—	—	—	—	0.297	0.641	0.604
Mahogany, Honduras	23	0.54	8.5	—	—	—	—	—	0.314	0.533	0.6
Maple, Bigleaf	23	0.48	10	—	—	—	—	—	—	—	—
Maple, Red	23	0.48	11.3	1.58	0.76	1.5	0.84	—	0.434	0.509	0.762
Maple, Sugar	23	0.63	12.6	1.66	0.82	1.4	0.8	—	0.424	0.476	0.774
Oak, Red	23	0.69	13.1	2.02	1.07	1.17	1.06	—	0.35	0.448	0.56
Oak, White	23	0.68	12.3	2	0.89	1.06	—	—	0.369	0.428	0.618
Oak, Willow	23	0.69	13	—	—	—	—	—	—	—	—
Pine, Loblolly	23	0.51	12.3	1.39	0.96	1.01	1	0.16	0.328	0.292	0.382
Pine, Lodgepole	23	0.41	9.2	0.94	0.63	0.451	0.42	0.046	0.316	0.347	0.469
Pine, Longleaf	23	0.59	13.7	1.4	0.754	0.97	0.82	0.164	0.332	0.365	0.384
Pine, Pond	23	0.56	12.1	0.86	0.5	0.61	0.544	0.11	0.28	0.364	0.389
Pine, Ponderosa	23	0.4	8.9	1.09	0.74	1.23	1.024	0.151	0.337	0.4	0.426
Pine, Red	23	0.46	11.2	0.99	0.493	1.08	0.91	0.123	0.347	0.315	0.408
Pine, Slash	23	0.59	13.7	1.01	0.62	0.754	0.73	0.137	0.392	0.444	0.447
Pine, Sugar	23	0.36	8.2	1.074	0.71	1.02	0.93	0.16	0.356	0.349	0.428
Pine, White	23	0.35	10.1	0.79	0.384	0.54	0.49	0.051	0.329	0.344	0.410
Poplar, Yellow	23	0.42	10.9	1	0.47	0.82	0.75	0.12	0.318	0.392	0.703
Redwood	23	0.41	9.2	0.8	0.82	0.61	0.71	0.1	0.36	0.346	0.373
Spurce, Engelmann	23	0.35	8.9	1.14	0.525	1.1	1.07	0.09	0.422	0.462	0.53
Spruce, Sitka	23	0.44	11	0.77	0.46	0.63	0.60	0.03	0.372	0.467	0.435
Tamarack	23	0.53	11.3	—	—	—	—	—	—	—	—
Walnut, Black	23	0.55	11.6	1.23	0.65	0.99	0.72	0.24	0.495	0.632	0.718

Notes: $\nu_{ij} E_{jj} = \nu_{ji} E_{ii}$ ($i = 1, 2, 3$; $j = 1, 2, 3$; $i \neq j$).

Table 134.2　Hydrothermal（Thermal+Hygroscopic）Properties of Wood［USA DOA- Forest Products Laboratory］

Specification	$T/℃$	α_{11}	α_{22}	α_{33}	k_{11}	k_{22}	k_{33}	γ	β_{11}	β_{22}	β_{33}
Balsa	23	—	16.3	24	—	0.06	0.06	—	—	—	—
Birch, Yellow	23	3.4	31	38	—	—	—	—	—	—	—
Cedar	23	4.5	—	—	—	0.12	0.12	—	—	—	—
Cottonwood	23	2.9	23	33	—	—	—	—	—	—	—
Fir, Douglas	23	3.2	28	43	—	—	—	—	—	—	—
Fir, White	23	3.3	22	33	—	—	—	—	—	—	—
Oak, Red	23	5.3	42.3	55	0.17	—	—	—	—	—	—
Maple, Sugar	23	3.8	27	35	0.16	—	—	—	—	—	—
Pine, White	23	—	—	—	0.23	0.12	0.12	2300	—	—	—
Pine, Yellow	23	4.3	24	35	0.22	0.15	0.15	2300	—	—	—
Poplar, Yellow	23	3.2	28	30	—	—	—	—	—	—	—
Redwood	23	4.3	24	35	0.16	—	—	—	—	—	—
Spruce, Sika	23	3.2	24	32	—	—	—	2300	0.009	0.17	0.31

Table 134.3　Orthotropic Tensile and Yield Strengths（$\varepsilon_y = 0.2\%$）of Wood at 12% Moisture Content ［DOA- Forest Products Laboratory］

Material	$T/℃$	$(\sigma_{11u}, \varepsilon_{11u})$	$(\sigma_{22u}, \varepsilon_{22u})$	$(\sigma_{33u}, \varepsilon_{33u})$	$(\sigma_{12u}, \varepsilon_{12u})/(\sigma_{23u}, \varepsilon_{23u})/(\sigma_{13u}, \varepsilon_{13u})$
Ash, White	23	$\sigma_{11c}=-51$ $\sigma_{11t}=103$	$\sigma_{22c}=-8$ $\sigma_{22t}=6.5$	$\sigma_{33c}=-8$ $\sigma_{33t}=6.5$	$\sigma_{12u}=13.2$ —
Aspen, Quaking	23	$\sigma_{11c}=-29.3$ $\sigma_{11t}=58$	$\sigma_{22c}=-2.6$ $\sigma_{22t}=1.8$	$\sigma_{33c}=-2.6$ $\sigma_{33t}=1.8$	$\sigma_{12u}=5.9$ —
Balsa ($\rho=0.08$)	23	$\sigma_{11t}=4.7$ $\sigma_{11c}=-7.6$	—	—	—
Balsa ($\rho=0.16$; Nominal)	23	$\sigma_{11t}=12$ $\sigma_{11c}=-20$	—	—	$\sigma_{12u}=2.1$
Balsa ($\rho=0.23$)	23	$\sigma_{11t}=19.5$ $\sigma_{11c}=-32$	—	$\sigma_{33c}=-1.5$	—

continued

Material	$T/°C$	$(\sigma_{11u}, \varepsilon_{11u})$	$(\sigma_{22u}, \varepsilon_{22u})$	$(\sigma_{33u}, \varepsilon_{33u})$	$(\sigma_{12u}, \varepsilon_{12u})/(\sigma_{23u}, \varepsilon_{23u})/(\sigma_{13u}, \varepsilon_{13u})$
Bamboo-Moso (Failed at node; 5^+ years; Averaged)	23	$\sigma_{11c} = -108$; (50, 0.2%) (125, 0.8%)	—	—	$\sigma_{12u} = 1.8$
Bamboo Fiber (Outer, Fig. 132.1; Sakaray et al.)	23	(140, 0.2%) $\sigma_{11t} = 265$	—	—	$\sigma_{12u} = 29$
	160	$\sigma_{11t} = 170$	—	—	—
	180	$\sigma_{11t} = 84.5$	—	—	—
	200	$\sigma_{11t} = 23$	—	—	—
Basswood	23	$\sigma_{11c} = -33$ $\sigma_{11t} = 60$	$\sigma_{22c} = -2.6$ $\sigma_{22t} = 2.4$	$\sigma_{33c} = -2.6$ $\sigma_{33t} = 2.4$	$\sigma_{12u} = 6.83$ —
Beech	23	$\sigma_{11c} = -50.3$ $\sigma_{11t} = 86.2$	$\sigma_{22c} = -7$ $\sigma_{22t} = 7$	$\sigma_{33c} = -7$ $\sigma_{33t} = 7$	$\sigma_{12u} = 13.9$ —
Birch, Yellow	23	$\sigma_{11c} = -56.3$ $\sigma_{11t} = 114$	$\sigma_{22c} = -6.7$ $\sigma_{22t} = 6.3$	$\sigma_{33c} = -6.7$ $\sigma_{33t} = 6.3$	$\sigma_{12u} = 13$ —
Cedar, Red Western	23	$\sigma_{11c} = -31.4$ $\sigma_{11t} = 45.5$	— $\sigma_{22t} = 1.5$	— $\sigma_{33t} = 1.5$	$\sigma_{12u} = 6.8$ —
Cherry, Black	23	$\sigma_{11c} = -49$ $\sigma_{11t} = 85$	$\sigma_{22c} = -4.8$ $\sigma_{22t} = 3.9$	$\sigma_{33c} = -4.8$ $\sigma_{33t} = 3.9$	$\sigma_{12u} = 11.7$ —
Chestnut	23	$\sigma_{11c} = -36.7$ $\sigma_{11t} = 59$	$\sigma_{22c} = -4.3$ $\sigma_{22t} = 3.2$	$\sigma_{33c} = -4.3$ $\sigma_{33t} = 3.2$	$\sigma_{12u} = 7.45$ —
Cotton Wood	23	$\sigma_{11c} = -27.7$	—	—	$\sigma_{12u} = 7.2$
Cypress, Bald	23	$\sigma_{11t} = 58.6$	$\sigma_{22t} = 1.9$	$\sigma_{33t} = 1.9$	$\sigma_{12u} = 6.9$
Elm, American	23	$\sigma_{11c} = -38.1$ $\sigma_{11t} = 81$	$\sigma_{22c} = -4.8$ $\sigma_{22t} = 4.6$	$\sigma_{33c} = -4.8$ $\sigma_{33t} = 4.6$	$\sigma_{12u} = 6.4$ —
Elm, Rock	23	$\sigma_{11c} = -49$ $\sigma_{11t} = 102$	$\sigma_{22c} = -8.5$ $\sigma_{22t} = 4.6$	$\sigma_{33c} = -8.5$ $\sigma_{33t} = 4.6$	$\sigma_{12u} = 10.4$ —
Fir, Douglas	23	$\sigma_{11c} = -43$ $\sigma_{11t} = 100$	$\sigma_{22c} = -5.9$ $\sigma_{22t} = 2.3$	$\sigma_{33c} = -5.9$ $\sigma_{33t} = 2.3$	$\sigma_{12u} = 8.3$ —
Fir, Subalpine	23	$\sigma_{11c} = -34$ $\sigma_{11t} = 59$	$\sigma_{22c} = -2.7$ —	$\sigma_{33c} = -2.7$ —	$\sigma_{12u} = 7.4$ —

continued

Material	$T/^{\circ}\text{C}$	$(\sigma_{11u}, \varepsilon_{11u})$	$(\sigma_{22u}, \varepsilon_{22u})$	$(\sigma_{33u}, \varepsilon_{33u})$	$(\sigma_{12u}, \varepsilon_{12u})/(\sigma_{23u}, \varepsilon_{23u})/$ $(\sigma_{13u}, \varepsilon_{13u})$
Gum, Sweet	23	$\sigma_{11c} = -43.6$ $\sigma_{11t} = 93.8$	— $\sigma_{22t} = 5.2$	— $\sigma_{33t} = 5.2$	$\sigma_{12u} = 11$
Helmlock, Western	23	$\sigma_{11c} = -44$ $\sigma_{11t} = 80$	$\sigma_{22c} = -5.2$ $\sigma_{22t} = 2.3$	$\sigma_{33c} = -5.2$ $\sigma_{33t} = 2.3$	$\sigma_{12u} = 8.9$ —
Hickory, Shagbark	23	$\sigma_{11c} = -63$	—	—	$\sigma_{12u} = 16.8$
Hickory, Pecan	23	$\sigma_{11c} = -54$ —	— $\sigma_{22t} = 3$	— $\sigma_{33t} = 3$	$\sigma_{12u} = 14.3$ —
Hickory, Pignut	23	$\sigma_{11c} = -63.4$	—	—	$\sigma_{12u} = 14.8$
Larch, Western	23	$\sigma_{11t} = 112$	$\sigma_{22t} = 3$	$\sigma_{33t} = 3$	$\sigma_{12u} = 9.4$
Locust, Black	23	$\sigma_{11c} = -70$	—	—	$\sigma_{12u} = 17$
Locust, Honey	23	$\sigma_{11c} = -52$	—	—	$\sigma_{12u} = 15.5$
Maple, Bigleaf	23	$\sigma_{11c} = -41$	—	—	$\sigma_{12u} = 11.9$
Maple, Red	23	$\sigma_{11c} = -45$ $\sigma_{11t} = 92$	$\sigma_{22c} = -7$ —	$\sigma_{33c} = -7$ —	$\sigma_{12u} = 12.8$ —
Maple, Sugar	23	$\sigma_{11c} = -54$ $\sigma_{11t} = 109$	$\sigma_{22c} = -10$ —	$\sigma_{33c} = -10$ —	$\sigma_{12u} = 16$ —
Oak, Red	23	$\sigma_{11c} = -46$ $\sigma_{11t} = 110$	$\sigma_{22c} = -7$ $\sigma_{22t} = 5.5$	— $\sigma_{33t} = 3.7$	$\sigma_{12u} = 12.3$ —
Oak, White	23	$\sigma_{11c} = -51.3$	—	—	$\sigma_{12u} = 11.9$
Oak, Willow	23	$\sigma_{11c} = -48.5$	—	—	$\sigma_{12u} = 11.4$
Pine, Loblolly	23	$\sigma_{11c} = -51.3$ $\sigma_{11t} = 80$	— $\sigma_{22t} = 3.2$	— $\sigma_{33t} = 3.2$	$\sigma_{12u} = 11.9$ —
Pine, Pitch	23	$\sigma_{11c} = -59$ $\sigma_{11t} = 105$	$\sigma_{22c} = -6.9$ —	$\sigma_{33c} = -6.9$ —	$\sigma_{12u} = 9.4$ —
Pine, Ponderosa	23	$\sigma_{11t} = 57.9$	$\sigma_{22t} = 2.9$	$\sigma_{33t} = 2.9$	$\sigma_{12u} = 7.8$
Pine, Red	23	$\sigma_{11c} = -42$	—	—	$\sigma_{12u} = 8.3$
Pine, White	23	$\sigma_{11t} = 73.1$	$\sigma_{22t} = 2.1$	$\sigma_{33t} = 2.1$	$\sigma_{12u} = 7.2$

continued

Material	$T/^\circ\text{C}$	$(\sigma_{11u},\ \varepsilon_{11u})$	$(\sigma_{22u},\ \varepsilon_{22u})$	$(\sigma_{33u},\ \varepsilon_{33u})$	$(\sigma_{12u},\ \varepsilon_{12u})/(\sigma_{23u},\ \varepsilon_{23u})/$ $(\sigma_{13u},\ \varepsilon_{13u})$
Poplar, Yellow	23	$\sigma_{11c}=-38$ $\sigma_{11t}=110$	$\sigma_{22c}=-3.4$ $\sigma_{22t}=3.7$	— $\sigma_{33t}=3.7$	$\sigma_{12u}=8.3$ —
Redwood (Grown-up)	23	$\sigma_{11c}=-42$ $\sigma_{11t}=67$	$\sigma_{22c}=-4.8$ $\sigma_{22t}=1.7$	$\sigma_{33c}=-4.8$ $\sigma_{33t}=1.7$	$\sigma_{12u}=6.5$ —
Redwood (Young)	23	$\sigma_{11c}=-36$ —	— —	— —	$\sigma_{12u}=7.7$
Spruce, Black	23	$\sigma_{11c}=-41$ $\sigma_{11t}=74$	$\sigma_{22c}=-3.8$ —	$\sigma_{33c}=-3.8$ —	$\sigma_{12u}=8.5$ —
Spruce, Engelmann	23	$\sigma_{11c}=-31$ $\sigma_{11t}=64$	$\sigma_{22c}=-2.8$ $\sigma_{22t}=2.4$	$\sigma_{33c}=-2.8$ $\sigma_{33t}=2.4$	$\sigma_{12u}=8.3$ —
Spruce, Red	23	$\sigma_{11c}=-38.2$ $\sigma_{11t}=74$	$\sigma_{22c}=-3.8$ $\sigma_{22t}=2.4$	$\sigma_{33c}=-3.8$ $\sigma_{33t}=2.4$	$\sigma_{12u}=8.9$ —
Spruce, Sika	23	$\sigma_{11c}=-38.7$ $\sigma_{11t}=76$	$\sigma_{22c}=-4$ $\sigma_{22t}=2.6$	$\sigma_{33c}=-3$ $\sigma_{33t}=1.7$	$\sigma_{12u}=7.9$ —
Spruce, White	23	$\sigma_{11c}=-37.7$ $\sigma_{11t}=68$	$\sigma_{22c}=-2.8$ $\sigma_{22t}=2.5$	$\sigma_{33c}=-2.8$ $\sigma_{33t}=2.5$	$\sigma_{12u}=6.7$ —
Tamarack	23	$\sigma_{11c}=-49.4$ $\sigma_{11t}=80$	$\sigma_{22c}=-5.5$ $\sigma_{22t}=2.8$	$\sigma_{33c}=-5.5$ $\sigma_{33t}=2.8$	$\sigma_{12u}=8.8$ —
Walnut, Black	23	$\sigma_{11c}=-52.3$	—	—	$\sigma_{12u}=9.4$

Chapter 135

Roads

135.1   Introduction

Roads are made of durable materials laid on an area intended to sustain vehicular or foot traffic, including asphalt, concrete, gravels, cobblestones, granite setts, and bricks. Bricks are porous porcelains (ceramics). Asphalt, concrete, rock, and soil are discussed here in detail. Fatigue cracking resistance of a pavement subject to thermal or mechanical loadings may be improved using rubber- and or polymer- binders in asphalt mixtures.

135.2   Asphalt Pavements

Asphalt occurs naturally or is obtained through the distillation of petroleum crude oil. Grade PG76-22 for most intersections means that the grade performance (PG) has an averaged 7-day maximum pavement design temperature of 76 ℃ and minimum pavement design temperature of 22 ℃.

135.2.1   Hot/Warm Mix Asphalt

An asphalt surface, i.e. top layer of an asphalt road, is generally laid on a gravel base. Its viscous nature of bitumen keeps asphalt pavement to sustain a significant amount of plastic deformation. Mechanical properties of HMA (Hot Mix Asphalt) and its foundation layers are given in Table 135.1. According to the mixture, an asphalt can be classified into three categories:

(a) DGA (Dense Grade Aggregate)- More Asphalt;
(b) OGFC (Open-graded Friction Course);
(c) SMA (Stone Mastic Aggregate)- Less Asphalt.

More asphalt provides road fatigue (durability) and flexibility, while more stability and friction come from "not so much" asphalt. Fatigue from repeated loading is the most common failure mechanism of HMA.

135.2.2   Porous Asphalt

Porous Asphalt (PA) is used worldwide for its favorable splash and spray properties and its reduction of aquaplaning under rainy conditions as well as its noise reduction properties. Many trial sections show lower noise levels on porous asphalt, which may be 6 dB lower than concrete layers or 2 to 6 dB lower than the HMA or HRA. Mechanical properties of porous asphalt pavements are given in Table 135.2.

135.2.3 Pitch Composites

Mechanical properties of pitch-composite asphalt pavements are given in Table 135.3.

135.3 Concrete Pavements

A concrete mixture for a road surface pavement consists mainly of cement, fine aggregate, coarse aggregate, and water. Three different concrete composites are listed as follows:

Ingredients	Mix A	Mix B	Mix C
Cement content (kg/m^3), Portland	380	439	439
Fine aggregate (kg/m^3) Coarse aggregate (kg/m^3)	673	621	621
19 mm	678	788	788
9.5 mm	438	340	340
Total	1162	1128	1128
Aggregate type	Siliceous	Carbonate	Carbonate
Water (kg/m^3)	167	161	161
Water-cement ratio	0.44	0.37	0.37
Retarding admixture (mL/m^3)	745	—	—
Superplasticizer (mL/m^3)	2500	300	1200
Steel fiber (kg/m^3)	42	—	42
28-day compressive strength (MPa)	39.9	32.6	43.2
Compressive strength at test date (MPa)	40.9	37.1	43.3

The modulus of elasticity of a concrete composite is a function of the modulus of the aggregates and cement matrix and their relative proportion. Typical mechanical properties of concrete pavements are given in Table 135.4.

Diamond grinding has been used for reducing noise and/or enhancing (restoring) skid resistance of (old) concrete pavement.

135.4   Soils, Rocks, and Other Construction Materials

135.4.1   Soils

Soil is an assembly of small "rock particles" with little cementation, while rock is an assembly of particles that are strongly cemented by chemical bonds. Rocks may be broken into small particles to create soils. Silt, sand, and gravels are little pieces of rocks of different sizes as their effective diameters are 0.002 mm, 0.05 mm, and 2 mm, respectively. Clay is "silt with high plasticity index and liquid limit". Typically the modulus of elasticity of silt soil falls between 35 and 135 MPa, so does clay soil. Crushed stones fall between 150 and 300 MPa. Soil with closely packed particles or being consolidated has a higher modulus. The shear strength and stiffness are usually used to determine the soil deformation and stability.

Soil tends to have a higher modulus with low water contents. If chemical cementation develops between particles at low water contents, the modulus of elasticity goes higher. Pavement over which on-ground vehicles will travel requires a soil bed with a higher elastic modulus than a muddy road. Material properties of soils are given in Table 135.5.

The Duncan-Chang Hyperbolic constitutive model [Duncan and Chang, (1970)] is widely used for the modeling of soil behavior, and is capable of modeling the non-linear, stress-dependent and inelastic behavior of cohesive and cohesionless soils. The tangential Young's modulus and Poisson's ratio based on the Duncan-Chang Hyperbolic model in conjunction with the Mohr-Coulomb failure criterion are, respectively,

$$E_t = K_e P_{atm} \left(\frac{\sigma_3}{P_{atm}} \right)^n \left\{ 1 - R_f \left[\frac{(1 - \sin \phi)(\sigma_1 - \sigma_3)}{2 c \cos \phi + 2 \sigma_3 \sin \phi} \right] \right\}^2 \tag{135.1}$$

and $\nu_t = 1/2 \left(1 - \dfrac{E_t}{B_t} \right)$ (135.2)

where:

E_t(MPa): Tangential Young's modulus;

ν_t: Poisson's ratio corresponding to tangential Young's modulus;

σ_1 & σ_3(MPa): Principal stresses-major and minor;

ϕ: Friction angle, a Mohr-Coulomb strength parameter that is soil cohesion-dependent;

c (MPa): a Mohr-Coulomb strength parameter;

K_e: Dimensionless modulus of elasticity, ranging from 350 to 1120;

n: Modulus exponent, ranging from 0 to 1;

P_{atm}(MPa): Atmospheric pressure, as a denominator to normalize stress input;

R_f: Failure ratio, defining the shape of the stress-strain curve, ranging from 0.6 to 0.95;

K_u: Unloading dimensionless modulus of elasticity;

B_t(MPa): Bulk modulus.

The Poisson's ratio (ν_t) can be either constant or stress-dependent. If the Poisson's ratio is stress-dependent, the following bulk modulus can be applied

$$B_t = K_b\, P_{atm} \left(\frac{\sigma_3}{P_{atm}}\right)^m \qquad (135.3)$$

of which K_b and m are dimensionless coefficients and exponent, respectively. Parameter K_b is used to denote the volumetric change and its numerical value generally ranges from 200 to 700.

In the unloading and reloading stage, instead of Eq. (135.1) the tangential Young's modulus is to be re-calculated using the following equation,

$$E_t = K_u\, P_{atm} \left(\frac{\sigma_3}{P_{atm}}\right)^n \qquad (135.4)$$

The eight pseudo-material parameters (ϕ, c, K_e, n, R_f, K_u, K_b, m) can be determined with a set of conventional triaxial tests. In practice, a curved Mohr-Coulomb failure envelop is obtained by setting $c = 0$ and letting ϕ vary with confining pressure according to the following equation,

$$\phi = \phi_o - \Delta\phi\, \log\left(\frac{\sigma_3}{P_{atm}}\right) \qquad (135.5)$$

Parameters c and ϕ in Eqs. (3.1)—(3.3) are thus to be replaced by ϕ_o and $\Delta\phi$ in practical applications. Example data of the new eight pseudo-material parameters (K_e, n, R_f, K_u, K_b, m, ϕ_o, $\Delta\phi$) for building a dam given by [Dong et al.] are listed as follows:

Dam Materials	K_e	n	R_f	K_u	K_b	m	ϕ_o	$\Delta\phi$
Rockfill I	1450	0.3	0.73	2800	550	0.13	55.8	12.3
Rockfill II	1360	0.43	0.74	2500	600	0.08	54.3	12.1
Gravel/Clay (Anti-seepage)	520	0.42	0.77	900	250	0.25	39.3	9.8

135.4.2　Rocks

Small rocks are basic ingredients used for asphalt and concrete pavements, as well as soils. Material properties of rocks are given in Table 135.6. The strength of rock material is often related to density and porosity. There are three different kinds of rocks:

(a) Igneous;

(b) Sedimentary;

(c) Metamorphic.

For most rocks, the thermal conductivity varies between 0.5 and 4.2 W/m/℃ and the specific heat capacity varies between 500 and 1000 J/kg/℃ [Berest]. While seismic wave velocity gives a physical measurement of the rock material, it is also used to estimate the pseudoelastic moduli of the rock material including porosity. The seismic modulus of elasticity is generally related to longitudinal P-wave velocity (v_p) and material density (ρ) as

$$E_s = \rho \, v_p^2 \tag{135.6}$$

where:

E_s(MPa): Seismic modulus of elasticity;

ρ (kg/mm^3): Density;

v_p(m/s): Longitudinal P-wave velocity.

Seismic modulus of elasticity should not be mistaken as the modulus of elasticity, which is a material property obtained by the uniaxial compression test. The value of the seismic modulus is generally slightly higher than the modulus determined from static compression tests. Similarly, seismic shear modulus G_s may be determined from shear s-wave velocity as

$$G_s = \rho \, v_s^2 \tag{135.7}$$

where:

G_s(MPa): Seismic Shear modulus;

V_s(m/s): Shear s-wave velocity.

Seismic Poisson's ratio v_s can be determined from

$$v_s = 1/2 \, E_s / \, G_s - 1 \tag{135.8}$$

References

BASTAMI M, 2010. High-Temperature Mechanical Properties of Concrete[J]. International Journal of Civil Engineering, 8(4): 337-351.

BAZANT Z, 1988. Mathematical Modeling of Creep and Shrinkage of Concrete[M]. John Wiley and Sons, New York, NY, USA.

BECQUART F, et al, 2009. Monotonic Aspects of the Mechanical Behavior of Bottom Ash from Municipal Solid Waste Incineration and Its Potential Use for Road Construction[J]. Waste Management, 29(4): 1320-1329.

BEREST P, VOUILLE G, 1988. Notions de base de la thermomécanique, in La Thermomecanique des Roches [J]. BRGM Manuels et Methods, 16: 68-101.

BRANSON D, 1977. Deformation of Concrete Structures[M]. McGraw-Hill, New York, NY, USA.

BRENNAN B J, 1981. Linear Viscoelastic Behavior in Rocks[M]. American Geophysical Union, Washington D. C., USA.

BROZOVSKY J, et al, 2006. Using Non-destructive Methods for Strength Detection on Blended Cements and Paving Blocks[J]. International Journal of Microstructure and Materials Properties, 1(3-4): 282-296.

CHANG Y F, et al, 2006. Residual Stress-Strain Relationship for Concrete after Exposure to High Temperatures [J]. Cement and Concrete Research, 36(10): 1999-2005.

COUGHLIN R, et al, 2011. Fatigue Testing and Analysis of Aluminum Welds under In-Service Highway Bridge Loading Conditions[J]. Journal of Bridge Engineering, 17(3): 409-419.

CREUS G J, 1986. Viscoelasticity-Basic Theory and Applications to Concrete Structures[M]. Springer Verlag, Berlin, Germany.

DAHAB M H, MOHAMED M D, 2002. Tractor Tractive Performance as Affected by Soil Moisture Content, Tire Inflation Pressure and Implement Type[J]. Agricultural Mechanization in Asia, Africa and Latin America, 33(1): 29-34.

DONG W, et al, 2013. Comparison between Duncan and Chang's EB Model and the Generalized Plasticity Model in the Analysis of a High Earth-Rockfill Dam[J]. Journal of Applied Mathematics, 709430.

FRIGIO F, PASQUINI E, PARTL M, et al, 2014. Use of Reclaimed Asphalt in Porous Asphalt Mixtures: Laboratory and Field Evaluations[J]. Journal of Materials in Civil Engineering, 27(7): 04014211.

FURUMURA F, et al, 1995. Mechanical Properties of High Strength Concrete at High Temperatures[J]. Journal of Structural and Construction Engineering, 64(515): 163-168.

GREENE J, et al, 2009. Impact of Wide-base Single Tires on Pavement Damage[J]. Transportation Research Record: Journal of the Transportation Research Board, 2155(1): 82-90.

GUBLER R, PARTL M, CANESTRARI F, et al, 2005. Influence of Water and Temperature on Mechanical Properties of Selected Asphalt Pavements[J]. Materials and Structures, 38(279): 523-532.

HESP S, et al, 2009. Asphalt Pavement Cracking: Analysis of Extraordinary Life Cycle Variability in Eastern and Northeastern Ontario[J]. International Journal of Pavement Engineering, 10(3): 209-227.

ILIUTA S, et al, 2004. Improved Approach to Low-temperature and Fatigue Fracture Performance Grading of Asphalt Cements[J]. Transportation Research Record: Journal of the Transportation Research Board, 1875: 14-21.

JOSEPH P G, 2014. Generalized Soil Deformation Model Based on Dynamical Systems Theory[J]. Geotechnical Research, 1(1): 32-42.

KAHRAMAN S, 2012. Predicting the Compressive and Tensile Strength of Rocks from Indentation Hardness Index[J]. The Journal of The Southern African Institute of Mining and Metallurgy, 112(5): 331-339.

KING M S, 1969. Static and Dynamic Elastic Moduli of Rocks under Pressure[J]. The 11th US Symposium on Rock Mechanics, USRMS 1969(1969): 329-351.

KLÜPPEL M, HEINRICH G, 2000. Rubber Friction on Self-Affine Road Tracks[J]. Rubber Chemistry and Technology, 73(4): 578-606.

KODUR V, 2014. Properties of Concrete at Elevated Temperatures[J]. ISRN Civil Engineering, 2014: 468510.

LESUEUR D, et al, 1996. A Structure Related Model to Describe Asphalt Linear Viscoelasticity[J]. Journal of Rheology, 40(5): 813-836.

L'HERMITE R, 1959. What Do We Know about the Plastic Deformation and Creep of Concrete[J]. Bulletin of RILEM, 1: 22-51.

LI Z, 1994. Effective Creep Poisson's Ratio for Damaged Concrete[J]. International Journal of Fracture, 66: 189-196.

LIE T T, KODUR V R, 1996. Thermal and Mechanical Properties of Steel-Fiber-Reinforced Concrete at Elevated Temperatures[J]. Canadian Journal of Civil Engineering, 23(4): 511-517.

LOSA M, BONOMO G, LICITRA G, et al, 2003. Performance Degradation of Porous Asphalt Pavements[J]. Maintenance and Rehabilitation of Pavements and Technological Control.

MASON W P, 1971. Internal Friction in Moon and Earth Rocks[J]. Nature, 234: 461-463.

MEI Z, CHUNG D, 2002. Improving the Flexural Modulus and Thermal Stability of Pitch by the Addition of Silica Fume[J]. Journal of Reinforced Plastic Composites, 21(1): 91-95.

MITCHELL J K, SOGA K, 2005. Fundamentals of Soil Behavior[M]. 3rd edition, John Wiley & Sons, Inc., New York, NY.

NARAINE K, 1989. Loading and Unloading Stress-Strain Curves for Brick Masonry[J]. Journal of Structural Engineering, 115(10): 2631-2644.

PERSSON B, TARTAGLINO U, ALBOHR O, et al, 2005. Rubber Friction on Wet and Dry Road Surfaces: The Sealing Effect[J]. Physics Review, B 71, 035428.

POULIKAKOS L D, TAKAHASHI S, PARTL M N, 2003. Evaluation of Improved Porous Asphalt by Various Test Methods[J]. Empa Report No. 113/13 Empa No 860076, 2003.

PUCCI T, DUMONT A G, DI BENEDETTO H, 2004. Thermomechanical and Mechanical Behavior of Asphalt Mixes at Cold Temperature: Road and Laboratory Investigations[J]. Journal of Road Materials and Pavement Design, 5: 45-72.

SHIBIB K S, et al, 2013. Enhancement in Thermal and Mechanical Properties of Bricks[J]. Thermal Science, 17(4): 1119-1123.

SIRATOVICH P A, et al, 2012. Physical and Mechanical Properties of the Rotokawa Andesite from Production Wells RK 27_L2, RK 28, and RK 30 [J]. New Zealand Geothermal Workshop Proceedings, 19-21 November 2012.

SOLEIMANI A, WALSH S, HESP S, 2009. Asphalt Cement Loss Tangent as Surrogate Performance Indicator for Control of Thermal Cracking[J]. Transportation Research Record: Journal of the Transportation Research Board, 2126: 39-46.

SULEM J, CERROLAZA M, 2002. Finite Element Analysis of the Indentation Test on Rocks with Microstructure[J]. Computers and Geotechnics, 29(2): 95-117.

TESORIERE G, CANALE S, VENTURA F, 1989. Analysis of Draining Pavements from a Point of View of Phono-Absorption[J]. Proc. 4th Europian Symp., Madrid, 878-881.

TRCKVOK J, 2005. Physical, Mechanical, and Deformation Properties of Metabasalts, Amphibolites and Gneisses from KSDB-3 Compared with Surface Analogue[J]. Acta Geodyn. Geomater., 2(4): 39-47.

WEN S H, CHUNG D D L, 2004. Effects of Carbon Black on the Thermal, Mechanical and Electrical Properties of Pitch-Matrix Composites[J]. Carbon, 42, 2393-2397.

Table 135.1 Mechanical Properties of Example Hot/Warm Mix Asphalt （HMA/WMA） Pavements （Top Down from Road Surface）

Material-DAM	$T/℃$	E_T	ρ	ν	(σ, ε)	α	k	γ	$\tan \delta$	K_{IC}
HMA-dense （Top layer, 50 mm thick）	23	4.8	2.275	0.35	—	—	2.5	920	—	—
	75	—	—	—	—	—	2.2	—	—	—
PG76-22 （Mid layer I, 90 mm thick; 06-101）	−10	—	2.3	—	$\sigma_{uts}=5.6$ （Porosity=4%） $\sigma_{uts}=4.6$ （Porosity=6.5%） $\sigma_{uts}=4.2$ （Porosity=9%）	—	—	—	—	—
	−4.4	—	2.3	—	$\sigma_{uts}=3.8$ （Porosity=4%）; $\sigma_{uts}=3.3$ （Porosity=6.5%）; $\sigma_{uts}=2.9$ （Porosity=9%）	—	—	—	—	—
	23	4.8	2.28	0.35	$\sigma_{uts}=1.31$ （Porosity=4%）; $\sigma_{uts}=1.17$ （Porosity=6.5%）; $\sigma_{uts}=1$ （Porosity=9%）	—	1.6	—	—	—
	75	—	—	—	—	—	1.3	—	—	—
Limerock base （Mid layer II; 265 mm thick）	23	0.55	1.842	0.4	—	—	—	—	—	—
	75	—	—	—	—	—	—	—	—	—
Granular base （Bottom layer; 205 mm thick）	23	0.131	1.81	0.45	—	—	—	—	—	—
	75	—	—	—	—	—	—	—	—	—

Table 135.2 Mechanical Properties of Example Porous Asphalt Pavements

Material-DAM	$T/℃$	E_T	ρ	ν	(σ,ε)	α	k	γ	$\tan\delta$	K_{IC}
Asphalt/VD7 (Porous; $V_v =$ 23%; VD7; Minerals/ styrelf)	−30	—	—	—	(0.8, 60%) (1.2, 100%) (2.1, 200%) (2.5, 270%)	—	—	—	—	—
	−20	—	—	—	(0.8, 100%) (1.8, 200%) (1.9, 300%) (2.3, 450%)	—	—	—	—	—
	−15	—	—	—	(0.6, 100%) (1.1, 200%) (2, 600%) (2, 750%)	—	—	—	—	—
	23	—	—	0.35	—	—	—	—	—	—

Table 135.3 Mechanical Properties of Pitch Composites (Asphalt + Particles)

Material-DAM	$T/℃$	E_T	ρ	ν	(σ,ε)	α	k	γ	$\tan\delta$	K_{IC}
(A) *Loaded at* 0.2 **Hz**:										
Asphalt	23	0.824	1.04	—	—	—	0.173	1686	0.145	—
	40.1 (Softening temperature)									
	121 (T_m)	—	—	—	—	—	—	—	—	—
Asphalt/7CB	23	1.77	—	—	—	—	—	—	0.081	—
	55.6 (Softening temperature)									
Asphalt/Sand	23	1.3	—	—	—	—	—	—	—	—
	44.2 (Softening temperature)									
Asphalt/7CB/ Sand	23	2.1	—	—	—	—	—	—	0.054	—
	80.9 (Softening temperature)									
(B) *Loaded at* 2 **Hz**:										
Asphalt	23	1.45	—	—	—	—	—	—	0.154	—
	40.1 (Softening temperature)									

continued

Material-DAM	$T/^\circ C$	E_T	ρ	ν	(σ, ε)	α	k	γ	$\tan\delta$	K_{IC}
Asphalt/7CB	23	3.38	—	—	—	—	—	—	0.068	—
	55.6 (Softening temperature)									
Asphalt/Sand	23	1.8	—	—	—	—	—	—	—	—
	44.2 (Softening temperature)									
Asphalt/7CB/ Sand	23	3.61	—	—	—	—	—	—	0.034	—
	80.9 (Softening temperature)									

Notes：CB = Carbon black；

E_D(GPa) = Dynamic modulus；Storage modulus $E_S = E_D / (1 + \tan\delta)^{\frac{1}{2}}$；

$\tan\delta$ = Loss tangent (damping capacity).

Table 135.4　Mechanical Properties of Concrete Pavement

Material-DAM	$T/^\circ C$	E_T	ρ	ν	(σ, ε)	α	k	γ	$\tan\delta$	K_{IC}
Cement (Type 1) (Portland; after 1 month)	23	30/10	2.31	—	$\sigma_{ucs} = -24$; $\sigma_{uts} = -2.4$	10	1.4	658	—	0.8
Cement (Type 2) (Portland; after 1 month)	23	30/10	2.31	—	$\sigma_{ucs} = -24$; $\sigma_{uts} = -2.3$	10	1.4	658	—	0.8
Cement (Type 3) (Portland; after 1 month)	23	30/10	2.31	—	$\sigma_{ucs} = -21$; $\sigma_{uts} = -2.6$	10	1.4	658	—	0.8
Cement (Type 4) (Portland; after 1 month)	23	30/10	2.31	—	$\sigma_{ucs} = -14$; $\sigma_{uts} = -2.1$	10	1.4	658	—	0.8
Cement (Type 5) (Portland; after 1 month)	23	30/10	2.31	—	$\sigma_{ucs} = -21$; $\sigma_{uts} = -2.3$	10	1.4	658	—	0.8
Cement (Portland; after 3 years)	23	30/10	2.31	—	$\sigma_{ucs} = -50$	10	1.4	658	—	0.8
Mortar (Pure)	23	24	1.5	0.22	—	—	0.862	880	—	0.8
	100									

continued

Material-DAM	$T/℃$	E_{T}	ρ	ν	(σ, ε)	α	k	γ	$\tan\delta$	K_{IC}
Concrete, Carbonate Aggregate (No fiber; 72 MPa)	0	—	—	—	—	—	2	800	−0.001	—
	23	—	—	—	(−5, −0.75%) (−18, −0.4%) (−40, −0.2%) (−27, −0.1%); (2.3, 0.01%) (4.5, 0.02%) (1, 0.2%) (0.5, 0.4%)	—	1.96	1200	−0.0009	—
	100	—	—	—	$\sigma_{\mathrm{ucs}}=-39$; (2.3, 0.015%) (4.3, 0.025%) (1.6, 0.1%) (1, 0.2%) (0.5, 0.4%)	—	1.82	1200	−0.0002	—
	200	—	—	—	(−5, −0.8%) (−38, −0.25%) (−23, −0.1%)	—	—	—	—	—
	250	—	—	—	(2.1, 0.02%) (3.2, 0.03%) (0.8, 0.2%) (0.5, 0.4%)	—	—	—	—	—
	300	—	—	—	$\sigma_{\mathrm{ucs}}=-37$	—	1.47	700	0.002	—
	400	—	—	—	$\sigma_{\mathrm{ucs}}=-37$	—	1.29	1000	0.003	—
	600	—	—	—	$\sigma_{\mathrm{ucs}}=-30$	—	1.05	800	0.005	—
Concrete, Carbonate Aggregate (No fiber; 72 MPa)	700	—	—	—	(−15, −0.95%) (−16, −7.5%) (−15.6, −0.6%) (−7, −0.2%)	—	—	—	—	—
	785	—	—	—	$\sigma_{\mathrm{ucs}}=-15$	—	—	1400	—	—
	830	—	—	—	—	—	—	3000	—	—
	900	—	—	—	$\sigma_{\mathrm{ucs}}=-2$	—	—	—	—	—
	1000	—	—	—	—	—	0.82	500	0.025	—

continued

Material-DAM	$T/℃$	E_{T}	ρ	ν	(σ, ε)	α	k	γ	$\tan\delta$	K_{IC}
Concrete, Siliceous Aggregate (No fiber)	0	—	—	—	—	—	3.22	708	−0.001	—
	23	27	—	0.18	$\sigma_{\mathrm{ucs}}=-33$	—	3.06	756	−0.0008	—
	100	—	—	—	$\sigma_{\mathrm{ucs}}=-32$	—	2.52	1200	−0.0004	—
	300	—	—	—	$\sigma_{\mathrm{ucs}}=-28$	—	1.61	1000	−0.005	—
	400	—	—	—	$\sigma_{\mathrm{ucs}}=-25$	—	1.4	1000	−0.005	—
	500	—	—	—	$\sigma_{\mathrm{ucs}}=-21$	—	—	—	—	—
	600	—	—	—	$\sigma_{\mathrm{ucs}}=-16$	—	1.4	1000	0.0135	—
	800	—	—	—	$\sigma_{\mathrm{ucs}}=-5$	—	—	—	—	—
	1000	—	—	—	$\sigma_{\mathrm{ucs}}=-2.3$	—	1.4	950	0.0135	—
Composite (Portland Concrete)	23	50/30	2.4	—	$\sigma_{\mathrm{ucs}}=-120$; $\sigma_{\mathrm{uts}}=50$	10	3.9/ 1.4	—	—	—
	100									
Composite (Reactive Powder)	23	50/30	2.4	—	$\sigma_{\mathrm{ucs}}=-190$	10	3.9/ 1.4	—	—	—
	100									
Mortar (Pure; Cement)	23	24	1.5	0.22	—	12	—	880	0.862	0.8
	400	—	—	—	—	14	—	—	—	—
	500	—	—	—	—	19	—	—	—	—
	800	—	—	—	—	11	—	—	—	—
	1000	—	—	—	—	10	—	—	—	—
47.6cement- 0.45plasticier- 3.84G- 38.5Wollastonit- 9.61Vermiculite	23	—	—	—	—	11	—	—	—	—
	200	—	—	—	—	8	—	—	—	—
	300	—	—	—	—	7	—	—	—	—
	500	—	—	—	—	5	—	—	—	—
	700	—	—	—	—	4	—	—	—	—

Table 135.5   Mechanical Properties of Soils and Construction Materials

Material-DAM	$T/℃$	E_{T}	ρ	ν	(σ, ε)	α	k	γ	$\tan\delta$	K_{IC}
Brick, Dense	23	—	2.243	—	—	—	1.3	927	—	—
Brick, General	23	—	1.78	—	$\sigma_{\mathrm{ucs}}=-44$	—	0.9	—	—	—
Brick, Hollow	23	—	1.36	—	$\sigma_{\mathrm{ucs}}=-31$	—	0.64	—	—	—
Tile, Ceramic	23	38.1	—	0.18	—	—	—	—	—	—
Silt	23	0.08	1.44	—	—	—	—	290	—	—

continued

Material-DAM	$T/℃$	E_T	ρ	ν	(σ, ε)	α	k	γ	$\tan \delta$	K_{IC}
Clay	23	0.08	1.44	—	—	—	1.4	1100	—	—
Sand，Dry	23	—	1.5	—	—	—	0.33	800	—	—
Gravel	23	0.22	—	—	—	—	0.7	—	—	—

Table 135.6 Mechanical Properties of Rocks

Material-DAM	$T/℃$	E_T	ρ	ν	(σ, ε)	α	k	γ	$\tan \delta$	K_{IC}
Amphibolite（闪岩；Surfaced）	23	97	3.1	0.25	$\sigma_{ucs}=-250$	—	3.3	1130	—	—
Amphibolite（闪岩；Deep Sea）	23	61	3.1	0.17	$\sigma_{ucs}=-170$	—	3.3	1130	—	—
Andesite（安山岩）	23	30	2.65	0.2	$\sigma_{ucs}=-200$；$\sigma_{uts}=10$	—	2.3	—	—	—
Andesite	23	30	2.54	0.2	$\sigma_{ucs}=-128$；$\sigma_{uts}=15.4$	—	2.3	—	—	—
Argillite（泥岩）	23	—	2.5	—	—	—	2.3	840	—	—
Basalt（玄武岩）	23	50	2.6	0.15	$\sigma_{ucs}=-350$；$(20, 0.35\%)$	5.4	1.7	—	—	0.41
Diorite（闪长岩）	23	—	—	—	—	—	2.7	1000	—	—
	800	—	—	—	—	—	1.7			
Dolerite（粗玄武岩）	23	85	—	0.15	$\sigma_{ucs}=-225$；$(18, 0.3\%)$	—	—	—	—	0.41
Dolomite（白云石）	23	50	2.45	0.15	$\sigma_{ucs}=-60$；$(10,0.17\%)$	—	2.1	800	—	—
Gabbro（辉长岩）	23	70	2.86	0.27	$\sigma_{ucs}=-200$；$(18,0.3\%)$	—	2.2	980	—	0.41
Gneiss（片麻岩；Surfaced）	23	88	2.8	0.27	$\sigma_{ucs}=-164$；$(14, 0.12\%)$	—	—	1020	—	—
Gneiss（片麻岩；Deep Sea）	23	41	2.75	0.27	$\sigma_{ucs}=-127$	—	—	1020	—	0.26
Granite（花岗岩）	23	50/2	2.68	0.17	$\sigma_{ucs}=-175$；$(16,0.25\%)$	9.2	2.7	810	—	0.26
Greywacke	23	10/14	—	—	—	—	—	—	—	—

continued

Material-DAM	$T/\text{℃}$	E_T	ρ	ν	(σ, ε)	α	k	γ	$\tan\delta$	K_{IC}
Lava （火山熔岩）	23	—	—	—	—	—	—	840	—	—
Limestone （石灰岩）	23	27/3	2.44	0.3	$\sigma_{ucs}=-140$; $\sigma_{uts}=16$	11	2.2	850	—	0.034
Marble （大理石）	23	50	2.6	0.22	$\sigma_{ucs}=-125$; $(18, 0.4\%)$	6.2	2.5	885	—	0.26
Metabasalt （Surfaced）	23	80	3.0	0.25	$\sigma_{ucs}=-294$	—	—	—	—	—
Metabasalt （Deep Sea）	23	109	3.05	0.26	$\sigma_{ucs}=-257$	—	—	—	—	—
Mica（云母）	23	7.6	2.96	—	$(27, 3.3\%)$	—	0.7	840	—	—
Mudstone （泥岩）	23	37	2.24	0.15	$\sigma_{ucs}=-55$; $(17, 0.15\%)$	—	—	—	—	—
Philite	23	48	2.74	0.26	$\sigma_{ucs}=-77$; $\sigma_{uts}=13$	—	—	—	—	—
Quartzite （石英）	23	80/28	2.64	0.17	$\sigma_{ucs}=-225$; $(13, 0.2\%)$	—	5.0	860	—	0.41
Rhyolite （流纹岩）	23	30	2.5	0.3	$\sigma_{ucs}=-120$; $\sigma_{uts}=7$	—	—	—	—	—
Sandstone （沙石）	23	32	2.24	0.14	$\sigma_{ucs}=-85$; $(15, 0.2\%)$	10	1.7	900	—	0.034
Salt	23	—	—	—	—	40	—	—	—	—
Shale （页岩）	23	17	2.2	0.1	$\sigma_{ucs}=-52$; $\sigma_{uts}=6$	—	1.6	—	—	0.034
Schist （板岩）	23	40/10	2.72	0.2	$\sigma_{ucs}=-110$; $\sigma_{uts}=7$	—	—	1100	—	0.016
Silstone	23	14/3	—	—	—	—	2.2	800	—	—
Slate （板石）	23	55	2.75	0.25	$\sigma_{ucs}=-115$; $(14, 0.35\%)$	—	—	—	—	0.034
Talc （滑石/云母）	23	4	1.27	—	$\sigma_{uts}=35$	—	—	—	—	—

Chapter 136

Human Beings

136.1　Introduction

Crashworthiness is the ability of a vehicle to protect its occupants during a crash or collision. All vehicles are tested for crashworthiness before being released to the public. Positively speaking, crashworthiness is the science of preventing or minimizing injuries or death following an accident through the rational deployment of safety systems, including airbags, seat belts, bumpers, and so on. Besides testing, nonlinear explicit finite element methods have been explored to predict the potential crash or collision damage to occupants. Material data of human beings, especially bones, are so needed for such an analysis.

136.2　Structural Bone

A structural bone is comprised of several different parts that work together to provide each bone with its mechanical function and use. Each individual bone is a composite of the bio-polymer collagen and the bio-ceramic hydroxyapatite, while the collagen is plied in various directions around the bone. A bone is comprised of a rigid matrix of calcium salts deposited around protein fibers, of which minerals provide rigidity and proteins provide elasticity and strength and connective tissue has the potential to repair and regenerate. Mechanical properties of a bone component are generally orthotropic, inhomogeneous, density-dependent, and age-dependent.

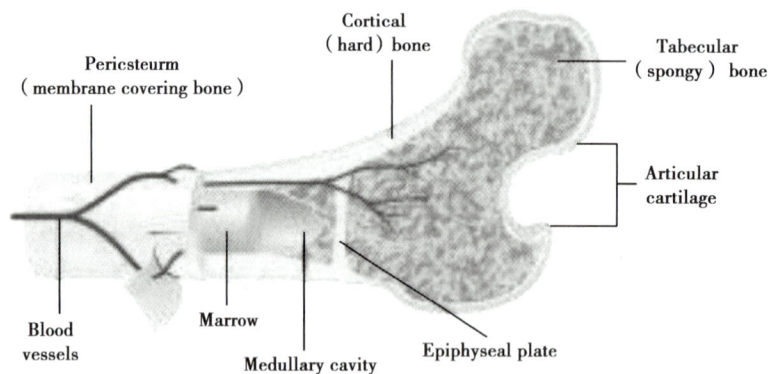

Fig. 136.1　Bone Cross-Section

Mechanical properties, thermal properties, and material strengths of bone materials are given in Tables 136.1—136.3, respectively. Cortical bone and trabecular bone are the two major physical forms that make up the entire structure of the bone (Fig. 136.1).

136.2.1   Cortical bone

The cortical bone is the load-carrying outer part that is much denser, stiffer and stronger than the trabecular bone. Mechanical properties of cortical bone decline with age. Both tensile strength and modulus of elasticity of the femur cortical bone decrease at about 2% per decade for the age range from 20 years to 90 years old [Burstein et al.].

136.2.2   Trabecular bone

The trabecular bone, also known as the cancellous bone or a spongy bone, is an important part of human anatomy that is responsible for carrying out a variety of regenerative and regular functions. The volume fraction of solid material may range from 5% to 70% in a cancellous bone (a structure with open cells) as the interstices in living bone are filled with marrow. The compressive strength of a cancellous bone depends very much on the density ρ (in g/cm^3) and also varies with the strain rate (s^{-1}) as follows [Carter and Hayes]:

$$\sigma_{\text{ucs}} = -68\left(\frac{d\varepsilon}{dt}\right)^{0.06} \rho^n \tag{136.1}$$

where exponent $n = 2$ for cancellous bones in general. The compressive failure of the cancellous bone proceeds at approximately constant stress until the cell walls touch each other; at this point any further compression causes the stress to rise rapidly [Gibson]. By contrast, fracture of cancellous bone in tension proceeds abruptly and catastrophically [Kaplan et al.].

136.3   Viscoelasticity of Bone

Bone exhibits viscoelastic behavior and the behavior may manifest itself as a creep due to its collagen and bone voids.

The loss tangent ($\tan \delta$) reaches as low as 0.01 at loading frequencies ranging from 1 to 100 Hz, while it is greater at a high or low frequency, e.g. 0.08 at 1 MHz or 10^{-6} Hz. Dynamic properties of bio-materials including damping are listed in Table 136.4.

136.4   Medical Implants

To design against premature mechanical failures, most implant devices such as coronary and endovascular stents [Marrey et al.] are assessed on the basis of survival, i.e., if a fatigue life of

108 cycles is met. Analysis and testing are performed to ascertain whether the device will survive 10^8 cycles under accelerated in vitro loading conditions. Frequently used medical implants are outlined in Table 136.5.

136.5 Hazardous Materials

Heavy metals such as Pb (Lead), Cr_6^+ (Hexavalent Chromium), Hg (Mercury), and Cd (Cadmium) mentioned in the IMDS (International Material Data System) are not permitted. Their maximum allowable percentages of the chemical composition of each part are listed as follows:

Material	Maximum Amount Allowed (ppm)
Pb (Lead)	0.09% (900 ppm) by weight
Cr_6^+ (Hexavalent Chromium)	0.09% (900 ppm) by weight
Hg (Mercury)	0.09% (900 ppm) by weight
Cd (Cadmium)	0.009% (90 ppm) by weight

References

BENSAMOUN S, et al, 2008. Assessment of Mechanical Properties of Human Osteon Lamellae Exhibiting Various Degrees of Minerialzation by Nanoindentation[J]. Journal of Musculoskeletal Research, 11(3): 135-148.

BETTELHEIM F A, WANG T, 1976. Dynamic Viscoelastic Properties of Bovine Vitreous[J]. Experimental. Eye Research, 23(4): 435-441.

BURSTEIN A H, REILLY D T, MARTENS M, 1976. Ageing of Bone Tissue: Mechanical Properties[J]. The Journal of Bone and Joint Surgery. American volume, 58(1): 82-86.

CALER W E, CARTER D R, 1989. Bone Creep-fatigue Damage Accumulation[J]. Journal of Biomechanics, 22(6-7): 625-635.

CARTER D R, HAYES W C, 1979. Bone Compressive Strength: the Influence of Density and Strain Rate[J]. Science, 194: 1174-1175, 1976.

CHAICHANASIRI E, et al, 2009. Finite Element Analysis of Bone around a Dental Implant Supporting a Crown with a Premature Contact[J]. Journal of Medical Association, Thai, 92(10): 1336-1344.

CHEN M, et al, 2006. Mechanical Behavior of Bovine Tendon with Stress-Softening and Loading-Rate Effects [J]. Journal of Advanced Theoretical and Applied Mechanics, 2, 59-74.

COHEN M L, 1977. Measurement of the Thermal Properties of Human Skin: A Review[J]. Journal of Invest. Dermatol., 69(3): 333-338.

COOPER T E, TREZEK G J, 1971. Correlation of Thermal Properties of Some Human Tissue with Water Content[J]. Aerospace Medicine, 42(1): 24-27.

CURREY J, 1984. The Mechanical Adaptations of Bones[M]. Princeton University Press, Princeton, NJ, USA.

DANESI V, 2012. Mechanical Properties of the Human Metasrsal Bones[J]. Journal of Mechanics in Medicine and Biology, 12(4): 1250062-1250062-15.

DAVIES J L, et al, 2011. An Efficient Method of Modeling Material Properties Using a Thermal Diffusion Analogy: An Example Based on Craniofacial Bone[J]. Plos One, 6(2), e17004.

FRASCA P, HARPER R A, KATZ J L, 1981. Micromechanical Oscillators and Techniques for Determining the Dynamic Moduli of Micro Samples of Human Cortical Bone at Microstrains[J]. Journal of Biomechanical Engineering, 103(3): 146-150.

GARNER E, et al, 2000. Viscoelastic Dissipation in Compact Bone: Implications for Stress- Induced Fluid Flow in Bone[J]. Transactions of the ASME, 122(2): 166-172.

GIANNINI M, SOARES C, DE CARVALHO R, 2004. Ultimate Tensile Strength of Tooth Structures[J]. Dental Materials,20(4): 322-329.

GIBSON L J, 1985. The Mechanical Behavior of Cancellous Bone[J]. Journal of Biomechanics, 18: 317-328.

GOLDSTEIN S A, 1987. The Mechanical Properties of Trabecular Bone: Dependence on Anatomic Location and Function[J]. Journal of Biomechanics, 20(11-12): 1155-1161 .

GONG X, et al, 2011. Fatigue to Fracture: An Informative, Fast, and Reliable Approach for Assessing Medical Implant Durability[J]. Journal of ASTM International, 6(7), Paper ID JAI102412.

GOSS S A, et al, 1978. Comprehensive Complication of Empirical Ultrasonic Properties of Mammalian Tissues [J]. The Journal of the Acoustical Society of America, 64(2): 423-457.

GU Y D, et al, 2010. Computer Simulation of Stress Distribution to Metatarsals at Different Inversion Landing Angles Using the Finite Element Method[J]. Journal of International Orthopaedics, 34(5): 669-676.

HELGASON B, et al, 2008. A Modified Method for Assigning Material Properties to FE Models of Bones[J]. Medical Engineering and Physics, 30(4): 444-453.

IATRIDIS J C, et al, 1996. Is the Nucleus Pulpous a Solid or a Fluid? Mechanical Behaviors of the Nucleus Pulpous of the Human Intervertebral Disc[J]. Spine, 21(10): 1174-1184.

KAPLAN S, HAYES W C, STONE J L, et al, 1985. Tensile Strength of Bovine Trabecular Bone[J]. Journal of Biomechanics, 18(9): 723-725, 727.

KASRA M, SHIRAZI-ADL A, DROUIN G, 1992. Dynamics of Human Lumbar Intervertebral Joints: Experimental and Finite Element Investigations[J]. Spine, 17(1): 93-102.

KEAVENY T M, et al, 1997. Systematic and Random Errors in Compression Testing of Trabecular Bone[J]. Journal of Orthopaedic Research, 15(1): 101-110.

KER R F, et al, 1987. The Spring in the Arch of the Human Foot[J]. Nature, 325(6100): 147-149.

LAKES R S, KATZ J L, 1979. Viscoelastic Properties of Wet Cortical Bone. Ⅲ. A Nonlinear Constitutive Equation[J]. Journal of Biomechanics, 12(9): 689-698.

LAKSARI K, SHAFIEIAN M, DARVISH K, 2012. Constitutive Model for Brain Tissue under Finite Compression[J]. Journal of Biomechanics, 45(4): 642-646.

LESLIE W D, NIX L M, 2011. Absolute Fracture Risk Assessment using Lumbar Spine and Femoral Neck Bone Density Measurements: Derivation and Validation of a Hybrid System[J]. Journal of Bone and Mineral Research, 26(3): 460-467.

MCELHANEY J H, et al, 1970. Mechanical Properties of Cranial Bone[J]. Journal of Biomechanics, 3(5): 495-511.

MARREY R V, et al, 2006. Fatigue and Life Prediction for Cobalt-Chromium Stents: A Fracture Mechanics Analysis[J]. Biomaterials, 27(9): 1988-2000.

MARTINS J, et al, 1998. A Numerical Model of Passive and Active Behavior of Skeletal Muscles[J]. Computer Methods in Applied Mechanics and Engineering, 151(3-4): 419-433.

MAUCH M, CURREY J D, SEDMAN A J, 1992. Creep Fracture in Bones with Different Stiffness[J]. Journal of Biomechanics, 25(1): 11-16.

MCELHANEY J H, 1970. Mechanical Properties of Cranial Bone[J]. Journal of Biomehnzics, 3(5): 495-511.

MOSES W M, et al, 1995. Measurement of the Thermal Conductivity of Cortical Bone by an Inverse Technique[J]. Experimental Thermal and Fluid Science, 11(1): 34-39.

OKAMOTO K, et al, 2008. Three-dimensional Finite Element Analysis of Stress Distribution in Composite Resin Cores with Fiber Posts of Varying Diameters[J]. Dental Materials Journal, 27(1): 49-55.

OSHIMA H, et al, 1989. Water Diffusion Pathway, Swelling Pressure, and Biomechanical Properties of Intervertebral Disc during Compression Load[J]. Spine, 14(11): 1234-1244.

PAPADOGIANIS Y, BOYER D B, LAKES R S, 1984. Creep of Conventional and Microfilled Dental Composites[J]. Journal of Biomedical Materials Research, 18(1): 15-24.

PAYNE P A, 1991. Measurement of Properties and Function of Skin[J]. Clinical Physics and Physiological Measurement, 12(2): 105-129.

RANU H S, 1987. The Thermal Properties of Human Cortical Bone: An in Vitro Study[J]. Engineering in Medicine, 16(3): 175-176.

RHO J, et al, 1999. Young's Modulus of Trabecular and Cortical Bone Material: Ultrasonic and Microtensile Measurements[J]. Journal of Biomechanics, 26(2): 111-119.

RHO J, KUHN S L, ZIOUPOS P, 1998. Mechanical Properties and the Hierarchical Structure of Bone[J]. Medical Engineering and Physics, 20(2): 92-102.

RITCHIE R O, BUEHLER M J, HANSMA P, 2009. Plasticity and Toughness in Bone[J]. Physics Today, 62, 41-47.

SAFARI M, et al, 1990. Clinical Assessment of Rheumatic Disease Using Viscoelastic Parameters for Synovial Fluid[J]. Biorheology, 27, 659-674.

SALADIN K, 2012. Anatomy and Physiology: The Unity of Form and Function[M]. McGraw-Hill, New York, NY, USA.

SETTON L A, MOW V C, HOWELL D S, 1995. Mechanical Behavior of Articular Cartilage in Shear is Altered by Transaction of the Anterior Cruciate Ligament[J]. Journal of Orthopaedics Research, 13(4): 473-482.

SINGER K, et al, 1995. Prediction of Thoracic and Lumbar Vertebral Body Compressive Strength: Correlations with Bone Mineral Density and Vertebral Region[J]. Bone, 17(2): 167-174.

SOERGEL F, et al, 1995. Dynamic Mechanical Spectroscopy of the Cornea for Measurement of Its Viscoelastic Properties in Virto[J]. German Journal of Ophthalmology, 4(3): 151-156.

STAINES M, ROBINSON W, HOOD J, 1981. Spherical Indentation of Tooth Enamel[J]. Journal of Materials Science, 16 (9): 2551-2556.

STRAIT D S, et al, 2008. Craniofacial Strain Patterns during Premolar Loading: Implications for Human Evolution[J]. Primate Craniofacial Function and Biology, (Edited by Vinyard, Ravosa, & Wall) Springer, New York: Springer, NYU, 173-198.

WILLIAMS J L, LEWIS J L, 1982. Properties and an Anisotropic Model of Cancellous Bone from the Proximal Tibial Epiphysis[J]. Journal of Biomechanical Engineering, 104(1): 50-56.

XU H, LIU W, WANG T, 1989. Measurement of Thermal Expansion Coefficient of Human Teeth[J]. Aust Dent Journal, 34(6): 530-535.

ZHANG L, SZERI A Z, 2009. Transport of Neutral Solute in Articular Cartilage: Effect of Microstructure Anisotropy[J]. Journal of Biomechanics, 41(2): 430-437.

Table 136.1 Mechanical Properties of Human Parts and Related Materials

Material	$T/°C$	ρ	E_{11}	E_{22}	E_{33}	G_{12}	G_{13}	G_{23}	ν_{12}	ν_{13}	ν_{23}
Blood:											
Whole	23	1.06	—	—	—	—	—	—	—	—	—
Femur:											
Cancellous	23	0.2	1	1	1	—	—	—	0.28	0.28	—
Collagen (Dry)	23	—	6	6	6	—	—	—	—	—	—
Cortical (25y)	23	1.85	17	9	9	—	—	—	—	—	—
Cortical (45y)	23	1.85	17.7	9	9	—	—	—	—	—	—
Cortical (85y)	23	—	15.6	—	—	—	—	—	—	—	—
Hydroxyapatite (Bone Mineral)	23	—	80	80	80	—	—	—	—	—	—
Trabecular	23	—	0.64	0.64	0.64	—	—	—	0.28	0.28	—
(Trabecular bone, depending on anatomic location and function [Goldstein])											
Metatarsal:											
Bone	23	—	7.3	7.3	7.3	—	—	—	0.3	0.3	0.3
Cartilage	23	—	0.001	0.001	0.001	—	—	—	0.4	0.4	0.4
Ligament	23	—	0.26	0.26	0.26	—	—	—	0.4	0.4	0.4
Plantar Fascia	23	—	0.35	0.35	0.35	—	—	—	0.4	0.4	0.4
Slip Plantar Facia	23	—	0.35	0.35	0.35	—	—	—	0.4	0.4	0.4
Tendon	23	—	1.2	1.2	1.2	—	—	—	0.4	0.4	0.4
Tissue (Hyper)	23 ($C_{10}=0.0856$, $C_{01}=-0.0584$, $C_{20}=0.039$, $C_{11}=-0.0232$, $C_{02}=0.0085$, $D_1=3.65$, $D_2=0$)										
Skull:											
Alveolus (M2-M3)	23	—	20.6	20.6	—	—	—	—	0.27	0.27	—
Alveolus (P3-M1)	23	—	16.7	16.7	—	—	—	—	0.34	0.34	—
Cranial Bone	23	0.38	5.6	5.6	2.4	—	—	—	0.2	0.2	—
Frontal Squama	23	—	14.9	14.9	—	—	—	—	0.31	0.31	—
Frontal Torus	23	—	13.1	13.1	—	—	—	—	0.25	0.25	—

continued

Material	$T/°C$	ρ	E_{11}	E_{22}	E_{33}	G_{12}	G_{13}	G_{23}	ν_{12}	ν_{13}	ν_{23}
Galabella	23	—	14.4	14.4	—	—	—	—	0.27	0.27	—
Media Orbital Wall	23	—	14.6	14.6	—	—	—	—	0.36	0.36	—
Palate Anterior	23	—	15.3	15.3	—	—	—	—	0.34	0.34	—
Palate Posterior	23	—	18.8	18.8	—	—	—	—	0.32	0.32	—
Premaxilla	23	—	18.5	18.5	—	—	—	—	0.21	0.21	—
Postorbital Bar	23	—	19.8	19.8	—	—	—	—	0.27	0.27	—
Rostrum, Dorsal	23	—	19.9	19.9	—	—	—	—	0.22	0.22	—
Rostrum, Lateral	23	—	18.1	18.1	—	—	—	—	0.25	0.25	—
Zygoma Arch-Posterior	23	—	12.5	12.5	—	—	—	—	0.28	0.28	—
Zygoma Arch-Anterior	23	—	20.8	20.8	—	—	—	—	0.26	0.26	—
Zygoma-Root	23	—	17.9	17.9	—	—	—	—	0.34	0.34	—
Vertebra:											
T7 & T8	23	—	19.7	—	—	—	—	—	—	—	—
L4	23	—	17.6	—	—	—	—	—	—	—	—
Tooth:											
Dentin	23	—	18.3	—	—	—	—	—	—	—	—
Enamel	23	—	84	—	—	—	—	—	—	—	—
Skin:											
Epidermis (Human)	23	2.2	—	—	—	—	—	—	—	—	—

Notes: $\nu_{ij} E_{jj} = \nu_{ji} E_{ii} (i = 1, 2, 3; j = 1, 2, 3; i \neq j)$;

1-Longitudinal direction of a bone;

2-Latitudinal direction;

3-Radial direction;

25y, 45y, 85y: 25, 45, and 85 years old.

Table 136.2   Thermal Properties of Human Parts and Related Materials

Material-DAM	$T/°C$	α_1	α_2	α_3	k_1	k_2	k_3	γ	β_1	β_2	β_3
Aorta:											
Whole	23	—	—	—	0.476	0.476	0.476	—	—	—	—
Blood:											
Whole	23	—	—	—	0.492	0.492	0.492	—	—	—	—
Plasma	23	—	—	—	0.57	0.57	0.57	—	—	—	—
Fat:											
Whole	23	—	—	—	0.204	0.204	0.204	—	—	—	—
Femur:											
Cortical (Dry)	23	27.3	27.3	27.3	0.7	0.7	0.7	—	—	—	—
Cortical (Saturated)	23	—	—	—	0.8	0.8	0.8	—	—	—	—
Heart:											
Whole	23	—	—	—	0.54	0.54	0.54	—	—	—	—
Kidney:											
Whole	23	—	—	—	0.543	0.543	0.543	—	—	—	—
Cotex	23	—	—	—	0.5	0.5	0.5	—	—	—	—
Medulla	23	—	—	—	0.5	0.5	0.5	—	—	—	—
Liver:											
Whole	23	—	—	—	0.517	0.517	0.517	—	—	—	—
Skin:											
Dermis	23	2.2	—	—	0.307	0.307	0.307	—	—	—	—
Epidermis	23	2.2	—	—	0.209	0.209	0.209	—	—	—	—
Spleen:											
Whole	23	—	—	—	0.543	0.543	0.543	—	—	—	—
Tooth:											
Dentin	23	17	17	17	0.57	0.57	0.57	—	—	—	—
Enamel	23	10.6	—	—	0.93	0.77	0.77	—	—	—	—

Notes: α_1, α_2, α_3(μm/m/°C): Coefficents of linear thermal expansion of a unidirectional lamina;

k_1, k_2, k_3(W/m/°C): Thermal conductivities of a unidirectional lamina;

β_1, β_2, β_3(μm/m/%): Swelling coefficients of linear moisture expansion;

γ (J/kg/°C): Specific heat capacity.

Table 136.3   Orthotropic Mechanical Strengths of Human Parts and Related Materials

Material	$T/^\circ\text{C}$	$(\sigma_{11}, \varepsilon_{11})$	$(\sigma_{22}, \varepsilon_{22})$	$(\sigma_{33}, \varepsilon_{33})$	$(\sigma_{12}, \varepsilon_{12})/(\sigma_{23}, \varepsilon_{23})/$ $(\sigma_{13u}, \varepsilon_{13})$
Femur:					
Cancellous	23	Eq. (136.1)	—	—	—/—/—
Cortical (25 years old)	23	$\sigma_{ucs}=-209$; $(120, 0.2\%)$ $\sigma_{uts}=140$	—	—	—/—/—
Cortical (55 years old)	23	$\sigma_{ucs}=-192$; $(111, 0.2\%)$ $\sigma_{uts}=131$	—	—	—/—/—
Cortical (85 years old)	23	$\sigma_{ucs}=-180$; $(104, 0.2\%)$ $\sigma_{uts}=120$	—	—	—/—/—
Trabecular	23	—	—	—	—/—/—
Hydroxyapatite (Bone Mineral)	23	$\sigma_{uts}=65$	$\sigma_{uts}=50$	$\sigma_{uts}=50$	—/—/—
Skull:					
Bone	23	$(70, 9\%)$	$(70, 9\%)$	—	—/—/—
Cranial Bone	23	$(-98, -0.05\%)$	$(-98, -0.05\%)$	$(-74, -0.2\%)$	—/—/—
Vertebra:					
Trabecular Bone	23	$\sigma_{uts}=0.73$	$\sigma_{uts}=0.46$	$\sigma_{uts}=0.23$	—/—/—
Tooth:					
Dentin- Outer	23	$\sigma_{uts}=62$	$\sigma_{uts}=62$	$\sigma_{uts}=62$	—/—/—
Dentin- Mid	23	$\sigma_{uts}=49$	$\sigma_{uts}=49$	$\sigma_{uts}=49$	—/—/—
Dentin- Inner	23	$\sigma_{uts}=34$	$\sigma_{uts}=34$	$\sigma_{uts}=34$	—/—/—
Enamel	23	$\sigma_{uts}=42.1$	$\sigma_{uts}=11.5$	$\sigma_{uts}=11.5$	—/—/—
Skin:					
(Human)	23	$(15, 0.2\%)$ $\sigma_{uts}=20$	$(15, 0.2\%)$ $\sigma_{uts}=20$	—	—/—/—

Table 136.4 Dynamic Properties of Human Parts and Related Materials, Tested at 10 Hz

Material-DAM	$T/°C$	G'	ρ	ν	(σ, ε)	α	k	γ	$\tan \delta$	K_{IC}
Compact Bone	23	4000	—	—	—	—	—	—	0.01	—
Spinal Motion	23	45	—	—	—	—	—	—	0.1	—
Articular cartilage	23	0.8	—	—	—	—	—	—	0.23	—
Meniscus	23	0.1	—	—	—	—	—	—	0.40	—
Nucleaus pulposus	23	0.011	—	—	—	—	—	—	0.45	—
Synovial Fluid	23	$2×10^{-5}$	—	—	—	—	—	—	0.29	—
Vitreous Humor	23	$2×10^{-6}$	—	—	—	—	—	—	1.12	—

Notes: G'(MPa) = Complex shear modulus.

Table 136.5 Materials for Medical Implants

Parts	Biomaterial	Annual Implants
Catheter	Silicone; Teflon	200 million
Contact Lens	Silicone Acrylate	30 million
Renal Dialyzer	Cellulose	16 million
Intraocular Lens	PMMA	2.7 million
Stent (Cardiovascular)	Stainless Steel; NiTi; Co-Cr	>1.0 million
Hip & Knee Prosthesis	Titanium; Co-Cr; PE	0.5 million
Pacemaker	Polyurethane	0.43 million
Dental Implant	Titanium	0.3 million
Vascular Graft	PTFE; PET	0.25 million
Heart Valve	Pig Valve; PyC; Ti; Co-Cr	0.2 million
Breast Implant	Silicone	0.192 millions

Notes: Co-Cr = Haynes 25.

Automobile Fluids

Chapter 137

Powertrain Lubricants

137.1 Introduction

The functional requirement of hydraulic fluids is to assure a smooth relative motion. Load and speed are the two major technical factors that predominate a selection of lubricants. A lubricant typically contains $90\% \sim 95\%$ base oil (e.g. mineral or synthetic oils) and lesser than 10% additives.

Special characteristics of lubricants must adhere to the following:

(a) Viscosity for film-pressurizing;

(b) Antiwear characteristics;

(c) Low-temperature fluidity;

(d) Thermal stability;

(e) Oxidation stability (resistance to oxidation);

(f) Hydrolytic stability (water handling ability);

(g) Cleanliness and filterability;

(h) Demulsibility (Carrying away dust, dirt etc.);

(i) Defoaming (air handling ability);

(j) Corrosion prevention/control.

The measurement and prediction procedures of fluid properties under high-pressure conditions at various working temperatures are increasing interest in many automotive systems, including fuel injection, power transmission, braking, steering, and hydraulic systems.

137.1.1 Mineral Oils

Additives are used to modify performance characteristics fo lubricants. The depletion of the additives, dependent on the service duty of the engine, may tell when oil should be changed. According to the main constituents, traditionally called base oils, liquid mineral lubricants can be divided into the following three groups:

(a) Paraffinic Oils: High paraffin content resulting in high viscosity index, widely used;

(b) Naphthenic Oils: Low viscosity index, but low pour point (temperature);

(c) Aromatic Oils.

137.1.2   Synthetic Oils

Each synthetic (man-made) oil is generally superior in extreme service conditions to conventional mineral oils, as made for its special application. Commonly used synthetic lubricants include:

(a) Polyalphaolefins (PAO): Excellent for internal combustion engines;

(b) Polio Ester Oils: Fire-resistant hydraulic fluids and jet engine oils;

(c) Polyalkaline glycols (PAG or Polyglycols): Dissolving deposits (for turbine engines);

(d) Silicones: Stable at high temperatures and not water-soluble (for brakes).

137.2   Dynamic Viscosity

Dynamic Viscosity is defined as a fluid's resistance to deforming (flow) when subjected to shear stress. Consider the engine operation. The viscosity will determine how fast the engine oil is pumped up through the engine components in working condition, such as passing through filters, rinsing the engine pistons/camshaft, dragging at bearing, and eventually draining back to the crankcase. In other words, the higher the viscosity the more the potential power loss. On the other hand, the higher the viscosity the more load can be supported at the crankshaft bearings.

The selection of engine oil is hence a multi-tasking decision-making process.

Dynamic viscosity is commonly reported in PaS (Poise) or cP (Centipoise), as 1 cP = 1 MPa · s = 10^{-3} Pa · s. Some simple measurement devices for viscosity [Janna] are given as follows:

(a) Orifice rheometer [ASTM D445]: gravity flow of a fluid through an opening;

(b) Rotating-cup viscometer [ASTM D2893]: frictional drag of surface against a fluid;

(c) Falling sphere viscometer: gravity flow of an object in the fluid;

(d) Capillary rheometer: pressure flow of a fluid.

A rheological diagram (the shear stress versus strain rate) obtained from the measured data can be described by the following equation:

$$\tau = \tau_0 + \mu_d \left(\frac{dU}{dy}\right)^n \tag{137.1}$$

where:

τ: Shear stress;

τ_0: Initial shear stress;

μ_d: Dynamic viscosity;

U: Speed in the x-direction;

y: y-coordinate;

n: Exponent.

It may exhibit one of the following phenomena:

      (1) Newtonian fluid (e.g. water): $\tau_0 = 0$, $\mu_d \neq \mu_d(t)$, and $n = 1$;

      (2) Dilatant fluid (e.g. nanofluid- high volume of particles): $\tau_0 = 0$, $\mu_d \neq \mu_d(t)$, and $n > 1$;

      (3) Pseudo-plastic fluid (e.g. grease): $\tau_0 = 0$, $\mu_d \neq \mu_d(t)$, and $n < 1$;

      (4) Bingham plastic fluid (e.g. toothpaste): $\tau_0 > 0$, $\mu_d \neq \mu_d(t)$, and $n = 1$;

      (5) Rheopetic fluid (e.g. gypsum suspension): $\tau_0 = 0$ & $\mu_d = \mu_d(t) > \mu_d(0)$, as $t > 0$;

      (6) Thixotropic fluid (e.g. gypsum suspension): $\tau_0 = 0$ & $\mu_d = \mu_d(t) < \mu_d(0)$, as $t > 0$.

Phenomena (2), (3), and (4) are non-Newtonian time-independent fluids, while phenomena (5) and (6) are non-Newtonian time-dependent fluids. Note that τ_0, μ, and n can be functions of temperature and pressure. One easy-to-use equation relating the viscosity to pressure (P) and temperature (T) for lubricants and hydraulic fluids is given as

$$\mu_d(P, T) = \mu_{d0}\, e^{\alpha_\mu(P - P_o)}\, e^{-\beta_\mu(T - T_o)}$$

$$= \mu_{d0}\, e^{\alpha_\mu(P - P_o) - \beta_\mu(T - T_o)} \qquad\qquad (137.2a)$$

$$\approx \mu_{d0}\, e^{\alpha_\mu P - \beta_\mu(T - T_o)} \qquad (\text{Elastohydrodynamic Lubrication}) \qquad (137.2b)$$

where:

$\mu_{d0}(\text{Pa} \cdot \text{s} = \text{N} \cdot \text{s/m}^2)$: Dynamic viscosity, at the reference temperature and ambient pressure;

α_μ: Pressure-viscosity coefficient, though it is an exponent;

β_μ: Temperature-viscosity coefficient, though it is an exponent;

T and T_o: Working and reference temperatures;

P and P_o: Working and reference pressure, as $P_o \ll P$ for elastohydrodynamic lubrication.

The reciprocal of dynamic viscosity is fluidity. For example, water at 20 ℃ has a dynamic viscosity of 1.002×10^{-3} Pa $\cdot$ s (= 1.002 MPa $\cdot$ s = 1.002 centipoise = 1.002 CP) and its fluidity is 998 Pa$^{-1} \cdot$ s^{-1}.

137.3   Kinematic Viscosity

As the density is a function of temperature independent of viscosity, it is sometimes more convenient to define the viscosity in a kinematic, called kinematic viscosity, as

$$\mu_k = \frac{\mu_d}{\rho} \tag{137.3}$$

where:

$\mu_k (m^2/s$ or $mm^2/s)$: Kinematic viscosity;

$\rho \ (kg/m^3)$: Density.

Water at 20 ℃ has a kinematic viscosity of 1 mm^2/s, i.e. $10^{-6} \ m^2/s$. The kinematic viscosity of a lubricant is quoted at 40 ℃ by ISO, with a viscosity index to identify its variation with respect to temperature change. For example, an oil quoted as conforming to ISO VG-320 will have a viscosity of 320 centistokes (i.e. cSt $\equiv mm^2/s$) at 40 ℃.

Assume that a lubricant has a specific gravity of ρ_1 (i.e. density = $\rho_1 \ g/cm^3$) and it has a kinematic viscosity of μ_{k1} centistoke, then the dynamic viscosity can be calculated as

$$\mu_{d1} = \mu_{k1}(mm^2/s) \times \rho_1(g/cm^3) = \mu_{k1}\rho_1[(mm^2/s) \times (g/cm^3)]$$

$$= \mu_{k1}\rho_1[(10^{-6} \ m/s) \times 10^{-3} \ kg/(10^{-6} \ m^3)]$$

$$= \mu_{k1}\rho_1[10^{-3} \ kg/m^2/s]$$

$$= \mu_{k1}\rho_1[10^{-3} \ kg/m^2/s]$$

$$= \mu_{k1}\rho_1[10^{-3} \ N \cdot s/m^2]$$

$$= \mu_{k1}\rho_1 \times 10^{-3} \ Pa \cdot s$$

Note that 1 N (Newton) = 1 $kg \cdot m/s^2$ and 1 Pa (Pascal) = N/m^2. Given that ρ_1 = 1.0 and μ_{k1} = 15 cSt, then μ_{d1} = 15 × 1.0 × 10^{-3} Pa · s = 15 × 10^{-3} Pa · s. The specific gravity of mineral oils is typically around 0.87 (g/cm^{-3}), while synthetic oils usually have a specific gravity around 1.2 (g/cm^{-3}).

137.4 Viscosity Versus Temperature Variation

Viscosity varies with respect to temperature variation nonlinearly. A high flash point (T_f) means good fire resistance and thermal stability, while a low pour point (T_p) means great pumpability and lubrication at low temperatures. VI (Viscosity Index) is a surrogate for many good characteristics of lubricants as a function of temperature variation.

137.4.1 Viscosity Index (VI)

Although the sensitivity of viscosity thinning on increasing temperature may be described mathematically by Eq. (137.2), traditionally VI (Viscosity Index) based on kinematic viscosity is used to denote the viscosity-temperature relation, defined as [ASTM D2270]

$$VI = \frac{\mu_{kL} - \mu_{kU}}{\mu_{kL} - \mu_{kH}} \times 100\% \qquad (137.4)$$

where:
$\mu_{kU}(\mathrm{mm^2/s})$: Kinematic viscosity at 40 ℃;
$\mu_{kL}(\mathrm{mm^2/s})$: Kinematic viscosity at 40 ℃ for oil of VI = 0 [ASTM D2270];
$\mu_{kH}(\mathrm{mm^2/s})$: Kinematic viscosity at 40 ℃ for oil of VI = 100 [ASTM D2270].

The smaller the value of the VI, the greater the change in viscosity in response to a temperature variation, and vice-versa. Lubricant viscosities are divided into four categories: Low (0~35), Medium (35~80), High (80~100), and Very High (> 100). PAO and PAG lubricants perform well at high operating temperatures than minerals. The viscosity index of synthetic oils ranges from 80 to over 400.

Although silicone lubricants come with a high viscosity index (e.g. VI = 320), they usually have a relatively weak temperature-viscosity relationship. The VI system suffers a major drawback in that it is undefined for lubricants with a kinematic viscosity less than 2cSt at 100 ℃, though it has been widely used.

137.4.2 Viscosity Number (VN)

Given the kinematic viscosities at 40 ℃ and 100 ℃ of a lubricant, the kinematic viscosity at these two temperatures can be substituted into the following regression model [Walther] [MaCabe].

$$\log\left[\log(\mu_k + 0.7)\right] = A + B \log(T) \qquad (137.5)$$

to solve for constant A and coefficient B, where μ_k is the kinematic viscosity and T the temperature. Once the coefficient B has been determined from the above equation the VN can be obtained using the equation

$$VN = 100 \left[1 + (3.55 + B) / 3.55 \right] \tag{137.6}$$

137.5　Automotive Powertrain Lubricants

The maximum and minimum viscosities of automotive transmission/differential oils are identified in SAE J306, as shown in Table 137.2. Cleanliness of lubricants can be classified using unwanted particle counts identified in ISO 4406, which shows code ranges pertaining to particle counts per 100 mL of fluid. Base oil types are classified into the following five categories by API (American Petroleum Institute):

Category (Base Oil)	Saturate (%wt)	Sulfur (%wt)	Visco. Index	Viscosity Range
I	Saturate<90%	or S > 0.03%	80 < VI<120	$10 \leqslant \mu_k \leqslant 1500$
II (High iso-paraffinic)	Saturate≥90%	& S≤0.03%	80≤VI≤120	$22 \leqslant \mu_k \leqslant 100$
III (High iso-paraffinic)	Saturate≥90%	& S≤0.03%	VI≥120	$22 \leqslant \mu_k \leqslant 68$
IV	PAO (Polyalphaolefin)	—	VI~140	$5 \leqslant \mu_k \leqslant 1000^+$
V (e.g. PAG)	Not included above	—	—	—

PAO base oils (Group IV) have the best thermal stability, oxidation stability, viscosity index, and other properties. Oxidation means a chemical reaction between the oil and oxygen, usually caused by heat, water and debris (e. g. wear metals). Thermal stability stands for resistance to forming deposits at high temperatures. The thermomechanical properties of commonly used engine oils for passenger vehicles and highway trucks are listed in Table 137.1.

137.5.1　Monograde Engine Oils

Monograde engine oils are designated by one number (5, 10, 20, 30, 40, 50, etc.), which designates the level of the oil viscosity at a specified temperature. The higher the grade number, the higher the oil viscosity. "W", as attached to the number, is used to designate its applicability at a low ambient temperature.

Aviation engine oils are ashless dispersant monograde oils (e.g. SAE 50 and SAE 60 with specialty additives) specifically developed for aviation piston engines.

Maine diesel engine oils (e.g. SAE 30, SAE 40, and SAE 50) have high TBN levels with enhanced detergency and disperse capability in order to reduce deposits especially in the ring belt area- preventing corrosive wear due to higher sulphur fuels.

137.5.2 Multigrade Engine Oils

Multigrade engine oils are designated by two temperature levels, at which the oil viscosity is specified such as SAE 5W30 (for sedans) and 15W40 (for highway trucks). Such an engine oil is called multigrade, used in a wide temperature range. The first number specifies the oil viscosity at the cold temperature, while the second number specifies the oil viscosity at the high temperature. SAE 5W30 oil has a low-temperature viscosity similar to that of SAE 5W, but it has a high-temperature viscosity similar to that of SAE 30.

The fuel consumption of a diesel engine using multigrade engine oils is better than its corresponding monograde viscosity oil, as tested under various loading conditions by [De Carvalhoa et al.]. By the same test, it was shown that the specific fuel consumption can be correlated linearly to the "high shear viscosity" at the high temperature.

SAE Grade 15W-40 (Table 137.1) has been a popular engine oil for heavy-duty diesel engines. The properties of the engine oil can be interpreted as:

(a) 15W: This oil will have a cranking viscosity no greater than 7 Pa · s in a cold engine crankcase at -20 ℃. Even if its temperature should drop to -25 ℃ at night, the pumping viscosity should be less than 60 Pa · s. Note that "W" means winter.
(b) 40: The engine oil has a kinematic viscosity in the range 12.5~16.3 mm^2/s at 100 ℃ (near the high operating temperature of engine oil) and a high-shear dynamic viscosity no less than 3.7×10^{-3} Pa · s at 150 ℃ (near the point of overheating) in the high pressurized parts of an engine.

137.6 Transmission/Transaxle Fluids

Automatic transmission fluid (ATF) has multi-functional requirements to meet during service. It operates the hydraulics, lubricates the moving parts, dissipates heat through the transmission cooler, and acts as the fluid medium for the torque converter. Hydraulic fluid is used as automatic transmission fluid in most automatic transmission systems. Automatic transmission fluid typically operates at higher temperatures than general gear oils typically, and thus more viscous. The transmission fluid is dissipated into the engine's coolant through a heat exchanger. The thermomechanical properties of lubricants for automotive transmissions and axles are listed in Table 137.2.

Many final drive (transaxle) fluids are silicone-based gear oils, which feature superior heat dissipation to accommodate high temperatures. The typical operating temperature for a roller bearing assembly (gear flank, bearing ring, and rollers) is about 80 ℃.

137.7   Surface Tension and Oiliness

The surface tension of a fluid is defined as the strength of the attractive mechanism formed between the surface molecules of the liquid. In general, the fluid of low specific gravity exhibits low surface tension. The surface tension of a lubricant, in combination with its viscosity, affects the spread rate of the lubricant over water or a solid surface. The lower the surface tension is, the greater its spread rate is. The surface tension decreases with increasing temperature.

Oiliness is the property of an oil (lubricant) to spread and attach itself firmly with the bearing surfaces. Oiliness of a lubricating oil ought to be high for better lubrication.

137.8   Key Temperature Parameters

137.8.1   Critical Temperature, Critical pressure, and Super Critical Fluid

The highest temperature and pressure along the liquid-vapor equilibrium line, at which the substance can exist as a vapor and liquid in equilibrium, are called the critical temperature and critical pressure, respectively. A Super Critical Fluid (SCF) is defined as a substance above its critical temperature (T_C) and critical pressure (P_C).

When the temperature and pressure reach a point, at which the substance can exist as a vapour, liquid, and solid in equilibrium, it is called the triple point.

137.8.2   Ignition

The flash point (T_f) is the minimum temperature, at which the lubricant (oil) gives off enough vapor so that a momentary flame is obtained in the presence of a naked flame. The fire point is the minimum temperature, at which an oil continuously burns. The fire point is always higher than the flash point. The flash point of the lubricating oil should be significantly higher than the operating temperature of the bearing.

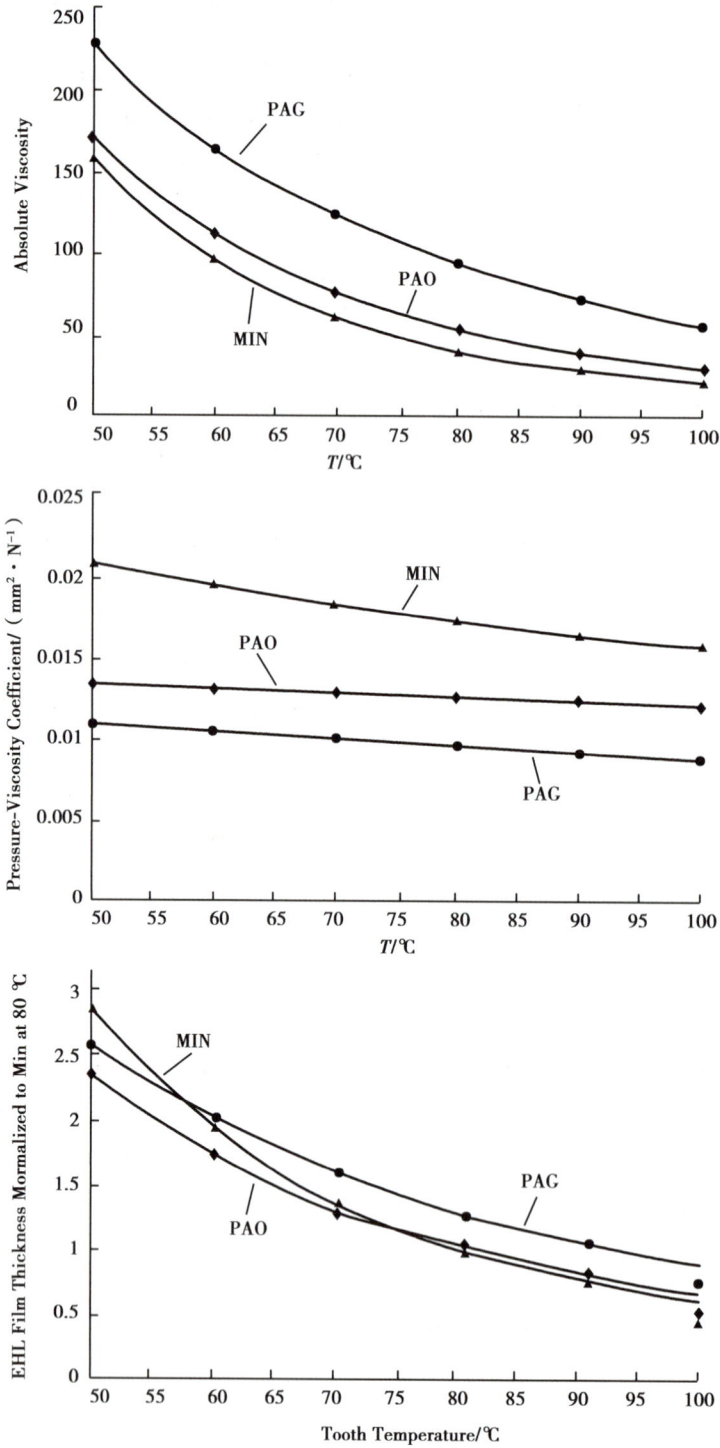

T/℃	Mineral	Synthetic PAO	Synthetic PAG
50	2.84345	2.34348	2.57309
60	1.92036	1.71324	1.99154
70	1.35868	1.29388	1.57558
80	1.00000	1.00496	1.27097
90	0.76114	0.79986	1.04306
100	0.59620	0.65022	0.86916

137.9 Effect of Water in Lubricants

When the amount of water dissolved in a lubricant exceeds the saturation point, the lubricant is no longer able to absorb more water molecules, resulting in emulsified water. The phenomenon is characterized by a hazy appearance of the oil and furthermore forming separate levels between oil and "free water". This emulsified water results in higher viscosity, reduced load-carrying ability, corrosion on metal surfaces, part wear, cavitation, and filter plugging.

137.10 Wear Reduction

Friction modifiers are additives that reduce friction by increasing the adhesive film strength to avoid surface to surface contact. In other words, these additives provide a cushioning effect and keep metal surfaces apart from each other.

137.11 Foaming Prevention

Agitation and aeration during operation can generate foam in the lubricant. Foaming slows down flow rate and heat transfer, as well as increases oxidation. Foam inhibitors, such as long-chain silicone polymers (0.05% ~ 0.5% by weight), may be added to the lubricant to reduce the surface tension between the air and liquid to the point where bubbles collapse.

137.12 Thermal Conductivity

Excessive water content leads to insufficient lubrication and subsequently to abrasive wear and corrosion in the case of lubrication oil, while increased water content results in a considerable reduction of the breakdown voltage the case of insulation oils (e.g. transformer oil). That water ($k = 0.6$ W/m/℃) contamination in mineral oil ($k = 0.14$ W/m/℃) can lead to an increased thermal conductivity. It indicates the potential application of thermal conductivity sensors in the field of oil conditions as a preventive action [Kuntner et al.].

References

ASTM D2270. 2010. Standard Practice for Calculating Viscosity Index from Kinematic Viscosity at 40 and 100 ℃[S]. ASTM International, Conshohocken, PA, USA.

AGMA, 2003. Effect of Lubrication on Gear Surface Distress[S]. AGMA 925-A03 Information Sheet.

AGMA/ANSI 9005 – E02 (2002. Industrial Gear Lubrication[S]. American Gear Manufacturers Association, Alexandria, VA, USA.

BAIR S, KOTTEKE P, 2003. Pressure-Viscosity Relationships for Elastohydrodynamcs [J]. Tribology Transactions, 46(3): 289-295.

BAIR S, et al, 2001. The Temperature, Pressure and Time Dependence of Lubricant Viscosity[J]. Tribology International, 34(7): 461-468.

BRENDAN, CASEY, 2011. Hydraulic Oil Can Make a Major Difference to Power Consumption[J]. Machinery Lubrication.

CERNY J, STRNAD Z, SEBOR G, 2001. Composition and oxidation stability of SAE 15W-40 engine oils[J]. Tribology International, 34(2): 127-134.

DECARVALHOA M J S, et al, 2010. Lubricant Viscosity and Viscosity Improver Additive Effects on Diesel Fuel Economy[J]. Tribology International, 43(12): 2298-2302.

HSIAO H, SHARMA S, HAMROCK B, 1992. Pressure-Temperature-Viscosity and Elastohydrodynamic Characteristics of Two Perfluoropolyalkylether Fluids[J]. SAE 922344.

ISO 3448:1992, 1992. Industrial Liquid Lubricants- ISO Viscosity Classification[S]. International Organization for Standardization, Geneva.

JANNA W S, 1993. Introduction to Fluid Mechanics[J]. PWS-KENT Publishing Company, Boston, MA, USA.

KEMP S, LINDEN J, 1990. Physical and Chemical Properties of a Typical Automatic Transmission Fluid[J]. SAE Technical Paper Series, 22-25.

KUNTNER J, et al, 2005. Oil Condition Monitoring Using a Thermal Conductivity Sensor[J]. Proceedings of the GMe Forum 2005, 203-209.

LISTON T V, 1992. Engine Lubricant Additives. What They Are and How They Function? [J]. Lubrication Engineering, 48(5): 389-397.

MACABE C, et al, 2001. Characterizing the Viscosity-Temperature Dependence of Lubricants by Molecular Simulation[J]. Fluid Phase Equilibria, 183(4): 363-370.

OWRANG F, MATTSSON H, OLSSON J, et al, 2004. Investigation of Oxidation of a Mineral and a Synthetic Engine Oil[J]. Thermochim Acta, 413(1-2): 241-248.

RUDNICK L, 2006. Synthetics, Mineral Oils and Bio-based Lubricants[M]. CRC Press, NY.

SAE J300, 2009. Engine Oil Viscosity Classification[S]. Society of Automotive Engineers, Warrendale, PA, USA.

SAE J306, 2005. Automotive Gear Lubricant Viscosity Classification[S]. Society of Automotive Engineers, Warrendale, PA, USA.

STACHOWIAK G W, BACHELOR A W, 2001. Engineering Tribology [M]. 2nd Edition, Butterworth-Heinemann, Boston.

TOTTEN G, 2003. Fuels and Lubricants Handbook[M]. ASTM International.

VAN D W, KLEIJWEGT P, TORREMAN M, et al, 2009. The Lubricant Contribution to Improved Fuel Economy in Heavy Duty Diesel Engines[J]. SAE 2009-01-2856.

Table 137.1 Typical Thermomechanical Characteristics of Engine Oils [SAE J300]

Material	$T/°C$	ρ	$\mu_d/(Pa \cdot s)$	α_μ	β_μ	α_v	k	γ	$k_\rho \times 10^3$	e_s
Monogrades for Low Ambient Temperatures:										
SAE 0W	−40	—	< 60 (Pumping)	—	—	—	—	—	—	—
	−35	—	< 6.2 (Cranking)	—	—	—	—	—	—	—
	40	ρ	$> 3.8 \times 10^{-3} \rho$	—	—	—	—	—	—	—
SAE 5W	−35	—	< 60 (Pumping)	—	—	—	—	—	—	—
	−30	—	< 6.6 (Cranking)	—	—	—	—	—	—	—
	40	ρ	$> 3.8 \times 10^{-3} \rho$	—	—	—	—	—	—	—
SAE 10W	−30	—	< 60 (Pumping)	—	—	—	—	—	—	—
	−25	—	< 7 (Cranking)	—	—	—	—	—	—	—
	−17.8	—	< 1.295	—	—	—	—	—	—	—
	40	ρ	$> 4.1 \times 10^{-3} \rho$	—	—	—	—	—	—	—
SAE 15W	−25	—	< 60 (Pumping)	—	—	—	—	—	—	—
	−20	—	< 7 (Cranking)	—	—	—	—	—	—	—
	−17.8	ρ	$1.3 \times 10^{-3} \rho < \mu_d$ $< 2.59 \times 10^{-3} \rho$	—	—	—	—	—	—	—
	40	ρ	$> 5.6 \times 10^{-3} \rho$	—	—	—	—	—	—	—
SAE 20W	20	—	< 60 (Pumping)	—	—	—	—	—	—	—
	−15	—	< 9.5 (Cranking)	—	—	—	—	—	—	—
	40	ρ	$> 5.6 \times 10^{-3} \rho$	—	—	—	—	—	—	—

continued

Material	$T/°C$	ρ	$\mu_d/(\text{Pa}\cdot\text{s})$	α_μ	β_μ	α_v	k	γ	$k_\rho\times10^3$	e_s
SAE 25W	−15	—	< 60 (Pumping)	—	—	—	—	—	—	—
	−10	—	< 13 (Cranking)	—	—	—	—	—	—	—
	40	ρ	$>9.3\times10^{-3}\rho$	—	—	—	—	—	—	—
Monogrades for High Ambient Temperatures:										
SAE 10	20	0.87	65×10^{-3}	—	—	—	—	—	—	—
SAE 20	20	0.88	—	—	—	—	—	—	—	—
	100	ρ	$5.6\times10^{-3}\rho< \mu_d$ $< 9.3\times10^{-3}\rho$	—	—	—	—	—	—	—
	150	—	$> 2.6\times10^{-3}$(HS)	—	—	—	—	—	—	—
SAE 30	20	—	—	—	—	—	—	—	—	—
	100	ρ	$9.3\times10^{-3}\rho < \mu_d$ $< 12.5\times10^{-3}\rho$	—	—	—	—	—	—	—
	150	—	$> 2.9\times10^{-3}$(HS)	—	—	—	—	—	—	—
SAE 30 (Xcel Marine; VI = 100)	−15 (T_p)	—	—	—	—	—	—	—	—	—
	40	ρ	$102\times10^{-3}\rho$	—	—	—	—	—	—	—
	100	ρ	$11.5\times10^{-3}\rho$	—	—	—	—	—	—	—
	210 (T_f)	—	—	—	—	—	—	—	—	—
SAE 40	20	0.88	319×10^{-3}	—	—	—	—	—	—	—
	100	ρ	$12.5\times10^{-3}\rho <\mu_d$ $< 16.3\times10^{-3}\rho$	—	—	—	—	—	—	—
	150	—	$> 3.7\times10^{-3}$(HS)	—	—	—	—	—	—	—
SAE 40 (Xcel Marine; VI = 100)	−12 (T_p)	—	—	—	—	—	—	—	—	—
	40	ρ	$140\times10^{-3}\rho$	—	—	—	—	—	—	—
	100	ρ	$14.5\times10^{-3}\rho$	—	—	—	—	—	—	—
	220 (T_f)	—	—	—	—	—	—	—	—	—
SAE 50	23	0.88	—	—	—	—	—	—	—	—
	100	ρ	$16.3\times10^{-3}\rho <\mu_d$ $< 21.9\times10^{-3}\rho$	—	—	—	—	—	—	—
	150	—	$> 3.7\times10^{-3}$(HS)	—	—	—	—	—	—	—
SAE 50 (Xcel Aviation; VI = 100)	−45 (T_p)	—	—	—	—	—	—	—	—	—
	40	ρ	$185\times10^{-3}\rho$	—	—	—	—	—	—	—
	100	ρ	$17.5\times10^{-3}\rho$	—	—	—	—	—	—	—
	280 (T_f)	—	—	—	—	—	—	—	—	—

continued

Material	$T/°C$	ρ	$\mu_d/(\text{Pa}\cdot\text{s})$	α_μ	β_μ	α_v	k	γ	$k_\rho\times10^3$	e_s
SAE 50 (Xcel Marine; VI = 100)	-12 (T_p)	—	—	—	—	—	—	—	—	—
	40	ρ	$190\times10^{-3}\rho$	—	—	—	—	—	—	—
	100	ρ	$18\times10^{-3}\rho$	—	—	—	—	—	—	—
	230 (T_f)	—	—	—	—	—	—	—	—	—
SAE 60	23	—	—	—	—	—	—	—	—	—
	100	ρ	$21.9\times10^{-3}\rho<\mu_d<26.1\times10^{-3}\rho$	—	—	—	—	—	—	—
	150	—	$>3.7\times10^{-3}(\text{HS})$	—	—	—	—	—	—	—
SAE 60 (Xcel Aviation; VI = 100)	-45 (T_p)	—	—	—	—	—	—	—	—	—
	40	ρ	$300\times10^{-3}\rho$	—	—	—	—	—	—	—
	100	ρ	$24\times10^{-3}\rho$	—	—	—	—	—	—	—
	295 (T_f)	—	—	—	—	—	—	—	—	—

Multigrades:

Material	$T/°C$	ρ	$\mu_d/(\text{Pa}\cdot\text{s})$	α_μ	β_μ	α_v	k	γ	$k_\rho\times10^3$	e_s
SAE 0W-20 (Mineral; SAE J300)	15.6	0.85	—	—	—	—	—	—	—	—
	40	0.84	36.4×10^{-3}	—	—	—	—	—	—	—
	100	ρ	$5.6\times10^{-3}\rho<\mu_d<9.3\times10^{-3}\rho$	—	—	—	—	—	—	—
	150	—	$>2.6\times10^{-3}(\text{HS})$	—	—	—	—	—	—	—
SAE 0W-30 (Viscopedia)	0	0.863	475×10^{-3}	—	—	—	—	—	—	—
	20	0.85	142×10^{-3}	—	—	—	—	—	—	—
	40	0.837	56×10^{-3}	—	—	—	—	—	—	—
	60	0.825	27×10^{-3}	—	—	—	—	—	—	—
	80	0.812	15.1×10^{-3}	—	—	—	—	—	—	—
	100	0.799	9.35×10^{-3}	—	—	—	—	—	—	—
SAE 0W-30 (Penn Grade 1; Typical data; VI = 170)	-48 (T_p)	—	—	—	—	—	—	—	—	—
	-40	—	20.6 (Pumping)	—	—	—	—	—	—	—
	-35	—	6 (Cranking)	—	—	—	—	—	—	—
	40	0.845	$63.5\times10^{-3}\rho$	—	—	—	—	—	—	—
	100	—	$11\times10^{-3}\rho$	—	—	—	—	—	—	—
	150	—	$3.38\times10^{-3}(\text{HS})$	—	—	—	—	—	—	—
	196 (T_f)	—	—	—	—	—	—	—	—	—
SAE 0W-40 (Mineral)	15.6	—	—	—	—	—	—	—	—	—
	40	—	—	—	—	—	—	—	—	—
	150	—	$>2.9\times10^{-3}(\text{HS})$	—	—	—	—	—	—	—

continued

Material	$T/°C$	ρ	$\mu_d/(\text{Pa} \cdot \text{s})$	α_μ	β_μ	α_v	k	γ	$k_\rho \times 10^3$	e_s
SAE 0W-60 (Synthetic; NASA)	40	—	—	—	—	—	—	—	—	—
SAE 5W-20 (Mineral)	−40 (T_p)	—	—	—	—	—	—	—	—	—
	15.6	0.85	—	—	—	—	—	—	—	—
	40	0.841	38×10^{-3}	—	—	—	—	—	—	—
	100	ρ	$5.6 \times 10^{-3}\rho < \mu_d < 9.3 \times 10^{-3}\rho$	—	—	—	—	—	—	—
	150	—	$> 2.6 \times 10^{-3}$ (HS)	—	—	—	—	—	—	—
	214 (T_f)	—	—	—	—	—	—	—	—	—
SAE 5W-30 (Mineral)	−36 (T_p)	—	—	—	—	—	—	—	—	—
	−35	—	<60 (Pumping)	—	—	—	—	—	—	—
	−30	—	<6.6 (Cranking)	—	—	—	—	—	—	—
	15.6	0.86	—	—	—	—	—	—	—	—
	40	0.846	53.4×10^{-3}	0.016	0.042	734	0.126	2000	—	—
	100	ρ	$9.3 \times 10^{-3}\rho < \mu_d < 12.5 \times 10^{-3}\rho$	—	—	—	—	—	—	—
	150	—	$> 2.9 \times 10^{-3}$ (HS)	—	—	—	—	—	—	—
	220 (T_f)	—	—	—	—	—	—	—	—	—
SAE 5W-30 (Synthetic)	−46 (T_p)	—	—	—	—	—	—	—	—	—
	−35	—	< 60 (Pumping)	—	—	—	—	—	—	—
	−30	—	< 6.6 (Cranking)	—	—	—	—	—	—	—
	15.6	0.865	—	—	—	—	—	—	—	—
	40	0.86	48.7×10^{-3}	—	—	—	—	—	—	—
	100	0.84	$9.3 \times 10^{-3}\rho < \mu_d < 12.5 \times 10^{-3}\rho$	—	—	—	—	—	—	—
	150	—	$> 2.9 \times 10^{-3}$ (HS)	—	—	—	—	—	—	—
	218 (T_f)	—	—	—	—	—	—	—	—	—
SAE 5W-30 (Penn Grade 1; Typical data; VI = 161)	−42 (T_p)	—	—	—	—	—	—	—	—	—
	−35	—	24 (Pumping)	—	—	—	—	—	—	—
	−30	—	6.2 (Cranking)	—	—	—	—	—	—	—
	40	0.858	$65.6 \times 10^{-3}\rho$	—	—	—	—	—	—	—
	100	—	$11.1 \times 10^{-3}\rho$	—	—	—	—	—	—	—
	150	—	3.2×10^{-3} (HS)	—	—	—	—	—	—	—
	202 (T_f)	—	—	—	—	—	—	—	—	—

continued

Material	$T/℃$	ρ	$\mu_d/(\mathrm{Pa \cdot s})$	α_μ	β_μ	α_v	k	γ	$k_p \times 10^3$	e_s
SAE 5W-40 (Synthetic or Blend)	-35	—	<60 (Pumping)	—	—	—	—	—	—	—
	-30	—	<6.6 (Cranking)	—	—	—	—	—	—	—
	15.6	0.87	—	—	—	—	—	—	—	—
	100	ρ	$12.5\times10^{-3}\rho < \mu_d < 16.3\times10^{-3}\rho$	—	—	—	—	—	—	—
	150	—	$> 2.9\times10^{-3}$ (HS)	—	—	—	—	—	—	—
SAE 5W-40 (Viscopedia)	0	0.867	753.5×10^{-3}	—	—	—	—	—	—	—
	20	0.855	207×10^{-3}	—	—	—	—	—	—	—
	40	0.842	76.6×10^{-3}	—	—	—	—	—	—	—
	60	0.83	35.4×10^{-3}	—	—	—	—	—	—	—
	80	0.817	19.2×10^{-3}	—	—	—	—	—	—	—
	100	0.805	11.6×10^{-3}	—	—	—	—	—	—	—
SAE 5W-50 (Synthetic)	-46 (T_p)	—	—	—	—	—	—	—	—	—
	-35	—	< 60 (Pumping)	—	—	—	—	—	—	—
	-30	—	< 6.6 (Cranking)	—	—	—	—	—	—	—
	15.6	0.911	—	—	—	—	—	—	—	—
	40	0.845	112.4×10^{-3}	—	—	—	—	—	—	—
	100	ρ	$16.3\times10^{-3}\rho < \mu_d < 21.9\times10^{-3}\rho$	—	—	—	—	—	—	—
	238 (T_f)	—	—	—	—	—	—	—	—	—
SAE 10W-30 (Mineral)	-33 (T_p)	—	—	—	—	—	—	—	—	—
	-30	—	< 60 (Pimping)	—	—	—	—	—	—	—
	-25	—	< 7 (Cranking)	—	—	—	—	—	—	—
	15.6	0.875	—	—	—	—	—	—	—	—
	40	0.865	57×10^{-3}	—	—	—	k	—	$k_p\times10^3$	—
	100	ρ	$9.3\times10^{-3}\rho < \mu_d < 12.5\times10^{-3}\rho$	—	—	—	—	—	—	—
	150	—	$> 2.9\times10^{-3}$ (HS)	—	—	—	—	—	—	—
	210 (T_f)	—	—	—	—	—	—	—	—	—
SAE 10W-30 (Penn Grade 1: Typical data; VI = 138; Partial synthetic)	-33 (T_p)	—	—	—	—	—	—	—	—	—
	-30	—	26.7 (Pumping)	—	—	—	—	—	—	—
	-25	—	6.5 (Cranking)	—	—	—	—	—	—	—
	40	0.875	$68.6\times10^{-3}\rho$	—	—	—	—	—	—	—
	100	—	$10.8\times10^{-3}\rho$	—	—	—	—	—	—	—
	150	—	3.54×10^{-3} (HS)	—	—	—	—	—	—	—
	204 (T_f)	—	—	—	—	—	—	—	—	—

continued

Material	$T/°C$	ρ	$\mu_d/(\text{Pa}\cdot\text{s})$	α_μ	β_μ	α_v	k	γ	$k_\rho\times10^3$	e_s
SAE 10W-40 (SAE J300)	$-33\ (T_p)$	—	—	—	—	—	—	—	—	—
	-30	—	< 60 (Pumping)	—	—	—	—	—	—	—
	-25	—	<7 (Cranking)	—	—	—	—	—	—	—
	40	0.851	79.3×10^{-3}	—	—	—	—	—	—	—
	100	0.813	$12.5\times10^{-3}\rho<\mu_d$ $<16.3\times10^{-3}\rho$	—						
	150	—	$>2.9\times10^{-3}$(HS)	—	—	—	—	—	—	—
	$220\ (T_f)$	—	—	—	—	—	—	—	—	—
SAE 10W-40 (Viscopedia)	0	0.876	735.4×10^{-3}	—	—	—	—	—	—	—
	20	0.863	208.9×10^{-3}	—	—	—	—	—	—	—
	40	0.851	79.3×10^{-3}	—	—	—	—	—	—	—
	60	0.838	36.1×10^{-3}	—	—	—	—	—	—	—
	80	0.824	19.7×10^{-3}	—	—	—	—	—	—	—
	100	0.813	12.7	—	—	—	—	—	—	—
SAE 10W-40 (Penn Grade 1: Typical data; VI = 154; Partial synthetic)	$-33\ (T_p)$	—	—	—	—	—	—	—	—	—
	-30	—	28.15 (Pumping)	—	—	—	—	—	—	—
	-25	—	6.3 (Cranking)	—	—	—	—	—	—	—
	40	—	$109\times10^{-3}\rho$	—	—	—	—	—	—	—
	100	—	$15.6\times10^{-3}\rho$	—	—	—	—	—	—	—
	150	—	4.23×10^{-3}(HS)	—	—	—	—	—	—	—
	$204\ (T_f)$	—	—	—	—	—	—	—	—	—
SAE 10W-60 (Viscopedia)	0	0.863	1.454	—	—	—	—	—	—	—
	20	0.85	381.1×10^{-3}	—	—	—	—	—	—	—
	40	0.838	135.5×10^{-3}	—	—	—	—	—	—	—
	60	0.826	60.6×10^{-3}	—	—	—	k	γ	—	e_s
	80	0.813	31.95×10^{-3}	—	—	—	—	—	—	—
	100	0.801	19×10^{-3}	—	—	—	—	—	—	—
SAE 15W-40 (SAE J300)	-25	—	<60 (Pumping)	—	—	—	—	—	—	—
	-20	—	<7.0 (Cranking)	—	—	—	—	—	—	—
	40	0.866	91.1×10^{-3}	—	—	—	—	—	—	—
	100	ρ	$12.5\times10^{-3}\rho<\mu_d$ $<16.3\times10^{-3}\rho$	—						
	150	—	$>3.7\times10^{-3}$(HS)	—	—	—	—	—	—	—

continued

Material	$T/℃$	ρ	$\mu_d/(\text{Pa}\cdot\text{s})$	α_μ	β_μ	α_v	k	γ	$k_\rho\times10^3$	e_s
SAE 15W-40 (SAE J300; Viscopedia)	0	0.892	1.328	—	—	—	—	—	—	—
	10	0.885	583×10^{-3}	—	—	—	—	—	—	—
	20	0.879	287×10^{-3}	—	—	—	—	—	—	—
	40	0.866	91.1×10^{-3}	—	—	—	—	—	—	—
	60	0.854	38.11×10^{-3}	—	—	—	—	—	—	—
	67	—	53×10^{-3}	—	—	700	0.139	2080	—	—
	80	0.841	19.4×10^{-3}	—	—	—	—	—	—	—
	100	0.829	11.3×10^{-3}	—	—	—	—	—	—	—
	127	—	9×10^{-3}	—	—	700	0.134	2340	—	—
	150	—	$>3.7\times10^{-3}(\text{HS})$	—	—	—	—	—	—	—
SAE 15W-40 (Penn Grade 1; Typical data; VI = 145; Partial synthetic)	$-42\ (T_p)$	—	—	—	—	—	—	—	—	—
	-30	—	28.15 (Pumping)	—	—	—	—	—	—	—
	-25	—	6.3 (Cranking)	—	—	—	—	—	—	—
	40	0.877	$113\times10^{-3}\rho$	—	—	—	—	—	—	—
	100	—	$15.5\times10^{-3}\rho$	—	—	—	—	—	—	—
	150	—	$4.52\times10^{-3}(\text{HS})$	—	—	—	—	—	—	—
	$204\ (T_f)$	—	—	—	—	—	—	—	—	—
SAE 20W-40	-20	—	<60 (Pumping)	—	—	—	—	—	—	—
	-15	—	<9.5 (Cranking)	—	—	—	—	—	—	—
	23	—	—	—	—	—	—	—	—	—
	100	ρ	$12.5\times10^{-3}\rho<\mu_d<16.3\times10^{-3}\rho$	—	—	—	—	—	—	—
	150	—	$>3.7\times10^{-3}(\text{HS})$	—	—	—	—	—	—	—
SAE 20W-40 (Xcel Railroad; VI = 120)	$-36\ (T_p)$	—	—	—	—	—	—	—	—	—
	40	ρ	$100\times10^{-3}\rho$	—	—	—	—	—	—	—
	100	ρ	$15.25\times10^{-3}\rho$	—	—	—	—	—	—	—
	$210\ (T_f)$	—	—	—	—	—	—	—	—	—
SAE 20W-50	-20	—	<60 (Pumping)	—	—	—	—	—	—	—
	-15	—	<9.5 (Cranking)	—	—	—	—	—	—	—
	40	0.872	144.8×10^{-3}	—	—	—	—	—	—	—
	100	ρ	$16.3\times10^{-3}\rho<\mu_d<21.9\times10^{-3}\rho$	—	—	—	—	—	—	—
	150	—	$>3.7\times10^{-3}(\text{HS})$	—	—	—	—	—	—	—

continued

Material	$T/°C$	ρ	$\mu_d/(Pa \cdot s)$	α_μ	β_μ	α_v	k	γ	$k_\rho \times 10^3$	e_s
SAE 20W-50 (Penn Grade 1: Typical data; VI = 140; Partial synthetic)	-27 (T_p)	—	—	—	—	—	—	—	—	—
	-20	—	35.7 (Pumping)	—	—	—	—	—	—	—
	-15	—	4.6 (Cranking)	—	—	—	—	—	—	—
	40	0.88	$159 \times 10^{-3}\rho$	—	—	—	—	—	—	—
	100	—	$20 \times 10^{-3}\rho$	—	—	—	—	—	—	—
	150	—	6.2×10^{-3} (HS)	—	—	—	—	—	—	—
	216 (T_f)	—	—	—	—	—	—	—	—	—
SAE 25W-40	-15	—	< 60 (Pumping)	—	—	—	—	—	—	—
	-10	—	< 13 (Cranking)	—	—	—	—	—	—	—
	23	—	—	—	—	—	—	—	—	—
	100	ρ	$12.5 \times 10^{-3}\rho < \mu_d < 16.3 \times 10^{-3}\rho$	—	—	—	—	—	—	—
	150	—	$> 3.7 \times 10^{-3}$ (HS)	—	—	—	—	—	—	—

Notes: W = Winter;

γ (J/kg/°C) = Specific heat capacity at 0.1 MPa (100 kPa) constant pressure;

μ_d(Pa $\cdot$ s) = Dynamic viscosity as averaged at the ambient pressure;

α_μ(MPa^{-1}) = Pressure-dynamic viscosity coefficient, Eq. (137.2);

β_μ(°C^{-1}) = Temperature-dynamic viscosity coefficient, Eq. (137.2);

α_v(mm^3/m^3/°C) = Coefficient of volumetric thermal expansion;

Cranking = Low-temperature cranking;

Pumping = Low-temperature pumping;

(HS) = High temperature (150 °C here) high shear.

Table 137.2   Typical Thermomechanical Characteristics of Axle, Manual Transmission, and other Gear Lubricants [SAE J306] [ASTM D2983] [ASTM D445]

Material	$T/°C$	ρ	$\mu_d/(Pa \cdot s)$	α_μ	β_μ	α_v	k	γ	$k_\rho \times 10^3$	e_s
Monogrades for Low Ambient Temperatures:										
SAE 70W	-55	—	< 150	—	—	—	—	—	—	—
	100	ρ	$> 4.1 \times 10^{-3}\rho$	—	—	—	—	—	—	—
SAE 75W	-40	—	< 150	—	—	—	—	—	—	—
	100	ρ	$> 4.1 \times 10^{-3}\rho$	—	—	—	—	—	—	—
SAE 80W	-26	—	<150	—	—	—	—	—	—	—
	100	ρ	$> 7 \times 10^{-3}\rho$	—	—	—	—	—	—	—
SAE 85W	-12	—	< 150	—	—	—	—	—	—	—
	100	ρ	$> 11 \times 10^{-3}\rho$	—	—	—	—	—	—	—

continued

Material	$T/°C$	ρ	$\mu_d/(\text{Pa}\cdot\text{s})$	α_μ	β_μ	α_v	k	γ	$k_p\times10^3$	e_s
SAE 30 (Viscopedia)	0	0.894	1.124	—	—	—	—	—	—	—
	20	0.882	239.4×10^{-3}	—	—	—	—	—	—	—
	40	0.869	74.6×10^{-3}	—	—	—	—	—	—	—
	60	0.857	30.6×10^{-3}	—	—	—	—	—	—	—
	80	0.844	15.3×10^{-3}	—	—	—	—	—	—	—
	100	0.832	8.8×10^{-3}	—	—	—	—	—	—	—
SAE 80	100	ρ	$7\times10^{-3}\rho < \mu_d < 11\times10^{-3}\rho$	—	—	—	—	—	—	—
SAE 85	100	ρ	$11\times10^{-3}\rho < \mu_d < 13.5\times10^{-3}\rho$	—	—	—	—	—	—	—
SAE 90	100	ρ	$13.5\times10^{-3}\rho < \mu_d < 18.5\times10^{-3}\rho$	—	—	—	—	—	—	—
SAE 110	100	ρ	$18.5\times10^{-3}\rho < \mu_d < 24\times10^{-3}\rho$	—	—	—	—	—	—	—
SAE 140	100	ρ	$24\times10^{-3}\rho < \mu_d < 32.5\times10^{-3}\rho$	—	—	—	—	—	—	—
SAE 190	100	ρ	$32.5\times10^{-3}\rho < \mu_d < 41\times10^{-3}\rho$	—	—	—	—	—	—	—
SAE 250	100	ρ	$> 41\times10^{-3}\rho$	—	—	—	—	—	—	—

Multigrades:

Material	$T/°C$	ρ	$\mu_d/(\text{Pa}\cdot\text{s})$	α_μ	β_μ	α_v	k	γ	$k_p\times10^3$	e_s
SAE 75W-90 (Synthetic PAO)	$-42\ (T_p)$	—	—	—	—	—	—	—	—	—
	15.6	0.887	—	—	—	—	—	—	—	—
	40	—	97×10^{-3}	—	—	—	0.152	1740	—	—
	100	—	17×10^{-3}	—	—	—	0.14	1900	—	—
	200	—	—	—	—	—	0.119	2200	—	—
	$195\ (T_f)$	—	—	—	—	—	—	—	—	—
SAE 80W-90	$-27\ (T_p)$	—	—	—	—	—	—	—	—	—
	15.6	0.887	—	—	—	—	—	—	—	—
	40	—	120×10^{-3}	—	—	—	—	—	—	—
	100	—	13×10^{-3}	—	—	—	—	—	—	—
	$218\ (T_f)$	—	—	—	—	—	—	—	—	—

continued

Material	$T/℃$	ρ	$\mu_d/(\text{Pa} \cdot \text{s})$	α_μ	β_μ	α_v	k	γ	$k_p \times 10^3$	e_s
SAE 85W-140	−12 (T_p)	—	—	—	—	—	—	—	—	
	15.6	0.901	—	—	—	—	—	—	—	—
	40	—	366×10^{-3}	—	—	—	—	—	—	—
	100	—	27×10^{-3}	—	—	—	—	—	—	—
	200 (T_f)	—	—	—	—	—	—	—	—	—

Note: SAE 5 W, 10 W, 75 W, 80 W and 85 W viscosities are specified at the corresponding low-temperatures application, while ISO and AGMA viscosities are specified at 40 ℃.

Chapter 138

Hydraulic Fluids

138.1   Introduction

The functional requirement of hydraulic fluids is to convey power. The technical demand placed on hydraulic systems becomes more and more stringent as the automotive industry requires greater operating efficiency and speed at high temperatures and pressures than most industrial applications. Special characteristics of such hydraulic fluids must adhere to the following:

(a) Incompressibility;

(b) Rapid air release;

(c) High water rejection;

(d) Negligible volatility;

(e) Low tendency of foaming;

(f) No chemical corrosiveness;

(g) Retarding fire and flash tendency.

Nominal thermomechanical characteristics of hydraulic fluids for industrial gear fluids and compressor oils are listed in Table 138.1. The four principal categories of hydraulic fluids are:

(a) Minerals: General Applications;

(b) Polyalphaolefins (PAO): Fire-resistant;

(c) Organophosphate Esters: Fire-resistant;

(d) PAG: Fire-resistant, wear-resistant, thermo-oxidative stability.

Approximately 85% of hydraulic oils are made from minerals. Others are environment-friendly bio-based solutions or fire-resistant formulae. A common international standard for viscosity measurement, defining a number of classes for viscous industrial fluids, as listed in Table 138.2, is described in ISO 3448. The viscosity of hydraulic fluid is typically measured at 40 ℃.

There are two types of PAG-based hydraulic fluids that provide wonderful benefits in hydraulic equipment [Totten and Bishop]:

(a) Water glycol hydraulic fluid (HF-C): PAG is used as a viscosity modifier and to provide friction control;

(b) PAG-based hydraulic fluid: Used as the primary base oil in synthetic PAG-based hydraulic fluids (HF-DU or HEPG), it improves the hydraulic system's reliability such as friction control, deposit control, and thermo-oxidative stability, in addition to fire resistance.

138.2   Brake Fluids

Brake fluids used in hydraulic brakes and clutches in automobiles are a type of hydraulic fluids (Table 138.2). Brake fluids are incompressible and non-corrosive, and expected to maintain a steady viscosity over a wide range of temperatures. Most brake fluids used are glycol-ether-based oils though mineral and silicone oils are also in use.

Brake fluids are classified by DOT (Department of Transportation, USA) as follows: DOT3, DOT4, DOT5, and DOT5.1, according to the dry boiling point, wet boiling point (with 3.7% H_2O by weight), and sustainability of viscosity.

138.3   Hydraulic Power Steering Fluids

Power steering fluid belongs to the family of hydraulic fluids. Most are mineral oils or silicone-based fluids, as given in Table 138.3. Automatic transmission fluids (synthetic base oils) are sometimes used instead.

138.4   Electrorheological Fluids in Shock Absorber

One major application is the active-controlled shock absorber, which is configured as a closed hydraulic system where the "ride shock" is used to try to pump fluid through a hydraulic valve. The shock absorbers of a vehicle's suspension system are filled with electrorheological fluid (ER fluid) that is made of a suspension of extremely non-conducting but electrically active fine particles (< 50 mm in diameter) in an electrically insulating fluid. The valve channels in the shock absorber, allowing the damping fluid to flow between the two chambers, are surrounded by electromagnets.

Once the shear stress of the ER fluid goes beyond the yield point, the fluid becomes non-Newtonian and its incremental shear stress is proportional to the rate of shear, called Winslow effect, and hence the apparent viscosity and critical frequency of the damper can be varied according to the vehicle's weight and its ride performance. It can also be dynamically altered in order to provide stability control across vastly different road conditions, with response times on the order of milliseconds.

An ER fluid, with a suspension of nanometer-sized urea-coated barium titanium oxalate in silicone oil, exhibits its high yield strength due to the high dielectric constant of the particles [Monkman].

It is called giant ER fluid, of which the relationship between the electrical field strength and the yield strength is linear after the electric field reaches 1 kV/mm.

138.5   Seal of Hydraulic Fluids

In general, NBR (Nitrile) or FPM (Fluorocarbon) is used as a seal material for static and dynamic seals of mineral-based hydraulic fluids. Air, considered as contamination since it results in cavitations at low pressure, typically enters the circuit through the suction line if the seals and fittings are not tight. Air bubbles trapped in the hydraulic fluid may also result in a spongy foaming system, slowing response time and retarding controllability. The water content for continuous operation must not exceed 0.1 % by weight [ISO 3733] unless otherwise specified.

138.6   Debris

Wear metals are the result of corrosive wear due to water and acids in the hydraulic fluid, but also abrasive wear due to surface roughness metal contact leading to welding. Typically particles smaller than 5 μm are detected. The particle size of debris is the equivalent diameter estimated using the projected square area (A) as

$$A = \frac{1}{4} \pi d_p^2$$

For example, if the area $A = 78.5$ (μm)^2, $d_p = (4A / \pi)^{1/2} = 10$ μm. Typical values (by weight) for traces of wear metal in hydraulic systems [Turolla]: Fe (30 mg/kg), Sn (10 mg/kg), Ni (2 mg/kg), Pb (15 mg/kg), Cr (10 mg/kg), Al (10 mg/kg), Cu (50 mg/kg), Mo (5 mg/kg).

References

AGMA, 2003. Effect of Lubrication on Gear Surface Distress[S]. AGMA 925-A03 Information Sheet.

AGMA/ANSI 9005-E02, 2002. Industrial Gear Lubrication[S]. American Gear Manufacturers Association, Alexandria, VA, USA.

BOYDE S, 2000. Hydrolytic Stability of Synthetic Ester Lubricants[J]. Journal of Syn. Lub., 16(4): 297-312.

DAVIN T, PELLÉ J, HARMAND S, et al, 2015. Experimental Study of Oil Cooling Systems for Electric Motors[J]. Applied Thermal Engineering, 75: 1-13.

EASTER J, JARRETT C, PESPISA C, et al, 2014. An Area Average Correlation for Oil–Jet Cooling of Automotive Pistons[J]. J. Heat Transf., 136(12): 124501.

ISO 3448:1992, 1992. Industrial Liquid Lubricants- ISO Viscosity Classification[S]. International Organization for Standardization, Geneva.

KAO M, TIEN D, TING C, et al, 2006. Hydrophilic Characterization of Automotive Brake Fluid[J]. Journal of Testing and Evaluation, 34(5): 400-404.

KHANICHEH A, MINTZOPOULOS D, 2008. Evaluation of Electrorheological Fluid Dampers for Applications at 3-T MRI Environment[J]. IEEE/ASME Transitions on Mechatronics, 13(3): 286-294.

KHEMCHANDANI G, GREAVES M, 2010. Novel Polyalkylene Glycol-Based Hydraulic Fluids[J]. Iron and Steel Technology, 7(12): 66-71.

LIM D H, KIM S C, 2014. Thermal Performance of Oil Spray Cooling System for in-Wheel Motor in Electric Vehicles[J]. Applied Thermal Engineering, 63(2): 577-587.

MONKMAN G J, 1991. Addition of Solid Structures to Electrorheological Fluids[J]. Journal of Rheology, 35, 1385-1387.

Rydberg Karl E, 2010. Hydraulic Fluids- TMHP02[M]. Sweden: Linköping University.

SAE J306, 2005. Automotive Gear Lubricant Viscosity Classification[S]. Society of Automotive Engineers, Warrendale, PA, USA.

TOTTEN G E, BISHOP R, 2000. Anhydrous Polyalkylene Glycol Hydraulic Fluids[J]. SAE 2000-01-2557.

TUROLLA, 2013. Hydraulic Fluids & Lubricant-Technical Information[J].Revision, Sep. 30, 2013.

WEN W, HUANG X, YANG S, et al, November 2003. The Giant Electrorheological Effect in Suspensions of Nanoparticles[J]. Nature Materials, 2(11): 727-730.

WINSLOW W M, 1949. Induced Vibration of Suspensions[J]. Journal of Applied Physics, 20(12): 1137-1140.

Table 138.1 Nominal Thermomechanical Characteristics of Industrial Gear Fluids and Compressor Oils [ISO 3448] [AGMA Standard 251.02]

Material	$T/{}^\circ\mathrm{C}$	ρ	$\mu_\mathrm{d}/(\mathrm{Pa \cdot s})$	α_μ	β_μ	α_v	k	γ	$k_\rho \times 10^3$	e_s
ISO 3448 VG-2	40	ρ	$2.2 \times 10^{-3}\rho$	—	—	—	—	—	—	—
ISO 3448 VG-3	40	ρ	$3.2 \times 10^{-3}\rho$	—	—	—	—	—	—	—

continued

Material	$T/°C$	ρ	$\mu_d/(\text{Pa}\cdot\text{s})$	α_μ	β_μ	α_v	k	γ	$k_\rho \times 10^3$	e_s
ISO 3448 VG-5	40	ρ	$4.6\times10^{-3}\rho$	—	—	—	—	—	—	—
ISO 3448 VG-7	40	ρ	$6.8\times10^{-3}\rho$	—	—	—	—	—	—	—
ISO 3448 VG-10	40	ρ	$10\times10^{-3}\rho$	—	—	—	—	—	—	—
ISO 3448 VG-15	15.6	0.86	—	—	—	—	—	—	—	—
	40	ρ	$15.6\times10^{-3}\rho$	—	—	—	—	—	—	—
	100	ρ	$4.1\times10^{-3}\rho$	—	—	—	—	—	—	—
	185 (T_f)	—	—	—	—	—	—	—	—	—
ISO 3448 VG-22	-36 (T_p)	—	—	—	—	—	—	—	—	—
	-21 (Low service temperature)									
	15.6	0.864	—	—	—	—	—	—	—	—
	40	0.854	18.8×10^{-3}	—	—	—	—	—	—	—
	60 (High service temperature)									
	100	—	3.5×10^{-3}	—	—	—	—	—	—	—
	208 (T_f)	—	—	—	—	—	—	—	—	—
ISO 3448 VG-32 (AGMA 0 & 0S;	-33 (T_p)	—	—	—	—	—	—	—	—	—
	-30	—	4.5	—	—	—	—	—	—	—
	-25	—	1.2	—	—	—	—	—	—	—
	-15 (Low service temperature)									
	4.44	0.877	218×10^{-3}	—	—	—	—	—	—	—
	10	0.873	145×10^{-3}	—	—	—	—	—	—	—
	15.6	0.864	101×10^{-3}	—	—	—	—	—	—	—
	20.5	—	70.2×10^{-3}	—	—	—	—	—	—	—
	40	0.850	27.0×10^{-3}	—	0.034	1020	0.13	2000	—	—
	48.9	0.847	19.5×10^{-3}	—	—	—	—	—	—	—
	77 (High service temperature)									
	100	—	4.7×10^{-3}	—	—	—	—	—	—	—
	160	0.772	—	—	—	—	—	—	—	—
	212 (T_f)	—	—	—	—	—	—	—	—	—
	288	0.690	—	—	—	—	—	—	—	—

continued

Material	$T/^\circ\text{C}$	ρ	$\mu_\text{d}/(\text{Pa} \cdot \text{s})$	α_μ	β_μ	α_v	k	γ	$k_\text{p} \times 10^3$	e_s
ISO 3448 VG-46 (AGMA 1 & 1S)	-30 (T_p)	—	8.0	—	—	—	—	—	—	—
	-25	—	3.0	—	—	—	—	—	—	—
	-9 (Low service temperature)									
	15.6	0.871	—	—	—	—	—	—	—	—
	20.5	—	125.7×10^{-3}	—	—	—	—	—	—	—
	40	0.856	39.4×10^{-3}	—	—	—	—	1020	—	—
	88 (High service temperature)									
	100	—	6×10^{-3}	—	—	—	—	—	—	—
	160	0.779	—	—	—	—	—	—	—	—
	220 (T_f)	—	—	—	—	—	—	—	—	—
	288	0.697	—	—	—	—	—	—	—	—
ISO 3448 VG-68 (AGMA 2, 2S & 2EP)	-26 (T_p)	—	—	—	—	—	—	—	—	—
	-1 (Low service temperature)									
	15.6	0.878	—	—	—	—	—	—	—	—
	20.5	—	192.8×10^{-3}	—	—	—	—	—	—	—
	40	0.868	59×10^{-3}	0.023	0.034	—	0.126	—	—	—
	88 (High service temperature)									
	100	—	7.4×10^{-3}	—	—	—	—	—	—	—
	242 (T_f)	—	—	—	—	—	—	—	—	—
HVL68 (Mineral)	15	0.879	—	—	—	—	—	—	—	—
	20.5	—	108.5×10^{-3}	—	—	—	—	—	—	—
	40	—	40.8×10^{-3}	—	—	—	—	—	—	—
	100	—	6.81×10^{-3}	—	—	—	—	—	—	—
ISO 3448 VG-100 (AGMA 3, 3S & 3EP)	-24 (T_p)	—	—	—	—	—	—	—	—	—
	15.6	0.88	—	—	—	—	—	—	—	—
	40	0.87	87×10^{-3}	—	—	—	—	—	—	—
	100	—	9.7×10^{-3}	—	—	—	—	—	—	—
	250 (T_f)	—	—	—	—	—	—	—	—	—
ISO 3448 VG-150 (AGMA 4, 4S & 4EP)	-24 (T_p)	—	—	—	—	—	—	—	—	—
	15.6	0.884	—	—	—	—	—	—	—	—
	40	—	130×10^{-3}	—	—	—	—	—	—	—
	100	—	13×10^{-3}	—	—	—	—	—	—	—
	256 (T_f)	—	—	—	—	—	—	—	—	—

continued

Material	$T/^\circ\text{C}$	ρ	$\mu_\text{d}/(\text{Pa}\cdot\text{s})$	α_μ	β_μ	α_v	k	γ	$k_\rho\times10^3$	e_s
ISO 3448 VG-220 (AGMA 5, 5S & 5EP)	$-18\ (T_\text{p})$	—	—	—	—	—	—	—	—	—
	15.6	0.9	—	—	—	—	—	—	—	—
	40	—	205×10^{-3}	—	—	—	—	—	—	—
	100	—	17×10^{-3}	—	—	—	—	—	—	—
	$258\ (T_\text{f})$	—	—	—	—	—	—	—	—	—
ISO 3448 VG-320 (AGMA 6, 6S & 6EP; Mineral)	$-15\ (T_\text{p})$	—	—	—	—	—	—	—	—	—
	15.6	0.907	—	—	—	—	—	—	—	—
	40	0.906	290×10^{-3}	—	—	—	—	—	—	—
	50	—	158.6×10^{-3}	0.0207	—	—	—	—	—	—
	60	—	94.98×10^{-3}	0.0193	—	—	—	—	—	—
	70	—	60.44×10^{-3}	0.0182	—	—	—	—	—	—
	80	—	40.50×10^{-3}	0.0173	—	—	—	—	—	—
	90	—	28.35×10^{-3}	0.0164	—	—	—	—	—	—
	100	—	20.61×10^{-3}	0.0157	—	—	—	—	—	—
	$220\ (T_\text{f})$	—	—	—	—	—	—	—	—	—
ISO 3448 VG-460 (AGMA 7, 7S, 7EP & 7Composite)	15.6	0.913	—	—	—	—	—	—	—	—
	$-15\ (T_\text{p})$	—	—	—	—	—	—	—	—	—
	40	0.91	419×10^{-3}	—	—	—	—	—	—	—
	100	—	27×10^{-3}	—	—	—	—	—	—	—
	$215\ (T_\text{f})$	—	—	—	—	—	—	—	—	—
ISO 3448 VG-680 (AGMA 8, 8S, 8EP & 8Composite)	40	0.912	620×10^{-3}	—	—	—	—	—	—	—
ISO 3448 VG-1000 (AGMA 8A EP & 8A Composite)	40	0.92	920×10^{-3}	—	—	—	—	—	—	—
ISO 3448 VG-1500 (AGMA 9, 9S & 9EP)	40	ρ	$1500\times10^{-3}\rho$	—	—	—	—	—	—	—
AGMA 10, 10S & 10EP	40	ρ	$3200\times10^{-3}\rho$	—	—	—	—	—	—	—

continued

Material	$T/℃$	ρ	$\mu_{\rm d}/({\rm Pa \cdot s})$	α_μ	β_μ	$\alpha_{\rm v}$	k	γ	$k_{\rm p}\times10^3$	$e_{\rm s}$
AGMA 12, 12S & 12EP	40	ρ	$6800\times10^{-3}\rho$	—	—	—	—	—	—	—
AGMA 13, 13S & 13EP	100	ρ	$205\times10^{-3}\rho$	—	—	—	—	—	—	—
AGMA 14R	100	ρ	$642.5\times10^{-3}\rho$	—	—	—	—	—	—	—
AGMA 15R	100	ρ	$1285.5\times10^{-3}\rho$	—	—	—	—	—	—	—
Synthetic PAG-25 (VI=132; Turbine [Dow])	-49 ($T_{\rm p}$)	—	—	—	—	—	—	—	—	—
	40	0.985	25.84×10^{-3}	—	—	—	0.145	2017	—	—
	100	—	5.11×10^{-3}	—	—	—	—	—	—	—
	242 ($T_{\rm f}$)	—	—	—	—	—	—	—	—	—
Synthetic PAG-46 (Compressor Oil)	-39 ($T_{\rm p}$)	—	—	—	—	—	—	—	—	—
	15.6	1.035	—	—	—	—	—	—	—	—
	40	—	46×10^{-3}	—	—	—	—	—	—	—
	100	—	8×10^{-3}	—	—	—	—	—	—	—
	263 ($T_{\rm f}$)	—	—	—	—	—	—	—	—	—
Synthetic PAG-46 Anhydrous (Fire-resistant) (VI=200; [Khemchandani & Greaves])	-48 ($T_{\rm p}$)	—	—	—	—	—	—	—	—	—
	15.6	—	—	—	—	—	—	—	—	—
	40	—	46×10^{-3}	—	—	—	—	—	—	—
	100	—	—	—	—	—	—	—	—	—
	295 ($T_{\rm f}$)	—		—	—	—	—	—	—	—
	315 (Fire Point)	—	—	—	—	—	—	—	—	—
Synthetic PAG-100 (Compressor Oil)	-35 ($T_{\rm f}$)	—	—	—	—	—	—	—	—	—
	15.6	1.048	—	—	—	—	—	—	—	—
	40	—	100×10^{-3}	—	—	—	—	—	—	—
	100	—	16.2×10^{-3}	—	—	—	—	—	—	—
	275 ($T_{\rm f}$)	—	—	—	—	—	—	—	—	—
Synthetic PAG-220 (Compressor Oil)	-33 ($T_{\rm p}$)	—	—	—	—	—	—	—	—	—
	15.6	1.072	—	—	—	—	—	—	—	—
	40	—	220×10^{-3}	—	—	—	—	—	—	—
	100	—	34×10^{-3}	—	—	—	—	—	—	—
	280 ($T_{\rm f}$)	—	—	—	—	—	—	—	—	—

continued

Material	$T/°C$	ρ	$\mu_d/(\text{Pa} \cdot \text{s})$	α_μ	β_μ	α_v	k	γ	$k_\rho \times 10^3$	e_s
Synthetic PAG-320	15.6	—	—	—	—	—	—	—	—	—
	40	—	320×10^{-3}	—	—	—	—	—	—	—
	50	—	228.8×10^{-3}	0.011	—	—	—	—	—	—
	60	—	164.6×10^{-3}	0.0105	—	—	—	—	—	—
	70	—	121.8×10^{-3}	0.01	—	—	—	—	—	—
	80	—	92.42×10^{-3}	0.0096	—	—	—	—	—	—
	90	—	71.69×10^{-3}	0.0092	—	—	—	—	—	—
	100	—	56.71×10^{-3}	0.0089	—	—	—	—	—	—
	280 (T_f)	—	—	—	—	—	—	—	—	—
Synthetic PAG-460 (Compressor Oil)	−30 (T_p)	—	—	—	—	—	—	—	—	—
	15.6	1.035	—	—	—	—	—	—	—	—
	40	—	460×10^{-3}	—	—	—	—	—	—	—
	100	—	69×10^{-3}	—	—	—	—	—	—	—
	280 (T_f)	—	—	—	—	—	—	—	—	—
Synthetic PAG-1000 (Compressor Oil)	−20 (T_p)	—	—	—	—	—	—	—	—	—
	15.6	1.07	—	—	—	—	—	—	—	—
	40	—	1000×10^{-3}	—	—	—	—	—	—	—
	100	—	146×10^{-3}	—	—	—	—	—	—	—
	275 (T_f)	—	—	—	—	—	—	—	—	—
Synthetic PAO-320	−34 (T_p)	—	—	—	—	—	—	—	—	—
	15.6	0.876	—	—	—	—	—	—	—	—
	40	—	294×10^{-3}	0.0134	—	—	—	—	—	—
	50	—	170.8×10^{-3}	0.0134	—	—	—	—	—	—
	60	—	110.4×10^{-3}	0.0131	—	—	—	—	—	—
	70	—	74.7×10^{-3}	0.0129	—	—	—	—	—	—
	80	—	52.55×10^{-3}	0.0126	—	—	—	—	—	—
	90	—	38.24×10^{-3}	0.0124	—	—	—	—	—	—
	100	—	28.66×10^{-3}	0.0122	—	—	—	—	—	—
	220 (T_f)	—	—	—	—	—	—	—	—	—
Synthetic PAO-460	−27 (T_p)	—	—	—	—	—	—	—	—	—
	15.6	0.878	—	—	—	—	—	—	—	—
	40	—	423×10^{-3}	—	—	—	—	—	—	—
	100	—	—	0.0122	—	—	—	—	—	—
	220 (T_f)	—	—	—	—	—	—	—	—	—

continued

Material	$T/^{\circ}\mathrm{C}$	ρ	$\mu_{\mathrm{d}}/(\mathrm{Pa\cdot s})$	α_{μ}	β_{μ}	α_{v}	k	γ	$k_{\rho}\times10^{3}$	e_{s}
Synthetic PAO-680	-27 (T_{p})	—	—	—	—	—	—	—	—	—
	15.6	0.88	—	—	—	—	—	—	—	—
	40	—	626×10^{-3}	0.0134	—	—	—	—	—	—
	100	—	51.5×10^{-3}	0.0122	—	—	—	—	—	—
	220 (T_{f})	—	—	—	—	—	—	—	—	—
Turbine Oils	ISO 3448 VG 32, 46, 68, and 100 may be applied.									

Notes: ISO 3448 VG & AGMA 0~12 = The upper limit is 110% of the nominal value;

ISO 3448VG & AGMA 0~12 = The lower limit is 90% of the nominal value;

$\mu_{\mathrm{d}}(\mathrm{Pa\cdot s})$ = Dynamic viscosity as averaged at the ambient pressure;

$\alpha_{\mu}(\mathrm{MPa}^{-1})$ = Pressure-dynamic viscosity coefficient, Eq. (137.2) with $P_{\mathrm{o}}=0$;

$\beta_{\mu}(^{\circ}\mathrm{C}^{-1})$ = Temperature-dynamic viscosity coefficient, Eq. (137.2) with $T_{\mathrm{o}}=0$;

$\alpha_{\mathrm{v}}(\mu\mathrm{m}^{3}/\mathrm{m}^{3}/^{\circ}\mathrm{C})$ = Coefficient of volumetric thermal expansion;

γ (J/kg/°C) = Specific heat capacity at 0.1 MPa (100 kPa) constant pressure (C_{p});

15 °C^{pl} = Pressurized liquid-Liquid at 15 °C and its corresponding equilibrium pressure;

$k\rho$ (MPa^{-1}) = Compressibility;

VG: Viscosity grade.

Table 138.2　Low Limits of Kinematic Viscosity for Brake Fluids

Material	$T/^{\circ}\mathrm{C}$	ρ	$\mu_{\mathrm{d}}/(\mathrm{Pa\cdot s})$	α_{μ}	β_{μ}	α_{v}	k	γ	$k_{\rho}\times10^{3}$	e_{s}
DOT3 (Glycol Ether; Small/me & medium cars)	-40	—	1.5ρ	—	—	—	—	—	—	—
	23	1.1	—	—	—	—	—	—	—	—
	100	—	$1.5\times10^{-3}\rho$	—	—	—	—	—	—	—
	140 (Wet T_{b})	—	—	—	—	—	—	—	—	—
	205 (Dry T_{b})	—	—	—	—	—	—	—	—	—
DOT4 (Glycol Ether /Borate Ester; For Sedans)	-40	—	1.8ρ	—	—	—	—	—	—	—
	23			—	—	—	—	—	—	—
	100	—	$1.5\times10^{-3}\rho$	—	—	—	—	—	—	—
	155 (Wet T_{b})	—	—	—	—	—	—	—	—	—
	230 (Dry T_{b})	—	—	—	—	—	—	—	—	—
DOT5.1 (Borate Ester /Glycol Ether; Large, sports & ABS-equipped cars)	-40	—	0.9ρ	—	—	—	—	—	—	—
	23	—	—	—	—	—	—	—	—	—
	100	—	$1.5\times10^{-3}\rho$	—	—	—	—	—	—	—
	180 (Wet T_{b})	—	—	—	—	—	—	—	—	—
	260 (Dry T_{b})	—	—	—	—	—	—	—	—	—

continued

Material	$T/°C$	ρ	$\mu_d/(Pa \cdot s)$	α_μ	β_μ	α_v	k	γ	$k_p \times 10^3$	e_s
DOT5 (Silicon-based; Special vehicles e.g. Hummer)	−40	—	0.9ρ	—	—	—	—	—	—	—
	23	—	—	—	—	—	—	—	—	—
	100	—	$1.5 \times 10^{-3}\rho$	—	—	—	—	—	—	—
	180 (Wet T_b)	—	—	—	—	—	—	—	—	—
	260 (Dry T_b)	—	—	—	—	—	—	—	—	—

Notes: γ (J/kg/°C) = Specific heat capacity at 0.1 MPa (100 kPa) constant pressure;

μ_d(Pa · s) = Dynamic viscosity as averaged at the ambient pressure;

α_μ(MPa^{-1}) = Pressure-dynamic viscosity coefficient, Eq. (137.2) with $P_o = 0$;

β_μ(°C^{-1}) = Temperature-dynamic viscosity coefficient, Eq. (137.2) with $T_o = 0$;

α_v(μm^3/m^3/°C) = Coefficient of volumetric thermal expansion;

T_b(°C) = Boiling point;

μ_k(mm^2/s) = kinematic viscosity;

pH value = 7.0 < pH value < 11.5 for all brake fluids.

Table 138.3   Typical Thermomechanical Characteristics of Power Steering Fluids

Material	$T/°C$	ρ	$\mu_d/(Pa \cdot s)$	α_μ	β_μ	α_v	k	γ	$k_p \times 10^3$	e_s
Power Steering Fluid (Prestone; MSD020)	−51 (T_p)	—	—	—	—	—	—	—	—	—
	−40	—	45	—	—	—	—	—	—	—
	15	0.868	—	—	—	—	—	—	—	—
	23	0.866	—	—	—	—	—	—	—	—
	40	0.86	39×10^{-3}	—	—	—	—	—	—	—
	100	0.84	6.3×10^{-3}	—	—	—	—	—	—	—
	220 (T_f)	—	—	—	—	—	—	—	—	—
	260 (T_b)	—	—	—	—	—	—	—	—	—

Notes: γ (J/kg/°C) = Specific heat capacity at 0.1 MPa (100 kPa) constant pressure;

μ_d(Pa · s) = Dynamic viscosity as averaged at the ambient pressure;

α_μ(MPa^{-1}) = Pressure-dynamic viscosity coefficient, Eq. (137.2) with $P_o = 0$;

β_μ(°C^{-1}) = Temperature-dynamic viscosity coefficient, Eq. (137.2) with $T_o = 0$;

α_v(mm^3/m^3/°C) = Coefficient of volumetric thermal expansion;

T_b(°C) = Boiling point;

μ_k(mm^2/s) = kinematic viscosity.

Chapter 139

Coolants

139.1   Introduction

A coolant is a fluid, which flows through or around a subject to prevent the subject from overheating. A good coolant has high thermal capacity and low viscosity. Ideally it is non-toxic, chemically inert, and corrosion-preventive. The thermomechanical properties of air, water, coolants, and related fluids are listed in Table 139.1, while those of hydrogen are given in Table 140.1.

The heat transfer coefficient (h) of a coolant is directly proportional to the thermal conductivity, the specific heat capacity, and the density of the fluid, and is inversely proportional to the dynamic viscosity (μ_d), as shown by the following empirical equation

$$h = \frac{0.1 \, k^{0.6} \, C_p^{0.4} \, \rho^{0.8}}{\mu_d^{0.4}}$$

where

k (W/m/℃): Thermal conductivity;

C_p(kJ/kg/℃): Specific heat capacity;

ρ (kg/m^3): Density;

μ_d(MPa · s): Dynamic viscosity.

139.2   Gaseous-Air and H$_2$

Air is a natural form of a coolant widely used in daily life (e.g. electric fans in the house and cooling fans of car engine radiators), while H$_2$(Hydrogen) is used as a high-performance gaseous coolant that is commonly used for electrical generators in large power plants. The thermomechanical properties of hydrogen are given in Table 140.1.

139.3   Engine Coolants

Water with antifreeze and corrosion inhibitors is the most common engine coolant. An engine coolant is a heat transfer fluid designed to remove excess heat from an internal combustion engine. Antifreeze is required for water to withstand temperatures below 0 ℃ and/or raise its boiling point (> 100 ℃). Organic Ethylene glycol (EG), diethylene glycol, and propylene glycol (PG) are typical chemicals, working as antifreezes in automobiles.

139.4   Nanofluids

Nanofluids are an emerging new class of coolants, which consist of a carrier liquid, such as water and/or ethylene glycol (EG), dispersed with nanoparticles. Nanoparticles including copper oxide (CuO), aluminum oxide (Al_2O_3), titanium dioxide (TiO_2), carbon nanotubes, silica (SiO_2), copper nanorods, silver nanorods, have been of great interest to researchers [Leong et al.] [Minsta et al.] [Sarkar et al.].

139.5   Refrigerant: HFO-1234yf ($CF_3 CF = CH_2$)

The SAE (Society of Automotive Engineers) promoted a new fluorochemical refrigerant HFO-1234yf ($CF_3CF = CH_2$ or 2,3,3,3-Tetrafluoropropene) in automobile air-conditioning systems, replacing R-134a (1,1,1,2-tetrafluoroethane). It has been in use for most GM passenger vehicles in the USA since 2013.

139.6   Refrigerant: 1,1,1,2-tetrafluoroethane (R-134a)

R-134a (1, 1, 2-Tetrafluoroethane) is a non-flammable gas, used primarily as a "high-temperature" refrigerant for domestic refrigeration systems and some automobile air conditioners.

139.7   Refrigerant: Freon 12 (R-12)

Dichlorodifluoromethane (R-12), also called Freon 12, is only allowed to be used as a fire retardant in submarines and aircraft due to the concern that it may do damage to the ozone layer.

139.8   Refrigerant: CO_2 (R-744)

Carbon dioxide (R-744) is used as a working fluid in climate control systems for cars. Solid carbon dioxide (Melting point) is always below $-78.5\ ℃$ at regular atmospheric pressure, regardless of the air temperature. Its thermomechanical characteristics are given in Table 139.1. As a refrigerant CO_2 lowers the temperature by undergoing phase change between liquid and gas.

139.9 Liquid N_2

Gaseous nitrogen (N_2) gas is inert and it makes up 78% of the Earth's atmosphere. Liquid nitrogen, which boils at about $-196\ ℃$ ($77\ K$), is a common and inexpensive natural coolant, in use especially in automotive laboratories.

139.10 Transformer Oils

The functional requirement of transformer oils is to insulate, work as a coolant, and suppress arcing/corona. They must have excellent high dielectric strength, chemical stability, and thermal conductivity at a wide range of temperatures for a prolonged period. Mineral-based oils are widely used as transformer oils. Transformer oils are pronounced by the four-letter designation system as

1st (Internal cooling medium):	O- Oil with flash point $\leqslant 300\ ℃$;
	K- Oil with flash point $> 300\ ℃$;
	L- Oil with no measurable flash point.
2nd (Internal cooling mechanism):	N- Natural convection through the cooling equipment and natural convection through windings;
	F- Forced circulation through the cooling equipment, while natural convection in windings;
	D- Forced circulation through the cooling equipment, with directed flow in main windings.
3rd (External cooling medium):	A- Air;
	W- Water.
4th (External cooling mechanism):	N- Natural convection;
	F- Forced circulation.

For example, ONAF means that the oil with a flash point $\leqslant 300\ ℃$ is naturally convected (via thermosiphon effect) in the transformer and the transformer exterior is cooled by the air in a forced circulation. Thermomechanical properties of an example motor oil are given in Table 139.1. Transformer oils are also used in capacitors and switches/circuit breakers for high-voltage applications.

There are two kinds of transformer oils: (a) Paraffin based and (b) Naphtha based.

References

ALSHAMANI K, 2003. Equations for Physical Properties of Automotive Coolants[J]. SAE 2003-01-0532.

ARCHER D, WANG P, 1990. The Dielectric Constant of Water and Debye-Hückel Limiting Law Slopes[J]. Journal of Physical and Chemical Reference Data, 19(2): 371-411.

CARTER W P L, 2009. Investigation of the Atmospheric Ozone Impacts of Trans 2,3,3,3- Tetrafluoropropene [J]. Final Report to Honeywell International Inc. Contract UCR-09010016.

CARTER W P L, 2009. Investigation of the Atmospheric Ozone Impacts of Trans 1,3,3,3-Tetrafluoropropene [J]. Final Report to Honeywell International Inc. Contract UCR-09010016.

CHALGREN Jr. R, BARRON Jr. L, 2003. Development and Verification of a Heavy Duty 42/14V Electric Powertrain Cooling System[J]. SAE 2003-01-3416.

CHASTAIN J, WAGNER J, 2006. Advanced Thermal Management for Internal Combustion Engines-Valve Design, Component Testing and Block Redesign[J]. SAE 2006-01-1232.

CHOUKROUN A, CHANFREAU M, 2001. Automatic Control of Electric Actuators for an Optimized Engine Cooling Thermal Management[J]. SAE 2001-01-1758.

FILHO Z A, et al, 2011. Rheology and Fluid Dynamics Properties of Sugarcane Juice [J]. Biochemical Engineering Journal, 53(3): 260-265.

HARR L, GALLAGHER J, KELL G, 1984. NBS/ NRC Steam Tables[J]. Chemie Ingenieur Technik, 57(9): 812.

HONG H, et al, 2004. Review and Analysis of Variable Valve Timing Strategies-Eight Ways to Approach[J]. Journal of Automobile Engineering, 218(10): 1179-1200.

HURLEY M D, WALLINGTON T J, JAVADI M S, et al, 2008. Atmospheric Chemistry of $CF_3CF = CH_2$: Products and Mechanisms of Cl Atom and OH Radical Initiated Oxidation[J]. Chemical Physics Letters, 450 (4-6): 263-267.

LASANCE C, SIMONS R, 2005. Advances in High Performance Cooling for Electronics [J]. Electronics Cooling, 11(4): 22-39.

LEONG K Y, et al, 2010. Performance Investigation of an Automotive Car Radiator Operated with Nanofluid-based Coolants (Nanofluid as a Coolant in a Radiator) [J]. Applied Thermal Engineering, 30(17-18): 2685-2692.

MARQUIS F, CHIBANTE L, 2005. Improving the Heat Transfer of Nanofluids and Nanolubricants with Carbon Nanotubes[J]. JOM, 57(12): 32-43.

MCSHANE C P, 2001. Relative Properties of the New Combustion-resistant Vegetable Oil-based Dielectric Coolants for Distribution and Power Transformers[J]. IEEE Transactions on Industry Applications, 37(4): 1132-1139.

MINSTA H A, et al, 2009. New Temperature Dependent Thermal Conductivity Data for Water-based Nanofluids [J]. International Journal of Thermal Sciences, 48(2): 363-371.

SARKAR J, et al, 2015. A Review on Hybrid Nanofluids: Recent Research, Development and Applications [J]. Renewable & Sustainable Energy Reviews, 43(C): 164-177.

SENGERS J V, WATSON J T R, 1986. Improved International Formulations for the Viscosity and Thermal Conductivity of Water Substance[J]. Journal of Physical and Chemical Reference Data, 15(4): 1291-1314.

TORREGROSA A J, et al, 2008. Assessment of the Influence of Different Cooling System Configurations on Engine Warm-up, Emissions and Fuel Consumption[J]. International Journal of Automotive Technology, 9, 447-458.

UKRAINCZYK N, KURAJICA S, SIPUSIE J, 2010. Thermophysical Comparison of Five Commercial Paraffin Sways as Latent Heat Storage Materials[J]. Chemical and Biochemical Engineering Quarterly, 24(2): 129-137.

VAISI A, et al, 2011. Experimental Investigation of Geometry Effects on the Performance of a Compact Louvered Heat Exchanger[J]. Applied Thermal Engineering, 31(16): 3337-3346.

VARGAFTIK N B, et al, 1983. International Tables of the Surface Tension of Water[J]. Journal of Physical and Chemical Reference Data, 12(3): 817-820.

YAN W M, SHEEN P J, 2000. Heat Transfer and Friction Characteristics of Fin and Tube Heat Exchangers [J]. International Journal of Heat & Mass Transfer, 43(9): 1651-1659.

ZALBA B, MARIN J, CABEA L, et al, 2003. Review on Thermal Energy Storage with Phase Change: Materials, Heat Transfer Analysis and Application[J]. Applied Thermal Engineering, 23(3): 251-283.

Table 139. 1   Typical Thermomechanical Characteristics of Air, Water/Ice, Coolants and Related Fluids

Material	$T/℃$	ρ	$\mu_d/(Pa \cdot s)$	α_μ	β_μ	α_v	k	$\gamma(C_p)$	$k_\rho \times 10^3$	e_s
Air (Dry)	-20	0.00137	15.1×10^{-6}	—	—	—	—	—	—	—
	0	0.00127	17.2×10^{-6}	—	—	—	—	—	—	—
	23	0.00119	18.2×10^{-6}	—	—	—	0.024	1005	—	—
	60	0.00107	20.0×10^{-6}	—	—	—	0.029	—	—	—
	100	0.000954	21.7×10^{-6}	—	—	—	—	—	—	—
	140	0.000838	23.4×10^{-6}	—	—	—	—	—	—	—
	180	0.000765	25.0×10^{-6}	—	—	—	—	—	—	—
	200	0.000732	25.7×10^{-6}	—	—	—	—	—	—	—
Ammonia (NH_3)	-78 (T_m)	—	—	—	—	—	—	—	—	—
	-33 (T_b)	—	—	—	—	—	—	—	—	—
	0	—	—	—	—	—	—	4600	—	—
	15 ℃^{pl}	0.697	266×10^{-6}	—	—	2400	0.507	—	0.71	—
	20	—	9.82×10^{-6}	—	—	—	—	—	—	—
	40	—	—	—	—	—	—	4860	—	—
	80	—	—	—	—	—	—	5400	—	—
	100	—	—	—	—	—	—	6200	—	—
	115	—	—	—	—	—	—	6740	—	—
Argon (Ar)	-189.4 (T_m)	—	—	—	—	—	—	—	—	—
	-186 (T_b)	—	—	—	—	—	—	—	—	—
	15 ℃^{pl}	1.3954	0.24×10^{-3}	—	—	4700	0.13	625	2.1	—
	23	0.0016	20×10^{-6}	—	—	—	—	523	—	—
Blood	37	1.06	3.5×10^{-3}	—	—	—	0.492	—	—	—
Blood Plasma	37	—	1.5×10^{-3}	—	—	—	—	—	—	—
Carbon Dioxide (CO_2)	-78.5	1.562	(Dry Ice)	—	—	—	—	—	—	—
	-56.6 (T_m/T_b)	—	—	—	—	—	—	—	—	—
	0	0.00198	—	—	—	—	0.0147	—	—	—
	10	—	—	—	—	—	0.0157	—	—	—
	15 ℃^{pl}	1.18	0.26×10^{-3}	—	—	3100	0.18	1950	0.88	—
	15	—	—	—	—	—	—	—	—	—
	23	0.00182	—	—	—	—	—	876	—	—
	50	—	—	—	—	—	0.0184	—	—	—

continued

Material	$T/°C$	ρ	$\mu_d/(Pa \cdot s)$	α_μ	β_μ	α_v	k	$\gamma(C_p)$	$k_\rho \times 10^3$	e_s
Carbon Monoxide (CO)	-205 (T_m)	—	—	—	—	—	—	—	—	—
	-192	0.789	—	—	—	—	—	—	—	—
	-191.5 (T_b)	—	—	—	—	—	—	—	—	—
	0	0.00125	—	—	—	—	—	—	—	—
	15	—	117.2×10^{-6}	—	—	—	—	—	—	—
	25	0.00115	—	—	—	—	—	—	—	—
Glycol, Ethylene (EG; $C_2H_6O_2$)	-17.8	1.16	310×10^{-3}	—	—	—	—	2260	—	—
	4.4	—	48×10^{-3}	—	—	—	—	2350	—	—
	15	1.12	20×10^{-3}	—	—	650	0.26	—	0.33	—
	25	—	16.1×10^{-3}	—	—	—	—	—	—	—
	50	—	—	—	—	—	—	2570	—	—
	100	—	2×10^{-3}	—	—	—	—	—	—	—
	115.6	1.067	1.8×10^{-3}	—	—	—	—	2885	—	—
	121 (T_f)	—	—	—	—	—	—	—	—	—
	125	—	—	—	—	—	—	—	—	—
	137.8	1.05	1.4×10^{-3}	—	—	—	—	2980	—	—
	142 (T_f)	—	—	—	—	—	—	—	—	—
	197 (T_b)	—	—	—	—	—	—	—	—	—
	427 (T_a)	—	—	—	—	—	—	—	—	—
EG/40% H_2O (by volume)	-52.8 (T_m)	—	—	—	—	—	—	—	—	—
	-40	—	170×10^{-3}	—	—	—	—	—	—	—
	-28.9	—	63×10^{-3}	—	—	—	—	—	—	—
	-17.8	1.11	32×10^{-3}	—	—	—	—	3027	—	—
	4.4	1.1	9×10^{-3}	—	—	—	—	3132	—	—
	26.7	1.09	3.8×10^{-3}	—	—	—	—	3215	—	—
	48.9	1.077	2×10^{-3}	—	—	—	—	3299	—	—
	93.3	1.049	0.88×10^{-3}	—	—	—	—	3475	—	—
	110 (T_b)	—	—	—	—	—	—	—	—	—

continued

Material	$T/℃$	ρ	$\mu_d/(Pa \cdot s)$	α_μ	β_μ	α_v	k	$\gamma(C_p)$	$k_\rho \times 10^3$	e_s
EG/50% H$_2$O (Engine Coolant; 50% by volume)	-36.8 (T_m)	—	—	—	—	—	—	—	—	—
	-17.8	1.1	22×10^{-3}	—	—	—	—	3266	—	—
	4.4	1.088	6.5×10^{-3}	—	—	—	—	3328	—	—
	20	1.08	3.8×10^{-3}	—	—	—	0.37	—	—	—
	26.7	1.077	2.8×10^{-3}	—	—	—		3412	—	—
	37.8	1.056	2.3×10^{-3}	—	—	—		—	—	—
	48.9	—	1.5×10^{-3}	—	—	—		3483	—	—
	93.3	1.038	0.7×10^{-3}	—	—	—		3622	—	—
	107.2 (T_b)	—	—	—	—	—	—	—	—	—
EG/60% H$_2$O (by volume)	-23.5 (T_m)	—	—	—	—	—	—	—	—	—
	-17.8	1. 08	15×10^{-3}	—	—	—	—	3475	—	—
	4.4	1.07	48×10^{-3}	—	—	—	—	3538	—	—
	26.7	1.06	2.2×10^{-3}	—	—	—	—	3600	—	—
	48.9	1.05	1.3×10^{-3}	—	—	—	—	3663	—	—
	93.3	1.026	0.6×10^{-3}	—	—	—	—	3789	—	—
	104.4 (T_b)	—	—	—	—	—	—	—	—	—
EG/70% H$_2$O	-7.9 (T_m)	—	—	—	—	—	—	—	—	—
	4.4	1.057	3.5×10^{-3}	—	—	—	—	—	—	—
	26.7	1.048	1×10^{-3}	—	—	—	—	—	—	—
	93.3	1.013	0.5×10^{-3}	—	—	—	—	—	—	—
	104.4 (T_b)	—	—	—	—	—	—	—	—	—
Glycol, Propylene (PG; C$_3$H$_8$O$_2$; Engine Coolant)	-57 (T_p)	—	—	—	—	—	—	—	—	—
	25	1.032	48.6×10^{-3}	—	—	730	0.206	2510	—	—
	60	1.066	8.42×10^{-3}	—	—	—	—	—	—	—
	104 (T_f)	—	—	—	—	—	—	—	—	—
PG/40% H$_2$O	-40	—	1.5	—	—	—	—	—	—	—
	-28.9	—	400×10^{-3}	—	—	—	—	—	—	—
	-17.8	—	103×10^{-3}	—	—	—	—	—	—	—
PG/50% H$_2$O (Engine Coolant; 50% by volume)	-37.8 (T_m)	—	—	—	—	—	—	—	—	—
	20	1.062	6.4×10^{-3}	—	—	—	0.36	3400	—	—
	37.8	1.026	3×10^{-3}	—	—	—	—	—	—	—
	48.9	—	—	—	—	—	—	—	—	—
	93.3	—	—	—	—	—	—	—	—	—

continued

Material	$T/℃$	ρ	$\mu_d/(\text{Pa}\cdot\text{s})$	α_μ	β_μ	α_v	k	$\gamma(C_p)$	$k_\rho\times10^3$	e_s
Glass	23	—	$10^{18}\sim10^{21}$	—	—	—	—	—	—	—
H$_2$O (Ice)	−30	0.983854	—	—	—	—	—	—	—	—
	−20	0.993547	—	—	—	—	—	—	—	—
	−10	0.998117	—	—	—	—	—	—	—	—
	0 (Ice)	—	—	—	—	2.18	2050	—	—	—
H$_2$O (Water)	0	0.998395	1.793×10^{-3}	—	—	—	0.561	4218	—	—
	4	0.999973	1.567×10^{-3}	—	—	—	—	—	—	—
	10	0.9997	1.307×10^{-3}	—	—	—	0.580	4192	—	—
	20	0.9982	1.002×10^{-3}	—	—	—	0.598	4182	4.5×10^{-4}	—
	23	0.9975	0.94×10^{-3}	—	—	—	—	—	—	—
	25	—	0.89×10^{-3}	—	—	—	—	—	4.6×10^{-4}	—
	30	0.9957	0.7975×10^{-3}	—	—	—	0.615	4178	—	—
	40	0.9922	0.6529×10^{-3}	—	—	—	0.631	4179	—	—
	50	0.9881	0.5468×10^{-3}	—	—	—	0.644	4181	—	—
	60	0.9832	0.4665×10^{-3}	—	—	—	0.654	4184	—	—
	70	0.9778	0.4042×10^{-3}	—	—	—	0.663	4190	—	—
	80	0.9718	0.3537×10^{-3}	—	—	—	0.67	4196	—	—
	90	0.9668	0.3147×10^{-3}	—	—	—	0.675	4205	—	—
	100	0.9584	0.2818×10^{-3}	—	—	—	0.679	4216	—	—
H$_2$O (Steam)	100	—	—	—	—	—	—	2080	—	—
	125	—	—	—	—	—	0.016	—	—	—
H$_2$O (Sea Water)	10	1.025	1.35×10^{-3}	—	—	—	—	—	—	—
	15	1.025	1.21×10^{-3}	—	—	—	—	—	—	—
	20	1.03	1.07×10^{-3}	—	—	—	—	3930	—	—
	104 (T_b)	—	—	—	—	—	—	—	—	—

continued

Material	$T/°C$	ρ	$\mu_d/(Pa \cdot s)$	α_μ	β_μ	α_v	k	$\gamma(C_p)$	$k_\rho \times 10^3$	e_s
Nitrogen (N_2)	$-259.2\ (T_m)$	—	—	—	—	—	—	—	—	—
	Liquid 0.071	—	—	—	—	—	—	—	—	—
	$-252.8\ (T_b)$	—	—	—	—	—	—	—	—	—
	$-210\ (T_m)$	—	—	—	—	—	—	—	—	—
	-196	—	15.8×10^{-3}	—	—	—	0.15	—	—	—
	$-195.8\ (T_b)$	—	—	—	—	—	—	—	—	—
	0	—	16.7×10^{-6}	—	—	—	—	—	—	—
	$15\ °C^{pl}$	0.807	0.161×10^{-3}	—	—	5600	0.145	2040	3.2	—
	27	—	17.8×10^{-6}	—	—	—	—	—	—	—
Refrigerant: R-12 $(CCl_2F_2;$ Fluorine$)$	$-157.7\ (T_m)$	—	—	—	—	—	—	—	—	—
	-40	—	—	—	—	—	—	880	—	—
	$-29.8\ (T_b)$	—	—	—	—	—	—	—	—	—
	-18	—	—	—	—	—	—	910	—	—
	$15\ °C^{pl}$	1.486	0.20×10^{-3}	—	—	1970	0.071	886	2.5	—
	21	ρ	$0.27 \times 10^{-3}\rho$	—	—	—	—	—	—	—
	48	—	—	—	—	—	—	1020	—	—
Refrigerant: R-134a (CF_3CH_2F)	$-96\ (T_m)$	—	—	—	—	—	—	—	—	—
	-27	1.38	—	—	—	—	—	—	—	—
	$-26.3\ (T_b)$	—	—	—	—	—	—	—	—	—
	$15\ °C^{pl}$	1.38	0.38×10^{-3}	—	—	2190	0.1	1280	1.3	—
	25	0.00425	—	—	—	—	—	—	—	—
Refrigerant: R-410A	$-153\ (T_m)$	—	—	—	—	—	—	—	—	—
	$-51\ (T_b)$	—	—	—	—	—	—	—	—	—
	$15\ °C^{pl}$	1.35	—	—	—	2190	0.17	1368	1.7	—
Silicone Oil $(DMS-10)$	15	0.95	9.5×10^{-3}	—	—	900	0.11	1800	0.6	—
	55	0.91	4.6×10^{-3}	—	—	—	—	—	—	—
	$301\ (T_f)$	—	—	—	—	—	—	—	—	—
Sulfur Dioxide (SO_2)	$-76\ (T_m)$	—	—	—	—	—	—	—	—	—
	$-10\ (T_b)$	—	—	—	—	—	—	—	—	—
	$15\ °C^{pl}$	1.455	0.55×10^{-3}	—	—	1800	0.2	—	0.98	—
	20	—	12.54×10^{-6}	—	—	—	—	—	—	—

continued

Material	$T/°C$	ρ	$\mu_d/(\mathrm{Pa \cdot s})$	α_μ	β_μ	α_v	k	$\gamma(C_p)$	$k_\rho \times 10^3$	e_s
Transfromer Oil (Mineral)	$-50\ (T_p)$	—	—	—	—	—	—	—	—	—
	15.6	0.88	—	—	—	750	0.162	1860	—	—
	40	0.864	19×10^{-3}	—	—	—	—	—	—	—
	100	0.846	2.2×10^{-3}	—	—	—	—	—	—	—
	$160\ (T_f)$	—	—	—	—	—	—	—	—	—
	$280\ (T_a)$	—	—	—	—	—	—	—	—	—

Notes: $\alpha_\mu(\mathrm{MPa^{-1}})$ = Pressure-dynamic viscosity coefficient, Eq. (137.2) with $P_o = 0$;

$\beta_\mu(°C^{-1})$ = Temperature-dynamic viscosity coefficient, Eq. (137.2) with $T_o = 0$;

$\alpha_v(\mu m^3/m^3/°C)$ = Coefficient of volumetric thermal expansion;

γ (J/kg/°C) = Specific heat capacity at 0.1 MPa (100 kPa) constant pressure (C_p);

15 °C^{pl} = Pressurized liquid-Liquid at 15 °C and its corresponding equilibrium pressure;

$k_\rho(\mathrm{MPa^{-1}})$ = Compressibility.

Chapter 140

Fuels

140.1 Introduction

Hydrocarbon fuels are molecular combinations of carbon and hydrogen atoms. Among thousands of hydrocarbon compounds, the commonly used hydrocarbon fuels are listed as follows:

Name	Molecular Structure
Hydrogen	H_2
Methane	CH_4
Ethane	C_2H_6
Propane	C_3H_8
Butane	C_4H_{10}
Heptane	C_7H_{16}
Methanol	CH_3OH
Ethanol	CH_3CH_2OH

Petroleum crude oil can be converted into transportation fuels, such as diesel fuel, gasoline, jet fuel and others, depending on the refining process.

140.2 Alcohols

Common alcohol fuels are methanol (CH_3OH) and ethanol (CH_3CH_2OH).

140.2.1 Ethanol (CH_3CH_2OH)

Ethanol (CH_3CH_2OH), also known as ethyl alcohol or EtOH, is a clear liquid (drinking alcohol). Though denatured ethanol (98% ethanol) contains about 30% less energy than gasoline, ethanol has a higher octane number than gasoline. It provides premium blending properties for gasoline to meet octane number requirements, reducing engine knocking and ensuring drivability.

Ethanol exhibits a positive net fossil energy value (i.e. less fossil energy used to produce ethanol than the energy available in ethanol). While corn-based ethanol can achieve moderate reductions in GHG (Greenhouse Gas), cellulosic ethanol can produce much greater energy and GHG benefits [Wang et al.] [Searchinger et al.].

140.2.2 Methanol (CH_3OH)

Methanol (CH_3OH), also called methyl alcohol, is the simplest alcohol. This industrial methanol is produced in a catalytic process directly from carbon monoxide, carbon dioxide, and hydrogen. Methanol is sometimes used to fuel internal combustion engines especially for supercharged engines in race cars.

140.3   Diesel Fuels

Diesel fuel, a mixture of hydrocarbons, is mainly comprised of consitalkanes (paraffinic), cycloalkanes (naphthenic), and aromatic. The relevant metric for diesel engines is the cetane number which is a measure of ease of combustion. In terms of combustion quality, cetane number is a measure of a fuel's ignition delay (the time period between the start of injection and the actual start of fuel combustion in a pre-combustion chamber type compression ignition test engine) and thus the related cold start performance. Generally, fuels with higher cetane numbers provide a shorter ignition delay and are of higher quality.

140.3.1 Petroleum Diesel Fuels

The petroleum industry is producing ultra-low sulfur diesel (ULSD) fuel, a cleaner diesel (ULSD) fuel in order to meet USA EPA requirements. Clean-burning diesel fuel contains no more than 15 ppm (parts per million) sulfur.

140.3.2 Bio-Diesel Fuels

Biodiesel refers to vegetable oils and animal fat-based diesel fuel. It consists of long-chain alkyl (methyl, ethyl, or propyl) esters. Biodiesel fuel has higher brake-specific fuel consumption compared with petroleum diesel fuel at the same engine performance. Nevertheless, biodiesel can be used alone or blended with petrodiesel in any proportions [Omidvarborna et al.].

140.3.3 Diesel-based Marine Fuels

Petroleum marine fuels (Diesel-based) are designated by a code that consists of [ISO 8216] [ISO 8217]:

(a) Initial: ISO;

(b) Letter F: for petroleum fuels;

(c) Fuel name consisting of three letters:

　　1st letter: Family letter (D for distillate or R for residual);

　　2nd letter: M for "Marine";

　　3rd letter: Classification based on ISO 8217, i.e. X, A, B, C, ..., or K;

(d) Maximum kinematic viscosity (mm^2/s) at 50 ℃.

For example, RMB 20 (or F-RMB 20) means petroleum-based residual marine (class B) having the maximum kinematic viscosity of 20 cSt (mm^2/s) at 50 ℃.

140.4　Gasoline

140.4.1　Automobile Gasoline

Gasoline is the dominant fuel for powering passenger vehicles in the USA. Specifications of automobile gasoline are given in ASTM D4814. Gasoline, when used in high-compression internal combustion engines, tends to autoignite (detonate), causing damaging engine knocking. The relevant metric for gasoline engines is the octane rating, of which the octane number (reference no. = 100) describes the anti-knock properties of gasoline fuel. Knock occurs, if the operating temperature exceeds the autoignition temperature.

140.4.2　Aviation Gasoline

Specifications of aviation gasoline (also called Avgas) for internal combustion engine-based aircraft are given in ASTM D4814. Avgas is high octane gasoline.

140.5　Helium

Helium is the second lightest and second most abundant element in the observable universe. Its boiling temperature (T_b) is the lowest among all elements.

140.6　Hydrogen (H_2)

The global energy system's transition from fossil fuel to hydrogen utilization attracts more and more researchers. Liquid hydrogen fuel has higher specific energy (energy per unit mass) than gasoline does, but a much lower volumetric energy density. Hydrogen (H_2) can be obtained from natural gas, methanol, and electrolysis of water. Hydrogen has the second-lowest boiling point and melting point of all elements, second only to helium.

140.7   Jet Fuels

Jet fuel, also called aviation turbine fuel, is a mixture of a large number of different hydrocarbons (paraffin, olefins, naphthenes, and aromatics) developed for turbine engines. There are two major groups of jet fuel:

- (a) Jet A and Jet A-1: Unleaded kerosene, mainly for commercial jets;
- (b) Jet B: Naphtha-kerosene blends, for its improved performance at cold temperatures. Wide-cut fuel is a blend of approximately 30% kerosene and 70% gasoline for extremely cold areas (e.g. Alaska).

JP (Jet Propellant) is used to designate USA military jet fuels, ranging from JP1 to JP10.

140.8   Kerosene

Kerosene has been widely used to power jet engines of aircraft as jet fuel, and some rocket engines [API]. The heat of combustion of kerosene is about 44.6 MJ/kg, similar to that of diesel fuel. There are two grades of kerosene:

- (a) 1-K Kerosene: less than 0.04% sulfur (weight);
- (b) 2-K Kerosene: 0.3% sulfur (weight).

140.9   Methane (CH_4 ; Natural Gas)

As described by [Cornell] that compressed natural gas is touted as the "cleanest burning" alternative fuel available, since the simplicity of the methane molecule reduces tailpipe emissions of different pollutants by 35% to 97%. Not quite as dramatic is the reduction in net greenhouse-gas emissions, which is about the same as corn-grain ethanol at about a 20% reduction over gasoline [Cornell]. The main advantage of natural gas is that it is significantly cheaper to run than gasoline.

LPG (Liquefied Petroleum Gas) fuel is compatible with petroleum gasoline engines while LNG (Liquefied Natural Gas) and CNG (Compressed Natural gas) with heavy-duty diesel vehicles, as argued in [Envocare].

140.10　Propane（$C_3H_8 + C_4H_{10}$）

Propane consists mainly of C_3H_8, with C_4H_{10} as a minor ingredient. It is made from petroleum, corn or sugarcanes and has a higher energy density than ethanol. Although it is often used in its gaseous form, propane is the cleanest-burning liquid fuel [Bourzac]. It is a by-product of petroleum refining or natural gas processing.

References

ABRAMOVIC K C, 1998. The Temperature Dependence of Dynamic Viscosity for Some Vegetable Oils[J]. Acta Chimica Slovenica, 45 (1): 69-77.

American Petroleum Institute, 1976. Alcohols: A Technical Assessment of Their Application as Motor Fuels, API Publication No. 4261, Washington, DC, USA.

ALTIN R, et al, 2001. The Potential of Using Vegetable Oil Fuels as Fuel for Diesel Engines[J]. Energy Conversion and Management, 42(5): 529-538.

BABU A K, DEVARADJANE G, 2003. Vegetable Oils and Their Derivatives as Fuels for CI: An Overview[J]. SAE 2003-01-0767.

BAILEY, 2005. Industrial Oil & Fat Products[M]. 6th Edition, Wiley-Interscience, New York, NY.

BAIR S, 2013. The Pressure and Temperature Dependence of Volume and Viscosity of four Diesel fuels[J]. Fuel, 135(1): 112-119.

BOŽIKOVÁ M, HLAVÁ P, 2013. Thermal Conductivity and Thermal Diffusivity of Biodiesel and Bioethanol Samples[J]. Acta technologica agriculture-Nitra: SUA in Nitra, 16(4): 88-92.

BROCK, et al, 2008. Experimental Determination of Viscosity and Thermal Conductivity of Vegetable Oils[J]. Revista Ciência e Tecnologia de Alimentos , 28(3): 564-570.

DEMIRBAS A, 2009. Biofuels Securing the Planet's Future Energy Needs [J]. Energy Conversion and Management, 50(9): 2239-2249.

ESTEBAN B, et al, 2012. Temperature Dependence of Density and Viscosity of Vegetable Oils[J]. Biomass and Bioenergy, 42(jul.): 164-171.

ESTELA-URIBE J F, JARAMILLO J, 2005. Generalized Virial Equation of State for Natural Gas Systems[J].

Fluid Phase Equilibria, 231(1): 84-98.

FASINA O, COLLEY Z, 2008. Viscosity and Specific Heat of Vegetable Oils as a Function of Temperature: 35 ℃ to 180 ℃[J]. International Journal of Food Properties, 11(4): 738-746.

FAZAL M A, et al, 2011. Biodiesel Feasibility Study: An Evaluation of Material Compatibility; Performance; Emission and Engine Durability[J]. Renewable and Sustainable Energy Reviews, 15(2): 1314-1324.

FRANCO Z, NGUYEN Q D, 2011. Flow Properties of Vegetable Oil-diesel Fuel Blends[J]. Fuel, 90(2): 838-843.

GAWRILOWM I, 2004. Vegetable Oil Usage in Lubricants[J]. inform, 15(11): 702-705.

GOERING C E, et al, 1982. Fuel Properties of Eleven Vegetable Oils[J]. Transactions of the ASAE, 25(6): 1472-1483.

HALDERMAN J D, MARTIN T, 2009. Hybrid and Alternative Fuel Vehicles, Pearson/Prentice Hall, New York, NY.

HANLEY H J, MCCARTY R D, HAYNES W N, 1975. Equation for the Viscosity and Thermal Conductivity Coefficients of Methane[J]. Cryogenics, 15(7): 413-417.

JAESCHKE M, SCHLEY P, 1995. Ideal Gas Thermodynamic Properties for Natural Gas Applications[J]. International Journal of Thermophysics, 16(6):1381-1392.

JAICHANDARL S, ANNAMALAI K, 2011. The Status of Biodiesel as an Alternative Fuel for Diesel Engine-An Overview[J]. Journal of Sustainable Energy & Environment, 2: 71-75.

KARAOSMANOGLU F M, TUTER, et al, 1999. Fuel Properties of Cottonseed Oil[J]. Energy Sources, Part A: Recovery, Utilization, and Environmental Effects, 21(9): 821-828.

KRISNANGKURA K, et al, 2006. An Empirical Approach in Predicting Biodiesel Viscosity at Various Temperatures[J]. Fuel, 85(1): 107-113.

LABECKAS G, SLAVINSKAS S, 2006. Performance of Direct-injection Off-road Diesel Engine on Rapeseed Oil[J]. Renewable Energy, 31(6): 849-863.

LEE S W, TANAKA D, KUSAKA J, et al, 2002. Effects of Diesel Fuel Characteristics on Spray and Combustion in a Diesel Engine[J]. JSAE Reviews, 23(4): 407-414.

MACEDO T, et al, 2013. Viscosity of Vegetable Oils and Biodiesel and Energy Generation[J]. International Journal of Chemical, Molecular, Nuclear, Materials and Metallurgical Engineering, 7(5).

MASON E A, SAXENA S C. Approximate Formula for the Thermal Conductivity of Gas Mixtures[J]. The

Physics of Fluids, 1(5): 361-369.

MCCARTHY P P, RASUL M G, MOAZZEM S S, 2011. Analysis and Comparison of Performance and Emissions of an Internal Combustion Engine Fuelled with Petroleum Diesel and Different Bio-diesels[J]. Fuel, 90(6): 2147-2157.

MOMIRLANA M, VEZIROGLUB T N, 2005. The Properties of Hydrogen as Fuel Tomorrow in Sustainable Energy System for a Cleaner Planet[J]. International Journal of Hydrogen Energy, 30(7): 795-802.

MONYEM A, VAN G J, 2001. The Effect of Biodiesel Oxidation on Engine Performance and Emissions[J]. Biomass Bioenergy, 20, 317-325.

MURALIDHARAN K K, VASUDEVAN D D, 2011. Performance, Emission and Combustion Characteristics of a Variable Compression Ratio Engine Using Methyl Esters of Waste Cooking Oil and Diesel Blends[J]. Applied Energy, 88(11): 3959-3968.

NOUREDDINI H, et al, 1992. Viscosities of Vegetable Oils and Fatty Acids[J]. Journal of the American Oil Chemists Society, 69(12): 1189-1191.

OMIDVARBORNA, et al, 2014. Characterization of Particulate Matter Emitted from Transit Buses Fueled with B20 in Idle Modes[J]. Journal of Environmental Chemical Engineering, 2(4): 2335-2342.

PEREIRA R G, et al, 2007. Exhaust Emissions and Electric Energy Generation in a Stationary Engine Using Blends of Diesel and Soybean Biodiesel[J]. Renewable Energy, 32(14): 2453-2460.

RAHMOUNI C, LE CORRE O, TAZEROUT M, 2003. Online Determination of Natural Gas Properties[J]. Comptes Rendus Mecanique, 331(8): 545-550.

REGUEIRA T, 2011. Compressibilities and Viscosities of Reference and Vegetable Oils for Their Use as Hydraulic Fluids and Lubricants[J]. Green Chemistry, 13, 1293-1302.

RIGDEN J S, 2002. Hydrogen: The Essential Element, Harvard University Press, Cambridge, MA, USA.

RODENBUSH C M, HSIEH F H, VISWANATH D D, 1999. Density and Viscosity of Vegetable Oils[J]. Journal of the Americal Oil Chemists Society, 76(12): 1415-1419.

SEARCHINGER T, et al, 2008. Use of U.S. Croplands for Biofuels Increases Greenhouse Gases through Emissions from Land Use Change[J]. Staff General Research Papers Archive, 319(5867): 1238-1240.

SCHASCHKE C, et al, 2013. Density and Viscosity Measurement of Diesel Fuels at Combined High Pressure and Elevated Temperature[J]. Processes, 1(2): 30-48.

THOMAS G, 2000. Overview of Storage Development DOE Hydrogen Program [J]. Sandia National Laboratories, Livermore, CA.

TUTTLE J, von KUEGELGEN T, 2004. Biodiesel Handling and Use Guidelines [M]. 3rd Edition, National Renewable Energy Laboratory.

VOGEL E, WILHELM J, KÜCHENMEISTER C, et al, 2000. High-precision Viscosity Measurements on Methane [J]. High Temperatures-High Pressures, 32(1): 73-81.

WANG M, WU M, HONG H, 2007. Life-Cycle Energy and Greenhouse Gas Emission Impacts of Different Corn Ethanol Plant Types [J]. Environmental Research Letter, 2: 024001.

YUAN W, et al, 2005. Temperature-dependent Kinematic Viscosity of Selected Biodiesel Fuels and Blends with Diesel Fuel [J]. Journal of the American Oil Chemists' Society, 82(3): 195-199.

Table 140. 1　Typical Thermomechanical Characteristics of Fuels [ASTM D975] [ASTM 6751] [ASTM D1665]

Material	T/℃	ρ	μ_d/(Pa·s)	α_μ	β_μ	α_v	k	γ	$k_\rho \times 10^3$	e_s
BD 100 (Bio-Diesel)	-14 (T_p)	—	—	—	—	—	—	—	—	—
	10	0.886	$9 \times 10^{-3} \rho$	—	—	—	—	—	—	—
	15	0.882	—	—	—	—	—	—	—	—
	40	0.864	$4.26 \times 10^{-3} \rho$	—	721×10^{-6}	—	—	—	—	42
	100	0.823	$1.69 \times 10^{-3} \rho$	—	—	—	—	—	—	—
	130 (T_f)	—	—	—	—	—	—	—	—	—
	140	0.791	$1.13 \times 10^{-3} \rho$	—	—	—	—	—	—	—
	262 (T_b)	—	—	—	—	—	—	—	—	—
Butane (C_4H_{10})	-60 (T_f)	—	—	—	—	—	—	—	—	—
	0 (T_b)	—	—	—	—	—	2300	—	—	—
	15	0.0025	—	—	—	—	—	—	—	—
	23	—	—	—	—	—	—	—	—	49.1
	288 (T_a)	—	—	—	—	—	—	—	—	—
Diesel Fuel (No.1; Petroleum; $C_{12}H_{16}$)	25	0.877	—	—	—	—	0.13	—	—	44
	38 (T_f)	—	—	—	—	—	—	—	—	—
	40	—	$1.3 \times 10^{-3} \rho < \mu_d < 2.4 \times 10^{-3} \rho$	—	—	—	—	—	—	—
	100	0.776	—	—	—	—	—	—	—	—
	140	0.752	$0.78 \times 10^{-3} \rho$	—	—	—	—	—	—	—
	256 (T_a)	—	—	—	—	—	—	—	—	—

continued

Material	$T/^\circ\text{C}$	ρ	$\mu_\text{d}/(\text{Pa}\cdot\text{s})$	α_μ	β_μ	α_v	k	γ	$k_\rho\times10^3$	e_s
Diesel Fuel (No.2; Petroleum)	$-24\ (T_\text{m})$	—	—	—	—	—	—	—	—	—
	$-18\ (T_\text{p})$	—	—	—	—	—	—	—	—	—
	20	0.830	$6\times10^{-3}\rho$	—	—	—	—	—	—	—
	23	—	—	—	—	—	—	1750	—	—
	25	—	—	—	—	—	0.13	—	—	44
	40	0.818	$1.9\times10^{-3}\rho<\mu_\text{d}<4.1\times10^{-3}\rho$	—	—	—	—	—	—	—
	$52\ (T_\text{f})$	—	—	—	—	—	—	—	—	—
	100	0.776	—	—	—	—	—	—	—	—
	140	0.752	$0.78\times10^{-3}\rho$	—	—	—	—	—	—	—
	$256\ (T_\text{a})$	—	—	—	—	—	—	—	—	—
Diesel Fuel (No.4; Petroleum)	-40	—	$<48\times10^{-3}\rho$	—	—	—	—	—	—	—
	10	0.838	—	—	—	—	—	—	—	—
	15	0.833	—	—	—	—	—	—	—	—
	23	—	—	—	—	—	—	1750	—	—
	25	—	—	—	—	—	0.13	—	—	44
	37.8	—	$<29.8\times10^{-3}\rho$	—	—	—	—	—	—	—
	40	0.818	$5.5\times10^{-3}\rho<\mu_\text{d}<24\times10^{-3}\rho$	—	—	—	—	—	—	—
	54.4	—	$<13.1\times10^{-3}\rho$	—	—	—	—	—	—	—
	100	0.776	—	—	—	—	—	—	—	—
	140	0.752	$0.78\times10^{-3}\rho$	—	—	—	—	—	—	—
	$256\ (T_\text{a})$	—	—	—	—	—	—	—	—	—
Diesel Fuel (No.6; Petroleum)	10	0.838	—	—	—	—	—	—	—	—
	15	0.833	—	—	—	—	—	—	—	—
	23	0.85	—	—	—	—	—	1750	—	—
	25	—	—	—	—	—	0.13	—	—	44
	100	0.776	—	—	—	—	—	—	—	—
	140	0.752	$0.78\times10^{-3}\rho$	—	—	—	—	—	—	—
	$256\ (T_\text{a})$	—	—	—	—	—	—	—	—	—

continued

Material	$T/°C$	ρ	$\mu_d/(Pa \cdot s)$	α_μ	β_μ	α_v	k	γ	$k_p \times 10^3$	e_s
Diesel Fuel (Commercial; Schaschke et al.)	25	0.845 $+561\times10^{-6}p$ $-0.7\times10^{-6}p^2$	2.80×10^{-3}	0.0122	—	—	—	—	—	44
	50	0.829 $+590\times10^{-6}p$ $-0.7\times10^{-6}p^2$	1.82×10^{-3}	0.0102	—	—	—	—	—	—
	75	0.813 $+632\times10^{-6}p$ $-0.8\times10^{-6}p^2$	1.26×10^{-3}	0.0088	—	—	—	—	—	—
	140	0.752	$0.78\times10^{-3}\rho$	—	—	—	—	—	—	—
Ethanol (CH_3CH_2OH; Alcohol, Ethyl)	0	—	—	—	—	—	—	2300	—	—
	20	—	1.1×10^{-3}	—	—	—	—	—	—	—
	25	0.787	1.074×10^{-3}	—	—	1100	0.171	2440	—	30
	37.8	—	$1.2\times10^{-3}\rho$	—	—	—	—	—	—	—
	40	—	—	—	—	—	—	2720	—	—
	78 (T_b)	—	—	—	—	—	—	—	—	—
Gasoline-a (C_8H_{18})	−43 (T_f)	—	—	—	—	—	—	—	—	—
	15.6	0.74	$0.88\times10^{-3}\rho$	—	—	—	—	2220	—	—
	25	—	—	—	—	—	—	—	—	46.4
	37.8	—	$0.71\times10^{-3}\rho$	—	—	—	—	—	—	—
	280 (T_a)	—	—	—	—	—	—	—	—	—
Gasoline-b (C_8H_{18})	−43 (T_f)	—	—	—	—	—	—	—	—	—
	15.6	0.72	$0.64\times10^{-3}\rho$	—	—	—	—	2220	—	—
	25	—	—	—	—	—	—	—	—	46.4
	37.8	—	$0.64\times10^{-3}\rho$	—	—	—	—	—	—	—
	280 (T_a)	—	—	—	—	—	—	—	—	—
Gasoline-c (C_8H_{18})	−43 (T_f)	—	—	—	—	—	—	—	—	—
	15.6	0.68	$0.46\times10^{-3}\rho$	—	—	—	—	2220	—	—
	25	—	—	—	—	—	—	—	—	46.4
	37.8	—	$0.40\times10^{-3}\rho$	—	—	—	—	—	—	—
	280 (T_a)	—	—	—	—	—	—	—	—	—
Gasoline (Avgas)	25	—	—	—	—	—	—	—	—	47

continued

Material	$T/℃$	ρ	$\mu_d/(\text{Pa}\cdot\text{s})$	α_μ	β_μ	α_v	k	γ	$k_p\times10^3$	e_s
Helium	-272.20 (T_m)	—	—	—	—	—	—	—	—	—
	-272	0.145	—	—	—	—	—	—	—	—
	-269	0.125	3.33×10^{-3}	—	—	—	—	—	—	—
	-268.93 (T_b)	—	—	—	—	—	—	—	—	—
	0	0.000179	18.6×10^{-6}	—	—	—	—	—	—	—
	15	0.000125	20×10^{-6}	—	—	20000	0.02	5000	—	—
	23	—	20×10^{-6}	—	—	—	0.151	5188	—	—
	-260	0.0763	—	—	—	—	—	—	—	—
	-259.15 (T_m)	—	—	—	—	—	—	—	—	—
	-253 (T_f)	—	—	—	—	—	—	—	—	—
Heptane (C_7H_{16})	-17.8	—	$0.683\times10^{-3}\rho$	—	—	—	—	—	—	—
	15.6	0.664	—	—	—	—	—	—	—	—
	25	—	—	—	—	—	0.14	2240	—	48
	37.8	—	$0.511\times10^{-3}\rho$	—	—	—	—	—	—	—
Hexane (C_6H_{14})	0	0.678	0.387×10^{-3}	—	—	—	—	—	—	—
	30	0.649	0.28×10^{-3}	—	—	—	0.124	2260	—	—
	50	—	0.235×10^{-3}	—	—	—	—	—	—	—
	≈60 (T_b)	—	—	—	—	—	—	—	—	—
Hydrogen (H_2)	-252.9	0.0708	—	—	—	—	—	—	—	—
	-252.88 (T_b)	—	—	—	—	—	—	—	—	—
	0	90×10^{-6}	8.42×10^{-6}	—	—	—	—	—	—	—
	15 ℃ pl	—	—	—	—	—	—	—	—	141.9
	15	71×10^{-6}	10×10^{-6}	—	—	8700	0.12	—	—	—
	20	—	—	—	—	—	—	14223	—	—
	23	—	—	—	—	—	—	14310	—	—
	585 (T_a)	—	—	—	—	—	—	—	—	—

continued

Material	$T/℃$	ρ	$\mu_\mathrm{d}/(\mathrm{Pa \cdot s})$	α_μ	β_μ	α_v	k	γ	$k_\rho \times 10^3$	e_s
Jet A Fuel	-55	0.8693	14.11×10^{-3}	—	—	—	—	—	—	—
	-50	0.8659	10.73×10^{-3}	—	—	—	—	—	—	—
	-45	0.8624	8.39×10^{-3}	—	—	—	—	—	—	—
	<-40 (T_m)	—	—	—	—	—	—	—	—	—
	-40	0.8586	6.7×10^{-3}	—	—	—	—	—	—	—
	-30	0.8514	4.81×10^{-3}	—	—	—	—	—	—	—
	-20	0.8443	3.41×10^{-3}	—	—	—	—	—	—	—
	15	0.820	—	—	—	—	—	—	—	—
	25	—	—	—	—	—	—	—	—	43
	>38 (T_f)	—	—	—	—	—	—	—	—	—
	210 (T_a)	—	—	—	—	—	—	—	—	—
Jet A-1 Fuel	-55	0.8107	9.92×10^{-3}	—	—	—	—	—	—	—
	-50	0.8069	7.74×10^{-3}	—	—	—	—	—	—	—
	<-47 (T_m)	—	—	—	—	—	—	—	—	—
	-40	0.7999	4.97×10^{-3}	—	—	—	—	—	—	—
	-30	0.7928	3.56×10^{-3}	—	—	—	—	—	—	—
	-20	0.7857	2.71×10^{-3}	—	—	—	—	—	—	—
	15	0.804	—	—	—	—	—	—	—	—
	25	—	—	—	—	—	—	—	—	42.8
	>38 (T_f)	—	—	—	—	—	—	—	—	—
	210 (T_a)	—	—	—	—	—	—	—	—	—
Jet N-2B Fuel	-55	0.859	56.95×10^{-3}	—	—	—	—	—	—	—
	-50	0.856	38.26×10^{-3}	—	—	—	—	—	—	—
	-40	0.849	20.06×10^{-3}	—	—	—	—	—	—	—
	-30	0.842	11.95×10^{-3}	—	—	—	—	—	—	—
	-20	0.835	7.76×10^{-3}	—	—	—	—	—	—	—
	>-23 (T_f)	—	—	—	—	—	—	—	—	—
	15	0.787	—	—	—	—	—	—	—	—
	25	—	—	—	—	—	—	—	—	43.2
	210 (T_a)	—	—	—	—	—	—	—	—	—

continued

Material	$T/\text{°C}$	ρ	$\mu_d/(\text{Pa·s})$	α_μ	β_μ	α_v	k	γ	$k_\rho \times 10^3$	e_s
JP-5 Fuel (Diesel; Certane=42)	40	ρ	$1.5\times10^{-3}\rho$	—	—	—	—	—	—	—
	62 (T_f)	—	—	—	—	—	—	—	—	—
JP-8 Fuel (Diesel; Certane=45)	40	ρ	$1.2\times10^{-3}\rho$	—	—	—	—	—	—	—
	45 (T_f)	—	—	—	—	—	—	—	—	—
Kerosene ($C_{12}H_{24}$)	-143 (T_m)	—	—	—	—	—	—	—	—	—
	-47 (T_p)	—	—	—	—	—	—	—	—	—
	-40	—	$<16\times10^{-3}\rho$	—	—	—	—	—	—	—
	15	0.82	2.4×10^{-3}	—	—	—	—	—	—	—
	25	0.823	1.64×10^{-3}	—	—	—	0.145	2090	—	44.6
	40 (T_f)	—	—	—	—	—	—	—	—	—
	177 (T_b)	—	—	—	—	—	—	—	—	—
	220 (T_a)	—	—	—	—	—	—	—	—	—
Methane (CH_4; Natural Gas)	-182.5 (T_m)	—	—	—	—	—	—	—	—	—
	-182	0.423	—	—	—	—	0.215	—	—	—
	-161.5 (T_b)	—	—	—	—	—	—	—	—	—
	-188 (T_f)	—	—	—	—	—	—	—	—	—
	15 °C^{pl}	0.74	—	—	—	—	—	—	—	55.6
	23	0.00068	—	—	—	—	—	2208	—	—
	27	—	11.2×10^{-6}	—	—	—	—	—	—	—
	537 (T_a)	—	—	—	—	—	—	—	—	—
Methanol (CH_3OH; Alcohol, Methyl)	-98 (T_m)	—	—	—	—	—	—	—	—	—
	0	ρ	$1.04\times10^{-3}\rho$	—	—	—	—	—	—	—
	11 (T_f)	—	—	—	—	—	2470	—	—	—
	15	0.791	0.593×10^{-3}	—	—	1490	0.202	2510	—	—
	25	0.789	0.544×10^{-3}	—	—	—	—	—	—	19.7
	65 (T_b)	—	—	—	—	—	—	—	—	—

continued

Material	$T/°C$	ρ	$\mu_d/(Pa \cdot s)$	α_μ	β_μ	α_v	k	γ	$k_p \times 10^3$	e_s
Octane-*n* (C_8H_{18})	-56 (T_m)	—	—	—	—	—	—	—	—	—
	-17.8	ρ	$1.266 \times 10^{-3}\rho$	—	—	—	—	—	—	—
	15.6	0.707	0.56×10^{-3}	—	—	—	—	—	—	—
	25	—	—	—	—	—	0.147	2150	—	48
	37.8	ρ	$0.807 \times 10^{-3}\rho$	—	—	—	—	—	—	—
	126 (T_b)	—	—	—	—	—	—	—	—	—
Oxygen (O_2)	-218.78 (T_m)	—	—	—	—	—	—	—	—	—
	-182	1.1412	—	—	—	—	—	—	—	—
	-182.1 (T_b)	—	—	—	—	—	—	—	—	—
	-182	0.00447	—	—	—	—	—	—	—	—
	0	—	18.1×10^{-6}	—	—	—	0.0244	—	—	—
	20	0.00135	20.2×10^{-6}	—	—	—	—	916	—	—
	23	0.00131	20.0×10^{-6}	—	—	—	—	920	—	—
Propane	-188 (T_m)	—	—	—	—	—	—	—	—	—
	-104 (T_f)	—	—	—	—	—	—	—	—	—
	-42.2 (T_b)	—	—	—	—	—	—	—	—	—
	0	0.002	—	—	—	—	—	2400	—	—
	15 °C[pl]	0.52	—	—	—	—	—	—	—	—
	25 °C[pl]	0.495	0.11×10^{-3}	—	—	—	—	2090	—	49.6
	490 (T_a)	—	—	—	—	—	—	—	—	—
Vegetable Oil (Almond)	35	—	44.0×10^{-3}	—	—	—	—	2354	—	—
	50	—	26.9×10^{-3}	—	—	—	—	2388	—	—
	80	—	12.4×10^{-3}	—	—	—	—	2477	—	—
	110	—	7.51×10^{-3}	—	—	—	—	2576	—	—
	140	—	5.0×10^{-3}	—	—	—	—	2715	—	—
	180	—	3.62×10^{-3}	—	—	—	—	2823	—	—

-218.79 (Triple point, at pressure of 0.0015 bar)

-118.57 (Critical point, at pressure of 50.43 bar)

continued

Material	$T/℃$	ρ	$\mu_{\mathrm{d}}/(\mathrm{Pa \cdot s})$	α_μ	β_μ	α_v	k	γ	$k_\rho \times 10^3$	e_s
Vegetable Oil (Canola, from Rapeseed; VI=211)	$-18\ (T_\mathrm{p})$	—	—	—	—	—	—	—	—	—
	4	—	163×10^{-3}	—	—	—	—	—	—	—
	10	0.921	115×10^{-3}	—	—	—	—	—	—	—
	20	0.915	71.6×10^{-3}	—	—	—	0.184	1913	—	—
	35	—	42.5×10^{-3}	—	—	—	—	2208	—	—
	40	0.903	31×10^{-3}	—	—	—	—	—	—	39.7
	50	—	25.8×10^{-3}	—	—	—	—	2245	—	—
	80	—	12.1×10^{-3}	—	—	—	—	2333	—	—
	110	—	7.77×10^{-3}	—	—	—	—	2413	—	—
	140	0.841	5.01×10^{-3}	—	—	—	—	2559	—	—
	180	—	4.65×10^{-3}	—	—	—	—	2640	—	—
	$282\ (T_\mathrm{f})$	—	—	—	—	—	—	—	—	—
Vegetable Oil (Castor)	$-40\ (T_\mathrm{p})$	—	—	—	—	—	—	—	—	—
	20	—	1.0	—	—	—	—	—	—	—
	25	0.96	985×10^{-3}	—	—	956	0.18	1800	—	—
	30	—	450×10^{-3}	—	—	—	—	—	—	—
	40	0.951	233×10^{-3}	—	—	—	—	—	—	39.5
	50	—	128×10^{-3}	—	—	—	—	—	—	—
	80	0.926	—	—	—	—	—	—	—	—
	100	0.914	—	—	—	—	—	—	—	—
	$277\ (T_\mathrm{f})$	—	—	—	—	—	—	—	—	—
Vegetable Oil (Coconut; VI=175)	15	0.928	—	—	—	—	—	—	—	—
	20	0.917	—	—	—	—	—	—	—	—
	30	—	39×10^{-3}	—	—	—	—	—	—	—
	40	0.914	26×10^{-3}	—	—	—	—	—	—	—
	50	—	19×10^{-3}	—	—	—	—	—	—	—
	90	—	—	—	—	—	—	—	—	—
	100	—	5.22×10^{-3}	—	—	—	—	—	—	—
	110	—	4.36×10^{-3}	—	—	—	—	—	—	—
	$288\ (T_\mathrm{f})$	—	—	—	—	—	—	—	—	—

continued

Material	$T/℃$	ρ	$\mu_{\mathrm{d}}/(\mathrm{Pa \cdot s})$	α_μ	β_μ	α_v	k	γ	$k_\rho \times 10^3$	e_s
Vegetable Oil (Corn)	-10 (T_{m})	—	—	—	—	—	—	—	—	—
	10	0.924	105×10^{-3}	—	—	—	—	—	—	—
	35	—	37.9×10^{-3}	—	—	—	—	1673	—	—
	40	0.905	31×10^{-3}	—	—	—	—	—	—	39.5
	50	—	23.3×10^{-3}	—	—	—	—	1702	—	—
	60	—	18×10^{-3}	—	—	—	—	—	—	—
	80	—	11×10^{-3}	—	—	—	—	1783	—	—
	110	—	6.83×10^{-3}	—	—	—	—	1866	—	—
	140	0.842	4.95×10^{-3}	—	—	—	—	1999	—	—
	180	—	3.33×10^{-3}	—	—	—	—	2045	—	—
	335 (T_{f})	—	—	—	—	—	—	—	—	—
Vegetable Oil (Cotton Seed)	-15 (T_{p})	—	—	—	—	—	—	—	—	—
	0	ρ	$213 \times 10^{-3} \rho$	—	—	—	—	—	—	—
	10	ρ	$121.4 \times 10^{-3} \rho$	—	—	—	—	—	—	—
	15	0.924	—	—	—	—	—	—	—	—
	20	0.918	80×10^{-3}	—	—	—	—	—	—	—
	30	—	55×10^{-3}	—	—	—	—	—	—	—
	40	0.91	38×10^{-3}	—	—	—	—	—	—	41.8
	50	—	27×10^{-3}	—	—	—	—	—	—	—
	90	—	—	—	—	—	—	2200	—	—
	234 (T_{f})	—	—	—	—	—	—	—	—	—
	320 (T_{b})	—	—	—	—	—	—	—	—	—
Vegetable Oil (Croton; Certaine = 40.7)	20	0.92	—	—	—	—	—	—	—	—
	40	—	30.3×10^{-3}	—	—	—	—	—	—	39.7

continued

Material	$T/℃$	ρ	$\mu_d/(\text{Pa}\cdot\text{s})$	α_μ	β_μ	α_v	k	γ	$k_\rho\times10^3$	e_s
Vegetable Oil (Grape Seed)	10	0.93	93.6×10^{-3}	—	—	—	—	—	—	—
	15	0.927	—	—	—	—	—	—	—	—
	20	0.924	55×10^{-3}	—	—	—	—	—	—	—
	35	0.91	41.5×10^{-3}	—	—	—	—	1572	—	—
	50	—	25.3×10^{-3}	—	—	—	—	1595	—	—
	80	—	12×10^{-3}	—	—	—	—	1654	—	—
	100	0.87	—	—	—	—	—	—	—	—
	110	—	10.4×10^{-3}	—	—	—	—	1735	—	—
	140	0.844	7.5×10^{-3}	—	—	—	—	1862	—	—
	180	—	4.78×10^{-3}	—	—	—	—	1949	—	—
Vegetable Oil (Hazelnut)	20	—	71×10^{-3}	—	—	—	—	—	—	—
	35	—	45.6×10^{-3}	—	—	—	—	1726	—	—
	50	—	27.4×10^{-3}	—	—	—	—	1742	—	—
	80	—	12.5×10^{-3}	—	—	—	—	1803	—	—
	110	—	7.56×10^{-3}	—	—	—	—	1876	—	—
	140	—	5.25×10^{-3}	—	—	—	—	1953	—	—
	180	—	3.48×10^{-3}	—	—	—	—	2045	—	—
Vegetable Oil (Karanja)	40	0.93	54×10^{-3}	—	—	—	—	—	—	36.5
	>200 (T_f)	—	—	—	—	—	—	—	—	—
Vegetable Oil (Linseed)	−15 (T_p)	—	—	—	—	—	—	—	—	—
	15	0.93	—	—	—	—	—	—	—	—
	20	0.93	48×10^{-3}	—	—	—	—	1840	—	—
	25	0.93	—	—	—	—	—	—	—	—
	30	—	33×10^{-3}	—	—	—	—	—	—	—
	40	—	25×10^{-3}	—	—	—	—	—	—	39.4
	50	—	18×10^{-3}	—	—	—	—	—	—	—
	71	—	—	—	—	—	—	2050	—	—
	264 (T_f)	—	—	—	—	—	—	—	—	—
	287 (T_b)	—	—	—	—	—	—	—	—	—

continued

Material	$T/℃$	ρ	$\mu_d/(\text{Pa}\cdot s)$	α_μ	β_μ	α_v	k	γ	$k_\rho\times10^3$	e_s
Vegetable Oil (Olive)	15	0.92	—	—	—	—	—	—	—	—
	20	0.912	80×10^{-3}	—	—	700	—	—	—	—
	35	—	46.3×10^{-3}	—	—	—	—	1746	—	—
	40	—	40×10^{-3}	—	—	—	—	—	—	39.5
	50	—	27.2×10^{-3}	—	—	—	—	1742	—	—
	80	—	12.6×10^{-3}	—	—	—	—	1783	—	—
	110	—	7.43×10^{-3}	—	—	—	—	1796	—	—
	140	—	5.29×10^{-3}	—	—	—	—	1804	—	—
	180	—	3.44×10^{-3}	—	—	—	—	1787	—	—
Vegetable Oil (Palm; VI=188)	20	0.89	—	—	—	—	0.173	1845	—	—
	30	0.885	43×10^{-3}	—	—	—	0.172	1975	—	—
	40	0.88	29×10^{-3}	—	—	—	0.171	1902	—	39.5
	50	0.875	20×10^{-3}	—	—	—	0.170	1930	—	—
	100	0.852	7.1×10^{-3}	—	—	—	0.166	2081	—	—
	140	0.833	3.7×10^{-3}	—	—	—	0.163	2214	—	—
	180	0.826	2.5×10^{-3}	—	—	—	0.161	2358	—	—
	314 (T_f)	—	—	—	—	—	—	—	—	—
Vegetable Oil (Peanut)	−6.7 (T_p)	—	—	—	—	—	—	—	—	—
	10	0.92	142×10^{-3}	—	—	—	—	—	—	—
	15	0.918	—	—	—	—	—	—	—	—
	25	0.912	—	—	—	—	—	—	—	—
	35	—	45.6×10^{-3}	—	—	—	—	2045	—	—
	40	0.903	36×10^{-3}	—	—	—	—	—	—	39.8
	80	—	12.7×10^{-3}	—	—	—	—	2147	—	—
	110	—	7.47×10^{-3}	—	—	—	—	2226	—	—
	140	—	5.14×10^{-3}	—	—	—	—	2300	—	—
	180	—	3.26×10^{-3}	—	—	—	—	2328	—	—
	315 (T_f)	—	—	—	—	—	—	—	—	—
Vegetable Oil (Safflower)	35	—	42.5×10^{-3}	—	—	—	—	2076	—	—
	50	—	22.3×10^{-3}	—	—	—	—	2110	—	—
	80	—	11.2×10^{-3}	—	—	—	—	—	—	—
	110	—	6.73×10^{-3}	—	—	—	—	2292	—	—
	140	—	4.95×10^{-3}	—	—	—	—	2384	—	—
	180	—	3.42×10^{-3}	—	—	—	—	2469	—	—

continued

Material	$T/°C$	ρ	$\mu_d/(\mathrm{Pa \cdot s})$	α_μ	β_μ	α_v	k	γ	$k_p \times 10^3$	e_s
Vegetable Oil (Sesame)	$-9.4\ (T_p)$	—	—	—	—	—	—	—	—	—
	15	0.922	—	—	—	—	—	—	—	—
	20	0.92	65×10^{-3}	—	—	—	—	—	—	—
	40	0.91	32.8×10^{-3}	—	—	—	—	—	—	39.3
	50	—	24.8×10^{-3}	—	—	—	—	2148	—	—
	80	—	11.9×10^{-3}	—	—	—	—	2224	—	—
	110	—	7.2×10^{-3}	—	—	—	—	2317	—	—
	140	—	4.95×10^{-3}	—	—	—	—	2409	—	—
	180	—	3.43×10^{-3}	—	—	—	—	2528	—	—
	$260\ (T_f)$	—	—	—	—	—	—	—	—	—
	$380\ (T_b)$	—	—	—	—	—	—	—	—	—
Vegetable Oil (Soybean; VI = 246)	$-9\ (T_p)$	—	—	—	—	—	—	—	—	—
	0	0.93	172×10^{-3}	—	—	—	—	—	—	—
	10	0.9254	99.6×10^{-3}	—	—	—	—	—	—	—
	20	0.92	60.5×10^{-3}	—	—	—	—	—	—	—
	30	—	45×10^{-3}	—	—	—	—	—	—	—
	35	—	38.6×10^{-3}	—	—	—	—	1675	—	—
	40	0.906	33×10^{-3}	—	—	—	—	—	—	39.6
	50	—	25×10^{-3}	—	—	—	—	1715	—	—
	80	—	11.5×10^{-3}	—	—	—	—	1798	—	—
	100	0.869	—	—	—	—	—	—	—	—
	110	—	7.17×10^{-3}	—	—	—	—	1906	—	—
	140	0.843	4.58×10^{-3}	—	—	—	—	1973	—	—
	180	—	3.3×10^{-3}	—	—	—	—	2079	—	—
	$325\ (T_f)$	—	—	—	—	—	—	—	—	—
Vegetable Oil (Sunflower; VI = 211)	$-12\ (T_p)$	—	—	—	—	—	—	—	—	—
	10	0.925	110×10^{-3}	—	—	—	—	—	—	—
	20	0.92	68×10^{-3}	—	—	—	—	—	—	—
	30	—	47×10^{-3}	—	—	—	—	—	—	—
	35	—	41.6×10^{-3}	—	—	—	—	2244	—	—

continued

Material	$T/°C$	ρ	$\mu_d(\text{Pa} \cdot \text{s})$	α_μ	β_μ	α_v	k	γ	$k_\rho \times 10^3$	e_s
Vegetable Oil (Sunflower; VI = 211)	40	0.904	35×10^{-3}	—	—	—	—	—	—	39.6
	50	—	25×10^{-3}	—	—	—	—	2276	—	—
	80	—	12×10^{-3}	—	—	—	—	2319	—	—
	100	0.867	6.75×10^{-3}	—	—	—	—	—	—	—
	110	—	—	—	—	—	—	2455	—	—
	140	0.841	5×10^{-3}	—	—	—	—	2558	—	—
	180	—	3.52×10^{-3}	—	—	—	—	2672	—	—
	316 (T_f)	—	—	—	—	—	—	—	—	—
Vegetable Oil (Walnut)	35	—	33.7×10^{-3}	—	—	—	—	2034	—	—
	50	—	21.2×10^{-3}	—	—	—	—	2068	—	—
	80	—	10.5×10^{-3}	—	—	—	—	2150	—	—
	110	—	6.71×10^{-3}	—	—	—	—	2243	—	—
	140	—	4.8×10^{-3}	—	—	—	—	2321	—	—
	180	—	3.46×10^{-3}	—	—	—	—	2377	—	—

Notes: $\mu_d(\text{Pa} \cdot \text{s} = \text{N}/\text{m}^2 \cdot \text{s}) = $ Dynamic viscosity as averaged at the ambient pressure;

$\alpha_\mu(\text{MPa}^{-1}) = $ Pressure-dynamic viscosity coefficient, Eq. (137.2) with $P_o = 0$;

$\beta_\mu(°C^{-1}) = $ Temperature-dynamic viscosity coefficient, Eq. (137.2) with $T_o = 0$;

$\alpha_v(\mu\text{m}^3/\text{m}^3/°C) = $ Coefficient of volumetric thermal expansion;

$\gamma(\text{J}/\text{kg}/°C) = $ Specific heat capacity at 0.1 MPa (100 kPa) constant pressure;

$e_s(\text{MJ}/\text{kg}) = $ Specific energy (combustion).

Chapter 141

IMDS (International Material Data System)

IMDS (International Material Data System) is a database created by the automotive industry to collect and report part structures and material composition data for vehicle components, as illustrated in Fig. 141.1. It meets the requirements of the European Directive on End-of-life Vehicles.

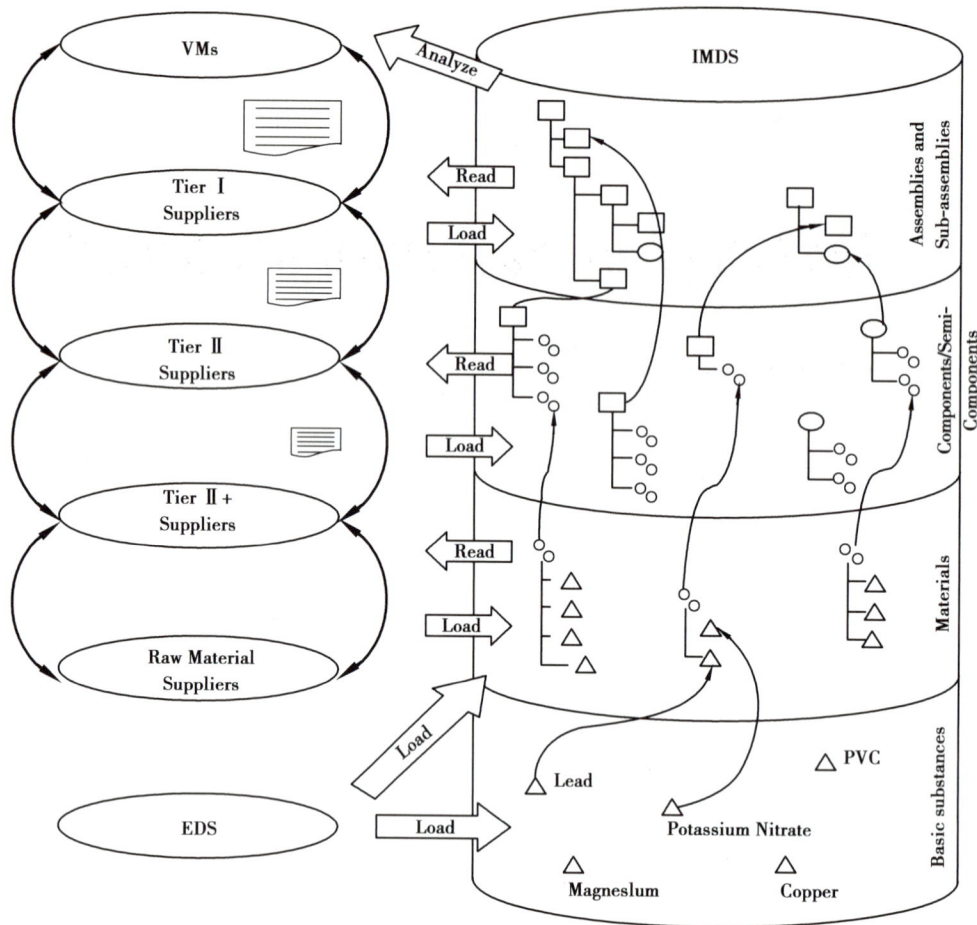

Fig. 141.1 IMDS Routing from Raw Material Suppliers to Vehicle Manufacturers (VMs)

RoHS (Restriction of Hazardous Substances Directive 2002/95/ECI) is the directive on the restriction of the use of certain hazardous substances in electrical and electronic equipment. RoHS is often referred to (inaccurately) as the "lead-free directive", while it restricts the use of the following six substances: Lead (Pb), Mercury (Hg), Cadmium (Cd), Hexavalent chromium (Cr^{6+}), Polybrominated biphenyls (PBB), Polybrominated diphenyl ether (PBDE). RoHS restricted substances have been used in a broad array of consumer electronics products.

Examples of leaded components include:

(a) Paints and pigments;

(b) PVC (vinyl) cables as a stabilizer (e.g., power cords and USB cables);

(c) Solders;

(d) Printed circuit board finishes, leads, internal and external interconnects;

(e) Glass in television and photographic products (e.g., CRT television screens and camera lenses);

(f) Metal parts;

(g) Lamps and bulbs;

(h) Batteries.

国家出版基金项目
NATIONAL PUBLICATION FOUNDATION

汽车材料的热机械性能 （中）

Automotive Engineering Materials–Thermomechanical Properties

江永瑞 著

重庆大学出版社

图书在版编目(CIP)数据

汽车材料的热机械性能 = Automotive Engineering
Materials-Thermomechanical Properties:上中下:
英文 / 江永瑞著. -- 重庆:重庆大学出版社,2022.4

(自主品牌汽车实践创新丛书)

ISBN 978-7-5689-3293-6

Ⅰ.①汽…　Ⅱ.①江…　Ⅲ.①汽车—工程材料—热机
械效应—性能—英文　Ⅳ.①U465

中国版本图书馆 CIP 数据核字(2022)第 080037 号

汽车材料的热机械性能

QICHE CAILIAO DE REJIXIE XINGNENG

（中）

江永瑞　著

策划编辑:杨粮菊　孙英姿　鲁　黎

责任编辑:陈　力　苟荟羽　　版式设计:杨粮菊
责任校对:姜　凤　　　　　　责任印制:张　策

*

重庆大学出版社出版发行

出版人:饶帮华

社址:重庆市沙坪坝区大学城西路 21 号

邮编:401331

电话:(023)88617190　88617185(中小学)

传真:(023)88617186　88617166

网址:http://www.cqup.com.cn

邮箱:fxk@cqup.com.cn(营销中心)

全国新华书店经销

重庆升光电力印务有限公司印刷

*

开本:889mm×1194mm　1/16　印张:34.5　字数:1123 千
2022 年 4 月第 1 版　　2022 年 4 月第 1 次印刷
ISBN 978-7-5689-3293-6　总定价:498.00 元

Ferrous

Chapter 71　Cast Irons

Chapter 72　Plain Carbon Steels

Chapter 79   Spring Steels

Chapter 80   Tool, Die, and Mold Steels

Chapter 81   Heat-Resistant Steels

Non-Ferrous

Chapter 82　Ag（Silver）

Chapter 83　Al（Aluminum）

Chapter 84　Au（Gold）

Ferrous

Chapter 71

Cast Irons

71.1　Introduction

Due to high carbon content, all cast irons contain graphite. There are five types of cast iron and their mechanical properties are listed in Tables 71.1—71.5:

(a) GCI (Gray Cast Iron)-lamellar graphite flakes, Table 71.1;
(b) DI (Ductile Iron)/NDI (Nodular Cast Iron)-nodular (spheroidal) graphite, Table 71.2;
(c) MCI (Malleable Cast Iron)-temper carbon graphite, Table 71.3;
(d) CGI (Compacted Graphite Iron)-compacted graphite, Table 71.4;
(e) ADI (Austempered Ductile Iron)-austempered nodular graphite, Table 71.5.

In general, iron castings won't lose their rigidity (Young's modulus) and strength unless the temperature exceeds 320 ℃. Ultimate tensile strengths of iron castings and low carbon steels decay linearly from the nominal room-temperature value at 400 ℃ down to almost zero at 650 ℃ [SAE J125 May88]. Mechanical properties of iron castings may vary with the following heat treatments:

(a) Annealed;
(b) Normalized;
(c) Normalized and tempered;
(d) Quenched and tempered.

Due to flexible-design and low-cost requirements, cast iron parts are used increasingly for very high loadings in a wide range of applications. But for highly dynamic loads with a significant failure behavior, e.g. in a car crash and an impeller burst, a standard material law defined only by a tension test is no longer sufficient. Particularly for cast iron parts, the different behaviors in tension and compression must be taken into the constitutive stress-strain curves as well as in the failure behavior.

71.2　Gray Cast Irons (GCI or GJL)

GCI (Gray Cast Iron) contains lamellar graphite flakes. The tensile strength (MPa) of high ended gray cast irons, i.e. ASTM 30, 35, and 40 grades can be approximated by the following conservative model [Loper and Shturmakov] regressed against the alloying ingredients,

$$\sigma_{uts} = 1083.7 - 220.9\ C - 30.26\ Si - 9.839\ Mn + 114.8\ S - 24.3\ P + 66.71\ Cr -$$

$$25.98\ Ni + 16.68\ Cu + 477.2\ Al - 1519.4\ Ti - 209.5\ V - 65.64\ Sn +$$

$$93.9\ Mo \hfill (71.1)$$

Gray iron castings are the primary low-cost material for cylinder heads and cylinder blocks for medium-and heavy-duty diesel engines. Material ASTM G3500 (SAE G3500), namely ASTM No. 35 or China GB HT250 or EN-GJS-250, is a popular choice. Stress-strain curves of three different gray iron castings at the room temperature are depicted in Fig. 71.1. Note that the compressive strength of a gray iron casting is much stronger than its tensile strength. The data given in Fig. 71.1 can be used for a nonlinear elastic finite element analysis. Stress-strain curves for gray iron castings of other grades can be approximated scaling G4000's stress-strain curve proportionally to their ultimate tensile strength, with the same ultimate tensile strength strain. The thermal of grey iron decreases with increasing temperature. A dynamic (cyclic) stress-strain curve of an example grey iron (GJL 150) is depicted in Fig. 71.2. The full response of a grey iron in the compressive mode during a dynamic stress-strain cycling consists of three different distinct forcing functions:

(a) Bulk effect, resembling the full response in tension;

(b) Reinforcement effect by graphite flakes;

(c) Crack closure effect between bulk Fe-material and graphite flakes.

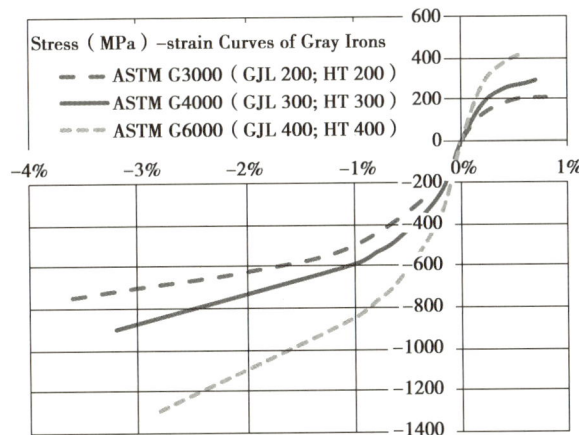

Fig. 71.1   **Stress-Strain Curves of Gray Iron Castings at the Room Temperature.**

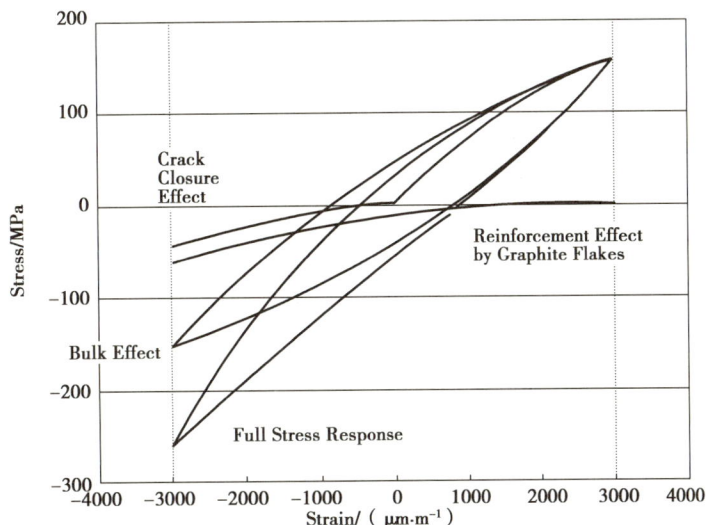

Fig. 71.2   **Schematic Cyclic Stress-strain Curve of Gray Cast Irons (Strain-Controlled Test).**

71.3 Ductile Irons (GJS)

DI (**D**uctile **I**ron) is a composite material. Its metal matrix is a controlled mixture of pearlite and ferrite, while the contained particulates are mainly spheroidal graphites with few flake-shaped types of graphites. Spherical nodules, rather than "sharp" flakes inhibit the creation of cracks and provide the enhanced ductility which gives the alloy its name.

When the solidification rate and the subsequent cooling rate leave inadequate opportunity for the carbon to form the equilibrium graphitic structure exclusively, some carbon may form a pearlitic structure. The nature of this process is well known that faster solidification and postsolidification cooling rates favor the formation of pearlite in preference to ferrite in the matrix by limiting the diffusion of the carbon in solution in the matrix to the second phase graphite which formed during solidification. A cyclic stress-strain curve of an example ductile iron with normalized stress is depicted in Fig. 71.3.

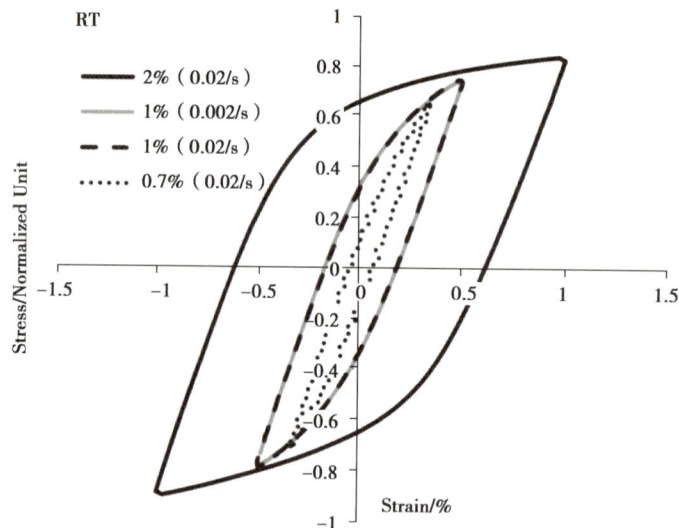

Fig. 71.3   Typical Normalized Stress-Strain Curve of Ductile Irons

A small percentage of manganese may be used as an alloying matter. Ductile irons are good in both tensile and compressive strengths, but they are poorer than gray irons in heat transfer as lacking a lattice work of heat-conducting graphites running through.

71.4　Malleable Cast Irons

MCI (**M**alleable **c**ast **i**rons) consist of ferrite and graphite particles with free carbons. Graphites of malleable iron castings exist in temper carbon nodules by heat treating. Malleable cast irons can be machined.

71.5　Compacted Graphite Irons (CGI; GJV)

CGI (Compacted graphite irons), also called vermicular graphite irons, are mixtures of gray irons and ductile irons. By changing the graphite nodularity from lamellar flakes (for gray iron) and spheroidal flakes (for ductile iron) to compacted one (short and thicker) with 20% graphite nodularity, another type of cast iron is formed and it is called CGI (compacted graphite iron). Its graphite occurs as blunt "worm-shaped" flakes which interconnected within each cell inhibit crack initiation and growth. This graphite structure and the resulting properties of the iron are the intermediate between grey and ductile irons. They have several advantages to grey iron such as better castability, strength, machinability, wear resistance, vibration and noise reduction. CGI consists of shorter and thicker graphite particles, and it provides greater strength relative to grey irons. Except for damping capacity, CGI's properties are far superior compared to gray cast irons. CGI has better thermal conductivity and damping capacity than ductile SGI (Spherical Graphite Iron) at the same level of hardness and slightly lower fatigue strength.

The microstructure dentition of CGI is formally specified by ASTM Standard A842 as a cast iron which contains a minimum of 80% of the graphite particles in compacted form. This means that at least 80% of the graphite particles must be individual vermicular or "worm-shaped" on a metallographic plane of polish with fewer than 20% of the particles in spheroidal form. The grades of CGI are 250, 300, 350, 400 and 450, based on their tensile strength, shown in Table 71.5. The lowest strength is ferritic, and the highest strength is pearlitic.

CGI grades have been somewhat optimized to achieve better mechanical properties, such as degree of nodularity (Fig. 71.4), content of pearlite, and low amount of alloy elements such as Ti. Higher nodularity means higher strength, as shown by EN GJV-450 material data given in Table 71.4. CGI used for engine cylinder blocks may contain low nodularity (e.g.10%) in thick walls;

but high nodularity (e.g.60%) in thin walls (e.g. ribs, water jackets and crankcase housings) can result in increasing strength and stiffness.

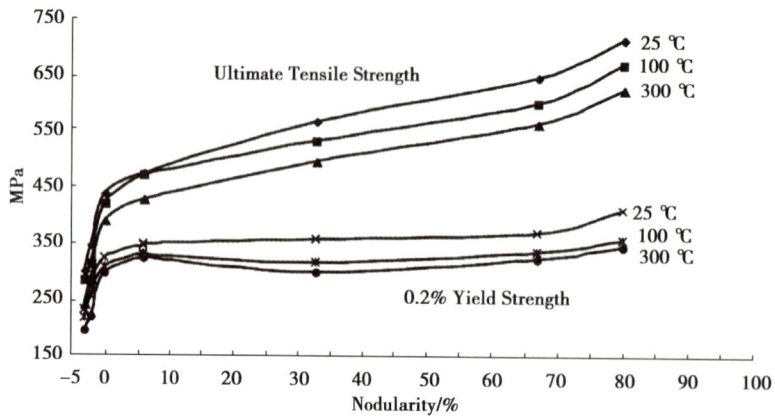

Fig. 71.4 Strength of CGI as a Function of Nodularity

Thermal conductivity of CGI and nodular cast irons slightly increases with an increasing temperature up to 400 ℃. A comparative analysis of thermal conductivity (W/℃/m) between the GJL's (GCI) and GJV's (CGI) for cylinder engine heads are given as follows [Guesser et al.]:

$T/℃$	GJL 250	GJL 300	CGI 350	CGI 450
100	50	45.5	37	33.6
200	46.6	43.2	37.4	34.2
300	43.6	41.2	37.2	34.3
400	40.9	39.7	36.5	33.9

Note that the unit for the thermal conductivities given above is W/℃/m. During thermal cycling, the maximum value of the compressive stress continuously decreases while the value of the maximum tensile stress continuously increases. Nevertheless, adding (molybdenum) to CGI improves the fatigue resistance by lowering the stress relaxation rate in the temperature range of 350~600 ℃ [Diaconu et al.].

71.6 Austempered Ductile Irons (ADI)

ADI (**A**ustempered **D**uctile **I**rons) are ductile irons alloyed using Ni, Cu, and Mo with austempering heat treatments. They are characterized by its higher tensile strength, toughness, and wear resistance relative to other iron castings.

71.7 Cast Steels

The role of the alloying elements in cast steel has a similar effect on traditional alloy steels and may be summarized as follows:

(a) All elements, except cobalt, increase harden ability;
(b) All carbide-forming elements retard softening during tempering;
(c) Nickel improves toughness;
(d) Chromium improves oxidation resistance;
(e) Molybdenum retards temper embrittlement and increases strength at high temperature;
(f) Vanadium and tungsten improve elevated temperature strength;
(g) Manganese plus sulfur improves machinability;
(h) Sulfur causes hot cracks;
(i) Carbon increases strength but decreases toughness;
(j) Phosphorous, arsenic, antimony;
(k) Tin accelerates temper embrittlement.

Structural carbon and low alloy cast steels enjoy a wide application for load-carrying applications. Material properties of cast steel are listed in their corresponding carbon and alloy steel categories.

Since porosity in cast steels varies from location to location, the modulus of elasticity (E) has to be estimated using the following approximating function of the porosity fraction at the applicable location as [Hardin & and Beckermann]

$$E = E_o \left(\frac{1 - \phi}{0.5} \right)^{2.5} \tag{71.2}$$

where:
E_o: Modulus of elasticity with zero porosity;
ϕ: Volume fraction of porosity.

The Poisson ratio, v, as a function of the porosity fraction, can be obtained from a relationship developed by [Roberts & Garboczi].

$$v = v_s + \frac{(v_\infty - v_s)\phi}{\phi_\infty} \qquad (71.3)$$

where $v_\infty = 0.14$; $v_s = 0.3$, and $\phi_\infty = 0.472$, according to [Roberts & Garboczi].

It is shown in the image analysis done by [Sigl et al.] on polished metallographic sections of SAE 8630 cast steel specimens microporosities exist with an averaged pore volume fraction of 0.7% and the mean distance between them ranging from 177 μm to 344 μm. Given the volume fraction of porosities and mean distance between two porosities, one can calculate the number of porosities per unit volume (n_p) that falls between 2.4×10^{10} and 1.8×10^{11}. By assuming that porosities are spherical and have a uniform mean radius, one can estimate the pore volume fraction by the following equation

$$\phi = n_p \left(\frac{4\pi}{3}\right) R_p^3 \qquad (71.4)$$

Using these values for ϕ and n_p, a mean pore radius of as 21 μm$< R_p <$41 μm can be obtained from the above equation, which was varied by the image analysis [Sigl et al.]. However, images of the fractured surface of the microporosity specimens revealed that failure always initiated from large isolated pores with a radius of 100 μm [Sigl et al.], which would have thinner walls between porosities.

71.8 Fatigue of Cast Irons

Each cast iron is a composite consisting of steel matrix and graphite particulates (flakes or nodules). The stress-strain response in cast iron is controlled by the properties of the steel matrix and, more importantly, the details of the graphite morphology.

Nodular irons when stressed remain linearly elastic over a considerable range of stress, and tensile and compressive behavior is nearly identical. The stress thus comes from steel matrix (called bulk stress) and reinforcement by nodular graphite (called graphite stress).

It is shown that gray iron under tensile stresses, in which well-oriented graphite flakes crack and debond from the matrix. The gray iron exhibits highly asymmetrical behavior and neither tensile nor compressive stress/strain curves show definable elastic limits. Another stress component, called compressive crack closure stress, has thus to be considered in addition to bulk stress and graphite stress.

71.8.1   Cyclic Loading

Crack-like defects (debonded graphite) can be detected on the surface of cast iron specimens loaded in tension. This behavior results in reduction in material stiffness at a high tensile stress than a lower one. Decreases in the unloading modulus from tensile peaks of flake iron hysteresis loops are evidence of these changes. Three different kinds of stresses depicted in Fig. 71.3 include

(a) Bulk stress;
(b) Graphite stress;
(c) Compressive crack close stress.

The cyclic deformation model presented accurately predicts the initial stress/strain response of cast iron under variable loading. Eight material parameters (m_T, K_T, n_T, m_C, K_C, n_C, m_U and E_o) are needed for cast irons, rather than four needed for wrought materials that share the same properties in tension and compression. The cyclic stress-strain curve (Ramberg-Osgood equation) can be written here for tensile and compressive strains, respectively, as

$$\varepsilon = \frac{\sigma}{E_T} + \left(\frac{\sigma}{K_T'}\right)^{\frac{1}{n_T'}} \tag{71.5}$$

$$\text{and} \quad \varepsilon = \frac{\sigma}{E_C} + \left(\frac{\sigma}{K_C'}\right)^{\frac{1}{n_C'}} \tag{71.6}$$

where
K_T' and K_C': Cyclic hardening coefficients in tension and compression, respectively;
n_T' and n_C': Cyclic hardening exponents in tension and compression, respectively;
E_T and E_C: Moduli of elasticity in tension and compression, respectively.

Note that the modulus of elasticity is here assumed to be linear in reference to the initial modulus of elasticity (E_o) as

$$E_T = E_o + m_T\sigma \qquad (\text{In Tension}) \tag{71.7}$$

$$\text{or} \quad E_C = E_o + m_C\sigma \qquad (\text{In Compression}) \tag{71.8}$$

Substituting the above two equations into Eqs.(71.5) and (71.6) leads to

$$\varepsilon = \frac{\sigma}{E_o + m_T\sigma} + \left(\frac{\sigma}{K_T'}\right)^{\frac{1}{n_T'}} \tag{71.9}$$

$$\text{and} \quad \varepsilon = \frac{\sigma}{E_o + m_C\sigma} + \left(\frac{\sigma}{K_C'}\right)^{\frac{1}{n_C'}} \tag{71.10}$$

There are seven parameters, i.e. m_T, K_T, n_T, m_C, K_C, n_C, and E_o, to be decided for the stressstrain cycling without considering crack closure. As the eighth parameter, a dimensionless parameter A_{eff} is defined as the fraction of cross-sectional area unaffected by surface cracking. For an unstressed cast iron specimen, $A_{\text{eff}} = 1$. Assume that surface cracking is presented by another decreased unloading modulus (E_u). A_{eff} is then expressed by

$$A_{\text{eff}} = \frac{E_u}{E_o} \tag{71.11}$$

The total flow stress for cast iron under cyclic loading is given by

$$\sigma = A_{\text{eff}}(\sigma_B + \sigma_G) + (1 - A_{\text{eff}})\sigma_{CC} \tag{71.12}$$

where

σ_B: Bulk stress;

σ_G: Graphite stress;

σ_{CC}: Compressive crack closure stress.

The first term on the right side, $A_{\text{eff}}(\sigma_B + \sigma_G)$, represents the bulk and graphite stresses acting over the fraction of cross-sectional area unaffected by surface cracking. The second term, $(1 - A_{\text{eff}})\sigma_{CC}$ is the compressive crack closure stress acting over the remaining area. Note that $A_{\text{eff}} = 1$ for a ductile cast iron, since its $\sigma_{CC} = 0$, as shown in Fig. 71.4.

71.8.2 Fatigue Strength

Fatigue properties of iron castings are listed in Table 71.6. If being not available in the open literature, the fatigue strength of an iron casting with a fatigue cutoff cycle of 10^6 based on the tension-compression test mode can be approximated by the following:

$$\sigma_f = 0.25 \; \sigma_{\text{uts}} \qquad \text{(Gray Cast Irons)} \tag{71.13}$$
$$\sigma_f = 0.3 \; \sigma_{\text{uts}} \qquad \text{(Compact Graphite Irons)} \tag{71.14}$$
$$\sigma_f = 0.7 \; \sigma_{\text{uts}} \qquad \text{(Ductile Iron)} \tag{71.15}$$

71.9 Coefficients of Linear Thermal Expansion of Cast Irons

Based on measured thermal expansions of CGI (Compacted Graphite Iron) and SGI (Spheroidal Graphite Iron) in the temperature range of 25 °C and 500 °C using push-rod type dilatometer, [Matsushita et al.] obtained the following regression model:

$$\alpha = 13.8 \times 10^{-6} + 0.0538 \times 10^{-6} N - 0.585 \times 10^{-6} G + 0.0185 \times 10^{-6} T - 2.41 \times 10^{-6} R_{\frac{p}{F}} -$$
$$0.0128 \times 10^{-6} N \, G - 0.297 \times 10^{-6} G \, R_{\frac{p}{F}} + 0.00465 \times 10^{-6} T \, R_{\frac{p}{F}} +$$

$$0.108 \times 10^{-6} G^2 - 0.000048 \times 10^{-6} T^2$$

where

N: Nodularity;

G: Area fraction of graphite, %;

T: Temperature, ℃;

$R_{\frac{P}{F}}$: Pearlite/Ferrite ratio in the matrix.

71.10   Creep of Cast Irons

Cast irons may also creep like other metals. Creep parameters of cast irons are given in Table 71.7.

71.11   Applications

Good mechanical properties and relatively low production costs lead to a common interest in cast irons for various technical applications. Besides cylinder heads and cylinder blocks, gray iron castings have a great deal of applications in diesel engines such as exhaust manifolds, cylinder liners, pistons, transmission cases, gear boxes, and camshafts. Gray iron, with proper hardening, is also the material for drum brakes and clutch plates. Ductile iron may be used for crankshafts, differential cases, differential carriers, and automotive suspension parts, which need more ductility in combination of strength. Malleable iron castings provide similar applications of ductile iron castings, but easier for machining.

Turbocharger housings and exhaust manifold demand materials with high resistance to thermomechanical loads. The influence of elevated temperatures (550 ℃ and 850 ℃) on micro-structure and resistance to oxidation of cast irons was analyzed utilizing samples made of different materials such as EN-GJL-250 (gray iron), EN-GJS-400-18 (ferritic ductile iron), ENGJS-500-7 (pearlitic ductile iron), EN-GJS-SiMo4-1, and EN-GJS-AXNiCr20-2 (ductile Irons) by [Unkic, F, et al.(2009)]. According to the resistance to oxidation and microstructure changes at a temperature between 550 ℃ and 850 ℃, materials are ranked as follows: EN-GJSAXNiCr20-2 (austenitic ductile iron) and EN-GJS-SiMo4-1(ferritic ductile iron). During oxidation of those cast irons at elevated temperatures, two oxide layers over the test sample surfaces were formed. The outer layer consisting of iron oxide is detachable. The inner layer is tightly attached to metal matrix while preventing progression of oxidation into the core body. This oxide layer consists of $Fe_2\text{-}SiO_4$(fayalite) or complex oxides (Fe, Cr, Ni, Si, and O) and is suitable for making thermo-mechanical loaded parts of an automotive engine, such as turbocharger housings and exhaust manifolds. EN-GJS-400-18, EN-GJS-500-7, and EN-GJL250 did not show adequate resistance to oxidation and microstructure changes at 550 ℃ and 850 ℃.

Another successful commercial application of CGI (Compacted Graphite Irons) is for the brake discs for high-speed trains; and then for the Diesel engine blocks, which demand high firing pressure for clean emission and noise reduction.

References

AKIHARO S, et al, 2004. Analysis of Residual Deformation of Spheroidal Graphite Cast Iron by Elastoplastic VOXEL-FEM[J]. Journal of Japan Foundry Engineering Society, 76(5): 359-365.

AMANO K, et al, 1997. Improvement in Thermal Fatigue Resistance of Cast Iron Piston[J]. SAE 978317.

BAER W, et al, 2003. Dynamic Fracture Toughness Behavior of Ductile Cast Iron with Respect to Structural Integrity Assessment [J]. Transactions of the 17th International Conference on Structural Mechanics in Reactor Technology (SMiRT 17), Prague, Czech Republic, Aug. 17-22.

BAHMANI M, ELLIOT R, VARAHRAM N, 1997. Austempered Ductile Iron: a Competitive Alternative for Forged Induction-Hardened Steel Crankshafts[J]. International Journal of Cast Metals Research, 9: 249-257.

CANZAR P, et al, 2012. Microstructure Influence on Fatigue Behavior of Nodular Cast Iron [J]. Material Science and Engineering, 556: 88-99.

CHATTERLEY T C, MURRELL P, 1998. ADI Crankshafts- An Appraisal of Their Production Potential[J]. SAE 980686.

CORONEL V F, BESHERS D N, 1988. Magnetomechanical Damping in Iron[J]. Journal of Applied Physics, 64: 2006-2015.

DAWSON S, 2009. Compacted Graphite Iron- A Modern Diesel Engine Cylinder Block and Cylinder Head Material[J]. China Foundry, 6(3): 241-246.

DELA'O J D, GUNDLACH R B, TARTAGLIA J M, 2001. Strain-Life Fatigue Data for Cast Iron: Survey of Data in the Public Domain[J]. AFS Research Report: 40, Des Plaines, IL.

DIACONU V L, et al, Stress Relaxation of Compacted Graphite Iron Alloyed with Molybdenum[J]. International Journal of Cast Metals Research, 26(1): 51-57.

DOONG J, et al, 1986. The influence of Pearlite Fraction on Fracture Toughness and Fatigue Crack Growth in

Nodular Cast Iron[J]. Journal of Materials Science, 21: 871-878.

DORAZIL E, 1986. Mechanical Properties of Austempered Ductile Iron[J]. Foundry Management & Technology, 1986: 36-45.

DUNLAP W, DRUSCHITZ A, 2010. Preliminary Evaluation of a Low-Cost Cast Iron for Exhaust Manifold and Turbocharger Applications[J]. International Journal of Materials and Manufacturing, 3(1): 413-424.

ERFAN O, ELMABROUK O, 2014. Influence of Section Thickness on the Thermal Conductivity of Compacted Graphite Cast Iron at Elevated Temperatures [J]. International Journal of Engineering and Innovative Technology, 3(7): 29-34.

GARRESTSON B, et al, 2003. Monotonic tension, Strain Controlled Fatigue and Fracture Toughness Properties of a Ductile Iron[J]. SAE 2003-01-0832.

GERMANN H, et al, 2010. Fatigue Behavior and Lifetime Calculation of the Cast Irons ENGJL-250 EN-GJS-600 and EN-GJV-400[J]. Procedia Engineering, 2(1): 1087-1094.

GHODRAT S, et al, 2011. Microstructural Evolution of Compacted Graphite Iron under ThermoMechanical Fatigue Conditions[J]. Advanced Materials Research, 409: 757-762.

GOO B, LIM C, 2012. Thermal Fatigue of Cast Iron Brake Materials[J]. Journal of Mechanical Science and Technology, 26(6): 1719-1724.

GUESSER W L, et al, 2005. Thermal Conductivity of Gray Iron and Compacted Graphite Iron Used for Cylinder Heads[J]. Revista Matéria, 10(2): 265-272.

GUO B, et al, 2014. Failure Analysis of a Modern High Performance Diesel Engine Cylinder Head[J]. Advances in Mechanical Engineering, 6: 862853.

GURDOGA O, et al, 1996. Mold Filling Analysis for Ductile Iron Lost Foam Castings[J]. Transactions of the American Foundrymen's Society, 104: 451-459.

GUESSER W L, et al, 2005. Thermal Conductivity of Gray Iron and Compacted Graphite Iron Used for Cylinder Heads[J]. Revista Matéria, 10(2): 265-272.

GUZIK E, DZIK S, 2009. Structure and Mechanical Properties of Vermicular Cast Iron in Cylinder Head Casting[J]. Archives of Foundry Engineering, 9: 175-180.

HARDIN R, BECKERMANN C, 2009. Prediction of the Fatigue Life of Cast Steel Containing Shrinkage Porosity[J]. Metallurgical and Materials Transactions, 40: 581-597.

HAYASHI M, MOURI H, 2007. Monosemousness of Thermal Plastic Strain on Thermal Fatigue Life in Ferrite Ductile Cast Iron[J]. Journal of Solid Mechanics and Materials Engineering, 1(5): 711-718.

HECHT R, DINWIDDIE R, PORTER W, et al, 1996. Thermal Transport Properties of Grey Cast Irons[J]. SAE 962126.

JANOWAK J. F, et al, 1990. Fatigue Strength of Commercial Ductile Irons[J]. Transactions, American Foundrymen's Society, 98: 90-123.

JUNICHIRO Y, et al, 2007. Evaluation of Fatigue Strength of Ductile Cast Iron Composed of Ferrite-pearlitic Structures with As-cast Surfaces (Effect of Surface Roughness, Microstructure Transition Layers, Defects and Residual Stress on Fatigue Strength[J]. Journal of Solid Mechanics and Materials Engineering, 1(2): 211-222.

KIM S, et al, 2009. Mechanical, Wear and Heat Exposure Properties of Compacted Graphite Cast Iron at Elevated Temperatures[J]. Journal of Alloys and Compounds, 487(1-2): 253-257.

KIM Y J, et al, 2008. Investigation into Mechanical Properties of Austempered Ductile Cast Iron (ADI) in Accordance with Austemperating Temperature[J]. Materials Letters, 62(3): 357-360.

KURIKUMA T, et al, 1998. Effects of Graphite Morphology and Matrix Microstructure on Damping Capacity, Tensile Strength and Young's Modulus of Casting Irons[J]. Journal of Japan Engineering Society, 68: 876-882.

LEE S, et al, 1998. Influence of Casting Size and Graphite Nodule Refinement on Fracture Toughness of Austempered Ductile Iron[J]. Metallurgical and Materials Transactions, A, 29: 2511-2521.

LEWIS R W, et al, 2006. A Finite Element Model of the Squeeze Casting Process[J]. International Journal of Numerical Methods for Heat & Fluid Flow, 16(5): 539-557.

LIN C, PAI Y, 1999. Low-cycle Fatigue of Austempered Ductile Irons at Various Strain Ratios [J]. International Journal of Fatigue, 21(1): 45-54.

LOPER C R JR, SHTURMAKOV A J, 2002. Predictive Analysis of Mechanical Properties in Commercial Gray Iron[J]. AFS Transactions, 99-94: 609-615.

MAIJER D, COCKCROFT S, JACOT A, 2000. Modeling of Microstructure and Residue Stress in Cast Iron Calendar Rolls[J]. Metallurgical and Materials Transactions, A, 31(4): 1201-1211.

MAJ M, 2013. Fatigue Life Assessment of Selected Engineering Materials Based on Modified Low-Cycle Fatigue Test[J]. Archives of Foundry Engineering, 13(1-2): 89-94.

MAMPAEY F, et al, 2010. On Line Oxygen Activity Measurements to Determine Optimal Graphite Form during Compacted Graphite Iron Production[J]. Int. J. Metalcasting, 4: 25-43.

MARAVEAS C, et al, 2015. An Experimental Investigation of Mechanical Properties of Structural Cast Iron at Elevated Temperatures and after Cooling Down[J]. Fire Safety Journal, 71: 340-352.

MATSUSHITA T, et al, 2015. On Thermal Expansion and Density of CGI and SGI Cast Irons[J]. Metals, 5 (2): 1000-1019.

MCCLORY B, et al, 2010. Effect of Simulated Material Properties and Residual Stresses on High Cycle Fatigue Prediction in a Compacted Graphite Iron Engine Block[J]. SAE 2010-01-0016.

MOURI1 H, HAYASHI M, WUNDERLICH W, 2009. Effect of Dynamic Strain Aging on Isothermal (473K) Low Cycle Fatigue of Ferritic Ductile Cast Iron[J]. Materials Transactions, 50(8): 1935-1940.

MROZIŃSKI S, GOLAŃSKI G, 2010. Elevated Temperature Low Cycle Fatigue Properties of Martensitic Cast Steel[J]. International Journal of Engineering & Technology, 13(1): 86-91.

PALMER K B, 1987. Mechanical Properties of Compacted-Graphite Irons[J]. BCIRA Journal, 24(12-13): 31-37.

PAN Y, et al, 2011. Effects of Graphite Shapes on Thermal Fatigue Properties of Ting-Walled Graphitic Cast Irons[J]. Key Engineering Materials, 457: 398-403.

RAMAZAN K, et al, 2009. A Model for Estimation of Mould Thermal Fatigue Life in Permanent Mould Casting [J]. Solid State Phenomena, 114: 145-150.

ROBINSON D, PALANINATHAN R, 2011. Thermal Analysis of Piston Casting using 3-D Finite Element Method[J]. Finite Elements in Analysis and Design, 37(2): 85-95.

RUFF G, 1981. Mechanical Properties of Compacted Graphite Cast Iron[J]. SAE 810209.

SALMAN S, FINDIK F, TOPUZ P, 2007. Effects of Various Austempering Temperatures on Fatigue Properties in Ductile Iron[J]. Materials and Design, 28(7): 2210-2214.

SANTNER J S, GOODRICH G M, 2006. Iron Alloys[J]. Engineering Casting Solutions: 17-21.

SEETHARAM K N, et al, 2001. Finite Element Modeling of Solidification Phenomena[J]. Sadhana, 26(1-2): 103-120.

SEIFERT T, RIEDEL H, 2010. Mechanism-based Thermomechanical Fatigue Life Prediction of Cast Iron. Part I: Models[J]. International Journal of Fatigue, 32(8): 1358-1367.

SELIN M, KÖNIG M, 2009. Regression Analysis of Thermal Conductivity based on Measurements of Compacted Graphite Irons[J]. Metallurgical and Materials Transactions, 40: 3235-3244.

SHAO S, et al, 1998. The Mechanical and Physical Properties of Compacted Graphite Iron[J]. Material Science and Engineering Technology, 29(8): 397-411.

SIGL K M, et al, 2004. International Journal of Cast Metals Research, 17(3): 130-146.

SINTERCAST D, 1999. Compacted Graphite Iron: Mechanical and Physical Properties for Engine Design[J]. VDI-Berichte, 1492: 85-105.

SJÖGREN T, VOMACKA P, SVENSSON I, 2004. Comparison of Mechanical Properties in Flake Graphite and Compacted Graphite Cast Irons for Piston Rings[J]. International Journal of Cast Met. Res, 17: 65-71.

STURM J C, BUSCH G, 2011. Cast Iron- a Predictable Material[J]. China Foundry, 1(8): 51-61.

TANAKA T, et al, 1998. Development of Ductile Cast Iron Flywheel Integrated with HotRolled Gear[J]. SAE 980568.

TARTAGLIA J M, 2012. Comparison of Monotonic and Cyclic Properties of Ductile Irons in the AFS/DOE Strain-Life Fatigue Database for Cast Iron[J]. International Journal of Metalcasting, 6(2): 7-22.

TARTAGLIA J M, RITTER P E, GUNDLACH R B, et al, 2000. Monotonic and Cyclic Property Design Data for Ductile Iron Castings[J]. SAE 2000-1-0758.

THOLL M, MAGATA A, DAWSON S, 1996. Practical Experience with Passenger Car Engine Blocks Produced in High Quality Compacted Graphite Iron[J]. SAE 960297.

TRAMPERT S, 2008. Thermomechanical Fatigue Life Prediction of Cylinder Heads in Combustion Engines[J]. J. Eng. Gas Turbines Power, 130(1): 012806.

TUCKER L, OLBERTS D, 1969. Fatigue Properties of Gray Cast Iron[J]. SAE 690471.

UNKIC F, et al, 2009. The Influence of Elevated Temperatures on Microstructure of Cast Irons for Automotive Engine Thermo-mechanical Loaded Parts[J]. Materials and Geoenvironment, 56(1): 9-23.

VATAVUK J, et al, 1997. Effects of Nitriding Process on Impact Resistance of Austempered Cast Irons and Quenched and Tempered Ones[J]. SAE 973108.

WILLIDAL T, BAUER W, SCHUMACHER P, 2005. Stress/strain Behavior and Fatigue Limit of Grey Cast Iron[J]. Materials Science and Engineering, 413-414: 578-582.

WILLIAMS J, FATEMI A, 2007. Fatigue Performance of Forged Steel and Ductile Cast Iron Crankshafts[J]. SAE 2007-01-1001.

WU X, QUAN T, SLOSS C, 2013. Failure Mechanisms and Damage Model of Ductile Cast Iron under Low-Cycle Fatigue Conditions[J]. SAE 2013-01-0391.

XUE H Q, et al, 2006. Fatigue Behavior and Energy Dissipation of a Nodular Cast Iron in Ultrasonic Fatigue Loading[J]. Journal of Achievements in Materials and Manufacturing Engineering, 18(1-2): 251-254.

ZAMBRANO H, et al, 2012. Fracture Toughness and Growth of Short and Long Fatigue Cracks in Ductile Cast Iron EN-GJS-400-18-LT[J]. Fatigue & Fracture of Engineering Materials & Structures, 35 (4): 374-388.

Table 71.1   Mechanical Properties of Gray Iron Castings

Material	$T/℃$	E_T	ρ	ν	(α, ε)	α	k	γ	β	K_{IC}
Fe (Pure)	23	211	7.874	0.29	(128,0.2%)	11.8	80.4	452	—	—
	200	—	—	—	—	13	—	—	—	—
	400	—	—	—	—	14.2	—	—	—	—
	770(T_c)	—	—	—	—	14.2	—	—	—	—
	800	—	—	—	—	14.6	—	—	—	—
	906 (bcc→fcc)		—	—	—	−70	—	—	—	—
	920	—	—	—	—	15	—	—	—	—
	1380	—	—	—	—	15	—	—	—	—
	1409(fcc→bcc)		—	—	—	160	—	—	—	—
	1450	—	—	—	—	16	—	—	—	—
	1538(T_m)	—		6.98 (Liquid)	—	—	—	—	—	—
GJL 150 (ASTM No.20; SAE G1800;As Cast)	23	81	7.05	0.2	(−572,−0.012); (100,0.2%) (150,0.9%)	10.6	54	460	—	—
	100	—	—	—	—	—	52.5	—	—	—
	300	—	—	—	—	—	50.5	—	—	—
	350	—	—	—	(−300,−1%) (−140,−0.2%); (95,0.2%) (120,0.6%)	—	—	—	—	—
	400	—	—	—	(−230,−1%) (−120,−0.2%); (85,0.2%) (110,0.7%)	—	49.5	—	—	—
	500	—	—	—	—	—	48.5	—	—	—
	1290(T_m)	—	—	—	—	—	—	—	—	—
GJL 180 (ASTM No.25; SAE G2500; As Cast)	23	114	7.1	0.19	(−758,−1%) (−420,−0.2%); (120,0.2%) (206,0.8%)	10.6	53	460	—	—
	100	—	—	—	—	—	52	—	—	—

continued

Material	$T/°C$	E_T	ρ	ν	(α, ε)	α	k	γ	β	K_{IC}
GJL 180 (ASTM No.25; SAE G2500; Annealed)	23	91	7.1	0.19	$(-670, -1\%)$ $(-409, -0.2\%)$; $(110, 0.2\%)$ $(180, 0.8\%)$	10.6	53	460	—	—
	100	—	—	—	—	—	52	—	—	—
	300	—	—	—	—	—	50	—	—	—
	400	—	—	—	—	—	47.8	—	—	—
	500	—	—	—	—	—	48	—	—	—
GJL 200 (ASTM No.30; SAE G3000; As Cast)	23	117	7.15	0.21	$(-890, -3.6\%)$ $(-750, -3\%)$ $(-635, -2\%)$ $(-500, -1\%)$ $(-200, -0.2\%)$; $(130, 0.2\%)$ $(200, 0.5\%)$ $(230, 0.8\%)$	10.6	52	460	—	19.1
GJL 200 (ASTM No.30; SAE G3000; Annealed)	23	101	7.15	0.21	$(-575, -3.6\%)$ $(-200, -0.2\%)$; $(80, 0.02\%)$ $(150, 0.2\%)$ $(200, 0.8\%)$	10.6	52	460	—	—
	100	—	—	—	—	—	51	—	—	—
	300	—	—	—	—	—	49	—	—	—
	400	—	—	—	—	—	47.8	—	—	—
	500	—	—	—	—	—	47	—	—	—
GJL 250 (ASTM No.35; SAE G3500; As Cast)	23	124	7.2	0.22	$\sigma_{uts} = -870$ $(-350, -0.2\%)$; $(50, 0.05\%)$ $(165, 0.2\%)$ $(240, 0.7\%)$	10.6	50	460	—	—
	100	—	—	—	—	—	49	—	—	—
	300	—	—	—	—	—	47	—	—	—
	400	—	—	—	$(-300, -0.2\%)$	—	45.8	—	—	—
	500	—	—	—	—	—	45	—	—	—

continued

Material	$T/°C$	E_T	ρ	ν	(α, ε)	α	k	γ	β	K_{IC}
GJL 280	23	124	7.2	0.22	$(-950,-3.4\%)$ $(-830,-2\%)$ $(-800,-1\%)$ $(-580,-0.2\%)$; $(183,0.2\%)$ $(280,0.7\%)$	10.6	49	460	—	—
	400	—	—	—	$(-800,-3\%)$ $(-750,-1.5\%)$ $(-700,-1\%)$ $(-500,-0.2\%)$	—	45	—	—	—
	500	—	—	—	$(-550,-3\%)$ $(-550,-1.5\%)$ $(-520,-1\%)$ $(-450,-0.2\%)$	—	—	—	—	—
GJL 300 (ASTM No.40; SAE G4000; As Cast)	23	126	7.25	0.24	$(-1070,-3.2\%)$ $(-600,-1\%)$ $(-535,-0.8\%)$ $(-470,-0.6\%)$ $(-250,-0.2\%)$; $(195,0.2\%)$ $(255,0.4\%)$ $(290,0.6\%)$ $(300,0.7\%)$	10.6	48	490	—	—
	100	—	—	—	—	—	47	—	—	—
	150	113	—	—	—	11.7	—	528	—	—
	300	—	—	—	—	—	45	—	—	—
	350	110	—	—	—	13.3	—	610	—	—
	400	—	—	—	—	—	44.4	—	—	—
	500	—	—	—	—	14.5	43.4	—	—	—
	600	—	—	—	—	—	—	750	—	—
GJL 350 (ASTM No.50; SAE G5000; As Cast)	23	143	7.3	0.26	$\sigma_{uts}=-1130$; $(228,0.2\%)$ $(360,0.6\%)$	10.6	47	460	—	—
	100	—	—	—	—	—	46	—	—	—
	300	—	—	—	—	—	44	—	—	—
	400	—	—	—	—	—	42.7	—	—	—
	500	—	—	—	—	—	41.7	—	—	—

continued

Material	$T/°C$	E_T	ρ	ν	(α, ε)	α	k	γ	β	K_{IC}
GJL 400 (ASTM No.60; SAE G6000; As Cast)	23	151	7.3	0.26	$(-1293,-2.8\%)$ $(-848,-1\%)$ $(-769,-0.8\%)$ $(-675,-0.6\%)$ $(-359,-0.2\%)$; $(276,0.2\%)$ $(380,0.4\%)$ $(430,0.6\%)$	10.6	45	460	—	—
	100	—	—	—	—	—	44	—	—	—
	300	—	—	—	—	—	42	—	—	—
	425	—	—	—	$\sigma_{uts}=255$	—	—	—	—	—
	500	—	—	—	—	—	40	—	—	—
	540	—	—	—	$\sigma_{uts}=173$	—	—	—	—	—
	650	—	—	—	$\sigma_{uts}=83$	—	—	—	—	—
GJL 450	23	—	7.3	0.26	$(443,0.2\%)$ $\sigma_{uts}=498$	10.6	45	460	—	—

Table 71.2　Mechanical Properties of Ductile Iron Castings

Material	$T/°C$	E_T	ρ	ν	(α, ε)	α	k	γ	β	K_{IC}
GJS-400-15 (Pearlite=8%)	-50	—	—	—	—	—	—	—	—	46
	-40	—	—	—	—	—	—	—	—	60
	-20	—	—	—	—	—	—	—	—	66
	23	—	7.1	0.29	$(270,0.2\%)$ $(400, 15\%)$	11	40	460	—	106
GJS-500-7 (Nodularity = 91%)	23	—	7.1	0.29	$(300,0.2\%)$ $(500,7\%)$	11	40	460	—	23
GJS-500-14 (Better wear than 500-7; Nodularity = 82%)	23	—	7.1	0.29	$(300,0.2\%)$ $(500,14\%)$	11	40	460	—	28

continued

Material	$T/℃$	E_T	ρ	ν	(α, ε)	α	k	γ	β	K_{IC}
D4018(60-40-18;Ferritic;As Cast)	23	164	7.1	0.29	$(329,0.2\%)$ $(480,21\%)$	11	40	460	—	80
	100	—	—	—	—	11.5	40.2	—	—	—
	200	155	—	—	$(250,0.2\%)$ $\sigma_{uts}=360$	—	43.3	—	—	—
	300	—	—	—	—	—	41.5	—	—	—
	500	—	—	—	—	—	36	515	—	—
	600	—	—	—	—	13.5	—	536	—	—
	700	—	—	—	—	—	—	603	—	—
D4018(60-40-18; Ferritic; Annealed)	23	160	7.1	0.28	$(288,0.2\%)$ $(443,25\%)$	11	40	460	—	—
	425	—	—	—	$\sigma_{uts}=276$	—	—	—	—	—
	500	—	—	—	—	—	36	515	—	—
	540	—	—	—	$\sigma_{uts}=173$; $\sigma_{crs,1000}=57$	—	—	—	—	—
	650	—	—	—	$\sigma_{uts}=90$	—	—	—	—	—
D4512(65-45-12; Ferritic-Pearlitic; As Cast)	23	164	7.1	0.29	$(-525,-13\%)$ $(-370,0.2\%)$; $(340,0.2\%)$ $(479,13\%)$	11	36	460	—	70
	100	—	—	—	—	11.5	38.5	—	—	—
	500	—	—	—	—	—	—	515	—	—
	600	—	—	—	—	13.5	536	—	—	—
D5010 (75-50-10; Ferritic-Pearlitic; As Cast)	23	163	7.1	0.29	$(350,0.2\%)$ $(520,10\%)$	11	35	460	—	65
	100	—	—	—	—	11.5	36	—	—	—
	200	—	—	—	—	—	38.8	—	—	—
	300	—	—	—	—	—	37.4	—	—	—
	500	—	—	—	—	—	33.5	515	—	—
	600	—	—	—	—	13.5	—	536	—	—
GJS-SiMo4-1	23	163	7.1	0.29	$(350,0.2\%)$ $(520, 10\%)$	11	35	460	—	

continued

Material	$T/℃$	E_T	ρ	ν	(α, ε)	α	k	γ	β	K_{IC}
D5506(80-55-06; EN GJS 600; Pearlitic-Ferritic; As Cast)	23	174	7.1	0.29	(358,0.02%) (480,0.2%) (560,6%)	11	32	460	—	60
	100	—	—	—	—	11.5	32.9	—	—	—
	200	—	—	—	—	—	35.4	—	—	—
	300	—	—	—	—	—	34.2	—	—	—
	500	—	—	—	—	—	31.6	515	—	—
	600	—	—	—	—	13.5	—	536	—	—
	700	—	—	—	—	—	—	603	—	—
Crankshaft (As cast)	23	174	7.1	0.29	(336,0.2%) (536,13%)	11	35	460	—	—
Crankshaft (Annealed)	23	174	7.1	0.29	(316,0.2%) (431,24%)	11	35	460	—	—
Crankshaft (Q:860 ℃ & T:860 ℃)	23	174	7.1	0.29	(581,0.2%) (748, 9.4%)	11	35	460	—	—
Crankshaft (Q:860 ℃ & T:480 ℃)	23	174	7.1	0.29	(792,0.2%) (1051,4%)	11	35	460	—	—
D7003(100-70-03;EN GJS-700; Pearlitic; e.g. as cast gears)	23	174	7.1	0.29	(487,0.2%) (836,8.2%)	11	29	460	—	30
	100	—	—	—	—	11.5	30	—	—	—
	200	—	—	—	—	12	32	—	—	—
	300	—	—	—	—	12.6	31	—	—	—
	500	—	—	—	—	13.4	30	515	—	—
	600	—	—	—	—	13.5	—	536	—	—
D7003(100-70-03; Pearlitic; Normalized; Thin Plate)	23	177	7.1	0.29	(513,0.2%) (883,8.2%)	11	29	461	—	—
	300	—	—	—	—	12.6	31	—	—	—
	500	—	—	—	—	13.4	30	515	—	—
	600	—	—	—	—	13.5	—	536	—	—

continued

Material	$T/℃$	E_T	ρ	ν	(α, ε)	α	k	γ	β	K_{IC}
D7003(100-70-03;Pearlitic; Normalized; Thick Plate)	23	171	7.1	0.29	(549,0.2%) (893, 4.7%)	11	29	460	—	—
D9002(120-90-02; 100% Tempered Martensitic)	23	177	7.1	0.28	(750,0.2%) (922,6.8%)	11	25	460	—	25
	100	—	—	—	—	11.5	25.1	—	—	—
	200	—	—	—	—	—	27.2	—	—	—
	300	—	—	—	—	—	28.1	—	—	—
	500	—	—	—	—	—	29	515	—	—

Table 71.3 Mechanical Properties of Malleable Iron Castings

Material	$T/℃$	E_T	ρ	ν	(α, ε)	α	k	γ	ρ_E	K_{IC}
M3210 (Annealed)	23	172	7.2	0.3	(225,0.2%) (345,10%)	12	55	460	—	—
M4504 (Air Q&T)	23	179	7.2	0.3	(310,0.2%) (450,4%)	12	55	460	—	—
M5003 (Air Q&T)	23	179	7.2	0.3	(345,0.2%) (515,3%)	12	55	460	—	—
M5503 (Liquid Q&T)	23	179	7.2	0.3	(380,0.2%) (520,3%)	12	55	460	—	—
M7002 (Liquid Q&T)	23	179	7.2	0.3	(480,0.2%) (620,2%)	12	55	460	—	—
M8501 (Liquid Q&T)	23	179	7.2	0.3	(590,0.2%) (725,1%)	12	55	460	—	—

Table 71.4 Mechanical Properties of Compact Graphite Iron Castings（Namely, CGI, GJV, VG, JV, or GGV）

Material	$T/℃$	E_T	ρ	ν	(α, ε)	α	k	γ	ρ_E	K_{IC}
EN GJV-250 (Nodularity ≈ 10%)	23	110	7.1	0.26	(175,0.2%) (250,3%)	10.8	47	475	—	—
	300	—	—	—	—	—	—	—	—	—

continued

Material	$T/{}^\circ\mathrm{C}$	E_T	ρ	ν	(α, ε)	α	k	γ	ρ_E	K_{IC}
EN GJV-300 (Ferritic)	23	115	7.1	0.26	(220,0.2%) (245,0.4%) (265,0.7%) (320,3%)	10.8	46	475	—	—
EN GJV-350 (Nodularity ≈ 10%)	23	125	7.1	0.26	(290,0.2%) (370,2.5%)	10.8	43	475	—	—
	100	—	—	0.26	(255,0.2%) (345,2%)	11	—	—	—	—
	200	—	—	—	—	—	37.4	—	—	—
	300	—	—	—	—	—	37.2	—	—	—
	400	—	—	0.27	(230,0.2%) (300,1.5%)	12.5	36.5	—	—	—
EN GJV-400 (Pearlitic=70%; Nodularity ≈ 10%)	23	145	7.1	0.26	(−400,−0.2%); (305,0.2%) (440,3%)	10.8	38	475	—	—
	100	140	—	0.26	(280,0.2%) (410,1.5%)	11	38	475	—	—
	400	135	—	0.27	(−330,−0.2%); (255,0.2%) (340,1%)	12.5	37	—	—	—
EN GJV-420 (Nodularity ≈ 10%)	23	147	7.1	0.26	(315,0.2%) (450,1.4%)	10.8	37	475	—	—
	100	—	—	—	—	11	—	—	—	—
	300	140	7.0	0.27	(284,0.2%) (375,1%)	12	36	—	—	—
EN GJV-450 (Pearlitic=90%; Nodularity ≈ 10%)	23	145	7.1	0.26	(−784,−2%) (−425,−0.2%); (440,0.2%) (495,1.4%)	10.8	34	475	—	31.4
	100	—	—	0.26	—	11	33.6	—	—	—
	200	—	—	—	—	—	34.2	—	—	—
	300	144	7.0	—	(320,0.2%) (410,1%)	12	34.3	—	—	—
	400	140	—	0.27	(−370,−0.2%); (290,0.2%) (390,1%)	12.5	33.9	—	—	—

continued

Material	$T/℃$	E_T	ρ	ν	(α, ε)	α	k	γ	ρ_E	K_{IC}
EN GJV-450 (Pearlitic=87%; Nodularity≈33%)	23	151	7.1	0.26	(360,2%) (570,4.3%)	10.9	33	475	—	—
	100	—	—	—	(320,2%) (530,3%)	11	—	—	—	—
	300	136	—	—	(300,2%) (500,3.3%)	—	—	—	—	—
	400	—	—	—	—	—	32	—	—	—
EN GJV-450 (Pearlitic=90%; Nodularity≈50%)	23	155	7.1	0.26	(390,0.2%) (590,3%)	11.1	31	475	—	—
	100	—	—	—	—	11.2	—	—	—	—
	300	—	—	—	(310,0.2%) (530,3%)	—	—	—	—	—
	400	—	—	—	—	—	31	—	—	—
EN GJV-450 (Pearlitic=90%; Nodularity≈67%)	23	155	7.1	0.26	(370,0.2%) (650,5.8%)	11.4	29	475	—	—
	100	—	—	—	(337,0.2%) (600,6.9%)	11.5	—	—	—	—
	300	—	—	—	(325,0.2%) (566,5%)	—	—	—	—	—
	400	—	—	—	—	—	32	—	—	—
EN GJV-450 (Pearlitic=90%; Nodularity≈80%)	23	162	7.1	0.26	(412,0.2%) (715,5.8%)	11.5	27	475	—	—
	100	161	—	—	(360,0.2%) (672,6.6%)	12	—	—	—	—
	300	158	—	—	(350,0.2%) (626,4.2%)	—	—	—	—	—
	400	—	—	—	—	—	31	—	—	—
EN GJV-450 (Pearlitic=90%; Nodularity≈90%)	23	168	7.1	0.26	(412,0.2%) (715,5.8%)	11.5	25	475	—	—
	100	161	—	—	(360,0.2%) (672,6.6%)	12	—	—	—	—
	300	158	—	—	(350,0.2%) (626,4.2%)	—	—	—	—	—
	400	—	—	—	—	—	31	—	—	—

continued

Material	$T/°C$	E_T	ρ	ν	(α, ε)	α	k	γ	ρ_E	K_{IC}
EN GJV-450 (Pearlitic=99%; Nodularity≈ 0%)	23	148	7.1	0.26	$(-437,-0.2\%)$	10.8	38	475	—	—
	100	147	—	—	$(308,0.2\%)$ $(422,1.1\%)$	—	—	—	—	—
	300	142	7.0	—	$(300,0.2\%)$ $(491,0.9\%)$	12	—	—	—	—
	400	—	—	—	$(-370,-0.2\%)$	—	36	—	—	—
EN GJV-500 (Mo-alloyed)	23	160	7.1	0.26	$(-480,-0.2\%)$; $(380,0.2\%)$ $(500,0.5\%)$	12	36	475	—	—
	400	—	—	—	$(-390,-0.2\%)$	—	36	—	—	—

Notes: GJV-400 = Pearlitic ≈ 70%;

GJV-450 = Pearlitic ≥ 90%.

Table 71.5　Mechanical Properties of Austempered Ductile Iron Castings (ASTM)

Material	$T/°C$	E_T	ρ	ν	(σ,ε)	α	k	γ	ρ_E	K_{IC}
Grade 1	23	163	7.1	0.25	$(760,0.2\%)$ $(960,11\%)$	14.6	22.1	461	—	105
Grade 2	23	160	7.09	0.25	$(890,0.2\%)$ $(1140,10\%)$	14.3	21.8	461	—	81
Grade 3	23	163	7.08	0.25	$(1100,0.2\%)$ $(1310,7\%)$	14.0	21.5	461	—	58
Grade 4	23	150	7.07	0.25	$(1240,0.2\%)$ $(1520,1\%)$	13.8	21.2	461	—	50
Grade5	23	155	7.06	0.25	$(1450,0.2\%)$ $(1650,1\%)$	13.5	20.9	461	—	42

Table 71.6　Fatigue ε-N Properties of Cast Irons

Material	$T/°C$	$d\varepsilon/dt$	σ_f'	ε_f'	b	c	K'	n'	$\sigma_f@2N_f$	R
Gray Cast Iron:										
GJL150 (G1800)	23	—	—	—	—	—	—	—	69@ 10^6	—
GJL180 (G2500)	23	—	—	—	—	—	—	—	79@ 10^6	—

continued

Material	$T/^\circ C$	$d\varepsilon/dt$	σ_f'	ε_f'	b	c	K'	n'	$\sigma_f @ 2N_f$	R
GJL200（G3000）	23	—	—	—	−0.113	−0.4	—	—	97@ 10^6	—
GJL250（G3500）	23	—	704	0.01	−0.175	−0.543	468	0.11	110@ 10^6	—
GJL300（G4000）	23	—	—	—	—	—	—	—	128 @ 10^6	—
GJL350（G5000）	23	—	—	—	—	—	—	—	148 @ 10^6	—
GJL400（G6000）	23	—	—	—	—	—	—	—	169 @ 10^6	—
Nodular Ductile Cast Iron:										
GJS-500-7	23	—	—	—	—	—	—	—	$\sigma_f = 224$	RB
GJS-500-14	23	—	—	—	—	—	—	—	$\sigma_f = 225$	RB
GJS-600-3	23	—	—	0.01	−0.096	−0.45	100	0.1	$\sigma_f = 190$	RB
GJS-600-10	23	—	—	—	—	—	—	—	$\sigma_f = 275$	RB
D4018（As Cast; 60-40-18；100% ferritic）	23	—	700	0.51	−0.06	−0.68	680	0.073	290@ 10^6 336@ 10^5 444@ 10^3	— — —
D4018（Annealed; 60-40-18；100% ferritic）	23	—	690	0.963	−0.061	−0.76	670	0.074	276@ 10^6 320@ 10^5 430@ 10^3	— — —
D4018（Annealed; 60-40-18；80% ferritic）	23	—	690	0.963	−0.061	−0.76	590	0.053	285@ 10^6 330@ 10^5 433@ 10^3	— — —
D4512（As Cast; 65-45-12；54% ferritic）	23	—	760	0.45	−0.064	−0.65	790	0.094	300@ 10^6 345@ 10^5 464@ 10^3	— — —
Crankshaft	23	—	927	0.202	−0.087	−0.696	1061	0.114	263@ 10^6	—
D5506（As Cast; 80-55-06）	23	—	1020	0.263	−0.082	−0.648	—	—	—	—
D5506（As Cast; 80-55-06）	23	5 Hz	667	—	−0.078	—	—	—	250@ 10^6	$R=-1$
	23	150 Hz	775	—	−0.082	—	—	—	190@ 2×10^7	$R=-1$
D7003（As Cast; 100-70-30；91% Pearlitic）	23	—	927	0.59	−0.067	−0.72	945	0.087	350@ 10^6 410@ 10^5 557@ 10^3	— — —

continued

Material	$T/^\circ\text{C}$	$\mathrm{d}\varepsilon/\mathrm{d}t$	σ_f'	ε_f'	b	c	K'	n'	$\sigma_\mathrm{f}@2N_\mathrm{f}$	R
D7003(Normalized; 100-70-30; 92% Pearlitic)	23	—	1130	0.665	−0.088	−0.668	1080	0.105	315@ 10^6 386@ 10^5 580@ 10^3	— — —
D7003(Normalized; 98% Pearlitic)	23	—	1140	0.273	−0.091	−0.64	1230	0.122	306@ 10^6 377@ 10^5 570@ 10^3	— — —
D9002 (Q&T;120-90-02; 100% Tempered Martensitic)	23	—	1320	0.37	−0.09	−0.7	1190	0.09	353@ 10^6 660@ 10^3	— —
Compact Graphite Iron (*CGI*):										
GJV-250	23	—	—	—	—	—	—	—	—	—
GJV-300(Ferritic)	23	—	—	—	—	—	—	—	178@ 10^6	—
GJV-350	23	—	—	—	—	—	—	—	—	—
GJV-400	23	—	—	—	—	—	—	—	—	—
GJV-420 (70% Pearlitic)	23	—	—	—	—	—	—	—	185@ 10^6	—
GJV-450 (90% Pearlitic)	23	10 Hz	—	—	—	—	—	—	195@ 10^7 210@ 10^7	−1 RB
	225	10 Hz	—	—	—	—	—	—	170@ 10^7 205@ 10^7	−1 RB
Austempered Ductile Iron (*ADI*)-*ASTM*:										
ADI Grade 1	23	—	1455	0.115	−0.090	−0.594	1744	0.133	367@ 10^6	—
ADI Grade 2	23	—	2720	0.178	−0.146	−0.628	—	0.138	—	—
ADI Grade 3	23	—	3100	0.396	−0.160	−0.752	—	0.147	370@ 10^6	—
ADI Grade 4	23	—	5020	0.488	−0.205	−0.848	—	0.16	385@ 10^6	—
ADI Grade 5	23	—	—	—	—	—	—	—	—	—
Cast Irons	23	—	Eq. (6.14)	Eq. (6.15)	—	—	$\sigma_\mathrm{f}'/(\varepsilon_\mathrm{f}')^{n'}$	b/c	Eq.(71.1) Eq.(71.2)	— —

Table 71.7 Mechanical Creep Parameters of Cast Irons

Material	$T/\degree C$	Stress/MPa	Strain Rate/s^{-1}	$A/(MPa^{-n} \cdot s^{m-1})$	$Q/(J \cdot mol^{-1})$	n	m
Grey 280	25	$E=1$	—	—	90	—	—

Notes: Creep equation $=\dfrac{d\varepsilon_{creep}}{dt}=A\left(\dfrac{\sigma-\sigma_{th}}{E}\right)^{n}t^{m}\exp\left(\dfrac{-Q}{RT_{k}}\right)$, $\sigma>\sigma_{th}$;

$\sigma_{th}=$ Stress threshold and $\sigma_{th}=0$, if not specified;

$E=$ Young's modulus; If given that $E=1$, it means E is not specified.

Chapter 72

Plain Carbon Steels

72.1 Introduction

Steel is a hard, strong malleable alloy of iron and carbon. It contains 0.2% up to 1.5% carbon, with other constituents such as manganese, chromium, nickel, molybdenum, copper, tungsten, cobalt, and silicon. Steel is the most used material for a passenger vehicle by weight. Mechanical properties of plain carbon steels are listed in Tables 72.1 and 72.2. Their related fatigue properties and creep strain rates are given in Tables 72.3 and 72.4, respectively. SAE and AISI share the 4-digit code system for naming carbon steels. The first two digits identify the major alloying elements, while the last two digits indicate the carbon content. For example, 10××, 11××, 12××, and 14×× are plain carbon steels with a different mix of manganese, sulfur, and sulphor:

    10××: Plain carbon steels;
    11××: Resulphurized plain carbon steels;
    12××: Resulphurized/rephosphorized plain carbon steels.

72.2 Mechanical Strength of Plain Carbon Steels

Plain carbon steels are divided into three categories according to carbon contents: low carbon (0.0%~0.25%), medium carbon (0.25%~0.55%), and high carbon (0.55%~1.0%). In general, ultimate strength increases and stretchability decreases with increasing carbon content. Processing is another factor affecting the strength and stretchability of steels. For example, yield strengths of hot-rolled (HR) and cold drawn (CD) SAE 1008 steels (containing 0.08% of carbon) are 170 MPa and 290 MPa (engineering stresses), respectively. SAE 1008HR is more stretchable than SAE 1008CD. Not knowing the ultimate tensile strength (MPa) of the applied carbon steel, one may use the following equation [Roessle et al.] for plain carbon steels as the first approximation from the Brinell hardness (H_B),

$$\sigma_{uts} = 0.0012(H_B)^2 + 3.3(H_B) \tag{72.1}$$

Note that the unit for the ultimate tensile strength is MPa.

The fatigue limit of plain carbon steel, σ_f, varies according to its surface preparation, size, loading, and temperature. It is the best if there is a fatigue limit available in the literature while analyzing the fatigue life of a component. Without knowing the fatigue strength (endurance limit) of the applied carbon steel, one may use the following equation [Roessle et al.] for plain carbon steels as the first approximation

$$\sigma_{\mathrm{f}} = 0.38\sigma_{\mathrm{uts}} \tag{72.2}$$

Fatigue failures of carbon steels are mostly contributed from the tensile failure mode. Compressive residual stresses in the part surface may improve the fatigue limit where residual stresses in tension affect it adversely. Mechanical operations build compressive residual stresses such as shot peening, hammering, and cold rolling improve the fatigue limit of steel significantly.

72.3　Crack Propagation

Material parameters on fatigue crack growth of plain carbon steels in opening mode are given in Table 72.5.

72.4　Oxidation of Plain Carbon Steels

Thermomechanical oxidation parameters of plain carbon steel are given in Table 72.6. Plain carbon steels are generally weak in oxidation resistance.

72.5　Applications

Carbon Content	Typical Applications
0.05%~0.1%	Stamping, rivets, wires, and cold-drawn parts
0.10%~0.2%	Structural shapes, machine parts, and carburized parts
0.2%~0.3%	Gears, shafts, levers, cold-forged, tubing, and carburized parts
0.3%~0.4%	Gears, shafts, connecting rods, crane hooks, and seamless tubing
0.4%~0.5%	Gears, shafts such as crankshafts, screws, and forgings
0.5%~0.7%	Wire springs, lock washers, and locomotive wheels
0.7%~0.9%	Leaf springs, plow shares, shovels, and hand tools
0.9%~1.2%	High-strength springs and cutters (knives/drills/taps/milling cutter)
1.2%~1.4%	Wire-drawn dies and cutters (files/knives/razors/saws)

The endurance limit of SAE 1045 steel for engine crankshafts (as forged) varies with respect to the loading frequency [Gyansah and Simmons], as shown in Table 72.3.

References

ABULUWEFA H T, 2005. Kinetics of High Temperature Oxidation of High Carbon Steels in Multi-component Gases Approximating Industrial Steel Reheat Furnace Atmospheres[J]. Lecture Notes in Engineering and Computer Science, 2196(1): 1664-1668.

ALVARENGA H D, et al, 2009. Influence of Carbide Morphology and Microstructure on the Kinetics of Superficial Decarburization of C-Mn Steels[J]. Metallurgical and Materials Transactions, A, 46(1): 123-133.

GYANSAH L, SIMMONS A, 2010. Investigation into the Fatigue Performance of 1045 Steel: Paper 1[J]. European Journal of Technology and Advanced Engineering Research, 1: 3039.

HAGGAG F M, et al, 1990. The Use of Miniatured Tests to Predict Flow Properties and Estimate Fracture Toughness in Deformed Steel Plates[J]. Journal of Testing and Evaluation, 1(1): 62-69.

HAGGAG F M, LUCAS G E, 1989. Determination of Luders Strains and Flow Properties in Steels from Hardness/Microhardness Tests[J]. Metallurgical Transactions, A, 14: 1607-1613.

HUADSON C M, FERRAINOLO J J, 1991. A Compendium of Sources of Fracture Toughness and Fatigue-crack Growth Data for Metallic Alloys-Part IV[J]. International Journal of Fracture, 48(2): R19-R43.

JANG D, ATZMON M, 2003. Grain-size Dependence of Plastic Deformation in Nanocrystalline Fe[J]. Journal of Applied Physics, 93(11): 9282.

LI Y, 2014. Segregation Stabilizes Nanocrystalline Bulk Steel with Near Theoretical Strength[J]. Physical Review Letters, 113(10): 106-104.

NAYEBI A, et al, 2002. New Procedure to Determine Steel Mechanical Parameters from the Spherical Indentation Techniques[J]. Mech. Mater., 68: 218.

ROESSLE M, FETIMI A, 2000. Strain-controlled Fatigue Properties of Steels and Some Simple Approximations[J]. International Journal of Fatigue, 22: 495-511.

SHANG D G, WANG D J, 2007. A New Multiaxial Fatigue Damage Model Based on the Critical Plane Approach[J]. International Journal of Fatigue, 20(3): 241-245.

WEHNER T, FATEMI A, 1991. Effects of Mean Stress Fatigue Behavior of a Hardened Carbon Steel, International Journal of Fatigue, 13: 241-248.

WILLIAMS K R, TAYLOR M, 1984. Creep of Mild Steel at Low Temperatures[J]. Mechanics of Materials, 3(1): 1-10.

ZHANG J, JIANG Y, 2005. An Experimental Study of Inhomogeneous Plastic Deformation of 1045 Steel under Multiaxial Cyclic Loading[J]. International Journal of Plasticity, 21: 2174-2190.

ZINEB A, et al, 2010. Analysis of Thermomechanical Fatigue by using Finite Element PostProcessing[J]. Australian Journal of Basic and Applied Sciences, 4(10): 4857-4869.

WEHNER T, FATEMI A, 1991. Effects of Mean Stress Fatigue Behavior of a Hardened Carbon Steel[J]. International Journal of Fatigue, 13: 241-248.

Table 72.1　Mechanical Properties of Plain Carbon Steels

Material	$T/°C$	E_T	ρ	ν	(σ,ε)	α	k	γ	ρ_E	K_{IC}
1006 (HR)	23	206	7.87	0.29	(170,0.2%) (390,26.2%)	12	51.5	480	—	—
1006 (CD)	23	206	7.87	0.29	(290,0.2%) (396,18.2%)	12	51.5	480	—	—
1008 (HR)	23	206	7.87	0.29	(170,0.2%) (394,26.2%)	12	51.5	480	—	—
	100	—	—	—	—	12.6	—	500	—	—
	400	—	—	—	—	13.7	45	620	—	—
	1426(T_m)	—	—	—	—	13.7	45	620	—	—
1008(CD)	23	206	7.87	0.29	(290,0.2%) (408,18.2%)	12	51.5	480	—	—
1009(HR)	23	206	7.87	0.29	(175,0.2%) (402,18.2%)	12	51.5	480	—	—
1009(CD)	23	206	7.87	0.29	(295,0.2%) (424,18.2%)	12	51.5	480	—	—
1010(HR)	23	206	7.87	0.29	(180,0.2%) (410,24.7%)	11.5	51.5	480	—	—
1010 (CD)	23	206	7.87	0.29	(300,0.2%) (440,18.2%)	11.5	51.5	480	—	—
1012 (HR)	23	206	7.87	0.29	(180,0.2%) (422,24.7%)	11.5	51.5	480	—	—
1012 (CD)	23	206	7.87	0.29	(310,0.2%) (440,18.4%)	11.5	51.5	480	—	—
1015 (HR)	23	206	7.87	0.29	(180,0.2%) (435,24.7%)	11.5	51.5	480	—	—
1015(CD)	23	206	7.87	0.29	(324,0.2%) (455,17%)	11.5	51.5	480	—	—

continued

Material	$T/{}^{\circ}C$	E_T	ρ	ν	(σ,ε)	α	k	γ	ρ_E	K_{IC}
1016(HR)	23	206	7.87	0.29	(210,0.2%) (475,22.3%)	11.5	51.5	480	—	—
1016 (CD)	23	206	7.87	0.29	(350,0.2%) (496,16.6%)	11.5	51.5	480	—	—
1018 (HR)	23	206	7.87	0.29	(220,0.2%) (500,22.3%)	11.5	51.5	480	—	—
1018(CD)	0	—	—	—	—	—	52	—	—	—
	23	206	7.87	0.29	(370,0.2%) (506,14%)	11.5	51.5	480	—	—
	100	—	—	—	—	11.7	—	—	—	—
	400	170	—	—	—	11.7	—	—	—	—
	600	—	—	—	(190,0.2%)	13.5	—	900	—	—
	740	120	—	—	—	15	20	2080	—	—
	800	—	—	—	(42,0.2%)	13.5	20	1000	—	—
	1200	—	—	—	—	—	20	1000	—	—
	1400	—	—	—	—	—	20	1000	—	—
	$1450(T_m)$	—	—	—	—	—	20	5500	—	—
	1500 (Liquid)	—	—	—	—	15.9	31.2	1000	—	—
	1600 (Liquid)	—	—	—	—	23.5	—	—	—	—
	2500 (Liquid)	—	—	—	—	23.5	125	1000	—	—
	5000 (Liquid)	—	—	—	—	—	156	1000	—	—
1020 (HR)	23	206	7.87	0.29	(210,0.2%) (475,22.3%)	11.5	51.5	480	—	—
	175	—	—	—	—	—	—	—	—	51.6
	200	—	—	—	—	—	48	—	—	—
	250	—	—	—	—	12.6	—	—	—	—
	375	—	—	—	—	—	—	599	—	—
	400	—	—	—	—	—	42	599	—	—
	500	—	—	—	—	13.9	—	—	—	—
1020 (CD)	23	206	7.87	0.29	(350,0.2%) (483,14%)	11.5	51.5	480	—	—

continued

Material	$T/℃$	E_T	ρ	ν	(σ,ε)	α	k	γ	ρ_E	K_{IC}
1020 (Cast; Annealed)	23	—	—	—	$\sigma_{uts}\geq414$	—	—	—	—	—
1020 (As TIG-welded to Invar 36; Filler wire: W)	−253	—	—	—	(593,0.2%) (710,5%)	—	—	—	—	—
	−196	—	—	—	(545,0.2%) (848, 12%)	—	—	—	—	—
	23	—	—	—	(317,0.2%) (469, 19%)	—	—	—	—	—
1020 (As TIG welded to Invar 36;Filler wire: 92)	−253	—	—	—	(703,0.2%) (779,2%)	—	—	—	—	—
	−196	—	—	—	(655,0.2%) (903,14%)	—	—	—	—	—
	23	—	—	—	(317,0.2%) (469, 19%)	—	—	—	—	—
1025 (HR)	23	206	7.86	0.29	(220,0.2%) (500,22.3%)	11.5	51.5	480	—	—
1025 (CD)	23	206	7.86	0.29	(370,0.2%) (506,14%)	11.5	51.5	480	—	—
1030 (HR)	23	206	7.85	0.29	(260,0.2%) (564,18.2%)	11.5	51.5	480	—	—
1030 (CD)	23	206	7.85	0.29	(440,0.2%) (582,11.3%)	11.5	51.5	480	—	—
1030 (Cast; Annealed)	23	—	—	—	(340,0.2%) (450,11%)	—	—	—	—	—
1035 (HR)	23	205	7.85	0.29	(270,0.2%) (590,16.6%)	11.5	51.5	480	—	—
	175	—	—	—	—	—	—	519	—	—
	250	—	—	—	—	12.6	—	—	—	—
	375	—	—	—	—	—	—	586	—	—
	500	—	—	—	—	13.9	—	—	—	—
1035 (CD)	23	205	7.85	0.29	(460,0.2%) (616,11.3%)	11.5	51.5	480	—	—
	175	—	—	—	—	—	—	519	—	—
	250	—	—	—	—	12.6	—	—	—	—
	375	—	—	—	—	—	—	586	—	—
	500	—	—	—	—	13.9	—	—	—	—

continued

Material	$T/℃$	E_T	ρ	ν	(σ,ε)	α	k	γ	ρ_E	K_{IC}
1040（HR）	0	—	—	—	—	—	52	—	—	—
	23	206	7.85	0.29	（290,0.2%） （614, 16.6%）	11.5	51.5	480	—	—
	100	—	—	—	—	—	50.7	—	—	—
	175	—	—	—	—	—	—	515	—	—
	500	—	—	—	—	14.3	38.2	—	—	—
	675	—	—	—	—	—	—	770	—	—
	725	—	—	—	—	—	—	1583	—	—
	1000	—	—	—	—	14.7	32.9	—	—	—
	1200	—	—	—	—	—	29.8			
1040（CD；Annealed）	23	206	7.85	0.29	（490,0.2%） （661,11.3%）	11.5	51.5	480	—	—
1040（As Cast）	23	—	—	—	$\sigma_{uts}\geqslant517$	—	—	—	—	—
1040（100 μm Boriding）	23	206	7.85	0.29	（650,0.2%） （814,9.5%） （1030,19.1%）	—	—	—	—	—
1040（5 μm Vanadium carbide coating）	23	206	7.85	0.29	（720,0.2%） （869,9.5%） （1238, 25.5%）	—	—	—	—	—
1045（HR）	23	206	7.85	0.29	（510,0.2%） （661, 14.8%）	11.5	51.5	480	—	—
	175	—	—	—	—	—	—	515	—	—
	375	—	—	—	—	—	—	586	—	—
1045（CD）	23	206	7.85	0.29	（530,0.2%） （706, 11.3%）	11.5	51.5	486	—	—
1045（ACD）	23	206	7.85	0.29	（500,0.2%） （661, 11.3%）	11.5	51.5	480	—	—
1045（Forged for Crankshaft）	23	221	7.85	0.29	（625,0.2%） （827, 54%）	11.5	51.5	480	—	—
1045-495（Q&T；Leaf Spring）	23	207	7.85	0.29	（1515,0.2%） $\sigma_{uts}=1584$	11.5	51.5	480	—	—
1045-595（Q&T；Leaf Spring）	23	207	7.85	0.29	（1860,0.2%） $\sigma_{uts}=2239$	11.5	51.5	480	—	—

continued

Material	$T/℃$	E_T	ρ	ν	(σ,ε)	α	k	γ	ρ_E	K_{IC}
1050 (HR)	23	206	7.85	0.29	(340,0.2%) (713,14%)	11.5	51.5	480	—	—
1050 (CD)	23	206	7.85	0.29	(580,0.2%) (759,9.5%)	11.5	51.5	480	—	—
1050 (ACD)	23	206	7.85	0.29	(550,0.2%) (726,9.5%)	11.5	51.5	480	—	—
1050 (Cast; Annealed)	23	—	—	—	$\sigma_{uts}\geqslant621$	—	—	—	—	—
1055 (HR)	23	206	7.85	0.29	(360,0.2%) (728,11.3%)	11.5	51.5	480	—	—
1055 (ACD)	23	206	7.85	0.29	(560,0.2%) (748,9.5%)	11.5	51.5	480	—	—
1060 (HR)	23	206	7.85	0.29	(370,0.2%) (762,11.3%)	11.5	51.5	480	—	—
1060 (SACD)	23	206	7.84	0.29	(480,0.2%) (682,9.5%)	11.5	51.5	480	—	—
1065 (HR)	23	206	7.85	0.29	(380,0.2%) (773,11.3%)	11.5	51.5	480	—	—
1070 (HR)	23	206	7.84	0.29	(390,0.2%) (784,11.3%)	11.5	51.5	480	—	—
	200	212	—	—	—	12.5	—	—	—	—
	400	220	—	—	—	14	—	—	—	—
	600	150	—	—	—	14	—	—	—	—
1070 (HR; Induction- hardened Case)	23	206	7.85	0.29	(1950,0.2%) (2069,2.3%)	11.5	51.5	480	—	—
1070 (SACD)	23	206	7.85	0.29	(500,0.2%) (704,9.5%)	11.5	51.5	480	—	—
1075 (HR)	23	206	7.85	0.29	(400,0.2%) (807,11.3%)	11.5	51.5	480	—	—
1080 (HR)	23	206	7.85	0.29	(420,0.2%) (847,9.5%)	11.5	51.5	480	—	—

continued

Material	$T/{}^\circ\text{C}$	E_{T}	ρ	ν	(σ,ε)	α	k	γ	ρ_{E}	K_{IC}
1080 (SACD)	23	206	7.85	0.29	(520,0.2%) (748,9.5%)	11.5	51.5	480	—	—
1085 (HR)	23	206	7.85	0.29	(460,0.2%) (913,9.5%)	11.5	51.5	480	—	—
1090 (HR)	23	206	7.85	0.29	(460,0.2%) (924,9.5%)	11.5	51.5	480	—	—
1090 (SACD)	23	206	7.85	0.29	(540,0.2%) (770,9.5%)	11.5	51.5	480	—	—
1095 (HR)	23	206	7.85	0.29	(460,0.2%) (913,9.5%)	11.5	51.5	480	—	—
1095 (Hardened from 900 ℃ & T:400 ℃; Spring grade)	-198	—	—	—	$\sigma_{\text{uts}}=2275$	—	—	—	—	—
	23	206	7.85	0.29	(1790,0.2%) (1940,6%)	11.5	51.5	480	—	—
	100	—	—	—	$\sigma_{\text{uts}}=1920$	—	—	—	—	—
	200	—	—	—	$\sigma_{\text{uts}}=1850$	—	—	—	—	—
	400	—	—	—	$\sigma_{\text{uts}}=850$	—	—	—	—	—

Notes: HR = Hot rolled;

CD = Cold drawn;

ACD = Annealed cold drawn;

SACD = Spheroidized annealed cold drawn;

T = Tempered;

(σ,ε) = True stress-strain data, from ultimate compression ($-$) to tension ($+$);

Typical mechanical properties varying with respect to temperature are demonstrated using SAE1018 (CD) steel.

Table 72.2 Mechanical Properties of Resulfurized Carbon Steels

Material	$T/{}^\circ\text{C}$	E_{T}	ρ	ν	(σ,ε)	α	k	γ	ρ_{E}	K_{IC}
1108 (HR)	23	206	7.86	0.29	(190,0.2%) (442, 26.2%)	11.5	51	473	—	—
	300	—	—	—	—	12.2	—	586	—	—
	500	—	—	—	—	13.9	—	—	—	—
1108 (CD)	23	206	7.86	0.29	(320,0.2%) (468,18.2%)	11.5	51	473	—	—
1117 (HR)	23	206	7.86	0.29	(230,0.2%) (529,20.7%)	11.5	51	473	—	—

continued

Material	$T/°C$	E_T	ρ	ν	(σ,ε)	α	k	γ	ρ_E	K_{IC}
1117 (CD)	23	206	7.86	0.29	(400,0.2%) (552,13.8%)	11.5	51	473	—	—
1132 (HR)	23	206	7.86	0.29	(310,0.2%) (661,14.8%)	11.5	51	473	—	—
1132 (CD)	23	206	7.86	0.29	(530,0.2%) (706,11.3%)	11.5	51	473	—	—
1137 (HR)	23	206	7.86	0.29	(380,0.2%) (800,24.5%)	11.5	52	472	—	—
	300	—	—	—	—	12.2	—	—	—	—
	500	—	—	—	—	13.9	—	—	—	—
1137 (CD)	23	206	7.86	0.29	(620,0.2%) (766,10%)	11.5	52	472	—	—
1137(Q:855 ℃ T:540 ℃; bulk)	23	207	7.86	0.29	(405,0.2%) (848,20.5%)	11.5	52	472	—	—
1137 (Q & T: 430 ℃)	23	207	7.86	0.29	(986,0.2%) (1103,14%)	11.5	52	472	—	—
1137 (Q & T: 204 ℃)	23	207	7.86	0.29	(1165,0.2%) (1500,5%)	11.5	52	472	—	—
1140 (HR)	23	206	7.86	0.29	(300,0.2%) (626,14.8%)	11.5	51	473	—	—
1140(CD)	23	206	7.86	0.29	(510,0.2%) (683,11.3%)	11.5	51	473	—	—
1141(HR)	23	206	7.86	0.29	(360,0.2%) (748,14%)	11.5	51	472	—	—
1141 (CD)	23	206	7.86	0.29	(610,0.2%) (728,11.3%)	11.5	51	472	—	—
1141 (Q & T: 650 ℃)	23	207	7.86	0.29	(593,0.2%) (701,23%)	11.5	51	472	—	—
1141 (Q & T: 430 ℃)	23	207	7.86	0.29	(1034,0.2%) (1165,12%)	11.5	51	472	—	—
1141 (Q & T: 204 ℃)	23	207	7.86	0.29	(1214,0.2%) (1634,6%)	11.5	51	472	—	—

continued

Material	$T/℃$	E_T	ρ	ν	(σ,ε)	α	k	γ	ρ_E	K_{IC}
1144 (HR)	23	206	7.86	0.29	(370,0.2%) (771,14%)	11.5	51	473	—	—
1144 (CD)	23	206	7.86	0.29	(620,0.2%) (814,9.5%)	11.5	51	473	—	—
1144 (Q & T: 651 ℃)	23	207	7.86	0.29	(503,0.2%) (724,23%)	11.5	51	473	—	—
1144 (Q & T: 430 ℃)	23	207	7.86	0.29	(607,0.2%) (850,18%)	11.5	51	473	—	—
1144 (Q & T: 204 ℃)	23	207	7.86	0.29	(627,0.2%) (876,17%)	11.5	51	473	—	—
1146 (HR)	23	206	7.86	0.29	(320,0.2%) (679,14%)	11.5	51	473	—	—
1146 (CD)	23	206	7.86	0.29	(550,0.2%) (728,11.3%)	11.5	51	473	—	—
1151 (HR)	23	206	7.86	0.29	(340,0.2%) (725,14%)	11.5	51	473	—	—
1151 (CD)	23	206	7.86	0.29	(590,0.2%) (770,9.5%)	11.5	51	473	—	—
1211 (HR)	23	206	7.86	0.29	(230,0.2%) (475,22.3%)	11.5	51	473	—	—
1211(CD)	23	206	7.86	0.29	(400,0.2%) (594,9.5%)	11.5	51	473	—	—
1212(HR)	23	206	7.86	0.29	(230,0.2%) (488,22.3%)	11.5	51	473	—	—
1212(CD)	23	206	7.86	0.29	(410,0.2%) (594,9.5%)	11.5	51	473	—	—
1213(HR)	23	206	7.86	0.29	(230,0.2%) (488,22.3%)	11.5	51	473	—	—
1213 (CD)	23	206	7.86	0.29	(410,0.2%) (594,9.5%)	11.5	51	473	—	—
1215 (CD)	23	206	7.86	0.29	(415,0.2%) (594,9.5%)	11.5	51	473	—	—

continued

Material	$T/℃$	E_T	ρ	ν	(σ,ε)	α	k	γ	ρ_E	K_{IC}
12L14（HR）	23	206	7.86	0.29	（230,0.2%） （476,19.9%）	11.5	51	473	—	—
12L14（CD）	23	206	7.86	0.29	（410,0.2%） （595,9.5%）	11.5	51	473	—	—
	1000	—	—	—	—	14.7	51	473	—	—

Notes：(σ,ε) = True stress-strain data；positive-tension，negative-compression.

Table 72.3   Fatigue ε-N Properties of Plain Steels

Material	$T/℃$	$d\varepsilon/dt$	σ_f'	ε_f'	b	c	K'	n'	$\sigma_f@2N_f$	R
1008（HR）	23	—	641	0.10	−0.11	−0.39	462	0.12	228	—
1008（CD）	23	—	538	0.11	−0.073	−0.408	490	0.11	248	—
1010（HR）	23	—	499	0.104	−0.10	−0.408	867	0.244	223	—
1012（HR）	23	—	—	—	—	—	738	0.19	—	—
1012（CD）	23	—	586	0.241	−0.075	−0.481	629	0.168	—	—
1015（HR）	23	—	884	0.729	−0.124	−0.581	—	—	—	—
1015（Normalized）	23	—	827	0.95	−0.11	−0.64	945	0.22	241	—
1020（HR）	23	—	896	0.41	−0.12	−0.51	772	0.18	208@ 10^8	—
1025（HR）	23	—	934	0.59	−0.107	−0.52	—	—	—	—
1025（CD；S25C）	23	—	821	0.216	−0.096	−0.458	1140	0.21	—	—
1030 （Normalized）	23	—	902	0.17	−0.12	−0.42	1545	0.29	—	—
1030（Cast）	−45	—	834	0.18	−0.089	−0.506	710	0.13	320@ 10^8	—
	23	—	655	0.28	−0.083	−0.552	710	0.13	320@ 10^8	—
1035（HR）	23	—	1491	1.56	−0.152	−0.73	838	0.09	—	—
1038（HR） （Normalized）	23	—	1040	0.309	−0.107	−0.48	1340	0.22	223@ 10^6	—
1038（HR；Q&T）	23	—	1009	0.225	−0.097	−0.46	1330	0.208	—	—
1038（CD）	23	—	1004	0.202	−0.098	−0.44	1420	0.222	—	—

continued

Material	$T/^{\circ}C$	$d\varepsilon/dt$	σ'_f	ε'_f	b	c	K'	n'	$\sigma_f @ 2N_f$	R
1040 (CD)	23	—	1311	0.848	−0.103	−0.612	915	0.131	—	—
1045 (HR; CK45)	23	—	948	0.26	−0.092	−0.445	1258	0.208	280@ 10^6	—
1045 (HR; Annealed)	23	—	912	0.486	−0.079	−0.52	1022	0.152	—	—
1045-495 (Q&T)	23	—	1684	0.79	−0.06	−0.83	1974	0.09	—	—
1045(HR; Q&T)	23	—	3372	0.038	−0.103	−0.47	3082	0.075	—	—
1045-595 (Q&T)	23	—	2261	0.196	−0.093	−0.643	3371	0.145	—	—
1045 (Forged Crankshaft)	23	—	1124	0.671	−0.079	−0.597	1159	0.128	359@ 10^8	—
1045 (CD; S45C)	23	—	1400	0.449	−0.107	−0.564	1150	0.152	—	—
1045 (25 Hz)	23	—	1667	—	−0.112	—	—	—	302@ 10^6	—
1045 (50 Hz)	23	—	1377	—	−0.12	—	—	—	288@ 10^6	—
1045 (75 Hz)	23	—	1301	—	−0.139	—	—	—	159@ 10^6	—
1045 (100 Hz)	23	—	964	—	−0.144	—	—	—	120@ 10^8	—
1047 (HR)	23	—	—	—	—	—	—	—	320@ 10^8	—
1050 (CD)	23	—	—	—	—	—	—	—	345@ 10^8	—
1050 (Normalized)	23	—	1109	0.292	−0.1	−0.456	—	—	—	—
1050 (Q&T)	23	—	1346	2.0	−0.062	−0.725	—	—	—	—
1050 (Induction Hardened)	23	—	4974	0.53	−0.152	−0.91	—	—	—	—
1070 (HR)	23	—	958	0.1	−0.093	−0.464	—	—	—	—
1090(Normalized at 900 ℃)	23	—	1310	0.25	−0.091	−0.496	1611	0.174	307@ 10^6	—
1090 (Q&T; Hot-formed)	23	—	1878	0.7	−0.12	−0.6	1873	0.176	—	—
1095 (Hardened from 900 ℃ & T: 400 ℃)	23	—	—	—	—	—	—	—	750@ $2×10^6$	—

continued

Material	$T/^\circ\text{C}$	$d\varepsilon/dt$	σ_f'	ε_f'	b	c	K'	n'	$\sigma_f @ 2N_f$	R
1141 (Normalized at 900 ℃ ; alloyed with fine-grained Vanadium)	23	—	1255	0.43	−0.102	−0.529	1467	0.191	—	—
1141 (Q&T; Alloyed with fine-grained Vanadium)	23	—	1162	0.534	−0.086	−0.555	1270	0.154	—	—
1144	23	—	1000	0.32	−0.08	−0.58	—	—	—	—
Steel (Generic)	23	—	Eq. (6.14)	Eq. (6.15)	−0.09	−0.6	$\sigma_f'/(\varepsilon_f')^{n'}$	b/c	Eq.(72.1)	—

Table 72.4   Mechanical Creep Parameters of Plain Carbon Steel

Material	$T/^\circ\text{C}$	Stress/MPa	Strain Rate/s^{-1}	$A/(\text{MPa}^{-n} \cdot s^{m-1})$	$Q/(\text{J} \cdot \text{mol}^{-1})$	n	m
Mild Steel (Generic)	360~400	$E=1 ; \sigma \leqslant 410$	—	250	217000	3.7	0

Notes: Creep equation $= \dfrac{d\varepsilon_{\text{creep}}}{dt} = A\left(\dfrac{\sigma - \sigma_{\text{th}}}{E}\right)^n t^m \exp\left(\dfrac{-Q}{RT_k}\right)$, $\sigma > \sigma_{\text{th}}$;

σ_{th} = Stress threshold and $\sigma_{\text{th}} = 0$, if not specified;

E = Young's modulus; If given that $E = 1$, it means E is not specified.

Table 72.5   Material Parameters on Fatigue Crack Growth of Plain Carbon Steels in Opening Mode

Material	$T/^\circ\text{C}$	σ_y	σ_{uts}	K_{IC}	$f(R)$	m	ΔK_{th}	$\Delta \sigma_{\text{fat}}$
SAE 1010 (HR)	23	302	450	—	$f(-1) = 3.807 \times 10^{-12}$	3.034	—	—

Notes: $\dfrac{da}{dN_p} = f(R) \mid \Delta K - \Delta K_{\text{fat}} \mid^m$;

σ_y(MPa) = Yield strength;

σ_{uts}(MPa) = Ultimate tensile strength;

$f(R)$ = Parameter as a function of load ratio (R) ;

m = Exponent;

ΔK_{th}(MPa $\cdot$ m$^{\frac{1}{2}}$) = Threshold stress intensity range;

$\Delta \sigma_{\text{fat}}$(MPa) = Fatigue strength range.

Table 72.6 Thermomechanical Oxidation Parameters of Plain Carbon Steels

Material	Period	$T/°C$	k_0	$Q_o/(\text{J} \cdot \text{mol}^{-1})$	n	m	Δm_{in}	t_{in}/h
1018	Steady	1000~1200	256.4	238179	2	1	0	0
1032	Steady	1000~1200	486.8	242128	2	1	0	0

Notes: $\text{Oxidation} = (\Delta m - \Delta m_{in})^n = k_0 (t - t_{in})^m \text{Exp}\left(\dfrac{-Q_o}{R\,T_k}\right)$;

Δm & $\Delta m_{in} = \text{kg/m}^2 (= 0.1 \text{ g/cm}^2)$.

Chapter 73

Alloy Steels

73.1   Introduction

One distinct category of steels is the family of alloy steels with high ultimate strength and reasonable stretchability. Most alloy steels are carbon steels hardened using alloying elements. The first two digits indicate the type of alloy according to alloying elements, described as follows:

13××: Manganese 1.75%;

25××: Nickel 5%;

40××: Molybdenum 0.2% or 0.25%;

41××: Chromium 0.5%, 0.8%, or 0.95% and Molybdenum 0.12%, 0.2%, or 0.3%;

43××: Nickel 1.83%, Chromium 0.5% or 0.8%, and Molybdenum 0.25%;

44××: Molybdenum 0.53%;

46××: Nickel 0.85% or 1.83%, and Molybdenum 0.2% or 0.25%;

47××: Nickel 1.05% and Chromium 0.45%;

48××: Nickel 3.5% and Molybdenum 0.25%;

50××: Chromium 0.4%;

51××: Chromium 0.8%, 0.88%, 0.93%, 0.95%, or 1%;

5×××× (52095-52101): Carbon 1.04%, and Chromium 1.03% or 1.45%;

6×××: Chromium and Vanadium;

61××: Chromium 0.6% or 0.95%, and Vanadium 0.13% or 0.15%;

86××: Nickel 0.55%, Chromium 0.5%, and Molybdenum 0.25%;

87××: Nickel 0.55%, Chromium 0.5%, and Molybdenum 0.35%;

88××: Nickel 0.55%, Chromium 0.5%, and Molybdenum 0.20%;

92××: Silicon 2%;

97××: Nickel 0.55%, Chromium 0.5%, and Molybdenum 0.35%;

98××: Nickel 0.55%, Chromium 0.5%, and Molybdenum 0.35%.

"××" indicates the carbon content. For example, the carbon content of SAE 4340 is 0.4%. Roles of alloying elements (carbon, chromium, cobalt, manganese, nickel, molybdenum, sulfur, tungsten, vanadium, boron, phosphorous, arsenic, antimony, tin) in steel are summarized as follows:

(a) Boron increases the hardenability of the material and this is done with having little effect on the ductility or ferrite strength of the steel.

(b) Calcium contributes toward imparting the steel with a non-scaling property, as it deoxidizes steels.

(c) Carbon increases strength but lessens toughness. This alloying element determines the level of hardness or strength attained by quenching.

(d) Chromium improves oxidation resistance. High chromium-alloyed steels have high temperature strength and they are quite resistant to high-pressure hydrogenation.

(e) Cobalt-based alloys are corrosion, heat and wear-resistant. The temperature stability of these alloys makes them suitable for use in turbine blades for gas turbines and jet aircraft engines.

(f) Manganese plus sulfur improves machinability. A small amount of manganese improves the workability of steel at high temperatures because it forms a high melting sulfide and therefore prevents the formation of a liquid iron sulfide at the grain boundaries.

(g) Molybdenum retards temper embrittlement. A small amount (0.15% to 0.25%) of Mo used in combination with chromium, increases the ultimate tensile strength of steel without affecting ductility or workability. The ability of molybdenum to withstand extreme temperatures without significantly expanding or softening makes it useful in applications that involve intense heat. The success of Mo-Si-B materials for turbineblade and other high-temperature applications (>1100 ℃), replacing Ni-based superalloys, depends on a compromise between several mechanical properties and the oxidation resistance [Kruzic et al.].

(h) Nickel improves toughness and hardenability. It also enhances strength at elevated temperatures.

(i) Nitrogen improves hardness, tensile strength and yield strength of steel, but it may cause a considerable decrease in toughness and ductility.

(j) Phosphorous, arsenic, antimony, and tin accelerate temper embrittlement.

(k) Silicon increases heat resistance and imparts good casting fluidity.

(l) Sulfur causes hot cracks.

(m) Titanium helps increase the effectiveness of boron as an alloying element of steel.

(n) Tungsten provides good toughness and inhibits grain growth for steels.

(o) Vanadium improves strength at elevated temperatures, as it helps control the grain growth during heat treatment.

(p) All carbide-forming elements retard softening during tempering.

Alloy steels have been used in the automotive industry for a variety of major structural parts such as valves, bolts, bearings, springs, gears, shafts, brakes/clutches, transmission parts, engines parts, sheet steels for body, and crash-resisting members. Major automotive power transmission components like gears, shafts and bearings have to be able to withstand operations. Steels would need to be case hardened if it is used for highly loaded gears.

73.2   Operations

Alloyed steels are made mainly by adding a small percentage of alloying metals to liquid steel to subsequently alter the hardness, fracture toughness, elasticity, fatigue, creep, and chemical behaviors once solidified. These material properties can be altered using different chemical and mechanical operations. Namely,

(a) **Normalizing**: Normalizing consists of uniform heating to a temperature slightly above the point at which grain structure is affected (known as the critical temperature), followed by cooling in still air to room temperature. This produces a uniform structure and hardness throughout.

(b) **Anneal**: Annealing consists of heating to and holding at a suitable temperature, then cooling slowly, when not preceded by a descriptive adjective. Annealing removes stresses, reduces hardness, increases ductility and produces a structure favorable for formability. Five distinct levels of annealing are addressed as follows:

1. **Full Anneal**-This term is synonymous with annealing and is used to differentiate anneal from bright annealing, stress relief anneal, soft anneal, and others.
2. **Spherodize Anneal**-This treatment is similar to full annealing except the steel is held at an elevated temperature for a prolonged period of time, followed by slow cooling in order to produce a microstructure where carbides exist in a globular or spheroidal form.
3. **Soft Anneal**-When maximum softness and ductility are required without change in grain structure, steel should be soft annealed. This process consists of heating to a temperature slightly below the critical temperature and cooling in still air.
4. **Stress Relief Anneal**-Stress relieving is intended to reduce the residual stresses imparted to the steel in the drawing operation. It generally consists of heating the steel to a suitable point below the critical temperature followed by slow cooling.
5. **Bright Anneal**-This process consists of annealing in a closely controlled furnace atmosphere which will permit the surface to remain relatively bright.

(c) **Quenching**: Quenching consists of heating steel above the critical range, then hardening by immersion in an agitated bath of oil, water, brine or caustic. Quenching increases tensile strength, yield point and hardness. It reduces ductility and impact resistance. By subsequent tempering some ductility and impact resistance may be restored, but at some sacrifice of tensile strength, yield point and hardness.

(d) **Tempering**: Tempering is the reheating of steel, after quenching, to the specified temperature below the critical range, then air cooling. It is done in furnaces, oil or salt baths, at temperatures varying from 150 ℃ to 700 ℃. Low tempering temperatures give maximum hardness and wear resistance. Maximum toughness is achieved at higher temperatures.

(e) **Cryogenic Treatment**: It is to subject material to a very low temperature such as 90 °K. It can be carried out by treating the material in a liquid nitrogen gas chamber. The cooling is done gradually and then allowed to come back to the room temperature naturally after a certain soaking period. Tool steels show an increase in hardness [Molinari et al.], carburized steels (e.g. AISI

4340 steel) show an increase in hardness and tensile strength with a slight decrease in impact strength [Zhirafar et al.], and austenitic stainless steels (e.g. AISI 304) show an improvement in fatigue limit and fatigue life and without any significant changes in hardness and ultimate tensile strength [Baldissera and Delprete].

Mechanical properties of structural alloy steels are listed in Table 73.1. Three popular structural steels used for automotive structural frames/beams, buildings, and constructions are ASTM A26, ASTM A572 Grade 50, and ASTM A992. HSLA (High Strength Low Alloy) and RHA (Rolled Homogeneous Armor), addressed in this chapter, are two promising structural alloy steels used for ground vehicles. Other alloy steels are given in other individual chapters according to their applications.

Strain hardening based on quenching and tempering is a promising way to make alloy steels stronger, especially on the outer surface (usually $2 \sim 3$ mm in thickness), which bears bending loads. Example true stress-strain curves of the inner core (unhardened) and outer shell (induction hardened) of 4140H steel (quenched and tempered) are given in Fig. 73.1 to demonstrate the effectiveness of strain hardening.

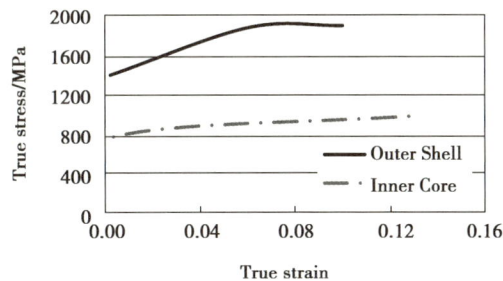

Fig. 73.1   Enhancement of Material Strength (4140 H Steel) by Induction Hardening

SAE 8620 alloy steels, belonging to HSLA-80 grade steels, are often used as the raw materials for carburization to raise their surface hardness. These carburized SAE 8620 steels are widely used as the wear-resistant parts of bearing, gears, lifting chains, and yoke fittings. 20CrMnTi is a low carbon alloy steel for gears massively used in China. Hardness will be much higher just below the surface ($0.8 \sim 1.8$ mm typically), with a surface hardness between 58 and 62 HRC (650750 HV) approximately. It has become a low-cost replacement of SAE 8620.

73.3   Railway Rails

Steels for railway rails are strong and tough. Even after years of service and high stress, there is no difference between the grain structure of a used rail and a new rail. Age, traffic and weather do not change their basic properties. Compositions of railway rail steels in percentage by weight are given as follows [Scutti]:

Steel	C	Si	Mn	Ni	Mo	Cr	V	B	Al	Ti
Bainitic Rail	0.04	0.2	0.75	2.0	0.25	2.8	—	0.01	0.03	0.03
Pearlitic	0.55	0.25	1.0	—	—	—	—	—	—	—
Pearlitic	0.8	0.3	1.0	—	—	—	—	—	—	—
Pearlitic	0.7	1.9	1.5	—	—	—	—	—	—	—
Pearlitic (Cr, V)	0.75	0.7	1.0	—	—	1.0	0.1	—	—	—
Pearlitic (Tire)	0.65	0.25	0.7	—	—	—	—	—	—	—
Roller Rail	1.0	0.25	0.25	—	—	1.5	—	—	—	—

All stresses are relieved through heating prior to being re-rolled. Mechanical properties of typical rail steels are given in Table 73.2. Typically, rail steels are produced in large BOS vessels and vacuum-degassed prior to being continuously cast into large blooms.

73.4   Fatigue Strength of Medium and High Carbon Steels

Medium and high carbon steels are applied to components, which requires high strength and fatigue life. Fatigue ε-N properties of alloy steels are presented in Table 73.3. In case of no data are available for a specific steel, the empirical models for estimating fatigue strength (endurance limit) of these steels given here can be used as the first approximation to evaluating the product life span of concern.

73.4.1   Fatigue of Quenched and Tempered Medium and High Carbon Steels

According to the data provided in the AISI Bar Steel Fatigue Database, the following regression equation is adequate to predict the fatigue strength of quenched and tempered alloy steels at 10^6 cycles with a tolerance range of ±40.18 MPa,

$$\sigma_f = 1.52\ H_B + 45.68\%\ C + 298.0\%\ Mn - 2301\%\ S - 25.63\%\ Si + 98.08\%\ Cr -$$

$$753.7\%\ Mo + 488.6\%\ Ni + 380.7\%\ Al - 261.5 \tag{73.1}$$

73.4.2   Fatigue of Normalized Medium and High Carbon Steels

According to the data provided in the AISI Bar Steel Fatigue Database, the following regression equation is adequate to predict the fatigue strength of quenched and tempered alloy steels at 10^6 cycles with a tolerance range of ±4.6 MPa,

$$\sigma_f = 0.18 \ H_B + 53.48\% \ C + 218.3\% \ Mn - 2053\% \ S - 46.4\% \ Si - 56.56\% \ Cr -$$

$$380.4\% \ Mo + 1337\% \ Ni + 36.1 \tag{73.2}$$

73.4.3   General Approximation to Fatigue Strength

Not knowing the fatigue strength (endurance limit) of the applied carbon steel and the detailed composition, one may use the following equation [Mischke] for alloy steels as the first approximation

$$\sigma_f = 0.504 \ \sigma_{uts}, \ \text{if} \ \sigma_{uts} < 1400 \ \text{MPa} \tag{73.3}$$

and

$$\sigma_f = 700 \ \text{MPa}, \ \text{if} \ \sigma_{uts}^3 \geqslant 1400 \ \text{MPa} \tag{73.4}$$

Alloy steels may be carburized to improve the fatigue strength of the surface. At long life, the case/core composite exhibited fatigue properties very close to those shown by the high hardness simulated case. At short life, however, the case/core composite fatigue properties of the case/core composite were between those of the simulated case and core.

73.4.4   Creep Fatigue

Creep fatigue of high-strength steels at an elevated temperature is of great concern. For example, AISI 4140 may fail due to creep rather than fracture when working at 730 ℃ or above as presented by the creep parameters in Table 73.4.

73.5   Crack Propagation

Material parameters on fatigue crack growth of alloy steels in opening mode are listed in Table 73.5.

73.6   Corrosion

The following equation has been used for the prediction of potential corrosion due to an alloy steel's exposure to the atmospherical environment [ASTM 2002b]

$$\text{Index} = 26.01\% \ Cu + 3.88\% \ Ni + 1.2\% \ Cr + 1.49\% \ Si + 17.28\% \ P -$$

$$7.29\% \text{ Cu Ni} - 9.1\% \text{ P Ni} - 33.39\% \text{ (Cu)}^2 \qquad\qquad (73.5)$$

The higher the index, the more corrosion-resistant the steel is.

References

AHMED R, LOVELOCK H, 2009. A Comparison of the Tribo-Mechanical Properties of a Wear Resistant Cobalt-Based Alloy Produced by Different Manufacturing Processes[J]. Journal of Tribology, 129(3): 25-33.

BALDISSERA P, DELPRETE C, 2010. Deep Cryogenic Treatment of AISI 302 Stainless Steel[J]. Materials and Design, 31: 4731-4737.

BALDISSERA P, 2009. Fatigue Scatter Reduction through Deep Cryogenic Treatment on the 18NiCrMo$_5$ Carburized Steel[J]. Materials and Design, 30: 3636-3642.

BARTHA B, et al, 2005. Wear of Hard-Turned AISI 52100 steel[J]. Metallurgical and Materials Transactions, A, 36(6): 1417-1425.

BERETTA S, et al, 2008. An Investigation of the Effects of Corrosion on the Fatigue Strength of AlN Axle Steel [J]. Journal of Rail and Rapid Transit, 222(2): 129-143.

CHIEN W Y, et al, 2005. Fatigue Analysis of Crankshaft Sections Under Bending with Consideration of Residual Stresses[J]. International Journal of Fatigue, 27: 1-19.

CHOI Y, LIU R, 2006. Rolling Contact Fatigue Life of Finish Hard Machined Surfaces[J]. Wear, 261 (5-6): 429-499.

DENG X, et al, 2011. Numerical and Experimental Investigation of Cold Rotary Forging of a 20CrMnTi Alloy Spur Bevel Gear[J]. Materials and Design, 32: 1376-1389.

DENNIS W H, 2010. Cobalt[J]. Metallurgy, 1863/1963: 254-256.

DIMIDUK D, PEREPEZKO J, 2003. Mo-Si-B Alloys: Developing a Revolutionary TurbineEngine Material[J]. MRS Bulletin, September, 28: 639-645.

DOBRZANSKI L A, BOREK W, 2009. Processes Forming the Microstructure Evolution of High-Manganese Austenitic Steel in Hot-Working Conditions[J]. Journal of Achievements in Materials and Manufacturing Engineering, 37(2): 397-402.

DUTTON T, et al, 1999. The Effect of Forming on the Crashworthiness of Vehicles with Hydroformed Frame Side Rails[J]. SAE 1999-01-3208.

GHOSH S, XIE C, 2003. Computational Modeling of HSLA Steel for Tensile and Fatigue Tests[J]. SAE 2003-01-0481.

GOKEN M, et al, 2001. Microstructural Mechanical Properties and Yield Point Effects in Mo Alloys[J]. Material Science and Engineering, A, 319-321: 902-908.

HUI W, et al, 2008. High-cycle Fatigue Fracture Behavior of Ultrahigh Strength Steels[J]. Journal of Materials Science and Technology, 24(5): 787-792.

KANKANAMGE N D, MAHENDRENN M, 2011. Mechanical Properties of Cold-Formed Steels at Elevated Temperatures[J]. Thin-Walled Structures, 49(1): 26-44.

KRUZIC J, et al, 2009. Ambient- to Elevated-Temperature Fracture and Fatigue Properties of Mo-Si-B Alloys: Role of Microstructure[J]. Metallurgical and Materials Transactions, A, 36: 2393-2402.

LAGODA T, MACHA E, 1997. Estimated and Experimental Fatigue Lives of 30CrNiMo8 Steel under In- and Out-of-phase Combined Bending and Torsion with Variable Amplitudes [J]. Fatigue & Fracture of Engineering Materials & Structures, 17: 1307-1318.

LIN H, et al, 2006. Mechanical Properties of Gear Steels and Other Perspective Light Weight Materials for Gear Applications[J]. SAE 2006-01-3578.

LIU Y, et al, 2009. Fatigue Properties of Two Case Hardening Steels after Carburization[J]. International Journal of Fatigue, 31: 292-299.

MASUMOTO H, et al, 1984. Damping Capacity and Pitting Corrosion Resistance of FE-Mo-Cr Alloys[J]. Transaction of Japanese Institute of Metallurgy, 25: 891-899.

MOLINARI A, et al, 2001. Effect of Deep Cryogenic Treatment on Mechanical Properties of Tool Steel[J]. Journal of Materials Processing Technology, 118: 350-355.

MROZIŃSKI, S, GOLAŃSKI, G, 2011. Low Cycle Fatigue of GX12CrMoVNbN9-1 Cast Steel at Elevated Temperature[J]. Journal of Achievements of Materials and Manufacturing Engineering, 49(1): 7-16.

PEREIRA H, et al, 2008. Influence of Loading Sequence and Stress ratio on Fatigue Damage Accumulation of a Structural Component[J]. Ciência e Tecnologia dos Materiais, 20(1-2): 60-67.

QURAISHI I M, HARNE M S, 2013. Fatigue Strength and Residual Stress Analysis of Deep Rolled Crankshafts [J]. International Journal of Engineering and Technology, 4(6): 466-473.

REISBICK M H, CAPUTO A A, 1978. Influence of Loading Rates on Mechanical Properties of Cobalt-Chromium Alloys[J]. British Dental Journal, 138(8): 295-298.

RINGSBERG J W, et al, 2000. Rolling Contact Fatigue of Railway Rails- Finite Element Modeling of Residual Stresses, Strains and Crack Initiation[J]. Proc IMechE, Part F, Journal of Rail and Rapid Transit, 214: 7-19.

SCHNEIDER W, et al, 1981. Damping Capacity of FE-Cr and Fe-Cr-based High Damping Alloys[J]. Journal of Physics, 42(C5): 635-639.

SHPAK A P, et al, 2009. Inherent Tensile Strength of Molybdenum Nanocrystals[J]. Science and Technology of Advanced Materials, 10: 045004.

SCUTTI J J, et al, 1984. Fatigue of Behavior of Rail Steel[J]. Fatigue and Fracture of Engineering Materials and Structures, 7(2): 121-135.

VAMSI KRISHNA P, 2013. Effect of Austempering and Martempering on the Properties of AISI 52100 Steel [J]. ISRN Tribology, 2013: 1-6.

WANG Q Y, ZHANG H, SRIRAMAN M R, 2005. Very Long Life Fatigue Behavior of Bearing Steel AISI 52100[J]. Key Engineering Materials, 297-300 (1- 4): 1846-1851.

WILDER A T, 2005. Power Frequency Magnetic Properties and Aging of 4130 Steel[J]. Journal of Magnetism and Magnetic Materials, 300(2): L257-L261.

ZHIRAFAR S, REZAEIAN A, PUGH M, 2007. Effect of Cryogenic Treatment on the Mechanical Properties of 4340 steel[J]. Journal of Materials Processing Technology, 186: 298-303.

ZOROUFI M, FATEMI A, 2004. Fatigue Life Comparison of Competing Manufacturing Processes: A Study of Steering Knuckle[J]. SAE 2004-01-0628.

Table 73.1 Mechanical Properties of Alloy Steels (AISI)

Material (AISI)	$T/^\circ\text{C}$	E_T	ρ	ν	(σ, ε)	α	k	γ	ρ_E	K_{IC}
1330 (HR; Q& T; 30Mn)	23	206	7.85	0.29	(1034, 0.2%) (1332, 14%)	11.5	50	475	—	—
1330 (Q & T: 650 ℃)	23	207	7.85	0.29	(570, 0.2%) (731, 23%)	11.5	50	475	—	—
1330 (Q & T: 430 ℃)	23	207	7.85	0.29	(1034, 0.2%) (1158, 15%)	11.5	50	475	—	—
1330 (Q & T: 204 ℃)	23	207	7.85	0.29	(1455, 0.2%) (1600, 9%)	11.5	50	475	—	—
1335 (Q & T; 35Mn$_2$)	23	200	7.85	0.29	(1034, 0.2%) (1332, 14%)	11.5	50	475	—	—
1340 (HR; Annealed)	23	206	7.85	0.29	(440, 0.2%) (710, 25.5%)	11.5	50	475	—	—
1340(HR; Normalized at 870 ℃)	23	206	7.85	0.29	(565, 0.2%) (840, 22%)	11.5	50	475	—	—
1340 (Q & T: 650 ℃)	23	207	7.85	0.29	(620, 0.2%) (800, 22%)	11.5	50	475	—	—

continued

Material (AISI)	$T/℃$	E_T	ρ	ν	(σ,ε)	α	k	γ	ρ_E	K_{IC}
1340 (Q & T: 430 ℃)	23	207	7.85	0.29	(1150,0.2%) (1260,14%)	11.5	50	475	—	—
1340 (Q & T: 204 ℃)	23	207	7.85	0.29	(1593,0.2%) (1806,11%)	11.5	50	475	—	—
1524 (HR)	23	206	7.85	0.29	(280,0.2%) (612,18.2%)	11.5	50	475	—	—
1524 (CD)	23	206	7.85	0.29	(480,0.2%) (638,11.3%)	11.5	50	475	—	—
1527 (HR)	23	206	7.85	0.29	(280,0.2%) (614,16.6%)	11.5	50	475	—	—
1527 (CD)	23	206	7.85	0.29	(480,0.2%) (638,11.3%)	11.5	50	475	—	—
1536 (HR)	23	206	7.85	0.29	(310,0.2%) (661,14.8%)	11.5	50	475	—	—
1536 (CD)	23	206	7.85	0.29	(530,0.2%) (693,9.5%)	11.5	50	475	—	—
1541 (HR)	23	206	7.85	0.29	(350,0.2%) (725,14%)	11.5	50	475	—	—
1541 (CD)	23	206	7.85	0.29	(600,0.2%) (781,9.5%)	11.5	50	475	—	—
1541 (ACD)	23	206	7.85	0.29	(550,0.2%) (715,9.5%)	11.5	50	475	—	—
1541H (Q & T)	23	206	7.85	0.29	(910,0.2%) $\sigma_{uts}=970$	11.5	50	475	—	—
	540	—	—	—	(330,0.2%) $\sigma_{uts}=420$	—	—	—	—	—
1547(Q & T)	23	206	7.85	0.29	(1140,0.2%) $\sigma_{uts}=1240$	11.5	50	475	—	—
1548(HR)	23 1510 (T_m)	206	7.85	0.29	(370,0.2%) (752,13.1%)	11.5	50	475	—	—

continued

Material (AISI)	$T/℃$	E_T	ρ	ν	(σ, ε)	α	k	γ	ρ_E	K_{IC}
1548 (CD)	23	206	7.85	0.29	(620,0.2%) (803,9.5%)	11.5	50	475	—	—
1548 (ACD)	23	206	7.85	0.29	(540,0.2%) (704,9.5%)	11.5	50	475	—	—
1552 (HR)	23	206	7.85	0.29	(410,0.2%) (829,11.3%)	11.5	50	475	—	—
1552 (ACD)	23	206	7.85	0.29	(570,0.2%) (738,9.5%)	11.5	51	475	—	—
3140 (HR; Annealed)	23	206	7.85	0.29	(423,0.2%) (690,24.5%)	11.5	45	475	—	—
3140 (HR; Normalized)	23	206	7.85	0.29	(520,0.2%) (790,19.7%)	11.5	45	475	—	—
	540	—	—	—	(110,0.2%) $\sigma_{uts}=140$	—	—	—		
	650	—	—	—	(57,0.2%) $\sigma_{uts}=86$	—	—	—	—	—
4037 (Q & T; 650 ℃)	23	207	7.85	0.29	(420,0.2%) (700,29%)	11.5	45	475	—	—
4037 (Q & T; 430 ℃)	23	207	7.85	0.29	(730,0.2%) (880,20%)	12	45	475	—	—
4037 (Q & T; 204 ℃)	23	207	7.85	0.29	(760,0.2%) (1015,6%)	11.5	45	475	—	—
4042 (Q & T; 650 ℃)	23	207	7.85	0.29	(690,0.2%) (793,28%)	11.5	45	475	—	—
4042 (Q & T; 430 ℃)	23	207	7.85	0.29	(1170,0.2%) (1290,15%)	11.5	45	475	—	—
4042 (Q & T; 204 ℃)	23	207	7.85	0.29	(1660,0.2%) (1800,12%)	11.5	45	475	—	—
4118 (Q & T; Carburized)	23	206	7.85	0.29	(650,0.2%) (986,18%)	11.5	45	475	—	—

continued

Material (AISI)	$T/℃$	E_T	ρ	ν	(σ,ε)	α	k	γ	ρ_E	K_{IC}
4130 (HR; Annealed)	23	206	7.85	0.29	(460,0.2%) (560,22%)	11.5	45	475	—	—
	200	—	—	—	—	—	41	523	—	—
	800	—	—	—	—	—	34	837	—	—
	1200	—	—	—	—	—	30.1	—	—	—
4130 (HR; Normalized at 870 ℃)	23	206	7.85	0.29	(436,0.2%) (669,26%)	11.5	45	475	—	—
	800	—	—	—	—	—	34	837	—	—
	1200	—	—	—	—	—	30.1	—	—	—
4130 (Q & T; 650 ℃)	23	207	7.85	0.29	(700,0.2%) (814,22%)	11.5	45	475	—	—
4130 (Q & T; 430 ℃)	23	207	7.85	0.29	(1193,0.2%) (1282,13%)	11.5	45	477	—	—
4130 (Q & T; 204 ℃)	23	207	7.85	0.29	(1460,0.2%) (1630,10%)	11.5	45	475	—	—
4130 (CD)	23	206	7.85	0.29	(535,0.2%) (675,25%)	11.5	45	475	—	—
4130 (Cast; Q & T)	23	—	—	—	$\sigma_{uts}\geqslant 1030$	—	—	—	—	—
4135 (CD)	23	206	7.85	0.29	(450,0.2%) (765,16%)	11.5	45	475	—	—
4140 (HR; Annealed; 42CrMo4)	23	206	7.85	0.29	(417,0.2%) (655,25.7%)	11.5	45	475	—	50
	300	190	—	—	—	13.2	39.4	590	—	—
	400	182	—	—	—	13.7	38	607	—	—
	600	—	—	—	—	—	33	—	—	—
	1416(T_m)	—	—	—	—	—	—	—	—	—

continued

Material (AISI)	$T/℃$	E_T	ρ	ν	(σ,ε)	α	k	γ	ρ_E	K_{IC}
4140 (HR; Normalized at 870 ℃)	23	206	7.85	0.29	(485,0.2%) (814,22.2%)	11.5	45	475	—	—
	300	190	—	—	—	13.2	39.4	590	—	—
	400	182	—	—	—	13.7	38	607	—	—
	600	—	—	—	—	33	—	—	—	—
4140 (Q & T: 650 ℃)	23	206	7.85	0.29	(655,0.2%) (758,22%)	11.5	45	475	—	—
4140(Q:845 ℃ & T:540 ℃)	23	206	7.85	0.29	(685,0.2%) (883,19.2%)	11.5	45	475	—	44
	300	190	—	—	—	13.2	39.4	590	—	—
	400	182	—	—	—	13.7	38	607	—	—
	600	—	—	—	—	33	—	—	—	—
4140 (Q & T: 430 ℃)	23	207	7.85	0.29	(1138,0.2%) (1248,13%)	11.5	45	475	—	—
4140 (Q & T: 204 ℃)	23	207	7.85	0.29	(1640,0.2%) (1772,8%)	11.5	45	475	—	—
4140 (Cast; Q & T)	23	—	—	—	$\sigma_{uts}\geqslant1241$	—	—	475	—	—
4140 H (Annealed)	23	206	7.85	0.29	(415,0.2%) (655,25%)	11.5	45	475	—	—
4140 H(Normalized: 870 ℃)	23	206	7.85	0.29	(675,0.2%) (1020,17%)	11.5	45	475	—	—
4140H (Q: 845 ℃& T: 540 ℃)	23	206	7.85	0.29	(685,0.2%) (883,19%)	11.5	45	475	—	—
	500	—	—	—	(390,0.2%) $\sigma_{uts}=500$	—	—	—	—	—
4140H (Q & T; Induction-Hardened)	23	206	7.85	0.29	(1400,0.2%) (1900,6%)	11.5	45	475	—	—

continued

Material (AISI)	$T/℃$	E_{T}	ρ	ν	(σ,ε)	α	k	γ	ρ_{E}	K_{IC}
4142 (HR; Annealed)	23	206	7.85	0.29	(415,0.2%) (655,25%)	11.5	45	475	—	—
	600	—	—	—	—	14.6	33	—	—	—
4142 (CD; Annealed)	23	206	7.85	0.29	(755,0.2%) (655,20%)	11.5	45	475	—	—
4142 (Q & T: 540 ℃)	23	207	7.85	0.29	(931,0.2%) (1069,16%)	11.5	45	475	—	—
4142 (Q & T: 260 ℃)	23	206	7.85	0.29	(1584,0.2%) $\sigma_{\text{uts}}=1757$	11.5	45	475	—	—
4147 (HR; Annealed)	23	206	7.85	0.29	(482,0.2%) (672,25%)	11.5	45	475	—	—
4150 (HR & Annealed; 50CrMo4)	23	206	7.85	0.29	(485,0.2% (730,20%)	11.9	45	475	—	—
4150 (HR; Normalized at 870 ℃)	23	206	7.85	0.29	(740,0.2%) (1160,11.7%)	11.5	45	475	—	—
4150 (Q & T: 650 ℃)	23	207	7.85	0.29	(840,0.2%) (958,19%)	11.5	45	475	—	—
4150 (HR; Q: 830 ℃; T:540 ℃)	23	206	7.85	0.29	(1100,0.2%) (1207,15%)	11.5	45	475	—	—
	300	190	—	—	—	13.2	39.4	590	—	—
	400	182	—	—	—	13.7	38	607	—	—
4150 (Q & T: 430 ℃)	23	207	7.85	0.29	(1380,0.2%) (1517,12%)	11.5	45	475	—	—
4150 (Q & T: 204 ℃)	23	207	7.85	0.29	(1724,0.2%) (1931,10%)	11.5	45	475	—	—
4150 (Q & T; HRC=56)	23	206	7.85	0.29	(1700,0.2%) (2020,2%) (2300,4%) (2355,5.8%)	11.5	45	475	—	—

continued

Material (AISI)	$T/°C$	E_T	ρ	ν	(σ,ε)	α	k	γ	ρ_E	K_{IC}
4160 (60CrMnMo; Roller Steel)	23	210	7.85	0.29	—	11.5	45	475	—	—
	200	206	—	—	—	13.9	42	502	—	—
	600	145	—	—	—	16.7	32.3	586	—	—
	1000	97	—	—	—	16.7	26.5	674	—	—
	1400	—	—	—	—	16.7	29.4	670	—	—
	1600	—	—	—	—	16.7	29.4	670	—	—
4317 (Q & T; HRc=52)	23	206	7.85	0.29	(850,0.2%) (1125,8%)	11.5	45	475	—	89
4320 (HR; Annealed)	23	206	7.85	0.29	(425,0.2%) (580,29%)	11.5	45	475	—	—
4320 (HR; Normalized)	23	206	7.85	0.29	(465,0.2%) (793,20.8%)	11.5	45	475	—	—
4320 (Q & T; Core after Carburization, Special)	23	206	7.85	0.29	(920,0.2%) $\sigma_{uts}=994$	11.5	45	475	—	—
4320 (Q & T; Carburized Case; Special)	23	206	7.85	0.29	(1344,0.2%) $\sigma_{uts}=1705$	11.5	45	475	—	—
4330 (Annealed)	23	206	7.85	0.29	(690,0.2%) (860,15%)	11.5	45	475	—	—
4330V (Q & T: 316°C; Austenitized)	23	206	7.85	0.29	(1330,0.2%) (1550,11%)	11.5	45	670	—	—
4330V (Q & T: 282°C; Austenitized)	23	206	7.85	0.29	(1345,0.2%) (1620,11%)	11.5	45	670	—	—
4330 (Cast; Q & T)	23	—	—	—	$\sigma_{uts}\geq1030$	—	—	—	—	—
4340 (HR; Annealed)	23	206	7.85	0.29	(470,0.2%) (745,22%)	11.5	45	475	—	50
	500	—	—	—	—	14.5	—	—	—	—

continued

Material（AISI）	$T/℃$	E_{T}	ρ	ν	(σ,ε)	α	k	γ	ρ_{E}	K_{IC}
4340（HR；Normalized at 870 ℃）	23	206	7.85	0.29	（710,0.2%） （1110,13%）	11.5	45	475	—	—
	500	—	—	—	—	14.5	—	—	—	—
4340（Q & T：650 ℃）	23	207	7.85	0.29	（800,0.2%） （814,19%）	11.5	45	475	—	—
4340（Q：870 ℃ & T：540 ℃）	23	206	7.85	0.29	（1000,0.2%） （1138,15%）	11.5	45	475	—	65.4
	500	—	—	—	—	14.5	—	—	—	—
4340（Q & T：430 ℃）	23	207	7.85	0.29	（1310,0.2%） （1420,10%）	11.5	45	475	—	—
4340（Q & T：260 ℃）	23	207	7.85	0.29	—	11.5	45	475	—	50
4340（Q & T：204 ℃）	23	207	7.85	0.29	（1730,0.2%） （1944,10%）	11.5	45	475	—	—
4340H（Q：845 ℃ & T：650 ℃）	23	207	7.85	0.29	—	11.5	45	475	—	—
4615（HR）	23	206	7.85	0.29	（400,0.2%） （552,30%）	11.5	45	475	—	—
4615（CD）	23	206	7.85	0.29	（550,0.2%） （655,17%）	11.5	45	475	—	—
4620（HR；Annealed）	23	206	7.85	0.29	（366,0.2%） （512,29%）	11.5	45	475	—	—
4620（HR；Normalized）	23	206	7.85	0.29	（372,0.2%） （574,20.8%）	11.5	45	475	—	—
4620（HR；Carburized Core；HRC=30,Mixed bainite-martensite microstructure）	23	206	7.85	0.29	（892,0.2%） （964,15%）	11.5	45	475	—	—
4620（HR；Carburized Case；HRC=54,Martensite）	23	206	7.85	0.29	（1169,0.2%） $\sigma_{\mathrm{uts}}=1776$	11.5	45	475	—	—

continued

Material (AISI)	$T/^\circ C$	E_T	ρ	ν	(σ, ε)	α	k	γ	ρ_E	K_{IC}
4815 (HR)	23	206	7.85	0.29	(483, 0.2%) (724, 25%)	11.5	45	475	—	—
4815 (Q; HT; Carburized Core)	23	207	7.85	0.29	(896, 0.2%) (1034, 16%)	11.5	45	475	—	—
4820 (HR; Annealed)	23	206	7.85	0.29	(464, 0.2%) (681, 31%)	11.5	45	475	—	—
4820 (HR; Normalized)	23	206	7.85	0.29	(484, 0.2%) (755, 29%)	11.5	45	475	—	—
5046 (Q & T: 650 ℃)	23	207	7.85	0.29	(655, 0.2%) (786, 24%)	11.5	45	475	—	—
5046 (Q & T: 540 ℃)	23	207	7.85	0.29	(765, 0.2%) (938, 18%)	11.5	45	475	—	—
5046 (Q & T: 430 ℃)	23	207	7.85	0.29	(930, 0.2%) (1040, 13%)	11.5	45	475	—	—
5046 (Q & T: 204 ℃)	23	207	7.85	0.29	(1407, 0.2%) (1744, 9%)	11.5	45	475	—	—
5115 (HR; 16 MnCr5; 15CrMn; 16MnCr5E; Fe-0.16C-0.25Si-1.15Mn-0.95 Cr-...)	23	206	7.85	0.29	(415, 0.2%) (520, 17%)	11.5	45	460	—	—
5115 (Annealed)	23	206	7.85	0.29	(415, 0.2%) (650, 25%)	11.5	45	475	—	—
5115 (Q:880 & T:200 ℃)	23	206	7.85	0.29	(590, 0.2%) (785, 10%)	11.5	45	475	—	—
5115 (Q & T)	23	206	7.85	0.29	(600, 0.2%) (880, 8%)	11.5	45	475	—	—
5120 (Q & T)	23	205	7.85	0.29	(635, 0.2%) (834, 14%)	11.5	45	475	—	—
5130 (Q & T: 650 ℃)	23	207	7.85	0.29	(690, 0.2%) (793, 20%)	11.5	45	475	—	—

continued

Material (AISI)	$T/^\circ C$	E_T	ρ	ν	(σ, ε)	α	k	γ	ρ_E	K_{IC}
5130 (Q & T: 540 ℃)	23	207	7.85	0.29	(938, 0.2%) (1034, 15%)	11.5	45	475	—	—
5130 (Q & T: 430 ℃)	23	207	7.85	0.29	(1207, 0.2%) (1276, 12%)	11.5	45	475	—	—
5130 (Q & T: 204 ℃)	23	207	7.85	0.29	(1517, 0.2%) (1613, 10%)	11.5	45	475	—	—
5140 (HR; Annealed; 40Cr)	23	205	7.85	0.29	(290, 0.2%) (570, 29%)	11.5	45	475	—	—
5140 (HR; Normalized at 870 ℃)	23	205	7.85	0.29	(472, 0.2%) (793, 23%)	11.5	45	475	—	—
5140 (Q & T: 650 ℃)	23	207	7.85	0.29	(662, 0.2%) (758, 25%)	11.5	45	475	—	—
5140 (Q & T: 540 ℃)	23	207	7.85	0.29	(870, 0.2%) (999, 17%)	11.5	45	475	—	—
5140 (Q & T: 430 ℃)	23	207	7.85	0.29	(1170, 0.2%) (1310, 13%)	11.5	45	475	—	—
5140 (Q & T: 204 ℃)	23	207	7.85	0.29	(1640, 0.2%) (1730, 9%)	11.5	45	475	—	—
5150 (HR; Annealed)	23	205	7.85	0.29	(357, 0.2%) (676, 22%)	11.5	45	475	—	—
5150 (HR; Normalized at 870 ℃)	23	205	7.85	0.29	(529, 0.2%) (870, 21%)	11.5	45	475	—	—
5150 (Q & T: 650 ℃)	23	207	7.85	0.29	(800, 0.2%) (814, 20%)	11.5	45	475	—	—
5150 (Q & T: 430 ℃)	23	207	7.85	0.29	(1310, 0.2%) (1420, 9%)	11.5	45	475	—	—
5150 (Q & T: 204 ℃)	23	207	7.85	0.29	(1730, 0.2%) (1944, 5%)	11.5	45	475	—	—
5150H (Q & T)	23	207	7.85	0.29	(910, 0.2%) $\sigma_{uts} = 990$	11.5	45	475	—	—

continued

Material (AISI)	$T/°C$	E_T	ρ	ν	(σ, ε)	α	k	γ	ρ_E	K_{IC}
5155 (HR; Annealed; JIS-SUP9)	23	205	7.85	0.29	—	11.5	45	475	—	—
5160 (HR; Annealed; Leaf Spring: Fe-0.56C-0.75Mn-0.7Cr-.)	23	205	7.85	0.29	(275,0.2%) (724,17.2%)	11.5	47	475	—	—
5160 (HR; Normalized)	23	205	7.85	0.29	(485,0.2%) (925,14.8%)	11.5	47	475	—	—
5160 (Q & T: 650 ℃)	23	206	7.85	0.29	(800,0.2%) (896,20%)	11.5	47	475	—	—
5160 (Q & T: 540 ℃)	23	206	7.85	0.29	(1141,0.2%) (1165,12%)	11.5	47	475	—	—
5160 (Q & T: 427 ℃; Leaf Spring Grade)	23	205	7.85	0.29	(1462,0.2%) (1607,10%)	11.5	47	475	—	—
5160 (Q & T: 316 ℃)	23	207	7.85	0.29	(1772,0.2%) (2000,9%)	11.5	47	475	—	—
5160 (Q & T: 204 ℃)	23	207	7.85	0.29	(1790,0.2%) (2220,4%)	11.5	47	475	—	—
5210 (Annealed)	23	207	7.85	0.29	(560,0.2%) (730,25%)	11.5	47	475	—	—
5210 (Q & T; Bearings)	23	210	7.85	0.29	(500,0.2%) (1292,12%)	11.5	47	475	—	—
5280 (Q & T; Bearings)	23	210	7.85	0.29	—	11.5	47	475	—	—
6150 (HR; Annealed; JIS-SUP10)	23	207	7.85	0.29	(412,0.2%) (670,23%)	11.5	47	475	—	—
6150 (HR; Normalized)	23	207	7.85	0.29	(616,0.2%) (940,21.8%)	11.5	47	475	—	—

continued

Material (AISI)	$T/℃$	E_{T}	ρ	ν	(σ,ε)	α	k	γ	ρ_{E}	K_{IC}
6150 (Q & T: 650 ℃)	23	207	7.85	0.29	(840,0.2%) (945,17%)	11.5	47	475	—	—
6150 (Q & T: 430 ℃; Leaf Spring Grade: Fe-0.48C-0.7 Mn-0.8Cr-0.15 V-...)	23	207	7.85	0.29	(1300,0.2%) (1470,9%)	11.5	47	475	—	—
6150 (Q & T: 204 ℃)	23	207	7.85	0.29	(1690,0.2%) (1930,8%)	11.5	47	475	—	—
8620 (HR)	23	205	7.85	0.29	(413,0.2%) (603,22%)	11.5	47	475	—	—
8620 (HR; Annealed)	23	205	7.85	0.29	(380,0.2%) (530,31%)	11.5	47	475	—	—
8620 (Normalized)	23	205	7.85	0.29	(360,0.2%) (630,26%)	11.5	47	475	—	—
8620 (Q & T; Carburized)	23	205	7.85	0.29	(1420,0.2%) $\sigma_{\mathrm{uts}}=1683$	11.5	47	475	—	—
8620 (Q & T; Carburized: Case=0.8 mm)	23	205	7.85	0.29	(1125,0.2%) (1869,<1%)	11.5	47	475	—	—
8620H (Q & T;Carburized)	23	205	7.85	0.29	(833,0.2%) (1157,14.3%)	11.5	47	475	—	—
8630 (Annealed)	23	207	7.85	0.29	(550,0.2%) (620,15%)	11.5	47	475	—	—
8630 (Normalized)	23	207	7.85	0.29	(1102,0.2%) (1144,3%)	11.5	47	475	—	—
8630 (Cast)	23	207	7.85	0.29	(980,0.2%) (1140,3%)	11.5	47	475	—	—
8640 (HR; Normalized)	23	207	7.85	0.29	(985,0.2%) (1144,3%)	11.5	47	475	—	—
8640 (Q & T: 650 ℃)	23	207	7.85	0.29	(800,0.2%) (900,20%)	11.5	47	475	—	—

continued

Material (AISI)	$T/℃$	E_T	ρ	ν	(σ,ε)	α	k	γ	ρ_E	K_{IC}
8640 (Q & T: 430 ℃)	23	207	7.85	0.29	(1300,0.2%) (1380,12%)	12	47	475	—	—
8640 (Q & T: 204 ℃)	23	207	7.85	0.29	(1670,0.2%) (1860,10%)	11.5	47	475	—	—
8642 (HR)	23	207	7.85	0.29	(414,0.2%) (724,20%)	11.5	47	475	—	—
8642 (CD; Annealed)	23	206	7.85	0.29	(724,0.2%) (860,16%)	11.5	47	475	—	—
8642 (Q & T: 540 ℃)	23	207	7.85	0.29	(845,0.2%) (1008,17%)	11.5	47	475	—	—
8645 (HR)	23	207	7.85	0.29	(448,0.2%) (793,20%)	11.5	47	475	—	—
8645 (HR; Annealed)	23	207	7.85	0.29	(379,0.2%) (723,23%)	11.5	47	475	—	—
8645 (Q & T: 540 ℃)	23	207	7.85	0.29	(784,0.2%) (965,17%)	11.5	47	475	—	—
8645 (HR; Normalized)	23	207	7.85	0.29	(1140,0.2%) (1240,3%)	11.5	47	475	—	—
86B45 (Q & T:650 ℃)	23	206	7.85	0.29	(876,0.2%) (903,19%)	11.5	47	472	—	—
86B45 (Q & T:430 ℃)	23	206	7.85	0.29	(1317,0.2%) (1380,11%)	11.5	47	472	—	—
86B45 (Q & T:204 ℃)	23	206	7.85	0.29	(1640,0.2%) (1980,9%)	11.5	47	472	—	—
8650 (HR; Annealed)	23	206	7.85	0.29	(386,0.2%) (716,22.5%)	11.5	47	475	—	—
8650 (HR; Normalized)	23	206	7.85	0.29	(688,0.2%) (1024,14%)	11.5	47	475	—	—
8650 (Q & T: 650 ℃)	23	207	7.85	0.29	(830,0.2%) (965,20%)	11.5	47	475	—	—
8650 (Q & T: 430 ℃)	23	207	7.85	0.29	(1320,0.2%) (1450,12%)	11.5	47	475	—	—

continued

Material (AISI)	$T/°C$	E_T	ρ	ν	(σ,ε)	α	k	γ	ρ_E	K_{IC}
8650 (Q & T: 204 ℃)	23	207	7.85	0.29	(1675,0.2%) (1937,10%)	11.5	47	475	—	—
8660 (Q & T: 650 ℃)	23	207	7.85	0.29	(952,0.2%) (1070,20%)	11.5	47	475	—	—
8660 (Q & T: 430 ℃)	23	207	7.85	0.29	(1550,0.2%) (1634,13%)	11.5	46	475	—	—
8740 (HR; Annealed)	23	206	7.85	0.29	(415,0.2%) (695,22.2%)	11.5	47	475	—	—
8740 (HR; Normalized)	23	206	7.85	0.29	(607,0.2%) (929,16%)	11.5	47	475	—	—
8740 (Q & T: 650 ℃)	23	207	7.85	0.29	(900,0.2%) (986,20%)	11.5	47	475	—	—
8740 (Q & T: 430 ℃)	23	207	7.85	0.29	(1360,0.2%) (1434,13%)	11.5	47	475	—	—
8740 (Q & T: 204 ℃)	23	207	7.85	0.29	(1655,0.2%) (2000,10%)	11.5	47	475	—	—
8742 (HR)	23	206	7.85	0.29	(414,0.2%) (810,20%)	11.5	47	475	—	—
8742 (CD; Annealed)	23	206	7.85	0.29	(690,0.2%) (776,14%)	11.5	47	475	—	—
8742 (Q & T: 540 ℃)	23	207	7.85	0.29	(880,0.2%) (1034,17%)	11.5	47	475	—	—
9254 (Q & T)	23	206	7.85	0.29	(1034,0.2%) (1158,9%)	11.5	50	475	—	—
9254(Q & T; Automotive Coil Spring Grade)	23	206	7.85	0.29	(2270,0.2%) (2950,4.1%)	11.5	50	475	—	—
9255(HR; Annealed)	23	206	7.85	0.29	(486,0.2%) (774,21.7%)	11.5	50	475	—	—
9255 (HR; Normalized)	23	206	7.85	0.29	(579,0.2%) (933,19.7%)	11.5	50	475	—	—

continued

Material (AISI)	$T/℃$	E_T	ρ	ν	(σ,ε)	α	k	γ	ρ_E	K_{IC}
9255 (Q & T: 650 ℃)	23	206	7.85	0.29	(814,0.2%) (990,20%)	11.5	50	475	—	—
9255 (Q & T: 430 ℃)	23	206	7.85	0.29	(1490,0.2%) (1600,8%)	11.5	50	475	—	—
9255 (Q & T: 204 ℃)	23	206	7.85	0.29	(2050,0.2%) (2100,1%)	11.5	50	475	—	—
9260 (Q & T: 650 ℃)	23	206	7.85	0.29	(814,0.2%) (980,20%)	11.5	50	475	—	—
9260 (Q & T: 430 ℃; Coil Spring;JIS-SUP7;Fe-0.6C-2Si-0.88Mn-...)	23	206	7.85	0.29	(1503,0.2%) (1758,8%)	11.5	50	475	—	—
	500	—	—	—	—	13.9	—	—	—	—
	1000	—	—	—	—	14.7	—	—	—	—
9262 (Annealed)	23	206	7.85	0.29	$\sigma_{uts}=524$	11.5	50	475	—	—
9262 (Q & T; HB=280)	23	206	7.85	0.29	$\sigma_{uts}=650$	11.5	50	475	—	—
9262 (Q & T)	23	206	7.85	0.29	(980,16%)	11.5	50	475	—	—
9262 (Q & T; HB=410)	23	206	7.85		$\sigma_{uts}=1050$	11.5	50	475	—	—
9310 (Annealed)	23	206	7.85	0.29	(440,0.2%) (820,17.3%)	11.5	50	475	—	—
9310 (Normalized)	23	206	7.85	0.29	(570,0.2%) (907,18.8%)	11.5	50	475	—	—
9310(Q & T: 425 ℃)	23	206	7.85	0.29	(1034,0.2%) (1158,15%)	11.5	50	475	—	115
94B30 (Q & T:650 ℃)	23	206	7.85	0.29	(725,0.2%) (827,21%)	11.5	50	475	—	—
94B30(Q & T:430 ℃)	23	206	7.85	0.29	(1207,0.2%) (1345,13%)	11.5	50	475	—	—
94B30 (Q & T:204 ℃)	23	206	7.85	0.29	(1550,0.2%) (1725,12%)	11.5	50	475	—	—

continued

Material (AISI)	$T/\text{℃}$	E_T	ρ	ν	(σ,ε)	α	k	γ	ρ_E	K_{IC}
52100 (Fe-1C-1.71Cr-0.31Mn-0.28Si-0.21Ni-0.013P−0.003S;Bearing properties depend on heat treatment)										
GP91(Cast Steel; Fe-8.22Cr-0.12C -0.9Mo-0.47Mn 0.31Si-0.12V -0.07Nb-0.04N- 0.004S)	23	207	7.8	0.28	(503,0.2%) (663,38.3%)	12	—	475	—	—
	400	182	—	—	(419,0.2%) (536,29%)	—	—	—	—	—
	550	161	—	—	(339,0.2%) (395,47.3%)	—	—	—	—	—
	600	146	—	—	(303,0.2%) (338,63.5%)	—	—	—	—	—
ASTM A36(HR)	23	206	7.85	0.29	(248,0.2%) $\sigma_{uts}=486$	11.5	50	475	—	—
ASTM A572 (HR; 50)	23	206	7.85	0.29	(345,0.2%) $\sigma_{uts}=448$	11.5	50	475	—	—
ASTM A992 (HR)	23	206	7.85	0.29	(345,0.2%) $\sigma_{uts}=448$	11.5	50	475	—	—
20CrMnTi	23	226	7.85	0.29	(326,0.2%) (521,10%)	11.5	50	475	—	—
Crankshaft (Forged; Hardened Crankshaft Surface; Fe- 0.39C-0.67Si- 1.38Mn- 0.01P-0.05S- 0.12Cr-0.14V)	23	210	7.85	0.29	(625,0.2%) (827,54%)	11.5	50	475	—	—
Crankshaft (Microalloyed: Fe-0.37C-0.62 Si-1.3Mn-0.01 P-0.05S-0.12 Cr-0.12V)	23	210	7.85	0.29	—	11.5	50	475	—	—

continued

Material (AISI)	$T/℃$	E_T	ρ	ν	(σ,ε)	α	k	γ	ρ_E	K_{IC}
Crankshaft (Microalloyed: Fe-0.4C-0.29 Si-0.84Mn-0.02 P-0.01S-1.1Cr-0.2Mo)	23	210	7.85	0.29	—	11.5	50	475	—	—

Notes: H = Hot-formed;

HR = Hot-rolled;

CD = Cold-drawn;

Q & T = Quenched and tempered;

HSLA = High strength low alloy (SAE J1392 JUN 84);

RHA = Rolled homogeneous armor steel for military applications;

(σ,ε) = True stress-strain data; positive-tension, negative-compression.

Table 73.2   Mechanical Properties of Railway Rails

Material	$T/℃$	E_T	ρ	ν	(σ,ε)	α	k	γ	ρ_E	K_{IC}
UIC 900A:										
R260 (Railway rail)	23	210	0.783	0.29	(430,0.2%) (760,2.9%)	—	—	—	—	—
	600	210	—	—	(240,0.2%) (340,3.2%)	—	—	—	—	—
	1470(T_m)	—	—	—	—	—	—	—	—	—
UIC 860- 0 (1986—2008):										
Grade 700	23	210	0.783	0.29	(680,0.2%) (830,14%)	—	—	—	—	—
Grade 800	23	210	0.783	0.29	(825,0.2%) (923,13%)	—	—	—	—	—
Grade 900	23	210	0.783	0.29	(880,0.2%) (1030,10%)	—	—	—	—	—

Table 73.3   Fatigue ε-N Properties of Alloy Steels

Material	$T/℃$	$d\varepsilon/dt$	σ_f'	ε_f'	b	c	K'	n'	$\sigma_f @ 2N_f$	R
1541 (Normalized at 900 ℃)	23	—	1622	0.515	−0.135	−0.548	1416	0.194	—	—
1541 (CD)	23	—	1044	0.513	−0.083	−0.557	950	0.114	—	—

continued

Material	$T/℃$	$\mathrm{d}\varepsilon/\mathrm{d}t$	σ'_f	ε'_f	b	c	K'	n'	$\sigma_f@2N_f$	R
1548（HR）	23	—	—	—	—	—	—	—	$275@10^8$	-1
4130（Annealed）	23	—	1261	0.985	−0.077	−0.648	—	—	$138@10^8$ $497@10^6$	—
4137（Q&T;SCM 435;34CrMo4）	23	—	1100	0.996	−0.067	−0.708	1070	0.089	—	—
4140（Q&T; 42CrMo4）	23	—	1154	0.18	−0.061	−0.53	1420	0.12	—	—
4140（Seawater）	23	—	—	—	—	—	—	—	$293@10^7$	—
4140H（Q&T; Induction-Hardened）	23	—	2850	0.1348	−0.087	−0.58	3135	0.15	$720@10^8$	—
4142（Q&T）	23	—	2143	0.637	−0.094	−0.716	2260	0.124	—	—
4340（HR）	23	—	1198	0.522	−0.095	−0.563	1337	0.168	—	—
4340（SNCM439）	23	—	1380	1.89	−0.072	−0.801	1000	0.066	—	—
4340（Normalized）	23	—	—	—	—	—	—	—	$520@10^8$	—
4340（Q&T）	23	—	—	—	—	—	—	—	$620@10^8$	—
5115（Annealed）	23	—	—	—	—	—	—	—	$275@10^8$	—
5140（Q&T）	23	—	1306	0.388	−0.12	−0.56	1592	0.173	—	—
5160	23	—	1930	0.4	−0.071	−0.57	—	—	—	—
5160H	23	—	2063	0.56	−0.08	−1.05	2060	0.1	—	—
	−45	—	1785	0.35	−0.1	−0.66	2542	0.197	$293@10^7$ $293@10^8$	−1 −1
8630（Cast Steel）	23	—	1936	0.42	−0.121	−0.693	2267	0.195	$365@10^7$ $365@10^8$	— —
8630（Normalized）	23	—	2390	0.11	−0.176	−0.908	2550	0.167	—	—
9254	23	—	—	—	—	—	—	—	$610@10^6$	—
9260（Coil Spring）	23	—	—	—	—	—	—	—	$687@10^7$	—
9260（Cavitation Shotless Peened）	23	—	—	—	—	—	—	—	$968@10^7$	—

continued

Material	$T/°C$	$d\varepsilon/dt$	σ_f'	ε_f'	b	c	K'	n'	$\sigma_f@2N_f$	R
9262 (Annealed; HB=260)	23		1041	0.16	−0.07	−0.47	1379	0.15	524	—
9262 (Q&T; HB=280)	23		1220	0.41	−0.07	−0.60	1358	0.12	648	—
9262 (Q&T; HB=410)	23		1855	0.38	−0.071	−0.47	2013	0.09	1048	—
GP91(Fe-9Cr-1Mo; Cast Steel)	23	—	880	0.124	−0.067	−0.484	—	—	69@ 10^6	—
	400	—	659	0.346	−0.06	−0.585	763	0.0956	319@ 8990 / 855@ 3786	— / —
	550	—	526	0.814	−0.055	−0.728	416	0.0743	249@ 4533 / 278@ 773	— / —
	600	—	248	2.11	−0.022	−0.851	496	0.1384	193@ 3548 / 236@ 683	— / —
SNCM630	23	—	1270	1.54	−0.073	−0.823	1060	0.054	—	—
SCM440	23	—	1400	0.675	−0.088	−0.650	1040	0.094	—	—
SFNCM85S	23	—	1040	0.316	−0.092	−0.522	1320	0.18	—	—
SF60	23	—	978	0.187	−0.082	−0.439	1350	0.186	—	—
Crankshaft (Forged; Hardened Crankshaft Surface; Fe-0.39C-0.67Si-1.38Mn-0.01P-0.05S-0.12Cr-0.14V)	23	—	1124	0.671	−0.079	−0.597	1158	0.128	—	—
Steel (Generic)	23	—	Eq. (6.14)	Eq. (6.15)	−0.09	−0.6	$\sigma_f'/(\varepsilon_f')^{n'}$	b/c	Eq.(71.1)	—

Notes: * =If there is no data available, use the following equations:

    a. $\sigma_f@10^6$ Cycles (MPa; Normalized Alloy Steels)

      = 0.18BHN+0.5348C+2.183Mn−20.53S−0.464Si+

        13.37Ni−0.5656Cr−0.3804Mo+36.1 (±4.6)

    b. $\sigma_f@10^6$ Cycles (MPa; Quench and Tempered Alloy Steels)

      = 2.52BHN+6.744C+3.886Mn−40.62S−12.25Si+3.55Ni+

        2.101Cr−22.6Mo+5.702Al−5.9V−476.48 (± 27.94)

Table 73.4　Mechanical Creep Parameters of Alloy Steels

Material	$T/{}^\circ\mathrm{C}$	Stress/MPa	Strain Rate/s^{-1}	$A/(\mathrm{MPa}^{-n}\cdot\mathrm{s}^{m-1})$	$Q/(\mathrm{J}\cdot\mathrm{mol}^{-1})$	n	m
4140 (Bolt Grade)	727	$E=1$	—	3×10^{-18}	0	4	0

Notes：Creep equation $=\dfrac{\mathrm{d}\varepsilon_{\mathrm{creep}}}{\mathrm{d}t}=A\left(\dfrac{\sigma-\sigma_{\mathrm{th}}}{E}\right)^{n}t^{m}\exp\left(\dfrac{-Q}{RT_{\mathrm{k}}}\right)$, $\sigma>\sigma_{\mathrm{th}}$;

$\sigma_{\mathrm{th}}=$ Stress threshold and $\sigma_{\mathrm{th}}=0$, if not specified;

$E=$ Young's modulus; If given that $E=1$, it means E is not specified.

Table 73.5　Material Parameters on Fatigue Crack Growth of Alloy Steels in Opening Mode

Material	$T/{}^\circ\mathrm{C}$	σ_{y}	σ_{uts}	K_{IC}	$f(R)$	m	ΔK_{th}	Δ_{fat}
EN19 (Steel, Camshaft)	23	591	750	—	$f(-1)=3.37\times10^{-10}$	3.37	13.23	—
SAE 4340	23	1456	1548	—	$f(-1)=2.05\times10^{-11}$	2.167	2.651	800
SAE 8630	-45	—	—	—	$f(0.05)$	—	7.2	—
	23	—	—	—	$f(0.05)$	—	8.5	—
SAE 8630	-45	—	—	—	$f(0.5)$	—	4.7	—
	23	—	—	—	$f(0.5)$	—	3.3	—
UIC 860-0 (Grade 800 Railway Steel)	23	—	—	—	$f(0.1)=2.63\times10^{-12}$	3.29	—	—

Notes：$\dfrac{\mathrm{d}a}{\mathrm{d}N_{\mathrm{p}}}=f(R)\,|\,\Delta K-\Delta K_{\mathrm{th}}\,|^{m}$;

$\sigma_{\mathrm{y}}(\mathrm{MPa})=$ Yield strength;

$\sigma_{\mathrm{uts}}(\mathrm{MPa})=$ Ultimate tensile strength;

$f(R)=$ Parameter as a function of load ratio (R);

$m=$ Exponent;

$\Delta K_{\mathrm{th}}(\mathrm{MPa}\cdot\mathrm{m}^{\frac{1}{2}})=$ Threshold stress intensity factor range;

$\Delta_{\mathrm{fat}}(\mathrm{MPa})=$ Fatigue strength range.

Chapter 74

Stainless Steels

74.1　Introduction

One special category of steel is stainless steel. A high content of chromium, 11% or more by weight, as the predominant alloying element makes the steel stainless. A higher concentration of chromium, preferably greater than 15% by weight, A thin (Cr_2O_3) impervious oxide film in the alloy forms, which protects the surface from corrosion and pitting. Addition of Ni (Nickel) provides ductility while improving strength, as it makes face-centered austenite structurally stable. Mechanical properties of stainless steels are listed in Tables 74.1—74.4. Stainless steels are classified into five categories with an approximate upper service temperature limit as follows (AISI):

Series	Alloys	Service Temp.	$\alpha/(\times 10^{-6} ℃)$
200 series	Austenitic (Fe-Cr-Ni-Mn)	Up to 650 ℃	17
300 series	Austenitic (Fe-Cr-Ni-Mn)	Up to 540 ℃	17
400 series	Ferritic (Fe-Cr)	Up to 250 ℃	10
400 series	Martensitic (Fe-Cr-C)	Up to 650 ℃	10
Duplex	PHed Fe-Cr-Ni-Cu-Nb	Up to 300 ℃	14

Notes: pH-Precipitation hardening;
　　　　α-Reference coefficient of linear thermal expansion.

Iron-based super alloys generally the contain composition of 32% ~ 67% iron, 15% ~ 22% chromium and 9% ~ 38% nickel.

74.1.1　Austenitic Stainless Steel (Table 74.1)

Austenitic stainless steel contains at least 18% chromium and 8% nickel, and thus it is the wellknown designation: 18/8 steel. In contrast to the pure chromium steels (e.g. ferritic stainless steel), steel being alloyed with Ni results in enhanced mechanical properties, such as increased workability and ductility, better resistance to thermal stress and improved weldability. Austenitic stainless steels are the strongest steel class for services above 540 ℃, but not exceeding 815 ℃. The highest service limit for oxidation resistance of stainless steels is achieved by the highly alloyed type 330 grade (Fe-19Cr-25Ni-1.0Si), which is suitable for continuous service at a temperature up to 1150 ℃. In the evolution of austenitic steels, Nb and Ti are added to improve creep rupture strength and to stabilize the steel from corrosion. The low carbon versions of the standard austenitic grades (Grades 304L and 316L) have reduced strength at high temperatures and are not generally used for structural applications at elevated temperatures. "H" versions of each grade, e.g. 304H, have higher carbon contents for these applications, which results in significantly higher creep strengths. At temperatures above 500 ℃, creep rupture strength of an austenitic stainless steel has to be taken into consideration for design. Austenitic stainless steels are not magnetic.

74.1.2   Martensitic Stainless Steel (Table 74.2)

A martensitic stainless steel can be hardened according to the tempering temperature. The brittleness of an individual martensitic stainless steel generally increases with an increasing grade number. Stress corrosion cracking resistance is low with martensitic stainless steels. The fracture toughness of stainless steel 420 reduces from 60 $MPa\text{-}m^{\frac{1}{2}}$ in the air to 12 $MPa\text{-}m^{\frac{1}{2}}$ when immersed in water with 3% NaCl, as shown in Table 74.2. Martensitic steels are magnetic.

74.1.3   Ferritic Stainless Steel (Table 74.3)

Ferritic stainless steels are brittle and magnetic. Stress corrosion cracking resistance of ferric stainless steels is excellent.

74.1.4   Suplex (Duplex) Stainless Steel (Table 74.4)

Duplex stainless steels are called duplex (or suplex) in short because they have a two-phased (or more) microstructure consisting of grains of ferritic and austenitic stainless steel. When duplex stainless steel is melted, it solidifies from the liquid phase to a completely ferritic structure. As the material cools to the room temperature, about 50% of the ferritic grains transform to austenitic grains. Hence a duplex (suplex) stainless steel is a composite that has two equilibrium phases-ferrite as the matrix and austenite as particulates. Its yield strength is about twice as high as that of austenitic stainless steels. Precipitation-hardening stainless steels have the highest room-temperature strength of all the stainless steels. When applied at an elevated temperature, enrichment with Mo throughout the oxidation layer of duplex stainless steels may be observed as Mo oxides less rapidly than Fe or Cr.

74.2   Coefficient of Linear Thermal Expansion

The magnitude of thermal expansion of stainless steel is greater than carbon steel. However, the rate of thermal expansion of stainless steel remains relatively constant up to 1200 ℃ compared to carbon steel because stainless steel does not experience phase transformation.

If no data is available, the Coefficient of linear thermal expansion for austenitic stainless steel as a function of temperature may be estimated using the following equation:

$$\alpha = 16 + 0.00479\ T - 0.000001243\ T^2\ \mu m/m/^\circ C \tag{74.3}$$

where

$\alpha\ (\mu m/m/^\circ C)$: Coefficient of linear thermal expansion at 20 ℃;

$T(^\circ C)$: Temperature of stainless steel.

Austenitic stainless steels are sensitive to thermal fatigue due to the unfavorable combination of high thermal expansion rate and low thermal conductivity.

74.3 Specific Heat (J/kg/℃)

The specific heat of stainless steel increases slightly at elevated temperatures, compared to carbon steel, which has a huge increase in specific heat at 730 ℃ due to a chemical transformation from ferrite-pearlite to austenite. If no data is available, the specific heat of stainless steel as a function of temperature may be estimated using the following equation:

$$\gamma = 450 + 0.28\ T - 0.000291\ T^2 + 0.000000134\ T^3\ J/kg/^\circ C \tag{74.4}$$

where

$\gamma(J/kg/^\circ C)$: the specific heat capacity and $T\ (^\circ C)$ is the temperature.

74.4 Thermal Conductivity

At the room temperature, stainless steel has a much lower thermal conductivity compared to carbon steel. However, the thermal conductivity of stainless steel increases at elevated temperatures, which exceeds the value of carbon steel if the operating temperature is above 1000℃. If no data is available, the thermal conductivity of stainless steel as a function of temperature may be estimated using the following equation:

$$k = 14.6 + 0.0127\ T \tag{74.5}$$

where

$k\ (W/m/^\circ C)$: the thermal conductivity and $T\ (^\circ C)$ is the temperature.

74.5   Fatigue Limit

Fatigue of stainless steels is complex. Fatigue properties of some stainless steels are given in Table 74.5. Without knowing the fatigue limit of a certain stainless steel, one may use the following equation for stainless steels with polished smooth surface as the first approximation

$$\sigma_f = 0.35 \, \sigma_{uts}, \text{ if } \sigma_{uts} < 1400 \text{ MPa} \tag{74.1}$$

and

$$\sigma_f = 490 \text{ MPa}, \text{ if } \sigma_{uts} \geqslant 1400 \text{ MPa} \tag{74.2}$$

It is difficult to generalize laboratory test data on corrosion fatigue due to the added dimension of corrosion environment in addition to stressing regime. As corrosion is time dependent, high fluctuating stress rates may result in fatigue failure before corrosion damage occurs.

74.6   Creep of Stainless Steels

Thermomechanical creep parameters of stainless steel are given in Table 74.6.

74.7   Crack Propagation

Material Parameters on Fatigue Crack Growth of Stainless Steels in Opening Mode are given in Table 74.7.

74.8   Pitting and Crevice Corrosion Resistance

In order to increase the pitting and crevice resistance of stainless steels, Cr (Chromium), Mo (Molybdenum) and N (Nitrogen) are used as alloying elements, especially that resistance to localized corrosion in seawater requires at least 6% molybdenum. One way of combining the effect of alloying elements is via the PRE (Pitting Resistance Equivalent) index which takes into account the varying effects of chromium, molybdenum, and nitrogen. One commonly used formula is given as follows:

$$PRE = \%Cr + 3.3 * \%Mo + 16 * \%N \tag{74.6}$$

Note that $\%Cr + \%Mo + \%N = 1 = 100\%$.

74.9 Oxidation and Scaling

Stainless steels are particularly resistant to oxidation effects. Material parameters on oxidation of stainless steels are given in Table 74.8. The chromium that provides the passive corrosion-resisting film at the room temperature also helps resist oxidation at elevated temperatures. More details are introduced in Chapter 8.

74.10 Applications

Grade 304 is a typical first choice for an application in a corrosive environment. Nevertheless, an alternative may be used in light of the following reasons:

301L: Higher work hardening rate such as roll formed or stretched formed parts;

302HQ: Lower work hardening rate needed such as cold forged screws and rivets;

303: Easy machining needed;

316: High resistance to pitting and crevice corrosion, typically in a chloride environment;

321: High operating temperature expected ($600 \sim 900$ ℃);

3Cr12: Lower cost, while discoloring accepted;

430: Lower cost, while slight corrosion accepted.

The most widely used stainless steel grades are the austenitic stainless steels, especially AISI 304 and 304L, which takeup more than 50% of the global production of stainless steel. The next most widely used grades are the ferritic steels such as AISI 410, followed by the molybdenum-alloyed austenitic steels AISI 316/316L. Together these stainless steel grades (304, 304L, 310, 316, and 316L) make up over 80% (by weight) of the total consumed stainless steels. Typical applications are listed as follows:

AISI Grade	Applications
301	General
302	Stainless springs
303	Fastening parts-bolts, nuts, and aircraft fittings
304	Welded structural members, springs, bolts
310	Parts with good thermal conductivity-turbine and heat exchangers
316	Stainless bolts
321	Parts long exposed in the sensitization range of 425-815
330	Suitable for continuous service at a temperature as high as 1150 ℃
347, 348	Parts requiring high temperature-jet engine & nuclear energy parts

AISI Grade	Applications
384	Extremely cold-worked parts including fasteners
409	Exhaust manifold
410	Shafts, bolts, and cutlery
414	Stainless springs, bolts, and cutlery
416	Fasteners, screws, tools, and cutlery
431	Bolts and aircraft fitting
440	Bearings, nozzles, and cutlery
430	Parts subject to elevated-temperature corrosion-screw & mufflers
446	Furnace parts and thermocouple protection tubes, where there are severe oxidation and low stresses
631	Springs
660	High temperature application, e.g. bolts

High carbon grades (AISI 304H) and thermal-stabilized steels (AISI 321, 347 and 316Ti) or nitrogen-alloyed steels (AISI 304LN and 316LN) are used at elevated temperatures depending on the service temperature and environment. At high temperatures (around 750 ℃ and above) special heat resistant grades are needed, such as AISI 310, S30415 (153MA), S30815 (253MA), and S35315 (353MA).

References

ANDRADE-CAMPOS A, et al, 2005. Modeling the Effect of Strain Rate on Thermo-mechanical Behavior of AISI 304 Stainless Steel[J]. Material Science and Engineering Technology, 36: 566-571.

AVERY K, et al, 2014. Fatigue Behavior of Stainless Sheet Specimens at Extremely High Temperatures[J]. SAE Int J Engines, 7(3): 560-566.

ATZORI B, et al, 2011. Analysis of the Fatigue Strength under Two Load Levels of a Stainless Steel Based on Energy Dissipation[J]. Frattura ed Integrità Strutturale, 17: 15-22.

BERGENGREN, LARSON, MELANDER, 1995. Fatigue Properties of Stainless Steels in Air at Room Temperature[J]. IM 3112, Material Science and Technology, 11: 1275-1279.

BRNIC J, et al, 2012. Martensitic Stainless Steel AISI 420-Mechanical Properties, Creep and Fracture Toughness[J]. Mechanics of Time-Dependent Materials, 15(4): 341-352.

BRNIC J, et al, 2009. Behavior of AISI 316L Steel Subjected to Uniaxial State of Stress at Elevated

Temperatures[J]. Journal of Material Science and Technology, 25(2): 175-180.

CHEN J, YOUNG B, 2006. Stress-Strain Curves for Stainless Steel at Elevated Temperatures[J]. Engineering Structures, 28(2): 229-239.

CHEN X, et al, 2006. Fatigue Life Prediction of Type 304 Stainless Steel under Sequential Biaxial Loading[J]. International Journal of Fatigue, 28: 289-299.

CHOPRA O, GAVENDA D, 1998. Effects of LWR Coolant Environments on Fatigue Lives of Austenitic Stainless Steels[J]. Journal of Pressure Vessel Technology, 120: 116-121.

COBB, HAROLD, 2007. The naming and Numbering of Stainless Steels[J]. Advanced Materials & Processes, 165(9): 39-44.

COLIN J, et al, 2010. Fatigue Behavior of Stainless Steel 304L Including Strain Hardening, Prestraining, and Mean Stress Effects[J]. Journal of Engineering Materials and Technology, 132(2): 8-21.

FAN Y N, SHI H J, TOKUDA K, 2015. A Generalized Hysteresis Energy Method for Fatigue and Creep-fatigue Life Prediction of 316L (N)[J]. Materials Science and Engineering, A, 625: 205-212

GULLAPALLI H, et al, 2011. Graphene Growth via Carburization of Stainless Steel and Application in Energy Storage[J]. Small, 7: 1697-1700.

HE X, et al, 2011. Statistical Thermal Fatigue-Creep Modeling of 316 Stainless Steel Materials[J]. Scientific Research and Essays, 6 (20): 7172-7178.

HUANG J, et al, 2006. High-Cycle Fatigue Behavior of Type 316L Stainless Steel[J]. Materials Transactions, 47(2): 409-417.

HAYHURST D R, et al, 2003. Constitutive Equations for Time Independent Plasticity and Creep of 316 Stainless Steel at 550 ℃[J]. International Journal of Pressure Vessels and Piping, 80: 97-109.

IDO T, KOMOTORI J, 2011. Effect of Static Pre-Strain on Low Cycle Fatigue Life of AISI 316L Stainless Steel [J]. Key Engineering Materials, 462-463: 65-69.

ITOH T, et al, 1995. Nonproportional Low Cycle Fatigue Criterion for Type 304 Stainless Steel[J]. Journal of Engineering Materials and Technology, 117(3): 285-292.

JASKE C, FREY N, 1982. Long-Life Fatigue of Type 316 Stainless Steel at Temperatures up to 593 ℃[J]. Journal of Engineering Materials and Technology, 104(2): 137-144.

JOHANSSON B, et al, 1984. Properties of High Strength Steels[J]. International Compressor Engineering Conference: 474.

KABIR S M K, et al, 2012. Fatigue Behavior of an Austenitic steel of 300-series under NonZero Mean Loading [J]. Journal of Mechanical Science and Technology, 26(1): 63-71.

LASEBIKAN B, et al, 2013. The Mechanical Behavior of a 25Cr Super Duplex Stainless Steel at Elevated Temperature[J]. Journal of Materials Engineering & Performance, 22(2): 598.

LEE W S, et al, 2011. Dynamic Mechanical Response of Biomedical 316L Stainless Steel as Function of Strain Rate and Temperature[J]. Bioinorganic Chemistry and Applications, 2011(8): 173-782.

MÄKELÄINEN P, OUTINEN J, 1998. Mechanical Properties of an Austenitic Stainless Steel at Elevated Temperatures[J]. Journal of Constructional Steel Research, 46(1-3): 455.

NARUSHIMA1 T, 2005. Fatigue Properties of Stainless Steel Wire Ropes for Electrodes in Functional Electrical Stimulation Systems[J]. Materials Transactions, 46(9): 2083-2088.

RAMAN S G S, JAYAPRAKASH M, 2007. Plain Fatigue and Fretting Fatigue Behavior of AISI 304 Austenitic Stainless Steel[J]. Materials Science and Technology, 23(1): 45-54.

RAMESH M, et al, 2011. Thermomechanical and Isothermal Fatigue Behavior of 347 and 316L Austenitic Stainless Tube and Pipe Steels[J]. International Journal of Fatigue, 33(5): 683-691.

ROY A K, et al, 2005. Tensile Properties of Martensitic Stainless Steels at Elevated Temperatures[J]. Journal of Materials Engineering and Performance, 14(2): 212-218.

STOUT M G, FOLLANSHEE P S, 1986. Strain Rate Sensitivity and Yield Behavior of 304L Stainless Steel[J]. Transactions of ASME, 108: 344.

VINCENTA L, 2012. On the High Cycle Fatigue Behavior of a Type 304L Stainless Steel at Room Temperature [J]. International Journal of Fatigue, 38: 84-91.

WRIGHT R N, 1976. The High Cycle Fatigue Strength of Commercial Stainless Steel Strip[J]. Materials Science and Engineering, 22: 223-230.

XUAN F Z, et al, 2004. Evaluation of the Time Dependent Failure Assessment Curves for 10CrMo910 and 316 SS at 550 oC[J]. ACTA Metallurgical Sinica, 17(4): 443-449.

ZHANG G, et al, 2006. Fatigue Strength of Small-Scaled Type 304 Stainless Steel Thin Films[J]. Materials Science and Engineering, A 426, (2006): 95-100.

ZHOUAIN A, et al, 1999. Fatigue Life Parameter for Type 304 Stainless Steel under Biaxial-Tensile Loading at Elevated Temperature[J]. Journal of Engineering Materials and Technology, 121: 305-312.

Table 74.1　Mechanical Properties of Austenitic Stainless Steels

Material	$T/℃$	E_T	ρ	ν	(σ,ε)	α	k	γ	ρ_E	K_{IC}
201 (Annealed)	23	199	7.8	0.27	(380,0.2%) (790,55%)	15.2	15	500	—	—
	100	—	—	—	—	16.6	16.9	—	—	—
	500	—	—	—	—	18.4	21.5	—	—	—
	1400(T_m)	—	—	—	—	—	—	—	—	—
201 (1/2 Hard)	23	199	7.8	0.27	(760,0.2%) (1030,10%)	15.2	15	500	—	—
	500	—	—	—	—	18.4	21.5	—	—	—
201 (Hard)	23	199	7.8	0.27	(965,0.2%) (1275,4%)	15.2	15	500	—	—
	500	—	—	—	—	18.4	21.5	—	—	—
202 (Annealed)	23	199	7.8	0.27	(379,0.2%) (724,55%)	16.5	15	500	—	—
	400	—	—	—	(200,0.2%) $\sigma_{uts}=530$	—	—	—	—	—
	500	—	—	—	—	19.2	21.5	—	—	—
	600	—	—	—	(170,0.2%) $\sigma_{uts}=430$	—	—	—	—	—
	1400(T_m)	—	—	—	—	—	—	—	—	—
202 (1/4 Hard)	23	199	7.8	0.27	(520,0.2%) (860,12%)	16.5	15	500	—	—
	500	—	—	—	—	18.4	21.5	—	—	—
	870	—	—	—	—	20.3	—	—	—	—
205 (HRB=98)	23	—	7.8	0.27	(480,0.2%) (830,58%)	—	—	—	—	—
216 (HRB=92)	23	—	7.8	0.27	(379,0.2%) (690,45%)	—	—	—	—	—

continued

Material	$T/℃$	E_T	ρ	ν	(σ,ε)	α	k	γ	ρ_E	K_{IC}
ASTM A 297 HH(ACI HH Ⅱ)	23	—	7.8	0.27	(275,0.2%) (550,15%)	16.5	14.2	—	—	—
	200	—	—	—	—	—	20.8	—	—	—
	600	—	—	—	—	17.1	—	—	—	—
	760	—	7.8	0.27	(136,0.2%) (258,16%)	—	—	—	—	—
	980	—	7.8	0.27	(50,0.2%) (75,31%)	—	—	—	—	—
	1090	—	—	—	—	19.3	30.3	—	—	—
301(1.4310; X12CrNi17-7; Annealed)	23	199	7.9	0.27	(230,0.2%) (750,55%)	16.3	15	500	—	—
	100	—	—	—	—	16.6	16.2	—	—	—
	400	—	—	—	(210,0.2%) (480,45%)	—	—	—	—	—
	500	—	—	—	—	18.6	21.5	—	—	—
	600	—	—	—	(140,0.2%) (360,40%)	—	—	—	—	—
	800	—	—	—	(120,0.2%) (200,35%)	—	—	—	—	—
	870	—	—	—	—	19.8	—	—	—	—
	1400(T_m)	—	—	—	—	—	—	—	—	—
301 (1/4 Hard)	23	199	7.9	0.27	(520,0.2%) (860,25%)	16.3	15	500	—	—
	100	—	—	—	—	16.6	16.2	—	—	—
	400	—	—	—	(430,0.2%) (630,30%)	—	—	—	—	—
	500	—	—	—	—	18.6	21.5	—	—	—
	600	—	—	—	(250,0.2%) (500,25%)	—	—	—	—	—
	800	—	—	—	(200,0.2%) (260,20%)	—	—	—	—	—

continued

Material	$T/^\circ\text{C}$	E_T	ρ	ν	(σ,ε)	α	k	γ	ρ_E	K_{IC}
301 (1/2 Hard)	23	199	7.9	0.27	(760,0.2%) (1030,18%)	16.3	15	500	—	—
	100	—	—	—	—	16.6	16.2	—	—	—
	400	—	—	—	(650,0.2%) (810,12%)	—	—	—	—	—
	500	—	—	—	—	18.6	21.5	—	—	—
	600	—	—	—	(370,0.2%) (550,16%)	—	—	—	—	—
	800	—	—	—	(200,0.2%) (250,14%)	—	—	—	—	—
301 (3/4 Hard)	23	199	7.9	0.27	(930,0.2%) (1210,12%)	16.3	15	500	—	—
	100	—	—	—	—	16.6	16.2	—	—	—
	500	—	—	—	—	18.6	21.5	—	—	—
301 (Hard)	23	199	7.9	0.27	(1263,0.2%) (1276,9%)	16.3	15	500	—	—
	100	—	—	—	—	16.6	16.2	—	—	—
	500	—	—	—	—	18.6	21.5	—	—	—
301 (Hardened from 900 ℃ & T:400 ℃)	-198	—	—	—	$\sigma_{uts}=2050$	—	—	—	—	—
	23	199	7.9	—	(1260,0.2%) (1290,23%)	16.3	15	500	—	—
	100	—	—	—	$\sigma_{uts}=1200$	16.6	—	—	—	—
	200	—	—	—	$\sigma_{uts}=1150$	—	—	—	—	—
	400	—	—	—	$\sigma_{uts}=1050$	—	—	—	—	—
	500	—	—	—	—	18.6	—	—	—	—
301M (Annealed)	23	199	7.9	0.27	(245,0.2%) (615,50%)	16.3	15	500	—	—

continued

Material	$T/°C$	E_T	ρ	ν	(σ,ε)	α	k	γ	ρ_E	K_{IC}
301Si (Annealed)	23	199	7.9	0.27	$(275,0.2\%)$ $(965,25\%)$	16.3	15	500	—	—
301Si (Hard)	23	199	7.9	0.27	$(1137,0.2\%)$ $(1681,1\%)$	16.3	15	500	—	—
302 (Annealed)	23	193	8	0.27	$(205,0.2\%)$ $(515,60\%)$	16.5	16.2	503	—	—
	400	—	—	—	$(240,0.2\%)$ $\sigma_{uts}=440$	—	—	—	—	—
	500	—	—	—	— $\sigma_{uts}=350$	18.2	21.5	—	—	—
	600	—	—	—	$(100,0.2\%)$	—	—	—	—	—
	$1400(T_m)$	—	—	—	—	—	—	—	—	—
302 (1/2 Hard)	23	193	8	0.27	$(520,0.2\%)$	16.5	16.2	503	—	—
	500	—	—	—	—	18.4	21.5	—	—	—
302 (30% CW)	23	193	8	0.27	$(896,0.2\%)$ $(1130,16\%)$	16.5	16.2	503	—	—
302B (Annealed)	23	193	7.9	0.27	$(275,0.2\%)$ $(655,50\%)$	16.5	15.9	500	—	—
	500	—	—	—	—	19.4	21.6	—	—	—
303	23	199	7.9	0.27	$(240,0.2\%)$ $(620,50\%)$	16	16.2	500	—	—
	500	—	—	—	—	18.4	21.5	—	—	—
303Se (Annealed)	23	199	7.9	0.27	$(240,0.2\%)$ $(620,50\%)$	16	16.2	500	—	—
	−196	—	—	—	$(400,0.2\%)$ $\sigma_{uts}=1600$	—	—	—	—	—
	−78	—	—	—	$(300,0.2\%)$ $\sigma_{uts}=1100$	—	—	—	—	—

continued

Material	$T/℃$	E_T	ρ	ν	(σ,ε)	α	k	γ	ρ_E	K_{IC}
304(1.4301; Annealed;Fe-18Cr-10Ni(363, 2%)-0.08c-...; e.g. Gasket)	23	199	7.9	0.27	$(290,0.2\%)$ $(326,1\%)$ $(363,2\%)$ $(640,53\%)$	16	15	502	—	200
	100	—	—	—	—	16.2	—	—	—	—
	150	186	—	—	$(185,0.2\%)$ $(475,50\%)$	—	—	—	—	—
	370	170	—	—	$(135,0.2\%)$ $(430,50\%)$	—	—	—	—	—
	500	160	—	—	$(123,0.2\%)$ $(410,36\%)$	18	21.4	—	—	—
	538	—	—	—	$\sigma_{crs,100000}=150$	—	—	—	—	—
	600	—	—	—	$(98,0.2\%)$ $(360,35\%)$; $\sigma_{crs,10000}=150$, $\sigma_{crs,100000}=75$	—	—	—	—	—
	700	142	—	—	$\sigma_{crs,10000}=60$, $\sigma_{crs,100000}=33$	—	—	—	—	—
	816	138	—	—	—	—	—	—	—	—
	800	—	—	—	$(71.4,0.2\%)$ $(119,80\%)$	—	—	—	—	—
	900	—	—	—	$\sigma_{uts}=90$	—	—	—	—	—
	$1400(T_m)$	—	—	—	—	—	—	—	—	—
304(Annealed, then exposed to 42% $MgCl_2$; Stress-corrosion Cracking)	23	193	8	0.27	—	16	15	502	—	10
304 (1/4 Hard)	23	199	8	0.3	$(550,0.2\%)$ $(795,15\%)$	16	15	500	—	—

continued

Material	$T/°C$	E_T	ρ	ν	(σ, ε)	α	k	γ	ρ_E	K_{IC}
304 (1/2 Hard)	23	199	8	0.27	$(760, 0.2\%)$ $(1100, 10\%)$	16	15	502	—	—
	500	160	—	—	—	17.5	21.4	—	—	—
304(CF)	23	199	8	0.27	$(592, 0.2\%)$ $(667, 1\%)$ $(695, 2\%)$ $(736, 27.4\%)$	16	15	502	—	—
	500	160	—	—	—	17.5	21.4	—	—	—
304H (Annealed)	23	199	8	0.27	$(244, 0.2\%)$ $(250, 1\%)$ $(585, 45\%)$	16	17	450	—	—
	100	—	—	—	$(157, 0.2\%)$ $(191, 1\%)$ $\sigma_{uts} = 440$;	—	—	—	—	—
	300	—	—	—	$(108, 0.2\%)$ $(137, 1\%)$ $\sigma_{uts} = 375$	—	—	—	—	—
	500	160	—	—	$(88, 0.2\%)$ $(118, 1\%)$ $\sigma_{uts} = 360$; $\sigma_{crs, 10000} = 250$, $\sigma_{crs, 100000} = 192$	17.5	21.4	—	—	—
	550	—	—	—	$\sigma_{crs, 10000} = 186$	—	—	—	—	—
	600	150	—	—	$(78, 0.2\%)$ $(108, 1\%)$ $\sigma_{uts} = 300$; $\sigma_{crs, 10000} = 134$, $\sigma_{crs, 100000} = 89$	18.5	—	—	—	—
	650	—	—	—	$\sigma_{crs, 10000} = 94$	—	—	—	—	—
	700	—	—	—	$\sigma_{crs, 10000} = 55$, $\sigma_{crs, 100000} = 28$	—	—	—	—	—
	800	—	—	—	—	19.4	26	—	—	—
	1000	—	120	—	—	19.8	—	—	—	—
	$1400(T_m)$	—	—	—	—	—	—	—	—	—

continued

Material	$T/\mathrm{℃}$	E_T	ρ	ν	(σ,ε)	α	k	γ	ρ_E	K_IC
304HCu (Annealed)	23	199	8	0.27	$(235,0.2\%)$ $(720,40\%)$	16	17	—	—	—
	−196	—	—	—	$(386,0.2\%)$ $(1620,40\%)$	—	—	—	—	—
	−40	—	—	—	$(331,0.2\%)$ $(1000,60\%)$	—	—	—	—	—
304L(Annealed; 18Cr-8Ni)	23	193	8	0.27	$(290,0.2\%)$ $(340,1\%)$ $(555,50\%)$	16	15	502	—	—
	100	—	—	—	—	16.6	—	—	—	—
	300	—	—	—	—	17.3	—	—	—	—
	425(High service temperature)									
	500	160	—	—	$(103,0.2\%)$ $(405,37\%)$ $\sigma_{\mathrm{crs},10000}=240$	18.3	21.4	—	—	—
	550	—	—	—	$\sigma_{\mathrm{crs},10000}=156;$ $\sigma_{\mathrm{crs},100000}=92$	—	—	—	—	—
	600	—	—	—	$\sigma_{\mathrm{crs},10000}=97;$ $\sigma_{\mathrm{crs},100000}=59$	—	—	—	—	—
	650	—	—	—	$\sigma_{\mathrm{crs},10000}=64;$ $\sigma_{\mathrm{crs},100000}=36$	—	—	—	—	—
	700	—	—	—	$\sigma_{\mathrm{crs},10000}=38;$ $\sigma_{\mathrm{crs},100000}=18$	—	—	—	—	—
	760	—	—	—	$(76,0.2\%)$ $(200,36\%)$	19.5	—	—	—	—
	$1400(T_\mathrm{m})$	—	—	—	—	—	—	—	—	—

continued

Material	$T/^{\circ}C$	E_T	ρ	ν	(σ,ε)	α	k	γ	ρ_E	K_{IC}
304LN (Annealed)	23	199	8	0.27	$(340,0.2\%)$ $(480,1\%)$ $(650,52\%)$	16	15	472	—	—
	580	—	—	—	$\sigma_{crs,10000}=162$	—	—	—	—	—
	600	—	—	—	$\sigma_{crs,10000}=139$; $\sigma_{crs,100000}=86$	—	—	—	—	—
	650	—	—	—	$\sigma_{crs,10000}=89$; $\sigma_{crs,100000}=49$	—	—	—	—	—
	700	—	—	—	$\sigma_{crs,10000}=53$; $\sigma_{crs,100000}=28$	—	—	—	—	—
	750	—	—	—	$\sigma_{crs,10000}=31$	—	—	—	—	—
	800	—	—	—	$\sigma_{crs,10000}=20$	—	—	—	—	—
304N (Annealed)	23	199	8	0.27	$(350,0.2\%)$ $(400,1\%)$ $(670,54\%)$	16	15	472	—	—
305(1.4303; Annealed)	23	199	7.9	0.27	$(255,0.2\%)$ $(586,50\%)$	16	15	500	—	—
	100	—	—	—	—	16.6	—	—	—	—
	500	—	—	—	—	18.4	21.5	—	—	—
308 (Annealed)	23	193	8.0	0.27	$(240,0.2\%)$ $(586,50\%)$	16.5	15.3	503	—	—
309 (Annealed)	23	193	7.9	0.27	$(310,0.2\%)$ $(620,45\%)$	15.6	15	500	—	—
	370	—	—	—	$(215,0.2\%)$ $(510,42\%)$	—	—	—	—	—
	500	—	—	—	$\sigma_{crs,10000}=385$	17.6	—	—	—	—
	600	—	—	—	$(170,0.2\%)$ $(410,38\%)$; $\sigma_{crs,10000}=165$, $\sigma_{crs,100000}=100$	—	—	—	—	—

continued

Material	$T/℃$	E_T	ρ	ν	(σ,ε)	α	k	γ	ρ_E	K_{IC}
309 (Annealed)	700	—	—	—	$(150,0.2\%)$ $(300,37\%)$; $\sigma_{crs,10000}=53$, $\sigma_{crs,100000}=40$	—	—	—	—	—
	800	—	—	—	$\sigma_{crs,10000}=35$, $\sigma_{crs,100000}=20$	—	—	—	—	—
	870	—	—	—	$\sigma_{uts}=174$	—	—	—	—	—
309S (Annealed)	23	199	7.9	0.27	$(210,0.2\%)$ $(250,1\%)$ $(500,35\%)$	15.5	13	472	—	—
	100	—	—	—	$(140,0.2\%)$ $(185,1\%)$ $\sigma_{uts}=470$	—	16.2	—	—	—
	300	—	—	—	$(100,0.2\%)$ $(139,1\%)$ $\sigma_{uts}=410$	17.3	—	—	—	—
	500	—	—	—	$(85,0.2\%)$ $(121,1\%)$ $\sigma_{uts}=370$	17.6	19.4	—	—	—
	600	150	—	—	$(82,0.2\%)$ $(114,1\%)$ $\sigma_{uts}=320$; $\sigma_{crs,10000}=120$	18.8	—	—	—	—
	800	—	—	—	$\sigma_{crs,10000}=18$	19.4	24.7	—	—	—
	870	—	—	—	$\sigma_{uts}=140$	—	—	—	—	—
	1000	120	—	—	—	20	—	—	—	—
310 (Annealed)	23	199	7.9	0.27	$(350,0.2\%)$ $(625,50\%)$	15.5	14.2	503	—	—
	370	—	—	—	$(205,0.2\%)$ $(525,35\%)$	16.1	—	—	—	—
	500	—	—	—	$(180,0.2\%)$ $(470,36\%)$	17.3	18.7	—	—	—
	600	—	—	—	$(150,0.2\%)$ $(420,38\%)$; $\sigma_{crs,10000}=137$, $\sigma_{crs,100000}=92$	—	—	—	—	—

continued

Material	$T/°C$	E_T	ρ	ν	(σ, ε)	α	k	γ	ρ_E	K_{IC}
310 (Annealed)	650	—	—	—	$\sigma_{crs,100000}=72$, $\sigma_{crs,100000}=47$	—	—	—	—	—
	700	—	—	—	$(132, 0.2\%)$ $(315, 31\%)$; $\sigma_{crs,10000}=42$, $\sigma_{crs,100000}=28$	—	—	—	—	—
	750	—	—	—	$\sigma_{uts}=280$; $\sigma_{crs,10000}=28$, $\sigma_{crs,100000}=18.5$	—	—	—	—	—
	800	—	—	—	$\sigma_{crs,10000}=19.5$, $\sigma_{crs,100000}=12.5$	—	—	—	—	—
	850	—	—	—	$\sigma_{uts}=180$; $\sigma_{crs,10000}=14$	—	—	—	—	—
	950	—	—	—	$\sigma_{uts}=90$	—	—	—	—	—
	1000	—	—	—	—	18.9	—	—	—	—
310MoLN (Annealed)	23	199	8.0	0.27	$(295, 0.2\%)$ $(777, 30\%)$	15	14	500	—	—
	200	—	—	—	—		15.7	—	—	—
	400	—	—	—	—		17.0	—	—	—
310N (Annealed)	23	199	7.9	0.27	$(295, 0.2\%)$ $(777, 30\%)$	15.5	15	500	—	—
310S (Annealed)	23	199	7.9	0.27	$(290, 0.2\%)$ $(330, 1\%)$ $(575, 50\%)$	15	14	500	—	—
	100	—	—	—	$(140, 0.2\%)$ $(185, 1\%)$ $\sigma_{uts}=470$	16	—	—	—	—
	300	—	—	—	$(100, 0.2\%)$ $(139, 1\%)$ $\sigma_{uts}=410$	17	—	—	—	—
	500	—	—	—	$(85, 0.2\%)$ $(121, 1\%)$ $\sigma_{uts}=370$; $\sigma_{crs,10000}=280$	18.3	19	—	—	—

continued

Material	$T/°C$	E_T	ρ	ν	(σ, ε)	α	k	γ	ρ_E	K_{IC}
310S (Annealed)	600	150	—	—	$(82, 0.2\%)$ $(114, 1\%)$ $\sigma_{uts} = 320$; $\sigma_{crs,10000} = 130$, $\sigma_{crs,100000} = 80$	18.8	—	—	—	—
	650	—	—	—	$\sigma_{crs,10000} = 70$	—	—	—	—	—
	700	—	—	—	$\sigma_{crs,10000} = 36$ $\sigma_{crs,100000} = 18$	—	—	—	—	—
	800	—	—	—	$\sigma_{crs,10000} = 18$, $\sigma_{crs,100000} = 7.5$	19.4	24.3	—	—	—
	870	—	—	—	$\sigma_{uts} = 153$	—	—	—	—	—
	900	—	—	—	$\sigma_{crs,10000} = 3$	—	—	—	—	—
	1000	120	—	—	—	20	—	—	—	—
314 (Annealed)	23	199	7.9	0.27	$(230, 0.2\%)$ $(270, 1\%)$ $(650, 30\%)$	15	15	500	—	—
	100	—	—	—	—	—	—	—	—	—
	300	—	—	—	$(100, 0.2\%)$ $(139, 1\%)$ $\sigma_{uts} = 410$	17.3	—	—	—	—
	400	—	—	—	$(91, 0.2\%)$ $(126, 1\%)$ $\sigma_{uts} = 400$	—	—	—	—	—
	500	—	—	—	$(85, 0.2\%)$ $(121, 1\%)$ $\sigma_{uts} = 370$	18.3	18.7	—	—	—
	600	150	—	—	$(82, 0.2\%)$ $(114, 1\%)$ $\sigma_{uts} = 320$ $\sigma_{crs,10000} = 130$, $\sigma_{crs,100000} = 80$	18.8	—	—	—	—
	700	—	—	—	$\sigma_{crs,10000} = 40$	—	—	—	—	—
	800	—	—	—	$\sigma_{crs,10000} = 20$	19.4	24.8	—	—	—
	900	—	—	—	$\sigma_{crs,10000} = 10$	—	—	—	—	—
	1000	120	—	—	—	20	—	—	—	—
	−196	—	—	—	$(580, 0.2\%)$ $\sigma_{uts} = 1300$	—	—	—	—	—
	−78	—	—	—	$(400, 0.2\%)$ $\sigma_{uts} = 820$	—	—	—	—	—

continued

Material	$T/°C$	E_T	ρ	ν	(σ,ε)	α	k	γ	ρ_E	K_{IC}
316(Annealed; (1.4401;S31600; Fe-17Cr-12Ni- 2.5Mo-2Mn- 0.75Si-0.1N- 0.03S-0.08C)	23	199	8	0.27	$(240,0.2\%)$ $(586,55\%)$	16	15	500	—	—
	370	—	—	—	$(160,0.2\%)$ $(500,47\%)$	—	—	—	—	—
	425(High service temperature if aqueous corrosion resistance required)									
	500	165	—	—	$(145,0.2\%)$ $(480,45\%)$; $\sigma_{crs,10000}=344,$ $\sigma_{crs,100000}=280$	17.5	21.5	—	—	—
	550	—	—	—	$\sigma_{crs,10000}=247,$ $\sigma_{crs,100000}=188$	—	—	—	—	—
	600	—	—	—	$\sigma_{uts}=460;$ $\sigma_{crs,10000}=168,$ $\sigma_{crs,100000}=118$	—	—	—	—	—
	650	—	—	—	$\sigma_{crs,10000}=109,$ $\sigma_{crs,100000}=70$	—	—	—	—	—
	700	142	—	—	$(131,0.2\%)$ $(345,43\%)$; $\sigma_{crs,10000}=68,$ $\sigma_{crs,100000}=40$	—	—	—	—	—
	760	138	—	—	$(212,26\%)$	—	—	—	—	—
	800	—	—	—	$\sigma_{uts}=190$	—	—	—	—	—
	870	138	—	—	$(124,47\%)$	—	—	—	—	—
316(T6; // rolling direction)	23	199	8	0.27	$(258,0.2\%)$ $\sigma_{uts}=560$	16	15	500	—	—
316(T6; ⊥ rolling direction)	23	199	8	0.27	$(298,0.2\%)$ $\sigma_{uts}=608$	16	15	500	—	—
316(T6;Weld // rolling direction)	23	199	8	0.27	$(253,0.2\%)$ $\sigma_{uts}=558$	16	15	500	—	—
316(T8; // rolling direction)	23	199	8	0.27	$(379,0.2\%)$ $\sigma_{uts}=612$	16	15	500	—	—
316(T8; ⊥ rolling direction)	23	199	8	0.27	$(334,0.2\%)$ $\sigma_{uts}=605$	16	15	500	—	—

continued

Material	$T/°C$	E_T	ρ	ν	(σ,ε)	α	k	γ	ρ_E	K_{IC}
316(Hard)	23	199	8	0.27	(415,0.2%) (620,30%)	16	15	500	—	—
	500	—	—	—	(207,0.2%) (427,43%)	17.5	21.5	—	—	—
316F(Annealed)	23	200	8,06	0.27	—	16	14.4	486	—	—
316H(Annealed)	23	193	8	0.27	(205,0.2%) (590,40%)	15.5	16.3	500	—	—
316L(1.4404; S31603;Fe-17Cr- 12Ni-0.03C-.)	23	195	8.03	0.27	(310,0.2%) (350,1%) (600,54%)	15.7	14.5	500	—	—
	200	185	—	—	—	16.9	16	—	—	—
	400	170	—	—	—	—	18.6	—	—	—
	500	159	—	—	(180,0.2%) (450,36%); $\sigma_{crs,10000}=321$, $\sigma_{crs,100000}=265$	18	20	—	—	—
	550	—	—	—	$\sigma_{crs,10000}=228$, $\sigma_{crs,100000}=177$	—	—	—	—	—
	600	151	—	—	$\sigma_{uts}=405$; $\sigma_{crs,10000}=155$, $\sigma_{crs,100000}=112$	—	—	—	—	—
	650	—	—	—	$\sigma_{crs,10000}=101$, $\sigma_{crs,100000}=67$	—	—	—	—	—
	700	142	—	—	$\sigma_{uts}=326$; $\sigma_{crs,10000}=64$	—	—	—	—	—
	760	—	—	—	(152,0.2%) (290,25%) $\sigma_{crs,10000}=35$	—	—	—	—	—
	850	—	—	—	(95,0.2%) $\sigma_{uts}=165$	—	—	—	—	—
	1000	—	—	—	—	—	19.5	—	—	—
316L (Weld)	23	195	8	0.27	(306,0.2%) (538,23%)	—	—	—	—	—
	300	—	—	—	(288,0.2%) (441,15.7%)	—	—	—	—	—

Material	$T/℃$	E_T	ρ	ν	(σ,ε)	α	k	γ	ρ_E	K_{IC}
316L (1/2 Hard)	23	195	8	0.27	(1000,0.2%) (1203,8%)	15.9	15	500	—	—
316L(Bio-Medical Grade; $d\varepsilon/dt=1000\ s^{-1}$)	23	195	8	0.27	(700,0.2%) (1040,10%) (1150,20%) (1250,44%)	15.9	15	500	—	—
	400	—	—	—	(600,0.2%) (900,10%) (1000,20%) (1150,55%)	—	—	—	—	—
	800	—	—	—	(500,0.2%) (650,10%) (700,20%) (900,72%)	—	—	—	—	—
SS-316L (Sintered; Density-dependent)	23	140	6.6	0.25	(138,0.2%) (207,18.5%)	—	—	—	—	—
	23	140	6.9	0.27	(283,0.2%) (393,21%)	—	—	—	—	—
316LN	23	196	8	0.27	(280,0.2%) (680,40%)	16	15	500	—	—
	550	—	—	—	$\sigma_{crs,10000}=300$, $\sigma_{crs,100000}=234$	—	—	—	—	—
	600	—	—	—	$\sigma_{crs,10000}=221$, $\sigma_{crs,100000}=151$	—	—	—	—	—
	650	—	—	—	$\sigma_{crs,10000}=143$, $\sigma_{crs,100000}=80$	—	—	—	—	—
	700	—	—	—	$\sigma_{crs,10000}=78$, $\sigma_{crs,100000}=42$	—	—	—	—	—
	750	—	—	—	$\sigma_{crs,10000}=42$	—	—	—	—	—
316LNB	23	196	8	0.27	—	16	15	500	—	—
	600	—	—	—	$\sigma_{crs,10000}=205$, $\sigma_{crs,100000}=141$	—	—	—	—	—
	650	—	—	—	$\sigma_{crs,10000}=135$, $\sigma_{crs,100000}=83$	—	—	—	—	—
	700	—	—	—	$\sigma_{crs,10000}=84$, $\sigma_{crs,100000}=52$	—	—	—	—	—

continued

Material	$T/℃$	E_T	ρ	ν	(σ,ε)	α	k	γ	ρ_E	K_{IC}
316N(N:0.1% Nitrogen)	23	196	8	0.27	(313,0.2%) (621,48%)	16	15	502	—	—
	300	—	—	—	(193,0.2%) (513,46%)	—	—	—	—	—
316Ti(1.4571; Annealed)	23	199	8	0.27	(250,0.2%) (330,1%) (620,54%)	16.2	14.6	500	—	—
	204	—	—	—	(180,0.2%) (455,28%)	—	—	—	—	—
	316	—	—	—	(160,0.2%) (445,26%)	—	—	—	—	—
	500	—	—	—	—	18.2	—	—	—	—
	540	—	—	—	(150,0.2%) (425,23%)	—	—	—	—	—
	580	—	—	—	$\sigma_{crs,10000}=198$, $\sigma_{crs,100000}=144$	—	—	—	—	—
	600	—	—	—	$\sigma_{crs,10000}=168$, $\sigma_{crs,100000}=118$	—	—	—	—	—
	650	—	—	—	(146,0.2%) (375,20%) $\sigma_{crs,10000}=109$, $\sigma_{crs,100000}=70$	—	—	—	—	—
	700	—	—	—	$\sigma_{crs,10000}=68$	—	—	—	—	—
	760	—	—	—	(150,0.2%) (260,23%)	—	—	—	—	—
	800	—	—	—	$\sigma_{crs,10000}=25$	—	—	—	—	—
	870	—	—	—	(112,0.2%) (155,48%)	—	—	—	—	—
	1000	—	—	—	—	19.5	—	—	—	—
317(1.4439; S31700; Annealed)	23	193	8.0	0.27	(205,0.2%) (515,35%)	16	16.3	500	—	—
	500	—	—	—	—	17.5	21.5	—	—	—
	760	—	—	—	(218,33%)	—	—	—	—	—
317 (1/2 Hard)	23	193	8.0	0.27	(985,0.2%) (1100,6%)	16	16.3	500	—	—

continued

Material	$T/℃$	E_T	ρ	ν	(σ,ε)	α	k	γ	ρ_E	K_{IC}
317L(1.4438; S31703; Annealed)	23	199	8.0	0.27	(300,0.2%) (350,1%) (610,53%)	16	14	500	—	—
	100	—	—	—	—	16.5	—	—	—	—
	500	—			(175,0.2%) (475,36%)	18.2	21.5	—	—	—
	760	—			(157,0.2%) (310,33%)	—	—	—	—	—
	1000	—		—	—	—	19.5	—	—	—
317L (1/2 Hard)	23	193	8.0	0.27	(990,0.2%) (1200,8.7%)	16.5	14	500	—	—
321(1.4541;Fe-18Cr-9Ni-Ti; Annealed)	23	193	7.9	0.24	(221,0.2%) (620,45%)	16	15	500	—	—
	100	—	—	—	—	—	16	—	—	—
	150	—	—	—	(190,0.2%) (465,52%)	—	—	—	—	—
	370	169	—	—	(157,0.2%) (414,40%)	—	—	—	—	—
	500	—	—	—	(140,0.2%) (380,37%); $\sigma_{crs,10000}=280$, $\sigma_{crs,100000}=200$	17.1	22	—	—	—
	650	146	—	—	(130,0.2%) (380,28%); $\sigma_{crs,10000}=104$, $\sigma_{crs,100000}=50$	19.3	—	—	—	—
	700	—	—	—	(113,0.2%) (265,28%); $\sigma_{crs,10000}=64$, $\sigma_{crs,100000}=15$	—	—	—	—	—
	815	—	—	—	(90,0.2%) (160,70%)	—	—	—	—	—
	1000	—	—	—	—	20.5	—	—	—	—
	1425(T_m)	—	—	—	—	—	—	—	—	—
321 (Quenched)	23	193	7.9	0.24	(275,0.2%) (550,55%)	16	15	500	—	—

continued

Material	$T/°C$	E_T	ρ	ν	(σ, ε)	α	k	γ	ρ_E	K_{IC}
321 (Quenched & Solution-Treated)	23	193	7.9	0.24	$(310, 0.2\%)$ $(650, 55\%)$	16	17	500	—	—
321/Aged SiC	600	193	7.9	0.24	$(178, 0.2\%)$ $(336, 34.4\%)$	16	15	500	—	—
321/Aged $Cr_{23}C_6$	600	193	7.9	0.24	$(160, 0.2\%)$ $(337, 34.4\%)$	16	15	500	—	—
	−160	—	—	—	$(986, 12\%)$	—	—	—	—	—
321 (W73; Test in He)	23	193	7.9	0.24	$(200, 0.2\%)$ $(579, 63\%)$	16	15	500	—	—
	−160	—	—	—	$(972, 12\%)$	—	—	—	—	—
321 (W73; Test in H_2)	23	193	7.9	0.24	$(255, 0.2\%)$ $(593, 64\%)$	16	15	500	—	—
321H (Solution annealed at 1010 ℃)	23	—	—	—	—	—	—	—	—	—
	600	—	—	—	$\sigma_{crs, 10000} = 140$	—	—	—	—	—
	650	—	—	—	$\sigma_{crs, 10000} = 88$	—	—	—	—	—
	700	—	—	—	$\sigma_{crs, 10000} = 49$	—	—	—	—	—
321H (Solution annealed at 1110 ℃)	23	193	7.92	0.24	$(195, 0.2\%)$ $(230, 1\%)$ $(585, 40\%)$	16	15	500	—	—
	100	—	—	—	$(162, 0.2\%)$ $(201, 1\%)$ $\sigma_{uts} = 410$	—	—	—	—	—
	300	—	—	—	$(132, 0.2\%)$ $(172, 1\%)$ $\sigma_{uts} = 350$	17.3	—	—	—	—
	500	—	—	—	$(113, 0.2\%)$ $(152, 1\%)$ $\sigma_{uts} = 330$	18.3	—	—	—	—
	550	—	—	—	$\sigma_{crs, 10000} = 230,$ $\sigma_{crs, 100000} = 170$	—	—	—	—	—

continued

Material	$T/°C$	E_T	ρ	ν	(σ, ε)	α	k	γ	ρ_E	K_{IC}
321H(Solution annealed at 1110 ℃)	600	150	—	—	$(103, 0.2\%)$ $(141, 1\%)$ $\sigma_{uts}=300$; $\sigma_{crs,10000}=160$, $\sigma_{crs,100000}=100$	18.8	—	—	—	—
	650	—	—	—	$\sigma_{crs,10000}=100$, $\sigma_{crs,100000}=62$	—	—	—	—	—
	700	—	—	—	$\sigma_{crs,10000}=60$, $\sigma_{crs,100000}=35$	—	—	—	—	—
	800	—	—	—	$\sigma_{crs,10000}=15$	19.4	25.8	—	—	—
	1000	120	—	—	—	—	—	—	—	—
330 (Annealed)	23	196	8	0.27	$(210, 0.2\%)$ $(550, 40\%)$	14.4	12.5	550	—	—
	500	150	—	—	—	16.7	21.6	—	—	—
	850	130	—	—	$(9, 0.2\%)$ $(150, 83\%)$	18	28.5	—	—	—
	980	130	—	—	$(50, 0.2\%)$ $(80, 90\%)$	20	31.2	—	—	—
	$1425(T_m)$	—	—	—	—	—	—	—	—	—
347(Solution annealed at 960 ℃)	23	—	—	—	—	—	—	—	—	—
	600	—	—	—	$\sigma_{crs,10000}=162$	—	—	—	—	—
	650	—	—	—	$\sigma_{crs,10000}=113$	—	—	—	—	—
	700	—	—	—	$\sigma_{crs,10000}=71$	—	—	—	—	—
347(1.4550; Fe-18Cr-10Ni; Sol. annealed at 1100 ℃)	23	199	7.9	0.27	$(241, 0.2\%)$ $(621, 50\%)$	16	15	500	—	—
	200	186			$(250, 0.2\%)$ $(510, 36\%)$	—	—	—	—	—
	430	—	—	—	$(200, 0.2\%)$ $(470, 30\%)$; $\sigma_{crs,10000}=400$	17.7	—	—	—	—
	500	160	—	—	—	18.6	22.2	—	—	—
	550	—	—	—	$\sigma_{crs,10000}=237$, $\sigma_{crs,100000}=172$	—	—	—	—	—

continued

Material	$T/^\circ\mathrm{C}$	E_{T}	ρ	ν	(σ,ε)	α	k	γ	ρ_{E}	K_{IC}
347(1.4550; Fe-18Cr-10Ni; Sol. annealed at 1100 ℃)	600	—	—	—	$(150,0.2\%)$ $(390,1\%)$; $\sigma_{\mathrm{crs,10000}}=166$, $\sigma_{\mathrm{crs,100000}}=115$	—	—	—	—	—
	650	148	—	—	$(165,0.2\%)$ $(360,26\%)$; $\sigma_{\mathrm{crs,10000}}=112$, $\sigma_{\mathrm{crs,100000}}=90$	—	—	—	—	—
	700	143	—	—	$(141,0.2\%)$ $(279,49\%)$; $\sigma_{\mathrm{crs,10000}}=74$	—	—	—	—	—
	815	—	—	—	$(125,0.2\%)$ $(180,50\%)$	—	—	—	—	—
	1000	—	—	—	—	20.5	—	—	—	—
347(CF)	23	199	7.9	0.27	$(448,0.2\%)$ $(758,40\%)$	16	15	500	—	—
	500	—	—	—	—	18.6	22.2	—	—	—
	−130	—	—	—	$(720,0.2\%)$ $(1579,12\%)$	—	—	—	—	—
347(H73;Test in He)	23	199	7.9	0.27	$(461,0.2\%)$ $(695,37\%)$	16	15	500	—	—
	500	—	—	—	—	18.6	22.2	—	—	—
	−130	—	—	—	$(664,0.2\%)$ $(1540,12\%)$	—	—	—	—	—
347(H73;Test in H_2)	23	199	7.9	0.27	$(455,0.2\%)$ $(752,40\%)$	16	15	500	—	—
	677	—	—	—	$(397,0.2\%)$ $(693,16\%)$	—	—	—	—	—
347(L72;Test in He)	23	199	7.9	0.27	$(206,0.2\%)$ $(572,60\%)$	16	15	500	—	—
	677	—	—	—	$(397,0.2\%)$ $(713,19\%)$	—	—	—	—	—
347(L72;Test in H_2)	23	199	7.9	0.27	$(200,0.2\%)$ $(520,38\%)$	16	15	500	—	—
347H (Annealed)	23	193	8.0	0.27	$(205,0.2\%)$ $(625,40\%)$	16	16.1	500	—	—

continued

Material	$T/℃$	E_T	ρ	ν	(σ,ε)	α	k	γ	ρ_E	K_{IC}
347HFG (Annealed)	23	193	8.0	0.27	(205,0.2%) (650,40%)	16	16.1	500	—	—
347N(Annealed N: 0.1% Nitrogen)	23	193	7.8	0.27	(241,0.2%) (621,50%)	16	16.1	500	—	—
	300	—	—	—	(202,0.2%) (469,38%)	—	—	—	—	—
348	23	193	7.8	0.27	(241,0.2%) (621,50%)	16.5	16.1	500	—	—
	500	—	—	—	—	18.6	22.2	—	—	—
348(CF)	23	193	7.8	0.27	(448,0.2%) (758,40%)	16.5	18.6	500	—	—
	500	—	—	—	—	18.4	21.5	—	—	—
384 (Annealed)	23	193	7.8	0.27	(241,0.2%) (517,55%)	16.5	16.3	503	—	—
	500	—	—	—	—	18.4	21.5	—	—	—
660(PH;0Cr15Ni 25Ti2MoAlVB; ST/Oil Q./Aged; Stainless Bolt; Incoloy A-286)	23	201	7.92	0.3	(655,0.2%) (1050,24%)	16.5	12.6	419	—	—
	200	—	—	—	(645,0.2%) (986,21%)	16.7	17.9	—	—	—
	400	175	—	—	(600,0.2%) (950,21%)	17.2	19.8	—	—	—
	538	—	—	—	(580,0.2%) (900,18%); $\sigma_{crs,1000}=600$	17.5	21.8	—	—	—
	600	—	—	—	(570,0.2%) (840,16%); $\sigma_{crs,1000}=490$	17.7	24	—	—	—
	650	—	—	—	(560,0.2%) (780,13%); $\sigma_{crs,1000}=290$	17.7	24.7	—	—	—
	700	—	—	—	(495,0.2%) (660,15%); $\sigma_{crs,1000}=210$	17.7	—	—	—	—

continued

Material	$T/℃$	E_T	ρ	ν	(σ,ε)	α	k	γ	ρ_E	K_{IC}
660(PH;0Cr15Ni 25Ti2MoAlVB; ST/Oil Q./Aged; Stainless Bolt; Incoloy A-286)	760	—	—	—	(395,0.2%) (500,18%); $\sigma_{crs,1000}=120$	—	—	—	—	—
	800	—	—	—	(220,0.2%) (250,19%); $\sigma_{crs,1000}=70$	—	—	—	—	—
	900	—	—	—	—	19.4	—	—	—	—
	1425(T_m)	—	—	—	—	—	—	—	—	—
904L (1.4539)	23	200	7.9	0.3	(260,0.2%) (310,1%) (490,35%) (600,49%)	15	13	500	—	—
	200	—	—	—	—	15.7	15.1	—	—	—
	500	—	—	—	—	16.9	—	—	—	—
(Fe-19Cr-11Ni-2Mn-1Si-0.045P-0.03S-0.03C)	23	195	7.9	0.29	(383,0.2%) (560,12%)	16	12.7	460	—	—
CF8C	23	—	7.9	—	(205,0.2%) (485,30%)	—	—	—	—	—
CF8C-plus(Fe-19Cr-12.5Ni-4Mn-0.8Nb-0.5Si-0.3Mo-0.24N-0.08Cu; ASM)	23	—	7.9	—	(276,0.2%) (587,43%)	—	—	—	—	—
	400	—	—	—	(169,0.2%) (476,40%)	—	—	—	—	—
	600	—	—	—	(143,0.2%) (398,40%)	—	—	—	—	—
	700	—	—	—	(135,0.2%) (324,32%)	—	—	—	—	—
	800	—	—	—	(136,0.2%) (255,27%)	—	—	—	—	—
	900	—	—	—	(120,0.2%) (170,50%)	—	—	—	—	—

continued

Material	$T/°C$	E_T	ρ	ν	(σ,ε)	α	k	γ	ρ_E	K_{IC}
S30415 (Annealed; 153MA)	23	200	7.9	0.27	$(380,0.2\%)$ $(410,1\%)$ $(700,50\%)$	16.5	15	500	—	—
	300	—	—	—	$(150,0.2\%)$ $(186,1\%)$ $\sigma_{uts}=475$	—	—	—	—	—
	500	155	—	—	$(135,0.2\%)$ $(165,1\%)$ $\sigma_{uts}=435$	—	—	—	—	—
	550	—	—	—	$(125,0.2\%)$ $(155,1\%)$ $\sigma_{uts}=410;$ $\sigma_{crs,10000}=250$	—	—	—	—	—
	700	—	—	—	$(120,0.2\%)$ $(135,1\%)$ $\sigma_{uts}=300;$ $\sigma_{crs,10000}=63$	—	—	—	—	—
	800	—	—	—	—	19.0	25.5	—	—	—
	1000	120	—	—	—	19.5	—	—	—	—
S30815 (Annealed; Fe-21Cr-11Ni-1.6Si-C-N-Ce; 253MA)	23	200	7.8	0.27	$(410,0.2\%)$ $(440,1\%)$ $(720,52\%)$	16.5	15.0	500	—	—
	300	—	—	—	$(170,0.2\%)$ $(200,1\%)$ $\sigma_{uts}=535$	—	—	—	—	—
	500	—	—	—	$(150,0.2\%)$ $(180,1\%)$ $\sigma_{uts}=495$	—	—	—	—	—
	550	—	—	—	$(145,0.2\%)$ $(175,1\%)$ $\sigma_{uts}=472;$ $\sigma_{crs,10000}=208,$ $\sigma_{crs,100000}=149$	—	—	—	—	—

continued

Material	$T/℃$	E_T	ρ	ν	(σ,ε)	α	k	γ	ρ_E	K_{IC}
S30815(Annealed;Fe-21Cr-11Ni-1.6Si-C-N-Ce;253MA)	600	155	—	—	$(140,0.2\%)$ $(170,1\%)$ $\sigma_{uts}=445;$ $\sigma_{crs,10000}=138,$ $\sigma_{crs,100000}=88$	18.5	—	—	—	—
	650	155	—	—	$\sigma_{crs,10000}=92$	—	—	—	—	—
	700	—	—	—	$(130,0.2\%)$ $(155,1\%)$ $\sigma_{uts}=360;$ $\sigma_{crs,10000}=61,$ $\sigma_{crs,100000}=35$	—	—	—	—	—
	760	115	—	—	$(110,0.2\%);$ $\sigma_{crs,10000}=38$	—	—	—	—	—
	800	—	—	—	$\sigma_{crs,10000}=28$	19.0	25.5	—	—	—
	1000	—	—	—	$\sigma_{crs,10000}=7.8$	19.5	—	—	—	—
S31254	23	200	7.8	0.27	$(340,0.2\%)$ $(690,50\%)$ $(380,1\%)$	16.5	12.7	460	—	—
S31726	23	200	7.8	0.27	$(320,0.2\%)$ $(650,52\%)$ $(360,1\%)$	16.5	12.7	460	—	—
S32654	23	200	7.8	0.27	$(520,0.2\%)$ $(890,55\%)$ $(560,1\%)$	16.5	12.7	460	—	—
S35315 (353MA)	23	200	7.8	0.27	$(360,0.2\%)$ $(400,1\%)$ $(720,50\%)$	16.5	15.0	500	—	—

Table 74.2 Mechanical Properties of Martensitic Stainless Steels

Material	$T/℃$	E_T	ρ	ν	(σ,ε)	α	k	γ	ρ_E	K_{IC}
403 (Annealed)	23	200	7.7	0.27	$(275,0.2\%)$ $(520,30\%)$	10.5	25	460	—	—
	-100	—	—	—	—	—	—	—	—	50
	-50	—	—	—	—	—	—	—	—	80

continued

Material	$T/℃$	E_{T}	ρ	ν	(σ,ε)	α	k	γ	ρ_{E}	K_{IC}
403 (T:760 ℃)	23	200	7.7	0.27	(415,0.2%) (620,30%)	10.5	25	460	—	190
403 (T:204 ℃)	23	200	7.7	0.27	(1000,0.2%) (1310,15%)	10.5	25	460	—	—
410 (Annealed)	23	200	7.7	0.27	(276,0.2%) (550,30%)	10.5	30	460	—	—
	150	—	—	—	(245,0.2%) (510,31%)	—	—	—	—	—
	500	—	—	—	(220,0.2%) (310,35%)	12.4	33.5	—	—	—
	540	—	—	—	(210,0.2%) (280,36%); $\sigma_{\text{crs},10000}=130$	—	—	—	—	—
	650	—	—	—	(120,0.2%) (160,47%); $\sigma_{\text{crs},10000}=19$	—	—	—	—	—
	700	—	—	—	(66,0.2%) (105,73%); $\sigma_{\text{crs},10000}=8$	—	—	—	—	—
	760	—	—	—	(55,0.2) (76,66%); $\sigma_{\text{crs},10000}=4$	13	—	—	—	—
	816	—	—	—	(62,800%)	—	—	—	—	—
410 (CF)	23	200	7.7	0.27	(724,0.2%) (834,17%)	10.4	30	460	—	—
	500	—	—	—	—	12.4	33.5	—	—	—
410 (T:760 ℃)	23	200	7.7	0.27	(414,0.2%) (620,30%)	10.5	30	460	—	—
410 (T:650 ℃)	23	200	7.7	0.27	(585,0.2%) (760,23%)	10.5	30	460	—	—
	500	—	—	—	(375,0.2%) $\sigma_{\text{crs}}=5$	12.4	33.5	—	—	—
	650	—	—	—	(276,0.2%) $\sigma_{\text{uts}}=310$	—	—	—	—	—
	760	—	—	—	(97,0.2%) $\sigma_{\text{uts}}=124$	13	—	—	—	—

continued

Material	$T/℃$	E_T	ρ	ν	(σ,ε)	α	k	γ	ρ_E	K_{IC}
410 (T:204 ℃)	23	200	7.7	0.27	(1200,0.2%) (1460,13%)	10.5	30	460	—	—
	200	—	—	—	(1180,0.2%) (1450,14%)	—	—	—	—	—
	430	—	—	—	(1050,0.2%) (1350,24%); $\sigma_{crs,10000}=330$	—	—	—	—	—
	480	—	—	—	(970,0.2%) (1200,24%); $\sigma_{crs,10000}=225$	—	—	—	—	—
	540	—	—	—	(510,0.2%) (540,15%); $\sigma_{crs,10000}=115$	—	—	—	—	—
	590	—	—	—	(320,0.2%) (350,30%); $\sigma_{crs,10000}=70$	12.5	—	—	—	—
	650	—	—	—	(190,0.2%) (220,39%); $\sigma_{crs,1000}=40$	—	—	—	—	—
HT-9(410+Mo+V+W;Fe-12Cr-0.5Ni-0.6Mn-0.4Si-0.2C-1Mo-0.3V-0.5W)	23	200	7.7	0.27	—	10	30	460	—	—
414 (Annealed)	23	200	7.78	0.27	(621,0.2%) (786,25%)	10	25	460	—	—
	550	—	—	—	—	12.5	28.7	—	—	—
414 (CF)	23	200	7.78	0.27	(758,0.2%) (896,15%)	10	25	460	—	—
	550	—	—	—	—	12.5	28.7	—	—	—
414 (HT)	23	200	7.78	0.27	(863,0.2%) (1103,17%)	10	25	460	—	—
	550	—	—	—	—	12.5	28.7	—	—	—
414 (Annealed)	23	200	7.7	0.27	(655,0.2%) (827,17%)	10	25	460	—	—

continued

Material	$T/$℃	E_T	ρ	ν	(σ,ε)	α	k	γ	ρ_E	K_{IC}
414 (T:650 ℃)	23	200	7.7	0.27	(720,0.2%) (830,20%)	10	25	460	—	—
414 (T:204 ℃)	23	200	7.7	0.27	(1034,0.2%) (1380,15%)	10	25	460	—	—
416 (Annealed)	23	215	7.7	0.27	(276,0.2%) (517,30%)	10.5	30	460	—	—
	550	—	—	—	—	12.5	33.5	—	—	—
416 (CF)	23	215	7.7	0.27	(586,0.2%) (690,13%)	10.5	30	460	—	—
	550	—	—	—	—	12.5	33.5	—	—	—
416 (T:650 ℃)	23	215	7.7	0.27	(586,0.2%) (758,20%)	10.5	30	460	—	—
	550	—	—	—	—	12.5	33.5	—	—	—
416 (T:430 ℃)	23	215	7.7	0.27	(1100,0.2%) (1400,11%)	10.5	30	460	—	—
416 (T:204 ℃)	23	215	7.7	0.27	(1200,0.2%) (1450,11%)	10.5	30	460	—	—
420 (S42000; Annealed)	23	200	7.75	0.24	(345,0.2%) (655,25%)	10.3	25	460	—	—
	500	—	—	—	—	11.5	28.7	—	—	—
420 (T:650 ℃)	23	200	7.75	0.24	(680,0.2%) (895,20%)	10.3	25	460	—	—
420 (T:540 ℃)	23	200	7.75	0.24	(1090,0.2%) (1300,15%)	10.3	25	460	—	—
	−198	—	—	—	$\sigma_{uts}=2000$	—	—	—	—	—
420(Hardened from 1020 ℃ & T:320 ℃)	23	—	—	—	(1320,0.2%) (1600,14%)	10.5	25	460	—	—
	100	—	—	—	$\sigma_{uts}=1720$	—	—	—	—	—
	200	—	—	—	$\sigma_{uts}=1800$	—	—	—	—	—
	400	—	—	—	$\sigma_{uts}=1450$	—	—	—	—	—
420 (T:200 ℃)	23	200	7.75	0.24	(1350,0.2%) (1600,12%)	10.3	25	460	—	—

continued

Material	$T/℃$	E_{T}	ρ	ν	(σ,ε)	α	k	γ	ρ_{E}	K_{IC}
420(3% NaCl Stress-Corrosion Cracking)	23	200	7.7	0.24	—	10.5	25	460	—	12
420L (Annealed)	23	200	7.7	0.24	(780,0.2%) (980,16%)	10.5	25	460	—	60
422 (Tempered)	23	215	7.78	0.24	(820,0.2%) (990,21%)	10.5	23.9	460	—	—
	300	—	—	—	(710,0.2%) (805,18%)	—	—	—	—	—
	400	—	—	—	(640,0.2%) (805,19%)	—	—	—	—	—
	600	—	—	—	(435,0.2%) (455,45%)	—	—	—	—	—
430(1.4016;Fe-17Cr-0.7Mn-0.6 Si-0.024S-0.021 P-0.12C; Annealed)	23	215	7.7	0.27	(360,0.2%) (530,25%)	10	25	460	—	—
	150	—	—	—	(234,0.2%) (455,32%)	—	—	—	—	—
	370	—	—	—	(230,0.2%) (400,30%)	—	—	—	—	—
	480	—	—	—	(191,0.2%) (335,35%); $\sigma_{\mathrm{crs},10000}=180$	—	—	—	—	—
	600	—	—	—	(130,0.2%) (205,42%); $\sigma_{\mathrm{crs},10000}=44$	—	—	—	—	—
	700	—	—	—	(55,0.2%) (105,82%); $\sigma_{\mathrm{crs},10000}=14$	—	—	—	—	—
430Ti (1.4510)	23	—	—	—	—	—	—	—	—	—
431 (Annealed)	23	215	7.7	0.27	(655,0.2%) (862,20%)	10	25	460	—	—
	550	—	—	—	—	12.5	28.7	—	—	—

continued

Material	$T/℃$	E_T	ρ	ν	(σ,ε)	α	k	γ	ρ_E	K_{IC}
431 (CF Wire)	23	215	7.7	0.27	(795,0.2%) (930,10%)	10	25	460	—	—
	550	—	—	—	—	12.5	—	—	—	—
431 (CF Bar)	23	215	7.7	0.7	(655,0.2%) (860,20%)	10	25	460	—	—
	500	—	—	—	—	12.5	—	—	—	—
431 (HT)	23	200	7.7	0.27	(862,0.2%) (1138,17%)	10	25	460	—	—
	550	—	—	—	—	12.5	—	—	—	—
431 (T:204 ℃)	23	215	7.7	0.27	(1034,0.2%) (1380,15%)	10	25	460	—	—
439 (Annealed)	23	210	7.7	0.27	—	10.2	—	—	—	—
	500	157	—	—	—	11.6	—	—	—	—
	760	115	—	—	—	12.3	—	—	—	—
440A(Fe-17 Cr-1Mn-1Si- 0.75Mo-0.7C- 0.04P-0.03S; Annealed)	23	210	7.7	0.28	(414,0.2%) (724,14%)	10.1	30	460	—	24
	550	—	—	—	—	12.5	—	—	—	—
440A (T:316 ℃)	23	210	7.7	0.28	(1655,0.2%) (1793,5%)	11	30	460	—	17.6
	200	—	—	—	—	10.8	—	—	—	—
	600	—	—	—	—	12.2	—	—	—	—
440A (CF)	23	210	7.7	0.28	(621,0.2%) (793,7%)	10.1	30	460	—	24
	200	—	—	—	—	10.8	—	—	—	—
	600	—	—	—	—	12.2	—	—	—	—
440B (Annealed)	23	210	7.7	0.28	(427,0.2%) (738,18%)	10.1	15	460	—	24
440B (T:204 ℃)	23	210	7.7	0.28	(1860,0.2%) (1930,3%)	10.1	15	460	—	17.6
	550	—	—	—	—	12.5	—	—	—	—

continued

Material	$T/°C$	E_T	ρ	ν	(σ,ε)	α	k	γ	ρ_E	K_{IC}
440C (Annealed; Fe-17Cr-1.2C-1 Mn-1Si-0.75Mo-0.04P-0.03S)	23	210	7.7	0.28	(450,0.2%) (760,14%)	10	24	460	—	24
	100	—	—	—	—	—	24.2	—	—	—
	200	—	—	—	—	10.1	—	—	—	—
	550	—	—	—	—	12.5	—	—	—	—
440C (T:371 °C)	23	210	7.7	0.28	(1660,0.2%) (1790,4%)	10	24	460	—	17.6
	550	—	—	—	—	12.5	—	—	—	—
440C (T:316 °C)	23	210	7.7	0.28	(1740,0.2%) (1860,4%)	10	24	460	—	17.6
	550	—	—	—	—	12.5	—	—	—	—
440C (T:260 °C)	23	210	7.73	0.28	(1830,0.2%) (1960,3%)	10	23.9	460	—	17.6
	550	—	—	—	—	12.5	—	—	—	—
440C (T:204 °C)	23	210	7.7	0.28	(1900,0.2%) (2030,2%)	10	24	460	—	17.6
	550	—	—	—	—	12.5	—	—	—	—
440F (Annealed)	23	210	7.7	0.28	(448,0.2%) (758,13%)	10	24	460	—	24
465 (13-8 Mo; PH at 566 °C; Fe-13Cr-8Ni-...)	23	200	7.7	0.3	(1351,0.2%) (1468,17%)	11	25	460	—	125
465 (13-8 Mo; PH at 482 °C)	23	200	7.7	0.3	(1613,0.2%) (1772,12%)	11	25	460	—	64
501 (Annealed)	23	200	7.7	0.27	(207,0.2%) (483,28%)	11	25	460	—	—
502 (Annealed)	23	200	7.7	0.27	(207,0.2%) (483,30%)	11	25	460	—	—
PH13-8 Mo (H950)	23	200	7.76	0.27	(1450,0.2%) (1550,12%)	10.5	14	460	—	—
	430	—	—	—	—	11.3	—	—	—	—
PH13-8 Mo (H1050)	23	200	7.76	0.27	(1240,0.2%) (1310,15%)	10.5	14	460	—	—
	430	—	—	—	—	11.3	—	—	—	—

continued

Material	$T/°C$	E_T	ρ	ν	(σ,ε)	α	k	γ	ρ_E	K_{IC}
PH13-8 Mo (H1150)	23	200	7.76	0.27	$(724,0.2\%)$ $(1000,20\%)$	10.5	14	460	—	—
	430	—	—	—	—	11.3	—	—	—	—
PH15-7 Mo (H950)	23	200	7.76	0.27	$(1550,0.2\%)$ $(1650,6\%)$	9	15.1	460	—	—
	480	—	—	—	—	10.8	21.7	—	—	—
PH15-7 Mo (H1050)	23	200	7.76	0.27	$(1380,0.2\%)$ $(1450,7\%)$	9	15.1	460	—	—
	480	—	—	—	—	10.8	21.7	—	—	—
	−198	—	—	—	$\sigma_{uts}=2050$	—	—	—	—	—
SS716(Hardened from 1020 ℃ & T:320 ℃)	23	200			$(1580,0.2\%)$ $(1870,8\%)$			460	—	—
	100	—	—	—	$\sigma_{uts}=1900$	—	—	—	—	—
	200	—	—	—	$\sigma_{uts}=2000$	—	—	—	—	—
	400	—	—	—	$\sigma_{uts}=1450$	—	—	—	—	—
S30815	23	200	7.7	0.27	$(410,0.2\%)$ $(440,1\%)$ $(720,52\%)$	11	23.9	460	—	—
AK 11Cr-Cb	23	210	7.7	0.27	$(372,0.2\%)$ $(538,29\%)$	11	17.2	451	—	—
	371	—	—	—	$(234,0.2\%)$ $(405,25\%)$	—	23	550	—	—
	593	—	—	—	$(175,0.2\%)$ $(348,16\%)$	—	25.2	790	—	—
	816	—	—	—	$(26,0.2\%)$ $(41,140\%)$	—	—	—	—	—
AK 18Cr-Cb	23	206	7.7	0.27	$(345,0.2\%)$ $(503,33\%)$	11	17.2	451	—	—
	371	—	—	—	$(232,0.2\%)$ $(418,25\%)$	—	550	550	—	—
	593	—	—	—	$(176,0.2\%)$ $(400,16\%)$	—	25.5	790	—	—
	816	—	—	—	$(41,0.2\%)$ $(54,70\%)$	—	—	—	—	—

Table 74.3 Mechanical Properties of Ferritic Stainless Steels

Material (AISI)	$T/℃$	E_{T}	ρ	ν	(σ,ε)	α	k	γ	ρ_{E}	K_{IC}
405(1.4002; Annealed)	23	200	7.73	0.27	(275,0.2%) (483,30%)	10.4	26.1	460	—	—
	$1530(T_{\mathrm{m}})$	—	—	—	—	—	—	—	—	—
409(1.4512; Annealed)	23	208	7.6	0.27	(205,0.2%) (480,20%)	10.4	25.8	460	—	—
	370	—	—	—	(152,0.2%) (330,28%)	11.5	—	—	—	—
	500	168	—	—	(146,0.2%) (260,33%)	12.4	27.5	—	—	—
	700	—	—	—	$\sigma_{\mathrm{crs},1000}=29$	—	—	—	—	—
	760	114	—	—	(39,0.2%) (61,69%)	13	—	—	—	—
	$1530(T_{\mathrm{m}})$	—	—	—	—	—	—	—	—	—
409M (Annealed)	23	208	7.6	0.27	(310,0.2%) (530,26%)	10.4	25	460	—	—
410(1.4006; Annealed)	23	200	7.75	0.27	(245,0.2%) (515,30%)	10.4	25	460	—	—
	400	185	—	—	—	—	—	—	—	—
	500	—	—	—	—	11.5	28.7	—	—	—
410 (T:650 ℃)	23	200	7.75	0.27	(575,0.2%) (755,23%)	10.4	25	460	—	—
410 (T:540 ℃)	23	200	7.75	0.27	(730,0.2%) (985,16%)	10.4	25	460	—	—
410 (T:200 ℃)	23	200	7.75	0.27	(1000,0.2%) (1310,16%)	10.4	25	460	—	—
410S(1.4000) (Annealed)	23	200	7.7	0.27	(1225,0.2%) (1525,14%)	10	25	460	—	—
	400	185	—	—	—	—	—	—	—	—
	500	—	—	—	—	11.5	28.7	—	—	—
	$1530(T_{\mathrm{m}})$	—	—	—	—	—	—	—	—	—
429 (Annealed)	23	200	7.78	0.27	(275,0.2%) (483,31%)	10	26	460	—	—

continued

Material (AISI)	$T/℃$	E_T	ρ	ν	(σ,ε)	α	k	γ	ρ_E	K_{IC}
430(1.4016; Annealed)	23	200	7.7	0.27	(310,0.2%) (517,32%)	9.5	25	460	—	—
	400	—	—	—	(240,0.2%) (400,17%)	—	—	—	—	—
	500	—	—	—	(240,0.2%) (390,10%)	—	—	—	—	—
	550(High work temperature)					11.6	28.7	—	—	—
	600(Steady-state Creep)				(150,0.2%) (190,25%)	—	—	—	—	—
430(CF)	23	200	7.7	0.27	(483,0.2%) (586,20%)	9.5	25	460	—	—
	550	—	—	—	—	11.6	28.7	—	—	—
430F (Annealed)	23	200	7.7	0.27	(380,0.2%) (586,25%)	10	25	460	—	—
430Ti	23	—	—	—	—	—	—	—	—	—
433	23	200	7.7	0.27	(325,0.2%)	—	—	—	0.65	—
	760	—	—	—	(80,0.2%)	—	—	—	—	—
434 (Annealed)	23	200	7.7	0.27	(280,0.2%) (540,18%)	10	25	460	—	—
436 (Annealed)	23	200	7.7	0.27	(300,0.2%) (520,25%)	10	25	460	—	—
439 (Annealed)	23	200	7.7	0.28	(310,0.2%) (510,21%)	10.4	24.2	460	0.63	—
	700	—	—	—	$\sigma_{crs,1000}=28$	—	—	—	—	—
	760	—	—	—	(48,0.2%)	—	—	—	—	—
	816	—	—	—	$\sigma_{crs,1000}=7$	—	—	—	—	—
441(1.4509; Annealed)	23	205	7.7	0.28	(320,0.2%) (490,16%)	—	—	—	0.587	—
	500	—	—	—	(340,13%)	—	—	—	—	—
	600	—	—	—	(270,9%)	—	—	—	—	—
	700	—	—	—	(200,8%) $\sigma_{crs,1000}=35$	—	—	—	—	—
	750(Steady-state Creep)				—	—	—	—	—	—
	760	—	—	—	(58,0.2%)	—	—	—	—	—
	816	—	—	—	$\sigma_{crs,1000}=11$	—	—	—	—	—

continued

Material (AISI)	$T/℃$	E_T	ρ	ν	(σ,ε)	α	k	γ	ρ_E	K_{IC}
442 (Annealed)	23	205	7.8	0.28	(290,0.2%) (530,20%)	9.7	21.7	460	—	—
443	23	200	7.7	0.27	(345,0.2%)	—	—	—	0.65	—
	760	—	—	—	(41,0.2%) $\sigma_{crs,1000}=41$	—	—	—	—	—
444(1.4521; Annealed)	23	200	7.7	0.3	(390,0.2%) (560,30%)	10	26.8	420	—	—
	500	—	—	—	(240,0.2%) $\sigma_{uts}=360$	11.4	—	—	—	—
	600	—	—	—	(190,0.2%)	—	—	—	—	—
	700	—	—	—	(135,0.2%) $\sigma_{uts}=225$	—	—	—	—	—
446 (Annealed)	23	200	7.7	0.3	(340,0.2%) (540,25%)	10.4	17	500	0.67	—
	400	—	—	—	(300,0.2%) $\sigma_{uts}=460$	—	—	—	—	—
	500	—	—	—	—	11.4	23	—	—	—
	600	—	—	—	(200,0.2%) $\sigma_{uts}=250$	—	—	—	—	—
	760	—	—	—	(55,0.2%); $\sigma_{crs,1000}=13.5$	—	—	—	—	—
	1000	—	—	—	—	13.0	—	—	—	—
446(CF)	23	200	7.73	0.3	(483,0.2%) (586,20%)	10.4	17	500	0.67	—
	500	—	—	—	—	11.4	23	—	—	—
	1000	—	—	—	—	13.0	—	—	—	—
447(1.4592)	23	200	—	—	—	—	—	—	—	—
453	23	200	—	—	(310,0.2%)	—	—	—	0.733	—
	760	—	—	—	(39,0.2%)	—	—	—	—	—
468	23	200	—	—	(282,0.2%)	—	—	—	—	—
	760	—	—	—	(62,0.2%)	—	—	—	—	—

continued

Material (AISI)	$T/℃$	E_{T}	ρ	ν	(σ,ε)	α	k	γ	ρ_{E}	K_{IC}
630(Fe-17Cr-4Ni-;1.4542;S17400;Annealed)	23	200	7.8	0.3	(760,0.2%) (1100,10%)	10.8	18.4	460	—	—
	316	—	—	—	—	11.2	—	—	—	—
	500	—	—	—	—	11.6	22.7	—	—	—
630(17-4 PH at 620 ℃;H1150)	23	200	7.8	0.3	(860,0.2%) (1000,19%)	10.8	16.4	460	—	53
630(17-4 PH at 550 ℃;H1025)	23	200	7.8	0.3	(1135,0.2%) (1215,15%)	10.8	16.4	460	—	—
630(17-4,PH at 480 ℃;H900)	23	200	7.8	0.3	(1270,0.2%) (1380,14%)	10.8	16.4	460	—	53
	316	—	—	—	—	11.3	—	—	—	—
631(17-7 PH;Fe-17Cr-7Ni;Annealed)	23	203	7.8	0.3	(276,0.2%) (896,35%)	15.1	16.4	460	—	—
	370	—	—	—	—	16.5	21.8	—	—	—
	−198	—	—	—	$\sigma_{\text{uts}}=2100$	—	—	—	—	—
631(17-7 PH;TH1050)	23	200	7.7	0.3	(1275,0.2%) (1380,9%)	10.1	16.4	460	—	—
	150	—	—	—	(1170,0.2%) (1234,8%)	—	—	—	—	—
	260	—	—	—	(1100,0.2%) (1150,4%)	11.2	18.5	—	—	—
	370	—	—	—	(1007,0.2%) (1075,4%); $\sigma_{\text{crs},1000}=841$	11.6	—	—	—	—
	482	—	—	—	(690,0.2%) (855,10%); $\sigma_{\text{crs},1000}=358$	—	21	—	—	—
631(17-7 PH;RH950)	23	200	7.7	0.3	(1517,0.2%) (1620,6%)	10.1	16.4	460	—	—
	150	—	—	—	(1324,0.2%) (1434,4%)	—	—	—	—	—
	260	—	—	—	(1213,0.2%) (1345,4%)	11.2	18.5	—	—	—

continued

Material (AISI)	$T/℃$	E_T	ρ	ν	(σ,ε)	α	k	γ	ρ_E	K_{IC}
631(17-7 PH; RH950)	370	—	—	—	(1117,0.2%) (1248,7%); $\sigma_{crs,1000}=1007$	11.6	—	—	—	—
	427	—	—	—	(945,0.2%) (1103,12%); $\sigma_{crs,1000}=634$	—	—	—	—	—
	482	—	—	—	(786,0.2%) (917,15%); $\sigma_{crs,1000}=303$	—	21	—	—	—
25Cr2MoVA (Stainless Collar)	23	200	7.84	0.3	(665,0.2%) (780,16%)	11.3	40	460	—	—
	300	—	7.75	—	—	12.8	36.9	—	—	—
	500	—	7.7	—	—	14.2	34.8	—	—	—

Table 74.4 Mechanical Properties of Duplex (Ferritic-Austenitic) Stainless Steels

Material	$T/℃$	E_T	ρ	ν	(σ,ε)	α	k	γ	ρ_E	K_{IC}
255	23	200	7.8	0.29	(530,0.2%) (830,25%)	12	15	500	—	—
329	23	200	7.8	0.29	—	13	15	500	—	—
S31803(1.4462; Annealed)	23	200	7.8	0.29	(500,0.2%) (590,1%) (770,36%)	12.5	16	500	—	—
	100	190	—	—	—	13	17	—	—	—
	370	—	—	—	(375,0.2%) $\sigma_{uts}=640$	—	—	—	—	—
	400	160	—	—	—	14.5	21	—	—	—
	500	150	—	—	—	15	22	—	—	—
	−20	210	—	—	—	14.1	—	—	—	—

continued

Material	$T/℃$	E_T	ρ	ν	(σ,ε)	α	k	γ	ρ_E	K_{IC}
S32001	23	208	7.8	—	$(450,0.2\%)$ $(620,25\%)$	14.4	15.9	471	—	—
	100	208	—	—	—	15.0	—	—	—	—
	260	—	—	—	—	—	18.9	548	—	—
	538	—	—	—	—	—	22.9	684	—	—
	−110	—	—	—	—	—	—	—	—	105
	−80	—	—	—	—	—	—	—	—	170
	−60	—	—	—	—	—	—	—	—	220
S32101	23	200	7.8	0.29	$(450,0.2\%)$ $(650,30\%)$	12.5	15	500	—	—
	100	194	—	—	—	13	16	—	—	—
	300	180	—	—	—	14	18	—	—	—
	−110	—	—	—	—	—	—	—	—	80
	−80	—	—	—	—	—	—	—	—	120
	−50	—	—	—	—	—	—	—	—	180
S32101(1.4162; Weld Material)	23	—	—	—	—	—	—	—	—	—
	−110	217	—	—	—	—	—	—	—	160
	−80	21	—	—	—	—	—	—	—	260
	−60	213	—	—	—	—	—	—	—	370
S32205(1.4462; Fe-22Cr-5Ni-3Mo-2Mn-1Si-...;Most used duplex)	23	207	7.85	0.29	$(450,0.2\%)$ $(620,25\%)$	13	16	470	—	—
	100	195	—	—	$(365,0.2\%)$ $\sigma_{uts}=630$	13.5	17	500	—	—
	200	185	7.8	0.29	$(315,0.2\%)$ $\sigma_{uts}=580$	—	19	530	—	—
	400	165	7.8	0.29	$(275,0.2\%)$ $\sigma_{uts}=550$	14.5	21	600	—	—
	500	155	—	—	—	15	22	—	—	—
	−110	—	—	—	—	—	—	—	—	85
	−80	—	—	—	—	—	—	—	—	130
	−50	—	—	—	—	—	—	—	—	215

continued

Material	$T/℃$	E_T	ρ	ν	(σ,ε)	α	k	γ	ρ_E	K_{IC}
S32205(1.4462; Weld Material)	23	200	—	—	—	—	—	—	—	—
	100	190	—	—	—	—	—	—	—	—
S32304 (1.4362)	23	200	7.8	0.29	(470,0.2%) (540,1%) (730,36%)	12.5	16	500	—	—
	100	190	—	—	—	13	17	—	—	—
	400	160	—	—	—	14.5	21	—	—	—
	500	150	—	—	—	15	22	—	—	—
S32520	23	205	7.8	0.29	—	12.5	17	500	—	—
	100	185	—	—	—	13	18	—	—	—
	300	170	—	—	—	13.5	20	—	—	—
S32550	23	210	7.8	0.29	—	12	13.5	500	—	—
	100	200	—	—	—	12.1	15.1	—	—	—
	300	192	—	—	—	13	21	—	—	—
	400	182	—	—	—	13.3	21	—	—	—
	500	170	—	—	—	13.6	22.5	—	—	—
S32750 (1.4410)	23	200	7.8	0.29	(600,0.2%) (670,1%) (850,35%)	12.5	16	500	—	—
	100	190	—	—	—	13	17	—	—	—
	400	160	—	—	—	14.5	21	—	—	—
	500	150	—	—	—	15	22	—	—	—
S32760(1.4501)	23	200	7.8	0.29	—	12.5	15	500	—	—
S32850	23	200	7.8	0.29	(550,0.2%) (795,15%)	12.5	15	500	—	—
S82441(1.4662)	23	200	7.8	0.29	—	12.5	15	500	—	—

Notes: L=Low Carbon;

H (or C)= High Carbon;

Se=Se Added;

Si=Si Added;

CF=Cold-work finish; in general, σ_Y and σ_{uts} increase while ε_{uts} decreases;

CR=Cold-rolled;

HF=Hot-finished;

HT=Hardened-tempered; σ_y & σ_{uts} increase much; applicable to Martensitic only.

Table 74.5   Fatigue ε-N Properties of Stainless Steels

Material	$T/{}^\circ\!C$	$d\varepsilon/dt$	σ_f'	ε_f'	b	c	K'	n'	$\sigma_f@2N_f$	R
301（Annealed）	23	—	—	—	—	—	—	—	240@ 10^7	−1
301（Hard）	23	—	—	—	—	—	—	—	552@ 10^7	−1
301（Cold-rolled）	23	—	—	—	—	—	—	—	580@ 2×10^6	−1
302（Annealed）	23	—	—	—	—	—	—	—	240@ 10^7	−1
303（Annealed）	23	—	534	0.052	−0.07	−0.292	2450	0.35	240@ 10^7	−1
304（Annealed）	23	—	1267	0.174	−0.139	−0.415	2275	0.334	240@ 10^7	−1
	427	—	465	0.37	−0.087	−0.45	—	—	—	—
	650	—	120	0.09	−0.087	−0.45	—	—	—	—
	816	—	31	0.09	−0.087	−0.45	—	—	—	—
304（3/4 Hard）	23	—	—	—	—	—	—	—	640@ 10^7	−1
304（CD）	23	—	2047	0.554	−0.112	−0.635	2270	0.176	490@ 10^7	−1
	427	—	800	0.186	−0.146	−0.43	1928	0.41	—	−1
304LN	23	—	212	0.114	−0.127	−0.362	454	0.351	—	—
304V	23	—	705	0.68	−0.06	−0.6	733	−0.1	240@ 10^7	−1
310（Annealed）	23	—	—	—	—	—	—	—	215@ 10^7	—
316（Annealed）	23	—	1280	0.12	−0.097	−0.45	—	—	270@ 10^7	—
316（3H）	23	—	—	—	—	—	1004	0.187	—	—
316（4H）	23	—	—	—	—	—	1384	0.224	—	—
316（6H）	23	—	—	—	—	—	1125	0.193	—	—
316（9H）	23	—	—	—	—	—	583	0.066	—	—
316（10H）	23	—	—	—	—	—	870	0.155	—	—
316L（Annealed）	23	—	586	0.18	−0.037	−0.433	677	0.085	184@ 10^7	−1
								—	161@ 10^7	0.1^+
								—	330@ 10^3	0.1^+
	300	—	—	—	—	—	—	—	123@ 10^7	−1
	565	—	—	—	—	—	—	—	60@ 10^7	0.1^+
317（Annealed）	23	—	—	—	—	—	—	—	260@ 10^7	—
321（Annealed）	23	—	—	—	—	—	—	—	260@ 10^7	—
420（Hardened）	23	—	—	—	—	—	—	—	774@ 2×10^6	—

continued

Material	$T/°C$	$d\varepsilon/dt$	σ'_f	ε'_f	b	c	K'	n'	$\sigma_f @ 2N_f$	R
347 (Annealed)	23	—	—	—	—	—	—	—	270@ 10^7	—
Fe-0.03C-19Cr-11 Ni-2Mn-1Si-0.045P-0.03S	23	—	3552	0.224	−0.248	−0.615	2105	0.22	—	—
409 (Annealed)	23	—	—	—	—	—	—	—	—	—
	704	—	—	—	—	—	—	—	45@ 10^7	—
420 (Hardened from 1020 ℃ & T: 320 ℃)	23	—	—	—	—	—	—	—	774@ $2×10^6$	—
439 (Annealed)	23	—	—	—	—	—	—	—	—	—
	704	—	—	—	—	—	—	—	28@ 10^7	—
630(17-4 PH)	23	—	1414	—	—	—	—	—	—	—
631(17-7 PH)	23	—	1414	—	—	—	—	—	600@ $2×10^6$	—
SS716(Hardened from 1020 ℃ & T: 320 ℃)	23	—	—	—	—	—	—	—	820@ $2×10^6$	RB
S32001 (Alloy 19d)	23	—	—	—	—	—	—	—	—	—
Steel (Generic)	23	—	Eq. (6.14)	Eq. (6.15)	−0.09	−0.6	$\sigma'_f/(\varepsilon'_f)^{n'}$	b/c	Eq.(71.1)	—

Table 74.6 Thermomechanical Creep Parameters of Stainless Steel

Material	$T/°C$	Stress/MPa	Strain Rate/s^{-1}	$A/(MPa^{-n} \cdot s^{m-1})$	$Q/(J \cdot mol^{-1})$	n	m
310S (Annealed)	700 ~ 800	$E=1;60 \sim 100$	—	—	340000	6.5	0
316	550	$E=1$	—	$3.171×10^{-5}$	0	1.494	0
316(Prestain = 5%)	550	$E=1$	—	$5.968×10^{-5}$	0	1.468	0

Notes: Creep equation $= \dfrac{d\varepsilon_{creep}}{dt} = A\left(\dfrac{\sigma-\sigma_{th}}{E}\right)^n t^m \exp\left(\dfrac{-Q}{RT_k}\right)$, $\sigma > \sigma_{th}$;

σ_{th} = Stress threshold and σ_{th} = 0, if not specified;

E = Young's modulus; If given that $E=1$, it means E is not specified.

Table 74.7 Material Parameters on Fatigue Crack Growth of Stainless Steels in Opening Mode

Material	$T/°C$	σ_y	σ_{uts}	K_{IC}	$f(R)$	m	ΔK_{th}	Δ_{fat}
304LN	23	318	617	—	$f(-1)=2.33\times10^{-12}$	3.00	—	—
SAE 1010HR	23	302	450	—	$f(-1)=3.807\times10^{-12}$	3.034	—	—

Notes: $\dfrac{\mathrm{d}a}{\mathrm{d}N_p}=f(R)\,|\,\Delta K-\Delta K_{th}\,|^{m}$;

$\sigma_y(\mathrm{MPa})=$ Yield strength;

$\sigma_{uts}(\mathrm{MPa})=$ Ultimate tensile strength;

$f(R)=$ Parameter as a function of load ratio (R);

$m=$ Exponent;

$\Delta K_{th}(\mathrm{MPa}\cdot\mathrm{m}^{\frac{1}{2}})=$ Threshold stress intensity factor range;

$\Delta_{fat}(\mathrm{MPa})=$ Fatigue strength range.

Table 74.8 Thermomechanical Oxidation Parameters of Stainless Steel

Material	Period	$T/°C$	k_0	$Q_o/(\mathrm{J}\cdot\mathrm{mol}^{-1})$	n	m	Δm_{in}	t_{in}/h
310S(Annealed)	Steady	700~900	—	210000	2	1	0	0

Notes: $\mathrm{Oxidation}=(\Delta m-\Delta m_{in})^{n}=k_0(t-t_{in})^{m}\exp\left(\dfrac{-Q_o}{R\,T_k}\right)$;

$\Delta m\ \&\ \Delta m_{in}=\mathrm{kg/m^2}\,(=0.1\ \mathrm{g/cm^2})$.

Chapter 75

Powder Steels

75.1   Introduction

Structural parts such as gears, bearings, and bushings may be made from powder metal. The density of a PM (**P**owder **M**etal) part is lower than the counterpart bulk metal. An important factor affecting the properties of structural PM parts is their porosity. PM parts are stiff but relatively weak in fatigue strength and ductility than counterpart bulk metal. Design engineers and other material scientists in organizations that are interested in PM components ought to be aware of the Global Powder Metallurgy Property Database.

75.2   Density-Dependent Material Properties

In general, increasing the density of a PM part will increase its stiffness, tensile strength, compressive strength, fatigue strength, and ductility. Mechanical properties of powder metallurgy steel depend on its density, sintering temperature, and after-treatment, as shown in Table 75.1. A part sintered at a high temperature (e.g. 1260 ℃) has a higher density but may have a higher degree of shrinkage from the die size that sintered at a lower temperature (e.g. 1120 ℃).

Thermal conductivity (k) and specific heat capacity (γ) of powder metal can be rationalized by the proportionality of the density ratio of the compacted powder preform to its bulk counterpart.

75.3   Fatigue of PM Parts

Fatigue properties of PM parts are listed in Table 75.2.

75.4   Applications

Powder Metallurgy (PM), due to its low cost and high volume production capacity, is a favored technique for net-shape manufacturing automotive components. Manufacturing through the PM route is attractive due to its low energy consumption and high raw material utilization. Structural steel parts such as gears, bushings/bearings and engine connecting rods may be made from powder. They are addressed as follows:

(a) PM Gears: Material properties of high-end PM (Powder Metal) gears made from MPIF

FLN4-4405 are shown in Table 75.1 [MPIF]. Typical gear preforms made of MPIF FLN4-4405 premix are compacted to a nominal value of 6.8 g/cm^3 in density and sintered at a temperature between 1120 ℃ and 1260 ℃. The follow-up heat treatment (HT) is essential to enhancing of its ultimate strength and the rolling-contact fatigue strength can be improved with densified surface [Jandeska et al.].

(b) PM Bushing/Bearing: PM bearings (Specifications B438 and B439) are self-lubricating because their porosity is impregnated with lubricants. Under vacuum, customer-specific oil products are impregnated into the remaining porosity of the completed part during the manufacturing process. In use, heat causes the lubricant to expand out of the pores forming a film between mating parts. When the operation is suspended, the lubricant cools and is drawn back into the pores for subsequent reuse. Low coefficients of friction, minimal maintenance and trouble-free service life, low cost, and simple installation are the major advantages of PM bearings.

References

COUBE O, RIEDEL H, 2000. Numerical Simulation of Metal Powder Die Compaction with Special Consideration of Cracking[J]. Powder Metallurgy, 43(2): 123-131.

CHAWLA N, et al, 2001. Axial Fatigue Behavior of Binder-Treated Versus Diffusion Alloyed Powder Metallurgy Steels[J]. Material Science Engineering, A, 308(1-2): 180-188.

HANEJKO F, TAYLOR A, 2002. Advanced Sintering Materials and Practices [J]. Advances in Powder Metallurgy and Particulate Materials, Part 13: 13-29.

HANEJKO F, TAYLOR A, 2002. Advances in P/M Gear Materials[J]. SAE 2002-01-340.

ILIA E, et al, 2003. Development of a Main Bearing Cap for an Inline 6 Cylinder Engine[J]. Advances in Powder Metallurgy and Particulate Materials, Part 9: 22-35.

JANDESKA W, et al, 2005. Rolling Contact Fatigue of Surface Densified FLN2-4405[J]. International Journal of Powder Metallurgy, 41(3): 49-61.

ULUS B S, 2011. Tribological and Mechanical Properties of PM Journal Bearings[J]. Powder Metallurgy, 54 (3): 338-342.

WIKMAN B, et al, 2000. Wall Friction Coefficient Estimation through Modeling of Powder Die Pressing Experiment[J]. Powder Metallurgy, 43(2): 132-138.

Table 75.1   Mechanical Properties of Powder Steels as a Function of Density

Material	$T/℃$	E_T	ρ	ν	(σ,ε)	α	k	γ	ρ_E	K_{IC}
F-0005(AS; Fe-0.5C)	23	125	6.9	0.25	(195,0.2%) (260,1.5%)	—	*	*	—	—
F-0008 (AS; Fe-0.8C)	23	130	7.0	0.25	(275,0.2%) (395,1%)	—	*	*	—	—
FC-0208 (AS; Fe-2Cu-0.8C)	23	86	5.8	0.25	(241,0.2%) (242,1%)	—	*	*	—	—
	23	114	6.3	0.25	(310,0.2%) (345,1%)	—	*	*	—	—
	23	121	6.7	0.25	(379,0.2%) (414,1%)	—	*	*	—	—
	23	155	7.2	0.28	(448,0.2%) (483,1%)	—	*	*	—	—
FC-0208(HT; Fe-2Cu-0.8C)	23	103	6.1	0.25	(345,0.2%) (448,1%)	—	*	*	—	—
	23	121	6.4	0.27	(448,0.2%) (517,1%)	—	*	*	—	—
	23	128	6.8	0.27	(552,0.2%) (621,1%)	—	*	*	—	—
	23	148	7.1	0.27	(655,0.2%) (724,1%)	—	*	*	—	—
F-0408 (AS)	23	135	6.9	0.25	(345,0.2%) (450,1%)	—	*	*	—	—
FL-4405 (AS)	23	186	7.46	0.28	(488,0.2%) (582,0.9%)	—	*	*	—	—
FL-4405 (HT)	23	153	7.46	0.28	(1178, 0.86%)	—	*	*	—	—
FL-5305	23	191	7.1	0.28	(1372,0.2%) (1627,2.3%)	—	*	*	—	—

continued

Material	$T/℃$	E_T	ρ	ν	(σ,ε)	α	k	γ	ρ_E	K_{IC}
FL-5305(HT; Low Alloy)	23	114	6.6	0.25	(724,0.2%) (793,1%)	12	*	*	—	—
	23	128	6.8	0.27	(827,0.2%) (896,1%)	12	*	*	—	—
	23	141	7.0	0.27	(931,0.2%) (1000,1%)	11	*	*	—	—
	23	155	7.2	0.28	(1034,0.2%) (1034,1%)	10	*	*	—	—
FLN2-4400C	23	180	7.4	—	—	—	*	*	—	—
FLN2-4405 (AS)	23	143	7.11	0.28	(452, 0.2) (553,2.4%)	—	*	*	—	—
FLN2-4405 (HT)	23	114	6.6	0.25	(621,0.2%) (690,0.5%)	12	*	*	—	—
	23	128	6.8	0.27	(827,0.2%) (896,0.5%)	12	*	*	—	—
	23	145	7.05	0.27	(1103,0.2%) (1172,0.5%)	11	*	*	—	—
	23	162	7.3	0.28	(1310,0.2%) (1448,0.5%)	10	*	*	—	—
FLN2-4408 (PF)	23	—	—	—	—	—	*	*	—	—
FLN4-4405 (HT)	23	114	6.6	0.25	(621,0.2%) (690,0.5%)	12	*	*	—	—
	23	128	6.8	0.27	(827,0.2%) (896,0.5%)	12	*	*	—	—
	23	145	7.05	0.27	(1138,0.2%) (1207,0.5%)	11	*	*	—	—
	23	162	7.3	0.28	(1345,0.2%) (1482,0.5%)	10	*	*	—	—

continued

Material	$T/\mathrm{°C}$	E_{T}	ρ	ν	(σ, ε)	α	k	γ	ρ_{E}	K_{IC}
FLNC-4405 (Sintered at 1260 ℃)	23	—	6.8	0.26	(655, 0.2%) (755, 1.3%)	12	*	*	—	—
	23	—	7.0	0.27	(745, 0.2%) (933, 1.8%)	12	*	*	—	—
	23	—	7.15	0.27	(780, 0.2%) (980, 1.9%)	12	*	*	—	—
FLNC-4405 (Sintered at 1120 ℃)	23	—	6.76	—	(510, 0.2%) (635, 1.3%)	—	*	*	—	—
	23	—	7.0	—	(565, 0.2%) (740, 1.5%)	—	*	*	—	—
	23	—	7.1	—	(615, 0.2%) (795, 1.6%)	—	*	*	—	—
FLNC-4408 (Sintered at 1260 ℃)	23	—	6.77	—	(745, 0.2%) (855, 1.4%)	—	*	*	—	—
	23	—	6.99	—	(850, 0.2%) (975, 1.4%)	—	*	*	—	—
	23	—	7.09	—	(880, 0.2%) (1035, 1.3%)	—	*	*	—	—
FLNC-4408 (Sintered at 1120 ℃)	23	—	6.78	—	(550, 0.2%) (635, 1.2%)	—	*	*	—	—
	23	—	6.98	—	(625, 0.2%) (710, 1.2%)	—	*	*	—	—
	23	—	7.08	—	(677, 0.2%) (790, 1.3%)	—	*	*	—	—
FN-0205 (AS; Fe-2Cu-0.5C)	23	125	6.9	0.25	(205, 0.2%) (345, 2.5%)	—	*	*	—	—
	23	165	7.4	0.25	(275, 0.2%) (480, 5.5%)	—	*	*	—	—

continued

Material	$T/℃$	E_T	ρ	ν	(σ,ε)	α	k	γ	ρ_E	K_{IC}
FN-0208 (AS; Fe-2Ni-0.8C)	23	86	5.8	0.25	(241,0.2%) (310,1%)	—	*	*	—	—
	23	114	6.3	0.25	(276,0.2%) (379,1%)	—	*	*	—	—
	23	121	6.7	0.25	(310,0.2%) (483,1%)	—	*	*	—	—
	23	155	7.2	0.28	(345,0.2%) (552,1%)	—	*	*	—	—
	23	169	7.4	0.28	(379,0.2%) (621,1%)	—	*	*	—	—
FN-0208 (HT; Fe-2Ni-0.8C)	23	121	6.7	0.25	(552,0.2%) (621,1%)	—	*	*	—	—
	23	134	6.9	0.25	(724,0.2%) (827,1%)	—	*	*	—	—
	23	141	7.0	0.25	(896,0.2%) (1000,1%)	—	*	*	—	—
	23	155	7.2	0.28	(1034,0.2%) (1172,1%)	—	*	*	—	—
	23	169	7.4	0.28	(1241,0.2%) (1345,1%)	—	*	*	—	—
FN-0405 (AS)	23	135	6.9	0.25	(275,0.2%) (415,3%)	—	*	*	—	—
	23	165	7.4	0.25	(345,0.2%) (620,4.5%)	—	*	*	—	—
FN-0408 (AS)	23	125	6.9	0.25	(345,0.2%) (450,1%)	—	*	*	—	—
Fe-0.85Mo-1.5 Cu-1.75Ni-0.6 Graphite	23	121	6.7	0.25	(526,0.2%) (650,1%) (774, 1.83%)	12	*	*	—	—

Notes：Bushings＝FC-0208 & FN-0208；

Gears＝FLN2-4405 HT & FLN4-4405 HT；

HT＝Heat treated, Mainly Q & T；

AS＝As sintered；

PF＝Powder forged；

* ＝Thermal conductivity (k) and specific heat capacity (γ) of powder steel can be；

rationalized by the proportionality of the density ratio of the compacted powder preform to its bulk counterpart.

Table 75.2 Fatigue ε-N Properties of Powder Steels

Spec.(Density)	$T/°C$	$\mathrm{d}\varepsilon/\mathrm{d}t$	σ_f'	ε_f'	b	c	K'	n'	$\sigma_f@2N_f$	R
F-0005 (AS):										
Density = 6.9	23	—	—	—	—	—	—	—	95@ 10^7	—
Density = 7.0	23	—	—	—	—	—	—	—	150@ 10^7	—
FN-0408(AS) Density = 6.9	23	—	—	—	—	—	—	—	170@ 10^7	—
FC-0205 (AS):										
Density = 6.9	23	—	1095	0.094	−0.111	−0.7	1612	0.164	130@ 10^7	—
Density = 7.4	23	—	1249	0.078	−0.123	−0.5	2338	0.246	185@ 10^7	—
FC-0208 (AS) [Abedin]:										
Density = 5.8	23	—	—	—	—	—	—	—	70@ 10^7	—
Density = 6.32	23	—	503	—	−0.108	—	7927	0.488	82@ 10^7 173@ 10^4	—
Density = 6.62	23	—	670	—	−0.108	—	5695	0.402	110@ 10^7	—
Density = 6.94	23	—	837	—	−0.107	—	3467	0.316	138@ 10^7 290@ 10^4	—
Density = 7.2	23	—	—	—	—	—	—	—	228@ 10^7	—
FC-0208 (HT):										
Density = 6.1	23	—	—	—	—	—	—	—	172@ 10^7	—
Density = 6.4	23	—	—	—	—	—	—	—	207@ 10^7	—
Density = 6.8	23	—	—	—	—	—	—	—	241@ 10^7	—
Density = 7.1	23	—	—	—	—	—	—	—	276@ 10^7	—
FN-0205 (AS):										
Density = 7.1	23	—	770	0.28	−0.153	−0.7	1003	0.207	—	—
Density = 7.4	23	—	852	0.096	−0.103	−0.5	1371	0.203	—	—
FN-0208 (AS):										
Density = 5.8	23	—	—	—	—	—	—	—	110@ 10^7	—
Density = 6.3	23	—	—	—	—	—	—	—	138@ 10^7	—

continued

Spec. (Density)	$T/°C$	$d\varepsilon/dt$	σ'_f	ε'_f	b	c	K'	n'	$\sigma_f @ 2N_f$	R
Density = 6.7	23	—	—	—	—	—	—	—	172@ 10^7	—
Density = 7.2	23	—	—	—	—	—	—	—	193@ 10^7	—
Density = 7.4	23	—	—	—	—	—	—	—	235@ 10^7	—
FN-0208 (HT):										
Density = 6.7	23	—	—	—	—	—	—	—	200@ 10^7	—
Density = 6.9	23	—	—	—	—	—	—	—	262@ 10^7	—
Density = 7.0	23	—	—	—	—	—	—	—	317@ 10^7	—
Density = 7.2	23	—	—	—	—	—	—	—	372@ 10^7	—
Density = 7.4	23	—	—	—	—	—	—	—	428@ 10^7	—
FC-0405 (AS):										
Density = 6.9	23	—	—	—	—	—	—	—	160@ 10^7	—
Density = 7.4	23	—	—	—	—	—	—	—	235@ 10^7	—
FN-0408										
Density = 6.9	23	—	—	—	—	—	—	—	170@ 10^7	—
Density = 7.4	23	—	—	—	—	—	—	—	235@ 10^7	—
FL-4405 (AS):										
Density = 7.46	23	—	834	0.106	−0.102	−0.5	1071	0.1573	—	—
FL-4405 (HT):										
Density = 7.46	23	—	1727	—	−0.141	—	—	—	—	—
FL-5305 (AS)	23	—	3265	—	−0.177	—	—	—	—	—
Density = 7.1	23	—	3265	—	−0.177	—	—	—	—	—
FL-5305 (HT):										
Density = 6.6	23	—	—	—	—	—	—	—	159@ 10^7	—
Density = 6.8	23	—	—	—	—	—	—	—	221@ 10^7	—
Density = 7.0	23	—	—	—	—	—	—	—	283@ 10^7	—

continued

Spec. (Density)	$T/^{\circ}C$	$d\varepsilon/dt$	σ_f'	ε_f'	b	c	K'	n'	$\sigma_f@2N_f$	R
Density = 7.2	23	—	—	—	—	—	—	—	345@ 10^7	—
FLNC-4408 (Sintered at 1120 ℃) :										
Density = 7.1	23	—	—	—	—	—	—	—	307@ 10^7	—
Density = 7.2	23	—	—	—	—	—	—	—	318@ 10^7	—
FLNC-4408 (Sintered at 1260 ℃) :										
Density = 7.1	23	—	—	—	—	—	—	—	372@ 10^7	—
FLN2-4400 (AS ; Sintered at 1120 ℃) :										
Density = 7.4	23	—	819	0.063	−0.089	−0.5	1300	0.177	217@ 10^7	—
FLN2-4400C (Sintered at 1120 ℃) :										
Density = 7.4	23	—	2561	—	−0.136	—	—	—	—	—
FLN2-4405 (AS) :										
Density = 7.11	23	—	728	0.017	−0.114	−0.3	2960	0.34	—	—
FLN2-4405 (HT) :										
Density = 6.6	23	—	—	—	—	—	—	—	221@ 10^7	—
Density = 6.8	23	—	—	—	—	—	—	—	283@ 10^7	—
Density = 7.1	23	—	—	—	—	—	—	—	345@ 10^7	—
Density = 7.3	23	—	—	—	—	—	—	—	407@ 10^7	—
FLN4-4405 (HT) :										
Density = 6.6	23	—	—	—	—	—	—	—	179@ 10^7	—
Density = 6.8	23	—	—	—	—	—	—	—	255@ 10^7	—
Density = 7.1	23	—	—	—	—	—	—	—	338@ 10^7	—
Density = 7.3	23	—	—	—	—	—	—	—	434@ 10^7	—
FLN2-4408 (PF) :										
Density = 7.8	23	—	725	1.11	−0.042	−0.7	776	0.074	221@ 10^7	—
Fe-0.5Mo−...	23	—	—	—	—	—	—	—	145@ 10^7	—

continued

Spec.(Density)	$T/℃$	$\mathrm{d}\varepsilon/\mathrm{d}t$	σ_{f}'	$\varepsilon_{\mathrm{f}}'$	b	c	K'	n'	$\sigma_{\mathrm{f}}@2N_{\mathrm{f}}$	R
Fe-0.85Mo-1.5Cu-1.75Ni-0.6 Graphite	23	—	—	—	—	—	—	—	175@ 10^7	—
PM(Conrod)	23	—	1093	0.20	−0.103	−0.53	2005	0.192	282@ 10^7	—

Notes：HT＝Heat Treated, Mainly Q & T；

　　　　AS＝As Sintered；

　　　　PF＝Powder Forge.

Chapter 76

Fe (Ferrous)-Strip Steels

76.1 Introduction

General strip steels generally accepted that the transition from mild steel to high strength steel occurs at a yield strength of about 210 MPa. For yield strength levels below 350 MPa, a simple C-Mn (carbon-manganese) steel is typically used. The composition of these steels is similar to low-carbon plain steels, except they have more carbon and manganese to increase the strength to the desired level. This approach is not usually practical for steels with yield strengths greater than 350 MPa because of a drop-off in elongation and weldability. Other alloying elements are thus used. Strip steels are generally denoted by yield strength with the following notations (SAE SAE J1442):

A: C and Mn as alloying elements;
B: C, Mn, and N as alloying elements;
C: C, Mn, and P as alloying elements;
F: Sulfide inclusion controlled, as killed (i.e. made to a fine grain practice);
K: Killed, i.e. made to a fine grain practice;
L: Low carbon content as C<0.13%;
W: Weathering composition, with Si, P, Cu, Ni, and Cr as optional alloying elements.

Since drawability declines progressively with increasing yield strength, forming limit curves may be used to define maximum strains without necking for different deformation paths.

Strip steels, in forms of plates and bars, are characterized by their special mechanical properties as obtained through special mechanical rolling processes under temperature control, not intended for any heat treatment in practice. Their material properties are quite thickness-dependent. They can be classified into the following groups according to applications:

(a) Structural steels;
(b) Strip steels for pressure vessels, boilers, and pipings;
(c) Rolled Homogeneous Armor (RHA) steel.

76.2 Structural Steels

Structural steels are strip steels produced in a wide range of forms, including plate, sheet, bar, and direct structural shapes for construction.

76.2.1   Structural Steels for Automobiles

Structural steels in automotive applications are generally of high strength to weight ratio, and weldable. Mechanical properties of structural steels used in the automotive industry (e.g. truck chassis and frames) are listed in Table 76.1. Their fatigue properties are given in Table 76.3.

One group of specialty structural steels used in USA is called HSLA (High Strength Low Alloy), of which the alloying elements are generally less than 5% namely according to SAE J1392. HSLA steels contain a low level of carbon (0.05% ~ 0.25% C) and up to 2% manganese. They are generally in sheet or plate form. Small quantities of chromium, nickel, molybdenum, copper, nitrogen, vanadium, niobium, titanium, and zirconium are used in various combinations in order to have adequate formability and weldability. HSLA steels are not only lighter than carbon steels with the same mechanical properties but also have better corrosion resistance.

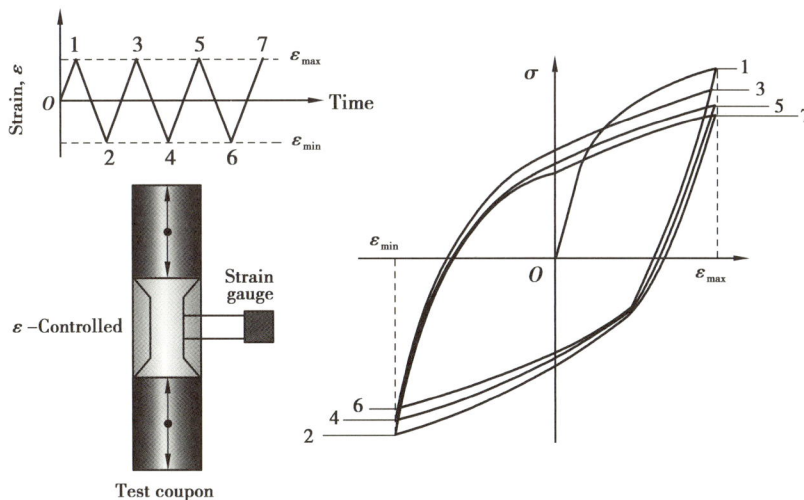

Fig. 76.1   Cyclic Softening of HSLA Steel during Strain-Controlled Fatigue Test (Courtesy of Dr. Steve Tipton, University of Tulsa, Arizona, USA)

Most HSLA steels are furnished in the as-hot-rolled condition with ferritic-pearlitic microstructure. The two exceptions are the controlled-rolled steels with an acicular ferrite microstructure and the dual-phase steels with martensite dispersed in a matrix of polygonal ferrite (detailed in the next chapter).

Because of their high endurance limits, HSLA steels are particularly well-suited to parts subject to fatigue loading. Nevertheless, the cyclic softening of an HSLA steel corresponding to a reduction in the yield strength as shown in Fig. 76.1 was reported by [Tipton]. The stable form of hysteresis loops eventually reaches a steady condition, termed as "cyclic stabilization" of the material. In the conventional low-cycle axial fatigue tests conducted on the HSLA material, cyclic stabilization appears to occur when the accumulated fatigue damage is within 20% to 40% of expended cycle life.

High strength low alloy (HSLA) steels are by far the most widely utilized metallic materials. When HSLA steels come with low carbon content but contain Nb, V, and Ti and they are called micro-alloyed high strength low alloy (HSLA) steels. The mechanical properties of hot rolled HSLA steels and their excellent cold-forming performance and low-temperature brittle fracture resistance support cost-effective solutions for many parts and sub-assemblies, for which weight, thickness and size reduction are sought such as vehicle chassis components, wheels, slide rails, and cross members. Truck frame rails are commonly made of high strength low alloy (HSLA) or heat-treated steels.

76.2.2 Structural Steels for Pressure Vessels and Boilers

Mechanical properties of structural steels for pressure vessels and boilers, and pipings are listed in Table 76.2. Oxidation, creep, and corrosion are of great concern to pressure vessels and boiler steels. General HSLA steels are restricted to the maximum operating temperature of 400 ℃, while Cr-, Mo-, and Nb-alloyed steels display favorable scaling and creep resistance properties at a high operating temperature of 500 ℃. Material properties of typical pressure vessels and boilers are given in Table 76.2. Again, material properties are thickness-dependent and affected by heat treatment and forming operations.

76.2.3 Shipbuilding

DH 32 (BV) is the most exclusively utilized structural steel in ship-buildings and offshore platforms. The typical material composition is Fe-0.18C-0.3Si-1.35Mn-0.035P-0.035S-0.35Cu 0.4Ni-0.2Cr-0.08Mo-0.075V-0.015Al-0.02Ti-0.035Nb.

76.2.4 RHA (Rolled Homogeneous Armor)

RHA steel has been developed traditionally for armor vehicle bodies.

76.3 Structural Steels as Practiced in Europe

Naming of structural steels addressed in European standard is straightforward, such as S+yield strength (MPa)+Minor Chemical Composition Variation. Generally,

Notation	Meaning
S	Structural steel
355	The minimum yield strength (MPa), tested at a thickness of 16 mm
J2/K2/JR/JO	Material toughness, resulting from Charpy impact or "V" notch tests
W	Weathering Steel (Atmospheric Corrosion Resistant)
Z	Structural steel with improved strength perpendicular to the surface
C	Cold-formed

For example, S355K2W is a structural steel that has been hardened (K2) and designed with a chemical composition to withstand increased weathering (W).

76.4   Welding

On welding, in order to restore the fatigue strength of base metal adjacent to welds in areas subjected to severe cyclic loading, a post-weld treatment such as TIG (Gas Tungsten Arc) melting, hammering, peening or grinding should be applied to weld toes.

76.5   Surface Protection

Electrogalvanized, galvannealed, and extragal coatings are three levels of surface protection against corrosion. Galvanizing (i. e. electrogalvanizing), using Zn-based coating, produced essentially no changes in tensile or fatigue properties of the base strip steels except in the extreme low-cycle fatigue regime where galvanizing caused a reduction in the fatigue ductility coefficient, ε'_f [Risbeck].

76.6   Fatigue Crack Growth of Strip Steels

Material parameters on fatigue crack growth of strip steels are given in Table 76.4.

References

ALKHADER M, BODELOT L, 2011. Large Strain Mechanical Behavior of HSLA-100 Steel Over a Wide Range of Strain Rates[J]. Journal of Engineering Materials and Technology, 134(1): 011005.

BASAN R, 2011. Estimation of Cyclic Stress-strain Curves for Low-Alloy Steel from Hardness[J]. Metalurgija, 49(2): 83-86.

CHEN J, YOUNG B, 2008. Design of High Strength Steel Columns at Elevated Temperatures[J]. Journal of Construction Steel Research, 64(6): 689-703.

CHINARAJ, 2011. Effect of Bolt Hole Residual Stresses on Fatigue Performance of Truck Frame Rail Structures [J]. Applied Mechanics of Materials, 300-301: 1089-1098.

CHOUNG J M, CHO S R, 2008. Study on True Stress Correction from Tensile Test[J]. Journal of Mechanical Science and Technology, 22(16): 1039-1051.

HUA S K, et al, 2001. Effect of Tempering Temperatures on the Mechanical Properties and Microstructures of HSLA-100 Type Copper-Bearing Steels[J]. Material Science and Engineering, A, 318(1-2): 197-210.

EWING K, et al, 1980. Fatigue of Welded High Strength Low Alloy Steels[J]. SAE 800374.

FEKETE J, STIBICH A, SHI M, 2001. A Comparison of the Response of HSLA and Dual Phase Sheet Steel in Dynamic Crush[J]. SAE 2001-01-3101.

GORAL T, et al, 2005. Automotive Front End Structures Constructed by Over Molding Hydroform Metal Tubes to Engineering Thermoplastic Structures[J]. SAE 2005-01-1680.

KUNDE N D, MICHAI G M, PAYER J H, 1997. Performance Evaluation of Prephosphated Galvannealed Steel Sheet for Automotive Applications[J]. SAE 970152.

MÄKELÄINEN P, OUTINEN J, KESTI J, 1998. Fire Design Models for Structural Steel S420M Based upon Transient State Tensile Test Results[J]. Journal of Constructional Steel Research, 48(1): 47-57.

MI C, et al, 2012. Frame Fatigue Life Assessment of a Mining Dump Truck Based on Finite Element Method and Multibody Dynamic Analysis[J]. Engineering Failure Analysis, 23(4): 18-26.

OUTINEN J, MAKELAINEN P, 2002. Mechanical Properties of Structural Steel at Elevated Temperatures and after Cooling Down[J]. The 2nd International Workshop-Structures in Fire, Christchurch, (2002): 1103-1100.

PEREIRA H F, et al, 2009. Cyclic and Fatigue Behavior of the P355NL1 Steel under Block Loading[J]. Journal of Pressure Vessel Technology, 131(2): 021210.

RISBECK T, 1978. The Effect of Galvanizing on the Fatigue Characteristics of an HSLA Steel[J]. SAE 780042.

SHERMAN M, 1975. Fatigue Properties of High Strength Low Alloy Steels[J]. Metallurgical Transactions, A, 6: 1035-1040.

SINHA S, GHOSH S, 2006. Modeling Cyclic Ratcheting Based Fatigue Life of HSLA Steels Using Crystal Plasticity FEM Simulation and Experiments[J]. International Journal of Fatigue, 28: 1690-1704.

TAKAGI S, et al, 2005. Stress-Strain Curves of High Strength Steel Sheets at Strain Rates from 10-3 to 103/S Obtained With Various Types of Tensile Testing Machines[J]. SAE 2005-01-0494.

TIWARI S, DUBEY A, 2011. FEA Based Durability Evaluation of HD Tipper Chassis and Cab Through Correlated Transient and Fatigue Analysis[J]. SAE 2011-26-0013.

VALLEJO R, 2008. Full Frame Fatigue Test on Heavy Trucks and Their Set up Using Finite Element Simulation [J]. SAE 2008-01-2667.

XU W, et al, 2013. Tensile and Fatigue Properties of Fiber Laser Welded High Strength Low Alloy and DP980 Dual-Phase Steel Joints[J]. Materials and Design, 43: 373-383.

Table 76.1　Mechanical Properties of Structural Steels

Material	$T/$℃	E_T	ρ	ν	(σ,ε)	α	k	γ	ρ_E	K_{IC}
SAE J 1392:										
HSLA 260/340 (CD; HC260LA)	23	200	7.8	0.29	(260,0.2%) (340,28%)	11	38	490	—	—
HSLA 280/360 (CD; HC280LA)	23	200	7.8	0.29	(280,0.2%) (360, 27%)	11	38	490	—	—
HSLA 300/390 (CD; HC300LA)	23	200	7.8	0.29	(300,0.2%) (390,26%)	11	38	490	—	—
HSLA 310/410 (CD; HC310LA)	23	200	7.8	0.29	(310,0.2%) (410, 24%)	11	38	490	—	—
HSLA 350/420 (CD; HC350LA)	23	200	7.8	0.29	(350,0.2%) (425,5%) (490, 10%) (530, 20%)	1138	490	—	—	—
HSLA 380 CD (CD; HC380LA)	23	200	7.8	0.29	(380,0.2%) (460, 20%)	11	38	490	—	—
HSLA 420/470 (CD; HC420LA)	23	200	7.8	0.29	(420,0.2%) (470,17%)	11	38	490	—	—
HSLA 475/545 (CD; ASTM A500)	23	200	7.8	0.29	(475,0.2%) (545,14%)	11	38	490	—	—
HSLA 240/310 (HR; S240MC)	23	200	7.8	0.29	(240,0.2%) (310, 28%)	11	38	490	—	—

continued

Material	$T/℃$	E_T	ρ	ν	(σ,ε)	α	k	γ	ρ_E	K_{IC}
HSLA 280/340 (HR; S280MC)	23	200	7.8	0.29	(280,0.2%) (340, 27%)	11	38	490	—	—
HSLA 310 HR (HR; S310MC)	23	200	7.8	0.29	(310,0.2%) (380, 24%)	11	38	490	—	—
HSLA 320/410 (HR; S320MC)	23	200	7.8	0.29	(320,0.2%) (410, 24%)	11	38	490	—	—
HSLA 340/430 (HR; S340MC)	23	200	7.8	0.29	(340,0.2%) (420,5%) (490, 10%) (530, 22%)	11	38	490	—	—
HSLA 350/450 (HR; S350MC)	23	200	7.83	0.29	(350,0.2%)	11	38	490	—	—
	300	—	—	—	(562,22.3%) (260,0.2%) (350, 10%)	—	—	—	—	—
	500	—	—	—	(180,0.2%) (230, 10%)	—	—	—	—	—
	600	—	—	—	(130,0.2%) (140, 10%)	—	—	—	—	—
	700	—	—	—	(60,0.2%) (70, 10%)	—	—	—	—	—
HSLA 360/470 (HR; S360MC)	23	200	7.8	0.29	(360,0.2%) (470, 22%)	11	38	490	—	—
HSLA 410/500 (HR; S410MC)	23	200	7.8	0.29	(410,0.2%) (510,26%)	11	38	490	—	—
HSLA 420/510 (HR; S420MC)	23	200	7.83	0.29	(420,0.2%) (620, 21.5%)	11	38	490	—	—
HSLA 460/550 (HR; S460MC)	23	200	7.8	0.29	(460,0.2%) (550, 21%)	11	38	490	—	—
HSLA 480/560 (HR; S480MC)	23	200	7.8	0.29	(480,0.2%) (604, 28%)	11	38	490	—	—

continued

Material	$T/℃$	E_T	ρ	ν	(σ,ε)	α	k	γ	ρ_E	K_{IC}
HSLA 490/600 (HR; S490MC)	23	200	7.83	0.29	(490,0.2%) (735, 20%)	11	38	490	—	—
HSLA 500/620 (HR; S500MC)	23	200	7.8	0.29	(500,0.2%) (620, 19%)	11	38	490	—	—
HSLA 550/650 (HR; S550MC)	23	200	7.8	0.29	(550,0.2%) (700,3%) (710,5%) (786, 13%)	11	38	490	—	—
HSLA 600/680 (HR; S600MC)	23	200	7.8	0.29	(600,0.2%) (786, 10%)	12	49	461	—	—
HSLA 710/790	23	200	7.8	0.29	(710,0.2%) (790, 19%)	12	49	461	—	—
SAE J 1442 HR (*Named after Yield Strength*):										
290A	23	200	7.8	0.29	(290,0.2%) (415, 20%)	11	38	490	—	—
345A	23	200	7.8	0.29	(345,0.2%) (450, 18%)	11	38	490	—	—
415A	23	200	7.8	0.29	(415,0.2%) (515,16%)	11	38	490	—	—
450A	23	200	7.8	0.29	(450,0.2%) (550, 15%)	11	38	490	—	—
345W	23	200	7.8	0.29	(345,0.2%) (485, 18%)	11	38	490	—	—
	−50	—	—	—	—	—	—	—	—	64
350WT	23	200	7.8	0.29	(350,0.2%) (461, 13%)	11	38	490	—	72
440W	23	200	7.8	0.29	(440,0.2%)	11	38	490	—	—
485W (Longitudinal)	23	200	7.8	0.29	(485,0.2%) (700, 13%)	11	38	490	—	—
485W (Longitudinal)	23	200	7.8	0.29	(485,0.2%) (550, 10%)	11	38	490	—	—

continued

Material	$T/℃$	E_T	ρ	ν	(σ, ε)	α	k	γ	ρ_E	K_{IC}
440C	23	200	7.8	0.29	(440, 0.2%)	10	24	490	—	22
	400(High service temperature)									
345F	23	200	7.8	0.29	(345, 0.2%) (415, 20%)	11	38	490	—	—
415F	23	200	7.8	0.29	(415, 0.2%) (515, 17%)	11	38	490	—	—
485F	23	200	7.8	0.29	(485, 0.2%) (550, 14%)	11	38	490	—	—
550F	23	200	7.8	0.29	(550, 0.2%) (620, 12%)	11	38	490	—	—
DH32 (BV)(Fe-0.14C-0.28Si-1.06 Mn-0.012P-0.003 S-003Cu-0.02Ni-0.03Cr-0.01Mo; Choung & Cho)	23	200	7.8	0.29	(355, 0.2%) (640, 10%) (600, 20%) (710, 40%) (800, 60%) (1000, 100%)	11	38	490	—	—
A36 (ASTM; General-purpose)	23	200	7.8	0.26	(240, 0.2%) (414, 23%)	11	38	490	—	—
European Standard:										
S235	23	200	7.8	0.26	(235, 0.2%) $\sigma_{uts} = 435$	11	38	490	—	—
S275	23	200	7.8	0.26	(275, 0.2%) $\sigma_{uts} = 450$	11	38	490	—	—
S355	23	205	7.8	0.26	(355, 0.2%) (385, 1%) (397, 2%) (506, 24%)	11	38	490	—	—
	300	170	—	—	—	—	—	—	—	—
	600	60	—	—	—	—	—	—	—	—
	700	30	—	—	—	—	—	—	—	—
	800	20	—	—	—	—	—	—	—	—

continued

Material	$T/{}^\circ\text{C}$	E_T	ρ	ν	(σ,ε)	α	k	γ	ρ_E	K_IC
S350GD+Z	23	200	7.8	0.26	(350,0.2%) (375,1%) (405,2%) (470,24%)	11	38	490	—	—
S355J2H	23	205	7.8	0.26	(355,0.2%) (520,1%) (540,2%) (600,24%)	11	38	490	—	—
	500	126	—	—	(250,0.2%) (268,0.5%) $\sigma_\text{uts}=350$	—	—	—	—	—
	600	65	—	—	(117,0.2%) $\sigma_\text{uts}=172$	—	—	—	—	—
	700	27.3	—	—	(50,0.2%) (90,1%) (105,2%)	—	—	—	—	—
S420M	23	205	7.8	0.26	(420,0.2%) (437,1%) (457,2%) (555,20%)	11	38	490	—	—
S460M	23	209	7.8	0.26	(451,0.2%) (445,1%) (440,2%) (563,17%)	11	38	490	—	—
UNS N06617 (Alloy 617)	23	200	7.8	0.29	(314,0.2%) (768,54%)	11	38	490	—	—
	650	—	7.8	0.29	(209,0.2%) (584,59%)	11	38	490	—	—
	750	—	7.8	0.29	(208,0.2%) (406,54%)	11	38	490	—	—
	850	—	7.8	0.29	(186,0.2%) (216,95%)	11	38	490	—	—
	950	—	7.8	0.29	(119,0.2%) (124,78%)	11	38	490	—	—

continued

Material		$T/°C$	E_T	ρ	ν	(σ,ε)	α	k	γ	ρ_E	K_{IC}
UNS N08810 (Alloy 800H)		23	200	7.8	0.29	(234,0.2%) (553,43%)	11	38	490	—	—
		650	—	7.8	0.29	(146,0.2%) (407,26%)	11	38	490	—	—
		750	—	7.8	0.29	(140,0.2%) (234,37%)	11	38	490	—	—
		850	—	7.8	0.29	(100,0.2%) (109,58%)	11	38	490	—	—
RHA-	Class I	23	210	7.8	0.28	(980,0.2%) (1078,11%)	11	38	490	—	—
	Class II	23	210	7.8	0.28	(784,0.2%) (882,15%)	11	38	490	—	—

Notes: H = Hot-formed;

HR = Hot-rolled;

CD = Cold-drawn;

Q & T = Quenched and tempered;

HSLA = High Strength Low Alloy (SAE J1392 JUN 84);

RHA = Rolled homogeneous armor steel for military applications;

A = C and Mn as alloying elements;

B = C, Mn, and N as alloying elements;

C = C, Mn, and P as alloying elements;

F = Sulfide inclusion controlled, as killed (i.e. made to a fine grain practice);

K = Killed, i.e. made to a fine grain practice;

L = Low carbon content as $C<0.13\%$;

W = Weathering composition, with Si, P, Cu, Ni, and Cr as optional alloying elements;

$(\sigma_{ucs}, \sigma_{ucs})\cdots(\sigma_{uts}, \varepsilon_{uts})$ = True stress-strain data; positive-tension, negative-compression.

Table 76.2　Mechanical Properties of Pressure Vessel and Boiler Steels, and Pipings

Material	$T/°C$	E_T	ρ	ν	(σ,ε)	α	k	γ	ρ_E	K_{IC}
P265GH ($h<16$ mm; Normalized)	23	200	7.8	0.29	(265,0.2%) (470, 22%)	11	—	490	—	—
P265GH ($60<h<100$ mm; Normalized)	23	200	7.8	0.29	(215,0.2%) (470, 22%)	11	—	490	—	—

continued

Material	$T/℃$	E_T	ρ	ν	(σ,ε)	α	k	γ	ρ_E	K_{IC}
P265GH(150<h<250 mm)	23	200	7.8	0.29	(185,0.2%) (460, 22%)	11	—	490	—	—
P355NH (h<16 mm)	23	200	7.8	0.29	(355,0.2%)	11	—	490	—	—
	200	—	—	—	(275,0.2%)	—	—	—	—	—
	400	—	—	—	(202,0.2%)	—	—	—	—	—
P355NH(16<h<40 mm)	23	200	7.8	0.29	(345,0.2%)	11	—	490	—	—
	200	—	—	—	(267,0.2%)	—	—	—	—	—
	400	—	—	—	(196,0.2%)	—	—	—	—	—
P355NH(40<h<60 mm)	23	200	7.8	0.29	(335,0.2%)	11	—	490	—	—
	200	—	—	—	(259,0.2%)	—	—	—	—	—
	400	—	—	—	(190,0.2%)	—	—	—	—	—
P355NH(60<h<100 mm)	23	200	7.8	0.29	(315,0.2%)	11	—	490	—	—
	200	—	—	—	(244,0.2%)	—	—	—	—	—
	400	—	—	—	(179,0.2%)	—	—	—	—	—
P355NH(100<h<150 mm)	23	200	7.8	0.29	(305,0.2%)	11	—	490	—	—
	200	—	—	—	(236,0.2%)	—	—	—	—	—
	400	—	—	—	(173,0.2%)	—	—	—	—	—
P355NH(150<h<160 mm)	23	200	7.8	0.29	(355,0.2%)	11	—	490	—	—
	200	—	—	—	(2280.2%)	—	—	—	—	—
	400	—	—	—	(167,0.2%)	—	—	—	—	—
P355GH, or P355N, or P355NL1	0	—	—	—	(360,0.2%)	—	—	—	—	—
	23	200	7.8	0.29	(355,0.2%)	11	—	490	—	—
	200	—	—	—	(290,0.2%)	—	—	—	—	—
	450	—	—	—	(195,0.2%)	—	—	—	—	—

continued

Material	$T/℃$	E_T	ρ	ν	(σ,ε)	α	k	γ	ρ_E	K_{IC}
P690Q（or P690QH，or P690QL1，or P690QL2）	0	—	—	—	(700,0.2%)	—	—	—	—	—
	23	200	7.8	0.29	(690,0.2%)	11	—	490	—	—
	200	—	—	—	(630,0.2%)	—	—	—	—	—
	420	—	—	—	(530,0.2%)	—	—	—	—	—
15NiCuMoNb5 （WB36）	0	—	—	—	(470,0.2%)	—	—	—	—	—
	23	200	7.8	0.29	(460,0.2%)	11	—	490	—	—
	200	—	—	—	(410,0.2%)	—	—	—	—	—
	470	—	—	—	(330,0.2%)	—	—	—	—	—
13CrMo4-5/-4	0	—	—	—	(300,0.2%)	—	—	—	—	—
	23	200	7.8	0.29	(295,0.2%)	11	—	490	—	—
	200	—	—	—	(275,0.2%)	—	—	—	—	—
	500	—	—	—	(160,0.2%)	—	—	—	—	—
10CrMo9-10	0	—	—	—	(310,0.2%)	—	—	—	—	—
	23	200	7.8	0.29	(295,0.2%)	11	—	490	—	—
	200	—	—	—	(245,0.2%)	—	—	—	—	—
	420	—	—	—	(170,0.2%)	—	—	—	—	—
16Mo3	0	—	—	—	(280,0.2%)	—	—	—	—	—
	23	200	7.8	0.29	(275,0.2%)	11	—	490	—	—
	200	—	—	—	(250,0.2%)	—	—	—	—	—
	500	—	—	—	(140,0.2%)	—	—	—	—	—
X20	23	206	7.83	0.29	(490,0.2%) (690,17%)	—	—	—	—	—
X60	23	206	7.83	0.29	(523,0.2%) (609,44%)	—	—	—	—	—
X70	23	206	7.83	0.29	(529,0.2%) (650,45%)	—	—	—	—	—

Table 76.3   Fatigue ε-N Properties of Strip Steels

Material	$T/°C$	$d\varepsilon/dt$	σ'_f	ε'_f	b	c	K'	n'	$\sigma_f @ 2N_f$	R
HSLA 240/310	23	—	492	0.18	−0.094	−0.576	706	0.164	—	—
HSLA 350/450	23	—	860	1.92	−0.098	−0.668	671	0.133	203@ 10^7	—
HSLA 475/545(CD)	23	—	1170	0.95	−0.12	−0.61	1070	0.187	230@ 10^7	—
PN355NL1	23	—	841	0.3034	−0.081	−0.602	777	0.1068	300	—
440W	23	—	841	0.468	−0.105	−0.513	966	0.198	209@ 10^7	—
485W(Longitudinal)	23	—	851	0.775	−0.07	−0.7	690	0.058	300@ 10^7	—
485W(Transverse)	23	—	741	1.917	−0.052	−0.83	956	0.113	265@ 10^7	—
Steel (Generic)	23	—	Eq. (6.14)	Eq. (6.15)	−0.09	−0.6	$\sigma'_f/(\varepsilon'_f)^{n'}$	b/c	Eq. (77.1)	—

Table 76.4   Material Parameters on Fatigue Crack Growth of Structural Steels in Opening Mode

Material	$T/°C$	σ_y	σ_{uts}	K_{IC}	$f(R)$	m	ΔK_{th}	Δ_{fat}
SAE 485W	23	485	600	—	$f(-1)=2.27\times10^{-10}$	3.26	—	—
		485	600	—	$f(0)=3.06\times10^{-10}$	3.12	—	—
		485	600	—	$f(0.5)=5.48\times10^{-9}$	3.14	—	—
Structural Steel (Generic)	23	—	—	—	$f(-1)=9.5\times10^{-12}$	3	6−4.56r (>2)	—

Notes: $\dfrac{da}{dN_p}=f(R)\,|\,\Delta K-\Delta K_{th}\,|^m$;

$\sigma_y(MPa)$ = Yield strength;

$\sigma_{uts}(MPa)$ = Ultimate tensile strength;

$f(R)$ = Parameter as a function of load ratio (R);

m = Exponent;

$\Delta K_{th}(MPa \cdot m^{\frac{1}{2}})$ = Threshold stress intensity factor range, $\Delta K_{th} \approx 6-4.5\ r$ and >2; or

$\Delta K_{th}(N \cdot mm^{-\frac{3}{2}})$ = Threshold stress intensity factor range, $\Delta K_{th} \approx 190-144\ r$ and >62;

r = Radius of notch;

$\Delta_{fat}(MPa)$ = Fatigue strength range.

Chapter 77

Sheet Steels

77.1   Introduction

Based on metallurgical designation, automotive sheet steels are divided into the following four categories [IISI]: ①low-strength steels, ②high-strength steels, ③advanced high strength steels, and ④others, including FB (ferritic-bainitic), TWIP (twinning-induced plasticity), HF (hot-formed), and post-forming heat treated steels. Mechanical properties and fatigue characteristics of sheet metals are presented in Tables 77.1 and 77.2, respectively.

77.2   Low Strength Sheet Steels

Mild and IF (interstitial free) steels fall into this category. Experimental results from fatigue tests of IF steels show that the fatigue limit is approximately corresponding to 40% of tensile strength and 80% of the yield strength of IF steels [Islam & Tomota].

B170P (P for Phosphorus) and SPCE steels have been used for outside and inner sedan doors, respectively.

77.3   High Strength Sheet Steels

Carbon & manganese-alloyed HSLA (high-strength low-alloy), BH (bake hardenable), and high strength IF (interstitial free) steels fall into this category.

77.4   Advanced High Strength Steel (AHSS)

AHSS (advanced high strength steel) is a family of steels with multi-phase microstructures that typifies the steel industry's response to automotive applications, including underbody, body panels, pillars, and other structural parts with sheet metals. The goal for IISI (International Iron and Steel Institute) to develop AHSS as new formable steels is to build ultra-light steel auto bodies, in response to the invasion of lightweight materials such as plastics and aluminum in the automotive body market. DP (dual phase), TRIP (transformation-induced plasticity), CP (complex phase), and MS (martensitic) steels fall into this category.

77.5   Ultra High Strength Steel (UHSS)

In hot stamping of UHSS (Ultra High Strength Steel), the blank is heated in a furnace to its austenitization temperature (about 900 ℃), formed in an internally cooled die set, and quenched under pressure at a minimum cooling rate of 27 ℃/s. This minimum cooling rate ensures the formation of martensitic microstructure in the part, which gives it a strength of about 1500 MPa.

The use of UHSS (ultrahigh-strength steel) in the automotive industry has increased in the last few years as manufacturers try to improve crash safety and reduce weight. Parts such as Bpillars, side impact reinforcement beams, and bumpers are increasingly manufactured from UHSS by hot stamping.

77.6   Boron Steels

Boron steel is also one kind of Ultra High Strength Steel (UHSS). Boron in its atomic state is added to steel through a specific heating procedure. Low-carbon high-boron may be used for enhancing the steel strength, decreasing cracking, and lowering the possibility of distortion. Boron steels are one of the strongest weldable materials. Boron steels (e. g. 22MnB5) are used for bumpers, A-pillar and B-pillar reinforcements, roof rails, and other safety components.

As taught by example, 22MnB5 boron steel is addressed here. It is a cold-rolled high-strength steel product with good ductility, suitable for products requiring formability in delivery conditions and high strength as a final product. The steel's strength and hardness are achieved by quench hardening after forming. If the homogenization temperature of low-carbon high-boron steel is less than 1000 ℃, the wear rate decreases with an increasing temperature. The wear rate does not display any obvious change, while the homogenization temperature exceeds 1000 ℃.

77.7   Flow Stress of Sheet Metals

Sheet metals of automotive body experience extreme strain-hardening rates as crash develops. The essential material properties include emissivity and flow stress as a function of temperature, strain, and strain rate. Also required are Young's modulus, Poisson's ratio, thermal conductivity, specific heat capacity, and coefficient of linear thermal expansion, each as a function of temperature. A quadratic term may be added to the flow stress of the Johnson-Cook constitutive equation for sheet metal of automotive body as follows:

$$\sigma = \left[A + B \left(\varepsilon_{eq}^{p} \right)^{n} \right] \left\{ 1 + C_1 \ln\left(\frac{d\varepsilon_{eq}^{p}}{dt} \right) + C_2 \left[\ln\left(\frac{d\varepsilon_{eq}^{p}}{dt} \right) \right]^{2} \right\} \left[1 + \left(\frac{T - T_{room}}{T_m - T_{room}} \right)^{m} \right] \quad (77.1)$$

Material parameters of the modified Johnson-Cook model for sheet metal of different grades are listed in Table 77.3 [Kang et al.]. A comparative study was carried out by [Yan et al.] on the plastic strain rate sensitivity of different high strength steels. The influence of strain rate on the stress-strain performance is demonstrated in Fig. 77. 1. The study indicates that the ultimate strengths of both DP and TRIP steels at a strain rate of 100/s are about 10% higher than under quasi-static loading conditions. A more pronounced effect is observed at strain rates above 100/s. The influence of environmental temperature on the stress-strain performance is also significant even in a small range of variation from −40 ℃ to 93 ℃, as shown in Fig. 77.2.

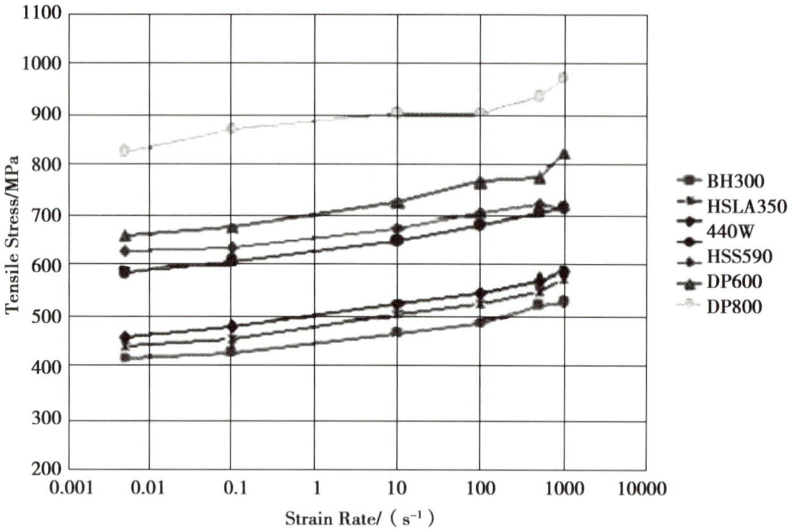

Fig. 77.1   Influence of Strain Rate on Ultimate Tensile Strength

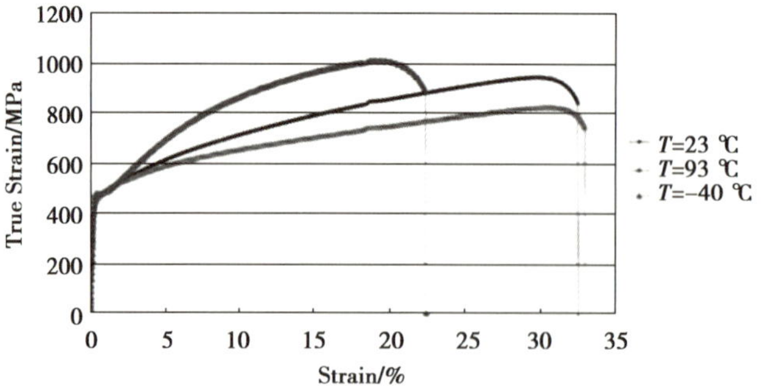

Fig. 77.2   Influence of Environmental Temperature on True Stress-Strain Curve of TRIP 800 Steel

References

ALTAN T, 2006. Hot-stamping Boron Alloyed Steels for Automotive Parts, part 1: Process Methods and Uses [J]. Stamping Journal, December: 40-41.

BLUMEL K W, GERLACH J, 1998. Biaxial Experimental Approach to Characterize Formability of Steel Sheet Metals[J]. SAE 980957.

CHEN F, LIAO Y, 2007. Analysis of Draw-Wall Wrinkling in the Stamping of a Motorcycle Oil Tank[J]. Journal of Materials Processing Technology, 192/193: 200-203.

CHOI K, et al, 2011. Loading Path Dependence of Forming Limit Diagram of a TRIP800 Steel[J]. SAE 2011-01-0019.

CORJETTE D, et al, 2005. Ultra High Strength FeMn TWIP Steels for Automotive Safety Parts[J]. SAE 2005-01-1327.

DUKUI K, et al, 1997. Development of High Strength Steels for Crashworthiness[J]. SAE 978421.

FISCHER F D, et al, 2000. A New View on Transformation Induced Plasticity (TRIP)[J]. International Journal of Plasticity, 16(7-8): 723-748.

FISCHER F D, SUN Q P, TANAKA K, 1996. Transformation-Induced Plasticity (TRIP)[J]. Applied Mechanics Reviews, 49(6): 317-364.

FLEHMIG T, et al, 2001. Thin Walled Steel Tube Prebending for Hydroformed Component-Bending Boundaries and Presentation of a New Mandrel Design[J]. SAE 2001-01-0642.

FU H, et al, 2009. Effect of Homogenization Temperature on Microstructure and Mechanical Properties of Low-carbon High-Boron Cast Steel[J]. Metals and Materials International, 15(3): 345-352.

GEIGER M, et al, 2005. A New Approach for Optimization of Sheet Metal Components[J]. Advanced Materials Research, 6-8: 255-262.

GERLACH J, BLUMEL K, KNEIPHOFF U, 1999. Material Aspects of Tube-hydroforming[J]. SAE 1999-01-3204.

GOKLU S, et al, 1999. The Influence of Corrosion and Fatigue Strength of Joined Components from Coated Steel Plate[J]. Materials and Corrosion, 50: 1.

HARIHARAN K, PRASKASH R, 2012. Modification of Fatigue Strain-Life Equation for Sheet Metals Considering Anisotropy due to Crystallographic Texture[J]. Fatigue and Fracture of Engineering Materials and Structures, 35(5): 458-465.

HARDELL J, KASSFELDT E, PRAKASH B, 2008. Friction and Wear Behavior of High Strength Boron Steel at Elevated Temperatures of up to 800 ℃[J]. Wear, 264(9-10): 788-799.

HEYER R H, NEWBY J R, 1968. Effects of Mechanical Properties of Biaxial Stretchability of Low Carbon Steels[J]. SAE 680094.

HILL S, KUHLMAN S, WANG K, et al, 2009. Bake-Hardening Effect of Dual Phase Steels[J]. SAE 2009-01-0796.

HILL R, HUTCHINSON J W, 1992. Differential Hardening in Sheet Metal under Biaxial Loading: A Theoretical Framework[J]. Journal of Applied Mechanics, 59: S1-S9.

HOSFORD W, DUNCAN J, 1999. Metal Forming-a Review[J]. Journal of Materials, 51(11): 39-44.

HOSHINO K, et al, 2011. Properties of a Newly Developed Galvannealed Steel Sheet with Modified Surface [J]. SAE 2011-01-1056.

HU X, et al, 2008. Numerical Analysis and Experimental Study on the Weld-line Movement of Tailor-welded Blank[J]. Advanced Materials Research, 97-101: 357-360.

ISLAM M, TOMOTA Y, 2005. Fatigue Strength and Fracture Mechanisms of IF28 Steels [J]. Advanced Materials Research, 15-17: 804-809.

KAMURA M, et al, 2003. Formability and Springback Characterization of Advanced High Strength Steel[J]. SAE 2003-01-0522.

KAMURA M, UTSUMI Y, OMIYA Y, et al, 2001. Crashworthiness and Spot Weldability of Galvannealed DP800 Steel Sheet[J]. SAE 2001-01-3094.

KANG W J, et al, 1999. Modified Johnson-Cook Model for Vehicle Body Crashworthiness Simulation [J]. International Journal of Vehicle Design, 21(4-5): 424-435.

KANG W J, et al, 1998. Identification of Dynamic Behavior of Sheet Metals for an Autobody with Tension Split Hopkinson Bar[J]. SAE 981010.

KIM C H, et al, 2010. A Study on the CO2 Laser Welding Characteristics of High Strength Steel up to 1500 MPa for Automotive Application[J]. Journal of Achievements in Materials and Manufacturing Engineering, 39(1): 79-86.

KONIECZNY A A, 2003. On the Formability of Automotive TRIP Steels[J]. SAE 2003-01-0521.

KONIECZNY A A, 2001. On Formability Assessment of the Automotive Dual Phase Steels[J]. SAE 2001-01-3075.

LE Q, et al, 2009. Modified Strain-Life Equation to Consider the Effect of Different Prestrain Paths for Dual Phase Sheet Steel[J]. Journal of Materials Processing Technology, 209(7): 3525-3531.

LI B, et al, 2003. Flow Stress and Microstructure of Cold-Rolled IF-steel [J]. Material Science and

Engineering: A, 356(1-2): 37-42.

LI Y, et al, 2011. Experimental Assessment of High Temperature Formability of Boron Steel Sheet Manufactured With a Spring Compound Bending Die[J]. Journal of Engineering Materials and Technology, 134(2): 021019.

LINK T M, HANCE B M, 2003. Effects of Strain Rate on the Work Hardening Behavior of High Strength Sheet Steels[J]. SAE 2003-01-0516.

MAHAGAONKAR N S, et al, 2011. Evaluation of Fatigue Properties and Effect of Stress Concentration on Fatigue Life of Dual Phase Steel Grade DP800[J]. SAE 2011-26-0120.

MIURA K, TAKAGI S, FURUKIMI O, et al, 1996. Dynamic Deformation Behavior of Steel Sheet for Automobile[J]. SAE 960019.

NADERI M, DURENBERGER L, MOLINARI A, et al, 2008. Constitutive Relationships for 22MnB5 Boron Steel Deformed Isothermally at High Temperatures[J]. Journal of MaterialsScience and Engineering, A, 478 (1-2): 130-139.

NOSOVA L V, SEREBRYAKOV V G, ESTRIN E L, 1991. Dependence of the Plasticity of Dual-Phase Austenite-Martensite Steels on Phase Composition [J]. Physics of Metals and Metallography (English Translation of Fizika Metallov i Metallovedenie), 71(5): 191-194.

PADMANABHAN R, OLIVEIRA M, MENEZES L, 2006. Deep Drawing of Aluminum-Steel Tailor-Welded Blanks[J]. Materials and Design, 29(1): 154-160.

RINGSBERG J, et al, 2006. Sheet Metal Fatigue near Nuts Welded to Thin Sheet Structures[J]. International Journal of Fatigue, 30(5): 877-887.

SHI M, et al, 2002. Formability Performance Comparison between Dual Phase and HSLA Steels[J]. Iron and Steel Society, 29(3): 27-32.

TAKAHASHI M, 2003. Development of High Strength Steels for Automobiles [J]. Nippon SteelTechnical Report, 88: 295-415.

TIMOTHY B, et al, 2009. Cyclic Deformation of Advanced High-Strength Steels: Mechanical Behavior and Microstructural Analysis[J]. Metallurgical and Materials Transactions, A, 40: 342-353.

TUNGTRONGPAIROJ J, et al, 2009. Determination of Yield Behavior of Boron Alloy Steel at High Temperature [J]. Journal of Metals, Materials and Minerals, 19(1): 29-38.

TURETTA A, BRUSCHI S, GHIOTTI A, 2006. Investigation of 22MnB5 Formability in Hot Stamping Operations[J]. Journal of Materials Processing Technology, 177(1-3): 396-400.

WEI D Y, 2004. Fatigue Behavior of 1500 MPa Bainite/Martensite Duplex-Phase High Strength Steel [J]. International Journal of Fatigue, 26: 437-442.

YAN B, et al, 2001. Effect of Forming Strain on Fatigue Performance of a Mild Automotive Steel[J]. SAE 2001-01-0083.

ZHANG G B, 2010. Die Structure Analysis of Stress Distribution during High-strength Steel Stamping Process and Experimental Validation[J]. International Journal of Materials and ProductTechnology, 38(2-3): 184-197.

Table 77.1   Mechanical Properties of Advanced High Strength Sheet Steels

Material	$T/°C$	E_T	ρ	ν	(σ,ε)	α	k	γ	ρ_E	K_{IC}
IISI Specification:										
BH 210/340	23	206.8	7.83	0.29	(210,0.2%) (469, 32.2%)	—	—	—	—	—
BH 260/370	23	206.8	7.83	0.29	(260,0.2%) (496, 29.3%)	—	—	—	—	—
BH 280/400	23	206.8	7.83	0.29	(280,0.2%) (528, 27.8%)	—	—	—	—	—
CP 500/800	23	206.8	7.83	0.29	(500,0.2%) (896, 11.3%)	—	—	—	—	—
CP 800/1000	23	206.8	7.83	0.29	(800,0.2%) (1105, 10%)	—	—	—	—	—
CP 1000/1200	23	206.8	7.83	0.29	(1000,0.2%) (1308,8.6%)	—	—	—	—	—
DP 300/500	23	206.8	7.83	0.29	(300,0.2%) (660, 27.8%)	—	—	—	—	—
DP 350/600	23	206.8	7.83	0.29	(350,0.2%) (630,5%) (710, 10%) (762, 23.9%)	—	—	—	—	—
DP 400/700	23	206.8	7.83	0.29	(400,0.2%) (854,19.9%)	—	—	—	—	41
DP 500/800	23	206.8	7.83	0.29	(500,0.2%) (780,3%) (930, 10%) (970,14%)	—	—	—	—	34.5

continued

Material	$T/℃$	E_T	ρ	ν	(σ,ε)	α	k	γ	ρ_E	K_IC
DP 700/1000	23	206.8	7.83	0.29	$(700,0.2\%)$ $(1000,3\%)$ $(1050,5\%)$ $(1190,8.6\%)$	—	—	—	—	—
FB 330/450	23	206.8	7.83	0.29	$(330,0.2\%)$ $(567,23.1\%)$	—	—	—	—	—
FB 450/600	23	206.8	7.83	0.29	$(450,0.2\%)$ $(732,19.9\%)$	—	—	—	—	—
HF 340/480	23	206.8	7.83	0.29	$(340,0.2\%)$ $(600,22.3\%)$	—	—	—	—	—
HF 1050/1500	23	206.8	7.83	0.29	$(1050,0.2\%)$ $(1590,5.8\%)$	—	—	—	—	—
IF 260/410	23	206.8	7.83	0.29	$(260,0.2\%)$ $(553,30\%)$	—	—	—	—	—
IF 300/420	23	206.8	7.83	0.29	$(300,0.2\%)$ $(556,28.1\%)$	—	—	—	—	—
MS 950/1200	23	206.8	7.83	0.29	$(950,0.2\%)$ $(1272,5.8\%)$	—	—	—	—	—
MS 1150/1400	23	206.8	7.83	0.29	$(1150,0.2\%)$ $(1477,5.3\%)$	—	—	—	—	—
MS 1250/1520	23	206.8	7.83	0.29	$(1250,0.2\%)$ $(1588,4.4\%)$	—	—	—	—	K_IC
TRIP 350/600	23	206.8	7.83	0.29	$(350,0.2\%)$ $(560,5\%)$ $(645,10\%)$ $(786,27\%)$	—	—	—	—	—
TRIP 400/700	23	206.8	7.83	0.29	$(450,0.2\%)$ $(882,23.1\%)$	—	—	—	—	—
TRIP 450/800	23	206.8	7.83	0.29	$(500,0.2\%)$ $(1032,25.5\%)$	—	—	—	—	—
TWIP 450/1000	23	206.8	7.83	0.29	$(450,0.2\%)$ $(1520,42\%)$	—	—	—	—	—

continued

Material	$T/℃$	E_T	ρ	ν	(σ,ε)	α	k	γ	ρ_E	K_{IC}
Boron Steel(Fe-22Mn-5B)	23	206.8	7.83	0.29	(1375,0.2%) $\sigma_{uts}=1500$	—	—	—	—	—
	600	—	—	—	(200, 20%)	—	—	—	—	—
	800	—	—	—	(90, 20%)	—	—	—	—	—
Bao Steels（宝钢）Specification:										
BR330/580(DP)	23	206.8	7.83	0.29	(330,0.2%) (580, 19%)	—	—	—	—	—
BR450/780(DP)	23	206.8	7.83	0.29	(450,0.2%) (780,14%)	—	—	—	—	—
BR400/590(TR)	23	206.8	7.83	0.29	(400,0.2%) (590, 24%)	—	—	—	—	—
BR450/780(TR)	23	206.8	7.83	0.29	(450,0.2%) (780, 20%)	—	—	—	—	—
BR300/450(HE)	23	206.8	7.83	0.29	(300,0.2%) (450, 24%)	—	—	—	—	—
BR440/580(HE)	23	206.8	7.83	0.29	(440,0.2%) (580,14%)	—	—	—	—	—
BR600/780(HE)	23	206.8	7.83	0.29	(600,0.2%) (780, 12%)	—	—	—	—	—
BR900/1200 (MS)	23	206.8	7.83	0.29	(900,0.2%) (1200,5%)	—	—	—	—	—
BR650/780(CP)	23	206.8	7.83	0.29	(650,0.2%) (780,5%)	—	—	—	—	—
BR720/950(CP)	23	206.8	7.83	0.29	(720,0.2%) (950,5%)	—	—	—	—	—
JIS Specification:										
SAPH(HR)	23	206.8	7.83	0.29	(180,0.2%) (310, 46%)	—	—	—	—	—
SAPH 370 (HR)	23	206.8	7.83	0.29	(225,0.2%) (370, 46%)	—	—	—	—	—

continued

Material	$T/℃$	E_T	ρ	ν	(σ,ε)	α	k	γ	ρ_E	K_{IC}
SAPH(HR)	23	206.8	7.83	0.29	(285,0.2%) (400, 39%)	—	—	—	—	—
SAPH(HR)	23	206.8	7.83	0.29	(305,0.2%) $\sigma_{uts}=440$	—	—	—	—	—
SPCC 300	23	206.8	7.83	0.29	(168,0.2%) (307, 47%)	—	—	—	—	—
SPCC 390	23	206.8	7.83	0.29	$\sigma_{uts}=390$	—	—	—	—	—
SPCC 440	23	206.8	7.83	0.29	$\sigma_{uts}=440$	—	—	—	—	—
SPFC 370	23	206.8	7.83	0.29	$\sigma_{uts}=370$	—	—	—	—	—
SPFC 440	23	206.8	7.83	0.29	$\sigma_{uts}=440$	—	—	—	—	—
SPFC 590Y (Cold-Rolled)	23	206.8	7.83	0.29	(354,0.2%) (612, 28%)	—	—	—	—	—
SPFH 490 (HR)	23	206.8	7.83	0.29	(325,0.2%) (490, 24%)	—	—	—	—	—
SPFH 540 (HR)	23	206.8	7.83	0.29	(355,0.2%) (540,23%)	—	—	—	—	—
SPFH 590 (HR)	23	206.8	7.83	0.29	(420,0.2%) (590, 21%)	—	—	—	—	—
Stress-Hardening Subject to Strain Rate:										
SPCC (0.001 s^{-1})	23	206.8	7.83	0.29	(400, 30%)	—	—	—	—	—
SPCC (1 s^{-1})	23	206.8	7.83	0.29	(460, 30%)	—	—	—	—	—
SPCC (2500 s^{-1})	23	206.8	7.83	0.29	(660, 30%)	—	—	—	—	—
SPCC (3500 s^{-1})	23	206.8	7.83	0.29	(680, 30%)	—	—	—	—	—
SPCEN (0.001 s^{-1})	23	206.8	7.83	0.29	(360, 30%)	—	—	—	—	—
SPCEN (1 s^{-1})	23	206.8	7.83	0.29	(400, 30%)	—	—	—	—	—
SPCEN (3500 s^{-1})	23	206.8	7.83	0.29	(610, 30%)	—	—	—	—	—
SPCEN (5000 s^{-1})	23	206.8	7.83	0.29	(620, 30%)	—	—	—	—	—

continued

Material	$T/°C$	E_T	ρ	ν	(σ, ε)	α	k	γ	ρ_E	K_{IC}
SPRC ($0.001\ s^{-1}$)	23	206.8	7.83	0.29	(470, 30%)	—	—	—	—	—
SPRC ($1\ s^{-1}$)	23	206.8	7.83	0.29	(500, 30%)	—	—	—	—	—
SPRC ($2500\ s^{-1}$)	23	206.8	7.83	0.29	(650, 30%)	—	—	—	—	—
SPRC ($3500\ s^{-1}$)	23	206.8	7.83	0.29	(660, 30%)	—	—	—	—	—

Notes: T = True stress-strain data;

BH = Bake hardenable;

CP = Complex phase;

DP = Dual phase;

FB = Ferritic-Bainitic;

HF = Hot-formed;

IF = Interstitial free;

MS = Martensitic;

TRIP = Transformation-induced plasticity;

TWIP = TWinning-Induced Plasticity.

Table 77.2 Fatigue ε-N Properties of Sheet Steels

Material	$T/°C$	$d\varepsilon/dt$	σ_f'	ε_f'	b	c	K'	n'	$\sigma_f@2N_f$	R
B170P (Electrogalvanized)	23	—	796	0.425	−0.129	−0.513	716 &	0.207	138@ 10^7	—
BH300	23	—	549	0.97	−0.063	−0.614	530	0.097	193	—
HSS590 (CR)	23	—	886	0.48	−0.095	−0.538	980	0.173	230	—
DP600 (GI)	23	—	983	0.211	−0.101	−0.457	1363	0.219	228	—
IF Steels	23	—	—	—	—	—	—	—	$\sigma_f = 0.4\sigma_y$	—
TRIP590 (EG)	23	—	813	0.496	−0.063	−0.572	871	0.109	336	—
TRIP780 (CR)	23	—	1400	0.365	−0.115	−0.51	1750	0.223	336	—
DP800 (GA)	23	—	1205	0.104	−0.101	−0.394	2104	0.253	307	—
DP980 (CR)	23	—	2900	0.06	−0.15	−0.33	3465	0.43	—	—
MS1024/1178	23	—	1270	1.54	−0.112	−0.895	802	0.288	483@ 10^7	—
MS1150/1400	23	—	2130	27.93	−0.086	−1.21	1692	0.072	669@ 10^7	—
Steel (Generic)	23	—	Eq. (6.14)	Eq. (6.15)	−0.09	−0.6	$\sigma_f'/(\varepsilon_f')^{n'}$	b/c	Eq. (77.1)	—

Table 77.3 Parameters of Johnson-Cook Stress Model for Sheet Metals of Automotive Body

Material	$A/$MPa	$B/$MPa	n	C or (C_1 & C_2)	m	$T_m/$℃
SPCEN	208	350	0.48	0.14(0.08 & 0.007)	0.31	1400
SPCC	214	433	0.45	0.15	0.25	1400
SPRC	221	483	0.43	0.13	0.26	1400
B170P	170	—	—	—	—	—
60TRIP	432	800	0.59	0.075(0.03 & 0.012)	0.55	1400
60C	463	800	0.63	0.036(0.037 & 0.004)	0.63	1400

Chapter 78

Bolt Steels

78.1 Introduction

All quality fasteners have rolled threads produced via rolling or sliding dies. The mechanical and physical properties of steel bolts are characterized by the following:

- Elastic Elongation: Elongation from which the fastener will recover when unloaded.
- Plastic Elongation: Permanent elongation that renders the fastener non-reusable.
- Necking Elongation: Elongation past the tensile strength of the fastener.
- Proof Load: The minimum point prior to permanent elongation.
- Yield Point: The point at which elasticity is lost and permanent elongation commences.
- Tensile Strength: The maximum load-carrying point prior to fracture.

The minimum tension used for design purposes is usually between 65% and 70% of proof load and it is the theoretical minimum tension the recommended tightening torque should achieve. The top three configurations of frequently used bolted joints are given in Fig. 78.1.

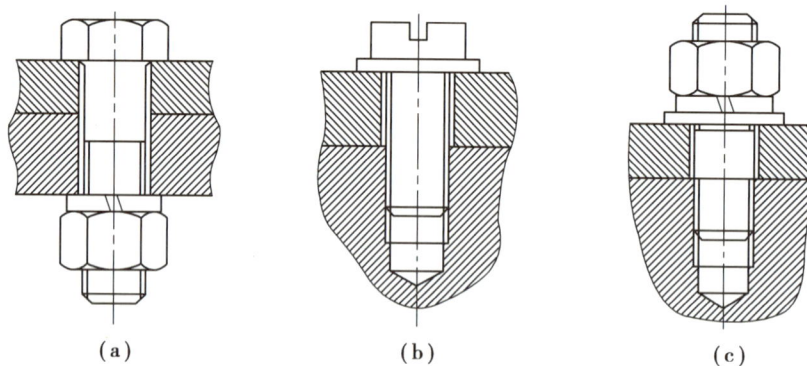

(a)   (b)   (c)

Fig. 78.1   Bolt Fastening: (a) Bolted Joint, (b) Screw Joint, and (c) Stud Joint

Applicability of externally threaded steel bolts, screws and studs is designated in Table 78.1. Proof loads of threaded steel bolts, screws and studs are identified in Table 78.2 and 78.3, respectively for fine and coarse pitches.

78.2 SAE Descriptive Symbol

Metric bolt descriptive symbols are demonstrated using an M 12 bolt as follows:

```
M  12  ×  1.75  –  6 g  ×  80   –  8.8
                                         Strength Class ( See Table 78.1 )
                                    Length ( mm )
                              Fit Symbol
                       Pitch ( mm )
               Major Diameter ( mm )
           ISO Metric Thread
```

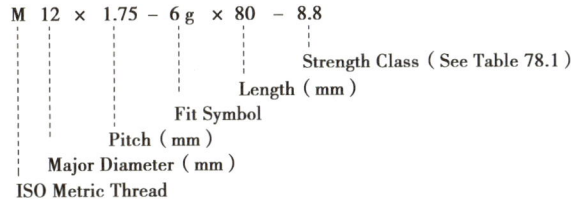

Approximately, the first digit stands for the multiplier of 100 MPa for the ultimate tensile strength and the second digit means the yield strength. For example, SAE J1199 Class 9.8 means that it has an ultimate tensile strength of 900 ($= 9 \times 100$) MPa and a yield strength of 720 ($= 900 \times 80\%$) MPa. Their corresponding true stress-strain relationships are plotted in Fig. 78.2.

A Mark is put on the bolt or head if its material is Class 8.8 or above. SAE Class 10.9 and Class 9.8 are the most used two materials for automotive bolts. Mechanical properties of standard SAE bolts are given in Table 78.4.

78.3   DIN17005 Specification

Material properties of bolts specified by DIN17005 are listed in Table 78.5.

78.4   ASTM Specification

Material properties of bolts specified by ASTM are listed in Table 78.6.

78.5   Bolt Strength

True stress-strain curves for bolts of various SAE material grades are depicted in Fig. 78.2. As a conservative approach to designing automotive bolts, the proof stress of a bolt or screw, σ_{proof}, can be estimated from the yield strength as follows:

$$\sigma_{proof} = 90\% \sigma_Y \tag{78.1}$$

Suggested tightening torques are listed in Table 78.7. In general, the stress level of the first thread root is of great concern. The first three or four threads may take most axial loading. If the variation of stress level due to operating loads is small, a bolt can be designed using σ_{proof} as the maximum stress in pretension. As the variation of stress level is significant, the stress level of a bolt pretension at the first thread root may be designed to be less than 70% of the proof load or proven by fatigue strain-life predictive models or Goodman's equation.

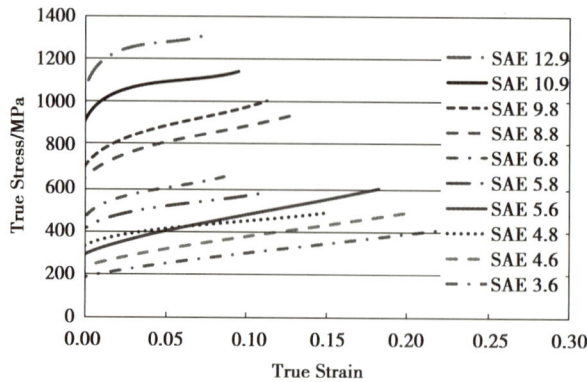

Fig. 78.2   True Stress-Strain Curves of SAE Bolt Materials

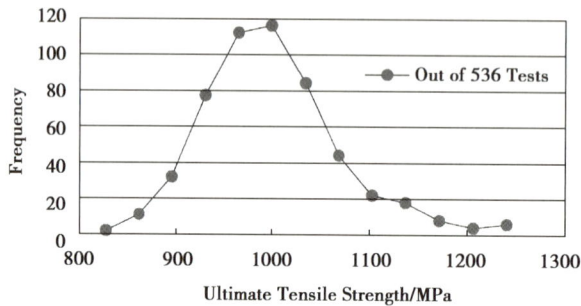

Fig. 78.3   Tensile Strength Histogram of J1199 Class 9.8 Bolts under Axial Tension

The statistical nature of bolt material strength is demonstrated based on axial tensile tests. A tensile strength histogram of SAE J1199 class 9.8, demonstrated in Fig. 78.3, shows that it corresponds to the Weibull distribution function with two parameters ($\eta = 1090$ MPa, $\beta = 8.82$), as

$$R(t) = \exp\left[-\left(\frac{t}{\eta}\right)^{\beta}\right] = \exp\left[-\left(\frac{t}{1090}\right)^{8.82}\right] \tag{78.2}$$

The above equation reveals that the tensile strength is 768.4 MPa with a reliability of 90% at a confidence level of 90%. This is still higher than its nominal yield strength of 720 MPa.

78.6   Tightening by What?

One major impact on the bolt-fastening force (axial load) in the bolt is the method of assembly. Variation in bolt-fastening force varies very much according to the tightening method as shown below [VDI 2230: Systematic Calculation of High Duty Bolted Joints]:

Tightening Method	Fastening Force Variation
By yield strength	±9% ~ ±17%
By angle of rotation	±9% ~ ±17%
Hydraulic tensioning	±9% ~ ±23%
Torque wrench	±17% ~ ±43%
Impact wrench or spanner	±43% ~ ±60%

Elastic interactions due to tightening order may loosen the load. When the first bolt is tightened, the fastener is stretched and the joint is partially compressed. When an adjacent bolt is tightened, the joint in the vicinity of the first bolt is further compressed. This allows the first bolt to relax somewhat.

On flanged joints, for instance, the bolts are tightened in stages using a crossing pattern. The first pass is tightened to approximately 30% of the final desired preload. The next two passes would be at 60% and 100% of the desired preload. It is also necessary to conduct an extra pass at 100% in reverse of the crossing patterns employed in the first three passes.

When a bolt is fastened using a torque wrench, an annoying bending moment (i.e. force * arm length, Fig. 78.4) is also created in addition to the torque provided for. Torque should be applied with a properly calibrated torque wrench.

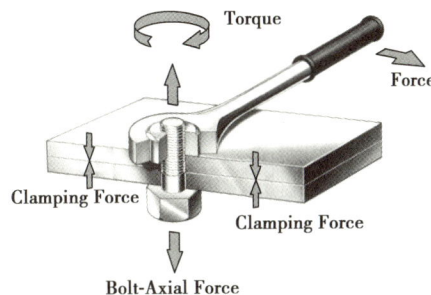

Fig. 78.4   Torquing

78.7   Rolled Threads

When a thread is rolled into a specimen, however, the grain flow of the material remains continuous and follows the contour of the thread. Rolling leaves the surface of the threads and roots pre-stressed in compression. These compressive stresses must be overcome before the tensile stresses can reach a level that will cause fatigue failure. On the other hand, the grain flow of the material is severed if the threads are cut. Therefore, rolled threads better resist tooth stripping (shear failures).

78.8　Surface Treatment of Fasteners

Heat-treatment is usually conducted before rolling the bolts. Threads that get hardened from HRc = 36 to HRc = 40 hardness may show increased fatigue strength.

78.9　Creep and Relaxation of Bolts/Fasteners

In the process of trying to return to its "at rest" length, the bolt tension relaxes (mainly due to creeps) a bit, as

(a) Fastened part/material creeps;

(b) Bolt shank creeps;

(c) Bolt threads seat in;

(d) Nut and bolt head dig into the connected, contacting each other only on microscopic high spots;

(e) Coatings on the connected material, such as paint or zinc, are compressible.

The strain creep rate is high at first, and then slows down quickly. Though the material failure due to creep is much related to secondary creep mode, the primary creep mode is also a major concern during a bolt-torquing process.

78.9.1　Creep of Fastened Materials

All materials and solids are subject to creep to some extent. The creep effect is most obvious and dramatic right after the clamping force has been applied. In many tightening applications, the majority of the creep, the reduction of clamp load (and sometimes static torque), appears within the first 0.01~0.05 second. The following techniques can be used to reduce the effect of creep and relaxation:

(a) Torque the fastener down, then un-tighten the joint and retighten it.

(b) Redesign the fastening joint, e.g. replacing soft gaskets with a sealing compound.

(c) Torque the fastener, wait briefly and then torque again; may be repeated in several steps.

(d) Use a power assembly tool with a low RPM setting to apply the final torque.

Thermal effects and creep behaviors of fastened parts must be taken into consideration, should the operating temperature goes beyond 1/3 of the melting point of any part material. Some materials can also experience creep and relaxation at the room temperature such as plastics, aluminum-, magnesium-, tin-, and zinc-based parts.

If the joint is a flange with a gasket, the losses become more severe over time. This is especially true if it is subjected to wide temperature cycles. As the joint members expand, the tension on the bolts increases, which further stresses the gasket. The increase in gasket stress will cause it to be compressed more than it was at assembly. When the system cools down, all of the joint members will return to their original thickness. Since the gasket is not fully elastic, it will not return to its initial compressed thickness. This will result in some loss of preload. The amount lost depends on the stiffness of the fastener system, gasket type, temperature and the rate of rising, and the number of cycles.

78.9.2   Creep of Bolts

When a steel bolt/nut joint is tightened, the effect of creep relaxation cannot be neglected once the temperature goes above 200 ℃. At a working temperature above 300 ℃ a carbon bolt experiences creep deformation-a permanent deformation loosening the bolt and its tensile strength decreases rapidly. A comparison of remaining fastening forces (percentage of the original fastening force) with different bolt materials after 1000 h stress relaxation at elevated temperatures is given below [GKN Bolts 1970]:

Material (ASTM)	100 ℃	200 ℃	300 ℃	350 ℃	400 ℃	500 ℃	550 ℃	600 ℃	650 ℃	700 ℃	750 ℃
Carbon Steel	83%	82%	71%	40%	10%	—	—	—	—	—	—
SAE 10.9	98%	95%	91%	85%	77%	45%	35%	18%	11%	8%	—
B4C	—	—	—	—	—	—	48%	21%	—	—	—
B7	95%	87%	83%	68%	60%	5%	—	—	—	—	—
B8	—	90%	90%	89%	85%	70%	70%	63%	10%	—	—
B8M	92%	92%	92%	87%	83%	73%	60%	46%	10%	—	—
B16	100%	90%	83%	72%	68%	36%	5%	—	—	—	—
B17	—	—	—	—	—	—	83%	60%	25%	2%	—
304 (Stainless)	100%	100%	98%	—	90%	75%	73%	65%	15%	—	—
316 (Stainless)	100%	100%	98%	—	86%	77%	65%	50%	15%	—	—
Nim 80A	—	—	—	—	—	—	—	—	52%	37%	20%

78.10   Friction

Friction between engaging threads and friction between the bolt head/nut and fastened parts are additional deciding factors on the quality of the bolt joint. A significant amount of work is done on tightening the bolt to overcome the friction between threads and between the bolt and part. Some experimental data are listed in Tables 78.8 and 78.9.

78.11   Hydrogen Embrittlement

Hydrogen embrittlement is induced by the absorption of hydrogen ions, which will later combine to form hydrogen molecules, trapped within grain boundaries, promoting enhanced de-cohesion of the steel, primarily as an intergranular phenomenon. In most cases, hydrogen embrittlement causes fasteners failures in high hardness and high strength fasteners that are electroplated. A bolt of SAE 8.8 or below usually has a low hardness (HRc<32) and does not have a problem with hydrogen embrittlement. Another necessary condition is that a bolt must have come into contact with acid during the manufacturing process.

78.11.1   Hydrogen Absorption

Thus, hydrogen embrittlement of fasteners is a major factor in the choice of material or coating for such components. Hydrogen can be introduced during heat treatment, pickling, cleaning, electroplating, phosphating, and in the service environment as a result of cathodic protection reactions or corrosion reactions. Hydrogen can also be introduced during fabrication, for example, during roll forming, machining and drilling due to the breakdown of unsuitable lubricants as well as during welding or brazing operations. Hydrogen release may occur with zinc deposition. The diffusion and accumulation of the hydrogen in metals are favored by cold working, as is the case of the head-to-shank transition region.

78.11.2   Hydrogen Desorption

Hydrogen absorption is not a permanent condition. If cracking does not occur and the environmental conditions have changed so that no hydrogen surrounds the surface of the metal, the hydrogen can re-diffuse out of the steel, and ductility is restored.

78.12 Washers

Washers are primarily used as a seat to distribute the load, but they may also provide spring tension, span oversize holes, insulate, seal, or provide electrical connection. Various kinds include flat, conical, and helical-spring washers, tooth or ribbed lock washers, and special-purpose washers.

78.13 Al-based Bolts

Aluminum alloys such as 2017A (T6), 5019, 6013 (T8), 6082 (T6), 7050 (T73), and 7075 (T73) are also used for corrosion-resistant bolts and nuts.

78.14 Cu-based Bolts

Copper alloys such as C10100 (Oxygen-free Cu), C11000 (ETP), Cu-37Zn (Brass), Cu-12Ni-24Zn (Nickel Silver), C17300 (C-1.9Be-...) are also used for electricity-conductive bolts and nuts.

78.15 Stainless Steel Bolt

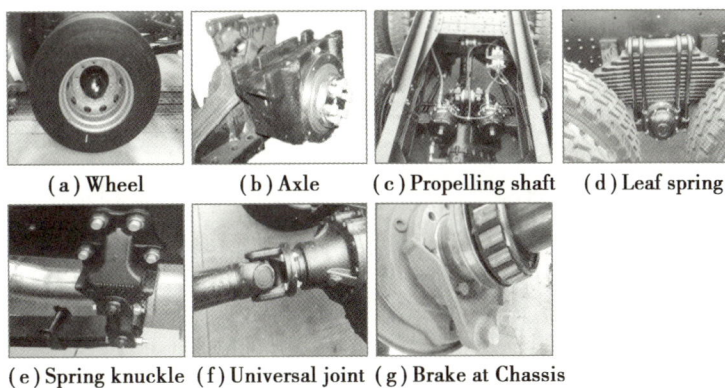

(a) Wheel   (b) Axle   (c) Propelling shaft   (d) Leaf spring

(e) Spring knuckle   (f) Universal joint   (g) Brake at Chassis

Fig. 78.5 Heavy-duty Truck Bolts as Assembled (Fig. a-g: Left to Right & Top-down)

78.16   Applications

There are more than 3000 bolts and screws used in a sedan and approximately 3 million fasteners in a Boeing 747 airplane. Crucial bolted-joints of a heavy-duty truck are demonstrated in Fig. 78.5.

References

ABID M, HUSSAIN S, 2010. Relaxation Behavior of Gasketed Joints during Assembly using Finite Element Analysis[J]. Sadhana, 35(1): 31-43.

CHIANG Y J, BARBER G C, 1997. Self-Threading Bolts Tapped into Temperature Dependent Plastic Bosses [J]. International Journal of Materials and Product Technology, 12(2-3): 110-123.

CHIANG Y J, ROWLANDS R E, 1991. Finite Element Analysis for Mixed-Mode Fracture of Bolted Composite Joints[J]. Journal of Composites Technology and Research, 13(4): 227-235.

CHIANG Y J, ROWLANDS R E, 1987. Fracture Analysis of Cracks Emanating from a PinLoaded Hole in Composites[J]. Developments in Mechanics, 14(b): 581-586.

CHO S S, CHANG H, LEE K W, 2009. Dependence of Fatigue Limit of High Tension Bolts on Mean Stress and Ultimate Tensile Strength[J]. International Journal of Automotive Technology, 10(4): 475-479.

DEJACK M, MA Y, CRAIG R, 2010. Bolt Load Relaxation and Fatigue Prediction in Threads with Consideration of Creep Behavior for Die Cast Aluminum[J]. SAE 2010-01-0965.

FUKUOKA T, et al, 2011. Finite Element Analysis of the Cyclic Stress Amplitude of Threaded Fasteners Using Helical Thread Models[J]. Journal of Pressure Vessel Technology, 133(6): 061201.

GRIZA S, BERTONI F, ZANON G, et al, 2009. Fatigue in Engine Connecting Rod Bolt due to Forming Laps Original Research Article[J]. Engineering Failure Analysis, 16(5): 1542-1548.

IBRAHIM R A, PETTIT C L, 2005. Uncertainties and Dynamic Problems of Bolted Joints and other Fasteners [J]. Journal of Sound and Vibration, 279: 857-936.

JAGLINSKI T, et al, 2007. Study of Bolt Load Loss in Bolted Aluminum Joints[J]. Journal of Engineering Materials and Technology, 129(1): 48-54.

KIRBY B R, 1995. The Behavior of High-Strength Grade 8.8 Bolts in Fire[J]. Journal of Constructional Steel Research, 33(1-2): 3-38.

KODUR V, et al, 2011. Effect of Temperature on Thermal and Mechanical Properties of Steel Bolts[J]. Journal of Materials in Civil Engineering, doi:10.1061/(ASCE)MT.1943-5533.0000445.

MALEK S S, CHIANG Y J, MASON J F, 1993. Multivariable Effects on an Automatic Screw-Torquing Process [J]. Journal of Manufacturing Systems, 12(6): 457-462.

NECHACHE A, BOUZID A, 2007. Creep Analysis of Bolted Flange Joints[J]. InternationalJournal of Pressure Vessels and Piping, 84(3): 185-194.

RAHMAN M U, CHIANG Y J, ROWLANDS R E, 1991. Stress and Failure Analysis of Double-Bolted Joints in Douglas Fir/Sitka Spruce[J]. Wood and Fiber Science, 23(4): 567-589.

REID J D, HISER N R, 2005. Detailed Modeling of Bolted Joints with Slippage[J]. Finite Elements in Analysis and Design, 41: 547-562.

ROWLANDS R E, RAHMAN M U, WILKINSON T L, et al, 1982. Single-and Multiple-Bolted Joints in Orthotropic Materials[J]. Composites: 273-279.

WENTZEL H, OLSSON M, 2008. Mechanisms of Dissipation in Frictional Joints-Influence of Sharp Contact Edges and Plastic Deformation[J]. Wear, 265(11-12): 1814-1819.

Table 78.1　Mechanical Properties of Externally Threaded Steel Bolts, Screws and Studs Often Used in Automotive Industry

Specification (Class)	Major Diameter	Strengths (Yield and Tensile) and Ultimate Strain
SAE J1199 (4.6)	M5 ~ M36	$\sigma_Y \geqslant 240$ MPa, $\sigma_{uts} \geqslant 400$ MPa, and $\varepsilon_{uts} \geqslant 22\%$
SAE J1199 (4.8)	M1.6 ~ M16	$\sigma_Y \geqslant 340$ MPa, $\sigma_{uts} \geqslant 420$ MPa
SAE J1199 (5.8)	M5 ~ M24	$\sigma_Y \geqslant 420$ MPa, $\sigma_{uts} \geqslant 520$ MPa
SAE J1199 (8.8)	M17 ~ M36	$\sigma_Y \geqslant 660$ MPa, $\sigma_{uts} \geqslant 830$ MPa, and $\varepsilon_{uts} \geqslant 12\%$
SAE J1199 (9.8)	M1.6 ~ M16	$\sigma_Y \geqslant 720$ MPa, $\sigma_{uts} \geqslant 900$ MPa
SAE J1199 (10.9)	M6 ~ M36	$\sigma_Y \geqslant 940$ MPa, $\sigma_{uts} \geqslant 1040$ MPa, and $\varepsilon_{uts} \geqslant 9\%$
SAE J1199 (12.9)	M1.6 ~ M36	$\sigma_Y \geqslant 1100$ MPa, $\sigma_{uts} \geqslant 1220$ MPa, and $\varepsilon_{uts} \geqslant 8\%$

Table 78.2　Proof Loads of Threaded Steel Bolts, Screws & Studs with Fine Pitches

Metric Threads	Fine Pitch								
Major Diameter	Pitch-Fine	Tensile Stress Area	Proof Load SAE 12.9	Proof Load SAE 10.9	Proof Load SAE 9.8	Proof Load SAE 8.8	Proof Load SAE 5.8	Proof Load SAE 4.8	Proof Load SAE 4.6
mm	mm	mm²	kN	kN	kN	kN	kN	kN	kN
No fine threads for bolts with small major diameters									
8	1	39.37	39.0	33.3	25.5	23.4	14.9	12.0	8.50
10	1.25	61.51	60.9	52.0	39.9	36.5	23.3	18.8	13.3
12	1.25	92.46	91.5	78.2	59.9	54.9	34.9	28.3	20.0
14	1.5	125.1	124	106	81.1	74.3	47.3	38.3	27.0
16	1.5	167.9	166	142	109	99.7	63.5	51.4	36.3
18	1.5	216.9	215	184	141	129	82.0	66.4	46.9
20	1.5	272.3	270	230	176	162	102.9	83.3	58.8
24	2	385.7	382	326	250	229	146	118	83.3
30	2	622.8	617	527	404	370	235	191	135
36	2	916.5	907	775	594	544	346	280	198
42	2	1267	1254	1072	821	752	479	388	274
48	2	1673	1657	1416	1084	994	633	512	361
56	2	2304	2281	1949	1493	1368	871	705	498
64	2	3035	3004	2567	1966	1803	1147	929	655
72	2	3866	3827	3271	2505	2296	1461	1183	835
80	2	4798	4750	4059	3109	2850	1814	1468	1036
90	2	6104	6043	5164	3956	3626	2307	1868	1319
100	2	7568	7492	6402	4904	4495	2861	2316	1635

Table 78.3　Proof Loads of Threaded Steel Bolts, Screws & Studs with Coarse Pitches

Metric Threads	Coarse Pitch									
Major Diameter	Pitch-Coarse	Tensile Stress Area	Proof Load SAE 12.9	Proof Load SAE 10.9	Proof Load SAE 9.8	Proof Load SAE 8.8	Proof Load SAE 5.8	Proof Load SAE 4.8	Proof Load SAE 4.6
mm	mm	mm²	kN	kN	kN	kN	kN	kN	kN
1.6	0.35	1.28	1.27	1.09	0.831	0.762	0.485	0.392	0.277
2	0.4	2.09	2.07	1.77	1.36	1.24	0.791	0.640	0.452
2.5	0.45	3.42	3.38	2.89	2.21	2.03	1.29	1.05	0.74
3	0.5	5.07	5.02	4.29	3.28	3.01	1.92	1.55	1.09
3.5	0.6	6.83	6.76	5.77	4.42	4.05	2.58	2.09	1.47
4	0.7	8.85	8.76	7.48	5.73	5.25	3.34	2.71	1.91
5	0.8	14.3	14.1	12.1	9.25	8.48	5.40	4.37	3.08
6	1	20.3	20.1	17.1	13.1	12.0	7.66	6.20	4.38
8	1.25	36.9	36.5	31.2	23.9	21.9	13.9	11.3	7.96
10	1.5	58.4	57.8	49.4	37.8	34.7	22.1	17.9	12.6
12	1.75	84.8	83.9	71.7	54.9	50.4	32.0	25.9	18.3
14	2	116	115	98.2	75.3	69.0	43.9	35.5	25.1
16	2	157	156	133	102	93.5	59.5	48.2	34.0
18	2	205	203	174	133	122	77.5	62.8	44.3
20	2.5	246	244	208	159	146	93.0	75.3	53.1
24	3	354	351	300	230	210	134	108	76.5
30	3.5	563	558	477	365	335	213	172	122
36	4	820	812	694	532	487	310	251	177
42	4.5	1126	1114	952	729	669	426	344	243
48	5	1479	1464	1251	959	879	559	453	320
56	5.5	2038	2018	1724	1321	1211	770	624	440
64	6	2686	2659	2272	1740	1595	1015	822	580
72	6	3471	3436	2936	2249	2062	1312	1062	750
80	6	4357	4313	3686	2823	2588	1647	1333	941
90	6	5605	5549	4742	3632	3329	2119	1715	1211

Notes: (a) Minor diameter (mm), $d = D - 1.226869 P$;

(b) Pitch diameter (mm), $d_P = D - 0.649519 P$;

(c) Tensile stress area is calculated as $\pi [1/2 (d_P + d)] [1/2 (d_P + d)]/4$;

(d) Tensile force as installed should be less than 70% of the proof load.

Table 78.4   Mechanical Properties of Steel Bolts

Material	$T/^\circ\!C$	E_T	ρ	ν	(σ,ε)	α	k	γ	ρ_E	K_{IC}
Class 3.6 (Low Carbon)	23	207	7.83	0.29	(190,0.2%) (330, 25%)	12	16.2	480	—	—
	1400(T_m)	—	—	—	—	—	—	—	—	—
Class 4.6 (Low Carbon)	23	207	7.83	0.29	(240,0.2%) (400, 22%)	12	16.2	480	—	—
	300	—	—	—	—	12	17.9	548	—	—
	400	—	—	—	—	12	19.2	561	—	—
Class 4.8	23	207	7.83	0.29	(340,0.2%) (420,16%)	12	16.2	—	—	—
Class 5.6	23	207	7.83	0.29	(330,0.2%) (500, 20%)	12	16.2	—	—	—
	100	—	—	—	(300,0.2%)	—	—	—	—	—
	200	—	—	—	(255,0.2%)	—	—	—	—	—
	300	—	—	—	(215,0.2%)	—	—	—	—	—
Class 5.8 (Low-Medium Carbon)	23	207	7.83	0.29	(420,0.2%) (520, 12%)	12	16.2	—	—	—
Class 6.8	23	207	7.83	0.29	(480,0.2%) (600,9%)	12	16.2	—	—	—
Class 8.8 (Medium Carbon; Q&T)	23	207	7.83	0.29	(710,0.2%) (830,14%)	12	16.2	—	—	—
	100	200	—	—	(655,0.2%)	—	—	—	—	—
	200	186	—	—	(600,0.2%)	—	—	—	—	—
	300	165	—	—	(530,0.2%) $\sigma_{uts}=810$	—	—	—	—	—
	400	145	—	—	$\sigma_{uts}=660$	—	—	—	—	—
	650	30	—	—	(165,1%) (180,3%) (180, 12%)	—	—	—	—	—
Class 9.8	23	207	7.83	0.29	(720,0.2%) (900, 12%)	12	16.2	—	—	—

continued

Material	$T/°C$	E_T	ρ	ν	(σ,ε)	α	k	γ	ρ_E	K_{IC}
Class 10.9 (Medium Carbon; Q&T)	23	207	7.83	0.29	(940,0.2%) (1000,0.5%) (1040, 10%)	12	16.2	—	—	—
	300	—	—	—	(860,0.2%) (900,0.8%) (1032, 21%)	—	—	—	—	—
	400	—	—	—	(776,0.2%) (871,26%)	—	—	—	—	—
	500	—	—	—	(399,0.2%) (561, 30%)	—	—	—	—	—
	600	—	—	—	(156,0.2%) (282, 60%)	—	—	—	—	—
	700	—	—	—	(54,0.2%) (128, 87%)	—	—	—	—	—
Class 12.9 (Medium Carbon; Q&T)	23	207	7.83	0.29	(1100,0.2%) (1220,8%)	12	16.2	—	—	—
	100	—	—	—	(1040,0.2%)	—	—	—	—	—
	200	—	—	—	(1005,0.2%)	—	—	—	—	—
	300	—	—	—	(915,0.2%)	—	—	—	—	—

Notes: From 300 °C upwards a creep effect is visible and not further negligible for steel bolts.

Table 78.5   Mechanical Properties of Steel Bolts

Material	$T/°C$	E_T	ρ	ν	(σ,ε)	α	k	γ	ρ_E	K_{IC}
1.1181	23	211	7.85	0.29	(300,0.2%)	10.5	42	460	—	—
	200	196	—	—	(229,0.2%)	12.1	—	—	—	—
	300	186	—	—	(192,0.2%)	12.9	—	—	—	—
	400	177	—	—	(173,0.2%)	13.5	—	—	—	—
	500	164	—	—	—	13.9	—	—	—	—
	600	127	—	—	—	—	—	—	—	—

continued

Material	$T/°C$	E_T	ρ	ν	(σ, ε)	α	k	γ	ρ_E	K_{IC}
1.4301 (X5CrNi18-10)	23	200	7.83	0.29	$(350, 0.2\%)$ $\sigma_{uts} = 500$	16	15	500	—	—
	200	197	—	—	$(127, 0.2\%)$	16.5	—	—	—	—
	300	186	—	—	$(110, 0.2\%)$	17	—	—	—	—
	400	172	—	—	$(98, 0.2\%)$	17.5	—	—	—	—
	500	165	—	—	$(92, 0.2\%)$	18	—	—	—	—
	550	—	—	—	$(90, 0.2\%)$; $\sigma_{cts, 10000} = 121$	—	—	—	—	—
	600	—	—	—	$\sigma_{cts, 10000} = 94$	—	—	—	—	—
	700	—	—	—	$\sigma_{cts, 10000} = 35$	—	—	—	—	—
1.4401 (X5CrNi Mo17-12-2)	23	200	7.83	0.29	$(250, 0.2\%)$ $\sigma_{uts} = 500$	16	15	500	—	—
	200	197	—	—	$(145, 0.2\%)$	16.5	—	—	—	—
	300	186	—	—	$(127, 0.2\%)$	17	—	—	—	—
	400	172	—	—	$(1158, 0.2\%)$	17.5	—	—	—	—
	500	165	—	—	$(110, 0.2\%)$	18	—	—	—	—
1.4923 (X21Cr NiV12-1)	23	216	7.83	0.29	$(600, 0.2\%)$ $\sigma_{uts} = 800$	10.5	24	—	—	—
	200	200	—	—	$(530, 0.2\%)$	11	—	—	—	—
	300	190	—	—	$(480, 0.2\%)$	11.5	—	—	—	—
	400	179	—	—	$(420, 0.2\%)$	12	—	—	—	—
	450	—	—	—	$\sigma_{cts, 10000} = 436$	—	—	—	—	—
	500	167	—	—	$(335, 0.2\%)$ $\sigma_{cts, 10000} = 289$	12.3	—	—	—	—
	550	—	—	—	$(280, 0.2\%)$	—	—	—	—	—
	600	127	—	—	$\sigma_{cts, 10000} = 79$	12.5	—	—	—	—

continued

Material	$T/℃$	E_{T}	ρ	ν	(σ,ε)	α	k	γ	ρ_{E}	K_{IC}
1.4980(X5Ni CrTi26-15)	23	211	7.83	0.29	$(635,0.2\%)$ $\sigma_{\mathrm{uts}}=900$	17	12	—	—	—
	200	200	—	—	$(560,0.2\%)$	17.5	—	—	—	—
	300	192	—	—	$(540,0.2\%)$	18.7	—	—	—	—
	400	183	—	—	$(520,0.2\%)$	18	—	—	—	—
	500	173	—	—	$(490,0.2\%)$; $\sigma_{\mathrm{cts},10000}=580$	18.2	—	—	—	—
	600	162	—	—	$(430,0.2\%)$; $\sigma_{\mathrm{cts},10000}=320$	18.5	—	—	—	—
	650	—	—	—	$(380,0.2\%)$; $\sigma_{\mathrm{cts},10000}=190$	—	—	—	—	—
1.5511(35B2)	23	211	7.83	0.29	$(300,0.2\%)$ $\sigma_{\mathrm{uts}}=500$	12	42	—	—	—
	200	196	—	—	$(229,0.2\%)$	12.1	—	—	—	—
	300	186	—	—	$(192,0.2\%)$	12.9	—	—	—	—
	350	186	—	—	$\sigma_{\mathrm{cts},10000}=208$	—	—	—	—	—
	400	177	—	—	$(173,0.2\%)$; $\sigma_{\mathrm{cts},10000}=147$	13.5	—	—	—	—
	500	164	—	—	$\sigma_{\mathrm{cts},10000}=35$	13.9	—	—	—	—
	600	127	—	—	—	14.1	—	—	—	—
1.7218 (25CrMo)	23	211	7.83	0.29	$(440,0.2\%)$ $\sigma_{\mathrm{uts}}=600$	12	—	—	—	—
	200	196	—	—	$(412,0.2\%)$	12.1	—	—	—	—
	300	186	—	—	$(363,0.2\%)$	12.9	—	—	—	—
	400	177	—	—	$(304,0.2\%)$	13.5	—	—	—	—
	420	—	—	—	$\sigma_{\mathrm{cts},10000}=274$	—	—	—	—	—
	500	164	—	—	$(235,0.2\%)$; $\sigma_{\mathrm{cts},10000}=147$	13.9	—	—	—	—
	550	—	—	—	$\sigma_{\mathrm{cts},10000}=64$	—	—	—	—	—
	600	127	—	—	—	14.1	—	—	—	—

continued

Material	$T/℃$	E_{T}	ρ	ν	(σ,ε)	α	k	γ	ρ_{E}	K_{IC}
1.7225	23	211	7.83	0.29	$(730,0.2\%)$	12	—	—	—	—
	200	196	—	—	$(640,0.2\%)$	12.1	—	—	—	—
	300	186	—	—	$(562,0.2\%)$	12.9	—	—	—	—
	400	177	—	—	$(475,0.2\%)$	13.5	—	—	—	—
	500	164	—	—	$(375,0.2\%)$	13.9	—	—	—	—
1.7709 (21CrMoV5-7)	23	211	7.83	0.29	$(550,0.2\%)$ $\sigma_{\mathrm{uts}}=700$	12	33	—	—	—
	200	196	—	—	$(500,0.2\%)$	12.1	—	—	—	—
	300	186	—	—	$(460,0.2\%)$	12.9	—	—	—	—
	400	177	—	—	$(410,0.2\%)$	13.5	—	—	—	—
	420	—	—	—	$\sigma_{\mathrm{cts},10000}=429$	—	—	—	—	—
	500	164	—	—	$(350,0.2\%)$; $\sigma_{\mathrm{cts},10000}=238$	13.9	—	—	—	—
	550	—	—	—	$\sigma_{\mathrm{cts},10000}=116$	—	—	—	—	—
	600	127	—	—	—	14.1	—	—	—	—
1.7711 (40CrMoV4-7)	23	211	7.83	0.29	$(700,0.2\%)$ $\sigma_{\mathrm{uts}}=850$	12	33	460	—	—
	200	196	—	—	$(631,0.2\%)$	12.1	—	—	—	—
	300	186	—	—	$(593,0.2\%)$	12.9	—	—	—	—
	400	177	—	—	$(554,0.2\%)$	13.5	—	—	—	—
	450	—	—	—	$\sigma_{\mathrm{cts},10000}=381$	—	—	—	—	—
	500	164	—	—	$(470,0.2\%)$ $\sigma_{\mathrm{cts},10000}=242$	13.9	—	—	—	—
	550	—	—	—	$\sigma_{\mathrm{cts},10000}=138$	—	—	—	—	—
	600	127	—	—	$(293,0.2\%)$	14.1	—	—	—	—

continued

Material	$T/°C$	E_T	ρ	ν	(σ,ε)	α	k	γ	ρ_E	K_{IC}
2.4952 (NiCr20TiAl; Nomonic 80a)	23	216	7.83	0.29	$(600,0.2\%)$ $\sigma_{uts}=1000$	12	13	—	—	—
	200	208	—	—	$(568,0.2\%)$	12.6	—	—	—	—
	300	202	—	—	$(560,0.2\%)$	13.1	—	—	—	—
	400	196	—	—	$(540,0.2\%)$	13.5	—	—	—	—
	500	189	—	—	$(520,0.2\%)$; $\sigma_{cts,10000}=624$	13.7	—	—	—	—
	600	179	—	—	$(500,0.2\%)$; $\sigma_{cts,10000}=398$	14	—	—	—	—
	650	—	—	—	$(480,0.2\%)$	—	—	—	—	—
	700	161	—	—	$\sigma_{cts,10000}=173$	—	—	—	—	—

Table 78.6   Mechanical Properties of Steel Bolts

Material	$T/°C$	E_T	ρ	ν	(σ,ε)	α	k	γ	ρ_E	K_{IC}
B5	23	200	7.83	0.29	$(550,0.2\%)$ $(690,16\%)$	—	—	—	—	—
B6	23	200	7.83	0.29	$(585,0.2\%)$ $(760,15\%)$	—	—	—	—	—
B6X	23	200	7.83	0.29	$(485,0.2\%)$ $(620,16\%)$	—	—	—	—	—
B7(M64 & under)	23	200	7.83	0.29	$(725,0.2\%)$ $(860,16\%)$	—	—	—	—	—
B7M(M100 & under)	23	200	7.83	0.29	$(550,0.2\%)$ $(690,18\%)$	—	—	—	—	—
B16(M64 & under)	23	200	7.83	0.29	$(720,0.2\%)$ $(860,18\%)$	—	—	—	—	—

Table 78.7　Suggested Torques（NM）for High Strength Bolts

Metric	SAE Class 8.8		SAE Class 10.9		SAE Class 12.9	
	Dry	Lubricated	Dry	Lubricated	Dry	Lubricated
M4	3.4	1.8	4.5	2.6	5.4	3.4
M5	6.4	3.8	8.8	5.2	11.2	6.6
M6	10.6	6.4	15.2	9.0	18.6	11.4
M7	17.6	10.6	25.5	15.2	31.5	18.6
M8	25.5	15.4	36.5	22	46	27.5
M10	51	30.5	72.5	43.5	89	54
M12	88	53	126	75.5	157	95
M14	141	84	200	121	252	150
M16	220	132	315	188	390	234
M18	310	187	430	258	535	320
M20	440	266	610	365	760	455
M24	565	460	1058	635	1320	790
M30	1517	911	2099	1260	2610	1570
M36	2651	1590	3667	2200	4572	2743

Table 78.8　Bolt Thread Friction

Steel Bolt	Steel-Self Finish	Steel-Zn Plated	Cast Iron	Aluminum
Self Finish：Dry	0.13±0.03	0.15±0.03	0.13±0.03	0.15±0.05
Self Finish：Oiled	0.12±0.04	0.14±0.04	0.13±0.05	0.14±0.04
Phosphate：Dry	0.13±0.03	0.15±0.03	0.13±0.03	0.15±0.05
Phosphate：Oiled	0.12±0.04	0.14±0.04	0.13±0.05	0.14±0.04
Zn Plated：Dry	0.16±0.04	0.17±0.05	0.135±0.035	0.16±0.04
Zn Plated：Oiled	0.14±0.04	0.14±0.04	0.13±0.03	0.14±0.04
Adhesive Applied	0.21±0.03	0.21±0.03	0.21±0.03	0.21±0.03

Table 78.9   Bolt Head and Nut Friction

Steel Bolt	Steel-Self Finish	Steel-Zn Plated	Cast Iron	Aluminum
Self Finish: Dry	0.14±0.04	0.14±0.04	0.12±0.04	—
Self Finish: Oiled	0.14±0.04	0.14±0.04	0.16±0.05	0.14±0.06
Phosphate: Dry	0.14±0.04	0.14±0.04	0.12±0.04	—
Phosphate: Oiled	0.14±0.04	0.14±0.04	0.16±0.05	0.14±0.06
Black Oxide: Dry	0.14±0.04	0.14±0.04	0.12±0.04	—
Black Oxide: Oiled	0.14±0.04	0.14±0.04	0.16±0.05	0.14±0.06
Zn Plated: Dry	0.16±0.04	0.19±0.03	0.15±0.05	—
Zn Plated: Oiled	0.14±0.04	0.14±0.04	0.14±0.04	—

Chapter 79

Spring Steels

79.1 Introduction

Coil spring steels can be classified into three groups, i.e. carbon steels, specialty steels, and stainless steels. Spring materials of different qualifications are well addressed in ASTM specifications as follows:

ASTM Specification	Wire Material	Cost Reference
A227	Cold-drawn steel (plenty of surface defects)	0.5
A228	Music wire steel (most used small springs)	1 (Base)
A229	Oil-tempered steel	0.65
A230	Oil-tempered valve spring-carbon steel	1.25
A313 (type 302)	302 stainless steel	3.1
A313 (type 631)	631 stainless steel	5
A401	Valve spring-chrome silicon steel	2
B159	Phosphor bronze	3.7
B197	Beryllium copper	11
—	Inconel (X-750)	19

The majority of springs are cold wound from cold-drawn carbon steel. The ultimate tensile strength of a spring wire reduces with an increasing wire radius, as shown in Figs.79.1—79.3. Mechanical properties and fatigue data are given in Tables 79.1 and 79.2, respectively. Required tolerances to the wire diameter and wire roundness are given as follows [SAE 1999]:

Wire Diameter	Diameter Tolerance	Wire Roundness
If $d \leqslant 0.70$ mm	$d \pm 0.02$ mm	± 0.02 mm
If 0.70 mm $< d \leqslant 2.00$ mm	$d \pm 0.03$ mm	± 0.03 mm
If 2.00 mm $< d \leqslant 9.00$ mm	$d \pm 0.05$ mm	± 0.05 mm
If $d \geqslant 9.00$ mm	$d \pm 0.08$ mm	± 0.08 mm

79.1.1 Coil Springs-Carbon Steel (Fig. 79.1 and Table 79.1)

79.1.2 Coil Springs-Stainless Steel (Fig. 79.2 and Table 79.1)

79.1.3 Coil Springs-Specialty Steels (Fig. 79.3 and Table 79.1)

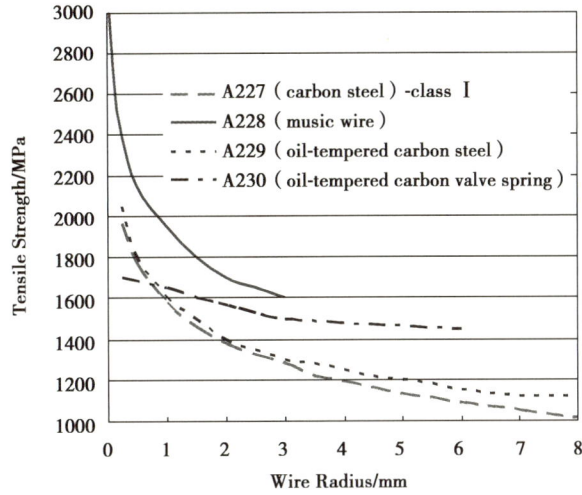

Fig. 79.1   Tensile Strength of Carbon Steel Springs as a Function of Wire Radius

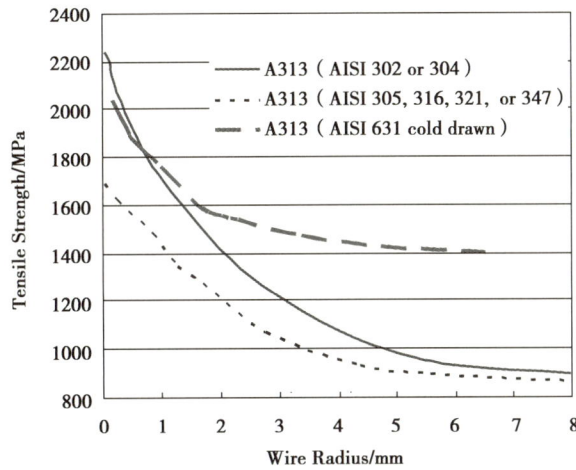

Fig. 79.2   Tensile Strength of Stainless Steel Springs as a Function of Wire Radius

Fig. 79.3   Tensile Strength of Specialty Steel Springs as a Function of Wire Radius

79.2   Types of Coil Spring End Types

There are four basic end types for compression springs, as shown in Fig. 79.4, which affect the total number of coils (N), active coils (N_a), pitch, free length (p), solid length, and seating. The solid length of an open-ended spring is N d, while it is $(N+1)$ d for a spring with closed endings, where N is the total number of spring coils. The number of active coils and solid length (L_s) is calculated according to its end types as follows:

End Type	N & N_a	Solid Height
Open	$N=N_a$	$L_s=(N+1)$ d
Closed	$N=N_a+2$	$L_s=(N+1)$ d
Open & Ground	$N=N_a+1$	$L_s=N$ d
Closed, Squared & Ground	$N=N_a+2$	$L_s=N$ d

The solid length for ground springs given above for a ground spring is more conservative for the design purpose. The more competent estimate is

$$L_s = (N - 0.5)(1.01\ d)$$

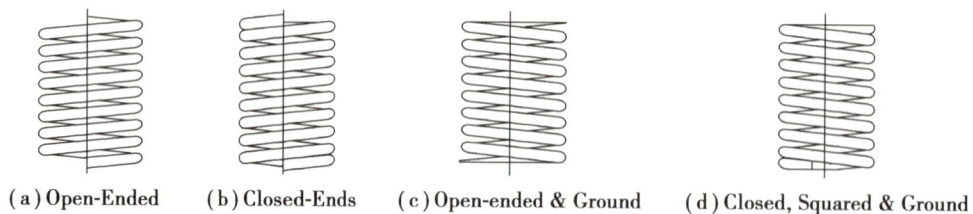

(a) Open-Ended   (b) Closed-Ends   (c) Open-ended & Ground   (d) Closed, Squared & Ground

Fig. 79.4   Four Basic End Types of Compression Springs

79.3   Loading of Coiled Springs

79.3.1   Shear Stress

The maximum allowable shear stress of a circular wire helical compression spring can be calculated as

$$\tau_{max} = \frac{8C_f F D_m}{\pi d^3} \tag{79.1}$$

where

d: Wire diameter;

C_f: Wah's factor, Eq.(79.2);

F: Applied axial force;

D_m: Mean diameter of the spring coils, $D_m = (D_o + D_i)/2$;

D_o: Outside diameter, or spring diameter generally;

D_i: Inner diameter, $D_i + 2d = D_o$.

The Wah's factor, C_f, is defined as

$$C_f = \frac{\dfrac{D_m}{d} - \dfrac{1}{4}}{\dfrac{D_m}{d} - 1} + \frac{0.615}{\dfrac{D_m}{d}} = \frac{C - \dfrac{1}{4}}{C - 1} + \frac{0.615}{C} \tag{79.2}$$

and $\quad C = \dfrac{D_m}{d}$ $\tag{79.3}$

79.3.2   Fatigue Crack Initiation of Springs

Failure analysis may be conducted in order to determine the fatigue crack initiation point and a comparison of that location with the most damaged zone predicted by numerical analysis can be made [Del Llano-Vizcaya et al.]. Among applied fatigue theories, it has been discovered that the Fatemi-Socie critical plane approach gives a good prediction of fatigue life, while the Wang-Brown criterion overestimates spring fatigue life and the Coffin-Mason model gives conservative results.

79.3.3   Axial Deflection and Spring Rate

Under an applied axial load, the spring got deflected. The axial deflection of the compression spring can be determined by

$$Z = \frac{8FD_m^3 N_a}{d^4 G} \tag{79.4}$$

where

Z: Axial deflection;

N_a: Active coil numbers;

G: Shear modulus.

Thus the spring rate can be calculated as

$$K \equiv \frac{F}{Z} = \frac{Gd^4}{8D_m N_a}$$

(79.5)

79.3.4 Maximum Twisting Moment Calculation

The maximum twisting moment (T) of the helical compression spring can be calculated using the following equation:

$$T = \frac{\pi \tau_{max} D_m^3}{16}$$

(79.6)

79.3.5 Buckling of Compression Springs

Slender compression springs are prone to buckling. In a traditional way, the length of a compression spring decreases under the effect of an axial loading. Below a critical length, some springs can be bend laterally instead of continuing to decrease the length and it is buckling. The length below which the phenomenon appears is called critical buckling length. The ratio of the critical buckling length to the original length corresponding to different fixity parameters (ψ) at both ends can be calculated as

$$\frac{L_{critical}}{L_o} = 1 - \left(\frac{1+\nu}{1+2\nu}\right) \left[1 - \left(\frac{1+2\nu}{2+\nu}\right) \left(\frac{\pi D_m}{\psi L_o}\right)^2\right]^{\frac{1}{2}}$$

(79.7)

where

$L_{critical}$: Critical length;

L_o: Original length of spring;

D_m: Mean diameter of the spring coils;

y: Fixity parameter;

n: Poisson's ratio and $G = \dfrac{E}{2(1+\nu)}$;

E: Young's modulus;

G: Shear modulus.

Note that ψ is a parameter depending on boundary conditions at the spring ends shown as follows:

> $\psi = 0.5$, if both ends are supported by flat parallel surfaces;
> $\psi = 0.707$, if one end is supported by flat surface and the other end hinged;
> $\psi = 1.0$, if both ends are hinged;
> $\psi = 1.0$, if both ends are supported by flat parallel surfaces & one end may slide laterally;
> $\psi = 2.0$, if one end is clamped and the other end free.

There is no buckling if the square-rooted term is less than or equal to zero, i.e.

$$\frac{D_m}{L_o} > \frac{\psi}{\pi}\left|\left(\frac{2+\nu}{1+2\nu}\right)^{\frac{1}{2}}\right|\qquad(79.8)$$

The critical length of buckling is independent of the stress level, but a function of the slenderness ratio of the spring (L_o/D_m) and boundary conditions at the spring ends. The basic concept to remember here in buckling is that as long as the spring free length is less than 4.4 times the mean diameter of the spring based on $\psi = 0.5$ and $\psi = 0.0$, the spring is safe from buckling. The minimum axial force (F_{buckle}) required to buckle an axial spring can be calculated as

$$F_{buckle} = \psi K L_o \qquad(79.9)$$

The direction of loading on a compression spring is not perfectly coincident with the spring axis. The eccentricity of the loading direction creates additional bending and twisting moments and the minimum load to cause buckling will be significantly lessened by the eccentric behavior. Prediction of buckling loads by Euler formula, i.e. Eq.(79.9), is only reasonable for long slender column with few geometric imperfections. In practice, structures may suffer from plastic knockdown and buckling loads obtained experimentally are less than the prediction by the Euler formula. The following semi-empirical formula, including the crushing strength of the material is proposed by [Rankine & Gordon]

$$\frac{1}{F_R} = \frac{1}{F_{buckle}} + \frac{1}{F_{uts}}\qquad(79.10)$$

where
F_R is the maximum endurable load, called Rankine-Gordon load, and

$$F_{uts} = \frac{1}{2}\pi d^2 \tau_{max}\qquad(79.11)$$

of which τ_{max} is obtained from Eq.(79.1).

79.3.6 Diameter Expansion as Compressed

The outside diameter of a compression coil spring increases when compressed mainly due to its pitch as

$$D_{o,compressed} = \left[D_m + \frac{p^2 - d^2}{\pi^2}\right]^{\frac{1}{2}}\qquad(79.12)$$

Since $D_{o,compressed} > D_{o,original}$, the dimensional tolerances related to the hole opening containing the spring have to be checked. On the other hand, the outside diameter of an extension spring decreases when extended.

79.3.7 Permanent Set of a Helical Spring

In order to assure that the permanent set of a helical spring is less than 2% of its original length, the maximum operating stress should be limited as follows [Associated Spring Corporation]:

Spring Material	Presetting	τ_{max}
Ferrous	No	$<0.45\ \sigma_{uts}$
Austenitic Stainless	No	$<0.35\ \sigma_{uts}$
Nonferrous	No	$<0.35\ \sigma_{uts}$
Ferrous	Yes	$<0.65\ \sigma_{uts}$
Austenitic Stainless	Yes	$<0.55\ \sigma_{uts}$
Nonferrous	Yes	$<0.55\ \sigma_{uts}$

79.3.8 Natural Frequency of Compression Springs

An empirical equation for predicting the natural frequency of compression is given as follows:

$$\omega_n = \frac{3.53 \times 10^5 d}{N_a D_m^2} \quad (d \text{ and } D_m \text{ in mm}) \tag{79.13}$$

79.4 Leaf Springs

Leaf springs have been the beloved structural parts for truck suspensions. SAE 5160 and SAE 6150 steels are used for leaf springs for trucks. A leaf spring can either be attached directly to the frame at both ends or attached directly at one end, usually the front, with the other end attached through a shackle that is a short swinging arm, as shown in Fig. 79.5. The shackle takes up the tendency of the leaf spring to elongate when compressed and thus makes for softer springiness.

Steel leaf springs are popular while composite springs are gaining the market share gradually. The natural frequency of a composite leaf spring for composite springs (14.3 Hz) is generally higher than a steel leaf spring (6.3 Hz) in comparison to that for road bumps at 12 Hz due to road irregularities. The result of the accelerated test for fatigue life by [Kumar et al.] shows that the life of a composite leaf spring is much higher than its steel counterpart.

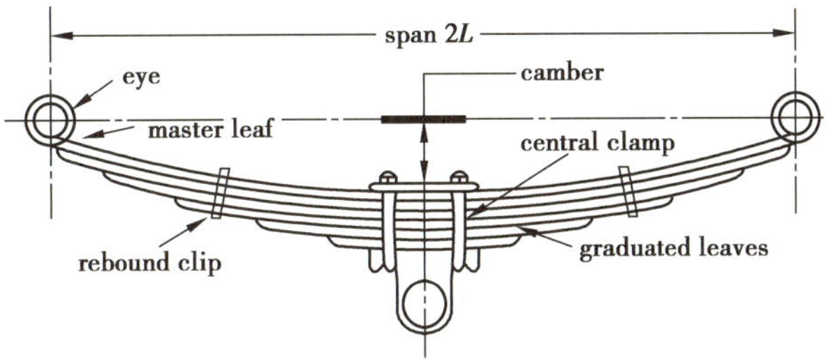

Fig. 79.5　Multi-leaf Spring for Heavy-duty Trucks

79.5　Spring Fatigue Life and Shot Peening

Fatigue parameters of spring materials are listed in Table 79.2. The fatigue life of springs, especially coil springs, may be enhanced by shot penning. Shot-peening springs increase compression spring fatigue life by at least 30 percent and have often increased the life from 2 to 10 times. Shot peening is basically used on compression springs with a wire thickness of 1.5 mm and above. Thinner wire can be shot-peened, but there is a risk that the wire may deform in the process.

The steel shot is flung at a great force at the surface of the spring. The steel shot is in a turbine wheel that flings it repeatedly at the material surface at high speed.

References

ARUN K, SWETHA K, 2011. Influence of Material Condition on the Dry Sliding Wear Behavior of Spring Steel [J]. Journal of Minerals and Material Characterization and Engineering, 10(4): 323-337.

BECKER L E, CLEGHORN W L, 1992. On the Buckling of Helical Compression Springs [J]. International Journal of Mechanical Science, 34(4): 276-282.

BOCKWOLDT T, MUNSIK G, 2013. Correction to Design Equation for Spring Diametral Growth Upon Compression[J]. Journal of Mechanical Design, 135(12): 209-219.

CHASSIE G G, et al, 1997. On the Buckling of Helical Springs under Combined Compression and Torsion[J]. International Journal of Mechanical Science, 39(6): 697-704.

DEL LLANO-VIZCAYA L, et al, 2006. Multiaxial Fatigue and Failure Analysis of Helical Compression Springs [J]. Engineering Failure Analysis, 13(8): 1303-1313.

DRAGONI E, STROUI A, 1989. Measuring the Load Eccentricity in Helical Compression Springs[J]. Strain, 25(3): 89-84.

KUMAR M S, VIJAYARANGAN S, 2007. Analytical and Experimental Studies on Fatigue Life Prediction of Steel and Composite Multi-leaf Spring for Light Passenger Vehicles Using Life Data Analysis[J]. Material Science, 13(2): 2.

LANDGRAF R W, FRANCIS R C, 1979. Material and Processing Effects on Fatigue Performance of Leaf Springs[J]. SAE 790407.

LI D M, KIM K W, LEE C S, 1997. Low Cycle Fatigue Data Evaluation for a HighStrength Spring Steel[J]. International Journal of Fatigue, 19(8-9): 607-612.

PRAWOTO Y, IKEDA, M, MANVILLE S, et al, 2008. Design and Failure Modes of Automotive Suspension Springs[J]. Engineering Failure Analysis, 15: 1155-1174.

RAMAKANTH U S, SOWJANYA K, 2013. Design and Analysis of Automotive Multi-Leaf Springs Using Composite Materials [J]. International Journal of Mechanical Engineering Production Research and Development, 3(1): 155-162.

SOROKIN S V, 2009. Linear Dynamics of Elastic Helical Springs: Asymptotic Analysis of Wave Propagation [J]. Proceedings of the Royal Society, A, Mathematical Physical and Engineering Sciences, 465(2105): 1513-1537.

SUSTARSIC B, et al, 2011. Fatigue Strength and Microstructural Features of Spring Steels [J]. Structural Integrity and Life, 11(1): 27-34.

Table 79.1   Mechanical Properties of Spring Steels ($T_m = 1400$ ℃)

Material	T/℃	E_T	ρ	ν	(σ, ε)	α	k	γ	ρ_E	K_{IC}
Coil Springs:										
ASTM A227	23	197	7.8	0.29	Fig. 79.1	15.7	16.2	500	—	—
	500	—	—	—	—	18.4	21.5	—	—	—
ASTM A228	23	197	7.8	0.29	Fig. 79.1	15.7	16.2	500	—	—
ASTM A229	23	197	7.8	0.29	Fig. 79.1	15.7	16.2	500	—	—
ASTM A230	23	197	7.8	0.29	Fig. 79.1	15.7	16.2	500	—	—
ASTM A232	23	197	7.8	0.29	Fig. 79.3	15.7	16.2	500	—	—

continued

Material	$T/^\circ C$	E_T	ρ	ν	(σ,ε)	α	k	γ	ρ_E	K_{IC}
ASTM A313	23	193	7.9	0.29	Fig. 79.2	16.9	16.2	500	—	—
ASTM A401	23	197	7.8	0.29	Fig. 79.3	15.7	16.2	500	—	—
ASTM A679	23	197	7.8	0.29	Fig. 79.3	15.7	16.2	500	—	—
Leaf Springs-Steels:										
DIN 51CrV4 (//)	23	207	7.8	0.29	(1500,0.2%) (1600, 9.9%)	12	16.2	500	—	—
DIN 51CrV4 ($\perp$)	23	207	7.8	0.29	(1500,0.2%) (1600,5.2%)	12	16.2	500	—	—
(Fe-0.52C-0.35Si-0.96Mn-0.94Cr-0.05Mo-0.12V-0.011P-0.004S; austenizing/cooling N_2/tempering 415 $^\circ C$)										
DIN 51CrV4 (//)	23	207	7.8	0.29	(1370,0.2%) (1450,10.6%)	12	16.2	500	—	—
DIN 51CrV4 ($\perp$)	23	207	7.8	0.29	(1370,0.2%) (1450,7%)	12	16.2	500	—	—
(Fe-0.52C-0.35Si-0.96Mn-0.94Cr-0.05Mo-0.12V-0.011P-0.004S; austenizing/cooling N_2/tempering 475 $^\circ C$)										
SUP9	23	207	7.85	0.27	(1158,0.2%) $\sigma_{uts}=1272$	12	16.2	500	—	—
(Fe-0.271C-0.265Si-0.762Mn-0.012P−0.213Ni-0.867Cr-0.048Mo-0.004Al-0.197Cu-0.025Co-0.003Nb -0.004V-0.001Ti)										
EN45	23	204	7.85	0.27	$\sigma_{uts}=621$	12	16	500	—	—
55Si2Mn90	23	207	7.86	0.27	(1479,0.2%) $\sigma_{uts}=1962$	12	16.2	500	—	—

Notes: // = along the longitudinal direction of leaf spring;

$\perp$ = Perpendicular to the longitudinal direction of leaf spring.

Table 79.2   Fatigue ε-N Properties of Spring Steels

Material-DAM	$T/^\circ C$	$d\varepsilon/dt$	σ_f'	ε_f'	b	c	K'	n'	$\sigma_f@2N_f$	R
Coil Springs:										
ASTM A227	23	—	—	—	—	—	—	—	$0.336\sigma_{uts}$	—
ASYM A228	23	—	—	—	—	—	—	—	$0.388\sigma_{uts}$	—

continued

Material-DAM	$T/℃$	$d\varepsilon/dt$	σ'_f	ε'_f	b	c	K'	n'	$\sigma_f @ 2N_f$	R
ASTM A229	23	—	—	—	—	—	—	—	$0.336\sigma_{uts}$	—
SAE 9254	23	—	4108	1.13	−0.109	−0.954	3322	0.088	—	—
(Q&T; Coil spring grade for automotive suspension)										
Leaf Springs :										
SAE 5160 (Tempered Martensite)	23	—	2050	1.24	−0.09	−0.79	2000	0.1	—	—
SAE 5160(Q&T; Special)	23	—	1930	0.56	—	—	1895	0.046	—	—
DIN 51CrV4 (//)	23	—	—	—	—	—	—	—	$416@ 10^7$	—
DIN 51CrV4 (⊥)	23	—	—	—	—	—	—	—	$382 @ 10^7$	—
(Fe-0.52C-0.35Si-0.96Mn-0.94Cr-0.05Mo-0.12V-0.011P-0.004S; austenizing/cooling N_2/tempering 415 ℃)										
DIN 51CrV4 (//)	23	—	—	—	—	—	—	—	$479@ 10^7$	—
DIN 51CrV4 (⊥)	23	—	—	—	—	—	—	—	$386 @ 10^7$	—
(Fe-0.52C-0.35Si-0.96Mn-0.94Cr-0.05Mo-0.12V-0.011P-0.004S; austenizing/cooling N_2/tempering 475 ℃)										
SUP9	23	—	2063	9.56	−0.08	−1.05	—	—	—	—
EN45	23	—	948	0.26	−0.092	−0.445	—	—	—	—
Steel (Generic)	23	—	Eq. (6.14)	Eq. (6.15)	−0.09	0.6	$\sigma'_f/(\varepsilon'_f)^{n'}$	b/c	Eq.(78.1)	— —

Chapter 80

Tool, Die, and Mold Steels

80.1　Introduction

High strength, toughness, and hardness at elevated temperature are the general requirements for tool, die, and mold steels. Classification of these special steels according to [SAE] & [AISI] is given as follows:

SAE/AISI Grade	Characteristics
A	Cold hardening; Air hardening (Medium alloys)
D	Cold hardening; (High carbon, high chromium)
F	Water hardened carbon tungsten steel tool; wear-resistant
H1-H19	Chromium base (Hot work), e.g. H13 provides better hardenability and better wear resistance than common alloy steels such as 4140
H20-H39	Tungsten-based alloys (Hot work)
H40-H59	Molybdenum-based alloys (Hot work)
L	Low alloy special purpose tool steel; L6 is extremely tough
M	Molybdenum-based high speed tool steel
O	Oil hardening (Cold hardening)
P	Plastic molds
S	Shock resistance tool steel
T	Tungsten-based high speed tool steel
W	Water-quenched high carbon plain steel

Their mechanical properties, fatigue strengths, and creep parameters are given in Tables 80.1—80.3, respectively. The change of mechanical properties of the tool, die and mold steels is accelerating of many causes, mainly due to degradation processes like creep, cyclic thermal stress (start-ups and going down) and many other influences. For example, the continuous operating temperature for T23 steel is below 580 ℃ while for steels P91 and P92 up to 610 ℃.

80.2　Tool Steels

Tool steels are high-carbon steel alloys (having carbon content between 0.7% and 1.5%), containing chromium (Cr), molybdenum (Mo), vanadium (V), and tungsten (W). Their suitability comes from their distinctive hardness, resistance to abrasion, ability to hold a cutting edge, and/or resistance to deformation at elevated temperatures (red-hardness). High speed steels also use cobalt to increase heat and wear resistance. Tool steels are generally used in a heat-treated state. Tool steels are used for common tools like screwdrivers and wrenches, and for machine parts that apply patterns or indentations onto other materials.

A2 is commonly used for blanking and forming punches, trimming dies, thread rolling dies, and injection molding dies. A6 air-hardens at a relatively low temperature (approximately the same temperature as oil-hardening grades) and is dimensionally stable. Therefore it is commonly used for dies, forming tools, and gauges that do not require extreme wear resistance but do need high stability. A10 contains a uniform distribution of graphite particles to increase machinability and provide self-lubricating properties. It is commonly used for gauges, arbors, shears, and punches.

D-grade tool steels contain between 10% and 18% chromium. These steels retain their hardness up to a temperature of 425 ℃. Common applications for D-grade of tool steel are forging dies, die-casting die blocks, and drawing dies. D2 is very wear-resistant but not as tough as lower alloyed steels. It is widely used for punches, shear blades, planer blades and industrial cutting tools, sometimes used for knives.

H-grade tool steels were developed for strength and hardness during prolonged exposure to elevated temperatures.

S-grade tool steels (low-carbon steel) displays very high impact toughness and relatively low abrasion resistance, and it can attain relatively high hardness (HRC 58/60). This type of steel is used in applications such as jackhammer bits and punches per 58 HRC (hardness Rockwell C).

T-grade tool steels and M-grade tool steels are used for cutting tools where strength and hardness must be retained at temperatures up to or exceeding 760 ℃. The elastoplastic behavior of M-50 can be described [Nelias] by the following equation

$$\sigma = 1280(4 + 10^6 \varepsilon_p)^{0.095} \text{ MPa}$$

M-50 is also an excellent material for bearings. Tungsten carbide steel (Fe-WC-6%Co) is a hard and wear-resistant carbide compound used for lathe, milling, and drilling cutters.

80.3   Die Steels

Die steels are a specific type of high-strength steel that is produced primarily for tools and machine parts. It is formed in one whole piece with a mold and then hardened. Die components may be classified into the following: die block, punch plate, blank punch, pierce punch, stripper plate, pilot, guide/back gage/finger stop, setting block, blanking die, and piercing die.

AISI D2 (Fe-1.5C-1Mo-12Cr-1V) has been used for drawing dies and cutlery. H13 tool steel is used extensively in aluminum extrusion, aluminum die casting and forging die applications. Its exceptional toughness and inherent resiliency have also made this a popular material for die casting in the cold heading field.

80.4 Mold Steels

A very special category of steel is mold steel. Mold steels can be used for molding of nonferrous metals such as aluminum-, magnesium-, and nickel-based alloys, plastics, fiber-reinforced plastics, rubber, and fiber-reinforced rubber.

NAK 80, NAK 55, P-20, PX5, and AISI 4140 are popular mold steels for the extrusion of plastics. P-grade tool steel is short for plastic mold steels. They are designed to meet the requirements of zinc die casting and plastic injection molding dies. P20 is for general purpose applications, while PX5 is a 30 HRc, P20-typed pre-hardened steel that can be used for all plastic molding.

The combination of machinability and weldability is the main reason mold makers select NAK (NAK 80 and NAK 55 for plastics) over P-20 for prehardened mold steels (for making large plastic injection molds) in spite of its higher cost.

References

ARIF A, et al, 2003. Modes of Die Failure and Tool Complexity in Hot Extrusion of Al-6063[J]. Journal of Materials Processing Technology, 134 (3): 318-328.

BAÁA P, 2010. New Tool Materials Based on Ni Alloys Strengthened by Intermetallic Compounds with a High Carbon Content[J]. Archives of Materials Science and Engineering, 42(1): 5-12.

BARRAU O, BOHER C, GRAS R, et al, 2003. Analysis of the Friction and Wear Behavior of Hot Work Tool Steel for Forging[J]. Wear, 255: 1444-1454.

CARVALHO M A, et al, 2002. Microstructure, Mechanical Properties and Wear Resistance of High Speed Steel Rolls for Hot Rolling Mills[J]. Iron and Steel Maker, 29(1): 27-32.

CORNACCHIA G, et al, 2008. Influence of Aging on Microstructure and Toughness of Die-Casting Die Steels [J]. International Journal of Microstructure & Materials Properties, 3(2-3): 195-205.

COWIE J G, PETERS D T, BRUSH Jr. E F, et al, 2001. Materials and Modifications to Die Cast the Copper Conductors of the Induction Motor Rotor[J]. Die-Casting Engineer, 45(5): 38-47.

DEGARMO E, PAUL, BLACK J T, et al, 2003. Materials and Processes in Manufacturing[M]. 9th edition. NewYork: John Wiley and Sons.

DEJESUS A, et al, 2006. Low and High Cycle Fatigue and Cyclic Elastoplastic Behavior of the P355NL1 Steel [J]. Journal of Pressure Vessels Technology, 128(3): 298-304.

DENG Y K, CHEN J R, WANG S Z, 2002. High Speed Tool Steel[M]. Beijing: Metallurgical Industry Press.

DOBRZAĚSKI J, et al, 2009. Microstructure, Properties Investigations and Methodology of the State Evaluation of T23 (2.25Cr-0.3Mo-1.6W-V-Nb) Steel in Boiler Application[J]. Journal of Achievements in Materials and Manufacturing Engineering, 32(2): 142-153.

ENGELMANN P, et al, 1997. Improved Product Quality and Cycle times Using Copper Alloy Mold Cores[J]. Journal of Injection Molding Technology, 1 (1): 18-24.

FU H G, et al, 2009. Effect of Quenching Temperature on Structure and Properties of Centrifugal Casting High Speed Steel Roll[J]. China Foundry, 6(1): 15-19.

FUSSELL P S, et al, 1991. A Sprayed Steel Tool for Permanent Mold Casting of Aluminum[J]. SAE 911114.

HALMOS, GEORGE T, 2006. Roll Forming Handbook[M]. Boca Raton: CRC Press.

HARDELL J, PRAKASH B, 2008. High-temperature Friction and Wear Behavior of Different Tool Steels during Sliding against Al-Si-coated High-strength Steel[J]. Tribology International, 41(7): 663-671.

IM Y T, et al, 2009. Research Activities of Computer-aided Materials Processing Laboratory[J]. Journal of Achievements in Materials and Manufacturing Engineering, 24(1): 219-229.

JACKSON M J, ROBISON G M, MORRELL J S, 2008. Microfinishing Quenched and Tempered M42 Tool Steels[J]. International Journal of Nanomanufacturing, 2(1-2): 174-180.

MAR S, LI Y, XU K, 2001. The Composite of Nitrided Steel of H13 and TiN Coatings by Plasma Duplex Treatment and the Effect of Pre-nitriding[J]. Surface Coating Technology, 137: 116-121.

MATSUDA A, 2004. Evaluation for Mechanical Properties of Laminated Rubber Bearings Using Finite Element Analysis[J]. Journal of Pressure Vessel Technology, 126(1): 134-140.

MEBARKI N, et al, 2004. Relationship between Microstructure and Mechanical Properties of a 5% Cr Tempered Martensitic Tool Steel[J]. Materials Science and Engineering: (A) 387-389: 171-175.

NELIAS D, JACQ C, LORMAND G, et al, 2005. New Methodology to Evaluate the Rolling Contact Fatigue Performance of Bearing Steels with Surface Dents: Application to 32CrMoV13 (Nitrided) and M50 Steels [J]. Journal of Tribology, 127: 611-622.

NOGUEIRA R A, FILHO F A, DE L M, et al, 2001. Microstructural Evaluation of AISI T-15 High Speed Steel [J]. Key Engineering Materials, 189/191: 401-407.

OBERG, ERIK, JONES, et al, 2004. Machinery's Handbook[M]. 27th edition. Berlin: Industrial Press.

QAMAR S Z, et al, 2009. Effect of Heat Treatment on Mechanical Properties of H11 Tool Steel[J]. Journal of

Achievements in Materials and Manufacturing Engineering, 35(2): 115-120.

TARNEY E, BECKMAN J, 2001. Material Properties and Performance Considerations for High-Speed Steel Gear-Cutting Tools[J]. Gear Technology, 18(4): 17-21.

WILCZYNSKI J S, GREGOIRE C A, 1991. The Effects of Die Materials and Electro-Etching on Frictional Characteristics of Automotive Sheet Steels[J]. SAE 920635.

YAMAMOTO K, et al, 2000. Effects of Alloying Elements in Hardenability for High C High Speed Steel Type Alloy[J]. Journal of Japan Foundry Engineering, 72(2): 90-95.

Table 80.1　Mechanical Properties of Tool, Die, and Mold Steels

Material	$T/°C$	E_T	ρ	ν	(σ,ε)	α	k	γ	ρ_E	K_{IC}
Fremax 45 (Q&T)	23	206	7.83	0.29	(420,0.2) $\sigma_{uts}=700$	11.5	42.3	481	—	—
SAE 4130 (Q&T)	23	206	7.83	0.29	(1210,0.2%) $\sigma_{uts}=1340$	11.5	42.3	481	—	—
SAE 4140 (HT)	23	206	7.83	0.29	(735,0.2%) (932,14%)	11.5	42.3	481	—	—
	300	190	—	—	—	13.2	39.4	590	—	—
	400	182	—	—	—	13.7	38	607	—	—
SAE 4140 (Q&T)	23	206	7.83	0.29	(1210,0.2%) $\sigma_{uts}=1380$	11.5	42.3	481	—	—
SAE 4340 (Q&T)	23	206	7.83	0.29	(1440,0.2%) $\sigma_{uts}=1680$	11.5	42.3	481	—	—
SAE 6150 (Q&T)	23	206	7.83	0.29	(1100,0.2%) $\sigma_{uts}=1310$	11.5	42.3	481	—	—
SAE 8620 (Q&T)	23	206	7.83	0.29	(630,0.2%) $\sigma_{uts}=745$	11.5	42.3	481	—	—
A2 (Q&T)	23	190	7.75	0.29	(1050,0.2%) $\sigma_{uts}=1200$	11.5	26	460	—	—
	200	185	7.7	0.29	—	11.6	27	—	—	—
	400	170	7.65	0.29	—	—	28.5	—	—	—

continued

Material	$T/℃$	E_T	ρ	ν	(σ,ε)	α	k	γ	ρ_E	K_{IC}
D2 (Q&T)	23	210	7.7	0.29	$(1220,0.2\%)$ $\sigma_{uts}=1400$	10.4	20	460	—	—
	200	200	—	—	—	11.2	21	—	—	—
	400	180	—	—	—	12	23	—	—	—
	$1421(T_m)$	—	—	—	—	—	—	—	—	—
D3	23	210	7.7	0.29	—	10.5	20	460	—	—
	$1421(T_m)$	—	—	—	—	—	—	—	—	—
D6 (Q&T)	23	210	7.83	0.29	$(1500,0.2\%)$	10.5	—	460	—	44
D6 (Q:950 ℃ & T:500 ℃)	23	210	7.83	0.29	$(2100,0.2\%)$	10.5	—	460	—	26
H11 (Q & T: 600 ℃)	23	207	7.8	0.29	$(950,2\%)$ $(1300,4\%)$ $(1420,6\%)$ $(1500,14\%)$	11	24.6	460	—	—
	200	190	—	—	—	12.4	—	—	—	—
	538	159	—	—	—	—	—	—	—	—
	$1427(T_m)$	—	—	—	—	—	—	—	—	—
H11 (Q & T: 500 ℃)	23	207	7.8	0.29	$(1170,0.2\%)$ $\sigma_{uts}=2100$	11	24.6	460	—	—
	200	190	—	—	—	12.4	—	—	—	—
H12 (Q&T)	23	207	7.8	0.29	$(1390,0.2\%)$ $\sigma_{uts}=1800$	10.4	23	460	—	—
H13 (HRC60)	23	207	7.8	0.29	$(415,0.2\%)$ $(520,17\%)$	10.4	23	460	—	—
	200	200	—	—	—	11.3	23.4	520	—	—
	400	—	—	—	—	—	588	—	—	46
	500	—	—	—	—	—	—	—	—	30

continued

Material	$T/℃$	E_{T}	ρ	ν	(σ,ε)	α	k	γ	ρ_{E}	K_{IC}
H13 (HRC60)	550	—	—	—	—	—	—	—	—	26
	600	197	—	—	—	14	26	726	—	32
	700	—	—	—	—	—	905	—	—	78
	760	—	—	—	—	—	1151	—	—	—
	800	190	—	—	—	—	885	—	—	—
	1000	160	—	—	—	—	733	—	—	—
H13 (Q&T)	23	207	7.8	0.29	$(1400,0.2\%)$ $\sigma_{\mathrm{uts}}=1750$	10.4	23	460	—	—
M2 (Q&T)	23	220	8.17	0.29	$(1220,0.2\%)$ $\sigma_{\mathrm{uts}}=1400$	11	24	420	—	—
M4	23	207	8	0.29	$(287,0.2\%)$ $\sigma_{\mathrm{uts}}=650$	9.5	—	—	—	—
M42	23	207	8	0.29	$(415,0.2\%)$ $(520,17\%)$	10	—	—	—	—
M50(Cr4MoV; Fe-0.8C-0.25Mn-0.015P-0.015S -0.25Si-4Cr-0.1 Ni-4.5Mo-1V)	23	203	7.85	0.29	$(450,0.2\%)$ $(770,16\%)$	10.6	25	460	—	18
	415(High service temperature)									
M50 Nil (Case)	23	203	7.85	0.29	$(1250,0.2\%)$ $(1060,16\%)$	10.6	25	460	—	52
M50 Nil (Core)	23	203	7.85	0.29	$(450,0.2\%)$ $(770,16\%)$	10.6	25	460	—	63
M54 (Railway)	23	203	7.85	0.29	$(530,0.2\%)$ $(844,10\%)$	10.1	26.3	460	—	65
M54, Ferrium (Martensitic; Secondary Hardening)	23	203	7.85	0.29	$(1724,0.2\%)$ $(2027,14\%)$	10.1	26.3	460	—	—
	100	—	—	—	—	10.2	27.9	480	—	—
	400	—	—	—	—	11.1	—	570	—	—
	500	—	—	—	—	11.5	33	—	—	—

continued

Material	$T/°C$	E_T	ρ	ν	(σ, ε)	α	k	γ	ρ_E	K_{IC}
M250	23	203	7.85	0.29	$(586, 0.2\%)$ $\sigma_{uts} = 827$	10.6	25	460	—	52
M300 (HRc = 53)	23	203	7.85	0.29	$(1690, 0.2\%)$ $\sigma_{uts} = 1990$	10.6	25	460	—	52
(HRc = 60 at induction-hardened surface; Gears, conrod, cranshafts, & torsional bars)										
NAK 80	23	207	7.83	0.29	$(1018, 0.2\%)$ $(1255, 16\%)$	11.3	—	—	—	—
	100	—	—	—	—	12.6	41.4	—	—	—
	200	—	—	—	—	12.6	42.2	—	—	—
	300	—	—	—	—	13.5	—	—	—	—
O1 (Q&T)	23	206	7.83	0.29	$(1220, 0.2\%)$ $\sigma_{uts} = 1400$	10.7	32	460	—	—
P2 (Carburized)	23	206	7.86	0.29	—	11.9	50	460	—	—
P20 (Nitrided or Carburized)	23	205	7.85	0.29	$(845, 0.2\%)$ $(998, 20\%)$	11.9	29	460	—	—
	300	192	—	—	—	12.7	—	527	—	—
	400	185	—	—	—	13	—	787	—	—
P22	23	206	7.83	0.29	$(205, 0.2\%)$ $(415, 30\%)$	—	—	—	—	—
P91 (Weld, New; Martensite)	23	206	7.83	0.29	$(450, 0.2\%)$ $(500, 2\%)$ $(615, 4\%)$ $(650, 6\%)$	—	—	—	—	97
	500	—	—	—	$\sigma_{crs,10000} = 289$	—	—	—	—	—
	600	—	—	—	$(425, 2\%)$ $(510, 5\%)$; $\sigma_{crs,10000} = 123$	—	—	—	—	—
	650	—	—	—	$(405, 2\%)$ $(430, 3\%)$; $\sigma_{crs,100000} = 50$	—	—	—	—	—

continued

Material	$T/℃$	E_{T}	ρ	ν	(σ,ε)	α	k	γ	ρ_{E}	K_{IC}
P91 (Weld) (After 350000 h exposure to 590 ℃)	23	—	—	—	$(396,0.2\%)$ $\sigma_{\mathrm{uts}}=482$	—	—	—	—	—
P92	23	206	7.83	0.29	$(430,0.2\%)$ $(520,5.5\%)$	10.5	—	—	—	—
	600	—	—	—	$\sigma_{\mathrm{crs},10000}=140$ $\sigma_{\mathrm{crs},50000}=119$	15.3	—	—	—	—
	625	—	—	—	$\sigma_{\mathrm{crs},10000}=106$ $\sigma_{\mathrm{crs},50000}=89$	—	—	—	—	—
	650	—	—	—	$\sigma_{\mathrm{crs},10000}=79$ $\sigma_{\mathrm{crs},50000}=63$	—	—	—	—	—
P92 (Weld)	23	206	7.83	0.29	$(430,0.2\%)$ $(520,5.5\%)$	—	—	—	—	—
	600	—	—	—	$\sigma_{\mathrm{crs},10000}=121$ $\sigma_{\mathrm{crs},50000}=95$	—	—	—	—	—
	625	—	—	—	$\sigma_{\mathrm{crs},10000}=87$ $\sigma_{\mathrm{crs},50000}=60$	—	—	—	—	—
	650	—	—	—	$\sigma_{\mathrm{crs},10000}=53$ $\sigma_{\mathrm{crs},50000}=31$	—	—	—	—	—
P195	23	206	7.83	0.29	—	—	—	—	—	—
	400	—	—	—	$\sigma_{\mathrm{crs},10000}=182$ $\sigma_{\mathrm{crs},100000}=141$	—	—	—	—	—
	500	—	—	—	$\sigma_{\mathrm{crs},10000}=58$ $\sigma_{\mathrm{crs},100000}=32$	—	—	—	—	—
P235	23	206	7.83	0.29	—	—	—	—	—	—
	400	—	—	—	$\sigma_{\mathrm{crs},10000}=182$ $\sigma_{\mathrm{crs},100000}=141$	—	—	—	—	—
	500	—	—	—	$\sigma_{\mathrm{crs},10000}=58$ $\sigma_{\mathrm{crs},100000}=32$	—	—	—	—	—

continued

Material	$T/°C$	E_T	ρ	ν	(σ,ε)	α	k	γ	ρ_E	K_{IC}
P265	23	206	7.83	0.29	—	—	—	—	—	—
	400	—	—	—	$\sigma_{crs,10000}=182$ $\sigma_{crs,100000}=141$	—	—	—	—	—
	500	—	—	—	$\sigma_{crs,10000}=58$ $\sigma_{crs,100000}=32$	—	—	—	—	—
P355	23	206	7.83	0.29	—	—	—	—	—	—
	400	—	—	—	$\sigma_{crs,10000}=243$ $\sigma_{crs,100000}=179$	—	—	—	—	—
	500	—	—	—	$\sigma_{crs,10000}=74$ $\sigma_{crs,100000}=41$	—	—	—	—	—
P355NL1 (Annealed)	23	205	7.8	0.28	$(418,0.2\%)$ $(568,30\%)$	—	—	—	—	—
P355NL1 (Q&T)	23	205	7.8	0.28	$(1034,0.2\%)$ $(1158,15\%)$	—	—	—	—	—
P510L	23	205	7.8	0.28	$(355,0.2\%)$ $(510,24\%)$	—	—	—	—	—
	600	—	—	—	$(180,0.2\%)$ $\sigma_{uts}=230$	—	—	—	—	—
	800	—	—	—	$(75,0.2\%)$ $\sigma_{uts}=100$	—	—	—	—	—
P510L (Annealed)	23	205	7.8	0.28	$(355,0.2\%)$ $(510,24\%)$	—	—	—	—	—
	600	—	—	—	$(180,0.2\%)$ $\sigma_{uts}=230$	—	—	—	—	—
	800	—	—	—	$(75,0.2\%)$ $\sigma_{uts}=100$	—	—	—	—	—
PX 5	23	207	7.83	0.29	$(865,0.2\%)$ $\sigma_{uts}=981$	11.9	42.4	481	—	—
	300	193	—	—	—	13.1	39.2	553	—	—
	400	185	—	—	—	13.5	38.8	628	—	—

continued

Material	$T/^\circ C$	E_T	ρ	ν	(σ,ε)	α	k	γ	ρ_E	K_{IC}
S1	23	207	7.83	0.29	—	11	32	460	—	—
S7	23	207	7.83	0.29	(380,0.2%) (640,25%)	11	29	460	—	—
S420M	23	207	7.83	0.29	(460,2%) (640,12%)	11	29	460	—	—
	300	—	—	—	(350,2%) (490,9%)	—	—	—	—	—
	500	—	—	—	(340,2%) (400,7%)	—	—	—	—	—
S420M（Weld）	100	—	—	—	(420,1%) (440,2%)	—	—	—	—	—
	300	—	—	—	(360,1%) (380,2%)	—	—	—	—	—
	500	—	—	—	(250,1%) (300,2%)	—	—	—	—	—
T1	23	207	8.67	0.29	(205,0.2%) (380,30%)	9.7	20	460	—	28
T15	23	214	8.15	0.29	—	10	21	460	—	—
T23	23	214	8.15	0.29	—	10	21	460	—	—
T91(Fe-9Cr-1Mo-V-Nb)	23	197	7.85	0.29	—	10	21	460	—	—
T92(Fe-9Cr-0.5Mo-2W-V-Nb)	23	197	7.85	0.29	(445,0.2%) $\sigma_{uts}>620$	11	28	420	—	21
	500	150	—	—	(350,0.2%)	14	32	580	—	—
	600	120	—	—	(260,0.2%)	15.5	30	640	—	—
	650	—	—	—	(220,0.2%)	16	—	650	—	—

continued

Material	$T/°C$	E_T	ρ	ν	(σ,ε)	α	k	γ	ρ_E	K_{IC}
T92(Super304H; Weld joint)	23	207	—	0.29	(450,0.2%) $\sigma_{uts}=781$	—	—	—	—	—
	550	—	—	—	(200,0.2%) $\sigma_{uts}=428$	—	—	—	—	—
	600	—	—	—	(200,0.2%) $\sigma_{uts}=343$	—	—	—	—	—
	650	—	—	—	(175,0.2%) $\sigma_{uts}=268$	—	—	—	—	—
TIG (Weld for tool steels)	23	207	—	0.29	(620,0.2%) (840,30%)	—	—	—	—	—
W1	23	205	7.83	0.29	(415,0.2%) (520,17%)	10.4	—	460	—	—
W1 (Q&T)	23	205	7.83	0.29	(1080,0.2%) $\sigma_{uts}=1220$	10.4	—	460	—	—
W360(Asutentizing Q & T: 580 °C; Gears, Crankshafts)	23	205	7.83	0.29	(1860,0.2%) $\sigma_{uts}=2000$	10.4	—	460	—	—
DIN 1.2367 (X38CrMoV5; Tool Steel)	23	202	—	0.29	(1625,0.2%) (2088,21.7%)	—	—	—	—	—
	540(1 h tempering×2 times)									
	1030(Heat-treated)									
DIN 1.2367 (X38CrMoV5; Tool Steel)	23	204	—	0.29	(1585,0.2%) (1995,19.5%)	—	—	—	—	—
	580(1 h tempering×2 times)									
	1030(Heat-treated)									
DIN 1.2367 (X38CrMoV5; Tool Steel)	23	203	—	0.29	(1375,0.2%) (1612,21.8%)	—	—	—	—	—
	620(1 h tempering×2 times)									
	1030(Heat-treated)									

continued

Material	$T/℃$	E_{T}	ρ	ν	(σ,ε)	α	k	γ	ρ_{E}	K_{IC}
DIN 1.2367 (X38CrMoV5; Tool Steel)	23	205	—	0.29	(1350,0.2%) (1711,10.1%)	—	—	—	—	—
	500(7 h Surface-Nitriding)									
	540(Heat-treated, T2)									
DIN 1.2367 (X38CrMoV5; Tool Steel)	23	203	—	0.29	(1220,0.2%) (1593,5.5%)	—	—	—	—	—
	500(7 h Surface-Nitriding)									
	580(Heat-treated, T2)									
DIN 1.2367 (X38CrMoV5; Tool Steel)	23	204	—	0.29	(1135,0.2%) (1367,6.7%)	—	—	—	—	—
	500(7 h Surface-Nitriding)									
	620(Heat-treated, T2)									

Notes: HT=Heat-treated.

Table 80.2　Fatigue ε-N Properties of Tool, Die, and Mold Steels

Material	$T/℃$	$d\varepsilon/dt$	σ_{f}'	$\varepsilon_{\mathrm{f}}'$	b	c	K'	n'	$\sigma_{\mathrm{f}}@2N_{\mathrm{f}}$	R
1Cr18Ni9Ti	23	—	1124	0.807	−0.091	−0.665	—	—	—	—
M-50	23	—	—	—	—	—	—	—	275@ 10^7	—
P355NL1	23	—	841	0.3034	−0.081	−0.602	777	0.107	—	—
P91	23	—	—	—	—	—	750	0.07	—	—
P92	23	—	—	—	—	—	954	0.11	—	—
W360 (Asutentizing Q & T=580 ℃)	23	—	—	—	—	—	—	—	950@ 10^7	—
DIN 1.2367	23	—	4405	0.8	−0.139	−1.027	—	—	—	—
(Tool Steel X38CrMoV5, Heat-treated as: 1030 ℃→540 ℃×1 h tempering×2 times)										
DIN 1.2367	23	—	2543	0.144	−0.08	−0.734	—	—	—	—
(Tool Steel X38CrMoV5, Heat-treated as: 1030 ℃→580 ℃×1 h tempering×2 times)										

continued

Material	$T/℃$	$\mathrm{d}\varepsilon/\mathrm{d}t$	σ'_f	ε'_f	b	c	K'	n'	$\sigma_f@2N_f$	R
DIN 1.2367	23	—	3673	0.142	−0.126	−0.67	—	—	—	—
(Tool Steel X38CrMoV5, Heat-treated as: 1030 ℃→620 ℃×1 h tempering×2 times)										
DIN 1.2367	23	—	2446	0.025	−0.093	−0.584	—	—	—	—
(Tool Steel X38CrMoV5, Heat-treated as: 540 ℃ T2→500 ℃×7 h Surface-nitriding)										
DIN 1.2367	23	—	2288	0.053	−0.088	−0.595	—	—	—	—
(Tool Steel X38CrMoV5, Heat-treated as: 580 ℃ T2→500 ℃×7 h Surface-nitriding)										
DIN 1.2367	23	—	1968	0.035	−0.075	−0.523	—	—	—	—
(Tool Steel X38CrMoV5, Heat-treated as: 620 ℃ T2→500 ℃×7 h Surface-nitriding)										
Steel (Generic)	23	—	Eq. (6.14)	Eq. (6.15)	−0.09	−0.6	$\sigma'_f/(\varepsilon'_f)^{n'}$	b/c	—	—

Table 80.3   Mechanical Creep Parameters of Tool, Die, and Mold Steels

Material	$T/℃$	Stress/MPa	Strain Rate/s^{-1}	$A/(\mathrm{MPa}^{-n}\cdot s^{m-1})$	$Q/(\mathrm{J}\cdot\mathrm{mol}^{-1})$	n	m
P91	625	$E=1$	—	9.016×10^{-27}	1.258	10.286	0

Notes: Creep equation $=\dfrac{\mathrm{d}\varepsilon_{creep}}{\mathrm{d}t}=A\left(\dfrac{\sigma-\sigma_{th}}{E}\right)^n t^m \exp\left(\dfrac{-Q}{RT_k}\right)$, $\sigma>\sigma_{th}$;

$\sigma_{th}=$ Stress threshold and $\sigma_{th}=0$, if not specified;

$E=$ Young's modulus; If given that $E=1$, it means E is not specified.

Chapter 81

Heat-Resistant Steels

81.1   Introduction

One distinct category of automotive steels is the family of alloy steels for engine valves, valve seat inserts and valve guides. Intake valve temperatures up to 700 ℃ have been observed, while 810 ℃ is a generally requested minimum design target for exhaust valves under a harsh environment at the full load and a high operating speed, as shown in Fig. 81.1.

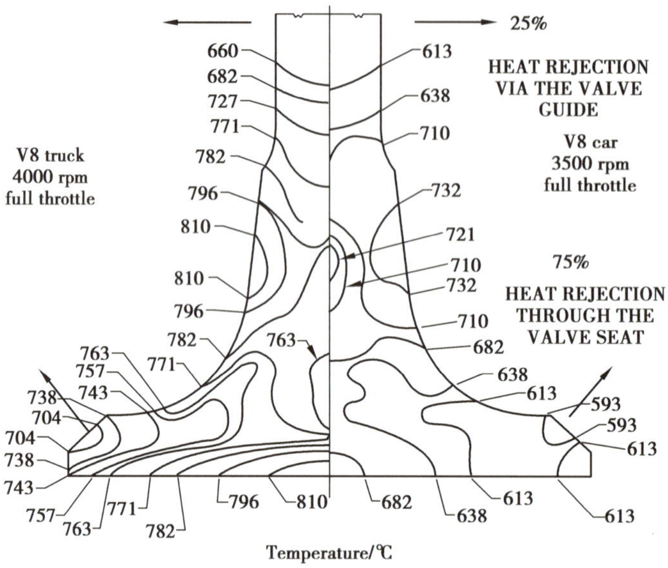

Fig. 81.1   Reference Temperature Distribution of an Exhaust Valve at 2 Different Operations: V8 Truck and V8 Car

81.2   Poppet Valves for Internal Combustion Engines

Materials that may be used for performance valve applications include carbon steel alloys, stainless steels, high-strength nickel-chromium-iron alloys, and titanium-based alloys. SAE classifies valve alloys with a prefix-code system as follows:

(a) NV: Low-alloy intake valve;

(b) HNV: high-alloy intake valve material;

(c) EV: Austenitic exhaust valve alloy such as 21-4N (EV-8);

(d) HEV: High-strength exhaust valve alloy such as Inconel 751.

Austenitic nitrogen-enhanced steels have been used extensively in internal combustion engine valve applications. They include 21-2N (Fe-21Cr-8Mn-2Ni-N), 21-4N (Fe-21Cr-9Mn-4Ni-N), 21-12N(Fe-21Cr-12Ni-1.25Mn-N), and 23-8N(Fe-21Cr-8Ni-3.5Mn-N). The nitrogen contents in these alloys range from 0.2% to 0.5%. Their mechanical properties are listed in Table 81.1. These engine valve grades are used at temperatures up to 760 ℃, but their strengths start to decay at the upper end of their temperature capabilities.

Inconel refers to a family of trademarked high-strength austenitic nickel-chromium-iron alloys that are sometimes used for exhaust valves because of their superior high temperature strength. More exactly, it is a "nickel-based superalloy" material. Inconel 751 is classified as an HEV3 alloy by SAE. This alloy has been used for the exhaust valves in some late model GM medium duty truck engines.

Titanium alloys are the ultimate valve alloy material because of their high-temperature strength and lightness. Titanium is about 40% lighter than steel, making it a good alternative for high revving engines.

In the later applications, exhaust materials are being used with facing alloys on the intake. New EGR requirements on the heavy-duty vehicles have driven this due to the excessive heat, new low sulfur diesel and changes to fluids and oils. Engine valves of a high-performance engine typically operate at the following temperatures:

(a) Intake valves: 650~700 ℃;
(b) Exhaust valves: 800~815 ℃.

81.3   Valve Seat Inserts

A valve seat insert is retained via an interference fit into a counterbore of the cylinder head. It is employed to resist wear and mechanical impact in a hot harsh environment. Some materials for valve seat inserts are given in Table 81.2. Higher temperatures (>700 ℃) cause unacceptable wear between exhaust valves and seat inserts, and reduce durability. Concerns about the valve seat design are given below:

(a) Alignment between valve/seat;
(b) Wear-in of the valve face;
(c) Wear-in of the seat;
(d) Progressive lateral displacement of material;
(e) Thermal cycling during start-up/shut-down/idle;
(f) Aging of the alloys;
(g) Surface/sub-surface oxidation in the presence of repetitive contact;
(h) External material sources: ash and other deposits;
(i) Mechanical mixing of surface material: effects of scales, debris, and transferred material on damage accumulation.

81.4　Valve Guides

The primary functional requirement of a valve guide is to guide the valve stem coaxial to the cylinder head and block as an axial sliding bearing, usually lubricated. Its secondary functional requirement is to get the heat dissipated. Mechanical properties of valve guides are given in Table 81.3. Though traditional cast irons are still widely used, new proprietary cast irons are popping up everywhere in order to combat the wear encountered on engines such as heavy-duty diesel and natural gas-based engines. With these engines, EGR applications, low sulfur diesel fuels and lubricants have driven this trend. Special coatings such as phosphate and added heat treatments are also becoming the norm for the heavy-duty engines.

81.5　Valve Guide Liners

Valve guide liners, usually made of phosphor bronze, have excellent lubricating and heatconduction properties.

81.6　Fatigue with Creep and Oxidation

Fatigue ε-N properties of valve/seat/guide/guideliner materials are given in Table 81.4. When fatigue of steels in this category is conducted at an elevated temperature, the complication from creep and oxidation must be taken into consideration. Of course the heat radiation can be an important factor.

81.7　Valvestem Seals

Valvestem seals play a critical role in controlling valve lubrication as well as oil consumption. If the seal does not fit properly or is not installed correctly, the guide may be either starved for lubrication or flooded with oil. Increased oil consumption due to worn or leaky valve stem seals will also increase hydrocarbon (HC) emissions in the exhaust, which may cause a vehicle to fail an emissions test. Debris from deteriorating seals is another concern that can cause additional problems.

Depending on the application and the design of the seal, the material used may be NBR (nitrile), ACM (polyacrylate), PA (nylon), FKM (fluoroelastomer), silicone, or Teflon. The materials given above are listed in the application temperature-ascending order. A higher temperature material is used for exhaust valves.

A positive seal is pressed in place on the end of the valve guide and wipes the oil off the valve stem as the stem moves up and down. The seal does not actually make direct contact with the stem but rides on a thin film of oil creating a hydrodynamic seal. This allows a small amount of oil to slip past the seal to lubricate the guide. A precise fit is extremely important with a positive seal to get accurate oil metering. Thus, the outside diameter of the guide chimney needs to be concentric with the inside diameter of the guide for a good seal.

References

CAMPO E, QUARANTA S, PIERAGOSTINI F, 1982. High Temperature Mechanical Properties of SAE EV11 Engine Valve Steel[J]. SAE 821085.

CHUN K, KIM J, HONG J, 2007. A Study of Exhaust Valve and Seat Insert Wear Depending on Cycle Numbers[J]. Wear, 263(7-12): 1147-1157.

GÖKSENLI A, et al, 2008. Failure Analysis of Diesel Engine Intake Valve[J]. Key Engineering Materials, 29: 385-387.

LANE M, SMITH P, 1982. Developments in Sintered Valve Seat Inserts[J]. SAE, 820233.

LEWIS R, DWYER-JOYCE R S, 2002. Wear of Diesel Engine Inlet Valves and Seat Inserts[J]. Journal of Automotive Engineering, 216(3): 205-216.

LIU R, WU X, KAPOOR S, et al, 2015. Effects of Temperature-Dependence on the Hardness and Wear Resistance of High-Tungsten Stellite Alloys[J]. Metallurgical and Materials Transactions A, 46(2): 587-599.

MACIEJEWSKI G, MROZ Z, 2013. Optimization of Functionally Gradient Materials in Valve Design under Cyclic Thermal and Mechanical Loading[J]. Computer Assisted Methods in Engineering and Science, 20: 99-112.

OOTANI T, et al, 1995. Impact Wear Characteristics of Engine Valve and Valve Seat Insert Materials at High Temperature (Impact Wear Tests of Austenitic Heat-resistant Steel SUH36 against Fe-based Sintered Alloy using Plane Specimens)[J]. Wear, 188(1-2): 175-184.

ONODA M, KUROISHI N, MOTOOKA N, 1988. Sintered Valve Seat Insert for High Performance Engine[J]. SAE 880668.

RAMALHO A, et al, 2009. Effect of Temperatures up to 400 ℃ on the Impact-Sliding of Valve Seat Contacts [J]. Wear, 267(5-8): 777-780.

ROTH G, 2003. Fatigue Analysis Methodology for Predicting Engine Valve Life[J]. SAE 200301-0726.

SAGI S, JAGDISH D, RAJAN B, 2008. Stress Analysis and Fatigue Life Determination of Engine Valves[J]. SAE 2008-28-0078.

SATO K, et al, 1998. Development of Low-Nickel Superalloys for Exhaust Valves[J]. SAE 980703.

SHOJAEFARD M, NOORPOOR A, BOZCHALOE D, et al, 2005. Transient Thermal Analysis of Engine Exhaust Valve[J]. Numerical Heat Transfer, 48(7): 627-644.

SUNULAHPA R, ORU M, 2011. Effect of Temperature on Mechanical Properties on Mechanical Properties and Type of Fracture of Superalloys Nimonic 80A[J]. METABK, 50(3): 155-158.

UMINO S, et al, 1998. New Fe-Based Exhaust Valve Material for Higher Heat Resistance[J]. SAE 980704.

ZRAHIA U, YOSEPH P, 1994. Alternative Designs towards Thermal Optimization of Coated Valves using Space-Time Finite Elements[J]. International Journal of Numerical Methods for Heat & Fluid Flow, 5(3): 189-206.

Table 81.1   Mechanical Properties of Valve Steels/Irons (SAE J775; for Engine and Other High Temperature Applications)

Material	$T/℃$	E_T	ρ	ν	(σ, ε)	α	k	γ	ρ_E	K_{IC}
EN52 (401S45; Intake valve)	23	210	7.71	0.29	$\varepsilon_{uts} = 14\%$	—	42	—	—	—
	500	—	—	—	$(500, 0.2\%)$ $\sigma_{uts} = 400$; $\sigma_{crs,1000} = 190$	—	—	—	—	—
	650	—	—	—	$(120, 0.2\%)$ $\sigma_{uts} = 170$; $\sigma_{crs,1000} = 40$	—	—	—	—	—
EV-4 (21-12N) (X20CrNiN20-8; 20Cr21Ni12N)	23	206	7.71	0.29	$(430, 0.2\%)$ $(820, 26.2\%)$	—	42	—	—	—
	650	—	—	—	$(230, 0.2\%)$ $\sigma_{uts} = 420$	—	—	—	—	—
	760	—	—	—	$(220, 0.2\%)$ $(300, 13.3\%)$	18.4	—	—	—	—

continued

Material	$T/^\circ C$	E_T	ρ	ν	(σ, ε)	α	k	γ	ρ_E	K_{IC}
EV-8 (21-4N; X53CrMnNiN219; 1.4871;53Cr21Mn 9Ni4N; Austenitic; Diesel intake valve)	23	205	7.6	0.29	$(740, 0.2\%)$ $(1140, 8\%)$	14.5	42	—	—	—
	600	—	—	—	$\sigma_{uts} = 590$	—	—	—	—	—
	650	—	—	—	$(330, 0.2\%)$ $\sigma_{uts} = 550$; $\sigma_{crs,1000} = 200$	—	—	—	—	—
	725	—	—	—	$\sigma_{crs,1000} = 110$	—	—	—	—	—
	760	—	—	—	$(260, 0.2\%)$ $(430, 18\%)$	18.4	—	—	—	—
	800	—	—	—	$\sigma_{uts} = 300$; $\sigma_{crs,1000} = 50$	—	—	—	—	—
	816	—	—	—	$\sigma_{uts} = 225$	—	—	—	—	—
21-4NWNb (X50CrMnNiN 21-9;1.4882; 53Cr21Mn9Ni 4N;401S45)	23	205	7.71	0.29	$\varepsilon_{uts} = 12\%$	—	42	—	—	—
	500	—			$(680, 0.2\%)$ $\sigma_{uts} = 350$	—	—	—	—	—
	650	—	—	—	$(550, 0.2\%)$ $\sigma_{uts} = 285$; $\sigma_{crs,1000} = 220$	—	—	—	—	—
	725	—	—	—	$\sigma_{crs,1000} = 120$	—	—	—	—	—
	750	—	—	—	$(410, 0.2\%)$ $\sigma_{uts} = 240$	—	—	—	—	—
	800	—	—	—	$(340, 0.2\%)$ $\sigma_{uts} = 220$; $\sigma_{crs,1000} = 55$	—	—	—	—	—
EV-12 (21-2N; X55CrMnNi20-8; 1.4875;55Cr 21Mn8Ni2N)	23	206	7.6	0.29	$(700, 0.2\%)$ $\sigma_{uts} = 1080$	—	—	—	—	—
	650	—	—	—	$(340, 0.2\%)$ $\sigma_{uts} = 59$	—	—	—	—	—
	760	—	—	—	$(280, 0.2\%)$ $\sigma_{uts} = 390$	18.4	—	—	—	—

continued

Material	$T/°C$	E_T	ρ	ν	(σ,ε)	α	k	γ	ρ_E	K_{IC}
21-2 Valve Steel (Fe-21Cr-8Mn-2Ni-0.5C-0.3N)	23	206	7.6	0.29	—	—	—	—	—	—
EV-13(X55Cr MnNi20-8)	23	206	7.6	0.29	$(520,0.2\%)$ $\sigma_{uts}=1080$	—	—	—	—	—
	650	—	—	—	$(350,0.2\%)$ $\sigma_{uts}=940$	—	—	—	—	—
	760	—	—	—	$(330,0.2\%)$ $\sigma_{uts}=430$	—	—	—	—	—
EV-16 (23-8N; X33CrNiMnN238; 1.4866;33Cr23 Ni8Mn3N)	23	206	7.6	0.29	$(580,0.2\%)$ $(1010,26\%)$	—	42	—	—	—
	650	—	—	—	$(270,0.2\%)$ $\sigma_{uts}=580$	—	—	—	—	—
	760	—	—	—	$(260,0.2\%)$ $\sigma_{uts}=470$	—	—	—	—	—
HEV-3 (751) (NiCr157FeTiAl; 2.4952; GH4751; ≈ Inconel 751)	23	206	8.06	0.29	$(630,0.2\%)$ $\sigma_{uts}=1120$	—	42	—	—	—
	650	—	—	—	$(570,0.2\%)$ $\sigma_{uts}=830$	—	—	—	—	—
	760	—	—	—	$(450,0.2\%)$ $(550,10\%)$	15	—	—	—	—
HEV-5 (80A; NiCr20CrTiAl; 2.4952; GH4080A; 2-staged HT: 2 min/1150 °C + 4 h/750 °C; ≈ Nimonic 80 A)	23	206	8.1	0.29	$(600,0.1\%)$ $(630,0.2\%)$ $(1066,44\%)$	12	25	430	—	—
	550	—	—	—	$(600,0.2\%)$ $(850,35\%)$	—	—	—	—	—
	650	—	—	—	$(550,0.2\%)$ $\sigma_{uts}=790$; $\sigma_{crs,10000}=348$	—	—	—	—	—
	700	—	—	—	$\sigma_{crs,10000}=225$; $\sigma_{crs,100000}=126$	—	—	—	—	—

Material	$T/{}^\circ\mathrm{C}$	E_{T}	ρ	ν	(σ,ε)	α	k	γ	ρ_{E}	K_{IC}
HEV-5（80A；NiCr20CrTiAl；2.4952；GH4080A；2-staged HT：2 min/1150 ℃+4 h/750 ℃；≈ Nimonic 80 A）	750	—	—	—	$\sigma_{\mathrm{crs},10000}=128$；$\sigma_{\mathrm{crs},100000}=66$	—	—	—	—	—
	760	—	—	—	$(500,0.2\%)$ $\sigma_{\mathrm{uts}}=590$	15	—	—	—	—
	800	—	—	—	$\sigma_{\mathrm{crs},1000}=83$	—	—	—	—	—
	850	—	—	—	$\sigma_{\mathrm{crs},1000}=50$	—	—	—	—	—
	$1365(T_{\mathrm{m}})$	—	—	—	—	—	—	—	—	—
HEV-8	23	206	7.87	0.29	$(770,0.2\%)$ $\sigma_{\mathrm{uts}}=1300$	—	42	—	—	—
	650	—	—	—	$(750,0.2\%)$ $\sigma_{\mathrm{uts}}=1150$	—	—	—	—	—
	760	—	—	—	$(730,0.2\%)$ $\sigma_{\mathrm{uts}}=850$	15.7	—	—	—	—
HNV-3（X45CrSi9-3；1.4731；42Cr9Si2）	23	206	7.44	0.29	$(690,0.2\%)$ $(920,22\%)$	13	42	—	—	—
	650	—	—	—	$(150,0.2\%)$ $\sigma_{\mathrm{uts}}=210$	—	—	—	—	—
	760	—	—	—	$(62,0.2\%)$ $\sigma_{\mathrm{uts}}=69$	—	—	—	—	—
HNV-6（XB；X80CrNiSi20；80Cr20Si2Ni）	23	206	7.42	0.29	$(840,0.2\%)$ $(940,15.5\%)$	13.3	42	—	—	—
	650	—	—	—	$(160,0.2\%)$ $\sigma_{\mathrm{uts}}=200$	—	—	—	—	—
	760	—	—	—	$(75,0.2\%)$ $(100,72\%)$	—	—	—	—	—
HNV-8（X85CrMoV18-2）	23	206	7.55	0.29	$(860,0.2\%)$ $\sigma_{\mathrm{uts}}=1030$	—	42	—	—	—
	650	—	—	—	$(310,0.2\%)$ $\sigma_{\mathrm{uts}}=360$	—	—	—	—	—

continued

Material	$T/℃$	E_T	ρ	ν	(σ, ε)	α	k	γ	ρ_E	K_{IC}
NV-8	23	206	7.44	0.29	$(690, 0.2\%)$ $(920, 22\%)$	13	42	—	—	—
	540	—	—	—	$(220, 0.2\%)$ $\sigma_{uts}=270$	—	—	—	—	—
	650	—	—	—	$(110, 0.2\%)$ $\sigma_{uts}=130$	—	—	—	—	—
Stellite 1 (57Co-30Cr-12W-1Fe-1Ni-2.5C-1.5Si)	23	230	8.69	0.3	$(1050, 0.2\%)$ $(1195, 1\%)$	—	—	—	—	—
Stellite 3 (Powder M.)	23	—	8.4	0.3	$(650, 0.2\%)$ $(863, 1\%)$	12	14.5	—	—	—
	500	—	—	—	—	13.0	—	—	—	—
	700	—	—	—	$\sigma_{uts}=660$	13.4	—	—	—	—
	900	—	—	—	—	14.5	—	—	—	—
	$1285(T_m)$	—	—	—	—	—	—	—	—	—
Stellite 4 (51Co-30Cr-14W-1C-1Fe-2Ni-0.5Si; Powder M.)	23	235	8.8	0.3	$\sigma_{uts}=171$; $(710, 0.2\%)$ $(940, 1\%)$	12.5	14.7	—	—	—
	700	—	—	—	—	14.7	—	—	—	—
	900	—	—	—	—	15.7	—	—	—	—
	$1356(T_m)$	—	—	—	—	—	—	—	—	—
Stellite 6 (Powder M.)	23	—	8.2	0.3	$(911, 1\%)$	13.5	14.8	—	—	—
	600	—	—	—	—	14.5	—	—	—	—
	650	—	—	—	$(676, 2\%)$	15.5	—	—	—	—
	700	—	—	—	—	14.7	—	—	—	—
	760	—	—	—	$(552, 5\%)$	—	—	—	—	—
	900	—	—	—	—	15.5	—	—	—	—
	$1357(T_m)$	—	—	—	—	—	—	—	—	—

continued

Material	$T/℃$	E_T	ρ	ν	(σ,ε)	α	k	γ	ρ_E	K_{IC}
Stellite 12 (Powder M.; Valve seat & valve seat coating)	23	208	8.52	0.3	$(900,0.2\%)$ $(1200,2\%)$	11	14.6	—	—	—
	500	—	—	—	—	13.3	—	—	—	—
	900	—	—	—	—	15.6	—	—	—	—
	$1341(T_m)$	—	—	—	—	—	—	—	—	—
Stellite 12 (As cast; 51Co-32 Cr-9.5W-2Fe-2Ni-1.3C-1.3 Mn-1Si)	23	226	8.69	0.3	$(580,0.2\%)$ $(740,1\%)$	11	14.6	—	—	—
	500	—	—	—	—	13.1	—	—	—	—
Stellite 21 (Powder M.; HIP)	23	245	8.31	0.3	$(650,0.2\%)$ $(1000,20\%)$	10.8	14.5	—	—	—
	500	—	—	—	—	13.1	—	—	—	—
	600	—	—	—	—	13.6	—	—	—	—
	700	—	—	—	—	14.3	—	—	—	—
	800	—	—	—	—	14.7	—	—	—	—
	900	—	—	—	—	15.2	—	—	—	—
	$1366(T_m)$	—	—	—	—	—	—	—	—	—
Stellite 21 (As Cast)	23	250	8.69	0.3	$(565,0.2\%)$ $(710,9\%)$	10.8	14.5	—	—	—
	500	—	—	—	—	13.1	—	—	—	—
Stellite 25 (As Cast; $\approx$ Haynes 25; 20% CW)	23	225	—	—	$(725,0.2\%)$ $(1070,41\%)$	9.4	—	—	—	—
	400	197	—	—	—	13	—	—	—	—
	500	188	—	—	—	18.7	—	—	—	—
	650	—	—	—	$(825,0.2\%)$ $(945,2\%)$	21.5	—	—	—	—

continued

Material	$T/℃$	E_T	ρ	ν	(σ,ε)	α	k	γ	ρ_E	K_{IC}
Stellite 25 (As Cast; ≈ Haynes 25; 20% CW)	760	—	—	—	$(660,0.2\%)$ $(740,2\%)$	—	—	—	—	—
	800	163	—	—	—	24.7	—	—	—	—
	980	147	—	—	$(205\ 0.2\%)$ $(285,4\%)$	29	—	—	—	—
Ti-834	See Chapter 96 (IMI 834)									
XEV-F	23	206	7.87	0.29	$(880,0.2\%)$ $\sigma_{uts}=1190$	—	42	—	—	—
	650	—	—	—	$(570,0.2\%)$ $\sigma_{uts}=720$	—	—	—	—	—
	760	—	—	—	$(280,0.2\%)$ $\sigma_{uts}=340$	17.3	—	—	—	—
XEV-H	23	206	7.87	0.29	$(1030,0.2\%)$ $\sigma_{uts}=1280$	—	42	—	—	—
	650	—	—	—	$(860,0.2\%)$ $\sigma_{uts}=1000$	—	—	—	—	—
XEV-J	23	—	—	—	—	—	—	—	—	—
	760	—	—	—	—	10.4	—	—	—	—

Notes: (1) NV-Low-alloy intake valve;

(2) HNV-High-alloy intake valve material;

(3) EV-Austenitic exhaust/intake valve alloy such as 21-4N (EV-8);

(4) HEV-High-strength exhaust valve alloy such as Inconel 751.

Table 81.2 Mechanical Properties of Materials for Valve Seat Inserts in Heat Treated Condition (SAE J1692)

Material	$T/℃$	E_T	ρ	ν	(σ,ε)	α	k	γ	ρ_E	K_{IC}
EH-2	23	120	5.8	0.27	$(600,0.2\%)$ $(750,0.8\%)$	—	29.3	—	—	—
	200	—	—	—	$\sigma_{uts}=720$	—	33.5	—	—	—
	300	—	—	—	$\sigma_{uts}=700$	10.2	—	—	—	—
	400	—	—	—	$\sigma_{uts}=680$	12.1	—	—	—	—

continued

Material	$T/°C$	E_T	ρ	ν	(σ,ε)	α	k	γ	ρ_E	K_{IC}
EH-8	23	126	6.7	0.27	$(500,0.2\%)$ $(600,0.7\%)$	11.3	21	—	—	—
	200	—	—	—	$\sigma_{uts}=500$	—	25.1	—	—	—
	300	—	—	—	—	12.0	—	—	—	—
	400	—	—	—	$\sigma_{uts}=400$	13.7	—	—	—	—
EH-9	23	138	6.8	0.27	$(310,0.2\%)$ $(380,0.5\%)$	—	16.7	—	—	—
	200	—	—	—	$\sigma_{uts}=380$	—	16.7	—	—	—
	300	—	—	—	—	13.8	20.9	—	—	—
	400	—	—	—	$\sigma_{uts}=390$	15.4	—	—	—	—
EH-10	23	127	6.8	0.27	$(350,0.2\%)$ $(400,0.3\%)$	11.6	25.1	—	—	—
	200	—	—	—	$\sigma_{uts}=380$	—	29.3	—	—	—
	400	—	—	—	$\sigma_{uts}=370$	12.8	—	—	—	—
	600	—	—	—	—	13.8	—	—	—	—
EH-11	23	148	8.2	0.28	$(350,0.2\%)$ $(400,0.3\%)$	10.8	25.1	—	—	—
	200	—	—	—	$\sigma_{uts}=480$	—	29.3	—	—	—
	400	—	—	—	$\sigma_{uts}=450$	12.5	—	—	—	—
	600	—	—	—	—	13.2	—	—	—	—
PL12M	23	180	—	—	$(650,0.2\%)$ $(800,2\%)$	12	29.3	—	—	—
PL33M	23	180	—	—	$(700,0.2\%)$ $(800,1\%)$	11	41.9	—	—	—
PL7N	23	120	—	—	$\sigma_{uts}=250$	12	41.9	—	—	—
	200	—	—	—	$\sigma_{uts}=400$	—	—	—	—	—

continued

Material	$T/°C$	E_T	ρ	ν	(σ,ε)	α	k	γ	ρ_E	K_{IC}
PL 476	23	180	—	—	(880,0.2%) (900,1%)	12	20.9	—	—	—
PLS 100	23	110	7.2	—	(250,0.2%) (350,5%)	13	41.9	—	—	—
PLS 250	23	130	8.0	—	(380,0.2%) (400,1%)	13	41.9	—	—	—
PLS 300	23	130	8.0	—	(380,0.2%) (450,2%)	13	41.9	—	—	—
PLS 301	23	130	8.0	—	(380,0.2%) (450,2%)	13	41.9	—	—	—
31V	816	—	—	—	(470,0.2%); $\sigma_{crs,100}=210$	—	—	—	—	—

Table 81.3 Mechanical Properties of Materials for Valve Guides and Guideliners in Heat Treated Condition（SAE J1682）

Material	$T/°C$	E_T	ρ	ν	(σ,ε)	α	k	γ	ρ_E	K_{IC}
EB-4	23	101	6.5	0.22	(280,0.2%) $\sigma_{uts}=340$	7.4	29.3	—	—	—
	100	101	—	—	(270,0.2%) $\sigma_{uts}=340$	10.4	28.1	—	—	—
	200	101	—	—	(270,0.2%) $\sigma_{uts}=340$	10.7	26.8	—	—	—
	400	101	—	—	(230,0.2%) $\sigma_{uts}=250$	12.5	23.0	—	—	—
PL 105	23	110	7.1	0.3	$\sigma_{uts}=250$	10	50.2	—	—	—
PL 106	23	120	7.1	0.3	$\sigma_{uts}=250$	10	50.2	—	—	—
PLS 103	23	100	6.6	0.3	(250,0.2%) (300,2%)	13	41.9	—	—	—
PLS 105	23	80	—	0.3	(250,0.2%) (300,2%)	13	41.9	—	—	—

Table 81.4   Fatigue *ε-N* Properties of Valve/Seat/Guide Steels/Irons（for Engine and Other High Temperature Applications）

Material	$T/℃$	$d\varepsilon/dt$	σ'_f	ε'_f	b	c	K'	n'	$\sigma_f @ 2N_f$	R
EV 8（21-4N）	23	—	—	—	—	—	—	—	337@ $1.85×10^5$ 280@ 10^6 250@ 10^7	— — —
	538	—	—	—	—	—	—	—	490@ 10^5 450@ 10^6 420@ 10^7	— — —
	700	—	—	—	—	—	—	—	345@ $3×10^8$	—
HEV 8	23	—	—	—	—	—	—	—	—	—
HNV-3（X-45Cr-Si9-3）	23	—	—	—	—	—	—	—	900@ $7×10^4$ 800@ 10^6	— —
Steel（Generic）	23	—	Eq.（6.14）	Eq.（6.15）	-0.09	-0.6	$\dfrac{\sigma'_f/}{(\varepsilon'_f)^{n'}}$	b/c	Eq.（77.1）	—

Non-Ferrous

Chapter 82

Ag (Silver)

82.1　Introduction

Ag (Silver) has the highest thermal conductivity of all natural materials and thus it is a heat sink. Its electric resistivity is low, yet increasing linearly from 0.016 $\mu\Omega$ m at room temperature to 0.055 $\mu\Omega$ m at 650 ℃. Elastoplastic and fatigue properties of silver and its related alloys are given in Tables 82.1 and 82.2. Ag (Silver) is one of the eight noble metals (silver, gold, platinum, palladium, rhodium, ruthenium, iridium, and osmium).

A creep test of silver was conducted at 450 ℃ by [Goods and Nix] and the plot from the resulting data is plotted in Fig. 82.1. Creep paths of regular polycrystalline silver and of silver with voids at grain boundary are identical at low strain (i.e. $\varepsilon < 2\%$). As the strain increases, the voided silver fractures prematurely at high strain.

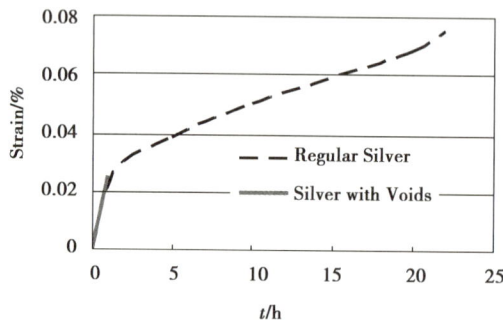

Fig. 82.1　Creep Behaviors of Silver versus Silver with Voids (1 μm) at 24 MPa and 450 ℃

82.2　Applications

Silver is commonly used in microelectronic packages due to its high electric and thermal relatively. Nanoscale silver sintered (with particles of 30 nanometers in size) at a relatively low temperature such as 280 ℃ is an option to be a lead-free soldering material suitable for bonding semiconductor devices to metallic substrates.

References

BAI J, et al, 2005. Low-Temperature Sintered Nanoscale Silver as a Novel Semiconductor Device-Metalized Substrate Interconnect Material[J]. IEEE Transactions on Components and Packaging Technologies, 29(3): 589-593.

FUNG M C, BOWEN D L,1996. Silver Products for Medical Indications: Risk-Benefit Assessment[J]. Journal of Toxicology, Clinical Toxicology, 34(1): 119-126.

OLIVIERI K, et al, 2007. Mechanical Properties and Microstructural Analysis of an AgPd Alloy Cast under Different Temperatures[J]. Cienc Odonto Brasil, 10(1): 6-11.

SCHWAIGER R, KRAFT O, 2003. Size Effects in the Fatigue Behavior of Thin Ag Films[J]. Acta Materialia, 51(1): 195-206.

SMITH D, FICKETT F, 1995. Low Temperature Properties of Silver[J]. Journal of Research of the National Institute of Standards and Technology, 100(2): 119-171.

Table 82.1 Mechanical Properties of Ag (Silver) and Related Alloys

Material	$T/℃$	E_T	ρ	ν	(σ,ε)	α	k	γ	ρ_E	K_{IC}
Silver(>99.9%) (Annealed)	−270	91.35	10.63	—	—	0.15	—	0.06	—	—
	−263	—	—	—	—	—	—	1.698	—	—
	−253	—	—	—	—	—	—	15.32	—	—
	−243	—	—	—	—	—	—	44.21	—	—
	−173	—	—	—	—	15	—	180	—	—
	23	76	10.49	0.364	(54,0.2%) (125, 48%)	18.9	418	235	0.0159	—
	962(T_m)	—	9.3	—	—	—	—	—	—	—
	1300	—	9.0	—	—	—	—	—	—	—
Silver(>99.9%) (1/2 Hard)	23	76	10.49	0.364	(235,8%)	18.9	418	235	—	—
Silver(>99.9%) (Hard)	23	76	10.49	0.364	(275,3%)	18.9	418	235	—	—
Silver(>99.9%) (Spring Hard; Trus s-s)	23	76	10.49	0.364	(300,0.5%) (340,1%) (375,1.5%)	18.9	418	235	—	—
Silver(>99.99%) (Polycrystalline; Cold-worked)	23	76	10.49	0.364	(240, 46%)	18.9	418	235	—	—
Ag (film; $h=0.2$ μm)	23	—	—	—	(300,0.2%)	—	—	—	—	—
Ag (film; $h=0.8$ μm)	23	—	—	—	(250,0.2%)	—	—	—	—	—
Ag (film; $h=1.5$ μm)	23	—	—	—	(155,0.2%)	—	—	—	—	—

continued

Material	$T/℃$	E_T	ρ	ν	(σ,ε)	α	k	γ	ρ_E	K_{IC}
Ag-nano (Sintered)	23	—	—	—	—	—	238	233	—	—
Ag-5Cu-1.25 Ti-1Al (Silver-ABA)	23	77	10	0.33	(136,0.2%) (282,37%)	20.7	344	—	—	—
Ag-7.5Cu (Sterling Silver Annealed)	23	75	10.4	0.33	(124,0.2%) (207,41%)	18	410	245	—	—
	893(T_m)	—	—	—	—	—	—	—	—	—
Ag-7.5Cu(CD; Annealed:700 ℃)	23	75	10.4	0.33	(275,30%)	18	410	245	—	—
	893(T_m)	—	—	—	—	—	—	—	—	—
Ag-7.5Cu (CD; Annealed:250 ℃)	23	75	10.4	0.33	(400,9%)	18	410	245	—	—
	893(T_m)	—	—	—	—	—	—	—	—	—
Ag-7.5Cu (Annealed Wire)	23	75	10.4	0.33	(124,0.2%) (283,40%)	18	410	245	—	—
Ag-7.5Cu(10% Hard; Wire)	23	75	10.4	0.33	(310, 20%)	18	410	245	—	—
Ag-7.5Cu(1/2 Hard; Wire)	23	75	10.4	0.33	(386,9%)	18	410	245	—	—
Ag-7.5Cu Hard; Wire)	23	75	10.4	0.33	(496,5%)	18	410	245	—	—
Ag-7.5Cu(Spring Hard; Wire)	23	75	10.4	0.33	$\sigma_{uts}=552$	18	410	245	—	—
Ag-20Pd-14.5 Cu-12Au(Dental Application)	23	95	—	0.33	(412,0.2%) (472,7.3%)	16	140	—	—	—
Ag-28Pd-11Cu-1.1Au (Dental Application)	23	95	—	0.33	(412,0.2%) (472,7.3%)	16	140	—	—	—

Notes: ρ_E($\mu\Omega$m) = Electric resistivity.

Table 82.2   Fatigue ε-N Properties of Ag（Silver）Alloys

Material	$T/^{\circ}\mathrm{C}$	$\mathrm{d}\varepsilon/\mathrm{d}t$	σ_{f}'	$\varepsilon_{\mathrm{f}}'$	b	c	K'	n'	$\sigma_{\mathrm{f}}@2N_{\mathrm{f}}$	R
Silver（>99%）	−253	—	—	—	—	—	—	—	150@ 10^6 166@ 10^5	— —
	−183	—	—	—	—	—	—	—	110@ 10^6 126@ 10^5	— —
	23	—	—	—	—	—	—	—	68@ 10^6 90@ 10^5	— —

Chapter 83

Al (Aluminum)

83.1　Introduction

Aluminum alloys are widely used in engineering structures and components where light weight or corrosion resistance is required. Aluminum's resistance to corrosion is excellent as protected by a natural-born hard thin oxide surface film in an oxidizing atmosphere. Pure aluminum is low in strength as being a member of the metal family. Cu, Mg, Mn, Si, Ni, and Zn are the top six elements used for hardening aluminum to make alloys. It means that as the strain rate increases, both yield strength and tensile strength decrease. Aluminum alloys are divided into three categories: die casting [Madan, Rao, and Kundra], sand casting, and wrought material. Wrought materials are designated by four digits, and cast aluminum alloys designated by three digits according to International Alloy Designation System (IADS), which is basically the same as what defined by Aluminum Association (AA) of the United States.

Temper designation system is established by the International Alloy Designation System, based on the classification developed by the Aluminum Association of the United States, as given in Table 83.1. Temper conditions for Al alloys (also for Mg alloys) have a great influence on their mechanical properties and they are listed as follows:

(F)- Fabricated, as it is
(H)- Hardening; the following digit x, ranging from 1 to 9, is the degree of hardening:
    (a) H1x- No heat treatment after hardening
    (b) H2x- Partially annealed after hardening
    (c) H3x- Stabilized (heated slightly above service temperature) after hardening.
(O)- Annealed to relieve strain-hardening and improve ductility; strength lowered.
(T)- 10 temper conditions with heat treatments other than (F), (H), and (O), i.e. T1, T2, T3, T4, T5, T6, T7, T8, T9, T10.
(W)- Solution heat treatment, for alloys that age-harden in service.

Mechanical properties of the frequently used cast (sand/die), wrought, and sintered aluminum alloys are listed in Tables 83.2—83.4. Fatigue properties of cast and wrought aluminum alloys are given in Tables 83.5 and 83.6, respectively.

83.2　Cast Aluminum

A cast aluminum alloy is designated by a four-digit number with a decimal point separating the 3rd and 4th digits, i.e. each cast aluminum alloy is given an ×××. × number, of which the first number indicates the major alloying elements, shown as follows:

1××. × series-Pure aluminum with a minimum 99% aluminum content by weight;

2××. × series-Alloyed with copper;

3××. × series-Alloyed with copper, silicon, and/or magnesium;

4××. × series-Alloyed with silicon;

5××. × series-Alloyed with magnesium;

6××. × series-Unused;

7××. × series-Alloyed with zinc;

8××. × series-Alloyed with tin or lithium;

9××. × series-Others.

The digit after decimal indicates the product form: 0-casting; 1 or 2-ingot. Cast aluminum alloys yield cost effective products due to the low melting point, although they generally have lower tensile strengths than wrought alloys. One important cast aluminum alloy system is Al-Si, where the high levels of silicon (4.0% to 13%) contribute to giving good casting characteristics. The wear resistance of Al-Si alloys increases with the increasing of the silicon content. Creep damage to an aluminum alloy has to be considered for the purpose of design, especially at an elevated temperature, such as cast Al-12Si-Cu-Ni-Mg pistons. Relevant factors affecting the selection of casting processes for alloys are given as follows:

Factor	Sand Casting(SC)	Perm ant Mold Casting(PM)	Die Casting (DC)
Tooling cost	Low(×)	Moderate(5×)	High(10×)
Casting rate	Low	Moderate	High
Size	Large	Moderate	Limited
Inner feature	Limited	Flexible	Limited
Wall Thick	>4.8 mm	>4.8 mm	>2 mm
Tolerance	Loose	Medium	Good
Finish	Rough	Medium	Smooth

83.2.1   Sand-Cast Aluminum

Molten metal is poured into a mould cavity formed out of sand (natural or synthetic). The sand cavity is usually formed by using a wooden pattern. The pattern resembles the real casting part. The upper part of the sand mould box is called cope and the lower part is called drag. The pattern is made slightly oversize to allow the metal contraction as it cools down. The liquid flows into the gap between the two parts, called the mold cavity. Sand castings have a rough surface and are machined later. The metal from the spruce and risers is cut from the rough casting. The riser is a surge reservoir of liquid metal to supply a contracting, cooling casting with make-up metal. It is used to prevent internal or external voids due to shrinkage.

Cast aluminum has scattered fatigue life due to the effects of porosity. The fatigue strength (endurance limit) of cast aluminum may be approximated, with a cutoff fatigue cycle of 10^8, using the following equations

$$\sigma_f = 0.16 \, \sigma_{uts} \tag{83.1}$$

A letter may be prefixed to the number of an aluminum alloy. Such a letter, which precedes an alloy number, distinguishes itself as an alternative that is only slightly in percentages of impurities from the original alloy and comes with minor alloying elements. For example, 356.0, A356.0, B356.0, and F356.0.

83.2.2　Permanent Mold Casting

The permanent mold process involves the pouring of molten metal into reusable metal molds (e. g. steel) of a higher melting utilizing a gravity or tilt pour method. Permanent mold castings are sounder, as they can be produced at lower tooling costs and be made with sand cores to yield shapes not available via die-casting. It is a precision technique produced by pouring molten aluminum into precisely (e.g. by CNC) machined steel molds under gravity, centrifugal force, or pressure. Due to the rapid heat transfer from the molten aluminum to the mold itself, the castings have finer grain structures and better strength properties than casts made by sand casting method. Permanent mold aluminum casting permits casting designs with thinner walls and less weight. Typically the tolerance is 1.5% for the first 25 mm and 0.2% for the additional thickness, but 0.25 mm has to be added in if crossing the parting line. Permanent mold castings are less subject to shrinkage and gas porosity than sand castings and do not contain the entrapped gas often found in die castings.

83.2.3　Die-Cast Aluminum

Die-casting is similar to permanent mold casting except that the molten metal is injected into the mold under high pressure, resulting in very uniform parts with good surface finish and dimensional accuracy. Die casting is a near-net-shape manufacturing process used extensively for realizing mass productions for nonferrous materials such as zinc (420 ℃), magnesium (649 ℃), aluminum (660 ℃), and copper (1083 ℃) alloys. Note that the temperature given in the parenthesis for each metal is its corresponding melting point. Design guidelines for aluminum alloys discussed here may be extended to copper, magnesium, and zinc alloys in principles. Diecasting utilizes two steel mold haves, known as core and cavity. Molten aluminum is injected into the assembled core and cavity under high pressure. Solid side cores may be used for forming some features, which are hard to make using the main mold core and cavities only. After solidification, mold core and cavity molds are separated, applying an ejector mechanism.

Many aluminum casting alloys display good fluidity for casting thin sections and fine details, but material shrinkage during casting is large as ranging from 3.5% to 8.5%. Die casting is less tolerant of varying alloys. Only highly castable alloys are used. Die casting usually requires a higher tooling charge relative to permanent-mold and sand castings, but also the lowest piece price on large quantities. Die castings of aluminum alloys are not usually solution heat-treated. Low-temperature aging treatments may be used for stress relief or enhancing dimensional stability.

83.3   Wrought Aluminum (Extruded Aluminum)

Extrusion of spray-formed deposits leads to a significant reduction of the porosity level of aluminum alloys and partial recrystallization, resulting in a material with enhanced ductility. Each wrought aluminum alloy is given a four-digit number (International Alloy Designation System), of which the first number indicates, the major alloying elements, shown as follows:

(a) 1000 series-pure aluminum with a minimum 99% aluminum content by weight;
(b) 2000 series-alloyed with copper;
(c) 3000 series-alloyed with manganese;
(d) 4000 series-alloyed with silicon;
(e) 5000 series-alloyed with magnesium;
(f) 6000 series-alloyed with magnesium and silicon;
(g) 7000 series-alloyed with zinc;
(h) 8000 series-a category used for lithium alloys.

The 1000 series is not heat treatable.

Al-Si-based alloys have been used for moderate heat-resistance components in the automotive industry such as engine pistons, cylinder blocks, and cylinder heads.

6×××series alloys achieve their properties by thermal treatment, which can be adjusted to provide combinations of strength and formability conditions with good corrosion resistance and weldability.

Aluminum-lithium alloys (Al-Li), such as 8090 (Al-1.3Cu-2.45Li-0.12Zr, by weight), were developed primarily as direct replacements for existing aluminum alloys for weight-sensitive aircraft and aerospace structures. They have become attractive candidate materials to replace the traditionally used 2×××- and 7××× series aluminum alloys for aircraft structural applications because of their superior properties such as reduced density, improved elastic modulus, higher specific strength, enhanced resistance to fatigue crack propagation and superior strengthtoughness combinations at cryogenic temperatures.

Another available category of aluminum alloys is scandium aluminum (Al_3Sc). These alloys contain scandium and other elements such as Zr and have excellent fatigue endurance at elevated temperatures [Wirtz et al.]. Aluminum-scandium alloys have been used for high temperature applications(> 300 ℃) , e.g. aerospace craft components.

An aluminum alloy does not have a definite fatigue limit, as it continues to weaken with continuous strain cycles. The fatigue strength (endurance limit) of wrought aluminum may be approximated, with a fatigue cutoff cycle of 5×10^8, using the following equations

$$\sigma_f = 0.45 \ \sigma_{uts} , \ \text{if} \ \sigma_{uts} < 340 \ \text{MPa} \tag{83.2}$$

and

$$\sigma_f = 133 \ \text{MPa}, \ \text{if} \ \sigma_{uts} \geqslant 340 \ \text{MPa} \tag{83.3}$$

Both tensile strength and fatigue limit of aluminum alloys decrease with thermal exposure to an elevated temperature. For example, the 7050 (T7451) alloy has a 19% reduction in its yield strength after being exposed to a working environment at 177 ℃ for 8 hours [Liu et al.].

By introducing insoluble particles such as silicon carbide into an aluminum matrix, 6063 (O)/ 15%SiC ($V_f = 15\%$) , the metal or alloy can be dispersion-strengthened and thereby retain its properties to a temperature well above the normal softening temperature because dislocations are impeded from moving and softening by recrystallization and grain growth is prevented by the pinning effect of the particles. Furthermore, the mismatch in the coefficient of thermal expansion between these two phases of silicon carbide particulates and the aluminum alloy matrix, generates thermal stresses that can be sufficient to deform this matrix plastically [Arsenault & Taya]. This leads to a high dislocation density which invariably strengthens the composite material. This can be likened to the effect of cold work done on the metal/alloy.

83.4 ε-N Fatigue Parameters of Aluminum Alloys

Based on the properties of 81 aluminum alloys, [Meggiolaro and Castro 2004] gave the following approximating formulae for ε-N fatigue parameters:

$$\sigma'_f = 1.9 \ \sigma_{uts} \tag{83.4}$$
$$\varepsilon'_f = 0.28 \tag{83.5}$$
$$b = -0.11 \tag{83.6}$$
$$c = -0.66 \tag{83.7}$$

83.5   Creep of Aluminum Alloys

Thermomechanical creep parameters of aluminum alloys are shown in Table 83.7. Fatigue lifetimes of most aluminum alloys, such as 3003 (AA wrought), are reduced by creep at a temperature above 150 ℃ (423 K).

In the CAF (Creep-Age Forming) process, the aging cycle of the alloy is used to relax external loads imposed on the part through creep mechanisms. Those relaxed stresses impose a new curvature to the part. At the end of the process, a significant springback (sometimes about 70%) is observed and the success in achieving the desired form depends on how the springback can be predicted in order to compensate it by tooling changes. Constitutive equations that combine creep and precipitation hardening simultaneously have been established, such as the use of the CAF process to shape aircraft wing skin panels that demand the use of alloys that exhibit high relaxation rates combined with high strength and toughness after the forming cycle.

83.6   Crack Propagation

Crack propagation data of aluminum alloys in the opening mode are listed in Table 83.8.

83.7   Aluminum-Based Composites

Mechanical properties, thermal properties, and material strengths of aluminum-based composites are given in Tables 83.9—83.11, respectively. Reinforcing fibers or particulates modify aluminum alloys' properties for some special durability and wear demands. Effects of normal load and sliding speed on tribological properties of an aluminum alloy/aluminum oxide-reinforced composite pin on sliding over EN36 steel disc were evaluated for friction and wear [Kathiresan & Sornakumar]. The wear rate increases with increasing normal load and sliding speed. The specific wear rate marginally decreases with the normal load. The coefficient of friction decreases with increasing normal load and sliding speed. The wear and coefficient of friction of the aluminum alloy/ aluminum oxide composite are lower than the plain aluminum alloy.

83.8   Applications

Aluminum alloys are widely used in engineering structures and components where light weight or corrosion resistance is required. Aluminum alloys have been successfully used for automotive structural parts such as engine blocks, suspension components, space frames, and vehicle bodies. Typical example applications of aluminum alloys are

242.0: Pistons, cylinder heads, and generator housings;

319.0, A319: Crankcases, engine oil pans, axle housings;

354.0: Automotive disk brake caliper;

355.0: Air compressor pistons, water jackets, and crankcases;

356.0: Automotive wheels, flywheels, transmission cases, pumps, and chassis;

357.0: High-strength aerospace castings, automotive disk brake caliper;

380.0, A380: Transmission gear casings, brake castings, and engine brackets;

390.0/A390: Hypereutectic version for cylinder blocks and pistons;

535.0: Aircraft components, as dimensionally stable, ductile, and strong;

712.0, 713.0: Automotive trailer parts, pumps, and marine castings;

2008: Automotive body panels;

2036: Automotive hoods;

3003: Truck panels and heat exchanger tube;

5083: Automotive inner body;

5182: Automobile frames (formed);

5456: Truck and trailer body panels;

5754: Automotive inner body and automobile frames (formed);

6016: Automobile hoods;

6061: Automobile frames (extruded) and gas cylinders for scuba diving;

6063: Automobile frames (extruded);

6111: Automotive external body panels and hoods;

6351: Gas cylinders for scuba diving;

7075: Aircraft/aerospace aluminum.

$6\times\times\times$ alloys used for autobody sheets are 6009, 6010, 6016, and 6111, and more recently, 6181 was added for recycling aspects. Alloy 6016 has good formability with low spring back, good hemming capability, high weldability, strong corrosion resistance, stretcher-strain-free surfaces, and stabilized formability in the T4 temper. It has been used for car body in gages of $1.0 \sim 1.2$ mm.

Aluminum alloys are a representative class of structural metals working at subzero temperatures. Retention of toughness and tensile strength.5083(O) is widely used for cryogenic applications due to its retention of fracture toughness, though 2219(T87) has the best combination of both properties at-195 ℃ (boiling point of N_2).

References

AHMAD Z, 2003. The Properties and Application of Scandium-Reinforced Aluminum[J]. Journal of Materials, 55(2): 35-39.

ALEXOPOUPOS N, TIRAYAKIOGLU M, 2009. Relationship between Fracture Toughness and Tensile Properties of A357 Cast Aluminum Alloy[J]. Metallurgical and Materials Transactions A, 40(3): 702.

AMOLD B, ALTENHOF W, 2005. Finite Element Modeling of Axial Crushing of AA6071-T4 and AA6063-T5 Structural Square Tube with Circular Discontinuity[J]. SAE 2005-01-0703.

ARSENAULT R J, TAYA M, 1989. Metal Matrix Composites, Thermo Mechanical Behavior[M]. Oxford: Pergamon Press.

BAHAIDEEN F B, et al, 2009. Fatigue Behavior of Aluminum Alloy at Elevated Temperature[J]. Modern Applied Science, 3(4): 52-61.

BAKHTIYAROV S, et al, 2001. Electrical and Thermal Conductivity of A319 and A356 Aluminum Alloys[J]. Journal of Materials Science, 36(19): 4643-4648.

CHAN T K, PORTER GOFF R F D, 2000. Welded Aluminum Alloy Connections: Test Results and BS8118 [J]. Thin-Walled Structures, 36(4): 265-287.

CHENG C H, 2005. Determination of True Stress-strain Curve for the Weldment of Aluminum Laser-welded Blanks[J]. Journal of Laser Applications, 17(3): 159-170.

CLAUSEN A D, et al, 1999. Stretch Bending of Aluminum Extrusions: Effect of Geometry and Alloy[J]. Journal of Engineering Mechanics, 125(4): 392-400.

COSTA J D, 2004. Comparative Analysis of Fatigue Life Predictions in Central Notched Specimens of Al-Mg-Si Alloys[J]. Fatigue and Fracture Engineering Materials & Structures, 27(9): 837-848.

COURVAL G, et al, 2003. Development of an Improved Cosmetic Corrosion Test by the Automotive and Aluminum Industries for Finished Aluminum Auto-body Panels[J]. SAE 200301-1235.

DANIEL D, HOFFMANN J, PLASSART G, et al, 2002. Optimization of 6016 Aluminum Alloy Selection for Outer Panels[J]. SAE 2002-01-2012.

DARRAS B M, et al, 2013. Analysis of Damage in 5083 Aluminum Alloy Deformed at Different Strain Rates [J]. Materials Science & Engineering A, 568: 143-149.

DAVIS G, WHISNANT P, VENABLES J, 1995. Subadhesive Hydration of 924 Aluminum Adherents and Its Detection by Electrochemical Impedance Spec 925 Troscopy [J]. Journal of Adhesives Science and

Technology, (9): 433-442.

DUFFY W, 1990. Acoustic Quality Factor of Aluminum Alloys from 40 mK to 300 K[J]. Journal of Applied Physics, (68): 5601-5609.

DUPRAT D, et al, 1996. Fatigue Damage Calculation in Stress Concentration Fields under Variable Uniaxial Stress[J]. International Journal of Fatigue, 18(4): 245-253.

FATEMI A, et al, 2005. Application of Bi-linear Log-Log S-N Model to Strain-controlled Fatigue Data of Aluminum Alloys and Its Effect on Life Predictions[J]. International Journal of Fatigue, 27(9): 1040-1050.

FENGA M D, et al, 2010. Effect of Microstructural Features on Fatigue Behavior in A319-T6 Aluminum Alloy [J]. Materials Science and Engineering, (527): 3420-3426.

FULLER C B, MURRAY J, 2005. Temporal Evolution of the Nanostructure of Al(Sc,Zr) Alloys: Part I - Chemical Compositions of Al3(Sc1-xZrx) Precipitates[J]. Acta Mater, 53(20): 5401-5413.

GUESSER W L, MASIERO I, 2005. Thermal Conductivity of Gray Iron and Compacted Graphite Iron Used for Cylinder Heads[J]. Revista Materia, 10(2): 265-272.

GUNGGOR S, EDWARDS L. Effect of Surface Texture on Fatigue Life in Squeeze Cast 6082 Aluminum Alloy [J]. Fatigue Fracture of Engineering Materials and Structures, 16(4): 391-403.

HAFIZ M, KOBAYASHI T, 1996. Fracture Toughness of Eutectic Al-Si Casting Alloy with Different Microstructural Features[J]. Journal of Materials Science, 31: 6195-6200.

HARLOW D G, 2003. The Effect of Statistic Variability in Material Properties on Springback[J]. International Journal of Materials and Product Technology, 20(1/3): 180-192.

HÉNAFF G, et al, 2010. Influence of Corrosion and Creep on Intergranular Fatigue Crack Path in 2×× × Aluminum Alloys[J]. Engineering Fracture Mechanics, 77(11): 1975-1988.

HÉNAFF G, ODEMER G, TONNEAU-MOREL A, 2007. Environmentally-assisted Fatigue Crack Growth Mechanisms in Advanced Materials for Aerospace Applications[J]. International Journal of Fatigue, 29(9-11): 1927-1940.

HOPPERSTAD O S, et al, 1999. Reliability-Based Analysis of a Stretch-Bending Process for Aluminum Extrusions[J]. Computers and Structures, (71): 63-75.

HSIEH W H, et al, 2004. Experimental Investigation of Heat-Transfer Characteristics of Aluminum-Foam Heat Sinks[J]. International Journal of Heat and Mass Transfer, 47(23): 5149-5157.

JABRA J, et al, 2006. The Effect of Thermal Exposure on the Mechanical Properties of 2099t83 Extrusions, 7075-T7651 Plate, 7075-T7452 Die Forgings, 7085-T7651 Plate, and 2397-T87 Plate Aluminum Alloys

[J]. Journal of Materials Engineering and Performance, 15(5): 601-607.

JAGADESH S K, et al, 2010. Prediction of Cooling Curves during Solidification of Al 6061SiCp Based Metal Matrix Composites Using Finite Element Analysis[J]. Journal of Materials Processing Technology, 210(4): 618-623.

JAGLINSKI T, et al, 2007. Study of Bolt Load Loss in Bolted Aluminum Joints[J]. Journal of Engineering Materials and Technology, 129: 48-54.

JIANG Y, HERTEL O, VORMWALD M, 2007. An Experimental Evaluation of Three Critical Plane Multiaxial Fatigue Criteria[J]. International Journal of Fatigue, 29(8): 1490-1502.

JOYCE C F, 1991. A Weibull Model to Characterize Lifetimes of Aluminum Alloy Electrical Wire Connections. IEEE Transaction on Components, Hybrids, and Manufacturing Technology, 14(1): 124-133.

KAHL S, et al, 2014. Tensile, Fatigue, and Creep Properties of Aluminum Heat Exchanger Tube Alloys for Temperatures from 293 K to 573 K (20 ℃ to 300 ℃)[J]. Metallurgical and Materials Transactions A, 44(11): 663-681.

KATHIRESAN M, SORNAKUMAR T, 2010. Friction and Wear Studies of Die Cast Aluminum Alloy-Aluminum Oxide-Reinforced Composites[J]. Industrial Lubrication and Tribology, 62(6): 361-371.

KAUFMAN J G, et al, 1971. Fracture Toughness of Structural Aluminum Alloys[J]. Engineering Fracture Mechanics, 2(3): 197-210.

KHAN S, VYSHNEVSKYY A, MOSLER J, 2010. Low Cycle Life Time Assessment of Al 2024 Alloy[J]. International Journal of Fatigue, (32): 1270-1277.

KHALIFA T A, MAHMOUD T S, 2009. Elevated Temperature Mechanical Properties of Aluminum Alloy AA6063/SiCp MMCs[J]. Proceedings of the World Congress on Engineering, (Ⅱ): 1557-1562.

KLUGER K, 2015. Fatigue Life Estimation for 2017A-T4 and 6082-T6 Aluminum Alloys Subjected to Bending-torsion with Mean Stress[J]. International Journal of Fatigue, (80): 22-29.

KOSTRIVAS A, LIPPOLD J C, 1999. Weldability of Li-bearing Aluminum Alloys[J]. International Materials Reviews, 44(6): 217.

KUMAI S, et al, 2004. Tear Toughness of Permanent Mold Cast DC A356 Aluminum Alloys[J]. Materials Transactions, 45(5): 1706-1713.

KWON Y, et al, 2007. Fracture Toughness and Fracture mechanisms of Cast A356 Aluminum Alloy[J]. Key Engineering Materials, 345/346: 633-636.

LAWSON B L, OZDOGANLAR O B, 2008. Effects of Crystallographic Anisotropy on Orthogonal Micromachining of Single-Crystal Aluminum[J]. Journal of Manufacturing Science and Engineering, 130(3): 031116.

LIM Y Y, et al, 1999. Accurate Determination of the mechanical Properties of Thin Aluminum Films Deposited on Sapphire Flats Using Nanoindentation[J]. Journal of Materials Research, 14(6): 2314.

LINDER J, et al, 2006. The Influence of Porosity on the Fatigue Life for Sand and Permanent Mould Cast Aluminum[J]. International Journal of Fatigue, 28(12): 1752-1758.

LIU Q, JUUL JENSEN D, HANSEN N, 1998. Effect of Grain Orientation on Deformation Structure in Cold-rolled Polycrystalline Aluminum[J]. ACTA Materials, 46(16): 5819-5838.

LIU X, et al, 2009. Fatigue Behavior and Dislocation Substructures for 6063 Aluminum Alloy under Nonproportional Loadings[J]. International Journal of Fatigue, (31): 1190-1195.

MADAN J, RAO P V M, KUNDRA T K, 2007. Computer-aided Manufacturability Analysis of Die-cast Parts [J]. Computer-Aided Design & Applications, 4(1-4): 147-158.

MEGGIOLARO M A, CASTRO J T P, 2004. Statistical Evaluation of Strain-Life Fatigue Crack Initiation Predictions[J]. International Journal of Fatigue, 26(5): 463-476.

MISSORI S, SILI A, 2000. Mechanical Behavior of 6082-T6 Aluminum Alloy Welds[J]. Metallurgical Science and Technology, 18(1): 12-18.

MRÓWKA-NOWOTNIK G, SIENIAWSKI J, 2005. Influence of Heat Treatment on the Microstructure and Mechanical Properties of 6005 and 6082 Aluminum Alloys[J]. Journal of Materials Processing Technology, 162/163: 367-372.

MUTOH Y, GAIR G, WATERHOUSE R, 1987. The Effect of Residual Stresses Induced by Shot Peening on Fatigue Crack Propagation in Two High Strength Aluminum Alloys[J]. Fatigue Fract. Engng. Mater. Struct., 10(4): 261-272.

NANNINGA N E, 2008. High Cycle Fatigue of AA6082 and AA6063 Aluminum Extrusions[D]. Houghton: Michigan Technological University.

NES E, 2005. Modeling Grain Boundary Strength in Ultra-fine Grained Aluminum Alloys[J]. Material Science and Engineering A- Structures, 410/411: 178-182.

NIELSEN K L, 2010. Modeling of plastic flow localization and damage development in friction stir welded 6005A aluminum alloy using physics based strain hardening law [J]. International Journal of Solids and Structures, 47(18-19): 2359-2370.

PICHLER A, WELLER M, ARZT C A, 1994. High Temperature Damping in Dispersion Strengthened Aluminum Alloys[J]. Journal of Alloys and Compounds, 211-212(1): 414-418.

RANDALL B H, ZENER C, 1940. Internal Friction of Aluminum[J]. Physics Review, (58): 472-483.

RAO K T, YU W, RITCHIE R O, 1989. Cryogenic Toughness of Commercial Aluminum Lithium Alloys: Role of Delamination Toughing[J]. Metallurgical Transactions, (20A): 485-497.

SALERNO G, et al, 2007. Mean Strain Influence in Low Cycle Fatigue Behavior of AA7175-T1 Aluminum Alloy[J]. International Journal of Fatigue, 29(5): 829-35.

SAMUEL A M, SAMUEL F H, 1995. Effect of Alloying Elements and Dendrite Arm Spacing on the Microstructure and Hardness of an Al-Si-Cu-Mg-Fe-Mn (380) Aluminum Die-Casting Alloy[J]. Journal of Materials Science, 30: 1698-1708.

SANDERS, ROBERT E Jr., 2001. Technology Innovation in Aluminum Products[J]. Journal of Materials, 53 (2): 21-25.

SCOTT M H, GITTOS M F, 1983. Tensile and Toughness Properties of Arc-welded 5083 and 6082 Aluminum Alloys[J]. Welding Journal Research Supplement, (62): 243s-252s.

SHETTY R, et al, 2008. Finite Element Modeling of Stress Distribution in Cutting Path in Machining of Discontinuously Reinforced Aluminum Composites[J]. APRN Journal of Engineering and Applied Sciences, 3(4): 25-31.

SHAKERI H, et al, 2002. Study of Damage Initiation and Fracture in Aluminum Tailor Welded Blanks Made via Different Welding Techniques[J]. Journal of Light Metals, (2): 95-110.

SNCHEZ-SANTANA U, RUBIO-GONZLEZ C, MESMACQUE G, et al, 2009. Effect of Fatigue Damage on the Dynamic Tensile Behavior of 6061-T6 Aluminum Alloy and AISI 4140T Steel[J]. International Journal of Fatigue, 31: 1928-1937.

SON D, et al, 2003. Film-thickness Considerations in Micro Cantilever-Beam Test in Measuring Mechanical Properties of Metal Thin Film[J]. Thin Solid Films, (437): 182-187.

SOYAMA H, SAITO K, SAKA M, 2002. Improvement of Fatigue Strength of Aluminum Alloy by Cavitation Shotless Peening[J]. Journal of Engineering Materials and Technology, 124(2): 135-139.

SPICE J J, 2007. Effects of Silicon and Boron Additions on the Susceptibility to Quench Embrittlement and Bending Fatigue Performance of Vacuum Carburized Modified 4320 Steel[J]. SAE 2007-01-1005.

STEPHENS R, MAHONEY B, FOSSMAN R, 1988. Low Cycle Fatigue of A356-T6 Cast Aluminum Alloy Wheels[J]. SAE 881707.

TAKAGI H, et al, 2006. Creep Characterization of Aluminum-Magnesium Solid-Solution Alloy through Self-Similar Microindentation[J]. Materials Transactions, 47(8): 2006-2014.

TAKAHASHI T, NAGAYOSHI T, KUMANO M, et al, 2002. Thermal Plastic-elastic Creep Analysis of Engine Cylinder Head[J]. SAE 2002-01-0585.

THORNTON P H, et al, 1996. The Aluminum Spot Weld[J]. Welding Research Supplement, 75(3): 101s-107s.

TIRAYAKIOGLU M, 2008. Fracture Toughness Potential of Cast Al-7%Si-Mg Alloys[J]. Materials Science and Engineering A, (497): 512-514.

TOHGO K, OKA M, 2004. Influence of Coarsening Treatment on Fatigue Strength and Fracture Toughness of Al-Si-Ma Alloy Castings[J]. Key Engineering Materials, 261/263: 1263-1268.

WANG L, TSAI C, 2014. Creep Resistance of 2024 Aluminum Alloy[J]. SAE 2013-32-9110.

WANG M Z, KASSNER M E, 2002. Tensile and Fatigue Properties of Aluminum Alloy Sheet 6022[J]. Journal of Materials Engineering and Performance, 11(2): 166-168.

WANG Q, et al, 2011. Modeling of Residual Stresses in Quenched Cast Aluminum Components[J]. SAE 2011-01-0539.

WANG Q G, et al, 2001. Fatigue Behavior of A356-T6 Aluminum Cast Alloys, Part I: Effect of Casting Defects [J]. Journal of Light Metals, 1(1): 73-84.

WANG Q G, et al, 2001. Fatigue Behavior of A356-T6 Aluminum Cast Alloys, Part II: Effect of Micro-structural Constituents[J]. Journal of Light Metals, 1(1): 85-97.

WANG Y Y, 2008. Fatigue Behaviors of LY12CZ Aluminum Alloy under Nonproportional Load[J]. Journal of Nanjing University of Aeronautics & Astronautics, (40): 484-488.

WIRTZ T, et al, 2000. Fatigue Properties of the Aluminum Alloys 6013 and Al-Mg-Sc[J]. Materials Science Forum, 331-337: 1489-1494.

WONG W, BUCCI R, STENTZ R, et al, 1987. Tensile and Strain-Controlled Fatigue Data for Certain Aluminum Alloys for Application in the Transportation Industry[J]. SAE 870094.

WUNDERLICH W, HAYASHI M, 2012. Thermal Cyclic Fatigue Analysis of Three Aluminum Piston Alloys [J]. International Journal of Material and Mechanical Engineering, 1(3): 57-60.

YE J C, et al, 2005. A Tri-Modal Aluminum Based Composite with Super-High Strength [J]. Scripta Materialia, 53: 481-486.

ZACHARIA T, AIDUN D, 1988. Elevated Temperature Mechanical Properties of Al-Li-Cu-Mg Alloy [J]. Welding Research Supplement: 281s-288s.

ZHANG J, ALPAS A, 1997. Transition between Mild and Severe Wear in Aluminum Alloys [J]. Acta Materialia, 45(2): 513-528.

ZHAO T, JIANG Y, 2008. Fatigue of 7075-T651 Aluminum Alloy[J]. International Journal of Fatigue, (30):
834-849.

Table 83.1   Temper Designations of Aluminum, Copper, and Magnesium Alloys

Letter	1st Digit (Operations)	2nd Digit (Hardening Level)
F-As Fabricated	—	—
O-Annealed	—	—
H-Hardened	0-No cold worked	1-Annealed
	1-Cold worked only	2-1/4 Hard
	2-Cold worked & annealed	4-1/2 Hard
	3-Cold worked & stabilized	6-3/4 Hard 8-Hard 9-Extra Hard
T-Heat Treated	T1-Cooled from elevated temperatures & natural aging T2-Cooled from elevated temperatures & artificial aging T3-Solution-heat-treated, cold worked, & naturally aged T4-Solution-heat-treated & naturally aged T5-Cooled from elevated temperatures & artificially aged T6-Solution-heat-treated & artificially aged T7-Solution-heat-treated & stabilized T8-Solution-heat-treated, cold worked, & artificially aged T9-Solution-heat-treated, artificially aged, & cold worked T10-Cooled from elevated temperatures, cold worked, & artificially aged	

Table 83.2   Mechanical Properties of Cast Aluminum Alloys

Material	$T/^\circ C$	E_T	ρ	ν	(σ,ε)	α	k	γ	ρ_E	K_{IC}
201.0(SC;F)	23	71	2.8	0.32	—	19	120	963	—	—
	300	—	—	—	—	25	—	—	—	—
	649(T_m)	—	—	—	—	—	—	—	—	—
201.0(SC;T4)	23	71	2.8	0.32	(215,0.2%) (365,20%)	19	120	963	—	—
201.0(SC;T6)	23	71	2.8	0.32	(435,0.2%) (485,7%)	19	120	963	—	—

continued

Material	$T/℃$	E_{T}	ρ	ν	(σ,ε)	α	k	γ	ρ_{E}	K_{IC}
201.0(SC;T7)	23	71	2.8	0.32	(345,0.2%) (414,3%)	19	120	963	—	—
	204	—	—	—	(314,0.2%) $\sigma_{\mathrm{uts}}=328$	23.2	—	—	—	—
204.0(PM;T4; Al-4Cu-Mg-Ti)	23	71	2.8	0.32	(200,0.2%) (331,8%)	19	120	963	—	—
	300	—	—	—	—	25	—	—	—	—
	649(T_{m})	—	—	—	—	—	—	—	—	—
204.0(SC;T4)	23	71	2.8	0.32	(193,0.2%) (310,6%)	19	120	963	—	—
204.0(PM;T6)	23	71	2.8	0.32	(230,0.2%) (390,20%)	19	120	963	—	—
204.0(SC;T6)	23	71	2.8	0.32	(250,0.2%) (390,14%)	19	120	963	—	—
206.0(SC;T7)	23	71	2.8	0.32	(350,0.2%) (436,12%)	19	126	920	—	43
	650(T_{m})	—	—	—	—	—	—	—	—	—
A206.0(SC;T6)	23	71	2.8	0.32	(350,0.2%) (440,5%)	19	120	963	—	—
	204	—	—	—	(285,0.2%) $\sigma_{\mathrm{uts}}=320$	23.2	—	—	—	—
208.0(SC;F)	23	71	2.8	0.32	(97,0.2%) (145,2.5%)	21	126	963	—	—
	627(T_{m})	—	—	—	—	—	—	—	—	—
208.0(PM;T4)	23	71	2.8	0.32	(103,0.2%) (228,5%)	21	126	963	—	—
208.0(PM;T6)	23	71	2.8	0.32	(152,0.2%) (241,2%)	21	126	963	—	—
208.0(PM;T7)	23	71	2.8	0.32	(110,0.2%) (228,3%)	21	126	963	—	—

continued

Material	$T/{}^\circ\text{C}$	E_T	ρ	ν	(σ,ε)	α	k	γ	ρ_E	K_IC
213.0(SC;F)	23	71	2.9	0.32	(105,0.2%) (160,1.5%)	21	126	963	—	—
213.0(SC;T2)	23	71	2.9	0.32	(140,0.2%) (190,1%)	21	126	963	—	—
	−80	—	—	—	(200,0.2%) (350,14%)	—	—	—	—	—
	−26	—	—	—	(200,0.2%) (345,10%)	—	—	—	—	—
218.0	23	71	2.9	0.32	(193,0.2%) (310,5%)	21	126	963	—	—
	100	—	—	—	(172,0.2%) (275,8%)	—	—	—	—	—
	200	—	—	—	(105,0.2%) (150,40%)	—	—	—	—	—
	260	—	—	—	(62,0.2%) (900,45%)	—	—	—	—	—
222.0(SC;F)	23	71	2.95	0.32	(71,0.2%) (160,2%)	21	130	963	—	—
	624(T_m)	—	—	—	—	—	—	—	—	—
222.0(SC;T6)	23	71	2.95	0.32	(127,0.2%) (207,2%)	21	130	963	—	—
222.0(PM;T65)	23	71	2.95	0.32	(127,0.2%) (276,2%)	21	130	963	—	—
224.0(PM;T7)	23	71	2.95	0.32	$\sigma_\text{uts}=425$	21	—	963	—	—
	100	—	—	—	$\sigma_\text{uts}=360$	—	—	—	—	—
	200	—	—	—	$\sigma_\text{uts}=275$	—	—	—	—	—

continued

Material	$T/°C$	E_T	ρ	ν	(σ,ε)	α	k	γ	ρ_E	K_{IC}
240.0(SC;F)	−200	—	—	—	$\sigma_{uts}=250$	—	—	—	—	—
	23	71	2.95	0.32	$\sigma_{uts}=245$	22	130	963	—	—
	93	—	—	—	$\sigma_{uts}=240$	—	—	—	—	—
	200	—	—	—	$\sigma_{uts}=225$	—	—	—	—	—
242.0(SC;F)	23	71	2.95	0.32	$(210,0.2\%)$ $(217,0.5\%)$	22	130	963	—	—
242.0(SC;O)	23	71	2.95	0.32	$(125,0.2\%)$ $(190,1\%)$	22	130	963	—	—
242.0(SC;T4)	23	71	2.95	0.32	$(110,0.2\%)$ $(220,8.5\%)$	22	130	963	—	—
242.0 (PM;T571)	−200	—	—	—	$\sigma_{uts}=295$	—	—	—	—	—
	23	71	2.95	0.32	$(238,0.2\%)$ $(285,1\%)$	21	130	963	—	—
	93	—	—	—	$\sigma_{uts}=280$	—	—	—	—	—
	200	—	—	—	$\sigma_{uts}=180$	—	—	—	—	—
242.0 (SC;T571)	23	71	2.95	0.32	$(210\ 0.2\%)$ $(223,0.5\%)$	21	130	963	—	—
	200	—	—	—	$\sigma_{uts}=180$	—	—	—	—	—
242.0 (PM;T61)	23	71	2.95	0.32	$(294,0.2\%)$ $(330,0.5\%)$	21	130	963	—	—
242.0 (SC;T61)	23	71	2.95	0.32	$(138,0.2\%)$ $(221,1\%)$	21	130	963	—	—
242.0(DC;T7)	23	71	2.95	0.32	$\sigma_{uts}=430$	21	—	963	—	—
	93	—	—	—	$\sigma_{uts}=380$	—	—	—	—	—
	200	—	—	—	$\sigma_{uts}=250$	—	—	—	—	—
295.0(SC;T4; $\approx$ZL203)	23	71	2.7	0.32	$(110,0.2\%)$ $(220,8.5\%)$	22	138	963	—	—
	300	—	—	—	—	25	—	—	—	—

continued

Material	$T/°C$	E_T	ρ	ν	(σ,ε)	α	k	γ	ρ_E	K_{IC}
295.0(SC;T6)	23	71	2.7	0.32	(165,0.2%) (250,5%)	22	138	963	—	—
	300	—	—	—	—	25	—	—	—	—
295.0(SC;T62)	23	71	2.7	0.32	(195,0.2%) (250,5%)	22	138	963	—	—
	300	—	—	—	—	25	—	—	—	—
295.0(SC;T7)	23	71	2.7	0.32	(110,0.2%) (200,5%)	22	138	963	—	—
296.0(T4)	23	71	2.7	0.32	(130,0.2%) $\sigma_{uts}=220$	22	—	—	—	—
296.0(T6)	23	71	2.7	0.32	(160,0.2%)	22	—	—	—	—
296.0(T61)	23	71	2.7	0.32	(140,0.2%) $\sigma_{uts}=275$	22	—	—	—	—
308.0(PM;F)	23	74	2.79	0.33	(162,0.2%) (195,2%)	21	109	963	—	—
319.0(PM;F;Al-3.5Cu-6Si-1Mg-1Zn-0.5Mn-0.25Ti)	23	74	2.79	0.33	(126,0.2%) (235,2%)	21	109	963	—	—
	400	—	—	—	—	23	155	—	—	—
	604(T_m)	—	—	—	—	—	—	—	—	—
319.0(SC; F;≈ZL107)	23	74	2.79	0.32	(133,0.2%) (190,2%)	21.4	109	963	—	—
319.0(SC;T5)	23	74	2.79	0.32	(162,0.2%) (210,2%)	21.4	109	963	—	—
319.0(DC;T6)	23	74	2.79	0.33	(185,0.2%) (234,2%)	21	109	963	—	—
319.0(PM;T6)	23	74	2.79	0.33	(190,0.2%) (280,3%)	21	109	963	—	—
319.0(SC;T6)	23	74	2.79	0.32	(168,0.2%) (250,2%)	21.4	109	963	—	—

continued

Material	$T/°C$	E_T	ρ	ν	(σ,ε)	α	k	γ	ρ_E	K_{IC}
319.0(DC;T7)	23	74	2.79	0.33	(190,0.2%) (250,0.4%) (300,1.2%) (317,1.8%)	21	109	963	—	—
	150	—	—	—	(205,0.2%) (241,0.45%) (274,2%)	—	—	—	—	—
	200	—	—	—	(200,0.2%) (221,0.27%) (253,2.4%)	—	—	—	—	—
	300	—	—	—	(71,0.2%) (86,0.4%) (96.4,1.4%) (99,2.3%)	—	—	—	—	—
320.0(DC;F; Al-7Si-3Cu- Mg)	23	73	2.77	0.33	(120,0.2%) (220,1%)	20.5	105	963	—	—
328.0(DC;F;Al- 8Si-1.5Cu-1.5Zn- 0.4Mg-0.35Cr- 0.25Ni-0.25Ti)	23	73	2.77	0.33	(110,0.2%) (160,2%)	20.5	105	963	—	—
	300	—	—	—	—	23.2	—	—	—	—
	621(T_m)	—	—	—	—	—	—	—	—	—
328.0(SC;F; ZL106)	23	70.3	2.71	0.32	(95,0.2%) (175,1%)	21.4	121	963	—	—
328.0(DC;T6)	23	73	2.77	0.33	(175,0.2%) (260,2.5%)	20.5	105	963	—	—
328.0(SC;T6)	23	70.3	2.71	0.32	(145,0.2%) (235,1%)	21.4	121	963	—	—
330.0(DC;F)	23	72.8	2.77	0.33	(150,0.2%) (193,1%)	20.5	105	963	—	—
330.0(DC;T5)	23	72.8	2.77	0.33	(172,0.2%) (234,1%)	20.5	105	963	—	—

continued

Material	$T/℃$	E_T	ρ	ν	(σ,ε)	α	k	γ	ρ_E	K_{IC}
330.0(DC;T6)	23	72.8	2.77	0.33	(207,0.2%) (290,1.5%)	20.5	105	963	—	—
332.0(DC;F)	23	72.8	2.77	0.33	—	—	—	—	—	—
	260	—	—	—	$\sigma_{uts}=90$	—	—	—	—	—
	370	—	—	—	$\sigma_{uts}=24$	—	—	—	—	—
333.0(PM;F;Al-9Si-3.5Cu-1Fe-1Zn-0.5Mg-0.5Ni-0.25Ti)	23	73.9	2.77	0.33	(135,0.2%) (235,2%)	20.5	105	963	—	—
	300	—	—	—	—	22.9	—	—	—	—
333.0(PM;T5)	23	73.9	2.77	0.33	(175,0.2%) (235,1%)	20.5	105	963	—	—
333.0(PM;T6)	23	73.9	2.77	0.33	(207,0.2%) (290,1.5%)	20.5	105	963	—	—
336.0(DC;T551)	23	73	2.77	0.33	(195,0.2%) (250,0.5%)	20.5	105	963	—	—
343.0(DC;F)	23	73	2.77	0.33	(140,0.2%) (245,6%)	20.5	105	963	—	—
354.0(DC;T4;Al-9Si-1.8Cu-0.5Mg-0.2Ti-0.1Zn;≈ZL111)	23	73.1	2.71	0.33	(198,0.2%) (242,3%)	20.9	126	963	—	—
	300	—	—	—	—	22.9	—	—	—	—
	596(T_m)	—	—	—	—	—	—	—	—	—
354.0(DC;T61)	23	73.1	2.71	0.33	(260,0.2%) (311,2%)	20.9	126	963	—	—
354.0(PM;T61)	23	73.1	2.71	0.33	(250,0.2%) (335,3%)	20.9	126	963	—	—
	204	—	—	—	(273,0.2%) $\sigma_{uts}=293$	23.2	—	—	—	—
354.0(DC;T62)	23	73.1	2.71	0.33	(281,0.2%) (289,2%)	20.9	126	963	—	—

continued

Material	$T/℃$	E_T	ρ	ν	(σ,ε)	α	k	γ	ρ_E	K_{IC}
355.0(DC;T6; Al-5Si-1.3Cu-0.5 Mg;≈ZL105)	23	70.3	2.71	0.33	(190,0.2%) (255,1.5%)	22.3	142	963	—	—
	300	—	—	—	—	24.7	—	—	—	—
	621(T_m)	—	—	—	—	—	—	—	—	—
355.0(DC;T7)	23	71	2.71	0.33	(205,0.2%) (248,2%)	22.3	163	963	—	—
355.0(SC;T6)	23	70.3	2.71	0.32	(138,0.2%) (221,3%)	22.3	142	963	—	—
356.0(DC;F;Al-7Si-0.2Mg-0.6Fe-0.35Mn-0.35Zn-0.25Ti;≈ZL101; ≈JIS-AC4C)	23	72	2.68	0.33	(120,0.2%) (133,0.25%) (150,1.7%) (155,3%)	21.2	167	963	—	17.3
	300	—	—	—	—	23.2	—	—	—	—
	400	—	—	—	—	24	213	—	—	—
	613(T_m)	—	—	—	—	—	140	—	—	—
356.0(PM;F)	23	72	2.68	0.33	(125,0.2%) (160,5%)	21.2	167	963	—	—
356.0(SC;F)	23	72.4	2.68	0.32	(125,0.2%) (165,6%)	21.4	155	963	—	17
356.0(F)/9% Al_2O_3/21%SiC (V_f=9% & 21%)	23	142	—	0.28	(166,0.2%) (231,1%) (249,1.5%) (256,1.7%)	—	—	—	—	—
356.0(PM;T51)	23	72	2.68	0.33	(140,0.2%) (190,2%)	21.2	167	963	—	—
356.0(SC;T51)	23	72	2.68	0.33	(140,0.2%) (175,2%)	21.2	167	963	—	—
356.0(DC;T6; Rheo-Cast)	23	72	2.68	0.33	(220,0.2%) (240,4%)	21.2	167	963	—	20.6

continued

Material	$T/℃$	E_T	ρ	ν	(σ,ε)	α	k	γ	ρ_E	K_{IC}
356.0(DC;T6; Cast-Forged)	23	72	2.68	0.33	(220,0.2%) (240,4%)	21.2	167	963	—	24.6
356.0(PM;T6)	23	72	2.68	0.33	(190,0.2%) (265,5%)	21.2	167	963	—	—
356.0(SC;T6)	23	72.4	2.68	0.32	(170,0.2%) (220,1%)	21.4	155	963	—	—
356.0(PM;T7)	23	72	2.68	0.33	(167,0.2%) (225,6%)	21.2	167	963	—	—
356.0(SC;T7)	23	72.4	2.68	0.32	(210,0.2%) (224,2%)	21.4	155	963	—	—
356.0(SC;T71)	23	72.4	2.68	0.32	(147,0.2%) (175,3.5%)	21.4	155	963	—	—
A356(PM;F)	23	72	2.7	0.33	(90,0.2%) (190,8%)	21	128	900	—	—
	100	—	—	—	—	—	—	963	—	—
	200	—	—	—	—	22.5		—	—	—
	300	—	—	—	—	23.5		—	—	—
	621(T_m)	—	—	—	—	—	—	—	—	—
A356(SC;F)	23	72	2.7	0.33	(85,0.2%) (160,6%)	21	128	900	—	—
	100	—	—	—	—	—	—	963	—	—
A356(DC;T6)	23	72	2.7	0.33	(220,0.2%) (240,4%)	21	128	900	—	—
	100	—	—	—	—	—	—	963	—	—
A356(PM;T6)	23	72	2.7	0.33	(210,0.2%) (286,4%)	21.0	128	900	—	—
	100	—	—	—	—	—	—	963	—	—
	204	—	—	—	(55,0.2%) $\sigma_{uts}=83$	23.2		—	—	—

continued

Material	$T/°C$	E_T	ρ	ν	(σ,ε)	α	k	γ	ρ_E	K_{IC}
A356(SC;T6)	23	72	2.7	0.33	(210,0.2%) (280,6%)	21	128	900	—	—
	100	—	—	—	—	—	—	963	—	—
	204	—	—	—	(55,0.2%) $\sigma_{uts}=83$	23.2	—	—	—	—
A356(PM;T61)	23	72	2.7	0.33	(210,0.2%) (285,10%)	21	128	900	—	—
	100	—	—	—	—	—	—	963	—	—
357.0(DC;F;Al-7Si-0.65Mg-0.2Ti-0.06Be)	23	72.4	2.67	0.33	(105,0.2%) (165,6%)	21	151	963	—	18
	100	—	—	—	—	21.4	—	—	—	—
	613(T_m)	—	—	—	—	23.2	—	—	—	—
357.0(PM;F)	23	72.4	2.67	0.33	(105,0.2%) (195,6%)	21	151	963	—	29
357.0(DC;T6)	23	72.4	2.67	0.33	(300,0.2%) (350,3%)	21	151	963	—	29
357.0(PM;T6)	23	72.4	2.67	0.33	(300,0.2%) (360,5%)	21	151	963	—	29
359.0(DC;T61)	23	72.4	2.68	0.33	(255,0.2%) (330,6%)	21.4	155	963	—	29
359.0(DC;T61)/20SiC(Brake Rotor; $W_f=$20%)	23	129	—	—	(290,0.2%) (350,5.5%)	—	—	—	—	—
	−80	—	—	—	(172,0.2%) (345,2%)	—	—	—	—	—
360.0(DC;F; Al-9.5Si-1.3Fe-0.6Cu-0.5Mg)	23	71	2.63	0.33	(170,0.2%) (300,2.5%)	18.5	113	963	—	—
	100	—	—	—	(170,0.2%) (300,3%)	—	—	—	—	—

continued

Material	$T/^\circ\text{C}$	E_T	ρ	ν	(σ,ε)	α	k	γ	ρ_E	K_IC
360.0(DC;F; Al-9.5Si-1.3Fe-0.6Cu-0.5Mg)	200	—	—	—	(100,0.2%) (155,8%)	—	—	—	—	—
	260	—	—	—	(52,0.2%) (83,20%)	—	—	—	—	—
	315	—	—	—	(31,0.2%) (48,35%)	—	—	—	—	—
	370	—	—	—	(21,0.2%) (31,40%)	—	—	—	—	—
	596(T_m)	—	—	—	—	—	—	—	—	—
A360.0 (≈YL104)	23	70	2.63	0.33	(170,0.2%) (317,3.5%)	18.5	113	963	—	—
	100	—	—	—	(166,0.2%) (300,3.5%)	—	—	—	—	—
	200	—	—	—	(90,0.2%) (150,14%)	—	—	—	—	—
	260	—	—	—	(45,0.2%) (76,20%)	—	—	—	—	—
	315	—	—	—	(28,0.2%) (45,45%)	—	—	—	—	—
	370	—	—	—	(15,0.2%) (30,45%)	—	—	—	—	—
	596(T_m)	—	—	—	—	—	—	—	—	—
363.0(DC; T4; Al-5Si-3Cu-0.85 Fe-0.4Mg)	23	71	2.63	0.33	(180,0.2%) (270,2.5%)	18.5	125	—	—	—
363.0(DC;T6)	23	71	2.63	0.33	(280,0.2%) (320,1%)	18.5	125	—	—	—
365.0(DC;F; Al-10Si-Mg-Mn)	23	71	2.63	0.33	(120,0.2%) (250,5%)	18.5	125	—	—	—
365.0(SC; F)	23	71	2.63	0.33	(80,0.2%) (150,2%)	18.5	125	—	—	—

continued

Material	$T/℃$	E_T	ρ	ν	(σ,ε)	α	k	γ	ρ_E	K_{IC}
365.0(DC; T5)	23	71	2.63	0.33	(150,0.2%) (270,4%)	18.5	125	—	—	—
365.0(SC; T6)	23	71	2.63	0.33	(180,0.2%) (220,1%)	18.5	125	—	—	—
365.0(DC;T7)	23	71	2.63	0.33	(120,0.2%) (200,12%)	18.5	125	—	—	—
	−80	—	—	—	(160,0.2%) (340,2.5%)	—	—	—	—	—
380.0(F;DC; Al-8Si-3.5Cu- 1.3Fe-3Zn-0.5 Mn-...;≈YL112)	23	71	2.74	0.33	(160,0.2%) (320,3%)	18.5	109	963	—	—
	100	—	—	—	(166,0.2%) (310,4%)	—	—	—	—	—
	200	—	—	—	(115,0.2%) (170,8%)	—	—	—	—	—
	260	—	—	—	(55,0.2%) (90,20%)	—	—	—	—	—
	315	—	—	—	(28,0.2%) (48,30%)	22.5	—	—	—	—
	370	—	—	—	(17,0.2%) (28,35%)	—	—	—	—	—
	593(T_m)	—	—	—	—	—	—	—	—	—
380.0 (Extruded)	23	71	2.74	0.33	(130,0.2%) (220,8.6%)	18.5	109	963	—	—
A380(DC;F)	23	71	2.74	0.33	(170,0.2%) (310,3%)	18.5	109	963	—	—
	100	—	—	—	(159,0.2%) (300,5%)	—	—	—	—	—
	150	—	—	—	(145,0.2%) (230,10%)	—	—	—	—	—

continued

Material	$T/℃$	E_T	ρ	ν	(σ,ε)	α	k	γ	ρ_E	K_{IC}
A380(DC;F)	200	—	—	—	(103,0.2%) (160,14%)	—	—	—	—	—
	260	—	—	—	(48,0.2%) (83,30%)	—	—	—	—	—
383.0(DC; F) Al-10Si-1.5Cu- 1.3Fe-3Zn-...; ≈YL113)	23	71	2.74	0.33	(150,0.2%) (310,3.5%)	18.5	96	963	—	—
	300	—	—	—	—	22.5	—	—	—	—
	543(T_m)	—	—	—	—	—	—	—	—	—
384.0(DC;F; Al-11Si-3.5Cu- 1.3Fe-3Zn-0.5 Mn...)	23	71	2.82	0.33	(165,0.2%) (331,2.5%)	18.5	92	963	—	—
	100	—	—	—	(162,0.2%) (330,2.5%)	—	—	—	—	—
	150	—	—	—	(160,0.2%) (262,5%)	—	—	—	—	—
	200	—	—	—	(130,0.2%) (180,6%)	—	—	—	—	—
	260	—	—	—	(62,0.2%) (97,25%)	—	—	—	—	—
	315	—	—	—	(28,0.2%) (48,45%)	22.5	—	—	—	—
	582(T_m)	—	—	—	—	—	—	—	—	—
Al-6Si-2Mg (DC; F)	23	—	—	0.32	(233,0.2%) (308,2.6%)	18	—	963	—	—
Al-6Si-2Mg (DC; T5)	23	—	—	0.32	(318,0.2%) (338,1%)	18	—	963	—	—
Al-12Si-5Cu- 0.6Mg-2.7Ni-... (DC;T5;Engine Piston)	23	84	2.72	0.32	(220,0.2%) $\sigma_{uts}=255$	18	130	963	—	—
	100	—	—	—	(203,0.2%) $\sigma_{uts}=240$	—	—	—	—	—

continued

Material	$T/℃$	E_T	ρ	ν	(σ,ε)	α	k	γ	ρ_E	K_{IC}
Al-12Si-5Cu-0.6Mg-2.7Ni-...(DC;T5;Engine Piston)	200	—	—	—	$(142,0.2\%)$ $\sigma_{uts}=180$	20.3	136	—	—	—
	250	—	—	—	$(100,0.2\%)$ $\sigma_{uts}=135$	—	—	—	—	—
	300	—	—	—	$(65,0.2\%)$ $\sigma_{uts}=95$	21.1	142	—	—	—
	350	—	—	—	$(48,0.2\%)$ $\sigma_{uts}=60$	—	145	—	—	—
	400	—	—	—	$(35,0.2\%)$ $\sigma_{uts}=45$	21.8	—	—	—	—
	450	—	—	—	$(31,0.2\%)$ $\sigma_{uts}=37$	—	—	—	—	—
Al-12.5Si-4.2 Cu-0.9Mg-2.2 Ni-...(T6;DC; Engine Piston)	23	84	2.77	0.32	$(200,0.2\%)$ $\sigma_{uts}=220$	18	130	963	—	—
	100	—	—	—	—	19.2	—	—	—	—
	200	78	—	—	$(176,0.2\%)$ $\sigma_{uts}=200$	20.3	136	—	—	—
	300	—	—	—	$(84,0.2\%)$ $\sigma_{uts}=110$	21.1	142	—	—	—
	360	70	—	—	$(55,0.2\%)$ $\sigma_{uts}=80$	—	146	—	—	—
390.0(DC;F; Al-17Si-4.5Cu-1.3Fe-1.5Zn-0.55Mg-0.5Mn-0.2Ti-0.2Sn)	23	81.3	2.73	0.33	$(250,0.2\%)$ $(317,1\%)$	21	134	963	—	—
	100	—	—	—	$(186,0.2)$ $(283,1\%)$	—	—	—	—	—
	150	—	—	—	$(255,1\%)$	—	—	—	—	—
	200	—	—	—	$(200,1\%)$	—	—	—	—	—
	260	—	—	—	$(131,2\%)$	—	—	—	—	—
	300	—	—	—	—	22.5	—	—	—	—
	370	—	—	—	$\sigma_{uts}=24$	—	—	—	—	—
	$649(T_m)$	—	—	—	—	—	—	—	—	—

continued

Material	$T/°C$	E_T	ρ	ν	(σ,ε)	α	k	γ	ρ_E	K_{IC}
390.0(SCF)	23	81	2.72	0.32	(195,0.2%) (200,1%)	21	134	963	—	—
390.0(DC;T5)	23	81.3	2.73	0.33	(260,0.2%) (295,1%)	21	134	963	—	—
390.0(SC;T6)	23	81.2	2.72	0.32	(350,0.2%) (360,1%)	21	134	963	—	—
390.0(SC;T7)	23	81.2	2.72	0.32	(250,0.2%) (260,1%)	21	134	963	—	—
A390(PM;F)	23	71	2.74	0.33	(205,0.2%) (205,1%)	21	134	963	—	—
A390(SC;F)	23	71	2.74	0.33	(162,0.2%) (162,1%)	21	134	963	—	—
A390(PM;T6)	23	71	2.74	0.33	(310,0.2%) (310,1%)	21	134	963	—	—
A390(SC;T6)	23	71	2.74	0.33	(280,0.2%) (280,1%)	21	134	963	—	—
A390(PM;T7)	23	71	2.74	0.33	(265,0.2%) (265,1%)	21	134	963	—	—
A390(SC;T7)	23	71	2.74	0.33	(250,0.2%) (250,1%)	21	134	963	—	—
B390(SC;F)	23	71	2.74	0.33	(175,0.2%) (245,1%)	16.2	134	963	—	—
398.0(DC;T5; Al-16Si-...; NASA 398; Engine Piston)	23	88.6	2.76	0.32	$\sigma_{uts}=360$	18.5	120	820	—	—
	300	—	—	—	$\sigma_{uts}=160$	19.72	129	952	—	—
	350	—	—	—	—	19.93	131.4	990	—	—
	400	—	—	—	$\sigma_{uts}=110$	—	—	—	—	—
	$620(T_m)$	—	—	—	—	—	—	—	—	—
413.0(DC;F; Al-12Si-1Cu-1.3 Fe-0.5Zn-0.5Ni- 0.35Mn-0.1Mg; ≈YL102)	23	71	2.66	0.33	(145,0.2%) (300,2.5%)	18.5	121	963	—	—
	260	—	—	—	$\sigma_{uts}=90$	—	—	—	—	—
	300	—	—	—	—	22.4	—	—	—	—
	370	—	—	—	$\sigma_{uts}=31$	—	—	—	—	—
	$582(T_m)$	—	—	—	—	—	—	—	—	—

continued

Material	$T/°C$	E_T	ρ	ν	(σ,ε)	α	k	γ	ρ_E	K_{IC}
A413.0 (DC;F)	23	71	2.66	0.33	(130,0.2%) (290,3%)	18.5	121	963	—	—
431.0(SC;T6)	23	95	2.6	0.32	(375,0.2%) (435,1%)	15.5	120	963	—	—
443.0(DC;F)	23	71	2.66	0.33	(70,0.2%) (160,6%)	21.1	146	963	—	—
443.0(SC;F)	23	72.4	2.68	0.32	(55,0.2%) (117,8%)	21.4	155	963	—	—
B443.0(DC;F)	23	72.4	2.68	0.32	(50,0.2%) (85,8%)	21.4	155	963	—	—
512.0(DC;F)	23	69	2.57	0.33	(90,0.2%) (140,2%)	22.1	138	963	—	—
512.0(SC;F)	23	69	2.57	0.33	(70,0.2%) (117,2%)	22.1	138	963	—	—
514.0(DC;F; ≈ZL302)	23	69	2.57	0.33	(80,0.2%) (175,9%)	22.1	138	963	—	—
518.0(DC;F) (Al-8Mg-1.8Fe-0.35Mn-0.25Cu)	23	69	2.57	0.33	(130,0.2%) (200,1%)	23.1	96	936	—	—
	621(T_m)	—	—	—	—	—	—	—	—	—
518.0(DC;T7)	23	69	2.57	0.33	(193,0.2%) (310,5%)	23.1	96	963	—	—
520.0(DC;T4; ≈ZL301)	23	69	2.57	0.33	(150,0.2%) (290,12%)	22.1	196	963	—	—
	100	—	—	—	—	24.7	—	—	—	—
	300	—	—	—	—	26.6	—	—	—	—
520.0(DC;T6)	23	69	2.57	0.33	(175,0.2%) (320,14%)	22.1	190	963	—	—
535.0(SC;F; Al-6.9Mg-0.005 Be;Almag 35)	23	69	2.57	0.33	(140,0.2%) (280,13%)	22.1	196	963	—	—
613.0(O)	23	69	2.57	0.33	(68,0.1%) (152,19%)	22.1	190	963	—	—

continued

Material	$T/℃$	E_T	ρ	ν	(σ,ε)	α	k	γ	ρ_E	K_{IC}
613.0(T4)	23	69	2.57	0.33	(153,0.1%) (297,27%)	22.1	190	963	—	—
613.0(T6)	23	69	2.57	0.33	(337,0.1%) (367,10%)	22.1	190	963	—	—
705.0(DC;T5)	23	71	2.76	0.33	(117,0.2%) (207,5%)	21.6	105	963	—	—
	638(T_m)	—	—	—	—	—	—	—	—	—
705.0(DC;T6)	23	71	2.76	0.33	(130,0.2%) (240,9%)	21.6	105	963	—	—
707.0(DC;T5)	23	71	2.81	0.33	(150,0.2%) (230,2%)	22.1	121	963	—	—
707.0(DC;T7)	23	71	2.81	0.33	(210,0.2%) (255,1%)	22.1	121	963	—	—
710.0(DC;T5)	23	71	2.81	0.33	(140,0.2%) (220,2%)	22.1	121	963	—	—
712.0(SC;T5)	23	71	2.81	0.33	(175,0.2%) (245,5%)	22.1	121	963	—	—
713.0(DC;F;Tenzaloy;Al-0.7Cu-0.4Mg-7.5Zn)	23	71	2.81	0.33	(152,0.2%) (221,3%)	22.1	121	963	—	—
	638(T_m)	—	—	—	—	—	—	—	—	—
713.0(DC;T5)	23	71	2.81	0.33	(175,0.2%) (235,4%)	22.1	121	963	—	—
771.0(DC;T5)	23	71	2.81	0.33	(262,0.2%) (290,1.5%)	22.1	121	963	—	—
771.0(DC;T51)	23	71	2.81	0.33	(186,0.2%) (221,3%)	22.1	121	963	—	—
771.0(DC;T52)	23	71	2.81	0.33	(207,0.2%) (248,1.5%)	22.1	121	963	—	—
771.0(DC;T6)	23	71	2.81	0.33	(280,0.2%) (350,5%)	22.1	121	963	—	—
771.0(DC;T71)	23	71	2.81	0.33	(310,0.2%) (330,5%)	22.1	121	963	—	—

continued

Material	$T/℃$	E_T	ρ	ν	(σ,ε)	α	k	γ	ρ_E	K_{IC}
850.0(SC;T5)	23	71	2.88	0.33	(75,0.2%) (110,5%)	21.7	180	963	—	—
	649(T_m)	—	—	—	—	—	—	—	—	—
851.0(DC;T5)	23	71	2.88	0.33	(75,0.2%) (140,8%)	21.7	167	963	—	—
851.0(SC;T5)	23	71	2.88	0.33	(75,0.2%) (120,3%)	21.7	167	963	—	—
852.0(DC;F)	23	71	2.88	0.33	(126,0.2%) (186,3%)	22	172	963	—	—
	635(T_m)	—	—	—	—	—	—	—	—	—
852.0(PM;T5)	23	71	2.88	0.33	(125,0.2%) (186,3%)	22	172	963	—	—
852.0(SC;T5)	23	71	2.88	0.33	(125,0.2%) (165,3%)	22	172	963	—	—

Notes: DC = Die castings of aluminum alloys are not usually solution heat-treated;

PM or PMC = Permanent mold castings;

SC = Sand castings.

Table 83.3　Mechanical Properties of Wrought Aluminum Alloys

Material	$T/℃$	E_T	ρ	ν	(σ,ε)	α	k	γ	ρ_E	K_{IC}
Al(Pure)	23	71	2.707	0.32	(12,0.2%) $\sigma_{uts}=47.4$	23.6	260	896	—	—
	400	—	—	—	—	—	230	—	—	—
	500	49	2.62	—	—	—	—	995	—	—
	600(T_m)	—	—	—	—	—	225	1034	—	—
	660	—	2.37	—	—	—	100	1274	—	—
Al(99.82% Purity of Al; True)	23	71	2.707	0.32	(26,0.2%) (80,30%) (100,60%)	23.6	260	896	—	—
Al (Film;$h=$ 0.2 μm)	23	74.6	2.707	0.32	(330,0.2%) (529,1.8%)	—	—	—	—	—
Al (Film;$h=$ 0.51 μm)	23	80.9	2.707	0.32	(200,0.2%)	—	—	—	—	—

continued

Material	$T/^\circ C$	E_T	ρ	ν	(σ,ε)	α	k	γ	ρ_E	K_{IC}
Al（Film；$h=$ 1.5 μm）	23	77.6	2.707	0.32	（114,0.2%）	—	—	—	—	—
1050（O；99.5% Purity of Al）	23	69	2.705	0.33	（28,0.2%） （76,39%）	21.8	231	900	—	—
	300	—	—	—	—	25.5	—	—	—	—
	657（T_m）	—	—	—	—	—	—	—	—	—
1050（H16）	23	69	2.71	0.33	（124,0.2%） （131,8%）	21.8	231	900	—	—
	-196	—	—	—	（33,0.2%） （150,53%）	—	—	—	—	—
	-80	—	—	—	（28,0.2%） （85,46%）	—	—	—	—	—
1060（O；99.6% Purity of Al）	23	69	2.71	0.33	（28,0.2%） （70,43%）	21.8	231	900	—	—
	205	—	—	—	（17,0.2%） （30,70%）	—	—	—	—	—
	260	—	—	—	（14,0.2%） （21,75%）	—	—	—	—	—
	315	—	—	—	（11,0.2%） （15,80%）	26	—	—	—	—
	370	—	—	—	（8,0.2%） （12,85%）	—	—	—	—	—
	660（T_m）	—	—	—	—	—	—	—	—	—
1060（H16）	23	69	2.71	0.33	（103,0.2%） （110,8%）	21.8	231	900	—	—
	-269	—	—	—	（58,0.2%） （315,37%）	—	—	—	—	—
	-196	—	—	—	（41,0.2%） （170,55%）	—	—	—	—	—
	-80	—	—	—	（38,0.2%） （105,43%）	—	—	—	—	—

continued

Material	$T/°C$	E_T	ρ	ν	(σ,ε)	α	k	γ	ρ_E	K_{IC}
1100 (O;99% Purity)	23	69	2.71	0.33	(34,0.2%) (90,35%)	21.8	222	904	—	21
	150	—	—	—	(29,0.2%) (59,55%)	—	—	—	—	—
	260	—	—	—	(18,0.2%) (21,75%)	—	—	—	—	—
	315	—	—	—	(14,0.2%) (20,80%)	26	—	—	—	—
	370	—	—	—	(11,0.2%) (14,85%)	28	—	—	—	—
	550	—	—	—	—	32	—	—	—	—
	660(T_m)	—	—	—	—	—	—	—	—	—
	−196	—	—	—	(115,0.2%) (195,46%)	—	—	—	—	—
	−80	—	—	—	(110,0.2%) (125,27%)	—	—	—	—	—
1100(H12)	23	69	2.71	0.33	(105,0.2%) (115,25%)	21.8	222	904	—	21
	150	—	—	—	(70,0.2%) (75,30%)	—	—	—	—	—
	260	—	—	—	(34,0.2%) (45,50%)	—	—	—	—	—
	315	—	—	—	(14,0.2%) (14,85%)	26	—	—	—	—
	370	—	—	—	(11,0.2%)	—	—	—	—	—
	−269	—	—	—	(160,0.2%) (345,34%)	—	—	—	—	—
	−196	—	—	—	(140,0.2%) (205,45%)	—	—	—	—	—
	−80	—	—	—	(125,0.2%) (140,24%)	—	—	—	—	—

continued

Material	$T/°C$	E_T	ρ	ν	(σ,ε)	α	k	γ	ρ_E	K_{IC}
1100(H14)	23	69	2.71	0.33	(115,0.2%) (125,20%)	21.8	222	904	—	—
	150	—	—	—	(85,0.2%) (95,23%)	—	—	—	—	—
	260	—	—	—	(23,0.2%) (45,35%)	—	—	—	—	—
	315	—	—	—	(14,0.2%) (20,80%)	26	—	—	—	—
	370	—	—	—	(11,0.2%) (14,85%)	28	—	—	—	—
1100(H16)	23	69	2.71	0.33	(138,0.2%) (145,6%)	21.8	222	904	—	—
	−196	—	—	—	(180,0.2%) (165,30%)	—	—	—	—	—
	−80	—	—	—	(160,0.2%) (180,16%)	—	—	—	—	—
1100(H18)	23	69	2.71	0.32	(150,0.2%) (165,15%)	21.8	222	904	—	—
	150	—	—	—	(95,0.2%) (125,24%)	—	—	—	—	—
	260	—	—	—	(21,0.2%) (38,55%)	—	—	—	—	—
	315	—	—	—	(14,0.2%) (20,80%)	26	—	—	—	—
	370	—	—	—	(11,0.2%) (14,85%)	28	—	—	—	—
1100(H112)	23	69	2.71	0.32	(66,0.2%) (105,37%)	21.8	222	904	—	—
	150	—	—	—	(55,0.2%) (70,69%)	—	—	—	—	—
1199(H18)	23	62	2.71	0.33	(110,0.2%) (115,5%)	21.8	240	900	—	21

continued

Material	$T/℃$	E_T	ρ	ν	(σ,ε)	α	k	γ	ρ_E	K_{IC}
1200(H112)	23	72	2.85	0.33	(66,0.2%)(105,37%)	21.8	151	873	—	—
	150	—	—	—	(55,0.2%)(70,69%)	—	—	—	—	—
	−253	—	—	—	(400,0.2%)(640,15%)	—	—	—	—	—
1210	23	72	2.85	0.33	(350,0.2%)(450,10%)	21.8	151	873	—	—
1350(O)	23	69	2.71	0.33	(30,0.2%)(83,23%)	21.8	222	904	—	—
1350(H19)	23	69	2.71	0.33	(165,0.2%)	21.8	222	904	—	—
1420(T6;Al-2Li-5Mg-0.12Zr-...)	23	69	2.47	0.33	(255,0.2%)(410,6%)	—	—	—	—	—
1421(T6;Al-Mg-Li-Sc-Zr)	23	69	2.47	0.33	(360,0.2%)(469,8%)	—	—	—	—	21
1424(T6)	23	69	2.56	0.33	(360,0.2%)(515,8%)	—	—	—	—	—
1441(T6;Al-2Li-1.6Cu-0.9Mg-...)	23	69	2.58	0.33	(323,0.2%)(420,6%)	—	—	—	—	—
	−253	—	—	—	(570,0.2%)(800,14%)	—	—	—	—	—
1460(Al-2Li-3Cu-...)	23	80	2.59	0.33	(490,0.2%)(570,8%)	22	86	860	—	—
2011(T3)	23	70	2.83	0.33	(296,0.2%)(379,15%)	22.3	151	880	—	—
2011(T6)	23	70	2.83	0.33	(280,0.2%)(403,15%)	22.3	151	880	—	—
2011(T8)	23	70	2.83	0.33	(310,0.2%)(407,12%)	22.3	151	880	—	—
2014(O;Al-4Cu-Si-Mg)	23	73	2.8	0.33	(97,0.2%)(185,18%)	22	193	880	—	—
	638(T_m)	—	—	—	—	—	—	—	—	—

continued

Material	$T/℃$	E_T	ρ	ν	(σ,ε)	α	k	γ	ρ_E	K_{IC}
2014(T4)	23	73	2.8	0.33	(290,0.2%) (425,20%)	22	193	880	—	—
	300	—	—	—	—	24.7	—	—	—	—
2014(T6)	23	73	2.8	0.33	(476,0.2%) (524,13%)	22	193	880	—	—
	−196	—	—	—	(555,0.2%) (630,14.3%)	—	—	—	—	—
	−80	—	—	—	(500,0.2%) (550,13%)	—	—	—	—	—
2014(T651)	23	73	2.8	0.33	(476,0.2%) (524,13%)	22	193	880	—	—
	100	—	—	—	(420,0.2%) (470,18%)	—	—	—	—	—
	150	—	—	—	(36,0.2%) (400,21%)	—	—	—	—	—
	300	—	—	—	—	24.7	—	—	—	—
2014(T6)/ 10% Al_2O_3 ($V_f=10\%$)	23	84	—	—	(496,0.2%) (531,3%)	—	—	—	—	—
2014(T6)/ 15% Al_2O_3 ($V_f=15\%$)	23	94	—	—	(503,0.2%) (531,2%)	—	—	—	—	—
2014(T6)/ 20% Al_2O_3 ($V_f=20\%$)	23	101	—	—	(503,0.2%) (517,1%)	—	—	—	—	—
2017(O)	23	72	2.79	0.33	(69,0.2%) (179,22%)	23	193	880	—	—
	641(T_m)	—	—	—	—	—	—	—	—	—
2017(T651)	23	72	2.79	0.33	(290,0.2%) (427,6%)	23	193	880	—	—
2018(T651)	23	72	2.79	0.33	(280,0.2%) (420,12%)	23	193	880	—	—

continued

Material	$T/°C$	E_T	ρ	ν	(σ, ε)	α	k	γ	ρ_E	K_{IC}
2020(O;Al-1.3Li-4.5Cu)	23	—	—	—	—	—	—	—	—	—
2024(O;Al-4 Cu-1Mg-0.6 Mn-0.3Fe)	23	73	2.78	0.33	(76,0.2%) (186,19%)	22.6	193	875	—	—
	493(T_m)	—	—	—	—	—	—	—	—	—
2024(T3) (True s-s)	23	73	2.78	0.33	(323,0.2%) (420,5%) (450,10%) (478,21%)	22.6	193	875	—	—
	200	—	—	—	(270,0.2%) (340,5%) (360,10%) (368,23%)	—	—	—	—	—
	300	—	—	—	$\sigma_{uts}=250$	—	—	—	—	—
	400	—	—	—	$\sigma_{uts}=130$	—	—	—	—	—
	500	—	—	—	$\sigma_{uts}=40$	—	—	—	—	—
2024(T351)	23	73	2.78	0.33	(366,0.2%) (473,18%)	22.6	193	875	—	36
2024(T361)	23	73	2.78	0.33	(393,0.2%) (496,13%)	22.6	193	875	—	—
2024(T4)	23	73	2.78	0.33	(325,0.2%) (470,19%)	22.6	193	875	—	—
	100	—	—	—	$\sigma_{crs,14604}=325$	—	—	—	—	—
2024(T6)	23	73	2.78	0.33	—	22.6	193	875	—	31
2024(T81)	23	73	2.78	0.33	(450,0.2%) (485,7%)	22.6	193	875	—	—
	−196	—	—	—	—	—	—	—	—	24
2090 (O)	23	76	2.59	0.33	(466,0.2%) (527,10%)	21.2	88	1203	—	22
2090(T351;Al-2.2Li-2.7Cu-0.12Zr)	23	76	2.59	0.33	(210,0.2%) (320,6%)	21.2	88	1203	—	—
	−269	—	—	—	(615,0.2%) (820,6.5%)	—	—	—	—	65/39
	−196	—	—	—	(600,0.2%) (725,6%)	—	—	—	—	52/34

continued

Material	$T/^\circ C$	E_T	ρ	ν	(σ,ε)	α	k	γ	ρ_E	K_{IC}
2090(T8)	23	76	2.59	0.33	$(525,0.2\%)$ $(565,5\%)$	21.2	88	1203	—	34/25
(Fracture toughness in longitudinal/transverse directions)										
2090(T83)	23	76	2.59	0.33	$(520,0.2\%)$ $(550,5\%)$	21.2	88	1203	—	44
2090(T84)	23	76	2.59	0.33	$(470,0.2\%)$ $(525,5\%)$	21.2	88	1203	—	49
2090(T86)	23	76	2.59	0.33	$(520,0.2\%)$ $(550,6\%)$	21.2	88	1203	—	—
2091(O;Al-2 Li-2Cu-1.5Mg-0.1Zr)	23	—	—	0.33	$\sigma_{uts}=180$	—	—	—	—	—
	300	—	—	—	$\sigma_{uts}=130$	—	—	—	—	—
	400	—	—	—	$\sigma_{uts}=80$	—	—	—	—	—
	550	—	—	—	$\sigma_{uts}=33$	—	—	—	—	—
	−196	—	—	—	$(442,0.2\%)$ $(596,10\%)$	—	—	—	—	41
2091(T351)	23	—	—	0.33	$(369,0.2\%)$ $(451,10\%)$	—	—	—	—	33
	300	—	—	—	$\sigma_{uts}=220$	—	—	—	—	—
	400	—	—	—	$\sigma_{uts}=100$	—	—	—	—	—
	550	—	—	—	$\sigma_{uts}=33$	—	—	—	—	—
	−196	—	—	—	$(483,0.2\%)$ $(610,14\%)$	—	—	—	—	44
2091(T8)	23	—	—	0.33	$(425,0.2\%)$ $(481,8\%)$	—	—	—	—	46
2095(T8)	23	—	—	0.33	$(585,0.2\%)$ $\sigma_{uts}=630$	—	—	—	—	—
2099(T6)	23	—	—	0.33	$(432,0.2\%)$ $(529,8\%)$	—	—	—	—	—
2099(T83)	23	—	—	0.33	$(502,0.2\%)$ $(561,7\%)$	—	—	—	—	—
2124(T851)	23	73	2.78	0.33	$(441,0.2\%)$ $(483,8\%)$	22.3	151	882	—	—
	$493(T_m)$	—	—	—	—	—	—	—	—	—

continued

Material	$T/℃$	E_T	ρ	ν	(σ,ε)	α	k	γ	ρ_E	K_{IC}
2124/17%SiC (Sintered; V_f = 17%)	23	—	2.85	—	(210,0.2%) (395,0.4%) (440,0.6%) (520,1.5%)	—	—	—	—	—
2124/25%SiC (Sintered; V_f = 25%)	23	—	2.89	—	(300,0.2%) (455,0.4%) (490,0.6%) (550,1.1%)	—	—	—	—	—
2195 (O; Al-1Li-4Cu-0.5Mg-0.12Zr)	23	—	2.71	0.33	—	—	—	—	—	—
2195(T8)	23	—	2.71	0.33	(600,0.2%) $\sigma_{uts}=630$	—	—	—	—	—
2219 (O)	23	73	2.84	0.33	(76,0.2%) (172,18%)	21.9	171	864	—	—
2219(T4)	23	73	2.84	0.33	(170,0.2%) (345,18%)	21.9	171	864	—	—
2219(T6)	23	73	2.84	0.33	(290,0.2%) (415,10%)	21.9	171	864	—	—
	100	—	—	—	(250,0.2%)	—	—	—	—	—
	200	—	—	—	(175,0.2%)	—	—	—	—	—
	300	—	—	—	(90,0.2%)	—	—	—	—	—
2219(T62)	23	73	2.84	0.33	(290,0.2%) (415,10%)	21.9	171	864	—	—
2219(T851)	23	73	2.84	0.33	(352,0.2%) (455,10%)	21.9	171	864	—	—
	535(T_m)	—	—	—	—	—	—	—	—	—
2297 (O; Al-1.5Li-2.8Cu-0.3Mn-0.12Zr)	23	—	2.65	—	—	—	—	—	—	—
2319(O)	23	72	2.84	0.33	(240,0.2%) (255,11%)	21.9	125	882	—	—
	300	56	—	—	—	24.7	—	—	—	—
	400	37	—	—	—	—	—	—	—	—
	643(T_m)	—	—	—	—	24.7	—	—	—	—

continued

Material	$T/^\circ\mathrm{C}$	E_T	ρ	ν	(σ,ε)	α	k	γ	ρ_E	K_IC
2397(T87)	23	—	—	0.33	$(423,0.2\%)$ $(473,7.5\%)$	—	—	—	—	—
2519(T87)	23	72	2.84	0.33	$(386,0.2\%)$ $(467,11\%)$	21.9	125	882	—	—
	100	—	—	—	$(315,0.2\%)$	—	140	930	—	—
	250	—	—	—	$(175,0.2\%)$	—	158	965	—	—
	300	56	—	—	$(130,0.2\%)$ $(150,15\%)$	24.7	155	950	—	—
	400	37	—	—	$(40,0.2\%)$	24.7	143	1060	—	—
	500	—	—	—	—	24.7	143	1060	—	—
	$668(T_\mathrm{m})$	—	—	—	—	—	300	—	—	—
	1000	—	—	—	—	—	300	1060	—	—
2618(T6)	23	72	2.8	0.33	$(370,0.2\%)$ $(440,7\%)$	21.6	—	—	—	—
	100	—	—	—	$(355,0.2\%)$	—	—	—	—	—
	150	—	—	—	$(275,0.2\%)$	—	—	—	—	—
	200	—	—	—	$(150,0.2\%)$	—	—	—	—	—
2618(T61)	23	72	2.8	0.33	$(370,0.2\%)$ $(440,7\%)$	21.6	—	—	—	—
	200	—	—	—	$(165,0.2\%)$ $\sigma_\mathrm{uts}=220$	—	—	—	—	—
Al2618/20Al$_2$O$_3$ (Al-2.3Cu-1.6Mg-1.1Fe-1Ni-0.07Ti-0.18Si ; Brake Rotor; $V_\mathrm{f}=20\%$)	23	97	—	—	$(293,0.2\%)$ $(295,0.5\%)$ $(310,1\%)$ $(328,2\%)$	—	—	—	—	—
2650(T6)	23	—	—	—	$(416,0.2\%)$	—	—	—	—	—
	100	—	—	—	$(390,0.2\%)$	—	—	—	—	—
	130	—	—	—	$(373,0.2\%)$	—	—	—	—	—
2650(T8)	23	—	—	—	—	—	—	—	—	—
	150	—	—	—	$\sigma_\mathrm{crs,10000}=210$	—	—	—	—	—
	180	—	—	—	$\sigma_\mathrm{crs,10000}=140$	—	—	—	—	—

continued

Material	$T/℃$	E_T	ρ	ν	(σ,ε)	α	k	γ	ρ_E	K_{IC}
3003(O) True s-s	23	69	2.73	0.33	(44,0.2%) (110,5%) (130,10%) (140,14%)	21.2	159	893	—	—
	100	—	—	—	(50,0.2%) (102,5%) (115,10%) (133,21%)	23.2	—	—	—	—
	200	—	—	—	(45,0.2%), (68,5%), (76,10%), (88,18%); $\sigma_{crs,1000}=45$, $\sigma_{crs,10000}=37$, $\sigma_{crs,100000}=32$	—	—	—	—	—
	250	—	—	—	$\sigma_{crs,1000}=27$, $\sigma_{crs,10000}=23$, $\sigma_{crs,100000}=18$	—	—	—	—	—
	300	—	—	—	(30,0.2%), (35,2%), (38,5%), (42,11%); $\sigma_{crs,1000}=15$, $\sigma_{crs,10000}=14$, $\sigma_{crs,100000}=12$	25	—	—	—	—
	$654(T_m)$	—	—	—	—	—	—	—	—	—
3003 (H12)	23	69	2.73	0.33	(117,0.2%) (150,20%)	21.2	159	893	—	—
3003(H14)	23	69	2.73	0.33	(145,0.2%) (250,8%)	21.2	159	893	—	—
	100	—	—	—	(130,0.2%) (145,16%)	23.2	—	—	—	—
	200	—	—	—	(62,0.2%) (96,20%)	—	—	—	—	—
	300	—	—	—	(30,0.2%) (40,36%)	25	—	—	—	—

continued

Material	$T/°C$	E_T	ρ	ν	(σ,ε)	α	k	γ	ρ_E	K_{IC}
3003(H18;Al-1Mn-Cu)	23	69	2.73	0.33	$(186,0.2\%)$ $(200,4\%)$	21.2	159	893	—	—
	100	26.8	—	—	$\sigma_{uts}=145$	—	—	—	—	—
	350	14.5	—	—	$\sigma_{uts}=26.5$	25.1	—	—	—	—
3004(O)	23	69	2.72	0.33	$(69,0.2\%)$ $(179,20\%)$	23.3	163	893	—	—
	535(T_m)	—	—	—	—	—	—	—	—	—
3004(H34)	23	69	2.72	0.33	$(180,0.2\%)$ $(234,12\%)$	23.3	163	893	—	—
3004(H38)	23	69	2.72	0.33	$(248,0.2\%)$ $(283,5\%)$	23.3	163	893	—	—
3005(O)	23	69	2.73	0.33	$(55,0.2\%)$ $(130,25\%)$	23.3	160	890	—	—
3005(H18)	23	69	2.73	0.33	$(225,0.2\%)$ $(240,4\%)$	23.3	160	890	—	—
3102(H112)	23	69	2.72	0.33	$(30,0.2\%)$ $(100,25\%)$	21.9	163	893	—	—
3105(O)	23	69	2.72	0.33	$(55,0.2\%)$ $(117,24\%)$	21.9	171	897	—	—
3105(H25)	23	69	2.72	0.33	$(159,0.2\%)$ $(179,8\%)$	21.9	171	897	—	—
4032(O)	23	79	2.68	0.33	$(317,0.2\%)$ $(379,9\%)$	18.8	154	850	—	—
	300	—	—	—	—	21	—	—	—	—
	571(T_m)	—	—	—	—	—	—	—	—	—
	−200	—	—	—	$(337,0.2\%)$ $(460,11\%)$	—	—	—	—	—
4032(T6)	23	79	2.68	0.33	$(320,0.2\%)$ $(380,9\%)$	18.8	154	850	—	—
	100	—	—	—	$(300,0.2\%)$ $(345,9\%)$	—	—	—	—	—
	200	—	—	—	$(62,0.2\%)$ $(90,30\%)$	20.2	—	—	—	—
	300	—	—	—	$(24,0.2\%)$ $(38,70\%)$	21	—	—	—	—

continued

Material	$T/{}^\circ\mathrm{C}$	E_T	ρ	ν	(σ, ε)	α	k	γ	ρ_E	K_IC
4043(O)	23	79	2.69	0.33	(70,0.2%) (145,22%)	21.5	163	850	—	—
	632(T_m)	—	—	—	—	—	—	—	—	—
4043(H18)	23	79	2.69	0.33	(270,0.2%) (285,0.5%)	21.5	163	850	—	—
4045(O)	23	—	2.67	0.33	—	20.5	171	—	—	—
	599(T_m)	—	—	—	—	—	—	—	—	—
4343(O)	23	—	2.68	0.33	—	21	180	—	—	—
	613(T_m)	—	—	—	—	—	—	—	—	—
5005(O)	23	69	2.7	0.33	(41,0.2%) (124,25%)	21	200	900	—	—
	300	—	—	—	—	25.6	—	—	—	—
	654(T_m)	—	—	—	—	—	—	—	—	—
5005(H12)	23	69	2.7	0.33	(131,0.2%) (138,10%)	21	200	900	—	—
5005(H38)	23	69	2.7	0.33	(186,0.2%) (200,5%)	21	200	900	—	—
5019(Al-5Mg)	23	69	2.7	0.33	(200,0.2%) (280,6%)	—	—	—	—	—
5050(O)	23	69	2.69	0.33	(55,0.2%) (145,24%)	21	193	900	—	—
5050(H38)	23	69	2.69	0.33	(200,0.2%) (221,6%)	21	193	900	—	—
	−196	—	—	—	(110,0.2%) (303,46%)	—	—	—	—	—
5052(O;Al-2.5 Mg)	23	70	2.68	0.33	(90,0.2%) (195,25%)	23	138	880	—	—
	100	—			(90,0.2%) (190,36%)	—	—	—	—	—
	150	—	—	—	(90,0.2%) (160,50%)	—	—	—	—	—
	200	—	—	—	(80,0.2%) (120,60%)	25	—	—	—	—
	260	—	—	—	(52,0.2%) (83,80%)	—	—	—	—	—
	371	—	—	—	(21,0.2%) (37,130%)	26	—	—	—	—
	649(T_m)	—	—	—	—	—	—	—	—	—

continued

Material	$T/℃$	E_T	ρ	ν	(σ, ε)	α	k	γ	ρ_E	K_{IC}
5052(H32)	23	70	2.68	0.33	(186,0.2%) (234,18%)	23	138	880	—	—
5052(H34)	23	70	2.68	0.33	(215,0.2%) (260,10%)	23	138	880	—	—
5052(H36)	23	70	2.68	0.33	(234,0.2%) (269,9%)	23	138	880	—	—
5052(H38)	23	70	2.68	0.33	(255,0.2%) (290,7%)	23	138	880	—	—
5056(O)	23	71	2.64	0.33	(150,0.2%) (290,25%)	23.5	117	904	—	—
5056(H18)	23	71	2.64	0.33	(415,0.2%) (440,10%)	23.5	117	904	—	—
5056(H38)	23	71	2.64	0.33	(348,0.2%) (418,15%)	23.5	117	904	—	—
5059(T6)	23	71	2.66	0.33	(280,0.2%) (400,16.2%)	21.8	117	900	—	—
5059(T6; As Welded by MIG)	23	—	—	—	(192,0.2%) (296,7.6%)	—	—	—	—	—
5081(O)	23	71	2.66	0.33	(130,0.2%) (270,23%)	23.2	117	900	—	—
5083(O)	23	70.4	2.66	0.33	(145,0.2%) (290,22%)	23.2	117	900	—	—
	300	—	—	—	—	26	—	—	—	—
5083(H111)	23	70.4	2.66	0.33	(165,0.2%) (275,23%)	23.2	117	900	—	—
5083(H112)	23	70.4	2.66	0.33	(110,0.2%) (268,23%)	23.2	117	900	—	—
5083(H321)	23	70.4	2.66	0.33	(228,0.2%) (317,16%)	23.2	117	900	—	—
5083(T6)	23	70.4	2.66	0.33	(270,0.2%) (346,20%)	23.2	117	900	—	—

continued

Material	$T/°C$	E_T	ρ	ν	(σ,ε)	α	k	γ	ρ_E	K_{IC}
5083(T6; As Welded by MIG)	23	—	—	—	(206,0.2%) (282,15%)	—	—	—	—	—
5086(O)	23	71	2.66	0.33	(117,0.2%) (262,12%)	23.3	125	900	—	—
5086(H111)	23	71	2.66	0.33	(165,0.2%) (275,12%)	23.2	125	900	—	—
5086(H112)	23	71	2.66	0.33	(110,0.2%) (270,12%)	23.3	125	900	—	—
5086(H32)	23	71	2.66	0.33	(207,0.2%) (290,12%)	23.3	125	900	—	—
5153(O)	23	70	2.66	0.33	(117,0.2%) (241,27%)	21.9	125	900	—	—
5153(H38)	23	70	2.66	0.33	(269,0.2%) (331,10%)	21.9	125	900	—	—
5154(O)	23	70	2.66	0.33	(117,0.2%) (241,27%)	23.3	125	900	—	—
5154(H38)	23	70	2.66	0.33	(331,0.2%) (269,10%)	23.3	125	900	—	—
5252(O)	23	69	2.67	0.33	(85,0.2%) (180,23%)	23.2	138	900	—	—
5252(H38)	23	69	2.67	0.33	(241,0.2%) (283,5%)	23.2	138	900	—	—
5254(O)	23	70	2.66	0.33	(117,0.2%) (241,27%)	23.3	125	900	—	—
5254(H38)	23	70	2.66	0.33	(269,0.2%) (331,10%)	23.3	125	900	—	—
5454(O)	23	70	2.69	0.33	(117,0.2%) (248,22%)	23	134	900	—	—
5454(H111)	23	70	2.69	0.33	(130,0.2%) (230,12%)	23	134	900	—	—
5454(H34)	23	70	2.68	0.33	(241,0.2%) (303,11%)	23	134	900	—	—

continued

Material	$T/℃$	E_{T}	ρ	ν	(σ,ε)	α	k	γ	ρ_{E}	K_{IC}
5456(O)	23	70	2.66	0.33	(159,0.2%) (310,24%)	23.3	117	900	—	—
5456(H111)	23	70	2.66	0.33	(180,0.2%) (290,12%)	23.3	117	900	—	—
5456(H321)	23	70	2.66	0.33	(255,0.2%) (352,16%)	23.3	117	900	—	—
5457(O)	23	69	2.69	0.33	(48,0.2%) (131,22%)	23.2	176	880	—	—
5457(H38)	23	69	2.69	0.33	(186,0.2%) (207,6%)	23.2	176	880	—	—
5652(O)	23	70	2.67	0.33	(90,0.2%) (193,25%)	23.2	138	900	—	—
5652(H38)	23	70	2.67	0.33	(255,0.2%) (290,7%)	23.2	138	900	—	—
5654(H25)	23	69	2.66	0.33	(145,0.2%) (185,9%)	21.9	125	900	—	—
5657(O)	23	69	2.69	0.33	(40,0.2%) (110,25%)	23.2	205	880	—	—
5657(H38)	23	69	2.69	0.33	(108,0.1%) (193,7%)	23.2	205	880	—	—
5754(O)	23	69	2.69	0.33	(108,0.1%) (165,0.2%) (236,16%)	23.2	205	880	—	—
6005(T3)	23	69	2.72	0.33	(240,0.2%) (260,8%)	21.9	163	893	—	—
6009(T4)	23	69	2.7	0.33	(125,0.2%) (230,25%)	21.4	180	890	—	—
	650(T_{m})	—	—	—	—	—	—	—	—	—
6009(T6)	23	69	2.7	0.33	(320,0.2%) (340,12%)	21.4	180	890	—	—
6010(T4)	23	69	2.7	0.33	(170,0.2%) (290,24%)	21.4	151	890	—	—
	649(T_{m})	—	—	—	—	—	—	—	—	—

continued

Material	$T/℃$	E_T	ρ	ν	(σ, ε)	α	k	γ	ρ_E	K_{IC}
6013(T651)	23	70	2.7	0.33	(360,0.2%) (380,9%)	22	164	900	—	—
6013(T8)	23	70	2.7	0.33	(370,0.2%) (400,10%)	22	164	900	—	—
6016(T4; Base; Al-0.42Mg-1.3Si)	23	69	2.7	0.33	(110,0.2%) (220,23%)	21.4	167	900	—	—
	655(T_m)	—	—	—	—	—	—	—	—	—
6016(T4;Stir weld-Conical)	23	—	—	—	(110,0.2%) (185,7%)	—	—	—	—	—
6016(T4;Stir weld-Scrolled)	23	—	—	—	(110,0.2%) (195,13%)	—	—	—	—	—
6016(T6)	23	69	2.7	0.33	(200,0.2%) (240,12%)	21.4	167	900	—	—
6022(T4)	23	68	2.7	0.33	(140,0.2%) (245,28%)	21.4	221	900	—	—
6022(T6)	23	68	2.7	0.33	(235,0.2%) (347,17%)	21.4	221	900	—	—
6053(O)	23	69	2.7	0.33	(55,0.2%) (110,35%)	22.4	171	890	—	—
6053(T6)	23	69	2.7	0.33	(220,0.2%) (255,13%)	22.4	171	890	—	—
6056(T6; Bolt for Mg alloy, e. g. AZ91)	23	70	2.7	0.33	$\sigma_{uts}=400$	—	—	—	—	—
6060 (T5 or T51)	23	70	2.7	0.33	(105,0.2%) (145,6%)	21.4	210	900	—	—
	615(T_m)	—	—	—	—	—	—	—	—	—
6060(T6)	23	70	2.7	0.33	(207,0.2%) (267,6%)	21.4	210	900	—	—
6061(O)	23	69	2.7	0.33	$\sigma_{uts}=-390$; (55,0.2%) (113,7.3%) (124,26%)	21.6	180	896	—	—
	250	—	—	—	—	25.2	—	—	—	—
	650(T_m)	—	—	—	—	—	—	—	—	—

continued

Material	$T/°C$	E_T	ρ	ν	(σ,ε)	α	k	γ	ρ_E	K_{IC}
6061(O)/15Fly Ash(Ash: 28.44 Al_2O_3-59.96SiO_2 -8.85Fe_2O_3-2.75 TiO_2-1.43Others)	23	69	2.71	0.33	$\sigma_{uts}=-520$; $\sigma_{uts}=132$	20	180	1256	—	—
6061(O)/8Fe_2O_3 ($W_f=8\%$)	23	69	2.71	0.33	$(-,0.2\%)$ $(141,5.64\%)$	—	—	—	—	—
6061(T1)	23	69	2.7	0.33	$(95,0.2\%)$ $(180,24\%)$	21.6	170	896	—	—
6061(T4)	23	69	2.7	0.33	$(110,0.2\%)$ $(207,22\%)$	21.6	170	896	—	—
6061(T51)	23	69	2.7	0.33	$(210,0.2\%)$ $(245,16\%)$	21.6	170	896	—	—
6061(T6)	23	69	2.7	0.33	$(276,0.2\%)$ $(310,12\%)$	21.8	170	896	—	29
	204	—	—	—	$(105,0.2\%)$ $\sigma_{uts}=152$	—	—	—	—	—
	232	—	—	—	$\sigma_{crs,1000}=62$	—	—	—	—	—
	260	—	—	—	$\sigma_{crs,1000}=50$	25.3	—	—	—	—
6061(T651)	23	69	2.7	0.33	$(276,0.2\%)$ $(310,10\%)$	21.8	170	896	—	29
6061(T6)/10% $Al_2O_3(V_f=10\%)$	23	81.4	—	—	$(296,0.2\%)$ $(352,8\%)$	—	—	—	—	—
6061(T6)/15% $Al_2O_3(V_f=15\%)$	23	89	—	—	$(324,0.2\%)$ $(365,6\%)$	—	—	—	—	—
6061(T6)/20% $Al_2O_3(V_f=20\%)$	23	97.2	—	—	$(353,0.2\%)$ $(372,4\%)$	—	—	—	—	—
6063(O)	23	70	2.7	0.33	$(45,0.2\%)$ $(90,30\%)$	21.8	219	900	—	—
	100	—	—	—	—	23.4	—	—	—	—
	300	—	—	—	—	25.6	—	—	—	—
	$654(T_m)$	—	—	—	—	—	—	—	—	—

continued

Material	$T/°C$	E_T	ρ	ν	(σ,ε)	α	k	γ	ρ_E	K_{IC}
6063(T1)	23	70	2.7	0.33	(90,0.2%) (150,20%)	21.8	218	900	—	—
6063(T4)	23	70	2.7	0.33	(120,0.2%) (190,21%)	21.8	218	900	—	—
	100	—	—	—	—	23.4	—	—	—	—
	300	—	—	—	—	25.6	—	—	—	—
6063(T5)	23	70	2.7	0.33	(145,0.2%) (185,12%)	21.8	218	900	—	—
	100	—	—	—	—	23.4	—	—	—	—
	300	—	—	—	—	25.6	—	—	—	—
	−196	—	—	—	(324,0.2%) $\sigma_{uts}=248$	—	—	—	—	—
6063(T6; Automobile Frames)	23	70	2.7	0.33	$\sigma_{uts}=-434$ (−276,−0.2%); (214,0.2%) (286,1%) (296,4%) (300,12%)	21.8	218	900	—	—
	100	—	—	—	(193,0.2%) (214,40%)	23.4	—	—	—	—
	204	—	—	—	(45,0.2%) (62,40%)	—	—	—	—	—
	315	—	—	—	(17,0.2%) (23,80%)	25.8	—	—	—	—
6063(T83)	23	70	2.7	0.33	(241,0.2%) (255,9%)	21.8	218	900	—	—
	100	—	—	—	—	23.4	—	—	—	—
	300	—	—	—	—	25.6	—	—	—	—
6063(O)/15% SiC($V_f=15\%$)	23	—	—	—	(120,0.2%) $\sigma_{uts}=180$	—	—	—	—	—
	100	—	—	—	(130,0.2%) $\sigma_{uts}=186$	—	—	—	—	—
	250	—	—	—	(135,0.2%) $\sigma_{uts}=196$	—	—	—	—	—
	400	—	—	—	(135,0.2%) $\sigma_{uts}=196$	—	—	—	—	—

continued

Material	$T/°C$	E_T	ρ	ν	(σ,ε)	α	k	γ	ρ_E	K_{IC}
6063(O)/0.75 CNT(W_f=0.75%)	23	—	—	—	(150,0.2%)	—	—	—	—	—
6066(O)	23	69	2.72	0.33	(83,0.2%) (152,18%)	22.6	154	887	—	—
6066(O)/20% Al$_2$O$_3$(Al-1Cu-1.1Mg-1.4Si; V_f=20%; Brake Rotor)	23	89	—	—	(313,0.2%) (320,0.5%) (330,1%) (340,2%)	—	—	—	—	—
6066(T6)	23	69	2.72	0.33	(359,0.2%) (393,12%)	22.6	154	887	—	—
6070(O)	23	69	2.71	0.33	(70,0.2%) (145,20%)	22.6	171	891	—	—
6070(T6)	23	69	2.71	0.33	(352,0.2%) (379,10%)	22.6	171	891	—	—
6082(O)	23	70	2.7	0.33	(60,0.2%) (130,27%)	21.8	180	894	—	—
	300	—	—	—	—	25.4	—	—	—	—
	650(T_m)	—	—	—	—	—	—	—	—	—
6082(T4)	23	71	2.7	0.33	(170,0.2%) (367,34%)	21.8	180	894	—	—
6082(T4;Seam weld-0°)	23	—	—	—	(174,0.2%) (377,31%)	—	—	—	—	—
6082(T4;Seam weld-45°)	23	—	—	—	(164,0.2%) (337,32%)	—	—	—	—	—
6082(T4;Seam weld-90°)	23	—	—	—	(170,0.2%) (360,28%)	—	—	—	—	—
6082(T6)	23	74	2.7	0.33	(250,0.2%) (300,4%) (350,8%) (375,11%)	21.8	180	894	—	—
6101(H111)	23	69	2.7	0.33	(76,0.2%) (97,30%)	22.8	220	895	—	—

continued

Material	$T/℃$	E_T	ρ	ν	(σ,ε)	α	k	γ	ρ_E	K_{IC}
6101(T6)	23	69	2.7	0.33	(193,0.2%) (221,15%)	22.8	220	895	—	—
6106(T4)	23	69	2.7	0.33	(130,0.2%) (150,12%)	21.6	160	900	—	—
6106(T6;Bulk)	23	69	2.7	0.33	(160,0.2%) (185,10%)	21.6	160	900	—	—
	650(T_m)	—	—	—	—	—	—	—	—	—
6106(T6;10 mm Thick)	23	69	2.7	0.33	(210,0.2%) (235,8%)	21.6	160	900	—	—
	650(T_m)	—	—	—	—	—	—	—	—	—
6110 (Quenched)	23	70	2.7	0.33	(155,0.2%) (302,33%)	21.8	180	900	—	—
6110(T6)	23	70	2.7	0.33	(420,0.2%) (455,22%)	21.8	180	900	—	—
6111(O)	23	71	2.76	0.33	(68,0.1%) (152,19%)	21.6	190	900	—	—
6111(T4)	23	71	2.76	0.33	(153,0.1%) (297,27%)	21.6	190	900	—	—
6111(T6)	23	71	2.76	0.33	(337,0.1%) (367,10%)	21.6	190	900	—	—
6151(T6)	23	69	2.71	0.33	(295,0.2%) (330,17%)	22.6	205	895	—	—
6201(T6)	23	69	2.7	0.33	(195,0.2%) (220,15%)	22.8	205	890	—	—
6201(T81)	23	69	2.7	0.33	(310,0.2%) (330,6%)	22.8	205	890	—	—
6261(T6)	23	69	2.7	0.33	(278,0.2%) (305,26%)	21.8	190	900	—	—
6351(T6)	23	68	2.7	0.33	(331,0.2%) (355,20.4%)	21.8	190	900	—	—
6463(O)	23	69	2.7	0.33	(50,0.2%) (90,28%)	22.8	200	890	—	—

continued

Material	$T/℃$	E_T	ρ	ν	(σ,ε)	α	k	γ	ρ_E	K_{IC}
6463(T6)	23	69	2.7	0.33	(214,0.2%) (241,12%)	22.8	200	890	—	—
6951(O)	23	69	2.7	0.33	(40,0.2%) (110,30%)	22.8	213	890	—	—
6951(T6)	23	69	2.7	0.33	(230,0.2%) (270,13%) (228,17%)	22.8	213	890	—	—
7001(O)	23	71	2.84	0.33	(150,0.2%) (255,14%)	22.8	150	860	—	—
	630(T_m)	—	—	—	—	—	—	—	—	—
7001(T6)	23	71	2.84	0.33	(625,0.2%) (675,9%)	22.8	150	860	—	—
7005(O)	23	70	2.84	0.33	(80,0.2%) (195,20%)	23	166	875	—	—
7005(T53)	23	70	2.84	0.33	(345,0.2%) (395,15%)	23	166	875	—	—
7005(T63)	23	70	2.84	0.33	(150,0.2%) (215,13%)	23	166	875	—	—
7010(T7)	23	72	2.82	0.33	(480,0.2%) (530,10%)	21.8	153	873	—	—
	630(T_m)	—	—	—	—	—	—	—	—	—
7016(T5)	23	71	2.7	0.33	(315,0.2%) (360,15%)	21.8	150	880	—	—
	630(T_m)	—	—	—	—	—	—	—	—	—
7020(T6)	23	70	2.78	0.33	(317,0.2%) (373,14%)	21.8	139	875	—	—
	300	—	—	—	—	25.0	—	—	—	—
7020(T6; As Welded by MIG)	23	—	—	—	(282,0.2%) (315,8.2%)	—	—	—	—	—
7021(T62)	23	72	2.78	0.33	(380,0.2%) (420,13%)	21.8	140	880	—	—
	300	—	—	—	—	25.3	—	—	—	—
	640(T_m)	—	—	—	—	—	—	—	—	—

continued

Material	$T/°C$	E_T	ρ	ν	(σ,ε)	α	k	γ	ρ_E	K_{IC}
7039(O)	23	70	2.74	0.33	(100,0.2%) (230,22%)	22.8	140	880	—	—
7039(T61)	23	70	2.74	0.33	(330,0.2%) (400,13%)	22.8	140	880	—	—
	635(T_m)	—	—	—	—	—	—	—	—	—
7050(T73)	23	69	2.81	0.33	(400,0.2%) (500,6%)	21.6	130	960	—	—
7050(T7451)	23	69	2.81	0.33	(455,0.2%) (540,10%)	21.6	130	960	—	—
7050(T7451; 8 h exposure to 177 ℃)	23	69	2.81	0.33	(370,0.2%) (470,10%)	21.6	130	960	—	—
7068(T6511; // Extruded;Engine conrod)	23	82.1	2.85	0.33	(683,0.2%) (710,9%)	21.6	190	—	—	—
	100	—	—	—	—	23.4	—	1050	—	—
	635(T_m)	—	—	—	—	—	—	—	—	—
7072(H12)	23	70	2.72	0.33	(100,0.2%) (230,22%)	23	222	893	—	—
7075(O)	23	71.7	2.81	0.33	(103,0.2%) (228,17%)	21.6	170	960	—	24
	635(T_m)	—	—	—	—	—	—	—	—	—
7075(T351)	23	71.7	2.81	0.33	(428,0.2%)	21.6	170	960	—	33
	−196	—	—	—	(634,0.2%) (703,9%)	—	—	—	—	—
7075(T6)	23	71.7	2.81	0.33	(532,0.2%) (585,11%)	21.6	170	960	—	33
	100	—	—	—	(448,0.2%) (483,14%)	—	—	—	—	—
	150	—	—	—	(180,0.2%) $\sigma_{uts}=210$	—	—	—	—	—
	200	—	—	—	(90,0.2%) (110,55%)	—	—	—	—	—
	315	—	—	—	(45,0.2%) (55,70%)	25.4	—	—	—	—
	−196	—	—	—	(634,0.2%) (703,9%)	—	—	—	—	—

continued

Material	$T/℃$	E_T	ρ	ν	(σ,ε)	α	k	γ	ρ_E	K_IC
7075(T651)	23	71.7	2.81	0.33	$(503,0.2\%)$ $(570,11\%)$	21.6	170	960	—	29
	100	—	—	—	$(448,0.2\%)$ $(483,14\%)$	—	—	—	—	—
	150	—	—	—	$\sigma_\mathrm{uts}=210$	—	—	—	—	—
	200	—	—	—	$(90,0.2\%)$ $(110,55\%)$	—	—	—	—	—
	315	—	—	—	$(45,0.2\%)$ $(55,70\%)$	25.4	—	—	—	—
7075(T73)	23	72	2.81	0.33	$(440,0.2\%)$ $(510,6\%)$	21.6	170	960	—	—
7075(T7651)	23	—	—	0.33	$(460,0.2\%)$ $(534,7.2\%)$	—	—	—	—	—
7085(T7452)	23	—	—	0.33	$(497,0.2\%)$ $(540,7.8\%)$	—	—	—	—	—
7085(T7651)	23	—	—	0.33	$(468,0.2\%)$ $(519,7.8\%)$	—	—	—	—	—
7150(T6511)	23	72	2.8	0.33	$(580,0.2\%)$ $(615,8\%)$	21.6	—	900	—	—
7175(T6)	23	71	2.7	0.33	$(525,0.2\%)$ $(595,12\%)$	21.6	177	860	—	31
	$635(T_\mathrm{m})$	—	—	—	—	—	—	—	—	—
7175(T7)	23	71	2.7	0.33	$(485,0.2\%)$ $(550,14\%)$	21.6	177	860	—	31
7175(T736)	23	71	2.7	0.33	$(510,0.2\%)$ $(560,14\%)$	21.6	177	860	—	31
	204	—	—	—	$(245,0.2\%)$ $\sigma_\mathrm{uts}=265$	25.4	—	—	—	—
7178(O)	23	72	2.83	0.33	$(100,0.2\%)$ $(228,15\%)$	21.7	150	856	—	—
	$630(T_\mathrm{m})$	—	—	—	—	—	—	—	—	—
	-196	—	—	—	$(650,0.2\%)$ $(730,5\%)$	—	—	—	—	—

continued

Material	$T/^\circ\text{C}$	E_T	ρ	ν	(σ, ε)	α	k	γ	ρ_E	K_{IC}
7178(T6)	23	72	2.83	0.33	(538,0.2%) (607,10%)	21.7	150	856	—	—
	100	—	—	—	(470,0.2%) (505,14%)	—	—	—	—	—
	150	—	—	—	(210,0.2%) (180,40%)	—	—	—	—	—
	200	—	—	—	(90,0.2%) (110,70%)	—	—	—	—	—
	315	—	—	—	(48,0.2%) (59,80%)	25.8	—	—	—	—
	−196	—	—	—	(650,0.2%) (730,10%)	—	—	—	—	—
7178(T76)	23	72	2.83	0.33	(505,0.2%) (570,11%)	21.7	150	856	—	—
	100	—	—	—	(440,0.2%) (475,17%)	—	—	—	—	—
	150	—	—	—	(185,0.2%) (215,40%)	—	—	—	—	—
	200	—	—	—	(83,0.2%) (105,70%)	—	—	—	—	—
	315	—	—	—	(48,0.2%) (59,80%)	25.8	—	—	—	—
	630(T_m)	—	—	—	—	—	—	—	—	—
7475(T6)	23	71.7	2.81	0.33	(510,0.2%) (586,13%)	21.6	138	880	—	—
	300	—	—	—	—	25.4	—	—	—	—
	635(T_m)	—	—	—	—	—	—	—	—	—
7475(T61)	23	71.7	2.81	0.33	(510,0.2%) (586,13%)	21.6	138	880	—	—
	200	—	—	—	(140,0.2%) $\sigma_{uts}=155$	25.4	—	—	—	—
	−196	—	—	—	(256,0.2%) (486,24%)	—	—	—	—	20
8090(T3;Al-2.4Li-1.3Cu-0.9Mg-0.12Zr)	23	77	2.54	0.33	(220,0.2%) (350,17%)	21.4	95.3	930	—	27

continued

Material	$T/^{\circ}\text{C}$	E_{T}	ρ	ν	(σ,ε)	α	k	γ	ρ_{E}	K_{IC}
8090(T6511)	23	77	2.54	0.33	$(370,0.2\%)$ $(480,4.5\%)$	21.4	95.3	930	—	—
	−196	—	—	—	—	—	—	—	—	38
8090(T8)	23	77	2.54	0.33	$(482,0.2\%)$ $(534,6.3\%)$	21.4	95.3	930	—	36
8090(T8151)	23	77	2.54	0.33	$(430,0.2\%)$ $(490,9\%)$	21.4	95.3	930	—	28
	$627(T_{\text{m}})$	—	—	—	—	—	—	—	—	—
	−196	—	—	—	$(382,0.2\%)$ $(572,14\%)$	—	—	—	—	28
8091(T351;Al-2.6Li-1.9Cu-0.9 Mg-0.12Zr)	23	—	—	—	$(309,0.2\%)$ $(417,11\%)$	—	—	—	—	38
	−196	—	—	—	$(574,0.2\%)$ $(697,12\%)$	—	—	—	—	38
8091(T8)	23	—	—	—	$(537,0.2\%)$ $(581,6\%)$	—	—	—	—	20
8092(O;Al-2.4 Li-0.65Cu-1.5 Mg-0.12Zr)	23	—	—	—	—	—	—	—	—	—
Al-8Fe-1.7Si-V	23	—	—	0.33	$(294,0.2\%)$ $(341,9.92\%)$	—	—	—	—	—
	300	—	—	0.33	$(226,0.2\%)$ $(237,12.3\%)$	—	—	—	—	—
Al-10Mg	23	70	—	0.33	$(140,0.2\%)$ $(220,10\%)$ $(325,20\%)$ $(395,50\%)$	—	—	—	—	—
Weldlite 049 (O)	23	—	2.6	0.33	$(330,0.2\%)$ $(480,24\%)$	21.4	95.3	930	—	—
Weldlite 049 (T6)	23	—	2.6	0.33	$(680,0.2\%)$ $(720,4\%)$	21.4	95.3	930	—	30
D16CzATW	23	68.4	2.6	0.33	$\sigma_{\text{uts}}=460$	—	—	—	—	—

continued

Material	$T/°C$	E_T	ρ	ν	(σ,ε)	α	k	γ	ρ_E	K_{IC}
Al-0.13Sc-8.9 Zn-2.1Cu-1.7 Mg-0.15Zr	23	70	2.6	0.33	(567,5%) (581,10%) (585,15%) (590,60%)	—	—	—	—	—

Notes: AA = Aluminum Association Number;

PWHT = Post-weld heat treatment;

Stir = Friction stir welding;

Conical = Conical shoulder;

Scrolled = Scrolled shoulder;

Seam weld−0°,−45°,&−90° = Directional angles measured from the seam weld line;

$\rho_E = 0.02828\ \mu\Omega m$ (Electric resistivity) for pure aluminum.

Table 83.4 Mechanical Properties of Sintered Aluminum Alloys

Material	$T/°C$	E_T	ρ	ν	(σ,ε)	α	k	γ	ρ_E	K_{IC}
A(T1)-sintered	23	61	—	—	(88,0.2%) (139,5%)	—	160	900	—	—
A(T4)-sintered	23	61	—	—	$\sigma_{ucs}=-174$; (114,0.2%) (172,5%)	—	160	900	—	—
A(T6)-sintered	23	61	—	—	$\sigma_{ucs}=-175$; (224,0.2%) (232,2%)	—	160	900	—	—
B(T1)-sintered	23	61	—	—	(170,0.2%) (201,5%)	—	134	900	—	—
B(T4)-sintered	23	61	—	—	$\sigma_{ucs}=-179$; (205,0.2%) (245,3.5%)	—	134	900	—	—
B(T6)-sintered	23	61	—	—	$\sigma_{ucs}=-205$; (322,0.2%) (323,0.5%)	—	134	900	—	—
E(T6)-sintered	23	—	—	—	(200,0.2%) (263,5%)	—	—	900	—	—
F(T6)-sintered	23	—	—	—	(276,0.2%) (310,2%)	—	—	900	—	—

Table 83.5   Fatigue ε-N Properties of Cast Aluminum Alloys

Material	$T/^{\circ}\mathrm{C}$	$\mathrm{d}\varepsilon/\mathrm{d}t$	σ_{f}'	$\varepsilon_{\mathrm{f}}'$	b	c	K'	n'	σ_{f}@ $2N_{\mathrm{f}}$	R
201.0(T7; SC)	23	—	—	—	—	—	—	—	98@ 10^8 130@ 6×10^5	— —
206.0(T7)	23	—	—	—	—	—	—	—	90@ 10^8 205@ 6×10^7 370@ 10^3	— — —
319.0(F; SC)	23	—	—	—	—	—	—	—	70@ 5×10^8	—
319.0(T6; SC)	23	—	—	—	—	—	—	—	75@ 5×10^8	—
319.0(T7; SC)	25	—	575.8	0.0072	−0.111	−0.902	—	—	—	—
	200	—	380.4	0.0154	−0.085	−0.443	—	—	—	—
	250	—	285	0.0076	−0.049	−0.599	—	—	—	—
	300	—	53.1	0.3474	−0.067	−0.664	—	—	—	—
330.0(T5; DC)	23	—	—	—	—	—	—	—	83@ 10^8	—
330.0(T6; DC)	23	—	—	—	—	—	—	—	103@ 10^8	—
354.0(T61; SC)	23	—	—	—	—	—	—	—	135@ 10^8 345@ 10^4	— —
A354.0(T6)	23	—	—	—	—	—	—	—	—	—
	260	—	—	—	—	—	—	—	52@ 10^8 70@ 10^7 133@ 10^6	RB RB RB
355.0(T6; DC)	23	—	—	—	—	—	—	—	69@ 10^8	—
355.0(T7; DC)	23	—	—	—	—	—	—	—	69@ 10^8	—
356.0(F)	23	—	—	—	—	—	—	—	100@ 10^8	—
356.0(F;Shot peening)	23	—	—	—	—	—	—	—	120@ 10^8	—
356.0(F;Cavitation shotless peening)	23	—	—	—	—	—	—	—	156@ 10^8	—
356.0(T7; SC)	23	—	—	—	—	—	—	—	62@ 10^8	—

continued

Material	$T/°C$	$d\varepsilon/dt$	σ_f'	ε_f'	b	c	K'	n'	$\sigma_f@2N_f$	R
356.0(T6; DC)	23	—	666	0.094	−0.117	−0.61	430	0.063	$72@10^6$ $100@10^5$	— —
A356(O)	23	—	594	0.027	−0.124	−0.53	379	0.043	—	—
A356(T6)	23	—	666	0.09	−0.117	−0.61	430	0.063	$172@10^8$	—
359.0(F)/20SiC (Brake Rotor; $V_f=20\%$)	23	—	558	0.011	−0.115	−0.61	—	—	$165@10^6$ $220@10^5$	0.1^+ 0.1^+
359.0(T6)/20SiC (Brake Rotor; $V_f=20\%$)	23	—	—	—	—	—	—	—	$177@10^6$ $215@10^5$	0.1^+ 0.1^+
360.0(F; DC)	23	—	—	—	—	—	—	—	$138@10^8$	—
380.0(F; SC)	23	—	328.5	0.085	−0.074	−0.42	522	0.2	$138@10^8$	—
380.0(F; DC)	23	—	306	0.125	−0.053	−0.904	410	0.058	$140@10^8$	—
383.0(F; DC)	23	—	—	—	—	—	—	—	$145@10^8$	—
384.0(F; DC)	23	—	—	—	—	—	—	—	$140@10^8$	—
390.0(F; SC)	23	—	—	—	—	—	—	—	$90@10^8$	—
390.0(T6; SC)	23	—	—	—	—	—	—	—	$115@10^8$	—
390.0(F; DC)	23	—	—	—	—	—	—	—	$140@5×10^8$	—
413.0(F; DC)	23	—	178	0.162	—	—	—	—	$130@10^8$	—
518.0(F; SC)	23	—	—	—	—	—	—	—	$130@10^8$	—
518.0(F; DC)	23	—	—	—	—	—	—	—	$160@10^8$	—
520.0(T4; SC)	23	—	—	—	—	—	—	—	$55@10^8$	—
713.0(F; DC)	23	—	—	—	—	—	—	—	$60@10^8$	—
Cylinder Head (Gravity Die Casting):										
Al-7Si-Mg-0.5Cu (T6)	23	—	—	—	—	—	—	—	—	—
	250	—	—	—	—	—	—	—	$72@2×10^7$	—

continued

Material	T/℃	dε/dt	σ_f'	ε_f'	b	c	K'	n'	σ_f@ $2N_f$	R
Al-8Si-3Cu(T5)	23	—	—	—	—	—	—	—	—	—
	250	—	—	—	—	—	—	—	55@ 2×10^7	—
Al-8Si-3Cu(T6)	23	—	—	—	—	—	—	—	—	—
	250	—	—	—	—	—	—	—	61@ 2×10^7	—
Al-10Si-Mg(T6)	23	—	—	—	—	—	—	—	—	—
	250	—	—	—	—	—	—	—	62@ 2×10^7	—
Engine Piston (Die Casting):										
	23	—	378	0.053	−0.071	−0.54	555	0.131	81@ 10^8	—
	100	—	342	0.074	−0.071	−0.53	487	0.122	74@ 10^8	—
	200	—	270	0.030	−0.071	−0.451	467	0.157	—	—
Al-12Si-5Cu-0.6 Mg-2.7Ni(DC; Engine Piston)	250	—	210	0.026	−0.071	−0.40	402	0.179	47@ 10^8	—
	300	—	163	0.051	−0.071	−0.424	268	0.167	—	—
	350	—	132	0.104	−0.071	−0.49	182	0.144	20@ 10^8	—
	400	—	108	0.197	−0.071	−0.57	132	0.124	—	—
	450	—	96	0.2	−0.071	−0.455	123	0.119	—	—
Al (control arm)	23	—	1002	0.35	−0.095	−0.69	966	0.11	—	—

Notes: 0.1^+ = Stress ratio $R=0.1$ and both high and low stress levels are positive.

Table 83.6   Fatigue ε-N Properties of Wrought Aluminum Alloys

Material	T/℃	dε/dt	σ_f'	ε_f'	b	c	K'	n'	σ_f@ $2N_f$	R
Al(Pure)	23	—	—	0.97	—	−0.61	102	0.093	—	—
1060(O)	23	—	—	—	—	—	—	—	21@ 10^8	—
1060(H16)	23	—	—	—	—	—	—	—	45@ 10^8	—
1100(O)	23	—	—	—	—	—	—	—	34@ 10^8	—

continued

Material	$T/℃$	$d\varepsilon/dt$	σ'_f	ε'_f	b	c	K'	n'	$\sigma_f @ 2N_f$	R
1100(T12)	23	—	—	—	—	—	—	—	42@ 10^8	—
1100(T14)	23	—	—	—	—	—	—	—	62@ 10^8	—
1100(T16)	23	—	—	—	—	—	—	—	65@ 10^8	—
1100(T18)	23	—	—	—	—	—	—	—	69@ 10^8	—
1421	23	—	—	—	—	—	—	—	185@ 10^7 280@ 10^5	— —
2011(T3)	23	—	—	—	—	—	—	—	125@ 10^8	—
2011(T6)	23	—	—	—	—	—	—	—	125@ 10^8	—
2014(O)	23	—	—	—	—	—	—	—	90@ 10^8	—
2014(T4)	23	—	1479	0	−0.147	0	—	—	130@ 10^8	—
2014(T4)	180	—	524	0	−0.086	0	—	—	—	—
2014(T6)	23	—	776	0.27	−0.091	−0.742	—	—	110@ $5×10^8$ 124@ 10^8	— —
2017(O)	23	—	—	—	—	—	—	—	90@ 10^8	—
2017(T4,T451)	23	—	632	0.125	−0.074	−1.4	556	0.0514	124@ $5×10^8$	—
2017A(T4)	23	—	607	0.678	−0.095	−0.713	640	0.135	—	—
2017(T651)	23	—	—	—	—	—	—	—	124@ 10^8	—
2018(T61)	23	—	—	—	—	—	—	—	118@ 10^8	—
2024(O)	23	—	—	—	—	—	—	—	90@ 10^8	—
2024(T3)	23	—	835	0.17	−0.1	−0.64	655	0.065	115@ 10^8	—
2024(T351)	23	—	—	—	—	—	770	0.086	—	—
2024(T4)	23	—	1069	—	−0.142	—	—	—	121@ 10^8	—
2024(T4)	180	—	524	—	−0.086	—	—	—	140@ $9.2×10^6$ 200@ $9×10^5$ 300@ 4000	— — —
2024(T6)	23	—	776	0.27	−0.091	−0.742	700	0.11	—	—

continued

Material	$T/℃$	$d\varepsilon/dt$	σ'_f	ε'_f	b	c	K'	n'	$\sigma_f @ 2N_f$	R
2024-DSC (Dispersion-Strengthed Composite)	23	—	—	—	—	—	—	—	—	—
	260	—	—	—	—	—	—	—	110@ 10^8 133@ 10^7 170@ 10^6	RB RB RB
2618/20%Al_2O_3(Brake Rotor; V_f=20%)	23	—	—	—	—	—	—	—	165@ 10^6 220@ 10^5	0.1^+ 0.1^+
2090(T83)	23	—	—	—	—	—	—	—	110@ 10^9 220@ 10^7	— —
2090(T86)	23	—	—	—	—	—	—	—	120@ 10^9 310@ 10^7	— —
2124(T351)	23	—	0.084	—	−0.53	—	890	0.113	—	—
2124/25SiC	23	—	—	—	—	—	1801	0.2	440@ $5×10^4$ 530@ 235	— —
2129(T851)	23	—	1172	—	—	—	—	—	125@ 10^8	—
2219(T851)	23	—	—	—	—	—	—	—	103@ 10^8	—
3003(O)	23	—	—	—	—	—	—	—	48@ 10^8 42@ 10^7	−1 0.1^+
	100	—	—	—	—	—	—	—	38@ 10^7	0.1^+
	180	—	—	—	—	—	—	—	34@ 10^7	0.1^+
	250	—	—	—	—	—	—	—	20@ 10^7	0.1^+
	300	—	—	—	—	—	—	—	14@ 10^7	0.1^+
3003(H12)	23	—	—	—	—	—	—	—	55@ 10^8	—
3003(H14)	23	—	—	—	—	—	—	—	62@ 10^9	—
3003(H18)	23	—	—	—	—	—	—	—	69@ 10^8	—
3004(H34)	23	—	—	—	—	—	—	—	105@ 10^8	—
4032(T6)	23	—	—	—	—	—	—	—	110@ 10^8	—
5050(O)	23	—	—	—	—	—	—	—	83@ 10^8	—

continued

Material	$T/℃$	$d\varepsilon/dt$	σ_f'	ε_f'	b	c	K'	n'	$\sigma_f@2N_f$	R
5050(H38)	23	—	—	—	—	—	—	—	97@ 10^8	—
5052(O)	23	—	—	—	—	—	—	—	110@ 10^8	—
5052(H32)	23	—	—	—	—	—	—	—	117@ 10^8	—
5052(H36)	23	—	—	—	—	—	—	—	124@ 10^8	—
5052(H38)	23	—	—	—	—	—	—	—	138@ 10^8	—
5056(O)	23	—	—	—	—	—	—	—	138@ 10^8	—
5056(H18)	23	—	—	—	—	—	—	—	152@ 10^8	—
5056(H38)	23	—	—	—	—	—	—	—	152@ 10^8	—
5083(O)	23	—	414	0.36	—	—	300	0.13	150@ 10^8	—
5083(H321)	23	—	780	1.15	−0.114	−0.86	544	0.75	159@ 10^8	—
5086(O)	23	—	—	—	—	—	—	—	145@ 10^8	—
5086(H32)	23	—	—	—	—	—	—	—	150@ 10^8	—
5154(O)	23	—	—	—	—	—	—	—	117@ 10^8	—
5154(H38)	23	—	—	—	—	—	—	—	145@ 10^8	—
5183(O)	23	—	421	0.4	—	—	313	0.113	—	—
5254(O)	23	—	—	—	—	—	—	—	117@ 10^8	—
5254(H38)	23	—	—	—	—	—	—	—	145@ 10^8	—
5454(O)	23	—	—	—	—	—	—	—	120@ 10^8	—
5454(H34)	23	—	—	—	—	—	—	—	125@ 10^8	—
5456(O)	23	—	—	—	—	—	—	—	150@ 10^8	—
5456(H311)	23	—	702	0.2	−0.102	−0.655	877	0.145	—	—
5754	23	—	455	9.19	0.074	−1.0	313	0.133	—	—
6009(T4)	23	—	—	—	—	—	—	—	120@ 10^6	—
6016(T6)	23	—	—	—	—	—	—	—	98@ 10^8	—
6053(O)	23	—	—	—	—	—	—	—	55@ 10^8	—

continued

Material	$T/°C$	$d\varepsilon/dt$	σ'_f	ε'_f	b	c	K'	n'	$\sigma_f @ 2N_f$	R
6053(T6)	23	—	—	—	—	—	—	—	$90@10^8$	—
6061(O)	23	—	—	—	—	—	—	—	$62@10^8$	—
6061(T6)	23	—	—	—	—	—	—	—	$97@10^8$	—
6066(T6)	23	—	—	—	—	—	—	—	$110@10^8$	—
6070(O)	23	—	—	—	—	—	—	—	$60@10^8$	—
6070(T6)	23	—	—	—	—	—	—	—	$96@10^8$	—
6101(T6)	23	—	—	—	—	—	—	—	$96@10^8$	—
6110(T6)	23	—	—	—	—	—	—	—	$310@10^4$ $230@10^5$ $170@10^6$	— — —
	160	—	—	—	—	—	—	—	$275@10^4$ $200@10^5$ $145@10^6$	— — —
	200	—	—	—	—	—	—	—	$250@10^4$ $180@10^5$ $125@10^6$	— — —
	250	—	—	—	—	—	—	—	$225@10^4$ $150@10^5$ $100@10^6$	— — —
6151(T6)	23	—	—	—	—	—	—	—	$85@10^8$	—
6061(O)	23	—	310	0.27	−0.105	−0.531	400	0.197	$62@10^8$	—
6061(T4)	23	—	332	0.15	−0.012	−0.52	514	0.23	—	—
6061(T6)	23	—	383	0.207	−0.053	−0.628	—	0.07	$97@10^8$	—
6061(T651)	23	—	394	0.634	−0.045	−0.723	509	0.239	$97@10^8$	—
6063(O)	23	—	556	0.74	−0.107	−0.83	249	0.07	$55@10^8$	—
6063(T6;tested in air)	23	—	—	—	—	—	384	0.067	$115@10^5$ $95@10^6$ $80@10^7$ $69@10^8$	— — — —

continued

Material	$T/^\circ C$	$d\varepsilon/dt$	σ_f'	ε_f'	b	c	K'	n'	$\sigma_f@2N_f$	R
6063(T6; in 3.5% NaCl solution)	23	—	—	—	—	—	—	—	60@ 5×10^5 55@ 10^6	—
6066/20%Al_2O_3 (Brake Rotor; $V_f=20\%$)	23	—	—	—	—	—	—	—	200@ 10^5 140@ 10^6	0.1^+ $0.1^{+\cdot}$
6082(T6; Tested in air)	23	—	487	0.21	−0.07	−0.593	596	0.126	110@ 10^6 100@ 10^7 73@ 10^8	— — —
6063(T6; in 3.5% NaCl solution)	23	—	—	—	—	—	—	—	50@ 10^6	—
6082	23	—	611	1.08	−0.1	−0.857	417	0.057	79@ 10^8	—
6201(T6; T651)	23	—	—	—	—	—	—	—	69@ 10^8	—
6201(T81)	23	—	—	—	—	—	—	—	105@ 10^8	—
6260	23	—	469	27.2	−0.09	−1.213	301	0.047	73@ 10^8	—
6463(T6)	23	—	—	—	—	—	—	—	69@ 10^8	—
7001(T6)	23	—	—	—	—	—	—	—	150@ 10^8	—
7005(T6)	23	—	—	—	—	—	—	—	150@ 10^8	—
7020(T6)	23	—	3672	0.48	−0.071	−0.69	3952	0.1	—	—
7021(T62)	23	—	—	—	—	—	—	—	140@ 10^8	—
7039(T61)	23	—	—	—	—	—	—	—	310@ 3×10^4 210@ 2×10^5 165@ 10^8 160@ 5×10^8	— — — —
7050(T7451)	23	10 Hz	—	—	—	—	—	—	157@ 10^6	0.1^+
7050(T7451;1 h exposure to 177 ℃)	23	10 Hz	—	—	—	—	—	—	157@ 5×10^5	0.1^+
7050(T7451;8 h exposure to 177 ℃)	23	10 Hz	—	—	—	—	—	—	157@ 2.5×10^5	0.1^+

continued

Material	$T/{}^\circ\text{C}$	$\mathrm{d}\varepsilon/\mathrm{d}t$	σ_f'	ε_f'	b	c	K'	n'	$\sigma_\mathrm{f}@2N_\mathrm{f}$	R
7068(T6;T6511)	23	—	—	—	—	—	—	—	159	—
7075(O)	23	—	—	—	—	—	—	—	$97@10^8$	—
7075(T6;Aged @ 204 ℃)	23	—	1315	0.19	−0.126	−0.52	852	0.074	$159@10^9$ / $330@2\times10^5$	— / —
	160	—	—	—	—	—	—	—	$285@4\times10^5$	—
	204	—	—	—	—	—	—	—	$195@4\times10^5$	—
7075(T651)	23	—	1231	0.26	−0.122	−0.806	852	0.074	—	—
7075(T7351)	23	—	989	6.81	−0.14	−1.2	695	0.094	$54@10^8$	—
7178(T6)	23	—	—	—	—	—	—	—	$150@10^8$	—
7178(T76)	23	—	—	—	—	—	—	—	$160@10^8$	—
7475(T761)	23	—	983	4.25	−0.11	−1.07	675	0.059	$107@10^8$	—
Al-Mg-4.5Mn	23	—	654	0.45	−0.09	−0.755	675	0.059	$103@10^8$	—
D16CzATW	23	—	791	1.456	−0.114	−1.072	—	—	—	—
Al Alloys	23	—	$1.9\sigma_\mathrm{uts}$	0.28	−0.11	−0.66	$\sigma_\mathrm{f}'/(\varepsilon_\mathrm{f}')^{n'}$	b/c	$0.45\sigma_\mathrm{uts}@10^8$	—

Notes：PM = Powder Metallurgy;

All the alloy compositions are in weight percentage unless stated otherwise;

0.1^+ = Stress ratio $R=0.1$ and both high and low stress levels are positive.

Table 83.7 Mechanical Creep Parameters of Al Alloys

Material	$T/{}^\circ\text{C}$	Stress/MPa	Strain Rate/s^{-1}	$A/(\mathrm{MPa}^{-n}\cdot\mathrm{s}^{m-1})$	$Q/(\mathrm{J}\cdot\mathrm{mol}^{-1})$	n	m
Al Foam (Syntactic)	500	—	—	3.95×10^{-8}	0	4.4	0
Al (Pure)	260	Low	—	—	—	4.5	—
	260	High	—	—	—	5	—
	371	—	—	—	—	4.5	—
	593	—	—	—	—	5	—

continued

Material	$T/^\circ\text{C}$	Stress/MPa	Strain Rate/s^{-1}	$A/(\text{MPa}^{-n} \cdot \text{s}^{m-1})$	$Q/(\text{J} \cdot \text{mol}^{-1})$	n	m
2011(Al-Cu-Bi-Pb)	625	95	—	—	142000	6	—
2618(T6)	215±15	138	—	—	49000	—	—
5083	350	—	—	—	—	5.4	—
	400	—	—	—	—	5.5	—
	450	—	—	—	—	5.7	—
	500	—	—	—	—	5.3	—
6061(O)	250	$E=1$	—	4.65×10^{-21}	0	4.37	0.76
	400	—	—	—	—	9.0	—
	450	—	—	—	—	8.9	—
	500	—	—	—	—	4.4	—
7075(T6)	300	$E=1$; $20\sim70$	—	—	—	5.9	—
7075(T651)	300	$E=1$;$20\sim70$	—	—	—	7.9	—
332	220	$E=1$;31.5	—	—	173000	—	1/3
	220	$E=1$; 56.5	—	—	246000	—	1/3
	220	$E=1$; 73	—	—	284000	—	1/3
333	220	$E=1$; 31.5	—	—	152000	—	1/3
	221	$E=1$; 56.5	—	—	125000	—	1/3
	220	$E=1$; 73	—	—	356000	—	1/3
Al-5.3Mg-... (Annealed)	317	$E=1$; $\sigma>52$ (Lattice diffusion)	—	—	137000	3.0	—
Al-5.3Mg-... (Annealed)	273	$E=1$; $\sigma>122$ (Mutual diffusion)	—	—	146000	4.9	—
Al-0.07Sc(New; $w_f=0.07\%$)	300	—	—	—	—	17	—

continued

Material	$T/°C$	Stress/MPa	Strain Rate/s^{-1}	$A/(MPa^{-n} \cdot s^{m-1})$	$Q/(J \cdot mol^{-1})$	n	m
Al-0.07Sc (Aged; $w_f = 0.07\%$)	300	—	—	—	—	16	—
Al-0.21Sc (New; $w_f = 0.21\%$)	300	—	—	—	—	12	—
Al-13Si-3Cu-0.2 Mg (Eutectic)	260~280	$E = 1$; 32	—	—	163000	—	—
		$E = 1$; 42	—	—	197000	—	—
		$E = 1$; 56	—	—	261000	—	—
B390 (Al-17Si-4Cu-0.5Mg)	260~280	—	—	—	—	12	—
Al-17Si-0.2Cu-0.5Mg-1.2Fe)	260~280	$E = 1$; 32	—	—	185000	12	—

Notes: Creep equation $= \dfrac{d\varepsilon_{creep}}{dt} = A\left(\dfrac{\sigma - \sigma_{th}}{E}\right)^n t^m \exp\left(\dfrac{-Q}{RT_k}\right)$, $\sigma > \sigma_{th}$;

$\sigma_{th} =$ Stress threshold and $\sigma_{th} = 0$, if not specified;

$E =$ Young's modulus; If given that $E = 1$, it means E is not specified.

Table 83.8   Material Parameters for Fatigue Crack Growth of Aluminum Alloys in Opening Mode

Material	$T/°C$	σ_y	σ_{uts}	K_{IC}	$f(R)$	m	ΔK_{th}	Δ_{fat}
2024 (T3)	23	360	490	—	$f(-1) = 4.94 \times 10^{-11}$	2.653	2.0	281
		360	490	—	$f(0) = 2.24 \times 10^{-10}$	—	1.146	200
		360	490	—	$f(0.1) = 2.603 \times 10^{-10}$	—	1.084	171
6082 (T6)	23	329	349	—	$f(-1) = 4.84 \times 10^{-10}$	3.37	9.54	—
7075 (T6)	23	520	575	—	$f(0) = 7.3 \times 10^{-10}$	2.34	0.520	227
		501	569	—	$f(-1) = 1.62 \times 10^{-10}$	—	1.003	403

Notes: $\dfrac{da}{dN_p} = f(R) \mid \Delta K - \Delta K_{th} \mid^m$

σ_y (MPa) = Yield strength;

σ_{uts} (MPa) = Ultimate tensile strength;

$f(R)$ = Parameter as a function of load ratio (R);

m = Exponent;

ΔK_{th} (MPa $\cdot$ m$^{\frac{1}{2}}$) = Threshold stress intensity factor range;

Δ_{fat} (MPa) = Fatigue strength range.

Table 83.9　Orthotropic Elastic Properties of Aluminum Composites

Material-DAM	$T/℃$	ρ	E_{11}	E_{22}	E_{33}	G_{12}	G_{13}	G_{23}	ν_{12}	ν_{13}	ν_{23}
Al/42% Al$_2$O$_3$ (V_f =42% Fibers)	23	2.5	342	—	—	—	—	—	—	—	—
(90Al-10Mg)/10CF (w_f = 10% ; Pitch-based)	23	2.43	—	—	—	—	—	—	—	—	—
(90Al-10Mg)/10CF (w_f = 10% ; PAN-based)	23	2.2	—	—	—	—	—	—	—	—	—

Table 83.10　Orthotropic Thermal Properties of Reinforced Aluminum Composites

Material-DAM	$T/℃$	α_1	α_2	α_3	k_1	k_2	k_3	γ	β_1	β_2	β_3
Al 6061/55% CF(PAN M40 V_f=55% ; As Cast)	23	0.3	2.3	2.3	—	—	—	—	—	—	—
	100	0.3	2.0	2.0	—	—	—	—	—	—	—
	200	0.3	1.5	1.5	—	—	—	—	—	—	—
	400	0.3	1.2	1.2	—	—	—	—	—	—	—
	450	0.3	1.4	1.4	—	—	—	—	—	—	—
Al 6061/55% CF(PAN M40 V_f=55% ; Annealed)	23	0.3	2.6	2.6	—	—	—	—	—	—	—
	100	0.3	2.7	2.7	—	—	—	—	—	—	—
	200	0.3	2.5	2.5	—	—	—	—	—	—	—
	400	0.3	1.6	1.6	—	—	—	—	—	—	—
	450	0.3	1.5	1.5	—	—	—	—	—	—	—
Al/42% Al$_2$O$_3$(V_f = 42% Fibers)	23	−0.49	—	—	—	—	—	—	—	—	—

Notes: α_1, α_2, α_3(μm/m/℃)= Coefficients of linear thermal expansion of a unidirectional lamina;

　　　k_1, k_2, k_3(W/m/℃)= Thermal conductivities of a unidirectional lamina;

　　　β_1, β_2, β_3(μm/m/%)= Swelling coefficients of linear moisture expansion;

　　　γ(J/kg/℃)= Specific heat capacity.

Table 83.11　Orthotropic Mechanical Strengths of Aluminum Composites

Lamina (Fiber Specification)	$T/^\circ\text{C}$	$(\sigma_{11},\varepsilon_{11})$	$(\sigma_{22},\varepsilon_{22})$	$(\sigma_{12},\varepsilon_{12})$	$(\sigma_{33},\varepsilon_{33})$
90Al-10Mg	23	(255,10%)	(255,10%)	—	(255,10%)
		(300,20%)	(300,20%)	—	(300,20%)
		(393,50%)	(393,50%)	—	(393,50%)
70%(90Al-10Mg)/30%CF($V_\text{f}=$ 30%; CF:PAN carbon fibers randomly on x-y plane)	23	(200,5%)	(200,5%)	$\sigma_{12\text{u}}=280$	(220,5%)
		(380,10%)	(380,10%)	—	(360,10%)
		(540,20%)	(540,20%)	—	(480,20%)
70%(90Al-10Mg)/30%CF($V_\text{f}=$ 30%; CF:Pitch carbon fibers randomly on x-y plane)	23	(100,2.5%)	(100,2.5%)	$\sigma_{12\text{u}}=220$	(130,5%)
		(170,5%)	(170,5%)	—	(180,10%)
		(225,8%)	(225,8%)	—	(190,14%)

Notes: σ_{ij}(MPa) & ε_{ij}=Stress and strain at failure in different directions and loading planes.

Chapter 84

Au (Gold)

84.1　Introduction

As solid bulk gold, the heavy metal has a density of 19.32 g/cm^3. Mechanical properties of gold vary according to its forming and processing are shown in Table 84.1. The size effect on the mechanical behavior of gold thin films and wires is also significant [Espinosa and Prorok] [Lee, et al.], as shown by the various Young's moduli and strengths among different shapes of gold. The "K" of K-Gold stands for karat, which is used to state how much pure gold is found in an item:

(a) 24 kt gold is pure gold.
(b) 18 kt gold contains 18-part gold and 6-part other metals, making it 75% gold.
(c) 14 kt gold contains 14-part gold and 10-part other metals, making it 58.3% gold.
(d) 12 kt gold contains 12-part gold and 12-part other metals, making it 50% gold.
(e) 10 kt gold contains 10-part gold and 14-part other metal(s), making it 41.7% gold.

Gold is ductile and one ounce can be drawn into an 80 km thin gold wire (5 μm in diameter) to make electrical contacts. The top three prominent properties of gold are:

(a) Chemical inertness: no oxidation;
(b) Excellent malleability;
(c) Yellow color.

84.2　Applications

Its low electric resistivity makes it the most efficient material for taking chemical reactions of fuel cells to electric power vehicles.

References

DEPASQUALE G, et al, 2008. Mechanical Fatigue Analysis on Gold MEMS Devices: Experimental Results [M]. DTIP 2008 Conference, Nice, France.

DIETIKER M, et al, 2008. Nanoindentation of Single-crystalline Gold Thin Films: Correlating Hardness and the Onset of Plasticity[J]. Acta Materialia, 56(15): 3887-3899.

ESPINOSA H D, PROROK B C, 2003. Size Effects on the Mechanical Behavior of Gold Thin Films[J]. Journal of Material Science, 38(20): 4125-4128.

GREER J R, OLIVER W, NIX W, 2006. Size Dependence in Mechanical Properties of Gold at Micron Scale in the Absent of Grain Gradients[J]. Acta Materialia, 54(6): 1705.

KIM K S, et al, 2006. Relationship between Mechanical Properties and Microstructure of Ultra-fine Gold Bonding Wires[J]. Mechanics of Materials, 38(2006): 119-127.

LEE D, et al, 2007. Micro-fabrication and Mechanical Properties of Nanoporous Gold at the Nanoscale[J]. Scripta Materialia, 56: 437-440.

LIN H, et al, 1993. Study of Vibrational Modes of Gold Nanostructures by Picosecond Ultrasonics[J]. Journal of Applied Physics, 73(1): 37-35.

SON D, et al, 2003. Film-thickness Considerations in Micro Cantilever-Beam Test in Measuring Mechanical Properties of Metal Thin Film[J]. Thin Solid Films, 437(1-2): 182-187.

REDDY A L, SHAIJUMON M M, GOWDA S R, et al, 2010. Multisegmented $AuMnO_2$/Carbon Nanotube Hybrid Coaxial Arrays for High-Power Supercapacitor Applications[J]. Journal of Physical Chemistry, C, 117(42): 658-663.

WEI T C, DAU A R, 2003. Mechanical and Electrical Properties of Au-Al and Cu-Al Intermetallics Layer at Wire Bonding Interface[J]. Journal of Electronic Packaging, 125(4): 617-620.

WU B, et al, 2005. Mechanical Properties of Ultrahigh-strength Gold Nanowires[J]. Nature Materials, (4): 525-529.

ZHANG, et al, 2010. Biotemplated Synthesis of Gold Nanoparticle-Bacteria Cellulose Nanofiber Nanocomposites and Their Application in Biosensing[J]. Advanced Functional Materials, 20: 1152-1160.

Table 84.1   Mechanical Properties of Gold (Au) and Gold Alloys

Material	$T/℃$	E_T	ρ	ν	(σ,ε)	α	k	γ	ρ_E	K_{IC}
Au(Pure)	−272	—	—	—	—	—	546	—	—	—
	−271	—	—	—	—	—	1090	—	—	—
	−268	—	—	—	—	—	2520	—	—	—
	−264	—	—	—	—	—	3270	—	—	—
	−258	—	—	—	—	—	2460	—	—	—
	−253	—	—	—	—	—	1580	—	—	—
	−243	—	—	—	—	—	755	—	—	—
	−213	—	—	—	—	—	374	—	—	—

continued

Material	$T/°C$	E_T	ρ	ν	(σ,ε)	α	k	γ	ρ_E	K_{IC}
Au(Pure)	23	79	19.32	0.42	(30,0.2%) (124,45%)	14.2	317	130	0.0023	—
	527	—	—	—		—	284	—	—	—
	927	—	—	—		—	255	—	—	—
	1064(T_m)	—	—	—		—	—	—	—	—
Au(Annealed)	23	79	19.32	0.42	(30,0.2%) (124,45%)	14.2	317	138	—	—
Au (Drawn)	23	79	19.32	0.42	(200,2%)	14.2	317	138	—	—
Au (Film;$h=$ 0.56 μm)	23	130	2.707	0.32	(391,0.2%)	—	—	—	—	—
Au (Film;$h=$ 0.99 μm)	23	109	2.707	0.32	(310,0.2%)	—	—	—	—	—
Au (Film;$h=$ 1.26 μm)	23	107	2.707	0.32	(115,0.2%)	—	—	—	—	—
Au (Nanowires)	23	385	19.32	0.42	(175,0.2%) (210,4%)	14.2	317	138	—	—
70Au-30Pt (Platinum Gold; Annealed)	23	114	19.92	—	(244,0.2%) (420,24%)	—	—	—	—	—
	1450(T_m)	—	—	—	—	—	—	—	—	—
22 K Gold:										
Au-10Cu (Coinage)	23	—	17.17	—	—	—	—	—	—	—
	940(T_m)	—	—	—	—	—	—	—	—	—
Au-3.2Ag-5.1 Cu(Annealed)	23	98.5	—	—	$\sigma_{uts}=275$	—	—	—	—	—
Au-3.2Ag-5.1 Cu (CW)	23	98.5	—	—	$\sigma_{uts}=463$	—	—	—	—	—
Au-5.5Ag-2.8 Cu(Annealed)	23	98.5	—	—	$\sigma_{uts}=220$	—	—	—	—	—

continued

Material	$T/℃$	E_T	ρ	ν	(σ,ε)	α	k	γ	ρ_E	K_{IC}
Au-5.5Ag-2.8 Cu（CW）	23	98.5	—	—	$\sigma_{uts}=390$	—	—	—	—	—
21 K Gold:										
Au-1.75Ag-10.75 Cu（Annealed）	23	98.5	—	—	$\sigma_{uts}=396$	—	—	—	—	—
Au-4.5Ag-8Cu （Annealed）	23	98.5	—	—	$\sigma_{uts}=363$	—	—	—	—	—
Au-4.5Ag-8Cu （CW）	23	98.5	—	—	$\sigma_{uts}=650$	—	—	—	—	—
18 K Gold:										
Au-4.5Ag-20.5 Cu（Annealed）	23	75	15.97	—	$(250,0.2\%)$ $\sigma_{uts}=550$	—	—	—	—	—
	$1040(T_m)$	—	—	—	—	—	—	—	—	—
Au-4.5Ag-20.5 Cu（CW）	23	75	15.97	—	$(700,0.2\%)$ $\sigma_{uts}=950$	—	—	—	—	—
	$1040(T_m)$	—	—	—	—	—	—	—	—	—
Au-12.5Ag-12.5 Cu（Annealed）	23	—	15.97	—	$\sigma_{uts}=520$	—	—	—	—	—
	$1040(T_m)$	—	—	—	—	—	—	—	—	—
Au-12.5Ag-12.5 Cu（CW）	23	—	15.97	—	$\sigma_{uts}=810$	—	—	—	—	—
	$1040(T_m)$	—	—	—	—	—	—	—	—	—
14 K Gold:										
Au-9Ag-32.5 Cu（Annealed）	23	75	13.18	—	$(250,0.2\%)$ $(580,26\%)$	—	—	—	—	—
	$875(T_m)$	—	—	—	—	—	—	—	—	—
Au-9Ag-32.5Cu （CW;Red Gold）	23	75	13.18	—	$(720,0.2\%)$ $\sigma_{uts}=1000$	—	—	—	—	—
	$875(T_m)$	—	—	—	—	—	—	—	—	—

continued

Material	$T/°C$	E_T	ρ	ν	(σ,ε)	α	k	γ	ρ_E	K_{IC}
58Au-30Ag-12Cu (Dental)	23	—	—	—	—	—	—	—	—	—
58Au-24Cu-18Pd(White Gold)	23	—	—	—	—	—	—	—	—	—
9 K Gold:										
37.4Au-62.6Ag (Nanoporous Film)	23	—	—	—	(111,0.2%) (190,10%)	—	—	—	—	—
Others (AU for solders listed in Chapter 127):										
Neyoro G(HT) (Au-Cu-Pt; Gyro gimbals)	23	102	11.8	0.4	(900,0.2%) (1100,5%)	—	—	—	—	—
Neyoro 28 (Au-Ag; Annealed; Potentiometer)	23	102	11.8	0.4	(350,0.2%) (490,6%)	—	—	—	—	—
Paliney 2000(HT; Au-Pd-Cu; Sensors)	23	102	11.8	0.4	(840,0.2%) (1200,4%)	—	—	—	—	—
49Au-5.5Ag-2.3Pd-26.9Cu-16.3Si	23	74	—	—	(−980,−2%)	—	—	—	—	—
	$130(T_g)$	—	—	—	—	—	—	—	—	—

Notes: ρ_E ($\mu\Omega m$) = Electric resistivity;

CW = Cold-worked;

HT = Heat-treated.

Chapter 85

Co (Cobalt)

▶ ▶ *Automotive Engineering Materials-Thermomechanical Properties*

85.1 Introduction

Metals alloyed with cobalt (Co) are of high value for their high wear resistance and hardness at elevated temperatures. Mechanical properties of cobalt and its related alloys are given in Table 85.1 and their fatigue properties in Table 85. 2. Cobalt-based superalloys generally contain the composition of 35%~65% cobalt, 19%~30% chromium, and 0%~35% nickel.

85.2 Applications

Casts alloys and wrought alloys are the two main types of cobalt-based alloys used for biomedical purpose. Co-28Cr-6Mo alloy is commonly used in dental and medical implants, and also for high-temperature engineering applications such as in aero engines.

Under the name "Stellite" by Elwood Haynes and Deloro Stellite Company, Co-Cr alloys have been used in various fields where high wear resistance has been in need, including automotive and aerospace industries.

Sm-Co magnets are extremely resistant to demagnetization and have high temperature stability up to 250 ℃. Their Curie temperatures range from 700 to 800 ℃. However, they are expensive and subject to price fluctuations.

References

AL JABBARI, YOUSSEF S, 2014. Physico-Mechanical Properties and Prosthodontic Applications of Co-Cr Dental Alloys: a Review of the Literature[J]. J. Adv. Prosthodont, 6(2): 138-145.

ANGELINI E, BONINO P, PEZZOLI M, et al, 1989. Tensile Strength of Cr-Co Dental Alloys Solder Joints [J]. Dent Mater, (5): 13-17.

CAREK A, BABIC J Z, SCHAUPERL Z, et al, 2011. Mechanical Properties of Co-Cr Alloys for Metal Base Framework[J]. Int. J. Prosthodont. Restor. Dent, 1: 13-19.

CHENG H, XU M, ZHANG H, et al, 2010. Cyclic Fatigue Properties of Cobalt-Chromium Alloy Clasps for Partial Removable Dental Prostheses[J]. J. Prosthetic Dent, (104): 389-396.

ISO 6871-1, 1994. Dental base metal alloys[M]. International Organization for Standardization.

LASSILA L V, VALLITTU P K, 1998. Effect of Water and Artificial Saliva on the Low Cycle Fatigue Resistance of Cobalt-Chromium Dental Alloy[J]. J Prosthet Dent, (80): 708-713.

MARTI A, 2000. Cobalt-base Alloys Used in Bone Surgery[J]. Injury, (31): 18-21.

SKOLOV L D, et al, 1969. Mechanical Properties of Cobalt at Different Temperatures and Deformation Rates [J]. Metal Science and Heat Treatment, 11(8): 626-628.

Table 85.1   Mechanical Properties of Cobalt (Co) and Related Alloys

Material	$T/°C$	E_T	ρ	ν	(σ, ε)	α	k	γ	ρ_E	K_{IC}
Co(Pure;Soft)	23	210	8.85	0.32	$(225, 0.2\%)$ $\sigma_{uts} = 760$	12	69	456	0.063	—
	$1495(T_m)$	—	—	—	—	—	—	—	—	—
Co(Pure;Hard Polycrystalline)	23	210	8.85	0.32	$(434, 0.2\%)$ $\sigma_{uts} = 1135$	12	69	456	0.063	—
	$1495(T_m)$	—	—	—	—	—	—	—	—	—
Co-28.5Cr-6Mo-... [ASTM F75]	23	220	8.29		$(>450, 0.2\%)$ $(>655, >8\%)$	—	—	—	—	—
Co-28Cr-6Mo	23	220	8.29		$(880, 0.2\%)$ $(1150, 9\%)$	12	13	—	—	—
	300	—	—	—	—	13	18	—	—	—
	500	—	—	—	—	14	22	—	—	—
	1000	—	—	—	—	16	33	—	—	—
	1150(Maximum service temperature)									
	$1390(T_m)$	—	—	—	—	—	—	—	—	—
Partial Denture Alloys[Al Jabbari 1]:										
Brealloy F400 (64.7Co-29Cr-5 Mo-0.5Si-0.4 Mn-0.4C...)	23	220	8.3	—	$(700, 0.2\%)$ $(900, 4\%)$	12	13	—	—	—
Suprachrome (63.6Co-28.5 Cr-6Mo-...)	23	200	8.3	—	$(600, 0.2\%)$ $(?, 9\%)$	12	13	—	—	—
Wironit LA(63.5 Co-29Cr-5Mo- 1.2Si-...)	23	220	8.3	—	$(640, 0.2\%)$ $(940, 10\%)$	12	13	—	—	—
Vitallium(63.4Co- 29Cr-5.2Mo-...)	23	200	8.3	—	$(680, 0.2\%)$ $(960, 10\%)$	12	13	—	—	—

continued

Material	$T/℃$	E_T	ρ	ν	(σ,ε)	α	k	γ	ρ_E	K_{IC}
Wironium Plus (62.5Co-29.5 Cr-5Mo-...)	23	220	8.3	—	(700,0.2%) (1000, 13%)	12	13	—	—	—
Metal-Ceramic Dental Restorative Alloys[Al Jabbari 1]:										
IPS d. SIGN 30 (60.2Co-30.1Cr-3.9Ga-3.2Nb-...)	23	180	—	—	(780,0.2%) (?, 10%)	13.4	—	—	—	—
Wirobond C(60.2 Co-25Cr-4.8Mo-6.2W-2.9Ga-...)	23	220	8.3	—	(540,0.2%) (680, 11%)	12	13	—	—	—
Vi-Comp(55.8 Co-25Cr-3Mo-5 W-7.5Ga-3Nb-...)	23	175	—	—	(448,0.2%) (695, 7.7%)	13.2	—	—	—	—
Genesis II(52.6 Co-27.5Cr-12W-2.5Ga-2.5Ru-...)	23	172	—	—	(517,0.2%) (?, 15%)	13.4	—	—	—	—
Callisto CP+ (40Co-21.4Cr-12.7Mo-25Pd-...)	23	180	—	—	(780,0.2%) (?, 10%)	13.4	—	—	—	—
Wirobond LFC (33.9Co-28.5Cr-5 Mo-30Fe-1Mn-...)	23	200	—	—	(660,0.2%) (950,16%)	14	—	—	—	—

Notes: $\rho_E(\mu\Omega m)$ = Electric resistivity.

Table 85.2　Fatigue ε-N Properties of Cobalt (Co) and Related Alloys

Material	$T/℃$	$d\varepsilon/dt$	σ_f'	ε_f'	b	c	K'	n'	$\sigma_f@2N_f$	R
Co-28Cr-6Mo	23	20 Hz	—	—	—	—	—	—	200@ 7.5×10^6	$R=0$
Co-28.5Cr-6Mo [ASTM F75]	23	—	—	—	—	—	—	—	610@ 10^7	RB

Chapter 86

Cr (Chromium)

86.1　Introduction

Metals alloyed with chromium (Cr) are of high value for their high corrosion resistance and hardness. Mechanical properties of chromium (Cr) and its related alloys are given in Table 86.1.

Chromium forms a passivation layer of chromium oxide (Cr_2O_3) when exposed to oxygen. The Cr_2O_3 layer is impervious to water and air, protecting the metal beneath. The base metal remains lustrous and smooth, because the Cr_2O_3 layer is thin and invisible.

Cr_2O_3 thin films are quite hard and have anti-corrosion and anti-wear properties.

86.2　Applications

Stainless steel differs from carbon steel by the amount of chromium content. When steel is alloyed with a minimum of 10.5% chromium content by mass, it may turn "stainless". Both the high-temperature strength and low-temperature ductility of stainless steel may be improved at the same time when it is alloyed by chromium simultaneously with magnesia and borides [Sul'zhenko, et al.].

Chromium is also widely used for plating purposes because of its excellent corrosion resistance.

References

ASHBY M F, JONES D R H, 1992. Engineering Materials 2 (with corrections ed.) [M]. Oxford: Pergamon Press.

BRANDES E A, GREENAWAY H T, STONE H E N, 1956. Ductility in Chromium[J]. Nature, 178(4533): 587.

HOLZWARTH U, STAMN H, 2002. Mechanical and Thermomechanical Properties of Commercially Pure Chromium and Chromium alloys[J]. Journal of Nuclear Materials, 300(2-3): 161-177.

KATZ, SIDNEY A, SALEM H, 1992. The Toxicology of Chromium with respect to Its Chemical Appreciation: A Review[J]. Journal of Applied Toxicology, 13: 217-224.

PANG X, et al, 2019. Investigation of Microstructure and Mechanical Properties of Multi-layer Cr/ Cr_2O_3 Coatings[J].Thin Solid Films, 517: 1922-1927.

SUL'ZHENKO V K, et al, 1981. Structure and Mechanical Properties of Chromium Alloyed with Magnesia and

Boron[J]. Soviet Powder Metallurgy and Metal Ceramics, 20(7): 505-509.

ZHAO J, XIA L, SEHGAL A, et al, 2001. Effects of Chromate and Chromate Conversion Coatings on Corrosion of Aluminum Alloy 2024-T3[J]. Surface and Coatings Technology, 140 (1): 51-57.

Table 86.1   Mechanical Properties of Chromium (Cr) and Related Alloys

Material	$T/°C$	E_T	ρ	ν	(σ, ε)	α	k	γ	ρ_E	K_{IC}
Cr(Pure; Soft)	23	—	7.19	0.21	$\sigma_{uts} = 103$	6.5	94	518	0.13	—
	$1857(T_m)$	—	6.3	—	—	—	—	—	—	—
Cr (Pure; Hard)	23	248	7.19	0.21	$(282, 0.2\%)$ $\sigma_{uts} = 689$	6.5	94	518	0.13	—
	$1857(T_m)$	—	6.3	—	—	—	—	—	—	—
Cr (Polycrystalline)	23	279	7.19	0.21	—	6.5	94	518	0.13	—
	$1857(T_m)$	—	6.3	—	—	—	—	—	—	—
Cr_2O_3(Bulk)	23	—	5.22	—	—	—	33	—	—	—
	$2435(T_m)$	—	—	—	—	—	—	—	—	—

Notes: $\rho_E(\mu\Omega m)$ = Electric resistivity.

Chapter 87

Cu (Copper)

87.1   Introduction

Copper alloys offer an excellent combination of material properties that makes them advantageous for many applications. They are widely used because of their excellent electric conductivity, thermal conductivity, strong fatigue resistance, ease of fabrication, high strength, and, outstanding resistance to corrosion. Copper alloys become stronger and more ductile as the temperature goes down. They also retain excellent impact resistance even down to -250 ℃. Copper alloys are often joined by welding in manufacturing.

87.2   Classification of Copper Alloys

Mechanical properties of copper-based alloys can be improved by applying cold work and solid solution. Copper lattice is able to dissolve a certain amount of atoms of other metals, e. g. Sn, Zn and Mg. These atoms take the lattice sites of copper atoms which are called solid solution. Copper alloys are designated by UNS (Unified Numbering System for Metals and Alloys) as C××××, of which each × is a digit ranging from 0 to 9, as shown in Table 87.1. Their mechanical properties are given in Table 87.2.

Copper, as well as silver and gold, is the most used metal for electric/electronic applications.

Pure copper has the highest electrical conductivity of all commercial metals, except silver. For electrical applications, the copper has to be extremely pure, at least 99.9% in purity, while silver is allowed and counted for copper content. Copper strengthened by silver has a higher better cold-working property at a high temperature.

Brass, a family of copper-zinc alloys, is the least expensive of all copper alloys. Mechanical properties depend on the content ratio of copper to zinc. As the zinc content increases, the color changes. Copper has sufficient strength, ductility and hardness for these applications at operating temperatures up to 100 ℃.

Bronze, mainly a combination of mainly copper and tin, is another large family of copper alloys. The strength of a bronze increases with the tin content, while its toughness and malleability decrease. Bronzes with 5%~8% of aluminum (Aluminum Bronze) in addition to copper and tin have been successfully applied to automotive structural parts, because of the high strength, corrosion resistance, and beloved classic brown color. Nickel Aluminum Bronze, with an addition of nickel to aluminum bronze, has been widely used in different kinds of machine parts where the superior resistance to corrosion and erosion in saltwater is needed. An addition of small amounts (0.01%~0.45%) of phosphorus (Phosphorous Bronze) to bronze further increases the hardness, fatigue resistance and wear resistance leading to applications such as springs, fasteners, masonry fixings, shafts, valve spindles, gears and bearings.

Beryllium copper is the hardest (HV 100-420) and strongest (tensile strength 410~1400 MPa) of any copper alloy as it is in the fully heat treated and cold worked condition.

Constantan (55% ~ 60% Cu-40% ~ 45% Ni-Mn-⋯) is a specialty alloy, of which its electric resistivity is quite constant over a wide range of temperatures or strain levels. Constantan is mostly used for strain gauges and thermocouples.

87.3 Fatigue of Copper Alloys

The fatigue strength (endurance limit) of a copper alloy, with a fatigue cutoff cycle of 10^8, falls between 25% and 50% of its ultimate tensile strength,

$$\frac{1}{4}\sigma_{uts} < \sigma_f < \frac{1}{2}\sigma_{uts} \tag{87.1}$$

Although it's not scientific to define the fatigue limit for copper for structural applications, the rule of thumb is to take 40% of its ultimate tensile strength. Fatigue parameters of copper alloys are given in Table 87.3, of which the fatigue strength for a copper alloy is reported for 10^8 cycles.

87.4 Creep of Copper Alloys

The creep rate of copper alloys in a steady state can be described by a power law, extended from creep equations from Chapter 8 as follows:

$$\frac{d\varepsilon_{creep}}{dt}A\sigma^n t^m \exp\left(\frac{-Q}{RT_k}\right) \tag{87.2}$$

where
ε_{creep}: Uniaxial equivalent creep strain;
t: Time;
σ (MPa): Equivalent stress;
A ($MPa^{-n}-s^{-m-1}$): Constant;
n: Stress creep exponent;
m: Time creep exponent;
T_k(K): Temperature;
Q(J/mol): Activation energy, independent of stress and temperature;

R(8.314 J/mol/℃): Universal gas constant.

Creep parameters of copper alloys are listed in Table 87.4 [Li et al.].

87.5　Cu Plating

The following equation [Wei and Hutchinson] can be used to estimate the yield strength of a Cu film corresponding to its plating thickness,

$$\sigma_Y = 230 \ (1 + 0.577 \ h^{\frac{1}{2}})\tag{87.3}$$

where h is the thin film thickness in microns. This information is extremely useful for the stress analysis of PCB.

87.6　Copper Composites

Copper-based metal matrix composites (MMC), mixed mainly with ceramic (e. g. aluminum oxide) particulates. The addition of small amounts of aluminum oxide has miniscule effects on the performance of the copper at the room temperature such as a minor decrease in thermal and electrical conductivity, but the copper alloy's resistance to thermal softening at an elevated temperature increases greatly.

The Cu/CF composite (MMC) is a candidate for electronic applications, e. g. packaging for high voltage chips, cooling plates for microwaves and heat sinks, which all serve for heat dissipation. Except for good thermal conductivity, it has the coefficient of linear thermal expansion (CTE) to match those of electronic materials. The composite can generally fulfill the following requirements:

  (a) Thermal conductivity: 200~300 W/m/K;
  (b) CTE matching the substrate material 5~8 μm/m/℃;
  (c) Good joinability;
  (d) Structural stability during thermal cycling in the application temperature range.

The highest in-plane axial and transverse conductivity achieved by a unidirectional Cu/40%CF composite (copper-coated C-Pan fibers; $V_f = 40\%$) at 100 ℃: $k_1 = 225$ W/m/℃ and $k_2 = 120$ W/m/℃ according to [Korábl, et al.]. Orthotropic elastic and thermal properties of copper composites are given in Tables 87.5 and 87.6. and mechanical strengths.

87.7 Applications

Copper for the automotive application is two folds. One is pure copper (in reddish pink color) for electrical conductivity such as conductor terminals and the other is its alloys for structural components. Copper is the preferred material for power and telecommunications cables, magnet (winding) wire, printed circuit board conductors, and a host of other electrical applications.

Alloy C11000, known as electrolytic tough pitch (ETP) copper, is used most in electric current carrying applications. Wire made of the precipitation-hardened high copper alloy such as UNS C70250 and UNS C70350 attracts more and more attention of electric-connector designers.

Beryllium coppers are costly and they are mostly used for durable components such as aircraft landing gear bearings, bushings, and springs.

Constantan is the most widely used material for strain gage alloy-high strain sensitivity (gage factor).

Nickel Aluminum Bronze (NAB) alloys have been widely used in different kinds of machine parts where the superior resistance to corrosion and erosion in saltwater is needed.

Once upon a time, copper alloys, welded using lead, were the most popular material for automotive heat exchangers. Due to the quest for a lead-free environment, aluminum alloys, which are weaker in strength and lower in thermal conductivity than copper alloys, have been used for heat exchangers. Recently, new brazing technology for some copper alloys such as Cu-Zn-Ni-P family has been developed [Cotton 2008]. OKC 600 (Cu-4.2Ni-15.6Zn-5.3P) and VZ 2255 (Cu-7Ni-9.3Zn-6.5P) are two derived products commercially available for heat-exchanger fins. As efficiency and downsizing of heat exchangers demand in the automotive industry, copper alloys may regain this market. Example materials for a copper-based heat exchanger are given in Table 87.7.

References

AINALI M, KORPINEN T, OCH FORSEN O, 2001. External Corrosion Resistance of CuproBraze Radiators [J]. SAE 2001-01-1718.

AYENSU A, LANGDON T G, 1996. The Inter-Relationship between Grain Boundary Sliding and Cavitation during Creep of Polycrystalline Copper[J]. Metallurgical Transactions A, 27:901-907.

THOMAS B, LI G, MOITRA A, et al, 1998. Analysis of Thermal and Mechanical Behavior of Copper Molds During Continuous Casting of Steel Slabs[J]. ISS Transactions, 25(10):125-143.

BESTERCI M, VELGOSOVA O, IVAN K, 2008. Mechanical Properties of Cu-Al$_2$O$_3$ System at Elevated Temperatures[J]. High Temperature Materials and Processes, 27(1):73-78.

BROYLES S, ANDERSON K, GROZA J, et al, 1995. Creep Deformation of Dispersion Strengthened Copper Alloys from Rapid Solidified Precursors: Part 2. Creep Behavior[J]. Metallurgical Transactions, 27:1217-1227.

CONRAD H, 2004. Grain-size Dependence of the Flow Stress of Cu from Millimeters to Nanometers[J]. Metallurgy and Materials Transaction A, 35(9):2681-2695.

COTTON N L, 2008. Back to the Future with Copper Brazing[J]. Machine Design, 2008:50-55.

FARID Z M, et al, 1989. On the Grain Boundary Internal Friction Peak of α-Brasses[J]. Material Science and Engineering A, 110: L31-L34.

FORMAN R G, HENKENER J A, 1990. An Evaluation of the Fatigue Crack Growth and Fracture Toughness Properties of Beryllium-Copper Alloy CDA172[R]. NASA Technical Memorandum 102166.

GUSTAFSSON B, SCHEEL J, 2000. CuproBraze Mobile Heat Exchanger Technology[J]. SAE 2000-01-3456.

FALKENÖ A, AINALI M, 2001. OCP-Materials[C]//SAE 2001 World Congress, SAE 01 HX-18.3.

JOVANOVIĆ M T, RAJKOVIĆ V, 2009. High Electrical Conductivity Cu-Based Alloys. Part I[J]. MJoM, 15(2):125-133.

KALNAUS S, JIANG Y, 2006. Fatigue Life Prediction of Copper Single Crystals Using a Critical Plane Approach[J]. Engineering Fracture Mechanics, 73:684-696.

KHATIBI G, et al, 2005. A Study of the Mechanical and Fatigue Properties of Metallic Microwires[J]. Fatigue Fract. Engng Mater. Struct. , 28:723-733.

KLEIN M, et al, 2001. The "Size Effect" on the Stress-Strain, Fatigue and Fracture Properties of Thin Metallic Foils[J]. Mater. Sci. Engn, A319/321:924-928.

KORAB J, KORB G, STEFANIK P, et al, (1988). Thermal Cycling of Copper Matrix-Continuous Fiber Reinforced Composites[J]. ISSE 98, 21st International Spring Seminar on Electronic Technology, Neusiedl am See, Austria, 1988:238-241.

KORPINEN T, 2001. Electrochemical Tests with Copper/Brass Radiator Tube Materials in Coolants[J]. SAE 2001-01-1754.

LEE W B, JUNG S B, 2004. The Joint Properties of Copper by Friction Stir Welding[J]. Materials Letters, 58(6):1041-1046.

LEE W B, TO S, CHEUNG C F, 2000. Effect of Crystallographic Orientation in Diamond Turning of Copper Single Crystals[J]. Scripta Materialia, 42:937-945.

LI G, THOMAS B, STUBBINS J, 2000. Modeling Creep and Fatigue of Copper Alloys[J]. Metallurgical and Materials Transactions A, 31(10):2491-2502.

MORRIS M A, JOYE J C, 1995. Effect of the Particle Distribution on the Mechanism Controlling Deformation of a Copper Alloy at Intermediate Temperature[J]. Acta Materialia, 43(1):69-81.

OZGOWICZ W, et al, 2008. The Influence of the Temperature of Tensile test on the Structure and Plastic Properties of Copper Alloy Type CuCr1Zr[J]. Journal of Achievements in Materials and Manufacturing Engineering, 29(2):143-146.

NAGORKA M S, LUCAS G E, LEVI C G, 1995. Novel Oxide-Dispersion-Strengthened Copper Alloys from Rapid Solidified Precursors: Part 2. Creep Behavior[J]. Metallurgical and Materials Transactions A, 26: 873-881.

RAJ S, LANGDON T, 1998. Creep Behavior of Copper at Intermediate Temperatures I. Mechanical Characteristics[J]. Acta Metall. , 37(3):843-852.

READ D T, CHENG Y W, GEISS R, 2004. Morphology, Microstructure, and Mechanical Properties of a Copper Electrodeposit[J]. Microelectronic Engineering, 75:63-70.

READ D T, 1998. Tension-Tension Fatigue of Copper Thin Films[J]. International Journal of Fatigue, 3:203-209.

ROBLES J, ANDERSON K, GROZA J, et al, 1994. Low-Cycle Fatigue of Dispersion-Strengthened Copper[J]. Metallurgical and Materials Transactions A, 25:2235-2245.

SHEN Y L, AMMAMURTY U R, 2003. Constitutive Response of Passivated Copper Films to Thermal Cycling [J]. Journal of Applied Physics, 93(3):1806-1812.

SOBHA B, MURTI Y, 1988. Low Frequency Internal Friction Spectra of $Cu_{0.81}Pd_{0.19}$ Alloy[J]. Bulletin of Material Science, 11:319-328.

SAKTHIVEL T, MUKHOPADHYAY J, 2007. Microstructure and Mechanical Properties of Friction Stir Welded Copper[J]. Journal of Materials Science, 42(19):8126-8129.

TAMBWE M F, et al, 1999. Hassen Plot Analysis of the Hall-Petch Effect in Cu-Nb Nanolayer Composites[J]. Journal of Materials Research, 14(2): 407.

TAPPER L, AINALI M, 2001. Interactions between the Materials in the Tube-Fin Joints in Brazed Copper-Brass Heat Exchangers[C]//1995 Vehide Thermal Management Systems Conference and Exhibition, SAE 2001-01-1726.

THOMAS B, et al, 1998. Analysis of Thermal and Mechanical Behavior of Copper Molds During Continuous Casting of Steel Slabs[J]. ISS Transactions, 25(10):125-143.

THOSSATHEPPITAK B, et al, 2013. Mechanical Properties at High Temperatures and Microstructures of a Nickel Aluminum Bronze Alloy[J]. Advanced Materials Research, 683: 82.

UEDA K, IWATA K, NAKAYAMA K, 1980. Chip Formation Mechanism in Single Crystal Cutting of β-Brass [J]. CIRP Annuals-Manufacturing Technology, 29(1):41-46.

VARANASI C V, et al, 2006. Biaxially Textured Constantan Alloy (55Cu-44Ni-1Mn) Substrates for YBa2Cu3O7-x Coated Conductors[J]. Superconductor Science and Technology, 19(9): 896.

XIE G M, et al, 2007. Development of a Fine-Grained Microstructure and the Properties of a Nugget Zone in Friction Stir Welded Pure Copper[J]. Scripta Mater, 57(2):73-76.

YIN Y G, et al, 2013. Study on Mechanical Properties of Cu-Bi Bearing Materials[J]. Advanced Materials Research, 756/759:89-92.

ZHANG J, JIANG Y, 2008. Constitutive Modeling of Cyclic Plasticity Deformation of a Pure Polycrystalline Copper[J]. International Journal of Plasticity, 24:1890-1915.

ZHU T, et al, 2004. Predictive Modeling of Nanoindentation Induced Homogeneous Defect Nucleation in Copper[J]. Journal of Mechanical Physics in Solids, 52:691-724.

Table 87.1   Classification of Cu (Copper) Alloys and Applications

Name	Alloy	UNS No.	Advantages	Example Applications
Pure Coppers(or Near-Pure)	Cu	C10100 −C12000	Electric conductivity	Conductors; Bus bars; Armatures; Rotor Bars; Commutators; Silver-bearing
Chromium-Zirconium Copper	Cu-Cr	C14500	Electric conductivity	Switchgears
Zirconium Coppers	Cu-Zr	C15000	Electric conductivity	Switchgears
Cadmium Coppers	Cu-Cd	C16200 −C16500	Electric conductivity	Connectors; Terminals
Beryllium Coppers	Cu-Be	C17000 −C17500	Strength; Electric conductivity; Corrosion resistance	Switchgears; Bearings
Chromium Coppers	Cu-Cr	C18100 −C18400	Electric conductivity	Spot Welding Electrodes; Seam Welding Wheels
Phosphor Bronze	Cu-Sn-P	C5××××	Fatigue resistance; Wear resistance	Springs, Fasteners Shafts, Bearings, Rears, Valve spindles, & Masonry fixings
Aluminum Bronze	Cu-Sn-Al	C60600 −C64200	Strength; Corrosion resistance	Structural parts

continued

Name	Alloy	UNS No.	Advantages	Example Applications
Silicon Bronze	Cu-Si	C64700~ C66100	Strength at elevated temperatures	Structural parts
Nickel Aluminum Bronze (NAB)	Cu-Al-Ni	C7××××	Resistance to saltwater erosion	Structural parts in seawater
—	Cu-Ag-P (Cu > 99.7%)	C80100~ C81200	Electric conductivity at high temperatures	Connectors; Hot Metal Handlings
Constantan resistivity	Cu-Ni-Mn & Strain gages		Constant electric resistivity	Thermocouples
Glidcop	Cu/Al$_2$O$_3$		Resistance to thermal softening	Structural parts

Table 87.2 Mechanical Properties of Cu (Copper) Alloys

Material(UNS)	$T/{}^\circ C$	E_T	ρ	v	(σ,ε)	α	k	γ	ρ_E	K_{IC}
Cu	23	107	8.93	0.33	(33,0.2%) (209, 60%)	15.4	401	391	—	—
Cu(Wire; $d=10$ μm)	23	120	8.93	0.33	(60,0.2%) (132,5%)	15.4	401	391	—	—
Cu(Wire; $d=20$ μm)	23	120	8.93	0.33	(36,0.2%) (107,8.6%)	15.4	401	391	—	—
C10100(Hard; 99.99% Cu; Oxygen-free Cu)	23	120	8.93	0.33	(350,0.2%) (385,6%)	15.4	401	391	—	—
	400	—	—	—	—	18.3	379	—	—	—
	450	—	—	—	(145,0.2%)	—	—	—	—	—
	600	—	—	—	(44,0.2%)	—	366	—	—	—
	700	—	—	—	(28,0.2%)	—	359	—	—	—
	1000	—	—	—	—	—	337	—	—	—
	1085(T_m)	—	—	—	—	—	160	—	—	—
	1200	—	—	—	—	—	158	—	—	—
C10100(Hard Cu Plated on PCB):										
2 μm thick	23	108	8.93	0.33	(350,0.2%)	15.4	386	391	—	—
1 μm thick	23	110	8.93	0.33	(375,0.2%)	15.4	386	391	—	—

continued

Material(UNS)	$T/℃$	E_T	ρ	υ	(σ,ε)	α	k	γ	ρ_E	K_{IC}
0.5 μm thick	23	125	8.93	0.33	(400,0.2%)	15.4	386	391	—	—
0.2 μm thick	23	133	8.93	0.33	(500,0.2%)	15.4	386	391	—	—
	1081(T_m)	—	—	—	—	—	—	—	—	—
C10100(Soft; 99.99% Cu)	23	120	8.93	0.33	(70,0.2%) (245,1%) (250,2%) (255, 45%)	15.4	401	391	—	—
C10200(O; 1 mm thick; 99.95% Cu)	23	117	8.93	0.33	(70,0.2%) (220, 45%)	15.4	387	385	—	—
	200	—	—	—	—	—	376	—	—	—
	300	—	—	—	—	—	17.5	370	—	—
C10200(H01; 1 mm thick)	23	117	8.93	0.33	(205,0.2%) (260, 25%)	15.4	387	385	—	—
	300	—	—	—	—	—	17.5	370	—	—
C10200(H02; 1 mm thick)	23	117	8.93	0.33	(250,0.2%) (290,14%)	15.4	387	385	—	—
	300	—	—	—	—	17.5	370	—	—	—
C10200(H04; 1 mm thick)	23	117	8.93	0.33	(310,0.2%) (345,6%)	15.4	387	385	—	—
	300	—	—	—	—	17.5	370	—	—	—
C10200(60% CW)	−196	−139	—	—	(375,0.2%) (458, 42%)	—	—	—	—	—
	−80	—	—	—	(345,0.2%) (365, 20%)	—	—	—	—	—
	23	117	8.93	0.33	(323,0.2%) (334,17%)	15.4	387	385	—	—
	300	—	—	—	—	17.5	370	—	—	—
C10200(H08; 1 mm thick)	23	117	8.93	0.33	(345,0.2%) (380,4%)	15.4	387	385	—	—
	300	—	—	—	—	17.5	370	—	—	—

continued

Material(UNS)	$T/^\circ C$	E_T	ρ	υ	(σ,ε)	α	k	γ	ρ_E	K_{IC}
C10200(H10; 1 mm thick)	23	117	8.93	0.33	(365,0.2%) (450,4%)	15.4	387	385	—	—
	300	—	—	—	—	17.5	370	—	—	—
C10400(H08;Cu-OFS, 84%CW)	23	117	8.93	0.33	(373,0.2%)	15.4	—	394	—	—
C10700(O)	23	117	8.93	0.33	(69,0.2%) (221, 50%)	17	287	376	—	—
C10700(H01)	23	117	8.93	0.33	(207,0.2%) (262, 35%)	17	287	376	—	—
C10700(H04)	23	117	8.93	0.33	(276,0.2%) (310, 20%)	17	287	376	—	—
C10700(H08)	23	117	8.93	0.33	(345,0.2%) (379,4%)	17	287	376	—	—
C10700(H10)	23	117	8.93	0.33	(365,0.2%) (393,4%)	17	287	376	—	—
	$1083(T_m)$	—	—	—	—	—	—	—	—	—
C11000(O; ETP; Bulk)	23	117	8.93	0.33	(69,0.2%) (221, 45%)	16	388	385	—	—
	300	—	—	—	—	17.5	370	—	—	—
	$1083(T_m)$	—	7.93	—	—	—	—	—	—	—
C11000(H04;Cu-ETP)	23	117	8.93	0.33	(250,0.2%) (290,14%)	16	388	385	—	—
	300	—	—	—	—	17.5	370	—	—	—
C11000(H08; ETP Copper)	23	117	8.93	0.33	(345,0.2%) (380,4%)	16	388	385	—	—
	300	—	—	—	—	17.5	370	—	—	—
C11000(H10; ETP Copper)	23	117	8.93	0.33	(350,0.2%) (390,5%)	16	388	385	—	—
	300	—	—	—	—	17.5	370	—	—	—

continued

Material(UNS)	$T/°C$	E_T	ρ	v	(σ, ε)	α	k	γ	ρ_E	K_{IC}
Cu-1Cr-0.19Zr-0.06Al	23	117	8.93	0.33	(99,0.2%) (280, 37%)	16	388	385	—	—
	100	—	—	—	(73,0.2%) (240, 46%)	—	—	—	—	—
	300	—	—	—	(67,0.2%) (205, 42%)	—	—	—	—	—
	500	—	—	—	(140,0.2%) (165, 28%)	—	—	—	—	—
	600	—	—	—	(130,0.2%) (140, 18%)	—	—	—	—	—
	700	—	—	—	(65,0.2%) (69, 44%)	—	—	—	—	—
C12200(O)	−269	137	—	—	(55,0.2%) (415, 65%)	—	—	—	—	—
	−196	126	—	—	(50,0.2%) (350, 62%)	—	—	—	—	—
	23	117	—	—	(45,0.2%) (215, 45%)	16	340	—	—	—
C12200(H2)	−269	137	—	—	(440,0.2%) (560, 44%)	—	—	—	—	—
	−196	126	—	—	(415,0.2%) (470, 28%)	—	—	—	—	—
	23	117	—	—	(340,0.2%) (355,17%)	16	340	—	—	—
C14415(O)	23	117	—	—	—	16	350	—	—	—
C15000(O; Cu-0.15Zr)	23	120	8.9	0.33	(90,0.2%) (250, 50%)	16.6	365	370	—	—
	1084(T_m)	—	—	—	—	—	—	—	—	—
C15000(H04)	23	120	8.9	0.33	(335,0.2%) (365,23%)	16.6	365	370	—	—

continued

Material(UNS)	$T/℃$	E_T	ρ	υ	(σ,ε)	α	k	γ	ρ_E	K_{IC}
C15000(H08)	−269	—	—	—	(445,0.2%) (590, 36%)	—	—	—	—	—
	−196	—	—	—	(450,0.2%) (535,26%)	—	—	—	—	—
	23	120	8.9	0.33	(410,0.2%) (445,16%)	16.6	365	370	—	—
Cu-0.22Zr-0.035 Si(H06)	23	—	8.9	0.33	(120,2%) (155,5%) (260, 20%) (380, 100%)	16.6	322	370	—	—
	300	—	—	—	(65,2%) (100,5%) (180, 20%) (300, 100%)	—	—	—	—	—
	700	—	—	—	(50,2%) (65,5%) (100, 20%) (150, 100%)	—	—	—	—	—
C15715(MMC; Cu-0.15Al/0.28 Al$_2$O$_3$) Glidcop 15)	23	130	8.9	0.34	(250,0.2%) (410,2%)	16.6	365	390	—	—
	250	—	—	—	(130,0.2%) (390,2%)	17.8	320	—	—	—
	400	—	—	—	(105,0.2%) (145,2%)	—	—	—	—	—
	500	—	—	—	(80,0.2%) (100,2%)	—	—	—	—	—
	600	—	—	—	(40,0.2%) (55,2%)	—	—	—	—	—
	1083(T_m)	—	—	—	—	—	—	—	—	—

continued

Material(UNS)	$T/^{\circ}C$	E_T	ρ	v	(σ,ε)	α	k	γ	ρ_E	K_{IC}
C15725(MMC; Cu-0.25Al/0.5 Al$_2$O$_3$)Glidcop 25)	23	130	8.86	0.34	(392,0.2%) (475, 5.5%)	16.6	344	390	—	—
	400	—	—	—	(152,0.2%) (172,1.2%)	—	—	—	—	—
	600	—	—	—	(48,0.2%) (66, 13.6%)	—	—	—	—	—
	1083(T_m)	—	—	—	—	—	—	—	—	—
C15760 (Tempered; Glidcop 60)	23	130	8.81	0.34	(621,0.2%) (689,9%)	16.6	322	390	—	—
	1083(T_m)	—	—	—	—	—	—	—	—	—
C15760 Cu/1.1 Al$_2$O$_3$;MMC; lidcop 60)	23	130	8.81	0.34	(413,0.2%) (525, 13%)	16.6	322	390	—	—
C16200(O;Cu-1Cd-...;Grain size: 0.050 mm)	23	117	8.89	0.34	(48,0.2%) (240, 57%)	16.7	360	380	—	—
	100	—	—	—	—	17	—	—	—	—
	300	—	—	—	—	17.7	—	—	—	—
	1076(T_m)	—	—	—	—	—	—	—	—	—
C16200(O;Grain size: 0.025 mm)	23	117	8.89	0.34	(83,0.2%) (250, 57%)	16.7	360	380	—	—
	100	—	—	—	—	17	—	—	—	—
	300	—	—	—	—	17.7	—	—	—	—
C16200(H01)	23	117	8.89	0.34	(310,0.2%) (400, 12%)	16.7	360	380	—	—
C16200(H04)	23	117	8.89	0.34	(474,0.2%) (505,9%)	16.7	360	380	—	—
C17000(ST;Cu-1.7Be)	23	128	8.4	0.3	(220,0.2%) (480, 45%)	16.7	107	420	—	—
	982(T_m)	—	—	—	—	—	—	—	—	—
C17000(TH04; Aged)	23	128	8.4	0.3	(1000,0.2%) (1035,7%)	16.7	107	420	—	—

continued

Material(UNS)	$T/°C$	E_T	ρ	υ	(σ,ε)	α	k	γ	ρ_E	K_{IC}
C17200(F;Cu-1.9Be-0.2Co-0.2 Al-0.2Si)	23	123	8.25	0.34	(221,0.2%) (483, 45%)	16.7	118	420	—	28
	200	—	—	—	—	17.0	131	—	—	—
	300	—	—	—	—	17.8	—	—	—	—
	980(T_m)	—	—	—	—	—	—	—	—	—
C17200 (TH02; Plate)	23	123	8.25	0.34	(1207,0.2%) (1344,3%)	16.7	118	420	—	28
	200	—	—	—	—	17.0	131	—	—	—
	300	—	—	—	—	17.8	—	—	—	—
C17200(TH04)	23	123	8.25	0.34	(1241,0.2%) (1379,2%)	16.7	118	420	—	28
C17200(TM00)	23	123	8.25	0.34	(565,0.2%) (724, 20%)	16.7	118	420	—	28
C17200(TM02)	23	123	8.25	0.34	(724,0.2%) (833, 15%)	16.7	118	420	—	28
C17200(TM05)	23	123	8.25	0.34	(860,0.2%) (1030,9%)	16.7	118	420	—	28
C17200(TM06)	23	123	8.25	0.34	(1020,0.2%) (1158,7%)	16.7	118	420	—	28
C17200(TM08)	23	123	8.25	0.34	(1103,0.2%) (1255,6%)	16.7	118	420	—	28
C17300(TH04; Cu-1.9Be)	23	117	8.25	0.34	(1000,0.2%) (1350,7%)	16.7	118	420	—	—
	980(T_m)	—	—	—	—	—	—	—	—	—
C17400(F)	23	117	8.75	0.3	(172,0.2%) (310, 28%)	16.7	118	420	—	—
	1029(T_m)	—	—	—	—	—	—	—	—	—
C17400(TH04; Cu-Be-Co)	23	117	8.75	0.3	(758,0.2%) (793,14%)	16.7	118	420	—	—
C17460(TH04; Cu-0.3Be-1.2Co-...)	23	117	8.75	0.3	(896, 15%)	16.7	222	420	—	—

continued

Material(UNS)	$T/℃$	E_T	ρ	v	(σ,ε)	α	k	γ	ρ_E	K_{IC}
C17500(Obsolete in automotive application)										
C17510(TF00; Cu-0.4Be-1.8Ni)	23	117	8.83	0.3	(620,0.2%) (790, 18%)	17	240	420	—	—
	1040(T_m)	—	—	—	—	—	—	—	—	—
C17510(TH04)	23	117	8.83	0.3	(740,0.2%) (845,14%)	17	240	420	—	—
C18000(H04)	23	128	8.82	0.3	(520,0.2%) (655,14%)	17	208	385	—	—
C18070(O)	23	117	—	—	—	—	310	—	—	—
C18100(H02)	23	117	8.82	0.33	(345,0.2%) (415, 25%)	17	323	385	—	—
C18135(TH01; Cu-Cr-Ag-Cd)	23	130	8.84	0.33	(483, 10%)	17	300	380	—	—
	1080(T_m)	—	—	—	—	—	—	—	—	—
C18150(TB00; Cu-1Cr-0.15Zr)	23	117	8.89	0.34	(380,0.5%)	17	323	386	—	—
	1070(T_m)	—	—	—	—	—	—	—	—	—
C18200(TB00; Cu-0.9Cr)	23	117	8.89	0.34	(130,0.2%) (235, 40%)	17	322	386	—	—
	1070(T_m)	—	—	—	—	—	—	—	—	—
C18200(TF00; Rod OD=100 mm)	23	117	8.89	0.34	(280,0.2%) (390, 30%)	17	322	386	—	—
C18200(TF00; Rod OD=12.7 mm)	23	117	8.89	0.34	(380,0.2%) (480, 20%)	17	322	386	—	—
C18200(84% Cold-worked≈ H08)	23	117	8.89	0.34	(520,0.2%)	17	322	386	—	—
C18400	23	117	8.89	0.34	—	17	175	—	—	—
	1070(T_m)	—	—	—	—	—	—	—	—	—
C19210(O)	23	117	—	—	—	—	350	—	—	—

continued

Material(UNS)	$T/℃$	E_T	ρ	υ	(σ,ε)	α	k	γ	ρ_E	K_{IC}
C19400(O)	23	117	8.9	0.34	(165,0.2%) (310, 32%)	16.3	262	380	—	—
	200	—	—	—	—	—	—	390	—	—
	300	—	—	—	—	17.6	—	410	—	—
C19400(H02)	23	130	8.9	0.34	(345,0.2%) (400,9%)	16.3	262	380	—	—
C21000(O; Cu-5Zn; Brass)	23	125	8.86	0.31	(75,0.2%) (240, 45%)	17	234	380	—	—
	$1065(T_m)$	—	—	—	—	—	—	—	—	—
C21000(H02)	23	125	8.86	0.31	(220,0.2%) (290, 25%)	17	234	380	—	—
	300	—	—	—	(37,0.2%) $\sigma_{uts}=160$	18	—	—	—	—
	500	—	—	—	(31,0.2%) $\sigma_{uts}=90$	—	—	—	—	—
C21000(H08)	23	125	8.86	0.31	(345,0.2%) (385,5%)	17	234	380	—	—
	300	—	—	—	(250,0.2%) (270, 15%)	18	—	—	—	—
C21000(H10)	23	125	8.86	0.31	(380,0.2%) (420,4%)	17	234	380	—	—
C22000(O;90Cu-10Zn)	−196	—	—	—	(91,0.2%) (385, 86%)	—	—	—	—	—
	23	123	8.8	0.33	(60,0.2%) (260, 56%)	17.2	180	377	—	—
	$1045(T_m)$	—	—	—	—	—	—	—	—	—
C22000(H00)	23	123	8.8	0.33	(100,0.2%) (310, 25%)	17.2	180	377	—	—
C22000(H08)	23	123	8.8	0.33	(400,0.2%) (600,2%)	17.2	180	377	—	—

continued

Material (UNS)	$T/°C$	E_T	ρ	v	(σ, ε)	α	k	γ	ρ_E	K_{IC}
C23000 (H00; 85Cu-15Zn)	−269	125	—	—	(130, 0.2%) (490, 82%)	—	—	—	—	—
	−196	123	—	—	(115, 0.2%) (430, 63%)	—	—	—	—	—
	23	120	8.75	0.33	(100, 0.2%) (280, 48%)	17.5	151	380	—	—
	1025 (T_m)	—	—	—	—	—	—	—	—	—
C23000 (H02)	23	120	8.75	0.33	(338, 0.2%) (393, 12%)	17.5	151	380	—	—
C23000 (H04)	23	120	8.75	0.33	(434, 0.2%) (580, 3%)	17.5	151	380	—	—
C23000 (H08)	23	120	8.75	0.33	(550, 0.2%) (725, 3%)	17.5	151	380	—	—
C24000 (H00; Cu-20Zn)	23	117	8.66	0.33	(50, 0.2%) (247, 52%)	17.8	140	380	—	—
	1025 (T_m)	—	—	—	—	—	—	—	—	—
C24000 (H02)	23	117	8.66	0.33	(138, 0.2%) (345, 46%)	17.8	140	380	—	—
C24000 (H04)	23	117	8.66	0.33	(345, 0.2%) (421, 18%)	17.8	140	380	—	—
C24000 (H08)	23	117	8.66	0.33	(600, 0.2%) $\sigma_{uts} = 860$	17.8	140	380	—	—
C26000 (O; Cu-30Zn)	23	114	8.53	0.33	(120, 0.2%) (340, 57%)	18.8	125	375	—	200
	955 (T_m)	—	—	—	—	—	—	—	—	—
C26000 (O; NH_4OH (pH7): Stress-corrosion Cracking)	23	114	8.53	0.33	—	18.8	125	375	—	1
C26000 (H00; HT at 200 °C)	23	114	8.53	0.33	(275, 0.2%) (700, 48%)	18.8	125	375	—	—

continued

Material(UNS)	$T/℃$	E_T	ρ	υ	(σ,ε)	α	k	γ	ρ_E	K_{IC}
C26000(H00; HT at 700 ℃)	23	114	8.53	0.33	(275,0.2%) (300, 48%)	18.8	115	375	—	—
C26000(H02)	23	114	8.53	0.33	(300,0.2%) (480, 30%)	18.8	125	375	—	—
	450	—	—	—	(45,0.2%)	—	—	—	—	—
	600	—	—	—	(15.5,0.2%)	—	—	—	—	—
	700	—	—	—	(7,0.2%)	—	—	—	—	—
C26000(Bearing Grade)	23	114	8.53	0.33	$\sigma_{uts}=-1000$; (450,0.2%) (500,16%)	18.8	125	375	—	—
C26000(H04)	23	114	8.53	0.33	(430,0.2%) (520,8%)	18.8	125	375	—	—
C26000(H08; Screw Brass)	23	114	8.53	0.33	(635,0.2%) (895,3%)	18.8	115	375	—	—
	300	—	—	—	—	19.9	—	—	—	—
C27000(O;65Cu-35Zn)	23	108	8.47	0.33	(150,0.2%) (360, 54%)	19.1	115	377	—	—
	930(T_m)	—	—	—	—	—	—	—	—	—
C27000(H04; Yellow Brass)	23	108	8.47	0.33	(414,0.2%) (510,8%)	19.1	115	377	—	—
C27200	23	105	8.45	0.33	—	19.2	121	380	—	—
C28000(O;60Cu-40Zn)	23	103	8.4	0.33	(145,0.2%) (372, 45%)	19.5	123	377	—	—
	905(T_m)	—	—	—	—	—	—	—	—	—
C28000(H04; Muntz Brass)	23	103	8.4	0.33	(345,0.2%) (480, 10%)	19.5	123	377	—	—
C35000(O)	23	103	8.5	0.31	(110,0.2%) (320, 54%)	20	115	377	—	—
	916(T_m)	—	—	—	—	—	—	—	—	—
C35000(H04)	23	103	8.5	0.31	(450,0.2%) (580,5%)	20	115	377	—	—

continued

Material(UNS)	$T/℃$	E_T	ρ	υ	(σ,ε)	α	k	γ	ρ_E	K_{IC}
C36000(O;Free-cut brass)	23	97	8.5	0.31	(125,0.2%) (340, 50%)	20	115	377	—	—
	899(T_m)	—	—	—	—	—	—	—	—	—
C36000(H04)	23	97	8.5	0.31	(310,0.2%) (390, 20%)	20	115	377	—	—
C42500	23	120	8.75	0.33	—	17.4	120	377	—	—
C43500(O;Cu-18Zn-0.9Sn)	23	110	8.66	0.33	(124,0.2%) (340, 50%)	19	110	377	—	—
	1004(T_m)	—	—	—	—	—	—	—	—	—
C43500(H04)	23	110	8.66	0.33	(470,0.2%) (550,7%)	19	110	377	—	—
C44300(O)	−269	112	—	—	(145,0.2%) (542, 92%)	—	—	—	—	—
	−196	107	—	—	(130,0.2%) (445, 98%)	—	—	—	—	—
	23	101	8.66	0.33	(45,0.2%) (310, 86%)	19	110	377	—	—
C46400(O;Cu-39Zn-0.7Sn)	−269	104	—	—	(300,0.2%) (685, 40%)	—	—	—	—	—
	−196	102	—	—	(262,0.2%) (554, 44%)	—	—	—	—	—
	23	100	8.41	0.33	(210,0.2%) (435, 37%)	21	116	377	—	—
	899(T_m)	—	—	—	—	—	—	—	—	—
C46400(H04)	23	100	8.41	0.33	(400,0.2%) (480,17%)	21	116	377	—	—
C50500(O;Cu-1.3Sn-0.19P)	23	117	8.89	0.33	(100,0.2%) (275, 48%)	17.8	208	377	—	—
	1077(T_m)	—	—	—	—	—	—	—	—	—
C50500(H04)	23	117	8.89	0.33	(345,0.2%) (450,8%)	17.8	208	377	—	—

continued

Material(UNS)	$T/^{\circ}C$	E_T	ρ	v	(σ,ε)	α	k	γ	ρ_E	K_{IC}
C51000(O;Cu-5Sn-0.2P)	23	110	8.86	0.33	(140,0.2%) (340, 18%)	17	90	377	—	—
	250	—	—	—	—	18.2	—	—	—	—
	1049(T_m)	—	—	—	—	—	—	—	—	—
C51000(H02)	23	110	8.86	0.33	(350, 35%)	17	90	377	—	—
C51000(CD; 85% spring)	−269	113	—	—	(690,0.2%) (800, 34%)	—	—	—	—	—
	−196	115	—	—	(615,0.2%) (725, 34%)	—	—	—	—	—
	23	110	8.86	0.33	(495,0.2%) (534, 18%)	17	90	377	—	—
C51000(H04)	23	110	8.86	0.33	(550,0.2%) (580,7%)	17	90	377	—	—
C51000(H08) (Spring temper; if wire diameter < 0.6 mm)	23	110	8.86	0.33	(850,0.2%) $\sigma_{uts}=965$	17	90	377	—	—
C51000(H08) (Spring temper; if 0.6 mm < wire diameter < 1.5 mm)	23	110	8.86	0.33	$\sigma_{uts}=895$	17	90	377	—	—
C51000(H08) (Spring temper; if wire diameter > 1.5 mm)	23	110	8.86	0.33	$\sigma_{uts}=860$	17	90	377	—	—
C51100(O; Cu-4Sn-0.2P)	23	115	8.85	0.33	(150,0.2%) (300, 47%)	17	113	377	—	—
	300	—	—	—	—	17.8	—	—	—	—
	1050(T_m)	—	—	—	—	—	—	—	—	—

continued

Material(UNS)	$T/{}^\circ\mathrm{C}$	E_T	ρ	υ	(σ,ε)	α	k	γ	ρ_E	K_IC
C51100(H02)	23	115	8.85	0.33	(310,0.2%) (345, 22%)	17	113	377	—	—
C51100(H04)	23	115	8.85	0.33	(520,0.2%) (550,8%)	17	113	377	—	—
C51100(H08)	23	115	8.85	0.33	(650,0.2%) (680,3%)	17	113	377	—	—
C51900(O;Cu-6Sn-0.2P-…)	23	112	8.84	0.33	(150,0.2%) (340, 45%)	17.5	70	377	—	—
	300	—	—	—	—	18	—	—	—	—
	930(T_m)	—	—	—	—	—	—	—	—	—
C51900(H02)	23	112	8.84	0.33	(385, 40%)	17.5	70	377	—	—
C51900(H04)	23	112	8.84	0.33	(580,0.2%) (610, 13%)	17.5	70	377	—	—
C52100(O;Cu-8Sn-0.2P)	23	110	8.8	0.35	(170,0.2%) (480, 70%)	17.5	65	377	—	—
	954(T_m)	—	—	—	—	—	—	—	—	—
C52100(H02)	23	110	8.8	0.35	(450,0.2%) (550, 33%)	17.5	65	377	—	—
C52100(H04)	23	110	8.8	0.35	(660,0.2%) (700,9%)	17.5	65	377	—	—
C52100(H06)	23	110	8.8	0.35	(930,0.2%) (965,6%)	17.5	65	377	—	—
C52100(10M)	23	110	8.8	0.35	(830,0.2%) (895,7%)	17.5	65	377	—	—
C52400(O)	23	110	8.77	0.35	(180,0.2%) (434, 68%)	18.2	50	377	—	—
	999(T_m)	—	—	—	—	—	—	—	—	—
C52400(H04)	23	110	8.77	0.35	(680,0.2%) (740, 10%)	18.2	50	377	—	—
C54400(O; Cu-4Sn-4Sn-4Pb)	23	105	8.89	0.35	(130,0.2%) (300, 50%)	17.2	87	377	—	—
	954(T_m)	—	—	—	—	—	—	—	—	—

continued

Material(UNS)	$T/℃$	E_T	ρ	υ	(σ,ε)	α	k	γ	ρ_E	K_{IC}
C54400(H04)	23	105	8.89	0.35	(275,0.2%) (400, 24%)	17.2	87	377	—	—
C54400(H08)	23	105	8.89	0.35	(400,0.2%) (475, 20%)	17.2	87	377	—	—
C61000(O;Cu-8Al-…)	23	117	7.78	0.31	(120,0.2%) (360, 45%)	17.8	69	375	—	—
	1041(T_m)	—	—	—	—	—	—	—	—	—
C61000(H04)	23	117	7.78	0.31	(190,0.2%) (415, 30%)	17.8	69	375	—	—
C61300(O)	23	115	8.93	0.31	(240,0.2%) (540, 42%)	16.2	56.5	375	—	—
C61300(H04;Cu-7Al-2.5Fe)	23	115	8.93	0.31	(400,0.2%) (585, 35%)	16.2	56.5	375	—	—
	1045(T_m)	—	—	—	—	—	—	—	—	—
C61400(O; Cu-7Al-2Fe)	−269	112	—	—	(565,0.2%) (930, 52%)	—	—	—	—	—
	−196	112	—	—	(480,0.2%) (730, 52%)	—	—	—	—	—
	23	110	7.7	0.33	(240,0.2%) (540, 42%)	16.2	68	377	—	—
	1046(T_m)	—	—	—	—	—	—	—	—	—
C61400(H04)	23	110	7.7	0.33	(370,0.2%) (550, 38%)	16.2	68	377	—	—
C62300(F; Cu-10Al-3Fe)	23	117	7.67	0.31	(240,0.2%) (520, 35%)	16.2	54	377	—	—
	1046(T_m)	—	—	—	—	—	—	—	—	—
C62300(H04)	23	117	7.67	0.31	(330,0.2%) (635, 28%)	16.2	54	377	—	—
C62400(H03)	23	117	7.67	0.31	(360,0.2%) (700,14%)	16.2	54	377	—	—

continued

Material(UNS)	$T/℃$	E_T	ρ	υ	(σ,ε)	α	k	γ	ρ_E	K_{IC}
C63000(F; Cu-10Al-3Fe-5Ni)	23	121	7.6	0.31	(415,0.2%) (690, 15%)	16.2	39	377	—	—
	1054(T_m)	—	—	—	—	—	—	—	—	—
C63000(H04)	23	121	7.6	0.31	(517,0.2%) (814, 15%)	16.2	39	377	—	
C64200(O; Cu-7Al-1.8Si)	23	110	7.7	0.33	(380,0.2%) (620, 28%)	18	45	377	—	—
	1004(T_m)	—	—	—	—	—	—	—	—	—
C64200(H04)	23	110	7.7	0.33	(470,0.2%) (700, 22%)	18	45	377	—	—
C64400(O)	23	110	7.7	0.33	(190,0.2%) (410, 22%)	18	45	377	—	—
	−269	163	—	—	(825,0.2%) (935, 31%)	—	—	—	—	—
	−196	160	—	—	(790,0.2%) (850, 24%)	—	—	—	—	—
C64700(Aged)	23	145	7.7	0.33	(720,0.2%) (780, 15%)	18	45	377	—	—
C65100(O)	23	117	8.75	0.34	(103,0.2%) (276, 50%)	17.8	57	377	—	—
	1004(T_m)	—	—	—	—	—	—	—	—	—
C65100(H08)	23	117	8.75	0.34	(460,0.2%) (620, 12%)	17.8	57	377	—	—
C65400(O)	23	117	8.55	0.33	(310,0.2%) (524, 45%)	17.5	36	377	—	—
	1018(T_m)	—	—	—	—	—	—	—	—	—
C65400(H08)	23	117	8.53	0.33	(690,0.2%) (786,5%)	17.5	36	377	—	—
	−269	121	—	—	(250,0.2%) (700, 70%)	—	—	—	—	—

continued

Material(UNS)	$T/\mathrm{°C}$	E_{T}	ρ	v	(σ,ε)	α	k	γ	ρ_{E}	K_{IC}
C65400(H08)	−196	111	—	—	(220,0.2%) (615, 70%)	—	—	—	—	—
C65500(O;Cu-3.3Si-0.9Mn)	23	105	8.53	0.33	(200,0.2%) (430, 55%)	18	36	377	—	—
	1027(T_{m})	—	—	—	—	—	—	—	—	—
C65500(H02)	23	103	8.53	0.33	(310,0.2%) (538,17%)	18	36	377	—	—
C65500(H08)	23	103	8.53	0.33	(410,0.2%) (720,6%)	18	36	377	—	—
C66420(H04;Cu-14Zn-0.9Fe)	23	122	8.75	0.33	(270,0.2%) (579,17%)	16.5	35	380	—	—
	300	—	—	—	—	19	—	—	—	—
C66420(H06)	23	122	8.75	0.33	(270,0.2%) (662,7%)	16.5	35	380	—	—
	300	—	—	—	—	19	—	—	—	—
C66420(Brazed)	23	122	8.75	0.33	(270,0.2%) (400, 30%)	17	30	380	—	—
C67300(Bearing)	23	110	8.93	0.33	(455,0.2%) (586,16%)	18	34	377	—	—
C68800	23	112	8.23	0.33	—	18.6	78	380	—	—
C70250(TM02;Cu-3Ni-Si-Mg)	23	131	8.82	0.33	(675,0.2%) (745,7%)	16.5	172	380	—	—
	100	—	—	—	—	16.7	—	—	—	—
	300	—	—	—	—	17.6	—	—	—	—
C70250(TM04)	23	131	8.82	0.33	(725,0.2%) (770,5%)	16.5	172	380	—	—
C70350(TM02;Cu-1Ni-1Co-Si)	23	131	8.82	0.33	(730,0.2%) (760,5%)	16.5	200	380	—	—
	100	—	—	—	—	16.7	—	—	—	—
	300	—	—	—	—	17.6	—	—	—	—
C70350(TM04)	23	131	8.82	0.33	(778,0.2%) (816,4%)	16.5	200	380	—	—

continued

Material(UNS)	$T/\mathrm{°C}$	E_{T}	ρ	υ	(σ,ε)	α	k	γ	ρ_{E}	K_{IC}
C70350(TM06)	23	131	8.82	0.33	(825,0.2%) (860,1%)	16.5	200	380	—	—
C70400(O;Cu-5.5Ni-1.5Fe-0.6Mn)	23	117	8.94	0.33	(83,0.2%) (260, 41%)	17.5	64	377	—	—
	$1121(T_{\mathrm{m}})$	—	—	—	—	—	—	—	—	—
C70400(H04)	23	117	8.94	0.33	(430,0.2%) (440,5%)	17.5	64	377	—	—
	−269	141	—	—	(172,0.2%) (556, 53%)					
	−196	134	—	—	(170,0.2%) (500, 50%)					
C70600(O;Cu-10Ni-1.4Fe-...)	23	124	8.94	0.33	(148,0.2%) (340, 37%)	17.1	45	377	—	—
	$1149(T_{\mathrm{m}})$	—	—	—	—	—	—	—	—	—
C70600(H04)	23	124	8.94	0.33	(390 0.2%) (415, 10%)	17.1	45	377	—	—
C71000(O; Cu-21Ni-...)	23	138	8.94	0.33	(90,0.2%) (352, 35%)	16.4	36	377	—	—
	$1199(T_{\mathrm{m}})$	—	—	—	—	—	—	—	—	—
C71000(H02)	23	138	8.94	0.33	(427,0.2%) (469,8%)	16.4	36	377	—	—
C71000(H04)	23	138	8.94	0.33	(490,0.2%) (505,5%)	16.4	36	377	—	—
C71000(H08)	23	138	8.94	0.33	(538,0.2%) (586,3%)	16.4	36	377	—	—
C71500(O;Cu-30Ni-1Mn-Fe)	−269	160	—	—	(275,0.2%) (720, 48%)					
	−196	159	—	—	(220,0.2%) (620, 52%)					
	23	152	8.93	0.33	(130,0.2%) (400, 47%)	16.4	29	380	—	—
	$1238(T_{\mathrm{m}})$	—	—	—	—	—	—	—	—	—
C71500(H04)	23	150	8.93	0.33	(390,0.2%) (414, 10%)	16.4	29	380	—	—

continued

Material(UNS)	$T/$℃	E_T	ρ	v	(σ,ε)	α	k	γ	ρ_E	K_{IC}
C71500(H08)	23	150	8.93	0.33	(480,0.2%) (580,3%)	16.4	29	380	—	—
C72150(O;Cu-44Ni-1Mn)	23	121	8.93	0.33	(125,0.2%) (315, 18%)	16.4	29	410	—	—
	1200(T_m)	—	—	—	—	—	—	—	—	—
C72200(O61)	23	118	8.94	0.33	(130,0.2%) (320, 45%)	15	35	—	—	—
C72200(H04; Bearing)	23	118	8.94	0.33	(450,0.2%) (490,6%)	15	35	—	—	—
C72900 (Spinodal- hardened)	23	128	8.94	0.32	(725,0.2%) (845,9%)	16.4	38	380	—	—
C74400(O;64Cu-3Ni-Fe-Pb-33Zn)	23	103	8.93	0.33	(115,0.2%) (350, 70%)	17	120	377	—	—
C74400(Brazed)	23	103	8.93	0.33	(105,0.2%) (340, 75%)	17	120	377	—	—
C74500(O;65Cu-10Ni-25Zn)	23	121	8.7	0.33	(140,0.2%) (365, 43%)	16.4	45	380	—	—
	1021(T_m)	—	—	—	—	—	—	—	—	—
C74500(H08)	23	121	8.7	0.33	(525,0.2%) (655,3%)	16.4	45	380	—	—
C75200(O;Cu-18Ni-17Zn)	23	124	8.75	0.33	(170,0.2%) (400, 40%)	16	33	380	—	—
	1110(T_m)	—	—	—	—	—	—	—	—	—
C75200(H08)	23	124	8.75	0.33	(510,0.2%) (590,3%)	16	33	380	—	—
C75400(O;65Cu-15Ni-20Zn)	23	124	8.7	0.33	(124,0.2%) (365, 43%)	16	36	380	—	—
	1077(T_m)	—	—	—	—	—	—	—	—	—

continued

Material(UNS)	$T/^\circ\text{C}$	E_T	ρ	υ	(σ,ε)	α	k	γ	ρ_E	K_IC
C75400(H08)	23	124	8.7	0.33	(545,0.2%) (635,2%)	16	36	380	—	—
C75700(O;Cu-12Ni-23Zn)	23	124	8.67	0.33	(125,0.2%) (360, 48%)	17	40	380	—	—
	1065(T_m)	—	—	—	—	—	—	—	—	—
C75700(H08)	23	124	8.67	0.33	(545,0.2%) (640,2%)	17	40	380	—	—
C76400(O;Cu-18Ni-20Zn)	23	130	8.73	0.33	—	16.7	30	380	—	—
	1105(T_m)	—	—	—	—	—	—	—	—	—
C77000(O;Cu-18Ni-27Zn)	23	130	8.7	0.33	(185,0.2%) (415, 40%)	16.7	30	380	—	
	1100(T_m)	—	—	—	—	—	—	—	—	—
C77000(H08)	23	130	8.7	0.33	(621,0.2%) (745,2%)	16.7	30	380	—	—
C80010(Mold cast;Cu>99.95%)	23	117	8.94	0.33	(60,0.2%) (170, 40%)	16.4	391	394	—	—
	1083(T_m)	—	—	—	—	—	—	—	—	—
C80410 Centrifugal-cast; Cu>99%)	23	117	8.94	0.33	(55,0.2%) (170, 25%)	16.6	315	394	—	—
	1083(T_m)	—	—	—	—	—	—	—	—	—
C81500(SC;ST & Aged)	23	132	8.1	0.33	(275,0.2%) (350,17%)	16.6	315	377	—	—
	1085(T_m)	—	—	—	—	—	—	—	—	—
C82000(O;Cu-6Be-2.6Co)	23	117	8.9	0.34	(140,0.2%) (345, 20%)	17.8	218	420	—	—
C82000(H04)	23	117	8.9	0.34	(517,0.2%) (689,8%)	17.8	218	420	—	—
C82700(SC;ST & Aged)	23	132	8.1	0.33	(895,0.2%) (1070,2%)	16.5	123	420	—	—
	954(T_m)	—	—	—	—	—	—	—	—	—

continued

Material(UNS)	$T/℃$	E_T	ρ	υ	(σ,ε)	α	k	γ	ρ_E	K_{IC}
C82800(F)	23	127	8.3	0.34	(345,0.2%) (550, 10%)	22	95	420	—	—
C83300(SC)	23	93	8.83	0.34	(70,0.2%) (215, 35%)	17.5	72	377	—	—
C83600(SC)	23	95	8.9	0.34	(115,0.2%) (255, 30%)	19	72	377	—	—
C84400(SC; Valve Copper)	23	90	8.7	0.33	(100,0.2%) (235,26%)	17.5	72	377	—	—
	1010(T_m)	—	—	—	—	—	—	—	—	—
C84800(SC; Plumbing)	23	90	8.69	0.33	(100,0.2%) (255, 35%)	17.5	72	377	—	—
	954(T_m)	—	—	—	—	—	—	—	—	—
C85400(SC)	23	83	8.44	0.33	(90,0.2%) (260, 35%)	20	88	377	—	—
	941(T_m)	—	—	—	—	—	—	—	—	—
C85200(SC)	23	76	8.5	0.33	(90,0.2%) (260, 35%)	20	84	377	—	—
C85400(SC)	23	83	8.44	0.33	(90,0.2%) (260, 35%)	20	88	377	—	—
	941(T_m)	—	—	—	—	—	—	—	—	—
C85500(SC)	23	103	8.33	0.34	(160,0.2%) (414, 40%)	20.5	116	377	—	—
	900(T_m)	—	—	—	—	—	—	—	—	—
C86100(SC)	23	103	8	0.33	(345,0.2%) (655, 20%)	21	36	375	—	—
	1199(T_m)	—	—	—	—	—	—	—	—	—
C86200(SC; Cu-25Zn-4Al-3Fe-3.7Mn)	23	103	8	0.34	(330,0.2%) (655, 20%)	21	36	377	—	—
	941(T_m)	—	—	—	—	—	—	—	—	—

continued

Material(UNS)	$T/{}^{\circ}\!C$	E_T	ρ	υ	(σ, ε)	α	k	γ	ρ_E	K_{IC}
C86300(SC;Cu-25Zn-6.2Al-3Fe-3.7Mn)	23	98	7.83	0.34	(427,0.2%) (754,14%)	21	36	377	—	—
	923(T_m)	—	—	—	—	—	—	—	—	—
C86400(SC)	23	97	8.33	0.34	(170,0.2%) (450, 15%)	20	88	377	—	—
C86500(SC)	23	103	8.33	0.34	(200,0.2%) (490, 30%)	20	86	377	—	—
	880(T_m)	—	—	—	—	—	—	—	—	—
C86700(SC)	23	103	8.33	0.34	(290,0.2%) (585, 20%)	19	86	377	—	—
	880(T_m)	—	—	—	—	—	—	—	—	—
C86800(SC)	23	100	8.1	0.32	(315,0.2%)	19	65	—	—	—
C87200(SC)	23	100	8.36	0.32	(175,0.2%)	17	28	—	—	—
C87400(SC)	23	106	8.3	0.33	(165,0.2%) (380, 30%)	19	28	377	—	—
	916(T_m)	—	—	—	—	—	—	—	—	—
C87500(SC)	23	106	8.3	0.33	(210,0.2%) (460, 21%)	18	28	377	—	—
	916(T_m)	—	—	—	—	—	—	—	—	—
C87600(SC)	23	117	8.3	0.33	(220,0.2%) (510,26%)	18	28	377	—	—
	150	—	—	—	(200,0.2%) (500,23%)	—	—	—	—	—
	300	—	—	—	(190,0.2%) (380,8%)	—	—	—	—	—
	971(T_m)	—	—	—	—	—	—	—	—	—
C87800(SC)	23	—	—	0.34	(260,0.2%) (580, 29%)	—	—	377	—	—

continued

Material(UNS)	$T/^\circ C$	E_T	ρ	v	(σ, ε)	α	k	γ	ρ_E	K_{IC}
C87850(SC)	23	105	8.3	0.33	(200,0.2%) (440, 37%)	18	38	377	—	—
	150	—	—	—	(190,0.2%) (430, 32%)	—	—	—	—	—
	300	—	—	—	(180,0.2%) (320, 28%)	—	—	—	—	—
	880(T_m)	—	—	—	—	—	—	—	—	—
C89320(SC)	23	98	8.8	0.32	(120,0.5%)	18	80	—	—	—
C89833(SC)	23	—	—	0.34	(120,0.2%) (250, 28%)	—	—	377	—	—
C90300(SC)	23	97	8.8	0.33	(145,0.2%) (310, 30%)	18	75	377	—	—
	1000(T_m)	—	—	—	—	—	—	—	—	—
C90500(SC)	23	103	8.72	0.33	(150,0.2%) (310, 25%)	20	75	377	—	—
	999(T_m)	—	—	—	—	—	—	—	—	—
C90700(SC)	23	103	8.77	0.33	(150,0.2%) (300, 20%)	18	71	377	—	—
	1015(T_m)	—	—	—	—	—	—	—	—	—
C91700(SC)	23	103	8.64	0.33	(150,0.2%) (300,16%)	16	71	377	—	—
	1015(T_m)	—	—	—	—	—	—	—	—	—
C92200(SC)	23	97	8.64	0.33	(130,0.2%) (280, 28%)	17.5	70	377		—
	150	—	—	—	(120,0.2%) (430,17%)	—	—	—		—
	300	—	—	—	(110,0.2%) (320,8%)	—	—	—		—
	988(T_m)	—	—	—	—	—	—	—	—	—

continued

Material(UNS)	$T/°C$	E_T	ρ	v	(σ,ε)	α	k	γ	ρ_E	K_{IC}
C92300(SC)	23	97	8.77	0.33	(131,0.2%) (276,16%)	17.5	75	377	—	—
	999(T_m)	—	—	—	—	—	—	—	—	—
C92700(SC)	23	110	8.78	0.33	(145,0.2%) (290, 20%)	17.5	47	377	—	—
	982(T_m)	—	—	—	—	—	—	—	—	—
C92900(SC)	23	97	8.9	0.33	(179,0.2%) (324, 20%)	17	58	377	—	—
	1039(T_m)	—	—	—	—	—	—	—	—	—
C93200(O; Bearing)	23	117	8.93	0.34	$\sigma_{ucs}=-315$; (125,0.2%) (240, 20%)	17	59	377	—	—
	100	—	—	—	—	18	—	—	—	—
C93400(SC)	23	76	8.87	0.33	(110,0.2%)	18	58	—	—	—
C93500(SC)	23	100	8.87	0.33	(110,0.2%)	18	70	—	—	—
C93600(SC)	23	77	9.05	0.33	(135,0.5%)	18.5	49	—	—	—
C93700(SC; Bearing)	23	76	8.86	0.33	(145,0.2%) (290, 20%)	17	47	377	—	—
	100	—	—	—	—	17.8	—	—	—	—
	929(T_m)	—	—	—	—	—	—	—	—	—
C93800(SC;Anti-acid)	23	73	9.25	0.33	(110,0.2%) (210, 18%)	18	52	377	—	—
	943(T_m)	—	—	—	—	—	—	—	—	—
C94100(SC)	23	75	9.3	0.33	(70,0.2%)	19	59	377	—	—
C94300(SC)	23	73	9.3	0.33	(90,0.2%) (190, 15%)	18	63	377	—	—
C95200(O;Cu-9Al)	23	105	7.64	0.33	(185,0.2%) (550, 35%)	16	50	377	—	—
	200	—	—	—	—	16.2	—	—	—	—
C95300(O)	23	106	7.6	0.33	(190,0.2%) (525, 25%)	16	—	—	—	—

continued

Material (UNS)	$T/\text{°C}$	E_T	ρ	υ	(σ,ε)	α	k	γ	ρ_E	K_IC
C95400 (O; 83Cu-11Al-4Fe-…)	23	107	7.5	0.32	(221, 0.2%) (586, 12%)	16	59	420	—	—
	200	—	—	—	—	16.2	—	—	—	—
	1038 (T_m)	—	—	—	—	—	—	—	—	—
C95400 (H04)	23	107	7.5	0.32	(310, 0.2%) (655, 10%)	16	59	420	—	—
C95500 (M02; Cu-11Al-4Fe-…)	23	120	7.53	0.34	$\sigma_\text{ucs}=-895$; (290, 0.2%) (655, 6%)	16	42	420	—	—
	300	—	—	—	—	16.2	—	—	—	—
C95800 (O)	23	114	7.64	0.32	(240, 0.2%) (585, 15%)	16	36	440	—	—
	200	—	—	—	—	16.2	—	—	—	—
	1040 (T_m)	—	—	—	—	—	—	—	—	—
C95800 (M01)	23	114	7.64	0.32	(260, 0.2%) (655, 25%)	16.2	36	440	—	—
C96200 (M01; Cu-10Ni-1.4Fe)	23	117	8.93	0.34	$\sigma_\text{ucs}=-255$; (172, 0.2%) (310, 20%)	16.2	45	385	—	—
C96300 (SC)	23	138	7.64	0.32	(380, 0.2%) (520, 10%)	16	37	375	—	—
	1199 (T_m)	—	—	—	—	—	—	—	—	—
C96400 (SC)	23	145	7.64	0.32	(260, 0.2%) (470, 28%)	16	29	375	—	—
	1238 (T_m)	—	—	—	—	—	—	—	—	—
C96900 (Spinodal-hardened)	23	128	8.94	0.32	(690, 0.2%) (735, 5%)	16	38	380	—	—
C96970 (Spinodal-hardened)	23	117	8.91	0.32	(655, 0.2%) (743, 8%)	16.2	65	380	—	—
C97300 (SC)	23	110	7.64	0.32	(120, 0.2%) (240, 10%)	16	29	375	—	—
	1040 (T_m)	—	—	—	—	—	—	—	—	—

continued

Material(UNS)	$T/℃$	E_T	ρ	υ	(σ,ε)	α	k	γ	ρ_E	K_{IC}
C97600(SC)	23	138	7.64	0.32	(165,0.2%) (310, 20%)	16	23	375	—	—
	1143(T_m)	—	—	—	—	—	—	—	—	—
C97800(SC)	23	131	8.86	0.32	(165,0.2%) (310, 20%)	17	25	375	—	—
	1180(T_m)	—	—	—	—	—	—	—	—	—
C98820(SC)	23	75	—	0.32	(65,0.2%)	16.2	80	—	—	—
C99300(SC; Incramet 800)	23	124	7.61	0.32	(380,0.2%) (655,2%)	16.2	43	420	—	—
	1077(T_m)	—	—	—	—	—	—	—	—	—
C99700(SC)	23	114	8.19	0.32	(170,0.2%) (380, 25%)	—	—	—	—	—
	902(T_m)	—	—	—	—	—	—	—	—	—
Cu-44.2Ni-1.5Mn-0.5Fe(Annealed Constantan)	23	162	8.92	0.34	(455, 45%)	14.9	23	410	—	—
	1210(T_m)	—	—	—	—	—	—	—	—	—
Cu-44.2Ni-1.5Mn-0.5Fe(CR Constantan)	23	168	8.92	0.34	(840,2%)	14.9	22.7	410	—	—
	1210(T_m)	—	—	—	—	—	—	—	—	—
Cu-0.57Co-0.32Si (H06)	23	—	8.9	0.33	—	17	322	390	—	—
	500	—	—	—	(150, 10%) (210, 60%)	—	—	—	—	—
	600	—	—	—	(210, 10%) (225, 20%)	—	—	—	—	—
Cu/2WC	23	—	—	—	(209, 10%)	—	—	—	—	—
Cu/8WC	23	—	—	—	(237,6%)	—	—	—	—	—

Notes: HT; TH=Heat-treated;

CR=Cold-rolled;

ST=Solution-treated;

F=As fabricated;

O, H02, H03, H04, H06, & H08=Annealed, ¼ hard,½ hard, hard, extra hard, & spring;

SC= Sand cast;

ETP= Electrolytic touch pitch copper, widely used copper for electronic products;

W_f= Weight fraction of particulates or fibers in a composite;

$\rho_E(\mu\Omega m)$= Electric resistivity; ρ_E= 0.0172 $\mu\Omega$m for pure copper.

Table 87.3   Fatigue ε-N Properties of Cu(Copper) Alloys

Material	$T/°C$	$d\varepsilon/dt$	σ_f'	ε_f'	b	c	K'	n'	$\sigma_f@2N_f$	R
Cu(Film; $h=$ 1.1 μm)	23	0.067 Hz	—	—	—	—	—	—	90@ 10^5	0.1
C10100(O)	−60	—	—	—	—	—	—	—	96@ $5×10^6$	—
									83@ $5×10^7$	—
									91@ $5×10^7$	—
	23	—	—	—	—	—	—	—	75@ 10^8	—
	130	—	—	—	—	—	—	—	74@ $5×10^5$	—
									69@ $5×10^6$	—
									57@ 10^7	—
C10100(H08)	−60	—	—	—	—	—	—	—	118@ $5×10^7$	—
	23	—	—	—	—	—	—	—	134@ 10^7	—
									143@ $5×10^6$	—
									166@ 10^6	—
									126@ 10^8	—
									142@ 10^7	—
									146@ $5×10^6$	—
									163@ 10^6	—
C10200(O)	23	—	—	—	—	—	—	—	75@ 10^8	—
									83@ 10^7	—
									89@ $5×10^6$	—
									99@ 10^6	—
	130	—	—	—	—	—	—	—	52@ $5×10^7$	—
									57@ 10^7	—
									60@ $5×10^6$	—
									70@ 10^6	—
C10200(H04)	23	—	—	—	—	—	—	—	90@ 10^8	—
C10200(H08)	23	—	—	—	—	—	—	—	117@ $3×10^8$	—
C10400(H08)	23	—	—	—	—	—	—	—	103@ $3×10^8$	—
C11000(H08)	23	—	—	—	—	—	—	—	117@ $3×10^8$	—
C15000(H08)	23	—	—	—	—	—	—	—	240@ $3×10^8$	—

continued

Material	$T/°C$	$d\varepsilon/dt$	σ_f'	ε_f'	b	c	K'	n'	$\sigma_f @ 2N_f$	R
C15715(H08)	23	—	—	—	—	—	—	—	$240@10^8$	—
C15715	23	—	503	0.5	−0.6	−0.085	—	—		—
C16200(TH04)	23	—	—	—	—	—	—	—	$205@3×10^8$	—
C17000(TH04)	23	—	—	—	—	—	—	—	$248@10^8$	—
C17200(TF00)	23	—	—	—	—	—	—	—	$248@10^8$	—
C17200(TH01)	23	—	—	—	—	—	—	—	$275@10^8$	—
C17200(TH02)	23	—	—	—	—	—	—	—	$300@10^8$	—
C17200(TH04)	23	—	—	—	—	—	—	—	$307@10^8$	—
C18200(H08)	23	—	—	—	—	—	—	—	$193@3×10^8$	—
C26000(O)	23	—	—	—	—	—	—	—	$97@10^8$	—
									$99@1.2×10^6$	—
									$128@4×10^5$	—
									$178@3×10^4$	—
C26000(H08)	23	—	—	—	—	—	—	—	$140@10^8$	—
C51000(H04)	23	—	—	—	—	—	—	—	$172@10^8$	—
C52100(O)	23	—	—	—	—	—	—	—	$172@10^8$	—
C52100(H04)	23	—	—	—	—	—	—	—	$200@10^8$	—
C52400(O)	23	—	—	—	—	—	—	—	$172@10^8$	—
C52400(H04)	23	—	—	—	—	—	—	—	$200@10^8$	—
C61300(H04)	23	—	—	—	—	—	—	—	$180@10^8$	—
C61400(O)	23	—	—	—	—	—	—	—	$172@10^8$	—
C62300(F)	23	—	—	—	—	—	—	—	$172@10^8$	—
C62300(H04)	23	—	—	—	—	—	—	—	$207@10^8$	—
C63000(F)	23	—	—	—	—	—	—	—	$248@10^8$	—
C63000(H04)	23	—	—	—	—	—	—	—	$255@10^8$	—
C64200(O)	23	—	—	—	—	—	—	—	$172@10^8$	—
C64200(H04)	23	—	—	—	—	—	—	—	$345@10^8$	—

continued

Material	$T/{}^\circ\mathrm{C}$	$\mathrm{d}\varepsilon/\mathrm{d}t$	σ_{f}'	$\varepsilon_{\mathrm{f}}'$	b	c	K'	n'	$\sigma_{\mathrm{f}}@2N_{\mathrm{f}}$	R
C64400(O)	23	—	—	—	—	—	—	—	$155@10^7$	—
									$196@10^6$	—
									$249@10^5$	—
									$398@10^3$	—
	300	—	—	—	—	—	—	—	$89@10^7$	—
									$127@10^6$	—
									$180@10^5$	—
									$365@10^3$	—
C84400(SC)	23	—	—	—	—	—	—	—	$76@10^8$	—
C84800(SC)	23	—	—	—	—	—	—	—	$76@10^8$	—
C86200(SC)	23	—	—	—	—	—	—	—	$100@10^8$	—
C86300(SC)	23	—	—	—	—	—	—	—	$100@10^8$	—
C86500(SC)	23	—	—	—	—	—	—	—	$138@10^8$	—
C90500(SC)	23	—	—	—	—	—	—	—	$90@10^8$	—
C90700(SC)	23	—	—	—	—	—	—	—	$172@10^8$	—
C92200(SC)	23	—	—	—	—	—	—	—	$76@10^8$	—
C93200(O)	23	—	—	—	—	—	—	—	$110@10^8$	—
C93700(SC)	23	—	—	—	—	—	—	—	$90@10^8$	—
C93800(SC)	23	—	—	—	—	—	—	—	$70@10^8$	—
C95200(O)	23	—	—	—	—	—	—	—	$150@10^8$	—
C95500(M02)	23	—	—	—	—	—	—	—	$210@10^8$	—
C95800(M01)	23	—	—	—	—	—	—	—	$214@10^8$	—
C96200(M01)	23	—	—	—	—	—	—	—	$90@10^8$	—
C96400(SC)	23	—	—	—	—	—	—	—	$124@10^8$	—
C97600(SC)	23	—	—	—	—	—	—	—	$107@10^8$	—
C97800(SC)	23	—	—	—	—	—	—	—	$108@10^8$	—
Cu Alloys	23	—	Eq. (6.14)	Eq. (6.15)	—	—	$\dfrac{\sigma_{\mathrm{f}}'}{(\varepsilon_{\mathrm{f}}')^{n'}}$	$\dfrac{b}{c}$	Eq. (87.1)	—

Notes: The fatigue strength for copper alloys is that reported for 10^8 cycles.

Table 87.4   Mechanical Creep Parameters of Cu Alloys

Material	$T/^\circ C$	Stress/MPa	Strain Rate/s^{-1}	$A/(MPa^{-n} \cdot s^{m-1})$	$Q/(J \cdot mol^{-1})$	n	m
C10100(Particle Size = 250 μm)	400	$E=1$; $15 \sim 105$	—	38.8	197000	4.8	0
C10700(Annealed; 400 μm < Particle Size < 650 μm)	193	$E=1$; $20 \sim 100$	—	1.16×10^5	197000	5.0	-0.5
C15715(MMC; Glidcop 15; Wrought; Cu-0.0028Al_2O_3)	250	$E=1$; $0 \sim 500$	$10^{-8} \sim 10^{-2}$	1.43×10^{10}	197000	2.5	-0.9
C15725(MMC; Glidcop 25; Annealed)	350	$E=1$; $70 \sim 130$	—	1.28×10^{-13}	197000	12.64	0
C17510(PH; 400 μm < Particle Size < 600 μm)	229	$E=1$; $180 \sim 372$	—	1.07×10^9	197000	2.5	-0.75
Cu-0.001Ag(Particle Size = 210 μm)	500	$E=1$; $35 \sim 65$	—	800	186000	3.8	-0.385
Cu-0.001Ag -0.005 Fe-0.015O; Particle Size = 250 μm)	600	$E=1$; $25 \sim 35$	—	6×10^{-3}	180000	4.8	-0.66
Cu-0.45Cr-0.19Zr	300	$E=1$; $110 \sim 213$	—	1.8×10^{-2}	197000	5.3	—
Cu-0.65Cr-0.1Zr (CCZ)	216	$E=1$; $\sigma_{th}=157$; $183 \sim 282$	—	7.56×10^{11}	197000	3.0	-0.92
Cu-2Cr-0.3Zr (Wought; 500 μm < Particle Size < 700 μm)	400	$E=1$; 98	—	3.25×10^{-25}	134000	15	0
Cu-2Cr-0.3Zr (Annealed; 500 μm < Particle Size < 700 μm)	400	$E=1$; 218	—	1.31×10^{-92}	112000	41	0

continued

Material	$T/°C$	Stress/MPa	Strain Rate/s^{-1}	$A/(\text{MPa}^{-n} \cdot \text{s}^{m-1})$	$Q/(\text{J} \cdot \text{mol}^{-1})$	n	m
Cu-2Cr-0.3Zr (Wrought; Particle Size = 0.7 μm)	450	$E=1$; 80~155	—	3.25×10^{-25}	235000	20	0
Cu-1.8Ni-0.4Be	229	$E=1$; 180~372	—	1.07×10^{-9}	197000	2.5	−0.75

Notes: Creep equation $= \dfrac{\mathrm{d}\varepsilon_{\text{creep}}}{\mathrm{d}t} = A\left(\dfrac{\sigma - \sigma_{\text{th}}}{E}\right)^{n} t^{m} \exp\left(\dfrac{-Q}{RT_{\text{k}}}\right), \sigma > \sigma_{\text{th}}$;

$\sigma_{\text{th}} = $ Stress threshold and $\sigma_{\text{th}} = 0$, if not specified;

$E = $ Young's modulus; If given that $E = 1$, it means E is not specified.

Table 87.5   Orthotropic Elastic Constants of Copper-based Composites

Material-DAM	$T/°C$	ρ	E_{11}	E_{22}	E_{33}	G_{12}	G_{13}	G_{23}	v_{12}	v_{13}	v_{23}
Cu/40%CF(V_f=40%; UD; Coated Pitch-Tolaran K1100)	23	6.11	—	—	—	—	—	—	—	—	—
	125	—	—	—	—	—	—	—	—	—	—

Table 87.6   Orthotropic Thermal Properties of Copper-based Composites

Material-DAM	$T/°C$	α_1	α_2	α_3	k_1	k_2	k_3	γ	β_1	β_2	β_3
Cu/40%CF(V_f=40%; UD; Coated Pitch-KT120)	23	—	—	—	215	150	150	—	—	—	—
	125	10	17	17	—	—	—	—	—	—	—
Cu/40%CF(V_f=40%; UD; Coated PAN-T300)	23	—	—	—	215	110	110	—	—	—	—
	50	—	—	—	—	—	—	450	—	—	—
	100	—	—	—	225	120	120	—	—	—	—
	250	—	—	—	240	140	140	520	—	—	—
Cu/50%Gr(V_f=50%; UD; Graphite: P100 Short Fibers)	23	—	—	—	—	—	—	—	—	—	—
	527	—	—	—	380	115	115	580	—	—	—
Cu/35%Gr(V_f=35%; UD; Graphite: P100 Short Fibers)	23	—	—	—	—	—	—	—	—	—	—
	527	—	—	—	350	110	110	650	—	—	—

Notes: α_1, α_2, α_3(μm/m/°C) = Coefficients of linear thermal expansion of a unidirectional lamina;

k_1, k_2, k_3(W/m/°C) = Thermal conductivities of a unidirectional lamina;

β_1, β_2, β_3(μm/m/%) = Swelling coefficients of linear moisture expansion;

γ (J/kg/°C) = Specific heat capacity.

Table 87.7 Mechanical Properties of a Generic Copper-Based Heat Exchanger

Material	$T/^\circ C$	E_T	ρ	v	(σ, ε)	α	k	γ	ρ_E	K_{IC}
Fins (Cu-0.2 Cr)	23	120	8.95	0.33	$\sigma_{uts} = 330$	16.5	377	377	—	—
	260	—	—	—	$\sigma_{uts} = 270$	—	—	—	—	—
	1083 (T_m)	—	—	—	—	—	—	—	—	—
Tubes (Cu-14Zn-1Fe)	23	113	8.53	0.33	$\sigma_{uts} = 435$	19.9	120	377	—	—
	260	—	—	—	$\sigma_{uts} = 290$	—	—	—	—	—
	925 (T_m)	—	—	—	—	—	—	—	—	—
Headers (Cu-33Zn-3Ni)	See C74400 in Table 87.2									
Tanks (Cu-33Zn-3Ni)	See C74400 in Table 87.2									
Supports (Cu-33Zn-3Ni)	See C74400 in Table 87.2									
Joints (74.9Cu-4.2Ni-15.6Sn-5.3P as Paste; or 77.2Cu-7Ni-9.3Sn-6.5P as Foil)										

Chapter 88

Li (Lithium)

88.1 Introduction

Li (Lithium) is used in lithium-based batteries because of its high electrochemical potential, as a typical Li cell can generate approximately 3.3 volts (nominal value), compared with 2.1 volts for lead/acid and 1.5 volts for zinc-carbon cells. Because of its low atomic mass, it has a high charge- and power-to-weight ratio. The energy of $LiFePO_4$ batteries is significantly lower than $LiCoO_2$, although much higher than nickel-metal hydride batteries with regard to safety and lifespan. A major competitor to $LiFePO_4$ is $LiMn_2O_4$ (lithium manganese spinel), which General Motor has chosen to use for the Chevrolet Volt, a gasoline-electric hybrid vehicle. The cathodes of lithium batteries are made with the above materials, and the anodes are generally made of carbon/ graphite. Performance comparisons of different Li-based battery properties are given as follows:

Cell Performance	$LiFePO_4$	$LiCoO_2$	$LiMn_2O_4$	$LiNiMnCoO_2$
Rated Voltage/V	3.2	3.7	3.8	3.6
Charging Voltage/V	3.7	4.2	4.2	4.2
Discharging End Voltage/V	2.0	3.0	2.5	2.5
Energy Density (Wh/kg)	90~110	140~145	105~115	140~155
Power-Weight Density	Acceptable	Good	Acceptable	Best
Life Cycles (Charge Times)	1800	700	500	700
Self-discharge Rate/%	0.05	1	5	1
High Temperature (> 55 ℃)	Excellent	Good	Acceptable	Good
Low Temperature (<−20 ℃)	OK	OK	OK	OK
High-rate Discharge (10 A)	Excellent	NA	Good	Good
Safety (e. g. Explosion)	Excellent	Bad	Good	Good

Lithium batteries are disposable (primary) batteries with lithium or its compounds as an anode. Lithium batteries are not to be confused with lithium-ion batteries. Newly developed rechargeable Li-based batteries include lithium polymer battery, lithium iron phosphate battery, and the nanowire thin-film battery. Lithium batteries are one of the great successes of modern materials electrochemistry. Mechanical properties of Li (Lithium) and Li-based compounds are listed in Tables 88.1 and 88.2, respectively for isotropic and orthotropic materials.

A lithium-ion battery consists of a lithium-ion intercalation negative electrode (anode)-such as graphite and binary lithium alloys and a lithium-ion intercalation positive electrode (cathode)- generally lithium metal oxides such as $Li(Fe, X)PO_4$, $Li(Ni, Mn)O_2$, and $LiCoO_2$. The overall electrochemical reaction follows the equation

$$Li_x C_6 + Li_{(1-x)} MO_2 \rightleftharpoons C_6 + LiMO_2$$

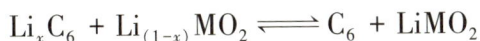

The discharge process is the lithium-ion moves out of the intercalated carbon and into another lithium intercalation compound.

88.2   LiCoO₂

Electrode sheets and the separator sheets are laminated onto each other, as cells are put in series.

Li-ion polymer sheets may delaminate due to expansion at a high level of state of charge (SOC). During discharge on load, the load has to be removed as soon as the voltage drops below a certain level of voltage (e. g.3.0 V per cell), or else the battery will subsequently no longer accept a full charge and may experience problems holding voltage under load. Electric circuitry for protective cut-off is required for both over-voltage and under-voltage. A typical Li-ion polymer battery is constructed as:

> Anode (Negative electrode): $LiCoO_2$ (or $LiMn_2O_4$);
> Separator: Conducting polymer electrolyte (e. g., polyethylene Oxide, PEO, PMMA);
> Cathode (Positive electrode): Li or carbon-Li intercalation compound.

Typical chemical reactions of a lithium-ion polymer battery are:

> Anode (Negative electrode): $Li_{1-x}CoO_2 + x\ Li^+ + xe^- \longrightarrow LiCoO_2$
> Separator: Li+conduction
> Cathode (Positive electrode): Carbon-$Li_x \longrightarrow C + xLi^+ + xe^-$

Small capacity Li-ion (polymer) batteries containing lithium cobalt oxide ($LiCoO_2$), also known as LCO batteries, offer a genuinely viable option for electronics and digital applications. Most lithium batteries (Li-ion) used in computers, communication, and consumer electronics, are mostly $LiCoO_2$ batteries. So far, the best choice for electrode reactions for commercial Li-ion batteries is Li intercalation compounds such as $LiCoO_2$ for cathode material and graphite for anode material. Performance indices of a Li-ion polymer battery are identified as follows:

> (a) Nominal cell voltage: 3.6 Volts, varying from 2.7 Volts (empty) to 4.23 Volts (full);
> (b) Specific energy: 130~200 Wh/kg;
> (c) Energy density: 300 Wh/L;
> (d) Specific power: 7.1 kW/kg;
> (e) Self-discharge rate: 5% per month;
> (f) Charge/discharge efficiency: 99.8%;
> (g) Cycle durability: 1000 times;
> (h) Time durability: 3 years.

Nanostructured porous materials based on Li (Lithium) for cathodes and anodes in advanced energy conversion and storage devices are promising alternatives-tuning the electrode material morphology or texture to obtain porous and high-surface-area electrodes constitutes another route to enhance electrode capacities. Nanostructured Li-Si and Li-Ge exhibit the highest reversible electrochemical capacities yet reported for an alloy electrode.

88.3 $LiFePO_4$

Lithium iron phosphate ($LiFePO_4$), also known as LFP, has become the material of choice in commercial batteries for large capacity and high power applications, such as power tools, e-wheel chairs, e-bikes, e-cars and e-buses. Under the stress of rapid charging or heavy use, a Li-ion battery may heat very quickly, causing a fire. Lithium iron batteries stay much cooler under the same stress. Some testing has shown that lithium iron phosphate batteries can last about 2000 charge/discharge cycles, compared to perhaps 1500 for Li-ion batteries. A typical lithium iron phosphate ($LiFePO_4$) battery is constructed as:

Anode (Negative electrode) : $LiFe(II)PO_4$;
Separator: Conducting polymer electrolyte (e. g., polyethylene Oxide, PEO, PMMA);
Cathode (Positive electrode) : Li or carbon-Li intercalation compound.

Typical chemical reactions of a typical lithium iron phosphate ($LiFePO_4$) battery are:

Anode (Negative electrode) : $Li_{1-x}CoO_2 + xLi^+ + xe^- \longrightarrow LiCoO_2$
Separator: Li+conduction
Cathode (Positive electrode) : Carbon-LiFe(II)$PO_4 \longrightarrow C + Fe(III)PO_4 + Li + e^-$

88.4 $LiNbO_3$ (Lithium Niobate)

Stoichiometric $LiNbO_3$ (Lithium Niobate) exhibits potentially attractive optical and piezoelectric properties at elevated temperatures. The combination of excellent electro-optical, acoustooptical and nonlinear optical properties makes an attractive host material for application in integrated optics.

88.5 Anodes

Silicon and carbon (graphite) are two widely used anode materials. Silicon electrodes swell to three times their normal size when ions flow into them during charging, then return to normal size upon release of the ions in discharge. Tests found that the electrodes lasted ten times longer when coated with a polymer, which repairs cracks in just a few hours.

References

ARČON D, et al, 2004. A Comparative Study of Magnetic Properties of $LiFePO_4$ and $LiMnPO_4$[J]. Journal of Physics: Condensed Matter, 16(30): 5531-5548.

ARICO, ANTONINO SALVATORE, et al, 2005. Nanostructured Materials for Advanced Energy Conversion and Storage Devices[J]. Nature Materials, 4(5):366-377.

ARVIND, 2009. Preparation, Structural and Thermo-Mechanical Properties of Lithium Aluminum Silicate Glass-Ceramics[J]. Ceramics International, 35(4):1661-1665.

BAZITO F, et al, 2007. Synthesis and Characterization of Two Ionic Liquids with Emphasis on Their Chemical Stability towards Metallic Lithium[J]. Electrochimica Acta, 52(23):6427-6437.

BORGES R S, MIQUITA D R, SILVA G G, 2011. Electrochemical Study of Double-Walled Carbon Nanotube Electrode/Block Polyether-Lithium Bis (trifluorosulphonyl) imide Salt Polymer Electrolyte Interface [J]. Electrochimica Acta, 56(12):4650-4656.

CHOI S, 2004. Fabrication and Characterization of a $LiCoO_2$ Battery-Supercapacitor Combination for a High-Pulse Power System[J]. Journal of Power Sources, 138(1-2):360-363.

DUDNEY N J, 2005. Solid-state Thin-film Rechargeable Batteries[J]. Materials Science and Engineering, B, 116(3):245-249.

FANG W, et al, 2010. Electrochemical-Thermal Modeling of Automotive Li-ion Batteries and Experimental Validation using a Three-Electrode Cell[J]. International Journal of Energy Research, 34(2):107-115.

FU L J, et al, 2006. Surface Modifications of Electrode Materials for Lithium Ion Batteries[J]. Solid State Sciences, 8(2):113-128.

GRAETZ J, et al, 2003. Highly Reversible Lithium Storage in Nanostructured Silicon[J]. Electrochemical and Solid-State Letters, 6(9):A194-A197.

GURGA A, et al, 2007. The Mechanical Properties of Lithium Tetraborate (100), (011) and (112) Faces [J]. Material Letters, 6(3):770-773.

HAMID N, et al, 2012. High-Capacity Cathodes for Lithium-ion Batteries from Nanostructured $LiFePO_4$ Synthesized by Highly-flexible and Scalable Flame Spray Pyrolysis[J]. Journal of Power Sources, 216:76-83.

HUGGINS R A, 2009. Advanced Batteries: Materials Science Aspects[M]. Springer.

JUNG Y, et al, 2010. Enhanced Stability of $LiCoO_2$ Cathodes in LithiumIon Batteries Using Surface Modification by Atomic Layer Deposition[J]. Journal of The Electrochemical Society, 157(1): A75-A81.

KAMAYA N, et al, 2011. A Lithium Superionic Conductor[J]. Nature Materials, 10(9):682-686.

KANG B, CEDER G, 2009. Battery Materials for Ultrafast Charging and Discharging[J]. Nature Materials, 458(12):190-193.

KUSHIBIK J, et al, 2005. Ultrasonic Microspectroscopy of Congruent $LiNbO_3$ Crystals[J]. Journal of Applied Physics, 98(12):123507.

MIZUSHIMA K, et al, 1981. $Li_xCoO_2(0<x<1)$: A New Cathode Material for Batteries of High Energy Density [J]. Solid State Ionics, 3-4:171-174.

NADHERNA M, et al, 2009. Electrochemical Behavior of Li_2FeSiO_4 with Ionic Liquids at Elevated Temperature [J]. Journal of Electrochemistry Society, 156(7), A619-A626.

PADHI A, et al, 1997. Phospho-olivines as Positive-Electrode Materials for Rechargeable Lithium Batteries [J]. Journal of Electrochemical Society, 144(4):1188-1194.

QI Y, et al, 2014. Lithium Concentration Dependent Elastic Properties of Battery Electrode Materials from First Principles Calculations[J]. Journal of Electrochemical Society, 161(11): F3010-F3018.

RUFFLO R, et al, 2009. Electrochemical Behavior of $LiCoO_2$ as Aqueous Lithium-Ion Battery Electrodes[J]. Electrochemistry Communications, 11(2):247-249.

SAITO YURIA, 2006. Lithium Electrolyte Design on the Basis of Ion Dynamics Measurements and Analyses [J]. Japan Journal of Polymer Science and Technology, 63(1):41-53.

SCROSATI B, GARCHE J, 2010. Lithium Batteries: Status, Prospects and Future [J]. Journal of Power Sources, 195(9):2419-2430.

TOKUDA H, et al, 2006. Design of Polymer Electrolytes to Realize High Lithium-Ionic Conductivity with Fast Interfacial Charge Transfer[J]. Japanese Journal of Polymer Science and Technology, 63(1):1-10.

WOODFORD W, CHIANG Y, CARTER W, 2010. Electrochemical Shock of Intercalation Electrodes: A Fracture Mechanics Analysis[J]. Journal of Electrochemical Society, 157(10):A1052-A1059.

YU S, et al, 2011. Physical and Electrochemical Properties of $LiFePO_4/C$ Cathode Material Prepared from a New Carbon Source[J]. Advanced Materials Research, 160/162:1654-1658.

ZHAO K J, PHARR M, VLASSAK J J, et al, 2010. Fracture of Electrodes in Lithiumion Batteries Caused by Fast Charging[J]. Journal of Applied Physics, 108(7):073517.

Table 88.1   Mechanical Properties of Li（Lithium）and Li-Based Compounds

Material	$T/^\circ\text{C}$	E_T	ρ	υ	(σ,ε)	α	k	γ	ρ_E	K_{IC}
Li（Bulk）	23	4.91	0.534	0.25	—	56	84.7	3600	—	—
	$180.7(T_m)$	—	—	—	—	—	—	—	—	—
Li（Nano BCC）	23	70	—	0.25	—	—	—	—	—	—
	$180.7(T_m)$	—	—	—	—	—	—	—	—	—
LiO_2	23	141	2.013	0.18	—	25.9	14.5	1686	—	—
	327	133	—	—	—	31.1	8.1	2485	—	—
	727	123	—	—	—	38	5.1	2767	—	—
	927	118	—	—	—	41.4	4.3	2860	—	—
	$1432(T_m)$	—	—	—	—	—	—	—	—	—
LiFePO_4（Cathode）	23	171	—	0.28	—	—	—	—	—	—
Mn_2O_4	23	231	—	0.22	—	—	—	—	—	—
LiMn_2O_4（Cathode）	23	253	—	0.26	—	—	—	—	—	—
LiNiMnCoO_2（Cathode）	23	—	—	—		—	—	—	—	—
LiCoO_2（Cathode）	23	325	—	0.23	—	—	—	—	—	—
Li(NiCo)O_2（Cathode）	23	—	—	—	—	—	—	—	—	—
LiNbO_3（LN；Cathode）	23	—	—	—	—	2.1	38	—	—	—
	$1160(T_c)$	—	—	—	—	—	—	—	—	—
	$1250(T_m)$	—	—	—	—	—	—	—	—	—
LiTi_2O_4（Cathode）	23	239	—	0.19	—	—	—	—	—	—
$\text{Li}_{2.25}$-Al（Bulk）	23	69	—	0.34	—	—	—	—	—	—
$\text{Li}_{3.5}$-Si（Nano）	23	—	—	—	（500,0.2%）（750, 12%）	—	—	—	—	—
$\text{Li}_{3.75}$-Si（Bulk）	23	83	—	0.18	—	—	—	—	—	—
$\text{Li}_{3.5}$-Sn（Bulk）	23	71	—	—	—	—	—	—	—	—
Silicon（Anode）	23	60	—	0.23	—	—	—	—	—	—

continued

Material	$T/°C$	E_{T}	ρ	υ	(σ,ε)	α	k	γ	ρ_{E}	K_{IC}
Separator(PP+ …)	23	—	—	—	—	—	—	—	—	—

Table 88.2   Orthotropic Mechanical Properties of Li-ion Batteries-Related Alloys

Specification	$T/°C$	ρ	E_{11}	E_{22}	E_{33}	G_{12}	G_{13}	G_{23}	υ_{12}	υ_{13}	υ_{23}
Graphite	23	0.6	615	334	48	—	—	—	0.19	0.2	0.32
LiC_6	23	—	566	129	44	—	—	—	0.18	0.19	0.24
CoO_2	23	—	156	93	26	—	—	—	0.34	0.32	0.22

Chapter 89

Mg (Magnesium)

89.1 Introduction

Magnesium alloys are designated by the top two alloying ingredients-aluminum and zinc, besides magnesium itself. For example, AZ31B means that the alloy contains 3% of aluminum and 1% of zinc. The possible first two letters are selected from the major alloying element as follows (ASTM):

A-Aluminum

B-Bismuth

C-Copper

D-Cadmium

E-Rare Earths

F-Iron

H-Thorium

J-Strontium

K-Zirconium

L-Lithium

M-Manganese

N-Nickel

P-Lead

Q-Silver

R-Chromium

S-Silicon

T-Tin

V-Gadolinium

W-Yttrium

X-Calcium

Y-Antimony

Z-Zinc

The last letter "B' in "AZ31B" is employed to present the variation of chemical ingredients or just chronological order of availability.

Mg (Magnesium) is the lightest structural metal of that the density is 1.74 g/cm^3. Its Young's modulus is 45 GPa which is relatively low as a family member of metal. Due to its low rigidity, magnesium parts can be formed using injection molding machines at elevated temperatures, ranging from 200 ℃ to 315 ℃. Mechanical properties of some magnesium alloys are listed in Table 89.1. Note that the strength data given in the table may be taken from thick specimens and the tensile strength is higher if derived from thinner test specimens. Magnesium alloys usually have lower compressive strength than their tensile strength.

When alloyed, Mg has the highest strength-to-weight ratio of all the structural metals. The fatigue strength (endurance limit) of a magnesium alloy with a fatigue cutoff cycle of 10^6 is approximately 35% of its ultimate tensile strength,

$$\sigma_f = 0.35\ \sigma_{uts} \tag{89.1}$$

Fatigue and creep parameters of Mg alloys are listed in Tables 89.2 and 89.3, respectively.

Thin-walled magnesium components optimize heat transfer with the excellent thermal conductivity of magnesium ($k = 72$ W/m · K), supporting the needs of miniaturization and efficient thermal management. Corrosion protection of such components made of magnesium-based alloys is required, as untreated magnesium has poor corrosion resistance.

89.2　Applications

Mg (Magnesium) is one of the earth's most abundant elements and recyclable. It is the third most commonly used structural metal, following steel and aluminum. Typical uses of magnesium and its alloys include seat frames, instrument panels, steering wheels, engine cradles, and transmission components. AZ91D is the most widely specified die casting alloy.

High strength magnesium alloys (e. g. WE43) are extensively used for helicopter gear casings at a working temperature up to 200 ℃.

References

AGNEW S R, DUYGULU O, 2005. Plastic Anisotropy and the Role of Non-Basal Slip in Magnesium Alloy AZ 31B[J]. International Journal of Plasticity, 21(6):1161-1193.

ALAN A, LUO, 2003. Recent Magnesium Alloy Development for Automotive Powertrain Applications[J]. Materials Science Forum, 419/422:57-66.

ALBINMOUSA J, JAHED H, LAMBERT S, 2011. Cyclic Behaviour of Wrought Magnesium Alloy under Multiaxial Loading[J]. International Journal of Fatigue, 33(11):1403-1416.

ALBINMOUSA J, et al, 2010. Monotonic and Fatigue Behavior of Magnesium Extrusion Alloy AM30: An International Benchmark Test in the Magnesium Front End Research and Development Project[J]. SAE 2010-01-0407.

ALBINMOUSA J, JAHED H, LAMBERT S, 2011. Cyclic Axial and Cyclic Torsional Behavior of Extruded AZ31B Magnesium Alloy[J]. International Journal of Fatigue, 33(8):1127-1139.

BAI J, et al, 2006. Microstructure and Tensile Creep Behavior of Mg-4Al Based Magnesium Alloys with Alkline Earth Elements Sr and Ca Additions[J]. Materials Science and Technology, A, 419(1-2):181-188.

BAG A, ZHOU W, 2011. Tensile and Fatigue Behavior of AZ91D Magnesium Alloy[J]. Journal of Material Sciences Letters, 20(5):457-459.

BAKKE P, et al, 2005. Powertrain Components-Opportunity for the Die Cast AE Family Alloys[J]. SAE 2004-01-0655.

BARRY N, et al, 2009. Effect of Shot Peening on the Fatigue Behavior of Cast Magnesium A8[J]. Materials Science and Engineering, A, 507 (2):50-57.

BEGUM S, et al, 2009. Low Cycle Fatigue Properties of an Extruded AZ31 Magnesium Alloy[J]. International Journal of Fatigue, 31(4):726-735.

BOEHLERT C J, 2007. The tensile and creep behavior of Mg-Zn Alloys with and without Y and Zr as ternary elements[J]. Journal of Materials Science, 42(10):3675-3684.

BOEHLERT C, KNITTEL K, 2006. The Microstructure, Tensile Properties, and Creep Behavior of Mg-Zn Alloys Containing 0-4.4% Zn[J]. Material Science and Engineering, A,417(1-2):315-321.

BRONFIN B, et al, 2007. High Performance HPDC Alloys as Replacements for A380 Aluminum Alloy[J]. Magnesium Technology, (Editors: Beals, Luo, Neelameggham, and Pekguleryuz), Warrendale, PA, USA: TMS, 2007:35-49.

CHAMOS A N, et al, 2008. Tensile and Fatigue Behavior of Wrought Magnesium Alloys AZ31 and AZ61[J]. Fatigue & Fracture of Engineering Materials & Structures, 31(9):812-821.

CHEN Z, et al, 2011. The Effect of Thermomechanical Processing on the Tensile, Fatigue, and Creep Behavior of Magnesium Alloy AM60[J]. Metallurgical and Materials Transactions, A, 42(5):1386-1399.

CHINO Y, et al, 2002. Mechanical Properties and Press Formability at Room Temperature of AZ31 Mg Alloy Processed by Single Roller Drive Rolling[J]. Materials Transactions, 43(10):2554-2560.

CIZEK L, et al, 2009. Structure and Mechanical Properties of Mg-Si Alloys at Elevated Temperatures[J]. Journal of Achievements in Materials & Manufacturing Engineering, 35(1):37-46.

CIZEK L, et al, 2006. Mechanical Properties of Magnesium Alloy AZ91 at Elevated Temperatures[J]. Journal of Achievements in Materials & Manufacturing Engineering,18(1):203-206.

CIZEK L, et al, 2006. Study of Selected Properties of Magnesium Alloy AZ91 after Heat Treatment and Forming [J]. Journal of Materials Processing Technology, 157-158:466-471.

COLE G S, 2007. Summary of "Magnesium vision 2020: A North American Automotive Strategic Vision for Magnesium"[C]. 2007 TMS Annual Meeting: Symposium on Magnesium Technology, 35-40.

DAUD M, AHADLIN M, 2012. Plane Strain Fracture Toughness Determination for Magnesium Alloy[J].

Journal of Mechanical Engineering and Technology, 4(2):45-51.

DEFORCE B, 2011. Cold Spray Al-5% Mg Coatings for the Corrosion Protection of Magnesium Alloys[J]. Journal of Thermal Spray Technology, 20(6):1352-1358.

DONG J, et al, 2011. Surface Characteristics and High Cycle Fatigue Performance of Shot Peened Magnesium Alloy ZK60[J]. Journal of Metallurgy, 2011:1-9.

ELIEZER A, et al, 2001. Corrosion Fatigue of Die-Cast and Extruded Magnesium Alloys[J]. Journal of Light Metals, 1(3):179-186.

ESPARZA J A, et al, 2002. Friction-Stir Welding of Magnesium Alloy AZ31B[J]. Journal of Material Science Letters, 21(12):917-920.

FENG A H, MA Z Y, 2007. Enhanced Mechanical Properties of Mg-Al-Zn Cast Alloy via Friction Stir Processing[J]. Scripta Mater, 56(5):397-400.

GU X, et al, 2010. Degradation and Cytoxicity of Lotus-Type Porous Pure Magnesium as Potential Tissue Engineering Scaffold Material[J]. Material Letters. , 64(17):1871-1874.

HASEGAWA S, TSUCHIDA Y, YANO H, et al, 2007. Evaluation of Low Cycle Fatigue Life in AZ31B-F Magnesium Alloy[J]. International Journal of Fatigue, 29(9-11):1839-1845.

ITOI T, et al, 2010. Tensile Property and Cold Formability of an Mg96Zn2Y2 Alloy Sheet with a Long-Period Ordered Phase[J]. Materials Letters, 64(21):2277-2280.

JAI POINERN G, BRUNDAVANAM S, FAWCETT D, 2012. Biomedical Magnesium Alloys: A Review of Material Properties, Surface Modifications and Potential as a Biodegradable Orthopaedic Implant [J]. American Journal of Biomedical Engineering, 2(6):218-240.

JONES, et al, 2007. Ballistic Evaluation of Magnesium Alloy AZ31B[J]. ARL-TR-4077, US Army Research Laboratory.

KOHLERA B, et al, 2011. Endurance Limit of Die-Cast Magnesium Alloys AM50hp and AZ91hp Depending on Type and Size of Internal Cavities[J]. International Journal of Fatigue, 44:51-60.

LABELLE P, 2002. New Aspects of Temperature Behavior of AJ52X, Creep Resistance Magnesium Alloys[J]. SAE 2002-01-0079.

LAPOVOK R, et al, 2005. Processing Routes Leading to Superplastic Behavior of Magnesium Alloy ZK60[J]. Materials Science and Engineering, A, 410/411:390-393.

LICHY P, CAGALA M, 2012. Microstructure and Thermomechanical Properties of Magnesium Alloys Castings [J]. Archives of Foundry Engineering, 12(2):49-54.

LIN J Z, LANKA S, RUDEN T, 2005. Physical and Virtual Prototyping of Magnesium Instrument Panel Structures[J]. SAE 2005-01-0726.

LIN X, CHEN D, 2008. Strain Controlled Cyclic Deformation Behavior of an Extruded Magnesium Alloy[J]. Materials Science and Engineering, A, 496:106-113.

LIU J, et al, 2009. Deformation Behavior of AZ31 Magnesium Alloy during Tension at Moderate Temperature [J]. Journal of Materials Engineering and Performance, 18(7):966-972.

LIU W C, et al, 2009. High Cycle Fatigue Behavior of As-extruded ZK60 Magnesium Alloy[J]. Journal of Materials Science, 44(11):2916-2924.

LULAY J, WERT C, 1957. Internal Friction in Alloys of Mg and Cd[J]. Acta Metallurgical Sinica, 4(6):627-631.

LV F, et al, 2011. Effect of Hysteresis Energy and Mean Stress on Low Cycle fatigue of Extruded Magnesium [J]. Scripta Materialia, 65(1):53-56.

MILLER W K, 1991. Creep of Die Cast AZ91 Magnesium at Room Temperature and Low Stress [J]. Metallurgical Transactions, A, 22(4):873-877.

MIRZA F A, 2013. Low Cycle Fatigue of a Rare-Earth Containing Extruded Magnesium Alloy[J]. Materials Science and Engineering, A, 575:65-73.

MORDIKE B, EBERT T, 2001. Magnesium Properties-Applications-Potential [J]. Material Science and Engineering, A,302(1):37-45.

MOSCOVITCH N, et al, 2005. The Effect of High Pressure Die Casting Process Characteristics on the Properties and Performance of Advanced Mg Alloys[J]. Magnesium Technology:357-363.

NODA M, et al, 2009. Evolution of Mechanical Properties and Microstructure in Extruded Mg96Zn2Y2 Alloys by Annealing[J]. Materials Transactions, 50(11):2526-2531.

NYBERG E A, et al, 2000. High Temperature-creep Resistant Magnesium Alloys: Advances in Thixomolding Automotive Components[J]. SAE 2000-01-1126.

PANTELAKIS S, ALEXOPOULOS N, CHAMOS A, 2007. Mechanical Performance Evaluation of Cast Magnesium Alloys for Automotive and Aeronautical Applications[J]. Journal of Engineering Materials and Technology, 129:422-430.

PEKGULERYYUZ M O, KAYA A A, 2003. Creep Resistant Magnesium Alloys for Powertrain Applications[J]. Advanced Engineering Materials, 5(12):866-878.

PERSHAUD-SHARMA D, et al, 2013. Mechanical Properties and Tensile Failure Analysis of Novel Bio-absorbable Mg-Zn-Cu and Mg-Zn-Se Alloys for Endovascular Applications[J]. Metals, 3(1):23-40.

RENNER F, ZENNER H, 2002. Fatigue Strength of Die-Cast Magnesium Components[J]. Fatigue & Fracture of Engineering Materials and Structures, 25(12):1157-1168.

SCHUMANN S, FRIEDRICH H, 2003. Current and Future Use of Magnesium in the Automobile Industry[J]. Material Science Forum, 419-422:50-51.

SCHWANEKE A E, NASH R W, 1971. Effect of Preferred Orientation on the damping Capacity on Magnesium Alloys[J]. Metallurgical Transaction, 2(12):3453-3457.

SHEN G, XU S, 2007. Finite Element Simulation of Bolted Joints and Magnesium Bolt-Load Retention Behavior [J]. SAE 2007-01-1032.

SHIH T, LIU W, CHEN Y, 2002. Fatigue of As-Extruded AZ61A Magnesium Alloy[J]. Materials Science and Engineering, A,325(1-2):152-162.

SHOOK S O, 1990. Fabricating a Magnesium Part-An Overview[J]. SAE 900790.

SOHN K Y, et al, 1998. Bolt-load Retention Behavior of Die-Cast AZ91D and AE42 Magnesium[J]. SAE 980090.

SKLENICKA V, et al, 2000. Damage and Fracture in Creep of Magnesium Alloy-based Composites[J]. Key Engineering Materials, 593:171-174.

SOMEKAWA H, MUKAI T, 2007. High Strength and Fracture Toughness Balance on the Extruded Mg-Ca-Zn Alloy[J]. Materials Science and Engineering, A, 459(1-2):366-370.

SONG G, ATRENS A, 1999. Corrosion Mechanisms of Magnesium Alloys[J]. Advanced Engineering Materials Reviews,1(1):11-33.

SONSINO C, DIETERICH K, 2006. Fatigue Design with Cast Magnesium Alloys under Constant and Variable Amplitude Loading[J]. International Journal of Fatigue, 28(3):183-193.

SUGIMOTO K, et al, 1977. A Study of Damping Capacity in Magnesium Alloys[J]. Transactions of Japan Institute of Metals, 18(3):277-288.

SUN Z Z, et al, 2008. Gating System Design for a Magnesium Alloy Casting[J]. Journal of Materials Science and Technology, 24(1):93-95.

TOKAJI K, et al, 2004. Fatigue Behavior and Fracture Mechanism of a Rolled AZ31 Magnesium Alloy[J]. International Journal of Fatigue, 26(11):1217-1224.

UNIGOVSKI Y, et al, 2003 "Corrosion Fatigue of Extruded Magnesium Alloys[J]. Materials Science and Engineering, A, 360(1-2):132-139.

WANG L, et al, 2010. XPS Study of the Surface Chemistry on AZ31and AZ91 Magnesium Alloys in Dilute NaCl Solution[J]. Applied Surface Science, 256(20):5807-5812.

WESTPHAL K, et al, 2005. Joining of Magnesium Components Using Al Fasteners (AL 6056)[J]. Light Metal Age, 63(2):1-3.

XIE G M, et al, 2007. Microstructural Evolution and Mechanical Properties of Friction Stir Welded Mg-Zn-Y-Zr Alloy[J]. Materials Science and Engineering, 471(1-2):63-68.

XUI S, et al, 2006. Bolt-load Retention Testing of Magnesium Alloys for Automotive Applications[J]. SAE

2006-01-0072.

XUE Y, et al, 2006. Micro-structure Based Fatigue Modeling of a Cast AE44 Magnesium Alloy[J]. International Journal of Fatigue, 29(4):666-676.

YU Q, et al, 2011. Multiaxial Fatigue of Extruded AZ61A Magnesium Alloy[J]. International Journal of Fatigue, 33(3):437-447.

ZELIN M G, et al, 1992. Interaction of High-Temperature Deformation Mechanisms in Magnesium Alloy with Mixed Fine and Coarse Grains[J]. Metallurgical Transactions, 23A:3135-3140.

ZHANG P, LINDEMANN J, 2005. Influence of Shot Peening on High Cycle Fatigue Properties of the High-Strength Wrought Magnesium Alloy AZ80[J]. Scripta Materialia, 52(6):485-490.

ZHANG P, 2004. Creep Behavior of the Die-cast Mg-Al Alloy AS21[J]. Scripta Materialia, 52(4):277-282.

Table 89.1　Mechanical Properties of Mg (Magnesium) Alloys

Material	$T/^\circ\text{C}$	E_T	ρ	υ	(σ,ε)	α	k	γ	ρ_E	K_{IC}
Mg (> 99%)	23	45	1.75	0.35	(41,0.2%) (165,14%)	27	171	1013	—	—
	150	—	—	—	(50,0.2%) $\sigma_{uts}=62$	—	—	—	—	—
	650(T_m)	—	—	—	—	—	—	—	—	—
AE42	23	45	1.79	0.35	(136,0.2%) (240, 11%)	26	84	1020	—	—
	150	—	—	—	(95,0.2%) (155,17%)	—	—	—	—	—
	175	—	—	—	(81,0.2%) (121,23%)	—	—	—	—	—
	200	—	—	—	$\sigma_{uts}=95$	—	—	—	—	—
AE44(Mg-4Al-...)	23	45	1.82	0.35	(136,0.2%) (240, 11%)	26	84	1020	—	—
	150	—	—	—	(115,0.2%) (162, 19%)	—	—	—	—	—
	175	—	—	—	(110,0.2%) (150, 25%)	—	—	—	—	—

continued

Material	$T/^\circ\mathrm{C}$	E_T	ρ	υ	(σ,ε)	α	k	γ	ρ_E	K_IC
AEM510(Mg-5Al-1RE-0.4 Mn)	23	45	—	0.35	$\sigma_\mathrm{ucs}=-310$ $(-66,-0.2\%)$; $(72,0.2\%)$ $\sigma_\mathrm{uts}=145$	—	—	—	—	—
AEM550(Mg-5Al-5RE-0.4 Mn)	23	45	—	0.35	$\sigma_\mathrm{ucs}=-327$ $(-96,-0.2\%)$; $(86,0.2\%)$ $\sigma_\mathrm{uts}=153$	—	—	—	—	—
AJ41(Mg-4Al-1Sr-0.3Mn)	23	45	—	0.35	$(82,0.2\%)$ $(166,\ 9.2\%)$	—	—	—	—	—
	175	—	—	—	$(62,0.2\%)$ $(137,\ 12.8\%)$	—	—	—	—	—
AJ42(Mg-4Al-2Sr-0.3Mn)	23	45	—	0.35	$(114,0.2\%)$ $(162,\ 5.1\%)$	—	—	—	—	—
	175	—	—	—	$(97,0.2\%)$ $(136,\ 9.8\%)$	—	—	—	—	—
AJ43(Mg-4Al-3Sr-0.3Mn)	23	45	—	0.35	$(88,0.2\%)$ $(129,\ 2.9\%)$	—	—	—	—	—
	175	—	—	—	$(57,0.2\%)$ $(105,\ 8.7\%)$	—	—	—	—	—
AJ62 (Inoculated)	23	45	—	0.35	$\sigma_\mathrm{uts}=100$		—	—	—	—
	150	—	—	—	$\sigma_\mathrm{uts}=85$		—	—	—	—
	250	—	—	—	$\sigma_\mathrm{uts}=100$		—	—	—	—
	300	—	—	—	$\sigma_\mathrm{uts}=70$		—	—	—	—
AJ62 (HPD)	23	45	—	0.35	$(119,0.2\%)$ $\sigma_\mathrm{uts}=245$	—	—	—	—	—
	150	—	—	—	$(105,0.2\%)$ $\sigma_\mathrm{uts}=165$	—	—	—	—	—
	250	—	—	—	$\sigma_\mathrm{uts}=80$	—	—	—	—	—

continued

Material	$T/°C$	E_T	ρ	υ	(σ,ε)	α	k	γ	ρ_E	K_{IC}
AJC411(Mg-4Al-1Sr-1Ca-0.3Mn)	23	45	—	0.35	(98,0.2%) (143,1.6%)	—	—	—	—	—
	175	—	—	—	(62,0.2%) (137,2.1%)	—	—	—	—	—
AJC421(Mg-4Al-2Sr-1Ca-0.3Mn)	23	45	—	0.35	(88,0.2%) (131,1.2%)	—	—	—	—	—
	175	—	—	—	(91,0.2%) (122,1.6%)	—	—	—	—	—
AM50A(DC; ASTM B93/B93M)	23	45	1.77	0.35	(120,0.2%) (260,6%)	26	65	1020	—	—
	150	—	—	—	(75,0.2%) (130, 19%)	—	—	—	—	—
AM50-7C-4Si	200	—	—	—	$\sigma_{uts}=123$		21/25	—	—	—
AM50-7C-4Si-Nd	200	—	—	—	$\sigma_{uts}=135$	—	—	—	—	—
AM60 (F;As Molded; Mg-6Al-0.1Zn-0.35Mn)	23	45	1.78	0.35	(131,0.2%) (204,6%)	26	61	1020	—	—
	150	—	—	—	(119,0.2%) (186,7%)	—	—	—	—	—
AM60 (Annealed)	23	45	1.8	0.35	(227,0.2%) (302, 19.4%)	26	61	1020	—	—
	150	—	—	—	(194,0.2%) (250, 27%)	—	—	—	—	—
AM60 (Tempered)	23	45	1.8	0.35	(336,0.2%) (367,4%)	26	61	1020	—	—
	150	—	—	—	(261,0.2%) (297,9%)	—	—	—	—	—
AM60A(DC; F)	23	45	1.8	0.35	(131,0.2%) (220,8%)	26	61	1020	—	—
AM60B(DC; ASTM B93/B93M)	23	45	1.8	0.35	(130,0.2%) (270,14%)	26	61	1020	—	—
	150	—	—	—	(90,0.2%) (145,16%)	—	—	—	—	—

continued

Material	$T/℃$	E_T	ρ	υ	(σ,ε)	α	k	γ	ρ_E	K_{IC}
AM100A（DC；As Cast）	23	45	1.78	0.35	$(83,0.2\%)$ $(150,2\%)$	25	73	1050	—	—
	$594(T_m)$	—	—	—	—	—	—	—	—	—
AM100A（DC；T6）	23	45	1.78	0.35	$(110,0.2\%)$ $(275,2\%)$	25	73	1050	—	—
AMZ（Inoculated）	23	—	—	—	$\sigma_{uts}=170$	—	—	—	—	—
	100	—	—	—	$\sigma_{uts}=155$	—	—	—	—	—
	200	—	—	—	$\sigma_{uts}=130$	—	—	—	—	—
	250	—	—	—	$\sigma_{uts}=100$	—	—	—	—	—
	300	—	—	—	$\sigma_{uts}=80$	—	—	—	—	—
AS31-1（Mg-3.43Al-0.82Si-0.31Mn-0.13Zn-…）	23	46	—	—	$(108,2\%)$	—	—	—	—	—
	100	—	—	—	$(81,1.6\%)$	—	—	—	—	—
	200	—	—	—	$(95,3.2\%)$	—	—	—	—	—
	300	—	—	—	$(62,4.2\%)$	—	—	—	—	—
	400	—	—	—	$(35,7.3\%)$	—	—	—	—	—
AS41	23	46	—	—	$(136,0.2\%)$ $(200,5.5\%)$	26	—	—	—	—
	150	—	—	—	$(94,0.2\%)$ $(153,17\%)$	—	—	—	—	—
	175	—	—	—	$(85,0.2\%)$ $(127,19\%)$	—	—	—	—	—
	200	—	—	—	$\sigma_{uts}=90$	—	—	—	—	—
AS41/20%CF（$V_f=20\%$）	23	74	1.8	—	$(155,0.2\%)$ $(187,0.5\%)$	19.5	—	—	—	—
	200	—	—	—	$(110,0.2\%)$ $(120,0.5\%)$	—	—	—	—	—
	250	—	—	—	$\sigma_{uts}=100$		—	—	—	—
AS41A（DC；F）	23	46	—	—	$(138,0.2\%)$ $(214,6\%)$	26	—	—	—	—

continued

Material	$T/℃$	E_T	ρ	υ	(σ,ε)	α	k	γ	ρ_E	K_{IC}
AZ31（O;Wrought;Mg-3Al-…）	−195	50.3	—	—	—		—	—	—	—
	−78	47.1	—	—	—		—	—	—	—
	23	44	1.74	0.35	（165,0.2%） （240,2%） （250, 10%） （260,16%）	26.8	77	1040	—	16
AZ31/（7C-4Si）	200	—	—	—	$\sigma_{uts}=127$		21/26	—	—	—
AZ31B（Extruded; F）	23	44	1.78	0.35	（136,0.2%） （252, 17.2%）	26.8	77	1040	—	16
	630（T_m）	—	—	—	—	—	—	—	—	—
AZ31B（Forged; F）	23	44	1.78	0.35	（105,0.2%） （220,17%）	26.8	77	1040	—	—
AZ31B（H24;Bulk）	23	44	1.78	0.35	（125,0.2%） （235,5%）	26.8	77	1040	—	19
AZ31B（H26;Bulk）	23	44	1.78	0.35	（145,0.2%） （240,5%）	26.8	77	1040	—	19
AZ31B（T1;Bulk）	23	44	1.78	0.35	（140,0.2%） （230, 15%）	26.8	77	1040	—	—
AZ31B（T5;Bulk）	23	44	1.78	0.35	（150,0.2%） （250, 13%）	26.8	77	1040	—	28
AZ61（O;Wrought;Mg-3Al-…）	23	43	1.8	0.35	（73,0.2%） （175,5%）	25	70	1050	—	13
AZ61（T4）	23	43	1.8	0.35	（75,0.2%） （237, 11%）	25	70	1050	—	—
AZ61A（O）	23	45	1.8	0.35	（−130,−0.2%） （230,0.2%） （310,16%）	25	70	1050	—	—
AZ63A（DC; F）	23	45	1.83	0.35	（97,0.2%） （200, 12%）	25	59	1050	—	—
	610（T_m）	—	—	—	—	—	—	—	—	—
AZ63A（DC;T4）	23	45	1.83	0.35	（97,0.2%） （270, 12%）	25	59	1050	—	—

continued

Material	$T/℃$	E_T	ρ	υ	(σ,ε)	α	k	γ	ρ_E	K_{IC}
AZ63A(FC; T6)	23	45	1.83	0.35	(130,0.2%) (275,5%)	26	59	1050	—	—
AZ63HP (DC)	23	45	1.83	0.35	(121,6%)	26	59	1050	—	—
AZ80A (O; Wrought; Mg-8.2Al-0.54Zn)	23	44	1.8	0.35	(230,0.2%) (330, 11%)	26	76	1050	—	—
	610(T_m)	—	—	—	—	—	—	—	—	—
AZ80A (T6)	23	44	1.8	0.35	(250,0.2%) (380,5%)	26	76	1050	—	—
AZ81A (SC; T4)	23	45	1.81	0.35	(69,0.2%) (234,7%)	—	—	1050	—	—
AZ91B (F; DC; Mg-9Al-1Zn-Si-Cu-Ni-...)	23	45	1.81	0.35	(159,0.2%) (234,3%)	26	65	1050	—	—
	595(T_m)	—	—	—	—	—	—	—	—	—
AZ91C (SC; F; Mg-9Al-0.7 Zn-0.3Mn-...)	23	45	1.81	0.35	(97,0.2%) (165,1.5%)	26	65	1050	—	—
	100	—	—	—	(115,1.6%)	—	—	—	—	—
	200	—	—	—	(69, 3.5%)	—	72	—	—	—
	300	—	—	—	(54, 7.5%)	—	—	—	—	—
	450	—	—	—	(25,1%)	—	—	—	—	—
AZ91C (T4)	23	45	1.81	0.35	(−90,−0.2%) (145,0.2%) (275, 15%)	26	65	1050	—	11
AZ91C(SC; T6)	23	45	1.81	0.35	(−130,−0.2%) (145,0.2%) (275,6%)	26	65	1050	—	11
	150	—	—	—	(97,0.2%) (185, 40%)	—	—	—	—	—
	240	—	—	—	(83,0.2%) (115, 40%)	—	—	—	—	—

continued

Material	$T/°C$	E_T	ρ	v	(σ,ε)	α	k	γ	ρ_E	K_{IC}
AZ91D(DC; F)	23	45	1.81	0.35	$(112,0.2\%)$ $(166,5\%)$	25.2	72	1050	—	—
	120	—	—	—	$\sigma_{crs,1380}=100$	—	—	—	—	—
	150	—	—	—	$\sigma_{crs,207}=90$	—	—	—	—	—
AZ91D (ST)	23	45	1.81	0.35	$(124,0.2\%)$ $(185,8\%)$	25.2	72	1050	—	—
AZ91D (T6; Mg-9Al-0.7Zn-0.3Mn)	23	45	1.81	0.35	$(160,0.2\%)$ $(220,5\%)$	25.2	72	1050	—	—
	150	—	—	—	$(105,0.2\%)$ $(160,16\%)$ $\sigma_{crs,1000}=80$	—	—	—	—	—
	175	—	—	—	$(89,0.2\%)$ $(138,21\%)$	—	—	—	—	—
	200	—	—	—	$\sigma_{uts}=70$; $\sigma_{crs,1000}=40$	—	—	—	—	—
	250	—	—	—	$\sigma_{uts}=110$; $\sigma_{crs,1000}=30$	—	—	—	—	—
	$596(T_m)$	—	—	—	—	—	—	—	—	—
AZ91D/20% Saffil(ST & Aged; $V_f=20\%$; Saffil:97% $Al_2O_3+3\%$ SiO_2)	23	69	—	—	$(230,0.2\%)$ $(290,2\%)$	20.5	—	—	—	—
	150	—	—	—	$\sigma_{crs,1000}=100$	—	—	—	—	—
	200	—	—	—	$\sigma_{crs,1000}=70$	—	—	—	—	—
	250	—	—	—	$\sigma_{uts}=157$; $\sigma_{crs,1000}=50$; $\sigma_{crs,10000}=40$	—	—	—	—	—
AZ91D/20% CF(T6; $V_f=20\%$)	23	63	1.9	—	$(220,0.2\%)$ $(242,0.5\%)$	19.5	140	—	—	—
	200	—	—	—	$(152,0.2\%)$ $(160,0.5\%)$	—	—	—	—	—
	250	—	—	—	$\sigma_{uts}=117$	—	—	—	—	—

continued

Material	$T/℃$	E_T	ρ	υ	(σ,ε)	α	k	γ	ρ_E	K_{IC}
AZ91E (ST; Aged)	23	45	1.81	0.35	$(175,0.2\%)$ $(245,6\%)$	26	65	1050	—	—
	$596(T_m)$	—	—	—	—	—	—	—	—	—
AZ91HP	23	45	1.81	0.35	$(175,0.2\%)$ $(245,6\%)$	26	65	1050	—	—
	$596(T_m)$	—	—	—	—	—	—	—	—	—
AZ91/Be (Inoculated)	23	45	—	0.35	$\sigma_{uts}=210$	—	—	—	—	—
	100	—	—	—	$\sigma_{uts}=200$	—	—	—	—	—
	150	—	—	—	$\sigma_{uts}=165$	—	—	—	—	—
	200	—	—	—	$\sigma_{uts}=110$	—	—	—	—	—
AZ92A(T6; SC)	23	45	1.81	0.35	$(124,0.2\%)$ $(234,1\%)$	—	—	1050	—	—
Elektron 21 (SC)	23	45	1.81	0.35	$(175,0.2\%)$ $\sigma_{uts}=280$	—	—	—	—	—
	150	—	—	—	$(185,0.2\%)$ $\sigma_{uts}=245$	—	—	—	—	—
	200	—	—	—	$(160,0.2\%)$ $\sigma_{uts}=230$	—	—	—	—	—
Elektron 675 (Wrought)	23	45	1.81	0.35	$(330,0.2\%)$ $\sigma_{uts}=434$	—	—	—	—	—
	150	—	—	—	$(290,0.2\%)$ $\sigma_{uts}=405$	—	—	—	—	—
	200	—	—	—	$(290,0.2\%)$ $\sigma_{uts}=400$	—	—	—	—	—
EZ33A (T5)	23	45	1.8	0.35	$(110,0.2\%)$ $(159,3\%)$	26.4	100	1040	—	—
	$643(T_m)$	—	—	—	—	—	—	—	—	—
HK31A (Annealed)	23	45	1.8	0.35	$(145,0.2\%)$ $(228,23\%)$	26.8	92	1000	—	—
	$651(T_m)$	—	—	—	—	—	—	—	—	—

continued

Material	$T/℃$	E_T	ρ	v	(σ, ε)	α	k	γ	ρ_E	K_{IC}
HM31A (F)	23	45	1.77	0.35	(230, 0.2%) (290, 11%)	26	104	1000	—	—
	650(T_m)	—	—	—	—	—	—	—	—	—
HM31A (T5)	23	45	1.77	0.35	(270, 0.2%) (300, 10%)	26	104	1000	—	—
Magnox(99Mg-1Al)	23	45	1.75	0.35	(41, 0.2%) (165, 14%)	27	171	1013	—	—
M1A(Mg-1.2 Mn Annealed)	23	45	1.77	0.35	(125, 0.2%) (230, 17%)	26	129	1000	—	—
	649(T_m)	—	—	—	—	—	—	—	—	—
M1A (CW; Wrought)	23	45	1.77	0.35	(180, 0.2%) (240, 7%)	26	129	1000	—	—
	649(T_m)	—	—	—	—	—	—	—	—	—
MRI 153M (Mg-Al-Ca-Sr)	23	45	1.8	0.35	(170, 0.2%) (250, 6%)	25.9	64	1090	—	—
	150	—	—	—	(135, 0.2%) (190, 17%)	—	—	—	—	—
	175	—	—	—	(125, 0.2%) (172, 22%)	—	—	—	—	—
MRI 201S (T6; Mg-Zr-Nd-Y)	23	45	1.79	0.35	(170, 0.2%) (255, 6%)	25.1	90	1050	—	—
	150	—	—	—	(165, 0.2%) (245, 10%)	—	—	—	—	—
	175	—	—	—	(165, 0.2%) (230, 11%)	—	—	—	—	—
	200	—	—	—	(155, 0.2%) (220, 15%)	—	—	—	—	—

continued

Material	$T/°C$	E_T	ρ	υ	(σ,ε)	α	k	γ	ρ_E	K_{IC}
MRI 202S(T6; Mg-Zr-Nd-Y)	23	45	1.79	0.35	(150,0.2%) (250,8%)	25.1	90	1050	—	—
	150	—	—	—	(145,0.2%) (220, 13%)	—	—	—	—	—
	175	—	—	—	(140,0.2%) (210, 11%)	—	—	—	—	—
	200	—	—	—	(135,0.2%) (200,16%)	—	—	—	—	—
MRI 230D (Mg-Al-Ca-Sr-Sn)	23	45	1.8	0.35	(180,0.2%) (245,5%)	25.1	77	1040	—	—
	150	—	—	—	(150,0.2%) (205,16%)	—	—	—	—	—
	175	—	—	—	(145,0.2%) (178, 18%)	—	—	—	—	—
QE22 (T6)	23	48	—	—	(185,0.2%) (262,5%)	26	—	—	—	—
	250	—	—	—	$\sigma_{uts}=210$; $\sigma_{crs,1000}=30$; $\sigma_{crs,10}=80$	—	—	—	—	—
QE22/20% Saffil (T6; $V_f=20\%$; Saffil: 97%Al_2O_3-3% SiO_2)	23	78	2.1	—	(270,0.2%) (290,1.2%)	20	—	—	—	—
	200	—	—	—	(215,0.2%) (245,1.5%)	—	—	—	—	—
	250	—	—	—	$\sigma_{crs,1000}=70$; $\sigma_{crs,10}=80$	—	—	—	—	—
QE22/20%SiC (T6; $V_f=20\%$)	23	74	—	—	(265,0.2%) (285,2.4%)	19.5	—	—	—	—
WE43 (F; Mg-4Y-0.15Zr-2.25Nd-...)	23	44.2	1.84	0.27	(160,0.2%) (260,6%)	25.2	51.3	1000	—	—
	200	—	—	—	—	27	—	—	—	—
	640(T_m)	—	—	—	—	—	—	—	—	—

continued

Material	$T/℃$	E_T	ρ	υ	(σ,ε)	α	k	γ	ρ_E	K_{IC}
WE43B (SC; T6)	23	44.2	1.84	0.27	$(160,0.2\%)$ $\sigma_{uts}=250$	25.2	51.3	1000	—	—
	150	—	—	—	$(185,0.2\%)$ $\sigma_{uts}=240$	—	—	—	—	—
	200	—	—	—	$(175,0.2\%)$ $\sigma_{uts}=230$	—	—	—	—	—
WE54A (SC; As cast)	23	44.2	1.84	0.27	$(210,0.2\%)$ $\sigma_{uts}=280$	—	—	—	—	—
	200	—	—	—	$(180,0.2\%)$ $\sigma_{uts}=245$	—	—	—	—	—
WE54A (Froged; T5)	23	44.2	1.84	0.27	$(210,0.2\%)$ $\sigma_{uts}=320$	—	—	—	—	—
	200	—	—	—	$(175,0.2\%)$ $\sigma_{uts}=245$	—	—	—	—	—
ZE41A (T5)	23	45	1.83	0.35	$(134,0.2\%)$ $(200,4\%)$	—	—	1000	—	—
ZE63A (T6)	23	45	1.83	0.35	$(186,0.2\%)$ $(275,5\%)$	—	—	1000	—	—
ZK30 (O;Mg-3Zn-0.6Zr)	23	45	1.82	0.35	$(215,0.2\%)$ $(300,9\%)$	25.2	72.3	1050	—	21
ZK30 (Forged Car wheel-rim; axial)	23	45	1.82	0.35	$(248,0.2\%)$ $(302,14\%)$	25.2	72.3	1050	—	21
ZK30 (Forged Car wheel-rim; tangential)	23	45	1.82	0.35	$(196,0.2\%)$ $(266, 12\%)$	25.2	72.3	1050	—	21
ZK30 (Forged Car wheel-spoke; axial)	23	45	1.82	0.35	$(157,0.2\%)$ $(260, 15\%)$	25.2	72.3	1050	—	21

continued

Material	$T/^\circ\mathrm{C}$	E_T	ρ	υ	(σ,ε)	α	k	γ	ρ_E	K_IC
ZK30（Forged Car Wheel-rim: tangential）	23	45	1.82	0.35	(203,0.2%) (265, 12%)	25.2	72.3	1050	—	21
ZK51A（T5; Mg-4.5Zn-0.7 Zr）	23	45	1.82	0.35	(165,0.2%) (276,3%)	26	110	1020	—	21
	640（T_m）	—	—	—	—	—	—	—	—	—
ZK60（O;Mg-6Zn-0.6Zr）	23	45	1.82	0.35	(235,0.2%) (315,8%)	25.2	120	1050	—	21
ZK60（T5;Mg-6Zn-0.6Zr）	23	45	1.82	0.35	(273,0.2%) (329,16%)	25.2	120	1050	—	21
ZK60A（F; Mg-5.5Zn-0.45Zr）	23	45	1.83	0.35	(260,0.2%) (340, 11%)	25.2	120	1000	—	—
ZK60A（T5; Mg-5.5Zn-0.45 Zr）	23	45	1.83	0.35	(305,0.2%) (365, 11%)	25.2	120	1000	—	—
ZK61A（T6）	23	45	1.83	0.35	(179,0.2%) (275,5%)	—	—	—	—	—
Mg-3Al-1Zn	23	—	1.7	—	(162,0.2%) (255,17%)	—	—	—	—	—
Mg-8Al-2Zn （Electrolytic）	23	—	1.75	—	—	—	66	—	—	—
Mg-20Cu-10Y-5Ag/3%ZrO$_2$ （V_f=3%; dε/ dt=0.0001）	23	—	—	—	(700, 7.5%)	—	—	—	—	—
	153	—	—	—	σ_uts=248	—	—	—	—	—
	163	—	—	—	σ_uts=267	—	—	—	—	—
Mg-8.7Li	23	40	1.51	0.35	(93,0.2%) (132, 52%)	—	—	—	—	—
Mg-8.8Li-6.4Al	23	39	1.53	0.35	(184,0.2%) (239, 33%)	—	—	—	—	—

continued

Material	$T/°C$	E_T	ρ	υ	(σ,ε)	α	k	γ	ρ_E	K_{IC}
Mg-8.2Li-6.9 Al-1.1Si	23	44	1.59	0.35	(145,0.2%) (225, 20%)	—	—	—	—	—
Mg-8.8Li-6.2Al-1.2Si-4.5Re	23	53	1.6	0.35	(200,0.2%) (260,14%)	—	—	—	—	—
Mg-10.7Li-1Zn	23	—	—	—	—	—	—	—	—	—
	250	—	—	—	(5.1, 213%)	—	—	—	—	—
Mg-12Li-2Nd/ 21% Steel fibers (Sheet; $V_f=$ 21%)	23	—	—	—	(330,8.6%)					
Mg-12Li-2Nd/ 21% Steel fibers (Rod; $V_f=$ 21%)	23	—	—	—	(325, 4.3%)	—	—	—	—	—
Mg-1Zn-1Cu (As cast)	23	41	1.76	0.27	(59,0.2%) (90,2%) (152, 13%)	—	—	—	—	—
Mg-1Zn-1Cu (Oxide layer)	23	60	—	—	—	—	—	—	—	—
Mg-1Zn-1Se (As cast)	23	38	1.75	0.39	(51,0.2%) (97,2%) (180, 10%)	—	—	—	—	—
Mg-1Zn-1Se (Oxide layer)	23	55	—	—	—	—	—	—	—	—
Mg-1.8Zn-0.3Ca	23	43.5	—	0.35	(291,0.2%) (329,16%)	—	—	—	—	28.3
Mg-2.9Zn	23	—	—	—	(84,0.2%) (220, 4.7%)	—	—	—	—	—
	150	—	—	—	(43,0.2%) (62,17%)	—	—	—	—	—

Material	$T/℃$	E_T	ρ	v	(σ,ε)	α	k	γ	ρ_E	K_{IC}
Mg-4.0Zn	23	—	—	—	(95,0.2%) (216, 4.1%)	—	—	—	—	—
	150	—	—	—	(84,0.2%) (111, 4.4%)	—	—	—	—	—
Mg-4.1Zn-0.2Y	23	—	—	—	(98,0.2%) (223,5%)	—	—	—	—	—
	150	—	—	—	(78,0.2%) (116, 5.4%)	—	—	—	—	—
Mg-4.4Zn	23	—	—	—	(68,0.2%) (155, 8.4%)	—	—	—	—	—
	150	—	—	—	(79,0.2%) (114, 5.2%)	—	—	—	—	—
Mg-5.4Zn-0.6Zr	23	—	—	—	(160,0.2%) (283, 15%)	—	—	—	—	—
	150	—	—	—	(107,0.2%) (130, 3.9%)	—	—	—	—	—

Notes: DC = Die casting;

HPD = High-pressure die cast;

SC = Sand casting;

CW = Cold-worked;

α (℃) = Coefficient of linear thermal expansion, along with/perpendicular to the flow direction.

Table 89.2   Fatigue ε-N Properties of Mg (Magnesium) Alloys

Material	$T/℃$	$d\varepsilon/dt$	σ'_f	ε'_f	b	c	K'	n'	$\sigma_f @ 2N_f$	R
Mg	23	—	—	—	—	—	—	—	156	—
AE42	23	—	—	—	—	—	—	—	80	—
AE44	23	—	—	—	—	—	—	—	73	—
AM50A (DC)	23	—	—	—	—	—	—	—	110@ 10^8	—
AM50B (DC)	23	—	—	—	—	—	—	—		—
AM100A (DC)	23	—	—	—	—	—	—	—		—

continued

Material	$T/\text{℃}$	$d\varepsilon/dt$	σ_f'	ε_f'	b	c	K'	n'	$\sigma_f@2N_f$	R
AM60HP	23	—	—	—	—	—	—	—	$43@10^9$	—
									$52@10^7$	—
AM50HP	23	—	489	0.058	−0.177	−0.495	440	0.242	—	—
AM100A (DC)	23	—	—	—	—	—	—	—	$70@10^8$	—
AM100A (T6)	23	—	—	—	—	—	—	—	$76@10^9$	—
AS21HP	23	—	—	—	—	—	—	—	$28@10^9$	—
									$40@10^7$	—
	125	—	—	—	—	—	—	—	$21@10^9$	—
									$25@10^7$	—
AZ31 (O)	23	—	467	0.0178	−0.13	−0.39	1621	0.33	$130@10^7$	—
									$160@3\times10^4$	—
AZ31B (F)	23	0.055 Hz	670	0.41	−0.178	−0.691	—	—	—	−1
AZ61 (O)	23	—	—	—	—	—	—	—	$160@10^7$	—
									$165@1.4\times10^5$	—
	−75	—	—	—	—	—	—	—	$110@3\times10^8$	RB
AZ61 (Forged)	23	—	—	—	—	—	—	—	$105@3\times10^8$	RB
AZ61A (F)	23	—	448.4	0.613	−0.16	−0.75	—	—	$108@10^7$	—
AZ61A (T4)	23	—	448.4	1.565	−0.16	−0.835	—	—	$160@10^7$	—
AZ91A (F)	23	—	—	—	—	—	—	—	$97@10^9$	—
AZ80A (T5)	23	—	—	—	—	—	—	—	$76@6.4\times10^6$	—
									$100@1.2\times10^6$	—
									$158@2\times10^4$	—
AZ80A (T6)	23	—	—	—	—	—	—	—	$100@10^6$	—
AZ91B (F)	23	—	—	—	—	—	—	—	$97@10^9$	—
AZ91C (F)	23	—	—	—	—	—	—	—	$80@10^8$	—
AZ91D (F)	23	—	—	—	—	—	—	—	$95@10^9$	—
AZ91E (F)	23	—	—	—	—	—	—	—	$80@10^8$	—
AZ91E (T6)	23	—	831	0.089	−0.148	−0.451	552	0.184	—	—

continued

Material	$T/℃$	$\mathrm{d}\varepsilon/\mathrm{d}t$	σ'_f	ε'_f	b	c	K'	n'	$\sigma_\mathrm{f}@2N_\mathrm{f}$	R
AZ91HP	23	—	599	0.04	−0.179	−0.493	496	0.206	$38@10^9$	—
									$52@10^7$	—
	125	—	—	—	—	—	—	—	$34@10^9$	—
									$42@10^7$	—
MRI153M	23	—	—	—	—	—	—	—	$110@10^7$	—
MRI230D	23	—	—	—	—	—	—	—	$105@10^7$	—
ZK60（F）	23	—	—	—	—	—	—	—	$150@10^7$	—
ZK60（T5）	23	—	—	—	—	—	—	—	$170@10^7$	—
GW 103K（Mg-10Gd-3Y-0.5Zr）	23	—	521	0.05	−0.11	−0.44	754	0.2	—	—
Magnesium Alloys	23	—	Eq.(6.14)	Eq.(6.15)	—	—	$\dfrac{\sigma'_\mathrm{f}}{(\varepsilon'_\mathrm{f})^{n'}}$	$\dfrac{b}{c}$	Eq.(89.1)	—

Table 89.3   Thermomechanical Creep Parameters of Mg Alloys

Material	$T/℃$	Stress/MPa	Strain Rate/s^{-1}	$A/(\mathrm{MPa}^{-n}\cdot\mathrm{s}^{m-1})$	$Q/(\mathrm{J}\cdot\mathrm{mol}^{-1})$	n	m
AZ91D	—	—	—	8×10^{-38}	0	4	−0.36
	120~130	120~130	—	—	190000	11	0
	150~160	120~130	—	—	220000	11	0
	160~170	120~130	—	—	105000	11	0
AJ42	175	50~60	—	—	—	5	0
		> 70	—	—	123300	12.4	0
AJ43	175	50~65	—	—	—	5	0
		> 70	—	—	91800	17.4	0
AJC411	175	50~65	—	—	83200	3.75	0
AJC421	175	50~65	—	—	69900	3.35	0
AS21	150	40~83	—	—	—	5	0

continued

Material	$T/^{\circ}C$	Stress/MPa	Strain Rate/s^{-1}	$A/(\mathrm{MPa}^{-n}\cdot \mathrm{s}^{m-1})$	$Q/(\mathrm{J}\cdot\mathrm{mol}^{-1})$	n	m
AS41	100	$\sigma<55$	—	—	—	2	0
	100	70	—	—	72	3.5	0
	100	90	—	—	100	3.5	0
	125	$\sigma<55$	—	—	—	1.3	0
	125	70	—	—	72	2	0
	125	90	—	—	100	2	0
	150	$\sigma<55$	—	—	—	3	0
	150	70	—	—	72	4	0
	150	90	—	—	100	4	0
	175	$\sigma<55$	—	—	—	2.7	0
	175	70	—	—	72	6	0
	175	90	—	—	100	6	0
QE22	150	40~83	—	—	—	7	0
Mg-5.4Zn-0.6Zr (DC) *	150	20~40	—	—	—	2.2	0
	150	40~83	—	—	—	6.8	0
	100~150	30	—	—	66000	—	0
	150~200	30	—	—	131000	—	0

Notes: Creep equation $=\dfrac{\mathrm{d}\varepsilon_{\mathrm{creep}}}{\mathrm{d}t}=A\sigma^{n}t^{m}\exp\left(\dfrac{-Q}{RT_{k}}\right)$;

Temp = Test temperature (℃), at which the data are obtained;

* = As temperature < 150 ℃, grain boundary sliding prevails;

As temperature > 150 ℃, the dislocation glide creep gets into control;

All the alloy compositions are in weight percentage unless stated otherwise.

Chapter 90

Mo (Molybdenum)

90.1 Introduction

Molybdenum increases lattice strain, thus increasing the energy required to dissolve iron atoms from the surface. Mo-based (Molybdenum) alloys have high strength at elevated temperatures, thermal conductivity, electric conductivity, and melting point. The main alloying elements are titanium, zirconium, tungsten, hafnium, and other rare elements. Molybdenum is also used in steel alloys without chromium for its high corrosion resistance and weldability. Mechanical properties of molybdenum alloys are listed in Table 90.1. Its combination of good thermal conductivity and low specific heat make it a natural choice for components to resist thermal shock and fatigue.

When the ferrous is alloyed by Mo (Molybdenum), its mechanical strength, hardenability, toughness, weldability, and corrosion resistance are enhanced very much, especially at elevated temperatures.

When added to Ni-based alloys, high-temperature creep and corrosion can be slowed significantly.

90.2 Applications

Mo-based alloys have been used for molds for thermal processing, molten metal processing, thermal spraying (e. g. engine pistons), and chemical treatment.

References

CHOE H, et al, 2000. Fracture and Fatigue-Crack Growth Behavior in Mo-12Si-8.5B Intermetallics at Ambient and Elevated Temperatures[M]. Chichester: John Willey & Sons, Ltd.

WINDER W, 1967. Molybdenum Disulfide as a Lubricant" A Review and Fundamental Knowledge[J]. Wear, 10(6): 422-452.

Table 90.1　Mechanical Properties of Molybdenum Alloys

Material	$T/℃$	E_T	ρ	υ	(σ,ε)	α	k	γ	ρ_E	K_{IC}
Mo (Pure)	23	320	10.28	0.31	$\sigma_{ucs}=-400$; $(330,0.2\%)$ $\sigma_{uts}=660$	5	140	254	—	15
	227	315	—	—	—	5.2	130	270	—	—
	727	292	—	—	$(161,0.2\%)$ $\sigma_{uts}=438$	5.5	112	295	—	—
	1227	270	—	—	$(80,0.2\%)$ $\sigma_{uts}=159$	6.1	98	330	—	—
	1727	242	—	—	$(20,0.2\%)$ $\sigma_{uts}=42$	6.8	90	380	—	—
	2227	—	—	—	—	7.7	86	460	—	—
	$2623(T_m)$	—	—	—	—	—	—	—	—	—
TZM (Mo-0.5 Ti-0.08Zr)	23	285	10.22	0.33	$(760,0.2\%)$	5.1	127	271	—	—
	227	265	—	—	—	5.2	123	272	—	—
	727	217	—	—	$(622,0.2\%)$	5.5	110	285	—	—
	1227	166	—	—	$(434,0.2\%)$	6.1	95	318	—	—
	1727	120	—	—	—	6.8	80	372	—	—
	2227	57	—	—	—	7.7	69	446	—	—
Mo-44.5Re (Annealed)	23	365	13.5	0.29	$\sigma_{uts}=990$	—	36.8	—	—	—
	500	—	—	—	—	5.7	—	—	—	—
	800	—	—	—	$(370,0.2\%)$ $\sigma_{uts}=660$	—	—	—	—	—
	1000	—	—	—	—	6.5	—	—	—	—
	1200	—	—	—	$(170,0.2\%)$ $\sigma_{uts}=220$	—	—	—	—	—
	$2450(T_m)$	—	—	—	—	—	—	—	—	—
Mo-47.5Re (Annealed)	23	365	13.5	0.29	$(845,0.2\%)$ $(1180,\ 22\%)$	—	36.8	—	—	—
	500	—	—	—	—	5.7	—	—	—	—
	800	—	—	—	$(415,0.2\%)$ $\sigma_{uts}=620$	—	—	—	—	—

continued

Material	$T/℃$	E_T	ρ	υ	(σ,ε)	α	k	γ	ρ_E	K_{IC}
Mo-47.5Re (Annealed)	1000	—	—	—	—	6.5	—	—	—	—
	1200	—	—	—	$(210,0.2\%)$ $\sigma_{uts}=240$	—	—	—	—	—
	1500	—	—	—	$\sigma_{uts}=147$	—	—	—	—	—
	1800	—	—	—	$\sigma_{uts}=50$	—	—	—	—	—
MoO_3	23	—	—	—	—	—	—	—	—	—
$MoSi_2$	23	—	—	—	—	—	—	—	—	3.5
Mo-12Si-8.5B	23	—	—	—	—	—	—	—	—	7
	1200	—	—	—	—	—	—	—	—	9.8
	1300	—	—	—	—	—	—	—	—	11.7

Chapter 91

Nb (Niobium)

91.1 Introduction

Nb (Niobium) is a ductile gray paramagnetic metallic element. It has the largest magnetic penetration depth of any element. The mechanical properties of niobium depend primarily on its purity and its oxygen, nitrogen, hydrogen, and carbon content. Even small concentrations of these elements can have a very significant effect. The manufacturing process, level of deformation, and heat treatment are other factors that modify the material properties of niobium. Adding niobium to the steel causes the formation of niobium carbide and niobium nitride within the structure of the steel. These compounds improve the grain refining, retardation of recrystallization, and precipitation hardening of the steel. Mechanical properties of Nb (Niobium) and its related alloys are listed in Table 91.1, while fatigue parameters are given in Table 91.2.

Nb_3Al (Niobium Aluminide), as well as Nb-Si-Al composites, has a low density and high strength at elevated temperatures but it is brittle. The addition of titanium to Nb-based composites, such as Nb-8Si-9Al-10Ti, improves the ultimate compressive strength at elevated temperatures, fracture toughness at room temperature, and oxidation resistance [Murayama and Hanada].

Niobium becomes a superconductor at cryogenic temperatures (<9.2 K). Superconducting alloys, e. g.50Nb-50Ti, are used in electromagnets, as well as energy storage and transmission.

Mechanical properties of Nb-1Zr alloys-based GTAW (Gas Tungsten Arc Weld) are listed in Table 91.1.

91.2 Applications

Nb (Niobium) is important in the production of high-temperature-resistant alloys. Nb is used in steel alloys, especially special stainless steel.

References

ALLAMEH S, et al, 2002. Interfaces and Dislocation Substructures in a Nb-Ti Base Alloy: Influence of Creep Deformation[J]. Journal of Materials Science, 37(4):2857-2864.

JIANG H, et al, 2003 "Mechanical Properties of Microstructure, and Texture of Electron Beam Butt Welds in High Purity Niobium[C]. IEEE Proceedings of the 2003 Particle Accelerator Conference.

KIM H Y, et al, 2004. Mechanical Properties and Shape Memory Behavior of Ti-Nb Alloys[J]. Materials

Transactions, 45(7):2443-2448.

KRAMER D P, et al, 1999. Mechanical Testing Studies on Niobium-1%zirconium in Association with Its Application as Cell Wall Material in an AMTEC Based Radioisotope Space Power System[J]. SAE 1999-01-2608.

MURAYAMA Y, HANADA S, 2002. High-Temperature Strength, Fracture Toughness and Oxidation Resistance of Nb-Si-Al-Ti Multiphase Alloys[J]. Science and Technology of Advanced Materials, 3(2):145-156.

RAO M G, KNEISEL P, 1994. Mechanical Properties of High RRR Niobium at Cryogenic Temperatures[J]. Advances in Cryogenic Engineering, 40:1383-1390.

SHIN H S, et al, 2002. RRR (Residual Resistivity Ratio) Behavior in NbTi Superconducting Cable due to Fatigue Damage[J]. Physica, C, 378/381:1148-1153.

Table 91.1 Mechanical Properties of Nb (Niobium) and Its Related Alloys

Material	$T/℃$	E_T	ρ	υ	(σ,ε)	α	k	γ	ρ_E	K_{IC}
Nb, Pure (Annealed)	−269	—	—	—	(658,0.2%) (929,16%)	—	—	—	—	46
	−263.8 (Superconductive)									
	−196	—	—	—	(618,0.2%) (642,30.5%)	—	—	—	—	55
	23	105	8.57	0.35	(67,0.2%) (172,58%)	7.2	53	270	—	1.84
	600	—	—	—	—	8.0	62	307	—	—
	1000	80	—	—	—	8.5	66	330	—	—
	1400	70	—	—	—	9.2	—	350	—	—
	2468(T_m)	—	—	—	—	—	—	—	—	—
Nb (Weld)	−269	—	—	—	(470,0.2%) (696,4.2%)	—	—	—	—	26
	−196	—	—	—	(445,0.2%) (639, 13.4%)	—	—	—	—	19
	23	—	8.57	0.35	(70,0.2%) (151, 28%)	—	—	—	—	—
Nb_2O_5	23	—	—	—	—	—	—	—	—	—
50Nb-50Ti	−268.8	—	—	—	(1300,1.7%)	—	—	—	—	—
	23	—	—	—	(700,1%)	—	—	—	—	—
Nb-5Si-9Al	23	—	—	—	—	—	—	—	—	—
	1300	—	—	—	$\sigma_{uts}=210$	—	—	—	—	10.6

continued

Material	$T/°C$	E_T	ρ	υ	(σ, ε)	α	k	γ	ρ_E	K_{IC}
Nb-0.7Si-3Al	23	—	—	—	—	—	—	—	—	—
	1300	—	—	—	$\sigma_{uts}=47$	—	—	—	—	9.3
Nb-1Zr	23	—	—	—	$\sigma_{uts}=280$	—	—	—	—	—
	400	—	—	—	$\sigma_{uts}=200$	—	—	—	—	—
	800	—	—	—	$\sigma_{uts}=220$	—	—	—	—	—
	527	—	—	—	—	—	60	—	—	—
	1000	—	—	—	$\sigma_{uts}=170$	—	—	—	—	—
	1200	—	—	—	$\sigma_{uts}=95$	—	—	—	—	—
Nb-1Zr (Weld; Ar-shielded)	23	—		—	$(208, 0.2\%)$ $(243, 30\%)$			—	—	—
Nb-1Zr (Weld; Ar-shielded & PWHT)	23	—	—	—	$(149, 0.2\%)$ $(201, 34\%)$	—	—	—	—	—
Nb-1Zr (Weld; He-shielded)	23	—	—	—	$(177, 0.2\%)$ $(225, 28.4\%)$	—	—	—	—	—
Nb-1Zr (Weld; He-shielded & PWHT)	23	—	—	—	$(151, 0.2\%)$ $(204, 36.6\%)$	—	—	—	—	—
Nb-1Zr (Weld; ASTM B393)	23	—	—	—	$(125, 0.2\%)$ $(195, 20\%)$	—	—	—	—	—

Notes: PWHT=Post-weld heat treatment.

Table 91.2 Fatigue ε-N Properties of Nb (Niobium) Alloys

Material	$T/°C$	$d\varepsilon/dt$	σ_f'	ε_f'	b	c	K'	n'	$\sigma_f@2N_f$	R
NbTi	23	—	—	—	—	—	—	—	$120@10^7$	—

Chapter 92

Ni (Nickel)

92.1 Introduction

Nickel is a naturally magnetostrictive material, meaning that in the presence of a magnetic field, the material undergoes a negative change in length, though small. Nickel and its alloys are characterized by their good corrosion resistance and high ductility. Mechanical elastoplastic properties, fatigue parameters, and creep parameters of nickel alloys are listed respectively in Tables 92.1—92.3. Their major alloying elements are given as follows:

(a) Nickel and Duranickel: Nickel>94%;
(b) Hastelloy: Ni-Mo & Ni-Mo-Cr (high-temperature applications);
(c) Inconel, Incoloy, Rene, and Udimet: Ni-Cr & Ni-Cr-Fe (for jet-engine applications);
(d) Invar: 64Fe-36Ni, notable for its low thermal expansion;
(e) Monel: Ni-Cu-Fe (for sub-zero temperature applications);
(f) Nitinol: Ni-Ti, Shape memory alloys.

The fatigue strength (endurance limit) of a nickel alloy with a fatigue cutoff cycle of 10^8 falls between 35% and 50% of its ultimate tensile strength, i.e.

$$0.35\,\sigma_{uts} < \sigma_f < 0.5\,\sigma_{uts} \tag{92.1}$$

Nickel alloys are as strong as iron, but have much better resistance to corrosion. Material parameters on fatigue crack growth of Ni-alloys in the opening mode are given in Table 92.4. The composition of nickel-based super alloys is from 38% to 76%; they also contain up to 27% chromium and 20% cobalt. Nickel-based super alloys generally contain a composition of 38% ~ 76% nickel, 0% ~ 27% chromium, and 0% ~ 20% nickel.

92.2 Hastelloy

Ni-Mo is the basic composition in this category of nickel alloys. Hastelloys are generally considered versatile corrosion-resistance alloys. For example, Hastelloy C276 and C22 are used in bleach plant mixers.

92.3 Inconel, Incoloy, Rene, and Udimet

Ni-Cr is the basic composition in this category of nickel alloys. Wrought nickel alloys of this category tend to be better known by trade names such as Monel, Hastelloy, Inconel (namely

Pyromet by UNS N07718), Incoloy, Rene, Udimet, etc. They offer good resistance to pitting, inter-granular corrosion, chloride-ion stress-corrosion cracking, and general corrosion in a wide range of oxidizing environments. Ni-Cr-Fe-Mo-Cu alloys are frequently used in applications involving sulfuric and phosphoric acids.

Inconel alloy 625 is an approved material of construction under the Boiler and Pressure Vessel Code of the ASME (American Society of Mechanical Engineers). It has good resistance to oxidation and scaling at high temperatures. Long-term (e.g. three months) exposure of Inconel 625 at an elevated temperature (e.g. 593 ℃) results in a minimal degradation of the room temperature ductility of a hot-rolled par but improves in fatigue life [Smith &Yates]. Inconel 738 is most commonly used for gas turbine blades and vanes for industrial use. After a long-time exposure (e.g. 4000 hours) to a working environment at an elevated temperature (e.g. 700 ℃ for Inconel 783 or 600 ℃ for Incoloy 909) may let such Ni-based alloys lower their high-temperature yield strengths.

Nichrome, a non-magnetic alloy that consists of 80% nickel and 20% chromium by weight, is widely used in heating elements because of its relatively high resistivity.

92.4   Invar

Invar is a Fe-Ni alloy. Invar 36 (Fe-36Ni-...) has constant dimensions over the range of normal operating temperatures and a low coefficient of linear thermal expansion from cryogenic temperatures to its Curie temperature (279 ℃). Variation of the coefficient of linear thermal expansion of invar over the Ni content is shown in Fig. 92.1.

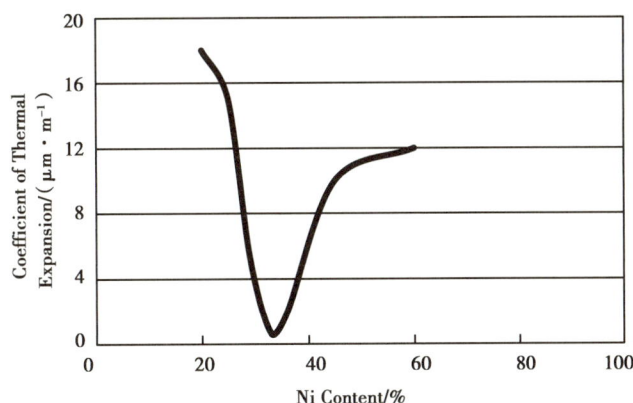

Fig. 92.1   The coefficient of linear thermal expansion of Invar (Ni-Fe alloys) plotted against the nickel content on a mass basis (Courtesy of National Electronic Alloys, Inc.)

Invar42 (Fe-42Ni-...) has a coefficient of linear thermal expansion similar to silicon and thus is widely used for integrated circuits and other electronic components. Kovar (Fe-Ni-Co) can be formulated to have the same thermal expansion behavior as borosilicate glass and thus is used for optical parts, which are expected to work in a wide range of temperature variations such as satellites.

92.5   Monel

Ni-Cu is the basic composition in this category of nickel alloys. These nickel alloys are used extensively because of their corrosion resistance, high-temperature strength, and their special magnetic and thermal expansion properties. One of its automotive applications is Monel 505 for engine valve seats, made of Ni-Cu-Fe alloy to the high nickel side.

92.6   Nitinol

The commercial importance of Ni-Ti is due to its closely related properties of shape memory and superelasticity. Ni-Ti alloys have the ability to undergo large deformation and return to their undeformed shape by heating or via stress removal (superelastic effect). Both properties result from the phase transformation between an austenitic (original) phase with a simple cubic structure to a martensite phase with a monoclinic structure. A schematic comparison of stress-strain curves of austenite and martensite is demonstrated in Fig. 92.2.

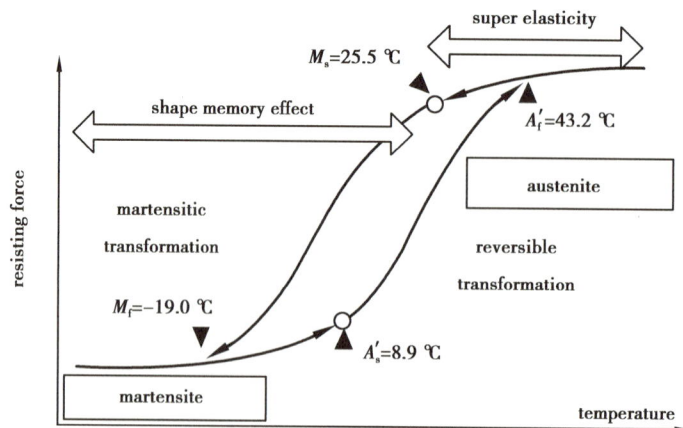

Fig. 92.2   Stress-strain Curves of Austenite and Martensite of Ni-Ti

The evolution of the stress-strain curve varies according to the stress-strain loading history (including strain level and loading frequency) and temperature, as illustrated in Fig. 92.3. In a reasonable working temperature range, the material is a shape memory alloy. Microscopic transformation can be demonstrated schematically as follows:

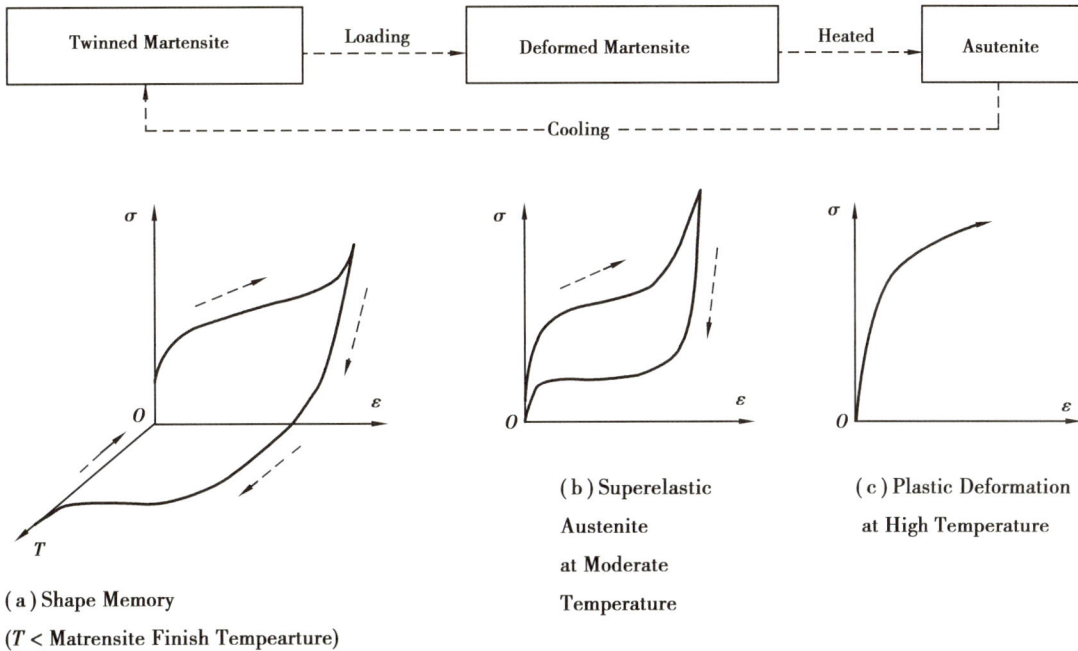

Fig. 92.3   Stress-strain-temperature Diagram for an Example NiTi Shape Memory Alloy (σ-Stress, ε-Strain, T-Temperature).

As the temperature increases and the material may turn into superelastic austenite with high damping, based on which the seismic resistant structure may be designed. Once the temperature goes beyond the maximum temperature at which martensite occurs, the material experiences general elastoplastic deformation.

Nitinol (Ni-Ti), as shape memory alloys, are also used for spring coils in solenoids, control valve, and linear motors.

References

ABU-HAIBA M S, et al, 2002. Creep Deformation and Monotonic Stress-strain Behavior of Haynes Alloy 556 at Elevated Temperatures[J]. Journal of Materials Science, 37(14), 2899-2907.

BAGDAHN J, SHARPE W N Jr., 2003. Reliability of Polycrystalline Silicon under Long-term Cyclic Loading

[J]. Journal of Sensors and Actuators, 103(1-2): 9-15.

BARBOSA C, et al, 2005. Microstructural Aspects of the Failure Analysis of Nickel-Base Superalloys Components[J]. Engineering Failure Analysis, 12(3): 348-361.

BERGER C, et al, 2001. Creep Rupture Behavior of Nickel Base Alloys for 700 ℃-Steam Turbines[J]. Super Alloys 718, 625, 706 and Various Derivatives, 489-199.

BOZORTH R M, et al, 1951.Frequency Dependence of Elastic Constants and Loss in Nickel[J]. Bell System Technology Journal, 30(4): 970-989.

BUSSO E P, et al, 2001. A Mechanical Study of Oxidation-Induced Degradation in a Plasma-Sprayed Thermal Barrier Coating System. Part I: Model Formulation[J]. Acta Materialia, 49(9): 1515-1528.

CAIRD S, TRELA D, 1981. High-Temperature Corrosion-Fatigue Test Method for Exhaust Valve Alloys[J]. SAE 810033.

CHEN L, et al, 1998. Fatigue and Creep-Fatigue Behavior of a Nickel-Based Superalloy at 850 ℃ [J]. International Journal of Fatigue, 20(7): 543-548.

CHEN Y, et al, 2012. Studies of Nanomechanical Properties and Fatigue Strength of Annealed Ni-Ti Shape Memory Alloy[J]. Materials Letters, 71(15): 84-87.

DESROCHES R, MCCORMICK J, DELEMONT M, 2004. Cyclic Properties of Superelastic Shape Memory Alloy Wires and Bars[J]. Journal of Structural Engineering, 130(1): 38-46.

DUCKI K, CIESLA M, 2008. Effect of Heat Treatment on the Structure and Fatigue Behavior of Austenitic Fe-Ni Alloy[J]. Journal of Achievements in Materials and Manufacturing Engineering, 30(1): 19-26.

FANG D, BERKOVITS A, 1994. Mean Stress Models for Low Cycle Fatigue of a Nickel-Based Superalloy[J]. International Journal of Fatigue, 16: 429-437.

GALL K, et al, 2008. Effect of Microstructure on the Fatigue of Hot-rolled and Cold-drawn NiTi Shape Memory Alloys[J]. Materials Science and Engineering, A, 486: 389-403.

GUO Z, et al, 2007. Modeling the Strain-Life relationship of Commercial Alloys[C]. Proceedings of CREEP8, July 22-26, 2007, San Antonio, Texas.

GUO Z, et al, 2007. Quantification of High-Temperature Strength of Nickel-Based Superalloys[J]. Materials Science Forum, 546/549: 1319-1326.

HECK K, SMITH J, SMITH R, 1998. INCONEL Alloy 783: An Oxidation Resistant, Low Expansion Superalloy for Gas Turbine Applications[J]. Journal of Engineering for Gas Turbine and Power, 120(2): 128-132.

HEMKER K J, LAST H R, 2001. Microsample Tensile Testing of LIGA Nickel for MEMS Applications[J]. Materials Science and Engineering, A, 319-321: 882-886.

HUGHES D A, HANSEN N, 2000. Microstructure and Strength of Nickel at Large Strains[J]. Acta Materials, 48(1): 2985-3004.

JONSTA P, JONSTA Z, SOJKA J, et al, 2007. Structural Characteristics of Nickel Superalloy Inconel 713LC after Heat Treatment[J]. Journal of Achievements in Materials and Manufacturing Engineering, 21(2): 29-32.

LAGAREC K, et al, 2001. Observation of a Composition-Controlled High-moment/low-moment Transition in the Face Centered Cubic Fe-Ni System: Invar Effect is an Expansion, Not a Contraction[J]. Journal of Magnetism and Magnetic Materials, 236: 107-130.

LAST H R, HEMKER K J, WITT R, 2000. MEMS Material Microstructure and Elastic Properties[J]. Materials Research Society Symposium, 605: 191-196.

LEE S, KIM S, KANG K, 2006. Effect of Heat Treatment on the Specific Heat Capacity of Nickel Based-alloys [J]. International Journal of Thermophysics, 27(1): 282-293.

LENG J S, et al, 2008. Electrical Conductivity of Thermoresponsive Shape-memory Polymer with Embedded Micron-Sized Ni Powder Chains[J]. Applied Physics Letters, 92(1): 014104.

LIN Z C, et al, 2000. The Study of Ultra-precision Machining and Residual Stress for NiP Alloy with Different Speeds and Depth of Cut[J]. Journal of Materials Processing Technology, 97(1-3): 200-210.

LU Y, CHEN L, WANG G, et al, 2004. Hold-time Effects on Low-cycle-fatigue Behavior of Hastelloy X Superalloy at High Temperatures [C]. 10th International Symposium on Superalloys, 19-23 September, Champion, Pennsylvania, 241-250.

MA L, CHANG K, MANNAN S. 2003. Oxide-Induced Crack Closure: An Explanation for Abnormal Time-Dependent Fatigue Crack Propagation Behavior in INCONEL alloy 783[J]. Scripta Materialia, 48: 583-588.

MALLET C, et al, 2011. Fatigue of Pseudoelastic NiTi within the Stress-Induced Transformation Regime: a Modified Coffin−Manson Approach[J]. Smart Materials and Structures, 21(11): 112001.

MARCHIONNI M, KLINGELHÜFFER H, KÜHN H, 2007. Thermo-mechanical Fatigue of the Nickel-Based Superalloy Nimonic 90[J]. Key Engineering Materials, 345/346: 347-350.

MAZUR Z, et al, 2005. Failure Analysis of a Gas Turbine Blade Made of Inconel 738LC Alloy[J]. Engineering Failure Analysis, 12: 474-486.

NATH C, RAHMAN M, 2008. Evaluation of Ultrasonic Vibration Cutting While Machining Inconel 718[J]. International Journal of Precision Engineering & Manufacturing, 9(2): 63-68.

NIRAJ N, et al, 2009. Effect of Mechanical Cycling on the Stress-Strain Response of a Martensitic Nitinol Shape Memory Alloy[J]. Materials Science & Engineering, A, 525(1-2): 60-67.

NORFLEET D, et al, 2009. Transformation-Induced Plasticity during Pseudoelastic Deformation in Ni-Ti Microcrystals[J]. Acta Materialia., 57(12): 3549-3561.

PARK J, et al, 2009. A Study on the Fatigue Behavior of Electro-Plated Nico Thin Film for Probe Tip Applications[J]. Material Science and Technology, 40(3): 187-191.

PELTON P, DUERIG T, STÖCKEL D, 2004. A Guide to Shape Memory and Superelasticity in Nitinol Medical Devices[J]. Minimally Invasive Therapy and Allied Technologies., 13(4): 218-221.

OPPENHEIMER S M, et al, 2007. Power-Law Creep in Near-Equiatomic Nickel-Titanium Alloys[J]. Scripta Materialia, 57(5): 377-380.

OTSUKA K, REN X, 2005. Physical Metallurgy of TiNi-based Shape Memory Alloys[J]. Progress in Material Science, 50(5): 511-678.

PARK S, KIM K, KIM H, 2007. Ratcheting Behavior and Mean Stress Considerations in Uniaxial Low Cycle Fatigue of Inconel 718 at 649 ℃[J]. Fatigue and Fracture of Engineering Materials and Structures, 30(11): 1076-1083.

PETRENEC M, et al, 2005. Fatigue Behavior of Cast Nickel-Based Superalloy Inconel 792-5A at Room Temperature[J]. Materials Engineering, 12: 21-24.

RANCOURT D G, DANG M. 1996. Relation between Anomalous Magneto-Volume Behavior and Magnetic Frustration in Invar Alloys[J]. Physical Review, B, 54(17): 12225-12231.

ROBERTSON S W, PELTONL A R, RITCHIE R O, 2012. Mechanical Fatigue and Fracture of Nitinol[J]. International Materials Reviews, 57(1): 1-37.

SAJJADI S, ZEBARJAD S, 2006. Study of Fracture Mechanisms of a Ni-Based Superalloy at Different Temperatures[J]. Journal of Achievements in Materials and Manufacturing Engineering, 18(1-2): 227-230.

SCHAFFER J E, PLUMLEY D L, 2009. Fatigue Performance of Nitinol Round Wire with Varying Cold Work Reductions[J]. Journal of Materials Engineering and Performance, 18(5-6): 563-568.

SHARGI-MOSHTAGHIN R, ASGARI S, 2004. The Influence of Thermal Exposure on the γ' Precipitates Characteristics and Tensile of Superalloy IN-738LC[J]. Journal of Materials Processing Technology, 147(3): 343-350.

SOCIE D F, et al, 1985. Biaxial Fatigue of Inconel 718 Including Mean Stress Effects[J]. ASTM STP 853: 463-481.

SONG K H, NAKATA K, 2009. Mechanical Properties of Friction-Stir-Welded Inconel 625 Alloy[J]. Materials Transactions, 50(10): 2498-2450.

STANKIEWICZ J M, ROBERTSON S W, RITCHIE R O, 2007. Fatigue-Crack Growth Properties of Thin-walled Superelastic Austenitic Nitinol Tube for Endovascular Stents [J]. Journal of Biomedical Materials Research., Part A, 81A(3): 685-691.

STARON P, et al, 2007. Characterization of Residual Stresses in IN 718 Turbine Discs by Neutron Diffraction and Finite Element Modeling[J]. Journal of Neutron Research, 15(3-4): 185-192.

SUWARIDE J, ARTIAGA R, MIER J, 2002. Thermal Characterization of a Ni-based Superalloy [J]. Thermochimica Acta, 392/393: 295-298.

TABANLI R M, et al, 2001. Mean Strain Effects on the Fatigue Properties of Superelastic NiTi [J]. Metallurgical and Materials Transactions, A, 32(7): 1866-1869.

TOTEMEIER T, TIAN H, 2007. Creep-Fatigue-Environment Interactions in Inconel 617[J]. Materials Science and Engineering, A, 468/470: 81-87.

YU J, et al, 2010. High-Temperature Creep and Low Cycle Fatigue of a Nickel-Based Superalloy[J]. Material Science and Engineering, A, 527: 2379-2389.

ZHAO P, et al, 2005. Nickel Foam and Carbon Felt Applications for Sodium Polysulfide/Bromine Redox Flow Battery Electrodes[J]. Electrochimica Acta, 51(6): 1091-1098.

ZHOU H, et al, 2004. Deformation Microstructures after Low-Cycle Fatigue in a Fourth-Generation Ni-based SC Superalloy TMS-138[J]. Materials Science and Engineering, A, 381(1-2): 20-27.

ZIELIŇSKA M, et al, 2010. Thermal Properties of Cast Nickel-Based Superalloys[J]. Archives of Materials and Manufacturing Engineering, 44(1): 35-38.

Table 92.1 Mechanical Properties of Ni (Nickel) Alloys

Material	$T/^\circ C$	E_T	ρ	ν	(σ, ε)	α	k	γ	ρ_E	K_{IC}
Nickel (>99%)	23	207	8.96	0.31	(138, 0.2%) (483, 40%)	13.3	90	540	—	—
	354 (T_c)	—	—	—	—	—	—	—	—	—
	1455 (T_m)	—	—	—	—	—	—	—	—	—
Nickel (Nanocrystalline)	23	—	—	—	(1400, 3.6%)	—	—	540	—	—

continued

Material	$T/°C$	E_T	ρ	ν	(σ, ε)	α	k	γ	ρ_E	K_{IC}
Nickel (LIGA; 400 μm thick) [Sharpe et al.]	23	201	—	—	(372,0.2%) (520,2.7%)	14	—	—	—	—
	200	—	—	—	(323,0.2%) (460,3%)	—	—	—	—	—
	300	—	—	—	(224,0.2%) (340,1.5%)	—	—	—	—	—
	400	—	—	—	(134,0.2%) (180,3%)	—	—	—	—	—
CMSX-4 (As cast)	23	—	—	0.3	—	—	—	—	—	—
	1000	—	—	—	(−690,−5%) (−675,−2%) (−640,−0.2%)	—	—	—	—	—
	1150	—	—	—	(−430,−5%) (−440,−2%) (−430,−0.2%)	—	—	—	—	—
CMSX-4 (HT)	23	—	—	0.3	—	—	—	—	—	—
	1050	—	—	—	(−580,−5%) (−570,−2%) (−540,−0.2%)	—	—	—	—	—
	1150	—	—	—	(−345,−5%) (−350,−2%) (−340,−0.2%)	—	—	—	—	—
GH4133 (China)	23	199	—	0.3	—	—	—	—	—	—
	530	177	—	—	—	—	—	—	—	—
Hastelloy B	0	—	—	—	—	—	11.1	373	—	—
	23	217	9.22	0.3	(396,0.2%) (914,55%)	10.3	11.5	380	—	—
	600	167	—	—	—	12	18.7	456	—	—
	1000	117	—	—	—	—	—	—	—	—
Hastelloy C276 (Ni-22Cr-9Mo-2W-18Fe; Annealed)	−200 (Low service temperature)									
	−168	—	—	—	—	—	7.2	—	—	—
	23	206	8.89	0.3	(365,0.2%) (867,59%)	11	10	427	—	—
	400 (High service temperature)									
	430	182	—	—	(240,0.2%) (655,65%)	13.2	17	—	—	—

continued

Material	$T/^\circ\mathrm{C}$	E_T	ρ	ν	(σ, ε)	α	k	γ	ρ_E	K_IC
Hastelloy C276 (Ni-22Cr-9Mo-2W-18Fe; Annealed)	540	176	—	—	$(233, 0.2\%)$ $(613, 60\%)$	13.4	19	—	—	—
	870	—	—	—	—	16	25	—	—	—
	1370 (T_m)	—	—	—	—	—	—	—	—	—
Hastelloy C276 (Ni-22Cr-9Mo-2W-18Fe; Spring Hard)	−200 (Low service temperature)									
	−168	—	—	—	—	—	7.2	—	—	—
	23	206	8.89	0.3	$\sigma_\mathrm{uts} = 1450$	10.2	—	427	—	—
	430	182	—	—	—	13.2	17	—	—	—
	540	176	—	—	—	13.4	19	—	—	—
	870	—	—	—	—	16	25	—	—	—
	1370 (T_m)	—	—	—	—	—	—	—	—	—
Hastelloy X (Heat-treated Sheet)	−100	—	—	0.33	—	—	—	—	—	—
	23	196	8.22	0.32	$(370, 0.2\%)$ $(780, 43\%)$	13	16.9	486	—	—
	650	—	—	—	$(270, 0.2\%)$ $(570, 37\%)$; $\sigma_\mathrm{crs, 1000} = 234$ $\sigma_\mathrm{crs, 10000} = 170$	15.3	—	582	—	—
	870	146	—	—	$(180, 0.2\%)$ $(250, 51\%)$; $\sigma_\mathrm{crs, 1000} = 45$ $\sigma_\mathrm{crs, 10000} = 28$	16.2	26.4	—	—	—
	982	—	—	—	$(110, 0.2\%)$ $(155, 45\%)$; $\sigma_\mathrm{crs, 1000} = 14$ $\sigma_\mathrm{crs, 10000} = 8$	16.6	28.7	799	—	—
	1000	139	—	—	$(80, 0.2\%)$ $(160, 64\%)$	—	—	—	—	—
	1355 (T_m)	—	—	—	—	—	—	—	—	—
Haynes 25 (ST Sheet)	23	211	—	0.3	$(65, 0.2\%)$ $(135, 60\%)$	12	10	—	—	—
	430	184	—	—	—	13.9	17	—	—	—
	540	181	—	—	$(39, 0.2\%)$ $(106, 72\%)$	14.4	20	—	—	—
	760	—	—	—	$(35, 0.2\%)$	16.9	—	—	—	—

continued

Material	$T/\text{°C}$	E_T	ρ	ν	(σ, ε)	α	k	γ	ρ_E	K_{IC}
Haynes 25 (ST Sheet)	870	—	—	—	$(85,28\%)$ $(18,0.2\%)$ $(34,40\%)$; $\sigma_{crs,1000}=25$	16.9	—	—	—	—
Haynes R41	23	—	—	—	—	—	—	—	—	—
	760	—	—	—	$(752, 0.2\%)$	—	—	—	—	—
	800	169	—	—	—	—	—	—	—	—
	816	—	—	—	$\sigma_{crs,1000}=165$	—	—	—	—	—
Haynes 150	23	—	—	0.3	—	—	—	—	0.87	—
	538	—	—	—	$(275, 0.2\%)$	—	—	—	—	—
	649	180	—	—	—	—	—	—	—	—
Haynes 188 (ST; Annealed)	-200	—	—	—	—	9.7	—	—	—	—
	23	170	8.98	0.3	$(460,0.2\%)$ $(940,53\%)$	11.3	10.7	—	1.01	—
	540	—	—	—	$(290,0.2\%)$ $(750,61\%)$	14.8	20	—	—	—
	760	—	—	—	$(270,0.2\%)$ $(620, 63\%)$; $\sigma_{crs,1000}=160$	16.2	24.1	—	—	—
	980	—	—	—	$(130,0.2\%)$ $(245,59\%)$; $\sigma_{crs,1000}=17$	17.8	—	—	—	—
Haynes 214	23	—	—	0.3	—	—	—	—	1.34	—
	760	—	—	—	$(640, 0.2\%)$	—	—	—	—	—
	800	162	—	—	—	—	—	—	—	—
Haynes 230 (HR; Annealed)	23	211	—	0.3	$(375,0.2\%)$ $(840,48\%)$	11.8	8.9	397	—	—
	500	184	—	—	—	13.6	18.4	473	—	—
	540	181	—	—	$(251, 0.2\%)$ $(690, 55\%)$	—	—	—	—	—
	650	—	—	—	$\sigma_{crs,1000}=250$ $\sigma_{crs,10000}=185$	—	—	—	—	—
	870	159	—	—	$(234, 0.2\%)$ $(308, 75\%)$; $\sigma_{crs,1000}=57$ $\sigma_{crs,10000}=39$	—	—	—	—	—

continued

Material	$T/℃$	E_T	ρ	ν	(σ, ε)	α	k	γ	ρ_E	K_{IC}
Haynes 230 (HR; Annealed)	980	—	—	—	$(118, 0.2\%)$ $(171, 96\%)$; $\sigma_{crs,1000}=18$ $\sigma_{crs,10000}=7.6$					
	1000	150	—	—	—	16.1	28.4	617	—	—
	1093	—	—	—	$(57, 0.2\%)$ $(120, 50\%)$	—	—	—	—	—
	1149	—	—	—	$(45, 0.2\%)$ $(90, 100\%)$	—	—	—	—	—
Haynes 230 (CR; Annealed)	23	211	—	—	$(422, 0.2\%)$ $(838, 47\%)$	11.8	8.9	397	—	—
	500	184	—	—	—	13.6	18.4	473	—	—
	538	181	—	—	$(303, 0.2\%)$ $(699, 54\%)$	—	—	—	—	—
	700	171	—	—	—	14.8	22.4	574	—	—
	871	159	—	—	$(242, 0.2\%)$ $(315, 100\%)$	—	—	—	—	—
	982	—	—	—	$(125, 0.2\%)$ $(172, 50\%)$	—	—	—	—	—
	1000	150	—	—	—	16.1	28.4	617	—	—
Haynes 242 (HR Plate; Annealed; Aged)	23	220	8.36	—	$(780, 0.2\%)$ $(1270, 38\%)$	10.6	11.7	386	—	—
	540	—	—	—	$(520, 0.2\%)$ $(1000, 47\%)$; $\sigma_{crs,1000}=825$	12.2	20.9	470	—	—
	650	—	—	—	$(480, 0.2\%)$ $(940, 38\%)$; $\sigma_{crs,1000}=515$	12.4	22.5	595	—	—
	705	—	—	—	$\sigma_{crs,1000}=240$	—	—	—	—	—
	760	—	—	—	$(290, 0.2\%)$ $(730, 66\%)$; $\sigma_{crs,1000}=115$	13.7	22.5	605	—	—
	870	—	—	—	$(275, 0.2\%)$ $(480, 56\%)$	14.5	24.2	610	—	—

continued

Material	$T/℃$	E_T	ρ	ν	(σ, ε)	α	k	γ	ρ_E	K_{IC}
Haynes 242 (CR; Annealed; Aged)	23	220	8.36	—	(930, 0.2%) (1365, 32%)	10.6	11.7	386	—	—
	540	—	—	—	(790, 0.2%) (1165, 31%)	12.2	20.9	470	—	—
	650	—	—	—	(680, 0.2%) (1045, 20%)	12.4	22.5	595	—	—
	760	—	—	—	(450, 0.2%) (760, 45%)	13.7	22.5	605	—	—
	870	—	—	—	(265, 0.2%) (445, 33%)	14.5	24.2	610	—	—
Haynes 263 (Annealed)	23	220	8.36	—	(265, 0.2%) (445, 33%)	11	11.7	461	—	—
	871	165	—	—	—	15.4	24.7	—	—	—
Haynes 556 (Annealed; Incoloy 556)	23	205	8.36	—	(376, 0.2%) (803, 51%)	—	—	—	—	—
	538	168	—	—	(211, 0.2%) (623, 60%)	15.7	—	—	—	—
	649	159	—	—	(211, 0.2%) (573, 57%)	16.1	—	—	—	—
	760	150	—	—	(220, 0.2%) (472, 53%)	16.4	—	—	—	—
	800	148	—	—	—	—	—	—	—	—
	871	144	—	—	(192, 0.2%) (340, 69%)	16.7	—	—	—	—
	982	139	—	—	(128, 0.2%) (212, 84%)	17	—	—	—	—
Incoloy 800 (Sol. annealed; Fe-33Ni-21Cr-0.4Ti-0.4Al-...)	−190	211	—	0.33	—		—	—	—	—
	23	196	7.95	0.34	(296, 0.2%) (600, 44%)	14.2	12	460	0.99	—
	430	—	—	—	(159, 0.2%) (228, 84%)	—	18.3	—	—	—
	600	158	—	0.37	$\sigma_{crs,10000} = 140$	17.1	—	—	—	—
	700	—	—	—	$\sigma_{crs,10000} = 69$	—	—	—	—	—
	760	—	—	—	(159, 0.2%) (228, 84%)	—	—	—	—	—

continued

Material	$T/°C$	E_T	ρ	ν	(σ, ε)	α	k	γ	ρ_E	K_{IC}
Incoloy 800 (Sol. annealed; Fe-33Ni-21Cr-0.4Ti-0.4Al-…)	800	141	—	0.39	—	18	—	—	—	—
	1000	—	—	—	—	18.7	—	—	—	—
	1357 (T_m)	—	—	—	—	—	—	—	—	—
Incoloy 800H (Sol. annealed)	23	196	7.95	0.34	$(296,\ 0.2\%)$ $(625,\ 40\%)$	14.2	12	460	—	—
	650	—	—	—	$(93,\ 0.2\%)$ $\sigma_{uts}=378$; $\sigma_{crs,10000}=121$ $\sigma_{crs,30000}=103$ $\sigma_{crs,100000}=90$	—	—	—	—	—
	760	154	—	—	$(90,\ 0.2\%)$ $\sigma_{uts}=236$; $\sigma_{crs,10000}=50$ $\sigma_{crs,30000}=43$ $\sigma_{crs,100000}=37$	—	—	—	—	—
	800	141	—	0.39	—	18	—	—	—	—
	1380 (T_m)	—	—	—	—	—	—	—	—	—
Incoloy 800HT (Annealed)	23	196	7.95	0.34	$(250,\ 0.2\%)$ $(560,\ 45\%)$	14.2	12	460	—	—
	650	—	—	—	$(93,\ 0.2\%)$ $\sigma_{uts}=378$; $\sigma_{crs,10000}=121$ $\sigma_{crs,30000}=103$ $\sigma_{crs,100000}=90$	—	—	—	—	—
	700	—	—	—	$\sigma_{crs,10000}=79$	—	—	—	—	—
	760	154	—	—	$(90,\ 0.2\%)$ $\sigma_{uts}=236$; $\sigma_{crs,10000}=50$ $\sigma_{crs,30000}=43$ $\sigma_{crs,100000}=37$	—	—	—	—	—
	800	141	—	0.39	$\sigma_{crs,10000}=39$		18	—	—	—
	900	—	—	—	$\sigma_{crs,10000}=19$	—	—	—	—	—
	1000	—	—	—	$\sigma_{crs,10000}=8.5$	—	—	—	—	—
	1385 (T_m)	—	—	—	—	—	—	—	—	—

continued

Material	$T/℃$	E_T	ρ	ν	(σ, ε)	α	k	γ	ρ_E	K_{IC}
Incoloy 801	23	197	—	—	(207, 0.2%)	—	—	—	1.01	—
	760	—	—	—	—	—	—	—	—	—
Incoloy 803	23	195	—	—	—	—	—	—	1.03	—
	760	—	—	—	(215, 0.2%)	—	—	—	—	—
Incoloy 825 (Annealed)	23	193	7.95	0.3	(300, 0.2%) (650, 44%)	14	11.1	460	1.13	—
	430	—	—	—	—	16.3	17.3	—	—	—
Incoloy 864	23	195	—	—	—	—	—	—	1.04	—
	760	—	—	—	(140, 0.2%)	—	—	—	—	—
Incoloy 901 (ST; Annealed; Aged)	23	207	8.14	0.26	(862, 0.2%) (1207, 15%)	13.3	—	430	—	—
	538	—	—	—	(779, 0.2%) (1076, 17%); $\sigma_{crs,1000}=689$	—	—	—	—	—
	650	—	—	—	(807, 0.2%) (1034, 14%); $\sigma_{crs,1000}=517$	—	—	—	—	—
	732	—	—	—	$\sigma_{crs,1000}=228$	—	—	—	—	—
	760	—	—	—	(707, 0.2%) (741, 9%)	—	—	—	—	—
	816	—	—	—	(545, 0.2%) (559, 13%); $\sigma_{crs,1000}=76$	—	—	—	—	—
Incoloy 909 (ST; Annealed; Aged)	23	207	8.8	0.3	(970, 0.2%) (1205, 8%)	4.5	14.8	427	—	—
	700	190	—	—	—	11	22.5	599	—	—
	1000	150	—	—	—	—	—	678	—	—
Incoloy 925	23	195	—	—	—	—	—	—	1.16	—
Incoloy MA956	23	175	7.25	0.3	(550, 0.2%) (650, 11%)	11	10.9	469	—	—
	300	160	—	—	(480, 0.2%) (585, 12%)	12	15.4	547	—	—
	600	125	—	—	(200, 0.2%) (280, 22%)	13	19.8	630	—	—
	700	118	—	—	(150, 0.2%) (195, 16%)	13.4	21.2	658	—	—

continued

Material	$T/°C$	E_T	ρ	ν	(σ, ε)	α	k	γ	ρ_E	K_{IC}
Incoloy MA956	800	110	—	—	$(115, 0.2\%)$ $(130, 12\%)$; $\sigma_{crs,1000}=92$	13.9	22.6	686	—	—
	900	98	—	—	$(100, 0.2\%)$ $(110, 8\%)$; $\sigma_{crs,1000}=80$	14.4	24.1	714	—	—
	1100	75	—	—	$(80, 0.2\%)$ $(85, 3\%)$; $\sigma_{crs,1000}=52$ $\sigma_{crs,10000}=42$	15.5	27	769	—	—
	1482 (T_m)	—	—	—	—	—	—	—	—	—
Inconel 22 (Ni-Cr-Fe-...; Plate)	23	209	8.6	0.3	$(365, 0.2\%)$ $(770, 65\%)$	12	8	380	—	—
	75 (Critical Crevice Temperature)									
	85 (Critical Pitting Temperature)									
	500	—	—	—	$(230, 0.2\%)$ $(690, 65\%)$	—	16.4	—	—	—
	600	—	—	—	$(210, 0.2\%)$ $(630, 65\%)$	—	17.9	—	—	—
	700	—	—	—	$(200, 0.2\%)$ $(560, 65\%)$	—	22.7	—	—	—
	800	—	—	—	—	—	24.6	—	—	—
	1387 (T_m)	—	—	—	—	—	—	—	—	—
Inconel 100 (As cast)	23	207	7.9	0.3	$(655, 0.2\%)$ $(790, 5\%)$	—	9.1	440	—	—
	1335 (T_m)									
Inconel 100 (ST; Annealed; Aged)	23	207	7.91	0.3	$(655, 0.2\%)$ $(1980, 30\%)$ $(790, 5\%)$	—	9.1	440	—	—
	300	—	—	—	—	—	13.7	503	—	—
	600	—	—	—	—	—	19.9	588	—	—
	650	—	—	—	$(650, 0.2\%)$ $(790, 5\%)$ $(1500, 27\%)$	—	—	—	—	—
	700	—	—	—	—	—	21.7	592	—	—

continued

Material	$T/℃$	E_T	ρ	ν	(σ, ε)	α	k	γ	ρ_E	K_{IC}
Inconel 100 (ST; Annealed; Aged)	732	—	—	—	$(875, 0.2\%)$ $(1095, 6.5\%)$; $\sigma_{crs,1000}=570$	—	—	—	—	—
	800	—	—	—	—	—	22.3	606	—	—
	816	—	—	—	$(815, 0.2\%)$ $(990, 6\%)$; $\sigma_{crs,1000}=380$	—	—	—	—	—
	927	—	—	—	$(500, 0.2\%)$ $(735, 6\%)$; $\sigma_{crs,1000}=170$	—	—	—	—	—
	1100	—	—	—	—	—	26.4	662	—	—
Inconel 556	23	207	7.91	0.3	—	—	9.1	440	—	—
	760	—	—	—	$\sigma_{uts}=220$	—	—	—	—	—
Inconel 600 (Ni-15.5Cr-2.5Fe; Annealed)	−150	—	—	—	—	10.9	12.5	—	—	—
	−124 (T_c)	—	—	—	—	—	—	—	—	—
	−50	—	—	—	—	12.3	—	—	—	—
	23	207	8.3	0.324	$(300, 0.2\%)$ $(660, 45\%)$	10.4	14.9	444	—	—
	500	187	—	0.300	$(200, 0.2\%)$ $(590, 48\%)$	14.9	22.1	536	—	—
	650	—	—	—	$(183, 0.2\%)$ $(448, 39\%)$	—	—	—	—	—
	732	—	—	—	$\sigma_{crs,1000}=65$	—	—	—	—	—
	760	166	—	—	$(120, 0.2\%)$ $(190, 46\%)$	16	26	587	—	—
	816	—	—	—	$\sigma_{crs,1000}=39$	—	—	—	—	—
	1000	143	—	0.339	—	16.7	—	—	—	—
	1354 (T_m)	—	—	—	—	—	—	—	—	—
Inconel 600 (Cold-Worked)	−150	—	—	—	—	10.9	12.5	—	—	—
	−124 (T_c)	—	—	—	—	—	—	—	—	—
	−50	—	—	—	—	12.3	—	—	—	—
	23	207	8.3	0.324	$(873, 0.2\%)$ $(1047, 15\%)$	10.4	14.9	444	—	—
	500	187	—	0.300	—	14.9	22.1	536	—	—
	650	—	—	—	$\sigma_{crs,1000}=100$	—	—	—	—	—

continued

Material	$T/℃$	E_T	ρ	ν	(σ, ε)	α	k	γ	ρ_E	K_{IC}
Inconel 600	760	166	—	—	$\sigma_{crs,1000}=39$	16	26	587	—	—
(Cold-Worked)	1000	143	—	0.339	—	—	—	—	—	—
Inconel 600H	23	207	8.3	0.324	$(283, 0.2\%)$ $(662, 45\%)$	10.4	14.9	444	—	—
Inconel 601 (HR; Ni-23Cr-1.35Al-...; Annealed Plate)	$-196\ (T_c)$	—	—	—	—	—	—	—	—	—
	23	206	8.11	0.27	$(350, 0.2\%)$ $(700, 45\%)$	13.5	11.2	448	—	—
	400	185	—	0.3	—	14.8	17.7	548	—	—
	500	178	—	0.31	—	15.2	19.5	578	—	—
	650	166	—	0.33	$\sigma_{crs,1000}=195$	15.9	21.9	617	—	—
	760	—	—	—	$\sigma_{crs,1000}=63$	—	—	—	—	—
	870	142	—	0.366	$\sigma_{crs,1000}=30$	—	—	—	—	—
	900	138	—	0.37	—	17.24	26.1	686	—	—
Inconel 601 (ST; 1150 ℃ rod)	23	206	8.11	0.27	$(235, 0.2\%)$ $(715, 50\%)$	13.5	11.2	448	—	—
	400	185	—	0.3	$(160, 0.2\%)$ $(620, 52\%)$	14.8	17.7	548	—	—
	500	178	—	0.31	$(150, 0.2\%)$ $(600, 50\%)$	15.2	19.5	578	—	—
	600	171	—	0.33	$(160, 0.2\%)$ $(550, 48\%)$	15.6	21	603	—	—
Inconel 617 (Annealed; Ni-22Cr-12.5Co-9Mo-1.5Fe-1.2Al-...)	23	205	8.36	0.3	$(350, 0.2\%)$ $(825, 40\%)$	11	13.4	419	1.22	—
	500	181	—	—	—	13.9	20.9	536	—	—
	538	175	—	—	$(250, 0.2\%)$ $(600, 71\%)$	—	—	—	—	—
	650	—	—	—	$\sigma_{crs,10000}=243$ $\sigma_{crs,100000}=179$	—	—	—	—	—
	700	151	—	—	$\sigma_{crs,10000}=163$ $\sigma_{crs,100000}=112$	14.8	23.9	586	—	—
	750	—	—	—	$\sigma_{crs,10000}=106$ $\sigma_{crs,100000}=68$	—	—	—	—	—
	800	—	—	—	$\sigma_{crs,10000}=67$ $\sigma_{crs,100000}=41$	—	—	—	—	—
	871	146	—	—	$(200, 0.2\%)$ $(300, 85\%)$	—	—	643	—	—

continued

Material	$T/°C$	E_T	ρ	ν	(σ, ε)	α	k	γ	ρ_E	K_{IC}
Inconel 617 (Annealed; Ni-22Cr-12.5Co-9Mo-1.5Fe-1.2Al-...)	1000	139	—	—	—	16.3	28.7	662	—	—
	1093	—	—	—	(40, 0.2%) (80, 70%)	—	—	—	—	—
	1149	—	—	—	(30, 0.2%) (60, 65%)	—	—	—	—	—
Inconel 617 (Tempered)	23	205	8.36	0.3	(500, 0.2%) (1100, 35%)	11	13.4	419	—	—
Inconel 617 (As Welded)	23	—	—	—	(510, 0.2%) (761, 43%)	—	—	—	—	—
Inconel 625 (HR; Ni-21.5Cr-2.5Fe-9Mo-3.6Nb-Ta)	23	206	8.44	0.28	(634, 0.2%) (1017, 46%)	11	10	410	—	—
	204	198	—	0.286	—	13.1	12.6	456	—	—
	650	—	—	—	(420, 0.2%) (900, 38%)	—	—	—	—	—
	760	160	—	—	—	—	—	—	—	—
	816	—	—	—	$\sigma_{crs,1000} = 96$	—	—	—	—	—
	1350 (T_m)	—	—	—	—	—	—	—	—	—
Inconel 625 (HR; Aged: 593 °C 3 months)	23	206	8.44	0.28	(776, 0.2%) (1158, 40%)	11	10	410	—	—
Inconel 625 (HR; Aged: 650 °C 3 months)	23	206	8.44	0.28	(945, 0.2%) (1258, 28%)	11	10	410	—	—
Inconel 625 (Annealed: 1040 °C; Rapidly cooled)	−157	—	—	—	—	7.3	7.2	—	—	—
	−18	—	—	—	—	—	9.2	402	—	—
	23	206	8.44	0.28	(496, 0.2%) (957, 38%)	12.5	10	410	—	—
	200	198	—	0.286	—	13.1	13	460	—	—
	400	185	—	—	—	13.8	17.6	500	—	—
	650	—	—	0.34	(393, 0.2%) (825, 47%); $\sigma_{crs,1000} = 414$	15.1	20.8	590	—	—

continued

Material	$T/^\circ\text{C}$	E_T	ρ	ν	(σ, ε)	α	k	γ	ρ_E	K_IC
Inconel 625 (Annealed: 1040 ℃; Rapidly cooled)	760	160	—	0.34	$(381, 0.2\%)$ $(585, 62\%)$; $\sigma_{\text{crs},1000} = 140$	15.7	20.8	590	—	—
	870	—	—	—	$(276, 0.2\%)$ $(285, 80\%)$	16.6	—	—	—	—
	982	—	—	—	—	17.3	25.3	645	—	—
Inconel 625 (Spring-tempered)	23	201	8.44	0.30	$\sigma_{\text{uts}} = 1450$	12.5	10	410	—	—
Inconel 657 (As Cast)	23	207	8.44	0.3	$(372, 0.2\%)$ $(600, 28\%)$	10.5	13	410	0.85	—
	540	—	—	—	$(320, 0.2\%)$ $(590, 16\%)$	13.3	23	—	—	—
	650	—	—	—	$(250, 0.2\%)$ $(545, 15\%)$; $\sigma_{\text{crs},100} = 210$	—	—	—	—	—
	760	—	—	—	$(200, 0.2\%)$ $(470, 15\%)$	—	—	—	—	—
	870	—	—	—	$(103, 0.2\%)$ $(250, 19\%)$	15	—	—	—	—
	$1316\ (T_\text{m})$	—	—	—	—	—	—	—	—	—
Inconel 671	23	—	—	—	—	—	—	—	0.87	—
	800	—	—	—	$(225, 0.2\%)$	—	—	—	—	—
Inconel 686 (Bolt-grade 1; Marine applications)	23	207	8.44	0.3	$(586, 0.2\%)$ $(850, 50\%)$	—	10	410	—	—
	85 (Critical Crevice Temperature)									
	85 (Critical Pitting Temperature)									
Inconel 686 (Bolt-grade 2; Marine applications)	23	207	8.44	0.3	$(862, 0.2\%)$ $(1000, 30\%)$	—	10	410	—	—
Inconel 686 (Bolt-grade 3; Marine applications)	23	207	8.44	0.3	$(1034, 0.2\%)$ $(1120, 23\%)$	—	10	410	—	—

continued

Material	$T/{}^\circ\mathrm{C}$	E_T	ρ	ν	(σ, ε)	α	k	γ	ρ_E	K_{IC}
Inconel 690 (HR)	23	207	8.19	0.3	(340, 0.2%) (690, 50%)	—	—	450	1.15	—
	100	200	—	—	—	14	13.5	471	—	—
	540	175	—	—	—	15.4	22	715	—	—
	640	165	—	—	(230, 0.2%) (430, 63%)	16.0	24	—	—	—
	760	155	—	—	(200, 0.2%) (350, 90%)	16.5	26	—	—	—
	800	155	—	—	(170, 0.2%)	—	—	—	—	—
Inconel 690 (CD)	23	207	8.19	0.3	(460, 0.2%) (760, 40%)	—	—	450	—	—
	100	200	—	—	—	14	13.5	471	—	—
	540	175	—	—	—	15.4	22	715	—	—
	640	165	—	—	—	16.0	24	—	—	—
	760	155	—	—	—	16.5	26	—	—	—
Inconel 706 (As Cast)	23	207	—	0.3	—	—	—	—	—	—
	650	—	—	—	$\sigma_{\mathrm{uts}} = 950$; $\sigma_{\mathrm{crs}, 100000} = 230$	—	—	—	—	—
Inconel 713C	23	207	7.91	0.3	(690, 0.2%) (770, 7.9%)	10.5	20	—	—	—
	540	—	—	—	(705, 0.2%) (866, 9.7%)	13.5	23.7	—	—	—
	649	—	—	—	(718, 0.2%) (867, 6.7%)	14.1	23.9	—	—	—
	871	—	—	—	(497, 0.2%) (727, 13.9%)	15.5	31.4	—	—	—
	982	—	—	—	(305, 0.2%) (472, 19.7%)	16.4	48.2	—	—	—
Inconel 713LC	23	207	7.95	0.3	—	9.82	9.8	444	—	—
	300	—	—	—	—	—	14.8	503	—	—
	600	—	—	—	—	—	21.6	590	—	—
	700	—	—	—	—	—	23	592	—	—
	800	—	—	—	—	—	23.5	606	—	—
	1000	—	—	—	—	—	26.1	637	—	—

continued

Material	$T/^\circ C$	E_T	ρ	ν	(σ, ε)	α	k	γ	ρ_E	K_{IC}
Inconel 718 (Hot-Worked; Ni-18.5Fe-19Cr-3Mo-5Nb-Ta; GH4169)	−184	216	—	0.25	—	—	—	—	—	—
	−86	211	—	0.3	—	—	—	—	—	—
	23	200	8.22	0.29	(1180, 0.2%) (1410, 21%)	12.8	11.4	435	—	—
	370	181	—	0.27	—	14.5	16.7	—	—	—
	540	179	—	—	(1069, 0.2%) (1276, 18%)	14.4	—	—	—	—
	600	—	—	—	(1040, 0.2%) (1270, 17%); $\sigma_{crs,1000}=890$	—	—	—	—	85
	650	172	—	0.283	(1027, 0.2%) (1158, 19%); $\sigma_{crs,1000}=590$	15.1	21.8	—	—	—
	760	162	—	0.31	(758, 0.2%) (758, 27%); $\sigma_{crs,1000}=172$	16	23.7	—	—	—
	982	120	—	0.34	—	—	27.4	—	—	—
	1093	99	—	0.402	—	—	—	—	—	—
Inconel 725 (Annealed; Age-hardened)	23	207	8.44	0.29	(896, 0.2%) (1250, 31%)	12	10	410	—	—
	650	—	—	—	(780, 0.2%) (1050, 38%)	—	—	—	—	—
	700	—	—	—	(720, 0.2%) (993, 22%)	—	—	—	—	—
Inconel 725 (HR; Annealed)	23	207	8.44	0.29	(690, 0.2%) (1050, 45%)	12	10	410	—	—
	540	—	—	—	(550, 0.2%) (850, 57%)	—	—	—	—	—
	650	—	—	—	(580, 0.2%) (860, 44%)	—	—	—	—	—
Inconel 738 (Most used gas turbines & vanes)	23	207	8.55	0.28	(952, 0.2%) (1096, 5.5%)	12.5	—	—	—	—
	650	170		0.27	(910, 0.2%) (1055, 7%)	15	—	—	—	—

continued

Material	$T/℃$	E_T	ρ	ν	(σ, ε)	α	k	γ	ρ_E	K_{IC}
Inconel 738 (Most used gas turbines & vanes)	760	160		0.3	(793, 0.2%) (965, 6.5%)	16	14.3	510	—	—
	871	127		0.3	(552, 0.2%) (772, 11%)	—	—	—	—	—
	982 (Sulfidation resistance up to)									
	1093 (Oxidation resistance up to)									
	1093 (T_m)	—	—	—	—	—	—	—	—	—
Inconel 738C	23	207	8.5	0.28	(952, 0.2%) (1096, 5.5%)	—	—	—	—	—
Inconel 738LC	23	207	8.55	0.28	(896, 0.2%) (1034, 57%)	—	—	—	—	—
	750	175.5	—	—	(840, 1.6%)	—	—	—	—	—
	850	151.4	—	—	(550, 1.4%)	—	—	—	—	—
	950	137	—	—	(300, 0.65%)	—	—	—	—	—
Inconel 740 (Annealed: 1200 ℃; Aged: 800 ℃)	23	207	8.5	0.28	(275, 0.2%) (515, 40%)	17.5	16.2	500	—	—
	816	—	—	—	$\sigma_{crs,2400} = 138$	—	—	—	—	—
Inconel 740 (Annealed: 1050 ℃)	23	207	8.5	0.28	—		17.5	16.2	500	—
	816	—	—	—	$\sigma_{crs,300} = 138$	—	—	—	—	—
Inconel X-750 (Annealed)	23	214	8.3	0.3	$\sigma_{uts} = 900$		12.6	17	431	—
	1430 (T_m)	—	—	—	—	—	—	—	—	—
Inconel X-750 (ST; Aged)	23	214	8.3	0.3	(634, 0.2%) (1110, 22%)	12.1	17	431	—	—
	538	172	—	—	(572, 0.2%) (965, 20%)	14.2	27		—	—
	650	145	—	—	(565, 0.2%) (827, 10%)	14.6	29		—	—
	816	128	—	—	(310, 0.2%) (324, 20%)	16	33	540	—	—
	1430 (T_m)	—	—	—	—	—	—	—	—	—

continued

Material	$T/\text{℃}$	E_T	ρ	ν	(σ,ε)	α	k	γ	ρ_E	K_{IC}
Inconel X-750 (Spring Hard; Precip. Hardened)	23	214	8.3	0.3	$(869, 0.2\%)$ $(1260, 30\%)$	12.6	17	431	—	—
	550 (High service temperature)									
	650	—	—	—	$(758, 0.2\%)$ $(986, 7\%)$	—	29	—	—	—
	1430 (T_m)	—	—	—	—	—	—	—	—	—
Inconel X-750 (Spring Hard; aged)	23	214	8.3	0.3	$\sigma_{cts}=1550$	12.6	17	431	—	—
	370 (High service temperature)									
	1430 (T_m)	—	—	—	—	—	—	—	—	—
Inconel 751 (HEV3; Valve; Ni-15Cr-7Fe-Ti-Al)	23	206	8.06	0.29	$(630, 0.2\%)$ $\sigma_{uts}=1120$	14.9	42	473	—	—
	650	—	—	—	$(570, 0.2\%)$ $\sigma_{uts}=830$					
	760	—	—	—	$(450, 0.2\%)$ $(550, 10\%)$					
Inconel 783	23	—	—	0.3	$(850, 0.2\%)$ $(1276, 21\%)$	—	—	—	—	—
	650	—	—	—	$(709, 0.2\%)$ $(984, 38\%)$					
Inconel 800H Or 800HT	−190	210.6	—	0.334	$(220, 0.2\%)$ $(550, 47\%)$	—	—	—	—	—
	−115 (T_c)	—	—	—	—	—	—	—	—	—
	23	196	7.94	0.34	$(240, 0.2\%)$ $(580, 50\%)$	14	11.5	460	—	—
	100	191	—	—	$(220, 0.2\%)$ $(550, 47\%)$	14.4	13	—	—	—
	500	165	—	0.367	$(125, 0.2\%)$ $(460, 48\%)$	16.8	19.5	—	—	—
	600	158	—	0.373	$(100, 0.2\%)$ $(450, 45\%)$	17.1	21.1	—	—	—
	650	—	—	—	$\sigma_{crs,10000}=121$ $\sigma_{crs,100000}=90$	—	—	—	—	—
	700	150	—	0.38	$(105, 0.2\%)$ $(355, 35\%)$; $\sigma_{crs,10000}=80$ $\sigma_{crs,100000}=60$	17.5	22.8	—	—	—

continued

Material	$T/℃$	E_T	ρ	ν	(σ, ε)	α	k	γ	ρ_E	K_{IC}
Inconel 800H Or 800HT	800	141	—	0.394	(110, 0.2%) (280, 70%)	18	24.7	—	—	—
	1385 (T_m)	—	—	—	—	—	—	—	—	—
Invar 32-5 (Super Invar; Inovco; Fe-32Ni-5Co-…; Heat-treated)	23	144	8.15	0.23	(276, 0.2%) (483, 40%)	0.6	—	—	—	—
	150	—	—	—	—	0.8	—	—	—	—
	260	—	—	—	—	2	—	—	—	—
Invar 36 (Fe-36Ni-…; Annealed)	−240	135	—	—	(700, 0.2%) (920, 41%)	2.2	—	—	—	—
	−100	140	—	—	(490, 0.2%) (760, 42%)	1.9	—	—	—	—
	23	144	8.05	0.26	(276, 0.2%) (492, 43%)	1.2	10.5	515	—	—
	200	—	—	—	(210, 0.2%) (427, 45%)	2	—	—	—	—
	250	—	—	—	—	3.4	—	—	—	—
	279 (T_c)	—	—	—	—	—	—	—	—	—
	300	—	—	—	(90, 0.2%) (407, 48%)	4.9	—	—	—	—
	400	—	—	—	(90, 0.2%) (352, 53%)	7.8	—	—	—	—
	500	—	8.2	—	(90, 0.2%) (290, 59%)	9.7	15	—	—	—
	600	—	—	—	(76, 0.2%) (207, 68%)	11.4	—	—	—	—
	1000	60	8.3	—	—	14	20	—	—	—
	1350	20	—	—	—	14.5	23	—	—	—
	1427 (T_m)	—	—	—	—	14.7	30	—	—	—
Invar 36 (1/4 Hard)	23	145	8.05	0.26	(617, 0.2%) (690, 9%)	1.3	11	515	—	—
Invar 36 (30% Hard)	23	145	8.05	0.26	(655, 0.2%) (730, 8%)	1.3	11	515	—	—
Invar 36 (1/2 Hard)	23	145	8.05	0.26	(770, 7%)	1.3	11	515	—	—

continued

Material	$T/℃$	E_T	ρ	ν	(σ, ε)	α	k	γ	ρ_E	K_{IC}
Invar 36 (Hard)	23	145	8.05	0.26	$\sigma_{uts} = 830$	1.3	11	515	—	—
Invar 36 (Fe-36Ni-…; Forged)	−180	—	—	—	(560, 0.2%) (840, 41%)	—	—	—	—	—
	−100	—	—	—	(400, 0.2%) (700, 41%)	—	—	—	—	—
	23	144	8.05	0.26	(276, 0.2%) (492, 41%)	1.2	10.5	515	—	—
	279 (T_c)	—	—	—	—	—	—	—	—	—
Invar 36 (As welded)	−253	—	—	—	(759, 0.2%) (869, 18%)	—	—	—	—	—
	−196	—	—	—	(612, 0.2%) (833, 23%)	—	—	—	—	—
	23	144	8.05	0.26	(308, 0.2%) (484, 28%)	1.2	10.5	515	—	—
Invar 36 (As welded & annealed)	−253	—	—	—	(727, 0.2%) (895, 20%)	—	—	—	—	—
	−196	—	—	—	(616, 0.2%) (844, 22%)	—	—	—	—	—
	23	144	8.05	0.26	(300, 0.2%) (495, 27%)	1.2	10.5	515	—	—
Invar 42 (Annealed)	23	150	8.12	0.26	(280, 0.2%) (448, 35%)	4	10.7	500	—	—
	380 (T_c)	—	—	—	—	—	—	—	—	—
	450	—	—	—	—	7	—	—	—	—
Invar 49 (Annealed)	23	155	8.18	0.26	(150, 0.2%) (500, 44%)	8.3	13	500	—	—
	475 (T_c)	—	—	—	—	—	—	—	—	—
Invar 49 (CD; Bar)	23	166	8.18	0.26	(552, 0.2%) (655, 25%)	8.3	13	500	—	—
Invar 49 (Cold-rolled Strip)	23	166	8.18	0.26	(552, 0.2%) (896, 5%)	8.3	13	500	—	—
Invar 49 (Deep-drawn Strip)	23	166	8.18	0.26	(450, 0.2%) (525, 32%)	8.3	13	500	—	—

continued

Material	$T/°C$	E_T	ρ	ν	(σ, ε)	α	k	γ	ρ_E	K_{IC}
Kovar (Fe-29Ni-17Co-C-Si-Mn-...)	23	207	8.36	0.32	(275, 0.2%) (518, 30%)	5.3	17	440	—	—
	400	—	—	—	—	5.1	—	—	—	—
	435 (T_c)	—	—	—	—	—	—	650	—	—
	700	—	—	—	—	9.1	—	—	—	—
	900	—	—	—	—	11.3	—	—	—	—
	1449 (T_m)	—	—	—	—	—	—	—	—	—
Monel 400 (Ni-31Cu-...; Annealed)	23	179	8.8	0.3	(240, 0.2%) (550, 50%)	13.9	21.8	427	—	—
	425	—	—	—	(170, 0.2%) (450, 48%)	—	—	—	—	—
	1350 (T_m)	—	—	—	—	—	—	—	—	—
Monel 400 (CD)	23	179	8.8	0.3	(768, 0.2%) (838, 8%)	13.9	21.8	427	—	—
Monel 401 (Annealed)	23	179	8.89	0.3	(134, 0.2%) (441, 51%)	13.9	19.2	427	—	—
	1350 (T_m)	—	—	—	—	—	—	—	—	—
Monel 404 (Annealed)	23	169	8.91	0.3	(172, 0.2%) $\sigma_{uts} = 483$	13.3	19.2	414	—	—
	300	—	—	—	—	15.3	—	—	—	—
	815	—	—	—	—	17.6	—	—	—	—
	1300 (T_m)	—	—	—	—	—	—	—	—	—
Monel 404 (Hard)	23	169	8.91	0.3	(689, 0.2%) $\sigma_{uts} = 758$	13.3	19.2	414	—	—
	300	—	—	—	—	15.3	—	—	—	—
Monel R405 (Annealed)	23	179	8.8	0.3	(240, 0.2%) (550, 40%)	13.7	21.8	427	—	—
	1350 (T_m)	—	—	—	—	—	—	—	—	—
Monel K500 (Precip. Hardened)	−65 (T_c)	—	—	—	—	—	—	—	—	—
	23	179	8.44	0.3	(790, 0.2%) (1100, 12%)	13.7	17.5	419	—	—
	425	—	—	—	(630, 0.2%) (860, 25%)	—	—	—	—	—
	1350 (T_m)	—	—	—	—	—	—	—	—	—
Monel 505 (Cast)	23	207	8.8	0.3	(1012, 3.2%)	14	—	—	—	—

continued

Material	$T/°C$	E_T	ρ	ν	(σ, ε)	α	k	γ	ρ_E	K_{IC}
Monel 505 (Hot Finished; Annealed)	23	207	8.8	0.3	(1300, 10%)	14	—	—	—	—
Mu-Metal (Ni-16Fe-5Cu-2Cr)	23	225	8.7	0.29	(280, 0.2%) $\sigma_{uts}=700$	12	19	460	—	—
	1440 (T_m)	—	—	—	—	—	—	—	—	—
Multimet (N155) (ST; Aged; 21Cr-20Ni-20Co-3Mo-2.5W-1.5Mn-0.12C-1Cb-0.15N-...)	23	202	8.3	0.3	(530, 0.2%) (795, 37%)	14	—	435	—	—
	200	—	—	—	—	15.5	14.6	—	—	—
	540	167	—	—	(400, 0.2%) (640, 38%)	—	19	—	—	—
	650	—	—	—	(380, 0.2%) (552, 39%) $\sigma_{crs,1000}=260$	17	21	—	—	—
	730	—	—	—	$\sigma_{crs,1000}=160$	—	—	—	—	—
	760	—	—	—	(262, 0.2%) (414, 35%)	—	—	—	—	—
	815	143	—	—	$\sigma_{crs,1000}=98$	—	—	—	—	—
	870	—	—	—	(179, 0.2%) (262, 37%)	19	—	—	—	—
	980	—	—	—	(125, 0.2%) (135, 38%)	—	—	—	—	—
	1354 (T_m)	—	—	—	—	—	—	—	—	—
Nickel 200 (Annealed)	23	207	8.89	0.30	(153, 0.2%) (453, 47%)	13	44	456	—	—
	1440 (T_m)	—	—	—	—	—	—	—	—	—
Nickel 200 (Cold-worked)	23	207	8.89	0.30	(642, 0.2%) (838, 8%)	13	44	456	—	—
	1440 (T_m)	—	—	—	—	—	—	—	—	—
Nimonic 75 (Ni-20Cr-0.4Ti-0.1C-...; Annealed)	23	—	—	—	(410, 0.2%) (790, 31%)	—	—	—	1.19	—
	540	—	—	—	(355, 0.2%) (725, 27%)	16	—	—	—	—
	650	—	—	—	(275, 0.2%) (475, 32%)	—	—	—	—	—

continued

Material	$T/℃$	E_T	ρ	ν	(σ,ε)	α	k	γ	ρ_E	K_{IC}
Nimonic 75 (Ni-20Cr-0.4Ti-0.1C-…; Annealed)	760	—	—	—	$(185, 0.2\%)$ $(285, 75\%)$	—	—	—	—	—
	870	—	—	—	$(140, 0.2\%)$ $(70, 90\%)$	—	—	—	—	—
Nimonic 80	23	—	—	—	—	12	—	—	1.24	—
	760	—	—	—	$(660, 0.2\%)$	—	—	—	—	—
Nimonic 80A (PH; Extruded Cold-rolled; HT: 8 h/1080 ℃ + 16 h/700 ℃; 3-staged heat treatment)	23	215	8.2	0.32	$(780, 0.2\%)$ $(1250, 30\%)$	12	11.2	448	1.17	—
	500	157	—	—	$(700, 0.2\%)$ $\sigma_{uts}=1050;$ $\sigma_{crs,10000}=834,$ $\sigma_{crs,100000}=713$	14.4	19.5	573	—	—
	550	—	—	—	$\sigma_{crs,10000}=680,$ $\sigma_{crs,100000}=544$	—	—	—	—	—
	600	150	—	—	$(650, 0.2\%)$ $\sigma_{uts}=1000;$ $\sigma_{crs,10000}=519,$ $\sigma_{crs,100000}=372$	—	20.8	600	—	—
	650	—	—	—	$(600, 0.2\%)$ $\sigma_{uts}=930;$ $\sigma_{crs,10000}=356,$ $\sigma_{crs,100000}=217$	—	—	—	—	—
	700	142	—	—	$(600, 0.2\%)$ $\sigma_{uts}=820$	—	22.3	628	—	—
	725	—	—	—	$\sigma_{crs,1000}=290$	—	—	—	—	K_{IC}
	760	—	—	—	$(504, 0.2\%)$	—	—	—	—	—
	800	—	—	—	$\sigma_{crs,1000}=150$	16.2	24.5	650	—	—
	$1365\ (T_m)$	—	—	—	—	—	—	—	—	—
Nimonic 81	23	—	—	—	—	11.1	—	—	1.27	—
Nimonic 90 (Annealed)	23	213	8.2	0.3	$\sigma_{uts}=900$	12.7	—	—	1.14	—
	760	—	—	—	$(538, 2\%)$	—	—	—	—	—
	$1370\ (T_m)$	—	—	—	—	—	—	—	—	—
Nimonic 90 (T: 650 ℃)	23	213	8.2	0.3	$\sigma_{uts}=1400$	12.7	—	—	—	—
	$1370\ (T_m)$	—	—	—	—	—	—	—	—	—

continued

Material	$T/°C$	E_T	ρ	ν	(σ, ε)	α	k	γ	ρ_E	K_{IC}
Nimonic 90 (T: 600 ℃; Aged)	23	213	8.2	0.3	$\sigma_{uts} = 1650$	12.7	—	—	—	—
	1370 (T_m)	—	—	—	—	—	—	—	—	—
Nimonic 95	23	—	—	—	—	13	—	—	1.1	—
Nimonic 101	23	—	—	—	—	11.1	—	—	1.11	—
	800	—	—	—	$(129, 0.2\%)$	—	—	—	—	—
Nimonic 105	23	220	8.0	0.29	$(788, 0.1\%)$ $(850, 0.2\%)$ $(988, 7\%)$	13	25	460	—	—
	400	—	—	—	$(800, 0.2\%)$	—	—	—	—	—
	760	—	—	—	$(750, 0.2\%)$	—	—	—	—	—
	900	—	—	—	$(400, 0.2\%)$	—	—	—	—	—
	1000	—	—	—	$(170, 0.2\%)$	—	—	—	—	—
Nimonic 115 (PH)	23	223	7.9	0.32	$(850, 0.2\%)$ $(1300, 25\%)$	12	10.6	444	—	—
	1345 (T_m)	—	—	—	—	—	—	—	—	—
Nimonic 263	23	—	—	—	—	—	—	—	1.15	—
	760	—	—	—	$(515, 0.2\%)$	—	—	—	—	—
	800	166	—	—	—	—	—	—	—	—
NiCrAlY (Bond Coat for TBS)	23	167	—	0.3	—	17.2	—	—	—	—
Ni-20Co-18Cr-12Al-0.2Y (Intermediate Coating)	23	200	—	0.3	$(426, 0.2\%)$	12.5	—	—	—	—
	200	—	—	—	$(412, 0.2\%)$	—	—	—	—	—
	400	—	—	—	$(396, 0.2\%)$	—	—	—	—	—
	600	160	—	—	Creep starts	15.2	—	—	—	—
	800	145	—	—	—	16.3	—	—	—	—
	1000	120	—	—	—	17.2	—	—	—	—
50.8Ni-49.2Ti (Superelastic Austenite Nitinol)	23	62	7	0.33	$(70, 0.2\%)$ $(150, 0.5\%)$ $(185, 1\%)$ $(195, 2\%)$ $(205, 4\%)$ $(325, 7\%)$	11	—	—	—	30
	1310 (T_m)	—	—	—	—	—	—	—	—	—

continued

Material	$T/℃$	E_T	ρ	ν	(σ, ε)	α	k	γ	ρ_E	K_{IC}
50.8Ni-49.2Ti (Annealed; Nitinol)	23	62	7	0.33	$(600, 0.2\%)$ $(1250, 23\%)$	11	—	—	—	—
50.8Ni-49.2Ti (30% CW; Nitinol)	23	62	7	0.33	$(700, 0.2\%)$ $(1450, 15\%)$	11	—	—	—	—
50.8Ni-49.2Ti (50% CW; Nitinol)	23	62	7	0.33	$(1400, 0.2\%)$ $(1900, 6\%)$	11	—	—	—	—
Nitinol 55 (55Ni-45Ti)	23	100	6.5	0.33	$\sigma_{uts} = 900$	10	9	—	—	—
55.7Ni-44.3Ti (HR; Heat-treated @ 300 ℃ 1.5 h; Gall et al.)	23	39	6.5	0.33	$(246, 0.2\%)$ $(300, 1\%)$ $(480, 1.5\%)$ $(420, 2\%)$ $(460, 4\%)$ $(880, 10\%)$ $(960, 15\%)$	—	—	—	—	—
	125	—	—	—	$(650, 1\%)$ $(800, 3\%)$ $(820, 5.6\%)$	—	—	—	—	—
55.7Ni-44.3Ti (HR; Heat-treated @ 550 ℃ 1.5 h)	23	62	6.5	0.33	$(185, 0.2\%)$ $(300, 1\%)$ $(280, 2\%)$ $(330, 4\%)$	—	—	—	—	—
	125	—	—	—	$(550, 10\%)$ $(700, 16\%)$ $(400, 1\%)$ $(550, 3\%)$ $(750, 14\%)$	—	—	—	—	—

continued

Material	$T/°C$	E_T	ρ	ν	(σ, ε)	α	k	γ	ρ_E	K_{IC}
55.7Ni-44.3Ti (CD; Heat-treated @ 300 ℃ 1.5 h; Gall et al.)	23	41	6.5	0.33	(304, 0.2%) (300, 1%) (470, 3%) (600, 5%) (1050, 7%) (1150, 11%)	—	—	—	—	—
	125	—	—	—	(550, 1%) (660, 5%) (800, 15%)	—	—	—	—	—
	150	—	—	—	(800, 1%) (1400, 5%) (1450, 7%)	—	—	—	—	—
55.7Ni-44.3Ti (CD; Heat-treated @ 550 ℃ 1.5 h)	23	27	6.5	0.33	(205, 0.2%) (190, 1%) (200, 2%) (190, 3%) (750, 10%) (850, 16%)	—	—	—	—	—
	125	—	—	—	(550, 1%) (660, 5%) (800, 15%)	—	—	—	—	—
Nitinol 60 (60Ni-40Ti)	23	114	6.7	0.33	—	10	18	—	—	—
Pyromet 680	23	—	—	0.33	—	—	—	—	—	—
	760	—	—	0.33	(241, 0.2%)	—	—	—	—	—
	816	144	—	0.33	$\sigma_{crs,1000} = 62$	—	—	—	—	—
Rene 41 (Precip. Hardened)	23	218	8.25	0.32	(1062, 0.2%) (1420, 14%)	12	11	452	—	—
	650	179		—	—	(1000, 0.2%) (1340, 14%); $\sigma_{crs,1000} = 690$	15	21	—	—	—
	760	171		—	—	(940, 0.2%) (1100, 11%); $\sigma_{crs,1000} = 275$	16	23	—	—	—
	815	—	—	—	$\sigma_{crs,1000} = 165$	—	—	—	—	—
	1345 (T_m)	—	—	—	—	—	—	—	—	—

continued

Material	$T/{}^\circ\mathrm{C}$	E_T	ρ	ν	(σ, ε)	α	k	γ	ρ_E	K_IC
Rene 77 (ST; Annealed; Aged)	23	207	—	0.3	$(760, 0.2\%)$ $\sigma_\mathrm{uts}=860$	16	—	—	1.3	—
	800	—	—	—	—	18	—	—	—	—
Rene 80	23	207	—	0.3	—	—	—	—	—	—
	850 (Transition from low to high creep rate)									
Rene 88 DT (Powder M.)	23	207	—	0.3	$(1250, 0.2\%)$	—	—	—	—	—
	200	—	—	—	$(1150, 0.2\%)$	—	—	—	—	—
	400	—	—	—	$(1080, 0.2\%)$	—	—	—	—	—
	600	—	—	—	$(1150, 0.2\%)$ $\sigma_\mathrm{uts}=1400$					
	650	—	—	—	$(1060, 0.2\%)$	—	—	—	—	—
Rene 95 (Forged)	23	207	8.8	0.3	$(1310, 0.2\%)$ $(1620, 15\%)$	—	—	—	—	—
	540	—	—	—	$(1255, 0.2\%)$ $(1551, 13\%)$	—	—	—	—	—
	650	—	—	—	$\sigma_\mathrm{uts}=1500$; $\sigma_\mathrm{crs,90}=1035$	—	—	—	—	—
	760	—	—	—	$\sigma_\mathrm{uts}=1150$; $\sigma_\mathrm{crs,55}=620$	—	—	—	—	—
Rene 220 (ST; Annealed; Aged)	23	207	—	0.3	$(830, 0.2\%)$ $(1105, 6\%)$	—	—	—	—	—
Udimet 500	23	—	—	0.3	—	13.3	—	—	1.2	—
	760	—	—	—	$(731, 0.2\%)$	—	—	—	—	—
Udimet 520	23	—	8.21	0.3	$(850, 0.2\%)$ $(1310, 99\%)$	—	—	—	—	—
	400	—	—	—	$(840, 0.2\%)$ $(1250, 99\%)$	—	—	—	—	—
	650	—	—	—	$\sigma_\mathrm{crs,1000}=585$	—	—	—	—	—
	700	—	—	—	$(700, 0.2\%)$ $(1150, 99\%)$; $\sigma_\mathrm{crs,1000}=470$	—	—	—	—	—
	760	—	—	—	$\sigma_\mathrm{crs,1000}=345$	—	—	—	—	—
	870	—	—	—	$\sigma_\mathrm{crs,1000}=150$	—	—	—	—	—
	1405 (T_m)	—	—	—	—	—	—	—	—	—

continued

Material	$T/°C$	E_T	ρ	ν	(σ, ε)	α	k	γ	ρ_E	K_{IC}
Udimet 720 (Grain~20 μm)	23	—	8.08	—	$(980, 0.2\%)$ $\sigma_{uts}=1580$	12.2	—	—	—	—
	650	—	—	—	$\sigma_{uts}=1400;$ $\sigma_{crs,1000}=700$	—	—	—	—	—
	700	—	—	—	$\sigma_{crs,1000}=500$	—	—	—	—	—
	760	—	—	—	$\sigma_{uts}=1050;$ $\sigma_{crs,1000}=480$	—	—	—	—	—
	870	—	—	—	$\sigma_{crs,1000}=220$	—	—	—	—	—
	980	—	—	—	$\sigma_{crs,1000}=68$	—	—	—	—	—
	1338 (T_m)	—	—	—	—	—	—	—	—	—
Waspaloy (Precipitation-Hardened; ST@ 1038 °C; Aged)	23	211	8.25	0.32	$(850, 0.2\%)$ $(1250, 33\%)$	12.2	11	520	—	—
	540	184	—	—	$(745, 0.2\%)$ $(1160, 31\%)$	13.9	18	540	—	—
	650	—	—	—	$\sigma_{uts}=1100;$ $\sigma_{crs,1000}=614$	—	—	—	—	—
	700	—	—	—	$\sigma_{crs,100000}=270$	—	—	—	—	—
	732	—	—	—	$\sigma_{crs,132}=517$	—	—	—	—	—
	815	156	—	—	$\sigma_{crs,47}=328$	15.7	23	570	—	—
	1360 (T_m)	—	—	—	—	—	—	—	—	—
Ni-Be Alloy 360 (Annealed)	23	200	8.27	0.30	$(380, 0.2\%)$ $(780, 30\%)$	14.5	48	461	—	—
	1200 (T_m)	—	—	—	—	—	—	—	—	—
Ni-Be Alloy 360 (1/2 Hard)	23	200	8.27	0.3	$(1380, 0.2\%)$ $(1690, 9\%)$	14.5	48	461	—	—
	1200 (T_m)	—	—	—	—	—	—	—	—	—
Ni-30Cr	23	—	8.1	0.29	$(875, 27\%)$	18	—	430	—	—

continued

Material	$T/°C$	E_T	ρ	ν	(σ, ε)	α	k	γ	ρ_E	K_{IC}
Ni-20Cr (Nichrome)	23	220	8.3	0.29	(350, 0.2%) (760, 30%)	13.4	11.3	435	—	135
	100	—	—	—	—	—	15	—	—	—
	400	—	—	—	(225, 0.2%) $\sigma_{uts}=670$	—	—	—	—	—
	600	—	—	—	(220, 0.2%) $\sigma_{uts}=585$	—	—	—	—	—
	800	—	—	—	(115, 0.2%) $\sigma_{uts}=285$	—	—	—	—	—
	1000	—	—	—	(25, 0.2%) $\sigma_{uts}=70$	—	—	—	—	—
	1400 (T_m)	—	—	—	—	—	—	—	—	—
Ni-10Cr (Chromel)	23	186	8.5	0.29	(700, 44%)	12.8	17	444	—	—
	1100 (High service temperature)									
	1420 (T_m)	—	—	—	—	—	—	—	—	—
Fe-10Ni	23	207	7.9	0.3	—	—	73	452	—	—
Fe-20Ni (HT & Aged)	23	207	8	0.3	(701, 0.2%) (1021, 27%)	13	19	460	—	—
	600	207	—	—	(611, 0.2%) (802, 12%)	—	—	—	—	—
Ni-2Co (High Strength)	23	—	—	0.33	(1250, 0.2%) (1350, 2%)	—	—	—	—	—
Ni-8Co (High Hardness)	23	—	—	0.33	(999, 0.2%) (1000, 1.5%)	—	—	—	—	—

Notes: HR-Hot Rolled;

CD-Cold Drawn;

HW-Hot Worked;

HT = Heat Treated;

Nickel 200 = more than 99.5% of Ni;

Monel 400 = 66Ni-32Cu;

Inconel 600 = 78Ni-15Cr-7Fe;

All the alloy compositions are in weight percent unless stated otherwise.

Table 92.2 Fatigue ε-N Properties of Ni（Nickel）Alloys

Material	$T/^\circ\mathrm{C}$	$\mathrm{d}\varepsilon/\mathrm{d}t$	σ'_f	ε'_f	b	c	K'	n'	$\sigma_\mathrm{f}@2N_\mathrm{f}$	R
Nickel（Nanocrystalline）	23	—	—	—	—	—	—	—	400@ 106	—
Ni-Ti	23	—	1267	0.174	−0.139	−0.415	2275	0.334	—	—
Fe-Ni	23	—	1233	0.092	—	—	—	—	—	—
GH4133	23	—	—	—	—	—	—	—	$\sigma_\mathrm{f}=420$	—
Hastelloy X	23	—	920	0.18	−0.07	−0.45	1048	0.13	—	—
	816	—	579	0.49	−0.07	−0.75	—	—	—	—
	982	—	257	0.77	−0.07	−0.75	—	—	—	—
Haynes 188	23	—	820	0.33	−0.105	−055	864	0.19	—	—
Haynes 230	23	—	—	—	—	—	—	—	—	—
	816	—	609	0.48	−0.07	−0.9	—	—	—	—
	982	—	255	0.77	−0.07	−0.9	—	—	—	—
Haynes 242（HR；Annealed）	650	—	—	—	—	—	—	—	550@ 3×10^5 650@ 3.3×10^4	0.05^+ 0.05^+
Incoloy 901	816	—	1977	0.125	−0.122	−0.648	1566	0.09	—	—
Incoloy 909（Annealed）	650	—	—	—	—	—	—	—	550@ 1.3×10^5 585@ 4.5×10	0.05^+ 0.05^+
Inconel 600（HR）	23	—	—	—	—	—	—	—	279@ 10^8	—
Inconel 600（CD）	23	—	—	—	—	—	—	—	310@ 10^8	—
Inconel 600（Annealed）	23	—	—	—	—	—	—	—	269@ 10^8	—
Inconel 625（Annealed）	23	59 Hz	—	—	—	—	—	—	552@ 1.9×10^6 621@ 3×10^5 758@ 600	−1 −1 −1
Inconel 625（Aged = 593 ℃ 300 h）	23	59 Hz	—	—	—	—	—	—	621@ 1×10^7 690@ 7×10^4 758@ 10^4	−1 −1 −1
Inconel 625（Aged = 704 ℃ 300 h）	23	—	—	—	—	—	—	—	621@ 1×10^7 690@ 10^5 758@ 2×10^4	−1 −1 −1

continued

Material	$T/°C$	$d\varepsilon/dt$	σ_f'	ε_f'	b	c	K'	n'	$\sigma_f @ 2N_f$	R
Inconel 686 (Annealed; Air)	23	—	—	—	—	—	—	—	$450@10^7$	—
Inconel 686 (Annealed; Seawater)	23	—	—	—	—	—	—	—	$360@10^7$	—
Inconel 686 (Bolt-Grade 3)	23	—	—	—	—	—	—	—	$310@10^7$ $350@10^6$ $490@10^5$	— — —
Inconel 713C	23	—	—	—	—	—	—	—	$224@10^8$	—
	650	—	—	—	—	—	—	—	$155@10^8$	—
	730	—	—	—	—	—	—	—	$179@10^8$	—
	815	—	—	—	—	—	—	—	$179@10^8$	—
	930	—	—	—	—	—	—	—	$155@10^8$	—
Inconel 718	23	—	780	1.15	−0.114	−0.86	544	0.075	—	—
Inconel 718	23	—	3950	1.5	−0.151	−0.761	1564	0.068	—	—
Inconel 718 (HT, Aged)	23	—	2295	3.637	−0.1	−0.894	1986	0.112	$896@10^7$ (Seawater)	—
Inconel 725 (HT, Aged)	23	—	—	—	—	—	—	—	$730@10^7$ (Seawater)	—
Inconel 738LC	23	—	—	—	—	—	—	—	$124@10^8$	—
	500	—	—	—	—	—	—	—	$117@10^8$	—
	800	—	—	—	—	—	—	—	$124@10^8$	—
	900	—	—	—	—	—	—	—	$117@10^8$	—
Inconel 751	23	—	1860	—	—	—	—	—	—	—
Inconel 925 (HT, Aged)	23	—	—	—	—	—	—	—	$500@10^7$ (Seawater)	—
Invar 36	−196	—	—	—	—	—	—	—	$273@10^7$	−1
	−73	—	—	—	—	—	—	—	$21@10^7$	−1
	23	—	—	—	—	—	—	—	$150@10^7$	−1
Rene 88 DT	23	20 kHz	—	—	—	—	—	—	$750@10^9$	0.05^+
	593	20 kHz	—	—	—	—	—	—	$950@10^7$ $1190@10^5$ $1400@10^3$	0.05^+ 0.05^+ 0.05^+
RR 1000	23	—	989.5	—	−0.082	—	—	—	—	—

continued

Material	$T/^\circ\text{C}$	$d\varepsilon/dt$	σ'_f	ε'_f	b	c	K'	n'	$\sigma_f@2N_f$	R
Ni Alloys (Generic)	23	—	Eq. (6.14)	Eq. (6.15)	—	—	$\sigma'_f/(\varepsilon'_f)^{n'}$	b/c	Eq. (92.1)	—

Table 92.3   Mechanical Creep Parameters of Ni Alloys

Material	$T/^\circ\text{C}$	Stress /MPa	Strain Rate /s^{-1}	$A/(\text{MPa}^{-n}\cdot\text{s}^{m-1})$	$Q/(\text{J}\cdot\text{mol}^{-1})$	n	m
Haynes 556	760~871	$E=1$; 40~100	—	1.18×10^{-5}	$Q/R=20850$	5.432	0
Haynes 230	—	$E=1$	—	591.5	410×10^3	6.885	0
Inconel 718	725	$E=1$;	—	4.5472×10^{-34}	0	9.71	−0.468
	825	$E=1$;	—	4.01344×10^{-33}	0	9.71	−0.468
Ni	950	$E=1$;	—	5.28	227×10^3	4.6	0
Ni (LIGA)	280	$E=1$;	—	—	279×10^3	6.5	0
Ni-Al	950	$E=1$;	—	3.7×10^{-3}	245×10^3	5.5	0
NiCrAlY (Bond Coat)	200~1100	$E=1$	—	3.237×10^7	298×10^3	3.0	0
50Ni-49.50Ti (HD wire)	600~900	$E=1$; 10~35	0.003~0.04	0.05	222×10^3	3.0	0
50.8Ni-49.2Ti (Annealed; 48 μm < grain < 140 μm)	950~1100	$E=1$; 4.7~11	$10^{-6}\sim10^{-5}$	0.05	155×10^3	2.66	0

Notes: Creep equation: $\dfrac{d\varepsilon_{creep}}{dt} = A\left(\dfrac{\sigma-\sigma_{th}}{E}\right)^n t^m \exp\left(\dfrac{-Q}{RT_k}\right)$, $\sigma > \sigma_{th}$;

σ_{th} = Stress threshold and σ_{th} = 0, if not specified;

E = Young's modulus; that $E = 1$ means E is not specified.

Table 92.4 Material Parameters on Fatigue Crack Growth of Ni-alloys in Opening Mode

Material	$T/°C$	σ_y	σ_{uts}	K_{IC}	$f(R)$	m	ΔK_{th}	$\Delta\sigma_{fat}$
Inconel 718	23	—	—	—	—	—	—	—
	600	—	—	—	$f(0.01)$	—	10	—
55.7Ni-44.3Ti (HR; Aged at 300 ℃ 1.5 h)	23	246	—	—	$f(-1) = 3.32\times10^{-11}$	2.76	2.42	—
55.7Ni-44.3Ti (HR; Aged at 550 ℃ 1.5 h)	23	185	—	—	$f(-1) = 1.02\times10^{-11}$	3.46	2.68	—
55.7Ni-44.3Ti (CD; Aged at 300 ℃ 1.5 h)	23	246	—	—	$f(-1) = 2.77\times10^{-10}$	3.3	0.65	—
55.7Ni-44.3Ti (CD; Aged at 550 ℃ 1.5 h)	23	185	—	—	$f(-1) = 4.6\times10^{-12}$	4.14	2.57	—

Notes: $da / dNp = f(R) \mid \Delta K - \Delta K_{th} \mid^m$

$\sigma_y(MPa)$ = Yield strength;

$\sigma_{uts}(MPa)$ = Ultimate tensile strength;

$f(R)$ = Parameter as a function of load ratio (R);

m = Exponent;

$\Delta K_{th}(MPa\ m^{\frac{1}{2}})$ = Threshold stress intensity factor range;

$\Delta\sigma_{fat}(MPa)$ = Fatigue strength range.

Chapter 93

Pb (Lead)

93.1 Introduction

Pb (Lead) is soft, malleable, and ductile. It can be easily worked into sheets. Mechanical properties of lead are given in Table 93.1.

Lead is a neurotoxin that accumulates in soft tissues and bones, damaging the nervous system and causing brain disorders [Hodge].

93.2 Applications

Lead and lead alloys are still widely used for car batteries, electronic solders, bearings, cable sheathing, pigments, ammunition, and radiation protection.

References

BEEMAN J W, et al, 2013. New Experimental Limits on the α Decays of lead Isotopes[J]. The European Physical Journal, A, 49: 50.

DE LA TORRE A, ADEVA P, ABALLE M, 1991. Indentation Creep of Lead and Lead-Copper Alloys[J]. Journal of Materials Science, 26(16): 4351-4354.

HODGET A. October 1981. Vitruvius, Lead Pipes, and Lead Poisoning[J]. American Journal of Archaeology, Archaeological Institute of America, 85(4): 486-491.

RIDDINGTON J, SAHOTA M, 2003. Mechanical Properties of Lead Alloys in Compression[J]. Journal of Materials in Civil Engineering, 5(4): 323-328.

RIEUWERTS J, 2015. Chapter 13. Lead[M]. The Elements of Environmental Pollution, Abingdon, UK: Routledge, 224-234.

THURMER K, et al, 2002. Autocatalytic Oxidation of Lead Crystallite Surfaces[J]. Science, 297(5589): 2033-2035.

Table 93.1 Mechanical Properties of Lead and Lead-Alloys

Material	$T/℃$	E_T	ρ	ν	(σ, ε)	α	k	γ	ρ_E	K_{IC}
Pb (>99%)	23	15	11.34	0.42	$\sigma_{uts}=17$	30	33	140	0.206	—
	327.5 (T_m)	—	—	—	—	—	—	—	—	—

Table 93.2 Fatigue ε-N Properties of Lead and Lead-Alloys

Material	$T/℃$	$d\varepsilon/dt$	σ_f'	ε_f'	b	c	K'	n'	$\sigma_f @ 2N_f$	R
Pb (>99%)	23	—	—	—	—	—	—	—	3.17	—

Chapter 94

Pd (Palladium)

94.1　Introduction

Pd (Palladium) is one of the four metals having ISO currency codes, besides platinum, gold, and silver. Its material properties are given in Table 94.1. All four metals are precious metals in jewelry.

One special characteristic of Pd (Palladium) is its absorption of hydrogen. A palladium hydride contains 900 times its volume of hydrogen in a reverse process at room temperature and atmospheric pressure.

94.2　Applications

Most palladium is used for catalytic converters in the automotive industry and multilayer chip capacitors for the electronic industry.

References

MEZGER P R, el al, 1988. Metallurgical Aspects of High-Palladium Alloys[J]. Journal of Dental Research, 67(10): 1307-1311.

WOLLASTON W H, 1804. On a New Metal Found in Crude Platina[J]. Philosophical Transactions of the Royal Society of London, 94: 419-430.

WATAHA J C, SHOR K, 2010. Palladium Alloys for Biomedical Devices[J]. Expert Review of Medical Devices, 7(4): 489-501.

VERMILYEA S G, et al, 1996. Metallurgical Structure and Microhardness of Four New Palladium-based Alloys [J]. Journal of Prosthod, 5(4): 288-294.

SUN Y, WANG H, XIA M, 2008. Single-walled Carbon Nanotubes Modified with Pd Nanoparticles: Unique Building Blocks for High-Performance, Flexible Hydrogen Sensors[J]. Journal of Physical Chemistry, C, 112(4): 1250-1259.

Table 94.1   Mechanical Properties of Pd（Palladium）Alloys

Material	$T/℃$	E_T	ρ	ν	(σ, ε)	α	k	γ	ρ_E	K_{IC}
Pd（Annealed; HV=37）	23	117	12.023	0.39	(180, 2%)	11.8	72	244	—	—
	1552 (T_m)	—	—	—	—	—	—	—	—	—
Pd（Hard; HV=100）	23	121	12.023	0.39	(205, 0.2%) $\sigma_{uts}=325$	11.8	72	244	—	—
	1552 (T_m)	—	—	—	—	—	—	—	—	—
Paliney 6（HT Pd-Ag-Cu; for Potentiometer）	23	115	10.8	0.4	(840, 0.2%) (1220, 6%)	13.5	—	—	—	—
Paliney 7 （HT; Aged Hardened Rod）	23	118	11.8	0.4	(999, 0.2%) (1250, 5%)	13	—	—	—	—
	1050 (T_m)	—	—	—	—	—	—	—	—	—
Paliney 7 （Annealed; Pd-Ag-Cu-Pt-Au; for Dental Rod）	23	118	11.8	0.4	(630, 0.2%) (840, 15%)	13	—	—	—	—
Pd-6Cu-17Si	23	96	—	0.41	$\sigma_{uts}=1530$	—	—	—	—	—
Pd-16Cu-20P	23	93	—	0.41	$\sigma_{uts}=1560$	—	—	—	—	—

Table 94.2   Fatigue ε-N Properties of Zinc Alloys

Material	$T/℃$	$\mathrm{d}\varepsilon/\mathrm{d}t$	σ_f'	ε_f'	b	c	K'	n'	$\sigma_f @ 2N_f$	R
Paliney 6	23	—	—	—	—	—	—	—	$315@\,10^8$	RB
Paliney 7	23	—	—	—	—	—	—	—	$350@\,10^8$	RB

Chapter 95

Pt (Platinum)

95.1 Introduction

Pt (Platinum) is one of the eight noble metals, highly resistant to corrosion and oxidation. Mechanical properties of Pt alloys are listed in Table 95.1.

95.2 Applications

The most common use of platinum is as a catalyst in chemical reactions. One interesting application of platinum in the automotive industry is for electric vehicles. It is used for electrical contacts and electrodes. It is also used for thermocouples to measure elevated temperatures.

The catalyst itself for an automotive emission catalytic converter is most often a precious metal. Platinum is the most active catalyst and is widely used. It is not suitable for all applications, however, because of unwanted additional reactions and/or cost. Palladium and rhodium are two other precious metals used. Platinum and rhodium are used as a reduction catalyst, while platinum and palladium are used as an oxidation catalyst.

References

FISCHER B, et al, 1999. High-Temperature Mechanical Properties of the Platinum Group Metals[J]. Platinum Metals Review, 43(1): 18-28.

HU X, NING Y, 2012. Physical Properties and Application Performance of Platinum-High-Temperature-Rhodium Alloys Modified with Cerium[J]. Platinum Metals Review, 56(1): 40-46.

JACKSON K M, LANG C, 2006. Mechanical Properties Data for Pt-5wt.%Cu and Pt-5wt.% Ru Alloys[J]. Platinum Metals Review, 50(1): 15-19.

LEE H, et al, 2009. Fabrication and Electric Properties of Platinum Nanofibers by Electrostatic Spinning[J]. Journal of Physics D: Applied Physics, 42(12): 125409.

Merker J, Lupton D, Topfer M, et al, 2001. High Temperature Mechanical Properties of the Platinum Group Metals[J]. Platinum Metals Review, 45(2): 74-82.

VOLKL R, et al, 2001. Finite Element Modeling of Strains and Stresses in Platinum Alloy Bushings for textile Glass Fiber production[J]. Glastech, Berlin Society of Glass Science and Technology, 74(5): 1-10.

Table 95.1　Mechanical Properties of Pt（Platinum）Alloys

Material	$T/℃$	E_T	ρ	ν	(σ, ε)	α	k	γ	ρ_E	K_{IC}
Pt（Annealed）	23	168	21.45	0.38	（172，3%）	8.8	70	130	—	—
	250	—	—	—	$\sigma_{uts}=177$	—	72	—	—	—
	500	—	—	—	$\sigma_{uts}=68$	9.6	—	—	—	—
	1000	—	—	—	$\sigma_{uts}=12.8$	10.2	—	—	—	—
	1250	—	—	—	$\sigma_{uts}=8.83$	—	—	—	—	—
	1600	—	—	—	$\sigma_{uts}=2.7$；$\sigma_{crs,10}=1.2$	—	—	—	—	—
	1769（T_m）	—	—	—	—	—	—	—	—	—
Pt（Cold-worked）	23	168	21.45	0.38	（180，0.2%）（380，3%）	8.8	70	130	—	—
Pt-5Au（Annealed）	23	96	21.33	—	$\sigma_{uts}=345$	—	—	—	—	—
	1760（T_m）	—	—	—	—	—	—	—	—	—
Pt-5Au（Hard）	23	96	21.33	—	$\sigma_{uts}=450$	—	—	—	—	—
Pt-5Co（Annealed）	23	96	20.02	—	$\sigma_{uts}=440$	—	—	—	—	—
	1765（T_m）	—	—	—	—	—	—	—	—	—
Pt-5Co（Hard）	23	96	20.02	—	$\sigma_{uts}=690$	—	—	—	—	—
Pt-5Cu（As cast）	23	96	20.05	—	（427，22%）	—	—	—	—	—
	1750（T_m）	—	—	—	—	—	—	—	—	—
Pt-5Cu（Annealed）	23	96	20.05	—	（400，30%）	—	—	—	—	—
	1750（T_m）	—	—	—	—	—	—	—	—	—
Pt-5Cu（Heat-Treated：800 ℃）	23	96	20.05	—	（360，0.2%）（530，36%）	—	—	—	—	—
	1750（T_m）	—	—	—	—	—	—	—	—	—
Pt-5Cu（90% Cold-worked）	23	96	20.05	—	（820，0.2%）（990，2%）	—	—	—	—	—
Pt-5Ir（Annealed）	23	96	21.5	0.38	$\sigma_{uts}=275$	—	—	—	—	—
	1795（T_m）	—	—	—	—	—	—	—	—	—
Pt-5Ir（Hard）	23	96	21.5	0.38	$\sigma_{uts}=475$	—	—	—	—	—
Pt-10Ir（Annealed）	23	96	21.55	0.38	（200，0.2%）（380，20%）	—	—	—	—	—
	1790（T_m）	—	—	—	—	—	—	—	—	—
Pt-5Ni（Annealed）	23	96	20.04	—	$\sigma_{uts}=450$	—	—	—	—	—
	1760（T_m）	—	—	—	—	—	—	—	—	—
Pt-5Ni（Hard）	23	96	20.04	—	$\sigma_{uts}=710$	—	—	—	—	—
Pt-6Ni-20P	23	96	20	0.42	（1860，3%）	—	—	—	—	—

continued

Material	$T/℃$	E_T	ρ	ν	(σ, ε)	α	k	γ	ρ_E	K_{IC}
Pt-4Pd-3.5Rh (Annealed at 900 ℃)	23	—	—	—	(240, 16%)	—	—	—	—	—
Pt-4Pd-3.5Rh (Annealed at 1000 ℃ Continuously)	23	—	—	—	(380, 10%)	—	—	—	—	—
	800	—	—	—	$\sigma_{uts}=75$	—	—	—	—	—
	1000	—	—	—	$\sigma_{uts}=48$	—	—	—	—	—
Pt-4Pd-3.5Rh-0.1Ce (Annealed at 900 ℃)	23	—	—	—	(240, 16%)	—	—	—	—	—
Pt-4Pd-3.5Rh-0.1Ce (Annealed at 1000 ℃ Continuously)	23	—	—	—	(380, 10%)	—	—	—	—	—
	800	—	—	—	$\sigma_{uts}=180$	—	—	—	—	—
	1000	—	—	—	$\sigma_{uts}=77$	—	—	—	—	—
Pt-5Pd (Annealed)	23	96	20.64	—	$\sigma_{uts}=450$	—	—	—	—	—
	1760 (T_m)	—	—	—	—	—	—	—	—	—
Pt-5Pd (Hard)	23	96	20.64	—	$\sigma_{uts}=710$	—	—	—	—	—
Pt-5Rh (Annealed)	23	96	20.7	—	$\sigma_{uts}=260$	—	—	—	—	—
	1795 (T_m)	—	—	—	—	—	—	—	—	—
Pt-5Rh (Hard)	23	96	20.7	—	$\sigma_{uts}=540$	—	—	—	—	—
Pt-5Rh (Annealed)	23	96	20.7	—	$\sigma_{uts}=260$	—	—	—	—	—
	1795 (T_m)	—	—	—	—	—	—	—	—	—
Pt-10Rh (Annealed at 900 ℃)	23	—	—	—	(260, 16%)	—	—	—	—	—
Pt-10Rh (Annealed at 1000 ℃)	23	—	—	—	(350, 14%)	—	—	—	—	—
	800	—	—	—	$\sigma_{uts}=135$	—	—	—	—	—
	1000	—	—	—	$\sigma_{uts}=72$	—	—	—	—	—
Pt-5Ru (Heat-Treated at 800 ℃)	23	96	20.67	—	(370, 0.2%) (540, 29%)	—	—	—	—	—
	1750 (T_m)	—	—	—	—	—	—	—	—	—
Pt-5Cu (90% Cold-worked)	23	96	20.67	—	(780, 0.2%) (960, 3%)	—	—	—	—	—
Pt-W (Annealed)	23	96	21.33	—	$\sigma_{uts}=540$	—	—	—	—	—
	1800 (T_m)	—	—	—	—	—	—	—	—	—
Pt-W (Hard)	23	96	21.33	—	$\sigma_{uts}=825$	—	—	—	—	—

Chapter 96

Sn (Tin)

96.1 Introduction

Sn (Tin) has an unusually low melting point of 232 ℃ and the unusually high boiling point of 2260 ℃ ; thus easy to form alloys without loss in vaporization. Sn becomes a superconductor below 3.72 K. β-Sn undergoes a ductile to brittle phase transition to α-Sn if the temperature goes below 13.2 ℃. Mechanical properties and fatigue parameters of Sn (Tin) alloys are listed in Tables 96.1 and 96.2, respectively.

96.2 Applications

Sn-based solders are used for integrating electronic circuits and joining pipes. The formation of tin whiskers causing electrical problems is a concern.

Sn (Tin) is used primarily to coat steel and some other metals to provide corrosion resistance. The coating can be only about 2.3 μm thick. The tin adheres strongly and uniformly to the steel, protecting it from attack.

The niobium-tin compound Nb_3Sn is commercially used as wires for superconducting magnets.

References

ALCHAGIROV B B, CHOCHAEVA A M, 2000. Temperature Dependence of the Density of Liquid Tin[J]. High Temperature, 38(1): 44-48.

CHALMERS B, 1936. Micro-plasticity in Crystals of Tin, Proceedings of the Royal Society of London, A[J]. Mathematics and Physical Science, 156(888): 427-443.

DEHAAS W, DEBOER J, VANDENBERG G, 1935. The Electric Resistance of Cadmium, Thallium, and Tin at Low Temperatures[J]. Physica, 2(1-12): 453-459.

HAMPSHIRE W B. 1993. The Search for Lead-free Solders[J]. Soldering and Surface Mount Technology, 5(2): 49-52.

IDOTA Y, et al, 1997. Tin-based Amorphous Oxides: a High-Capacity Lithium-Ion Storage Material[J]. Science, 276(5317): 1395-1397.

MAO O, DAHN J R, 1999. Mechanically Alloyed Sn-Fe(-C) Powders as Anode Materials for Li-Ion Batteries. III. Sn_2Fe: $SnFe_3C$ Active/Inactive Composites[J]. Journal of Electrochemical Society, 146(2): 405-413.

NAGASAKA M, 1999. Strain-rate and Temperature Dependence of Plastic Deformation in White Tin Single Crystals[J]. Japanese Journal of Applied Physics, 38(3): 171-175.

NAKAI K, et al, 2008. A Model for Nucleation of Tin Whisker through Dislocation Behavior[J]. Journal of Physics Conference Series, 165: 012089.

THOBURN J T, 1994. Tin in the World Economy[M]. Edinburgh: Edinburgh University Press.

Table 96.1   Mechanical Properties of Sn (Tin) Alloys

Material	$T/°C$	E_T	ρ	ν	(σ, ε)	α	k	γ	ρ_E	K_{IC}
Sn (Pure; Bulk)	−55	52.3	—	—	—	—	—	—	—	—
	23	43	7.3	0.36	(12, 0.2%) (21, 10%); $\sigma_{crs,1000} = 8.4$	22	64	227	—	
	50	41	—	—	—	—	—	—	—	—
	100	35.5	—	—	$\sigma_{crs,1000} = 2.2$	—	—	—	—	—
	232 (T_m)	—	—	—	—	—	—	—	—	—
	300 (Liquid)	7.0	—	—	—	30	—	—	—	—
Sn (Cast; Hammered)	23	43	7.35	0.36	(12, 0.2%) (21, 10%)	22	62.5	226	—	—
	232 (T_m)	—	—	—	—	—	—	—	—	—
Sn (Crysrtalline)	23	82.7	—	0.34	—	—	—	—	—	—

Notes: Sn-based solders and intermetallics are given in Chapter 127.

Table 96.2   Fatigue ε-N Properties of Sn (Tin) Alloys

Material	$T/°C$	$d\varepsilon/dt$	σ'_f	ε'_f	b	c	K'	n'	$\sigma_f @ 2N_f$	R
Sn	23	—	—	—	—	—	—	—	$13.7@ 10^3$	—
	100	—	—	—	—	—	—	—	$9@ 10^3$	—

Chapter 97

Ti (Titanium)

97.1   Introduction

It is the fifth most abundant metal in the earth's crust. Titanium with more than 99% concentration has similar material properties as HSLA (high strength low alloys) steel, but it is lighter (density = 4.5 g/cm^3). Titanium alloys are nonmagnetic and corrosion-resistant. There are four groups of titanium alloys: α alloys, near-α alloys, α + β alloys, and β alloys:

(A) α Alloys: They are non-heat treatable and are generally very weldable. The more highly alloyed alpha and near-alpha alloys offer optimum high temperature creep strength and oxidation resistance as well. CP Ti 99.5, CP Ti 99.0; IMI 115, IMI 155, IMI, 230, IMI 260, IMI 317; Ti35A, and Ti75A are α alloys.

(B) Near-α Alloys: IMI 679, IMI 685, IMI 829; Ti-8-1-1, Ti-6-2-4-2, Ti-11.

(C) α + β Alloys: They are heat treatable, and most are weldable. Their strength levels are medium to high. Their hot-forming qualities are good, but the high temperature creep strength is not as good as in most alpha alloys. IMI 318, IMI 550, IMI 551, IMI 680; Ti-6-4, Ti-6-6-2, Tu-6-2-4-6, and Ti-8Mn are α + β alloys.

(D) β Alloys: They are readily heated, generally weldable, and capable of high strengths and good creep resistance to intermediate temperatures. Excellent formability can be expected of the beta alloys in the solution treated condition. Ti-13-11-3, Ti8-8-2-3, Beta 111, Beta C, and Transage 129 are β Alloys.

A number of Ti alloys have been developed with superior properties, as shown in Table 97.1. It was shown that there is a 2%~6% strength reduction in welding zones [Balasubramanian et al.]. Their fatigue parameters, creep parameters and crack growth rates are given in Tables 97.2—97.4, respectively.

The fatigue strength (endurance limit) of a titanium alloy with a fatigue cutoff cycle of 10^8 falls between 45% and 65% of its ultimate tensile strength, i.e.

$$0.45 \, \sigma_{uts} < \sigma_f < 0.65 \, \sigma_{uts} \tag{97.1}$$

with a nominal value of 0.5 σ_{uts}. Ceramics conversion and shot peening can improve fatigue strength [Li, et al.].

Ti-Nb composites, ranging from Ti-20Nb to Ti-27Nb, possess shape memory. The maximum recovered strain of 3% was obtained at room temperature in solution-treated Ti-26Nb alloys [Kim, et al.]

97.2   Applications

Titanium is now used for high-performance vehicle components such as valves, valve springs, rocker arms, connecting rods, and frames due to its high strength, low weight, and corrosion resistance. Although there are few applications for passenger vehicles, titanium has gained more applications to military armor vehicles. Its high mechanical strength at a low density makes it very attractive to military applications.

Ti-6Al-4V is the most widely used of the titanium alloys as it can be heat-treated to different strength levels, is readily weldable, and is relatively easy to machine. The many uses of Ti-6Al-4V include blades and discs for aircraft turbines and compressors, rocket motor cases, marine components, steam turbine blades, structural forgings, and fasteners. Due to the high-temperature gradient and fast rate of solidification, Ti-6Al-4V products manufactured via 3D printing tend to have a more refined microstructure, resulting in good mechanical properties.

An extra-low interstitial (ELI) grade of Ti-6Al-4V titanium alloy in the annealed military condition, with an ultimate tensile strength around 1000 MPa and specific gravity of 4.5 (g/cm^3), makes the material ductile enough to take a ballistic threat. Mass efficiency for ballistic protection is defined as the weight per unit area of RHA (Rolled Homogeneous Armor) steel required to defeat a given ballistic threat divided by the weight per unit area of the subject material. Other competitive materials for military armors are ceramics and their composites.

References

AGHDAM M M, FALAHATGAR S R, GORJI M, 2008. Micromechanical Consideration of Interface Damage in Fiber Reinforced Ti-Alloy under Various Combined Loading Conditions [J]. Composites Science and Technology, 68: 3406-3411.

ALTENBERGER I, et al, 2012. On the Effect of Deep-Rolling and Laser-Peening on the Stress-Controlled Low- and High-Cycle Fatigue of Ti-6Al-4V at Elevated Temperature up to 550 ℃ [J]. International Journal of Fatigue, 44: 292-302.

ANDERSON D D, ROSAKIS A J, 2006. Dynamic Fracture Properties of Titanium Alloys [J]. Experimental Mechanics, 46: 399-406.

AZVEDO A F, et al, 2002. Chemical Vapor Deposition Diamond Thin Films Growth on Ti-6Al-4V Using Surfatron System [J]. Diamond Related Materials, 11: 550-554.

BALASUBRAMANIAN T, et al, 2011. Effect of Welding Processes on Fatigue Properties of Ti-6Al-4V Alloy

Joints[J]. Proceedings of World Academy of Science, Engineering and Technology, 50: 899-908.

BAUR H, WORTBERG D, CLEMENS H, 2003. Titanium Aluminides for Automotive Applications, in: Gamma Titanium Aluminides[C]. 2004 TMS Annual Meeting: 3rd International Symposium on Gamma Titanium Aluminides, 23-31.

BIALLAS G, et al, 2005. Influence of Environment on Fatigue Mechanisms in High-Temperature Titanium Alloy IMI 834[J]. International Journal of Fatigue, 27(10-12): 1485-1493.

BOEHLART C, et al, 2008. Fatigue and Wear Evaluation of Ti-Al-Nb Alloys for Biomedical Applications[J]. Journal of Materials Science and Engineering, 28(3): 323-330.

BYSTRZANOWSKI S, et al, 2005. Creep Behavior and Related High-Temperature Microstructural Stability of Ti-46Al-9Nb Sheet Material[J]. Intermetallics, 13(5): 515-524.

CAO J, 2006. High-Temperature Low Cycle Fatigue Behavior of Titanium Aluminide Ti-24Al-15Nb-1Mo Alloy [J]. Materials Science and Engineering, A, 424: 47-52.

COSTA M, et al, 2006. Evaluation of Shot Peening on the Fatigue Strength of Anodized Ti-6Al-4V Alloy[J]. Materials Research, 9(1): 107-109.

FOUVRY S, DUO P, PERRUCHAUT P, 2004. A Quantitative Approach of Ti-6Al-4V Fretting Damage: Friction, Wear and Crack Nucleation[J]. Wear, 257(9-10): 916-929.

FUJII H, et al, 2009. Application of Titanium and Its Alloys for Automobile Parts[J]. Nippon Steel Technical Report, 88(88): 70-75.

GANESH B, et al, 2012. Effect of Heat Treatment on Dry Sliding Wear of Titanium-Aluminum-Vanadium (Ti-6Al-4V) Implant Alloy[J]. Journal of Mechanical Engineering Research, 4(2): 67-74.

GLAESER W A, LAWLESS B H, 2001. Behavior of Alloy Ti-6Al-4V under Pre-Fretting and Subsequent Fatigue Conditions[J]. Wear, 250/251(1): 621-630.

GOLDEN P J, GRANDT Jr. A F, 2004. Fracture Mechanics Based Fretting Fatigue Life Predictions in Ti-6Al-4V[J]. Engineering Fracture Mechanics, 71(15): 2229-2243.

GROGLER T, et al, 1998. Microwave Plasma CVD Diamond Coatings onto Titanium and Titanium Alloys[J]. Surface Coating and Technology, 98(1-3): 1079-1091.

GUERRERO-TOVA A, et al, 2008. Fatigue of the Near-Alpha Ti-Alloy Ti6242[C]. Proceedings of the XIth International Congress and Exposition June 2-5, 2008 Orlando, Florida USA.

HAN W D, 1997. Adhesion of Diamond Films on Ti-6Al-4V[J]. Surface Coating and Technology, 91: 32-36.

HE G, et al, 2012. Porous Titanium Materials with Entangled Wire Structure for Load-Bearing Biomedical Applications[J]. Journal of the Mechanical Behavior of Biomedical Materials, 5(1): 16-31.

HECKEL T, CHRIST H, 2010. Thermomechanical Fatigue of the TiAl Intermetallic Alloy TNB-V2 [J]. Experimental Mechanics, 50(6): 717-724.

HÉNAFF G, GLOANEC A, 2005. Fatigue Properties of TiAl Alloys[J]. Intermetallics, 13(5): 543-558.

HOTTA Y, KANENO Y, TAKASUGI T, 2006. High-Temperature Environmental Embrittlement of Thermo-mechanically Processed TiAl-Based Intermetallic Alloys[J]. Metallurgical and Materials Transactions, A, 37(2): 361-369.

HUANG W M, et al, 2005. Pile-up and Sink-in in Micro-indentation of a NiTi Shape-Memory Alloy[J]. Scripta Materialia, 53: 1055-1057.

JHA A, SINGH S, KIRANMAYEE M. 2010. Failure Analysis of Titanium Alloy (Ti6Al4V) Fastener in Aerospace Application[J]. Journal of Engineering Failure Analysis, 17: 1457-1465.

JIN O, MALL S, 2002. Influence of Contact Configuration on Fretting Fatigue Behavior of Ti-6Al-4V under Independent Pad Displacement Condition[J]. International Journal of Fatigue, 24(12): 1243-1253.

KIM H S, et al, 2008. Microstructure, Elastic Modulus and Tensile Properties of Ti-Nb-O Alloy System[J]. Journal of Materials Science and Technology, 24(1): 33-36.

KIM H Y, et al, 2004. Mechanical Properties and Shape Memory Behavior of Ti-Nb Alloys[J]. Materials Transactions, 45(7): 2443-2448.

KOBAYASHI E, et al, 2006. Fatigue Life Prediction of Biomedical Titanium Alloys under Tensile/Torsional Stress[J]. Materials Transactions, 47(7): 1826-1831.

LEE W S, LIN C F, 1998. High-temperature Deformation Behavior of Ti-6Al-4V Alloy Evaluated by High Strain-rate Compression[J]. Journal of Materials Processing Technology, 75: 127-136.

LI C, et al, 2007. Effect of Ceramic Conversion Surface Treatment on Fatigue Properties of Ti-6Al-4V Alloy [J]. International Journal of Fatigue, 29(12): 2273-2280.

LI F, et al, 2006. Research on Low Cycle Fatigue Properties of TA15 Titanium Alloy Based on Reliability Theory[J]. Materials Science and Engineering, A, 430: 216-220.

LI R, SHIH A J, 2006. Finite Element Modeling of 3D Turning of Titanium[J]. International Journal of Advanced Manufacturing Technology, 29: 253-261.

LIU B, et al, 2008. Low Cycle Fatigue Improvement of Powder Metallurgy Titanium Alloy through Thermomechanical Treatment[J]. Transactions of Nonferrous Metals of China, 18: 227-232.

LONG M, RACK H J, 1998. Titanium Alloys in Total Joint Replacement-A Materials Science Perspective[J]. Biomaterials, 19: 1621-1639.

LOPZE J, et al, 2010. Pre-fatigue Influence on Quasi-Static Tensile Properties of Ti-6Al-4V in Thin-Sheet Form[J]. EPJ Web of Conferences, 6: 42022.

MAJUMDAR P, SINGH S, CHAKRABORTY M, 2008. Wear Response of Heat Treated Ti-13Zr-13Nb Alloy in Dry Condition and Simulated Body Fluid[J]. Wear, 264(11-12): 1015-1025.

MEDEKSHAS H, 2008. Effect of Elevated Temperature and Welding on Low Cycle Fatigue Strength of Titanium Alloys[J]. Mechanika, 35(2): 5-10.

MEYER Jr. H W, KLEPONIS D S, 2001. Modeling the High Strain Rate Behavior of Titanium Undergoing Ballistic Impact and Penetration[J]. International Journal of Impact Engineering, 26: 509-521.

MONTGOMERY J, WELLS M, ROOPCHAND B, et al, 1997. Low-cost Titanium Armors for Combat Vehicles [J]. Journal of Materials, 59(5): 45-47.

MOORE D, 1968. The Welding of Titanium and Its Alloys[J]. Aircraft Engineering and Aerospace Technology, 40(11): 12-18.

MORDYUK B N, PROKOPENKO G J, 2006. Fatigue Life Improvement of α-Titanium by Novel Ultrasonically Assisted Techniques[J]. Material Sciences and Engineering, A, 437(2): 396-405.

MOREHEAD M D, et al, 2006. Experimental Investigation of the Machinability of Equal Channel Angular Pressing Processed Commercially Pure Titanium[J]. Transactions of NAMRI, SME, 34: 539-546.

NIMA S, MAKSYM G. 2010. Multiaxial Fatigue of Titanium including Step Loading and Load Path Alteration and Sequence Effects[J]. International Journal of Fatigue, 21: 1862-1874.

OGAWA H, et al, 1997. Measurements of Mechanical Properties of Microfabricated Thin Films[C]. IEEE 10th International Workshop on Microelectromechanical Systems, 430-435.

PATHER R, MITTEN W A, HOLDWAY P, 2003. The Effect of High-Temperature Exposure on the Tensile Properties of γ-TiAl Alloys[J]. Intermetallics, 11: 1015-1027.

POTOZKY P, MAIER H J, CHRIST H J, 1998. Thermomechanical Fatigue Behavior of the High-Temperature Alloy IMI 834[J]. Metallurgical and Materials Trans., A, 29(12): 2995-3004.

QU J, et al, 2005. Friction and Wear of Titanium Alloys Sliding against Metal, Polymers and Ceramic Countersurfaces[J]. Wear, 258: 1348-1356.

RAO M G, KNEISEL P. Mechanical Properties of High RRR Niobium at Cryogenic Temperatures[J]. Advances in Cryogenic Engineering, 40: 1383-1390.

RECINA V, KARLSSON B, 1999. High-Temperature Low Cycle Fatigue Properties of Ti-48Al-2W-0.5Si Gamma Titanium Aluminide[J]. Materials Science and Engineering, A, 262(1): 70-81.

ROTH M, BIERMANN H, 2008. Thermo-mechanical Fatigue Behavior of a Modern γ-TiAl Alloy [J]. International Journal of Fatigue, 30: 352-356.

SCHOENFELD S E, KAD B, 2002. Texture Effects on Shear Response in Ti-6Al-4V Plates[J]. International Journal of Plasticity, 18: 461-486.

SEN I, et al, 2010. Fatigue in Ti-6Al-4V-B Alloys[J]. Acta Materialia, 58(20): 6799-6809.

HOSSEINI S, LIMOOEI M B, 2001. Investigation of Fatigue Behavior and Notch Sensitivity of Ti-6Al-4V[J]. Applied Mechanics and Materials, 80-81: 7-12.

SINGH N, GOUTHAMA, SINGH V, 2007. Low Cycle Fatigue Behavior of Ti Alloy Ti metal 834 at 873 K[J]. International Journal of Fatigue, 29: 843-851.

SOLIMINE P, LISSENDEN C, 2004. Fatigue of Beta Titanium Alloy at 20, 482 and 648 ℃[J]. Fatigue and Fracture of Engineering Materials and Structures, 27(10): 943-955.

SOMMER A W, et al, 1973. Relaxation Processes in Metastable Beta Alloys[J]. Acta Metallurgical Sinica, 21: 489-497.

SOMMER A W, KEIJZERS G C, 2003. Gamma TiAl and the Engine Exhaust Valve[C]. 2004 TMS Annual Meeting: 3rd International Symposium on Gamma Titanium Aluminides, 3-7.

TAKAHASHI K, SATO E, 2010. Influence of Surface Treatments on Fatigue Strength of Ti6Al4V Alloy[J]. Materials Transactions, 51(4): 694-698.

TAMIN M N, SUDIN I, MON T T, 2008. Thermal-mechanical Responses of Ti-6Al-4V during Orthogonal Cutting Process[J]. Diffusion and Defect Data. Part A Defect and Diffusion Forum, 273-276: 673-678.

TETSUI T, 2002. Development of a TiAl Turbocharger for Passenger Vehicles[J]. Materials Science and Engineering, A, 329/331: 582-588.

UMBRELLO D, 2008. Finite Element Simulation of Conventional and High-Speed Machining of Ti-6Al-4V Alloy[J]. Journal of Materials Processing Technology, 196: 79-87.

VENKATESH B, CHEN D, BHOLE S, 2009. Effect of Heat Treatment on Mechanical Properties of Ti-6Al-4V Alloy[J]. Materials Science and Engineering, 506: 117-124.

WAGNER M, NAYAN N, RAMAMURTY U, 2008. Healing of Fatigue Damage in NiTi Shape Memory Alloys [J]. Journal of Applied Physics, 41: 185408.

WANG R F, et al, 2012. Low Cycle Fatigue Behaviors of TI-6AL-4V Alloys Controlled by Strain and Stress[J]. Key Engineering Materials, 525/526: 441-444.

WOKULSKI Z, 2004. Mechanical Properties of TiN Whiskers[J]. Physica Status Solidi, 120(1): 175-184.

YAMAGUCHI M, et al, 2008. Importance of Microstructural Stability in Creep Resistance of Lamellar TiAl Alloys[J]. Materials Science and Engineering, A, 483/484: 517-520.

ZELLER A, DETTENWANGER F, SCHÜTZE M, 2002. Influence of Water Vapour on the Creep and Fatigue Properties of TiAl[J]. Intermetallics, 10(1): 33-57.

ZHANG Y, et al, 2008. Microstructural Characteristics and Mechanical Properties of Ti-6Al-4V Friction Stir

Welds[J]. Materials Science and Engineering, A, 485 (1-2): 448-455.

ZHECHEVA A, SHA W, MALINOV S, et al, 2005. Enhancing the Microstructure and Properties of Titanium Alloys through Nitriding and Other Surface Engineering Methods[J]. Journal of Surface Coating Technology, 200: 2192-2207.

ZHEREBTSOV S, et al, 2005. Mechanical Properties of Ti-6Al-4V Titanium Alloy with Submicrocrystalline Structure Produced by Severe Plastic Deformation[J]. Materials Transactions, 46(9): 2020-2025.

ZHU X, 2010. Fatigue Analysis of Wind Generator Bearing's Engineering Material-Ti-6Al-4V[C]. IEEE 2010 International Conf. on Computer Application and System Modeling (ICCASM).

Table 97.1 Mechanical Properties of Ti (Titanium) and Its Alloys

Material	$T/°C$	E_T	ρ	ν	(σ, ε)	α	k	γ	ρ_E	K_{IC}
Ti (> 99%)	23	104	4.51	0.37	(240, 0.2%) (330, 30%)	8.4	21.6	544	—	—
	1000	—	—	—	—	10.1	—	—	—	—
	1670 (T_m)	—	—	—	—	—	—	—	—	—
Ti, Porous (Porosity = 44.7%)	23	—	—	—	(75, 0.2%) $\sigma_{uts} = 108$	—	—	—	—	—
Ti, Porous (Porosity = 57.9%)	23	—	—	—	(24, 0.2%) $\sigma_{uts} = 47.5$	—	—	—	—	—
Ti (Film; $h = 0.5$ μm)	23	96	—	—	(—, 0.2%) (950, 1.3%)	—	—	—	—	—
Ti/SiC ($V_f = 8\%$) (//fiber direction; Aspect ratio = 10)	23	—	—	—	(610, 2%) (690, 6%)	—	—	—	—	—
Ti/SiC ($V_f = 8\%$) (⊥ fiber direction; Aspect ratio = 10)	23	—	—	—	(500, 2%) (550, 6%)	—	—	—	—	—
Ti/SiC ($V_f = 8\%$) (//fiber direction; Aspect ratio = 50)	23	—	—	—	(530, 0.5%) (610, 1%) (670, 2%) (780, 6%)	—	—	—	—	—
Ti/SiC ($V_f = 12\%$) (⊥ fiber direction; Aspect ratio = 10)	23	—	—	—	(570, 0.5%) (640, 1%) (690, 2%) (780, 6%)	—	—	—	—	—

continued

Material	$T/^\circ\text{C}$	E_T	ρ	ν	$(\sigma,\ \varepsilon)$	α	k	γ	ρ_E	K_IC
Ti-alloy (Grade 1)	23	104	4.51	0.37	(172, 0.2%) (241, 24%)	8.6	20.8	520	—	—
	100	—	—	—	(130, 0.2%) (260, 40%); $\sigma_{\text{crs},10000}=195$	—	—	—	—	—
	200	—	—	—	(100, 0.2%) (210, 38%); $\sigma_{\text{crs},10000}=152$	—	—	—	—	—
	250	—	—	—	$\sigma_{\text{crs},1000}=97$	—	—	—	—	—
	315	—	—	—	(83, 0.2%) (159, 48%)	9.2	—	—	—	—
	815	—	—	—	(83, 0.2%) (159, 48%)	9.9	—	—	—	—
	1670 (T_m)	—	—	—	—	—	—	—	—	—
Ti-alloy (Grade 2)	−269	—	—	—	(936, 0.2%) (1153, 36%)	—	—	—	—	75
	−196	—	—	—	(695, 0.2%) (936, 51%)	—	—	—	—	—
	23	104	4.51	0.37	(276, 0.2%) (345, 20%)	8.6	20.8	520	—	—
	150	—	—	—	$\sigma_{\text{crs},10000}=240$	—	—	—	—	—
	200	—	—	—	(166, 0.2%) (283, 41%)	—	—	—	—	—
	250	—	—	—	$\sigma_{\text{crs},1000}=117$	—	—	—	—	—
	300	78	—	—	—	9.5	15	595	—	—
	500	72	—	—	—	9.7	15	615	—	—
	815	—	—	—	—	10.1	—	—	—	—
	1670 (T_m)	—	—	—	—	—	—	—	—	—
Ti-alloy (Grade 2; Weld)	−269	—	—	—	(834, 0.2%) (1123, 27.6%)	—	—	—	—	<75
	−196	—	—	—	(681, 0.2%) (872, 34%)	—	—	—	—	—
	23	—	—	—	(332, 0.2%) (446, 14.3%)	—	—	520	—	—
	1677 (T_m)	—	—	—	—	—	—	—	—	—

continued

Material	$T/°C$	E_T	ρ	ν	$(\sigma,\ \varepsilon)$	α	k	γ	ρ_E	K_{IC}
Ti-alloy (Grade 3)	23	104	4.51	0.37	$(379,\ 0.2\%)$ $(448,\ 18\%)$; $\sigma_{crs,1000}=400$	8.6	19.7	520	—	—
	200	—	—	—	$\sigma_{crs,10000}=228$	—	—	—	—	—
	250	—	—	—	$\sigma_{crs,1000}=138$	—	—	—	—	—
	315	—	—	—	$(138,\ 0.2\%)$ $(262,\ 33\%)$	9.2	—	—	—	—
	426	—	—	—	$(117,\ 0.2\%)$ $(207,\ 22\%)$	—	—	—	—	—
	815	—	—	—	—	10.1	—	—	—	—
	1677 (T_m)	—	—	—	—	—	—	—	—	—
Ti-alloy (Grade 4)	23	105	4.54	0.37	$(483,\ 0.2\%)$ $(552,\ 15\%)$	8.6	17.3	540	—	—
	250	—	—	—	$\sigma_{crs,10000}=241$	—	—	—	—	—
	315	—	—	—	$(172,\ 0.2\%)$ $(283,\ 28\%)$; $\sigma_{crs,1000}=200$	9.2	—	—	—	—
	426	—	—	—	$(145,\ 0.2\%)$ $(214,\ 26\%)$	—	—	—	—	—
	815	—	—	—	—	10.1	—	—	—	—
	1660 (T_m)	—	—	—	—	—	—	—	—	—
Ti-alloy (Grade 5; α+β Ti-6Al-4V; Annealed 2 h at 700 ℃)	23	114	4.43	0.32	$\sigma_{ucs}=-897$; $(915,\ 0.2\%)$ $(965,\ 17\%)$	8.6	7	526	—	84
	250	—	—	—	—	9.2	—	—	—	—
	370	—	—	—	$(565,\ 0.2\%)$ $(690,\ 18\%)$	—	—	—	—	—
	400	—	—	—	$\sigma_{crs,1000}=620$	—	—	—	—	—
	527	—	—	—	—	—	45	—	—	—
	600	—	—	—	—	10.3	—	—	—	—
	1660 (T_m)	—	—	—	—	—	—	—	—	—

continued

Material	$T/℃$	E_T	ρ	ν	(σ, ε)	α	k	γ	ρ_E	K_{IC}
Ti-alloy (Grade 5; α+β; Ti-6Al-4V; Annealed 1 h at 500 ℃; Q; & Annealed 8 h at 500 ℃)	23	114	4.43	0.32	(970, 0.2%) (1080, 16%)	8.6	7	526	—	69
Ti-alloy (Grade 5; α+β Ti-6Al-4V; ST & Aged)	23	114	4.43	0.32	(1018, 0.2%) (1100, 10%) (1200, 50%)	8.6	7	526	—	60
	250 ℃	—	—	—	(650, 0.2%) (750, 10%) (800, 50%)	9.2	—	—	—	—
	400	—	—	—	—	9.6	—	—	—	—
	600	—	—	—	(500, 0.2%) (460, 10%) (400, 50%)	10.3	—	—	—	—
	1660 (T_m)	—	—	—	—	—	—	—	—	—
Ti-alloy (Grade 5; α+β Ti-6Al-4V; Post stress-Corrosion Cracking by 0.6M KCl)	23	114	4.43	0.32	—	8.6	7	—	—	20
Ti-alloy (Grade 6; Ti-5Al-2.5Sn-...)	23	107	4.48	0.34	(793, 0.2%) (827, 10%)	9.4	8.3	530	—	—
	315	—	—	—	(448, 0.2%) (565, 18%)	—	—	—	—	—
	430	—	—	—	(405, 0.2%) (535, 18%); $\sigma_{crs,1000}=415$	—	—	—	—	—
	540	—	—	—	(379, 0.2%) (462, 19%); $\sigma_{crs,1000}=140$	9.5	—	—	—	—
	1704 (T_m)	—	—	—	—	—	—	—	—	—

continued

Material	$T/^{\circ}C$	E_{T}	ρ	ν	(σ,ε)	α	k	γ	ρ_{E}	K_{IC}
Ti-alloy (Grade 7; Ti-0.15Pd)	23	103	4.51	0.34	$(276,0.2\%)$ $(345,20\%)$	8.6	20.8	520	—	—
	150	—	—	—	$\sigma_{\mathrm{crs},10000}=240$	—	—	—	—	—
	200	—	—	—	$(170,0.2\%)$ $(285,40\%)$	—	—	—	—	—
	250	—	—	—	$\sigma_{\mathrm{crs},1000}=117$	—	—	—	—	—
	315	—	—	—	$(103,0.2\%)$ $(221,20\%)$	9.2	—	—	—	—
	815	—	—	—	—	10.1	—	—	—	—
	1660 (T_{m})	—	—	—	—	—	—	—	—	—
Ti-alloy (Grade 9; Ti-0.3Al-2.5V)	23	103	4.48	0.34	$(483,0.2\%)$ $(620,15\%)$	9.2	8.3	544	—	—
	150	—	—	—	$(450,0.2\%)$	—	—	—	—	—
	250	—	—	—	$\sigma_{\mathrm{crs},1000}=421$ $(534,26\%)$	—	—	—	—	—
	540	—	—	—	—	9.5	—	—	—	—
	1704 (T_{m})	—	—	—	—	—	—	—	—	—
Ti-alloy (Grade 11; Ti-0.15Pd-...)	23	103	4.51	0.34	$(172,0.2\%)$ $(241,24\%)$	8.6	20.8	520	—	—
	200	—	—	—	$(100,0.2\%)$ $(205,38\%)$; $\sigma_{\mathrm{crs},10000}=152$	—	—	—	—	—
	250	—	—	—	$\sigma_{\mathrm{crs},1000}=97$	—	—	—	—	—
	315	—	—	—	$(83,0.2\%)$ $(159,48\%)$	9.2	—	—	—	—
	815	—	—	—	—	9.9	—	—	—	—
	1670 (T_{m})	—	—	—	—	—	—	—	—	—
Ti-alloy (Grade 12; Ti-0.3Mo-0.8Ni)	23	103	4.51	0.34	$(345,0.2\%)$ $(483,18\%)$	9.6	19	544	—	—
	150	—	—	—	$(365,0.2\%)$ $(424,18\%)$	—	—	—	—	—
	200	—	—	—	$(303,0.2\%)$ $(359,30\%)$	—	—	—	—	—
	1650 (T_{m})	—	—	—	—	—	—	—	—	—

continued

Material	$T/°C$	E_T	ρ	ν	(σ, ε)	α	k	γ	ρ_E	K_{IC}
Ti-alloy (Grade 16; Ti-0.05Pd-…)	23	103	4.51	0.34	(276, 0.2%) (345, 20%)	8.6	20.8	520	—	—
	150	—	—	—	$\sigma_{crs,10000} = 240$	—	—	—	—	—
	200	—	—	—	(280, 0.2%) (395, 41%)	—	—	—	—	—
	250	—	—	—	$\sigma_{crs,1000} = 117$	—	—	—	—	—
	315	—	—	—	(103, 0.2%) (221, 38%)	9.2	—	—	—	—
	815	—	—	—	—	10.1	—	—	—	—
	1660 (T_m)	—	—	—	—	—	—	—	—	—
Ti-alloy (Grade 17; Ti-0.05Pd-…)	23	103	4.51	0.34	(172, 0.2%) (241, 24%)	8.6	20.8	520	—	—
	200	—	—	—	(100, 0.2%) (200, 38%); $\sigma_{crs,10000} = 152$	—	—	—	—	—
	250	—	—	—	$\sigma_{crs,1000} = 97$	—	—	—	—	—
	315	—	—	—	(83, 0.2%) (159, 48%)	9.2	—	—	—	—
	815	—	—	—	—	9.9	—	—	—	—
	1670 (T_m)	—	—	—	—	—	—	—	—	—
Ti-alloy (Grade 18; Ti-3Al-2.5V-0.05Pd-…)	23	107	4.48	0.34	(483, 0.2%) (620, 15%)	9.5	8.3	544	—	—
	150	—	—	—	(448, 0.2%) (534, 26%)	—	—	—	—	—
	250	—	—	—	$\sigma_{crs,1000} = 421$	—	—	—	—	—
	540	—	—	—	—	9.9	—	—	—	—
	1704 (T_m)	—	—	—	—	—	—	—	—	—
Ti-alloy (Grade 23; Ti-6Al-4V; ELI)	23	114	4.48	0.34	(793, 0.2%) (862, 10%)	9.2	7.3	565	—	—
	150	—	—	—	(640, 0.2%) (770, 15%)	—	—	—	—	—
	260	—	—	—	(532, 0.2%) (678, 16%)	—	—	—	—	—
	540	—	—	—	—	10.1	—	—	—	—
	1650 (T_m)	—	—	—	—	—	—	—	—	—

continued

Material	$T/℃$	E_T	ρ	ν	(σ, ε)	α	k	γ	ρ_E	K_{IC}
Ti-alloy (Grade 26; Ti-0.1Ru-...)	23	103	4.51	0.34	(276, 0.2%) (345, 20%)	8.6	20.8	520	—	—
	150	—	—	—	$\sigma_{crs,10000}=240$	—	—	—	—	—
	200	—	—	—	(170, 0.2%) (285, 41%)	—	—	—	—	—
	250	—	—	—	$\sigma_{crs,1000}=117$	—	—	—	—	—
	315	—	—	—	(103, 0.2%) (221, 38%)	9.2	—	—	—	—
	815	—	—	—	—	10.1	—	—	—	—
	1660 (T_m)	—	—	—	—	—	—	—	—	—
Ti-alloy (Grade 27; Ti-0.1Ru-...)	23	103	4.51	0.34	(172, 0.2%) (241, 24%)	8.6	20.8	520	—	—
	200	—	—	—	(100, 0.2%) (200, 38%); $\sigma_{crs,10000}=152$	—	—	—	—	—
	250	—	—	—	$\sigma_{crs,1000}=97$	—	—	—	—	—
	315	—	—	—	(83, 0.2%) (159, 48%)	9.2	—	—	—	—
	815	—	—	—	—	9.9	—	—	—	—
	1670 (T_m)	—	—	—	—	—	—	—	—	—
Ti-alloy (Grade 28; Ti-3Al-2.5V-0.1Ru-...)	23	107	4.48	0.34	(483, 0.2%) (620, 15%)	9.5	8.3	544	—	—
	150	—	—	—	(448, 0.2%) (534, 26%)	—	—	—	—	—
	250	—	—	—	$\sigma_{crs,1000}=421$	—	—	—	—	—
	540	—	—	—	—	9.9	—	—	—	—
	1704 (T_m)	—	—	—	—	—	—	—	—	—
Ti-alloy (Grade 29; Ti-6Al-4V-0.1Ru-...)	23	114	4.48	0.34	(760, 0.2%) (830, 10%)	9.2	7.3	565	—	—
	150	—	—	—	(640, 0.2%) (770, 15%)	—	—	—	—	—
	260	—	—	—	(532, 0.2%) (678, 16%)	—	—	—	—	—
	540	—	—	—	—	10.1	—	—	—	—
	1650 (T_m)	—	—	—	—	—	—	—	—	—

continued

Material	$T/℃$	E_T	ρ	ν	(σ, ε)	α	k	γ	ρ_E	K_{IC}
TiB$_2$ (Purity>98%; Polycrystalline)	23	565	4.5	0.11	$\sigma_R = 400$	7.4	96	617	—	6.2
	500	550	4.45	0.11	$\sigma_R = 429$	7.9	81	1073	—	—
	1000	534	4.39	0.11	$\sigma_R = 459$	8.6	78	1186	—	—
	1500	—	4.322	—	—	—	—	—	—	—
	3160 (T_m)	—	—	—	—	—	—	—	—	—
TiO$_2$ (Purity = 99.6%)	23	259	4.01	0.28	(350, 0.2%)	—	—	690	—	2.8
	2113 (T_m)	—	—	—	—	—	—	—	—	—
Beta C (Ti-15Mo-3Nb- 3Al-0.2Si)	23	103	4.81	—	(993, 0.2%) (1035, 6%)	9.3	8.4	—	—	—
	100	—	—	—	—	9.4	—	—	—	—
	300	—	—	—	—	9.7	—	—	—	—
IMI 230 (Ti-2.5Cu)	23	107	4.56	0.31	(400, 0.2%) (540, 16%)	9	13	525	—	—
	300	—	—	—	—	9.1	—	—	—	—
	600	—	—	—	—	9.5	—	—	—	—
IMI 550 (Ti-4Al-4Mo- 2Sn-0.5Si)	23	114	4.60	0.31	(960, 0.2%) (1100, 9%)	8.6	7.9	525	—	—
	100	—	—	—	—	8.8	—	—	—	—
	300	—	—	—	—	9.2	—	—	—	—
IMI 679 (Ti-11Sn-5Zr- 2.5Al-1Mo)	23	115	4.84	0.31	(970, 0.2%) (1110, 8%)	8	8.3	500	—	—
	100	—	—	—	—	8.2	—	—	—	—
	300	—	—	—	—	9.3	—	—	—	—
	500	—	—	—	—	10	—	—	—	—
IMI 685 (Ti-6Al-5Zr- 0.5Mo-0.2Si)	23	125	4.45	0.31	(850, 0.2%) (990, 6%)	9.8	4.8	525	—	—
	100	—	—	—	—	9.8	—	—	—	—
	300	—	—	—	—	9.5	—	—	—	—
IMI 829(Ti-5.5Al- 3.5Sn-3Zr-1Nb- 0.3Mo-0.3Si)	23	120	4.54	0.31	(820, 0.2%) (960, 9%)	9.4	—	525	—	—
	100	—	—	—	—	9.5	—	—	—	—
	300	—	—	—	—	9.8	—	—	—	—
	1649 (T_m)	—	—	—	—	—	—	—	—	—

continued

Material	$T/°C$	E_T	ρ	ν	(σ, ε)	α	k	γ	ρ_E	K_{IC}
IMI 834 (Ti834) (Ti-5.8Al-4Sn-3.5Zr-0.7Nb-0.5Mo-0.3Si)	23	120	4.55	0.31	(910, 0.2%) (1030, 6%)	10.5	7.0	525	—	45
	300	—	—	—	—	10.9	—	—	—	—
	500	—	—	—	$\sigma_{uts}=771$	11	—	—	—	—
	600	—	—	—	(510, 0.2%) (654, 15%)	11	—	—	—	—
	1000	—	—	—	—	11.3	—	—	—	—
Ti-17 (Ti-5Al-4Mo-4Cr-2Sn-2Zr)	23	115	4.6	0.32	(1110, 0.2%) (1165, 12%)	9	7.5	634	—	60
	315	—	—	—	(807, 0.2%) (965, 12%)	9.7	—	—	—	—
	370	—	—	—	(745, 0.2%) (917, 13%)	—	—	—	—	—
	430	—	—	—	$\sigma_{crs,7500}=690$	—	—	—	—	—
Ti-550 (Ti-4Al-4Mo-2Sn-0.5Si)	23	115	4.6	0.32	(1020, 0.2%) (1145, 12%)	8.8	7.5	634	—	60
	315	—	—	—	(683, 0.2%) (876, 17%)	9.2	—	—	—	—
	400	—	—	—	$\sigma_{crs,100}=841$	10	—	—	—	—
Ti-1100 (Timetal-1100; Ti-6Al-4Zr-2.75Sn-0.4Mo-0.45Si)	23	—	4.55	0.32	(910, 0.2%) (1000, 8%)	8.8	6.6	640	—	—
	300	—	—	—	—	9.5	—	—	—	—
	500	—	—	—	—	9.5	—	—	—	—
	650	—	—	—	—	10.1	—	—	—	—
Ti-1100 (Cast Timetal-1100; Ti-6Al-4Zr-2.75Sn-0.4Mo-0.45Si)	23	—	4.5	0.32	(850, 0.2%) (920, 6%)	8.5	6.6	640	—	—
	300	—	—	—	—	9.5	—	—	—	—
	500	—	—	—	(690, 7%)	—	—	—	—	—
	650	—	—	—	—	10.1	—	—	—	—
Ti-2448	23	46	—	0.32	(700, 0.2%) (830, 15%)	—	—	—	—	—
Ti-5111	23	110	4.55	0.32	(745, 0.2%) (850, 13%)	8.8	6.6	640	—	—
Ti-5553 (Cast & HIP)	23	110	4.55	0.32	$\sigma_{ucs}=-1138$; (1055, 0.2%) (1160, 9%)	8.8	6.6	640	—	—

continued

Material	$T/℃$	E_T	ρ	ν	(σ, ε)	α	k	γ	ρ_E	K_{IC}
Ti-6242 (Ti-6Al-2Sn-4Zr-2Mo-0.1Si)	23	114	4.54	0.32	$(990, 0.2\%)$ $(1000, 1\%)$ $(1100, 8.5\%)$	7.7	7.7	460	—	—
	350	96.7	—	—	—	—	—	—	—	—
	480	89	—	—	$(600, 0.2\%)$ $(650, 1\%)$ $(730, 5\%)$	—	—	—	—	—
	550	84.4	—	—	—	—	—	—	—	—
	600	—	—	—	$(485, 0.2\%)$ $(560, 15\%)$	—	—	—	—	—
	1704 (T_m)	—	—	—	—	—	—	—	—	—
Ti-6246 $(\alpha+\beta)$	23	105	4.52	0.32	$(1050, 0.2\%)$ $\sigma_{uts}=1155$	9	7		—	—
Ti-6246 (β)	23	105	4.52	0.32	$(1055, 0.2\%)$ $\sigma_{uts}=1170$	9	7	—	—	—
Ti-6553 (Ti-6Al-5V-5Mo-3Cr)	23	105	4.52	0.32	$\sigma_{ucs}=-1389$; $(1055, 0.2\%)$ $(1159, 9\%)$	—	7	—	—	—
Ti-2.5Al-2V (Weld-HAZ)	23	—	—	—	$(686, 0.2\%)$ $\sigma_{uts}=747$	—	—	—	—	—
	350	—	—	—	$(392, 0.2\%)$ $\sigma_{uts}=437$	—	—	—	—	—
Ti-2.5Al-2Zr (Ti Alloy)	23	—	—	—	$(496, 0.2\%)$ $\sigma_{uts}=552$	—	—	—	—	—
	350	—	—	—	$(296, 0.2\%)$ $\sigma_{uts}=483$	—	—	—	—	—
Ti-2.5Al-2Zr (Weld)	23	112	—	—	$(458, 0.2\%)$ $\sigma_{uts}=543$	—	—	—	—	—
	350	—	—	—	$(240, 0.2\%)$ $\sigma_{uts}=298$	—	—	—	—	—
Ti-2.5Al-2Zr (Weld-HAZ)	23	—	—	—	$(442, 0.2\%)$ $\sigma_{uts}=539$	—	—	—	—	—
	350	—	—	—	$(227, 0.2\%)$ $\sigma_{uts}=288$	—	—	—	—	—

continued

Material	$T/^\circ\text{C}$	E_T	ρ	ν	(σ, ε)	α	k	γ	ρ_E	K_{IC}
Ti-2.5Al-2V (Ti Alloy)	23	—	—	—	$(669, 0.2\%)$ $\sigma_{uts}=733$	—	—	—	—	—
	350	—	—	—	$(372, 0.2\%)$ $\sigma_{uts}=474$	—	—	—	—	—
Ti-2.5Al-2V (Weld)	23	—	—	—	$(542, 0.2\%)$ $\sigma_{uts}=607$	—	—	—	—	—
	350	—	—	—	$(272, 0.2\%)$ $\sigma_{uts}=330$	—	—	—	—	—
Ti-3Al-13V-11Cr	23	110	4.5	0.32	$(1051, 0.2\%)$ $(1113, 4\%)$	—	—	—	—	—
Ti-4.8Al-1.5Fe-6.8Mo-1.2Nd (As Forged)	23	114	4.5	—	$(1203, 0.2\%)$ $(1298, 10.3\%)$	—	—	—	—	—
Ti-4.8Al-1.5Fe-6.8Mo-1.2Nd (As Sintered)	23	110	4.4	—	$(1109, 0.2\%)$ $(1172, 8.4\%)$	—	—	—	—	—
Ti Alloy: β-Cez (Ti-5.0Al-1.9Sn-4.5Zr-3.9Mo-2.2Cr-1.1Fe-...)	23	110	—	0.32	$(1190, 0.2\%)$ $\sigma_{uts}=1275$	—	—	—	—	—
Ti-5Al-2.5Sn (Eli)	-253	—	—	—	$(1420, 0.2\%)$ $(1580, 15\%)$	—	—	—	—	—
	-196	—	—	—	$(1210, 0.2\%)$ $(1310, 16\%)$	—	—	—	—	—
	23	110	4.48	—	$(690, 0.2\%)$ $(725, 10\%)$	9.4	7.8	530	—	—
	815	—	—	—	—	10.1	—	—	—	—
	$1600\,(T_m)$	—	—	—	—	—	—	—	—	—
Ti-Sf61 (Ti-5.9Al-2.7Sn)	23	121	4.52	0.32	$(1050, 0.2\%)$ $(1068, 11\%)$	—	8	—	—	—
	600	—	—	—	$(752, 0.2\%)$ $(655, 16\%)$	—	—	—	—	—
Ti-Sf61 (Ti-5.9Al-2.7Sn-4Zr-0.45Mo-0.35Si-0.22)	23	120	4.56	0.32	$(1050, 0.2\%)$ $(1068, 11\%)$	—	8	—	—	—
	600	—	—	—	$(752, 0.2\%)$ $(655, 16\%)$	—	—	—	—	—

continued

Material	$T/°C$	E_T	ρ	ν	(σ, ε)	α	k	γ	ρ_E	K_{IC}
Ti-6Al-6V-2Sn	23	105	4.52	0.32	(650, 0.2%) (1035, 9%)	9	5.5	635	—	—
	1704 (T_m)									
Ti-6Al-7Nb (Annealed)	23	105	4.52	0.32	(910, 0.2%) (1021, 15%)	—	—	—	—	—
	1800 (T_m)	—	—	—	—	—	—	—	—	—
Ti-24Al-15Nb-1Mo	23	92	—	—	(570, 0.2%) (727, 17.6%)	—	—	—	—	—
Ti-29Nb-1Ta-4.6Zr	23	62	—	—	(600, 0.2%) (640, 15%)	—	—	—	—	—
TNB-V2 (Ti-45Al-8Nb-0.2C; Intermetallic)	23	—	—	—	—	—	—	—	—	—
	550	146	—	—	—	—	—	—	—	—
	800 (Transition from brittle to ductile)									

Notes: STA = Solution treated and aged.

Table 97.2   Fatigue ε-N Properties of (Ti) Titanium Alloys

Material	$T/°C$	$d\varepsilon/dt$	σ_f'	ε_f'	b	c	K'	n'	$\sigma_f @ 2N_f$	R
Ti (>99%)	23	—	647	0.548	−0.033	−0.646	669	0.051	300@ 10^7	−1
cpTi (Polished Mechanically)	23	—	—	—	—	—	—	—	234@ 10^7	−1
cpTi (Polished Electrolytically)	23	—	—	—	—	—	—	—	200@ 10^7	−1
IMI 230	23	—	—	—	—	—	—	—	230@ 10^7	−1
IMI 834 (Timetal 834)	23	—	—	—	—	—	—	—	530@ 10^7	−1
	760	—	—	—	—	—	—	—	142@ 10^7	−1
Ti Alloy: β-Cez (Ti-5.0Al-1.9Sn-4.5Zr-3.9Mo-2.2Cr-1.1Fe-...)	23	—	—	—	—	—	—	—	625@ 10^7	−1
Ti-5553 (Cast HIP)	23	—	—	—	—	—	—	—	758@ 10^7	−1

continued

Material	$T/℃$	$d\varepsilon/dt$	σ_f'	ε_f'	b	c	K'	n'	$\sigma_f @ 2N_f$	R
Ti-6Al-4V ($\alpha+\beta$) (Surface Grinding)	23	—	—	—	—	—	—	—	427@ 10^7	−1
Ti-6Al-4V ($\alpha+\beta$) (Annealed 1 h at 700 ℃; Dia = 60 mm)	23	—	—	0.0186	—	−0.026	854	0.015	430@ 10^7 586@ 3.8×10^5 550@ 2×10^6 611@ 5×10^4	RB RB RB RB
Ti-6Al-4V ($\alpha+\beta$) (Polished; Dia < 20 mm)	23	—	—	—	—	—	—	—	596@ 10^7	RB
Ti-6Al-4V ($\alpha+\beta$) (Annealed; Submicro-crystalline)	23	—	—	—	—	—	—	—	690@ 10^7	RB
Ti-6Al-4V ($\alpha+\beta$) (Shot Peening)	23	—	—	—	—	—	—	—	725@ 10^7	RB
Ti-6Al-7Nb	23	—	—	0.0386	—	−0.098	—	—	600@ 10^6	—
Ti-6242 (Ti-6Al-2Sn-4Zr-2Mo-0.1Si)	23	—	—	—	—	—	—	—	—	—
	350	—	2687	—	−0.17	−0.28	—	—	400@ 33512	—
	450	—	2626	—	−0.19	−1.53	—	—	400@ 11700	—
	550	—	1693	—	−0.16	−0.76	—	—	400@ 4748	—
	760	—	—	—	—	—	—	—	138@ 10^7	—
Ti-6246 (Ti-6Al-2Sn-4Zr-6Mo-…)	23	—	—	—	—	—	—	—	575@ 10^7	—
Ti-24Al-15Nb-1Mo	23	—	—	—	—	—	—	—	350@ 10^7	—
	650	—	955.5	0.2145	−0.085	−0.82	976	0.097	—	—
Ti-4.8Al-1.5Fe-6.8Mo-1.2Nd:										
As forged	23	—	2537	0.0048	−0.198	−0.7	11855	0.286	—	—
As sintered	23	—	2512	0.0665	−0.132	−0.8	3253	0.142	—	—

continued

Material	$T/℃$	$d\varepsilon/dt$	σ_f'	ε_f'	b	c	K'	n'	$\sigma_f@2N_f$	R
Ti-4.5Al-3V-2Fe-2Mo (shot-peened)	23	—	—	—	—	—	—	—	660@ 10^7 700@ 10^7	RB RB
Ti-4.5Al-3V-2Fe-2Mo /40%SiC ($V_f=40\%$)	23	—	—	—	—	—	—	—	650@ 10^6	—
	400	—	—	—	—	—	—	—	600@ 10^6	—
Ti-Sf61	23	—	—	—	—	—	—	—	—	
	760	—	—	—	—	—	—	—	195@ 10^7	—
TNB-V2 (Ti-45Al-8Nb-0.2C; Heat-Treated)	23	—	—	—	—	—	—	—	1000@ 650	—
	550	—	2098	0.026	−0.15	−0.5	—	—	800@ 450	—
	750	—	—	—	—	—	—	—	650@ 250	—
	850	—	—	—	—	—	—	—	500@ 500	—
Ti Alloys	23	—	Eq. (6.14)	Eq. (6.15)	−0.095	−0.69	$\sigma_f'/(\varepsilon_f')^{n'}$	b/c	Eq. (97.1)	—

Table 97.3   Thermomechanical Creep Parameters of Ti Alloys

Material	$T/℃$	Stress/MPa	Strain Rate $/s^{-1}$	$A/$ $(MPa^{-n}\cdot s^{m-1})$	$Q/$ $(J\cdot mol^{-1})$	n	m
Ti Grade 5	150	$E=1$	—	4.65×10^{-21}	0	4.37	0.76
Ti-48Al-2Nb-2Cr	705	$E=1$; $\sigma<150$	—	—	0	3	0
		$E=1$; $\sigma>150$	—	—	0	7	0
	760	$E=1$; $\sigma<200$	—	—	0	3	0
		$E=1$; $\sigma>200$	—	—	0	7	0
	815	$E=1$; $\sigma=103$	—	—	300000	3	0
		$E=1$; $\sigma<220$	—	—	0	3	0
		$E=1$; $\sigma>220$	—	—	0	7	0
		$E=1$; $\sigma=241$	—	—	410000	7	0

Notes: Creep equation $=\dfrac{d\varepsilon_{creep}}{dt}=A\left(\dfrac{\sigma-\sigma_{th}}{E}\right)^n t^m \exp\left(\dfrac{-Q}{RT_k}\right)$, $\sigma>\sigma_{th}$;

$\sigma_{th}=$ Stress threshold and $\sigma_{th}=0$, if not specified;

$E=$ Young's modulus; If given that $E=1$, it means E is not specified.

Table 97.4　Material Parameters on Fatigue Crack Growth of Ti-alloys in Opening Mode

Material	$T/\text{℃}$	σ_y	σ_{uts}	K_{IC}	$f(R)$	m	ΔK_{th}	$\Delta\sigma_{fat}$
Ti-6Al-4V	23	1003	1014	—	$f(-1) = 7.36\times10^{-11}$	2.378	1.469	804
					$f(0.1) = 1.66\times10^{-10}$	—	1.043	502
					$f(0.5) = 2.23\times10^{-10}$	—	0.922	360

Notes：$\dfrac{\mathrm{d}a}{\mathrm{d}N_{p}} = f(R) \mid \Delta K - \Delta K_{th} \mid^{m}$；

$\sigma_y(\text{MPa}) = $ Yield strength；

$\sigma_{uts}(\text{MPa}) = $ Ultimate tensile strength；

$f(R) = $ Parameter as a function of load ratio R；

$m = $ Exponent；

$\Delta K_{th}(\text{MPa} \cdot \text{m}^{\frac{1}{2}}) = $ Threshold stress intensity factor range；

$\Delta\sigma_{fat}(\text{MPa}) = $ Fatigue strength range.

Chapter 98

V (Vanadium)

98.1   Introduction

V (Vanadium) is soft and ductile-resistant to corrosion by alkalis, sulfuric acid, and hydrochloric acid. In tool and spring steels, it is a powerful alloying agent; a small amount (less than 1%) adds strength, toughness, and heat resistance. Large steel forgings contain vanadium in the range between 0.050% and 0.25%, where vanadium acts as a grain refiner, and also improves the mechanical properties of the forgings. The physical properties of vanadium are susceptible to interstitial impurities. Mechanical properties of V (Vanadium) alloys are listed in Table 98.1.

Vanadium becomes a superconductor once the temperature goes below 4.5 K.

V (Vanadium) oxidizes vigorously, with the formation of vanadium pentoxide, V_2O_5, as well as lower oxides at a temperature between 600 ℃ and 700 ℃. Vanadium pentoxide, V_2O_5, is commercially important. However, all vanadium compounds are assumably considered toxic.

98.2   Applications

V (Vanadium) has good structural strength, having been used in rust-resistant high-speed tools, as a carbon stabilizer in some steels, as a titanium-steel bonding agent, or as a catalyst.

Nanotubes of VO_x have been prepared and investigated as Li-Fe-based cathodes. For V_2O_5, aerogels (disordered mesoporous materials with a high pore volume) were recently reported to have electroactive capacities greater than polycrystalline non-porous V_2O_5 powders. Note that V_2O_5 is poisonous orange solid.

References

DONG W, ROLISON D R, DUNN B, 2000. Electrochemical Properties of High Surface Area Vanadium Oxides Aerogels[J]. Electrochemical and Solid-State Letters, 3(10): 457-459.

FUKUMOTO K, et al, 2004. Varying Temperature Effects on Mechanical Properties of Vanadium Alloys during Neutron Irradiation[J]. Journal of Nuclear Materials, 329-333(1): 472-476.

Table 98.1 Mechanical Properties of V（Vanadium）Alloys

Material	$T/℃$	E_T	ρ	ν	(σ, ε)	α	k	γ	ρ_E	K_{IC}
V（Pure）	23	130	6. 1	0.36	（127, 0.2%） （200, 19%）	8.3	31	482	—	—
	1900（T_m）	—	—	—	—	—	—	—	—	—
V-45Cr-4Ti	23	—	—	0.36	$\sigma_{uts}=440$	—	—	—	—	—
	700	—	—	—	$\sigma_{uts}=395$	—	—	—	—	—
	800	—	—	—	$\sigma_{uts}=350$	—	—	—	—	—
V-15Cr-5Ti	23	126	6.2	0.36	（580, 0.2%） $\sigma_{uts}=680$	9.3	21	450	—	—
	700	112	—	0.36	（340, 0.2%） $\sigma_{uts}=540$	10.7	31	600	—	—
	1880（T_m）	—	—	—	—	—	—	—	—	—

Chapter 99

W (Tungsten)

99.1　Introduction

W (Tungsten) has the highest melting point, highest tensile strength, lowest coefficient of linear thermal expansion, and good creep resistance of all the non-alloyed metals. It has been used for the production of hard materials such as WC (tungsten carbide). W (Tungsten) is a good electrical conductor. Its electric resistivity (ρ_e) is

$$\rho_e = \rho_{ref}[1 + \alpha (T - T_{ref})] \tag{99.1}$$

where:

ρ_{ref} (ohm−m): Resistivity at reference temperature & $\rho_{ref} = 5.5 \times 10^{-8}$ ohm-m for tungsten;

α (℃−1): Temperature coefficient at 20 ℃ & $\alpha = 0.0045$ ℃$^{-1}$ for tungsten;

T & T_{ref} (℃): Temperature and reference temperature & $T_{ref} = 20$ ℃ for tungsten.

Mechanical properties and fatigue parameters of tungsten alloys are listed in Tables 99.1 and 99.2, respectively.

99.2　Applications

Alloying small quantities of tungsten with steel significantly increases its toughness. W is alloyed with C, the only element having a higher melting point than tungsten of all the pure materials, to make wear-resistant abrasives and cutters. WC is an efficient electrical conductor.

Having good mechanical properties, as well as superior thermal and electrical conductivities, WCu composites are suitable for die inserts and electrode facings, flash and butt welding dies, and hot upsetting.

References

ARORA A, 2004. Tungsten Heavy Alloy for Defense Application[J]. Materials Technology, 19(4): 210-216.

KOUTSOSPYROS A, et al, 2006. A Review of Tungsten: From Environmental Obscurity to Scrutiny[J]. Journal of Hazardous Materials, 136 (1): 1-19.

LASSNER E, SCHUBERT W D, 1999. Tungsten: Properties, Chemistry, Technology of the Element, Alloys, and Chemical Compounds[D]. Springer.

SUN H L, et al, 2010. Microstructure and Mechanical Properties of Nanocrystalline Tungsten Thin Films[J].
US Army Research Laboratory, USA, 49(12): 1.

Table 99.1   Mechanical Properties of W (Tungsten).

Material	$T/°C$	E_T	ρ	ν	(σ, ε)	α	k	γ	ρ_E	K_{IC}
W (Soft)	−40	—	—	0.28	—	4.3	186	—	—	—
	23	410	19.3	0.28	(550, 0.2%) (585, <1%)	4.4	164	133	—	8
	500	393	—	0.28	—	5.4	125	144	—	—
	1000	355	—	0.29	—	5.8	114	153	—	—
	2000	272	—	0.29	—	6.3	98	172	—	—
	3420 (T_m)	—	—	—	—	—	—	—	—	—
W (Hard; Annealed)	−40	—	—	0.28	—	4.3	186	—	—	—
	23	410	19.3	0.28	(750, 0.2%) (980, <1%)	4.4	164	133	—	5.5
	500	393	—	0.28	—	5.4	125	144	—	
	600	—	—	—	(480, 0.2%) (540, 20%)	—	—	146	—	7.5
	1000	355	—	0.29	(350, 0.2%) (400, 20%)	5.8	114	153	—	
	2000	272	—	0.29	—	6.3	98	172	—	—
	3420 (T_m)	—	—	—	—	—	—	—	—	—
W-26Ag	23	—	15.1	—	$\sigma_{uts}=483$	—	—	—	—	—
W-10Cu	23	330	16.8	0.29	$\sigma_{uts}=483$	6.5	147	163	—	—
	400	—	—	—	—	8.7	—	—	—	—
W-15Cu	23	310	15.2	0.29	$\sigma_{uts}=517$	7.1	175	174	—	—
W-20Cu	23	280	15.2	0.29	$\sigma_{uts}=662$	7.6	182	195	—	—
	400	—	—	—	—	9.2	—	—	—	—
W-25Cu	23	256	15.2	0.29	$\sigma_{uts}=620$	8.2	189	211	—	—
W-30Cu	23	245	13.8	0.29	$\sigma_{uts}=586$	8.7	201	225	—	—
W-35Cu	23	235	13.3	0.29	—	9.3	205	230	—	—
W-40Cu	23	225	12.8	0.29	—	9.8	230	240	—	—
W-45Cu	23	220	12.3	0.29	$\sigma_{uts}=434$	10.4	240	252	—	—
W-50Cu	23	210	11.9	0.29	—	11	—	—	—	—
W-3.5Ni-1.5Cu (Class 3; Inermet 180)	23	315	18.2	0.29	(595, 0.2%) (770, 7%)	4	138	—	—	—
	400	—	—	—	—	4.43	—	—	—	—

continued

Material	$T/°C$	E_T	ρ	ν	(σ, ε)	α	k	γ	ρ_E	K_{IC}
W-6Ni-4Cu (Class 1; Inermet 170)	23	276	17	0.29	(550, 0.2%) (760, 6%)	5	96	—	—	—
	400	—	—	—	—	5.4	—	—	—	—
92.5W-Ni-Fe-5Co (Die-metal) (Grade 925; True s-s)	23	315	18	0.29	(1275, 0.2%) (1320, 2%) (1340, 3%) (1420, 7.3%)	—	—	—	—	—
W-2.1Ni-0.9Fe	23	365	18.5	0.3	(590, 0.2%) (850, 7%)	5	126	—	—	—
	400	—	—	—	—	4.6	—	—	—	—
W-3.5Ni-1.5Fe	23	345	18	0.3	(620, 0.2%) (830, 7%)	4	109	—	—	—
	400	—	—	—	—	4.6	—	—	—	—
W-4Ni-2Fe-4Mo (Anviloy 1150)	23	340	19.3	0.3	(650, 0.2%) (950, 10%)	4	70.2	—	—	—
	650	—	—	—	$\sigma_{uts} = 724$	4.6	—	—	—	—
	815	—	—	—	$\sigma_{uts} = 517$	5.3	—	—	—	—
W-4.5Ni-2Fe-2.5Co	23	315	18	0.29	(1275, 0.2%) (1285, 9.4%)	—	—	—	—	—
	600	—	—	—	(450, 2%) (720, 20%)	—	—	—	—	—
	1000	—	—	—	(400, 2%) (470, 20%)	—	—	—	—	—
W-5Ni-2.5Fe (Diemetal; D176)	23	385	17.6	0.29	(630, 0.2%) (840, 4%)	4	—	—	—	6
	400	—	—	—	—	4.5	—	—	—	—
W-5.25Ni-2.25Fe (Class 2)	23	330	17.5	0.29	(590, 0.2%) (800, 7%)	4.4	84	200	—	—
	400	—	—	—	—	4.6	—	—	—	—
W-7Ni-3Fe (Class 1)	23	315	17.1	0.29	(610, 0.2%) (840, 10%)	4	75	180	—	60
	400	—	—	—	—	4.6	—	—	—	—
W-8Ni-2Mn	23	—	—	0.29	—	—	45	—	—	—
W-9Ni-1Mn	23	—	—	0.29	—	—	51	—	—	—
WO$_3$	23	—	—	—	—	—	—	—	—	—

continued

Material	$T/°C$	E_T	ρ	ν	(σ, ε)	α	k	γ	ρ_E	K_{IC}
W-5Re	23	405	19.57	0.3	(1517, 10%)	—	—	—	—	—
	3120 (T_m)	—	—	—	—	—	—	—	—	—
W-25Re (Annealed)	23	430	19.7	0.3	(1370, 20%)	—	—	140	—	—
	500	—	—	—	$\sigma_{uts} = 880$	4.48	—	—	—	—
	1000	—	—	—	$\sigma_{uts} = 550$	5.04	—	156	—	—
	1500	—	—	—	$\sigma_{uts} = 330$	—	—	—	—	—
	1800	—	—	—	$\sigma_{uts} = 200$	—	—	—	—	—
	3050 (T_m)	—	—	—	—	—	—	—	—	—
W-26Re	23	430	19.7	0.3	(1517, 10%)	—	—	—	—	—
	3120 (T_m)	—	—	—	—	—	—	—	—	—

Notes: $T_m(°C) = $ Melting point;

$E_T(GPa) = $ Tensile modulus of elasticity;

$\rho(g/cm^3) = $ Density;

$\nu = $ Poisson's ratio;

$\sigma_Y(MPa) = $ Yield strength is estimated at 0.2% in elongation;

$\sigma_{UTS}(MPa)$ & eUTS $=$ Ultimate tensile strength and strain;

$\alpha(mm/m/°C) = $ Coefficient of linear thermal expansion;

$k(W/m/°C) = $ Thermal conductivity;

$\gamma(J/Kg/°C) = $ Specific heat capacity;

$K_{IC}(MPa \cdot m^{\frac{1}{2}}) = $ Fracture toughness (Mode I).

Table 99.2 Fatigue ε-N Properties of Some W (Tungsten) Alloys

Material	$T/°C$	$d\varepsilon/dt$	σ_f'	ε_f'	b	c	K'	n'	$\sigma_f @ 2N_f$	R
W-3.5Ni-1.5Cu (Inermet 180)	23	—	1048	—	−0.11	—	—	—	210@ 4×10^6	—
W-5Ni-2.5Fe (Densimet 176)	23	—	3000	—	−0.13	—	1314	0.08	425@ 3×10^6	—

Notes: $\sigma_f'(MPa) = $ Fatigue strength coefficient;

$\varepsilon_f = $ Fatigue ductility coefficient;

$b = $ Fatigue strength exponent;

$c = $ Fatigue ductility exponent;

$\sigma_f = $ Fatigue strength (endurance limit);

$N_{cutoff} = $ Number of reversals at endurance limit or cutoff if no apparent knee point;

$K'(MPa) = $ Strain hardening coefficient;

$n' = $ Strain hardening exponent.

Chapter 100

Zn (Zinc)

100.1 Introduction

Zn (Zinc) is hard and brittle at normal operating temperatures but becomes malleable between 100 and 150 ℃. The metal becomes brittle again once heated above 210 ℃ and can be pulverized by beating. Zinc is the principal alloying element used for brass (copper-zinc) alloys, which were used to make utensils such as "ding" in China more than 3000 years ago. Besides zinc, lead and tin are the other two metals with low melting points.

Because of their low melting point, most zinc alloys are die-cast. Creep is expected to be the design challenge for a structural application due to its low melting point. When it works at a temperature above 40% of its melting point (measured in K), creep is often the dominant control factor. Any application at a temperature above 70% of its melting point (measured in K) should be avoided. Its Young's modulus, yield strength, ultimate tensile strength, and fatigue limit are creep-dependent. The ultimate compressive strength of zinc alloys is significantly higher than its ultimate tensile strength. Material properties listed in Table 100.1 is for reference only.

Fatigue and creep parameters are listed in Tables 100.2 and 100.3, respectively. Strictly speaking, zinc alloys do not have a single value for elastic modulus. Yield strength (allowable stress) under sustained loading is dependent on the allowable design strain over the required service life.

Orthotropic elasticities (stiffness tensor) of a single zinc crystal at room temperature are given in Table 100.2.

100.2 Zamak

Zamak stands for Zn-4Al-others, i.e. composites with 4% of Al by weight, i.e. composites with 4% of Al by weight. Zamak 3 is the most used zinc alloy. Zamak alloys are die-cast, and they perform fair structurally. They are used for simple automotive parts such as console, car door handles, car door lock housing, windshield mirror mount, steering column housing, gear shift bracket, throttle stop bracket, grille, and suspension control valve.

100.3 ZA Alloys

ZA stands for a zinc-aluminum alloy with more than 4% of aluminum. Typically Zn-based alloys such as ZA27, ZA12, and ZA8 are used as cost- and energy-effective substitutes for bronze, cast irons, and aluminum alloys. Dimensional instability is a concern.

100.4　Wear-Resistant Zinc Alloys

ACuZinc5 and ACuZinc10 are defined as wear-resistant materials. Nevertheless, they are comparable to those of more expensive materials, making them suitable for high-load applications and those at elevated temperatures. Also, Alzen 305 and Alzen 501 (from 30 to 50% of Al) perform pretty well in various tribological applications.

100.5　Zinc Coating

Pure zinc has one important application, i.e. galvanizing steel. Zinc coatings can be applied to steel by different methods, from zinc-containing simple paint to hot-dip galvanizing. All these methods can provide successful protection when exposed to a corrosive environment. In general terms, the life of a zinc coating is more or less proportional to its thickness. Generally speaking, there are five coating methods:

(a) Hot-dip galvanizing;
(b) Electroplating;
(c) Mechanical coatings;
(d) Zinc spraying;
(e) Zinc dust painting.

There are several the coating jobs, such as galvanization, self-repairing, passivation, and barrier protection.

100.5.1　Galvanization and Galvanneal

Galvanization, which is the coating of pure zinc onto ferrous metals to protect the metals against corrosion, is the most familiar form of using zinc in this way. The metal is protected by galvanic action. The formability and adhesion of continuous galvanized zinc coatings are excellent and, in most cases, match the formability of the underlying steel. The formability of galvanized steel-which is defined as the resistance to cracking and loss of adhesion of the zinc coating during forming-is inversely proportional to coating and steel substrate thickness. There are, however, some coatings that are more ductile than others, an important consideration for deep draw stamping applications. Therefore, it is necessary to balance the requirements for corrosion resistance and formability.

On flame spray coating, both tensile strength and hardness of a pure zinc coating increase with an increase in spray distance [Kobayashi et al.].

Galvanneal is a zinc-iron alloy coating (zinc/8-10% iron alloy) with improved paintability, weldability, and drivability relative to galvanization. Galvanneal is used in the automotive industry because of its improved manufacturing performance in models which use lighter and stronger grades of steel.

100.5.2 Self-Repairing

Zinc oxides and carbonates migrate to the damaged area of the coating to actively repair the coating and restore barrier protection.

100.5.3 Passivation

Metal oxides slow down the corrosion reaction of zinc and steel to provide three times greater corrosion protection than pure zinc.

100.5.4 Dacromet for Barrier Protection

Dacromet is comprised mainly of overlapping zinc and aluminum flakes in an inorganic binder. Overlapping zinc and aluminum flakes provide an excellent barrier between the steel substrate and the corrosive media, and it is called barrier protection.

100.6 Coating on Welds

Mechanical properties of sound welds made with the covered electrode shielded metal arc or submerged arc processes in zinc-coated steel are equivalent to the properties of sound welds in uncoated steel [Gregory]. It means zinc-coating has a negligible effect on welding.

References

ASTM Designation B86-98. Standard Specification for Zinc and Zinc-Aluminum (ZA) Alloy Foundry and Die Castings[S]. ASTM, West Conshohocken, PA, USA.

CAY F, KUMAZ S, 2005. Hot Tensile and Fatigue Behavior of Zinc-Aluminum Alloys Produced by Gravity and Squeeze Casting[J]. Materials and Design, 26(6): 479-485.

GAGNE M, 2011. Zinc Castings for Automotive Applications[J]. Die Casting Engineers, 55(3): 36-40.

GREGORY E N, 1971. The Mechanical Properties of Welds in Zinc Coated Steel[J]. Welding Research Supplement, 445s-450s.

HANNA M, et al, 1996. ACuZinc5 Applications in the Auto Industry[J]. SAE 960764.

HILLIER M, ROBINSON M, 2004. Hydrogen Embrittlement of High Strength Steel Electroplated with Zinc-Cobalt Alloys[J]. Corrosion Science, 46(3): 715-727.

KALLIEN L H, LEIS W, 2011. Ageing of Zinc Alloys[J]. International Foundry Research, 64(1): 1-23.

KOBAYASHI T, et al, 2003. Characterization of Pure Aluminum and Zinc Sprayed Coatings Produced by Flame Spraying[J]. Materials Transactions, 44(12): 2711-2717.

LI H, et al, 2007. Compressive and Fatigue Damage of Commercial Pure Zinc[J]. Materials Science and Engineering, A, 466: 38-46.

MIR A, MURPHY S, 1999. Kinetics of Compressive Creep in Sand Cast Commercial Zinc-Based Alloys No. 3 and No. 5[J]. Metallurgical Science and Technology, 17(2): 36-42.

OTANI T, et al, 1985. Damping Capacity of Zn-Al Alloy Castings[J]. Journal of Physics Colloques, 46 (C10): 417-420.

PARISOT R, 2000. Modeling the Mechanical Behavior of a Multicrystalline Zinc Coating on a Hot-Dip Galvanized Steel Sheet[J]. Computational Materials Science, 19(1-4): 189-204.

REGEV M, et al, 1998. Creep Studies of Coarse-Grained AZ91D Magnesium Castings[J]. Materials Science and Engineering, A, 252(1): 6-16.

RITCHIE I G, PAN Z L, GOODWIN F E, 1991. Characteristics of the Damping Properties of Zn-Al Alloys[J]. Metallurgical Transactions, A, 22: 617-622.

SONG G M, 2001. Interface Fracture Behavior of Zinc Coatings on Steels: Experiments and Finite Element Calculations[J]. Surface and Coating Technology, 201(7): 4311-4316.

VOORWALD H, et al, 2005. Effects of Electroplated Zinc-Nickel Alloy Coatings on the Fatigue Strength of AISI 4340 High-Strength Steel[J]. Journal of Materials Engineering and Performance, 14(2): 249-257.

WINTER R, 2011. EZAC-A Novel High Strength, Creep Resistant, Hot Chamber Zinc Die Casting Alloy[J]. SAE 2011-01-1084.

Table 100.1　Mechanical Properties of Zn（Zinc）Alloys

Material	$T/^\circ\mathrm{C}$	E_T	ρ	ν	(σ, ε)	α	k	γ	ρ_E	K_IC
Zn（Pure；Soft；Cast）	23	108	7.144	0.25	$(-85, -54\%)$ $(-62, -35\%)$ $(-54, -11\%)$ $(-45, -6\%)$ $(-32, -3\%)$ $(-13.8, -0.2\%)$; $(28, 65\%)$	31.2	113	382	—	—
	410	—	6.85	—	—	—	96	—	—	—
	419.5（T_m）	—	—	—	—	—	—	—	—	—
	420（Liquid）	—	6.63	—	—	—	164	—	—	—
	800（Liquid）	—	6.24	—	—	—	56	—	—	—
Zn（Coating）	23	108	7.14	0.25	$(75, 0.2\%)$ $(126, 5\%)$	30.2	116	394	—	—
	100	70	—	—	—	—	—	404	—	—
	400	—	6.85	—	—	—	96	455	—	—
	420（T_m）	—	6.57	—	—	—	164	—	—	—
Zn（Crystal）（//a-xis）	23	120	7.144	0.25	$(110, 0.2\%)$ $(295, 60\%)$	61	—	—	—	—
（//c-xis）	23	45	7.144	0.25	$(50, 0.2\%)$ $(114, 60\%)$	15	—	—	—	—
Zn（99.95%；Rolled；Soft Temper）	23	70	7.144	0.25	$(75, 0.2\%)$ $(126, 65\%)$	39.5	113	382	—	—
	100	—	—	—	—	39.7	—	404	—	—
	400	—	6.85	—	—	—	96	—	—	—
	420（T_m）	—	—	—	—	164	—	—	—	—
Zn（98.5%；Rolled；Hard Temper）	23	96.5	7.144	0.25	$(120, 0.2\%)$ $(246, 5\%)$	39.5	113	382	—	—
	100	—	—	—	—	39.7	—	404	—	—
	400	—	6.85	—	—	—	96	—	—	—
	420（T_m）	—	—	—	—	164	—	—	—	—
ACuZinc5（DC；Zn-5.5 Cu-2.9Al-0.038Mg；ASTM 894-3）	20	100	6.85	0.29	$(284, 0.2\%)$ $(355, 9.4\%)$	24.1	106	340	—	—
	50	—	—	—	—	26.4	108	360	—	—
	100	—	—	—	—	27.3	110.5	400	—	—
	140	—	—	—	$\sigma_{\mathrm{crs},212}=31$	—	—	—	—	—
	502（T_m）	—	—	—	—	—	—	—	—	—

continued

Material	$T/℃$	E_T	ρ	ν	(σ, ε)	α	k	γ	ρ_E	K_{IC}
EZAC (Zn-7.3Al-2.85 Cu-0.2Cr-0.3 Ti-0.03B)	23	—	—	—	(400, 0.2%) (420, 1%)	—	—	—	—	—
	140	—	—	—	(269, 0.2%) $\sigma_{uts} = 310$; $\sigma_{crs,731} = 31$	—	—	—	—	—
Zamak 2 (DC; AC 43A; Z0430)	−40	101	—	—	(−454, −6%) (−339, −0.2%); (376, 0.2%) $\sigma_{uts} = 386$	—	—	—	—	—
	−20	98	—	—	(−424, −5%) (−310, −0.2%); (378, 0.2%) $\sigma_{uts} = 399$	—	—	—	—	—
	0	96	—	—	(−403, −5%) (−304, −0.2%); (347, 0.2%) (367, 4%)	—	—	—	—	—
	23	96	6.7	0.27	(−379, −5%) (−257, −0.2%); (319, 0.2%) (350, 0.8%) (343, 7%)	27.4	105	420	—	—
	75	84	—	—	(−288, −5%) (−212, −0.2%); (193, 0.2%) $\sigma_{uts} = 235$	—	—	—	—	—
	135	65	—	—	(−192, −5%) (−138, −0.2%); (82, 0.2%) $\sigma_{uts} = 109$	—	—	—	—	—

continued

Material	$T/^{\circ}\mathrm{C}$	E_{T}	ρ	ν	(σ, ε)	α	k	γ	ρ_{E}	K_{IC}
Zamak 2 (DC; AC 43A; Z0430)	140	—	—	—	$\sigma_{\mathrm{crs},52} = 31$	—	—	—	—	—
	374 (T_{m})	—	—	—	—	—	—	—	—	—
Zamak 2 (DC; Aged)	23	83	6.7	0.27	$(241, 0.2\%)$ $(310, 10\%)$	27.4	105	420	—	—
	374 (T_{m})	—	—	—	—	—	—	—	—	—
Zamak 3 (DC; AG40; Z0400)	−40	102	—	—	$(-316, -5\%)$ $(-243, -0.2\%)$; $(276, 0.2\%)$ $(339, 3\%)$	—	—	—	—	—
	−20	101	—	—	$(-303, -5\%)$ $(-225, -0.2\%)$; $(269, 0.2\%)$ $\sigma_{\mathrm{uts}} = 327$	—	—	—	—	—
	0	103	—	—	$(-373, -5\%)$ $(-274, -0.2\%)$; $(255, 0.2\%)$ $\sigma_{\mathrm{uts}} = 299$	—	—	—	—	—
	23	95	6.6	0.27	$(-373, -5\%)$ $(-274, -0.2\%)$; $(232, 0.2\%)$ $(260, 1\%)$ $(271, 10\%)$	27.2	113	420	—	58
	75	85	—	—	$(-199, -5\%)$ $(-156, -0.2\%)$; $(152, 0.2\%)$ $\sigma_{\mathrm{uts}} = 179$	—	—	—	—	—
	100	8	—	—	$(194, 30\%)$	—	—	—	—	—
	135	61	—	—	$(-136, -5\%)$ $(-102, -0.2\%)$; $(72, 0.2\%)$ $\sigma_{\mathrm{uts}} = 81$	—	—	—	—	—
	387 (T_{m})	—	—	—	—	—	—	—	—	—

continued

Material	$T/℃$	E_T	ρ	ν	(σ, ε)	α	k	γ	ρ_E	K_{IC}
Zamak 5 (DC; AC41A; Z410)	-40	102	—	—	$(-377, -5\%)$ $(-284, -0.2\%)$; $(328, 0.2\%)$ $(355, 1\%)$ $(374, 2\%)$	—	—	—	—	—
	-20	103	—	—	$(-367, -5\%)$ $(-256, -0.2\%)$; $(318, 0.2\%)$ $(345, 1\%)$ $(357, 4\%)$	—	—	—	—	—
	0	100	—	—	$(-353, -5\%)$ $(-256, -0.2\%)$; $(353, 0.2\%)$ $\sigma_{uts} = 256$	—	—	—	—	—
	23	95	6.7	0.27	$(-266, -5\%)$ $(-199, -0.2\%)$; $(289, 0.2\%)$ $(310, 1\%)$ $(340, 7\%)$	27.2	109	420	—	65
	75	87	—	—	$(-243, -5\%)$ $(-185, -0.2\%)$; $(179, 0.2\%)$ $(210, 1\%)$ $(280, 14\%)$	—	—	—	—	—
	100	—	—	—	$(240, 23\%)$	—	—	—	—	—
	135	66	—	—	$(-153, -5\%)$ $(-109, -0.2\%)$; $(79, 0.2\%)$ $(95, 1\%)$ $(93, 4\%)$	—	—	—	—	—
	386 (T_m)	—	—	—	—	—	—	—	—	—
Zamak 7 (DC; AG40B)	23	83	6.6	0.27	$(221, 0.2\%)$ $(283, 13\%)$	27.2	113	420	—	—
	387 (T_m)	—	—	—	—	—	—	—	—	—

continued

Material	$T/°C$	E_T	ρ	ν	(σ, ε)	α	k	γ	ρ_E	K_{IC}
ZA 8 (DC; Zn-8.4Al-1Cu)	−40	90	—	—	$(-453, -5\%)$ $(-349, -0.2\%)$; $(373, 0.2\%)$ $\sigma_{uts}=441$	—	—	—	—	—
	−20	95	—	—	$(-446, -5\%)$ $(-337, -0.2\%)$; $(350, 0.2\%)$ $(412, 5.6\%)$	—	—	—	—	—
	0	84	—	—	$(-411, -5\%)$ $(-327, -0.2\%)$; $(328, 0.2\%)$ $\sigma_{uts}=383$	—	—	—	—	—
	23	90	6.3	0.29	$(-321, -5\%)$ $(-233, -0.2\%)$; $(284, 0.2\%)$ $(375, 1\%)$ $(385, 5\%)$	23.3	115	435	—	—
	75	86	—	—	$(-258, -5\%)$ $(-180, -0.2\%)$; $(154, 0.2\%)$ $\sigma_{uts}=206$	—	—	—	—	—
	135	57	—	—	$(-134, -5\%)$ $(-93, -0.2\%)$; $(60, 0.2\%)$ $\sigma_{uts}=80$	—	—	—	—	—
	404 (T_m)	—	—	—	—	—	—	—	—	—
ZA 8 (DC; Aged)	23	90	6.3	0.29	$(225, 0.2\%)$ $(297, 20\%)$	23.3	115	435	—	—
	404 (T_m)	—	—	—	—	—	—	—	—	—
ZA 12 (DC; Zn-11Al-0.9Cu-...)	23	83	6	0.3	$(320, 0.2\%)$ $(404, 5\%)$	24.2	116	448	—	—
	432 (T_m)	—	—	—	—	—	—	—	—	—
ZA 12 (SC)	23	83	6	0.3	$(211, 0.2\%)$ $(299, 1.5\%)$	24.2	116	448	—	—
ZA 12 (PM)	23	83	6	0.3	$(268, 0.2\%)$ $(328, 2.2\%)$	24.2	116	448	—	—

continued

Material	$T/°C$	E_T	ρ	ν	(σ, ε)	α	k	γ	ρ_E	K_{IC}
ZA 27 (DC; Zn-27Al- 2.2Cu-…)	23	83	5	0.32	$(-385, -0.2\%)$; $(371, 0.2\%)$ $(426, 2.5\%)$	26	126	534	—	—
	484 (T_m)	—	—	—	—	—	—	—	—	—
ZA 27 (SC)	23	83	5	0.32	$(371, 0.2\%)$ $(421, 4.6\%)$	26	126	534	—	—
ZA 27 (SC; Heat-treated)	23	83	5	0.32	$(317, 10\%)$	26	126	534	—	—
ZA 27 (PM)	23	83	5	0.32	$(376, 0.2\%)$ $(441, 2.5\%)$	26	126	534	—	—
Zn-27Al-2Cu- 0.035Ti-0.007B (Bearing)	23	135	5	0.32	$(365, 0.2\%)$ $(440, 7.8\%)$	26	126	534	—	—
Zn-5Al	23	—	—	—	$\sigma_{ucs} = -750$; $(190, 0.2\%)$ $(210, 3\%)$	—	—	—	—	—

Table 100.2   Fatigue ε-N Properties of Zinc Alloys

Material	$T/°C$	$d\varepsilon/dt$	σ_f'	ε_f'	b	c	K'	n'	$\sigma_f @ 2N_f$	R
ACuZinc5 (DC)	23	—	—	—	—	—	—	—	$84 @ 5 \times 10^8$	—
Zamak 2 (DC)	23	—	—	—	—	—	—	—	$59 @ 5 \times 10^8$	—
Zamak 3 (DC)	23	—	—	—	—	—	—	—	$48 @ 5 \times 10^8$	—
Zamak 5 (DC)	23	—	—	—	—	—	—	—	$57 @ 5 \times 10^8$	—
Zamak 7 (DC)	23	—	—	—	—	—	—	—	$47 @ 5 \times 10^8$	—
ZA 8 (DC)	23	—	—	—	—	—	—	—	$52 @ 5 \times 10^8$	—
ZA 8 (SC)	23	—	—	—	—	—	—	—	$50 @ 5 \times 10^8$	—
ZA 12 (DC)	23	—	—	—	—	—	—	—	$117 @ 5 \times 10^8$	—
ZA 12 (SC)	23	—	—	—	—	—	—	—	$103 @ 5 \times 10^8$	—
ZA 27 (DC)	23	—	—	—	—	—	—	—	$174 @ 5 \times 10^8$	—
ZA 27 (SC)	23	—	—	—	—	—	—	—	$172 @ 5 \times 10^8$	—

Notes: DC, SC, and PM = Die cast, sand cast, and permanent mold, respectively.

Table 100.3 Thermomechanical Creep Parameters of Zn Alloys

Material	$T/{}^{\circ}\mathrm{C}$	Stress/MPa	Strain Rate $/\mathrm{s}^{-1}$	$A/$ $(\mathrm{MPa}^{-n}\cdot\mathrm{s}^{m-1})$	$Q/$ $(\mathrm{J}\cdot\mathrm{mol}^{-1})$	n	m
AZ91D (DC)	140~150	$E=1$	—	—	200000	11	0
	150~160	$E=1$	—	—	220000	11	0
	160~170	$E=1$	—	—	105000	11	0
Zamak 2 (DC;Z0400)	70~160	$E=1$; 0~100	—	3.9×10^5	94000	4.15	0
Zamak 3 (DC; Z0410)	70~160	$E=1$; $-100\sim-20$	—	2.1×10^6	103000	5.1	0
Zamak 5 (DC; Z0430)	70~160	$E=1$; $-100\sim-20$	—	4.7×10^5	108000	4.2	0

Notes: Creep equation $=\dfrac{\mathrm{d}\varepsilon_{\text{creep}}}{\mathrm{d}t}=A\left(\dfrac{\sigma-\sigma_{\text{th}}}{E}\right)^{n}t^{m}\exp\left(\dfrac{-Q}{RT_{k}}\right),\sigma>\sigma_{\text{th}}$;

$\sigma_{\text{th}}=$ Stress threshold and $\sigma_{\text{th}}=0$, if not specified;

$E=$ Young's modulus; If given that $E=1$, it means E is not specified.

Table 100.4 Orthotropic Elasticities (Stiffness Tensor) of Zinc Single Crystal at the Room Temperature

Material	E_{1111}	E_{2222}	E_{3333}	E_{1212}	E_{2323}	E_{3131}	E_{1122}	E_{2233}	E_{3311}
Zn-Crystal	165	165	61.8	67	39.6	39.6	31.1	50	50

Notes: E_{11}(GPa) & E_{22}(GPa)= Young's moduli in axial and transverse directions, respectively;

$G12$ (GPa)= Shear modulus of elasticity in the lamina plane, i.e. (1, 2) plane;

$\nu_{12}=$ Poisson's ratio in the lamina plane, i.e. (1, 2) plane.

Chapter 101

Welding- Electric Resistance and Seam

101.1 Introduction

Welding is done by melting the workpiece and sometimes adding filler materials to form a pool of molten material, called weld pool, which cools to become a strong joint. This sculptural process causes convalescence to join materials, for most metals and thermoplastics. Pressure may be used in conjunction with heat to produce the weld. Spot welds and seam welds are commonly used in the automotive industry for the fabrication of all manner of bodies and structural components. Other useful thermal sources such as electric arc, laser, gas flame, electron beam, friction, and ultrasound for seam welding are briefed.

Welds can be geometrically prepared in many different ways according to the structural design of base materials. A welding joint consists of three distinct material zones: base material, heat-affected zone (HAZ), and a weld nugget. A weld nugget is composed of a thermomechanically affected zone (TMAZ) and fusion zone (FZ). Mechanical properties of welds are listed in Table 101.1. A picture detailing different material zones of a welding joint is demonstrated in Fig. 101.1.

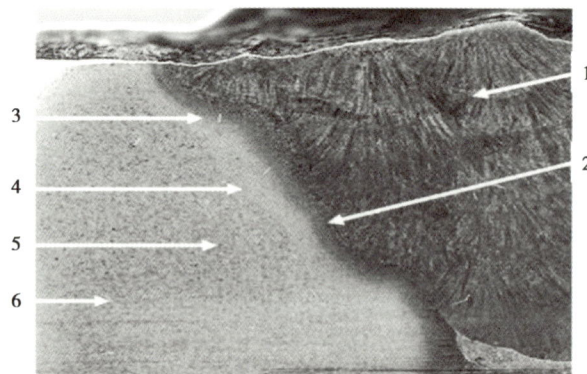

Fig. 101.1   Zoning of Welding Joint of an HSLA: 1-Weld Metal, 2-Fusion Line, 3-Coarse Grained Zone, 4-Fine Grained Zone, 5-Intercritical Zone, and 6-Base Metal

Consider a steel alloy. The tensile strength of nugget is higher than HAZ, which is also higher than the base metal, but vice versa the ductility is. This is because the microstructure of nugget and HAZ transforms into martensite.

Electric resistance spot welding is a popular method used to join overlapping metal sheets up to 3 mm thick such as automotive body sheet metals. Mechanical properties of tools and raw materials related to electric resistance welding are listed in Table 101.2. A specialized process, called shot welding, can be used to spot weld stainless steel.

When the fatigue strength assessment of a complex welded joint is considered using finite element methods, solid elements should be applied to the hot spot stress calculation because a shell model is not sufficient to provide the information required for a multiaxial fatigue analysis [Rucho] [Storsul].

101.2   Spot Welding

It takes more than 5000 spot welds to fasten various panels and components together in a typical unibody structure of a sedan. These spot welds are mostly made by industrial robots, sometimes by human hands. A schematic drawing of electric resistance welding setup is shown in Fig. 101.2. As moving electrodes approach and touching work pieces prior to welding, an impulsive forcing function is imparted to each electrode. A dynamic transient vibration is induced consequently and it oscillates until a steady state is reached. This load fluctuation results in high electrode wear, but indiscernible impact on weld quality as long as the electrode force is stabilized before current flow kicks in, i.e. the start of welding phase. In the welding phase, the electrodes move toward each other as the stiff workpiece materials get softened and transformed into plastic deformation and even melt. Especially in projection welding, the electrode force drops sharply in a short time due to the collapse of projection that causes oscillations of the load and even the loss of contact between the electrode and workpiece, resulting in poor weld quality. To ensure good weld quality, a fast compensating move of the electrode is thus essential to follow up for the deformation or collapse of the workpiece.

Mechanical properties of spot-welded joints relative to base materials are addressed in Table 101.3.

101.2.1   Heat Buildup

The electrical resistance of the material causes a heat buildup in the work pieces between the copper electrodes as

$$\text{Heat} \propto V I t \tag{101.1}$$

and

$$V = R I + L \left(\frac{\mathrm{d}I}{\mathrm{d}t}\right) \tag{101.2}$$

where:
V: Applied voltage;
R: Electric resistance;
I: Electric current;
L: Inductance;
t: Time duration.

Note that $R(T)$ and $L(t)$ are functions of temperature and $I(t)$ is a function of time. The rising temperature causes a rising resistance and results in a molten pool contained between the electrodes most of the time. As the heat dissipates throughout the workpiece in less than a second (resistance welding time is generally programmed as a quantity of AC cycles or milliseconds), the molten or plastic state grows to meet the welding tips. When the current stops, the copper tips cool the spot weld causing the metal to solidify under pressure.

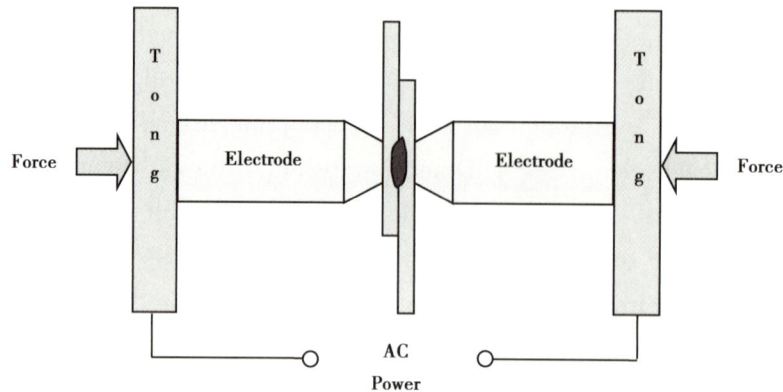

Fig. 101.2   Schematic Representation of Resistance Spot Welding.

101.2.2   Heat Transfer

101.2.3   Convection of Heat

The convective heat loss to the air via the exterior surface of electrodes or workpieces at temperature T to the air (or water) at temperature T_{air} (or T_{water}) can be estimated using Newton's Law of cooling as follows:

$$Q = h A (T - T_{air}) \tag{101.3}$$

where h is the convective heat transfer coefficient. Coolant is usually applied to electrodes for temperature control.

101.2.4   Radiation of Heat

The heat exchange through radiation from the outer surface of an ideal black body (mainly electrodes for electric resistance welding) at temperature T to its surroundings at an absolute temperature of T_{air}, is given by the Stefan-Boltzmann equation as

$$Q = 5.67 \times 10^{-8} \, \varepsilon \, A \, (T^4 - T_{air}^4) \tag{101.4}$$

where h is the convective heat transfer coefficient. Note that the unit for the heat exchange Q given in the above equation is $W/M^2/℃$. Parameter ε is the thermal emissivity and $\varepsilon = 1$ for an ideal black body. In the practice of electric resistance welding, the contribution of heat radiation to the electrode temperature distribution is less than 2 ℃, and considered negligible.

101.2.5 Contact Resistance

The electric resistance to account for the constrictive contact between workpieces has been of great interest to researchers, and so does for the constrictive contact between workpieces and electrodes. Heat conduction and electric conduction have the same type of governing differential equation and they flow through essentially the same pathway. Therefore an isothermal surface may also be a surface of equal electric potential [Holm and Holm]. Accordingly, for an infinitesimal differential element between two constrictive surfaces, thermal resistance dW is related to electrical resistance dR as

$$\frac{dW}{k} = \frac{dR}{\rho} \tag{101.5}$$

in which ρ and k are the electrical resistivity and thermal conductivity of the material, respectively.

The temperature differential between two adjacent isothermal surfaces can be obtained according to Fourier law of heat conduction as follows:

$$- dT = q \, dW = i \, v \, \frac{dR}{\rho k} = v \, \frac{dv}{\rho k} \tag{101.6}$$

where q is the quantity of heat supplied, i is the current and v is the electrical potential in reference to the contact interface. Assume that the materials including electrodes and workpieces, as per metals do, obey the Wiedemann-Franz-Lorentz law, i.e.

$$\rho \, k = L \, T \tag{101.7}$$

where L is the Lorentz constant and T is the temperature in K. Plugging Eq. (101.7) into Eq. (101.6) to eliminate $\rho \, k$, one has the differential equation between temperature T and electric voltage v as

$$v \, dv = LT \, dT \tag{101.8}$$

Integration of the above equation over a distance across the contact interface, of which the temperature reduces to the bulk temperature, yields

$$V^2 = L \left(T_S^2 - T_B^2 \right) \tag{101.9}$$

where V is the voltage drop due to constriction resistance on one side of the contact member, T_S is the contact temperature required to maintain solid contact, and T_B is the bulk temperature of the interface.

101.2.6 Performance of Electric Resistance Welding

The maximum amount of heat is produced where the electric resistance is at its maximum, which is on the surface between the sheets being joined, producing a molten nugget. Force is applied before, during and after electric current. This force is necessary in order to maintain the electric current continuity and to assure the pressure necessary to avoid defects in the joint. Affecting factors can be listed as follows:

(a) Weld current (3 to 100 Kiloamperes; generally 8.5 kA);
(b) Weld current frequency (low frequency: 50 or 60 Hz; high frequency: 150~450 kHz);
(c) Weld voltage (1 to 25 V);
(d) Resistance of the workpiece (material and thickness);
(e) Resistance between the electrode and its contact workpiece;
(f) Resistance in the faying zone (between workpieces);
(g) Pressing force and electrode movement;
(h) Electrode material (such as Cu, Cu-Cd, Cu-Cr, Cu-Zr, and Cu-Cr-Zr);
(i) Electrode geometry;
(j) Material of workpieces;
(k) Timing: Squeeze time;
(l) Timing: Weld time;
(m) Timing: Hold time;
(n) Timing: Off time;
(o) Proportions of workpieces;
(p) Workpiece surface-coating or no coating, treatment;
(q) Machine;
(r) Operator.

With regard to the optimization of electric resistance welding, the objective is a balance of the following functional goals:

(a) FZ size: The larger the FZ size, the higher the strength;
(b) Electrode indentation depth: It should be kept at a minimum value;
(c) Severe expulsion (i.e. ejection of molten metal from hot weld): It must be prevented;
(d) Carbide precipitation in the HAZ: It should be kept at the minimum value;
(e) Strength: Results from tension-shear tests must meet the engineering specifications.

101.2.7 Fracture-Interfacial Failure Mode or Pullout Failure Mode

Considering a nugget as a cylinder with diameter (d) and height ($2t$), failure load at the interfacial failure mode (P_{IF}) could be expressed assuming a uniform distribution of shear stress in the weld interface as follows:

$$P_{IF} = \frac{1}{4} \pi d^2 (\tau_{us})_{FZ} \tag{101.10}$$

of which $(\tau_{us})_{FZ}$ is the ultimate shear strength of the fusion zone (FZ).

On the other concern of failure in the pullout failure mode (P_{PF}), it is assumed that failure occurs when maximum radial stress at the circumference of half of the cylindrical nugget reaches the ultimate strength of the failure location. Namely,

$$P_{PF} = \pi d h (\sigma_{uts})_{FL} \tag{101.11}$$

where $(\sigma_{uts})_{FL}$ is the ultimate tensile strength at the pullout location. Failure is a competitive process, i.e. spot weld failure occurs in a mode, which needs less force. A critical fusion zone size (d_{Cr}) can be defined as the fusion zone that does not fail before the pullout. Spot welds with $d < d_{Cr}$ tend to fail via interfacial cracks while welds with $d > d_{Cr}$ tend to fail via pullout. Therefore,

$$d_{Cr} = \frac{4 h (\sigma_{uts})_{FL}}{(\tau_{us})_{FZ}} \tag{101.12}$$

It is difficult to measure the mechanical properties of the different regions of a spot weld. It is well known that there is a direct relationship between materials' tensile strength and their hardness. Also, the shear strength of materials can be related linearly to their tensile strength by a constant coefficient. According to Tresca's criterion that $(\tau_{us})_{FZ}/(\sigma_{uts})_{FL} = 0.5$, Eq. (9.13) for the critical diameter reduces to

$$d_{Cr} = 8 h \tag{101.13}$$

101.2.8 Fatigue Strength of Spot Welding

Fatigue resistance of these joints imparts a significant influence on the durability of a vehicle. Stress risers at welds such as irregular geometry, misalignment, post-welding residual stress, and corrosive environment are the major causes of fatigue crack initiations. Spot weld fatigue behavior is mainly controlled by the strain rate and geometric factors such as sheet thickness and weld diameter with given stress risers. No effect of paint-bake cycle on spot welding quality. Adhesive bonding and weld bonding significantly improve fatigue behavior over spot welding alone, although this improvement is in keeping with the actual increase in joint area gained by the addition of the adhesive layer.

Under a combined biaxial loading of normal stress and shear stress, a spot-weld joint (6~8 mm) can be evaluated using the following failure criterion based on Von-Mises Stress

$$\frac{(2\sigma^2 + 6\tau)^{\frac{1}{2}}}{3} = \frac{2^{\frac{1}{2}}}{3}\sigma_f \tag{101.14}$$

The fatigue strength of HAZ in steel, which is the crack initiation site of spot weld, is generally almost equal to the base. Utilizing applied stresses at the crack initiation site (HAZ) in combination with the residual stress, one can estimate the fatigue lifetime of the joint HAZ based on a fatigue theory (e.g. ε-N curves). See Section 7.5 for various approaches to material fatigue.

101.3 Seam Welding, Electric Resistance or Laser

While resembling the physics of resistance spot welding, the electrodes for seam welding appear to be disc-shaped and rotate as the material passes between them. This allows the electrodes to stay in constant contact with the material to make long continuous welds. The electrodes may also move or assist the movement of the to-be-welded material.

High-frequency resistance welding is used for applications of continuous seam or butt seam welding. High-frequency resistance welding for engineering structures requires minimal heat input, produces a narrow heat-affected zone (HAZ) as shown in Fig. 101.3, and results in improved weld properties. The solid-state weld process uses less heat input because high-frequency (150~400 kHz) electromagnetic energy is used in conjunction with high pressure to join two materials.

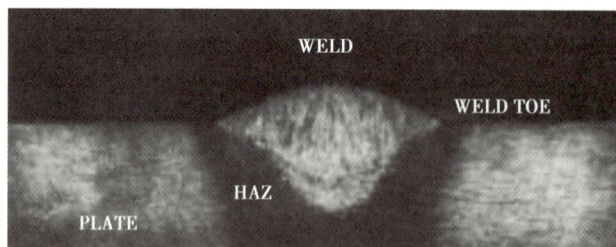

Fig. 101.3 Seam Welding: Base Material (Plate), HAZ (Heat-affected Zone), and Weld.

101.3.1 Seam and Charge Welds

As an example, welds in an A-pillar of a passenger car made of AA6082-T4 reveal that the observed extrusion weld is a composite of a seam weld (longitudinal weld) and a charge weld (transverse weld). To determine the mechanical properties of this weld region, tensile specimens are usually prepared with the weld located in the 0°, 45°, and 90° directions relative to the tensile axis [Loukus et al.], as well as no-weld regions. The specimens with 45° weld exhibited the lowest tensile strength, followed by the specimens with 90° weld, no-weld, and 0° weld specimens. Comparison of failure strains and fracture modes revealed that weld regions are more brittle than the no-weld regions.

101.3.2   Seam Weld- Butt Joint

The seam generally forms a butt joint or an overlap joint between two similar materials and the process is usually automated. Butt joints are commonly employed in the fabrication of welded pipe systems. During the prefab from a pipe on an elbow, a minimum gap of approximately 3 ~ 4 mm should be reserved, in order to obtain a proper weld penetration.

Butt joints, the idealized geometry shown in Fig. 101.4, result in a stress concentration factor as [Pedersen et al.]

$$K_t = 1.055 \, h^{0.216} \, K_m \tag{101.15}$$

where h is the thickness. As an example, $K_t \approx 1.65$ for h = 8 mm in thickness. K_m is the constant that accounts for the misalignment; K_m = 1.1 for most cases [Hobbacher]. In general, for welds in the as-welded condition, the average toe radius approximately ranges from 1 mm to 1.5 mm, i.e. 1 mm $\leqslant R \leqslant$ 1.5 mm.

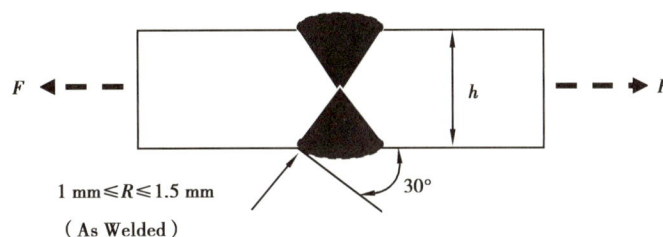

1 mm$\leqslant R \leqslant$1.5 mm   30°

(As Welded)

Fig. 101.4   2-D Schematic Butts Joint for Notch Stress Assessment.

101.3.3   Seam Weld: T-Welded Joints

Fillet welded joints, such as tee, lap, edge, and corner joints, are the most common connection in automotive frame fabrication, as schematically drawn in Fig. 101. 5. Others may be a combination of these basic types. The pseudo hot spot is traditionally identified at two distinct stress-concentrated locations as illustrated in Fig. 101.6:

Type a: Located at the plate edge (vertical plate);

Type b: Located at the plate surface (vertical plate).

In the assembly of the joint before welding, the pipe or tube shall be inserted into the socket to the maximum depth and then withdrawn back at a certain distance (approximately 1.6 mm as a general practice) away from contact between the end of the pipe and the shoulder of the socket [ASME B31.1 1998 127.3]. The bottoming clearance in a socket weld is to reduce the residual stress at the weld root that could occur during solidification of the weld metal, and also to accommodate the differential expansion between the mating elements.

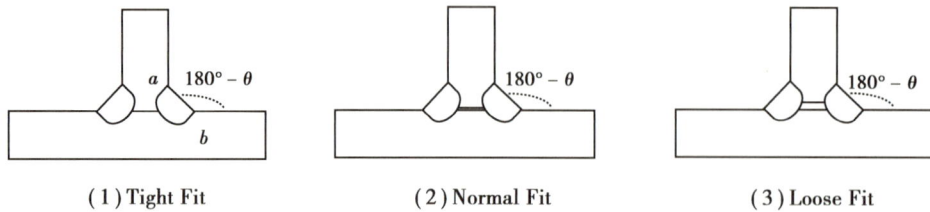

(1) Tight Fit　　　　(2) Normal Fit　　　　(3) Loose Fit

Fig. 101.5　Seam Weldment Fit-up and Angle with a Hot Spot Having 2 Stress Concentration Locations: Corner points *a* & *b*.

For one-sided fillet-welded joints, of which the idealized geometry is shown in Fig. 101.6(a), results in stress concentration factors under axial and bending loads at Point b, respectively as [Chattopadhyay et al.]

$$K_{t,axial} = 1 + \frac{1 - \exp\left[-0.9\,\theta\left(\dfrac{H}{2h_a}\right)^{\frac{1}{2}}\right]}{1 - \exp\left[-0.45\pi\left(\dfrac{H}{2h_a}\right)^{\frac{1}{2}}\right]} \left\{ \frac{\dfrac{h_a}{r_b}}{\left|\dfrac{2.8H}{h} - 2\right|} \right\}^{0.65} \tag{101.16}$$

$$\text{and} \quad K_{t,bending} = 1 + \frac{1 - \exp\left[-0.9\,\theta\left(\dfrac{H}{2h_a}\right)^{\frac{1}{2}}\right]}{1 - \exp\left[-0.45\,\pi\left(\dfrac{H}{2h_a}\right)^{\frac{1}{2}}\right]} \cdot \frac{0.247 + 1.235\left(1 - \dfrac{r_b}{h}\right)^4}{\left(\dfrac{r_b}{h}\right)^{\frac{1}{3}}}$$

$$\tanh \frac{\left(\dfrac{2h_a}{h}\right)^{\frac{1}{4}}}{1 - \dfrac{r_b}{h}} \left\{ \tanh\left[\frac{2h_\perp}{h + 2h_a} + \frac{2r_b}{h}\right] \right\}^{\frac{1}{2}} \tag{101.17}$$

of which $H = (h + 2h_a) + 0.3(h_\perp + 2h_b)$. The geometric dimensions of the *T*-welded joint given in the above equations for calculating the stress concentration factors are identified in Fig. 101.6.

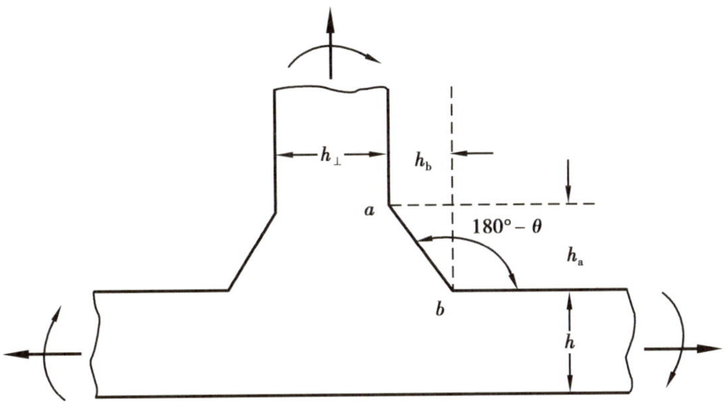

Fig. 101.6   T-Welded Joint Loaded by Both Axial and Bending Stresses.

The geometric combined peak stress, σ_{peak}, required for fatigue crack initiation is the sum of the axial (membrane) and pure bending load contributions, as

$$\sigma_{\text{peak}} = \sigma_{\text{axial}} K_{t,\text{axial}} + \sigma_{\text{bending}} K_{t,\text{bending}} \qquad (101.18)$$

101.3.4   Seam Weld: Cruciform-Welded Joints

Cruciform-welded joints, the idealized geometry shown in Fig. 101.7, result in stress concentration factors under axial and bending loads at Point b, respectively as [Chattopadhyay et al.]

$$K_{t,\text{axial}} = 1 + 2.2 \frac{1 - \exp\left[-0.9\,\theta\left(\dfrac{H}{2h_a}\right)^{\frac{1}{2}}\right]}{1 - \exp\left[-0.45\,\pi\left(\dfrac{H}{2h_a}\right)^{\frac{1}{2}}\right]} \left\{ \frac{\dfrac{h_a}{r_b}}{\left|\dfrac{2.8\,H}{h} - 2\right|} \right\}^{0.65} \qquad (101.19)$$

$$\text{and} \quad K_{t,\text{bending}} = 1 + \frac{1 - \exp\left[-0.9\,\theta\left(\dfrac{H}{2h_a}\right)^{\frac{1}{2}}\right]}{1 - \exp\left[-0.45\,\pi\left(\dfrac{H}{2h_a}\right)^{\frac{1}{2}}\right]} \frac{0.13 + 0.65\left(1 - \dfrac{r_b}{h}\right)^{4}}{\left(\dfrac{r_b}{h}\right)^{\frac{1}{3}}}$$

$$\tanh \frac{\left(\dfrac{2h_a}{h}\right)^{\frac{1}{4}}}{\left(1 - \dfrac{r_b}{h}\right)} \left\{ \tanh\left[\frac{2h_\perp}{h + 2h_a} + \frac{2r_b}{h}\right]^{\frac{1}{2}} \right\} \qquad (101.20)$$

of which r is the radius "at" Point b and $H = (h + 2h_a) + 0.3\,(h_\perp + 2h_b)$. The geometric dimensions of the cruciform-welded joint given in the above equations for calculating the stress concentration factors are identified in Fig. 101.7.

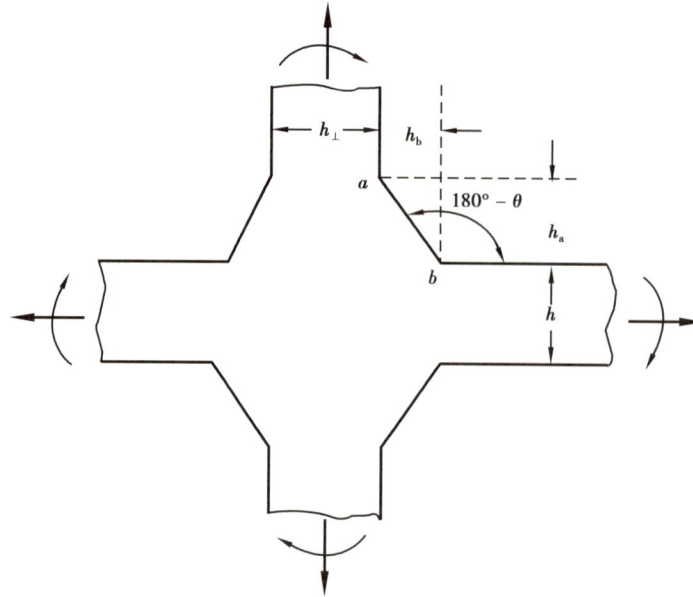

Fig. 101.7   Cruciform-Welded Joint Loaded by Both Axial and Bending Stresses.

101.4   Quality Control of Electric Resistance Welding

101.4.1   Potential Weld Defects

Frequently observed defects are listed as follows:

(a) Undercutting is one of the most common defects. A groove appears in the base metal directly along the edges of the weld. It is most common in lap joints, but can also be found in butt joints. This type of defect is most caused by improper welding parameters; especially welding speed and arc voltage.

(b) Lack of fusion is another common defect, also called cold lapping. This defect occurs when there is no fusion between the weld metal and the surfaces of the base metal. Cold laps often result when the arc does not melt the base metal sufficiently.

(c) Another defect is incomplete penetration, which is usually caused by insufficient flow of current, low welding speed, and/or an incorrect torch angle.

(d) Porosity is the presence of cavities in the weld metal, which may be caused by the cool-down of gas released from the weld pool while it solidifies.

(e) The welding pattern is not correct. It should be corrected using finite element analysis.

101.4.2   Inspection of Weld Quality

To test the quality of a weld, either destructive or nondestructive testing methods are commonly used to verify that welds are free of defects, have acceptable levels of residual stresses and distortion, and have an acceptable heat-affected zone (HAZ), including fusion zone (FZ), properties. Inspections can be done as follows:

(a) Visual Inspection;
(b) Liquid Penetrant Inspection;
(c) Magnetic-Particle Inspection;
(d) Radiography;
(e) Ultrasonic Inspection.

FZ (Fusion Zone) size is the most important parameter in the determination of mechanical properties of RSWs (Resistance Spot Welds). The larger the FZ size, the higher the strength. FZ size is governed by heat generated during the welding process which is in turn controlled by welding parameters. Generally, the higher the heat input (i.e. higher welding current, higher welding time, and lower electrode force), the higher is FZ size.

101.5   Strain Energy Fatigue Approach to Seam Welds

The fatigue life is affected by weldment material, base material, plate thickness, weldment size, fit-up between parts, weld toe radius, and weldment angle, e.g. $180°-\delta$ shown in Fig. 101.4. To apply traditional strain energy (e.g. ε-N curves) fatigue analysis to welds, an appropriate value of the stress concentration factor and residual stress must be taken into consideration.

101.5.1   Residual Stress

One major concern of a seam weld is the residual stress due to rapid heating and cooling of welds. Nonuniform tensile residual stresses at the weld toe and other critical locations are expected. Tensile and compressive residual stress distributions of a simple straight seam weld are schematically drawn in Fig. 101.8 [Barsoum & Barsoum]. Transverse residual stresses tend to have peak value at the same distance from toe location irrespective of material yield strength and plate thickness, but remain much below yield limit [Asgher].

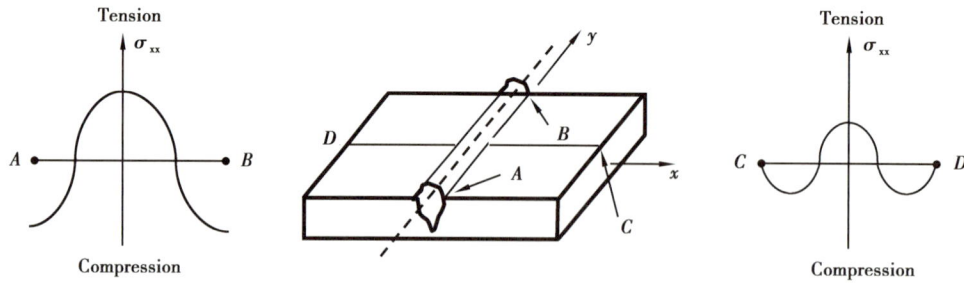

Fig. 101.8 Schematically Drawing of Transverse Residual Stresses at Butt Weld Toe *A-B* and In-plane Transversal *C-D* [Lassen & Recho].

As a function of weld shape and boundary conditions, induced residual stresses may be in tension or compression in the weld. Compressive residual stresses may be beneficial to fatigue life, but tensile stresses are detrimental and may significantly reduce the fatigue strength. Applying forging force properly may reduce the residual stress in the hot spot [Chang et al.].

101.5.2 Stress Concentration

The major influence on the stress concentration of a weld is local weld toe radius (Fig. 101.6 and Fig. 101.7), which varies along the length of the weld. There is a critical radius (not necessarily the smallest) for fatigue that can be used to compute the fatigue notch factor.

Stress concentration factor due to weld geometry and weld surface quality and discontinuity settles between 6 and 9. Generally speaking, stress intensity factor may be used instead. The K_t value (notch fatigue factor), which is employed to account for the stress intensity factor (and stress concentration) at the "almost zero radius" weld toe corresponding to the weldment angle $180°-\theta$ can be approximated by the following three possibilities (Fig. 101.7):

  (a) K_t = 3.6, if the two welded members are closely tight fit-up;
  (b) $3.6 < K_t < 6.4$, if the two welded members are normally fit-up;
  (c) K_t = 6.4, if the two welded members are loosely fit-up.

More precisely, with the weldment angle and material being taken into consideration, the fatigue life can be evaluated using the strain energy criterion for fatigue [Livieri and Lazzarin].

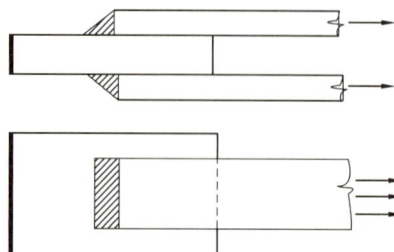

Fig. 101.9 Seam Weld Connection with End Fillet Loaded in Tension

When a connection with end fillets is loaded in tension as shown in Fig. 101.9, the weld may develop high strength and the stress developed in the weld is close to the value of the weld metal. However, the ductility is minimal. Finite element methods and experimental mechanics are suggested to resolve stress problems with a fillet weld, because a rigorous closed-form solution to predict the stress distribution in a fillet weld has not been possible so far. Potential failure modes are given in Fig. 101.10.

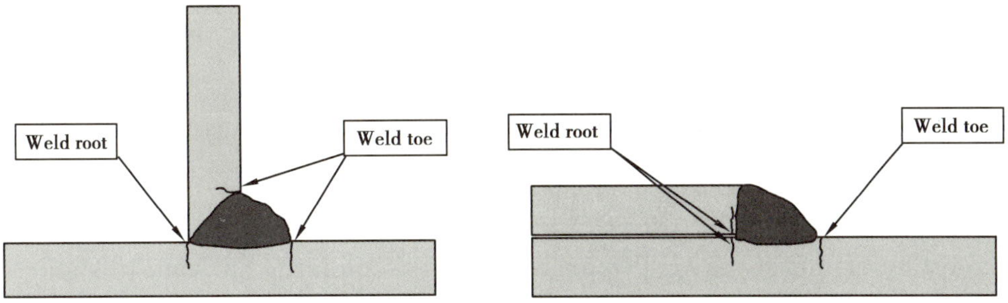

Fig. 101.10   Potential Failure Modes Weld Joints: (a) Fillet and (b) Overlap

101.6   Fatigue Crack Growth Approach to Weld Fatigue

Many weld details have planar lack of fusion defects. This is particularly true of fillet welds. In this case, fracture mechanics models for fatigue crack growth are more appropriate for the weld life prediction. A fatigue life curve ΔK-N is then needed for the fatigue life prediction. Consider now, therefore, the Paris law:

$$\frac{\mathrm{d}a}{\mathrm{d}N} = C \ (\Delta k)^{m} \tag{101.21}$$

Consider a weld between two shear-loaded sheet plates. The sharp notch between the sheets is assumed to be a crack tip without an apparent fatigue crack, and an initial equivalent stress intensity factor (SIF) can then be determined. This SIF is used as the fatigue parameter for the laser weld and adjacent sheets. The approximating equation given for overlap-welded joints (Fig. 101.10) of two plates of thickness h by [Radaj and Sonsino] leads to

$$\Delta K \approx 0.58 \ \Delta\sigma_{\text{inner}} \ h^{\frac{1}{2}} \tag{101.22}$$

where:

h (mm): thickness;

$\Delta\sigma_{\text{inner}}$(MPa): Stress fluctuation, i.e. structural stress-fluctuating range on the inside of the sheet
at the notch root (Fig. 101.10).

As an example, for a double cantilever beam loaded under a force or bending moment. the factor 0.58 is exactly for in-plane bending, K_{I}. For in-plane shear, K_{II}, the corresponding factor is 0.5 for decomposed stresses. However, the equivalent SIF, K_{eq}, by [Erdogan and Sih] is often used for overlap welded joints [Radaj and Sonsino] to account for the equivalent effect. For pure mode II, $K_{\mathrm{eq}} = 1.15 K_{\mathrm{II}}$ using the [Erdogan and Sih] approach, as $0.58 = 0.5 \times 1.15$.

101.7　Experimental Determination of Hot-Spot Stress Amplitude

Experimental determination of the structural stress is based on strain measurement, e.g. using strain gauges. Once the strain is measured, it is possible to infer (Hook law) the stress on the surface of the component. To avoid measuring any component of the notch stress (nonlinear portion of the stress), the measurement is undertaken some distance away from the weld toe.

The extrapolation procedure on hot spot type "b" is based on measurement of the strain at a fixed distance: i.e. 4 mm (strain gage A), 8mm (strain gage B), and 12 mm (strain gage C), empirically as shown in Fig. 101.11. The "hot-spot stress" can be derived from a quadratic extrapolation of the measured stresses at points A, B, and C to the weld toe as follows:

$$\sigma_{\text{hot-spot}} = 3\,\sigma_{4\,\text{mm}} - 3\,\sigma_{8\,\text{mm}} + \sigma_{12\,\text{mm}} \tag{101.23}$$

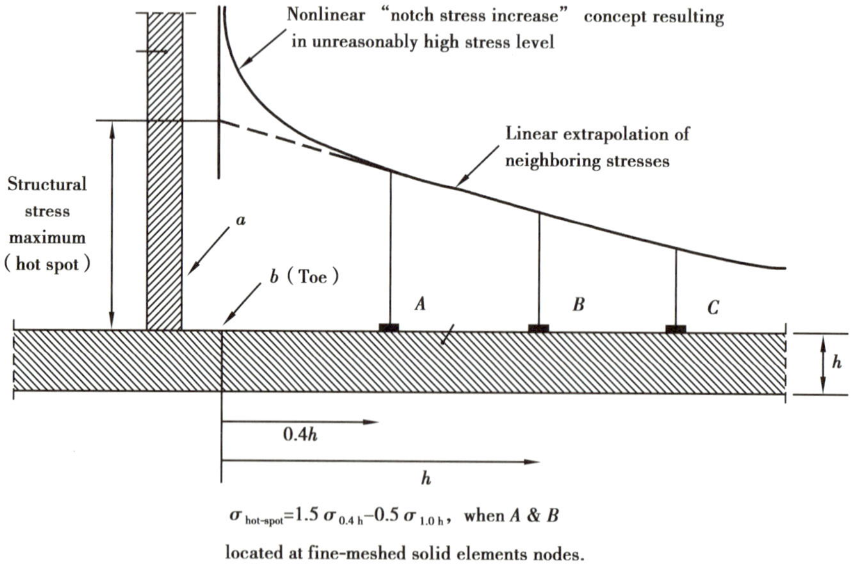

Figure 101.11　Linear Extrapolation Procedure for "Hot Spot Stress" (Type b)

101.8   Determination of Hot-Spot Stress Amplitude by Finite Element Methods

The use of 3-D solid elements to model the connection including the weld seam would allow determining the distribution of the stress at the weld toe by the linearization of the stress at that point, Figs. 101.11 and 101.12. However, this approach requires having a highly refined finite element mesh to represent the weld profile in detail. The foregoing is the reason why even using 3-D finite element models is common to use the extrapolation techniques to evaluate the hot spot stress. Two extrapolation schemes are suggested by IIW (International Institute of Welding) for finite element analysis based on solid elements as

(a) Coarse meshes (nominally $h \times h$, but less than $h \times L$) for hot spot type "a": The surface midpoints of related solid elements can be extrapolated to the hot-spot stress as

$$\sigma_{\text{hot-spot}} = 1.5 \ \sigma_{0.5 \ h} - 0.5 \ \sigma_{1.5 \ h} \tag{101.24}$$

(b) Coarse meshes (nominally 10 mm × 10 mm) for hot spot type "b": The surface midpoints of related solid elements can be extrapolated to the hot-spot stress as

$$\sigma_{\text{hot-spot}} = 1.5 \ \sigma_{5 \ \text{mm}} - 0.5 \ \sigma_{15 \ \text{mm}} \tag{101.25}$$

(c) Fine meshes (less than $0.4h \times h$ or $0.4h \times 0.5L$) for hot spot type "a": The nodal points can be used as extrapolations for the stress at the hot spot,

$$\sigma_{\text{hot-spot}} = 1.5 \ \sigma_{0.4 \ h} - 0.5 \ \sigma_{1.0 \ h} \tag{101.26}$$

(d) Fine meshes (less than 4 mm × 4 mm) for hot spot type "b": When the nodal points are used as extrapolations for the stress at the hot spot,

$$\sigma_{\text{hot-spot}} = 3 \ \sigma_{4 \ \text{mm}} - 3 \ \sigma_{8 \ \text{mm}} + \sigma_{12 \ \text{mm}} \tag{101.27}$$

Note that L is the seam weld length, i.e. attachment length perpendicular to the drawing plane as shown in Fig. 101.10. Each stress component (6 stress components for solid elements) has to be extrapolated individually to the hot spot (type a or type b) for resolving the stress flow (e.g. principal stress or von Mises stress) at the hot spot. Nevertheless, it is a common practice to extrapolate the stress flows at the calculated mid-points or nodal points directly to the hot spot. The IIW extrapolation scheme with non averaged FEM stress results works well if the first row of solid (tetrahedron) elements lies within $0.3 \ h$ (0.3 times the base material thickness).

Crack
nucleation
point

Fig. 101.12   Seam Weld Modeled Using 8-Noded Solid Elements

101.9   Arc Welding

Electric current is used to maintain an arc between the torch and the surface of the work piece in an arc welding process. Depending on how to protect the weld pool from atmospheric contamination, it can be divided into the following three being contaminated by the atmospheric.

101.9.1   Shielded Metal Arc Welding (SMAW)

An electric current is used to generate an electric arc between the consumable electrode and workpieces (metals). A molten weld pool forms a joint between workpieces after it cools down. Layered slag is also formed to encapsulate the weld area avoiding atmospheric contamination.

When the flux coating of the electrode degenerates, it gives off vapors that serve as a shielding gas as it is named It is called manual metal arc welding (MMA or MMAW) or flux shielded arc welding.

101.9.2   Gas Shielded Arc Welding (GSAW)

Gas is provided to cover and shield around the arc to make a weld that has the same properties as the base to prevent the atmosphere from contaminating the weld. Gas-shielded arc welding is the most widely used welding method. The intensity of the power input is around 10 W/mm^2. It is able to bridge relatively large gaps. Gas-shielded arc welding, including metal inert gas (MIG), metal active gas (MAG), and tungsten inert gas (TIG).

101.9.3   Submerged Arc Welding (SAW)

It is also called Flux-Cored Arc Welding (FCAW). The molten weld and the arc zone are protected from atmospheric contamination by being "submerged" under a blanket of granular fusible flux consisting of lime, silica, manganese oxide, calcium fluoride, and other compounds.

101.10   Ultrasonic Welding

High-frequency ultrasonic acoustic vibrations are locally applied to workpieces, which are pushed together under pressure, to create a weld. Ultrasonic welding has been used to assemble large plastic and electrical components such as instrument panels, door panels, lamps, air ducts, steering wheels, interior upholstery, and engine components.

101.11   Friction Stir Welding (FSW)

Friction stir welding (FSW) is a solid state joining technique, in which the joined material is plasticized by heat generated by friction between the surface of the plates and the contact surface of a special tool, composed of two main parts: shoulder and pin. The shoulder is responsible for the generation of heat and for containing the plasticized material in the weld zone, while the pin mixes the material of the components to be welded, thus creating a joint. During friction stir welding (FSW), temperatures remaining below the melting point result in a low shrinkage phenomenon and excellent mechanical properties, together with a reduction of residual stress within the weld zone. Mechanical properties of an FSW joint are quite good, and fatigue properties are practically the same as the parent metal.

Cast aluminum alloys are widely used in the transportation industries and can be arc welded in a protective atmosphere or joined by brazing. Unfortunately, the welding production cost is relatively high and some welding defects such as porosity and slag inclusion are easily formed in the weld. Friction stir welding (FSW) is a promising process that can produce high-quality, low-cost joints. This welding process is being extensively and intensively studied in order to weld various types of wrought aluminum alloys, especially heat treatable aluminum alloys that are difficult to fusion weld. It is also being developed to weld other materials such as magnesium, titanium, copper, steel, and aluminum matrix composites.

101.12   Laser Welding

Laser welding is an energy-concentrated fusion welding method, which is obtained by a high power density. The power is in the range of $0.3 \sim 3$ kW for Nd:YAG laser and $5 \sim 10$ kW for CO_2 laser, achieved by focusing a laser light beam to a very small spot, with a focused power density at the weld surface in the order of 10 kW/mm^2.

References

ABADI M, POURANVARI M, 2010. Correlation between Macro/Micro Structure and Mechanical Properties of Dissimilar Resistance Spot Welds of AISI 304 Austenitic Stainless Steel and AISI 1008 Low Carbon Steel[J]. MJoM, 16 (2): 133-146.

ANDREASSON F M, FRODIN B, 1998. Fatigue Life Prediction of MAG-Welded Thin Sheet Structures[J]. SAE transactions, 107(15): 1280-1286.

ASLANLAR S, et al, 2007. Effect of Welding Current on Mechanical Properties of Galvanized Chromided Steel Sheets in Electrical Resistance Spot Welding[J]. Materials and Design, 28(1): 2-7.

ASLANLAR S, et al, 2006. The Effect of Nucleus Size on Mechanical Properties in Electrical Resistance Spot Welding of Sheets Used in Automotive Industry[J]. Materials and Design, 27: 125-131.

BAE D H, et al, 2013. Assessing the Effects of Residual Stresses on the Fatigue Strength of Spot Welds[J]. Welding Journal, 82(1): 18s-23s.

BALTAZAR V H, et al, 2008. Influence of Microstructure and Weld Size on the Mechanical Behaviour of Dissimilar AHSS Resistance Spot Welds[J]. Science and Technology of Welding and Joining, 13(8): 769-776.

BARSOUM Z, BARSOUM I, 2009. Residual Stress Effects on Fatigue Life of Welded Structures Using LEFM [J]. Engineering Failure Analysis, 16(1): 449-467.

CAM G, et al, 1997. Determination of Mechanical and Fracture Properties of Laser Beam Welded Steel Joints [J]. Welding Journal Research Supplement, 78(6): 193s-201s.

CARY H B, HELZER S C, 2005. Modern Welding Technology[M]. Upper Saddle River, New Jersey, USA.

CELIK A, ALSARAN A, 1999. Mechanical and Structural Properties of Similar and Dissimilar Steel Joints[J]. Materials Characterization, 43(5): 311-318.

CHATTOPADHYAY A, et al, 2011. Stress Analysis and Fatigue of Welded Structures[J]. Welding in the World, 55(7-8): 2-21.

CHANG B, et al, 2007. Comparative Study of Small Scale and "Large Scale" Resistance Spot Welding[J]. Science and Technology of Welding and Joining, 12(1): 67-72.

CHANG B, LI M, ZHOU Y, 2001. Comparative Study of Small Scale and "Large Scale" Resistance Spot Welding[J]. Science and Technology of Welding and Joining, 6(5): 1-6.

CHAO Y, et al, 2009. Dynamic Failure of Resistance Spot Welds[J]. SAE 2009-01-0032.

DE A, THEDDEUS M P, 2002. Finite Element Analysis of Resistance Spot Welding Aluminum[J]. Science and Technology of Welding and Joining, 7(2): 111-118.

DE A, DORN L, GUPTA O, 2000. Analysis and Optimization of Electrode Life for Conventional and Compound Tip Electrodes during Resistance Spot Welding of Electrogalvanized Steels[J]. Science and Technology of Welding and Joining, 5(1): 49-57.

DONG P, 2006. A Structural Stress Definition and Numerical Implementation for Fatigue Analysis of Welded Joints[J]. International Journal of Fatigue, 23(10): 865-876.

DONG P, et al, 1998. Finite Element Analysis of Electrode Wear Mechanisms: Face Extrusion and Pitting Effects[J]. Science and Technology of Welding and Joining, 3(2): 59-64.

ERDOGAN F, SIH G C, 1963. On the Crack Extension in Plates under Plane Loading and Transverse Shear [J]. Journal of Basic Engineering, 85(4): 519-527.

ERICSSON M, SANDSTROM R, 2000. Fatigue of Friction Stir Welded AlMgSi-Alloy 6082 [J]. Material Science Forum, 331/337: 1787-1792.

ERTAS A H, et al, 2009. Measurement and Assessment of Fatigue Life of Spot-Weld Joints[J]. Journal of Engineering Materials and Technology, 131(1): 011011.

FERMER M, HENRYSSON H F, WALLMICHRATH M, et al, 2003. Low Cycle Fatigue of Spot Welds under Constant and Variable Amplitude Loading[J]. SAE 2003-01-0913.

FRICKE W. 2010. Guideline for the Fatigue Assessment by Notch Stress Analysis for Welded Structures[J]. International Institute of Welding, IIW Doc. XⅢ-2240-08/XⅤ-1289-08.

FRICKE W, KAHL A, 2005. Comparison of Different Structural Stress Approaches for Fatigue Assessment of Welded Ship Structures[J]. Marine Structures, 18: 473-488.

HAMADI M, PASHAZADEH H, 2008. Numerical Study of Nugget Formation in Resistance Spot Welding[J]. International Journal of Mechanics, 1(2): 11-15.

HASHMI M, MRIDH S, NAHER S, 2011. Investigation on Joint Strength of Dissimilar Resistance Spot Welds of Aluminum Alloy and Low Carbon Steel[J]. Advanced Materials Research, 264/265: 384-389.

HERNANDEZ V, et al, 2008. Influence of Microstructure and Weld Size on the Mechanical Behavior of Dissimilar AHSS Resistance Spot Welds[J]. Science and Technology of Welding and Joining, 13(8): 769-776.

HIRSCH R, 2007. Making Resistance Spot Welding Safer[J]. Welding Journal, 86(2): 32-37.

HOBBACHER A, 2007. Recommendations for Fatigue Design of Welded Joints and Components[J]. Welding Research Council Bulletin, TN · 520: ⅰ-ⅲ, ⅴ, ⅶ-ⅸ, 1-144.

HOBBACHER A, 1996. Fatigue Design of Welded Joints and Components[M]. The International Institute of Welding, England.

HOLM R, HOLM E, 1967. Electric Contacts: Theory and Application[M]. 4th edition, Springer-Verlag, New York, NY.

HOWE P, KELLEY S, 1988. A Comparison of the Resistance Spot Weldability of Bare, Hot-Dipped, Galvannealed, and Electrogalvanized DQSK Sheet Steels[J]. SAE 880280.

IVIO F, FERRACCI M, 2009. A Theoretical Model for the Elastic-Plastic Behavior of Spot Welded Joints[J]. SAE 2009-01-0026.

JOU M, 2003. Real Time Monitoring Weld Quality of Resistance Spot Welding for the Fabrication of Sheet Metal Assemblies[J]. Journal of Materials Processing Technology, 132(1-3): 102-113.

KANG H, BARKEY M E, LEE Y, 2000. Evaluation of Multiaxial Spot Weld Fatigue Parameters for Proportional Loading[J]. International Journal of Fatigue, 22: 691-702.

KASSAB R K, et al, 2012. Experimental and Finite Element Analysis of a T-Joint Welding[J]. Journal of Mechanical Engineering and Automation, 2(7): 411-421.

KAHN M I, et al, 2008. Microstructure and Mechanical Properties of Resistance Spot Welded Advanced High Strength Steels[J]. Materials Transaction, 49(7): 1629-1637.

KATSAOUNIS A, 1993. Heat Flow and Arc Efficiency at High Pressures in Argon and Helium Tungsten Arcs [J]. Welding Journal Research Supplement, 72(9): 447s-454s.

KHAN J A, XU L, CHAN Y J, et al, 2000. Numerical Simulation of Resistance Spot Welding Process[J]. Numerical Heat Transfer, Part A, 37: 425-446.

KIM D, et al, 2007. Estimation of Weld Quality in High-Frequency Electric Resistance Welding with Image Processing[J]. Welding Journal, 107(3): 67-72.

KURATANI F, MATSUBARA K, YAMAUCHI. Finite Element Model for Spot Welds Using Multi-Point Constraints and its Dynamic Characteristics[J]. SAE 2011-01-1697.

LABANOWSKI J, 2007. Mechanical Properties and Corrosion Resistance of Dissimilar Stainless Steel Welds [J]. Archives of Materials Science and Engineering, 28(1): 27-33.

LASSEN T, RECHO N, 2006. Fatigue Life Analyses of Welded Structures[M]. Great Britain and United States ISTE, Ltd.

LEE H, POLICE P, 2011. Application of Failure Plastic Strain to Quasi-Static Finite Element Analysis for Projection Weld and Strain-based Spot Weld Evaluation[J]. SAE 2011-01-1074.

LI V, DONG P, 1998. Modeling and Analysis of Microstructure Development in Resistance Spot Welds of High Strength Steels[J]. SAE 982278.

LIM S, KIM S, LEE C G, et al, 2004. Tensile Behavior of Friction-stir-welded Al 6061-T651[J]. Metall Mater Transactions, A, 35(9): 2829-2835.

LIN S H, et al, 2003. A General Failure Criterion for Spot Welds under Combined Loading Conditions[J]. International Journal of Solids and Structures, 40(21): 5539-5564.

LIPA M, 1992. Mechanical Properties of Resistance Spot and Projection Welding Machines[J]. Welding International, 6(8): 661-667.

LIU H J, et al, 2004. Microstructure and Mechanical Properties of Friction Stir Welded Joints of AC4A Cast Aluminum Alloy[J]. Materials Science and Technology, 20(3): 399-402.

LIVIERI P, LAZZARIN P, 2005. Fatigue Strength of Steel and Aluminum Welded Joints Based on Generalized Stress Intensity Factors and Local Strain Energy Values[J]. International Journal of Fatigue, 133(3): 247-176.

LOUKUS A, et al, 2004. Mechanical Properties and Microstructural Characterization of Extrusion Welds in AA6082-T4[J]. Journal of Materials Science, 39(21): 6561-6569.

LUO Y, LIU J, XU H, et al, 2009. Regression Modeling and Process Analysis of Resistance Spot Welding of Galvanized Steel Sheet[J]. Materials and Design, 30(7): 2547-2555.

MALCOLM S, O'HARA B, 2009. Application of Spot Weld and Sheet Metal Failure Prediction to Non-Linear Transient Finite Element Analysis of Automotive Structures[J]. SAE 2009-01-0352.

MARIN T, NICOLETTO G, 2009. Fatigue Design of Welded Joints Using the Finite Element Method and the 2007 ASME Div. 2 Master Curve[J]. Frattura ed Integrità Strutturale, 3(9): 76-84.

MARYA M, GAYDEN X, 2008. Development of Requirements for Resistance Spot Welding Dual-Phase (DP600) Steels Part 1-The Causes of Interfacial Fracture[J]. Welding Journal, 84(11): 172-182.

MATHIEU S, PATOU P, 1985. Zinc Coating Influence on Spot-Weldability of Hot-Dip Galvanized Steel Sheets [J]. SAE 850273.

MOCHIZUKI M, HATTORI T, NAKAKADO K, 2000. Residual Stress Reduction and Fatigue Strength

Improvement by Controlling Welding Pass Sequences[J]. Journal of Engineering Materials and Technology, 122 (1): 108-112.

MUKHOPADHYAYA G, BHATTACHARYA S, RAY K K, 2009. Strength Assessment of Spot-Welded Sheets of Interstitial Free Steels[J]. Journal of Materials Processing Technology, 209: 1995-2007.

NAKAYAMA E, et al, 2003. Prediction of Strength of Spot-Welded Joints by Measurements of Local Mechanical Properties[J]. SAE 2003-01-2830.

NIEMI E, FRICKE W, MADDOX S J, 2006. Fatigue Analysis of Welded Components: Designer's Guide to the Structural Hot Spot Approach[M]. Woodhead Publishing Limited, USA.

PAN N, SHEPPARD S, 2002. Spot Welds Fatigue Life Prediction with Cyclic Strain Range[J]. International Journal of Fatigue, 24: 519-528.

PARKER J, WILLIAMS N, HOLLIDAY R, 1998. Mechanisms of Electrode Degradation When Spot Welding Coated Steels[J]. Science and Technology of Welding and Joining, 3(2): 65-74.

PEDERSEN M, 2010. Re-analysis of Fatigue Data for Welded Joints Using the Notch Stress Approach[J]. International Journal of Fatigue, 32(10): 1620-1626.

PETTERSSON G, 2004. Fatigue Assessment of Welded Structures with Non-linear Boundary Conditions, Licentiate Thesis[M]. Dept. of Aeronautical and Vehicle Engineering, KTH, Sweden.

POURANVARI M, MARASHI S P H, 2010. Factors Affecting Mechanical Properties of Resistance Spot Welds [J]. Materials Science and Technology, 26(9): 1137-1144.

RADAKOVIC D J, TUMULURU M, 2008. Predicting Resistance Spot Weld Failure Modes in Shear Tension Tests[J]. Welding Journal, 87(4): 96s-105s.

RADAJ D, SONSINO C M, FRICKE W, 2009. Recent Developments in Local Concepts of Fatigue Assessment of Welded Joints[J]. International Journal of Fatigue, 31(1): 2-11.

RADAJ D, SONSINO C M, 1998. Fatigue Assessment of Welded Joints by Local Approaches[M]. Abington Publishing, Cambridge, UK.

RAHMAN M, et al, 2009. Fatigue Life Prediction of Spot-Welded Structures: A Finite Element Analysis Approach[J]. European Journal of Scientific Research, 22(3): 444-456.

RODRIGUES D M, et al, 2008. Influence of Friction Stir Welding Parameters on the Microstructural and Mechanical Properties of AA 6016-T4 Thin Welds[J]. Materials and Design, 30(6): 1913-1921.

RUCHO P, MAHERAULT S, CHEN W, 2001. Comparison of Measurements and Finite Element Analysis of Side Longitudinals [C]. Proceedings of the Eleventh International Offshore and Polar Engineering

Conference, Stavanger, Norway, ISOPE, 4: 73-80.

RUPP A, STORZEL K, GRUBISIC V, 1995. Computer Aided Dimensioning of Spot-Welded Automotive Structures[J]. SAE 950711.

SAHIN M, et al, 2007. Characterization of Mechanical Properties in AISI 1040 Parts Welded by Friction Welding[J]. Materials Characterization, 58(10): 1033-1038.

SANTELLA M, et al, 1999. Mechanical Properties of Nb-1Zr Weldments[J]. American Institute of Physics, 845-852.

SHEPPARD S D, STRANGE M E, 1992. Fatigue Life Estimation in Resistance Spot Welds: Initiation and Early Growth Phase[J]. Fatigue and Fracture of Engineering Materials and Structures, 15(6): 531-549.

SIN S, et al, 2011. Fatigue Analysis of Multi-Lap Spot Welding of High Strength Steel by Quasi Static Tensile-Shear Test[J]. Key Engineering Materials, 345/346: 251-254.

SONSINO C, et al, 2012. Notch Stress Concepts for the Fatigue Assessment of Welded Joints-Background and Applications[J]. International Journal of Fatigue, 34: 2-16.

SONSINO C M, 2009. A Consideration of Allowable Equivalent Stresses for Fatigue Design of Welded Joints According to the Notch Stress Concept with the Reference Radii rref = 1.00 and 0.05 mm[J]. Welding in the World, 53(3-4): R64-R75.

STOCCO D, VILELA D, BATALHA G, 2009. Spot Weld Fatigue and Durability Performance Evaluation through the Use of FEA[J]. SAE 2009-36-0189.

SUSMEL L, 2009. Three Different Ways of Using the Modified Wöhler Curve Method to Perform the Multiaxial Fatigue Assessment of Steel and Aluminum Welded Joints[J]. Engineering Failure Analysis, 16: 1074-1089.

SUN C X, et al, 2008. Effects of Fusion Zone Size and Failure Mode on Peak Load and Energy Absorption of Advanced High Strength Steel Spot Welds under Lap Shear Loading Conditions[J]. Engineering Failure Analysis, 15: 356-367.

SUN X, KAHLEEL M, 2004. Resistance Spot Welding of Aluminum Alloy to Steel with Transition Material: Part II: Finite Element Analyses of Nugget Growth[J]. Welding Journal, 83(7): 197s-202s.

SUN X, DONG P, 2000. Analysis of Aluminum Resistance Spot Welding Processes Using Coupled Finite Element Procedures[J]. Welding Journal, 79(8): 215s-221s.

SVENSSON F H, 2001. Industrial Experiences of FE-based Fatigue Life Predictions of Welded Automotive Structures[J]. Fatigue and Fracture of Engineering Materials and Structures, 24(7): 489-500.

TANG H, et al, 2003. Influence of Welding Machine Mechanical Characteristics on the Resistance Spot Welding Process and Weld Quality[J]. Welding Jamal, 82(5): 116s-224s.

THAKUR A G, 2010. Application of Taguchi Method for Resistance Spot Welding of Galvanized Steel[J]. ARPN Journal of Engineering and Applied Sciences, 5(11): 22-26.

TUMULURU M, 2010. Effects of Baking on the Structure and Properties of Resistance Spot Welds in 780 MPa Dual-Phase and TRIP Steels[J]. Welding Journal, 89: 91s-100s.

VURAL M, AKKUS A, ERYÜREK B, 2006. Effect of Welding Nugget Diameter on the Fatigue Strength of the Resistance Spot Welded Joints of Different Steel Sheets[J]. Journal of Materials Processing Technology, 176: 127-132.

VURAL M, AKKUS A, 2004. On the Resistance Spot Weldability of Galvanized Interstitial Free Steel Sheets with Austenitic Stainless Steel Sheets[J]. Journal of Materials Processing Technology, 153/154: 1-6.

WAHAB M, SAKANO M, 2001. Experimental Study of Corrosion Fatigue Behavior of Welded Steel Structures [J]. Journal of Materials Processing Technology, 118(1-3): 116-121.

WEMAN K, 2003. Welding Processes Handbook[M]. Floriad, CRC Press.

WU P, et al, 2005. Characterization of Dynamic Mechanical Properties of Resistance Welding Machines[J]. Welding Journal Research Supplement, 17s-21s.

YEUNG K, THORNTON P, 1999. Transient Thermal Analysis of Spot Welding Electrodes[J]. Welding Journal, 78(1): 1-6.

ZHANG C, LI L, 2009. A Friction-Based Finite Element Analysis of Ultrasonic Consolidation[J]. Welding Journal Research Supplement, 87(7): 187s-194s.

ZHANG W, 2003. Design and Implementation of Software for Resistance Welding Process Simulations[J]. SAE 2003-01-0978.

ZHANG Y, et al, 2009. Comparison of Mechanical Properties and Microstructure of Weld Nugget between Weld-Bonded and Spot-Welded Dual-Phase Steel[J]. Journal of Engineering Manufacture, 223(10): 1341-1350.

ZHIGANG H, et al, 2006. A Study on Numerical Analysis of the Resistance Spot Welding Process[J]. Journal of Achievements in Materials and Manufacturing Engineering, 14(12): 140-145.

ZIMMEY E J, et al, 2007. Correction Factors for 4-Probe Electrical Measurements with Finite Size Electrodes and Material Anisotropy: a Finite Element Study[J]. Measurement Science and Technology, 18(7): 2067-2073.

ZHOU M, ZHANG H, HU S J, 2003. Relationships between Quality and Attributes of Spot Welds[J]. Welding Journal, 82(4): 72-77.

Table 101.1   Mechanical Properties of Welded Joints

Material	$T/{}^\circ\text{C}$	E_T	ρ	ν	(σ, ε)	α	k	γ	ρ_E	K_IC
AC4A (Al-Si-...; Base)	23	71	2.7	0.32	(81, 0.2%) (150, 2%)	—	—	—	—	—
AC4A (Stir-Weld)	23	71	2.7	0.32	(87, 0.2%) (179, 5.3%)	—	—	—	—	—
AC4A (Stir-Weld Nugget)	23	71	2.7	0.32	(96, 0.2%) (251, 14%)	—	—	—	—	—
SAE1005 (Base)	23	205	7.85	0.29	(335, 80.5%)	12	51.5	480	—	—
SAE 1005 (HAZ)	23	205	—	—	(617, 47.5%)	12	51.5	480	—	—
SAE 1005 (Nugget)	23	205	—	—	(1003, 39.2%)	12	51.5	480	—	—
SAE 1018 (CD; Base; Dynamic)	23	205	—	0.33	(702, 0.2%) (729, 14%)	11.5	51.5	480	—	—
SAE 1018 (CD; Joint; Dynamic)	23	205	—	0.33	(455, 0.2%) (587, 10%)	11.5	51.5	480	—	—
SPFC 590 (Base)	23	205	7.85	0.29	(635, 60.7%)	12	42	473	—	—
SPFC 590 (HAZ)	23	205	—	—	(968, 44.7%)	12	42	473	—	—
SPFC 590 (Nugget)	23	205	—	—	(1245, 32.6%)	12	42	473	—	—
6016 (T4; Al)	Chapter 73									
6082 (T4; Al)	Chapter 73									

Notes: PWHT = Post-weld heat treatment;

Stir = Friction stir welding;

Conical = Conical shoulder;

Scrolled = Scrolled shoulder;

Seam weld −0°, −45°, & −90° = Directional angles measured from the seam weld line.

Table 101.2　Mechanical Properties of Tool and Raw Materials Related to Welding

Material	$T/°C$	E_T	ρ	ν	(σ, ε)	α	k	γ	ρ_E	K_{IC}
Cu-Cr-Zr (Electrode)	23	120	8.8	0.33	(592, 0.2%) (619, 51%)	17	322	390	—	—
	400	—	—	—	(382, 0.2%) (392, 45%)	—	—	—	—	—
	500	—	—	—	(309, 0.2%) (317, 46%)	—	—	—	—	—
	600	—	—	—	(194, 0.2%) (212, 60%)	—	—	—	—	—
	700	—	—	—	(46, 0.2%) (49, 277%)	—	—	—	—	—
	800	—	—	—	(23, 0.2%) (24, 148%)	—	—	—	—	—
	1085 (T_m)	—	—	—	—	—	—	—	—	—

Table 101.3　Fatigue ε-N Properties of Weld Joints

Material	$T/°C$	$d\varepsilon/dt$	σ'_f	ε'_f	b	c	K'	n'	$\sigma_f@2N_f$	R
SPFC 590 (HAZ) (Spot)	23	—	—	—	—	—	—	—	265@ 2×10^6	−1
									280@ 2×10^5	−1
									380@ 3.5×10^4	−1
									220@ 2×10^6	0.1
									240@ 10^5	0.1
									300@ 5×10^4	0.1
SAE 1005 (HAZ) (Spot)	23	—	—	—	—	—	—	—	265@ 2×10^6	−1
									315@ 10^5	−1
									360@ 5×10^4	−1
									190@ 2×10^6	0.1
									220@ 4×10^5	0.1
									250@ 3×10^4	0.1

国家出版基金项目
NATIONAL PUBLICATION FOUNDATION

汽车材料的热机械性能 （上）

Automotive Engineering Materials–Thermomechanical Properties

江永瑞　著

重庆大学出版社

图书在版编目(CIP)数据

汽车材料的热机械性能 = Automotive Engineering
Materials-Thermomechanical Properties：上中下：
英文／江永瑞著. -- 重庆：重庆大学出版社，2022.4
（自主品牌汽车实践创新丛书）
ISBN 978-7-5689-3293-6

Ⅰ.①汽…　Ⅱ.①江…　Ⅲ.①汽车—工程材料—热机
械效应—性能—英文　Ⅳ.①U465

中国版本图书馆 CIP 数据核字(2022)第 080037 号

汽车材料的热机械性能
QICHE CAILIAO DE REJIXIE XINGNENG
（上）

江永瑞　著
策划编辑:杨粮菊　孙英姿　鲁　黎
责任编辑:陈　力　苟荟羽　　版式设计:杨粮菊
责任校对:姜　凤　　　　责任印制:张　策

*

重庆大学出版社出版发行
出版人:饶帮华
社址:重庆市沙坪坝区大学城西路 21 号
邮编:401331
电话:(023)88617190　88617185(中小学)
传真:(023)88617186　88617166
网址:http://www.cqup.com.cn
邮箱:fxk@ cqup.com.cn（营销中心）
全国新华书店经销
重庆升光电力印务有限公司印刷

*

开本:889mm×1194mm　1/16　印张:31.75　字数:1034 千
2022 年 4 月第 1 版　　2022 年 4 月第 1 次印刷
ISBN 978-7-5689-3293-6　总定价:498.00 元

自主品牌汽车实践创新丛书

编委会

李克强(中国工程院院士,清华大学教授)

潘复生(中国工程院院士,重庆大学教授,国家镁合金材料工程技术研究中心主任)

李开国(中国汽车工程研究院股份有限公司董事长,研高工)

刘 波(重庆长安汽车股份有限公司原副总裁,研高工)

曹东璞(清华大学教授)

秦大同(长江学者,重庆大学教授)

郭 钢(重庆大学原汽车工程学院院长,重庆自主品牌汽车协同创新中心原执行副主任,教授)

赵 会(重庆长安汽车工程研究院总院副院长、博士)

朱习加(中国汽车工程研究院股份有限公司首席专家,博士)

江永瑞(重庆大学原外籍教授)

刘永刚(重庆大学教授)

付江华(重庆理工大学副教授)

    汽车产业是各国科技、经济的"主战场"。汽车产业是国家和区域经济发展中的支柱产业,具有科技含量高、经济产值大、产业链长、影响面广等诸多特征。特别是当今,随着信息技术、人工智能、新材料等高科技的广泛运用,电动化、智能化、网联化、共享化等"新四化"已成为全球汽车产业发展大趋势。当今的汽车产品也已经超出了交通工具的范畴,成为智能移动空间,是智能交通和智慧城市的重要组成部分,在国民经济与社会发展中扮演着更加重要的角色。汽车产业不仅是未来人们消费的热点,也是供给侧改革的重点。党的十九大报告指出,"深化供给侧结构性改革……把提高供给体系质量作为主攻方向"。作为 GDP 总量世界第二的中国,汽车产业不可缺席,中国自主品牌汽车企业必须参与到全球竞争中去,在竞争中不断崛起和创新发展。

    自主品牌汽车的发展是加快建设创新型国家、实施"创新驱动"国家战略的一个重要方面。党的十九大报告提出"加快建设创新型国家""建立以企业为主体、市场为导向、产学研深度融合的技术创新体系"。2016 年 5 月,中共中央、国务院发布的《国家创新驱动发展战略纲要》指出,推动产业技术体系创新、创造发展新优势,强化原始创新、增强源头供给,优化区域创新布局、打造区域经济增长极,从而明确企业、科研院所、高校、社会组织等各类创新主体功能定位,构建开放、高效的创新网络。发展新能源汽车是我国从汽车大国迈向汽车强国的必由之路,是应对气候变化、推动绿色发展的战略举措。2012 年国务院发布《节能与新能源汽车产业发展规划(2012—2020 年)》。为深入贯彻落实党中央、国务院重要部署,顺应新一轮科技革命和产业变革趋势,抓住产业智能化发展战略机遇,加快推进智能汽车创新发展,国家发改委 2020 年 2 月发布的《智能汽车创新发展战略》请各省、自治区、直辖市、计划单列市结合实际制定促进智能汽车创新发展的政策措施,着力推动各项战略任务有效落实。可见,我国汽车产业的发展,尤其是自主品牌汽车企业的发展是加快建设创新型国家、实现中国制造向中国创造转型的重要一环。

    重庆自主品牌汽车协同创新中心由重庆大学牵头,联合重庆长安汽车股份有限公司、中国汽车工程研究院股份有限公司、青山工业、超力高科、西南铝业、重庆理工大学、重庆邮电大学等核心企业、零部件供应商及院校共同组建。2014 年 10 月,教育部、财政部联合发文,认定"重庆自主品牌汽车协同创新中心"为国家级"2011 协同创新中心",成为三个国家级"2011 汽车协同创新中心"之一。"2011 计划"是继"211 工程""985 工程"之后,国家在高等教育系统又一项体现国家意志的重大创新战略举措,其建设以协同创新中心为基本载体,服务国家、行业、区域重大创新战略需求。汽车领域有 3 个国家级的"2011 协同创新中心",其中重庆自主品牌汽车协同创新中心面向区域汽车产业发展的前沿技术研发与创新人才培养共性需求,围绕汽车节能环保、安全舒适、智能网联三大方向开展协同创新和前沿技术研发,取得系列重要协同创新成果。其支撑长安汽车成为中国自主品牌汽车领头羊和自主研发技术标杆,支撑中国汽研成为国内一流汽车科技研发与行业服务机构,支撑重庆大学等高校成为汽车领域高层次创新人才培养基地。

重庆自主品牌汽车协同创新中心联合重庆大学出版社共同策划组织了大型、持续性出版项目"自主品牌汽车实践创新丛书",丛书选题涵盖节能环保、安全舒适、智能网联、可靠耐久 4 个大方向和 15 个子方向。3 个主要协同单位的首席专家担任总主编,分别是刘庆(重庆自主品牌汽车协同创新中心第一任主任)、刘波(重庆长安汽车股份有限公司原副总裁)、任晓常(中国汽车工程研究院股份有限公司原董事长)。系列丛书集中体现了重庆自主品牌汽车协同创新中心的核心专家、学者在多个领域的前沿技术水平,属汽车领域系列学术著作,这些著作主题从实际问题中来,成果也已应用到设计和生产实际中,能够帮助和指导中国汽车企业建设和提升自主研发技术体系,具有现实指导意义。

本系列著作的第一辑,包括 8 本著作(6 本中文著作,2 本英文著作),选题涉及智能网联汽车人机交互理论与技术、汽车产品寿命预测、汽车可靠性及可持续性设计、高塑性镁合金材料及其在汽车中的应用、动力总成悬置系统工程设计、汽车风洞测试、碰撞与安全等。中文著作分别是中国工程院院士、重庆大学潘复生教授团队撰写的《高塑性镁合金材料》、长安汽车赵会博士团队撰写的《汽车安全性能设计》、重庆大学郭钢教授团队撰写的《智能网联汽车人机交互理论与技术》、中国汽车工程研究院朱习加博士团队撰写的《汽车风洞测试技术》、重庆大学刘永刚教授团队撰写的《新能源汽车能量管理与优化控制》、重庆理工大学付江华副教授团队撰写的《动力总成悬置系统工程设计及实例详解》。

本系列著作具有以下特点:

1.知识产权的自主性。本系列著作是自主品牌汽车协同创新中心专家团队研究开发的技术成果,且由专家团队亲自撰写,具有鲜明的知识产权自主性。其中,一些著作以英文写作,出版社已与国际知名出版企业合作出版,拟通过版权输出的形式向全世界推介相关成果,这将有利于我国汽车行业自主技术的国际交流,提升我国汽车行业的国际影响力。

2.技术的前沿性。本系列著作立足于我国自主品牌汽车企业的创新实践,在各自领域反映了我国汽车自主技术的前沿水平,是专家团队多年科研的结晶。

3.立足于产学研的融合创新。本系列著作脱胎于"2011协同创新平台",这就决定了其具有"产学研融合"的特点。著作主题从工程问题中来,其成果已应用到整车及零部件设计和生产的实际中去,相关成果在进行理论梳理和技术提炼的同时,更突出体现在实践上的应用创新。

4.服务目标明确。本系列著作不过分追求技术上的"高精尖",而更注重服务于我国自主品牌汽车研发创新知识与技术体系的形成,对于相关行业的工程研究人员以及相关专业高层次人才的培养具有非常高的参考价值。

本系列著作若有不妥或具争议之处,愿与读者商榷。

《自主品牌汽车实践创新丛书》编委会

2021 年 9 月

Purpose This book is intended as a reference manual for practitioners in various areas of mechanical engineering design and manufacturing. Material properties are nonlinear in nature, so are technical principles involved in product design and manufacturing. Definitions and technical aspects of thermomechanical properties of materials are presented first for building up the reader's primary theoretical background. Mechanical characteristics of each material are then addressed briefly in an individual short chapter, to which the corresponding data of thermomechanical properties are attached as tables. As an engineer, the challenge going forward is not who provides the most technology but who best materialize (realize) that technology timely in a way that most excites and delights people.

Engineering Materials Material property data collected in this book are classified into the following categories: (1) elastomers/rubbers, (2) thermoplastics, (3) thermoset plastics, (4) metals, (5) diamond/graphite/carbon, (6) ceramics, (7) integrated electronic circuits and related packaging materials, and (8) natural materials. What listed in the book are typically nominal thermomechanical data for engineering analysis, not intended for use as limiting specifications.

Product Design and Validation Since the advent of 21st century, calculated products with minimal physical tests have prevailed in most industries including the automotive engineering. Realistic material data for proper nonlinear analyses rendering calculated products to the reality are scattered in the available literature. Here is an attempt to put them together to help practitioners speed up realizing their product design and validation.

Data Accuracy Material property data addressed here are obtained from various sources. Nominal values of true stress-strain curves are tabulated in contrast to engineering stresses and strains in paradox. Because thermomechanical properties of a material vary according to its chemical composition and production conditions, data given herein are approximate values. Exactly accurate property data of a specific material should be obtained or derived directly from its manufacturer.

Stochastic in Nature Material property data are statistically scattered. Weibull distribution functions and the lognormal distribution function are preferred for modeling material failure modes by scholars, while the normal distribution function is ostensible to most engineers' understanding. It is strongly recommended to take the nominal value of each material property and the related statistical properties, and then check the calculated result against the historical reliability data and physical test data of each product rather than taking the "absolute minimum strength" without a statistical description.

Living Reference Correction does much, but encouragement does more. Each chapter herein is as concise as possible such that a person can find the data he/she wants in minutes. Hopefully this book can be improved in future versions through readers' constructive criticisms and suggestions. It will be perfected accordingly.

Cost and Benefit Every couple of hours spent on searching for material-property data by an engineer or scientist may cost him/her more than this book.

Acknowledgements Authors of the technical papers containing original material-property data cited in the references are deeply appreciated for helping engineers bring calculated products into reality.

Young Chiang, PhD
College of Automotive Engineering
Chong Qing University

Nomenclature

A (MPa)	Yield strength at a strain rate of 1 s^{-1} and room temperature
A_f	Final cross-sectional area of the specimen center at fracture in tensile tests
A_r	Archimedes number
B	Strain hardening coefficient at a strain rate of 1 s^{-1} & 23 ℃ (mechanics)
$\boldsymbol{B}$	Magnetic flux density (electromagnetic engineering)
B_R	Retentivity, which is the B value when $H = 0$ (no magnetic field)
b, b_o	Normal and shear fatigue strength exponents, respectively
C	Strain-rate hardening coefficient at room temperature
c, c_o	Normal and shear fatigue ductility exponents, respectively
C_d	Aerodynamic drag coefficient
C_e	Equivalent damping coefficient
C_p	Specific heat capacity at constant pressure
C_v	Damping coefficient (viscous)
C_{10}, C_{01}, C_{20}, C_{30}	Hyper-elastic constants of Mooney-Rivilin's and Yeoh's material models
C_m	Moisture concentration
$C_{m,24}$	Moisture concentration after 24-hour immersion in the fluid
$C_{m,sat}$	Saturated moisture concentration
CNT	Carbon nano-tubes
D, d	Diameter
D_{min}	Cross-sectional diameter in the thinnest part of the neck in tensile tests
d_f (mm or μm)	Fiber diameter
E (GPa)	Modulus of elasticity (Young's modulus)
E_{11}, E_{22}, E_{33} (GPa)	Moduli of elasticity (Young's moduli) for orthotropic materials
E_T (GPa)	Tensile modulus of elasticity
E_C (GPa)	Compressive modulus of elasticity
E_D (GPa)	Dynamic modulus; $E_D = E_S(1 + \tan \delta)^{\frac{1}{2}}$
E_S (GPa)	Storage modulus; $E_S = E_D / (1 + \tan \delta)^{\frac{1}{2}}$
E^* (GPa)	Complex modulus
E' (GPa)	Storage modulus
E'' (GPa)	Loss modulus
F (N)	Force (Newton)

f (Hz or s^{-1})	Frequency
G (GPa)	Shear modulus of elasticity
G_r	Grashof number
g_x, g_y, g_z	Gravity per unit volume in X, Y, and Z directions, respectively
G'(GPa)	Storage shear modulus
G''(GPa)	Loss shear modulus
G^* (GPa)	Complex shear modulus
G_{12}, G_{23}, G_{31}(GPa)	Shear moduli of elasticity for orthotropic materials
H, h, hr	Hour
H (A/m)	Magnetic field intensity
H_C(A/m)	Coercivity, which is the H value when $B = 0$ (i.e. no magnetic flux)
H_r	Relative humidity
h ($W/m^2/℃$)	Heat convection coefficient
I_{zod}(kJ/m^2)	I_{zod} notched impact strength at 23 ℃ (ISO 180/1A)
K(MPa)	Bulk modulus
K_S	Surface factor
K_R	Residual stress factor
K_T	Treatment factor such as heat treatment and shot-peening
K_I, K_{II}, K_{III}($MPa \cdot m^{\frac{1}{2}}$)	Fracture toughness (Mode I, Mode II, and Mode III, respectively)
K_{IC}, K_{IIC}, K_{IIIC}($MPa \cdot m^{\frac{1}{2}}$)	Critical fracture toughness (Mode I, Mode II, and Mode III, respectively)
K' (MPa)	Cyclic Strain hardening coefficient
k (W/m/℃)	Thermal conductivity
k_x, k_y, k_z(W/m/℃)	Thermal conductivities in x-, y-, and z-directions, respectively
k_1, k_2, k_3(W/m/℃)	Thermal conductivities in 1-, 2-, and 3-directions, respectively
MAPP	Methyl Acetylene Propadiene Stabilized
MEMS	MicroElectroMechanical Systems
MS	Sprung mass
M_U	Unsprung mass
m	Strain softening exponent with respect to temperature variation
n	Strain hardening exponent at the room temperature
n'	Cyclic strain hardening exponent
N_b	Number of repeated blocks leading to failure
N_c	Number of cycles
N_{cutoff}	Number of reversals at cutoff as no apparent knee point is available
N_f	Number of reversals at endurance limit, or cutoff if no apparent knee point
$2N_f$	Number of loading cycles at endurance limit
N_{fi}	Number of fatigue cycles to failure corresponding to the stress level of σ_i
N_u	Nusselt number

$P_{er}(\mathrm{L/m^2/24\,h/atm})$	Permeability in He (Helium) at 4 ounces/yard^2.
pphr	Parts Per Hundred Rubber parts by weight
P_r	Prandtl number
P_T	Precipitation-Treated
Q (J)	Heat energy
R (mm or m)	Radius
R	Stress ratio (S-N fatigue) or strain ratio (ε-N fatigue);
	$R = -1$ for fully reversed tension-compression fatigue test
R_a	Rayleigh number
$R_a(\mu m)$	Surface roughness- Average
$R_{rms}(\mu m)$	Surface roughness- Root Mean Squared
$R_z(\mu m)$	Surface roughness- Maximum
R_e	Reynolds number
S	Multi-axial path-independent damage parameter
$S_e(\mathrm{MPa})$	Ideal fatigue strength (endurance limit)
SP	Solution- & Precipitation-Treated
ST	Solution-Treated
STA	Solution-treated and aged
T (℃) or T_k(K)	Temperature in ℃ or Temperature in K
$T(t)$	Mass for mm-sec-ton system
t (s)	Time
T_a(℃)	Auto-ignition point
T_c(℃)	Curie temperature, at which ferromagnetic becomes paramagnetic
Temp(℃)	Temperature in ℃
T_f(℃)	Flash point
T_g(℃)	Glass transition point (Temperature)
T_m(℃)	Melting point (Temperature)
T_p(℃)	Pour point
T_{room}(℃)	Room temperature (23 ℃)
$T_x, T_y, \& T_z(\mathrm{N\cdot m; N\cdot mm})$	Torques in the x-, y-, and z-direction, respectively
$\tan\delta$	Loss tangent, also called loss factor due to mechanical hysteresis
$\tan D$	Loss tangent, also called loss factor of dielectric permittivity
$u, v \& w$	Displacements in x, y, and z directions, respectively
V_f, V_F	Volume fraction of fibers- percentage by volume
V_p	Volume fraction of particulates/particles- percentage by volume
V_v	Volume fraction of voids
V_x, V_y, V_z	Speeds in x-, y-, and z-directions, respectively
W_A	Water absorption (24 h test), following ASTM D 570;
W_f, W_F	Weight fraction of fibers- percentage by weight
(X, Y, Z)	Cartesian coordinate system
(x, y, z)	Cartesian coordinate system

α	$\perp$ and $/\!/$ crystal (a, b, c) axes, as applied to crystal structures
α (μm/m/℃)	Coefficient of linear thermal expansion; $\perp$ and $/\!/$ to mold or casting flow
α_x, α_y, α_z (μm/m/℃)	Coefficients of linear thermal expansion in x-, y-, and z- directions
α_1, α_2, α_3 (μm/m/℃)	Coefficients of linear thermal expansion in 1-, 2-, and 3-directions
α_μ (MPa^{-1})	Pressure-dynamic viscosity coefficient
β (μm/m/%)	Swelling coefficients of linear moisture expansion
β_1, β_2, β_3 (μm/m/%)	Swelling coefficients of linear moisture expansion of a composite lamina
$\delta\sigma_N$	Stress recursion on the critical plane
Δ_{22}	Compression set, after 22 hours constantly under a 25% deflection
γ (J/kg/℃)	Specific heat capacity
μ	Coefficient of Coulomb friction (mechanics)
μ	Magnetic permeability (electromagnetic engineering)
μ_D	Dynamic coefficient of friction
μ_d	Dynamic viscosity (fluid only)
μ_{d0}	Dynamic viscosity at ambient pressure
μ_{dg}	Dynamic viscosity at glass transition temperature
μ_f	Frictional factor
μ_k	Kinematic viscosity
μ_o	Magnetic permeability of vacuum, i.e. $4\pi \times 10^{-7}$ H/m
μ_r	Relative magnetic permeability
μ_S	Static coefficient of friction
ε	Strain (mechanics)
ε	Dielectric permittivity (electromagnetic engineering)
ε_{creep}	Creep rupture strain
ε_{eq}	Equivalent strain
ε_{eq}^p	Equivalent plastic strain
$d\varepsilon_{eq}^p/dt$	Equivalent plastic strain rate obtained in reference to a strain rate of 1 s^{-1}
ε_f'	Fatigue ductility coefficient
ε_p	Plastic strain
ε_r	Relative dielectric permittivity
ε_{xx}, ε_{yy}, ε_{zz}	Normal strains
ε_{yz}, ε_{zx}, ε_{xy}	Shear strains
ε_{ucs}	Ultimate compressive strain
ε_{uts}	Ultimate tensile strain
ε_0	Dielectric permittivity of vacuum, i.e. 8.854×10^{-12} F/m
ε_1, ε_2, ε_3	Principal strains
ε_{11}, ε_{22}, ε_{33}	Normal strains defined in the (1, 2, 3) coordinate system
ε_{12}, ε_{23}, ε_{31}	Shear strains (tensor) defined in the (1, 2, 3) coordinate system
ε_{11c}, ε_{22c}, ε_{33c}	Ultimate compressive strains along the primary orthotropic material

axes

ε_{11t}, ε_{22t}, ε_{33t}	Ultimate tensile strains along the primary orthotropic material axes
ε_{12u}, ε_{23u}, ε_{31u}	Ultimate shear strains in primary orthotropic material coordinates (1, 2, 3)
$\Delta\varepsilon$	Fluctuating strain; $\Delta\varepsilon = \Delta\varepsilon^e + \Delta\varepsilon^p$
$\Delta\varepsilon^e$	Fluctuating (equivalent) elastic strain
$\Delta\varepsilon^p$	Fluctuating (equivalent) plastic strain
γ_f	Specific heat of fibers in a composite
γ_m	Specific heat of matrix in a composite
$\lambda_i (i = 1, 2, 3)$	Stretch ratio along axis, i.e. deviate principal stretches
ρ, ρ_f, $\rho_m (g/cm^3)$	Density, density of fiber, and density of matrix, respectively
ρ_E, $\rho_e (\Omega \cdot m \text{ or } \Omega \cdot mm)$	Electric resistivity
$\rho_{e,ref} (\Omega \cdot m \text{ or } \Omega \cdot mm)$	Resistivity at the reference temperature
σ (MPa)	Stress
σ_A(MPa)	Stress amplitude
$\sigma_{ccs,10000}$(MPa)	Creep compressive strength (rupture in compression) at 10000 h
$\sigma_{creep,1\%,1000}$(MPa)	Creep strength or limiting creep strength; creep = 1% at 1000 h
$\sigma_{creep,1\%,10000}$(MPa)	Creep strength or limiting creep strength; creep = 1% at 10000 h
$\sigma_{creep,5\%,1000}$(MPa)	Creep strength or limiting creep strength; creep = 5% at 1000 h
$\sigma_{creep,5\%,10000}$(MPa)	Creep strength or limiting creep strength; creep = 5% at 10000 h
σ_{crs}(MPa)	Creep rupture strength
$\sigma_{crs,1000}$(MPa)	Creep rupture strength at 1000 h (≈ 41.7 d)
$\sigma_{crs,10000}$(MPa)	Creep rupture strength at 10000 h (≈ 417 d)
$\sigma_{cts,10000}$(MPa)	Creep tensile strength in tension at 10000 h
$\sigma_E (\Omega \cdot m^{-1}; \Omega \cdot mm^{-1})$	Electric conductivity, also called specific conductance; $\sigma_E = 1/\rho_E$
σ_{eq}(MPa)	Equivalent stress, e.g. von Mises stress
σ_f(MPa)	Fatigue limit, also called endurance limit
σ_f'(MPa)	Fatigue strength coefficient
σ_M(MPa)	Mean stress
σ_R(MPa)	Rupture strength, resulting from 3-point bending tests for brittle materials
σ_Y or $\sigma_{0.2\%}$(MPa)	Yield strength; stress at strain = 0.2% in elongation
$\sigma_{100\%}$ & $\sigma_{300\%}$(MPa)	Stresses at 100% and 300% strains, respectively, used for rubbers
σ_{YT} and σ_{YC}(MPa)	Yield strengths in tension and compression, respectively
σ_{xx}, σ_{yy}, σ_{zz}(MPa)	Normal stresses
σ_{yz}, σ_{zx}, σ_{xy}(MPa)	Shear stresses
σ_{us}(MPa)	Ultimate strength
σ_{uts}(MPa)	Ultimate tensile strength
σ_{ucs}(MPa)	Ultimate compressive strength
$(\sigma_{ucs}, \varepsilon_{ucs}) \cdots (\sigma_{uts}, \varepsilon_{uts})$	Stress-strain curve data ranging from ultimate compression to tension
σ_1, σ_2, σ_3(MPa)	Principal stresses

σ_{11c}, σ_{22c}, σ_{33c} (MPa)	Ultimate compressive stresses along the primary orthotropic material axes
σ_{11t}, σ_{22t}, σ_{33t} (MPa)	Ultimate tensile stresses along the primary orthotropic material axes
σ_{12u}, σ_{23u}, σ_{31u} (MPa)	Ultimate shear stresses in primary orthotropic material coordinates (1,2,3)
τ, τ_{xy}, τ_{xz}, τ_{yz} (MPa)	Shear stresses
ξ	Damping factor
ν	Poisson's ratio
ν_{12}, ν_{23}, ν_{31}	Poisson's ratios for orthotropic materials
ν_{xy}, ν_{yz}, ν_{zx}	Poisson's ratios for composites
ω or Ω (Hz or s^{-1})	Frequency
ω_D or ω_d	Damped natural frequency
ω_N or ω_n	Undamped natural frequency

Acronyms

AFM	Atomic force microscope
AGMA	American Gear Manufacturers Association
AHSS	Advanced high strength steels
API	American Petroleum Institute
AS	As sintered
ASTM	American Society of Materials
BGA	Ball grid array
BH	Bake hardenable
BHN	Brinell hardness
BLDC	Brushless direct-current motor
BPA	Bisphenol-A
BPC	Bisphenol-C
BNNT	Boron nitride nanotube
C	Carbon
CB	Carbon black such as N110,..., N990 (ISO classification)
CD	Cold-drawn
CMOS	Complementary metal-oxide-semiconductor
CNT	Carbon nanotube
COB	Chip-on-board
COG	Chip-on-glass
CP	Complex phase
CR	Cold-rolled
CSM	Chopped strand mat; fibers laid randomly and held together by a binder
CVD	Chemical vapor deposit
CW	Cold-worked
DAM	Dry as molded
DBTT	Ductile-brittle transition temperature
DC	Die cast
DF or DOF	Degree of freedom
DFMEA	Design failure modes and effect analysis
DGEBA	Diglycidyl ether of Bisphenol A (commercial epoxy)
DIN	Deutsche Industrial Normale (German)
DP	Dual phase
DSC	Differential Scanning Calorimetry
EBPVD	Electron beam vapor deposition

ETP	Electrolytic touch pitch copper
Exp	Exponential
F	Force
F	As fabricated
FB	Ferritic-bainitic
FCBGA	Flip-chip ball grid array
FET	Field Effect Transistor
FZ	Fusion zone
G	Gravity
Gf or GF	Glass fiber
Gl	Glass
Gr	Graphite
GPa	Gega-pascals
GTAW	Gas tungsten arc welding
g	Gram
H	Hardening Symbol, such as H12, H14, H16, H18, H22, H24, H26, H28, H32, H34, H36, H38 for 1×××, 3×××, & 5××× series aluminum alloys:

1st digit:

     0- No cold worked

     1- Cold worked only

     2- Cold worked & annealed

     3- Cold worked & stabilized

2nd digit:

     1-Annealed

     2-$\frac{1}{4}$ Hard

     4-$\frac{1}{2}$ Hard

     6-$\frac{3}{4}$ Hard

     8-Hard

     9-Extra Hard

HAZ	Heat affected zone
HB	Brinell hardness- spherical indenter
HD	Hot-drawn
HF	Hot-formed
HIP	Hot Isostatic pressing
HK	Knoop hardness- pyramidal indenter
HM	Martens hardness
HR	Hot-rolled
H_R	Humidity, relative
HRc	Rockwell hardness (C scale)- spheroconical indenter
HSLA	High strength low alloy (SAE J1392 JUN 84)
HV	Vickers hardness- rectangular pyramidal indenter

Hz	Herz (cycles per second)
IF	Interstitial free
IGBT	Insulated gate bipolar transistor
ISO	International standards organization
J	Joule
kg	Kilogram
kPa	Kilo Pascals
M or m	Meter
MAG	Metal active gas welding
Max (Subscript)	Maximum
MCM	Multi-chip module
MIG	Metal inert gas welding
Min	Minute
Min (Subscript)	Minimum
MOE	Modulus of elasticity
MPa	Mega-Pascals
MS	Martensitic
MM or mm	Mini-meter
MOR	Modulus of rupture
MOSFET	Metal-oxide-semiconductor field-effect transistor
MWCNT or MWNT	Multi-walled carbon nanotubes
N	Newton
O	Annealed, soft (a heat treatment condition)
PCB	Printed circuit boards
PF	Powder forged
PH	Precipitation hardening
PM	Powder metallurgy
PM	Permanent mold cast
pphr	Parts per hundred rubber parts by weight
PTMG	Polyoxytetramethylene Glycol
PWHT	Post-weld heat treatment
Q&T	Quench and tempering
Q&T&C	Quench, tempering, and carburizing
Rad	Radian
RH	Relative humidity
RHA	Rolled homogeneous armor- steel for military applications, e.g. armors
Flexural B.	Flexural bending fatigue test via cantilever impact
RoHS	Restriction of Hazardous Substances Directive 2002/95/EC
Rotating B.	Rotating beam bending fatigue test
RRR	Residual Resistivity Ratio
RTM	Resin transfer molding
R-3p; 3p Bending	3-point bending fatigue test

R-4p; 4p Bending	4-point bending fatigue test
S, s, Sec, sec	Second
SC	Sand cast
SIP	System in package
ST	Solution-treated
SVO	Straight Vegetable Oil
SWNT	Single-walled nano-carbon tube
T	Temperature
t	Ton
T	Heat Treatment, such as T1, T2, T3, T4, T5, T6, T7, T8, T9, T10 for $2\times\times\times$, $4\times\times\times$, $6\times\times\times$, $7\times\times\times$, & $8\times\times\times$ aluminum alloys
T1	Cooled from elevated temperatures & naturally aged
T2	Cooled from elevated temperature & artificially aged
T3	Solution-heat-treated, cold worked, & naturally aged
T4	Solution-heat-treated & naturally aged
T5	Cooled from elevated temperatures & artificially aged
T6	Solution-heat-treated & artificially aged
T7	Solution-heat-treated & over-aged/stabilized
T8	Solution-heat-treated, cold worked, & artificially aged
T9	Solution-heat-treated, artificially aged, & cold worked
T10	Cooled from elevated temperatures, cold worked, & artificially aged
TGA	Thermogravimetric Analysis
TGMDA	Diglycidyl ether of Bisphenol A (epoxy for aerospace applications)
TGO	Thermally grown oxide
TIG	Tungsten inert gas welding
TM	Trade Mark
TPC	Thermoplastic copolyester
TPE	Thermoplastic elastomer
TPE-s	Styrenic block copolymers
TPG	Thermal pyrolytic graphite
TPI	Thermoplastic polyamides
TPO	Thermoplastic olefin (Polyolefin blends)
TPU	Thermoplastic polyurethanes
TPV (or TPE-v)	Thermoplastc vulcanizates, i.e. thermoplastic alloys
TRIP	Transformation-induced plasticity
TWIP	Twinning-induced plasticity
t	Time
VG	Viscosity Grade
W	Watt
W	Solution heat-treated only
$\times\times$A	Shore A durometer hardness, e.g. 70 A ($\times\times$ = 70) is Shore A hardness 70

Consistent Units ···

Units for engineering calculations such as finite element methods for structural analysis, thermal analysis, vibration, dynamics, fluid flow, and magnetic field have been complicated by the unit of length in the automotive industry. Universally mm (mini-meter) has been used for parts and their assemblies on automotive engineering drawings. Conversions of units between mm-based (mini-meter) systems and m-based (meter) systems are complicated by the fact of even-ordered differential equations for dynamics and odd-ordered differential equations for heat transfer by nature. Usage of consistent units for engineering analysis is more complex than it appears.

Units employed in Table 0.1, exhibited in next page, are based on the principle that the units of time, temperature, and force are always second (s), centigrade (℃), and Newton (N), respectively no matter whether mm (mini-meter) or m (meter) is used for length. The derivative units are illustrated using generic steel data as unit-conversion examples, shown in the last column of the table.

Table 0.1 Recommended Units for Automotive Engineering Practice

Variable	Unit/mm	Unit/m	Generic Steel (Example)
Time, t	s (second)	s	s
Temperature, T	℃ or K	℃ or K	℃
Force, F	N	N	N
Frequency, ω or f	Hz (s^{-1})	Hz	Hz
Angular velocity, ω or Ω	rad/s	rad/s	rad/s
Length, L	mm	m	1 mm = 10^{-3} m
Mass, M	t (Ton)	kg	1 t = 10^3 kg
Torque, T_x, T_y, T_z	N · mm	N · m	1 N · mm = 10^{-3} N · m
Velocity, V	mm/s	m/s	1 mm/s = 10^{-3} m/s
Acceleration, a; Gravity, g	mm/s^2	m/s^2	1 g = 9807 mm/s^2 = 9.807 m/s^2
Work	N · mm	J (N · m)	1 N · mm = 10^{-3} J
Power	N · mm/s	W (J/s)	1 N · mm/s = 10^{-3} W
Spring constant, K	N/mm	N/m	1 N/mm = 10^3 N/m
Stress, σ	MPa (N/mm^2)	Pa (N/m^2)	1 MPa = 10^6 Pa

continued

Variable	Unit/mm	Unit/m	Generic Steel (Example)
Body force	N/mm^3	N/m^3	$1\ N/mm^3 = 10^9\ N/m^3$
Strain, ε	—	—	—
Density, ρ	t/mm^3	kg/m^3	$7.83\times10^{-9}\ t/mm^3 = 7830\ kg/m^3$
Tensile modulus of elasticity, E_T	$MPa\ (N/mm^2)$	$Pa\ (N/m^2)$	$206\ GPa = 206\times10^3\ MPa = 206\times10^9\ Pa$
Ultimate tensile strength, σ_{uts}	MPa	Pa	$370\ MPa = 370\times10^6\ Pa$
Ultimate tensile strain, ε_{uts}	—	—	0.235 or 23.5%
Poisson's ratio, ν	—	—	0.29
Fatigue limit, σ_f	MPa	Pa	$190\ MPa = 190\times10^6\ Pa$
Damping coefficient (viscous), C_v	NS/mm	NS/m	$NS/mm = 10^3\ NS/m$
C. of linear thermal expansion, α	nm/mm/℃	nm/m/℃	$12\ nm/mm/℃ = 12\ \mu m/m/℃$
C. of linear moisture expansion, β	mm/mm/%	m/m/%	$(3.3\times10^{-3}\ mm/mm/℃\ for\ PA6)$
Specific heat capacity, γ	$N \cdot mm/T/℃$	J/kg/℃	$473\times10^6\ N \cdot mm/T/℃ = 473\ J/kg/℃$
Thermal conductivity, k	N/s/℃	W/m/℃	$42\ N/s/℃ = 42\ W/m/℃$
Heat convection coefficient, h	N/s/mm/℃	$W/m^2/℃$	$9\times10^{-3}\ N/s/mm/℃ = 9\ W/m^2/℃$

Automotive Engineering Materials

Elastomers

Thermoplastics

Thermoset Plastics

Ferrous

Ceramics

Carbon

Electromagnetic Materials

Natural Materials

Automobile Fluids

Contents

Automotive Engineering Materials

Chapter 6   Ceramics

Chapter 7   Diamond and Other Carbon Solids

Chapter 8   Electromagnetic Materials

Elastomers

Chapter 28   Hoses

Chapter 29   Seals

Thermoplastics

:

Thermoset Plastics

Automotive Engineering Materials

Chapter 1

Elastomers

1.1 Introduction

"Elastomer" is a contraction of elastic polymer. They are rubber-like polymers with cross-linked long chains. Elastomers be capable of being stretched many times their original length and quickly reverting to their original length (or almost) upon release. They are resilient and yet exhibit internal friction. Rubber is typical elastomeric material. Chemistry is involved in developing the elastomer and crosslinking it to create a usable 3-D structure. "Cross-linking" between the polymer chains is formed (covalently bonded) during the vulcanization process. To be useful as an elastomer, the chain typically must have at least 700 to 800 covalently bonded monomer units; 1000 units or more are required to develop adequate physical properties and 2000 to 3000 units for maximum ultimate properties. Cross-linking chemically bonds polymeric chains of an elastomer and bonding usually does not break at elevated temperatures. Elastomers can be further classified by the basic polymer family, from which they are made. In each elastomer family, individual elastomers vary in the fillers, softeners, processing aids, curing agents, accelerators, and other additives. Besides tires, elastomers are utilized to solve sealing and vibration-damping problems.

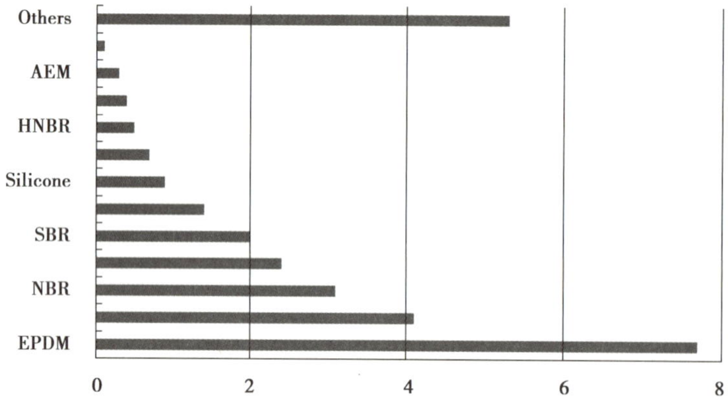

Fig. 1.1 Application of Rubbers (in Percentage) in a Typical Sedan (Mercedes E-Class) Excluding Tires

Typical application of rubbers in automotive industry may be demonstrated using Mercedes E-Class Sedan as shown in Fig. 1.1. Mechanical performance measures of different types of elastomers are listed in Table 1.1 and the influence of various environmental conditions is given in Table 1.2. Mechanical behaviors of elastomers depend strongly on crosslink density and fillers. The IRHD (international rubber hardness degrees) hardness is a relevant quick indicator. Modulus is defined as the engineering stress (original cross-section) in MPa required to produce a certain elongation. Data for rubber moduli of elasticity are often taken at 100% and 300% strain levels. For example, if the stress required to produce 100% is 3 MPa and 300% is 5 MPa, $\sigma_{100\%} = 3$ MPa and $\sigma_{300\%} = 5$ MPa respectively.

The Poisson's ratio of hyperelastic rubbers is 0.5, yet it is generally not true for rubbers at elevated temperatures. Strain-energy functions such as Mooney-Rivilin's material model and Yeoh's material model are used for describing the modulus of elasticity of rubber in a static finite element analysis (FEA). Most FEA codes, ABAQUS for instance, automatically take such calibrated test stress-strain data and curve-fit for the appropriate constitutive model parameters. There are several different ways to do a dynamic finite element analysis of rubber components, such as

(a) Viscous elastic model as a function of temperature and time;
(b) Complex shear modulus as a function of frequency and temperature.

1.2   Chemistry of Hyperelastic Rubbers

Hyperelastic rubbers are flexible long-chain polymers, which are capable of cross-linking. Polymeric chains of elastomers cross-linked by chemical covalent bonds cannot go back to non-cross-linked state any more, being different from no cross-linking in plastics of that the solid state will recover from its rubbery state after the temperature goes back from an elevated temperature as long as it is below its glass transition point. Cross-linking in hyperelastic rubbers provides the elastic resilience in such applications with large deformations as tires, hoses, seals, vibration isolators. Rubber is often vulcanized (also called cured. Vulcanization is a process by which it is heated at certain temperatures for certain time durations, while sulfur, peroxide or bisphenol are added to enhance its elasticity preventing it from perishing. The rubber modulus of elasticity roughly increases with increasing hardness as exhibited in Table 1.1. The relations between crosslink density and physical properties have been neatly summarized by [Coran] as redrawn in Fig. 1.2. The degree of cross-linking $\left(\frac{1}{2}C_{\mathrm{L}}\right)$ can be assessed using stress-strain measurements as

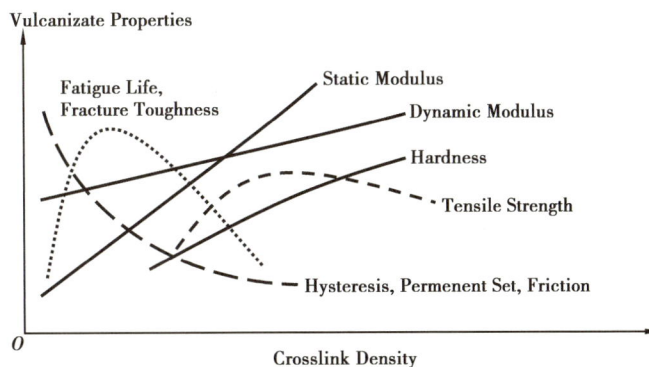

Fig. 1.2   Mechanical Properties of Generic Rubber versus Crosslink Density

$$F = \frac{\rho RTA_{\circ}}{C_{\mathrm{L}}}(\lambda - \lambda^{-2}) \tag{1.1}$$

where

F (N): Force;

ρ (t/mm^3): Density;

R: Gas constant;

T (K): Temperature;

A_0 (mm^2): Cross-sectional area;

λ: Extension ratio ($\lambda \equiv$ Instantaneous length/Original length);

C_L: Number of average molecular weight of the rubber chains between crosslinks;

$\frac{1}{2}C_L$: Degree of cross-linking, i.e. number of gram moles of crosslinks per gram of rubber.

Another assessment is to go through the state of cure. While vulcanization occurs, the modulus curve rises rapidly. The cure time is thus defined as the sum of scorch time and vulcanization time. Finite element methods combined with Weibull statistics have been a decisive tool for predicting the cure time of tires and other rubber products [Chiang et al.].

1.2.1 Reinforcement by Fillers

The stress-strain properties of many elastomeric compounds change with the addition of reinforcing fillers such as carbon black and silica. Modulus of elasticity and tensile values can increase substantially with such reinforcements, but they may decrease again if over-dozed. A proper amount of adhesive resin may enhance the material properties, too.

Carbon black has been used to improve the rubber strength, resilience, fatigue life, and other material properties as being the most effective additive [Isshiki et al.]. Carbon blacks are characterized by particle size, surface area, and shape. Optimal levels vary according to the rubber-filler system but usually fall in the range of between 30 and 60 pphr (Parts Per Hundred Rubber Parts by Weight). Carbon black is pure elemental carbon (black in color) in the form of colloid particles that are produced by incomplete combustion or thermal decomposition of gaseous or liquid hydrocarbons under controlled conditions. Caron black is classified into the following grades roughly in the descending order of surface area: N110, N121, S212, N219, N220, N230, N231, N234, N242, N293, N294, N299, N299, S315, N326, N327, N330, N332, N339, N341, N347, N351, N356, N363, N375, N472, N539, N550, N568, N601, N650, N660, N683, N741, N754, N762, N765, N774, N785, N787, N907, and N990. The first number is basically the surface area as measured by iodine adsorption. For example, the iodine adsorption is 145 mg/g for N110 and 8 mg/g for N990. A study was done on rubber reinforced by different carbon blacks including N990, N770, N550, N330 and N220. It is shown that the tensile stress at 100% extension (100% modulus) reaches the maximum when reinforced using N550. The "work" values at 20% extension continued to show an increase with N330 reinforcement and arrived at the maximum with N220 reinforcement.

1.2.2 Strength versus Hardness

As shown in Fig. 1.2, the tensile strength of rubber reaches its maximum at a certain level of cross-linking and then decays, while the hardness keeps growing. Applicable work ranges of hardness of rubbers and plastics are illustrated in Fig. 1.3. The Shore A durometer scale is the most prevalent for measuring rubber hardness in the United States. A conical indenter with a spring force that decreases with increasing indentation is used. The readings range from 30 to 95 points. Once the rubber is too hard for Shore A scale, it can be tested on Shore D durometer scale.

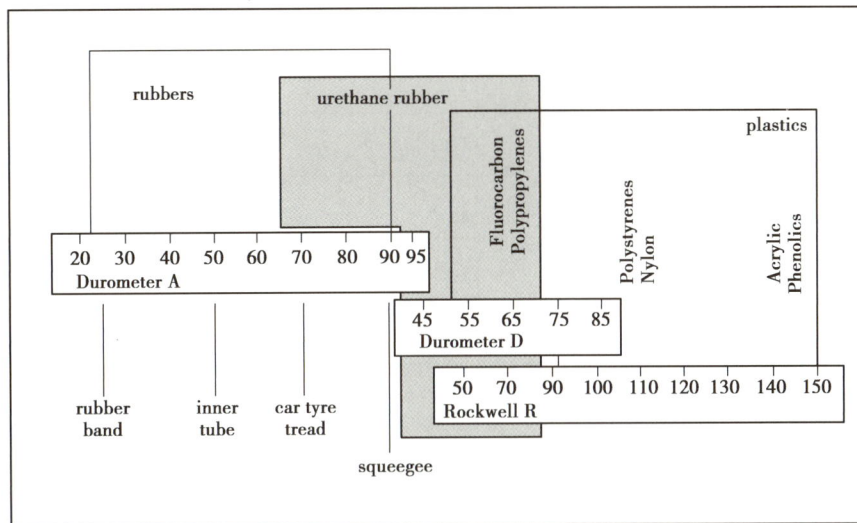

Fig. 1.3 Hardness Scales for Rubber and Plastics

1.2.3 Compression Set (Permanent Set), Creep, and Stress Relaxation of Rubber

Compression set tests, as described in ASTM D-395, are of two types. Method A is for compression set under constant load; while Method B for compression set at constant deflection of 25%. Method B of ASTM D-395 calls for the elastomer to be 25% compressed at a specified temperature (i.e. 23 ℃, 70 ℃, 121 ℃, and 150 ℃) for a given period of time (i.e. 22 h, 70 h, or 1000 h). Given 30 min recovery time, the sample is measured. For example, a compression set of 35% states that the elastomer regains only 65% of its compression thickness. Testing temperatures for different elastomers/plastics recommended [ASTM D2000] are listed according to their upper long-term service temperature as follows:

Polymer	Duration/h	Temperature/℃	ASTM D2000 Grade
NA, SBR	22	70	AA
SBR, EP	22	70	BA

continued

Polymer	Duration/h	Temperature/℃	ASTM D2000 Grade
CR	22	100	BC
NBR	22	100	BG
CA	22	100	CA
NBR, ECO	22	100	CH
EP	22	150	DA
HNBR	22	150	DH
AEM	22	150	EE
ACM	22	150	EH
VMQ	22	175	FC
PVMQ	22	175	FE
FVMQ	22	175	FK
Silicone	22	175	GE
FKM	22	175	HK
FFKM	22	200	KK

Rubbers deform under load and rarely return completely to their original dimensions when the load is removed. The difference between the original and final dimensions is known as compression set, also called permanent set. It is the residual deformation of an elastomer after it has been deformed and the applied forcing function (forces or hydrothermal effects) is removed. It has great impact on product performance, especially with elastomeric seals. It can be calculated as

$$\text{Permanent set} = \frac{\text{Original thickness} - \text{Thickness after recovery}}{\text{Original thickness} - \text{Height of the compression}}$$

Method A of ASTM D-395 calls for compression set under a constant load means strain relaxation similar to a creep behavior. It is important in applications such as engine mountings since it influences the alignment of various parts of the equipment. The creep characteristics of two urethane polymers, over a ten-month period, are shown on Fig. 1.4. After 3000 h creep reaches a plateau and becomes almost constant. The amount of creep is a function of stress level. Creep analysis based on stress-versus-strain behaviors (Chapter 6) can be carried out using data derived from the force-versus-deflection data obtained following Method A.

Creep in Compression

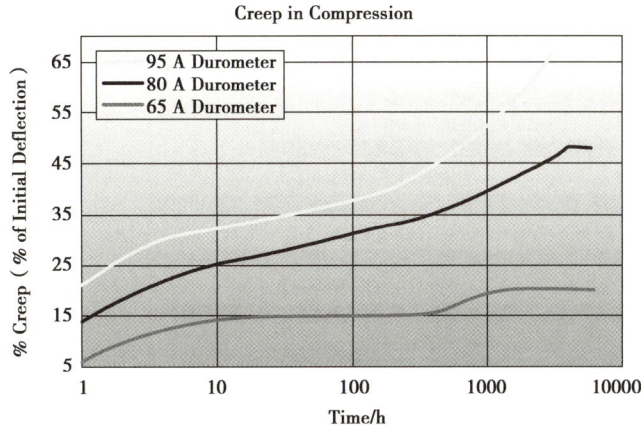

Fig. 1.4   Creep of Urethanes of Different Hardness as a Function of Loading Time

Stress Relaxation of 90 A Urethane
25% Extension @ 70 deg. F., 50% R. H.

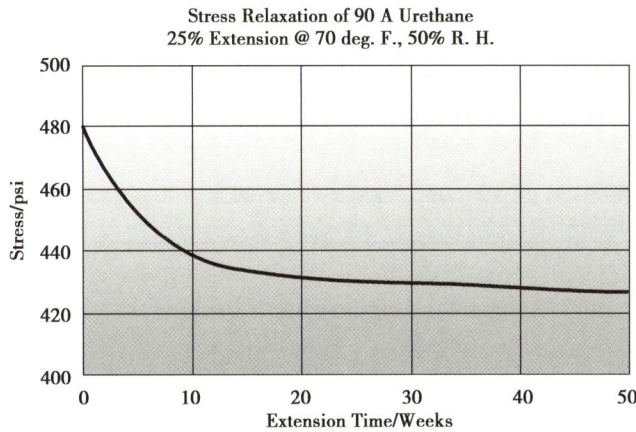

Fig. 1.5   Compression Stress Relaxation of Urethanes as a Function of Loading Time

Although compression set is used as a primary property in the rubber industry, many designers prefer to establishing compression stress relaxation (CSR) values to more fully characterize the sealing capability of material, Fig. 1.5. By the CSR method, the sample is compressed and aged in a manner similar to Method B of ASTM D-395. But after aging, it is maintained in its compressed condition, where sealing force is measured in a quasi-static condition. This sealing force value is compared to an initial measured value and is reported as a percentage of the retained sealing force (% RSF).

1.2.4   Behaviors at Cold and Hot Temperatures

The glass transition point (T_g) of an elastomer is generally below the ice point of water (0 ℃). Once a rubber material is cooled down below its T_g(glass transition point), it loses its elasticity and becomes brittle. A rubber material recovers slowly from its deformed shape if the working temperature is close to, even not below, its T_g. This is very damaging to elastomeric seals such as O-rings. The working temperature ranges for common engineering elastomers are given in Fig. 1.6.

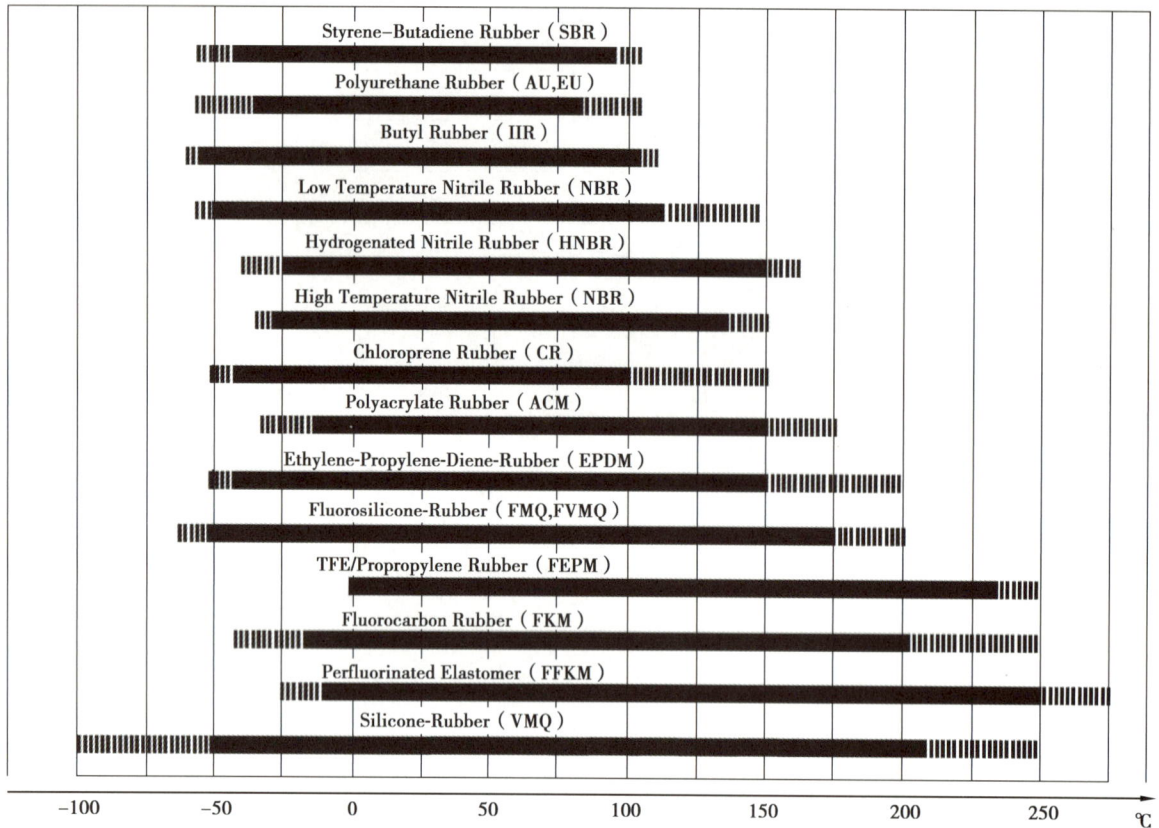

Fig. 1.6   Working Temperature Ranges for Engineering Elastomers

The modulus of elasticity and strength of an elastomer drops profoundly with increasing working temperature while the permanent set increases at elevated temperatures. A property of viscoelastic materials is that the time-temperature superposition technique (Chapter 9) is available. The transformation unifies apparently disconnected results into a composite master curve for the design purpose, but only applicable to viscoelastic properties.

1.3   TPE (Thermoplastic Elastomers) and TPV (Thermoplastic Vulcanizates)

Thermoplastic rubbers are copolymers produced by chemically joining two or more dissimilar polymers along the chain backbone. The pseudo-cross-linking in thermoplastic elastomers is dominated by weaker dipole or hydrogen bond, though there is covalent bond within an individual material phase. At working temperatures one polymer (i.e. hyper elastic rubber) is rubbery while others are glassy or even semi-crystalline thermoplastics. The two-phase or multiphase structure consists of aggregates of hard segments dispersed in a soft-segmented elastomeric matrix. The material of hard segments or blocks in glassy state serves as reinforced fillers as well as thermally reversible multifunctional crosslink. A thermoplastic elastomer may be processed by rapid thermoplastic forming process (such as injection molding and extrusion) at elevated temperatures, yet at low working temperatures they behave as a chemically cross-linked tuber. An increase in the content of hard segments generally increases the modulus of elasticity but reduces the elongation at break. A typical thermoplastic rubber is polyurethane elastomer.

A TPE (Thermoplastic Elastomer) is by nature a two-phase system-compounds with fully cross linked rubber in a continuous thermoplastic matrix of plastic and rubber compositions having excellent elastomeric properties. In this case the curing of the rubber phase occurs during the mastication with the thermoplastic resin. This process gives a useful elastomeric alloy with properties of a cured rubber but has the processing characteristics of a thermoplastic. A TPE is thought of made from a plastic phase and an elastomer phase. Most often the elastomer phase is dispersed in the matrix of the plastic phase. The elastomer phase is usually soft, elastic and not changing its behavior under the thermal effect (heat), i.e., it is not melted at an elevated temperature. The plastic phase is usually hard, serving as the crosslinking point, holding the elastomer phase in place. The phase can be thermally softened or melted at high enough temperature to make the whole polymer system fluidic.

TPEs improve soft-touch grips and handles-contributing to user comfort, stylish product appearance and safer nonslip control in wet environments. Direct over-molding and co-extrusion bonding options onto PP, ABS, PC and PC/ABS blends open the door to design flexibility, parts consolidation, and manufacturing cost efficiencies. TPEs are generally thermoset materials.

A TPV (Thermoplastic Vulcanizate) is one kind of TPE, of which the elastomeric phase is fully vulcanized-enhanced performance such as better mechanical, tribological properties, and high service temperature can be achieved. It is important that the mixing be continuous throughout the masticating step, or a thermoset material could result.

TPVs are an excellent choice for under the hood applications that demand both flexibility and durability-requiring material with excellent long term resistance to heat, automotive fluids, oils and road grime. Plugs and fasteners, boots and bellows, bumpers and mechanical stops, air management systems, mechanical cables, and various line jackets are example applications of TPV.

1.4　Hyperelastic Models

The general form of the stored energy function of stressed elastomeric material is

$$W = \sum_{m=0}^{\infty} \sum_{n=0}^{\infty} C_{ij}(I_1 - 3)^m (I_2 - 3)^n \tag{1.2}$$

The invariants given above are related to stretches along principal directions (1, 2, 3) as follows:

$$I_1 = \lambda_1^2 + \lambda_2^2 + \lambda_3^2 \tag{1.3}$$
$$I_2 = \lambda_1^2\lambda_2^2 + \lambda_2^2\lambda_3^2 + \lambda_3^2\lambda_1^2 \tag{1.4}$$

and $\quad I_3 = \lambda_1^2\lambda_2^2\lambda_3^2 (I_3 = 1$ for incompressible elastomers$)$ \tag{1.5}

$\lambda_i (i = 1, 2, 3)$ is the stretch ratio along the principal axes (1, 2, 3), i.e. the ratio of the length after deformation to the original length (= 1 + engineering strain), also called deviatorial principal stretches,

$$\lambda_i = \frac{L}{L_o} = 1 + \varepsilon_{ii} (i = 1, 2, \text{ or } 3) \tag{1.6}$$

1.4.1　Neo-Hookean's Material Model

The first term of Eq. (1.2) corresponding to $m = 1$ and $n = 0$, yields W the form derived from kinetic energy, which gives a reasonably good first approximation to the elastomeric stress-strain relation as

$$W = C_{10}(I_1 - 3) \tag{1.7}$$

1.4.2　Mooney-Rivilin's Material Model

Based on the assumption that the hyperelastic rubber is incompressible (Poisson's ratio = 0.5) and initially isotropic, [Rivilin and Sunders] extended Mooney's theory and gave the following strain energy potential for hyperelastic rubber

$$W = C_{10}(I_1 - 3) + C_{01}(I_2 - 3) + D^{-1}(J^{el} - 1)^2 \tag{1.8}$$

where C_{10} and C_{01} are called Mooney's material constants and J^{el} is the elastic volume ratio that is part of the total volume ratio J, i.e. 3rd invariant of the stretch tensor; $J = J^{el}J^{th}$, of which J^{th} is the thermal volume ratio. Constant D is the number used to describe the situation of being "almost incompressible". If the bulk modulus K of the specific elastomer is known, then $D = 2 K^{-1}$. Otherwise, $D \approx 1.0e^{-4}$ is a conventional wisdom for the purpose of numerical analysis of most hyperelastic rubbers.

The Mooney's material constants can be characterized using the following relationship described by Mooney-Rivlin equation, i.e. Eq. 1.1 as

$$\sigma_{ii} = 2(\lambda_i - \lambda_i^{-2})(C_{10} + C_{01}\lambda_i^{-1}) \tag{1.9}$$

where σ_{ii} is the stress applied, λ_i is the extension ratio, and C_{10} and C_{01} are Mooney's material constants. According to Eq. (1.2), the plot of $\sigma_{ii}/[2(\lambda_i-\lambda_i^{-2})]$ against λ_i^{-1} yields a straight line, from which C_{10} can be obtained by extrapolating the linear portion of the curve to horizontal axis, and C_{01} is the slope of the linear portion. A regression model may be required for fitting the straight line. If no material constants available, Mooney's C_{10} and C_{01} may be estimated from the hardness as the first approximation, Table 1.3. Mooney's material constants for some generic rubbers are given in Table 1.4.

Elastic response of rubber-like materials is often modeled based on the Mooney-Rivlin model. The constants are determined by the fitting predicted stress from the above equations to experimental data. The recommended tests are uniaxial tension, equibiaxial compression, equibiaxial tension, uniaxial compression, and for shear, planar tension and planar compression.

The two parameter Mooney's material model is usually valid for strains less than 100%, which is much larger than most vibration-isolation applications. However, elastomeric material constants are strain-rate (e.g. response frequency) dependent. The initial estimations of the material constants are achieved by using static uniaxial tensile test data. To ensure of the consistency of dynamic response of a real component, the frequency response function of several vibration isolators (e.g. similar engine mounts) is extracted from experimental modal data. The average of them is then used in the finite element analysis procedure.

1.4.3   Yeoh's Material Model

As the Mooney-Rivilin model is such a linear model that it is short of describing the nonlinear deflection of a stress strain curve of rubber, the following material of a higher order was proposed by [Yeoh]:

$$W = C_{10}(I_1 - 3) + C_{20}(I_1 - 3)^2 + C_{30}(I_1 - 3)^3 + \frac{J^{el} - 1}{D} \tag{1.10}$$

where C_{10}, C_{20} and C_{30} are material constants and D is the number used to describe the status of being "almost incompressible". If the bulk modulus K of the specific elastomer is known, $D = 2 K^{-1}$. Otherwise, $D \approx 1.0e^{-4}$ is a conventional wisdom for the purpose of numerical analysis of most hyperelastic rubbers. Though three terms are needed in Eq. (1.7) to make the equation a complete $N=3$ polynomial model. In practice, it is hard to get the subsequent D in addition to the initial D from test data. The rubber material parameter can be obtained approximately from the initial shear modulus. The approximate relations are given by the following equations:

$$C_{10} = \frac{E}{6} \tag{1.10a}$$

$$C_{20} = -\frac{E}{60} \qquad (1.10\mathrm{b})$$

$$\text{and} \quad C_{30} = \frac{E}{600} \qquad (1.10\mathrm{c})$$

Parameters C_{10} and C_{30} have influences on the behavior of the rubber at low and high strain rates, respectively.

1.4.4 Strain Energy Model with Fractional Exponents (Davis-De-Thomas Model)

In order to account for the reinforcement of carbon black and cross-linking behavior of rubber, [Davis-De-Thomas] formulated an equation of strain energy potential for hyperelastic rubber as follows:

$$W = \frac{A}{2\left(1 - \frac{1}{2}n\right)}(I_1 - 3 + C^2)^{1-\frac{n}{2}} + K(I_1 - 3)^2 \qquad (1.11)$$

where A, C, and n are material constants related to the content (amount and type) of black carbon and degree of cross linking. C is the initial strain beyond which the breakdown of the black carbon structure begins-incorporated to ensure a finite value of the modulus at zero strain; usually a small value is assumed, e.g. a value between 0.001 and 0.01. Exponent n indicates the rate at which the black carbon breaks down. The hardening (upswing) of the stress-strain curve is governed by K, which shows the finite extensibility of rubber cross-linking network. This model is valid for a strain value within the range of 0.1% to 100%. Most engineering applications of elastomers such as tires and engine mounting devices fall into this range. The strain energy model with fractional exponents is more accurate than Yeoh's equation and Mooney-Rivilin equation for modeling the stress-strain curve of a carbon black-reinforced rubber.

1.4.5 Odgen-Roxburgh Hyperelastic Model

Before Eq. (1.9) was published, Odgen had formulated a constitutive equation for elastomers as follows:

$$\sigma_{ii} = \sum_{i=1}^{N} \left\{ \frac{2G_i}{\alpha_i}\lambda_1^{\alpha i} + \lambda_2^{\alpha i} + \lambda_3^{\alpha i} - 3 + \frac{1}{D_i}(J^{\mathrm{el}} - 1)^{2i} \right\} \qquad (1.12)$$

Again, $D_i(i = 1, 2, \cdots, N)$ are parameters used to describe compressibility. The first one, D_1, can be related to initial bulk modulus K by $D_1 = 2 K^{-1}$, if the initial bulk modulus is given.

1.5　Hyperfoams

Hyperfoams are foams made of elastomers. Foams have low Poisson's ratios. Any material with a Poisson's ratio higher than 4.5 should be modeled using hyperelastic models (such as Mooney-Rivilin's and Yeoh's). For hyperfoams, e.g. polyurethane (PU) foam, a modified Ogden strain energy potential can be applied [Abaqus 6.10] to characterize the material properties, i.e.

$$\sigma_{ii} = \sum_{i=1}^{N} \frac{2G_i}{\alpha_i} \left[\lambda_1^{\alpha i} + \lambda_2^{\alpha i} + \lambda_3^{\alpha i} - 3 + \frac{1 - 2\nu_i}{\nu_i} (J_{el}^{\frac{-\alpha_i}{1-2\nu_i}} - 1) \right] \tag{1.13}$$

where J_{el} is the elastic volume ratio that is part of the total volume ratio J, i.e. 3rd invariant of the stretch tensor; $J = J_{el} J_{th}$, of which J_{th} is the thermal volume ratio. The degree of compressibility is determined by J_{el}, on which the Poisson's ratio ν_i has a great influence. The effect of thermal expansion is not given Eq. (1.10). The shear-modulus coefficients are related to the initial shear modulus G, by

$$G = \sum_{i=1}^{N} G_i \tag{1.14}$$

G_i, α_i, and $\nu_i (i = 1, 2, \cdots, 6)$ are the input data sets for the material model for Abaqus (6 sets most). By default, $\nu_i = 0$, if not known exactly.

1.6　Mullins' Effect-Modified Odgen-Roxburgh Damage Model

Structural properties of elastomers change significantly during the first several times of deformation. The behavior is referred to as the Mullins' effect. The degree of stress softening during the first few loading-unloading cycles depends on the maximum elongation achieved and the carbon content. Where the applied strain reaches another higher level, there is another Mullin's effect. Both the stress softening and residual strain increase with the carbon black content [Harbor et al.]. For most materials the initial loading and subsequent unloading and reloading follow a different path.

In order to capture this stress softening, Ogden and Roxburgh incorporated a damage parameter into the theory of incompressible isotropic elasticity, i.e. Eq. (1.11). The damage parameter controls the unloading response of the material based on the dissipation of energy and the previous point of maximum loading. The strain-energy density function modified with Mullins damage function η of a rubber is

$$W(I_1) \leftarrow \eta W(I_1) \tag{1.15}$$

In order to accommodate the new stress-strain path the damage parameter η is divided into three different working ranges:

(a) Initial loading: $\eta = 1$ (1.15a)

(b) Unloading: $\eta = 1 - \dfrac{1}{r_1} \tan h \left[\dfrac{W(I_{1,\,max}) - W(I_1)}{m_1} \right]$ (1.15b)

(c) Subsequent Reloading: $\eta = 1 - \dfrac{1}{r_2} \tan h \left[\dfrac{W(I_{1,\,max}) - W(I_1)}{m_2} \right]$ (1.15c)

$W(I_1)$ can be any of the Mooney-Rivilin's (with $C_{01} = 0$), Yeoh's, and Davis-De-Thomas' material models for elastomers. $W(I_{1,\,max})$ is the strain energy at the maximum stretch in the loading history. Parameters r_1, r_2, m_1, and m_2 are material properties, which can be derived from curve-fitting of biaxial testing while material constants for damaging parameters accounting for Mullins Effect listed in Table 1.5. Since the primary loading path is governed by a different strain energy function than the unloading path, this concept is referred to as pseudoelasticity.

1.7 Dynamic, Storage, and Loss Moduli

To determine the dynamic mechanical characteristics of elastomers, in most of the documented methods the elastic and storage moduli (or elastic modulus and loss factor) have been used as material properties where these properties are extracted from resonant tests. Dynamic applications of elastomers in automotive engineering such as tires and engine mounting devices utilize the material strain value within the range of -100% and 100%. Mooney-Rivilin's, Yeoh's, and Davis-De-Thoms', and Odgen models work fine in this range. The dynamic modulus of elasticity (Young's modulus) and shear modulus of a rubber are calculated using Mooney's material constants as, respectively

$$E \approx 6(C_{10} + C_{01}) \tag{1.16}$$

and

$$G = \frac{E}{2(1 + \nu)} = \frac{E}{3} \approx 2(C_{10} + C_{01}) \tag{1.17}$$

The stress-strain response for rubber materials exhibits significant inelastic effects. The observed inelastic effects were larger for SBR than NR. Hyperelastic material models do not account for inelastic effects. Inelastic effects are especially important for variable amplitude loading conditions since the peak strains applied to the material significantly affect the resulting stress-strain behavior of the material in rubbers. Loss tangent, also called loss factor, accounting for hysteresis loss is defined as the ratio of loss modulus E'' to storage modulus E' as

$$\tan \delta = \frac{E''}{E'} \tag{1.18}$$

Since the overall Young's modulus is the vector sum of storage modulus and loss modulus,

$$E = (E' + E'')^{\frac{1}{2}} \tag{1.19}$$

Thus for a given Young's modulus E, its associated storage modulus and loss modulus can be calculated according to the following two equations

$$E' = \frac{E}{(1 + \tan^2\delta)^{\frac{1}{2}}} \tag{1.20}$$

and

$$E'' = E \tan \delta \tag{1.21}$$

Complex Poisson's ratio ν may be estimated from the complex Young's modulus E and bulk modulus K based on the theory of elasticity as

$$\nu = 0.5 - \frac{E}{6K} \tag{1.22}$$

For rubbers, a numerical implementation of the above equation shows

$$\nu = 0.5 - \frac{E}{774} \quad (E \text{ in GPa}) \tag{1.23}$$

Note that most rubbers have Young's moduli lower than 10 MPa (0.01 GPa). The equation given above implies that the dynamic bulk modulus of rubber K is similar for most elastomers, i.e. very incompressible. It changes very slowly with temperature and frequency.

All of the hyperelastic material models (Arruda-Boyce, Blatz-Ko, Hyperfoam, Mooney-Rivilin, Neo-Hookean, Ogden, Van der Waals, Yeoh) can be used in conjunction with a finite strain viscoelastic model to account for the damping effect.

1.8   Viscoelastic and Viscoelastic Theories

Having been implemnted in most commercial FEA codes (Abaqus, Marc, Nastran, and Ansys), Prony series of N sets of Maxwell models is a simple but competent model to represent the viscoelastic model of elastomers using a normalized relaxation function,

$$E(t) = E_0 - \sum_{i=1}^{N} E_i \left[1 - \exp\left(\frac{-t}{\tau_i} \right) \right] \tag{1.24}$$

where

$E(t)$: Relaxation modulus, a function of time;

E_0: Initial modulus of elasticity;

E_i: Instantaneous modulus of elasticity in each stage;

τ_i: Time constant.

Dynamic properties of both rubber gum and filled rubber with filler content less than a critical amount are linear viscoelastic, while those of filled rubbers with filler content exceeding the critical amount are strongly strain-and strain-rate dependent, as well as nonlinear viscoplastic. Thus, viscoelastic models are of limited use for the purpose of rubber design, since inelastic permanent set does appear in stressed rubbers. Visco-elasto-plastic models for rubbers are in need as virtual product validation is in demand.

1.9 Specific Heat

It was reported [Furukawa and Reilly] [Wood and Bekkedahl] that the specific heat of rubbers in reference to 25 ℃ can be represented by, consistently,

$$C_p = 1947 + 4.37 (T - 25) + 0.00224 (T - 25)^2 \tag{1.25}$$

where C_p is the specific heat in joule/(kg · ℃) and T is the temperature in degrees Celsius.

1.10 Rubber Recycle

Rubber is a thermoset material and as such is generally considered difficult to recycle; therefore there is a demand for the development of rubber recycling technology to protect the environment and conserve resources. Some technologies exist to recycle vulcanized rubbers, but none of these has high enough productivity to produce reclaimed rubber. Re-vulcanized rubber does not have the same properties as virgin rubber materials.

1.11 Tires, Belts, Hoses, Seals, and Vibration Isolators

Top six elastomeric applications in the automotive industries are tires, timing belts, hoses, seals, bushings, and vibration isolators. They are mostly rubber composites.

References

ALI M, et al, 2010. Continuum Damage Mechanics Modeling for Fatigue Life of Elastomeric Materials[J]. International Journal of Structural Integrity, 1(1):63-72.

BANKS H T, et al, 2008. Modeling of Nonlinear Hysteresis in Elastomers under Uniaxial Tension[J]. Journal of Intelligent Materials and Structures, 10(2):116-134.

BARNETT C E, 1934. Thermal Properties of Rubber Compounds I. Thermal Conductivity of Rubber and Rubber Compounding Materials[J]. Industrial & Engineering Chemistry, 26(3):303-306.

BECHIR H, CHEVALIER L, CHAOUCHE M, et al, 2006. Hyperelastic Constitutive Model for Rubber-Like Materials Based on the First Seth Strain Measures Invariant[J]. European Journal of Mechanics, A, Solids, 25:110-124.

BISCHOFF J, et al, 2002. Finite Element Simulations of Orthotropic Hyperelasticity[J]. Finite Elements in Analysis and Design, 38(10):983-998.

BLOW C M, HEPBURN C, 1982. Rubber Technology and Manufacture[M]. 2nd edition. Butterworth Scientific, Boston, MA, USA.

CHIANG Y J, SHIH C D, LIN C C, et al, 2004. Examination of Tire Rubber Cure by Weibull Distribution Functions[J]. International Journal of Materials and Product Technology, 20(1-3):210-219.

DAVIES C, et al, 1994. Characterization of the Behavior of Rubber for Engineering Design Purposes (1) Stress and Strain Relations[J]. Rubber Chemistry and Technology, 67(4):716-728.

DORFMANN A, OGDEN R W, 2004. A Pseudo-Elastic Model for the Mullins Effect in Filled Rubber[J]. International Journal of Solids and Structures, 41:1855-1878.

DROBNY J G, 2006. Fluoropolymers in Automotive Applications[J]. Polymer Science and Engineering, 18(2):117-121.

EIRICH F R, CORAN A Y, 1994. Science and Technology of Rubber[M]. Academic Press, New York, NY, USA.

GENT A N, 1992. Engineering with Rubber[M]. Oxford University Press, New York, NY, USA.

GENT A N, 2012. A New Constitutive Relation for Rubber[J]. Rubber Chemistry and Technology, 69(1):59-61.

GUGLIELMOTTI A, et al, 2009. Production of Rubber Pads by Tire Recycling[J]. International Journal of Materials Engineering Innovation, 1(1):91-106.

HARTMANN S, NEFF P, 2003. Polyconvexity of Generalized Polynomial-type Hyperelastic Strain Functions for Near-Incompressibility[J]. International Journal of Solids and Structures, 40(11):2767-2791.

HOFER P, LION A, 2009. Modeling of Frequency-and Amplitude-Dependent Material Properties of Filler-Reinforced Rubber[J]. J. the Mechanics and Physics of Solids, 57(3):500-520.

HORGAN C O, SACCOMANDI G, 2004. Constitutive Models for Atactic Elastomers[J]. World Scientific:281-294.

JER-RUEY HUANG J R, et al, 2009. Antifouling Properties of Conductive Rubber Coating Used for Fishing Nets[J]. Journal of Marine Science and Technology, 17(3):173-179.

ISSHIKI N, et al, 2010. Preparation and Mechanical Properties of Rubber Composites Reinforced with Carbon Nanohorns[J]. Journal of Nanoscience and Nanotechnology, 10(6):3810-3814.

KARAK N, GUPTA B R, 2000. Effects of Different Ingredients and Cure Parameters on Physical Properties of a Tire Tread Compound[J]. Kautschuk Gummi Kunststoffe, 53(1):30-34.

KIM W I, et al, 2000. Kinetic Characterization of Thermal Degradation Process for Commercial Rubbers[J]. Journal of Industrial and Engineering Chemistry, 6(5):348-355.

KOHL J, et al, 2008. Determining the Viscoelastic Parameters of Thin Elastomer Based Materials Using Continuous Microindentation[J]. Polymer Testing, 27(6):679-682.

KONTOU G S, 2010. Modeling of Nonlinear Viscoelasticity at Large Deformations[J]. Journal of Materials Science, 43(6):2046-2052.

LI J, et al, 2008. A Constitutive Model Dealing with Damage due to Cavity Growth and the Mullins Effect in Rubber-Like Materials under Triaxial Loading[J]. Journal of Mechanics and Physics of Solids, 56(3):953-973.

LIN D C, DIMITRIADIS E K, HORKAY F, 2007. Elasticity of Rubber-Like Materials Measured by SFM Nanoindentation[J]. EXPRESS Polymer Letters, 1(9):576-584.

LION A, KARDELKY C, 2004. The Payne Effect in Finite Viscoelasticity [J]. International Journal of Plasticity, 20(7):1313-1345.

MARK J E, BURAK E, EIRICH F, 2005. The Science and Technology of Rubber[M]. 3rd edition, Elsevier, New York, NY, USA.

MARS W, FATEMI A, 2002. A Literature Survey on Fatigue Analysis Approaches for Rubber[J]. International Journal of Fatigue, 24(9):949-961.

MAZICK K A, SAMUS M A, 1990. Role of Entanglement Couplings in Threshold Fracture of a Rubber Network [J]. Macromolecules, 23(9):2478-2483.

MERCKEL Y, et al, 2011. Characterization of the Mullins Effect of Carbon-Black Filled Rubbers[J]. Rubber Chemistry and Technology, 84(3):402-414.

MOON S, et al, 2017. Study on the Determination of Fatigue Damage Parameter for Rubber Component under Multi-Axial Loading[J]. Elastomers and Composites, 47:194-200.

MOONEY M, 1940. A Theory of Large Elastic Deformation[J]. Journal of Applied Physics, 11(9):582-592.

MUHR A H, 2005. Modeling the Stress-Strain Behavior of Rubber[J]. Rubber Chemistry and Technology, 78 (3):391-425.

MULLINS S L, 2012. Softening of Rubber by Deformation[J]. Rubber Chemistry and Technology, 42(1):339-362.

OGDEN R W, ROXBURGH D G, 1999. A Pseudo-Elastic Model for the Mullins Effect in Filled Rubber[J]. Proceedings of the Royal Society London, Ser. A, 455:2861-2877.

OGDEN R W, 1972. Large Deformation Isotropic Elasticity -On the Correlation of Theory and Experiment for Incompressible Rubberlike Solids[J]. Proceedings of the Royal Society London. Series A, Mathematical and Physical Sciences, 326(1567):565-584.

OTSUKA S, et al, 2000. Development of Automotive Rubber Parts with New Recycling Technology[J]. SAE Technical Paper 2000-01-0015.

PUCCI E, SACCOMANDI G, 2002. A Note on the Gent Model for Rubber-like Materials [J]. Rubber Chemistry and Technology, 75:839-851.

QI H J, BOYCE M C, 2004. Constitutive Model for Stretch Induced-Softening of the Stress-Stretch Behavior of Elastomeric Materials[J]. J. of Mech. Phys. Solids, 52(10):2187-2205.

RIVILIN R S, THOMAS A G, 1953. Rupture of Rubber, I: Characteristic Energy for Tearing[J]. Journal of Polymer Science, 10(3):291-318.

RIVILIN R S, SAUNDERS D W, 1951. Large Elastic Deformation of Isotropic Materials, VII: Experiments on the Deformation of Rubber[J]. Philosophical Transactions, A243:251-288.

RIVLIN R S, 1948. Large elastic deformations of isotropic materials, IV. Further developments of the general theory[J]. Philosophical Transactions, A241:379-397.

SASSO M, et al, 2008. Characterization of Hyperelastic Rubber-like Materials by Biaxial and Uniaxial Stretching Tests Based on Optical Methods[J]. Polymer Testing, 27:995-1004.

SHUMSKAYA A G, et al, 1975. Temperature Dependence of Elastic Constants of Rubbers [J]. Journal of Polymer Science, Polymer Symposia, 53(1):219-230.

SMITH T L, 1964. Ultimate Tensile Properties of Elastomers, II. Comparison of Failure Envelopes for Unfilled Vulcanizates[J]. Journal of Applied Physics, 35:27-36.

SWANSON S R, 1985. A Constitutive Model for High Elongation Elastic Materials[J]. Journal of Engineering Materials and Technology, 107:110-114.

THWARDOWSKI T, GAYLORD R J, 1989. The Localization Model of Rubber Elasticity and the Stress-strain Behavior of a Network Formed by Cross-linking Deformed Melt, II-Equibiaxial and Pure Shear[J]. Polymer

Bulletin, 21:393-400.

TRELOAR L R G, 1975. Physics of Rubber Elasticity[M]. Claredon Press, Oxford, UK.

TURATSINZE A, GARROS M, 2008. On the Modulus of Elasticity and Strain Capacity of Self-compacting Concrete Incorporating Rubber Aggregates[J]. Resources, Conservation and Recycling, 52:1209-1215.

VAN KREVELEN D W, 1990. Properties of Polymers[M]. Elsevier, New York, NY, USA.

WOOD L, BEKKEDAHL N, 1968. Specific Heat of Natural Rubber and Other Elastomers above the Glass Transition Temperature[J]. Journal of Polymer Science, Part B: Polymer Letters, 5(2):169-175.

YEOH O H, FLEMING P H, 1997. A New Attempt to Reconcile the Statistical and Phenomenological Theories of Rubber Elasticity[J]. Journal of Polymer Science, B: Polymer Physics, 35:1919-1931.

YEOH O H, 1990. Characterization of Elastic Properties of Carbon-Black-Filled Rubber[J]. Rubber Chemistry and Technology, 63:92-805.

YEOH O H, 1993. Some Forms of the Strain Energy Function for Rubber[J]. Rubber Chemistry and Technology, 66(5):754-771.

ZHANG J, et al, 1998. Constitutive Modeling of Polymeric Foam Material Subjected to Dynamic Crash loading[J]. International Journal of Impact Engineering, 21(5):369-386.

Table 1.1 Mechanical Properties of Elastomers (A: Excellent, D: Poor)

Material	(ASTM D 1418/ISO DIN 1629)	Tensile	Set	Creep	Wear	Impact	Tear	Air	Fatigue
ACM	(Polyacrylate rubber)	C	B	B	C	B	D	—	—
AEM	(Ethylene Acrylic)	C	C	B	B	B	B	A	—
AU	(Polyester urethane)	A	D	D	A	B	A	—	—
BR	(Butadiene rubber)	B	B	B	A	A	B	—	B
CO	(Epichlorohydrin)	B	B	C	B	B	A	—	—
CR	(Chloroprene rubber or Neoprene)	B	B	B	B	B	B	C	—
CSM	(Chlorosulfonated Polyethylene)	C	C	A	D	B	—	—	—
ECO	(Ethylene oxide epichlorohydrin)	A	A	B	A	B	B	—	—
EPDM	(Ethylene propylene diene, sulfur)	B	C	B	B	B	C	—	—
EPDM	(Ethylene propylene diene, peroxide)	B	A	A	B	B	C	—	—
EU	(Polyether urethane)	A	D	B	A	B	A	—	—

continued

Material	(ASTM D 1418/ISO DIN 1629)	Tensile	Set	Creep	Wear	Impact	Tear	Air	Fatigue
FFKM/ FFPM	(Perfluoroelastomers)	B	B	C	—	—	—	—	—
FKM/ FPM	(Fluoroelastomers)	B	A	A	B	D	B	—	—
FVMQ	(Fluorosilicone rubber)	D	C	B	D	D	D	—	—
HNBR	(Hydrogenated acrylonitrile-butadiene)	A	A	A	A	B	B	—	—
IIR	(Butyl rubber)	B	B	B	C	D	B	A	A
IR	(Isoprene rubber)	A	—	—	A	B	A	—	C
NBR	(Acrylonitrile-butadiene; Nitrile)	B	B	B	B	B	B	B	—
NR	(Natural rubber)	A	A	A	A	A	A	D	C
SBR	(Styrene-butadiene rubber)	B	B	B	B	B	C	—	C
VMQ	(Silicone rubber)	D	B	A	B	B	C	—	—

Notes: Tensile = Tensile strength;

Set = Compression set-permanent deformation due to compression (ASTM D 395);

Creep = Resistance to creep;

Wear = Resistance to abrasion and wear;

Impact = Impact resilience/rebound;

Tear = Tear strength;

Air = Air impermeability;

Fatigue = Fatigue strength.

Table 1.2　Environmental Conditions for Elastomers (A: Excellent, B, C, D, E: Poor)

Material	(ASTM D 1418/ISO DIN 1629)	T/℃	Oil	Fuel	Water /℃	Aging	O_3	Weather
ACM	(Polyacrylate rubber)	−4~120	A	C	—	A	B	A
AEM	(Ethylene Acrylic)	−35~135	B	C	100	B	A	A
AU	(Polyester urethane)	−40~100	B	C	50	B	A	A
BR	(Butadiene rubber)	−40~80	D	D	—	C	E	D
CO	(Epichlorohydrin)	−15~125	A	B	—	B	A	B
CR	(Chloroprene rubber or Neoprene)	−40~100	C	C	80	B	A	B
CSM	(Chlorosulfonated Polyethylene)	−20~120	B	D	—	B	A	A

continued

Material	(ASTM D 1418/ISO DIN 1629)	$T/℃$	Oil	Fuel	Water /℃	Aging	O_3	Weather
ECO	(Ethylene oxide epichlorohydrin)	−35~125	A	B	—	A	A	B
EPDM	(Ethylene propylene diene, sulfur)	−50~150	E	E	130	B	A	A
EPDM	(Ethylene propylene diene, peroxide)	−50~150	E	E	150	B	A	A
EU	(Polyether urethane)	−40~100	B	C	50	B	A	A
FFKM/ FFPM	(Perfluoroelastomers)	−15~260	A	A	No water	A	A	A
FKM/FPM	(Fluoroelastomers)	−20~200	A	B	80	A	A	A
FVMQ	(Fluorosilicone rubber)	−55~175	B	B	100	A	A	A
HNBR	(Hydrogenated acrylonitrile-butadiene)	−30~150	A	C	100	B	A	A
IIR	(Butyl rubber)	−40~120	E	D	—	A	A	A
IR	(Isoprene rubber)	−30~80	E	D	—	C	D	C
NBR	(Acrylonitrile-butadiene; Nitrile)	−30~120	A	C	80	B	C	D
NR	(Natural rubber)	−30~70	E	D	—	C	D	C
SBR	(Styrene-butadiene rubber)	−40~105	E	D	—	B	E	D
VMQ	(Silicone rubber)	−50~230	C	D	100	A	A	A

Notes: Temperature (℃) = Recommended range of proper working temperature;

Oil = Resistance to oil and grease; A is the best and E is not qualified;

Fuel = Resistance to fuel; A is the best and E is not qualified;

Water = Resistance to hot water;

Aging = Chemical networks (main chains & crosslinking) change during heat aging;

O_3 = Ozone resistance;

Weather = Resistance to weather.

Table 1.3 Shore-A Hardness and Related Modulus of Elasticity (Young's Modulus, E) and Mooney's Material Constants (C_{10} and C_{01}) of Rubber

Shore-A Hardness	E/MPa	C_{10}/MPa	C_{01}/MPa
35	1.22	0.162	0.041
36	1.22	0.163	0.041
37	1.24	0.165	0.041
38	1.26	0.168	0.042
39	1.31	0.174	0.044

continued

Shore-A Hardness	E/MPa	C_{10}/MPa	C_{01}/MPa
40	1.36	0.181	0.045
41	1.42	0.189	0.047
42	1.49	0.198	0.050
43	1.57	0.209	0.052
44	1.65	0.220	0.055
45	1.74	0.232	0.058
46	1.84	0.245	0.061
47	1.94	0.259	0.065
48	2.05	0.273	0.068
49	2.15	0.287	0.072
50	2.27	0.302	0.076
51	2.38	0.317	0.079
52	2.50	0.333	0.083
53	2.62	0.349	0.087
54	2.74	0.366	0.091
55	2.87	0.382	0.096
56	3.00	0.400	0.100
57	3.13	0.417	0.104
58	3.27	0.436	0.109
59	3.41	0.454	0.114
60	3.56	0.474	0.118
61	3.71	0.494	0.124
62	3.87	0.516	0.129
63	4.03	0.538	0.135
64	4.21	0.561	0.140
65	4.40	0.586	0.147
66	4.59	0.612	0.153
67	4.80	0.640	0.160

continued

Shore-A Hardness	E/MPa	C_{10}/MPa	C_{01}/MPa
68	5.03	0.670	0.168
69	5.26	0.702	0.175
70	5.52	0.736	0.184

Notes: C_{10} & C_{01} (MPa): $W = C_{10}(I_1 - 3) + C_{01}(I_2 - 3)$;

E (MPa) $\approx 0.0788\,A - 0.003065\,A^2 + 0.00004895\,A^3$, where A = Shore-A hardness;

E (MPa) $\approx 6\,(C_{10} + C_{01})$ for incompressible rubber;

G (MPa) $= E/3$ (Young's Modulus) for incompressible rubber;

Data given above are for reference only;

To measure is to have actual data.

Table 1.4　Mooney's Material Constants for Different Rubbers

Elastomer	C_{10}, Nominal	Range	C_{01}, Nominal	Range
ACM (Polyacrylate)	1.2	0.6~1.6	1.8	0.9~4.8
BR	2.6	2.1~3.2	1.5	1.4~1.6
EPR/EPDM	2.6	2.1~3.1	2.5	2.2~2.9
EPDM/30pphr CB	0.493	—	0.123	—
EU/AU	3	2.4~3.4	2	1.8~2.2
NR	2.0	0.9~3.8	1.5	0.9~2.0
SBR	1.8	0.8~2.8	1.1	1.0~1.2
Silicone Rubber	0.75	0.3~1.2	0.75	0.3~1.1

Notes: C_{10}, C_{01}, C_{20}, C_{30} (MPa) $= W = C_{10}(I_1 - 3) + C_{01}(I_2 - 3) + C_{20}(I_1 - 3)^2 + C_{30}(I_1 - 3)^3$;

$C_{01} = C_{20} = C_{30} = 0$, and $C_{10} \neq 0$: Neo-Hookean's model;

$C_{20} = C_{30} = 0$, $C_{10} \neq 0$, and $C_{02} \neq 0$: Mooney's model;

$C_{01} = 0$, $C_{10} \neq 0$, $C_{20} \neq 0$, and $C_{30} \neq 0$: Yeoh's model;

E (MPa) $= E = 6\,(C_{10} + C_{01})$, equivalent Young's modulus.

Table 1.5　Material Constants for Damaging Parameters Accounting for Mullins Effect

Elastomer	T/℃	E/MPa	r_{OR}	m/MPa	β
NR (60 pphr N650)	23	4.8	2.25	0.5	0.1
SBR (75 pphr N234)	23	4.8	1.65	1.05	0

Notes: Modulus of elasticity, E(MPa) $\approx 6\,(C_{10} + C_{01})$ for incompressible rubber.

Chapter 2

Thermoplastics

2.1　Introduction

Plastics are polymers with long chains, which are not usually cross-linked. Individual molecules that make up a plastic are large and have an extended chain-like shape that results in an entangled structure. The relatively high levels of elongation that most polymers exhibit without breaking are due in large part to chain entanglement. On the other hand entanglement restricts the degree of freedom required at a molecular level to organize in crystals. Consequently, no polymer under normal processing conditions is fully crystalline, and some polymers do not crystallize to any significant degree. Plastics are further classified into two categories: thermoplastics and thermoset plastics. Thermoplastics can be heated and cooled without changing chemical structures and are thus environmentally friendly (Table 2.1). Thermoset resins are hardened via chemical reactions during curing.

In each plastic family, individual plastics vary in their fillers, softeners, processing aids, curing agents, accelerators, and other additives. Plastics and fiber-reinforced plastics have been successfully used for replacing metallic parts in order to reduce the product weight and cost. They are often supplied as granules and heated to permit fabrication by inexpensive methods such as molding or extrusion. Mechanical properties of plastics depend on the working temperature, strain, and strain rate. In order to satisfy functional, aesthetic, and economic design requirements of a plastic product, a specification must be addressed to embrace the following conditions [Du Pont]:

(a) Material brand name and grade, and generic name, e.g. Zytel 101, PA6,6 or 66 nylon;
(b) Surface finish;
(c) Parting line location desired;
(d) Flash limitations;
(e) Permissible gating and weld line areas;
(f) Locations where voids are intolerable;
(g) Allowable warpage;
(h) Tolerances;
(i) Color;
(j) Decorating considerations;
(k) Performance considerations.

A schematic softening of thermoplastic material based on its tensile modulus is shown in Fig. 2.1. There are four stages of material transformations as the working temperature arises: (a) glassy, (b) leathery, (c) rubbery, and (d) melt (viscous flow). Key critical temperatures are defined herein in this section.

2.1.1　Glass Transition Point (T_g)

Glass transition point (T_g) is the temperature point that when reached the material transforms from rigid glass-like state to rubbery state subject to reversible breakage of Van der Waals bonds between polymer molecular chains. The effect of T_g on the elastic modulus of a semicrystalline or amorphous polymer can be reduced by adding fillers and reinforcements. However, the transition temperatures do not change. The T_g is generally the upper limit for amorphous polymers to operate in an application environment.

(a) DMA (Dynamic Mechanical Analysis) is a method to measure mechanical stiffness physically. As heat is applied, when a rapid decrease in modulus properties occurs, the T_g has been reached.

(b) DSC (Differential Scanning Calorimetry) is the other method. This is a chemical analysis that detects energy absorption. A polymer requires a certain amount of energy to transition states, much like water requires a certain temperature to transition to steam.

When designing a structure with plastics or plastic composites, it is important to pay special attention to the situation, in which the T_g is lower than the temperature the material might ever be exposed to.

2.1.2　Melting Point (T_m)

Melting point (T_m) is the temperature, at which the material goes from solid to liquid. The T_m is generally the upper limit for semi-crystalline polymers to operate in an application environment.

2.1.3　Decomposition Temperature

Decomposition temperature is the temperature, at which a polymer irreversibly undergoes physical and chemical degradation, such as thermal destruction of cross-links, resulting in weight loss of material.

2.1.4　Deflection Temperature

Deflection temperature is the temperature, at which a polymer undergoes excessive unacceptable physical deformations under a certain amount of load. For example, The deflection temperature of PP (Polypropylene; $T_m = 170\ ℃$) is 100 ℃ under a 0.46 MPa load or 70 ℃ under a 1.8 MPa load, respectively, while the deflection temperature of PP/ 30 GF (Polypropylene reinforced with 30% of glass fibers by weight) is 170 ℃ under a 0.46 MPa load or 160 ℃ under a 1.8 MPa load, respectively.

2.2　Characteristics of Plastics

Plastics and fiber-reinforced plastics are extensively used in automotive applications. Exterior vehicle parts that have been replaced by plastic materials include front-end modules, beams and brackets, trunk lids, deck lids, body panels and floor panels. More plastics are being used in air-bag containers, pedals and seat components. Plastics are applied to the powertrain in the air inlet manifolds, air ducts and resonators, chain tensioners and belt pulleys, oil pans and sumps, cylinder head covers, and mechanical torsion damper components. Some gears and pump components are also becoming more plastics-friendly. An assembly with multiple metallic components may be replaced by a single plastic part.

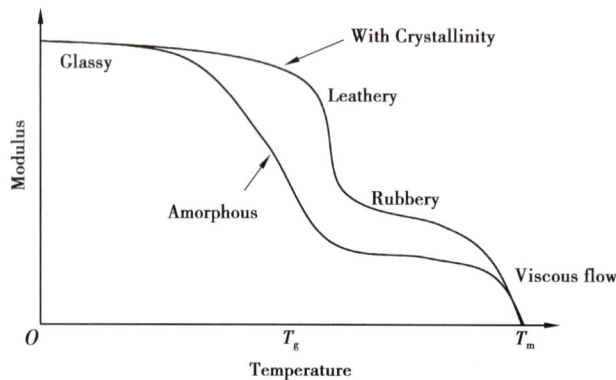

Fig. 2.1　Thermoplastic Tensile Modulus as a Function of Temperature

Plastics with bulkier molecular shapes are called amorphous such as PMMA, PS, ABS, and PEI. Plastics with spaghetti-like stringed molecular shapes are crystalline. Nevertheless thermoplastics usually exhibit semi-crystalline such as PP, PE, PA, PBT, PET, POM, PPS, PEEK, and LCP. Typical transformation of amorphous material as a function of temperature is given as the lower curve in Fig. 2.1, while with crystallinity a plastic can extend its glassy period as the given upper curve in Fig. 2.1. The tensile strength behaves in a similar manner. The coefficient of linear thermal expansion depends on the material's operating temperature, mold flow direction, reinforcement by fibers or particles, and thermal cycles. The glass transition temperature of plastic corresponds to the expansion of free volume, allowing greater chain mobility above this transition point. The coefficient of linear thermal expansion grows significantly after its glass transition point. A schematic thermal expansion curve of a typical thermoplastic is depicted in Fig. 2.2. Of course the coefficient of linear thermal expansion is also a function of mold flow as molded. It is low along the flow direction and high in the transverse direction, respectively.

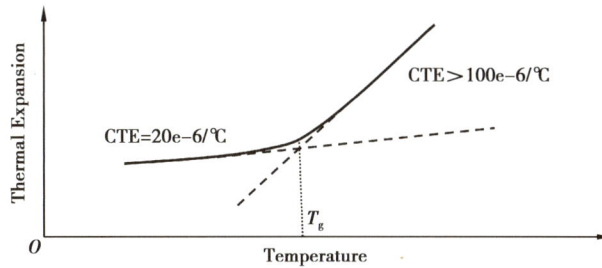

Fig. 2.2   Coefficient of Linear Thermal Expansion（CTE）of a Typical Plastic as a Function of Temperature

The surface of a molded part where flow fronts join during filling is called weld surface（or weld lines）or knit surface（knit lines）. A weld surface causes cosmetic flaws and reduction in mechanical performance, because few polymer chains cross the boundary of the weld surface as molded. Resulting notches（voids）on the weld surface also act as stress risers（stress concentration）, which further reducing its strength in bending, pull, and impact［Wu and Liang］. There are three ways to make an injection mold: chunk of metal, laminate mold, and subtractive pinned mold.

2.3   Molding of Plastics

The traditional mold is made from a chunk of metal. Thermal analyses and moldflow patterns of molding are conducted to locate the hot spots in the design stage. Gun-drilled cooling lines are then created to conform to the part geometry and ejectors are positioned. The following must be considered in the molding process:

（a）***Uniform Thin Walls***: Non-uniform wall thickness can cause warpage and create dimensional management problems. When enhancement in structural stiffness and strength is required, it is more economical to use ribs rather than to increase the wall thickness. However, sink marks may show up in the ribbing area. If aesthetics are of concern, then hide the sink mark by some decorating design, e.g. opposing ribs and texture surfaces. Coring is one way to create a uniform wall. If uniform wall thickness is impossible, a gradual transition from one thickness to the other one should be used ［DuPont］, as abrupt changes tend to increase the stress level. Sharp Corners should be rounded, as illustrated in Fig. 7.2.2. Finally, one should use the minimum wall thickness as long as it provides satisfactory structural performance. Thin wall sections solidify and cool down faster than thick ones. A schematic chart for cycle cost factor versus wall thickness is illustrated in Fig. 7.2.2.

（b）***Draft Angles and Knock-Out Pins/Rings/Plates***: Draft angles are designed to provide the smooth ejection of parts from a mold. The angle required for ejection depends mainly on the depth of draw and next on the roughness of interfacial surfaces between the part and the mold. Nominal draft angles for smooth luster finish are listed in Table 7.2.1 [DuPont]. Sometimes pins, rings, or plates can be used to knock out parts from the mold. Preventive actions, e.g. a larger pinning surface, are taken to avoid damages such as puncturing, distorting, or marking.

(c) **Fillets and Radii**: Smooth fillets or corners (with larger radii) provide streamlined mold flow path and result in easier ejection of parts. In general the minimum recommended radius is 0.5 mm. On the other consideration, usually a fillet radius should exceed one-half the wall thickness of the part in order to reduce the stress concentration.

(d) **Bosses**: Bosses are used for mounting purpose or to serve as reinforcement around holes. Contrasts of good to bad good design are shown in Fig. 7.2.3 [DuPont]. Bosses may serve as a suitable fastening device for self-tapping bolts, but they can cause sink marks on the surface.

(e) **Ribbing**: Ribs can be added to a part to improve the rigidity and strength for the purpose of structural reinforcement. Proper usage can reduce warpage.

(f) **Holes and Coring**: Holes can be produced in the molded part by inserting core pins in the mold cavity. Through holes are easier than blind holes due to the possible supports on both ends. Some design guidelines are given as follows: The depth of a blind hole should be no more than twice the core pin diameter. The bottom thickness of the blind hole should be no less than 1/6 the hole diameter. Core pins can be polished and draft can be added to improve the ejection of core pins.

(g) **Threads**: In consideration of stress and fastening forces, at least three threads must be provided to hold the fasteners and more than five threads are unnecessary [Chiang and Barber]. High thermal-stress level can be created due to the difference in the coefficients of thermal expansion between metallic fasteners and plastic bosses. For example, the coefficients of thermal expansion are 12×10^{-6} and 60×10^{-6} for steel and nylon 66, respectively. This thermal stress would result in creep or stress-relaxation of the plastic part in the long run. If the plastic has to be external to the metal, a back-up sleeve could reduce the creep.

(h) **Undercuts**: Undercuts are shaped ① using split cavity molds, ② using collapsible cores, ③ using separate core pins (for internal undercuts only), or ④ stripping the part from the mold (for small undercuts only). Finite element methods can be employed to estimate the potential damage during stripping, if necessary.

(i) **Mold-in Insert**: When bosses or ribs are not strong enough, mold-in insert could be the next resource for the structural rigidity, especially for threaded areas. A mold-in metal insert may destroy the plastic part due to the shrinkage of plastic and thermal stresses induced by non-uniform temperature variation on the insert surface. Inserts are often hard to align in the plastic melt and usually prolong the curing cycle.

Recently two innovative methods for making molds have been developed: laminate tooling and subtractive pin tooling. As to laminate tooling, CAD software slices the mold assembly into many layers in the virtual world. In the physical world, stainless steel (300 or 400 series) or aluminum (6061 T6) is then cut and punched for details of each mold slice. These metal sheets, as layered, are pressed and bonded together to form an approximating mold by laser beams. Fine finish of cavities, positioning of ejectors, flooding cooling channels, and additional required features are then added on through various machine processes.

In contrast to laminate mold, subtractive pinned mold is built using a grid of rectangular "pins" mounted on threaded rods. The height of each pin is adjusted to form an almost net-shape surface for part cavity. The pins are clamped by bolsters to take the cavity shape and then the final finish of the cavity is completed using milling equipment. Composites manufacturing, super-plastic forming, vacuum forming, and pattern making have been successfully realized using subtractive pinned mold.

2.3.1   Injection Molding

Injection molding is the most economical way to produce precise parts with complex shapes of small or medium sizes on a mass production scale. Thermoplastics, thermoset plastics, elastomers, and some metals can be injection molded.

2.3.2   Compression Molding

Compression molding is mostly used to make large flat and moderately curved parts such as hoods, fenders, scoops, spoilers, lift gates, and other automotive body parts. Bulk molding compound (BMC) or sheet molding compound (SMC), are conformed to the mold form by the applied pressure and heated until the curing reaction occurs. SMC feed material is usually cut to conform to the surface area of the mold. The mold is then cooled and the part removed.

2.4   Automotive Plastics

Thermoplastic molding compounds are used everywhere in every-day life and provide many unique design features to today's design engineers. More and more plastics are used for making vehicle parts. As of year 2001, the plastics market shares of automotive applications based on the weight percentage are shown in Fig. 2.3 and listed as follows: polypropylene (PP), polyurethane (PU), acrylonitrile-butadiene-styrenes (ABS), polyvinyl chlorides (PVC), polyester (PBT and PET), polyethylene (PE), polyamides (PA; nylon), and polycarbonate (PC). They are thermoplastic. Mechanical properties of these plastics without any fiber-reinforcement or special treatment are listed in Table 2.1. Statistically speaking, all the data should be a range for each parameter. Nevertheless a single number is given here for each parameter as an input for analyses based on a traditional nominal scale.

Engineering plastics such as fiber-reinforced PPS, PPA, and PEI are formulated for use in high temperature environments. Resins such as PEEK, LCP, and PAI are also capable of withstanding extremely high temperatures. These engineering plastics also meet stringent requirements of outgassing and flammability. The tensile modulus of elasticity and strength are functions of strain, strain rate, and temperature. Both increase at a higher loading speed. Plastics exhibit non-linear elastoplastic deformation. Usually, there is no linear portion to the initial stress-strain curve. Instead, the tangent modulus is seen to steadily decrease monotonically with increasing strain all the way to the yield point. Starting from the yield point, the plastic begins to take on irrecoverable plastic strain. The yield point may be identified using the recovery curves obtained with varying loads [Quinsen and Perez].

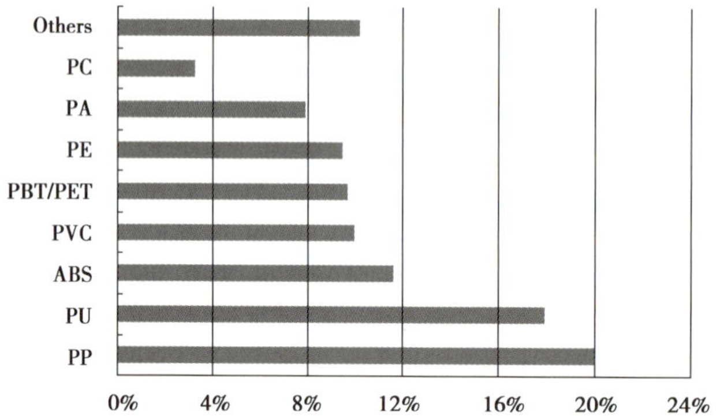

Fig.2.3　Automotive Application of Thermoplastics in Order of Weight Percentage

2.5　Directional Fiber-Reinforced Plastics

Fiber-reinforcement in plastics is able to improve most mechanical properties of plastics, e.g. modulus of elasticity, dimensional stability, hydrolytic stability, and fatigue resistance, by a factor of two or more. Directional fibers-reinforced plastics are used for strengthening structural performance. The fiber reinforces the plastics directionally. Popular fibers include glass, carbon/graphite, glass, Kevlar, and boron. Material properties of commonly used fibers are given in Tables 2.1. Material properties of fibers may be isotropic (e.g. E-glass) or orthotropic (e.g. Kevlar).

Glass-fiber reinforced plastics (GFRP) are inexpensive for automotive structural applications, while carbon-fiber reinforced plastics (CFRP) meets the high-rigidity and low-weight requirement at a higher cost. As glass fibers are transparent to radio frequency radiation, they may be used for radar antennas. Carbon fibers can cause galvanic corrosion when used adjacent to metals.

2.6   Random Fiber-Reinforced Plastics

Random fibers-reinforced plastics are used for general structural applications. It consists of discontinuous fibers. Fibers are directed as the mold flow pattern dictates. Fibers used for random reinforcement are short, ranging from 0.75 mm to 1.5 mm. Longer discontinuous fibers (ranging from 1.5 mm to 10 mm) are hard to mold, but may make the composite stronger if the glass content is not too high. Unlike a unidirectional fiber-reinforced plastic whose tensile strength shows a monotonic increase with increasing fiber content, the tensile strength of a random fibers-reinforced plastic reaches its maximum value at a certain level of fiber content and then decreases. Similarly the tensile modulus of a random-fibers-reinforced plastic reaches its maximum value at another certain level of fiber content and then decreases. In general, the fiber content for maximum tensile modulus is not the same as that for maximum tensile strength. Higher volume of voids and poor bonding between fibers and matrix are due to the cause. The fiber volume fraction is generally less than 40%, as limited by mass-production manufacturing processes.

2.7   Lubricants

Some thermoplastics such as nylon, acetal, and PTFE (polytetrafluoroethylene) are inherently lubricious. PTFE, silicon fluids, and graphite powder, and MoS_2 (molybdenum disulfide) are the primary lubricants being used for internally lubricated composites. PTFE has the lowest coefficient of friction of all plastics.

2.8   Nano-composites

Nano-composites consist of polymers reinforced by nanometer-scale particles dispersed throughout. A nano-composite can be easily extruded or molded to near-final shape and provide strength and rigidity approaching metallic or fibrous composite parts. Benefits include light weight, better corrosion resistance, integral parts with complex geometries, and recyclability.

2.9   Cellulosics

Cellulosics are a family of tough and hard thermoplastic materials, including the following five plastics: cellulose acetate, cellulose nitrate, propionate, acetate butyrate, and ethyl cellulose.

References

ABOT J L, et al, 2004. In-plane Mechanical, Thermal, and Viscoelastic Properties of a Satin Fabric/Epoxy Composite[J]. Composites Science and Technology, 64:263-268.

BERGER R C, STOCKSTILL R L, 1995. Finite Element Method for High-Velocity Channels[J]. Journal of Hydraulic Engineering, 121(10):710-716.

BOCIAGA E, JARUGA T, 2007. Experimental Investigation of Polymer Flow in Injection Mold[J]. Archives of Material Science and Engineering, 28(3):165-172.

CARDOZO D, 2008. Three Models of the 3D Filling Simulation for Injection Molding: A Brief Review[J]. Journal of Reinforced Plastics and Composites, 27(18):1963-1974.

CHAVKA N G, DAHI J S, 1999. P4: Glass Fibers Preforming Technology for Automotive Applications[J]. SAMPE, May 23-27, 1999, Long Beach, CA, USA.

CHIANG Y J, TANG C, 1995. Accuracy Assessment to Applying 20-Node Solid Elements to Pressurized Composite Shells[J]. Finite Elements in Analysis and Design, 20:219-231.

EDWARDS K L, 1998. Designer's Guide to Engineering Polymer Technology[J]. Materials and Design, 19 (2):57-67.

ERVIN V J, MILES W W, 2003. Approximation of Time-dependent Viscoelastic Fluid Flow[J]. SIAM Journal of Numerical Analysis, 41(2):457-486.

FERGUSON R F, et al, 1998. Determining the Through-thickness Properties of FRP Materials[J]. Composites Science and Technology, 58:1411-1420.

FISCHER G, EYERER P, 2004. Measuring Spatial Orientation of Short Fiber Reinforced Thermoplastics by Image Analysis[J]. Polymer Composites, 9(4):297-304.

FU S Y, LAUKE B, 1996. Effect of Fiber Length and Fiber Orientation Distributions on the Tensile Strength of Short-Fiber-Reinforced Polymers[J]. Composites Science and Technology, 56:1179-1190.

GASTON L, KAMARA A, BELLET M, 2000. An Arbitrary Lagrangian-Eulerian Finite Element Approach to Non-steady State Turbulent Fluid Flow with Application to Mold Filling in Casting[J]. International Journal for Numerical Methods in Fluids, 34(4):341-369.

GATES T S, et al, 1997. Creep and Physical Aging in a Polymeric Composite: Comparison of Tension and Compression[J]. Journal of Composite Materials, 32(24):2478-2505.

GENG T, LI D, ZHOU H, 2006. Three-dimensional Finite Element Method for the Filling Simulation of Injection Molding[J]. Engineering with Computer, 21(4):289-295.

GONG Z, MUJUMDAR A, 1998. Flow and Heat Transfer in Convection-dominated Melting in a Rectangular Cavity Heated from Below[J]. International Journal of Heat and Mass Transfer, 41(17):2573-2580.

GROSS R A, KALRA B, 2002. Biodegradable Polymers for the Environment[J]. Science, 297 (5582):803-807.

HAAGH G, et al, 2001. A 3-D Finite Element Model for Gas-assisted Injection Molding: Simulation and Experiments[J]. Polymer Engineering and Science, 41(3):449-465.

HAN X, et al, 2006. Visualization Analysis of the Filling Behavior of Melt into Microscale V-Groove during Filling Stage of Injection Molding[J]. Polymer Engineering and Science, 46(11):1590-1597.

HERU UTOMO B D, et al, 2007. High Speed Fracture Phenomena in Dyneema Composite [J]. Key Engineering Materials,353-358(Pt1):120-125.

HETU J F, et al, 1998. 3D Finite Element Method for the Simulation of the Filling Stage in Injection Molding [J]. Polymer Engineering and Science, 38(2):223-236.

HINE P J, DUCKETT R A, 2004. Fiber Orientation Structures and Mechanical Properties of Injection Molded Short Glass Fiber Reinforced Ribbed Plates[J]. Polymer Composites, 25(3):237-254.

HSIEH C C, OH K P, 1997. Simulation and Optimization of Assembly Processes Involving Flexible Parts[J]. International Journal of Vehicle Design, 18(5):455-465.

JAWORSKI M J, et al, 2003. Theoretical and Experimental Comparison of the Four Major Types of Mesh Currently Used in CAE Injection Molding Simulation Software[J]. ANTEC Conference:642-646.

KANAWADE D, JANDALI G, KRIDLI G T, et al, 2002. Cost-Benefit Analysis of Thermoplastic Matrix Composites for Structural Automotive Applications[J]. SAE 2002-01-1891.

KIM H C, et al, 1996. Creep Behavior of Long Glass Fiber Reinforced Thermoplastics [J]. Journal of Engineering and Applied Science, 2:2541-2545.

KIM M, PARK J, LEE W, 2003. A New VOF-based Numerical Scheme for the Simulation of Fluid Flow with Free Surface. Part II: Application to the Cavity Filling and Sloshing Problems[J]. International Journal for Numerical Methods in Fluids, 42(7):791-812.

KUO W, FANG J, LIN H, 2003. Failure Behavior of 3D Composites under Transverse Shear[J]. Composites, Part A, 34:561-575.

KURIGER R J, ALAM M K, 2001. Strength Prediction of Partially Aligned Discontinuous Fiber-reinforced Composites[J]. Journal of Material Science, 16(1):226-232.

MSFARLAND A, COLTON J S, 2004. Production and Analysis of Injection Molded Microoptic Components[J]. Polymer Engineering and Science, 44(3):564-580.

LEE C, JONES E, KINGSLAND R, 2003. Poisson's Ratios of Engineering Plastics[J]. Advances in Polymer

Technology, 6(1):85-90.

LOBO H, 2008. Simulating Plastics in Drop and Crash Tests[J]. Machine Design, (11):86-89.

MARGOLIS JAMES M, 2006. Engineering Plastics Handbook[M]. McGraw-Hill, New York, NY, USA.

MCKEEN L W, 2008. The Effect of Temperature and Other Factors on Plastics[M]. 2nd Edition. ChemTech Publishing.

PERKINS L R, LOBO H, 2005. A Novel Technique to Measure Tensile Properties of Plastics at High Strain Rates[M]. SPE ANTEC Proceedings, Boston, MA, USA.

QUINSON R, PEREZ J, 1996. Components of Non-elastic Deformation in Amorphous Glassy Polymers[M]. Journal of Material Science, 31:4387-4394.

QUINSON R, PEREZ J, 1997. Yield Criteria for Amorphous Glassy Polymers[J]. Journal of Material Science, 32(5):1371.

RABIO A, et al, 1992. Influence of the Processing Parameters in Glass Mat Reinforced Thermoplastic (GMT) Stamping[J]. Composites Manufacturing, 3(1):47-52.

REN X J, SILBERSCHMIDT V V, 2008. Numerical Modeling of Low-density Cellular Materials[J]. Computers in Material Science, 43:65-74.

SPOERRE J, ZHANG C, WANG B, et al, 1998. Integrated Product and Process Design for Resin Transfer Molded Parts[J]. Journal of Composite Materials, 32(2):1244-1272.

STOKES V K, NIED H F, 1986. Solid Phase Sheet Forming of Thermoplastics-Part I: Mechanical Behavior of Thermoplastics to Yield[J]. Journal of Engineering Materials and Technology, (108):107.

VANLANDINGHAM M R, et al, 2001. Nanoindentation of Polymers: an Overview [J]. Macromolecular Symposia, 167:15-43.

WANG T, YOUNG W, 2005. Study on Residual Stresses on Thin-walled Injection Molding[J]. European Polymer Journal, 41:2511-2517.

WU C H, et al, 2005. Weldlines in Injection-Molded Parts: A Review, Advances in Polymer Technology[J]. Polymer Engineering and Science, 45(7):1021-1030.

WU LIANG, 2005. Effects of Geometry and Injection Molding Parameters on Weld-line Strength[J]. Polymer Engineering and Science, 45(7):1021-1030.

XIAO X, 2007. Dynamic Tensile Testing of Plastic Materials[J]. Polymer Testing, 27(2):164-178.

YANG B, ZHOU H, LI D, 2007. Numerical Simulation of the Filling Stage for Plastic Injection Molding Based on Perkov-Galerkin Methods [J]. Proceedings of the Institution of Mechanical Engineers, Journal of Engineering Manufacture, 221(10):1573-1577.

ZHAO Z, SHAH J J, 2005. Domain Independent Shell for DFM and Its Application to Sheet Metal Forming and Injection Molding[J]. Computer-Aided Design, 37:881-898.

ZHOU H M, et al, 2004. Modeling and Prediction of Weldline Location and Properties Based on Injection Molding Simulation[J]. International Journal of Materials and Technology, 21(6):526-538.

ZHOU H M, LI D Q, 2003. Further Studies of the Gas Penetration Process in Gas-Assisted Injection Molding [J]. Polymer-Plastics Technology and Engineering, 42(5):911-923.

Table 2.1   Nominal Mechanical Properties of Thermoplastics at the Room Temperature

Material-DAM	ρ	E_T	σ_{uts}	$\tan\delta$	α	$C_{m,24}/\%$	$C_{m,sat}$	T_g	T_m	Phase
ABS	1.06	2.1	44	0.033	74	0.27	—	105	105	A
Cellulose Acetate	1.26	1.63	31.4	—	130	1.7	—	—	—	—
FEP	2.15	0.35	23	—	95	0.01	—	−35	260	—
LCP	1.4~2.0	8~17	53~185	—	0~30	0.03	—	145	282	LCP
PB (Polybutylene)	0.92	0.25	33	—	140	0.03	—	−21	135	SC
PA6	—	—	—	—	—	1.3	—	—	—	—
PA6,6 (Nylon 6,6)	1.11	2.8	83	—	81	1.24	—	57	258	SC
PA6,12 (Nylon 6,12)	1.2	2.0	61	—	90	0.25	—	46	222	SC
PA11	—	—	—	—	—	0.25	—	—	—	—
PAI	1.45	4.8	103	—	28	0.33	—	275	—	A
PAF	2.15	0.55	21	—	150	0.05	—	—	305	—
PBI	1.3	5.86	140	—	23	0.4	—	399	760	A
PBT	1.34	3.1	52	—	60~95	0.08	—	60	223	SC
PC	1.2	2.3	55	0.02	68	0.15	—	150	284	A
PE-LD	0.92	range	11	0.195	160	0.1	—	−110	122	SC
PE-HD	0.95	1.1	32	—	120	0.03	—	−90	135	SC
PE-UHMW	0.94	0.7	17.2	—	72	<0.01	—	−25	144	SC
PEEK	1.30	3.7	100	—	47~108	0.5	—	143	343	SC
PEI	1.27	3.3	105	—	56	0.25	—	215	370	A
PES	1.34	2.7	83	0.026	56	0.30	—	224	360	A
PET	1.37	2.95	62	—	65	0.16	—	73	256	SC
PFA	2.15	0.48	21	—	150	0.02	—	—	305	—
PK	1.24	1.5	55	—	110	0.5	—	15	220	—

continued

Material-DAM	ρ	E_T	σ_{uts}	$\tan \delta$	α	$C_{m,24}/\%$	$C_{m,sat}$	T_g	T_m	Phase
PMMA (Acrylics)	1.17	3.10	60	—	74	0.2	—	95	200	A
POM (Acetal)	1.41	3.0	70	—	106	0.25	—	−15	163	SC
PP	0.91	1.0	32	0.132	91	<0.01	—	−20	165	SC
PPA	1.13	2.2	62	—	93	0.21	—	134	303	SC
PPE	1.08	2.54	57	—	64	0.07	—	215	—	A
PPO (PPE-PA)	1.07	2.48	54	—	60	0.01	—	125	250	A
PPS	1.35	3.4	66	0.055	50	0.02	—	90	288	SC
PS (Solid)	1.05	3.2	41	—	75	0.07	—	95	270	A
PSU (Polysulfone)	1.25	2.5	71	—	56	0.3	—	190	—	A
PTFE (Teflon)	2.2	3.45	21	0.131	135	<0.01	—	100	327	SC
PU-solid	1.4	0.8	15	—	34	0.8	—	120	140	—
PVC-Unplasticized	1.37	2.8	51	—	110	0.06	—	82	172	A
PVC-flexible	1.3	0.006	15	—	—	—	—	—	—	—
PVDF	1.78	2.5	53	—	120	0.02	—	−35	175	SC
SAN	1.07	3.6	75	0.037	70	0.4	—	105	—	—
TPI (ThermoPolyimide)	1.37	2.42	90	—	53	0.29	—	250	388	SC
TPO	1.08	1.31	20	—	59 ~ 108	0.03	—	—	120	—

Notes: ρ (g/cm^3) = Density;

E_T(GPa) = Tensile modulus of elasticity;

σ_{uts}(MPa) and ε_{uts} = Ultimate tensile strength and strain;

α (μm/m/℃) = Coefficient of linear thermal expansion, averaged value;

$C_{m,24}$ = Moisture concentration after 24 h test (ASTM D 570 or ISO-62), i.e. water if not mentioned
   otherwise;

$C_{m,sat}$ = Saturated moisture concentration;

I_{zod}(kJ/m^2) = Izod unnotched impact strength at 23 ℃ (ISO 180/1A);

T_g(℃) = Glass transition point;

T_m(℃) = Melting point;

Phase A = Amorphous;

Phase SC (semi-crystalline) = Having crystalline region dispersed in amorphous material.

Chapter 3

Thermoset Plastics

3.1   Introduction

Thermoset plastics, also thermosets in brief, are stiff plastics which are defiant to higher temperatures than thermoplastics. A thermoset cannot go back to its original form after its initial heat-forming in contrast to thermoplastics. An irreversible change in the chemical network structure occurs with heat. The chemical structure of a thermoset at the room temperature is not the same as that at elevated temperatures.

Thermoset materials are usually liquid or malleable prior to curing and designed to be molded into their final form, or used as adhesives. The curing process transforms the resin into a plastic or rubber by cross-linking. Heat and catalysts are added to cause the molecular chains to link into a rigid 3-dimensional structure. A thermoset material cannot be melted and re-molded after it is cured. Thermoset polymers are the most widely used matrix material in composite materials. Different types of thermoset plastic matrices used in composites are Amino, BMI (Bis-Maleimides), EP (Epoxy), PCN (Polycyanurate), PF (Phenolics), PI (Polyimide), Polyester, PU (Polyurethane), Silicone, and Vinyester. Their general physical properties are given in Table 3.1. The top three resins used for composites with continuous fibers are epoxy, polyester, and vinylester.

3.2   Resin Transfer (Compression) Molding

RTM (Resin Transfer Molding) is a process that consists of injecting a thermosetting resin into a closed mold cavity. The resin wets through the reinforcement (preform) and solidifies to form a composite part. RTM is used to mold components with complex shapes, large surface areas and a smooth finish on both sides (class A) and reasonable dimensional tolerances (±1 mm) for applications like truck cabs and electrical cabinets. Transfer molding, unlike compression molding uses a closed mold, so smaller tolerances and more intricate parts can be achieved. In the semiconductor industry, package encapsulation is usually done with transfer molding due to the high accuracy of transfer molding tooling and low cycle time of the process. A resin with low viscosity such as epoxy, polyester, and vinylester can be done. Molding pressure is lower than in the compression molding process, so tooling and equipment capital costs are lower than high-volume compression molding, but higher than open molding processes.

VARTM (Vacuum-Assisted Resin Transfer Molding) or VIP (Vacuum Infusion Processing) is a single sided molding process where the dry preform (reinforcement or coring materials) is placed into the mold, a cover (or a vacuum bag) is placed over the top to form a vacuum-tight seal. A distribution medium (a mesh) is used and laid on top of the top release fabric to help maintain an even distribution of resin and to facilitate the flow of resin through the thickness of the panel. The low viscosity resin typically enters the preform through resin distribution and vacuum distribution lines with the aid of vacuum.

LRTM (Light Resin Transfer Molding) is really much more like VARTM, utilizing a vacuum process with only one rigid mold and a semi-rigid mold called a counter toll. Hence it is more cost-effective. LRTM shares a few good attributes with conventional RTM such as yielding two cosmetic surfaces per part and permitting a larger range of glass contents.

3.2.1   Preform

Preform is a continuous filament mats, complexes or fabrics that can be used in RTM as reinforcement.

3.2.2   Permeability

Permeability is defined as the flow of a fluid through a medium, usually porous. For example, the resin impregnates the preform in a resin transfer molding. Due to the complexity of geometry, permeability of a preform is obtained empirically. Permeability of resin flow through a glass fiber preform may be modeled by the Darcy's equation for anisotropic material as

$$\begin{Bmatrix} q_1 \\ q_2 \\ q_3 \end{Bmatrix} = \frac{1}{\mu_v} \begin{bmatrix} S_{11} & S_{12} & S_{13} \\ S_{12} & S_{22} & S_{23} \\ S_{13} & S_{23} & S_{33} \end{bmatrix} \begin{Bmatrix} \dfrac{\partial P_1}{\partial X_1} \\ \dfrac{\partial P_2}{\partial X_2} \\ \dfrac{\partial P_3}{\partial X_3} \end{Bmatrix} \tag{3.1}$$

where
μ_v: Fluid viscosity;
P_1, P_2, P_3: Pressure in the X_1, X_2, and X_3 directions, respectively;
S_{ij}: Permeability tensor, i = 1, 2, 3 and j = 1, 2, 3.

For an orthotropic material such as a layer of preform with unidirectional continuous fiber,

$$q_i = \frac{1}{\mu_v} S_{ii} \left(\frac{\partial P_i}{\partial X_i} \right), \ i = 1, 2, \text{ and } 3 \tag{3.2}$$

Permeability tensors of a preform depend on the following four factors: (a) wetting-surface treatment of fibers, (b) fiber volume, (c) fiber cross-section-size and shape, and (d) lamination.

3.3 Compression Molding

Compression molding is a method of molding in which the molding material, generally preheated, is first placed in an open heated mold cavity. The mold is closed with a top forcing member (e.g. hydraulic ram), pressure is applied to press the material into contact with all mold areas, while heat and pressure are maintained until the molding material has cured. BMC (bulk molding compound) or SMC (sheet molding compound), are conformed to the mold form by the applied pressure and heated until the curing reaction occurs. It has been used in manufacturing automotive parts such as hoods, fenders, scoops, spoilers. Materials that are typically manufactured through compression molding include Polyester (SMC & BMC), PAI (Polyamide-imide), PI (Polyimide), PPS (Poly(p-phenylene sulfide)), EP (Epoxy), and many grades of PEEK.

3.4 Thermoplastic elastomers (TPE)

TPE (**T**hermo **p**lastic **e**lastomers), also called thermoplastic rubbers, are thermoset materials. It is a polymer blend or compound which, above its melting temperature, exhibits a thermoplastic characteristic that enables it to be shaped into a fabricated article which, within its design temperature range, possesses elastomeric behavior without cross-linking during fabrication. This process is reversible and the products can be reprocessed and remolded. TPS is a class of materials that can be processed like thermoplastics but exhibit the physical properties of vulcanized rubbers. In other words, they have the following three distinct characteristics:

- (a) Stretchability at a moderate elongation (e.g. more than 100% in strain) and returning to its original shape or almost when unloaded;
- (b) Having Mullins' effect but little creep;
- (c) Processability as a melt at an elevated temperature.

TPEs are widely used to modify the properties of rigid thermoplastics, usually improving impact strength. This is quite common for sheet goods and general molding TPEs. There are six generic classes of commercial TPEs:

- (a) Thermoplastic Amide Elastomer (TPE-a);
- (b) Thermoplastic Polyester Elastomer (TPE-e);
- (c) Thermoplastic Olefinic Elastomer (TPE-o or TPO);
- (d) Styrenic Block Copolymers (TPE-s or SEBS);
- (e) Thermoplastic Polyurethane Elastomer (TPE-u or TPU);
- (f) Thermoplastic Vulcanizate or Elastomeric Alloys (TPE-v or TPV);

(g) Thermoplastic copolyester (TPE-e, COPE or TEEE);

(h) Thermoplastic Polyamides (TPI);

(i) Melt-Processable Rubbers (MPR).

Injection molding and extrusion are the two popular manufacturing ways of making TPEs, as manufacturing cost is of concern. Material properties of TPEs are listed in its corresponding chapter of its contributing plastic(s), which can be thermoplastics or thermoset plastics. For example, material properties of TPI (Thermoplastic Polyamides) are given in the PI (Polyamides) Chapter. Material properties of TPV's listed in Table 3.2 are classified according to the hardness. In general TPEs can be divided into two groups of materials:

(a) Block copolymers with "soft" elastomeric rubbers and "hard" thermoplastics: Since they possess physical crosslinks as copolymers, i.e. thermoplastics+elastomers, unlike vulcanized rubbers, elasticity is derived from an amorphous network interconnected by chemical crosslinks.

(b) Blends of rubbers with thermoplastics: The blends consist of rubber domains in a thermoplastic matrix like a particulate composite.

A TPE sometimes has its cost advantage. For example, a TPE bellow boot for the automotive constant-velocity joint is a cost-effective alternative to vulcanized rubber as a blow-molded TPE boot costs less than an injection-molded rubber boot. Additional advantages over thermoset rubber provided by TPEs include excellent colorability and a lower density. Applications include automotive window seals (TPE-s), lip seals (TPE-s), coextruded automotive gaskets (TPV), wire/cable (TPE-s or TPU), cable jacketing (TPE-a) fiber-reinforced touch surface for interior (TPO), spoilers (TPE-s), airbag covers (COPE), steering wheels, bushings, bellows, gear knobs, petrol tubes, rolling diaphragms, belts, coiled tubing, and fiber-reinforced hoses.

3.5   TPV (Thermoplastic Vulcanizates)

TPV (Thermoplastic Vulcanizates), a subset of TPE (Thermoplastic Elastomers), are compounds with fully cross linked rubber in a continuous thermoplastic matrix of plastic and rubber compositions having excellent elastomeric properties. In this case the curing of the rubber phase occurs during the mastication with the thermoplastic resin. The process produces a useful custom-made elastomeric alloy with properties of a cured rubber but has expected processing characteristics of the thermoplastic. If the elastomer phase is fully vulcanized, enhanced performance such as better mechanical, tribological properties, and high service temperature can be achieved. It is important that the mixing be continuous throughout the masticating step, or a "thermoset" phase could result.

Applications include bumpers, soft nose bumpers, window profiles & seals, protective covers, bellows, boots, floor mats, knobs, gear knobs, flexible grip, mirror case, tubes, extruded items like strap, co-extruded automotive gasket, trim, edge band, 2-shot molded ventilation flap, 2-shot molded gasket into car lamps, colored interior component as claimed by Synoprene Polymers Pvt. Ltd.

References

ADHIKARI R, GODEHARDT R, HUY T A, et al, 2003. Low Temperature Tensile Deformation Behavior of Styrene/Butadiene Based Thermoplastic Elastomer[J]. Kautschuk Gummi Kunststoffe (KGK), 56(11): 573-577.

BAUSANO J V, LESKO J J, CASE S W, 2006. Composite Life under Sustained Compression and One-sided Simulated Fire Exposure: Characterization and Prediction [J]. Composites, A, Applied Science and Manufacturing, 37(7):1092-1100.

BOYCE M C, et al, 2001a. Micromechanisms of Deformation and Recovery in Thermoplastic Vulcanizates[J]. Journal of Mechanical Physics, 49:1073-1098.

BOYCE M, et al, 2001b. Micromechanisms of the Cyclic Softening in Thermoplastic Vulcanizates[J]. Journal of Mechanical Physics, 49:1343-1360.

BOYCE M C, et al, 2001. Deformation of Thermoplastic Vulcanizates[J]. Journal of Mechanical Physics, 49: 1073-1098.

BROSTOW W, et al, 2010. Effect of Peroxides on Properties of Thermoplastic Vulcanizates [J]. Plastics Research Online, SPE, 10.1002/spepro.002598.

BUCKLEY C P, et al, 2001. Deformation of Thermosetting Resins at Impact Rates of Strain. Part I : Experimental Study[J]. Journal of Mechanics and Physics of Solids, 49:1517-1538.

CORREIA N C, et al, 2004. Use of Resin Transfer Molding Simulation to Predict Flow, Saturation, and Compaction, in the VARTM Process[J]. Journal of Fluids Engineering, 126(2):61-68.

DAVILA C G, CAMANHO P P, ROSE C A, 2005. Failure Criteria for FRP Laminates [J]. Journal of Composite Materials, Vol. 39:323-345.

EL-ASSAL A M, KHASHABA U A, 2009. Fatigue Analysis of Unidirectional GFRP Composites under Combined Bending and Torsional Loads[J]. Journal of Composite Structures, 79:599-605.

FERGUSON R F, et al, 1998. Determining the Through-Thickness Properties of FRP Materials[J]. Composites Science and Technology, 58:1411-142.

KHASHABA U, et al, 2007. Behavior of Notched and Unnotched [0/±30/±60/90]S GFR/Epoxy Composites under Static and Fatigue Loads[J]. Journal of Composite Structures, 81:606-613.

MAIMI P, et al, 2007. A Continuum Damage Model for Composite Laminates: Part Ⅱ-Computational Implementation and Validation[J]. Mechanics of Materials, 39:909-919.

MIYANO Y, et al, 1997. prediction of Flexural Fatigue Strength of CRFP Composites under Arbitrary Frequency, Stress Ratio, and Temperature[J]. Journal of Composite Materials, 31(6):619-638.

GOODMAN S H. 1999. Handbook of Thermoset Plastics[M]. 2nd edition, ChemTech Publishing.

SANGWICHIEN C, et al, 2008. Effect of Filler Loading on Curing Characteristics and Mechanical Properties of Thermoplastic Vulcanizate[J]. Chiang Mai Journal Science, 35(1):141-149.

SIMACEK P, ADVANI S, LOBST S, 2009. Modeling Flow in Compression Resin Transfer Molding for Manufacturing of Complex Lightweight High-Performance Automotive Parts [J]. Journal of Composite Materials, 42(23):2523-2545.

Table 3.1   Nominal Material Properties of Thermoset Plastics for Automotive Applications at the Room Temperature

Material	ρ	E_T	$(\sigma_{uts}, \varepsilon_{uts})$	α	$C_{m,24}/\%$	$C_{m,sat}$	T_g	T_m	Phase
BMI (Bismaleimides)	1.3	3.9	(104, 4.8%)	65	—	—	260	—	—
EP (Epoxy): DGEBA	1.3	3.1	(62, 2.4%)	63	0.03	—	155	—	—
PCN (Polycyanurate)	1.32	3.1	(83, 2.5%)	65	—	—	289	—	—
PF (Phenolic; injection molded)	1.452	3.0	(48, 1.7%)	36	0.65	—	—	—	—
PI (polyimide)	1.43	3.2	(83, 6%)	50	0.32	—	308	—	—
Silicone	0.97~2.5	—	(2~7, 20%~700%)	10~19	0.1	—	—	—	—
UP (unsaturated polyester)	1.12	3.4	(37, 1.4%)	31	0.88	—	140	250	—
VE (Vinylester)	1.1	3.2	(77, 17%)	19	0.36	—	118	—	—
Zylon (PBO)	1.55	174	(4200, —)	—	—	—	—	—	—

Notes: W_A = Water absorption (24 h test), ASTM D 570;

$C_{m,24}$ = Moisture concentration after 24 h test per ASTM D 570 or ISO-62, i.e. water if not mentioned otherwise;

$C_{m,sat}$ = Saturated moisture concentration;

$T_g(℃)$ & $T_m(℃)$ = Glass transition point and melting point, respectively;

Phase = "A" for amorphous and "SC" for semi-crystalline.

Table 3.2　Mechanical Properties of Generic TPV（Thermoplastic Vulcanizates）

Material-DAM	$T/^\circ\text{C}$	E_T	ρ	ν	(σ, ε)	α	k	γ	β	K_{IC}
TPV-55	−60（Brittleness Point）									
	23	—	0.95	—	（2.14, 100%） （4, 330%）	—	—	—	—	—
	125（High service temperature）									
TPV-73	−55（Brittleness Point）									
	23	—	0.95	—	（6.6, 340%）	—	—	—	—	—
	125（High service temperature）									
TPV-86	−50（Brittleness Point）									
	23	—	0.96	—	（4.7, 100%） （11, 340%）	—	—	—	—	—
	125（Service temperature）									
TPV-90	−50（Brittleness Point）									
	23	—	0.97	—	（100%） （18.5, 502%）	—	—	—	—	—
	125（Service temperature）									

Notes：DAM＝Dry as Molded；

　　　55, 73, 86, 90＝Shore A Durometer hardness.

Chapter 4

Metals: Ferrous

4.1 Introduction

A metal is a substance of crystalline luster with ions being surrounded by de-localized electrons. Most metals are good conductors of electricity and heat. Metals are mechanically malleable and chemically reactive. Metallic bonds are electrostatic interactions between ions and the surrounding clouds of electrons. Metals are still the most used materials for on-ground vehicles as measured by weight.

Balance between strength and ductility is the major outstanding metal performance index. Both strength and ductility are a function of intrinsic factors like composition, grain size, cell structure etc., as well as by external factors like hydrostatic pressure, temperature, plastic deformation already suffered etc. For a given strength, ductility may be improved by controlling the following factors:

(a) Cell Structure: Metals generally possess one of the following three cell structure-BBC (Body centered cubic structure), FCC (Face centered cubic structure), and HCP (Hexagonal closed packed structure). Metals with FCC and BCC crystal structure show higher ductility at high temperatures compared to those with HCP crystal structure.

(b) Grain Size: It has significant influence on ductility. Many alloys show super-plastic behavior when grain size is very small, up to a few microns or even nanometers.

(c) Oxygen: Steels with higher oxygen content show low ductility.

(d) Impurity: In some alloys, impurities even in very small percentages have significant effect on ductility. Ductility of carbon steels containing sulfur impurity as small as 0. 018%, drastically decreases ductility at around 1040 ℃. This can however be remedied if Mn content is high. In fact the ratio Mn/S is the factor which can alter ductility of carbon steels at 1040 ℃. With the value of this ratio 2 the percent elongation is only 12% ~ 15% at 1040 ℃ while with ratio of 14 it is 110%.

(e) Temperature: Temperature is a major factor that influences ductility and hence formability. In general it increases ductility while reduces the strength. However, ductility may decrease at certain temperatures due to phase transformation and micro-structural changes brought about by increase in temperature. It was shown that the ductility of stainless steel is low at 1050 ℃ and maximized 1350 ℃ [Sellars & Tegart], consequently having a very narrow hot working range.

(f) Duplexity: Duplex microstructures generally lead to lower ductility [Stout & Follanshee]. As an example, low carbon steel when tested in $(\alpha + \gamma)$ range shows lower ductility.

(g) Alloying Elements: Many pure metals are soft, corrode easily, or have other mechanical or chemical disadvantages that can be overcome if the metals are combined with other metals into alloys. This is called alloying. Alloying elements are expected to improve strength or ductility. Nevertheless, effects on strength and ductility may be contradictory to each other. The temperature for optimal ductility of an individual alloy is affected by the concentrations of alloying elements.

(h) Hydrostatic Pressure: Hydrostatic pressure increases ductility [Bridgeman]. In torsion tests the length of specimen decreases with an increase in torsion. When a specimen is subjected to an axial compressive stress in a torsion test it shows higher ductility than when there is no axial stress. If a tensile axial stress is applied, the ductility decreases still further.

(i) Strain Rate: It has been shown in tension tests that an increasing strain rate increases the elongation in uniform deformation region and decreases the same in the neck region. To obtain the effect of strain rate the observed values must be corrected for change in temperature, because at a high strain rate there is considerable increase in temperature of material that increases ductility.

4.2　Ferrous Metals

Ferrous metals are iron-based materials. Steel is a crystalline alloy of iron, carbon and several other elements, which hardens above its critical temperature. The four major ferrous products used in the automotive industry are

(a) Cast Irons;
(b) Plain Carbon Steels;
(c) Alloyed Steel;
(d) Stainless Steels.

An iron-carbon phase diagram that describes the iron-carbon system of alloys containing up to 6.67% of carbon is given here, disclosing the phase compositions and their transformations of the alloys as a function of temperature variations, as shown in Fig. 4.1.

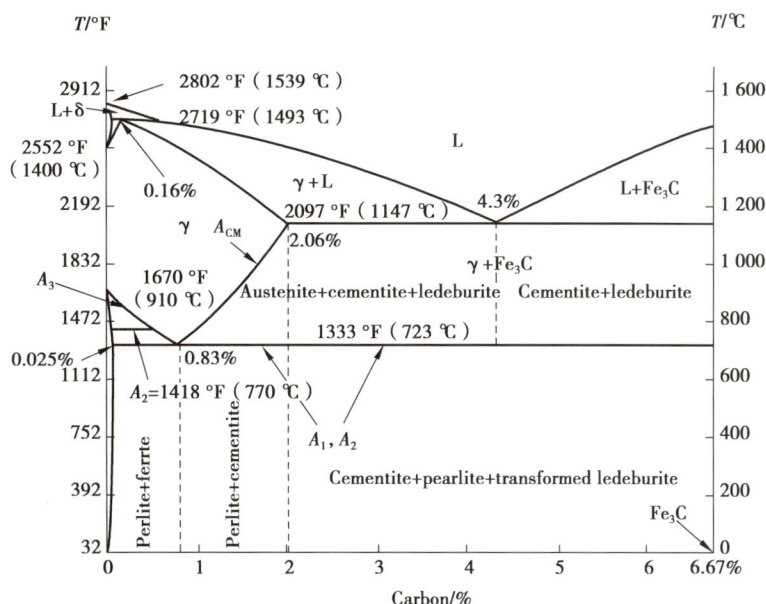

Fig. 4.1　Iron-Carbon Phase Diagram

4.3   Alloying Metals

Chromium (Cr) and Molybdenum (Mo) are two widely used alloying elements. Cr-alloyed steels are corrosion-resistant and Mo contributes further corrosion resistance to "chrome-moly" stainless steels.

4.4   Refractory Metals

Tungsten (W), Molybdenum(Mo), Niobium (Nb), Tantalum (Ta), and Rhenium (Re) are the five refractory metals. They all share certain material properties such as high melting points (above 2000 ℃), high hardness, being chemically inert, and having a relatively high density. As a group they provide a number of unique characteristics such as resistance to heat, corrosion and wear-making them useful in a multitude of applications. For example, tungsten-alloyed steel greatly increases its toughness of the base steel, even with small quantities of tungsten.

4.5   Noble Metals

The eight noble metals, namely silver (Ag), gold (Au), platinum (Pt), palladium (Pd), rhodium (Ro), ruthenium (Ru), iridium (Ir), and osmium (Os) have been used as conductors and other electronic applications in the automotive industry.

4.6   Metallic Glasses

A metallic glass containing nonmetallic alloying elements such as phosphorous and boron in the metal can be produced in noncrystalline form with solidification rates that are orders of magnitude less than those necessary to yield amorphous structure in the regular metal. Relative to its regular metallic forms, a noncrystalline metal is less compressible, higher in Poisson's ratios, lower in elastic moduli, but higher in tensile strength [Chen, Jackson, and Davis].

4.7   Rubber-to-Metal Bonding

Rubber-to-metal bonding is necessary in providing well bonded metal inserts and reinforcements in molded-elastomer products. The bond strength is generally greater than the strength of the elastomer, and the failure mode is usually within the elastomer. The main field of application for components made with rubber-to-metal bonds is in the automotive industry. Examples of auto products made via this route are engine mounts, shock absorbers, gaskets and shaft seals, v-belts, and reinforced tires.

The rubber-to-metal bonding process is also well suited for most molding operations and eliminates processes and materials that are necessary in post-vulcanization bonding.

4.8   Machinability of Metals

Machinability of metals is a function of thermal conductivity, area of reduction at fracture, and hardness as [Datsko]

$$V_{\mathrm{C}} \propto \frac{k(1 - A_{\mathrm{r}})^{\frac{1}{2}}}{H_{\mathrm{B}}}$$

where

k: Thermal conductivity;

A_{r}: Area of reduction at fracture;

H_{B}: Brinell hardness.

References

BRIDGEMAN P W, 1952. Studies in Large Plastic Flow and Fracture with Special Emphasis on the Effects of Hydrostatic Pressure[M]. McGraw-Hill, New York, NY, USA.

DASKO J, 1977. Materials in Design and Manufacturing[M]. Malloy, Ann Arbor, MI, USA.

DAVIS J R, 1998. Metals Handbook[M]. ASM International, Metals Park, OH, USA. Dieter, G. E. 1986, Mechanical Metallurgy, 3rd edition, McGraw-Hill, New York, NY, USA.

Chapter 5

Metals: Non-Ferrous

5.1   Introduction

A metal is a substance of crystalline luster with ions being surrounded by de-localized electrons. Most metals are good conductors of electricity and heat. Metals are mechanically malleable and chemically reactive. Metallic bonds are electrostatic interactions between ions and the surrounding clouds of electrons. Metals are still the most used materials for on-ground vehicles as measured by weight.

Balance between strength and ductility is the major outstanding metal performance index. Both strength and ductility are a function of intrinsic factors like composition, grain size, cell structure etc., as well as by external factors like hydrostatic pressure, temperature, plastic deformation already suffered etc. For a given strength, ductility may be improved by controlling the following factors:

(a) Cell Structure: Metals generally possess one of the following three cell structure-BBC (Body centered cubic structure), FCC (Face centered cubic structure), and HCP (Hexagonal closed packed structure). Metals with FCC and BCC crystal structure show higher ductility at high temperatures compared to those with HCP crystal structure.

(b) Grain Size: It has significant influence on ductility. Many alloys show super-plastic behavior when grain size is very small up to a few microns and even nanos.

(c) Oxygen: Steels with higher oxygen content show low ductility.

(d) Impurity: In some alloys, impurities even in very small percentages have significant effect on ductility. Ductility of carbon steels containing sulfur impurity as small as 0. 018%, drastically decreases ductility at around 1040 ℃. This can however be remedied if Mn content is high. In fact the ratio Mn/S is the factor which can alter ductility of carbon steels at 1040 ℃. With the value of this ratio 2 the percent elongation is only 12%~15% at 1040 ℃ while with ratio of 14 it is 110%.

(e) Temperature: Temperature is a major factor that influences ductility and hence formability. In general it increases ductility while reduces the strength. However, ductility may decrease at certain temperatures due to phase transformation and micro-structural changes brought about by increase in temperature. It is shown that the ductility of stainless steel is low at 1050 ℃ and maximized 1350 ℃ [Sellars & Tegart]; consequently having a very narrow hot working range.

(f) Duplexity: Duplex microstructures generally lead to lower ductility [Stout & Follanshee]. As an example, low carbon steel when tested in (α + γ) range shows lower ductility.

(g) Alloying Elements: Many pure metals are soft, corrode easily, or have other mechanical or chemical disadvantages that can be overcome if the metals are combined with other metals into alloys This is called alloying. Alloying elements are expected to improve strength or ductility. Nevertheless, effects on strength and ductility may be contradictory to each other. The temperature for optimal ductility of an individual alloy is affected by the concentrations of alloying elements.

(h) Hydrostatic Pressure: Hydrostatic pressure increases ductility [Bridgeman]. In torsion tests the length of specimen decreases with an increase in torsion. When a specimen is subjected to an axial compressive stress in a torsion test it shows higher ductility than when there is no axial stress. If a tensile axial stress is applied the ductility decreases still further.

(i) Strain Rate: It has been shown in tension tests that increase in strain rate increases the elongation in uniform deformation region and decreases the same in the neck region. For obtaining the effect of strain rate the observed values must be corrected for change in temperature, because at a high strain rate there is considerable increase in temperature of material that increases ductility.

5.2   Ferrous Metals

Ferrous metals are iron-based materials. Steel is a crystalline alloy of iron, carbon and several other elements, which hardens above its critical temperature. The four major ferrous products used in the automotive industry are

(a) Cast Irons;
(b) Plain Carbon Steels;
(c) Alloyed Steel;
(d) Stainless Steels.

An iron-carbon phase diagram that describes the iron-carbon system of alloys containing up to 6.67% of carbon is given here, disclosing the phase compositions and their transformations of the alloys as a function of temperature variations, as shown in Fig. 5.1.

5.3   Nonferrous Base Metals

Aluminum (Al), Magnesium (Mg), Zinc (Zn), Copper (Cu), Tin (Sn), and Nickel (Ni) are six top nonferrous metals.

Al-, Mg-, and Zn-based metals have been used for replacing automotive metallic parts for weight reduction. Cu-and Sn-based alloys find ample applications in automotive electronics and bearings. Ni-based alloys offer good resistance to pitting, inter-granular corrosion, chloride-ion stress-corrosion cracking, and general corrosion in a wide range of oxidizing environments at high temperatures.

5.4 Alloying Metals

Chromium (Cr) and Molybdenum (Mo) are two widely used alloying elements. Cr-alloyed steels are corrosion-resistant and Mo contributes further corrosion resistance to "chrome-moly" stainless steels.

5.5 Refractory Metals

Tungsten (W), Molybdenum(Mo), Niobium (Nb), Tantalum (Ta), and Rhenium (Re) are the five refractory metals. They all share certain material properties such as high melting points (above 2000 ℃), high hardness, being chemically inert, and having a relatively high density. As a group they provide a number of unique characteristics such as resistance to heat, corrosion and wear-making them useful in a multitude of applications. For example, tungsten-alloyed steel greatly increases its toughness of the base steel, even with small quantities of tungsten.

5.6 Noble Metals

The eight noble metals, namely silver (Ag), gold (Au), platinum (Pt), palladium (Pd), rhodium (Ro), ruthenium (Ru), iridium (Ir), and osmium (Os) have been used as conductors and other electronic applications in the automotive industry.

5.7 Metallic Glasses

A metallic glass containing nonmetallic alloying elements such as phosphorous and boron in the metal can be produced in noncrystalline form with solidification rates that are orders of magnitude less than those necessary to yield amorphous structure in the regular metal. Relative to its regular metallic forms, a noncrystalline metal is less compressible, higher in Poisson's ratios, lower in elastic moduli, but higher in tensile strength [Chen, Jackson, and Davis].

5.8　Rubber-to-Metal Bonding

Rubber-to-metal bonding is necessary in providing well bonded metal inserts and reinforcements in molded-elastomer products. The bond strength is generally greater than the strength of the elastomer, and the failure mode is usually within the elastomer. The main field of application for components made with rubber-to-metal bonds is in the automotive industry. Examples of auto products made via this route are engine mounts, shock absorbers, gaskets and shaft seals, v-belts, and reinforced tires.

The rubber-to-metal bonding process is also well suited for most molding operations and eliminates processes and materials that are necessary in post-vulcanization bonding.

5.9　Machinability of Metals

Machinability of metals is a function of thermal conductivity, area of reduction at fracture, and hardness as [Datsko]

$$V_C \propto \frac{k(1 - A_r)^{\frac{1}{2}}}{H_B}$$

where
k: Thermal conductivity;
A_r: Area of reduction at fracture;
H_B: Brinell hardness.

References

BRIDGEMAN P W, 1952. Studies in Large Plastic Flow and Fracture with Special Emphasis on the Effects of Hydrostatic Pressure[M]. McGraw-Hill, New York, NY, USA.

CHEN H S, JACKSON K A, DAVIS L A, 1978. Metallic Glasses, ASM International, Metals Park, OH, USA.

DASKO J, 1977. Materials in Design and Manufacturing, Malloy, Ann Arbor, MI, USA.

DAVIS J R, 1998. Metals Handbook, ASM International, Metals Park, OH, USA. Dieter, G. E, 1986. Mechanical Metallurgy, 3rd edition, McGraw-Hill, New York, NY, USA.

SAE, 1999. Ferrous Materials Manual, SAE International, Warrendale, PA, USA.

YANG Z G, 2002. Materials Properties Database for Selection of High-Temperature Alloys and Concepts of Alloy Design for SOFC Applications [C]. Pacific Northwest National Laboratory, Richland, Washington 99352.

Chapter 6

Ceramics

6.1   Introduction

Ceramics are composed of electrically charged cations and anions. Cations are positive charged ions such as Al^{3+} in Al_2O_3. Anions are negative charged ions such as O^{2-} in Al_2O_3. The crystal structure of a ceramic depends on the charge magnitude and radius of each ion. They withstand high heat and chemical erosion. Ceramics are inorganic oxide materials, usually ionic or covalent bonded. It is solid and inert at the room temperature. They are brittle, hard, strong in compression, and weak in shearing and tension.

They can be divided into two groups-amorphous ceramics and crystalline ceramics. Amorphous ceramics are generally referred to as glasses. Crystalline ceramics maintain their strength at elevated temperatures. Ceramics are the hardest material on the earth, except diamond. However, the inherent brittleness of ceramics makes special considerations necessary in designing with these materials. Ranked on the Knoop scale in hardness, ceramic materials are listed in Table 10.3. The most widely used structural ceramics is alumina (Al_2O_3). Both alumina and boron carbide have been in use for armor vehicles and ballistic-armored vests.

Mechanical properties of ceramics of interest include elasticity, plasticity, tensile strength, compressive strength, shear strength, fracture toughness, ductility (low in brittle materials), and indentation hardness. Traditional tensile tests do not produce consistent data for ceramics, as ceramics are so brittle and sensitive to porosities. The flexural strength is applied instead as a general practice in the industry, though higher than the tensile strength.

Fiber-reinforced ceramic composites are the efficient way of utilizing ceramics. Carbon-reinforced silicon carbide is used for nozzle flaps and seals in military jets. Its expansion into space shuttle, gas turbines, nuclear fission and fusion, on-ground armor vehicles, and human-body armors has been testified. Low cost and flexible manufacturing processes are the keys to commercial applications of fiber-reinforced ceramic composites.

6.2   Structural Ceramics

The reason why ceramics are built for structural parts is three folds. First of all, ceramics remain hard and resist deformation at high temperatures where metals soften or melt for applications such as metal cutting, metal filters, brake pads and rotors. Secondarily, ceramics resist cavitations and ablative wear for applications such as nozzles for water cutting, ink jet printing, and rocket engines. Finally, they are inert and bio-compatible (named bioceramics) for applications such as hip joints, knees, teeth, and other bone replacements. Two typical structural ceramics are ceramic armors and ceramic bearings.

6.2.1　Ceramic Armors

Ceramic armors are another kind of application in automobiles, used for protection of military personnel and vehicles from ballistic threat. Key design parameters in such an application are

(a) Density (specific weight) of protective material (g/cm^3);
(b) Tensile strength of protective material (MPa);
(c) Specific strength (MPa cm^3/g);
(d) Mass efficiency for ballistic protection (relative to RHA steel);
(e) Multi-hit capability;
(f) Edge effect on structural integrity.

Highly localized high-impact amortization, i.e. transformation to glassy state as observed in softer semiconductors and minerals, has been verified for some ceramics. It explains why crystal-structured boron carbide is great in blocking low-energy projectiles such as handgun bullets, but shatters when hit by powerful ammunition.

6.2.2　Ceramic Bearings

One important application of structural ceramics is ceramic bearing. Ceramic bearings don't need liquid lubricants (grease and oil), because they do not undergo cold welding or corrode during operations. Ceramics have lower densities, thermal expansions, and friction than stainless steel. A ceramic bearing set, which consists of ZrO_2 races, Si_3N_4 balls, a PTFE (polytetrafluoroethylene) retainer, and labyrinth non-contact seals (plain-weave fiberglass impregnated with 50% ~ 70% PTFE), consumes less than 14% energy of all stainless steel bearing set [Kay].

6.3　Electroceramics

Electroceramics are primarily used for their electrical properties, including ferroelectrics for high dielectric capacitors and non-volatile memories, ferrites for data and information storage, solid electrolytes for energy storage and conversion, and semiconducting oxides for environmental monitoring.

Varistor is the most widely application among all based on electroceramics. It exhibits the property that resistance drops sharply at a certain threshold voltage. Once the voltage across the device reaches the threshold, there is a breakdown of the electrical structure in the vicinity of the grain boundaries, which results in its electrical resistance dropping from several megaohms down to a few hundred ohms. After the voltage across the device drops below the threshold, its resistance returns to the high level (several megaohms). The major advantage of these is that they can dissipate a lot of energy, and they self reset.

Automotive ceramics include spark plug insulators, catalysts and catalyst supports for emission control devices, and sensors of various kinds. Ceramics are also employed as gas sensors due to the change of electric resistance according to the type of gas. Inexpensive ceramic devices can be fabricated, with tuning to the possible gas mixture.

Under some conditions, such as operating an extremely low temperature, some ceramics exhibit high superconductivity.

6.4   Piezoceramics

Piezoelectricity is a link between electrical and mechanical response. A piezoceramic element produces mechanical energy in response to electric signals, and conversely. Commercially used piezoceramics are primarily lead zirconate titanate (PZT), Barium titanate (BT), strontium titanate (ST), and quartz.

A piezoelectric actuator is a solid state device that uses the change in shape of a piezoelectric material when an electric field is applied to create motion. For example, Piezoceramic actuators have been used for fuel injection systems, in-jet printers, cameras, and acoustic transducers. One major advantage of piezoelectric actuators is the ability to generate 10 μm (micrometer) displacement in a time as short as 10 μs (microsecond) just subjected to a high stress such as 100 MPa [McMahon].

Ultrasonic piezoelectric motors use ultrahigh-frequency acoustic vibrations on a nanoscale to create linear or rotary motion.

6.5   Glass

Glasses, usually formed from melts, are amorphous ceramics. Glass is shaped when either fully molten by casting or when in a state of toffee-like viscosity by methods such as blowing to a mold.

6.6   Glass Ceramics

Glass ceramics are formed from molten glass and subsequently crystallized by heat treatment. The three common glass ceramics, lithium-aluminum-silicate (LAS, or beta spodumene), magnesium-aluminum-silicate (MAS, or cordierite), and aluminum-silicate (AS, or aluminous keatite), are stable at high temperatures, have a near-zero coefficient of linear thermal expansion, and resist various forms of high-temperature corrosion, especially oxidation.

6.7　Porcelains

Porcelains are ceramic material made by heating selected and refined materials often including clay in the form of kaolinite to high temperatures. The most used three porcelains are: Steatite (MgO-SiO_2), Cordierite ($2MgO$-$2Al_2O_3$-$5SiO_2$), and Mullite ($3Al_2O_3$-SiO_2).

6.8　Bricks

Clay is one of the earliest materials used to produce ceramics. Bricks made from clay-reinforced with fibers have been in use for thousands of years.

6.9　Creep of Ceramics

Slow deformation of ceramics can also occur when subjected to a constant stress at high temperature, e.g. homologous temperature $T/T_m > 50\%$.

References

BARNAKOV Y A, et al, 2007. The Progress towards Transparent Ceramics Fabrication[J]. Proc. SPIE, 6552: 65521B.1-65521B.7.

DAL MASCHIO R, NOBILE L, 1995. A Simplified Approach for Ceramic Fracture Toughness Evaluation by Indentation[J]. Engineering Fracture Mechanics, 51(2):209-215.

GIANNAKOPOULOS A E, 2000. Strength Analysis of Spherical Indentation of Piezoelectric Materials[J]. Journal of Applied Mechanics, 67(2):409-416.

HYNES A, DOREMUS R, 1996. Theories of Creep in Ceramics[J]. Critical Review of Solid State Material Science, 21(2):129-187.

JIS-R-1602, 1986. Testing Method for Elastic Modulus of Fine Ceramics, Japanese Standards Association.

MCMAHON J, 2010. Medical-Device Makers Warm up to Piezomotors[J]. Machine Design, 2010,20:72-77.

MOULSON A J, HERBERT J M, 1982. Electroceramics: Materials, Properties, and Applications[M]. 2nd edition. John Wiley and Sons, New York, NY, USA.

MUNZ D, FETT T, 2001. Ceramics: Mechanical Properties, Failure Behavior, Materials Selection, Springer Series in Materials Science[M]. New York, NY, USA.

QUINN J B, QUINN G D. 1997.Indentation Brittleness of Ceramics[J]. Journal of Material Science, 32:4331-4336.

RILEY F L, 2009. Structural Ceramics: Fundamentals and Case Studies[M]. Cambridge University Press, New York, NY, USA.

SAPUAN S M, et al, 2002. A Prototype Knowledge-based System for Material Selection of Ceramic Matrix Composites of Automotive Engine Components[J]. Materials and Design, 23(8):701-708.

SETTER N, WASER R, 2000. Electroceramic Materials[J]. Acta Materialia, 48:151-178.

SHETTY D K, RSENFIELD A R, MCGUIRE P, et al, Biaxial Flexural Test for Ceramics [J]. American Ceramics Society Bulletin, 59:1193−1197.

WACHTMAN J, CANNON W, MATHEWSON M, 2009. Mechanical Properties of Ceramics[M]. John Wiley & Sons, New York, NY, USA.

WAKAKI MORIAKI, et al, 2007. Physical Properties and Data of Optical Materials[M]. Taylor & Francis Inc, Bosa Roca, USA.

ZOK F, LEVI C, 2001. Mechanical Properties of Porous-Matrix Ceramic Composites[J]. Advanced Engineering Materials, 3(1-2):15-23.

Chapter 7

Diamond and Other Carbon Solids

7.1 Introduction

Carbon is the 4th most abundant element in the universe by mass, after hydrogen, helium and oxygen. It is the chemical basis of all known life. Carbon-based engineering materials used in automotive engineering can be classified as follows:

(a) Diamond;

(b) Graphene;

(c) Graphite;

(d) Amorphous Carbon (e.g. Carbon Black);

(e) Carbon Fiber;

(f) CNT (Carbon Nanotubes): SWNT and MWNT.

Although diamond and graphite are not ceramics by the chemical composition, they are sometimes considered pseudo-ceramic materials. Carbon has three natural crystalline allotropic forms: diamond, graphite and fullerene. Diamond crystallizes in the isometric system and graphite crystallizes in the hexagonal system. Diamond is hard and an excellent electric insulator, while graphite is soft a good electric conductor. Graphene sheets stack to form graphite. Carbon nanotubes, a special form of fullerenes, are carbon-based advanced engineering materials.

7.2 Diamond

Each carbon of diamond is bonded to four adjacent atoms by strong covalent bonds in the cubic crystal structure, called "diamond crystal structure". Diamond has an ideal tensile strength of 95 GPa and ideal shear strength of 95 GPa, respectively for diamond as identified by [Roundy and Cohen]. Note that the shear calculation is performed on the (1 1 1) slip plane sheared in a {1 1 2} direction and the tensile load is applied in the {1 1 1} direction.

The introduction of boron in single-crystal CVD diamond can significantly enhance the fracture toughness of this material without sacrificing its high hardness (~78 GPa).

Diamond tools are used for machining automotive components made of fiber-reinforced composites and aluminum alloys.

7.3   Graphene

Graphene, in which carbon atoms are packed in a regular sp^2-bonded atomic-scale in-plane-wire hexagonal) pattern, is regarded as a one-atom thick layer of graphite. It is the basic structural element of other allotropes, including graphite, charcoal, carbon nanotubes and fullerenes.

Graphene is seen as a promising candidate to replace silicon as the building block of nanocircuitry with smaller and more complex transistors.

7.4   Graphite

Each carbon is bonded to three adjacent coplanar atoms by strong covalent bonds in a layer, while interlayer bonds are of the weak van der Waals type. Facile interplanar cleavage of van der Waals bonds leads to good lubricative properties of graphite. A graphite structure has a self-lubricating ability, as compared to a deck of cards with individual layers able to easily slide off the deck.

Its electric conductivity is also anisotropic accordingly-significantly higher in crystallographic direction parallel to the hexagonal sheets. Natural graphite can be amorphous, flaky, and crystalline.

Mechanical applications of graphite include piston rings, thrust bearings, journal bearings, spherical ball bearings for automotive exhaust systems, and vanes. The main application for graphite as an electrical material is in the manufacture of carbon brushes in electric motors.

Graphite can be used for molds to cast some nonferrous parts such as zinc-aluminum alloys, if die casting is slow and machining is expensive.

Chemically aggressive applications represent another application niche for carbon-graphite composites. Carbon-based seals are used in the shafts and fuel pumps of many aircraft jet engines. Carbon-graphite and graphite are excellent materials for aircraft turbine engine mainshaft seals that prevent rotor support bearings from hot gases flowing through the engine and stopping the loss of lubricant in the bearing compartment.

7.5   Amorphous Carbon

Amorphous carbon exhibits a turbostratic disorder which makes the material extremely hard and resistant to wear.

A proper mixture of carbon and graphite is strong and hard with low friction. The combined composite has excellent corrosion resistance and is capable of operating at elevated temperatures.

7.6   Carbon Fiber

Carbon fiber-reinforced composite materials, especially carbon fiber-reinforced graphite composites, are most notably used structurally in high-temperature applications. The carbon can become further enhanced, as high modulus or high strength, by heat treatment processes: Carbon heated in the range of 1500~2000 ℃ (carbonization) exhibits the highest tensile strength (5650 MPa), while carbon fiber heated in the range of 2500~3000 ℃ (graphitizing) exhibits a higher modulus of elasticity (531 GPa). According to the types of precursors, Carbon fibers are divided into the following two groups:

(a) PAN carbon fiber: Having high strength, dominating the high-performance market;
(b) Pitch carbon fiber: Lower strength, while less expensive.

Carbon fibers are not only stronger and stiffer than glass fiber, but also have less stress corrosion. Continuous carbon fiber-reinforced plastics are used for a range of structural automotive components such as seatback shells, body panels, spoilers, roofs, driveshafts, and high-pressurized fuel tanks for hydrogen fuel-cell and compressed natural gas vehicles.

7.7   CNT (Carbon Nanotubes)

Since the discovery of carbon nanotubes by [Iijima] in 1991, the synthesis of tubular nanostructures has raised worldwide interest. Each sheet is comprised of hexagonal sets of carbon atoms as shown in Fig. 7.1. Nanotubes have been constructed with length-to-diameter ratio of up to 132000000 ∶ 1. The one-atom-thick form of carbon exhibits the quantum Hall effect and thermal conductive, as a result from relativistic electron current flow. It has been used as a filler for improving materials properties of elastomers, plastics, and others.

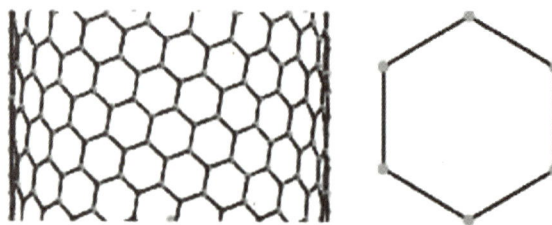

Fig. 7.1   Carbon Nanotube

7.7.1　SWNT (Single-Walled Carbon Nanotube)

A carbon nanotube can be thought of as a single layer graphite sheet in one carbon atom thickness, as rolled into a tube. Primarily SWNTs are synthesized via chemical vapor disposition (CVD). Defects can occur in the form of atomic vacancies. Thermal conductivity along the tube (k_1) as a function of defect concentration as [Hone et al.]

$$k_1 = 22.733 \, d_c^{-0.6418}$$

where d_c is the defect concentration per thousand parts. Promising applications of single-walled carbon nanotubes are their use in solar panels and paper batteries.

7.7.2　WWNT (Multi-walled Carbon Nanotube)

Multi-walled nanotubes (MWNT) consist of concentric tubes and/or multiple rolled layers of graphene. The interlayer distance in multi-walled nanotubes is close to the distance between graphene layers in graphite, approximately 3.4 Å. For a 2-layered double-walled nanotube (DWNT), it exhibits a striking tiny telescoping property whereby an inner nanotube core may slide, almost without friction, within its outer nanotube shell. There, it can be an atomically perfect linear or rotational bearing.

References

IRIFUNE T, KURIO A, SAKAMOTO S, et al, 2003. Ultrahard Polycrystalline Diamond from Graphite[J]. Nature, 421(6923):599-600.

KUMAR B, et al, 2013. Renewable and Metal-Free Carbon Nanofiber Catalysts for Carbon Dioxide Reduction [J]. Nature Communications, 4(1): 2819.

Pagel-Theisen, Verena, 2001. Diamond grading ABC: The Manual, 9th Edition, Rubin & Son n.v., Antwerp, Belgium:84-85,

PIERSON H O, 1993. Handbook of Carbon, Graphite, Diamond and Fullerenes: Properties, Processing, and Application[M]. Noyes Publications, Park Ridge, NJ, 1993.

ROUNDY D, COHEN M, 2001. Ideal Strength of Diamond, Si, and Ge[J]. Physics Review, B64,212103.

SHARPE W N JR, et al, 2004. Mechanical Properties of MEMS Materials[J]. AFRL-IF-RS-TR-2004-76 Final Technical Report, Airforce Research Lab., NY, USA.

Chapter 8

Electromagnetic Materials

8.1　Introduction

Electronic packaging techniques for on-ground vehicles include printed circuit assemblies, hermetic ceramics and metal/glass cases, sheet metals, cast metals, machined metals, potting, plastic molding, rubber curing, composites impregnation, conformal coating, and tolerance control. In light of high durability of BLDC (Brushless Direct-Current) and induction motors, more and more magnets are packaged into on-ground vehicles. The fundamental theory of electromagnetics underlining these devices is addressed herein.

8.2　Maxwell's Equations

Electromagnetic fields are governed by four Maxwell's equations [James Clerk Maxwell, 1873], by which bilateral couplings between electric and magnetic field quantities are [Ulaby] given as follows:

$$\nabla \cdot \boldsymbol{D} = \rho_{v} \qquad (8.1)$$

$$\nabla \times \boldsymbol{E} = \frac{-\partial \boldsymbol{B}}{\partial t} \qquad (8.2)$$

$$\nabla \cdot \boldsymbol{B} = 0 \qquad (8.3)$$

$$\nabla \times \boldsymbol{H} = \boldsymbol{J} - \frac{\partial \boldsymbol{D}}{\partial t} \qquad (8.4)$$

where

$\boldsymbol{D}$: Electric flux density vector;

$\boldsymbol{E}$ (V): Electric field intensity;

ρ_{v}: Electric charge density per unit volume;

$\boldsymbol{B}$ (T $=$ W/m^2): Magnetic flux density;

$\boldsymbol{H}$ (A/m $=$ W/m/H): Magnetic field intensity;

$\boldsymbol{J}$ (A/m^2): Current density per unit area.

Parameters such as ∇, $\boldsymbol{D}$, $\boldsymbol{E}$, $\boldsymbol{B}$, and $\boldsymbol{H}$ denoted by bold italic characters are vectors in the space. Note that ∇ is the operator of gradient, defined in the Cartesian coordinate system (x, y, z) as

$$\nabla = \left(\frac{\partial}{\partial x}\right)\boldsymbol{i} + \left(\frac{\partial}{\partial y}\right)\boldsymbol{j} + \left(\frac{\partial}{\partial z}\right)\boldsymbol{k} \qquad (8.5)$$

Note that $(\boldsymbol{i}, \boldsymbol{j}, \boldsymbol{k})$ are directional unit vectors corresponding to the (x, y, z) coordinates.

Electric fields and magnetic fields are coupled if they are not constant with respect to time, as given in Eqs. (8.2) and (8.4).

Another important equation in addition to the four Maxwell equations is the continuity equation, relating to the charge and current density, as

$$\nabla \cdot J + \left(\frac{\partial \rho}{\partial t}\right) = 0 \tag{8.6}$$

Note that there are only four independent equations among the following five governing equations of electromagnetics: Eqs. (8.1), (8.2), (8.3), (8.4) and (8.6). Vectors B and E are the fundamental electromagnetic field vectors, which define the electromagnetic force vector F acting on the electric charge q moving with a velocity V in an electromagnetic field according to Lorenz force equation, given as

$$F = q\ (E + V \times B) \tag{8.7}$$

8.3 Electric Permittivity

The two electric fields (D & E) are related to each other by the electric permittivity of material as

$$D = \varepsilon E \tag{8.8}$$

where ε_d is the electric permittivity of the dielectric material. Electric permittivity can be written on a relative basis as

$$\varepsilon = \varepsilon_0 \ \varepsilon_r \tag{8.9}$$

where
$\varepsilon_0 (8.854 \times 10^{-12}$ F/m): Electric permittivity of free space or vacuum;
ε_r: Relative permittivity of the material, also called dielectric constant if $\varepsilon_{dr} > 1$.

The relative permittivity, commonly called dielectric constant, quantifies how well a material is polarized in response to an applied electric field. It is a function of the operating temperature and frequency. It is typical to call any material with $\varepsilon_r > 1$ a dielectric material (e.g. air with $\varepsilon_r = 1.0006$), though even vacuum with $\varepsilon_r = 1$ is traditionally called a dielectric.

8.4 Magnetic Permeability

The two magnetic fields (B & H given in Fig. 8.1) are related to each other by the magnetic permeability of material as

$$B = \mu \ H \tag{8.10}$$

where μ (Henry/m, H/m, or volt sec/amp/m) is the magnetic permeability of the material. Magnetic permeability can be written on a relative basis as

$$\mu = \mu_0 \ \mu_r \tag{8.11}$$

where

$\mu_0 (4\pi \times 10^{-7} \ H/m)$: Magnetic permeability of free space or vacuum;

μ_r : Relative permeability, as a substance with $\mu_r > 1$ is referred to as magnetic material.

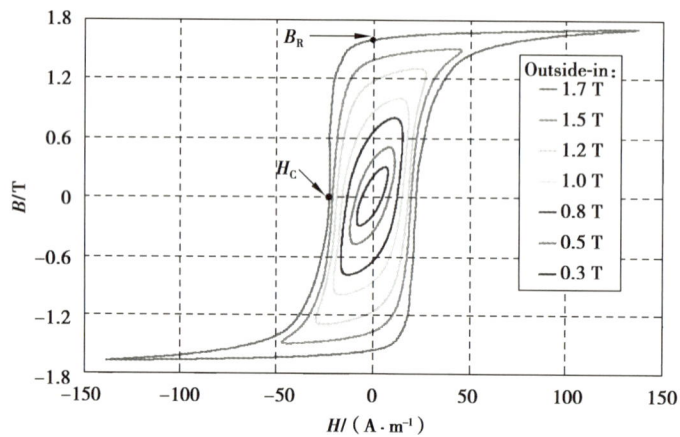

Fig. 8.1 *B-H* **Diagram to Show the** B_R **and** H_C (See Table 130.2 for B_R and H_C Values for Various Magnets)

Coercivity denoted by H_C and usually measured in the unit of A/m measures the resistance of a ferromagnetic material to becoming demagnetized. It is the H value (magnetic field intensity) when $B = 0$ (no magnetic flux).

Retentivity, denoted by B_R and measured in the unit of Tesla measures the resistance of magnetized ferromagnetic material. It is the B value (magnetic flux density) when $H = 0$ (no magnetic field).

8.5   Electric Conductivities

The electrical conductivity of a material quantifies how well it conducts current, and thus it is the inverse of its electric resistivity. The electric resistivities of some materials are listed in Table 8.1. Generally speaking, they are classified into the following five categories:

Material	Resistivity/$(\Omega \cdot m)$
Superconductors	≈ 0
Metals	10^{-7} and less
Semiconductors	Variable
Electrolytes	Variable
Insulators	10^{16} and above

An electric resistivity (ρ_e), as a function of temperature, is redeemable in a linear form as

$$\rho_e = \rho_{e,ref}[1 + \alpha (T - T_{ref})] \tag{8.12}$$

where

$\rho_{e,ref}(\Omega \cdot m)$: Resistivity at the reference temperature;

$\alpha (\text{℃}^{-1})$: Temperature coefficient at 20 ℃;

T & $T_{ref}(\text{℃})$: Temperature and reference temperature.

The material resistivity is usually measured under a steady-state DC (direct current) condition. However, it increases with increasing frequency.

8.6   Semiconductors

The group of chemical elements, which are semi-conductors including germanium, silicon, gray (crystalline) tin, selenium, tellurium, and boron.

8.7   Passive Components

Capacitors, resistors, inductors, and memristors are passive components for electronic equipments.

8.8   Solenoids

Consider a uniform wound solenoid of radius R and n turns per unit length (axially). The magnetic flux density at a point in the space is

$$\boldsymbol{B} = \mu n I \boldsymbol{k} \tag{8.13}$$

The directional vector $\boldsymbol{k}$ means that the magnetic flux density is directed axially in the solenoid cylinder.

8.9　Finite Element Methods for Induction Motors

Applications of finite element methods in electromagnetics include MRI machines, induction motors, BLDC motors, and electric circuits. Finite element methods do magnetic field calculations based on precise geometric dimensions and materials of assembled parts. The calculated magnetic field distribution consequently results in magnetic flux density, inductances, and electromagnetic torque. Spatial harmonic effects, split winding patterns, and nonlinear behaviors of ferromagnetic materials are considered in finite element analysis.

In order to account for the effects imposed by finite axial length, stator ending windings, rotor rings, and rotor slot skewing, it is necessary to conduct the finite element analysis in the 3-dimensional space. The governing equation in the magnetic field can be obtained by substituting Eqs. (8.6) and (8.7) into Eq. (8.4), as

$$\frac{1}{\mu} \nabla \times \boldsymbol{B} = \boldsymbol{J} + \varepsilon \frac{-\partial \boldsymbol{E}}{\partial t} \tag{8.14}$$

The nodal variable employed in finite element formulations is the magnetic vector potential, which is a vector consisting of three scalar variables in the 3-dimensional space and defined as the potential to generate magnetic flux density (a vector in the space) along a certain direction. Mathematically, the curl of the nodal variable yields the magnetic flux density

$$\boldsymbol{B} = \nabla \times \boldsymbol{A} \tag{8.15}$$

of which $\boldsymbol{A}$ is the magnetic vector potential. Substitution of Eq. (8.15) into Eq. (8.14) yields

$$\nabla \times \left(\frac{1}{\mu} \nabla \times \boldsymbol{A} \right) = \boldsymbol{J} - \sigma_{\mathrm{E}} \frac{\mathrm{d}\boldsymbol{A}}{\mathrm{d}t} \tag{8.16}$$

where

σ_{E} (amp/volt/meter = mhos/meter = ohm^{-1}/meter): Electric conductivity. As applied to permanent magnet-based induction motors, Eq. (8.16) may be modified as

$$\nabla \times \left(\frac{1}{\mu} \nabla \times \boldsymbol{A} - \boldsymbol{H}_{\mathrm{C}} \right) = \boldsymbol{J} - \sigma_{\mathrm{E}} \frac{\mathrm{d}\boldsymbol{A}}{\mathrm{d}t} \tag{8.17}$$

where

$\boldsymbol{H}_{\mathrm{C}}$(A/m): Coercivity (magnetic field intensity) of the permanent magnet.

The finite element mesh in the discredited domain has to extend off to infinity for an exact solution, unrealistic physically. It takes experience to judge the optimal size of the exterior region.

References

AL -DIN M, AL-MASHAKBEH A, 2010. Computation of Magnetic Losses in canned High-field PMSM Using Finite Element Method[J]. European Journal of Scientific Research, 40(3):341-351.

AL-NAEMI F, MOSES A, 2006. FEM Modeling for Motor Losses in PM Motors[J]. Journal of Magnetism and Magnetic Materials, 304:794-797.

BASARAN C, DESAI C S, KUNDU T, 1998. Thermo-mechanical Finite Element Analysis of Problems in Electronic Packaging Using State Concept: Part I -Theory and Formulation[J]. Journal of Electronic Packaging, 120:41-47.

BATOS J, SADOWSKI N, 2003. Electromagnetic Modeling of Finite Element Methods[M]. Marcel Dekker, New York, NY, USA.

BINNS K J, LAWRESON P J, TROWBRIDGE C W, 1982. The Analytical and Numerical Solution of Electric and Magnetic Fields[M]. John Wiley and Sons, New York, NY, USA.

CORONEL V F, BESHERS D N, 1988.Magnetomechanical Damping in Iron[J]. Journal of Applied Physics, 64:2006-2015.

DAI M, KEYHANI A, SBASTIAN T, 2005. Fault Analysis of a PM Brushless DC Motor Using Finite Element Method[J]. IEEE Transactions on Energy Conversion, 20(1):1-6.

DESAI C S, et al, 1995. Thermo-mechanical Response of Materials and Interfaces in Electronic Packaging, Part II: Unified Constitutive Models Variation and Design[J]. Journal of Electronic Packaging, 119:301-309.

ELIK M C, GENC C, 2008. Mechanical Fatigue of Electronic Componets under Random Vibration[J]. Fatigue and Fracture of Engineering Materials and Structures, 31(7):505-516.

DRIESEN J, BELMANS R, HAMEYER K, 1999. Coupled Magnetothermal Simulation of Thermally Anisotropic Electric Machine[C]. IEEE International Electric Machines and Drives Conference, 469-471.

FELIZIANI M, MARADEI F, 1999. Modeling of Electromagnetic Fields and Electronic Circuits with Lumped and Distributed Elements by the WETD Method[J]. IEEE Transactions on Magnetics, 35:1666-1669.

GIANCOLI DOUGLAS C, 1995. Physics[M]. 4th Edition, Prentice Hall, NY.

HSU L, et al, 2004. Tooth Shape Optimization of Brushless Permanent Magnet Motors for Reducing Torque Ripples[J]. Journal of Magnetism and Magnetic Materials, 282:193-197.

HUANG M C, TAI C C, 2001. The Effect Factor in the Warpage Problem of an Injection Molded Part with a Thin Shell Feature[J]. J. of Materials Processing Technology, 110:1-9.

IONEL D M, et al, 2007. Computation of Core Losses in Electrical Machines Using Improved Models for Laminated Steel[J]. IEEE Transactions on Industrial Applications, 43(6):1554-1564.

JABBAR M A, AZEMAN A, 2004. Fast Optimization of Electromagnetic Problems: the Reduced Basis Finite Element Approach[J]. IEEE Transactions on Magnetics, 40(4):2161-2163.

JABBARI A, et al, 2009. Shape Optimization of Permanent Magnet Motors Using Reduced Basis Technique [J]. World Academy of Science, Engineering, and Technology, 49:592-597.

JIAN L, CHAU K T, 2009. Analytic Calculation of Magnetic Field Distribution in Coaxial Magnetic Gear[J]. PIER 92:1-16.

LEE J Y, et al, 2007. Tooth Shape Optimization for Cogging Torque Reduction of Transverse Flux Rotary Motor Using Design of Experiments and Response Surface Methodology[J]. IEEE Transactions on Magnetics, 43 (4):1817-1820.

MADAWALA U, BOYS J, 2005. magnetic Field Analysis of an Ironless Brushless DC Machine[J]. IEEE Transactions on Magnetics, 41(8):2384-2390.

MOHAMMAD O A, et al, 2007. Internal Short Circuit Fault Diagnosis for PM Machines Using FE-based Phase Variable Mode and Wavelets Analysis[J]. IEEE Transactions on Magnetics, 43(4):1729-1732.

OKAFOR E, et al, 2009. Magnetic Field Mapping of a Direct Electrical Machine Using Finite Element Method [J]. Journal of Applied Science Research, 5(11):1889-1898.

PAKDEL M, 2009. Analysis of the Magnetic Flux Density, the Magnetic Force and Torque in a 3D Brushless DC Motor[J]. Journal of Electromagnetic Analysis & Applications, 1:1-5.

PASCA S, et al, 2008. Sequentially Coupled Finite Element Model of Transient Magneto-structural Phenomena in Electromagnetic Forming Processes[J]. Proceedings of Advanced Topics in Electrical Engineering, Bucharest:197-202.

PHAM T H, et al, 1999. Transient Finite Element Analysis of an Induction Motor with External Circuit Connections and Electromechanical Coupling[J]. IEEE Transactions on Energy Conversion, 14(4):1407-1412.

READ T, CHEN Y W, GEISS R, 2004. Morphology, Microstructure, and Mechanical Properties of a Copper Electrodeposit[J]. Microelectric Engineering, 75:63-70.

REFFAEE A, et al, 2007. Electrical and Mechanical Properties of Acrylonitrile Butadiene rubber/Styrene Butadiene Rubber Blends Filled with Carbon Black[J]. IEEE International Conference on Solid Dielectrics, July 2007, Winchester, UK:274-276.

TENHUNEN A, 2005. Calculation of Eccentricity Harmonic of the Airgap Flux Density in Induction Motor machine by Impulse Method[J]. IEEE Transactions on Magnetics, 41(5):1904-1907.

TUMBERGER B S, HRIBERNIK B, GORIC V, 2000. Flux Distortion and Iron Losses in Flux-weakened

Permanent Magnet Synchronous Motor[J]. Journal of Magnetism and Magnetic Materials, 215/216:753-755.

ULABY F T, 2007. Fundamentals of Applied Electromagnetic[M]. Pearson Education, Upper Saddle River, NJ, USA.

VASEGHI B, TAKORABET N, MEIBODY-TABAR F, 2009. Transient Finite Element Analysis of Induction Machines with Stator Winding Turn Fault[J]. PIER 95:1-18.

VOKOUN D, et al, 2009. Magnetostatic Interactions and Forces between Cylindrical Permanent Magnets[J]. Journal of Magnetism and Magnetic Materials, 321(22):3758-3763.

VU-QUOC L, et al, 2003. Finite Element Analysis of Advanced Capacitors[J]. International Journal of Numerical Methods in Engineering, 48:397-461.

WANG S, et al, 1999. Continuum Shape Design Sensitivity Analysis of Magnetostatic Field Using Finite Element Method[J]. IEEE Transactions on Magnetics, 35(3):1159-1162.

WANG S, KANG J, 2000. Shape Optimization of BLDC Motor Using 3-D Finite Element Method[J]. IEEE Transactions on Magnetics, 36(4):1119-1123.

WU H, CANGELLARIS A, 2005. Finite Element Analysis for of passive Electromagnetic Devices Including Electric Circuit Models[J]. IEEE Proceedings of Electronic Components and Technology, 1:231-236.

YEH C L, et al, 2007. Transient Analysis of Drop Responses of Response Spectra Incorporated with Modal Superstition[J]. Microelectronics Reliability, 47(8):626-636.

ZHU Z Q, et al, 2000. Analysis of Anisotropic Bonded NdFeB Halbach Cylinders Accounting for Partial Powder Alignment[J]. IEEE Transactions on Magnetics, 36(5):3575-3577.

Table 8.1   Electric Resistivity and Magnetic Permeability of Materials

Material	$T/℃$	$\rho_E/(\Omega \cdot m)$	μ /Hm^{-1}
Carbon (Graphene)	20	10^{-8}	—
Cabon Fiber (Nano)	20	1.45×10^{-8}	—
Ag (> 99%)	20	$1.59\times10^{-8}[1 + 0.0038 (T-20 ℃)]$	—
Ag-nano (Sintered)	23	3.8×10^{-8}	—
Ag-micro (Sintered)	23	6.6×10^{-8}	—
Cu	20	$1.68\times10^{-8}[1 + 0.003862 (T-20 ℃)]$	1.256629×10^{-6}
C11000-ETP	20	1.712×10^{-8}	—
Cu (Annealed)	20	$1.72\times10^{-8}[1 + 0.00393 (T-20 ℃)]$	—
C10200 (Cu-OF)	20	1.725×10^{-8}	—

continued

Material	$T/°C$	$\rho_E/(\Omega \cdot m)$	μ/Hm^{-1}
C10400 (Cu-OFS)	20	1.725×10^{-8}	—
C15000	20	1.86×10^{-8}	—
C16200	20	1.92×10^{-8}	—
C18200	20	2.15×10^{-8}	—
Constantan (Cu-44.2Ni-...)	20	$4.9 \times 10^{-7}[1 + 0.000008 (T-20 °C)]$	—
Au	20	$2.44 \times 10^{-8}[1+0.0034 (T-20 °C)]$	—
Al	20	$2.82 \times 10^{-8}[1+0.0039 (T- 20 °C)]$	1.256665×10^{-6}
Ca (Calcium)	20	$3.36 \times 10^{-8}[1+0.0041 (T-20 °C)]$	—
Be	23	3.56×10^{-8}	—
Mg	23	3.9×10^{-8}	—
Sodium	23	4.77×10^{-8}	—
W	20	$5.6 \times 10^{-8}[1+0.0045 (T-20 °C)]$	—
Co	23	5.81×10^{-8}	—
Zn	23	$5.9 \times 10^{-8}[1+0.0037 (T-20 °C)]$	—
Ni	20	$6.99 \times 10^{-8}[1+0.006 (T-20 °C)]$	$(1.26 \sim 7.54) \times 10^{-4}$
Ni-10Cr	20	$0.706 \times 10^{-6}[1+0.00032 (T-20 °C)]$	—
Ni-20Cr	20	$1.1 \times 10^{-6}[1+0.0004 (T-20 °C)]$	—
Ni-30Cr	20	1.18×10^{-6}	—
Ni-16Fe-5Cu-2Cr (Mu)	20	5.5×10^{-7}	0.044
In	23	8.37×10^{-8}	—
Pt	20	1.06×10^{-7}	1.25697×10^{-6}
Sn	23	1.24×10^{-7}	—
Pb	23	2.18×10^{-7}	—
Magnet (Fe-Cr-Co)	23	7×10^{-7}	—
Mercury	20	9.8×10^{-7}	—
Magnet (Nd-Fe-B)	23	1.6×10^{-6}	1.32×10^{-6}
Metglas (2605SA1)	20	1.3×10^{-6}	0.6
Bi	23	1.29×10^{-6}	1.25643×10^{-6}

continued

Material	$T/{}^\circ\!C$	$\rho_E/(\Omega \cdot m)$	$\mu\,/Hm^{-1}$
Potassium	23	1.06×10^{-5}	—
Pt	20	$1.06\times10^{-5}[1+0.00392\,(T-20\ {}^\circ\!C)]$	1.256970×10^{-6}
Sn	20	$1.09\times10^{-5}[1+0.0045\,(T-20\ {}^\circ\!C)]$	—
Pb	20	$2.2\times10^{-5}[1+0.0039\,(T-20\ {}^\circ\!C)]$	—
Ti	20	$4.2\times10^{-5}[1+0.0039\,(T-20\ {}^\circ\!C)]$	—
Manganin	20	$4.82\times10^{-5}[1+0.000002\,(T-20\ {}^\circ\!C)]$	—
Mercury	20	$9.8\times10^{-5}[1+0.0009\,(T-20\ {}^\circ\!C)]$	—
Li	20	$9.28\times10^{-4}[1+0.006\,(T-20\ {}^\circ\!C)]$	—
Fe (Iron)	20	$9.6\times10^{-4}[1+0.005\,(T-20\ {}^\circ\!C)]$	2.5×10^{-1}
SAE1010 Steel	20	1.43×10^{-5}	1.26×10^{-4}
C Fiber (AS-4; Long)	20	1.53×10^{-5}	—
C-Ni coated (AS-4)	20	7×10^{-6}	—
Ge	20	0.46	—
Silicon	20	10^{14}	—
PVC	20	10^{11}	—
Diamond	20	10^{12}	—
Epoxy	20	10^{12}	—
Epoxy-6 MWCNT	20	3.5×10^{-2}	—
Epoxy-4 MWCNT	20	9.55×10^{-2}	—
Epoxy-2 MWCNT	20	6.52×10^{-1}	—
Epoxy-1 MWCNT	20	5.34	—
Epoxy-0.5 MWCNT	20	1.92×10^{2}	—
Epoxy-0.25 MWCNT	20	1.57×10^{3}	—
Polydimethylsiloxane	20	10^{13}	—
PC	20	10^{14}	—
ABS	20	10^{14}	—
Fused Quarts (SiO_2)	20	7.5×10^{17}	—
PET	20	10^{21}	—

continued

Material	$T/{}^{\circ}C$	$\rho_E/(\Omega \cdot m)$	$\mu\,/Hm^{-1}$
Teflon	20	10^{24}	1.2567×10^{-6}
Sapphire	20	—	1.2566368×10^{-6}

Notes: $\rho_E(\Omega \cdot m)$ = Electric resistivity and $\rho_e = \rho_{ref}[1 + \alpha(T - T_{ref})]$;

μ (Hm^{-1} or $N \cdot A^{-2}$) = Magnetic permeability, also called electromagnetism as $\mu = B/H$;

(Eq. (121.10)), and $\mu_0 = 4\pi \times 10^{-7}\ Hm^{-1}$ in the vacuum;

T = Temperature in ${}^{\circ}C$;

MWCNT = 6% (by weight) of multi-walled nano-tube carbon ($D = 20$ nm & $L = 50$ μm).

Chapter 9

Natural Materials

9.1　Introduction

Some objects related to the study of automobile engineering come from nature. They are mainly cellulosics, wood and bamboo, roads, and human beings. Most of them are orthotropic materials by nature.

9.2　Cellulosics

Plastic composites reinforced by cellulose fibers from trees or other plants can be used in place of fiberglass or mineral reinforcements. Fibers used in the new composite are more and more taken from sustainably grown and harvested trees and related byproducts such as chips. The cellulose-based plastic composite material meets the requirements for stiffness, durability, and temperature resistance. However, in the process of fabricating the composite, it is difficult to impregnate the thermoplastic resin into reinforcement fibers because of the high melt viscosity. Surface treatment on continuous natural fiber may be performed by using PU (polyurethane) or EP (flexible epoxy) to improve the interfacial properties [Wongsriraksa et al.].

9.3　Wood and Bamboo

Wood, bamboo and other natural fibrous plants are natural composites with high strength-to-weight ratio useful for structures. They are used in old vehicles, and gain more attention as reinforcing fibers for plastics in the automotive applications.

9.4　Roads

Roads, intended to sustain vehicular or foot traffic, are made of durable materials such as asphalt, concrete, gravels, cobblestones, granite setts, and bricks. Interactions between vehicles and grounds have been a challenge to durability engineers.

9.5　Human beings

Protection of human beings is a necessity to vehicle design. The versatility of numerical simulation permits automotive engineers to systematically analyze the complex arrays of factors experienced by a biomechanical system such as a human being under various loading scenarios such as passenger damage induced in a car crash. Accuracy in taking material data from cone, skeletal muscle, cartilage, tendon and ligament, brain, and joints is of great concern to analysts.

Chapter 10

Automobile Fluids

10.1   Introduction

Engine oil lubricates and cools internal combustion engines as there are so many moving parts working like the lifeblood of a vehicle. Oil reduces friction and keeps the engine from overheating. This lubrication also prevents rust by preventing oxygen from getting to the metal. The general rule of thumb is to change your oil every 6000 kilometers for a passenger car, if not specified otherwise.

10.2   Hydraulic Fluid

Hydraulic fluid is the medium, by which power is transferred in hydraulic machinery. Common hydraulic fluids are based on mineral oil or water. Examples of passenger vehicles that might use hydraulic fluid include hydraulic brakes, power steering systems, and transmissions. Hydraulic fluids are also used in off-high machinery such as garbage trucks, forklifts, aircraft flight systems, excavators, and backhoes. Hydraulic systems in aircraft provide a means for the operation of aircraft components.

10.2.1   Transmission/Transaxle fluid

Transmission/Transaxle fluid performs many of the same functions as motor oil, such as lubrication and cooling. As transmission/Transaxle fluid moves through a transmission, it gets pressurized and provides the hydraulic power needed to perform the transmission/Transaxle's basic functions, like changing gear ratios.

10.2.2   Brake Fluid

Brake fluid gets pressurized and provides the hydraulic power needed to push brake pads (or shoes) against the disk (or drum). Brake fluid should be filled to the "full" line, or at least two-thirds full.

10.2.3   Power Steering Fluid

It is supposed to fill power steering fluid reservoir, if it is not an electric power steering system. Power steering fluid, pressurized by a small hydraulic pump powered by the engine, helps to make turning a vehicle easier.

10.3   Coolant

Coolants are needed for reducing the temperature rise in engines, transmissions, or electric motors. Adding antifreeze to the water lowers the freezing temperature of the water, which helps prevent freezing in cold weather. A 50/50 mix is recommended for coolant which is not diluted.

10.4   Window Washer Fluid

Washer fluid provides a fast means of clearing the window/windshield/lamp of dust, bug residue, and other particles while driving. Washer fluid may contain methanol that can break down bug guts, as well as ethylene glycol or other antifreeze fluids to lower the freezing temperature of the washer fluid.

10.5   Battery Fluid

Cars with maintenance-free batteries don't require checking the battery fluid. Other car batteries, however, must have their individual cells refilled from time to time.

10.6   Some Key Temperature Points

10.6.1   Flash Point

Flash point is the temperature, at which a liquid gives off vapor in sufficient quantity to ignite momentarily or flash when a flame is applied.

10.6.2   Fire Point

Fire point is the temperature at which a substance gives off vapor in sufficient quantity to ignite and continue to burn when exposed to a spark or flame.

10.6.3　Pour Point

Pour point is the temperature, at which the fluid stops flowing [ISO 3016].

References

BECALSKI A, BARTLETT K H, 2006. Methanol Exposure to Car Occupants from Windshield Washing Fluid: a Pilot Study[J]. Indoor Air, 16(2):153-157.

ESTEBAN B, 2012. Temperature-dependent of Density and Viscosity of Vegetable Oils [J]. Biomass and Bioenergy, 42:164-171.

Elastomers

Chapter 11

ACM (Polyacrylate Rubber)

11.1   Introduction

Polyacrylate rubber is also called Acrylic Co-Monomer (ACM). ACM has a good resistance to oil at an elevated temperature similar to, although not as good as, FKM, FFKM, and FVQM in the automotive applications. It is an inexpensive substitute for fluoro-polymers as low cost components providing acceptable performance. Mechanical properties of ACM (Polyacrylate Rubber) are listed in Table 11.1. Two example stress-strain curves are depicted in Fig. 11.1.

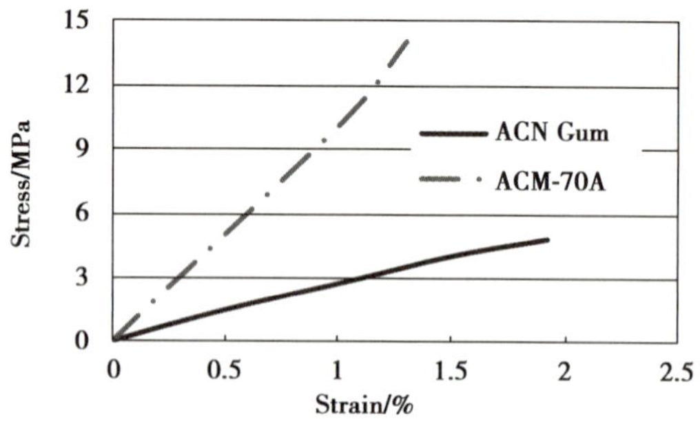

Fig. 11.1   Example Stress-Strain Curves of ACM Rubber

ACM is a saturated rubber and it is commercialized with different types of cure-site monomers [Vital]. These sites react with functional groups present in other polymers during the melt processing, producing graft copolymers or networks at the interface, which act as bridges between the phases. This process, known as reactive compatibilization, decreases the interfacial tension and increases the interfacial adhesion [Soares]. Consequently a fine morphology is usually achieved for these blends, which contributes to an improvement of the overall properties as demonstrated by ACM-based thermoplastic elastomers.

11.2   Applications

ACM (Polyacrylate Rubber) are oil resistant and high temperature resistant rubbers, which have important applications as oil seals and gaskets used in high performance engines. Its major applications in automotive industry are gaskets in engine valve covers, oil pans, rocker covers, transmissions, and hoses. Recently its application has been expanded to housings, tubes, and air ducts.

References

ABUDUL KADER M, BHOWMICJ K, 2003. Thermal Ageing, Degradation and Swelling of Acrylate Rubber,

Fluororubber and Their Blends Containing Polyfunctional Acrylates[J]. Polymer Degradation and Stability, 79(2):283.

CELESTINO M L, et al, 2009. Acrylic Rubber/Nitrile Rubber Blends: The Effect of Curatives on the Mechanical, Morphological, and Dynamic Mechanical Properties[J]. Journal of Applied Polymer Science, 113(2):721-729.

DING X, XU R, YU D, et al, 2003. Effect of Ultrafine, Fully Vulcanized Acrylate Powdered Rubber on the Mechanical Properties and Crystallization Behavior of Nylon 6[J]. Journal of Applied Polymer Science, 90: 3503-3511.

DOS SANTOS D, BATALHA G, 2010. Mechanical Behavior Characterizing and Simulation of Polyacrylate Rubber[J]. Journal of Achievements in Materials and Manufacturing Engineering, 38(1):33-40.

GIANNETTI E, MAZZOCCHI R, FIORE L, et al, 1983.Ammonium Salt Catalyzed Crosslinking Mechanism of Acrylic Rubbers[J]. Rubber Chemistry and Technology, 56:21-30.

JHA A, DUTTA B, BHOWMICK A K, 1999. Effect of Fillers and Plasticizers on the Performance of Novel Heat and Oil-Resistant Thermoplastic Elastomers from Nylon-6 and Acrylate Rubber Blends[J]. Journal of Applied Polymer Science, 74:1490-1501.

NAKAJIMA N, DEMARCO R D, 2001. Application of Polyacrylate Rubber for High Performance Automotive Gaskets and Seals[J]. J. of Elastomers and Plastics, 33(2):114-120.

SHIVAKUMAR E, SRIVASTAVA R, PANDEY K, et al, 2005. Compatibility Study of Blends of Acrylic Rubber (ACM), Poly(ethylene terephthalate) (PET), and Liquid Crystalline Polymer (LCP)[J]. Journal of Macromolecular Science, A: Pure and Applied Chemistry, 42:1181-1195.

SOARES B, et al, 2008. A Novel Thermoplastic Elastomer Based on Dynamically Vulcanized Polypropylene/Acrylic Rubber Blends[J]. Express Polymer Letters, 2(8):602-613.

VIAL T M, 1971. Recent Developments in Acrylic Elastomers[J]. Rubber Chemistry and Technology, 44:344-362.

VIJAYABASKAR V, et al, 2004. Electron Beam Initiated Modification of Acrylic Elastomer in Presence of Polyfunctional Monomers[J]. Radiation Physics and Chemistry, 71:1045-1058.

WIMOLMALA E, WOOTTHIKANOKKHAN J, SOMBATSOMPOP N, 2001. Effects of Composition and Temperature on Extrudate Characteristics, Morphology, and Tensile Properties of Acrylic Rubber-Blended PVC[J]. Journal of Applied Polymer Science, 80:2523-2534.

WONG-ON J, WOOTTHIKANOKKHAN J, 2003. Dynamic Vulcanization of Acrylic Rubber-Blended PVC[J]. Journal of Applied Polymer Science, 88:2657-2663.

WU C, OTANI Y, NAMIKI N, et al, 2001. Phase Modification of Acrylate Rubber/Chlorinated Polypropylene Blends by a Hindered Phenol Compound[J]. Polymer Journal, 33:322-329.

Table 11.1   Mechanical Properties of ACM（Polyacrylate Rubber）

Material-DAM	$T/℃$	ρ	(σ,ε)	α	k	γ	Set	$\tan\delta$
ACM	$-40(T_g)$	—	—	—	—	—	—	—
	$-20($ Low service temperature $)$							
	23	1.33	$(1.4,\ 50\%)$ $(2.7,\ 100\%)$ $(4,\ 150\%)$ $(4.8,\ 192\%)$	—	—	—	—	—
	70	—	—	—	—	—	$\Delta_{22}=20\%$	—
	$150($ High service temperature $)$							
ACM（75A;65 pphr N550）	$-40(T_g)$	—	—	—	—	—	—	—
	23	1.33	$(10,100\%)$ $(14,130\%)$	—	—	—	—	—
	$150($ High service temperature $)$							
ACM（90A）	$-40(T_g)$	—	—	—	—	—	—	—
	23	1.33	$(17.2,100\%)$	—	—	—	—	—
	$150($ High service temperature $)$							
ACM（65A; 100 pphr N990）	$-40(T_g)$	—	—	—	—	—	—	—
	23	1.33	$(5.4,100\%)$ $(7.2,175\%)$	—	—	—	—	—
	$150($ High service temperature $)$							
ACM（87A; 200 pphr N990）	$-40(T_g)$	—	—	—	—	—	—	—
	23	1.33	$(8.1,80\%)$	—	—	—	—	—
	$150($ High service temperature $)$							

Notes：pphr＝Parts of reinforcing material per hundred parts of rubber；

CB＝Carbon black such as N110, ⋯, N990（ISO classification）；

××A＝Shore A durometer hardness；

$\tan\delta$＝Loss factor ≡ loss modulus/storage modulus at 1 Hz.

Chapter 12

AEM (Ethylene Acrylic Rubber)

12.1　Introduction

AEM (Ethylene Acrylic Rubber) exhibits properties similar to those of ACM (Polyacrylate Rubber), but with enhanced mechanical properties such as working in an extended low temperature range.

AEM (Ethylene Acrylic Rubber) is an acrylic monomer. It is also called EAM (by ASTM and DIN). Ethylene-acrylate offers a high degree of ozone, sunlight, heat, oil swell, gas permeability, and weather resistance. Mechanical properties of AEM (Ethylene Acrylic Rubber) are listed in Table 12.1. Two example stress-strain curves are depicted in Fig. 12.1. One version of AEM is Vamac (DuPont Dow Elastomers).

Fatigue life of AEM (Ethylene Acrylic) is generally good, so are tearing, abrasion, and permanent-set-in-compression properties. It has the ability to absorb energy over a wide temperature range. The damping characteristics of AEM hold by quite constantly over a frequency range between 10 Hz and 10^3 Hz as long as the temperature is constant. The damping effect is more significant than IIR at elevated temperatures (above 40 ℃).

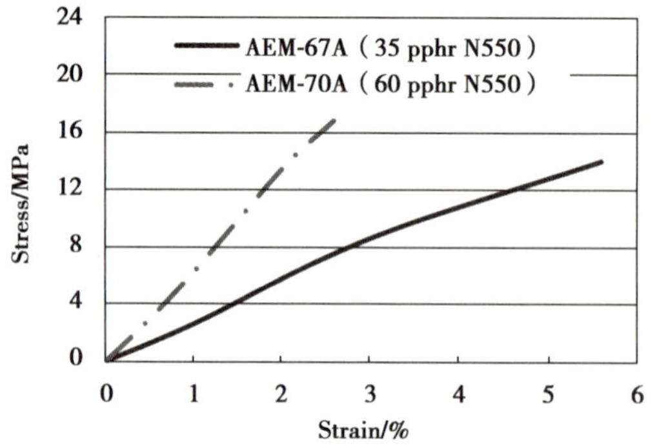

Fig. 12.1　Example Stress-Strain Curves of AEM Rubbers

12.2　Applications

AEM (Ethylene Acrylic) has been used in automotive applications requiring resistance to service fluids over a broad temperature range, such as power steering seals, turbocharger hoses, automatic transmission seals/gaskets/oil hoses, crankcase venting hoses, torsional vibration dampers, fuel hose covers, vacuum tubes, and vibration mount applications (e.g. engine mount). AEM rubber would be a suitable replacement for natural rubber or neoprene rubber in engine mounts where exposure to hydrocarbon fluids such as diesel fuel and lubricating oil is a concern.

References

HARRELL J R, et al, 2001. Ethylene/Acrylic Elastomers (AEM)-New Developments for Automotive Applications[J]. SAE Transactions, 110:624-628.

KUMAR E, et al, 2007. Viscoelastic Properties of In Situ Composite Based on Ethylene Acrylic Elastomer (AEM) and Liquid Crystalline Polymer (LCP) Blend[J]. Composites Science and Technology, 67(6): 1202-1209.

Table 12.1   Mechanical Properties of AEM (Ethylene Acrylic Rubber)

Material-DAM	$T/℃$	ρ	(σ,ε)	α	k	γ	Set	$\tan\delta$
AEM (67A;35 pphr N550)	−80	—	—	—	—	—	—	0.005
	−37(T_g)	—	—	—	—	—	—	0.05
	−20	—	—	—	—	—	—	0.37
	23	1.04	(2.6, 100%) (8.6, 300%) (14, 560%)	—	—	—	—	0.17
	40	—	—	—	—	—	—	0.25
	80	—	—	—	—	—	—	0.3
	120	—	—	—	—	—	—	0.18
	175(High service temperature)							
AEM-G (70A; 60 pphr N550)	−37(T_g)	—	—	—	—	—	—	—
	23	1.04	(1.7, 25%) (2.9, 50%) (6.2, 100%) (13.3, 200%) (16.8, 260%)	—	—	—	—	—
	175(High service temperature)							
AEM (64A;55 pphr N550; Vmac DP)	−37(T_g)	—	—	—	—	—	—	—
	23	1.04	(7.2, 100%) (18.2, 208%)	—	—	—	—	—
	175(High service temperature)							

continued

Material-DAM	$T/℃$	ρ	(σ, ε)	α	k	γ	Set	$\tan \delta$
AEM (73A; Vmac DP; Heat Aging 6 weeks at 150 ℃)	$-37(T_g)$	—	—	—	—	—	—	—
	23	1.04	(8.7, 100%) (17.2, 200%)	—	—	—	—	—
	175 (High service temperature)							
AEM (56A; Vmac DP; SF105 Oil Aging, 6 weeks at 150 ℃)	$-37(T_g)$	—	—	—	—	—	—	—
	23	1.04	(6.2, 100%) (15.2, 188%)	—	—	—	—	—
	175 (High service temperature)							
AEM (78A; Vmac G)	$-36(T_g)$	—	—	—	—	—	—	—
	23	1.03	(8.5, 100%) (16.3, 195%)	—	—	—	—	—
	175 (High service temperature)							
AEM (78A; Vmac Ultra IP)	$-37(T_g)$	—	—	—	—	—	—	—
	23	1.04	(7, 100%) (18, 261%)	—	—	—	—	—
	175 (High service temperature)							
AEM (63A; Vmac Ultra LT; 20 pphr Polyether/ester plasticizer + 66pphr N550)	$-54(T_g)$	—	—	—	—	—	—	
	23	1.04	(3.1, 100%) (11, 355%)	—	—	—	—	—
	80	—	—	—	—	—	—	—
	120	—	—	—	—	—	—	—
	175 (High service temperature)							
AEM (95A)	$-37(T_g)$	—	—	—	—	—	—	—
	23	1.04	(20, 200%)	—	—	—	—	—
	175 (High service temperature)							

Notes: pphr = Parts of reinforcing material per hundred parts of rubber;

CB = Carbon black such as N110, ⋯, N990 (ISO classification);

××A = Shore A durometer hardness;

$\tan \delta$ = Loss factor = loss modulus/storage modulus at 1 Hz.

Chapter 13

BR (Butadiene Rubber)

13.1 Introduction

BR (Butadiene Rubber) has good resistance to wear and maintain high resilience at low temperatures. BR is flexible, but has a low elongation at break since the interaction among BR molecules is not as intensive as other rubbers. BR has been used in combination with NR (or SBR) in order to compensate each other's physical performance. Mechanical properties of BR (Butadiene Rubber) are listed in Table 13.1. An example stress-strain curve is given in Fig. 13.1.

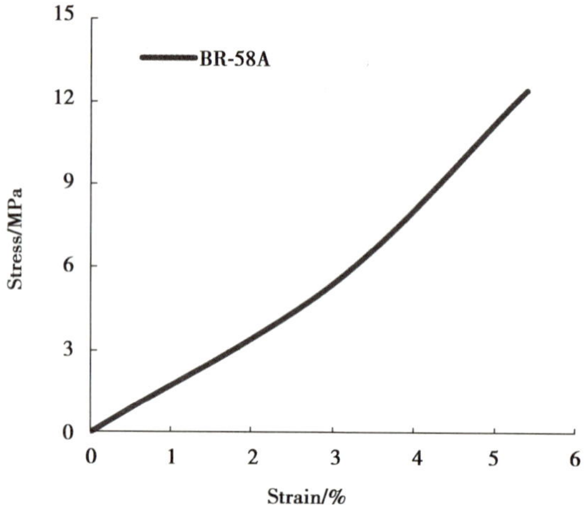

Fig. 13.1　Example Stress-Strain Curve of BR (Butadiene Rubber)

13.2 Applications

BR (Butadiene Rubber) is mixed with NR and SBR as an indispensable ingredient for tire components such as treads, sidewalls, and belts.

References

CHIU H, TSAI P, 2006. Aging and Mechanical Properties of NR/BR Blends [J]. Journal of Materials Engineering and Performance:15(1):88-94.

KARAK N, GUPTA B R, 2000. Effects of Different Ingredients and Cure Parameters on Physical Properties of a Tyre Tread Compound[J]. Kautschuk Gummi Kunststoffe, 53(1-2):30-34.

PALADE L, VERNEY V, ATTANE P, 1995. Time-Temperature Superposition and Linear Viscoelasticity of Polybutadienes[J]. Macromolecules, 28:7051-7057.

YANG BIN, et al, 2006. A Study of the Ozonolysis of Butadiene Rubber in the Presence of Ethanol[J].
Polymer Degradation and Stability, 95:852-858.

Table 13.1　Mechanical Properties of BR (Butadiene Rubber)

Material-DAM	$T/℃$	ρ	(σ,ε)	α	k	γ	Set	$\tan\delta$
BR (58A)	$-85(T_g)$	—	—	—	—	—	—	—
	23	0.93	(5.4, 300%) (12.4, 540%)	224	0.25	—	—	0.05
	107(High service temperature)							

Notes: pphr = Parts of reinforcing material per hundred parts of rubber;

CB = Carbon black such as N110, ⋯, N990 (ISO classification);

××A = Shore A durometer hardness.

Chapter 14

CO (Epichlorohydrin) and ECO (Ethylene Oxide Epichlorohydrin)

14.1   Introduction

CO (Epichlorohydrin) and ECO (Ethylene Oxide Epichlorohydrin) are aliphatic polyethers with chlorofunctional side chains, noted for their resistance to fuel oil, high (low) temperature, aging, impervious to gas and good shock-proof. Mechanical properties of CO (Epichlorohydrin) and ECO (Ethylene Oxide Epichlorohydrin) are listed in Table 14.1.

14.2   CO (Epichlorohydrin)

It is a homopolymer of Epichlorohydrin. Its air impermeability is excellent, even better than butyl rubber that is used for inner liners to seal the air in tires. However, it has limited flexibility at low temperatures (−20 ℃ or lower).

14.3   ECO (Ethylene Oxide Epichlorohydrin)

It is a copolymer of epichlorohydrin and ethylene oxide. This rubber has excellent ozone resistance. Epichlorohydrin (ECO) has properties similar to nitrile rubber but with better heat, oil and petrol resistance. It has a low gas permeability and better low temperature flexibility than NBR. Its resistance to acids, alkalis and ozone is excellent. Because it is electro-statically dissipative, ECO is useful for roll applications such as printer rollers. However, its poor resistance to compression set limits its use as a sealing material and its corrosive effect on metals can limit metal bonding applications. One example stress-strain curve is given in Fig. 14.1.

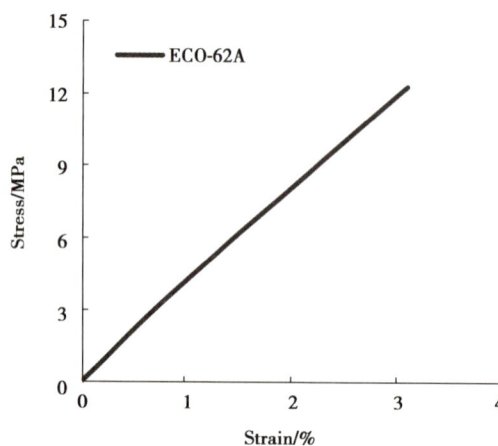

Fig. 14.1   Example Stress-Strain Curve of ECO (Ethylene Oxide Epichlorohydrin)

14.4   Applications

Applications of CO and ECO include automotive fuel hoses, emission tubings, bladders, air ducts, diaphragms, and air conditioner hoses.

Reference

CABLE C J, SMITH C T, 1996. Epichlorohydrine in Fuel Hoses [M]. Rubber Division Meeting, ACS, Louisville, KY, USA.

Table 14.1   Mechanical Properties of CO (Epichlorohydrin) and ECO (Ethylene Oxide Epichlorohydrin)

Material-DAM	$T/℃$	ρ	(σ, ε)	α	k	γ	Set	$\tan \delta$
CO (61A)	$-25(T_g)$	—	—	—	—	—	—	—
	-15	(T_b)	—	—	—	—	—	—
	23	1.27	(13.8, 550%)	222	—	—	—	—
	135(High service temperature)							
ECO (62A; 40 pphr N550)	$-46(T_g)$	—	—	—	—	—	—	—
	23	1.27	(4.2, 100%) (11.5, 300%) (12.3, 310%)	222	—	—	—	—
	135(High service temperature)							
ECO (78A)	$-46(T_g)$	—	—	—	—	—	—	—
	23	1.27	(15, 350%)	222	—	—	—	—
	135 (High service temperature)							

Notes: pphr = Parts of reinforcing material per hundred parts of rubber;

CB = Carbon black such as N110, ⋯, N990 (ISO classification);

××A = Shore A durometer hardness.

Chapter 15

CR (Chloroprene Rubber or Neoprene)

15.1 Introduction

CR (Chloroprene Rubber or Neoprene) is all-purpose rubber, being famous for its well balance of material properties such as good mechanical strength, high ozone resistance, good aging resistance, low flammability, good resistance to chemicals, moderate fuel/oil resistance, good adhesion to many substrates (eg. fabricated metals), and ease to be vulcanized using various accelerators over a wide temperature range. One major drawback is its limited flexibility at low temperatures. Mechanical properties of CR (Chloroprene rubber or Neoprene) are listed in Table 15.1. Typical stress-strain curve of CR with high hardness is shown in Fig. 15.1. Influence of working temperature and aging on rubber elasticity of CR is identified in Table 15.2. The typical delivery form of commercial CR is "chips".

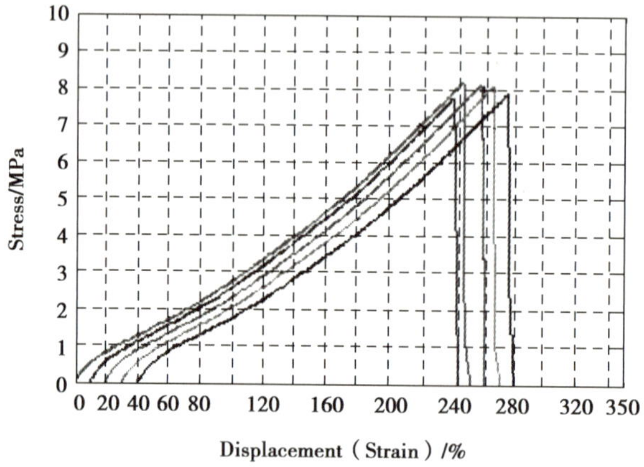

Fig. 15.1 **Typical Stress-Strain Curves of CR (Chloroprene Rubber) with High Hardness (5 Samples)**

15.2 Applications

CR (Chloroprene Rubber or Neoprene), has been used for automotive transmission belts, cables, and hoses.

References

HA ANH T, VU-KHANH T, 2005. Prediction of Mechanical Properties of Polychloroprene during Thermo-Oxidative Aging[J]. Polymer Testing, 24(6):775-780.

MARTINS A, et al, 2004. Mechanical and Dynamic Mechanical Properties of Chloroprene Rubber and Cellulose II Composites[J]. Journal of Applied Polymer Science, 92(4):2425-2430.

Table 15.1   Mechanical Properties of CR（Chloroprene Rubber or Neoprene）

Material-DAM	$T/℃$	ρ	(σ,ε)	α	k	γ	Set	$\tan\delta$
CR（40A）	$-43(T_{\mathrm{g}})$	—	—	—	—	—	—	—
	23	1.2	（5.5, 350%）	200	0.19	1120	—	0.11
	149（High service temperature）							
CR（50A）	$-43(T_{\mathrm{g}})$	—	—	—	—	—	—	—
	23	1.2	（5.5, 300%）	200	0.19	1120	—	0.11
	149（High service temperature）							
CR（60A）	$-43(T_{\mathrm{g}})$	—	—	—	—	—	—	—
	23	1.2	（6.2, 300%）	200	0.19	1120	—	0.11
	149（High service temperature）							
CR（70A）	$-43(T_{\mathrm{g}})$	—	—	—	—	—	—	—
	23	1.2	（6.9, 200%）	200	0.19	1120	—	0.11
	70	—	—	—	—	—	$\Delta_{22}=35\%$	—
	149（High service temperature）							
CR-Specialty（Fig. 15.1）	$-43(T_{\mathrm{g}})$	—	—	—	—	—	—	—
	23	1.2	（2.8, 100%） （6.4, 200%） （8, 240%）	200	0.19	1120	—	0.11
	149（High service temperature）							
CR（70A; 100 pphr N990）	$-43(T_{\mathrm{g}})$	—	—	—	—	—	—	—
	23	1.2	（7, 200%） （16, 390%）	200	0.19	1120	—	0.11
	149（High service temperature）							
CR（80A; 200 pphr N990）	$-43 (T_{\mathrm{g}})$	—	—	—	—	—	—	—
	23	1.2	（8.3, 200%） （9, 250%）	200	0.19	1120	—	0.11
	149（High service temperature）							

Notes：pphr＝Parts of reinforcing material per hundred parts of rubber；

CB＝Carbon black such as N110, ⋯, N990（ISO classification）；

××A＝Shore A durometer hardness.

Table 15.2 Influence of Working Temperature and Aging on Rubber Elasticity of CR (Neoprene)

$T/^{\circ}C$	Aging/h	E/MPa	C_{10}/MPa	C_{01}/MPa
100	0	3.41	0.169	0.443
100	48	3.69	0.199	0.413
100	96	3.68	0.214	0.454
100	168	4.84	0.299	0.541
120	0	3.41	0.169	0.443
120	48	4.74	0.243	0.619
120	96	6.96	0.343	0.834
120	168	10.9	1.588	1.329
130	0	3.41	0.169	0.443
130	48	5.14	0.293	0.607
130	96	3.68	0.214	0.454
130	168	24.6	1.186	3.189
140	0	3.41	0.169	0.443
140	24	6.78	0.345	0.786
140	48	10.5	0.523	1.221
140	96	24.3	1.129	2.920
150	0	3.41	0.169	0.443
150	24	5.92	0.429	0.631
150	48	11.81	0.74	1.435

Notes: $E(MPa) \approx 6(C_{10}+C_{01})$ for almost incompressible rubber;

Data given above are for reference only.

Chapter 16

CSM (Chlorosulfonated Polyethylene)

16.1 Introduction

CSM (Chlorosulfonated Polyethylene), also called CE or CSPE, and commercially named Hypalon by [DuPont], is rubber-like thermoset material; high molecular with polyethylene with sulphonyl chloride. It is usually formulated to produce self-vulcanizing membranes. CSM has demonstrated durability in harsh environment due to its good resistance to oxygen, ozone, water, alkalis, acids, and most chemicals. Mechanical properties of CSM are listed in Table 16.1. One example stress-strain curve is given in Fig. 16.1. Although CSM is flame retardant, it has limited flexibility at low temperatures. CSM has excellent abrasion resistance and excellent tensile and elongation, but it is not suitable for any dynamic sealing applications due to its large compression set.

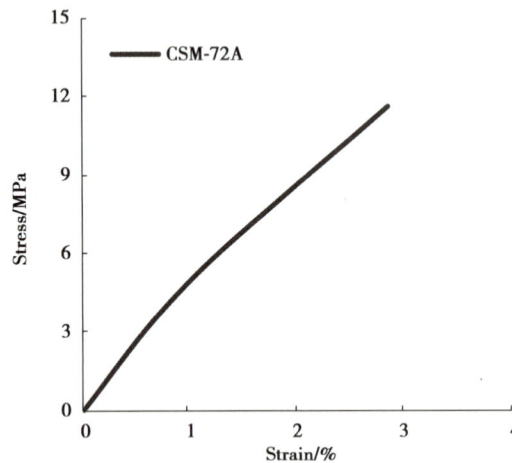

Fig. 16.1 Example Stress-Strain Curve of CSM (Chlorosulfonated Polyethylene)

16.2 Applications

Automotive applications include timing belts, hoses, tubing, and power steering. CSM (Chlorosulfonated Polyethylene), along with PVC, is one of the most common materials used to make inflatable boats and folding kayaks.

References

LEE J, et al, 2014. A Study on the Properties of CSPE According to Accelerated Thermal Aging Years[J]. Journal of Electric Engineering and Technology, 9(2):643-648.

MAIDAI A K, et al, 2012. Chlorosulfonated Polyethylene-Polypropylene Thermoplastic Vulcanizate: Mechanical, Morphological, Thermal, and Rheological Properties[J]. Journal of Applied Polymer Science, 127(2):1268-1274.

NANDA M, TRIPATHY D K, 2010. Influence of Different Curing Systems on the Physico-Mechanical and Rheological Properties of CSM Rubber[J]. Polymers and Polymeric Composites,18(8):417-427

NANDA M, TRIPATHY D K, 2008. Physico-Mechanical and Electrical Properties of Chlorosulfonated Polyethylene Vulcanizates[J]. Express Polymer Letters, 2(12):855-865.

NARUSE T, et al, 2009. Thermal Degradation of Chlorosulfonated Polyethylene Rubber and Ethylene Propylene Diene Terpolymer[J]. Materials and Design, 42:147-155.

TANRATTANAKUL V, PETCHKAEW A, 2007. Mechanical Properties and Blend Compatibility of Natural Rubber-Chlorosulfonated Polyethylene Blends[J]. Journal of Applied Polymers, 99(1):127-140.

Table 16.1   Mechanical Properties of CSM (Chlorosulfonated Polyethylene)

Material-DAM	$T/℃$	ρ	(σ,ε)	α	k	γ	Set	$\tan \delta$
CSM (50A)	$-38(T_g)$	—	—	—	—	—	—	—
	23	1.18	(7.6, 350%)	—	—	—	—	—
	130(High service temperature)							
CSM (60A)	$-38(T_g)$	—	—	—	—	—	—	—
	23	1.18	(10.3, 350%)	—	—	—	—	—
	130(High service temperature)							
CSM (72A; 85 pphr N650)	-38	(Tg)	—	—	—	—	—	—
	23	1.18	(4.9, 100%) (12, 286%)	—	—	—	—	—
	130(High service temperature)							
CSM (89A; Uncured)	$-38(T_g)$	—	—	—	—	—	—	—
	23	1.18	(5.3, 100%) (7.4, 510%)	—	—	—	—	—
	130(High service temperature)							

Notes:pphr = Parts of reinforcing material per hundred parts of rubber;

CB = Carbon black such as N110, ⋯, N990 (ISO classification);

××A = Shore A durometer hardness.

Chapter 17

EPDM (Ethylene Propylene Diene Monomer Copolymer)

17.1　Introduction

EPDM (Ethylene Propylene Diene Monomer Copolymer) rubbers are valuable for their excellent resistance to heat, oxidation, ozone, and water aging due to their stable saturated polymer backbone chains. The E refers to Ethylene, P to Propylene, D to diene and M refers to its classification in ASTM standard D-1418. Amorphous or low crystalline grades have excellent flexibility at low temperatures with glass transition point at −60 ℃. EPDM with sulfur acceleration systems may resist heat aging up to 130 ℃, while WPDM with peroxide cure system up to 160 ℃. EPDM rubbers have high electric resistivity and can be used for electricity insulation material. Mechanical properties of EPDM (Ethylene Propylene Diene Monomer Copolymer) rubbers are listed in Table 17.1. Viscoelastic properties of EPDM reinforced with silica are given in Table 17.2.

EPR (Ethylene Propylene Rubber) has good resistance to heat, polar fluids (water, ketones, and phosphate ester), ozone, sunlight, and weathering. It has low compression set and works fine at low temperatures, but cannot be used with petroleums and fuels.

Santoprene is a thermoplastic elastomer (TPE), which is the mixture of in-situ cross linking of EPDM rubber and polypropylene as pre-compound material that is able to process by conventional thermoplastic tools. Santoprene is a thermoplastic compound that is processed in much the same way as any type of plastic. The difference is that Santoprene possesses the same levels of flexibility and durability that are commonly found with natural rubber compounds. Because of the longer life of Santoprene in both extremely hot and cold environments, the material is often preferred over the use of rubber.

17.2　Applications

EPDM (Ethylene Propylene Diene Monomer Copolymer) rubbers are the most useful synthetic rubber family. EPDM rubbers are primarily used for weather seals such as door seals, window seals, trunk seals, and hood seals. Another automotive application is hoses or similar parts in a cooling system, where no expensive FKM or FFKM is required. They are also used for automotive brake seals, radiator hoses, and commercial aircraft hydraulic seals. One major nonautomotive application is housing roofs.

EPR has been the choice of material for electric insulation cables at elevated temperatures due to its good die-electric properties. However, noticeable degradation of dielectrics of EPR starts from a temperature above 200 ℃ and rapidly once above 400 ℃.

References

ANNADURAI P, et al, 2002. Studies on Microwave Shielding Materials Based on Ferrite-and Carbon Black-Filled EPDM Rubber in the X-Band Frequency[J]. Journal of Applied Polymer Science, 83:145-150.

BROSTOW W, et al, 2011. Thermal and mechanical properties of EPDM/PP + thermal shock-resistant ceramic composites[J]. Journal of Materials Science, 46:2445-2455.

CHATTERJEE K, NASKAR K, 2007. Development of Thermoplastic Elastomers Based on Maleated Ethylene Propylene Rubber (m-EPM) and Polypropylene (PP) by Dynamic Vulcanization[J]. Express Polymer Letters, 1:527-534.

CHEREMISINOFF N, 1982. Spotlight on EPDM Elastomers [J]. Polymers-Plastics Technology and Engineering, 31(7/8):713-744.

FELHOSI D, et al, 2008. Viscoelastic Characterization of an EPDM Rubber and Finite Element Simulation of Its Dry Rolling Friction[J]. Express Polymer Letters, 2(3):157-164.

FUKUMORI K, MATSUSHITA M, 2004. Material Recycling Technology of Crosslinked Rubber Waste[J]. R&D Review of Toyota CRDL, 38(1):39-47.

GHOSH P, CHAKRABARTI A, 2010. Conducting Carbon Black Filled EPDM Vulcanizates: Assessment of Dependence of Physical and Mechanical Properties and Conducting Character on Variation of Filler Loading [J]. European Polymer Journal, 10(5):1043-1054.

GUPTA N K, JAIN A K, SINGHAL R, et al, 2000. Effect of Dynamic Crosslinking on Tensile Yield Behavior of Polypropylene/Ethylene-Propylene-Diene Rubber Blends[J]. Journal of Applied Polymer Science, 78:2104-2121.

KARGER-KOCSIS J, MOUSAB A, MAJOR Z, et al, 2008. Dry Friction and Sliding Wear of EPDM Rubbers against Steel as a Function of Carbon Black Content[J]. Wear, 64:359-367.

KARGER-KOCSIS J, FELHÖS D, THOMANN R, 2008. Tribological Behavior of Carbon Nanofiber Modified, Santoprenes Thermoplastic Elastomer under Dry Sliding and Fretting Conditions against Steel[J]. Journal of Applied Polymer Science, 108:724-730.

KOMALAN C, et al, 2007. Dynamic Mechanical Analysis of Binary and Ternary Polymer Blends Based on Nylon Copolymer/EPDM Rubber and EPM Grafted Maleic Anhydride Compatibilizer[J]. Express Polymer Letters, 1:641-653.

MAHAPATRA S P, et al, 2008. AC Conductivity and Positive Temperature Coefficient Effect in Microcellular EPDM Vulcanizites[J]. Polymer Composites, 29:1125-1136.

MANCHADO M A L, ARROYO M, KENNY J M, 2002. New Developments in Dynamically Cured PP-EPDM

Blends[J]. Rubber Chemistry and Technology, 74:211-220.

PLACEK V, KOHOUT T, HANT V, et al, 2009. Assessment of EPDM Seal Lifetime on Nuclear Power Plants [J]. Polymer Testing, 28:209-214.

SONG B, CHEN W, CHENG M, 2004. Novel Model for Uniaxial Strain-rate-dependent Stress-strain Behavior of Ethylene Propylene Diene Monomer (EPDM) Rubber in Compression and in Tension[J]. Journal of Applied Polymer Science, 92(3):1553-1558.

SONG B, CHEN W, 2003. One-dimensional Dynamic Compressive Behavior of Ethylene Propylene Diene Monomer (EPDM) Rubber[J]. Journal of Engineering Materials and Technology, 125(3):294-301.

WU J, LIECHTI K M, 2000. Multiaxial and Time Dependent Behavior of a Filled Rubber[J]. Mechanics of Time-Dependent Materials, 4:293-331.

XIAO H, et al, 2004. Morphology, Rheology, and Mechanical Properties of Dynamically Cured EPDM/PP Blend: Effect of Curing Agent Dose Variation[J]. Journal of Applied Polymer Science, 92(1):357-362.

ZAHARESCU T, et al, 2007. Thermal Study on Binary Blends of Ethylene-Propylene Elastomers and Acrylonitrile-Butadiene Rubber[J]. Polymer Bulletin, 58(4):683-689.

Table 17.1 Mechanical Properties of EPDM Rubber (Ethylene Propylene Diene Monomer Copolymer)

Material-DAM	$T/℃$	ρ	(σ,ε)	α	k	γ	Set	$\tan\delta$
EPR	−40	—	—	—	—	1200	—	—
	23	—	—	—	0.33	2180	—	—
	50	—	—	—	0.32	2000	—	—
	150	—	—	—	0.30	1600	—	—
EPDM	−80	—	—	—	—	—	—	0.02
	−51(T_g)	—		—	—	—	—	0.5
	−25	—	—	—	—	—	—	0.365
	23	0.86	(11, 1036%)	875	0.293	2180	—	0.04
	70	—	—	—	—	—	$\Delta_{22}=25\%$	—
	80	—	—	—	—	—	—	0.5
	150(High service temperature)							
EPDM-10CF (10% carbon fiber)	−51(T_g)	—	—	—	—	—	—	—
	23	—	—	100	—	—	—	—
	80	—	—	1250	—	—	—	—
	150	—	—	>2000	—	—	—	—

continued

Material-DAM	$T/°C$	ρ	(σ,ε)	α	k	γ	Set	$\tan\delta$
EPDM(52A; 100 pphr N990)	$-51(T_g)$	—	—	—	—	—	—	—
	0	—	—	—	—	—	—	0.17
	23	0.86	(1.3, 100%) (2.2, 200%) (3, 300%) (7.4, 640%)	160	0.293	2180	—	0.14
	100	—	—	—	—	—	—	0.10
	150(High service temperature)							
EPDM (69A; 200 pphr N990)	$-51(T_g)$	—	—	—	—	—	—	—
	0	—	—	—	—	—	—	0.27
	23	0.86	(3, 100%) (4.6, 200%) (5, 300%) (5.7, 520%)	160	0.293	2180	—	0.25
	100	—	—	—	—	—	$\Delta_{22}<30\%$	0.17
	150(High service temperature)							
EPDM-Zn (No CB)	$-26(T_g)$	—	—	—	—	—	—	0.257
	23	0.86	(23, 691%)	—	—	—	—	0.04
	150(High service temperature)							
EPDM-Zn-CB10 (10 pphr CB)	$-26(T_g)$	—	—	—	—	—	—	0.232
	23	0.86	(21.1,526%)	—	—	—	—	0.044
	150(High service temperature)							
EPDM-Zn-CB20 (20 pphr CB)	$-26(T_g)$	—	—	—	—	—	—	0.203
	23	0.86	(22.5, 494%)	—	—	—	—	0.054
	150(High service temperature)							
EPDM-Zn-CB35 (35 pphr CB)	$-26(T_g)$	—	—	—	—	—	—	0.194
	23	0.86	(22.4,378%)	—	—	—	—	0.055
	150(High service temperature)							
EPDM-Zn-CB50 (50 pphr CB)	$-26(T_g)$	—	—	—	—	—	—	0.172
	23	0.86	(21.4, 260%)	—	—	—	—	0.072
	150(High service temperature)							

continued

Material-DAM	$T/°C$	ρ	(σ, ε)	α	k	γ	Set	$\tan \delta$
Santoprene	23	0.97	(2, 100%) (4.4, 330%)	—	—	—	—	0.0372
	135(High service temperature)							

Notes：pphr＝Parts of reinforcing material per hundred parts of rubber；

CB＝Carbon black such as N110, ⋯, N990 (ISO classification)；

××A＝Shore A durometer hardness；

EPDM-Zn＝Zinc sulfonated EPDM；

EPDM-Zn-CB20＝Zinc sulfonated EPDM reinforced with 20-phr HAF carbon black.

Table 17.2 Normalized Prony Parameters for Creep/Relaxation of EPDM (Ethylene Propylene Diene Monomer Copolymer)

Material	$T/°C$	$E_0 \parallel E_\infty/\mathrm{MPa}$	N	$[p_i/\mathrm{MPa}, T_i/\mathrm{H}]$, $i = 1, 2, \cdots, N$
Silicone Rubber (Liquid)	70	$E_0 = 0.7709$	3	[0.1688, 18.58] [0.1332, 254.1] [0.1769, 2500]
EPDM/Silica	23	$E_\infty = 0.1218$	14	[0.256, 4×10^{-4}] [0.19, 2×10^{-3}] [0.137, 2×10^{-2}] [0.114, 0.2] [0.0642, 2] [0.0347, 20] [0.0254, 200] [0.0177, 2×10^3] [0.012, 2×10^4] [0.0087, 2×10^5] [0.005, 2×10^6] [0.0057, 2×10^7] [−0.0011, 2×10^8] [0.0987, 2×10^9]
Santoprene (TPV 67A5)	23	—	3	[9.21×10^{-2}, 4.083] [0.1716, 71.2] [0.1664, 1044]
Santoprene (TPV 67A10)	23	—	3	[9.21×10^{-2}, 4.083] [0.1716, 71.2] [0.1664, 1044]
Santoprene (TPV 73A5)	23	—	4	[4.57×10^{-2}, 1.85] [8.0163, 11.986]
			3	[0.11, 66.8] [0.1158, 376.43] [0.1235, 2783]
Santoprene (TPV 73A10)	23	—	4	[4.57×10^{-2}, 1.85] [8.0163, 11.986] [0.11, 66.8] [0.1158, 376.43] [0.1235, 2783]

Chapter 18

FKM (Fluoroelastomers) and FFKM (Perfluoroelastomers)

18.1 Introduction

FKM (Fluoroelastomers) and FFKM (Perfluoroelastomers) are two kinds of fluorinated elastomers, which are made of long randomly coiled flexible macromolecules that allow them to undergo a large deformation upon stretching or compression. A crosslinking structure between the polymer chains provides a permanent three-dimensional network that ensures recovery [DuPont]. Mechanical properties of FKM (Fluoroelastomers) and FFKM (Perfluoroelastomers) are listed in Table 18.1.

18.2 FKM (Fluoroelastomers)

Fluorinated elastomers contain a partially fluorinated backbone are called FKM or FPM (Fluoroelastomers). FKM is the designation of most (>80%) of fluorocarbon elastomers. FKM and its derivative FFKM offer the best heat resistance of all conventionally processed rubbers, combined with an outstanding resistance to swell and permeation when exposed to chemicals including automotive fuels and its related additives. Seals made of FKM remain resilient and retain an effective compressive sealing force long after having been exposed to elevated temperatures. Representative stress-stress curves corresponding to soft and hard FKM's at the room temperature are plotted in Fig. 18. 1. Stress-strain curves of a standard FKM (Dupont Viton) at different temperatures are illustrated in Fig. 18.2. Viton is the registered trademark of DuPont fluoroelastomers.

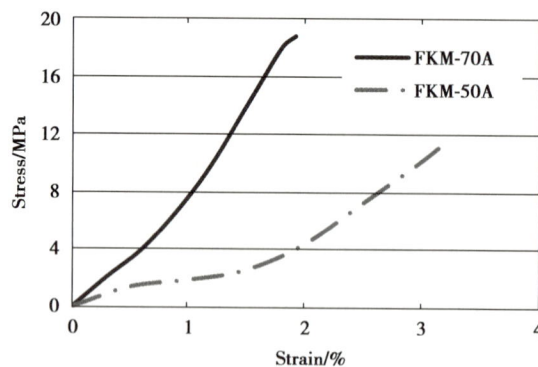

Fig. 18.1   Two Representative Stress-strain Curves (Soft versus Hard) of FKM (FPM)

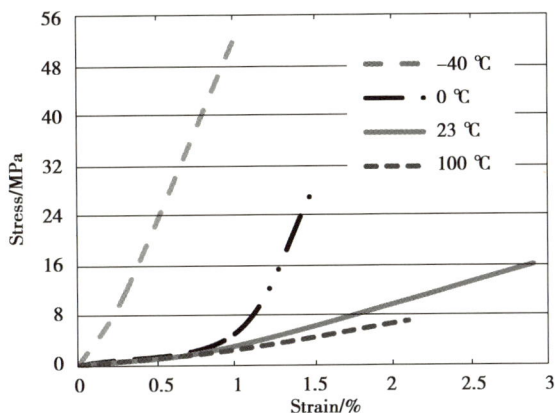

Fig. 18.2   Stress-Strain Curves of FKM-Standard（DuPont）at Different Temperatures

18.3   FFKM（Perfluoroelastomers）

Fluorinated elastomers containing a fully fluorinated backbone are called Perfluoroelastomers（FFKM）. FFKM（Perfluoroelastomers）has a better resistance to chemical attacks from acids and bases than FKM, especially at a working temperature as high as 200 ℃. As a seal, it has longer seal life than FKM and other rubber seals. Nevertheless, it deteriorates very fast if exposed to hot water or steam. It is normally not used due to the high cost, unless extremely temperature resistance is required.

18.4   Applications

18.4.1   FKM（Fluoroelastomers）

The primary use of FKM is for automotive fuel systems such as tank hoses/tubings/seals, filler neck hoses, fuel cap seals, fuel filter seals, fuel injector O-rings, fuel pump seals, rollover fuel valves, canister purge solenoid valve seals, pressure regulator seals, vapor recovery lines, air intake manifold gaskets, quick connector O-rings, on-board-diagnostics pressure sensor diaphragm, and emission control devices.

18.4.2   FFKM（Perfluoroelastomers）

As a derivative of FKM, FFKM tends to exhibit better resistance to chemical attack from strong acids and bases, suggesting potentially longer life. The primary use of FFKM is for automotive fuel systems such as tank hoses and tubings, filler neck hoses, fuel injector seals, fuel pump seals, diaphragms, air intake manifold gaskets, and emission control devices.

References

APOSTOLO M, TRIULZI F, 2004. Properties of Fuoroeleastomer/Semicrystalline Perfluoroelastomer Nano Bends[J]. Journal of Fluorine Chemistry, 125(2):303-314.

STAHL W M, STEVENS R D, 1992. Fuel-Alcohol Permeation Rate of Fluoroelastomers, Fluoroplastics, and other Fuel Resistant Materials[J]. SAE 920163.

THOMAS E W, FULLER R E, TERAUCHI K, 2007. Fluoroelastomer Compatibility with Biodiesel Fuels[J]. SAE 2007-01-4061.

THOMAS E W, 2003. Fluoroelastomer and Perfluoroelastomer Compatibility with Advanced Gas Turbine Lubricants[J]. SAE 2003-01-3029.

WANG S, LEGARE J, 2003. Perfluoroelastomer and Fluoroelastomer Seals for Semiconductor Wafer Processing Equipment[J]. Journal of Fluorine Chemistry, 122(1):113-119.

Table 18.1 Mechanical Properties of FKM (Fluoroelastomers) and FFKM (Perfluoroelastomers)

Material-DAM	$T/^{\circ}C$	ρ	(σ,ε)	α	k	γ	Set	$\tan\delta$
	$-23(T_g)$	—	—	—	—	—	—	—
FKM (50A)	23	1.82	(1.4, 50%) (1.9, 100%) (2.6, 150%) (4.3, 200%) (7.2, 250%) (10.1, 300%) (11, 315%)	160	0.25	—	—	—
	225(High service temperature)							
FKM (64A) (30 pphr N990)	$-23(T_g)$	—	—	—	—	—	—	—
	23	1.82	(4.7, 100%) (14.1, 230%)	160	0.25	—	—	—
	200(High service temperature)							
FKM (White)	$-23(T_g)$	—	—	—	—	—	—	—
	23	1.82	(15, 280%)	160	0.25	—	—	—
	225(High service temperature)							

Material-DAM	$T/℃$	ρ	(σ,ε)	α	k	γ	Set	$\tan\delta$
FKM (DuPont Standard; 70A)	-40	—	(11.5, 30%) (52, 100%)	—	—	—	—	0.05
	$-23(T_g)$	—	—	—	—	—	—	0.2
	0	—	(5, 100%) (28, 150%)	—	—	—	—	1.2
	23	1.82	(3, 100%) (16, 290%)	160	0.25	—	—	0.1
	50	—	(2, 100%) (10, 270%)	—	—	—	—	0.08
	70	—	—	—	—	—	$\Delta_{22}=35\%$	—
	100	—	(2.4, 100%) (7, 210%)	—	—	—	—	—
	150	—	(2.6, 100%) (6, 175%)	—	—	—	—	—
	200	—	(2.8, 100%) (5, 150%)	—	—	—	—	0.1
	225(High service temperature)							
FKM (70A)	$-23(T_g)$	—	—	—	—	—	—	—
	23	1.82	(16, 211%)	160	0.25	—	—	—
	225(High service temperature)							
FKM (75A)	$-23(T_g)$	—	—	—	—	—	—	—
	23	1.82	(2.1, 30%) (3.9, 60%) (6.6, 90%) (9.8, 120%) (13.8, 130%) (17.9, 180%) (18.8, 192%)	160	0.25	—	—	—
	225(High service temperature)							

continued

Material-DAM	$T/°C$	ρ	(σ, ε)	α	k	γ	Set	$\tan \delta$
FKM (90A)	$-23(T_g)$	—	—	—	—	—	—	—
	23	1.82	(7.1, 67%) (24.4, 160%)	160	0.25	—	—	—
	225(High service temperature)							
FFKM (73A)	$-23(T_g)$	—	—	—	—	—	—	—
	23	2.08	(4.3, 100%) (15, 200%)	230	0.19	—	—	—
	260(High service temperature)							

Notes: pphr = Parts of reinforcing material per hundred parts of rubber;

CB = Carbon black such as N110, ⋯, N990 (ISO classification);

××A = Shore A durometer hardness.

Chapter 19

IIR (Butyl Rubber) and Halobutyl Rubber

19.1　IIR（Butyl Rubber）

IIR（Butyl Rubber）is a synthetic rubber, which is a copolymer of isobutylene with a small amount of isoprene. Butyl rubber is impermeable to air and has good flex properties, resulting from low levels of instauration between long polyisobutylene segments. Pure IIR gum is self-reinforcing, with a high tensile strength (e.g. 25 MPa). The damping characteristic of IIR is quite constant over a frequency range between 10 Hz and 10^3 Hz when operating at a constant temperature. Its damping effect is more significant than AEM in the low temperature range (below 40 ℃). Stress-strain curves of IIR with and without fillers are depicted in Fig. 19.1. Mechanical properties of IIR (Butyl Rubber) are listed in Table 19.1.

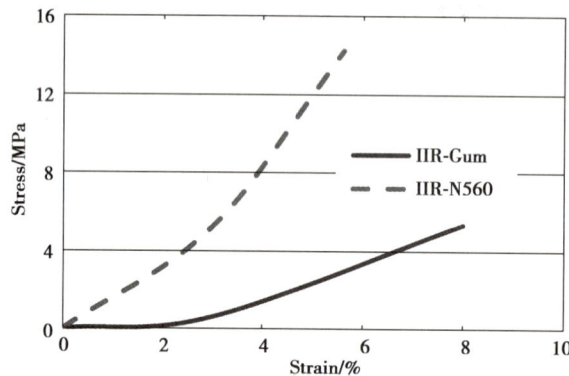

Fig. 19.1　Stress-Strain Curve of IIR Gum and IIR-70A（N560）

19.2　Halobutyl Rubber（Halogenated Butyl Rubber）

Halogenated butyl rubber, also called halo butyl rubber, is made by adding chlorine or bromine to butyl rubber. Halogenated butyl rubber takes shorter vulcanization time, while possessing the same material properties as butyl rubber.

19.3　Applications

The primary characteristic of IIR（Butyl Rubber）and Halobutyl Rubber is its low permeability to air that leads to common use for tire inner liners and air conditioner hoses. It also has excellent thermal-oxidative stability, as well as excellent moisture and chemical resistance. Tire inner liners used for sealing the tire air and tire inner tubes are by far the best automotive application for Halobutyl Rubber（Halogenated Butyl Rubber）. Bladders made of butyl rubber are used for shaping tires in the curing process. IIR (Butyl Rubber) is also used for airtight seals in many sporting goods such as bladders in basketballs, soccer balls, footballs, and tennis balls.

The secondary characteristic of IIR (Butyl Rubber) and Halobutyl Rubber is its high energy absorption that leads to use in automotive engine and body mounts and other vibration-damping applications. Butyl rubbers' unique combination of barrier properties, high damping, resistance to ozone and heat aging makes them ideal for many automotive mounts.

References

CHEMICAL W, 2009. Butyl Rubber: A Techno-commercial Profile[J]. Chemical Weekly, 55 (12):207-211.

LIANG Y, et al, 2008. New Strategy to Improve the Gas Barrier Property of Isobutylene-Isoprene Rubber/Clay Nanocomposites[J]. Polymer Testing, 27:270-276.

LIANG Y, et al, 2005. Preparation and Properties of Isobutylene-Isoprene Rubber (IIR)/Clay Nanocomposites [J]. Polymer Testing, 24:12-17.

MANUEL H J, 2000. Butyl Reclaim in Innerliner Applications [J]. Kautschuk Gummi Kunststoffe, 53, Jahrgang, Nr. 12:730-734.

TAKAHASHI S, et al, 2006. Gas Barrier Properties of Butyl Rubber/Vermiculite Nanocomposite Coatings[J]. Polymer, 47:3083-3093.

ZAHARESCU T, PODINA C, 1997.Thermal Degradation of Butyl Rubber[J]. Journal of Materials Science Letters, 16(9):761-762.

Table 19.1   Mechanical Properties of IIR (Butyl Rubber)

Material-DAM	$T/℃$	ρ	(σ,ε)	α	k	γ	Set	$\tan\delta$
IIR (31A; Gum)	$-73(T_g)$	—	—	—	—	—	—	—
	23	0.92	(0.4, 100%) (0.6, 300%) (5.3, 800%)	194	0.09	—	—	—
	210(High service temperature)							
IIR	$-73(T_g)$	—	—	—	—	—	—	—
	23	0.92	(5.5, 300%) (8, 350%)	194	0.09	—	—	—
	210(High service temperature)							

continued

Material-DAM	$T/\text{°C}$	ρ	(σ, ε)	α	k	γ	Set	$\tan \delta$
IIR(N560)	$-73(T_g)$	—	—	—	—	—	—	0.002
	-60 —	—	—	—	—	—	—	0.2
	-40 —	—	—	—	—	—	—	0.5
	-20 —	—	—	—	—	—	—	0.75
	23	0.92	(5.2, 300%) (14.2, 650%)	194	0.09	—	--	0.45
	40	—	—	—	—	—	—	0.15
	80	—	—	—	—	—	—	0.07
	120	—	—	—	—	—	—	0.05
	210(High service temperature)							
IIR (56A;75 pphr N990)	$-73(T_g)$	—	—	—	—	—	—	—
	0	—	—	—	—	—	—	—
	23	0.92	(1.5, 300%) (9.5, 700%)	—	0.09	—	—	—
	210(High service temperature)							
IIR (66A; 150 pphr N990)	$-73(T_g)$	—	—	—	—	—	—	—
	0	—	—	—	—	—	—	—
	23	0.92	(2.2, 300%) (4.6, 660%)	—	0.09	—	—	—
	210(High service temperature)							

Notes: pphr=Parts of reinforcing material per hundred parts of rubber;

CB=Carbon black such as N110, ⋯, N990 (ISO classification);

××A=Shore A durometer hardness.

Chapter 20

IR (Isoprene Rubber)

20.1　Introduction

IR (Isoprene Rubber) is a synthetic rubber, which has the same principal constituent (i.e. isoprene) as NR (Natural Rubber). Its material properties resemble NR, but with a more uniform quality since no natural impurities are involved. It does not contain proteins, fatty acids and other substances that are present in natural rubber. Synthetic polyisoprene exhibits good inherent tack, high compounded gum tensile, good hysteresis, and good hot tensile properties. However, the tensile strength and tear strength of IR are lower than NR, because it is not 100% the cis isomer. Mechanical properties of IR (Isoprene Rubber) are listed in Table 20.1.

20.2　Applications

Whatever is made of NR may be replaced by IR. However, IR costs more than NR. Recent reports about allergic reactions to proteins present in natural rubber have prompted increased usage of the more pure IR in various applications.

References

CHUNG B, FUNT J M, OUYANG G B, 1991. Effects of Carbon Black on Elastomer Ultimate Properties-IR Compounds[J]. Rubber World, 204:46-51.

EL-TAYEB N, NASIR R, 2007. Effect of Soft Carbon Black on Tribology of Deproteinised and Polyisoprene Rubbers[J]. Wear, 262:350-361.

ROLAND C M, SOBIESKI J W, 1989. Anomalous Fatigue Behavior in Polyisoprene[J]. Rubber Chemistry and Technology, 62:683-697.

Table 20.1　Mechanical Properties of IR (Isoprene Rubber)

Material-DAM	$T/{}^{\circ}\mathrm{C}$	ρ	(σ, ε)	α	k	γ	Set	$\tan \delta$
IR (Isoprene)	$-70(T_g)$	—	—	—	—	—	—	—
	23	0.915	(0.7, 100%) (28, 700%)	194	0.09	1550	—	—
	100(High service temperature)							

Notes: pphr = Parts of reinforcing material per hundred parts of rubber;

　　　　CB = Carbon black such as N110, ⋯, N990 (ISO classification);

　　　　××A = Shore A durometer hardness.

Chapter 21

Nitriles-NBR, HNBR, and XNBR

21.1　Introduction

Nitriles including NBR（Nitrile Butadiene Rubber）, HNBR（Hydrogenated acrylonitrile-butadiene）, and XNBR（Carboxylated Acrylonitrile-Butadiene）have excellent oil and fuel resistance. Mechanical properties of NBR（Nitrile Butadiene Rubber）, HNBR（Hydrogenated acrylonitrile-butadiene）, and XNBR（Carboxylated Acrylonitrile-Butadiene）are listed in Table 21.1. Normalized Prony parameters to account for creep or relaxation of nitrile are given in Table 21.2.

21.2　NBR（Nitrile Butadiene Rubber；Acrylonitrile-Butadiene）

NBR（Nitrile Butadiene Rubber）, also called nitrile, is a family of unsaturated copolymers of Acrylonitrile and butadiene. The acrylonitrile content of nitrile sealing compounds varies considerably（from 18% to 50%）and influences the physical properties of the finished NBR material. The higher the acrylonitrile content, the better the resistance to oil and fuel. At the same time, elasticity and resistance to compression set are adversely affected. Cross-linked phenolic resins may be used for improving NBR strength [Ye et al.]. Although silicone rubber almost matches NBR in oil resistance, it does not reach NBR's physical and mechanical properties. When used for O-rings, its property of compression set is nice as shown in Fig. 21.1.

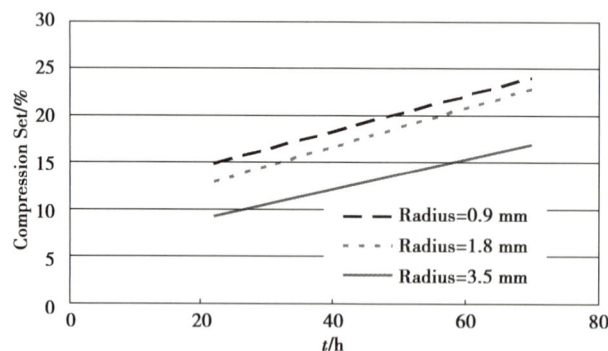

Fig. 21.1　Compression Set of NBR 36624 O-rings [ERIKS] at 100 ℃（per ASTM D 395）

21.3　HNBR（Hydrogenated Acrylonitrile-Butadiene）

NBR elastomers can be hydrogenated, called HNBR, for reducing the chemical reactivity of the polymer backbone. The reduction of double bonds due to hydrogenation improves its resistance to oil, fuel, and chemicals at elevated temperatures. Good physical properties and chemical resistance to most common hydraulic fluids makes HNBR an excellent sealing material. Stress-strain curves of HNBR with different levels of fillers are depicted in Fig. 21.2.

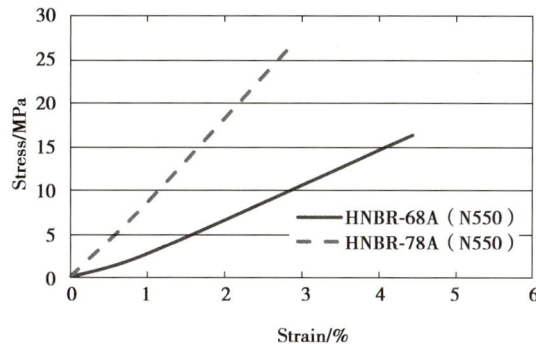

Fig. 21.2   Stress-Strain Curves of HNBR with Different Levels of Fillers

21.4   XNBR (Carboxylated Acrylonitrile-Butadiene)

Carboxylated NBR, called XNBR, is a terpolymer of NBR with acid organic monomer with carboxylic acid as the third monomer. The carboxyl group is added to significantly improve the abrasion resistance of NBR while retaining excellent oil and solvent resistance, as coming with higher hardness, abrasive resistance, and tear strength than NBR. HXNBR blends made of XNBR/HNBR (65/35) with low levels of zinc peroxide (3 pphr) has been applied in order to optimize compression set [Campomizzi].

21.5   Applications

NBR (Nitrile Butadiene Rubber), HNBR (Hydrogenated NBR), and XNBR (Carboxylated Acrylonitrile-Butadiene) are used for timing belts, fuel/oil handling hoses, air conditioning hoses, seals, and gasket grommets in the automotive industry. It is also used for water handling applications. HNBR is also proven to be used in the seals and moldings of car engines to be new fuels such as rapeseed oil methyl ester.

References

AIN Z, AZURA A, 2010. Effect of Different Types of Filler and Filler Loadings on the Properties of Carboxylated Acrylonitrile-Butadiene Rubber Latex Films[J]. Journal of Applied Polymer Science, 119(5): 2815-2823.

BIDHENDI A, KOHORNEN R, 2012. A Finite Element Study of Micropipette Aspiration of Single Cells: Effect of Compressibility[J]. Computational and Mathematical Methods in Medicine, 2012(3):192618.

BUDRUGEAC P, 1982. Thermooxdative Degradation of Some Nitride-Butadiene Rubbers [J]. Polymer Degradation and Stability, 38(2):165-172.

CAMPOMIZZI E, et al, 2000. New Developments for Surviving Aggressive Environments with HNBR[J]. SAE 2000-01-0746.

FELHÖS D, KARGER-KOCSIS J, XU D, 2008. Tribological Testing of Peroxide Cured HNBR with Different MWCNT and Silica Content under Dry Sliding and Rolling Conditions against Steel[J]. Journal of Applied Polymer Science, 108:2840-2851.

GEORGE S, VARUGHESE K T, THOMAS S, 1999. Dielectric Properties of Isotactic Polypropylene/Nitrile Rubber Blends: Effects of Blend Ratio, Filler Addition, and Dynamic Vulcanization[J]. Journal of Applied Polymer Science, 73:255-270.

HUANG X, et al, 2007. Friction and Wear Properties of NBR/PVC Composites [J]. Journal of Applied Polymer Science, 106(4):2565-2570.

HUSSIEN I, et al, 2004. Study of the Miscibility and Mechanical Properties of NBR/HNBR Blends [J]. Polymer Engineering and Science, 44(12):2346-2352.

ISSHIKI N, et al, 2010. Preparation and Mechanical Properties of Rubber Composites Reinforced with Carbon Nanohorns[J]. Journal of Nanoscience and Nanotechnology, 10(6):3810-3814.

KAWASHIMA T, OGAWA T, 2005. Prediction of the Lifetime of Nitrile-Butadiene Rubber by FT-IR[J]. Ana. Sci., 21(12):1475-1478.

KOH S, et al, 2001. Durability Analysis of Rubber Diaphragm (HNBR) for Vehicle Suspension Damper System [J]. Advanced Nondestructive Evaluation Ⅱ, 1:306-311.

LEE S, et al, 2008. New Strategy and Easy Fabrication of Solid-State Supercapacitor Based on Polypyrrole and Nitrile Rubber[J]. J. of Nanoscience and Nanotechnology, 8(9):4722-4725.

MOON S, 2009. Flame Resistance and Foaming Properties of NBR Compounds with Halogen-Free Flame Retardants[J]. Polymer Composites, 30(12):1732-1742.

NADERI G, et al, 1999. Studies on Dynamic Vulcanization of PP/NBR Thermoplastic Elastomer Blends[J]. Iranian Polymer Journal, 8:37-42.

PRAMANIK P K, KHASTGIR D, SAHA T N, 1991. Electromagnetic Interference Shielding by Conductive Nitrile Rubber Composites Containing Carbon Fillers[J]. Journal of Elastomers and Plastics, 23:345-361.

SAHOO S, BHOWMICK A K, 2007. Influence of ZnO Nanoparticles on the Cure Characteristics and Mechanical Properties of Carboxylated Nitrile Rubber[J]. Journal of Applied Polymer Science, 106(5):3077-3083.

SONG X, et al, 2009. Analysis and Optimization of Nitrile Butadiene Rubber Sealing Mechanism of Ball Valve [J]. Transactions of Nonferrous Metals Society of China, 19(S1):220-224.

TIAN M, et al, 2011. Mechanical Properties and Reinforcement Mechanisms of Hydrogenated Acrylonitrile Butadiene Rubber Composites Containing Fibrillar Silicate Nanofibers and Short Aramid Microfibers [J]. Journal of Applied Polymer Science, 120(3):1439-1447.

TIAN M, et al, 2005. The Anisotropy of Fibrillar Silicate/Rubber Nanocomposites [J]. Macromolecular Materials and Engineering, 290:681-687.

YANG J, et al, 2010. Mechanical and Functional Properties of Composites Based on Graphite and Carboxylated Acrylonitrile Butadiene Rubber[J]. Journal of Applied Polymer Science, 116(5):2706-2713.

YE L, et al, 2007. Mechanical Properties and Microstructure of Acrylonitrile-Butadiene Rubber Vulcanizates Reinforced by in Situ Polymerized Phenolic Resin[J]. Journal of Applied Polymer Science, 105(6):3583-3587.

ZAHARESCU T, et al, 2007. Thermal Study on Binary Blends of Ethylene-Propylene Elastomers and Acrylonitrile-Butadiene Rubber[J]. Polymer Bulletin, 58(4):683-689.

ZHANG X, HUANG H, ZHANG Y, 2002. Dynamically Vulcanized Nitrile Rubber/PP Thermoplastic Elastomers[J]. Journal of Applied Polymer Science, 85:2862-2866.

Table 21.1   Mechanical Properties of Nitriles-NBR, HNBR, and XNBR

Material-DAM	T/℃	ρ	(σ,ε)	α	k	γ	Set	$\tan\delta$
NBR (58A; 100 pphr N990)	$-26(T_g)$	—	—	—	—	—	—	—
	0	—	—	—	—	—	—	0.43
	23	0.98	(2, 100%) (4.5, 200%) (6.5, 300%) (14, 680%)	230	0.24	250	—	0.18
	100 —	—	—	—	—	—	—	0.14
	135(High service temperature)							
NBR (70A; N550)	$-26(T_g)$	—	—	—	—	—	—	—
	23	0.98	(17, 380%)	230	0.24	250	—	—
	70	—	—	—	—	—	$\Delta_{22}=25\%$	—
	135(High service temperature)							

continued

Material-DAM	$T/℃$	ρ	(σ, ε)	α	k	γ	Set	$\tan \delta$
NBR (76A; 200 pphr N990)	$-26(T_g)$	—	—	—	—	—	—	—
	0	—	—	—	—	—	—	0.5
	23	0.98	(5.6, 100%) (9.5, 200%) (9, 270%)	230	0.24	250	—	0.31
	100	—	—	—	—	—	—	0.2
	135 (High service temperature)							
NBR (85A)	$-26(T_g)$	—	—	—	—	—	—	—
	0	—	—	—	—	—	—	0.5
	23	1.32	(11, 100%) (17, 150%)	230	0.24	250	—	0.31
	100	—	—	—	—	—	—	0.2
	135 (High service temperature)							
HNBR (68A) (Seal)	$-25(T_g)$	—	—	—	—	—	—	—
	-20 (High service temperature)							
	23	1.32	(2.7, 100%) (16, 445%)	197	0.24	250	—	—
	65 (High service temperature, with water and glycol)							
	150 (High service temperature)				—	—	$\Delta_{70}=24\%$	—
HNBR (78A; 50 pphr N550)	$-25(T_g)$	—	—	—	—	—	—	—
	23	1.33	(8.6, 100%) (26.1, 280%)	197	0.24	250	—	—
	150 (High service temperature)							
HNBR (85A) (Seal)	$-25(T_g)$	—	—	—	—	—	—	—
	-20 (High service temperature)							
	23	1.32	(9.7, 100%) (21, 300%)	197	0.24	250	—	—
	65 (High service temperature, with water and glycol)							
	70	—	—	—	—	—	$\Delta_{24}=20\%$	—
	100	—	—	—	—	—	$\Delta_{22}=22\%$	—
	150 (High service temperature)				—	—	$\Delta_{70}=23\%$	—

continued

Material-DAM	$T/℃$	ρ	(σ,ε)	α	k	γ	Set	$\tan\delta$
XNBR (70A)	$-30(T_g)$	—	—	—	—	—	—	—
	23	—	—	—	—	—	—	—
	100(High service temperature)							
NBR/PVC (60A)	23	—	(9.7, 100%) (14, 400%)	—	—	—	—	—

Notes: pphr = Parts of reinforcing material per hundred parts of rubber;

CB = Carbon black such as N110, ⋯, N990 (ISO classification);

××A = Shore A durometer hardness.

Table 21.2   Normalized Prony Parameters for Creep/Relaxation of Nitrile

Material-Dam	$T/℃$	E_0 or E_∞ /MPa	N	$[p_i/\text{MPa}, T_i/\text{h}]$, $i = 1, 2, \cdots, N$
HNBR	23	$E_0 = 0.9$	1	[0.6, 0.000333]

Chapter 22

NR (Natural Rubber)

22.1   Introduction

NR (Natural Rubber) is a thermoelastic elastomer by nature, made from latex collected from rubber trees. It turns into a thermoset after it is vulcanized. When cooled below the glass transition temperature the natural rubber loses its elasticity abruptly, but the process is reversible. Stress-strain curves of NR with and without carbon black are shown in Fig. 22.1. Stress-induced crystallization of natural rubber vulcanizates with no carbon black is very significant. The self-reinforcing properties of NR result in high tensile strength and tear strength, so does synthetic counterpart IR. Both NR and IR have low heat buildup during flexing. Owing to the presence of a double bond between repeated units, natural rubber is sensitive to ozone cracking. Mechanical properties of NR (Natural Rubber) are listed in Table 22.1. Ogden model coefficients of hyperelastic NR are given in Table 22.2.

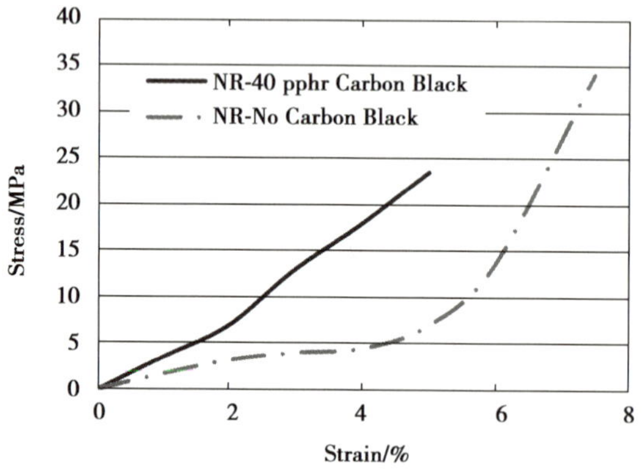

Fig. 22.1   Stress-Strain Curves of Natural Rubbers with and without Carbon Black

Viscoelastic properties of natural rubber compounds vary very much with the type and amount of carbon black used. Both the dilution effect (i.e. mobilized rubber content in the compound) and filler transient network are responsible for viscoelastic properties, depending on the state of vulcanization. Higher levels of polysulfidic crosslinks generally correlate with the higher mechanical property values [Nasir]. The hysteresis energy per cycle for SBR (with 60 pphr N560 carbon black) is related to loading strain energy density per cycle [Harbor et al.] as

$$H = 0.255 \, W_L \tag{22.1}$$

The damping factor of the uncured NR decreases with increasing carbon black loading, as attributed to the reduction of the dilution effect. However, in the case of the cured NR vulcanizates, the established filler transient network as cured is the dominant factor governing the damping factor of the vulcanize. With increasing black loading, the damping factor of the vulcanizate increases with increasing the loading of carbon black [Sajjayanukul et al.]. Under both cyclic compression and shear, HDR and NR exhibit significant rate-dependent phenomena in the loading phase whereas during unloading the rate-dependence is very weak [Amin et al.].

Monotonic responses obtained from tests conducted in natural rubber and high-damping rubbers demonstrate the prominent existence of the Fletcher-Gent effect, indicated by high stiffness at low strain levels.

22.2   Applications

NR is still used extensively in tires and dampers although synthetic rubbers of similar material properties are available.

References

AMIN A F M S, et al, 2006. Hyperelasticity Model for Finite Element Analysis of Natural and High Damping Rubbers in Compression and Shear[J]. Journal of Engineering Mechanics, 132(1):54-64.

ANDRÉ N, CAILLETAUD G, PIQUES R, 1999. Haigh Diagram for Fatigue Crack Initiation Prediction of Natural Rubber Components[J]. Kautschuk Und Gummi Kunstoffe, 52:120-123.

ASALETHA R, et al, 2008. Stress-relaxation Behavior of Natural Rubber/Polystyrene and Natural Rubber/Polystyrene/Natural Rubber-Graft-Polystyrene Blends[J]. Journal of Applied Polymer Science, 108:904-913.

BAKER C S, GELLING I R, NEWELL R, 1985. Epoxidized Natural Rubber[J]. Rubber Chemistry and Technology, 58(1):67-85.

BOONSTRA B, 1950. Stress-strain Properties of Natural Rubber under Biaxial Strain[J]. Journal of Applied Physics, 21(11):1098-1104.

BRISTOW G M, 1991. Influence of Grade of Natural Rubber on Reversion Behavior[J]. Journal of Natural Rubber Research, 6(3):137-151.

CHEN C H, et al, 1982. The Influence of Carbon Black on the Reversal Process in Sulfur-Accelerated Vulcanization of Natural Rubber[J]. Rubber Chemistry and Technology, 37:563-570.

CHENAL J M, et al, 2007. New Insights into the Cold Crystallization of Filled Natural Rubber[J]. Journal of Polymer Science, B, 45:955-962.

CHIU H T, et al, 1998. The Dynamic and Mechanical Properties and Anti-vibration Performance of NR/BR Blends[J]. Chinese Journal of Materials (in Chinese), 30(1):21-32.

DRAGONI E, MEDRI G, 1988. Fracture Toughness Evaluation of Natural Rubber[J]. Theoretical and Applied Fracture Mechanics, 10:79-83.

GORITZ D, KISS M, 1985. On the Origin of Strain-induced Crystallization [J]. Rubber Chemistry and Technology, 59:40-45.

HARBOR R J, et al, 2008. Constitutive Behavior and Temperature Effects in NR and SBR under Variable Amplitude and Multiaxial Loading Conditions [J]. Journal of EngineeringMaterials and Technology, 130: 011005.

KAMAL M M, CLARKE J, AHMAD M, 2009. Comparison of Properties of Natural Rubber Compounds with Various Fillers [J]. Journal of Rubber Research, 12:27-44.

KIM J H, JEONG H Y, 2005. A Study on the Material Properties and Fatigue Life of Natural Rubber with Different Carbon Blacks [J]. International Journal of Fatigue, 27:263-272.

KOSHY T A, KURIAKOSE B, THOMAS S, 1992. Studies on the Effect of Blend ratio and Cure System on the Degradation of Natural Rubber/Ethylene-Vinyl Acetate Rubber Blends [J]. Polymer Degradation and Stability, 36(2):137-147.

LAKE G J, LINDLEY P B, 1965. The Mechanical Fatigue Limit of Rubber [J]. Journal of Applied Polymer Science, 9:1233-1251.

LEE D J, DONOVAN J A, 1987. Mixed Mode I and II Fracture of Carbon Black-filled Natural Rubber [J]. Journal of Fracture, 34:41-55.

LIN GUI, et al, 2004. Study on Microstructure and Mechanical Properties Relationship of Short Fibers/Rubber Foam Composites [J]. European Polymer Journal, 40:1733-1742.

MARS W V, FATEMI A, 2004. Observations of the Constitutive Response and Characterization of Filled Natural Rubber under Monotonic and Cyclic Multiaxial Stress-States [J]. Journal of Engineering Materials and Technology, 126:19-28.

MARS W V, FATEMI A, 2004. Multiaxial Stress Effects on Fatigue Behavior of Natural Rubber [J]. International Journal of Fatigue, 28:521-529.

NASIR M, THE G K. 1988. The Effects of Various Types of Crosslinks on the Physical Properties of Natural Rubber [J]. European Polymer Journal, 24:733-736.

NGOLEMASANGO F, et al, 2008. Degradation and Life Prediction of a Natural Rubber Engine Mount Compound [J]. Journal of Applied Polymer Science, 110(1):248-355.

PAYNE A R, 1963. The Dynamic Properties of Carbon Black-loaded Natural Rubber Vulcanizates Part I [J]. Rubber Chemistry and Technology, 36 (2):432-443.

PAYNE A R, 1963. The Dynamic Properties of Carbon Black-loaded Natural Rubber Vulcanizates Part II [J]. Rubber Chemistry and Technology, 36 (2):444-450.

RATTANASOM N, et al, 2009. Comparison of the Mechanical Properties at Similar Hardness Level of Natural Rubber Filled with Various Reinforcing-Fillers" Polymer Testing, 28:8-12.

RIVILIN R S, THOMAS A G, 1953. Rupture of Rubber, I: Characteristic Energy for Tearing[J]. Journal of Polymer Science, 10(3):291-318.

SAINTIER N, CAILLETAUD G, PIQUES R, 2006. Multiaxial Fatigue Life Prediction for a Natural Rubber [J]. International Journal of Fatigue, 28:530-539.

SAJJAYANUKUL T, et al, 2005. Experimental Analysis of Viscoelastic Properties in Carbon Black-Filled Natural Rubber Compounds[J]. Journal of Applied Polymer Science, 97(6):2197-2203.

SOMA P, et al, 2010. A Fracture Mechanics Approach for Evaluating the Effects of Heat Aging on Fatigue Crack Growth of Vulcanized Natural Rubber[J]. Journal of Solid Mechanics and Engineering, 4(6):727-737.

THIELE J L, COHEN R E, 1980. Thermal Expansion Phenomena in Filled and Unfilled Natural Rubber Vulcanizates[J]. Rubber Chemistry and Technology, 53:313-320.

WANG Y, et al, 2005. Structure and Properties of Strain-Induced Crystallization Rubber-Clay Nanocomposites by Co-coagulating the Rubber Latex and Clay Aqueous Suspension[J]. Journal of Applied Polymer Science, Vol. 96:318-323.

WOO C, et al, 2008. A Study on the Materials Properties and Fatigue Life Prediction of Natural Rubber Component[J]. Materials Science and Engineering A, 483(1):376-381.

XU W, et al, 2003. Effect of Nano-zinc Oxide on Crosslinking and Thermal Stability of Natural Rubber[J]. Chinese Journal of Applied Chemistry:2002-2012.

YU W, et al, 2008. Uniaxial Ratcheting Behavior of Vulcanized Natural Rubber[J]. Polymer Engineering and Science, 48(1):191-197.

Table 22.1   Mechanical Properties of NR（Natural Rubber）

Material-DAM	$T/^\circ C$	ρ	(σ, ε)	α	k	γ	Set	$\tan \delta$
NR（Pure）	$-75(T_g)$	—	—	—	—	—	—	—
	23	0.92	(1.7, 100%) (3.2, 200%) (4, 300%) (4.5, 400%) (7, 500%) (13.6, 600%) (34, 750%)	220	0.14	1880	—	0.1
	70	—	—	—	—	—	$\Delta_{22}=25\%$	—
	120（High service temperature）							

continued

Material-DAM	$T/℃$	ρ	(σ,ε)	α	k	γ	Set	$\tan\delta$
	$-52(T_g)$	—	—	—	—	—	—	—
NR(40 pphr N330)	23	1.16	(3.5, 100%) (7, 200%) (13, 300%) (18, 400%) (23.5, 500%)	220	0.15	1880	—	0.14
	120(High service temperature)							
	-75	—	—	—	—	—	—	0.05
	$-49(T_g)$	—	—	—	—	—	—	0.85
	-25	—	—	—	—	—	—	0.32
NR(65 pphr N330)	23	1.16	(3, 50%) (7, 100%) (16, 200%) (21, 310%); $\sigma_{crs,10000}=14$	220	0.15	1880	—	0.25
	60	—	$\sigma_{crs,10000}=11$	—	—	—	—	0.22
	120(High service temperature)			—	—	—	—	0.15
	$-52(T_g)$	—	—	—	—	—	—	—
NR(60 pphr N650)	23	1.16	(1.6, 50%) (2.5, 100%) (4.5, 140%)	220	0.15	1880	—	0.14
	120(High service temperature)							
	-75	—	—	—	—	—	—	0.08
	$-51(T_g)$	—	—	—	—	—	—	0.78
	-25	—	—	—	—	—	—	0.2
NR(65 pphr N660)	23	1.16	(3, 50%) (6.9, 100%) (14.5, 200%) (20.5, 295%); $\sigma_{crs,10000}=12.4$	220	0.15	1880	—	0.14
	120(High service temperature)							

continued

Material-DAM	$T/℃$	ρ	(σ,ε)	α	k	γ	Set	$\tan\delta$
NR (65A;100 pphr N990)	$-52(T_g)$	—	—	—	—	—	—	—
	23	1.16	(6.5, 300%) (16, 560%)	220	0.15	1880	—	—
	120(High service temperature)							
NR (77A;200 pphr N990)	$-52(T_g)$	—	—	—	—	—	—	—
	23	1.16	(7.5, 300%) (9, 430%)	220	0.15	1880	—	—
	120(High service temperature)							
NR (47A;5 pphr ZnO_2)	$-52(T_g)$	—	—	—	—	—	—	—
	23	0.971	—	—	—	—	—	0.03
	120(High service temperature)							
NR(64A; 26 pphr N550 & 5 pphr ZnO_2)	$-52(T_g)$	—	—	—	—	—	—	—
	23	1.063	—	—	—	—	—	0.04
	120(High service temperature)							

Notes：pphr＝Parts of reinforcing material per hundred parts of rubber；

      CB＝Carbon black such as N110, ···, N990 (ISO classification)；

      ××A＝Shore A durometer hardness.

Table 22.2   Ogden Model Coefficients of Hyperelastic NR

Material-Dam	$T/℃$	ρ	(G_1,α_2,ν_3)	···	(G_N,α_N,ν_N)	α	k	γ	$\tan\delta$
NR (60 pphr CB)	$-50(T_g)$	—	—	—	—	—	—	—	—
	23	1.16	(−1.528,−1.012, 0) (0.223, 4.205, 0)	—	(−1134, −4.399, 0)	220	0.15	1880	—
	93(High service temperature)								

Notes：pphr＝Parts of reinforcing material per hundred parts of rubber；

      CB＝Carbon black such as N110, ···, N990 (ISO classification)；

      ××A＝Shore A durometer hardness；

      N＝Number of coefficients to be used in the Ogden Model.

Chapter 23

SBR (Styrene-Butadiene Rubber)

23.1　Introduction

SBR (Styrene-Butadiene Rubber) is a synthetic copolymer of styrene and butadiene. There are two major types of SBR, i.e. Emulsion SBR (E-SBR) and Solution SBR (S-SBR), based on the different manufacturing processes. SBR (Styrene-butadiene rubber) has a wide range of applications in the automotive industry due to its high durability, as well as resistance to abrasion, oils and oxidation. The glass transition point is around −55 ℃, but varies according to the styrene content. Mechanical properties of SBR (Styrene-butadiene rubber) are listed in Table 23.1. A plot of the monotonic stress-strain curves at −5 ℃, 23 ℃, and 50 ℃ are shown in Fig. 23.1.

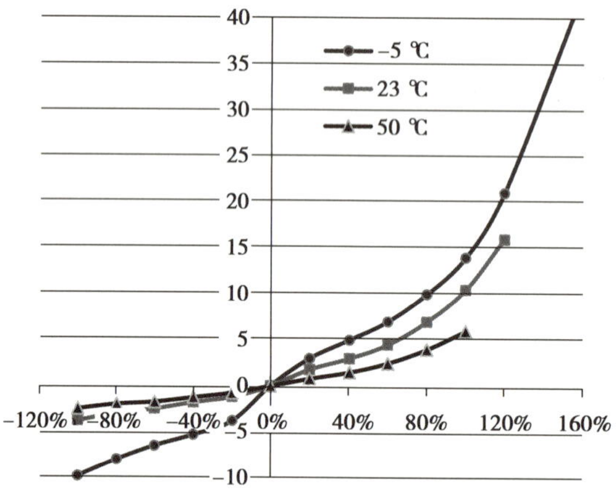

Fig. 23.1　Monotonic Str

The hardness and tensile strength increase with the content of carbon content. It can be seen that the cross-linking degrees of the vulcanizates increase gradually with the increment of carbon nanotubes. The tensile strength reaches its peak value of 12.7 MPa at 50 pphr (Parts per Hundred Parts of Rubber by Weight) of carbon nanotubes, and then tends to decrease with further increment of carbon nanotube content [Zhou et al.]. High-styrene resins may be used for improving SBR strength.

SBR is also used in tuned dampers, which aim to reduce and control the angular vibrations of crankshafts, acting as an isolator and energy absorber between the tune damper's hub and the inertia ring. The dynamic properties of this polymer are therefore important to be considered in developing an appropriate analytical model. The hysteresis energy per cycle for SBR (with 75 pphr N234 carbon black) is related to loading strain energy density per cycle [Harbor et al.],

$$H = 0.512\ W_L \tag{23.1}$$

One interesting property of SBR is its frequency dependent behavior. It was shown by [Lin et al.] experimentally that the low frequency stiffness changes rapidly up to 20 ~ 30 Hz, followed by a more gradual slope towards mid range frequencies, while the damping in the frequency range of practical use, is very similar to structural damping.

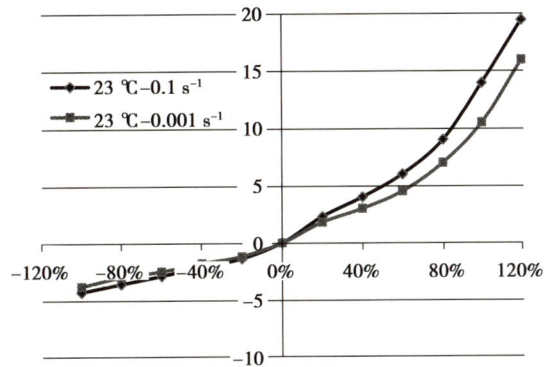

Fig. 23.2   Monotonic Stress (MPa)-Strain Curves at 23 ℃ with Two Loading Rates: $d\varepsilon/dt = 0.001$ s^{-1} and $d\varepsilon/dt = 0.1$ s^{-1}

The flex-fatigue life of carbon black-filled SBR can be improved significantly by incorporation of 2~5 pphr of nano-dispersed clay [Wu et al., 2006]. Addition of clay does not decrease the degree of crosslinking of the material but improves the hysteresis and tearing energy.

23.2   Applications

Solution SBR (Styrene-Butadiene Rubber) is the most widely used solid rubber. Its applications vary from tires to vibration isolators, as well as use for brake fluid seals and gaskets. SBR is also the most used synthetic rubber for automotive tires, where it may be blended with natural rubber.

The rubber used in the road wheel backer pads for tracked vehicles mainly consists of styrene butadiene rubber (SBR) along with reinforcing fillers, antiozonants and antidegradants[Brown et al.].

Emulsion SBR (Styrene-Butadiene rubber) is widely used to modify cement mortar. It has been shown that SBR-modified mortars have good mechanical properties, antipenetrability, and frost resistance. Styrene-Butadiene rubber (SBR) emulsion can be also used to make self-leveling materials for cement pavement [Mirza et al.].

References

AMIN M, et al, 1974. Conductivity of Carbon Black-loaded Styrene-Butadiene Rubber[J]. Journal of Polymer Science, Polymer Chemistry Edition, 12(11):2651-2657.

BOKOBZA L, et al, 2001. Silica Reinforcement of Styrene-Butadiene Rubbers [J]. Kautschuk Gummi Kunststoffe, 54(4), Jahrgang: 177-180.

CHEN K S, et al, 1997. On the Thermal Decomposition Kinetics of Styrene-Butadiene Rubber in Nitrogen Atmosphere[J]. Environmental Engineering Science. 14(3) : 175-181.

FITT M, OUYANG X, 2007. Three-Dimensional Constitutive Equations for Styrene Butadiene Rubber at High Strain Rates[J]. Mechanics of Materials, 40(1-2) : 1-6.

GAUTHIER C, et al, 2004. Analysis of the Non-linear Viscoelastic Behavior of Silica Filled Styrene Butadiene Rubber[J]. Polymer, 45 : 2761-2771.

HAMED G R, ZHAO J, 1999. Tensile Behavior after Oxidative Aging of Gum and Black-Filled Vulcanizates of SBR and NR[J]. Rubber Chemistry and Technology, 72(4) : 721-730.

HAO PHAM THI, ISMAIL H, HASHIM A, 2001. Study of Two Types of Styrene Butadiene Rubber in Tire Tread Compounds", Polymer Testing, Vol. 20 : 539-544.

HARBOR R, et al, 2008. Constitutive Behavior and Temperature Effects in NR and SBR under Variable Amplitude and Multiaxial Loading Conditions[J]. Journal of Engineering Materials and Technology, 130 (1) : 1075-1076.

HOANG G C, et al, 2004. Electrical Resistivity and Thermal Expansion Coefficient of Carbon-Black-Filled Compounds around T_g[J]. Journal of the Korean Physical Society, 44(4) : 962-966.

JAYASREE T, PREDEEP P, 2008. Effect of Fillers on Mechanical Properties of Dynamically Cross-linked Styrene Butadiene Rubber/High Density Polyethylene Blends[J]. Journal of Elastomers and Plastics, 40 (2) : 127-146.

JIA Z X, et al, 2009. Morphology, Interfacial Interaction and Properties of Styrene-Butadiene Rubber/Modified Halloysite Nanotube Nanocomposites[J]. Chinese Journal of Polymer Science, 27(6) : 857-864.

KHAIRY S A, ATEIA E, 1993. Thermoelasticity in Carbon Black-Filled Styrene-Butadiene Rubber[J]. Journal of Physics D: Applied Physics, 26 : 2272-2275.

LIN H, BENGISU T, MOURELATOS Z, 2009. Dynamic Properties of Styrene-Butadiene Rubber for Automotive Applications[J]. SAE 2009-01-2128.

MINETT S, FENWICK K, 1999. A Steel-Rubber Laminate That Can Quieten Cars & Other Machines[J]. Noise & Vibration Worldwide, 30 (2) : 12-13.

MIRZA J, et al, 2002. Laboratory and Field Performance of Polymer-Modified Cement-Based Repair Mortars in Cold Climates[J]. Construction and Building Materials, 16(6) : 365-374.

MOJANRAJ G, et al, 2006. AC Impedance Analysis and EMI Shielding Effectiveness of Conductive SBR Composites[J]. Polymer Engineering and Science, 46(10) : 1342-1349.

MONGRUEL A, CARTAULT M, 2006. Nonlinear Rheology of Syrene-Butadiene Rubber Filled with Carbon-Black or Silica Particles[J]. Journal of Rheology, 50(2):115-135.

NAKAZONO T, MATSUMOTO A, 2010. Mechanical Properties and Thermal Aging Behavior of Styrene-Butadiene Rubbers Vulcanized Using Liquid Diene Polymers as the Plasticizer[J]. Journal of Applied Polymer Science, 118(4):2314-2320.

RODRIDGUES E, FILLISKO F, 1986. Thermal Effect in SBR at High Hydrostatic Pressures[J]. Polymer, 27: 1943-1947.

SAKR E M, et al, 1995. Study of Stress-Strain Characteristics of SBR and Blended NR/SBR Rubber[J]. Czechoslovak Journal of Physics, 45(3):275-282.

WILIAM O S, et al, 2007. Non-Gaussian Effects in Styrene-Butadiene Rubber[J]. British Polymer Journal, 12 (1):19-23.

WU Y, et al, 2006. Improvement of Flex-Fatigue Life of Carbon-Black-Filled Styrene-Butadiene Rubber by Addition of Nano-Dispersed Clay[J]. Macromolecular Materials and Engineering, 291:944-949.

WU Y, et al, 2008. The Influence of In Situ Modification of Silica on Filler Network and Dynamic Mechanical Properties of Silica-Filled Solution Styrene-Butadiene Rubber[J]. Journal of Applied Polymer Science, 108: 112-118.

YANG Z, et al, 2009. Effect of Styrene-Butadiene Rubber Latex on the Chloride Permeability and Microstructure of Portland Cement Mortar[J]. Construction and Building Materials, 23(6):2283-2290.

ZHOU X, et al, 2010. New Fabrications and Mechanical Properties of Styrene-Butadiene Rubber/Carbon Nanotubes Nanocomposite[J]. Journal of Materials Science and Technology, 26(12):1127-1132.

Table 23.1   Mechanical Properties of SBR（Styrene-Butadiene Rubber）

Material-DAM	$T/℃$	ρ	(σ, ε)	α	k	γ	Set	$\tan \delta$
SBR（40A）	$-55(T_g)$	—	—	—	—	—	—	—
	23	0.94	(5.5, 400%)	221	0.23	1940	—	0.24
	80(High service temperature)							
SBR（50A）	$-55(T_g)$	—	—	—	—	—	—	—
	23	0.94	(8.3, 350%)	221	0.23	1940	—	0.24
	80(High service temperature)							
SBR（60A）	$-55(T_g)$	—	—	—	—	—	—	—
	23	0.94	(8.3, 300%)	221	0.23	1940	—	0.24
	80(High service temperature)							

continued

Material-DAM	T/℃	ρ	(σ,ε)	α	k	γ	Set	tan δ
SBR (70A)	−55(T_g)	—	—	—	—	—	—	—
	23	0.94	(10.3, 250%)	221	0.23	1940	—	0.24
	70	—	—	—	—	—	$\Delta_{22}=25\%$	—
	80(High service temperature)							
SBR-75A(50 pphr of CB)	−55(T_g)	—	—	—	—	—	—	—
	23	0.94	(12.7, 250%)	221	0.23	1940	—	0.24
	80(High service temperature)							
SBR(75 pphr N234)	−55(T_g)	—	—	—	—	—	—	—
	23	0.94	(1.7, 50%) (2.5, 100%) (3, 165%)	221	0.23	1940	—	0.24
	80(High service temperature)							
SBR (80A)	−55(T_g)	—	—	—	—	—	—	—
	23	0.94	(7.6, 150%)	221	0.23	1940	—	0.24
	80(High service temperature)							
SBR (65A; 100 pphr N990)	−55(T_g)	—	—	—	—	—	—	—
	23	0.94	(6.4, 300%) (9.6, 530%)	221	0.23	1940	—	0.24
	80(High service temperature)							
SBR (76A; 200 pphr N990)	−55(T_g)	—	—	—	—	—	—	—
	23	0.94	(8.1, 230%)	221	0.23	1940	—	0.24
	80(High service temperature)							
SBR-Zn (Tin-coupled SBR)	−100	—	—	70	—	—	—	—
	−50	—	—	65	—	—	—	—
	−24(T_g)	—	—	118	—	—	—	—
	0	—	—	190	—	—	—	—
	23	0.94	—	200	—	—	—	—
	80	—	—	195	—	—	—	—

continued

Material-DAM	$T/℃$	ρ	(σ,ε)	α	k	γ	Set	$\tan\delta$
SBR-Zn-CB50 (50 pphr N234)	−100	—	—	45	—	—	—	—
	−50	—	—	45	—	—	—	—
	−24(T_g)	—	—	55	—	—	—	—
	0	—	—	180	—	—	—	—
	23	0.94	—	200	—	—	—	—
	80	—	—	195	—	—	—	—
SBR (Tracked Vehicle Pad; [Brown et al.])	−40(T_g)	—	—	—	—	—	—	—
	−5	—	(−9.8, −100%) (−8.0, −80%) (−6.5, −60%) (−5.3, −40%) (−3.8, −20%) (0,0) (3, 20%) (5, 40%) (7, 60%) (10, 80%) (14, 100%) (21, 120%) (43, 160%)	—	—	—	—	—
SBR (Tracked Vehicle Pad; [Brown et al.])	23	—	(−3.8, −100%) (−3.0, −80%) (−2.5, −60%) (−1.8, −40%) (−1.2, −20%) (0,0) (1.8, 20%) (3.0, 40%) (4.5, 60%) (7.0, 80%) (10.5, 100%) (16, 120%)	—	—	—	—	—

continued

Material-DAM	$T/℃$	ρ	(σ,ε)	α	k	γ	Set	$\tan\delta$
SBR (Tracked Vehicle Pad; [Brown et al.])	50	—	$(-2.5,\ -100\%)$ $(-2.0,\ -80\%)$ $(-1.75,\ -60\%)$ $(-1.25,\ -40\%)$ $(-0.75,\ -20\%)$ $(0,0)$ $(0.8,\ 20\%)$ $(1,5,\ 40\%)$ $(2.5,\ 60\%)$ $(4.0,\ 80\%)$ $(6.0,\ 100\%)$	—	—	—	—	—

Notes: pphr = Parts of reinforcing material per hundred parts of rubber;

CB = Carbon black such as N110, ⋯, N990 (ISO classification);

××A = Shore A durometer hardness.

Chapter 24

Silicone Rubber-VMQ, PVMQ, and FVMQ

24.1 Introduction

Silicone is an inorganic polymer, and the technically correct term for the various silicone rubbers is polydimethylsiloxanes or polysiloxanes. Silicone rubber forms the matrix of the first autonomic self-healing elastomer [Keller]. The microcapsule-based material is capable of recovering almost all of the original tear strength. Mechanical properties of some silicone rubbers are listed in Table 24.1. Material models corresponding to Yeoh's strain energy density function for soft, medium, and hard silicone rubbers [Kosinski & Kosinski] are given in Table 24.2.

Silicone rubber is regarded as the best-in-class elastomer for applications at extreme temperatures and aging. All types of silicone rubber exhibited a second-order transition at about −123 ℃, the lowest temperature at which such a transition has been observed in a polymer. Silicone rubber compounds have several great inherent characteristics, such as a high degree of hydrophobicity and high resistance to ultraviolet energy.

Silicone rubber membranes have exceptional mechanical properties such as low modulus of elasticity, high elongation, good insulation properties, and promising sealing on rough surfaces. Typical silicones such as VMQ (Vinyl Methyl Siloxane) and PVMQ (Phenyl Vinyl Methyl Siloxane) are the most permeable elastomers.

24.2 VMQ (Vinyl Methyl Siloxane)

VMQ (Vinyl Methyl Siloxane) rubber gum has the lowest glass transition point (−123 ℃) of all elastomers. It is also called MVQ (by ASTM & DIN). VMQ tends to crystallize and becomes inflexible at −50 ℃ and below. Mechanical strength of VMQ is weak. Such deficiency may be improved with certain reinforcing fillers, such as carbon black, fumed nano silica (FNS), hydrophobic nano silica sol (HNSS), and precipitated nano silica and nano calcium carbonate. The tensile strength of VMQ can reach 11.7 MPa with its transmittance up to 90%, as it is reinforced by 40 pphr HNSS [Wang et al.]. Note that a material with a transmittance of 80% or higher is considered transparent.

24.3 PVMQ (Phenyl Vinyl Methyl Siloxane)

PVMQ (Phenyl Vinyl Methyl Siloxane), formulated with an addition of phenyl pendant groups to VQM, remains flexible until the temperature goes below its glass transition point (−123 ℃). Room temperature vulcanizing (RTV) PVMQ coating is a novel approach to electricity insulators.

24.4   FVMQ(Fluorosilicone Rubber)

FVMQ (Fluorosilicone rubber) provides an improved resistance to fuel and mineral oil, though bearing with similar physical properties to VMQ (Silicone rubber). It contains trifluoropropyl groups next to methyl groups in the chemical structure. Its resistance to fuel/oil and a wide operating temperature region (ranging from -55 to 175 ℃) make itself applicable to the under-the-hood environment, especially when exposed to hot water and steam. It is normally not used due to the high cost of FVMQ, unless extreme temperature resistance is essential. Fluorosilicone compounds, such as Dow Silastic ® LS-2860 and Silastic ® LS 5-2060, have tensile strength values at 200 ℃ similar to the fluorocarbon compounds.

24.5   Thermally Conductive VMQ and FVMQ

Silicone rubbers can be made thermally conductive by dispersing thermally conductive materials such as alumina platelets and titanium diboride. They offer excellent heat conductivity and have a damping (cushioning) effect. Thermally conductive VMQ is mostly used in power transistors, thermistors, or CPUs. The thermal conductivity of thermally conductive VQM falls between 0.6 and 2.5 W/m/℃. The use of larger particles of alumina is an effective way of increasing the thermal conductivity with an increasing particle size. It is shown in one case study by [Zhou et al., 2008] that the thermal conductivity is 1.14 W/m/℃, 1.28 W/m/℃, and 1.48 W/m/℃ as the particle size is 5 μm, 10 μm, and 30 μm, respectively. Nevertheless, the coefficient of linear thermal expansion of alumina-filled silicone rubbers decreases as 70 (ranging from 59 to 80) μm/m/℃, 67 (ranging from 56 to 78) μm/m/℃ and 64 (ranging from 53 to 75) μm/m/℃, respectively, for the three cases.

24.6   Electrically Conductive and EMI-shielding VMQ and FVMQ

Silicone rubbers can be made EMI-shielding by dispersing thermally conductive materials such as carbon (carbon fibers and/or carbon black), nickel-coated graphite, silver-coated aluminum, silver-coated copper, silver-coated glass, and silver-coated nickel. In the same item it can be the shielding of EMI (Electromagnetic Interference), EMP (Electromagnetic Pulse), ESD (Electrostatic Discharge), and RFI (Radio Frequency Interference). Shielding is an important application in vehicle communications and radar systems.

24.7 Applications of Silicone

Cured silicone elastomers can be formulated to produce a wide range of products, including micro thin coatings, flexible adhesives, soft cured gels, sponges, foams, and solid rubbers of varying hardness. Silicone Rubbers including VMQ, PVMQ, and FVMQ are also used in room temperature vulcanizing (RTV) sealants for joints.

The primary use of high temperature vulcanizates (HTV) such as VMQ, PVMQ, and FVMQ is for O-rings in automotive fuel systems and turbocharger hose liners. FVMQ is used for static applications only due to its low tear strength, low abrasion resistance, and high friction. FVMQ is much more expensive than VMQ. Thermally conductive adhesive tape is a powerful heatsinking mechanism for IC packaging even on a curved surface.

Silicone rubbers have become widely used by LED design engineers to provide improved light performance, extended product life and environmental protection.

References

CUI T, et al, 2011. Service Life Estimation of Liquid Silicone Rubber Seals in Polymer Electrolyte Membrane Fuel Cell Environment[J]. Journal of Power Sources, 196:1216-1221.

DOREMUS R H, 2002. Viscosity of Silica[J]. Journal of Applied Physics, 92(12):7619-7629.

HE Y, et al, 2009. Thermal Conductivity and Mechanical Properties of Silicone Rubber Filled with Different Particle Sized SiC[J]. Advanced Materials Research, Vol. 87/88:137-142.

HINRICHSEN G, et al, 1979. Mechanical Behavior of Cerclage Material Consisting of Silicone Rubber[J]. Graefe's Archive of Clinical and Experimental Ophthalmology, 211(3):251-258.

HOMMA H, MIRLEY C L, 2000. Field and Laboratory Aging of RTV Silicone Insulator Coating[J]. IEEE Transaction of Power Delivery, 15(4):1298-1303.

KELLER, et al, 2008. Torsion Fatigue Response of Self-Healing Poly(dimethylsiloxane) Elastomers [J]. Polymer, 49:3136-3145.

KELLER, et al, 2007. A Self-Healing Poly(dimethylsiloxane) Elastomer[J]. Advanced Functional Materials, 17:2399-2404.

KOROCHKINA T V, et al, 2008. Experimental and Numerical Investigation into Nonlinear Deformation of Silicone Rubber Pads during Ink Transfer Process[J]. Polymer Testing:778-791.

LEE K, LEE J, KOO B, 1998. Development of A Continuously Variable Speed Viscous Fan Clutch for Engine Cooling System[J]. SAE 980838.

LOEW R, MEIER P 2007. Simulation of Reiterated Mechanical Load of Silicone Rubber[J]. Finite Element Analysis and Design, 43(6-7):453-462.

LOTTERS J C, et al, 1997. The Mechanical Properties of the Rubber Elastic Polymer Polydimethylsiloxane for Sensor Applications[J]. Journal of Micromechanics and Microengineering, 797(3):145-147.

MARUNGSRI B, SHINOKUBO H, MATSUOKA R, et al, 2006. Effect of Specimen Configuration on Deterioration of Silicone Rubber for Polymer Insulators in Salt Fog Ageing Test[J]. IEEE Transactions on DEI, 13(1):129-138.

MUHR A, GOUGH J, GREGORY L, 1999. Experimental Determination of Model for Liquid Silicone Rubber: Hyperelasticity and Mullin's Effect[J]. Constitutive Models for Rubber, Dorfman and Muhr (editors), Balkema, Rotterdam:181-187.

SALEEM A, et al, 2010. Fabrication of Extrinsically Conductive Silicone Rubbers with High Elasticity and Analysis of Their Mechanical and Electrical Characteristics[J]. Polymer, 2:200-210.

SEREDA L, et al, 2003. Effect of Silica and Rice Husk Ash Fillers on the Modulus of Polysiloxane Networks [J]. Journal of Applied Polymer Science, 90(2):421-429.

TALEBI M A, et al, 2005. Technical & Economic Evaluation of Using Silicone Rubber RTV Coating for High Voltage Substation in Polluted Area[J]. 18th International Conference on Electricity Distribution, Turlin, June 6-9, 2005:1-4.

VIRANT M S, et al, 1991. The Effect of Alternative Fuels on Fluorosilicone Elastomers[J]. SAE 910102.

WANG P, DING T, 2010. Creep of Electrical Resistance under Uniaxial Pressures for Carbon Black Silicone Rubber Composites[J]. Journal of Materials Science, 45:3595-3601.

WANG Q, et al, 2008. Preparation of High-Temperature Vulcanized Silicone Rubber of Excellent Mechanical and Optical Properties Using Hydrophobic Nano Silica Sol as Reinforcement[J]. China Journal of Polymer Science, 26(4):495-500.

WEIR C E, et al, 1951. Crystallization and Second-Order Transitions in Silicone Rubbers [J]. Rubber Chemistry & Technology, 24(2):366-373.

ZHOU HUA, et al, 2009. Study on the Structure and Properties of Conductive Silicone Rubber Filled with Nickel-Coated Graphite[J]. J. of Applied Polymer Science, 115(5):2710-2717.

ZHOU W, et al, 2008. Effect of Filler Size Distribution on the Mechanical and Physical Properties of Alumina-Filled Silicone Rubber[J]. Polymer Engineering and Science, 48(7):1381-1388.

ZHOU W, et al, 2007. Thermally Conductive Silicone Rubber Reinforced with Boron Nitride Particle[J]. Polymer Composites, 28(1):23-28.

Table 24.1 Mechanical Properties of Silicone Rubber

Material-DAM	$T/℃$	ρ	(σ, ε)	α	k	γ	Set	$\tan \delta$
VMQ (70A; Unfilled)	$-123(T_g)$	—	—	—	—	—	—	—
	23	1.18	(11, 500%)	287	0.17	1280	—	—
	70	—	—	—	—	—	$\Delta_{22}=15\%$	—
	200(High service temperature)							
VMQ (52A; 50 pphr Silica)	$-123(T_g)$	—	—	—	—	—	—	—
	-30	—	—	400	—	—	—	—
	23	1.14	(1.7, 100%) (4.8, 300%) (5.6, 410%)	270	0.18	1256	—	—
	200(High service temperature)							
VMQ(40 pphr HNSS)	$-123(T_g)$	—	—	—	—	—	—	—
	23	1.2	(11.7, 500%)	70	0.2	—	—	—
	200(High service temperature)							
VMQ (84A; Thermally Conductive)	$-123(T_g)$	—	—	—	—	—	—	—
	23	2.7	(4.5, 50%)	70	1.3	—	—	—
	200(High service temperature)							
VMQ (25A; Electrically Conductive; 1.5% CF)	$-123(T_g)$	—	—	—	—	—	—	—
	23	1.17	(1.3, 50%) (1.56, 100%) (1.8, 135%)	140	—	—	—	—
	200(High service temperature)							
VMQ (43A; Electrically Conductive; 4% CF)	$-123(T_g)$	—	—	—	—	—	—	—
	23	1.1	(1, 12%) (1.5, 23%) (1.8, 45%)	140	—	—	—	—
	200(High service temperature)							
VMQ (Unfilled sponge)	$-123(T_g)$	—	—	—	—	—	—	—
	23	0.47	(0.6, 150%)	324	0.11	1256	—	—
	200(High service temperature)							

continued

Material-DAM	$T/℃$	ρ	(σ,ε)	α	k	γ	Set	$\tan\delta$
VMQ (Unfilled foam)	$-123(T_g)$	—	—	—	—	—	—	—
	23	0.19	(0.17, 60%)	—	0.061	1256	—	—
	200(High service temperature)							
PVMQ	-100		(2.9, 50%) (4, 100%) (5, 500%)	—	0.22		—	—
	23	1.3	—	—	—	—	—	—
	230(High service temperature)							
FVMQ (42A; Unfilled)	23	1.41	(0.9, 100%) (12.9, 513%)	200	0.25	—	—	0.03
	70	—	—	—	—	—	$\Delta_{22}=15\%$	—
	250(High service temperature)							
FVMQ (40A; Dow Corning Silastic FSR)	$-71(T_g)$	—	—	—	—	—	—	—
	-50	—	(18, 240%)	—	0.45	—	—	—
	0	—	(13, 325%)	—	0.23	—	—	—
	23	1.41	(6.7, 100%) (12.4, 320%)	—	0.17	—	—	—
	50	—	(10, 300%)	—	0.14	—	—	—
	100	—	(5.2, 100%) (7, 250%)	—	0.13	—	—	—
	150	—	(5, 100%) (6, 200%)	—	0.11	—	—	—
	200	—	(5, 140%)	—	0.08	—	—	—
	250(High service temperature)							

Notes：pphr=Parts of reinforcing material per hundred parts of rubber；

×× A=Shore A durometer hardness.

Table 24.2   Elastomeric Material Constants for Silicone Rubbers

Material-DAM	$T/℃$	ρ	C_{10}	C_{01}	C_{20}	C_{30}	α	k	γ	$\tan\delta$	$\sigma_{uts},\varepsilon_{uts}$
Silicone-soft	23	—	0.0231	0	-3.14×10^{-5}	0.000195	—	—	—	—	—
Silicone-medium	23	—	0.0335	0	-0.00191	0.000937	—	—	—	—	—

continued

Material-DAM	$T/°C$	ρ	C_{10}	C_{01}	C_{20}	C_{30}	α	k	γ	$\tan \delta$	$\sigma_{uts}, \varepsilon_{uts}$
Silicone-hard	23	—	0.0583	0	−0.00366	0.00178	—	—	—	—	—

Notes: C_{10}, C_{01}, C_{20}, C_{30}(MPa): $W = C_{10}(I_1 - 3) + C_{01}(I_2 - 3) + C_{20}(I_1 - 3)^2 + C_{30}(I_1 - 3)^3$;

$C_{01} = C_{20} = C_{30} = 0$, and $C_{10} \neq 0$: Neo-Hookean's model;

$C_{20} = C_{30} = 0$, $C_{10} \neq 0$, and $C_{02} \neq 0$: Mooney's model;

$C_{01} = 0$, $C_{10} \neq 0$, $C_{20} \neq 0$, and $C_{30} \neq 0$: Yeoh's model;

E (MPa): $E = 6 (C_{10} + C_{01})$, equivalent Young's modulus.

Chapter 25

Urethane-AU (Polyester Urethane) and EU (Polyether Urethane)

25.1 Introduction

Urethane rubbers have the highest available tensile strength among all elastomers and outstanding resistance to abrasion and tear at the room temperature, while providing good elongation characteristics. The ester-based urethanes (AU) provide slightly improved abrasion, heat, and oil swell resistance as compared with ether-based urethanes (EU). Nevertheless, EU rubber is directed toward low temperature flexibility applications. Mechanical properties of AU (Polyester Urethane Rubber) and EU (Polyether Urethane Rubber) are listed in Table 25.1 and their material properties of related composites are given in Table 25.2.

25.2 AU (Polyester Urethane)

AU (Polyester Urethane) Rubber is a thermoplastic elastomer, namely copolymer of polyester and urethane. Mechanical properties of AU rubber depend on the content of urethane. The volume fraction of urethane controls the modulus of elasticity, strength, glass transition point, and the high softening temperature behavior. The urethane segments reside primarily in solid domains, which serve both as viscoelastic filler particulates and physical crosslinks. Three example stress-strain curves of AU are depicted in Fig. 25.1.

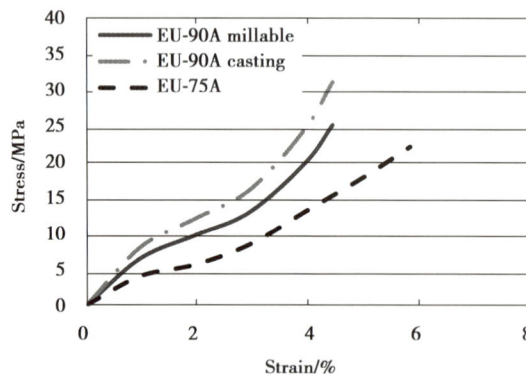

Fig. 25.1   Example Stress-Strain Curves of AU (Polyester Urethane) Rubber

25.3 EU (Polyether Urethane)

EU (Polyether Urethane) Rubber is a thermoplastic elastomer, namely copolymer of polyether and urethane. Mechanical properties of EU rubber are similar to AU rubber. Representative stress-stress curves corresponding to soft and hard EU Rubbers at the room temperature are plotted in Fig. 25.2.

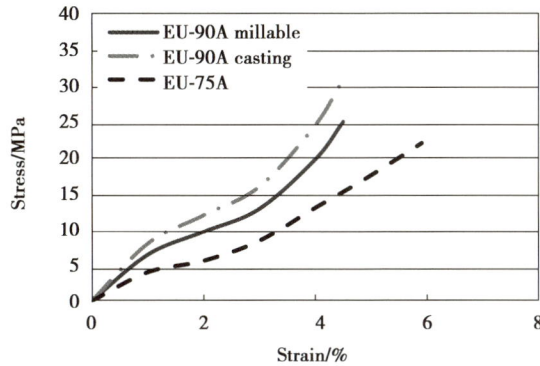

Fig. 25.2 Example Stress-Strain Curves of EU (Polyether Urethane) Rubber

25.4 PU Foam (Polyurethane Foam)

Mechanical properties of polyurethane foam depend on the microstructure, which is a function of foam density and deformation mechanics. The material parameters are calculated by curve-fitting experimental data using the modified Ogden model as given in Chapter 11. PU foams can be used to substitute helical springs as well as for energy absorption or damping in multiple applications. The main contrast between these and steel springs is that the elastomers are more reliable in emergency situations because of their longer life being unattended. Elastomers have a maximum load resistance as well as an excellent impact absorption capacity.

25.5 Applications

AU (Polyester Urethane) and EU (Polyether Urethane) rubbers are ideal materials for damping devices, such as automotive suspension (control arm) bushings, engine mounts, transmission mounts, driveline couplers, and bump stops.

References

BAHLOULI N, et al, 2004. Stress-strain Response of Biomaterials by a Digital Image Correlation Method, Application to Recoflex[J]. Journal of Material Science and Technology, 20(1):114-116.

DEL PIERO G, PAMPOLINI G, 2010. On the Rate-Dependent Properties of Open-Cell Polyurethane Foams [J]. Technische Mechanik, 30(1-3):74-84.

DENG R, DAVIES P, BAJAJ A, 2006. A Nonlinear Fractional Derivative Model for Large Uni-axial Deformation Behavior of Polyurethane Foam[J]. Signal Processing, 86:2728-2743.

ECEIZA A., et al, 2008. Structure-Property Relationships of Thermoplastic Polyurethane Elastomers based on Polycarbonate Diols", Journal of Applied Polymer Science, 108:3092-3103.

FALABELLA R, FARRIS R J, COOPER S L, 1984. Constitutive Equations for Orientation in Polyurethane Elastomers[J]. Journal of Rheology, 28(2):123-154.

GOODS S, NEUSCHWANGER C, WHINNERY L, 1999. Mechanical Properties of a Particle-Strengthened Polyurethane Foam[J]. Journal of Applied Polymer Science, 74:2724-2736.

MOTT P H, et al, 2002. Acoustic and Dynamic Mechanical Properties of a Polyurethane Rubber[J]. Journal of Acoustic Society America, 111(4):1782-1790.

PAMPOLINI G, DEL PIERO G, 2008. Strain Localization in Open-Cell Polyurethane Foams: Experiments and Theoretical Model[J]. Journal Mechanics Materials and Structures, 3:969-981.

PANKOKE S, WOLFEL H, 2003. Determination of the Deflected Contact Surface between Human Body and Seat under Realistic Individual Sitting Conditions-A Mixed Experimental and Numerical Approach[J]. SAE 2003-01-2209.

SPATHIS G D, 1991. Polyurethane Elastomers (AU) Studied by the Mooney-Rivilin Equation for Rubbers[J]. Journal of Applied Polymer Science, 43(3):613-620.

WHITE S W, KIM S K, BAJAJ A K, et al, 2000. Experimental Techniques and Identification of Nonlinear and Viscoelastic Properties of Flexible Polyurethane Foam[J]. Nonlinear Dynamics, 22(3):281-313.

YI J, BOYCE M, LEE G, et al, 2006. Large Deformation Rate-Dependent Stress-Strain Behavior of Polyurea and Polyurethanes[J]. Polymer, 47(1):319-329.

Table 25.1 Mechanical Properties of Urethane Rubbers-AU and EU

Material-DAM	$T/℃$	ρ	(σ, ε)	α	k	γ	Set	$\tan\delta$
AU (35A)	$-50(T_g)$	—	—	—	—	—	—	—
	23	1.25	(3.4, 900%)	180	0.16	1760	—	—
	93(High service temperature)							
AU (95A)	$-50(T_g)$	—	—	—	—	—	—	—
	23	1.25	(41, 250%)	170	0.16	1760	—	—
	70	—	—	—	—	—	$\Delta_{22}=45\%$	—
	93(High service temperature)							

continued

Material-DAM	$T/℃$	ρ	(σ,ε)	α	k	γ	Set	$\tan\delta$
EU (75A; Millable)	$-34(T_g)$	—	—	—	—	—	—	—
	23	1.2	(4, 100%) (5.6, 200%) (8.4, 300%) (13, 400%) (17.5, 500%) (22, 590%)	180	0.29	1760	—	—
	70	—	—	—	—	—	$\Delta_{22}=27\%$	—
	93(High service temperature)							
EU (90A; Casting)	$-34(T_g)$	—	—	—	—	—	—	—
	23	1.2	(8, 100%) (12, 200%) (16, 300%) (24.5, 400%) (31, 450%)	170	0.29	1760	—	—
	70	—	—	—	—	—	$\Delta_{22}=27\%$	—
	93(High service temperature)							
EU (90A; Millable)	$-34(T_g)$	—	—	—	—	—	—	—
	23	1.2	(6.5, 100%) (9.7, 200%) (12.9, 300%) (19.8, 400%) (25, 450%)	170	0.29	1760	—	—
	70	—	—	—	—	—	$\Delta_{22}=27\%$	—
	93(High service temperature)							
Backrest TPU (Foam, Seating)	$-50(T_g)$	—	—	—	—	—	—	—
	23	0.38	(−0.015, −70%) (−0.009, −60%) (−0.006, −50%) (−0.005, −40%) (−0.004, −30%) (−0.003, −10%) (−0.002, −5%)	—	—	—	—	—
	93(High service temperature)							

continued

Material-DAM	$T/℃$	ρ	(σ,ε)	α	k	γ	Set	$\tan\delta$
TPU[Bajsic et al.]	$-25(T_g)$	—	—	—	—	—	—	—
	23	0.02	(1.5, 20%) (3, 2500%)	—	—	—	—	—
TPU Seal(90A; Polyurethane)	-35(Low service temperature)							
	23	1.08	(−6.5, −25%) (−4.7, −20%) (−3.4, −15%) (−2.4, −10%) (−1.45, −5%); (7, 20%) (11.7, 100%) (11.4, 300%) (28, 450%)	—	—	—	—	—
	100	—	—	—	—	$\Delta_{22}=28\%$	—	
	65(High service temperature, with water and glycol)							
	110(High service temperature)							
TPU Seal(95A; Polyurethane)	-35(Low service temperature)							
	23	1.22	(10, 20%) (12, 100%) (22, 300%) (51, 440%)	—	—	—	—	—
	70	—	—	—	—	—	$\Delta_{22}=28\%$	—
	65(High service temperature, with water and glycol)							
	110(High service temperature)							
TPU Seal(60D; Polyurethane)	-31(Low service temperature)							
	23	1.16	(−28, −25%) (21, −20%) (−16, −15%) (11.4, −10%) (−6.9, −5%); (25, 100%) (33, 200%) (46, 290%)	—	—	—	—	—
	110(High service temperature)							

continued

Material-DAM	$T/°C$	ρ	(σ,ε)	α	k	γ	Set	$\tan\delta$
TPU Seal(72D; Polyurethane)	−31	(Low service temperature)						
	23	1.20	(−50, −25%) (41, −20%) (−32, −15%) (26, −10%) (−15, −5%); (36, 100%) (41, 200%) (49, 230%)	—	—	—	—	—
	110(High service temperature)							
TPU/20PP	−22(T_g)	—	—	—	—	—	—	—
	23	0.04	(1.5, 10%) (4.3, 84%)	—	—	—	—	—
TPU/40PP	−22(T_g)	—	—	—	—	—	—	—
	23	0.24	(6, 5%) (7, 8%)	—	—	—	—	—
TPU/60PP	−21(T_g)	—	—	—	—	—	—	—
	23	0.48	(13, 5%) (15, 19%)	—	—	—	—	—
TPU/80PP	−19(T_g)	—	—	—	—	—	—	—
	23	0.65	(16.7, 5%) (17.4, 7%)	—	—	—	—	—

Notes: pphr = Parts of reinforcing material per hundred parts of rubber;

CB = Carbon black such as N110, ⋯, N990 (ISO classification);

××A = Shore A durometer hardness;

$\tan\delta$ = Loss factor = loss modulus/storage modulus at 1 Hz, detailed in Chapter 4.

Table 25.2   Mechanical Properties of Urethane Reinforced by Straight Continuous Fibers

Material-DAM	$T/°C$	ρ	E_{11}	E_{22}	E_{33}	G_{12}	G_{13}	G_{23}	v_{11}	v_{22}	v_{23}
Urethane/GF ($V_f = 12.1\%$)	23	—	17.9	2.25	2.25	5.34	5.34	—	0.45	0.45	—

Notes: $v_{ij} E_{jj} = v_{ji} E_{ii} (i = 1, 2, 3; j = 1, 2, 3; i \neq j)$.

Table 25.3   Ogden Model Coefficients of Flexible Open-Celled Polyurethane Foam

Material-DAM	$T/℃$	ρ	(G_1, α_2, ν_3)	$\cdots$	(G_N, α_N, ν_N)	α	k	γ	$\tan \delta$
Backrest foam, Seating ($N=2$)	$-50(T_g)$	—	—	—	—	—	—	—	—
	23	0.38	(22.94, −3.14, 0)		(32.1, 0.064, 0)	—	—	—	—
	93 (High service temperature)								

Notes: pphr = Parts of reinforcing material per hundred parts of rubber;

　　　CB = Carbon black such as N110, $\cdots$, N990 (ISO classification);

　　　tan δ = Loss factor = loss modulus/storage modulus at 1 Hz.

Chapter 26

Tires

26.1　Introduction

Principal rubbers used for main tire components are NR (Natural Rubber), IR (Isoprene Rubber), SBR (Styrene Butadiene Rubber), BR (Butadiene Rubber), and Halo-IIR (Halogenated Butyl Rubber). IR is supposed to be a synthetic replacement for NR. The reinforcement materials include fillers (such as carbon black and silica), organic textile plies (such as polyester or rayon bodies, nylon or Kevlar cap), and steel wires for belts and bead cords. Mixtures of traditional tire rubbers for individual components are given in Table 26.1. A comparison of their durabilityrelated performance is listed in Table 26.2. Mechanical properties of typical passenger tire rubbers are in exhibition in Table 26.3. Each tire tread is a mix of NR, SBR, and/or BR, compounded for low loss tangents, as low as 0.05. Mechanical properties of tire treads are shown in Table 26.4 and individual stress-strain curves are depicted in Fig. 26.1.

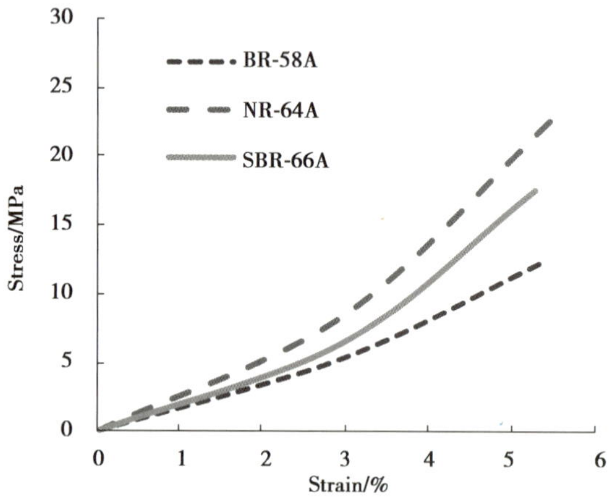

Fig. 26.1　Stress-Strain Curves of Rubbers Used for Tire Treads

26.2　Dynamic Rubber Properties

When a tire rotates, mechanical hysteresis losses in rubber compounds and their reinforcement materials are manifested in internal heat generation. The hysteresis loss per cycle per unit volume of material under a sinusoidal deformation is

$$H = \pi\sigma\varepsilon \sin \delta \tag{26.1}$$

where

H: Heat generated due to hysteresis;

σ: Stress;

ε: Strain;

$$\sin \delta = \frac{E''}{(E'^2 + E''^2)^{\frac{1}{2}}}.$$

A tire temperature increases due to the hysteresis loss. The operating load and speed of a tire are then limited to the speed of heat dissipation into the air to balance the internal heat generation. Nevertheless, the loss factor ($\tan \delta = E''/E'$) decreases with increasing temperature, so do the storage modulus and loss modulus.

The dynamic storage modulus of tire rubbers, E', usually range from 10 MPa to 18 MPa for a low-amplitude vibration of 60 Hz at the room temperature for a typical tread compound. Both storage and loss moduli decrease with an increase in temperature. This means that the viscoelastic effect prevails for a tire when it is in a running condition. The loss tangent is a function of temperature, strain amplitude, and strain rate; but more sensitive to the temperature variation than strain amplitude and strain rate. The loss tangent decreases as the temperature rises. For example, $\tan \delta = 0.28$ at 10 ℃, $\tan \delta = 0.214$ at 50 ℃, and $\tan \delta = 0.158$ at 100 ℃ based on the case study on rubber materials by [Song et al.]. Thus, a running tire would approach equilibrium in temperature rather than getting hotter and hotter.

It has been shown that increasing the "$\tan \delta$ at 0 ℃" measure of the tread compound correlates to improved wet traction. Conversely, lowering "$\tan \delta$ at 60 ℃" correlates to improved rolling resistance [Evans et al.]. Most treads fit a linear tradeoff between better predicted wet traction (higher $\tan \delta$ at 0 ℃) and better predicted rolling resistance (lower $\tan \delta$ at 60 ℃).

26.3   Tire-Shaping

A cured tire is cooled from the cure temperature to a point below the glass transition temperature of the fabric cords while being held at a constant inflation pressure. Due to thermal effects and creep/relaxation behaviors of the component materials, the shape of the tire will be different after the post cure inflation than before. This change in tire shape from that in the mold drawings should be accounted for in performing the finite element analysis to predict tire performance characteristics.

References

BALDWIN J M, BAUER D R, 2008. Rubber Oxidation and Tire Aging-A Review[J]. Rubber Chemistry and Technology, 81:338-359.

BIJARIMI M, ZULKAFLI H, BEG M, 2010. Mechanical Properties of Industrial Tyre Rubber Compounds[J]. Journal of Applied Sciences, 10:1345-1348.

Chiang Y J, Shih C D, Lin C C, et al, 2004. Examination of Tire Rubber Cure by Weibull Distribution Functions[J]. International Journal of Materials and Product Technology, 20(1-3):210-219.

CHIANG Y J, SHIH C D, LIN C C, et al, 2000. Multi-Variable Effects on Sealing Pressure between Tires and Rims[J]. International Journal of Vehicle Design, 23(1-2):78-93.

CHO J R, KIM K W, YOO W S, et al, 2004. Mesh Generation Consideration Detailed Tread Blocks for Reliable 3D Tire Analysis[J]. Adv. Eng. Software, 32:105-113.

CHUNG B, et al, 2002. Cure System and Carbon Black Effects on NR Compound Performance in Truck Tires [J]. Rubber World, 227:36-42.

CLARK S K, 1983. Mechanics of Pneumatic Tires[M]. USA-DOT-NHTA, U.S. Government Printing Office, Washington, D.C. 20402, USA.

GHOREISHY M H R, 2006. Finite Element Analysis of Steady Rolling Tyre with Slip Angle: Effect of Belt Angle[J]. Plast. Rubber Composites, 35:83-90.

HIROSHI Z, YOSHIHARO Y, 2004. Identification of Stress-strain Data of Rubber for Finite Element Analysis [J]. Journal of the Society of Rubber Industry (in Japanese), 77(9):306-311.

KARAK N, GUPTA B R, 2000. Effects of Different Ingredients and Cure Parameters on Physical Properties of a Tyre Tread Compound[J]. Kautschuk Gummi Kunststoffe, 53(1-2):30-34.

KINDT P, DE CONINCK F, SAS P, et al, 2007. Analysis of Tire/Road Noise Caused by Road Impact Excitations[J]. SAE 2007-01-2248.

KWON E, CASTALDI M J, 2009. Fundamental Understanding of the Thermal Degradation Mechanisms of Waste Tires and Their Air Pollutant Generation in a N2 Atmosphere[J]. Environ Sci Technol., 43(15): 5996-6002.

PACEJKA H B, BESSELINK I J M, 2008. Magic Formula Tire Model with Transient Properties [J]. Supplement to Vehicle System Dynamics, 27:234-249.

SHOOP S A, KESTLER K, HAEHNEL R. 2006. Finite Element Modeling of Tires on Snow[J]. Tire Science and Technology, 34(1):2-37.

SOMBATSOMPOP N, KUMNUANTIP C, 2003. Rheology, Cure Characteristics, Physical and Mechanical Properties of Tire Tread Reclaimed Rubber/Natural Rubber Compounds[J]. Journal of Applied Polymer Science, 87:1723-1731.

TONG J, YAN X, 2002. Finite Element Analysis of Tire Curing Process[J]. Journal of Reinforced Plastics and Composites, 22(11):983-1002.

YANG X, OLATUNBOSUN O, BOLARINWA E, 2010. Materials Testing for Finite Element Tire Model[J]. SAE Int. J. Mater. Manuf., 3(1):211-220.

ZHONG H, et al, 2009. Modification of EPDM with Alkylphenol Polysulfide for Use in Tire Sidewalls, I-Mechanical Properties[J]. Macromolecular Materials and Engineering, 295(1):67-75.

Table 26.1 Typical Mixtures of Traditional Tire Rubbers

Vehicle	Tire Component	NR/IR	SBR	BR	Halo IIR/IIR	CR	EPDM
Car Tires	Liner	Yes	Yes	No	Yes	No	No
	Carcass	Yes	Yes	No	No	No	No
	Tread, upper	Yes	Yes	Yes	No	No	No
	Under tread	Yes	Yes	Yes	No	No	No
	Sidewall-black	Yes	No	Y	No	No	Yes
	Sidewall-White	Yes	No	No	No	Yes	Yes
	Belt	Yes	No	No	No	No	No
Truck Tires	Liner	Yes	Yes	No	Yes	No	No
	Carcass	Yes	No	No	No	No	No
	Tread, upper	Yes	Yes	Yes	No	No	No
	Under tread	Yes	Yes	Yes	No	No	No
	Sidewall	Yes	No	No	No	No	No
	Belt	Yes	No	Yes	No	No	No

Table 26.2 Resistance of Tire Rubbers to Potential Failure Modes (A: Good; D: Bad)

Rubber	Impact	Tear	Wear	Fatigue	Air	Ozone	Aging	Weather
NR/IR	B	A	A	C	D	D	C	C
SBR	C	D	B	C	D	D	B	B
BR	A	C	A	B	D	B	B	B
Halo-IIR	D	C	C	A	A	A	A	A

Notes: Impact = Impact resilience;

Tear = Tear strength;

Wear = Wear Resistance;

Fatigue = Fatigue strength;

Air = Air impermeability;

Ozone = Ozone cracking;

Aging = Aging resistance;

Weather = Weather influence.

Table 26.3   Mechanical Properties of Typical Radial Passenger Tire Rubbers

Material-DAM	$T/℃$	ρ	C_{10}	C_{01}	C_{20}	C_{30}	α	k	γ	$\tan \delta$	$(\sigma_{uts}, \varepsilon_{uts})$
Line	23	1.15	0.5712	0	−0.178	0.0507	—	0.19	—	0.4	(7, 5)
	200	—	—	0	—	—	—	0.17	—	—	—
Cap	23	1.14	0.6786	0	-0.197	0.0566	—	0.23	—	—	—
	200	—	—	0	—	—	—	0.21	—	—	—
Carcass	23	1.14	0.6786	0	-0.197	0.0566	—	0.23	—	0.17	(21, 5.5)
	200	—	—	—	—	—	—	0.21	—	—	—
Tread, upper	23	1.15	0.6817	0	−0.217	0.1749	0.23	—	—	0.2	(17, 5)
	200	—	—	0	—	—	0.21	—	—	—	—
Tread, under	23	1.16	0.6817	0	−0.217	0.1749	—	0.23	—	0.05	(12, 5)
	200	—	—	0	—	—	—	0.21	—	—	—
Sidewall	23	1.12	0.685	0	−0.162	0.0388	—	0.21	—	0.25	(17, 5.5)
	200	—	—	0	—	—	—	0.19	—	—	—
Belt	1.20	1.20	1.0237	0	−0.31	0.111	—	0.24	—	0.25	(21, 2.5)
	200	—	—	0	—	—	—	—	0.22	—	—
Belt skim	23	1.20	1.0237	0	−0.31	0.111	—	0.24	—	0.25	(21, 2.5)
	200	—	—	0	—	—	—	0.22	—	—	—
Belt edge	23	1.20	1.0237	0	−0.31	0.111	—	0.24	—	0.25	(21, 2.5)
	200	—	—	0	—	—	—	0.22	—	—	—
Chafer	23	1.00	1.0348	0	−0.282	0.0822	—	—	—	—	—
Rim strip	23	1.00	1.0348	0	−0.282	0.0822	—	—	—	—	—
Apex (bead)	23	1.30	2.4613	0	−1.721	2.0383	—	0.25	—	—	(14, 2.5)
	200	—	—	0	—	—	—	0.23	—	0.4	—

Notes: C_{10}, C_{01}, C_{20}, C_{30} (MPa) $= W = C_{10}(I_1-3) + C_{01}(I_2-3) + C_{20}(I_1-3)^2 + C_{30}(I_1-3)^3$

ν (Poisson's ratio) $\rightarrow 0.5$;

E (Young's modulus) $\approx 6 (C_{10} + C_{01})$

G (initial shear modulus) $= E/3$.

Table 26.4   Mechanical Properties of Tire Treads-Related Rubber Compounds

Material-DAM	$T/℃$	ρ	(σ, ε)	α	k	γ	Set	$\tan \delta$
BR (58A)	23	1.16	(5.4, 300%) (12.5, 540%)	—	—	—	—	0.050

continued

Material-DAM	$T/℃$	ρ	(σ,ε)	α	k	γ	Set	$\tan\delta$
NR (64A)	23	1.16	(8.5, 300%) (23.5, 560%)	—	—	—	—	0.054
SBR (66A)	23	1.16	(6.6, 300%) (17.5, 527%)	—	—	—	—	0.056
50NR-50BR (61A)	23	1.16	(7.1, 300%) (20, 556%)	—	—	—	—	0.052
50NR-50SBR (65A)	23	1.16	(7.2, 300%) (19.5, 496%)	—	—	—	—	0.055
50SBR-50BR (65A)	23	1.16	(6.3, 300%) (15.5, 530%)	—	—	—	—	0.052

Chapter 27

Belts

27.1 Introduction

Neoprene, EPDM, and HNBR are the three main rubbers for making automotive timing belts. Elongation, belt slips, hydroplaning, misalignment (e.g. due to structural bending or alignment calibration error) are typical causes to fail an automotive timing belt. Failure modes of timing belts include cracking (sectioned), glazing, abrasion (generally due to misalignment), and pilling as shown in Fig. 27.1.

Neoprene (CR) belts have a life expectancy between 80000 km and 100000 km. As they wear out, cracks and chunk-outs may occur.

EPDM belts have a life expectancy up to 100000 km. When EPDM serpentine belts lose material in the valleys of the ribs, the space between the ribs widens without getting shorter. It means that material wears out, the pulleys ride deeper into the belt valleys resulting in slip, noise, and hydroplaning rather than chunk-outs.

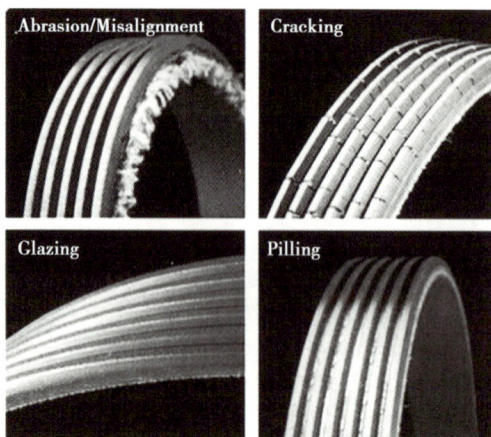

Fig. 27.1   Typical Failure Modes Multi-Grooved Belts

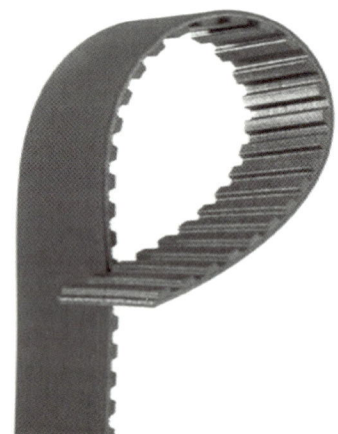

Fig. 27.2   Timing Belt

HNBR (Hydrogenated nitrile rubber) has some intriguing mechanical properties, such as resilience, high tensile strength, low permanent set, and good abrasion resistance. Automotive belts, mainly timing belts, currently account for more than 50% of HNBR use in Europe. Timing belts made of HNBR materials are expected to have a lifetime expectancy of more than 100000 km, and stretched up to 200000 km. The vast majority of timing belts nowadays are made from HNBR rather than traditional neoprene.

Power transmission is a function of belt tension and belt friction. Two belt structures are used most in the automotive applications: timing belts and conveying V-belts.

27.2   Timing Belts

Timing belts, as well as timing chains, are the devices that synchronize the rotations of the crankshaft and camshaft(s) of an internal combustion engine.   These belts have teeth that fit into a matching toothed pulley. When correctly tensioned, they have no slippage, run at a constant speed in accordance with the engine crankshaft speed, and are often used to transfer direct motion for indexing or timing purposes as named after. Timing belts need the least tension of all belts and are among the most efficient. In light of improving the transmission efficiency, reducing noises, and prolonging life, timing belts may have a helical offset tooth design [Ueda et al.] like helical gears, other than straight trapezoid-shaped teeth. Correct belt tension is crucial to preventing the engine valves from striking the piston.

Typically, a timing belt structure consists of three distinct materials, i.e. cord, the woven, and the bulk part as shown in Fig. 27.2. Their typical material properties are given in Table 27.1. Cords are made of helical glass fibers and their functional requirement is to take the tensile force in response to the applied load. The woven cover is the facing fabric in contact with the pulley during operation and is generally made of polyamide. The bulk part is rubber, which provides the flexibility to let the belt wrap around the pulley teeth smoothly in a continuous manner. The usual failure modes of timing belts are tooth-stripping and/or cord delamination/unraveling.

27.3   Conveying V-Belts

The "V" shape of the belt tracks in a mating groove in the pulley (or sheave), with the result that the belt cannot slip off. As a V-belt digs in, self-alignment is assured. Five or six V-belts make a multigroove V-belt, also called polygroove V-belts. A polygroove belt may be wrapped around a pulley on its back tightly enough to change its direction, or even to provide a light driving force. An idler pulley may be used for tensioning. Belt drive hardware may be one of the following:

(a) Gray Irons: G3500 and G4000;
(b) Ductile Irons: 65-45-12 and 80-55-06;
(c) Steel: SAE 1018 and SAE 1144;
(d) Stainless Steel: 304L and 416;
(e) Sintered Steel: FC-0208-50 and FC-0008-30;
(f) Aluminum: 2024-T3, 6061-T6, and 7075-T6.

27.4　Fibrous Reinforcement

The fibers may be of textile materials such as cotton, polyamides (e.g. Nylon), polyester, aramid (e.g. Twaron and Kevlar). The strengths of such reinforcing cords are greatly affected by water and antifreeze. Steel may be used as reinforcing fibers for increasing the carrying load.

References

ALCIATORE D G, et al, 2005. Multipulley Belt Drive Mechanics: Creep Theory versus Shear Theory[J]. Journal of Mechanical Design, 117(4):506-511.

BEIKMANN R S, et al, 1997. Design and Analysis of Automotive Serpentine Belt Drive Systems for Steady State Performance[J]. Journal of Mechanical Design, 119(2):162-168.

CHAMPLIAUD H, LAJMI A, VAN LÊ N, 2005. Finite Element Analysis of a Three-Point Belt Tension Tester [J]. SAE 2005-01-3137.

FURUKAWA Y, TOMONO K, TAKAHASHI H, et al, 1997. Analysis of Stress Distribution of Timing Belts by FEM[J]. SAE 970919.

HU J, et al, 2009. Finite Element Analysis of V-ribbed Belt/Pulley System with Pulley Misalignment Using a Neural-Network-Based Material Model[J]. Neural Computing & Applications, 18(8):927-938.

JOHANESSON T, et al, 2002. Dynamic Loading of Synchronous Belts[J]. Journal of Mechanical Design, 124 (1):79-85.

SHEN Y, et al, 2005. Finite Element Analysis of V-ribbed Belts using Neural Network Based Hyperelastic Material Model[J]. International Journal of Nonlinear Mechanics, 40(6):875-890.

SUNDARARAMAN S, et al, 2006. Mode-I Fatigue Crack Growth Analysis of V-Ribbed Belts[J]. Finite Elements in Analysis and Design, 43(11-12):870-878.

SROJANOCIC B, MILORADOVIC N, 2009. Development of Timing Belt Drives[J]. Mobility and Vehicle Mechanics, 25(2):31-36.

UEDA H, KAGOTANI M, KOYAMA T, et al, 1999. Noise and Life of Helical Timing Belt Drives[J]. Journal of Mechanical Design, 121(2):274-279.

Table 27.1 Mechanical Properties of Timing-Belt Constituents

Material	$T/℃$	E_T	ρ	υ	(σ, ε)	α	k	γ	$\tan \delta$
Cord	23	1.575	—	0.3	—	—	—	—	—
Woven	23	0.204	—	0.3	—	—	—	—	—
Rubber	23	—	—	—	$C_{10} = 11.6$, $C_{11} = -0.18$, $C_{01} = 3.5$, $C_{20} = 0.22$, $C_{02} = 0.0085$	—	—	—	—

Notes: The stress-strain relationship of rubber is represented by C_{10}, C_{11}, C_{01}, C_{11}, C_{20}, and C_{02}.

Chapter 28

Hoses

28.1 Introduction

High performance (i.e. high tensile strength and elongation) and low gas permeability are key product characteristics of rubber hoses. Automotive hoses are generally layered composite structures such as rubber reinforced with continuous fibers in addition to additives (e.g. carbon black). Each layer has its own mission, namely low permeability, oil resistance, water resistance, ozone resistance, and high strength.

28.2 Permeability

Permeability is a special characteristic of automotive hose materials and can be calculated as follows [Zhang]:

$$P_{er} = \frac{V\Delta}{At\,(P_1 - P_0)} \tag{28.1}$$

where

P_{er}: Permeability for a given fluid (air, gas, water, oil, & etc.) via a given membrane;

V: Volume of gas going through the membrane;

Δ: Thickness of membrane;

A: Area of membrane;

t: Time;

P_1: High fluid pressure on one side of the membrane;

P_0: Low fluid pressure on the other side.

Performance and labeling requirements for hydraulic, air, and vacuum brake hoses, brake hose assemblies, and brake hose fittings for all motor vehicles are established in the standard-FMVSS 106. Brake hoses demand low deformations in operation. Permeability test-outs can be carried out according to ASTM D1434-82 and ASTM E-961D-814. Hose permeability and leakage are influenced by the following factors:

  (a) Gas type: The smaller the size of the gas molecule, the faster the diffusivity.
  (b) Hose material: Amount of free volume and a high degree of chain mobility.
  (c) Temperature: Amount of free volume and degree of chain mobility changes according to its working temperature.
  (d) Pressure: Amount of gas that diffuses through membrane increases with an increasing pressure, though the permeability (normalized against the pressure by definition) remains unchanged.

(e) Thickness: Amount of gas that diffuses through membrane decreases with an increasing thickness, though the permeability (normalized against the thickness by definition) remains unchanged.

(f) Area: Amount of gas that diffuses through membrane increases with an increasing contact area, though the permeability (normalized against the contact area by definition) remains unchanged.

28.3   Brake Hoses

Vacuum brake and air brake tubes have to resist high pressures at high temperatures, while not being degraded by oils and greases. They also need to meet other strict industry regulations.

28.4   Air Conditioning Hoses

An air conditioning hose, typically composed of layers of rubber materials and reinforced braids, is used to supply a high-pressure refrigerant fluid between the engine and the air conditioner.

28.5   Radiator Hoses, Heater Hoses, and Surge/Degass Assemblies

Radiator hoses, heater hoses, and surge/degass assemblies are generally made of EPDM or silicone rubbers, although plasticized PA12/PA6 plastics are used sometimes for "not-so-high" temperature applications. Two possible degradations may happen to EPDM radiator hoses: (a) thermo-oxidative aging and electrochemical degradation. As a result of the thermo-oxidative aging tests, the hardness of the EPDM rubber increases while its elongation at break decreases much. A slight increase in crosslink density indicates that changes in the properties are caused by the concentration of carbonyl groups in the skin layer. For the electrochemical degradation (ECD), the weight of EPDM rubber increases whereas its elongation and hardness decreases drastically because water solution penetrates into the skin part.

28.6   Fuel Hoses

The inner tube of a fuel hose is made of fluorine rubber such as FKM compound that is gas/oil resistant, while the very outer cover is made of CPE (Chlorinated Polyethylene), CSM, CO, ECO, or AEM compound that is temperature friendly. Layers of materials settling down between them are Teflon film-sealing, tie layer-adhesion, and the layer reinforced by Kevlar fibers-pressure supportive, as shown in Fig. 28.1.

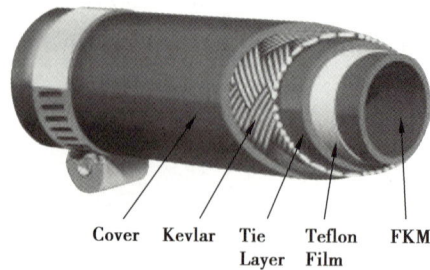

Cover Kevlar Tie Teflon FKM
Layer Film

Fig. 28.1 Automotive Fuel Hose with FKM in Direct Contact with Fuel

28.7 Power Steering Hoses

Inner tubes of power steering hoses are generally made of CSM compounds, while their covers are either CPE (Chlorinated Polyethylene) or CSM compounds.

28.8 Turbocharger Hoses

Turbocharged diesel engines expose hoses to a temperature above 165 ℃ and up to 220 ℃ and pressures of 0.25 MPa (≈ 2.5 Bars). ACM (Acrylic Ethylene Rubber) and FKM (Fluoroelastomers) offer the ideal temperature profiles and chemical resistant properties for turbocharger hoses.

References

BASSER H, 2007. Global Optimization of Length and Macro-Micro Transition of Fabric-Reinforced Elastomers with Application to Brake Hose[J]. Computational Material Science, 39:113-116.

BENNER S, COSTELLO F, SWANSON T, 1990. Fatigue Testing of Corrugated and Teflon Hoses[J]. SAE 901436.

BREIG W, 1993. Thermal-Mechanical Stresses Induced in the Fabrication and Curing of Multilayered Fabric and Wire Reinforced Elastomeric Hose[J]. SAE 931961.

DEMCHAK M D, CORTESE M E, 2005. Calculation of True Six-Sigma Hose Crimp Compression Ranges Using Probabilistic Design Techniques[J]. SAE 2005-01-1608.

KAWAHARA H, et al, 2008. FEM Analysis for Sealing Performance of Hydraulic Pressure Brake Hose Caulking Portion[J]. Key Engineering Materials, 385-387:169-172.

KAWASAKI M, et al, 1997. Low Gasoline Permeable Fuel Filler Hose[J]. SAE 971080.

KEIL M, et al, 2002. Modeling and Validation of Large Hydraulic Hose Deflections[J]. SAE 2002-01-2589.

KELLER R, 1990. Performance Studies of Ethylene-Propylene Rubber Automotive Coolant Hoses[J]. SAE 900576.

KONDO T, et al, 2000. Development of Thermoplastic Elastomeric Vacuum Hose for Engine Control[J]. SAE 2000-05-0150.

KWAK E, CHOI M, 2010. Degradation Mechanisms and Mechanical Property Variation of EPDM Rubbers for Automotive Radiator Hoses[J]. International Journal of Modern Physics B, 24(15-16):2597-2602.

LEE M, et al, 2000. Nonlinear CAE Mesh-free Simulation of a Truck-Based Radiator Hose/Fitting/Clamp Assembly Process[J]. SAE 2000-01-0295.

LIEVENS S, et al, 2000. Influence of Engine Coolant Composition on the Compatibility of EPDM Hose Materials[J]. SAE 2000-01-1975.

MU X, et al, 2005. Experimental Evaluation of R134a Emission with Various Hose Constructions[J]. SAE 2005-01-2032.

OGINO H, et al, 1991. Dynamic Characteristics Analysis of Brake Pipings[J]. SAE 910022.

PETT R A, 1995. Predicting the Life of Automotive Power Steering Hose Materials[J]. Rubber World, 211(6):27-28,30-31,58.

ROBB W L, 1968. Thin Silicone Membranes-Their Permeation Properties and Some Applications[J]. Annuals of the New York Academy of Science, Vol. 146:119-137.

ROBINSON K, 2005. Push-on Forces of Automotive Coolant Hoses[J]. SAE 2005-01-1053.

ROBINSON K, 1996. Coolant Hose Clamp Fitting Joint Design Guide[J]. SAE 960269.

SIVAKUMAR A, GOPAL R, 2011. Halogen Free Synthetic Elastomer Blend to Meet Properties of Fuel Hose Outer Cover (Return Line) Application[J]. SAE 2011-01-2233.

SMITH R, 1981. The Effect of Silicone Brake Fluid on Rayon Reinforced, Neoprene Tube and Cover Brake Hoses[J]. SAE 810802.

VAN AMERONGEN G J, 1946. The Permeability of Different Rubbers to Gases and Its Relation to Diffusivity and Solubility[J]. Journal of Applied Physics, 17(11):972-985.

WINTERS R, PRZYBYLA R, 1979. Silicone Rubber Oil Hose Development[J]. SAE 790662.

YU J, POPESCU S, 2001. Measurements of Transmission and Attenuation Characteristics of Fluid-borne Noise in Fluid Hoses with/without Tuning Cables[J]. SAE 2001-01-1610.

YU J, et al, 1999. Experimental Evaluation for Fluid-borne Noise Attenuation in Tuning Cables and Hoses of Automotive Power Steering Hydraulic Systems[J]. SAE 1999-01-1777.

ZWICKERT M, 1979. Improved Sour Gasoline Resistance of Epichlorohydrin (CO) Elastomer Fuel Hose[J]. SAE 790660.

Table 28.1　Mechanical Properties of Elastomers/Plastics for Automotive Hoses

Material-DAM	$T/°C$	ρ	(σ,ε)	α	k	γ	Set	$\tan\delta$	P_{er}
PVMQ	−100	—	—	—	—	—	—	—	130
	23	—	—	—	—	—	—	—	138
	50	—	—	—	—	—	—	—	206

Notes: P_{er}(L/m²/24 h/atm): Permeability in Helium at 4 ounces/yard²;

T_g(°C): Glass transition point.

Chapter 29

Seals

29.1   Introduction

Seals are simple high-precision products providing seal via compression. The application determines the rubber compound such that the primary deciding factor is the fluid to be sealed. NBR (Nitrile) is the most widely used elastomer in the seal industry today due to its excellent resistance to petroleum products and its ability to be compounded for service over a wide temperature range of -54 to $135\ ℃$. Typical sealants for automobiles are demonstrated in Fig.29.1 and seal materials required for various media are listed as follows:

Fluid	Retainer	Seal	$T/℃$
Acetone	Phenolic	EPDM	$0\sim27$
Air	G-10	Nitrile	$-54\sim107$
CO_2	G-10	Nitrile	$0\sim66$
Ethanol	G-10	EPDM	$0\sim38$
Fuel Oil	G-10	FKM	$-29\sim138$
Gas, Natural	Phenolic	Nitrile	$-40\sim104$
Gas, Sour	Phenolic	FKM	$-29\sim104$
Hydrogen	G-10	Nitrile	$-40\sim121$
Jet Fuel	G-10	FKM	$-29\sim107$
Nitrogen	Phenolic	Nitrile	$-40\sim104$
Oil, Crude	G-10	FKM	$-29\sim138$
Propane	G-10	Nitrile or Teflon	$0\sim27$
Propylene	G-10	FKM	$0\sim27$
Sewage	G-10	FKM	$-29\sim138$
Toluene	G-10	FKM or Teflon	$0\sim66$
Water (Hot)	G-10	EPDM	$79\sim138$
Water (Potable)	G-10	EPDM	$0\sim138$
Water (Sea)	G-10	EPDM	$0\sim138$

The softer the elastomer, the better the seal material conforms to the contact surfaces to be sealed. It takes a low pressure for soft elastomers to fulfill a sealing task. Nevertheless, a harder seal material offers greater resistance to external disturbances such as high fluid pressure and flow. The higher the compression, the higher the fluid pressure to be contained. Material properties of seals are given in Tables 29.1 and 29.2.

(a) O-Rings   (b) Molded Rubber   (c) Gaskets

Fig. 29.1   Automotive Sealants

29.2　Aging, Relaxation, and Creep of Seals

However, a seal will experience a permanent deformation in the squeeze direction and it is called a compression set (ASTM D 395) which also increases with the amount of compression. A low compression set means good remaining seal capacity. The compression set of a seal has to be smaller than its squeeze in its working environment and time frame. The compression set of seal material generally increases with increasing temperature and time. The retained sealing force after having been exposed to an elevated temperature is reduced resulting from a compression set due to the higher thermal expansion of the sealant than its housing. The seal rubber loses its elasticity gradually, behaves stiffer, and eventually becomes hard and brittle. Increasing carbon black loading improves the tensile strength of polysulfide sealants promptly, but compression performance increases slowly. The simultaneous use of carbon black and silicon dioxide filler in polysulfide sealants hardly changes the tensile strength of sealants, whereas the ultimate elongation and compression performance of sealants are enhanced remarkably [Lu et al.].

Elastomers rely on pressure exerted by a housing for their sealing properties. The compressive pressure decays over so much time that it may result in a phenomenon-accelerated aggressive fluids, especially at elevated temperatures. Chemical reactions present another challenge in analysis as the sealant is attacked by fluids in contact. After the sealing force decreases, at some point the seal leaks and fails. The process is commonly known as aging.

Stress relaxation and creep can significantly affect seal shape, deformation, and performance. Stress relaxation reduces the force or stress exerted by the seal on adjacent surfaces and it significantly influences compressive stress relaxation (CSR) and aging. CSR measures a material's stress relaxation in compression at a specified temperature over a period of time.

Aging is a general term describing changes in sealing stress or force, in part caused by stress relaxation. Creep and relaxation of seal materials are presented in Table 29.3.

29.3　Sealing Modeling by FEA

If a gap exists between the part and the gasket, the mesh of the gasket is connected directly to the part, this value will simulate the gap (Fig. 29.2). The gasket will compress the amount entered in this field without creating any pressure as set up in most FEA codes (e.g. Abaqus) , and then will start to follow the pressure-closure curve. The reason for using this input is to create a simpler model, i.e. surface to surface contact could be used between the part and gasket without a rigid-body motion.

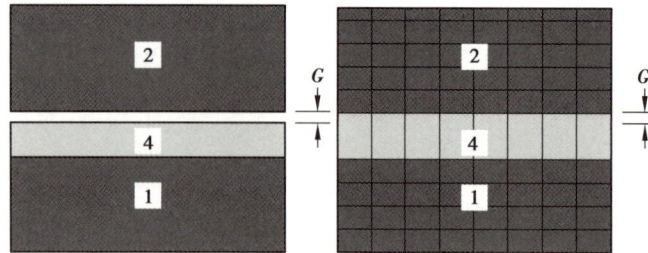

Fig. 29.2　Modeling of a Gasket Gap between the Part and Gasket in FEA

To simplify FEA to study creep and stress relaxation in seals, most case studies are focused on linear viscoelasticity. The material follows the principle of superposition where the relaxation (or creep) rate is proportional to the instantaneous stress (or strain), as discussed in Chapter 8.

29.4　Sealing Surface

A rough surface encourages seal slippage, adhesive wear, and foreign-object wear, and increases seal-generated heat. Traditional roughness measures including R_a (average roughness), R_{max} (maximum peak-to-valley roughness), and R_z (average peak-to-valley) are insufficient to relate the surface roughness to seal quality. Two different approaches to assessing how the surface roughness is related to seal quality: (a) Statistical method and (b) Deterministic method.

A bearing-area curve, also called Abbott-Firestone curve, describes an object's surface texture using statistical methods as surface profiles resemble white noise. In 1933, E.J. Abbott and F.A. Firestone introduced statistical methods to surface topography. According to [Stachowiak and Batchelor] they proposed a bearing-area curve to represent the surface profile, which can distinguish between different surfaces with the same value of R_a or other height characteristics. It is constructed by plotting the measured surface height over a length, then passing an infinitesimally thin plane (parallel to the base) through the surface, starting at the highest peak and ending at the lowest valley. The length of intersections with the material along the plane is measured, summed, and plotted as a proportion of total length; and the procedure is repeated through a number of slices. In other words, it plots the bearing area at different heights above the object's base. The resulting height will be a probability density function, which can be used for assessing damage evaluation according to its physical height and functional physics or chemistry in seals. Integrating the height distribution (assuming it is Gaussian) results in a classical cumulative statistical distribution function of the surface profile in terms of height. The curve starts from the highest projection, with 0% of the material, and ends at the lowest depression, where it includes 100% of the material as shown in Fig. 29.3.

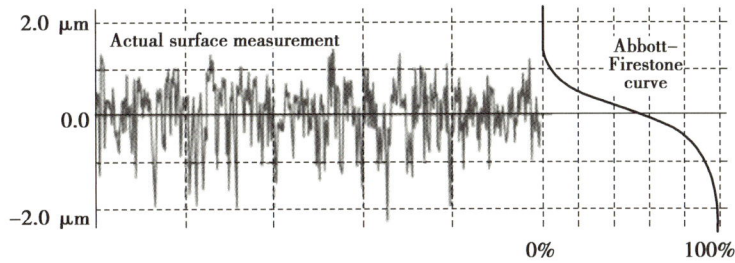

Fig. 29.3   A Bearing-Area Curve as a Statistical Distribution Function

Another approach is to assess the surface roughness deterministically. The deviation of a 2-dimensional surface profile from its mean value along x-axis is described by the following W-M model [Weierstrass & Mandelbrot]:

$$Z(x) = G^{D-1} \sum_{n=n_1}^{\infty} \frac{\cos(2\pi \gamma^n x)}{\gamma^{(2-D)n}} \qquad (29.1)$$

where

G: Characteristic length of the surface;

D: Fractal dimension, and $1 < D < 2$;

γ: Discrete frequency spectrum of the surface, and $\gamma > 1$ usually;

n_1: Low frequency cut-off determined by a low boundary of a non-scale range.

Compatibility between the seal and lubricant and amount of interference have to be checked out. Two types of carbonization at the interface between the seal and the rotating shaft can be assumed:

(a) Carbonized oil sticking to the seal surface-progressive damage;

(b) Oil penetrating the rubber bulk and carbonizing the inside of the rubber member-catastrophic failure mode. This is dangerous.

Shafts with worn sealing surfaces often need to be stripped, reground, and polished. Polishing with diamond-coated abrasive cloth may sometimes help restore roughened surfaces to the recommended finish.

29.5   O-rings

O-ring rubbers are simple high-precision products, providing sealing via compression, as shown in Fig. 29.1. Commonly used elastomers for O-ring seals are ACM (Polyacrylate), NBR (Nitrile), SCR (Styrene Butadiene Rubber), silicone (VQM and PVQM), FVQM (fluorosilicone), FKM (fluoroelastomer, also called FPM), and FFKM (perfluoroelastomer). Each of them represents a family of rubbers. Recommended application conditions are given as follows (Table 29.1):

Fluid	O-ring Material
Mineral (e.g. Engine & Transmission Oil) :	NBR 70A, NBR 90A
Gasoline :	NBR 70A
Bio Fuel :	SBR 70A
Coolant :	EPDM 70A
Brake Fluid :	SBR 70A
High-Temperature Applications :	ACM, VQM/FVQM, FKM, FFKM

A 25% squeeze of seal is suggested as the starting point for seal design iterations. Compression set of an O-ring is defined as the percentage of deflection in the loading direction that the elastomer fails to recover after a fixed period of time and under a specific squeeze. Compression set in percentage is calculated as follows:

$$\text{Set} = \frac{h_o - h_s}{h_o - h_1} \tag{29.2}$$

where

h_o : Original height;

h_s : Height after test and 30 min relaxation;

h_1 : Height after installation, i.e. squeeze employed.

For rubber O-rings the minimum squeeze is about 0.2 mm at the room temperature such that the effect from uneven contact conditions, size contraction at a cold temperature, compression set, and heat aging can be minimized. A good compression set resistant compound can be distinguished from a poor one with a simple paired 0.2 mm squeeze test. Frequently used standards for quantifying comparative compression set are ASTM D 395 and DIN 53517. Automotive fluids to be sealed by O-rings include

(a) Engine Fuels;

(b) Engine Lubricants (Oils) ;

(c) Engine Coolants;

(d) Transmission Fluids;

(e) Power Steering Fluids;

(f) Air Conditioning Refrigerants and Lubricants;

(g) Compressor Lubricants.

29.6 Automotive Weather Strips

Automotive weather strips include primary door seals, secondary door seals, air intake cowl seals, air intake lights seals, liftgate seals, ditch molding, outer waist belts, and sunroof seals. Primary automotive weather-stripping materials are EPDM/PP, PVC, TPE and TPO. Sunroof weather-stripping is made of silicone rubber due to the extreme heat that parts on automobile roofs commonly encounter.

Press-in-place seals are static face seals with rectangular cross sections and self-retaining features integrated into the OD and/or ID of the seal. This can be accomplished using proper interferences. These press-in-place seals offer a wider contact surface as well as greater seal retention in the groove [Parker Hannifin Corp.].

29.7   Bellow Boot for Constant Velocity Joints

A bellows-like boot is attached to a constant velocity universal joint used for power transmission in automobiles and various industrial machines in order to prevent intrusion of foreign objects such as dust and water into the joint and leakage of grease sealed in the joint. Key requirements include

(a) High-temperature performance up to at least 150 ℃;
(b) Low-temperature flexibility down to at least −40 ℃;
(c) Cracking and puncturing resistance;
(d) Mechanical stability to resist high-speed deformation;
(e) Resistance to internal pressure changes.

Frequently used polymeric and elastomeric materials of boots for constant velocity joints (CVJ) are listed as follows:

(a) VMQ (Silicone Rubber): Broad service temperature;
(b) FVMQ (Silicone Rubber): Broad service temperature and good grease compatibility;
(c) CR (Chloroprene): Good grease compatibility and lower cost;
(d) ACM (Acrylic Ethylene Rubber);
(e) CPE (Chlorinated Polyethylene);
(f) HNBR: Good resistance to heat and grease.

Most CVJ boots today are thermoplastic. The options include ethylene acrylic elastomers (AEM), thermoplastic elastomers (TPE), thermoplastic vulcanizates (TPV), thermoplastic urethanes (TPU) and some specialties [Jones et al.].

29.8   Boots for Shifters

Similar to the boot for a constant velocity universal joint, the boot for a shifter is to prevent intrusion of foreign objects such as dust and water into the joint and leakage of grease sealed in the joint, while the automotive console gear shift would provide a uniform moment when shifting.

29.9   Air Duct Kiss Seals

It provides two functional sealing requirements, i.e. no fluid leakage or wind noise, while avoiding a high closure force. Air ducts operate in hot and stressful environments that involve pressure, engine oil and blow-by-gases. These conditions can induce rapid heat aging in all but the highest performing plastic materials. Depending on product requirements, specific grades of thermoplastic elastomer with copolyester (e.g. DuPont Hytrel) and Nylon (e.g. DuPont Zytel) for air ducts deliver optimum results in terms of performance and processability.

29.10   Turbocharger Hose Seals

For hose seals, FKM is able to withstand temperatures from −40 ℃ to 230 ℃ in aggressive oils and highly concentrated acid environments for a vehicle's lifetime.

29.11   Crankshaft Seals

Sealing of rotating shafts such as engine crankshafts and turbocharger high-speed shafts is a challenge in the automotive industry. Seals have two functional requirements: (a) outer seal to protect the shaft from dust, dirt and contaminants and (b) inner seal to restrain the lubricant from leakage.

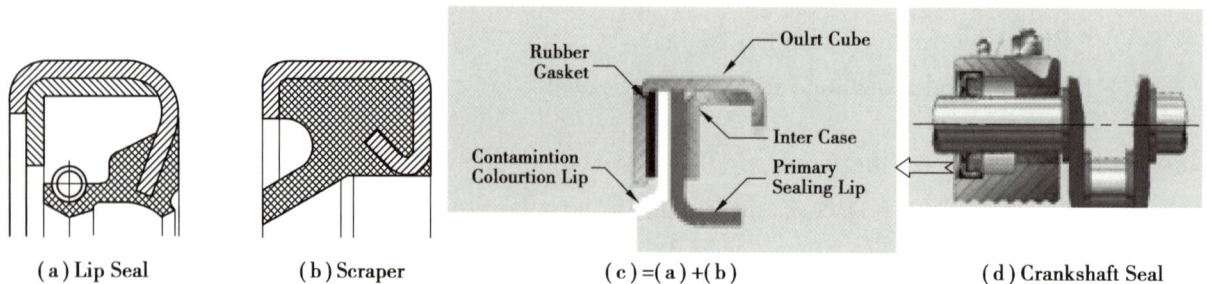

(a) Lip Seal   (b) Scraper   (c)=(a)+(b)   (d) Crankshaft Seal

Fig. 29.4   Seals for Oscillating Bearings (e.g. Crankshafts)

Crankshaft end seals are used for restricting lubricant leaks to the atmosphere and limiting the foreign debris to getting into internal combustion engine, as shown in Fig. 29.4(c). The sealing mechanism at a rotating shaft end may consist of the following functional seals:

(a) Stationery seal ring gasket;

(b) Rotating seal ring gasket;

(c) Labyrinth seal;

(d) Auxiliary O-rings-static seals.

The structural construction of a labyrinth seal for engine crankshaft is shown in Fig. 29.4. It consists of two sealing lips, one gasket, and their supporting steel cases:

(a) Primary sealing lip (TPFE+Fillers) with coined multi-grooves "pumping" back the engine oil. As the coined grooves are unidirectional, it can be used only if the shaft always rotates in one direction. The friction of an elastomer is characterized by contact normal force, temperature, and sliding velocity (rotation speed).

(b) The contamination-deterring lip (TPFE+Fillers) prevents the potential extruding foreign objects from getting in.

(c) A gasket sits between the contamination-deterring lip and the outer steel case, which prevents leakage between the inside of the case and the PTFE lips.

(d) Inner and outer steel cases provide the structural rigidity to constrain the sealing components mentioned above.

The inherent slickness of the PTFE compensates for poor lubrication and eliminates stick-slip, which in turn helps keep underlip temperature lower than rubbers. Furthermore, PTFE is also very resistant to chemical attack, making degradation of the lip by oil additives unlikely.

Besides unwanted leakage, one potential failure mode is the cutting of sealing lips into the crankshaft journals. Sealing lips of a labyrinth seal make a direct contact with the shaft, resulting in liquid film seal and/or wear. A coating of DLC (diamond-like carbon) on the steel shaft may slow the rubber's cutting into it.

29.12   Polymer Electrolyte Membrane Fuel Cell (PEMFC) Seals

Both mechanical and chemical degradations of gasket materials in the PEMFC (Polymer Electrolyte Membrane Fuel Cell) environment are of concern. Leachants from gasket materials dissolved in the liquid solution may be detrimental to the electrochemical reactions in fuel cells. Potential seal materials include silicone rubber, EPDM, and FKM. The stress relaxation behavior in the solution (fuel cell) at different temperatures has to be studied, as the liquid silicone rubber depicted in Fig. 29.5.

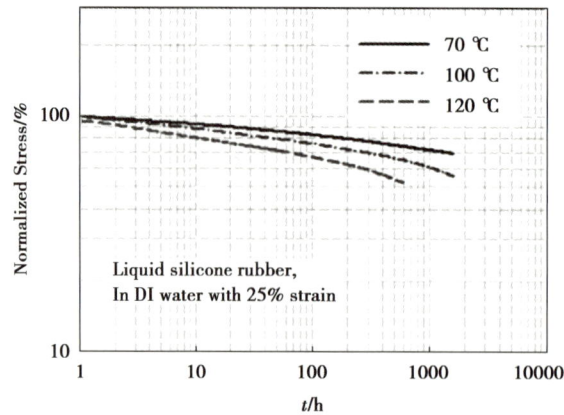

Fig. 29.5 Stress Relaxation of Liquid Silicone Rubber in the Polymer Electrolyte Membrane Fuel Cell Environment

References

AL -GHATHIAN F, et al, 2005. Friction Forces in O-ring Seals[J]. American Journal of Applied Science, 2 (3):626-632.

CUI T, et al, 2011. Service life Estimation of Liquid Silicone Rubber Seals in Polymer Electrolyte Membrane Fuel Cell Environment[J]. Journal of Power Sources, 196:1216-1221.

DRAGONI E, STROZZI A, 1988. Analysis of an Unpressurized Laterally Restrained, Elastomeric Rings[J]. Journal of Tribology, 110(2):193-199.

FERN A, MASON-JONES A, PHAM D, et al, 1998. Finite Element Analysis of a Valve Stem Seal[J]. SAE 980580.

GEORGE A F, STROZZI A, RICH J I, 1987. Stress Fields in Compressed Unconstrained Elastomer O-ring Seals and Comparison with Computer Predictions with Experimental Results[J]. Tribology International, 20: 237-247.

FENG X, GU B, 2007. Fractal Characterization of Sealing Surface Topography and Leakage Model of Metallic Gaskets[J]. Key Engineering Materials, 353-358(pt4):2977-2980.

FREITAS T, 2009. Rubber Sealing Study Applied to Ball Bearing Components Using Finite Element Method [J]. SAE 2009-36-0034.

GREEN I, ENGLISH C, 1944. Stresses and Deformation of Compressed Elastomeric O-Ring Seals[J]. 14th International Conference on Fluid Sealing, Bedford, UK:(83-95).

HARTLEY C, et al, 2011. Simulating the Static and Dynamic Response of an Automotive Weatherstrip Component[J]. SAE 2011-01-1602.

HERTZ D, 1993.Elastomers in Automotive Fuels, Oils & Fluids at High Temperatures[J]. SAE 930993.

JONES B A, KING K B, 2014. Development of New Silicone Rubber with High Flex-Fatigue Resistance[J]. Rubber World, 250(1):29-32,43.

LU Y, et al, 2011. Effect of Filler on the Compression Set, Compression Stress-Strain Behavior, and Mechanical Properties of Polysulfide Sealants[J]. Journal of Applied Polymer Science, 120(4):2001-2007.

MOON H, et al, 2011. Predicted Minimum Door-Closing Velocity Based on a 3-Dimensional Door-Closing Simulation[J]. Finite Element in Analysis and Design, 47(3):296-306.

NURAINI A, et al, 2009. Performance of Dual Lips Elastomeric Seal for Spigot-Socket Push Fit Joint Using Finite Element Method[J]. European Journal of Scientific Research, 32(1):66-76.

SALITA M. 1988.Simple Finite Element Analysis of O-rings Deformation and Activation during Squeeze and Pressurization[J]. Journal of Propulsion and Power, 4:497-511.

SONG X, et al, 2009. Analysis and Optimization of Nitrile Butadiene Rubber Sealing Mechanism of Ball Valve [J]. Transactions of Nonferrous Metals Society of China, 19(1):s220-s224.

STACHOWIAK B, 2005. Engineering Tribology[M]. 3rd Edition, Elsevier Science Publishers, NY.

STEVENS R D, 2001. Permeation and Stress Relaxation Resistance of Elastomeric Seals[J]. SAE 2001-01-1127.

STROZZI A, 1986. Experimental Stress-Strain Field in Elastomeric Seals[J]. Experimental Stress Analysis: 613-622.

UEDA R H, et al, 2010. Analysis of Automotive Liftgate Seals Using Finite Element Analysis[J]. Polímeros, 20(4):301-308.

WANG G, 2011. Nonlinear Finite Element Analysis and Optimization for the Rubber Boot of Shift Lever[J]. SAE 2011-01-0030.

WHITE C C, HUNSTON D L, 2008. Characterizing the Nonlinear Viscoelastic Properties of Sealant, Including Its Mullins Effect[J]. Polymer Engineering and Science, 48(12):2317-2328.

Table 29.1 Thermomechanical Compression Sets of Automotive O-Ring Seals

Material-DAM	T/℃	Wire Diameter/mm	Compression/%	Duration/h	Set
EPDM (70A)	100	3.53	25	22	$\Delta_{22}<30\%$
EPDM/PC (70A)	100	3.53	25	22	$\Delta_{22}<25\%$
FFKM (75A)	100	3.53	25	22	$\Delta_{22}<11\%$
FKM (70A)	100	3.53	25	22	$\Delta_{22}<19\%$

continued

Material-DAM	$T/℃$	Wire Diameter/mm	Compression/%	Duration/h	Set
FKM (90A)	100	3.53	25	22	$\Delta_{22} < 18\%$
NBR (70A)	100	1.78	25	22	$\Delta_{22} = 15\%$
	100	1.78	25	70	$\Delta_{70} = 24\%$
	100	3.53	25	22	$\Delta_{22} = 13\%$
	100	3.53	25	70	$\Delta_{70} = 23\%$
	100	6.99	25	22	$\Delta_{22} = 9\%$
	100	6.99	25	70	$\Delta_{70} = 17\%$
NBR (90A)	100	3.53	25	22	$\Delta_{22} < 30\%$
Neoprene (70A)	100	3.53	25	22	$\Delta_{22} < 25\%$
VQM (70A)	100	3.53	25	22	$\Delta_{22} < 40\%$

Table 29.2   Mechanical Properties of Automotive Rubber Seals

Material-DAM	$T/℃$	ρ	(σ, ε)	α	k	γ	Set	$\tan \delta$	P_{er}
Air Duct Seal	23	—	$(-1.45, -40\%)$ $(-1.19, -35\%)$ $(-1, -30\%)$ $(-0.84, -25\%)$ $(-0.73, -20\%)$ $(-0.61, -15\%)$ $(-0.46, -10\%)$ $(-0.25, -5\%)$ $(0, 0\%)$ $(0.91, 5\%)$ $(1.59, 10\%)$ $(2.05, 15\%)$ $(2.5, 20\%)$ $(4.1, 25\%)$ $(6.37, 30\%)$ $(8.7, 40\%)$	—	—	—	—	—	—

Table 29.3   Elastomeric Material Constants for Automotive Rubber Seals

Material-DAM	$T/℃$	ρ	C_{10}	C_{01}	C_{20}	C_{30}	α	k	γ	$\tan \delta$	$(\sigma_{uts}, \varepsilon_{uts})$
Boot Seal	23	—	0.752	0	0	0	—	—	—	—	—
Gasket, Rubber	23	—	0.35	0.25	0	0	—	—	—	—	—

Notes: C_{10}, C_{01}, C_{20}, C_{30}(MPa) = $W = C_{10}(I_1-3) + C_{01}(I_2-3) + C_{20}(I_1-3)^2 + C_{30}(I_1-3)^3$

$C_{01} = C_{20} = C_{30} = 0$, and $C_{10} \neq 0$: Neo-Hookean's model;

$C_{20} = C_{30} = 0$, $C_{10} \neq 0$, and $C_{02} \neq 0$: Mooney's model;

$C_{01} = 0$, $C_{10} \neq 0$, $C_{20} \neq 0$, and $C_{30} \neq 0$: Yeoh's model;

E (MPa) = $E = 6 (C_{10} + C_{01})$, equivalent Young's modulus.

Table 29.4   Normalized Prony Parameters for Creep/Relaxation of Seal Materials

Material-DAM	$T/℃$	E_0 or E_∞/MPa	N	$[p_i/\text{MPa}, T_i/\text{h}]$, $i = 1, 2, \cdots, N$
Silicone (Liquid)	70	$E_0 = 0.7709$	3	[0.1688, 18.58] [0.1332, 254.1] [0.1769, 2500]
Nitrile	—	—	—	—
FKM	—	—	—	—
PA6,6	—	—	—	—
PEEK	—	—	—	—
TPFE	—	—	—	—
TPFE/Bronze	—	—	—	—

Chapter 30

Vibration Isolators and Dampers

30.1　Introduction

Elastomeric materials are widely used in noise and vibration isolation mechanisms at different industries such as automotive, aerospace, building and so on. Rubbers, generally soft while showing large inherent damping, are a perfect choice of materials for use in vibration isolators. A representative rubber vibration isolator consists of one or more pieces of vulcanized rubber bonded to metal parts, facilitating load distribution and installation. The large difference in material bulk and Young's moduli (or shear modulus), i.e.

$$B = \frac{E}{3(1 - 2\nu)} = \frac{G}{1 - 2\nu} \tag{30.1}$$

enables people to design a variety of damping components by adjusting their geometry. For the application of elastomer actuators, the prestrain condition, ranging approximately from 50% to 100%, is a substantial factor in actuator design and application. Material properties of rubbers are given in Tables 30.1 and 30.2.

The purpose of damping in an isolator is to reduce or dissipate energy as rapidly as possible. Damping is also beneficial in reducing vibration amplitudes at resonance. The structural stiffness above and below a vibration isolation mount has an important effect on isolator performance. Unusually excessive engine vibrations may be caused by one of the following mishappenings:

(a) Faulty or poorly-adjusted fueling;
(b) Faulty timing belt or chain;
(c) Loose or disconnected hoses, especially vacuum hose;
(d) Broken engine mount;
(e) Worn-out plug (gas engines).

30.2　Engine Mounts

It is normal for an IC (Internal combustion) engine to produce a characteristic vibration spectrum signature. Vibration analysis of an IC engine mounted in a vehicle then must focus on "variations" from the "normal" vibration signature. An engine mount must meet two functional requirements: (a) supporting the static weight of the engine and (b) isolating the vibration caused by imbalances in the engine from the vehicle frame.

Each piston fires every other crankshaft revolution in a four stroke engine, and thus the fundamental spectral line will be at 1/2 the engine RPM (at crankshaft), namely 1/2 order vibration. The spectral lines of an firing engine will be at integer multiples of the firing rate of each piston and they are $0.5P$, $1P$, $1.5P$, $2P$, $2.5P$, $3P$, ..., and so on.

30.2.1   1/2-Order Vibration

If all of the pistons produce nearly identical combustion pulses, the 1/2 order vibrating speed will be very small, usually varying from 2.5 mm/s to 7.5 mm/s at 2500 RPM. When a cylinder produces less power than the others, the 1/2 order vibration will increase from 7.5 mm/s up to over 25 mm/s for a misfire.

1/2 order vibration are especially troublesome as they can be felt in the cabin by the aircraft pilot. Low frequency vibrations are not well isolated by most engine mounts, and the vibration will shake the entire aircraft. If not taken care of, a 1/2 order vibration can loosen rivets, hinges, and pivots all over the airframe, as well as causing premature pilot fatigue. This is a serious safety issue.

30.2.2   1P Vibration

$1P$ vibrations are usually dominated by propeller imbalance or unequal piston mass. Nevertheless, an out-of-balance propelling system will produce nearly equal vibrations in vertical and horizontal directions. In horizontally opposed engines, this will produce a $1P$ vibration in the horizontal plane, but little vibration in the vertical plane. If the rear of the engine has a high $1P$ vibration that is not corrected by balancing the propelling system, piston mass imbalance is the most likely cause. Pistons and cylinders are often replaced 1 jug at a time, and once in a great while the wrong weight piston is used due to error.

30.2.3   Interaction between Engine and Suspension

Two analytic models have been in use for different levels of understanding of an engine mount, which is supposed to isolate the load transfer between the engine and suspension:

(a) 6-DOF system module: able to explore the idle and the engine shake vibrations, including fore/aft, lateral, bounce, roll, pitch, and yaw motions.
(b) 16-DOF system module: able to detect vehicle mode analysis and bounce in suspension in addition to fore/aft, lateral, bounce, roll, pitch and yaw motions in engine.

30.2.4   Laminated Rubber-Steel shims

Laminated high-damping rubber reinforced with steel shims has evolved to be an automotive damper, as well as a vital seismic isolation device. The alternating steel shims constrain the rubber layers from moving laterally as a transversely isotropic material, while having high laminate stiffness in the out-of-plane direction without changing the in-plane shearing behavior.

30.2.5 Hydraulic Engine Mounts

Hydraulic damping has been successfully utilized in an engine mount, Fig. 30.1. Simultaneously, it controls motion of the engine due to vibrations transmitted from the frame of the vehicle. It fulfills the function requirements under harsh conditions, which prevail under the hood of the vehicle for a long period of time. These conditions include working at both high and low temperatures and exposure to automotive fluids.

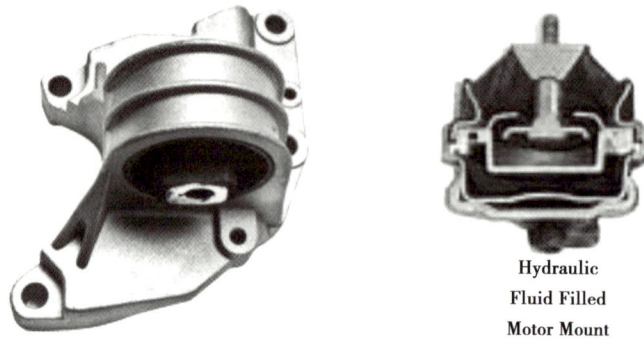

Hydraulic Fluid Filled Motor Mount

Fig. 30.1   Example Hydraulic Engine Mounts

Vibration isolation using hydraulically amplified magnetostrictive actuators for active powertrain mounts is a plus. The performance of the hydraulic engine mount due to variations in the excitation frequency and amplitude is of interest to the designer.

30.3 Battery Mounts for Electric Cars

High-voltage Li-based batteries for 5-seated electric sedans can weigh as much as 400 kg. The functional requirement of a battery mount is to control motion of the batteries due to vibrations transmitted from the frame of the vehicle. Laminated rubber-steel shims are recommended. High energy absorption of IIR leads to its advantage in automotive engine and body mounts, and other vibration isolators.

30.4 Electric Motor Mount

Data shown in the Fig. 30.2, for example, have to be given for calculation of the electric motor mount need.

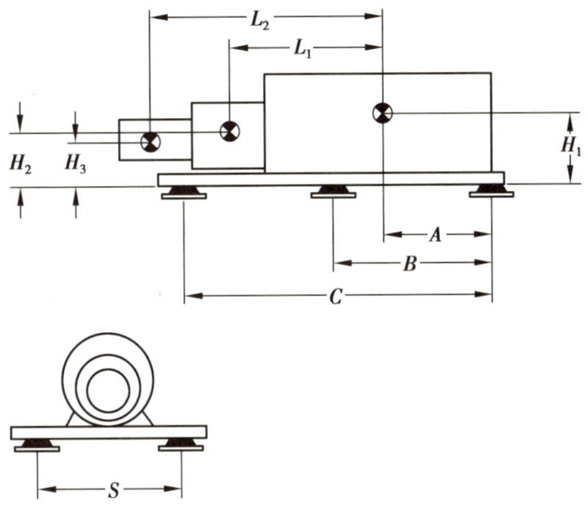

Fig. 30.2   Key Dimensional Parameters for Electric Motor Mount

30.5   Bushings

Bushings are used as soft joints between metallic parts, such as suspension bushings (Fig. 30.3), sway bar (antiroll bar) bushings, spring bushings, shock bushings, and steering bushings.

Fig. 30.3   Suspension Bushing Connecting Trailing Arm to Body Cross Member

30.6   Jounce Bumper

Jounce bumper is a member of vehicle vibration isolation system located above the coil spring (shock absorber or strut) that connects the wheel to the vehicle frame. A jounce bumper is press-fitted onto a solid mandrel, which is in it. Microcellular rubber foam is used due to its high compressibility and low Poisson's ratio.

30.7   Air Spring/Damper

Air springs are made of tough molded rubber composites such as polyurethane composites. Air springs may improve handling and braking, provides adjustable air pressure for custom tuning and offers load support to reduce body roll and prevent the suspension from bottoming out.

References

ALBERT A, HOWLE A, 2007. Design Issues in the Use of Elastomers in Automotive Tuned Mass Dampers[J]. SAE 2007-01-2198.

BEDNAREK S, 1999. The Giant Magnetostriction in Ferromagnetic Composites within an Elastomer Matrix[J]. Applied Physics, A:63-67.

BELLAN C, BOSSIS G, 2002. Field Dependence of Viscoelastic Properties of MR Elastomers[J]. International Journal of Modern Physics, B, 16(17-18):2447-2453.

BOSSIS G, ABBO C, CUTILLAS S, et al, 2001. Electroactive and Electrostructured Elastomers [J]. International Journal of Modern Physics, B, 15(6-7):564-573.

CARLSON J D, JOLLY M R, 2000. MR Fluid, Foam and Elastomer Devices[J]. Mechatronics, 10:555-569.

CHEN L, GONG X L, LI W H, 2008. Effect of Carbon Black on the Mechanical Performances of Magnetorheological Elastomers[J]. Polymer Testing, 27(3):340-345.

CHEN Z, 2011. Finite Element Analysis of Light Vehicle Cab's Hydraulic Mount Based on Fluid-Structure Interaction Method[J]. SAE 2011-01-1604.

CHIU H, et al, 2005. Dynamic Properties of Rubber Vibration Isolators and Anti-vibration Performance of Nanoclay-Modified PU/PEL Blends System[J]. Polymer Engineering and Science, 45(4):539-548.

DAVIS L C, 1999. Model of Magnetorheological Elastomers[J]. Journal of Applied Physics, 85(6):3348-3351.

DEMCHUK S A, KUZMIN V A, 2002. Viscoelastic Properties of Magnetorheological Elastomers in the Regime of Dynamic Deformation[J]. Journal of Engineering Physics Thermodynamics, 75(2):396-400.

DENG H X, GONG X L, 2007. Adaptive Tuned Vibration Absorber Based on Magnetorheological Elastomer [J]. Journal of Intelligent Material Systems and Structures, 18(12):1205-1210.

DHOBLE A, SHARMA R, 2001. Finite Element Analysis of Engine Mount for Multi Utility Passenger Vehicle [J]. SAE 2001-26-0046.

DICKENS J D, 2000. Dynamic Model of Vibration Isolator under Static Load[J]. Journal of Sound and Vibration, 236(2):323-337.

DORFMANN A, OGDEN R W, 2003. Magnetoelastic Modeling of Elastomers [J]. European Journal of Mechanics, A/Solids, 22:497-507.

FARSHAD M, BENINE A, 2004. Magnetoactive Elastomer Composites[J]. Polymer Testing, 23:347-353.

FUJINO M, et al, 2003. Flutter Characteristics of an Over-the-Wing Engine Mount Business-Jet Configuration [J]. AIAA 2003-1942.

GINDER J M, et al, 2002. Magnetostrictive Phenomena in Magnetorheological Elastomers [J]. International Journal of Modern Physics, B, 16(17-18):2412-2418.

GONG X L, CHEN L, LI J F, 2007. Study of Utilizable Magnetorheological Elastomers [J]. International Journal of Modern Physics, B, 21(28-29): 4875-4882.

GRIFFIN S, et al, 2002. Virtual Skyhook Vibration Isolation System[J]. Journal of Vibration and Acoustics, 124:63-67.

HORVATH A T, KLINGENBERG D J, SHKELM Y M, 2002. Determination of Rheological and Magnetic Properties for Magnetorheological Composites via Shear Magnetization Measurements [J]. International Journal of Modern Physics, B, 16(17-18):2690-2696.

IBRAHIM R A, 2008. Recent Advances in Nonlinear Passive Vibration Isolators[J]. Journal of Sound and Vibration, 314:371-451.

JOLLY M R, CARLSON J D, MUNOZ B C, et al, 1996. The Magnetoviscoelastic Response of Elastomers Composites Consisting of Ferrous Particles Embedded in a Polymer Matrix[J]. Journal of Intelligent Material Systems and Structures, 7:613-622.

KIM W, et al, 2004. Fatigue Life Estimation of an Engine Rubber Mount[J]. International Journal of Fatigue, 26:553-560.

KOVACIC I, BRENNAN M J, WATERS T P, 2008. A Study of a Nonlinear Vibration Isolator with a Quasi-Zero Stiffness Characteristics[J]. Journal of Sound and Vibration, 315:700-711.

LEE B S, RIVIN E I, 1996. Finite Element Analysis of Load-Deflection and Creep Characteristics of Compressed Rubber Components for Vibration Control Devices[J]. Journal of Mechanical Design, 118(3): 328-336.

LEE H W, et al, 2003. Finite Element Analysis of Diaphragm-type Air Springs with Fiber-Reinforced Rubber Composites[J]. Journal of Composite Materials, 37(14):1261-1274.

LEE J S, KIM J S, 2007. Optimal Design of Engine Mount Rubber Considering Stiffness and Fatigue Design [J]. Journal of Automobile Engineering, 22(7):823-835.

LERNER A A, CUNEFARE K A, 2008. Performance of MRE-based Vibration Absorbers[J]. Journal of Intelligent Material Systems and Structures, 19(5):551-563.

LI Q, et al, 2009. The Modeling and Road Simulation Test of a Hydraulic Engine Mount[J]. International Journal of Modeling, Identification and Control, 8(1):73-79.

LI Q, et al, 2009. Fatigue Life Prediction of a Rubber Mount Based on Test of Material Properties and Finite Element Analysis[J]. Engineering Failure Analysis, 16:2304-2310.

LI W, ZHANG X, 2008. Research and Application of MR Elastomers[J]. Recent Patents on Mechanical Engineering, 1:161-166.

LIN C, LEE Y, 1998. Effects of Viscoelasticity on Rubber Vibration Isolator Design[J]. Journal of Applied Physics, 83(12):8027-8035.

LOKANDER M, STENBERG B, 2003. Improving the Magnetorheological Effect in Isotropic Magnetorheological Rubber Materials[J]. Polymer Testing, 22:677-680.

NGUYEN Q, CHOI S, 2009. Optimal Design of a Vehicle Magnetorheological Damper Considering the Damping Force and Dynamic Range[J]. Smart Materials and Structures, 18(1):015013.

NORWOOD C, DICKENS J, 1998. The Effect of Vibration Isolator Properties and Structural Stiffness on Isolator Performance[J]. Journal of Vibration and Control, 4(3):253-275.

SAMAD M, et al, 2011. Durability of Automotive Jounce Bumper[J]. Materials and Design, 32(2):1001-1005.

SHEN Y, et al, 2004. Experimental Research and Modeling of Magnetorheological Elastomers[J]. Journal of Intelligent Material Systems and Structures, 15:27-35.

SHIGA T, OKADA A, KURAUCHI T, 1995. Magnetroviscoelastic Behavior of Composite Gels[J]. Journal of Applied Polymer Science, 58:787-792.

SJÖBERG M, KARI L, 2002. Nonlinear Behavior of a Rubber Isolator System Using Fractional Derivatives[J]. Vehicle System Dynamics, 37(3):217-236.

SU H, HUA Y, 2009. CAE Virtual Design Validation Tests of Automotive Engine Mount Systems[J]. SAE 2009-01-0404.

TARAGO M J, et al, 2009. Viscoelastic Models for Rubber Mounts: Influence on the Dynamic Behavior of an Elastomeric Isolated System[J]. International Journal of Vehicle Design, 49(4-5):303-317.

VERICK A M, 2003. Vibration Protection of Critical Components of Electronic Equipment in Harsh Environmental Conditions[J]. Journal of Sound and Vibration, 259(1):161-175.

WANG L R, et al, 2009. ALE Based Finite Element Method for Characteristic Simulation of Hydraulically Damped Rubber Mount[J]. SAE 2009-01-0358.

WILSON M J, FUCHS A, GORDANNEJAD F, 2002. Development and Characterization of Magnetorheological Polymer Gels[J]. Journal of Applied Polymer Science, 84:2733-2742.

WOO C, et al, 2012. Damage and Analysis of Rubber Components[J]. Advanced Structural Materials, 16(2): 289-306.

WOO C, et al, 2008. Fatigue Life Evaluation of Automotive Engine Mount Insulator[J]. Key Engineering Materials, Vol. 385/387:647-652.

WU J, et al, 2010. Anti-Vibration and Vibration Isolator Performance of Poly (Styrene-Butadiene-Styrene)/ Ester-Type Polyurethane Thermoplastic Elastomers[J]. Polymers for Advanced Technologies, 21(3):164-169.

YALCINTAS M, DAI H, 2004. Vibration Suppression Capabilities of Magnetorheological Materials Based Adaptive Structures[J]. Smart Materials and Structures, 13:1-11.

YILDIZ A et al, 2004. Optimal Design of Vehicle Components Using Topology Design and Optimization[J]. International Journal of Vehicle Design, 34(4):387-398.

YIN H M, et al, 2002. Micromechanics-based Hyperelastic Constitutive Modeling of Magnetostrictive Particle-Filled Elastomers[J]. Mechanics of Materials, 34:505-516.

YORK D, et al, 2007. A New MR (Magnetorheological) Fluid-Elastomer Vibration Isolator[J]. Journal of Intelligent Material Systems and Structures, 18(12):1221-1225.

YOSHIDA J, et al, 2003. Three-Dimensional Finite-Element Analysis of High Damping Rubber Bearings[J]. Journal of Engineering Mechanics, 130(5):607-620.

ZAVALA P G, et al, 2000. Experimental and Computational Simulation Approaches for Engine Mounting Development and Certification[J]. SAE 2000-01-3239.

ZHOU G Y, 2004. Complex Shear Modulus of a Magnetorheological Elastomer [J]. Smart Materials and Structures, 13:1203-1210.

Table 30.1   Elastomeric Material Constants of Rubber Components in Vibration Isolators and Dampers

Material-DAM	$T/\text{℃}$	ρ	C_{10}	C_{01}	C_{20}	C_{30}	α	k	γ	$\tan\delta$	$(\sigma_{\text{uts}}, \varepsilon_{\text{uts}})$
NB	23 100	—	0.298	0	−0.045	0.015	—	—	—	—	—
NB (65A; 50 pphr silica)	23 100	—	0.51	0	−0.064	0.012	—	—	—	—	—
NB (Engine Mount)	23	—	0.551	0	−0.32	0.02	—	—	—	—	—
Bushing	23	—	27.56	6.89	0	0	—	—	—	—	—

continued

Material-DAM	$T/℃$	ρ	C_{10}	C_{01}	C_{20}	C_{30}	α	k	γ	$\tan\delta$	$(\sigma_{uts},\varepsilon_{uts})$
Air Spring	23	—	3.2	0.8	0	0	—	—	—	—	—

Notes: C_{10}, C_{01}, C_{20}, C_{30}(MPa)$= W = C_{10}(I_1-3) + C_{01}(I_2-3) + C_{20}(I_1-3)^2 + C_{30}(I_1-3)^3$;

$C_{01} = C_{20} = C_{30} = 0$, and $C_{10} \neq 0$: Neo-hookean's model;

$C_{20} = C_{30} = 0$, $C_{10} \neq 0$, and $C_{02} \neq 0$: Mooney's model;

$C_{01} = 0$, $C_{10} \neq 0$, $C_{20} \neq 0$, and $C_{30} \neq 0$: Yeoh's model;

E (MPa)$= E = 6(C_{10}+ C_{01})$, equivalent Young's modulus.

Table 30.2　Ogden Model Coefficients of Flexible Hyperfoams as Dampers

Material-DAM	$T/℃$	σ	(G_1,α_1,v_1)	...	(G_N,α_N,v_N)	α	k	γ	$\tan\delta$
Backrest Foam, Seating ($N=2$)	$-50(T_g)$	—	—	—	—	—	—	—	—
	23	0.38	(22.94, -3.14, 0)		(32.1, 0.064, 0)	—	—	—	—
	93(High service temperature)								
Bumper, Jounce ($N=1$)	23	—	(3, 11.5, 0.1)		—	—	—	—	

Notes: $N=$ Number of coefficients to be used in the Ogden Model.

Thermoplastics

Chapter 31

ABS (Acrylonitrile-Butadiene-Styrenes)

31.1   Introduction

ABS (**A**crylonitrile-**B**utadiene-**S**tyrenes) is a family of "terpolymers", in that they involve the combination of three different monomers to form a single material that draws from the properties of all three thermoplastic copolymer, integrating the stiffness and strength of acrylonitrile and styrenes into the toughness of poly-butadiene rubber. These three monomers are typically added together in specific proportions: 15% ~ 35% **A**crylonitrile, 5% ~ 30% **B**utadiene and 40% ~ 60% **S**tyrene. Its chemical formula is $(C_8H_8 \cdot C_4H_6 \cdot C_3H_3N)_n$. A small change in one of the monomers may create drastic changes in the mechanical and physical properties of ABS.

ABS (Acrylonitrile-Butadiene-Styrenes) possesses outstanding impact strength, high mechanical strength, good toughness and rigidity, low creep, good dimensional stability, good electric insulating property, low weight, and a good resistance to acids and alkalis. It is recommended for applications at a working temperature between -25 ℃ and 80 ℃, as ABS is flammable. ABS plastic may be damaged by sunlight. One way to protect ABS against thermal degradation is the addition of carbon black (CB) that acts as a stabilizer.

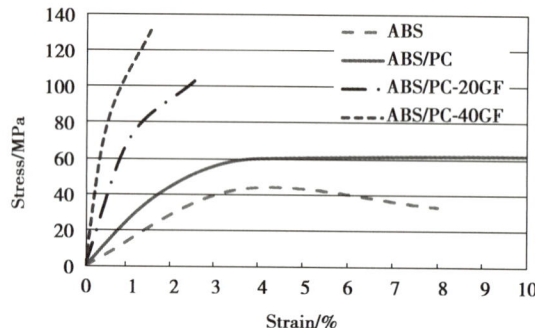

Fig. 31.1   Stress-Strain Curves of Generic ABS and ABS/PC Blend

ABS/PC (Acrylonitrile-Butadiene-Styrenes/Polycarbonate) blends and related composites are a specialty polymer group. Improvement of the tensile strength and toughness from ABS to ABS/PC is demonstrated in Fig. 31.1. Mechanical properties of general-purpose ABS and ABS/PC blends are given Table 31.1. Mode-Ⅰ fracture and Mode-Ⅱ fracture toughness of ABS are $K_{IC} = 4.32$ MPa/$m^{\frac{1}{2}}$ and $K_{IIC} = 1.42$ MPa/$m^{\frac{1}{2}}$, respectively, under the plain strain condition.

Fibers (usually glass fibers) and additives can be mixed in ABS resin pellets to make the final product strong and raise the operating range to as high as 80 ℃.

31.2   Applications

ABS (Acrylonitrile-Butadiene-Styrenes) shares 11.6% of automotive thermoplastics, including mobile phones, instrument panels, seat armrests, interior panel trims, seat belt retainers, glove compartment doors, liftgates, wheel covers, grilles (such as radiator and horn), headlight bezels, mirror housing, emblems, some decorative trims, and safety helmet (for auto workers).

One of the most common materials utilized by material extrusion 3D printing is ABS. The mechanical properties of extruded ABS can be enhanced by an addition of reinforcing materials.

References

AHN, et al, 2002. Mechanical Implementation Services for Rapid Prototyping[J]. Journal of Engineering Manufacture, 216(8):1193-1199.

ARSAD A, et al, 2010. Mechanical and Rheological Properties of PA6/ABS Blends -With and Without Short Glass Fiber[J]. Journal of Reinforced Plastics and Composites, 29(18):2808-2820.

CHIFOR V, et al, 2010. Mechanical, Thermal and Electrical Properties of Acrilonitril Butadiene Styrene (ABS) Composites Filled with Bronze Powder[J]. Material Science Forum, 672:179-182.

DREVAL V E, 2006. Rheological and Mechanical Properties of ABS Plastics Prepared by Bulk Polymerization [J]. Vysokomolekularnye Soedinenia, 48(3):524-533.

GURALP O, et al, 2005. Short Glass Fiber Reinforced ABS and ABS/PA6 Composites: Processing and Characterization[J]. Polymer Composites, 2005, 26(6):745-755.

ISITMAN N A, et al, 2010. Interfacial Strength in Short Glass Fiber Reinforced Acrylonitrile-Butadiene-Styrene/Polyamide 6 Blends." Polymer Composites, 31(3):392-398.

KEIJI O, et al, 2004. Mechanical Properties of ABS Resin Reinforced with Recycled CFRP (Carbon Fibers-Reinforced Epoxy)[J]. Advanced Composite Materials, 16(2):181-194.

KOONS G F, WILT M H, 1985. Design and Analysis of an ABS Pipe Compound Experiments, "Design, Analysis, and Interpretation of Results, ASQE, Milwaukee:111-117.

KRACHE R, DEBBAH I, 2011. Some Mechanical and Thermal Properties of PC/ABS Blends[J]. Materials Sciences and Applications, 2:404-410.

LEE J W, et al, 2010. Mechanical Properties and Sound Insulation Effect of ABS/Carbon-black Composites [J]. Journal of Composite Materials, 44(14):1701-1716.

LI H M, et al, 2008. Fracture Toughness of PC and PC/ABS Alloys[J]. Advanced Material Research, Vol. 33-37:567-572.

LI J, ZHANG Y, 2010. The Tensile Properties of Short Carbon Fiber Reinforced ABS and ABS/PA6 Composites[J]. Journal of Reinforced Plastics and Campsites [J]. Journal of Reinforced Plastics and Composites, 29(11):1727-1733.

MAS J, et al, 2002. Dynamic Mechanical Properties of Polycarbonate and Acrylonitrile-Butadiene-Styrene Copolymer Blends[J]. J. of Applied Polymer Science, 83(7):1507-1516.

MATCHIMAPIRO T, SORNTHUMMALEE P, POTHISIRI T, et al, 2008. Impact Behaviors and Thermomechanical Properties of TPP-Filled Polycarbonate/Acrylonitrile-Butadiene-Styrene Blends [J]. Journal of Metals, Materials and Minerals, 18(2):187-190.

NAGASAKA A, et al, 2006. Effect of Carbon Nano Fiber on Mechanical Properties of ABS Resin[J]. Tanso, 223:191-193.

OZKOC G, et al, 2005. Short-Fiber Reinforced ABS and ABS/PA6 Composites: Processing and Characterization[J]. Polymer Composites, 26(6):745-755.

RAMARAJ B, 2007. Mechanical, Thermal and Morphological Properties of Environmentally Degradable ABS and Poly(Vinyl Alcohol) Blends[J]. Journal of Applied Polymer Science, 106(2):1048-1052.

RODRIGUEZ J F, et al, 2001. Mechanical Behavior of Acrylonitrile Butadiene Styrene (ABS) Fused Deposition Materials. Experimental Investigation[J]. Rapid Prototyping Journal, 7(3):148-158.

SHENAVAR A, et al, 2009. Flow and Mechanical Properties of Carbon Black Filled ABS (Acrylonitrile-Butadiene-Styrene)[J]. Thermoplastic Composite Materials, 22(6):753-766.

SUAREZ H, BARLOW J, PAUL D, 1984. Mechanical Properties of ABS/Polycarbonate Blends[J]. Journal of Polymer Science, 29(11):3253-3259.

TAN Z Y, et al, 2006. Influence of Rubber Content in ABS in Wide Range on the Mechanical Properties and Morphology of PC/ABS Blends with Different Composition[J]. Polymer Engineering and Science, Oct. 1, 2006.

TANG C Y, et al, 2009. Mechanical and Thermal Properties of ABS-CaCO$_3$ Composites [J]. Journal of Reinforced Plastics and Composites, 21(15):1337-1345.

WANG W Y, et al, 2007. Study on the Micro Structure and Mechanical Properties of Nano-CaCO3/ABS Composites[J]. Solid State Phenomena, 121/123:1459-1462.

XU X, XU X, 2011. Mechanical Properties and Deformation Behaviors of Acrylonitrile-Butadiene-Styrene (ABS) under Izod Impact test and Uniaxial Tension at Various Strain Rates[J]. Polymer Engineering and Science, 51(5):902-907.

YILMAZER U, 1982. Tensile, Flexural and Impact Properties of a Thermoplastic Matrix Reinforced with Glass Fibers and Glass Bead Hybrids[J]. Composites Science and Technology, 44(2):119-125.

Table 31.1 Mechanical Properties of ABS（Acrylonitrile-Butadiene-Styrenes）and Related Composites, Depending on Grades

Material-DAM	$T/℃$	E_T	ρ	v	(σ, ε)	α	k	γ	β	K_{IC}
ABS	−25（Low service temperature）									
	−18	2.8	—	—	(−64, −3.4%) (36, 15%)	—	—	—	—	—
	23	2.3	1.07	0.35	(−63, −20%); (43, 3.5%) (39, 25%)	79/87	0.17	2050	—	2
	60（High service temperature）									
	107（T_g）	—				—	0.18	—	—	—
	240（T_m）	—								
ABS/10GF	23	3.7	1.14	0.35	(60, 3.1%) (60, 4%)	44	—	—	—	—
ABS/20GF	23	5.2	1.2	0.35	(74, 3%) (74, 3.1%)	37	—	—	—	—
ABS/30GF	23	7	1.3	0.35	(85, 2.6%) (85, 3%)	28	0.21	—	—	4.32
ABS/40GF	23	7	1.35	0.35	(88, 2.3%) (87, 3%)	—	—	—	—	—
ABS-PC	23	2.7	1.18	0.35	(60, 4%) (45, 70%)	76/80	—	—	—	—
ABS-PC/5GF	23	3.5	1.18	0.36	(72, 5%)	61/80	—	—	—	—
ABS-PC/10GF	23	4.8	1.22	0.36	(79, 4%)	57/80	0.2	—	—	—
ABS-PC/20GF	23	6.9	1.29	0.36	(70, 1%) (103, 2.5%)	41/80	0.16	1560	—	—
	240（T_m）	—	1.07							
ABS-PC/30GF	23	9.6	1.38	0.36	(114, 2%)	32/75	—	—	—	—
ABS-PC/40GF	23	10.3	1.48	0.36	(80, 0.5%) (131, 1.5%)	—	—	—	—	—
ABS/5TiO$_2$ (∥)	23	—	—	—	$\sigma_{uts} = 32.2$	—	—	—	—	—

continued

Material-DAM	$T/\mathrm{°C}$	E_T	ρ	υ	(σ,ε)	α	k	γ	β	K_IC
ABS/5TiO$_2$ ($\perp$)	23	—	—	—	$\sigma_\mathrm{uts}=18.4$	—	—	—	—	—

Notes: DAM = Dry as Molded;

GF (CF) = Reinforced with glass (carbon) fibers, by weight unless V_f is given;

$T_\mathrm{g}(\mathrm{°C})$ & $T_\mathrm{m}(\mathrm{°C})$ = Glass transition point and melting point, respectively;

TiO$_2$ = Reinforcement, by weight;

// & $\perp$ = Parallel and perpendicular to the extrusion direction, respectively.

Chapter 32

EVA (Ethylene Vinyl Acetate)

32.1　Introduction

EVA (**E**thylene **V**inyl **A**cetate) is the copolymer of ethylene and vinyl acetate. The weight percent of ethylene may vary from 60% to 90%. It is a thermoplastic, but soft and flexible like an elastomer. Mechanical properties of EVA are listed in Table 32.1. It has good clarity and gloss, low-temperature toughness, stress-crack resistance, hot-melt adhesive water proof properties, and resistance to UV radiation. EVA has a distinctive "vinegar" odor.

EVA foam exhibits good mechanical strength, excellent chemical resistance, high buoyancy, low water absorption, and good acoustic properties. EVA is one of the materials popularly known as expanded rubber or foam rubber.

32.2　Applications

EVA is competitive with rubber and vinyl products in many electrical applications. It is a polymer widely used as an encapsulant between the glass cover of a photovoltaic (PV) modules (i.e. solar modules) and the glass cover of the solar cells within the module.

EVA foam with closed cells is used in a variety of industrial and commercial gasket and sealing applications. It is also used for bicycle saddles and other similar shock-absorbing applications.

References

BANDYOPADHYAY G G, et al, 1999. Dynamic Properties of NR/EVA Polymer Blends : Model Calculations and Blend Morphology[J]. Journal of Applied Polymer Science, 72(2):165-174.

MÉSZÁROS, et al, 2012. Mechanical Properties of Recycled LDPE/EVA/Ground tire Rubber Blends: Effects of EVA Content and Post-irradiation[J]. Journal of Applied Polymer Science, 125(1):512-519.

VARGHESE H, et al, 1995. Morphology, Mechanical and Viscoelastic Behavior of Blends of Nitrile Rubber and Ethylene-Vinyl Acetate Copolymer[J]. European Polymer Journal, 31(10):957-967.

WU W, et al, 2013. Morphology and Mechanical Properties of Ethylene-Vinyl Acetate Rubber/Polyamide Thermoplastic Elastomers[J]. Journal of Applied Polymer Science, 130(1):338-344.

Table 32.1   Mechanical Properties of EVA (Ethylene Vinyl Acetate) and Related Composites

Material-DAM	$T/°C$	E_T	ρ	υ	(σ, ε)	α	k	γ	β	K_{IC}
EVA (Film Grade)	23	0.064	0.93	—	(7, 8%) (15, 500%)	180	0.34	1400	—	—
	90(T_m)	—								
EVA (Wire & Cable Grade)	23	—	1.2	—	(11, 860%)	180	0.34	1400	—	—
EVA (Coating Grade)	23	0.05	0.94	—	(6, 200%) (10, 770%)	180	0.34	1400	—	—
EVA (Sealant Grade)	23	0.07	0.94	—	(7.4, 670%)	180	0.34	1400	—	—
70EVA-30tPa (Shore A = 75; TPE)	23	—	—	—	(75, 360%)	—	—	—	—	—

Notes：DAM = Dry as Molded；

　　　　tPa = Ternary polyamide，30% by weight；

　　　　TPE = Thermoplastic Elastomer.

Chapter 33

FEP (Fluorinated Ethylene Propylene)

33.1 Introduction

FEP (**F**luorinated **E**thylene **P**ropylene) is a type of fluoropolymer. FEP resin is melt-processable using conventional injection molding and screw extrusion. FEP has high transparency, with good transmittance of ultra violet and visible wavelengths. It has long term weatherability and excellent resistance to ozone, sunlight and weather. FEP offers the lowest refractive index of all thermoplastics with low light reflection in the same order of water. Thermomechanical and fatigue properties of FEP (Fluorinated Ethylene Propylene) are given in Tables 33.1 and 33.2, respectively.

33.2 Applications

FEP (Fluorinated Ethylene Propylene), along with PFA, is routinely used for plastic labware and tubing that involves critical or highly corrosive processes due to its flexibility, extreme resistance to chemical attack and optical transparency. Thus, wire and cable insulation for computers and electronics systems in a harsh environment, as well as insulating bushings, is a major application.

Reference

PTFE, FEP, PFA Specifications, Boedeker Corp., 2007.

Table 33.1 Mechanical Properties o FEP (Fluorinated Ethylene Propylene)

Material-DAM	$T/{}^{\circ}\text{C}$	E_{T}	ρ	v	(σ, ε)	α	k	γ	β	K_{IC}
FEP (DuPont FEP100)	−251	—	—	—	$\sigma_y = 165$	—	—	—	—	—
	−196	—	—	—	$\sigma_y = 131$	—	—	—	—	—
	−73	—	—	—	$\sigma_y = 62$	—	—	—	—	—
	−40	—	—	—	(35, 225%)	—	—	—	—	—
	0	—	—	—	$\sigma_y = 14$, (29, 300%)	—	—	—	—	—
	23	0.4	2.15	0.48	(13.5, 5%) (14, 100%) (17, 200%) (23, 325%)	100	0.22	1170	—	—

continued

Material-DAM	$T/°C$	E_T	ρ	v	(σ, ε)	α	k	γ	β	K_{IC}
FEP (DuPont FEP100)	$60(T_g)$	—	—	—	—	—	—	—	—	—
	100	—	—	0.36	(7, 50%) (10, 100%) (12, 200%) (14, 300%)	—	—	1300	—	—
	121	—	—	—	$\sigma_Y = 3.5$	—	—	—	—	—
	150	—	—	—	—	237	—	1400	—	—
	204(High service temperature)				(3, 50%) (4, 100%) (5, 200%) (6, 300%)	270	—	—	—	—
	$260(T_m)$	—	—	—	—	—	—	—	—	—

Notes：DAM = Dry as Molded.

Table 33.2   Fatigue ε-N Properties of FEP（Fluorinated Ethylene Propylene）

Material	$T/°C$	$d\varepsilon/dt$	σ'_{f-}	ε'_{f-}	b	c	K'	n'	$\sigma_f @ 2N_f$	R
FEP (DuPont FEP100)	23	—	—	—	—	—	—	—	$6.9@7×10^6$	—
									10@1300	—
									10.3@960	—

Chapter 34

LCP (Liquid Crystal Polymers)

34.1　Introduction

LCP（**L**iquid **C**rystal **P**olymers）is partial crystalline aromatic polyesters based on phydroxybenzoic acid and related monomers. It can be present in liquid form such as LCD（liquid crystal display）or in solid form such as lystropic LCP（also known as Kevlar）. LCP has high chemical resistance, dimensional stability, moldability, heat-aging resistance, dielectric strength, abrasion resistance, creep resistance, and flame retardance. The weldline strength of LCPs is lower than most other engineering plastics, so it is necessary to limit gate locations to only one or two places to avoid excessive numbers of weld lines.

The properties of having low viscosity, low moisture absorption and good adhesion make it a good adhesive material. Thermomechanical material properties of solid LCP reinforced with randomly oriented short fibers are given in Table 34.1. Their fatigue properties are given in Table 34.2. Representative stress-strain curves of LCP/GF30 and LCP/CF30 reinforced with randomly oriented short-fiber glass and carbon at different temperatures are presented in Fig.34.1 and Fig. 34.2, respectively.

Fig. 34.1　Stress-Strain Curves of LCP/GF30, Reinforced with Randomly Oriented Short-Fiber Glass at Different Temperatures

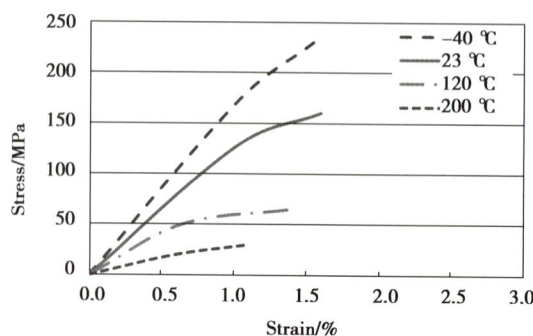

Fig. 34.2　Stress-Strain Curves of LCP/CF30, Reinforced with Randomly Oriented Short-Fiber Carbon at Different Temperatures

Mechanical properties of LCP are highly anisotropic-significantly stronger in the mold flow direction. LCP has a high coefficient of linear thermal expansion along the Z-axis than the inplane thermal expansion. It is weldable, but the strength of the heat affected zone is weaker than the original.

34.2   Applications

LCP (Liquid Crystal Polymers) has recently gained more attention in packaging of microelectromechanical systems (MEMS). A variety of integrated electronic circuits can be incorporated onto a thin flexible paper-like LCP plastic, which molds to a desired shape and performs well at high temperatures and in intense radiation. One application is flexible LCP antennas.

References

ADAMS P M, FARROW G, BEERS D, 1995. Advanced-fiber Applications: Properties and Applications of Fibers from Fully Aromatic Polyesters[J]. Tappi Journal, 78(11):169-173.

BASTIDA S, et al, 1995. Reprocessing of Liquid-Crystal Polymers: Effects on Structure and Mechanical Properties[J]. Journal of Applied Polymer Science, 56(11):1487-1494.

BLANAS A M, KONTOU E, SPATHIS G, 1999. A Mechanical Model for the Prediction of the Elastic Properties of Polymeric Resins Reinforced with Liquid Crystal Polymers[J]. Journal of Reinforced Plastics and Composites, 18(5):390-412.

BROADBENT H A, IVANOV S Z, FRIES D P, 2007. Fabrication of a LCP-based Conductivity Cell and Resistive Temperature Device via PCB MEMS technology[J]. Journal of Micromechanics and Microengineering, 17:722-729.

CHOY C L, LAU K W E, WONG Y W, 1996. Elastic Moduli of a Liquid Crystalline Polymer and its In-situ Composites[J]. Polymer Engineering and Science, 36(9):1256-1265.

DEJEAN G, et al, 2005. Liquid Crystal Polymer (LCP): A New Organic material for the Development of Multilayer Dual-Frequency/Dual-Polarization Flexible Antenna Arrays[J]. IEEE Transactions on Antenna and Wireless Propagation Letters, 4:22-26.

FAHEEM F, LEE Y C, 2009. Liquid Crystal Polymer for RF MEMS Packaging[J]. International Journal of Materials and Product Technology, 34(1-2):66-76.

HARRIS K D, et al, 2007. Physical Properties of Anisotropically Swelling Hydrogen-Bonded Liquid Crystal Polymer Actuators[J]. Journal of Microelectromechanical Systems, 16(2):480-488.

KULICHIKHIN V G. 1997. Rheological, Mechanical, and Adhesive Properties of Thermoplastic-LCP Blends

Filled by Glass Fibers[J]. Polymer Engineering and Science, 37(8):1314-1321.

LEE K, CHENG H, JOU W, et al, 2007. The influence of Carbon Fiber Orientation on the Mechanical and Tribological Behavior of Carbon Fiber/LCP Composites[J]. Materials Chemistry and Physics, 102(2):187-194.

LISINETSKAYA P, et al, 2009. Polarization Properties of Polymer-Dispersed Liquid-Crystal Film with Small Nematic Droplets[J]. Applied Optics, 48(17):3144-3253.

PEGORETTI A, ZANOLLI A, MIGLIARESI C, 2006. Preparation and Tensile Mechanical Properties of Unidirectional Liquid Crystalline Single-Polymer Composites[J]. Composites Science and Technology, 66:1970-1979.

THOMPSON D C, et al, 2004. Characterization of Liquid Crystal Polymer (LCP) Material and Transmission Lines on LCP Substrates from 30 to 100 GHz[J]. IEEE Transactions on Microwave Theory and Techniques, 52(4):1343-1352.

WANG X, ENGEL J, LIU C, 2003. Liquid Crystal Polymer (LCP) for MEMS: Processes and Applications [J]. Journal of Micromechanics and Microengineering, 13:628-633.

XIAO J, OTAIGBE J, 2000. Polymer Bonded Magnets. II. Effect of Liquid Crystal Polymer and Surface Modification on Magneto-Mechanical Properties[J]. Polymer Composites, 21(2):332-342.

ZHOU J, et al, 2004. Effect of Temperature on the Tribological and Dynamic Mechanical Properties of Liquid Crystal Polymers[J]. Polymer Testing, 24(3):270-274.

Table 34.1 Mechanical Properties of Representative LCP (Liquid Crystal Polymers) and Related Composites

Material-DAM	$T/℃$	E_T	ρ	υ	(σ,ε)	α	k	γ	β	K_{IC}
LCP (Average)	23	10	1.45	0.45	(100, 2.8%)	18/54	0.52	—	—	—
	145(T_g)									
	220(High service temperature)									
	282(T_m)									
LCP/30GF	−40	—	—	—	(167, 1%) (230, 1.5%)	—	—	—	—	—
	23	15	1.62	0.45	(125, 1%) (160, 1.6%)	14/36	0.32	800	—	—
	80	—	—	—	(77, 0.8%) (98, 1.4%)	—	—	—	—	—
	120(T_g)	—	—	—	(50, 0.65%) (65, 1.3%)	—	—	1100	—	—
	200	—	—	—	(20, 0.6%) (30, 1.1%)	—	0.45	1250	—	—

continued

Material-DAM	$T/°C$	E_T	ρ	υ	(σ,ε)	α	k	γ	β	K_{IC}
LCP/30CF	−40	—	—	—	(85, 0.2%) (180, 0.5%)	—	—	—	—	—
	23	23.5	1.5	0.45	(130, 0.4%) (200, 0.7%)	10/30	—	—	—	—
	80	—	—	—	(95, 0.4%) (160, 1.2%)	—	—	—	—	—
	120	—	—	—	(70, 0.4%) (99, 1.5%)	—	—	—	—	—
	200	—	—	—	(16, 0.4%) (22, 1 %)	—	—	—	—	—

Notes: DAM = Dry as Molded;

GF (CF) = Reinforced with glass (carbon) fibers, by weight unless V_f is given;

α (m/m/°C) = Coefficient of linear thermal expansion ∥ or ⊥ fiber direction;

T_g(°C) & T_m(°C) = Glass transition point and melting point, respectively.

Table 34.2   Fatigue ε-N Properties of LCP (Liquid Crystal Polymers) and Related Composites

Material	$T/°C$	$d\varepsilon/dt$	σ'_{f-}	ε'_{f-}	b	c	K'	n'	$\sigma_f@2N_f$	R
LCP/30GF	23	—		—	—	—	—	—	50	—
LCP/30CF	23	—		—	—	—	—	—	35	—

Chapter 35

PA (Polyamides-Nylon)

35.1　Introduction

Nylon, commercial name for typical PA (**Poly**amides), is a member of the polyamides family which consists of long-chain backbone with recurring amide groups. Polyamides are resistant to wear and abrasion, have good mechanical properties even at elevated temperatures, low permeability to gases, and good chemical resistance. Temperature and humidity have great influences on polyamides.

Chopped discontinuous glass and carbon fibers are two popular fillers used to reinforce PA (Polyamides). Evaluations and influences of fiberglass reinforcements on mechanical performance of injection-molded PA6 and PA6,6 were presented in [Thomason] and [Kagan], respectively. Mechanical properties of dry as molded (DAM) DuPont Zytel 101 (PA6,6), Zytel 70G (glass fiber-reinforced PA6,6), and Zytel 77G (glass fiber-reinforced PA6,12) are listed in Table 35.1. The mechanical properties reduce significantly in a humid environment as shown in Table 35.2. The fatigue and creep material properties are given in Tables 35.3 and 35.4, respectively.

PA6,6 produced by the reaction of adipic acid (a 6-carbon dibasic acid) and hexamethylene diamine (a 6-carbon aliphatic diamine) is the most popular polyamide product. Representative stress-strain curves of typical dry as molded PA6,6/33GF (33% glass fibers by weight) are given in Fig. 35.1. Their corresponding stress-strain curves at 50% relative humidity are presented in Fig. 35.2.

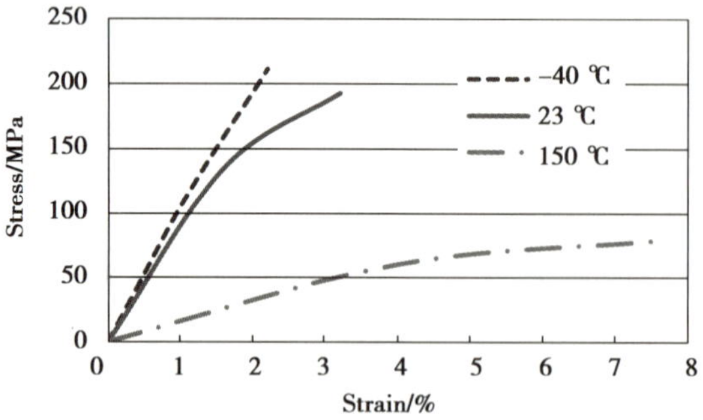

Fig. 35.1　Stress-Strain Curves of Dry-as-Molded PA6,6/33GF [DuPont] at Different Temperatures

35.2　Influence of Moisture on PA

Polyamides (PA) absorbs relatively more moisture than other thermoplastics. The moisture concentration (C_m) has a great influence on the mechanical properties of PA and PA-based composites like wind turbine blade made of PA6/glass fiber. Under a standard condition at 23 ℃, the moisture concentration (C_m) via water absorption varies with respect to the RH (Relative Humidity) in the working environment as follows [BASF]:

Type of PA	30% RH	50% RH	62% RH	100% RH
PA4,6	1.4%	3.8%	5.0%	15%
PA 6	1.1%	2.75%	3.85%	9.5%
PA 6,6	1.0%	2.5%	3.6%	8.5%

The swelling coefficient of linear moisture expansion of PA6, denoted by β, is 3.3×10^{-3} m/m/C_m at 23 ℃. According to the moisture concentration listed in the above table, the strain and stress induced by moisture in PA6 at 23 ℃ and 50% RH are, respectively,

$$\varepsilon_{hygro} = \frac{\Delta L}{L_{dry}} = \beta C_m = 3.3 \times 10^{-3} \times 2.75 \approx 0.0091$$

and $$\sigma_{11,hygro} = -\frac{E}{1-2\nu} \varepsilon_{hygro} = \frac{1150}{1 - 2 \times 0.37} \times 0.0091 = 40.3 \text{ MPa}$$

where

C_m: Moisture concentration;

ε_{hygro}: Strain due to moisture concentration;

$\sigma_{11,hygro}$: Stress due to moisture concentration.

The change of T_g resulting from moisture absorption is so significant that once the moisture increases from 0.15% (corresponding to a typical "dry-as-molded condition") to 1.36% (water absorption value after 24 h test) T_g decreases from 47 ℃ to 8 ℃.

35.3   PA6,6

PA6,6 (6,6 nylon) is the most used Polyamide. Representative stress-strain curves of typical dry as molded (DAM) PA6,6/33GF are depicted in Fig. 35.2. At −40 ℃, PA6,6 lost 10% of its tensile strength in a moderate to high RH environment, but other characteristics such as tensile strain and Young's modulus remained largely unchanged, especially within the elastic limit. At 80 ℃ and above, the tensile strength and Young's modulus decrease further, while the elongation or strain to failure increases. Fatigue and creep properties of polyamides are given in Tables 35.3 and 35.4, respectively.

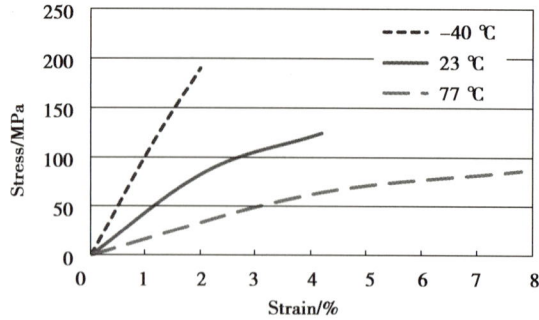

Fig. 35.2　Stress-Strain Curves of PA6,6/33GF〔DuPont〕at 50% Relative Humidity and Different Temperatures

35.4　PA6,12

PA6,12 has lower melting point, strength, and stiffness than PA6,6, but PA6,12 absorbs less water and thus has better dimensional stability and electric properties in a humid environment.

PA6,12 also has better chemical resistance than PA6,6. A stress-strain curve of PA6,12/33GF is plotted in Fig. 35.3.

Fig. 35.3　Stress-Strain Curves of Dry-as-Molded PA6,12/33GF〔DuPont〕at Different Temperatures

35.5　PA4,6

Another nylon that maintains good strength at elevated temperatures is PA4,6. However, it is limited by its high water absorption and thus not quite suitable for automotive applications.

35.6　PA Fibers

Polyamides (Nylons) are often formed into fibers and used for monofilaments and yarns. One famous family member of polyamide fibers is agamid. Kevlar is one of them and has been long used for structural applications. Kevlar-fiber-reinforced plastics can be as strong as steel when loaded in the fiber direction.

35.7   Applications

Polyamides share 7.9% of automotive plastics (Year 2001). Electric connectors, wire jackets, emission canisters, light-duty gears for windshield wipers, speedometers, engine fans, radiator headers, brake and power-steering fluid reservoirs, valve covers, door and liftgate handles, fender extensions, intake manifolds for engines, and linkage rods for suspension stabilizers (reinforced by glass fibers) are typical products. Relatively, polyamides can be discerned as follows:

(a) PA 6,6-General applications;
(b) PA 6-Copycat;
(c) PA 6,10-Less water absorption;
(d) PA 6,12-Flexibility and less water absorption;
(e) PA 2,2-Higher strength.

References

ABU-ISA I A, 2006. Mechanical, Thermal and Rheological Properties of Polymers Used in Plastic Fuel Tanks [J]. SAE 2006-01-0333.

BHATTACHARYYA D, MAITROT P, FAKIROV S, 2009. Polyamide 6 Single Polymer Composites[J]. Express Polymer Letters, 3:525-532.

CARLSON D, YAMAZAKI H, FUKUDA S, et al, 2003. Application of Nylon Composite Recycle Technology for Automotive Applications[J]. SAE 2003-01-0794.

CHANG L, ZHANG Z, SCHLORB A K, 2006. On the Sliding Wear of Nanoparticle Filled Polyamide 66 Composites[J]. Composites Science and Technology, 66:3188-3198.

CRUTIS P T, et al, 1978. The Stiffness and Strength of Polyamide Thermoplastic Reinforced with Glass and Carbon Fibers[J]. Journal of Material Science, 13:377-390.

GARRELL M G, SHIH A J, MA B M, et al, 2003. Mechanical Properties of Nylon Bonded Nd-Fe-B Permanent Magnets[J]. Journal of Magnetism and Magnetic Materials, 257(1):32-43.

GARRETT D, OWENS G, 1995. Polyphthalamide Resins for Use as Automotive Engine Coolant Components [J]. SAE 950192.

HE CHUNJIANG, et al, 2006. Effect of the Processing Molding Temperature on the Crystalline Structure and Properties of Acrylonitrile-Butadiene Rubber/Trinylon Thermoplastic Vulcanizates[J]. Journal of Applied Polymer Science, 102:1374-1379.

JIA N, KAGAN V. 1997. Effect of Time and Temperature on Tension-tension Fatigue Behavior of Short Fiber Reinforced Polyamides[J]. Polymer Composites, 19(4):408-414.

KAGAN V A, MCPHERSON R, CHUNG J S, 2001. An Advanced High Modulus (HMG) Short Glass-Fiber Reinforced Nylon 6: Part Ⅰ-Role and Kinetic of Fiberglass Reinforcements[J]. Journal of Reinforced Plastics & Composites, 22(11):1035-1044.

KAGAN V A, 2002. Understanding of a New Paradigm in High Modulus Nylon 6 Grades for a Load Bearing and Light Weight Applications[J]. Journal of Injection Molding Technology, 6(1):18-36, SPE.

KAGAN V A, MCPHERSON R, CHUNG J S, 2001. An Advanced High Modulus (HMG) Short Glass-Fiber Reinforced Nylon 6: Part Ⅱ-Mechanical Performance[J]. Journal of Reinforced Plastics & Composites, 22(12):1049-1058.

KUKUREKA S W, et al, 1999. The Effect of Fiber Reinforcement on the Friction and Wear of Polyamide 66 under Dry Rolling-Sliding Contact[J]. Tribology International, 66:107-116.

MACDONALD J, BATES P, LIANG H, 2001. Vibration Welding of Glass Filled Nylon 66 -Effect of Part Geometry[J]. SAE 2001-01-0440.

MATHEW B A, WIEBECK H, 1999. Automotive Air Intake Manifold Application using Nylon 6,6 Composite Material[J]. SAE 1999-01-3011.

MENCHACA C, et al, 2006. In Situ High-temperature Raman Study of Crystalline Nylon 6/12 Fibers Gamma-irradiated in Argon Atmosphere[J]. Journal of Physics and Chemistry of Solids, 67(9-10):2111-2118.

MOUHMID B, et al, 2006. A Study of the Mechanical Behavior of a Glass Fiber Reinforced Polyamide 6,6: Experimental Investigation[J]. Polymer Testing, 25:544-552.

NODA K, et al, 2001. Fatigue Failure Mechanisms of Short-fiber Glass-Reinforced Nylon 66 Based on Nonlinear Dynamic Viscoelastic Measurements[J]. Polymers, 42(13):5803-5811.

OKADA O, KESKKULA H, PAUL D R, 2004. Fracture Toughness of Nylon-6 Blends with Maleated Rubbers [J]. Journal of Polymer Science, Part B: Polymer Physics, 42(9):1739-1758.

POTENTE H, et al, 1993. The Vibration Welding of Polyamide 6,6[J]. Journal of Thermoplastic Composite Materials, 6:2-17.

RAJESH J, et al, 2001. Influence of Fillers on Abrasive Wear of Short Glass Fiber Reinforced Polyamide Composites[J]. Journal of Material Science, 36:351-356.

RETOLAZA A, et al, 2004. Structure and mechanical properties of polyamide-6, 6/poly (ethylene terephthalate) Blends[J]. Polymer Engineering and Science, 44(8):1405-1413.

SASAKI H, et al, 1998. Direct Adhesion of Nylon 899 Resin to Stainless Steel Plates Coated with Triazine Thiol Polymer by Elec-900 Tropolymerization during Injection-Molding[J]. Japanese Journal of Polymer Science and Technology, 55(8):470-476.

SEGUNPTA R, TIKKU V, SOMANI A, et al, 2005. Electron Beam Irradiated Polyamide 6-6 films -I: Characterization Wide Angle X-Ray Scattering and Infrared Spectroscopy [J]. Radiation Physics and Chemistry, 72:625-633.

STARKOVA O, YANG J, ZHANG Z, 2007. Application of Time-stress Superposition to Nonlinear Creep of Polyamide 66 Filled with Nanoparticles of Various Sizes[J]. Composites Science and Technology, 67:2691-2698.

THOMASON J L, 2007. Structure-property Relationships in Glass-reinforced Polymers, Parts 3: Effects of Hydrolysis aging on the Dimensional Stability and Performance of Short Glass-fiber-reinforced Polyamide 66 [J]. Polymer Composites, 28(3):344-354.

THOMASON J L, 2001. Micromechanical Parameters from Macromechanical Measurements of Glass-Reinforced Polyamide 66[J]. Composites Science and Technology, 61:2007-2016.

TSANG K Y, et al, 2005. Fatigue Strength of Vibration-Welded Unreinforced Nylon Butt Joints[J]. Polymer Engineering and Science, 45(7):935-944.

VAN DYKE J, GNATOWSKI M, BURCZYK A, 2008. Solvent Resistance and Mechanical Properties in Thermoplastic Elastomer Blends Prepared by Dynamic Vulcanization [J]. Journal of Applied Polymer Science, 109:1535-1546.

ZANETTO L E, et al, 2001. Fusion Bonding of Polyamide 12[J]. Polymer Engineering and Science, 41:890-897.

ZHOU Y, MALLICK P K, 2006. Fatigue Performance of an Injection-Molded Short E-glass Fiber-reinforced Polyamide 6,6. I. Effects of Orientation, Holes, and Weld Line[J]. Polymer Composites:230-237.

Table 35.1 Mechanical Properties of PA-DAM (Dry as Molded) and Related Composites

Material-DAM	$T/℃$	E_T	ρ	υ	(σ,ε)	α	k	γ	β	K_{IC}
PA4,6	23	—	—	—	(70,4%) (80, 5%) (95, 20%)	—	—	—	—	—
PA4,6/30GF	23	—	—	—	—	—	—	—	—	—
	149	—	—	—	(62, 2%) (98, 8%)	—	—	—	—	—

continued

Material-DAM	$T/°C$	E_T	ρ	υ	(σ, ε)	α	k	γ	β	K_{IC}
PA6	23	2.75	1.15	0.39	$\sigma_{ucs} = -90$; (50, 2.5%) (75, 5%) (80, 35%)	85	0.25	—	—	—
	$50(T_g)$	—	—	—	—	—	—	—	—	—
	$215(T_m)$	—	—	—	—	—	—	—	—	—
PA6/MoS$_2$ (Solid Lubricant)	23	3.3	1.16	—	(78, 25%)	80	0.3	—	—	—
	90(High service temperature)									
	$220(T_m)$	—	—	—	—	—	—	—	—	—
PA6/20Curaua Fiber	23	5.5	1.18	—	(83, 3%)	—	—	—	—	—
PA6/20Talc	23	6.5	1.27	—	(73, 6%)	—	—	—	—	—
	−40	—	—	—	(114, 15%)	63	0.25	1253	—	—
PA6,6	23	2.8	1.11	0.41	(−104, −10%) (−73, −4%); (50, 2%) (83, 5%)	81	0.25	1462	—	4
	$57(T_g)$	—	—	—	—	—	—	—	—	—
	77	—	—	—	(62, 300%)	90	0.25	1880	—	—
	121	—	—	—	(43, 300%)	125	0.25	2298	—	—
	$263(T_m)$	—	—	—	—	—	—	—	—	—
	−40	—	—	—	(−250, −4%) (−100, −2%); (105, 1%) (200, 3.5%)	—	—	—	—	—
PA6,6/30GF	23	10	1.38	0.35	(−180, −5%) (−90, −2%) (90, 1%) (170, 4.5%)	27/81	0.30	—	—	—
	80	—	—	—	(−110, −8.5%) (−60, −4%); (62, 4%) (120, 8.5%)	—	—	—	—	—
	$263(T_m)$	—	—	—	—	—	—	—	—	—

continued

Material-DAM	$T/^\circ\text{C}$	E_T	ρ	υ	(σ, ε)	α	k	γ	β	K_{IC}
PA6,6/30GF	−40	—	—	—	(110, 1.1%) (204, 2.2%)	23/63	—	—	—	—
PA6,6/33GF	23	10.8	1.4	0.35	(−190, −4.8%) (−100, −1.6%); (130, 1.6%) (186, 3.2%)	23/81	0.30	1670	—	—
	77	—	—	—	$\sigma_{\text{uts}} = 110$	23/90	—	—	—	—
	93	—	—	—	(62, 4%) (86, 7.8%)	—	—	—	—	—
	149	—	—	—	(−50, −6%) (−30, −2%); (58, 4%) (76, 7.6%)	—	—	—	—	—
	263(T_m)	—	—	—	—	—	—	—	—	—
PA6,6/43GF	−40	—	—	—	(156, 1.1%) (238, 2.2%)	22/63	—	—	—	—
	23	13.8	1.5	—	(133, 1.2%) (207, 2.4%)	22/81	—	—	—	—
	45	—	—	—	(175, 4.2%)	—	—	—	—	—
	65	—	—	—	(160, 5.4%)	—	—	—	—	—
	77	—	—	—	—	22/91	—	—	—	—
	85	—	—	—	(125, 5.5%)	—	—	—	—	—
	93	—	—	—	(88, 2.4%) (103, 4.8%)	—	—	—	—	—
	263(T_m)	—	—	—	—	—	—	—	—	—
PA6,6/30CF	23	24	1.28	—	(260, 3%)	14	0.51	—	—	—
	263(T_m)	—	—	—	—	—	—	—	—	—
	−40	—	—	—	(94, 8%) (94, 17%)	90	—	—	—	—

continued

Material-DAM	$T/°C$	E_T	ρ	υ	(σ, ε)	α	k	γ	β	K_{IC}
PA6,12	23	2.2	1.06	0.41	(61, 7%) (61, 100%)	115	—	—	—	—
	46(T_g)	—	—	—	—	—	—	—	—	—
	77	—	—	—	(30, 30%) (41, 230%)	170	—	—	—	—
	222(T_m)	—	—	—	—	—	—	—	—	—
PA6,12/33GF	−40	—	—	—	(140, 1%) (235, 2.2%)	—	—	—	—	—
	23	8.3	—	—	(140, 2.1%) (166, 3.2%)	—	—	—	—	—
	77	—	—	—	(70, 2%) (110, 5%)	—	—	—	—	—
	149	—	—	—	(55, 8%) (65, 13.5%)	—	—	—	—	—
	222(T_m)	—	—	—	—	—	—	—	—	—
	40									
PA6,12/43GF	23	8.3	—	—	(160, 2.1%) (200, 5.4%)	23/81	0.243	—	—	—
	80	—	—	—	—	23/90	—	—	—	—
	149	—	—	—	(65, 8%) (76, 13.5%)	—	—	—	—	—
	222(T_m)	—	—	—	—	—	—	—	—	—
PA6,12/30CF	23	15	—	—	(200, 3.0%)	—	—	—	—	—
	222(T_m)	—	—	—	—	—	—	—	—	—

Table 35.2   Mechanical Properties of PA Reinforced with Randomly Oriented Fibers at 50% Relative Humidity

Material-50%RH	$T/°C$	E_T	ρ	υ	(σ, ε)	α	k	γ	β	K_{IC}
PA4,6	23	—	—	—	(20, 5%) (40, 20%) (50, 35%)	—	—	—	—	—

continued

Material-50%RH	$T/℃$	E_T	ρ	υ	(σ, ε)	α	k	γ	β	K_{IC}
PA6	23	1.15	1.11	0.37	$\sigma_{ucs}=-45$; (20, 5%) (40, 35%)	85	0.19	—	—	—
	−40	—	—	—	(110, 20%)	63	0.25	—	—	—
PA6/20GF	23	6.5	1.27	—	(101, 3%)	—	—	—	—	—
PA6,6	23	1.2	1.11	0.37	(−80, −10%) (−50, −4%); (45, 6%) (59, 300%)	81	—	—	—	—
	77	—	—	—	(41 >300%)	90	—	—	—	—
	121	—	—	—	(38 >300%)	—	0.25	—	—	—
	−40	—	—	—	—	23/63	—	—	—	—
PA6,6/33GF	23	7.4	1.4	—	(85, 2.1%) (124, 4.2%)	23/81	—	—	—	—
	77	—	—	—	$\sigma_{uts}=86$	23/90	—	—	—	—
	−40									
PA6,6/43GF	23	11	1.5	—	(105, 1.3%) (155, 2.6%)	22/81	—	—	—	—
	77	—	—	—	$\sigma_{uts}=93$	22/90	—	—	—	—
	−40	—	—	—	(93, 10%) (93, 20%)	90	—	—	—	—
PA6,12	23	1.7	1.06	0.37	(51, 30%) (52, 250%)	115	—	—	—	—
	77	—	—	—	(35, 40%) (36, 300%)	170	—	—	—	—
PA6,12/33GF	−40	—	—	—	—	—	—	—	—	—
	23	6.2	—	—	(85, 2.1%) (138, 4.2%)	—	—	—	—	—
	77	—	—	—	$\sigma_{uts}=97$	—	—	—	—	—

Notes: DAM = Dry as Molded;

GF(CF) = Reinforced with glass (carbon) fibers, by weight unless V_f is given;

50% RH = 50% Relative Humidity;

$T_g(℃)$ & $T_m(℃)$ = Glass transition point and melting point, respectively.

Table 35.3 Fatigue ε-N Properties of PA（Polyamide）-Based Composites

Material	$T/{}^\circ\!\mathrm{C}$	$\mathrm{d}\varepsilon/\mathrm{d}t$	σ'_{f-}	ε'_{f-}	b	c	K'	n'	$\sigma_f@2N_f$	R
PA6/30%GF ($V_f=30\%$)	23	3 Hz	—	—	—	—	—	—	$60@\,5\times10^5$	0.1^+
									$63@\,10^5$	0.1^+
									$70@\,10^4$	0.1^+
									$80@\,10^3$	0.1^+
	50	3 Hz	—	—	—	—	—	—	$48@\,10^6$	0.1^+
									$54@\,10^5$	0.1^+
									$61@\,10^4$	0.1^+
									$66@\,2\times10^3$	0.1^+
PA6/50%GF ($V_f=50\%$)	23	3 Hz	—	—	—	—	—	—	$62@\,10^6$	0.1^+
									$70@\,2\times10^5$	0.1^+
									$74@\,10^5$	0.1^+
									$87@\,10^4$	0.1^+
	50	3 Hz	—	—	—	—	—	—	$53@\,10^6$	0.1^+
									$63@\,10^5$	0.1^+
									$75@\,10^4$	0.1^+
									$85@\,2\times10^3$	0.1^+
PA6,6/30GF (//Mold Flow Direction; DAM)	23	—	156	—	-0.057	—	—	—	$17@\,5\times10^8$	—
									$85@\,10^5$	—
									$92@\,10^4$	—
									$101@\,10^3$	—
PA6,6/30GF ($\perp$ Mold Flow Direction; DAM)	23	—	102	—	-0.06	—	—	—	$51@\,10^5$	—
									$56@\,10^4$	—
									$64@\,10^3$	—
PA6,6/30GF (Weldline; DAM)	23	—	82.5	—	-0.067	—	—	—	$40@\,10^5$	
									$45@\,10^4$	—
									$52@\,10^3$	—

Notes：0.1^+：Stress ratio $R=0.1$ and both high and low stress levels are positive.

Table 35.4 Normalized Prony Parameters for Creep/Relaxation of PA

Material-DAM	$T/{}^\circ\!\mathrm{C}$	E_0 or E_∞/MPa	N	$[\,p_i(\mathrm{MPa})\,,\ T_i(\mathrm{h})\,]\,,\ i=1,2,\cdots,N$
Zytel 101L (Dupont PA6,6)	23	$E_0=3.1$	1	$[\,0.7355,\ 2.388\,]$

Chapter 36

PAI (Polyamide-imide)

36.1 Introduction

PAI (**P**oly**a**mide-**i**mide) is a high performance amorphous thermoplastic. It has exceptional mechanical, thermal and chemical resistant properties among thermoplastics. The combined aromatic groups and imide linkages are responsible for the polymer's exceptional thermal stability with a glass transition temperature of 275 ℃. Resins for injection molding include unreinforced, glass-fiber reinforced, carbon fiber reinforced, and wear resistant grades. PAI (Polyamideimide) resins were first discovered by Amoco chemists in the 1960's.

Enameled wires are subjected to severe mechanical stress and enamel films are susceptible to damage and loss of insulating effectiveness when wound at a high speed. One countermeasure to this problem is the use of self-lubricating enameled wires with strong lubrication and abrasion resistance. Polyamideimide coatings on magnet wires offer the best performance in chemical resistance and toughness.

Mechanical properties of PAI and its related composites are listed in Table 36.1 and their fatigue properties are given in Table 36.2. Stress-strain curves of PAI reinforced with glass and carbon fibers at the room temperature are plotted in Fig. 36.1. Composites of PAI reinforced with glass fibers at different temperatures are plotted in Fig. 36.2. Composites of PAI reinforced with carbon fibers are electrically conductive and fatigue resistant.

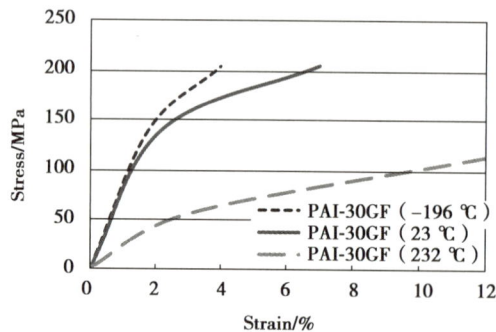

Fig. 36.1 **Stress-Strain Curves of PAI and Its Related Composites at the Room Temperature**

Fig. 36.2 **Stress-Strain Curves of PAI/30GF at Different Temperatures**

36.2   Applications

Polyamide-imide polymers can be processed into a wide variety of forms, ranging from injection or compression molded parts and ingots to coatings, films, fibers and adhesives. Its applications include, but not limited to, high temperature electrical connectors, labyrinth seals, and bearing cages. The thermal properties of polyamideimide coatings are outstanding when compared to polyimide resins. Coating applications include corona resistance enamels, self-lubricated, and high abrasion resistance coatings. The hybrid car industry offers opportunities for further innovations in magnet wire coatings.

References

FRITSCH D, PEINEMANN K V, 1995. Novel Highly Permselective 6F-Polyamideimidea as Membrane Host for Nano-sized Catalysts[J]. Journal of Membrane Science, 99(1):29-38.

KONING C, et al, 2001. Synthesis and Properties of α-, ω-diaminoalkane Based Polyamideimides [J]. Polymer, 42(17):7247-7256.

NICKOLS M E, et al, 1990. Creep and Physical Aging in a Polyamideimide Carbon Fiber Composite[J]. Journal of Macromolecular Science, Part B: Physics, 29(4):303-336.

Table 36.1   Mechanical Properties of PAI (Polyamide-imide) and Related Composites

Material-DAM	T/℃	E_T	ρ	υ	(σ, ε)	α	k	γ	β	K_{IC}
PAI	23	4.8	1.42	0.38	(100, 3%) (152, 7.6%)	31	0.26	1013	—	—
	275(T_g)	—	—	—	—	—	—	—	—	—
	−196	—	—	—	(155, 2%) (218, 6%)	—	—	—	—	—
PAI/TiO$_2$	23	4.9	1.45	0.45	(100, 3%) (145, 8%)	—	0.26	1013	—	2.2
	135	—	—	—	(80, 3%) (117, 21%)	—	—	—	—	—
	177	—	—	—	—	—	—	—	—	0.9

continued

Material-DAM	$T/℃$	E_T	ρ	v	(σ,ε)	α	k	γ	β	K_{IC}
PAI/TiO$_2$	232	—	—	—	(50, 3%) (66, 22%)	—	—	1640	—	—
	-196	—	—	—	(140, 1.8%) (204, 4%)	—	—	—	—	—
PAI/30GF	23	14.5	1.61	0.43	$\sigma_{ucs}=-264$; (140, 2%) (205, 2.3%)	16	0.37	959	—	2.6
	135	—	—	—	(70, 3%) (160, 15%)	—	—	—	—	—
	177	—	—	—	—	—	—	—	—	2.2
	232	—	—	—	(55, 3%) (113, 12%)	—	—	1470	—	—
	-196	—	—	—	(108, 1.5%) (158, 3%)	—	—	—	—	—
PAI/30CF	23	16.5	1.48	0.39	$\sigma_{ucs}=-254$; (160, 1%) (221, 1.5%)	9	0.53	963	—	3.2
	135	—	—	—	(80, 3%) (158, 14%)	—	—	—	—	—
	177	—	—	—	—	—	—	—	—	2.6
	232	—	—	—	(60, 3%) (108, 11%)	—	—	1560	—	—

Notes：DAM = Dry as Molded；

   GF（CF）= Reinforced with glass（carbon）fibers，by weight unless V_f is given；

   T_g（℃）& T_m（℃）= Glass transition point and melting point，respectively；

   TiO$_2$ = Reinforcement，by weight.

Table 36.2 Fatigue ε-N Properties of PAI（Polyamide-imide）and Related Composites

Material	$T/℃$	$d\varepsilon/dt$	σ'_{f-}	ε'_{f-}	b	c	K'	n'	$\sigma_f@2N_f$	R
PAI	23		—	—	—	—	—	—	33	—
PAI/TiO$_2$	23	—	—	—	—	—	—	—	33	—
	177	—		—	—	—	—	—	12	—

continued

Material	$T/℃$	$d\varepsilon/dt$	σ'_{f-}	ε'_{f-}	b	c	K'	n'	$\sigma_f@2N_f$	R
PAI/30GF	23	15 Hz		—	—	—	—	—	$84@2×10^5$	0.1
									$68@10^6$	0.1
									$63@6×10^6$	0.1
									$40\ (\sigma_f)$	
	177	—		—	—	—	—	—	33	—
PAI/30CF	23	30 Hz		—	—	—	—	—	$185@10^3$	0.1
									$75@10^6$	0.1
									$60@10^7$	0.1
									$45\ (\sigma_f)$	
	177	—		—	—	—	—	—	40	—

Chapter 37

PAN (Polyacrylonitrile)

37.1 Introduction

PAN (**Polya**cry**lo**nitrile) is a synthetic, semicrystalline organic polymer resin, with the linear formula $(C_3H_3N)_n$. Because PAN softens only slightly below its thermal degradation temperature, it must be processed by wet or dry spinning rather than melt spinning. Mechanical properties of PAN are given in Table 37.1.

Researchers used an electrospinning technique, i. e. applying high voltage to a solution until a small jet of liquid ejects, to make ultrafine continuous PAN nanofibers that are both stronger and tougher.

37.2 Applications

PAN (Polyacrylonitrile) is typically used in fiber form. It is a versatile polymer used to produce large variety of products such as ultra filtration membranes, sails for yachts, and fibers for textiles.

References

BAJAJ P, et al, 2001. Effect of Reaction Medium on Radical Polymerization of Acrylonitrile with Vinyl Acids [J]. Journal of Applied Polymer Science, 79(9):1640-1652.

PAPKOV D, et al, 2013. Simultaneously Strong and Tough Ultrafine Continuous Nanofibers[J]. ACS Nano, 7 (4):3324-3331.

Table 37.1 Mechanical Properties of PAN (Polyacrylonitrile) and Related Composites

Material-DAM	$T/°C$	E_T	ρ	υ	(σ, ε)	α	k	γ	β	K_{IC}
PAN	23	—	1.18	—	(15, 0.2%) (33, 340%)	140	0.22	1800	—	—
	$95(T_g)$	—	—	—	—	—	—	—	—	—
	$317(T_m)$	—	—	—	—	—	—	—	—	—

Chapter 38

PB (Polybutylene)

38.1   Introduction

PB (**P**oly**b**utylene) is a polyolefin with chemical formula $(C_4H_8)_n$, linear semicrystalline thermoplastic. It is flexible with good elastic recovery. Mechanical properties of PB are given in Table 38.1.

38.2   Applications

PB is used in pressure piping, flexible packaging, and hot melt adhesives. It is usable for hot and cold water. Only compression and band-typed joints are allowed due to their low rigidity.

Reference

FREEMAN A, MANTELL S C, DAVISON J H, 2005. Mechanical Properties of Polysulfone, Polybutylene, and Polyamide 6/6 in Hot Chlorinated Water[J]. Solar Energy, 79(6):624-637.

Table 38.1   Mechanical Properties of PB (Polybutylene) and Related Composites

Material-DAM	$T/\mathrm{°C}$	E_{T}	ρ	v	(σ,ε)	α	k	γ	β	K_{IC}
PB	$-21(T_{\mathrm{g}})$	—	—	—	—	—	—	—	—	—
	23	0.25	0.92	0.37	(15, 0.2%) (33, 340%)	140	0.22	1800	—	—
	100(High service temperature)									
	135(T_{m})									

Chapter 39

PBI (Polybenzimidazole)

39.1　Introduction

PBI (**P**oly**b**enz**i**midazole) offers the highest heat resistance and mechanical property retention over 205 ℃ among all unfilled plastics. It has better wear resistance and load carrying capabilities at extreme temperatures than any other reinforced or unreinforced engineering plastic. It also has an extremely low coefficient of linear thermal expansion up to 250 ℃ , inherent low flammability, low out-gassing in vacuum and high purity in terms of ionic contamination. According to tests conducted using ASTM D570, PBI's water absorption is 0.4% by the 24 h immersion test and its water absorption at saturation is 5%. Mechanical properties of PBI are rare in the public domain. Some obtained from research publications in the public domain are listed in Table 39.1.

It is shown that PBI reinforced with carbon nanotubes have higher storage modulus than pure PBI in the temperature range between the room temperature and 350 ℃ ; even holding storage modulus higher than 1.54 GPa at a temperature close to 300 ℃ [Zhang et al.].

PBI (Polybenzimidazole) based segmented block copolymers are used for high temperature fuel cell membranes. The separation of the polymer backbones caused by the doping acid makes it easier for the gases to diffuse through the acid doped membranes than through the dense pristine PBI membrane. Electric conduction properties of PBI membranes depend on the level of doping with phosphoric acid, temperature, and water content (moisture) [Xiao et al.] [Glipa et al.], as shown in Table 39.2. Conductivity of phosphoric acid-doped PBI membranes increases with increasing doping level and increasing temperature. High doping levels result in high proton conductivity, but mechanical properties of acid-doped membranes become poor at high doping levels [Li et al.]. High molecular weights of the polymers improve the mechanical strength but have little influence on the proton conductivity of the membranes [He et al.]. The sulphonated PBI membrane has a high conductivity (0.18 s/cm) at 125 ℃. Nevertheless, only the composite membrane with TiO_2 retained high conductivity values at the higher temperatures and this is a result of its high doping level and high water retention capacity. It is demonstrated that the PBI/ TiO_2 composite membrane can achieve a power density of 800 mWcm^{-1} at 150 ℃ [Lobato et al., 2011].

39.2　Applications

PBI (Polybenzimidazole) membranes have been suggested to be used as electrolytes in fuel cells with hydrogen, methanol and other types of fuels. Among various types of alternative high temperature polymer electrolyte membranes developed so far, phosphoric acid doped polybenzimidazole {poly (2,2-(m-phenylene)-5,5-bibenzimidazole) ; PBI} is one of the most promising candidates [Xiao et al., 2005].

Other engineering applications of PBI (Polybenzimidazole) include wafer retaining rings for gas plasma etching, vacuum tips, wafer carriers, contact seals, insulator bushings, thermal isolators, guide rollers.

PBI (Polybenzimidazole) is also used to fabricate high-performance protective apparel such as firefighter turnout coats and suits, astronaut space suits, high temperature protective gloves, welders' apparel, race driver suits, braided packings, and aircraft wall fabrics.

References

ANDRES T E, 1999. Polybenzimidazole Based Materials in Automotive Tribological Applications [J]. SAE 940552.

ASENSIO J, et al, 2002. Proton Conducting Polymers Based on Benzimidazole and Sulfonated Benzimidazoles [J]. Journal of Polymer Science, A, 40:3703-3710.

CAROLLO A, QUARTARONE E, TOMASI C, 2006. Developments of New Proton Conducting Membranes Based on Different Polybenzimidazole Structures for Fuel Cells Applications [J]. Journal of Power Sources, 160:175-180.

CHUANG S, HSU S, HSU C, 2007. Synthesis and Properties of Fluorine-Containing Polybenzimidazole/ Montmorillonite Nanocomposite Membranes for Direct Methanol Fuel Cell Applications [J]. Journal of Power Sources, 168(1):172-177.

GEORMEZI M, et al, 2008. Novel Pyridine-based Poly(ether sulfones) and Their Study in High Temperature PEM Fuel Cells [J]. Macromolecules, 41(23):9051-9056.

GLIPA X, et al, 1999. Investigation of the Conduction Properties of Phosphoric and Sulfuric Acid Doped Polybenzimidazole [J]. Journal of Mater. Chem., 9:3045-3049.

HASIOTIS C, et al, 2001. New Polymer Electrolytes Based on Blends of Sulfonated Polysulfones with Polybenzimidazole [J]. Electrochim Acta, 46:2401-2406.

HASIOTIS C, et al, 2001. Development and Characterization of Acid-Doped Polybenzimidazole Sulfonated Polysulfone Blend Polymer Electrolytes for Fuel Cells [J]. Journal of Electrochemical Society, 148:A513-A519.

HE R, et al, 2006. Physicochemical Properties of Phosphoric Acid Doped Polybenzimidazole Membranes for Fuel Cells [J]. Journal of Membrane Science, 277(1-2):38-45.

HOGARTH W, et al, 2005. Solid Acid Membranes for High Temperature (>140 ℃) Proton Exchange Membrane Fuel Cells [J]. Journal of Power Sources, 142(1-2):223-237.

IWAKURA Y, UNO K, IMAI Y, 1964. Polyphenylenebenzimidazoles[J]. Journal of Polymer Science, A, 2: 2605-2615.

KAWAHARA M, RIKUKAWA M, SANUI K, et al, 2000. Synthesis and Proton Conductivity of Sulfopropylated Poly(benzimidazole) Film[J]. Solid State Ionics, 136/137:1193-1196.

KONGSTEIN O, et al, 2007. Polymer Electrolyte Fuel Cells Based on Phosphoric Acid Doped Polybenzimidazole (PBI) Membranes[J]. Energy, 32(4):418-422.

KREUER K, FUCHS A, ISE M, et al, 1998. Imidazole and Pyrazole-Based proton Conducting Polymers and Liquids[J]. ElectrochimActa, 43:1281-1288.

LI M, SHAO Z, SCOTT K, 2008. A High Conductivity Cs2.5H0.5PMo12O40/Polybenzimidazole (PBI)/ H3PO4 Composite Membrane for Proton-Exchange Membrane Fuel Cells Operating at High Temperature[J]. Journal of Power Sources,183(1):69-75.

LI QINGFENG, HJULER H A, BJERRUM N J, 2001. Phosphoric Acid Doped Polybenzimidazole Membranes: Physiochemical Characterization and Fuel Cell Applications [J]. Journal of Applied Electrochemistry, 31(7):773-779.

LI Q, HE R, BERG R, et al, 2004. Water Uptake and Acid Doping of Polybenzimidazoles as Electrolyte Membranes for Fuel Cells[J]. Solid State Ionics, 168(1-2):177-185.

LOBATO J, et al, 2011. A Novel Titanium PBI-Based Composite Membrane for High Temperature PEMFCs [J]. Journal of Membrane Science, 369(1-2):105-111.

LOBATO J, et al, 2007. Improved Polybenzimidazole Films for H_3PO_4-Doped PBI-Based High Temperature PEMFC[J]. Journal of Membrane Science, 306(1-2):47-55.

NORES-PONDAL F J, et al, 2010. Thermal Properties of Phosphoric Acid-Doped Polybenzimidazole Membranes in Water and Methanol-Water Mixtures[J]. Journal of Power Sources, 195(19):6389-6397.

QUARTARONE E, et al, 2009. PBI Composite and Nanocomposite Membranes for PEMFCs: The Role of the Filler[J]. Fuel Cells, 9(3):231-236.

SCANLON E, BENICEWICZ B C, 2004. Polybenzimidazole Based Segmented Block Copolymers for High Temperature Fuel Cell Membranes[J]. Fuel Division Prepr., 49(2):522-523.

SCHMIDT T, BAURMEISTER J, 2008. Properties of High-Temperature PEFC Celtec-P 1000 MEAs in Start/ Stop Operation Mode[J]. Journal of Power Sources, 176(2):428-434.

WAINRIGHT J, et al, 1995. Acid-Doped Polybenzimidazoles: a New Polymer Electrolyte [J]. Journal of Electrochemical Society, 142(7):L121.

XIAO L, et al, 2005. Synthesis and Characterization of Pyridine-Based Polybenzimidazoles for High Temperature Polymer Electrolyte Membrane Fuel Cell Applications[J]. Fuel Cells, 5(2):287-295.

YU S, XIAO L, BENICEWICZ B, 2008. Durability Studies of PBI-Based High Temperature PEMFCs[J]. Fuel Cells, 8(3-4):165-174.

ZHANG Li, et al, 2010. Synthesis and Mechanical Properties of Polybenzimidazole Nanocomposites Reinforced by Vapor Grown Carbon Nanofibers[J]. Polymer Composites, 31(3):491-496.

ZHANG LI, et al, 2008. Mechanical Properties of Polybenzimidazole Reinforced by Carbon Nanofibers[J]. Advanced Materials Research, 47-50:302-305.

Table 39.1　Mechanical Properties of PBI (Polybenzimidazole) and Related Composites

Material-DAM	$T/^\circ C$	E_T	ρ	v	(σ,ε)	α	k	γ	β	K_{IC}
PBI (Bulk)	23	5.9	1.3	0.34	$(-345, -10\%)$; $(110, 2\%)$	23.4	0.4	—	—	—
	316(High service temperature)									
	$399(T_g)$	—	—	—	—	—	—	—	—	—
	$760(T_m)$	—	—	—	—	—	—	—	—	—
	−40									
PBI (Fiber) (Acid level = 0)	23	5.9	—	0.34	$(-400, -10\%)$; $(160, 3\%)$	23.4	0.41	—	—	—
	125	—	—	—	$\sigma_{uts}=150$	—	—	—	—	—
	180	—	—	—	$\sigma_{uts}=130$	—	—	—	—	—
	316(High service temperature)									
	−40									
PBI (Fiber) (Acid level = 2.3)	23	5.9	—	0.34	$(-400, -10\%)$; $(160, 3\%)$	23.4	0.41	—	—	—
	125	—	—	—	$\sigma_{uts}=160$	—	—	—	—	—
	180	—	—	—	$\sigma_{uts}=48$	—	—	—	—	—
	316(High service temperature)									
	−40									
PBI (Fiber) (Acid level = 5.7)	23	5.9	—	0.34	$(-400, -10\%)$; $(160, 3\%)$	23.4	0.41	—	—	—
	125	—	—	—	$\sigma_{uts}=10$	—	—	—	—	—
	180	—	—	—	$\sigma_{uts}=6$	—	—	—	—	—
	316(High service temperature)									

continued

Material-DAM	$T/℃$	E_T	ρ	υ	(σ,ε)	α	k	γ	β	K_{IC}
PBI (Fiber) (Acid level= 5.7)	23	5.9	—	0.34	(−400, −10%); (160, 3%)	23.4	0.41	—	—	—
	180	—	—	—	$\sigma_{uts}=12$	—	—	—	—	—
	316(High service temperature)									
2,5 PPBI(Film) (8.5% polymer)	23	—	—	—	(0.45, 26%) (1.82, 386%)	—	—	—	—	—
2,6 PPBI(Film; 17.8% polymer)	23	—	—	—	(1.92, 43%) (1.79, 153%)	—	—	—	—	—

Notes: DAM=Dry as Molded;

$T_g(℃)$ & $T_m(℃)$= Glass transition point and melting point, respectively;

ρ (MW)= Density or (Molecular Weight);

Proton (Scm^{-1})= Proton conductivity.

Table 39.2 Performance of PBI (Polybenzimidazole) Membrane

Material	$T/℃$	Molecular Weight	Moisture	Acid Type	Doping Level	Proton
PBI (Membrane)	23					
	140	21900	20% RH	H_3PO_4	6.6	0.061
	140	21900	30% RH	H_3PO_4	6.3	0.050
	140	25100	20% RH	H_3PO_4	6.2	0.057
	140	55000	20% RH	H_3PO_4	6.6	0.063
	200	21900	5% RH	H_3PO_4	6.6	0.09
	200	25100	5% RH	H_3PO_4	6.2	0.095
	200	55000	5% RH	H_3PO_4	6.6	0.098
	399(T_g)	—	—	—	—	—
	760(T_m)	—	—	—	—	—

Chapter 40

PBT (Poly-Butylene Terephthalate)

40.1   Introduction

PBT (**P**oly-**B**utylene **T**erephthalate) is a semi-crystalline thermoplastic polymer. Due to its excellent rigidity, high mechanical strength, flexible formability, low shrinkage (relative to other plastics), good heat stability, non-combustibility (with flame retardants as additives), strong resistance to solvents and oils, and good electric resistance, PBT has become a major material for electrical applications such as connectors. It is a cost-effective performance plastic, though strength degrades as temperature arises. It can withstand a temperature up to 150 ℃ with no distortion, and even 200 ℃ with no distortion if reinforced by fiberglass. However, it is recommended for applications with a continuous exposure to heat at 135 ℃ or below if there is a molded-in metal such as an electrical connector. Mechanical properties are shown in Table 40.1 and fatigue properties in Table 40.2. The representative stress-strain curves of PBT/30GF and PBT/40GF, randomly reinforced with 30% and 40% of short-fiber glass by weight, respectively, are given in Fig. 40.1 and Fig. 40.2.

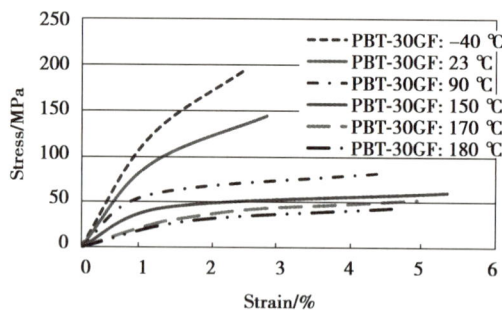

Fig. 40.1   Mechanical properties of PBT/30GF Composites

The polybutylene terephthalate (PBT) and polyethylene terephthalate (PET) polymer systems are based on a thermoplastic polyester or terephthalate system. Relative to PET (polyethylene terephthalate), PBT has slightly better impact resistance, but slightly lower strength and rigidity, and a slightly lower glass transition temperature.

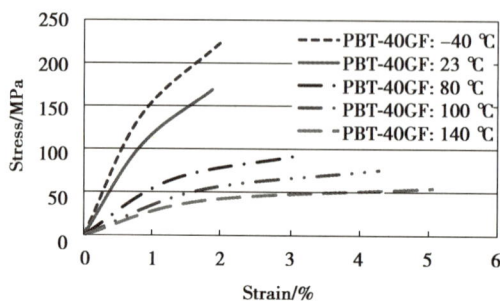

Fig. 40.2   Mechanical properties of PBT/40GF Composites

40.2   Applications

Polyesters (mainly PET, PBT, and thermoset polyester) share 9.7% of automotive plastics, including polyester fibers for tires, body panels, truck hoods, trailer panels, and seating.

References

ANIA F, et al, 2006. Micromechanical Properties of Poly(Butylene Terephthalate) Nanocomposites with Single-and Multi-Walled Carbon Nanotubes[J]. Composite Interfaces, 13(1):33-45.

BANIK K, 2008. Effect of Mold Temperature on Short and Long-Term Mechanical Properties of PBT[J]. Express Polymer Letters, 2(2):111-117.

BANIK K, MENNIG G, 2006. Influence of the Injection Molding Process on the Creep Behavior of Semicrystalline PBT during Aging Below Its Glass Transition Temperature[J]. Mechanics of Time-Dependent Materials, 9(4):45-55.

CARR P, et al, 1998. Tensile Drawing, Morphology, and Mechanical Properties of Poly(Butylene Terephthalate)[J]. Journal of Polymer Science, Part B: Polymer Physics, 35(15):2465-2481.

FUNG C, TIEN Y, 2005. Study of Multi-response Optimization for Fiber-reinforced Polybutylene Terephthalate [J]. Journal of Reinforced Plastics and Composites, 24(9):923-933.

GUERRICA-ECHEVARRIA G, EGUIAZABAL J, 2009. Structure and Mechanical Properties of Impact Modified Poly(butylene terephthalate)/Poly(ethylene terephthalate) Blends[J]. Polymer Engineering and Science, 49(5):1013-1021.

LAI M, LIU L, 2002. Thermal Conductivity, Thermo-Mechanical and Rheological Studies of Boron Nitride-Filled Polybutylene Terephthalate[J]. Materials Science Forum, 437/438:239-242.

LIU S, LIN M, WU Y, 2007. An Experimental Study of the Water-Assisted Injection Molding of Glass Fiber Filled Poly-Butylene-Terephthalate (PBT) Composites[J]. Composites Science and Technology, 67:1415-1424.

MARIES G R E, MIHALIA S, PANTEA I, 2008. A Study Concerning Mechanical Resistance and Domains of Usage of the Ultradur Polybutylene Terephthalate (PBT)[J]. Fascicle of Management and Technological Engineering, VII(XVII):1572-1578.

MATHEW G, HONG P, RHEE J, 2006. Preparation and Anisotropic Mechanical Behavior of Highly-Oriented Electrospun Poly(Butylene Terephthalate) Fibers[J]. Journal of Applied Polymer Science, 101(3):2017-2021.

NARKHEDE J, SHERTUKDE V, 2011. Mechanical Properties and Rheological Behavior of Poly(butylene terephthalate)/Clay Nanocomposites with Different Organoclays[J]. Journal of Applied Polymer Science, 119(2):1067-1074.

PARK C, et al, 2002. Crystallinity Morphology and Dynamic Mechanical Characteristics of PBT Polymer and Glass Fiber-reinforced Composites[J]. Journal of Applied Polymer Science, 86(2):478-488.

PARK J, PARK Y, 2005. Synthesis and Properties of Novel Flame Retardant Poly(butylene terephthalate)[J]. Macromolecular Research, 13(2):128-134.

THOMASON J L, 2002. Micromechanical Parameters from Macromechanical Measurements of Glass-filled Polybutylene Terephthalate[J]. Composites, Part A: Applied Science and Manufacturing, 33(3):331-339.

TSUKAMOTO K, et al, 2002. A Study on Poly Butylene Terephthalate Gears Filled with Glass Fibers[J]. Japanese Society of Mechanical Engineers, Part C, 68(3):935-940.

Table 40.1 Mechanical Properties of PBT (Poly-Butylene Terephthalate) and Related Composites

Material-DAM	$T/℃$	E_T	ρ	v	(σ,ε)	α	k	γ	β	K_{IC}
PBT	23	3.1	1.34	0.44	(52, 250%)	95	0.21	1210	—	—
	$60(T_g)$	—	—	—	—	—	—	—	—	—
	90	—	—	—	—	140	—	—	—	—
	$223(T_m)$	—	—	—	—	—	—	—	—	—
	−40	—	—	—	(85, 2%) (127, 4.1%)	—	—	—	—	—
PBT/10GF	23	4.5	1.42	—	(65, 2%) (90, 5%)	—	—	—	—	—
	80	—	—	—	(27, 2%) (67, 10.5%)	—	—	—	—	—
	140	—	—	—	(16, 2%) (32, 11.6%)	—	—	—	—	—
PBT/20GF	23	8	1.49	—	(80, 1%) (114, 3%)	23/97	—	—	—	—
	−40	—	—	—	(120, 1%) (195, 2.4%)	—	—	—	—	—

continued

Material-DAM	$T/\mathrm{°C}$	E_T	ρ	υ	(σ,ε)	α	k	γ	β	K_IC
PBT/30GF	23	9.7	—	—	(90, 1%) (144, 2.7%)	20/70	0.24	1830	—	—
	90	—	—	—	(57, 1%) (82, 4.4%)	—	—	—	—	—
	150	—	—	—	(43, 1.2%) (60, 5.3%)	—	—	—	—	—
	170	—	—	—	(32, 1.5%) (52, 4.9%)	—	—	—	—	—
	180	—	—	—	(29, 1.6%) (43, 4.5%)	—	—	—	—	—

Notes: DAM = Dry as Molded;

      GF (CF) = Reinforced with glass (carbon) fibers, by weight unless V_f is given;

      $T_\mathrm{g}(\mathrm{°C})$ & $T_\mathrm{m}(\mathrm{°C})$ = Glass transition point and melting point, respectively.

Table 40.2　Fatigue ε-N Properties of PBT（Poly-Butylene Terephthalate）and Related Composites

Material	$T/\mathrm{°C}$	$\mathrm{d}\varepsilon/\mathrm{d}t$	$\sigma'_\mathrm{f-}$	$\varepsilon'_\mathrm{f-}$	b	c	K'	n'	$\sigma_\mathrm{f}@2N_\mathrm{f}$	R
PBT	23 ℃	—	—	—	—	—	—	—	$19.5@10^7$	—
PBT/20GF	23 ℃	—	—	—	—	—	—	—	$27.5@10^7$	—
PBT/30GF	23 ℃	—	—	—	—	—	—	—	$34.4@10^7$	—

Chapter 41

PC (Polycarbonate)

41.1 Introduction

PC (**Poly**carbonate) is a thermoplastic polymer containing carbonate groups as named. It is a clear colorless polymer used extensively for engineering and optical applications. A balance of useful characteristics including temperature resistance, impact resistance, and optical properties positions polycarbonates at the low end of engineering plastics. It has low scratch resistance and so a hard coating is applied to exterior automotive components made of polycarbonate and other products such as polycarbonate eyewear lenses. Material properties of PC and its related composites are given in Table 41.1 and fatigue properties in Table 41.2. Representative stress-strain curves of PC (Polycarbonate) are presented in Fig. 41.1.

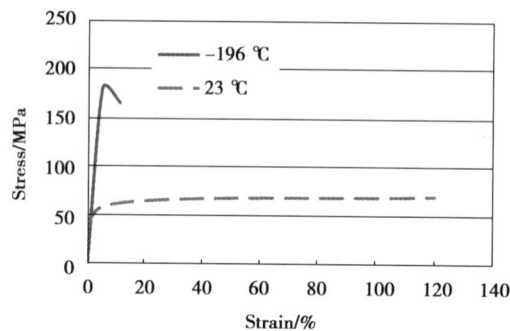

Fig. 41.1   Representative Stress-Strain Curves of PC (Polycarbonate) at Different Temperatures

The deficiencies of PC are creep tendency, low chemical resistance, poor weatherability, and chemical resistance, especially at elevated temperatures. The equation to generate isochronous stress-strain curves to account for PC (without reinforcement) creep at the room temperature is given as follows:

$$\varepsilon_{\text{creep}} = \left(4.734 \times 10^{-4} - 7.8314 \times 10^{-5} \exp\frac{-t}{662}\right)\sigma +$$

$$\left(-8.6842 \times 10^{-6} + 6.5748 \times 10^{-6} \exp\frac{-t}{873}\right)\sigma_2 +$$

$$\left(3.9907 \times 10^{-7} - 1.028 \times 10^{-7} \exp\frac{-t}{284} - 1.7059 \times 10^{-7} \exp\frac{-t}{5242}\right)\sigma_3 \quad (41.1)$$

of which t (time) is in seconds and σ (tensile stress) is in MPa.

41.2 Applications

It shares 3.2% of automotive plastics (Year 2001), including headlights, taillights, signal light lenses and housings, runway markers, blow-molded spoilers, instrument panels, seat back, glazing, decorative bezels, optical reflectors, light pipes, and bullet-resistant windows.

References

BISWAS K K, IKUEDA M, SOMIYA S, 2001. Study on Creep Behavior of Glass Fiber-Reinforced Polycarbonate[J]. Advanced Composite Materials, 10(2-3):265-273.

CHEN S C, et al, 2003. Investigations of the Tensile Properties on Polycarbonate Thin-wall Injection Molded Parts[J]. Journal of Reinforced Plastics and Composites, 22:479-494.

DIN K J, HASHEMI S, 1997.Influence of Short-Fiber Reinforcement on the Mechanical and Fracture Behavior of Polycarbonate/Acrylonitrile Butadiene Styrene Polymer Blend[J]. Journal of Material Science, 32:375-387.

EDWARDS M R, WATERFALL H, 2007. Mechanical and Ballistic Properties of Polycarbonate Apposite to Riot Shield Applications[J]. Plastics, Rubber and Composites, 36(10):1-5.

EITAN A, et al, 2006. Reinforcement Mechanisms in MWCNT-Filled Polycarbonate[J]. Composites Science and Technology, 66:1159-1170.

FACTOR A, ORLANDO C M, 1980. Polycarbonates from 1,1-dichloro-2,2-bis (4-hydroxyphenyl) Ethylene and Bisphenol A: A Highly Flame-Resistant Family of Engineering Thermoplastics[J]. Journal of Polymer Science, Polym. Chem., 18:579-592.

FANG Q, WANG T, BEOM H, et al, 2008. Effect of Cyclic Loading on Tensile Properties of PC and PC/ABS [J]. Polymer Degradation and Stability, 93:1422-1432.

GAO Y, et al, 2006. Improving the Mechanical Properties of Polycarbonate Nanocomposites with Plasma-Modified Carbon Nanofibers[J]. Journal of Macromolecular Science, B, 45(4):671-679.

GIRISH D V, MANJUNATH A, 2007. Effect of Short Fiber Reinforcement on Characteristic of Polymer Matrix (Polycarbonate)-An Experimental Study [J]. International Conference on Advanced Materials and Composites, 24-26:917-922.

HO K C, JENG M C, 1997. Tribological Characteristics of Short Fiber Reinforced Polycarbonate Composites [J]. Wear, 206:60-68.

HO K C, et al, 1996. Tensile Properties of Short Fiber Reinforced Polycarbonate Composites[J]. Polymers and Polymeric Composites, 4(8):563-575.

JAWALI N D, et al, 2008. Polycarbonate/Short Glass Fiber Reinforced Composites-Physicomechanical, Morphological and FEM Analysis[J]. Journal of Reinforced Plastics and Composites, 27(3):313-319.

KRACHE R, DEBAH I, 2011. Some Mechanical and Thermal Properties of PC/ABS Blends[J]. Materials Sciences and Applications, 2(5):404-410.

KRISHINA A, BERG E, 2011. Stress Cracking of Polycarbonate Exposed to Sunscreen[J]. SAE 2011-01-0037.

KUMAR V, WELLER J E. 1944.Production of Microcellular Polycarbonate Using Carbon Dioxide for Bubble Nucleation[J]. Journal of Engineering for Industry, ASME:413-420.

LIN T H, ISAYEV A I, 2008. Phtoviscoelastic Behavior and Residual Thermal Birefringence Optical-Grade Polycarbonates[J]. Acta Rheology, 47(9):977-988.

LUO W, JAZOULI S, VU-KHANH T, 2007. Modeling of Nonlinear Viscoelastic Creep of Polycarbonate[J]. e-Polymers, 7(1):191-201.

MACHIKO M, et al, 2008. Internal Structure and Mechanical Properties of Glass Fiber Reinforced PC/ABS Injection Moldings with Different Fiber Surface Treatments[J]. Polymers and Polymer Composites, 16(1): 27-33.

MAS J, et al, 2002. Dynamic Mechanical Properties of Polycarbonate and Acrylonitrile-Butadiene-Styrene Copolymer Blends[J]. Journal of Applied Polymer Science, 83(7):1507-1516.

PARSONS E, BOYCE M C, PARKS D M, 2004. An Experimental Investigation of the Large-Strain Tensile Behavior of Neat and Rubber-Toughened Polycarbonate[J]. Polymer, 45:2665-2684.

POTENTE H, et al, 2008. Simulation of the Residual Stresses in the Contour Laser Welding of Thermoplastics [J]. Polymer Engineering and Science, 48(4):767-773.

OLIVER A, et al, 2008. Mechanical Properties of Non-functionalized Multiwall Nanotube Reinforced Polycarbonate at 77 K[J]. Nanotechnology, 19(50):505702.

SCHARTEL S, et al, 2008. Mechanical, Thermal, and Fire Behavior of Bisphenol a Polycarbonate/Multiwall Carbon Nano-tube Nano-composites[J]. Polymer Science and Engineering, 48(1):149-158.

SIVIOUR C R, et al, 2005. The High Strain Rate Compressive Behavior of Polycarbonate and Polyvinylidene Difluoride[J]. Polymer, 46(26):12546-12555.

STOLIAROV S I, WESTMORELAND P R, 2003. Mechanism of the Thermal Decomposition of Bisphenol C Polycarbonate: Nature of Its Fire Resistance[J]. Polymer, 44(18):5469-5475.

TANAHASHI M, 2006. Fatigue-Fracture Surface of Polycarbonate Subjected to Heating/Cooling Cycles under Longitudinal Confinement[J]. Japanese Journal of Polymer Science and Technology, 63(12):767-773.

VICTOR A, et al, 2003. Physical Aging of Polycarbonate: Elastic Modulus, Hardness, Creep, Endo-thermic Peak, Molecular Weight Distribution, and Infrared Data[J]. Macro-Molecules, 36:7585-7597.

WANG C H, BROWN M W, 1993. A Path-Independent Parameter for Fatigue under Proportional and Non-

Proportional Loading[J]. Fatigue and Fracture of Engineering Materials and Structures, 16:1285-1298.

YANG Y K, 2006. Optimization of Injection Molding Process for Mechanical Properties of Short Glass Fiber and Polytetrafluoroethylene Reinforced Polycarbonate Composites: A Case Study [J]. Journal of Reinforced Plastics and Composites, 25(12):1279-1290.

ZHOU R, 2010. Mechanical and Optical Properties of Nanosilica-filled Polycarbonate Composites[J]. Journal of Thermoplastic Composite Materials, 23(4):487-500.

Table 41.1   Mechanical Properties of PC（Polycarbonate）and Related Composites

Material-DAM	$T/°C$	E_T	ρ	υ	(σ, ε)	α	k	γ	β	K_{IC}
PC	−196	—	—	—	(180, 5%) (165, 11.3%)	—	—	—	—	—
	23	2.3	1.21	0.38	(60, 7%) (70, 120%)	68	0.20	1250	—	2.4
	80	—	—	—	—	68	—	—	—	—
	120	—	—	—	$\sigma_{uts}=30$	—	—	—	—	—
	150(T_g)	—	—	—	—	—	0.18	—	—	—
	284(T_m)	—	—	—	—	—	0.24	1900	—	—
PC/30CF	23	18	—	0.35	(170, 2%)	14	0.7	—	—	—
PC/30GF	23	9	1.41	0.35	(135, 3.5%)	22	0.26	1080	—	—
	160	—	—	—	—	42	—	—	—	—
PC/30GF/ 15PTFE	23	8.3	1.55	—	$\sigma_{uts}=120$	—	—	—	—	—
PC/22PTFE	23	—	1.33	—	$\sigma_{uts}=45$	—	—	—	—	—

Notes: DAM = Dry as Molded;

$T_g(°C)$ & $T_m(°C)$ = Glass transition point and melting point, respectively;

GF, CF, TPFE = Reinforced with glass fiber, carbon fiber, & PTFE, respectively (weight).

Table 41.2   Fatigue ε-N Properties of PC（Polycarbonate）and Related Composites

Material	$T/°C$	$d\varepsilon/dt$	σ'_{f-}	ε'_{f-}	b	c	K'	n'	$\sigma_f@2N_f$	R
PC	23	—		—	—	—	—	—	24.5@1897	—
									31.5@858	—

Chapter 42

PE (Polyethylene)- LDPE, HDPE, UHMWPE, and XLPE

42.1   Introduction

PE (**P**olyethylene) is a family of resins derived from polymerizing ethylene ($H_2C = CH_2$) and it is the largest volume commercial polymer. Polyethylene (PE) and its conversions with higher molecular weight such as HDPE (High Density Polyethylene), HMW HDPE (High Molecular Weight High Density Polyethylene), and UHMWPE (Ultrahigh Molecular Weight Polyethylene), share 9.5% of automotive plastics (Year 2001). The density ranges from 0.92 g/cm^3 to 0.96 g/cm^3. The plastic is available in a range of flexibility with high density materials being the most rigid. Material properties of PE reinforced with fibers are given in Table 42.1. Their fatigue and creep properties are given in Tables 42.2 and 42.3, respectively. Two representative stress-strain curves at the room temperature for LDPE and HDPE, respectively, are plotted in Fig. 42.1.

Fig. 42.1   Example Stress-Strain Curves of LDPE (Low Density Polyethylene) and HDPE (High Density Polyethylene)

42.2   XLPE (Cross-linking PE; PEX)

XLPE obtained by cross-linking PE has improved thermal stability and mechanical properties over PE. It is also called PEX. Almost all XLPE is made from HDPE. XLPE is used for the insulation layer surrounding the copper conductor in high voltage (HV) and extra high voltage (EHV) cables, as shown in Fig. 42.2. Commercially available EPR and XLPE cable dielectrics typically have about the same thermal conductivity, although the thermal conductivity of XLPE above the melting point of the crystallites drops below that of the EPR dielectrics.

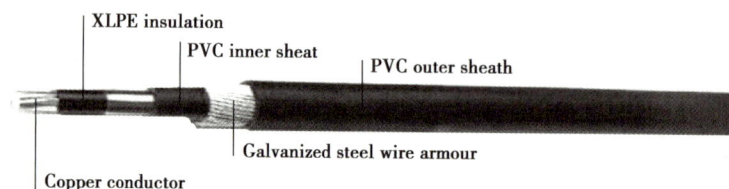

Fig. 42.2   XLPE as the Insulation Material Surrounding the Copper Conductor

42.3   Dyneema

Another product derived from PE (polyethylene) is Dyneema [DSM], which is a strong fiber. Its specific strength (strength per unit weight) is 15 times stronger than quality steel (bulk) and up to 40% stronger than aramid fibers. It is extremely resistant to abrasion, moisture, UV rays, and chemicals.

42.4   CPE (Chlorinated Polyethylene)

CPE (Chlorinated Polyethylene) is a flexible thermoplastic, which has good UV resistance, high tear strength, chemical resistance. It is mainly used as an impact modifier for PVC or compounded with LDPE and HDPE to improve toughness. Another application is bellow boots for automotive constant-velocity universal joints.

42.5   PEN (Polyethylene Naphthalate)

Polyethylene Naphthalate (PEN), as well as FEP, PEEK, PEI, PET, Polyimide (PI) and their copolymer films, has been used as the base material for the flexible PCB (Printed Circuit Board) laminate due to its blend of advantageous electrical, mechanical, chemical and thermal properties. The thickness of the base material usually ranges from 0.01 mm to 0.1 mm. The adhesive may be applied before metal foils (usually copper-based materials) are printed (either electro-deposited or rolled-up) onto it. Flexible printed circuits (FPC) are made with a photolithographic technology. Multilayered laminates are feasible. An alternative way of making flexible foil circuits or flexible flat cables (FFCs) is laminating very thin (e.g. 0.07 mm) copper strips in between two layers of polymer, which are typically 0.05 mm thick each and coated with adhesive that is thermosetting, and will be activated during the lamination process.

42.6   PEO (Polyethylene Oxide)

PEO (Polyethylene Oxide) consists of repeating $-O-CH_2-CH_2$ units.

42.7 Applications

PE (Polyethylene) is the most used plastic among all, although it shares only 9.5% of automotive plastics. Treadle pads of an automotive accelerator pedal may be made of regular PE, while a plastic fuel tank is an example application of HMW HDPE. One interesting application is bullets, fragments of exploding bombs and artillery shells-resistant armors made of Dyneema composites.

XLPE (Cross-linking PE; PEX) is a material of choice for electric cables due to its superior thermal resistance, dielectric properties, and tubings. The upper operating temperature for operation of XLPE cable is limited to 90 ℃ for continuous use and 105 ℃ for intermittent use, while the more expensive competitor EPR cable can be operated continuously and safely up to 140 ℃. On the tubing and piping, it has been adopted by installers of radiant-floor heating since it neither corrodes nor develops pinhole leaks. XLPE also resists chlorine and scaling, and uses fewer fittings than rigid plastic and metallic pipe. The piping is approved for potable hot-and cold-water plumbing systems as well as for hydronic heating systems in all plumbing and mechanical codes in the United States and Canada [Heavens].

References

ADHIKARY K B, PANG S, MARK P S, 2008. Dimensional Stability and Mechanical Behaviour of Wood-Plastic Composites Based on Recycled and Virgin High-Density Polyethylene (HDPE)[J]. Composites, B, 39(5):807-815.

AL-ROBADI, 2009. Synergistic Effect of TNPP and Carbon Black in Weathered XLPE Materials[J]. Journal of Polymers and the Environment, 17(4):267-272.

BISTOLFI A, et al, 2009. Tensile and Tribological Properties of High-Crystallinity Radiation Crosslinked UHMWPE[J]. Journal of Biomedical Materials Research, 90B(1):137-144.

CHAE D W, KIM K J, KIM B C, 2006. Effects of Silicalite-1 Nanoparticles on Rheological and Physical Properties of HDPE[J]. Polymer, 47(10):3609-3615.

CHONG Y, CHEN G, HOSIER I, et al, 2005. Heat Treatment of Cross-Linked Polyethylene and Its Effect on Morphology and Space Charge Evolution[J]. IEEE Transactions on Electrical Insulation, 12:1209-1221.

CRISSMAN J M, 1986. Creep and Recovery Behavior of a Linear High-density Polyethylene and an Ethylene-hexene Copolymer in the Region of Small Uniaxial Deformations[J]. Polymers Engineering and Science, 26 (15):1050-1059.

CRISSMAN J M, ZAPAS L J, 1985. The Mechanical Preconditioning of Ultrahigh-Molecular-Weight Polyethylene at Small Uniaxial Deformations[J]. Journal of Polymer Science, B, Polymer Physics, 23

（12）:2599-2610.

DENCHEV Z, et al, 2010. Nanostructure and Mechanical Properties Studied during Dynamical Straining of Microfibrillar Reinforced HDPE/PA Blends[J]. Journal of Polymer Science Part B: Polymer Physics, 48:237-250.

EDWARDS D B, DUVALL D E. 1993. Creep and Stress Rupture Testing of Polyethylene Sheet under Equal Biaxial Tensile Stresses[J]. Journal of Reinforced Plastics and Composites, 12(3):285-295.

EICHHORN R M, 1981. A Critical Comparison of XLPE and EPR for Use as Electrical Insulation on Underground Power Cables[J]. IEEE Transactions on Electrical Insulation, 6(6):469-482.

ELKSNITE I, et al, 2010. Effects of Small Additions of a Liquid Crystalline Polymer on the Mechanical Properties of Polyethylene[J]. Mechanics of Composite Materials, 46 (1):105-119.

FANG L, LENG Y, GAO P, 2006. Processing and Mechanical Properties of HA/UHMWPE Nanocomposites [J]. Biomaterials, 27:3701-3707.

FABRIS F W, 2009. Improving the Properties of LDPE/Glass Fiber Composites with Silanized-LDPE [J]. Polymer Composites, 30(7):872-879.

GENG H Z, et al, 2002. Fabrication and Properties of Composites of Poly(ethylene oxide) and Functionalized Carbon Nanotubes[J]. Advanced Materials, 14(19):1387-1390.

GENT A N, WANG C, 1996. Cutting Resistance of Polyethylene[J]. Journal of Polymer Science, Part B: Polymer Physics, 34(13):2231-2237.

GOTO T, YAMAZAKI T, 2004. Recycling of Silane Cross-linked Polyethylene for Insulation of Cables using Supercritical Alcohol[J]. Hitachi Cable Review, 23:24-27.

HILLMANSEN S, et al, 2000. The Effect of Strain rate, Temperature, and Molecular Mass on the tensile Deformation of Polyethylene[J]. Polymer Engineering and Science, 40(2):481-489.

HUANG W, et al, 2005. Water-driven Programmable Polyurethane Shape Memory Polymer: Demonstration and Mechanism[J]. Applied Physics Letters, 86:114105.

JAHAN A, et al, 2012. Comparative Study of Physical and Elastic Properties of Jute and Glass Fiber Reinforced LDPE Composites[J]. International Journal of Scientific & Technology Research, 1(10):68-72.

KABAMBA E T, RODRIGUE D, 2008. The Effect of Recycling on LDPE Foamability: Elongation Rheology [J]. Polymer Science and Engineering, 48(1):11-18.

KHELIF R, et al, 2008. Statistical Analysis of HDPE Fatigue Lifetime[J]. Mechanica, 43:567-576.

KHONAKDARA H A, JAFARIB S H, WAGENKNECHTC U, et al, 2006. Effect of Electron-Irradiation on Cross-link Density and Crystalline Structure of Low-and High-Density Polyethylene[J]. Radiation Physics and Chemistry, 75(1):78-86.

KHONAKDAR H A, et al, 2003. Thermal and Shrinkage Behavior of Stretched Peroxide-Crosslinked High-Density Polyethylene[J]. European Polymer Journal, 39: 1729-1734.

KRISHNASWAMY R K, 2005. Analysis of Ductile and Brittle Failures from Creep Rupture Testing of High-Density Poly-ethylene (HDPE) Pipes[J]. Polymer, 46(25):11664-11672.

KUBOKI T, et al, 2009. Mechanical Properties and Foaming Behavior of Cellulose Fiber Reinforced High-Density Polyethylene Composites[J]. Polymer Engineering and Science, 49(11):2179-2188.

LAZZERI A, et al, 2005. Filler Toughening of Plastics. Part 1-The Effect of Surface Interactions on Physico-Mechanical Properties and Rheological Behavior of Ultrafine CaCO₃/HDPE Nanocomposites[J]. Polymer, 46(3):827-844.

LENG J S, HUANG W M, LAN X, et al, 2008. Significantly Reducing Electrical Resistivity by Forming Conductive Ni Chains in a Polyurethane Shape-memory Polymer/Carbon-Black Composite[J]. Applied Physics Letters 92:204101.

LIU H, POLAK M, PENLIDIS A, 2008. A Practical Approach to Modeling Time-dependent Nonlinear Creep Behavior of Polyethylene for Structural Applications[J]. Polymer Science and Engineering, 48(1):159-167.

MOLDOVAN Z, et al, 2008. HDPE-EPDM Thermoplastic Vulcanizates-Mechanical and IR Spectrometric Properties[J]. Revue Roumaine de Chimie, 53(11):1051-1057.

PARK I H, et al, 2006. Development and Application of Conducting Shape Memory Polyurethane Actuators [J]. Smart Materials and Structures, 15(5):1476-1482.

PEJIS T, et al, 1944. Strain Rate and Temperature Effects on Energy Absorption of Polyethylene Fibers and Composites[J]. Applied Composite Materials, 1:35-54.

QI X, BOGGS S, 2006. Thermal and Mechanical Properties of EPR and XLPE Cable Compounds[J]. IEEE Electric Insulation Magazine, 22(3):19-24.

READER W T, MEGILL R W, 1991. Clorosulfonated Polyethylene: a Versatile Polymer for Damping Acoustic Waves[J]. Metallurgical Transactions, 22, A:633-640.

SERVER K, 2010. The Improvement of Mechanical Properties of Jute Fiber/LDPE Composites by Fiber Surface Treatment[J]. Journal of Reinforced Plastics and Composites, 29(13):1921-1929.

SUI G, et al, 2009. Structure, Mechanical Properties, and Friction Behavior of UHMWPE/HDPE/Carbon Nanofibers[J]. Materials Chemistry and Physics, 115 (1):404-412.

TON THAT P, TANNER K, BONFIELD W, 2003. Fatigue Characterization of a Hydroxyapatite-Reinforced Polyethylene Composite. I. Uniaxial Fatigue[J]. Journal of Biomedical Materials Research, 51(3):453-460.

WHITE C, et al, 2000. Separation, Size Reduction, and Processing of XLPE from Electrical Transmission and Distribution Cable[J]. Polymer Engineering and Science, 40(4):863-879.

WRÓBEL G, SZYMICZEK M, 2008. Influence of Temperature on Friction Coefficient of Low Density Polyethylene[J]. Journal of Achievements in Materials and Manufacturing Engineering, 28(1):31-44.

XIAO K, et al, 2007. Mechanical and Rheological Properties of Carbon Nanotube-Reinforced Polyethylene

Composites[J]. Composites Science and Technology, 67:177-182.

YAMANAKA A, et al, 2005. Thermal Conductivity of High Strength Polyethylene Fiber in Low Temperature [J]. Journal of Polymer Science, Part B, 43(12):1495-1503.

YANG B, HUANG W M, LI C, et al, 2006. Effects of Moisture on the Thermomechanical Properties of a Polyurethane Shape Memory Polymer[J]. Polymer, 47(4):1348-1356.

YANG B, HUANG W M, LI C, et al, 2005. Qualitative Separation of the Effects of Carbon Nano-powder and Moisture on the Glass Transition Temperature of Polyurethane Shape Memory Polymer [J]. Scripta Materialia, 53(1):105-107.

YODA B, MURAKI K, 1997. Development of EHV Crosslinked Polyethylene Insulated Power Cables[J]. IEEE Transactions on Power Apparatus and Systems, PA92:506-513.

ZAMAN H, et al, 2011. A Comparative Study on the Mechanical and Degradation Properties of Plant Fibers Reinforced Polyethylene Composites[J]. Polymer Composites, 32(10):1552-1560.

ZHANG C, MOORE I D, 1997. Nonlinear Mechanical Response of High Density Polyethylene, Part II: Uniaxial Constitutive Model[J]. Polymer Engineering and Science, 37:414-420.

Table 42.1   Mechanical Properties of PE (Polyethylene) and Related Composites

Material-DAM	$T/°C$	E_T	ρ	υ	(σ, ε)	α	k	γ	β	K_{IC}
LDPE	−150	—	—	—	—	—	0.36	840	—	—
	−110(T_g)	—	—	—	—	—	—	—	—	—
	−100	—	—	—	—	—	0.38	1100	—	—
	−40	—	—	—	(22, 2%) (27.5, 4%)	122	0.37	1500	—	—
	0	—	—	—	—	—	0.35	1900	—	—
	23	0.3	0.91	0.46	(6.5, 90%) (10, 200%) (8, 340%) (12.7, 850%)	172	—	—	—	—
	50	—	—	—	—	270	0.31	2730	—	—
	70(High service temperature)									
	100	—	—	—	—	—	0.24	—	—	—
	111(T_m)	—	—	—	—	—	—	—	—	—
LDPE/30GF	23	1.7	—	—	(39, 10%)	—	—	1510	—	—
LDPE/55GF	23	2.5	—	—	(86, 6%)	—	—	—	—	—
LDPE/30Jute	23	1.0	—	—	(33, 15%)	—	—	—	—	—

continued

Material-DAM	$T/\text{°C}$	E_T	ρ	υ	(σ,ε)	α	k	γ	β	K_{IC}
LDPE/44Jute	23	1.3	—	—	(54, 10%)	—	—	—	—	—
LDPE/30Doum	23	0.5			(9.5, 40%) (13, 100%)	—	—	—	—	—
HDPE	−150	—	—	—	—	68	0.62	840	—	—
	−110(T_g)	—	—	—	—	—	—	—	—	—
	−100	—	—	—	—	95	0.56	1100	—	—
	−50	—	—	—	—	124	0.50	1340	—	—
	0	—	—	—	—	—	0.44	1640	—	—
	23	1.1	0.95	0.46	(15, 50%) (25, 120%) (15, 350%) (16, 850%) (20, 1000%)	170	0.42	1900	—	—
	50	—	—	—	—	330	0.38	2050	—	—
	100	—	—	—	—	690	0.32	2860	—	—
	130(T_m)	—	—	—	—	—	0.29	—	—	—
UHMW PE	−110(T_g)	—	—	—	—	—	—	—	—	—
	23	0.75	0.935	0.46	(20, 5%) (28, 25%)	175	0.41	1750	—	—
	133(T_m)	—	—	—	—	—	—	—	—	—
	−40	—	—	—	—	—	—	1400	—	—
XLPE ($\rho=0.93$)	23	—	0.93	—	(19, 450%)	170	0.33	2400	—	—
	50	—	—	—	—	—	0.32	2900	—	—
	90(High service temperature)									
	105	—	—	—	—	—	0.39	12000	—	—
	120	—	—	—	—	—	0.265	—	—	—
	140	—	—	—	—	—	0.255	—	—	—
	−40	—	—	—	—	—	—	1400	—	—

continued

Material-DAM	$T/°C$	E_T	ρ	υ	(σ, ε)	α	k	γ	β	K_{IC}
XLPE ($\rho = 0.954$)	23	—	0.954	—	(26, 450%)	170	0.33	2400	—	—
	50	—	—	—	—	—	0.32	2900	—	—
	90 (High service temperature)									
	105	—	—	—	—	—	0.39	12000	—	—
	120	—	—	—	—	—	0.265	—	—	—
Dyneema (UHMWPE Fiber)	23	118	—	—	$\sigma_{uts} = 3800$	—	—	—	—	—
CPE	23	0.002	1.16	—	(12.5, 700%)	180	—	—	—	—
	150 (T_m)	—	—	—	—	—	—	—	—	—
PEO	23	0.06	—	—	(2, 7%) (3.5, 100%)	—	—	—	—	—
PEO-1F/ SWNT	23	0.147	—	—	(5.2, 10%) (9.5, 100%)	—	—	—	—	—

Notes: DAM = Dry as Molded;

GF (CF) = Reinforced with glass (carbon) fibers, by weight unless V_f is given;

T_g (°C) & T_m (°C) = Glass transition point and melting point, respectively;

Jute & Doum = Reinforcement, by weight.

Table 42.2   Fatigue ε-N Properties of PE (Polyethylene) and Related Composites

Material	$T/°C$	$d\varepsilon/dt$	σ'_{f-}	ε'_{f-}	b	c	K'	n'	$\sigma_f @ 2N_f$	R
PE	23	—		—	—		—	—	—	—
LDPE	23	—		—	—		—	—	—	—
HDPE	23	—	—	—	−0.118	—		—	11@ 106	—

Table 42.3   Mechanical Creep Parameters of PE

Material	$T/°C$	Stress/MPa	Strain Rate/s^{-1}	$A/(MPa^{-n} \cdot s^{m-1})$	$Q/(J \cdot mol^{-1})$	n	m
HDPE	25	$E = 1$	—	—	90	—	—

Notes: Creep equation $= \dfrac{d\varepsilon_{creep}}{dt} = A\left(\dfrac{\sigma - \sigma_{th}}{E}\right)^n t^m \exp\left(\dfrac{-Q}{RT_k}\right), \sigma > \sigma_{th}$;

σ_{th} = Stress threshold and $\sigma_{th} = 0$, if not specified;

E = Young's modulus; If given that $E = 1$, it means E is not specified.

Chapter 43

PEI (Polyetherimide)

43.1　Introduction

PEI (**P**oly**e**ther**i**mide) is an amorphous engineering thermoplastic characterized by high heat resistance, high strength and module, excellent electrical properties that remain stable over a wide range of temperatures and frequencies, and excellent processability. The molecular formula of the repeating unit of PEI is $C_{37}H_{24}O_6N_2$. Unmodified PEI resin is transparent and has inherent flame resistance and low-smoke evolution. Resistance to UV radiation and gamma radiation is good. It has a high dielectric strength. Another favorite characteristic of PEI is its high glass transition point (215 ℃), which is extremely high as a thermoplastic. Material properties of PEI reinforced with fibers are given in Table 43.1. It is prone to stress cracking in chlorinated solvents. Stress-strain curves of PEI and PEI/GF30 at different temperatures are depicted in Fig. 43.1.

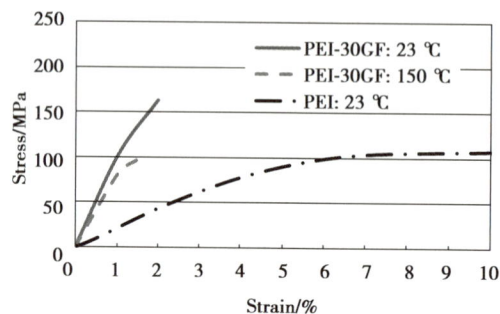

Fig. 43.1　Stress-Strain Curves of PEI and PEI/GF30 at Different Temperatures

43.2　Applications

Composites with random fibers such as PEI/40GF and PEI/30CF are good choices for applications at a temperature as high as 175 ℃, such as electrical connectors and position sensors for EGR (exhaust gas recirculation) valves.

References

ARJULA S, HARSHA A, GHOSH M, 2008. Erosive Wear of Unidirectional Carbon Fiber-Reinforced Polyetherimide Composite[J]. Materials Letters, 62(17-18):3246-3249.

CAI C, et al, 2011. The Tribological Properties of Thermoplastic Polyetherimide Composites Filled with Kevlar Pulp[J]. Applied Mechanics and Materials, 66/68:862-865.

CHANG L, et al, 2005. Effects of Nanoparticles on the Tribological Behavior of Short Carbon Fiber Reinforced Polyetherimide Composites[J]. Tribology International, 38(1):966-973.

KIM J, 2008. Polyetherimide Substrates for Future High Density Optical Data Storage[J]. Polymer Science and Engineering, 48(1):97-101.

KIM K, YE L, PHOA K, 2004. Interlaminar Fracture Toughness of CF/PEI and GF/PEI Composites at Elevated Temperatures[J]. Applied Composite Materials, 11(3):173-190.

KUMAR S, et al, 2009. Dramatic Property Enhancement in Polyetherimide using Low-Cost Commercially Functionalized Multi-Walled Carbon Nanotubes via a Facile Solution Processing Method [J]. Nanotechnology, 20(46):465708.

KUMAR S, et al, 2007. Study on Mechanical, Morphological and Electrical Properties of Carbon Nanofiber/ Polyetherimide Composites[J]. Materials Science and Engineering, Part B, 141(1-2):61-70.

LI B, et al, 2010. Effectual Dispersion of Carbon Nanofibers in Polyetherimide Composites and Their Mechanical and Tribological Properties[J]. Polymer Engineering and Science,50(10):1914-1922.

ROY S, et al, 2009. Improvement of Properties of Polyetherimide/Liquid Crystalline Polymer Blends in the Presence of Functionalized Carbon Nanotubes[J]. Journal of Nanoscience and Nanotechnology, 9(3):1928-1934.

SHARMA M, RAO I, BIJWE J, 2009. Influence of Orientation of Long Fibers in Carbon Fiber-Polyetherimide Composites on Mechanical and Tribological Properties[J]. Wear, 267(5-8):839-845.

SUI G, et al, 2009. Carbon Nanofiber/Polyetherimide Composite Membranes with Special Dielectric Properties [J]. Soft Matter, 5(19):3593.

VACCARO N, et al, 2010. Effects of Mixing and Loading of Carbon Nanofiber on Mechanical Properties of Polyetherimide Nanofoams[J]. Transactions of NAMRI/SME, 38:547-554.

WAGNER A H, YU J S, KALYON D M, 1989. Injection Molding of Engineering Plastics[J]. Advances in Polymer Technology, 9(1):17-32.

YUANG Q, et al, 2001. Resistance Welding of Carbon Fiber Reinforced Polyetherimide Composites [J]. Journal of Thermoplastic Composite Materials, 14(1):2-19.

Table 43.1 Mechanical Properties of PEI (Polyetherimide) and Related Composites

Material-DAM	$T/°C$	E_T	ρ	v	(σ,ε)	α	k	γ	β	K_{IC}
PEI	23	3.1	1.27	0.36	$\sigma_{ucs}=-150$; (105, 7.5%) (85, 60%)	56	0.22	2000	—	10
	170(High service temperature)									
	217(T_g)	—	—	—	—	—	—	—	—	—
	370(T_m)	—	—	—	—	—	0.22	2100	—	—
	−40									

continued

Material-DAM	$T/℃$	E_T	ρ	υ	(σ,ε)	α	k	γ	β	K_IC
PEI/30GF	23	9	1.51	0.35	$\sigma_\mathrm{ucs}=-210$; (9.5, 0.1%) (163, 3%)	20/56	0.29	—	—	—
	150	—	—	—	(80, 1%) (97, 1.5%)	—	—	—	—	—
PEI/40GF	23	16.8	1.58	0.35	(196, 1.7%)	16/56	0.3	—	—	—
PEI/30CF	23	18.2	1.39	0.35	(224, 1.5%)	—	—	—	—	—

Notes: DAM = Dry as Molded;

GF (CF) = Reinforced with glass (carbon) fibers, by weight unless V_f is given;

$T_\mathrm{g}(℃)$ & $T_\mathrm{m}(℃)$ = Glass transition point and melting point, respectively;

TiO_2 = Reinforcement, by weight;

α (℃) = Coefficient of linear thermal expansion, along with/perpendicular to the flow direction.

Chapter 44

PES (Polyethersulfone)

44.1   Introduction

PES (**Poly**ether**s**ulfone) is a thermoplastic polymer known for its strength, toughness, and dimensional stability at elevated temperatures. It has a very high resistance to mineral acids, alkali, and salt solutions. Resistance to detergents and hydrocarbon oils is good, even at elevated temperatures under moderate stress levels in a moist environment. The polymer is rigid and transparent and it retains the room-temperature properties quite well between − 100 ℃ and 150 ℃, as shown in Table 44.1. Fatigue properties are given in Table 44.2. Representative stress-strain curves of PES (Polyethersulfone) and glass fiber-reinforced composites are reconstructed using some discrete data obtained mainly from [Ultrason, BASF] as shown in Fig. 44.1.

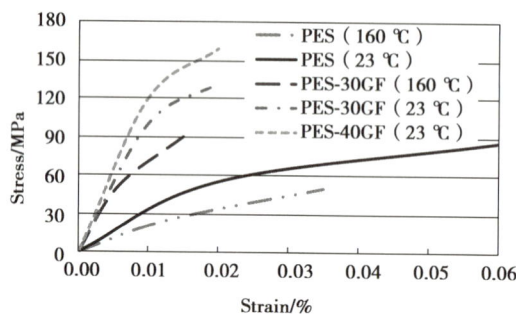

Fig. 44.1   Representative Stress-Strain Curves of PES (Polyethersulfone) and the Related Composites

44.2   Applications

PES (Polyethersulfone) may be partially fluorinated (F-PES) for thermally stabilizing the polymers when applied to proton exchange membrane fuel cells (PEMFCs) under humid conditions at high temperatures. It is also used for electrical connectors and as a dielectric in capacitors for applications at elevated temperatures. Another major application of PES (Polyethersulfone) is for aircraft interiors.

References

ARKHANGELSKY E, et al, 2007. Impact of Chemical Cleaning on Properties and Functioning of Polyethersulfone Membranes[J]. Journal of Membrane Science, 305:176-184.

BIJWE J, et al, 2004. Influence of Concentration of Aramid Fabric on Abrasive Wear Performance of Polyethersulfone Composite[J]. Tribology Letters, 17:187-194.

DI VONA M, et al, 2010. High Ionic Exchange Capacity Polyphenylsulfone (SPPSU) and polyethersulfone (SPES) Cross-Linked by Annealing Treatment: Thermal Stability, Hydration Level and Mechanical Properties[J]. Journal of Membrane Science, 354:134-141.

GUAN R, et al, 2006. Effect of Casting Solvent on the Morphology and Performance of Sulfonated Polyethersulfone Membranes[J]. Journal Membrane Science, 277 (1-2):148-156.

JIANG D, et al, 2011. Compatibility of Polyethersulfone/Polycarbonate Blends [J]. Advanced Materials Research, 217/218:1601-1605.

KIM I C, et al, 1999. Sulfonated Polyethersulfonebny Heterogeneous Method and Its Membrane Performances [J]. Journal of Applied Polymer Science, 74(8):2046-2055.

LIU X, et al, 2007. Study on the Polyethersulfone/Bismaleimide Blends: Morphology and Rheology during Isothermal Curing[J]. Journal of Material Science, 42:2150-2156.

QI K, HUANG R, 1944. Effect of Processing on the Structure and Properties of PES[J]. Polymer-Plastics Technology and Engineering, 33(2):121-133.

WANG M, WU L, ZHENG X, et al, 2006. Surface Modification of Phenolphthalein Poly (Ether Sulfone) Ultrafiltration Membranes by Blending with Acrylonitrile-Based Copolymer Containing Ionic Groups for Imparting Surface Electrical Properties[J]. Journal of Colloid Interface Sci., 300(1):286-292.

YOON K, et al, 2009. Formation of Functional Polyethersulfone Electrospun Membrane for Water Purification by Mixed Solvent and Oxidation Processes[J]. Polymer, 50(13):2893-2899.

Table 44.1 Mechanical Properties of PES (Polyethersulfone) and Related Composites

Material-DAM	$T/℃$	E_{T}	ρ	v	(σ,ε)	α	k	γ	β	K_{IC}
PES	−40	2.8	—	—	—	—	—	—	—	—
	23	2.6	1.34	0.4	(55, 2%) (88, 6%)	56	0.16	—	—	11
	150	—	—	—	$\sigma_{\mathrm{uts}}=60$ (50, 3.5%)	56	—	—	—	—
	160	2.1	—	—	(20, 1%)	56	—	—	—	—
	180(High service temperature)					56	—	—	—	—
	200	—	—	—	$\sigma_{\mathrm{uts}}=30$	56	—	—	—	—
	224(T_{g})	—	—	—	—	—	—	—	—	—
	341(T_{m})	—	—	—	—	—	—	—	—	—
	−40	10.5	—	—	—	—	—	—	—	—

continued

Material-DAM	$T/℃$	E_T	ρ	υ	(σ,ε)	α	k	γ	β	K_{IC}
PES/30GF	23	9.8	1.58	0.42	(100, 1%) (132, 2%)	17/56	0.2	—	30	30
	100	—	—	—	$\sigma_{uts}=113$	—	—	—	—	—
	150	—	—	—	$\sigma_{uts}=100$	—	—	—	—	—
	160	9.4			(50, 0.5%) (90, 1.5%)					
	200	—	—	—	$\sigma_{uts}=55$	—	—	—	—	—
	−40	—	—	—	—	—	—	—	—	—
PES/40GF	23	12.4	1.68	0.43	(159, 2.1%)	15/56	0.36	—	—	—

Notes: DAM = Dry as Molded;

GF (CF) = Reinforced with glass (carbon) fibers, by weight unless V_f is given;

$T_g(℃)$ & $T_m(℃)$ = Glass transition point and melting point, respectively;

TiO_2 = Reinforcement, by weight.

Table 44.2 Fatigue ε-N Properties of PES (Polyethersulfone) and Related Composites

Material	$T/℃$	$d\varepsilon/dt$	σ'_{f-}	ε'_{f-}	b	c	K'	n'	$\sigma_f@2N_f$	R
PES	23	—	—	—	—	—	—	—	9@107	—
PES/30GF	23	—	—	—	—	—	—	—	30@107	—

Chapter 45

PET (Polyethylene Terephthalate)

45.1   Introduction

PET (Polyethylene Terephthalate) is a linear saturated thermoplastic polyester-one of the most used plastics. It has high strength, toughness, shatter resistance, good barrier properties, low weight, and easy recyclability. Its mechanical stiffness and strength are relatively higher than PBT (the other thermoplastic polyester).

Due to creep in flexure and effect of air oven aging at an elevated temperature, the stress level for a PET-based part should stay within 60% of its applicable tensile strength in the working environment temperature. The material gets softened as temperature rises, as shown in Table 45.1. The influence of moisture on PET is smaller as compared with PA (nylon).

For glass-fiber-reinforced PET composites, the tensile modulus reaches its maximum at fiber content of 55% by weight, while its tensile strength reaches its maximum at fiber content of 52% by weight. It is recommended for applications with a continuous exposure to heat up to 135 ℃, especially where there is a molded-in metal such as an electrical connector. Stress-strain curves of representative PET/30GF and PET/45GF at different temperatures are presented in Figs. 45.1 and 45.2, respectively.

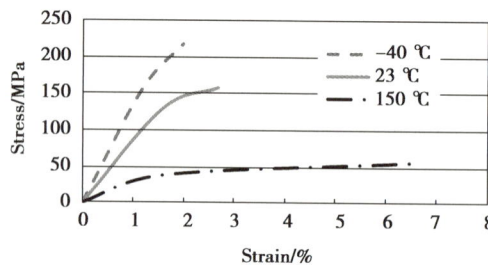

Fig. 45.1   Stress-Strain Curves of PET/30GF at Different Temperatures

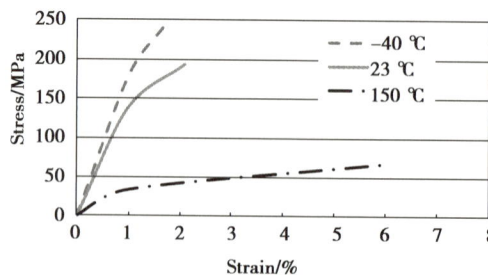

Fig. 45.2   Stress-Strain Curves of PET/45GF at Different Temperatures

PET (Polyethylene Terephthalate) can be reinforced by glass fibers or mineral/glass fiber combinations (DuPont Rynite) for structural applications such as chair shells, electronic connectors, transformer housings, and T-roof railings. Another popular application is food packaging such as bottles.

45.2   TPC-ET（Thermoplastic Copolyester-PET/PBT Elastomers）

TPC-ET（Thermoplastic Copolyester-PET/PBT Elastomers）serves as the benchmark for excellent balance of grease resistance, elevated temperature durability, and low-temperature flexibility. Its original length is identical to the maximum extended length in use, in such a way that kinking is avoided. A typical material based on Du Pont's polyester block copolymers, called Hytrel. Hytrel is a group of engineering thermoplastic elastomers, combining characteristics of high-performance elastomers and flexible thermoplastic polyesters (mainly PET/PBT).

TPC-ET（Thermoplastic Copolyester-PET/PBT Elastomers）are the ideal replacement for PVC in data, power and USB cable jackets, and DC power cable insulation and jacket.

45.3   Applications

Polyesters (mainly PET, PBT, and thermoset polyester) share 9.7% of automotive plastics, including polyester fibers for tires, body panels, truck hoods, trailer panels, and seating.

References

BALBAQ M Z, PAT S, 2011. Electrically Conductive and Optically Transparent Polyethylene Terephthalate Films Coated with Gold and Silver by Thermionic Vacuum Arc[J]. Journal of Plastic Film and Sheeting, 27 (3):209-222.

BANDYOPADHYAY J, et al, 2007. Thermal and Thermo-mechanical Properties of Poly (Ethylene Terephthalate) Nanocomposites[J]. Journal of Ind. Eng. Chemistry, 13(4):614-623.

CHEN J C, et al, 2011. Fabrication and Mechanical Properties of Self-Reinforced Poly (Ethylene Terephthalate) Composites[J]. Express Polymer Letters, 5(3):228-237.

DECHER G, HONG J, SCHMITT J, 1982. Buildup of Ultrathin Multilayer Films by a Self-Assembly Process. III. Consecutively Alternating Adsorption of Anionic and Cationic Polyelectrolytes on Charged Surface[J]. Thin Solid Films, 210:83-835.

FAKIROV S, et al, 2010. From PET Nanofibrils to Nanofibrillar Single-Polymer Composites [J]. Macromolecular Materials and Engineering, 295:515-518.

GIRALDI A, et al, 2005. Glass Fiber Recycled Polyethylene Terephthalate Composites: Mechanical and Thermal Properties[J]. Polymer Testing, 24:507-512.

HINE P J, WARD I M, 2004. Hot Compaction of Woven Poly(Ethylene Terephthalate) Multifilaments[J]. Journal of Applied Polymer Science, 91:2223-2233.

KAGAN V A, et al, 2004. Plastics Part Design: Low Cycle Fatigue Strength of Glass-fiber-reinforced Polyethlene Terephthalate (PET)[J]. Journal of Reinforced Plastics and Composites, 23(15):1607-1614.

KAMAL M, et al, 1983. Mechanical Properties of Injection Molded Blends of Poly(ethylene-terephthalate) and Poly(amide-6,6)[J]. Polymer Engineering and Science, 23(11):637-641.

LECHAT C, et al, 2006. Mechanical Behavior of Polyethylene Terephthalate & Polyethylene Naphthalate Fibers under Cyclic Loading[J]. Journal of Material Science, 41(6):1745-1756.

LEI YONG, et al, 2010. Phase Structure and Properties of Polyethylene Terephthalate/Polyethylene Based on Recycled Materials[J]. Journal of Applied Polymer Science, 113(3):1710-1719.

MALZHAN J C, SCHULTZ J M, 1986. Tension-tension and Compression-compression Fatigue Behavior of Injection-molded Short-glass-fiber/Polyethylene Terephthalate Composite [J]. Composites Science and Technology, 27:253-289.

MENARY G H, et al, 2011. Biaxial Deformation and Experimental Study of PET at Conditions Applicable to Stretch Blow Molding[J]. Polymer Engineering and Science, 52(3):671-688.

REZAEIAN I, 2009. An Investigation on the Rheology, Morphology, Thermal and Mechanical Properties of Recycled Poly (Ethylene Terephthalate) Reinforced with Modified Short Glass Fibers [J]. Polymer Composites, 30(7):993-999.

ROJANAPITAYAKORN P, et al, 2005. Optically Transparent Self-Reinforced Poly(Ethylene Terephthalate) Composites: Molecular Orientation and Mechanical Properties[J]. Polymer, 46:761-773.

SATAPATHY S, et al, 2009. Mechanical Properties and Fracture Behavior of Short PET Fiber-Waste Polyethylene Composites[J]. Journal of Reinforced Plastics and Composites, 27(9):967-984.

TORRES N, 2000. Study of Thermal and Mechanical Properties of Virgin and Recycled Poly (Ethylene Terephthalate) Before and After Injection Molding[J]. European Polymer Journal, 36(10):2075-2080.

TOSHIFUMI I, et al, 2005. Mechanical Properties of Poly(ethylene terephthalate) Fiber Drawn with CO_2 Laser Heating[J]. Fiber, 58(1):16-21.

VIANA J C, et al, 2004. Morphology and Mechanical Properties of Injection Molded Poly (Ethylene Terephthalate)[J]. Polymer Engineering and Science, 44(12):2174-2184.

XIAO HONG, et al, 2011. The Structures and Properties of PET (Polyethylene Terephthalate)/PTT (Polytrimethylene Terephthalate) Self-Crimp Filament at Different Temperatures[J]. Advanced Materials Research, 332/334:239-245.

Table 45.1   Mechanical Properties of PET（Polyethylene Terephthalate）and Related Composites

Material-DAM	$T/°C$	E_T	ρ	υ	(σ, ε)	α	k	γ	β	K_{IC}
PET	23	2.95	1.37	0.4	(62, 50%)	70	0.27	1275	—	—
	73(T_g)	—	—	—	—	—	—	—	—	—
	256(T_m)	—	—	—	—	—	—	—	—	—
	−40	—	—	—	(156, 1.2%) (218, 2%)	32/70	0.28	—	—	—
PET/30GF	23	10	—	—	(129, 1.6%) (158, 2.7%)	27/70	—	—	—	—
	93	—	—	—	(54, 1.6%) (83, 5.9%)	22/70	—	—	—	—
	150	—	—	—	(38, 1.6%) (56, 6.5%)	22/70	—	—	—	—
	−40	—	—	—	(177, 1%) (242, 1.7%)	24/70	—	—	—	—
PET/45GF	23	12.7	—	—	$\sigma_{ucs}=-191$; (137, 1%) (193, 2.1%)	24/70	—	—	—	—
	93	—	—	—	(50, 1%) (92, 4.5%)	16/70	—	—	—	—
	150	—	—	—	(33, 1%) (67, 6.0%)	16/70	—	—	—	—
PET/55GF	−40	—	—	—	(221, 1.3%)	14/70	—	—	—	—
	23	—	—	—	(196, 1.6%)	14/70	—	—	—	—
	93	—	—	—	(96, 4.0%)	7/70	—	—	—	—
	150	—	—	—	(71, 4.5%)	7/70	—	—	—	—

Table 45.2   Fatigue ε-N Properties of PET（Polyethylene Terephthalate）and Related Composites

Material	$T/°C$	$d\varepsilon/dt$	σ'_{f-}	ε'_{f-}	b	c	K'	n'	$\sigma_f@2N_f$	R
PET/45GF	23	—		—	—	—	—	—	40@ 10^4	0.1^+
									48@ $2×10^3$	0.1^+
									53@ 10^3	0.1^+

continued

Material	$T/℃$	$dε/dt$	$σ'_{f-}$	$ε'_{f-}$	b	c	K'	n'	$σ_f @ 2N_f$	R
PET/45GF	23	—		—	—	—	—	—	47@ $2×10^4$	0.1^-
									48@ 10^4	0.1^-
									53@ 10^3	0.1^-

Notes: 0.1^+ = Stress ratio $R = 0.1$ and both high and low stress levels are positive;

0.1^- = Stress ratio $R = 0.1$ with positive high stress and negative low stress.

Chapter 46

PFA (Perfluoroalkoxy)

46.1   Introduction

PFA (**Per**fluoro**a**lkoxy) is a type of fluoropolymer. Although PFA bears similar mechanical and electric properties to PTFE (polytetrafluoroethylene), its dielectric strength is almost four times higher. Furthermore, PFA resin is melt-processable using conventional injection molding and screw extrusion. PFA is also one of the few plastics, similar to PTFE and FEP, which is suitable for both high and low-temperature applications and can be used over a wide temperature domain ranging from -268 ℃ to 260 ℃. Mechanical properties of PFA are listed in Table 46.1. In many ways, PFA is similar to FEP but generally has better mechanical properties at higher temperatures.

46.2   Applications

PFA (Perfluoroalkoxy), along with FEP, are routinely used for plastic labware and tubing that involves critical or highly corrosive processes due to its flexibility, extreme resistance to chemical attack and optical transparency. Thus, wire and cable insulation for computers and electronics systems in a harsh environment, as well as insulating bushings, is a major application.

Reference

PTFE, FEP, PFA. Specifications, Boedeker Corp., 2007.

Table 46.1   Mechanical Properties o PFA (Perfluoroalkoxy) and Related Composites

Material-DAM	$T/℃$	E_T	ρ	υ	(σ, ε)	α	k	γ	β	K_{IC}
PFA	-95 (Low service temperature)									
	23	0.48	2.15	0.45	(5.5, 1%) (21, 300%)	150	195	1172	—	—
	100	—	—	—	—	160	—	—	—	—
	250	—	—	—	—	250	—	—	—	—
	260 (High service temperature)									
	305 (T_m)	—	—	—	—	—	—	—	—	—

Chapter 47

PK (Polyketones)-PEK, PEEK, and PEKK

47.1   Introduction

The polar ketone groups in the polymer backbone of PK (**Poly**ketones) give rise to a strong attraction between polymer chains. Polyketones are stronger and more rigid than most other engineering plastics. They are tough and impact-resistant over a wide range of temperatures. Polyketones have very high fatigue strength. Both coefficients of friction and coefficient of wear for polyketones are relatively low.

The modulus of polyketones remains almost constant until the temperature is close to the T_g. T_g (Glass transition temperatures) and T_m (Melting temperatures) for polyketones depend on the ratio of ketone to ether groups. With increasing ether groups, both temperatures decrease. Polyketones have comparatively low thermal coefficients of linear expansion and excellent resistance to burning, and very low flame spread. These materials have good dielectric properties, with high volume and surface resistivities, and high dielectric strength. Common solvents do not attack polyketones even at elevated temperatures. They have very good resistance to hydrolysis, even in hot water.

Commercially available polyketones are PAEK (Polyaryletherketones)/PEK (Polyetherketone), Polyetherketoneketones (PEEK), and Polyetherketoneketones (PEKK). Polyketones can be extruded to form sheets, cast-film, stock for machining, and wire coatings. Mechanical properties of them are presented in Tables 47.1~47.4.

Cross-linked PK-furan, which is a thermoset plastic, is thermally healable or called remendable. When exposed to heat, the polymers display the relevant properties of linear thermoplastics, such as remeltability, reprocessability, and recyclability because of the opening of the DA adduct. After slowly cooling to room temperature for 30 to 40 minutes, a rigid structural polymer network can be achieved because of the regeneration of the DA adduct. In this process, polymer chains are able to reorganize and therefore reconstruct or remodel themselves into any desired physical shape.

47.2   PAEK or PEK (Polyaryletherketones)

PAEK or PEK (**Poly** **a**ryl **e**ther **k**etones) has repeating ether and ketone groups combined by phenyl rings.

47.3 PEEK (Polyetherketoneketones)

PEEK (**P**oly**e**ther**k**etoneketones) has repeating monomers of two ether groups and a ketone group. It is a semi-crystalline material and its material properties depend on the degree of crystallinity.

Typical material properties of PEEK with 35% crystallinity are given in Table 47.1 and fatigue properties in Table 47.2. It has good mechanical strength, including tensile strength (especially when reinforced by glass or carbon fibers), impact resistance, and low wear rate (especially when lubricated by PTFE), over a wide range of temperatures.

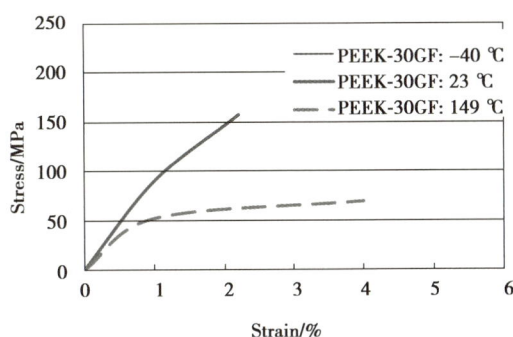

Fig. 47.1 Stress-strain Curves of PEEK/30GF Composite at Different Temperatures

One advantage of PEEK reinforced with glass fibers is its impact resistance, as compared with PAI and PPS. Representative stress-strain curves of PEEK/GF30 (randomly reinforced with 30% short-fiber glass by weight) are also given in Fig. 47.1. The orthotropic material properties and related strengths are given in Table 47.3 and Table 47.4, respectively.

47.4 PEKK (Polyetherketoneketones)

PEKK (**P**oly **e**ther **k**etone **k**etones) has repeating monomers of one ether group and two ketone groups. PEKK, unfilled or reinforced with glass or carbon fibers, displays superior chemical resistance, excellent thermal stability, and outstanding mechanical properties.

47.5 Applications

PEEK reinforced with carbon fibers is used for piston components and bearing linings. Electric connectors or cable couplings made of fiber-reinforced PEEK are suitable for high-temperature applications.

References

BRILLHART M, BOTSIS J. 1944.Fatigue Crack Growth Analysis in PEEK[J]. Fatigue, 16:134-140.

CHU X X, et al, 2010. Mechanical and Thermal Expansion Properties of Glass Fibers-reinforced PEEK Composites at Cryogenic Temperatures[J]. Cryogenics, 50(2):84-88.

COMYN J, et al, 1996. Corona-Discharge Treatment of Polyethertherketone for Adhesive Bonding[J]. Journal of Adhesion and Adhesives, 16(4):301-304.

CRICK R A, et al, 2005. Interlaminar Fracture Morphology of Carbon/PEEK Composites [J]. Journal of Material Science, 22(6):2094-2104.

DAVIM J P, CARDOSO R, 2005. Thermo-mechanical Model to Predict the Tribological Behavior of the Composite PEEK-CF30/Steel Pair in Dry Sliding Using Multiple Regression Analysis [J]. Industrial Lubrication Tribology, 57(5):181-186.

EDULJEE R F, et al, 2004. On the Application of Micromechanics to the Prediction of Macroscopic Thermal Residual Stress in Short-fiber Reinforced Poly ether ether ketone[J]. Polymer Engineering and Science, 31 (17):1257-1263.

HAMDAN S, SWALLOWE G M, 1996. The Strain-Rate and Temperature Dependence of the Mechanical Properties of Polyetherketone and Polyetherether ketone[J]. Journal of Materials Science, 31:1415-1423.

HSIAO B S, et al, 1991. Isothermal Crystallization Kinetics of Poly(ether ketone) and its Carbon-fiber-reinforced Composites[J]. Polymer, 32(15):2799-2805.

HSU S Y, et al, 1999. Inelastic Behavior of an AS4/PEEK Composite under Combined Transverse Compression and Shear, Part III: Modeling[J]. International Journal of Plasticity, 15:807-836.

HUANG R Y M, et al, 2001. Pervaporation Separation of Water/Isopropanol Mixture Using Sulfonated Poly (ether ether ketone) (SPEEK) Membranes: Transport Mechanism and Separation Performance[J]. Journal of Membrane Science, 192 (1-2):115-127.

KURTZ S M, DEVINE J N, 2007. PEEK Biomaterials in Trauma, Orthopedic, and Spinal Implants [J]. Biomaterials, 28(32):4835-4869.

MELO J, RADFORD D W, 2005. Viscoelastic Properties of PEEK-IM7 Related to Temperature[J]. Journal of Reinforced Plastics and Composites, 24(5):545-556.

NAGHIPOUR P, et al, 2010. Effect of Fiber Angle Orientation and Stacking Sequence on Mixed Mode Fracture Toughness of Carbon Fiber Reinforced Plastics: Numerical and Experimental Investigations[J]. Materials Science and Engineering, A, 527(3):509-517.

OKAWA, TOMOHIRO, et al, 2006. Polymerization of Polyetherketone and the Possibility for Self-repairing

Materials[J]. Japanese Journal of Polymer Science and Technology, 63(11):759-765.

PHILLIPS R, GLAUSER T, MÅNSON J A E, 1997. Thermal Stability of PEEK/Carbon Fiber in Air and its Influence on Consolidation[J]. Polymer Composites, 18(4):500-508.

PRATTE J F, BAI J M, LEACH D, 2002. Poly (Ether Ketone Ketone) Matrix Composites[J]. SAMPE 2002, Baltimore, MD, USA, 34:949-958.

RASHEVA Z, ZHANG G, BURKHART T, 2010. A Correlation between the Tribological and Mechanical Properties of Short Carbon Fibers Reinforced PEEK Materials with Different Fiber Orientations[J]. Tribology International, 43(8):1430-1437.

SALEEM A, FRORMANN L, IQBAL A, 2007. High Performance Thermoplastic Composites: Study on the Mechanical, Thermal, and Electrical Resistivity Properties of Carbon Fiber-Reinforced Polyetheretherketone and Polyethersulphone[J]. Polymer Composites, 28:785-796.

SGRECCIA E, et al, 2009. Self-Assembled Nanocomposite Organic-Inorganic Proton Conducting Sulfonated Poly-Ether-Ether-Ketone (SPEEK)-Based Membranes: Optimized Mechanical, Thermal and Electrical Properties[J]. Journal of Power Sources, 192:353-359.

SWIER S, et al, 2005. Sulfonated Poly(ether ketone ketone) Ionomers as Proton Exchange Membranes[J]. Polymer Engineering and Science, 45(8):1081-1091.

TANG S, et al, 2004. Tension Fatigue Behavior of Hydroxyapatite Reinforced Polyetheretherketone Composites [J]. International Journal of Fatigue, 26:49-57.

TOTH J, WANG M, ESTES B, et al, 2006. Polyetheretherketone as a Biomaterial for Spinal Applications[J]. Biomaterials, 27:324.

VASCONCELOS G, et al, 2010. Evaluation of Crystallization Kinetics of Poly (ether-ketone-ketone) and Poly (ether-ether-ketone) by DSC[J]. Journal of Aerospace Technology Management, 2(2):155-162.

VENTURA G, et al, 1999. Thermal Conductivity of PEEK at Low Temperatures[J]. Cryogenics, 39:481.

WANG W, et al, 1997. Dynamic Study of Crystallization-and Melting-Induced Phase Separation in PEEK/PEKK Blends[J]. Macromolecules, 30(16):4544-4550.

ZHANG, et al, 2009. Thermally Self-Healing Polymeric Materials: The Next Step to Recycling Thermoset Polymers? [J]. Macromolecules, 42(6):1906-1912.

Table 47.1 Mechanical Properties of PK (Polyketones)-PEK, PEEK, PEKK, and Their

Material-DAM	T/℃	E_T	ρ	v	(σ,ε)	α	k	γ	β	K_{IC}
PK	23	1.59	1.24	—	(55, 350%)	110	0.27	1800	—	—
	15(T_g)	—	—	—	—	—	—	—	—	—
	220(T_m)	—	—	—	—	—	—	—	—	—

continued

Material-DAM	$T/℃$	E_T	ρ	υ	(σ,ε)	α	k	γ	β	K_{IC}
PK (Furan; Thermally Healable)	23	4.0	—	—	$\sigma_{uts}=70$	—	—	—	—	—
PAEK	23	—	—	—	—	—	—	—	—	—
	$190(T_g)$	—	—	—	—	—	—	—	—	—
	$380(T_m)$	—	—	—	—	—	—	—	—	—
PEEK	23	3.7	1.31	0.38	$\sigma_{ucs}=-120$; (50, 2%) (75,4%) (90, 6%) (95, 37%)	47	0.25	2160	—	7.5
	$143(T_g)$	—	—	—	—	—	—	—	—	—
	150	—	—	—	$\sigma_{uts}=48$	—	—	—	—	—
	250	—	—	—	$\sigma_{uts}=17$	—	—	—	—	—
	$343(T_m)$	—	—	—	—	—	—	—	—	—
PEEK/30GF	23	10	1.5	0.45	$\sigma_{ucs}=-215$; (90, 1%) (157, 2.7%)	22	0.43	1710	—	—
	149	—	—	—	(52, 1%) (69, 4%)	—	—	—	—	—
PEEK/40GF	23	14.7	1.58	—	(196, 1.8%)	—	—	—	—	—
	−65 (Brittleness temperature)									
PEEK/30CF	23	22.3	1.41	0.44	$\sigma_{ucs}=-300$; (215, 1.6%)	14	0.92	1850	—	—
	$143(T_g)$	—	—	—	—	18	—	—	—	—
	250 (High service temperature)					30	—	—	—	—
PEEK/40CF	23	35.0	1.46	—	(273, 1.0%)	—				
PEEK/30PTFE	23	2.76	1.5	—	(52, 3.8%)	—				
PEEK/8 μm Al$_2$O$_3$(8 μm; $V_f=43\%$)	23	—	—	—	—	22	—	—	—	—

continued

Material-DAM	$T/°C$	E_T	ρ	υ	(σ,ε)	α	k	γ	β	K_{IC}
PEEK/39 nm Al_2O_3(V_f=12%)	23	—	—	—	—	23	—	—	—	—
PEKK	23	—	—	—	—	—	—	—	—	—
	156(T_g)	—	—	—	—	—	—	—	—	—
	306(T_m)	—	—	—	—	—	—	—	—	—

Notes: DAM = Dry as Molded;

GF (CF) = Reinforced with glass (carbon) fibers, by weight unless V_f is given;

T_g(°C) & T_m(°C) = Glass transition point and melting point, respectively;

PTFE & Al_2O_3 = Reinforcements by weight;

V_f = Volume fraction.

Table 47.2   Fatigue ε-N Properties of PK (Polyketones-PEK, PEEK, and PEKK) and Related Composites

Material	$T/°C$	$d\varepsilon/dt$	σ'_{f-}	ε'_{f-}	b	c	K'	n'	$\sigma_f@2N_f$	R
PEEK/30GF	23	—	—	—	—	—	—	—	50	—

Table 47.3   Mechanical Properties of PEEK Reinforced by Straight Continuous Fibers

Material-DAM	$T/°C$	ρ	E_{11}	E_{22}	E_{33}	G_{12}	G_{13}	G_{23}	υ_{12}	υ_{13}	υ_{23}
PEEK/60%CF (PEEK/AS4; V_f=60%)	23	—	128	10.3	—	6	3.45	—	0.32	—	—
PEEK/67CF (PEEK/AS4; W_f=67% or V_f=41%)	23	1.6	141	9.0	—	8.3	—	—	0.33	—	—

Table 47.4   Orthotropic Mechanical Strength of Unidirectional Fiber-Reinforced PEEK Composites

Material	$T/°C$	$\sigma_{11u},\varepsilon_{11u}$	$\sigma_{22u},\varepsilon_{22u}$	$\sigma_{33u},\varepsilon_{33u}$	$(\sigma_{12u},\varepsilon_{12u})/(\sigma_{23u},\varepsilon_{23u})/(\sigma_{13u},\varepsilon_{13u})$
PEEK/60%CF (V_f=60%)	23	σ_{11t}=2070	σ_{22t}=155	σ_{33t}=155	σ_{12u}=206/—/—
		σ_{11c}=-1360	σ_{22c}=-196	σ_{33c}=-196	—
PEEK/67%CF (V_f=67%)	23	σ_{11t}=2370	σ_{22t}=66	—	σ_{12u}=87/—/—
		σ_{11c}=-1100	—	—	—

Chapter 48

PMMA (Polymethylmethacrylate; Acrylics)

48.1 Introduction

PMMA (**P**oly**m**ethyl**m**eth**a**crylate) is the synthetic polymer of methyl methacrylate as named explicitly. As being famous for its transparency, PMMA (Polymethylmethacrylate) competes with glass for optical applications especially as a light shatter-resistant alternative to glass. Thus, it is sometimes called acrylic glass. PMMA is a strong and lightweight material with a density less than half that of glass and an impact strength higher than glass. Acrylic glass made of PMMA has good thermal stability, and insulation properties, low water absorption, and excellent weather resistance, while it is easy to polish. Disadvantages of acrylic glass are low chemical resistance and low impact fracture toughness (i.e. being brittle). Representative stress-strain curves of PMMA (Polymethylmethacrylate) are plotted in Fig. 48.1. Mechanical, fatigue, and creep properties of PMMA, and PMMA-based composites are listed in Tables 48.1—48.3, respectively.

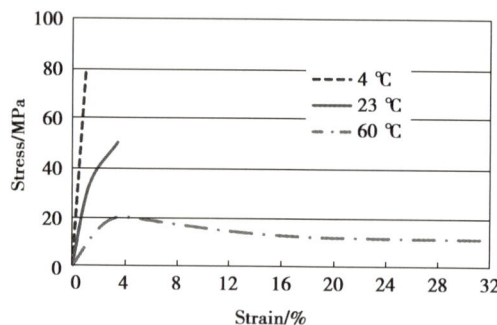

Fig. 48.1   Representative Stress-Strain Curves of PMMA (Polymethylmethacrylate) at Different Temperatures

PMMA (Polymethylmethacrylate) compounds containing relatively low loadings (under 6% by weight) of nano-meterized mineral particles show their competitive strength. The insulation and compressive mechanical properties of PMMA/CNT composite foams were found to improve those of neat PMMA foam substantially. In particular, 22.6% decrease in thermal conductivity, 19.7% decrease in dielectric constant and 160% increase in compressive modulus were observed with PMMA/0.3c-MWNT, i.e. PMMA reinforced with 0.3% of carboxyl-multi walled carbon nanotubes (c-MWNTs) by weight [Yeh et al.].

PMMA/1BNNT composite, i.e. PMMA reinforced with 1% of Boron nitride nanotubes (BNNTs) by weight, the elastic modulus of PMMA increases by 19%, and its thermal stability and glass transition temperature of PMMA are also positively affected. More importantly, the thermal conductivity of PMMA/1BNNT is three times as of PMMA's [Zhi et al.].

48.2   Applications

Major automotive applications of Polymethylmethacrylate (PMMA), under different trade names (Plexiglass, Perpex, or Lucite), are light lenses, shaped glazing, signs, and aircraft windows.

Composites of multi-walled carbon nanotubes (MWCNT) of various functionality (unconstrained and carboxyl and amine functionalized) with polymethyl methacrylate (PMMA) are used as bone cement.

Polymethyl methacrylate (PMMA) is one of the most widely used materials in prosthetic dentistry. The incorporation of zirconia in various dental materials is biocompatible, and it improves mechanical properties [Yoshida et al.].

References

AGRAWAL S, et al, 2011. Investigation of Temperature-Dependent Mechanical Properties of CdS/PMMA Nanocomposites[J]. Journal of Composite Materials, 45(24):2507-2514.

AJAXON I, PERSSON C, 2014. Compressive Fatigue Properties of Acrylic Bone Cement for Vertebroplasty[J]. European Cells and Materials, 28(S1):47.

ANTUNES F V, et al, 2002. Fatigue Life Predictions in Polymer Particle Composites[J]. International Journal of Fatigue, 24:1095-1105.

ALHAREB1 A O, AHMAD1 Z A, 2011. Effect of Al_2O_3/ZrO_2 Reinforcement on the Mechanical Properties of PMMA Denture Base[J]. Journal of Reinforced Plastics and Composites, 30(1):86-93.

ASH B, et al, 2002. Mechanical Properties of Al_2O_3/Polymethylmethacrylate Nanocomposites[J]. Polymer Composites, 23(6):1014-1025.

BALDACCHINI T, et al, 2004. Acrylic-based Resin with Favorable Properties for Three-dimensional Two-photon Polymerization[J]. Journal of Applied Physics, 95(11):6072-6076.

BUREK M, GREER J, 2009. Fabrication and Microstructure Control of Nanoscale Mechanical Testing Specimens via Electron Beam Lithography and Electroplating[J]. Nano Letters, 10(1):69-76.

CHEN FENG, et al, 2011. Mechanical and Thermal Properties of Attapulgite Clay Reinforced Polymethylmethacrylate Nanocomposites[J]. Polymers for Advanced Technologies, 22(12):1912-1918.

JIA Z, et al, 1999. Study on Poly(MethylMethacrylate)/Carbon Nanotube Composites[J]. Materials Science and Engineering, A, 271(1-2):395-400.

JIN Z, PRAMODA K, XU G, et al, 2001. Dynamic Mechanical Behavior of Melt-Processed Multi-Walled Carbon Nanotube/Poly(Methyl Methacrylate) Composites[J]. Chemical Physics Letters, 337(1-3):43-47.

KANE R J, et al, 2010. Improved Fatigue Life of Acrylic Bone Cements Reinforced with Zirconia Fibers[J]. Journal of the Mechanical Behavior of Biomedical Materials, 3:504-511.

KAUFMANN T, et al, 2002. Cardiovascular Effects of Polymethylmethacrylate Use in Percutaneous Vertebroplasty[J]. American Journal of Neuroradiology, 23(4):601-604.

KIM H, COLTON J S, 2005. Fabrication and Analysis of Plastic Hypodermic Needles[J]. Journal of Medical Engineering and Technology, 29(4):181-186.

LU H, et al, 1997. Uniaxial, Shear, and Poisson relaxation and Their Conversion to Bulk Relaxation: Studies on Poly(methyl methacrylate)[J]. Polymer Engineering and Science, 18(2):211-222.

MARIANI P, et al, 1996. Viscoelasticity of Rubber-Toughened PolyMethylmethacrrylate, Part I: Deformational Behavior[J]. Polymer Science and Engineering, 36(22):2750-2757.

MARIANI P, et al, 1996. Viscoelasticity of Rubber-Toughened PolyMethylmethacrylate, Part II: Fracture Behavior[J]. Polymer Science and Engineering, 36(22):2758-2764.

MARSHALL G P, WILLIAMS J G, 1973. The Correlation of Fracture data for PMMA[J]. Journal of Material Science, 8(1):138-140.

MAUZAC O, SCHIRRER R, 1989. Effect of Particle Volume Fraction on Crack-tip Crazes in High Impact Poly (methylmethacylate)[J]. Applied Polymer Science, 38(12):2289-2302.

ORMSBY R, et al, 2012. Fatigue and Biocompatibility Properties of a Poly(Methyl Methacrylate) Bone Cement with Multi-Walled Carbon Nanotubes[J]. Acta Biomater., 8(3):1201-1212.

PALM G, et al, 2006. Large Strain mechanical Behavior of PMMA near the Glass Transition Temperature[J]. Journal of Engineering Materials and Technology, 128(4):559-563.

PANYAYONG W, et al, 2002. Reinforcement of Acrylic Reins for Provisional Fixed Restoration. Part III: Effects of Addition of Titania and Zirconia Mixtures on Some Mechanical and Physical Properties[J]. Biomedical Materials and Engineering, 12(4):353-366.

SAHA N, et al, 2000. Tensile Behavior of Unidirectional Polyethylene Fibers PMMA and Glass Fibers-PMMA Composite Laminates[J]. Journal of Applied Polymer Science, 76(1):1489-1493.

SCHIRRER R, FOND C, LOBBRECHT A, 1996. Volume Change and Light Scattering during Mechanical Damage in Poly(methylmethacrylate) Toughened with Core Sell Rubber Particles[J]. Journal of Material Science, 31:6409-6422

SHIU P, OSTOJIC M, KNOPF G, et al, 2008. Rapid Fabrication of Polymethylmethacrylate Micro mold Masters using a Hot Intrusion Process[J]. Journal of Micro/Nanolithography, MEMS, and MOEMS, 7(4):043012.

STÉPHAN C, et al, 2000. Characterization of Single-walled Carbon Nanotubes-PMMA Composites [J]. Synthetic Metals, 108(2):139-149.

WANDRACZEK K, et al, 2004. Effect of Thermal Degradation on Glass Transition Temperature of PMMA[J]. Macromolecular Chemistry and Physics, 205(14):1858-1862.

WEON J, et al, 2010. Mechanical Behavior of Polymethylmethacrylate with Molecules Oriented via Simple Shear[J]. Polymer Engineering and Science, 45(3):314-324.

YAMAHADA C, et al, 2005. A PMMA Valveless Micropump Using Electromagnetic Actuation[J]. Microfluid Nanofluid, 1:197-207.

YEH J, et al, 2011. Enhancement in Insulation and Mechanical Properties of PMMA Nanocomposite Foams Infused with Multi-Walled Carbon Nanotubes[J]. Journal of Nanoscience and Nanotechnology, 11(8):6757-6764.

YOSHIDA K, GREENER E H, 1944. Effects of Coupling Agents on Mechanical Properties of Metal Oxide Polymethacrylate Composites[J]. Journal of Dent., 22(1):57-62.

ZHI C, et al, 2008. Mechanical and Thermal Properties of Polymethyl Methacrylate-BN Nanotube Composites [J]. Journal of Nanomaterials, 2008(1):145-152.

Table 48.1   Mechanical Properties of PMMA (Polymethylmethacrylate; Acrylics) and Related Composites

Material-DAM	$T/^{\circ}C$	E_T	ρ	υ	(σ, ε)	α	k	γ	β	K_{IC}
PMMA	−40	—	—	—	—	40	—	—	—	—
	4	—	—	—	(40, 0.5%) (80, 1%)	—	—	—	—	—
	23	2	1.17	0.37	(33, 1.3%) (50, 3.5%)	66	0.18	1466	—	1.6
	60	—	—	—	(15, 2%) (20, 4%) (12, 20%) (10, 130%)	85	—	—	—	—
	106(T_g)	—	—	—	—	—	—	—	—	—
	160(T_m)	—	—	—	—	—	—	—	—	—
	200(Boiling temperature)				—	—	0.21	2300	—	—
PMMA/5Al$_2$O$_3$ (Bone Cement, W_f=5%)	23	1.7	—	—	$\sigma_{uts}=42.7$; $\sigma_R=88.4$	—	—	—	—	1.98
PMMA-ATH (PMMA/48% Al$_2$O$_3$; V_f= 48%; Trihydrate)	23	—	—	—	(−63, −0.8%) (−25, −0.25%) (25, 0.25%) (46, 0.85%)	—	—	—	—	—
	90	—	—	—	(5, 0.2%) (13, 0.5%) (16, 1.2%) (15, 3%)	—	—	—	—	—

continued

Material-DAM	$T/℃$	E_T	ρ	υ	(σ,ε)	α	k	γ	β	K_{IC}
PMMA/3MWNT (Bone Cement)	23	1.92	—	—	—	—	—	—	—	—
	$160(T_m)$	—	—	—	—	—	—	—	—	
PMMA/1BNNT	23	2.47	—	—	$(54.5,\ 4\%)$	—	—	—	—	—
PMMA/5BNNT	23	2.47	—	—	—	—	0.35	—	—	—
PMMA/10BNNT	23	2.47	—	—	—	—	0.5	—	—	—
PMMA/SiO$_2$ (V_f=44%)	23	1.69	8.9	0.24	$\sigma_{uts}=65$	—	—	—	—	4.8
PMMA/SiO$_2$ (V_f=48%)	23	1.74	8.1	0.26	$\sigma_{uts}=38$	—	—	—	—	7.7
PMMA/SiO$_2$ (V_f=64%)	23	1.92	13.4	0.22	$\sigma_{uts}=22$	—	—	—	—	6
PMMA/5ZrO$_2$ (Bone Cement, W_f=5%)	23	1.72	—	—	$\sigma_R=48.7$; $\sigma_R=102$	—	—	—	—	2.06

Notes: DAM = Dry as Molded;

   GF (CF) = Reinforced with glass (carbon) fibers, by weight unless V_f is given;

   $T_g(℃)$ & $T_m(℃)$ = Glass transition point and melting point, respectively;

   BNNT, MWNT, Al$_2$O$_3$, SiO$_2$, TiO$_2$, & ZrO$_2$ = Reinforcements, by weight.

Table 48.2   Fatigue ε-N Properties of PMMA (Polymethylmethacrylate) and Related Composites

Material	$T/℃$	$d\varepsilon/dt$	σ'_{f-}	ε'_{f-}	b	c	K'	n'	$\sigma_f@2N_f$	R
PMMA	23	—	—	—	—	—	—	—	10	—
PMMA/45ZrO$_2$ (Bone Cement)	23	2 Hz	—	—	—	—	—	—	50@ 10^6	∞
									55@ 10^4	∞
									78@ 10^2	∞
									& 86@ 10	∞
	23	10 Hz	—	—	—	—	—	—	40@ 10^6	∞
									45@ 10^4	∞
									74@ 10^2	∞
									86@ 10	∞

Notes: ∞ = Stress ratio $R=∞$ with positive high stress and zero low stress.

Table 48.3　Thermomechanical Creep Parameters of PMMA

Material	$T/℃$	Stress/MPa	Strain Rate/s^{-1}	$A/(\text{MPa}^{-n} \cdot \text{s}^{m-1})$	$Q/(\text{J} \cdot \text{mol}^{-1})$	n	m
PMMA	—	$E=1$	—	—	—	—	—

Notes: Creep equation $= \dfrac{\text{d}\varepsilon_{\text{creep}}}{\text{d}t} = A\left(\dfrac{\sigma - \sigma_{\text{th}}}{E}\right)^{n} t^{m} \exp\left(\dfrac{-Q}{RT_{\text{k}}}\right)$, $\sigma > \sigma_{\text{th}}$;

$\sigma_{\text{th}} =$ Stress threshold and $\sigma_{\text{th}} = 0$, if not specified;

$E =$ Young's modulus; If given that $E = 1$, it means E is not specified.

Chapter 49

POM (Polyoxymethylene; Acetal)

49.1　Introduction

POM (**P**oly**oxym**ethylene) , also known as acetal or polyacetal , is notable for having a low coefficient of friction , excellent wear resistance , high modulus of elasticity and strength , good impact strength , high flexural fatigue , good creep performance , and resistance to many solvents and automotive fuels. Its low moisture absorption results in excellent dimensional stability and makes POM an excellent candidate for parts that must exhibit tight tolerances in moist environments. Mechanical properties of POM (Polyoxymethylene) are given in Table 49.1 and fatigue properties in Table 49.2. Stress-strain curves at different temperatures , as shown in Fig. 49.1. POM (Polyoxymethylene) is machinable.

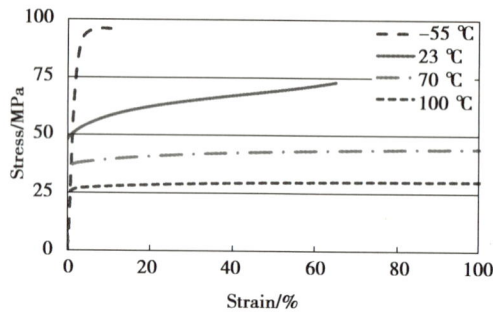

Fig. 49.1　Stress-Strain Curves of POM (Polyoxymethylene) at Different Temperatures

Homopolymers , POM (Polyoxymethylene) modified with formaldehyde , has better resistance to UV light and generally to acids and alkalis than pure POM (Polyoxymethylene) . The homopolymer is also more suitable for continuous use with hot water.

POM (Polyoxymethylene) can be chemically lubricated or filled with Teflon (PTFE) to create low friction material. An interesting application of acetal is rotating shafts and gears. Worms in nylon against gears in acetal have been a typical gear-ratio-reduction application for rotary (adjunct) actuators for automotive doors. Delrin 500AF , lubricated by Teflon (TPFE) , offers the lowest wear and coefficient of friction values among DuPont's acetal products. Representative stress-strain curves of some POM-based composites are presented in Fig. 49.2.

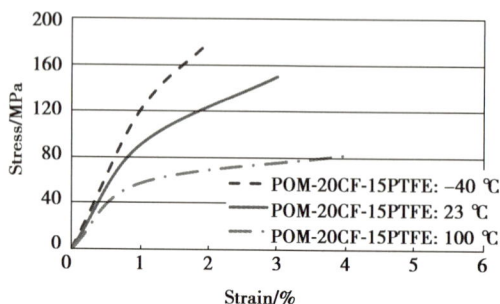

Fig. 49.2　Stress-Strain Curves of POM/20CF/15PTFE Composite (Reinforced with Short Glass Fibers and PTFE Particulates Randomly) at Different Temperatures

49.2   Applications

Its reasonable melting point (165 ℃) and low moisture absorption make it a good candidate for mechanical and structural components such as plastic bearings and gears. The material of plastic gear depends on the fatigue strength, impact ductility, and the material of its mating worm. Some compatible mating options for gearing applications are given in Table 49.3.

Other applications of POM and its composites are in fuel pumps and other fuel system components, control cables, windshield wipers, heater/air conditioner control systems, interior door handles, and seat belts.

References

BREEDS A R, et al, 1993. Wear Behavior of Acetal Gear Pairs[J]. Wear, 166:85-91.

GAO X, et al, 2004. Brittle-Ductile Transition and Toughening Mechanism in POM/TPU/CaCO$_3$ Ternary Composites[J]. Macromolecular Materials and Engineering, 289(1):41-48.

HUANG C, TSENG C, 2000. The Effect of Interface Modification between POM and PTFE on the Properties of POM/TPFE Composites[J]. Journal of Applied Polymer Science, 78(4):800-807.

JOSE A, ALAGAR M, 2011. Development and Characterization of Organoclay-Filled Polyoxymethylene Nanocomposites for High Performance Applications[J]. Polymer Composites, 32(9):1315-1324.

KUROKAWA A, et al, 2003. Tribological Properties of Polyoxymethylene Composites against Aluminum[J]. Journal of Tribology, 125(3):661-669.

LU J, et al, 2008. High-elongation Fiber Mats by Electrospinning of Polyoxymethylene[J]. Macromolecules, 41 (11):3762-3764.

MAO K, HOOKE C J, WALTON D, 1996. The Wear Behavior of Polymer Composite Gears[J]. Synthetic Lubrication, 12:337-342.

MOHANRAJ J, et al, 2006. The Effect of Strain Rate on the Die-drawing of Polyoxymethylene at Elevated Temperatures[J]. Journal de Physique IV, 134:1231-1237.

UTHAMAN R, et al, 2007. Mechanical, Thermal, and Morphological Characteristics of Compatibilized and Dynamically Vulcanized Polyoxymethylene/Ethylene Propylene Diene Terpolymer Blends [J]. Polymer Engineering and Science, 47(6):934-942.

NOVACO R, 2011. Determination of Molding Parameter Effects on the Physical Properties of a Carbon Powder Filled, Impact Modified Acetal Copolymer[J]. SAE 2011-01-0250.

PENICK K, et al, 2005. Performance of Plastic (POM) as a Component of a Tissue Engineering Bioreactor [J]. Journal of Biomedical Materials Research, (7591):168-174.

POSTAWA P, et al, 2008. Influence of the Method of Heating/Cooling Moulds on the Properties of Injection Molding Parts[J]. Archives of Materials Science and Engineering, 31(2):121-124.

SUN L, et al, 2008. Mechanical and Tribological Properties of Polyoxymethylene Modified with Nanoparticles and Solid Lubricants[J]. Polymer Engineering and Science, 48(9):1824-1832.

SUN T, et al, 2008. A New and Highly Efficient Formaldehyde Absorbent of Polyoxymethylene[J]. Polymers for Advanced Technologies, 19(9):1286-1295.

TIAN Y Q, et al, 2012. The Mechanical and Tribological Properties of Carbon Fiber Reinforced POM Composites[J]. Applied Mechanics and Materials, 182/183:135-138.

TSAI M H, TSAI Y C, 1999. A Method for Calculating Static Transmission Errors of Plastic Spur gears Using FEM Evaluation[J]. Finite Elements in Analysis and Design, 27(4):345-357.

WALTON D, et al, 2002. The Efficiency and Friction of Plastic Cylindrical Gears Part 2: Influence of Tooth Geometry [J]. Journal of Engineering Tribology, Proceedings of the Institution of Mechanical Engineers, 216(2):93-104.

YAMAGUCHI Y, et al, 2004. The Limiting Pressure-velocity (PV) of Plastics under Lubricated Sliding[J]. Polymer Science and Engineering, 22(4):248-253.

YELLE H, BURNS D J, 1981. Calculation of Contact Ratios for Plastic/Plastic and Plastic/Steel Spur Gear Pairs[J]. Journal of Mechanical Design, 103:528-542.

VAN MELICK H, 2007. Tooth-Bending Effects in Plastic Spur Gears[J]. Gear Technology, 24(7):58-66.

Table 49.1 Mechanical Properties of POM (Acetal) and Related Composites

Material-DAM	$T/^\circ C$	E_T	ρ	υ	(σ, ε)	α	k	γ	β	K_{IC}
POM (Medium Flow)	-55	—	—	—	$(90, 3\%)$ $(96, 13\%)$	82	—	—	—	49
	23	3	1.41	0.35	$\sigma_{ucs} = -125$; $(53, 3\%)$ $(73, 65\%)$	106	0.34	1500	—	35
	70 (High service temperature)				$(38, 3\%)$ $(46, 190\%)$	144	—	—	—	29
	100	—	—	—	$(27, 3\%)$ $(30, 250\%)$	172	—	—	—	15
	$165 (T_m)$	—	—	—	—	—	0.23	2300	—	—

continued

Material-DAM	$T/℃$	E_T	ρ	υ	(σ,ε)	α	k	γ	β	K_{IC}
POMH (Homopolymer)	−50(Low service temperature)									
	23	3.1	1.42	0.35	(70, 58%)	122	0.23	1500	—	—
	100(High service temperature)									
	165(T_m)	—	—	—	—	—	0.23	2300	—	—
POM/13PTFE	−50(Low service temperature)									
	23	3.1	1.52	0.36	(38.5, 2%) (55, 10%)	110	—	—	—	—
	100(High service temperature)									
POM/20PTFE	23	—	—	0.36	$\sigma_{ucs}=-90$	—	—	—	—	—
POM/25GF	−55	—	—	—	—	36/50	—	—	—	—
	23	9.2	—	—	$\sigma_{ucs}=-120$; (133, 3%)	40/56	0.41	—	—	—
	70	—	—	—	—	43/67	—	—	—	—
	100(High service temperature)				45/84	—	—	—	—	—
POM/30GF	−55	—	—	—	—	36/50	—	—	—	—
	23	10	—	—	—	40/56	—	—	—	—
	70	—	—	—	—	43/67	—	—	—	—
	100	—	—	—	—	45/84	—	—	—	—
POM/20CF	−40	—	—	—	(120, 1%) (180, 2%)	—	—	—	—	—
	23	13.3	—	0.4	(90, 1%) (150, 3%)	—	—	—	—	—
	100	—	—	—	(57, 1%) (82, 4%)	—	—	—	—	—

Notes: DAM = Dry as Molded;

GF (CF) = Reinforced with glass (carbon) fibers, by weight unless V_f is given;

T_g(℃) & T_m(℃) = Glass transition point and melting point, respectively;

TPFE = Reinforcement, by weight.

Table 49.2 Fatigue ε-N Properties of POM (Acetal) and Related Composites

Material	$T/°C$	$d\varepsilon/dt$	σ'_{f-}	ε'_{f-}	b	c	K'	n'	$\sigma_f@2N_f$	R
POM	−55	—	—	—	—	—	—	—	49@ 10^6	—
	23	—	—	—	—	—	—	—	35@ 10^6	—
	70	—	—	—	—	—	—	—	19@ 10^6	—
	100	—	—	—	—	—	—	—	15@ 10^6	—

Table 49.3 Recommended Plastic Material for Worm-Gear Mating Mechanisms

Worm	Gear	Applications
Steel-machined or rolled	Delrin 500CL	Counters
Steel-others	Delrin 100	Windshield wipers & power window
Metal-nonferrous	Delrin 500CL	Speedometer and counters
PA6/6 nylon	Delrin 500 or 100	Speedometer and counters

Chapter 50

PP (Polypropylene)

50.1　Introduction

PP (**P**olypropylene) is a thermoplastic material, and its specific weight of 0.90 makes it lighter than water. Because of its good processability, relatively high mechanical properties, great recyclability, and low cost, PP has been used for a wide range of automotive products, such as household goods and packaging. It is one of the most important commodity polymers widely used in technical applications. PP is hardly an engineering plastic due to the following weaknesses: poor fire resistance, sensitivity to sunlight and oxygen, a low modulus of elasticity, high notch sensitivity, and poor impact resistance. Elastomers, $CaCO_3$, and talc have been used for toughening PP.

Mechanical and fatigue properties of PP and its related composites with randomly-aligned fibers are given in Tables 50.1 and 50.2, respectively. Orthotropic mechanical properties and strengths of PP-composites with well-aligned fibers are given in Tables 50.3 and 50.4, respectively. Mechanical properties of the composite become more brittle (lower strain at break) with increasing fiber volume fraction, irrespective of the direction of measurement. For PP composites reinforced with glass fibers, the tensile modulus reaches its maximum at fiber content of 52% by weight, while its tensile strength reaches its maximum at fiber content of 38% by weight.

Polypropylene compounds containing relatively low loadings (under 6% by weight) of nanometalized mineral particles show their competitive fracture toughness relative to fiber-reinforced PP, in automotive exterior claddings such as sidebars. PP/3CaCO₃(PP reinforced by 3% nano-particles of calcium carbonate by weight) has a modulus higher than PP by about 10%, while its impact toughness increases by 60% over PP [Eiras and Pessan], Fig. 50.1. The tensile strength PP reinforced with nano-SiO_2 reaches its maximum with 4.0% of nano-SiO_2, and the notched impact toughness achieves its maximum with the 5.0% of nano-SiO_2[Huang et al.].

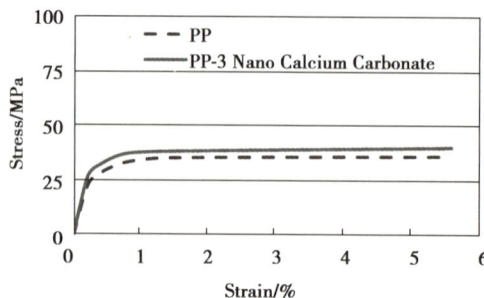

Fig. 50.1　Representative True Stress-Strain Curves of PP (Polypropylene) and PP/3CaCO₃(3% of CaCO₃ by weight)

50.2　TPO（Thermoplastic Olefin）

Olefins are products of the polymerization of propylene and ethylene gases. PP (Polypropylene) and PE (polyethylene) are the two most common members of the family. TPO (Thermoplastic Olefin or Thermoplastic Elastomer Polyolefin) is a blend of elastomer, PP (polypropylene), PE (Polyethylene), and block copolymer polypropylene, rubber, and fillers, achieving a balance of material properties via its compounded ingredients. Elastoplastic and creep properties of TPO and its fiber-reinforced composites are given in Tables 50.5 and 50.6. If PP and PE are the dominant components of a TPO blend, then the rubber fraction will be dispersed into a continuous matrix of "crystalline" PP (polypropylene). If the fraction of rubber is greater than 40%, phase inversion may be possible when the blend cools, resulting in a continuous amorphous phase and a dispersed crystalline phase. This type of material is non-rigid and is sometimes called TPR (Thermoplastic Rubber).

50.3　TPC-P-E（Thermoplastic Propylene-Ethylene Elastomer）

An initial "conditioning" extension to 800% strain resulted in a P-E (Propylene-Ethylene) elastomer with low initial modulus, strong strain hardening at high strain, and complete recovery over many cycles. Characterization of the structural changes at various strains during the conditioning process revealed the transformation of crystalline lamellae into shish-kebab fibers by melting and recrystallization [Poon et al.]. The shish-kebab fibers, accounting for only 5% of the bulk, are interconnected by a matrix of entangled, amorphous chains that constituted the remaining 95% in a Propylene-19.4 Ethylene Copolymer.

50.4　Applications

50.4.1　PP（Polypropylene）

PP (Polypropylene) is the most used automotive plastic (almost 20% of all). The applications include heating/air conditioning ductworks, fans, dashboard components, and seat backs.

A light-weighted sandwich panel may be composed of two polyethylene skins separated by lightweight polyethylene foam. The two polyethylene skins may be made of PP-based composites

[Mechraouli et al.]. Such a self-reinforced PP/honeycomb laminate load floor with carpets folded back in the sedan trunk reveals an easyclean surface.

Polypropylene fibers have been used as a filler material in Portland cement concrete (PCC) due to their advantageous properties-being chemically inert, stable in the alkaline environment of concrete, resistant to plastic shrinkage cracking and having hydro-phobic surfaces.

Nevertheless, the bonding strength between PP and concrete is weak without further treatment. Gamma irradiation has been used for curing PP in concrete. Dynamic elastic modulus of the reinforced concrete can be obtained in a non-destructive way of measuring the pulse velocity along the composite using electrical transducers located on the two opposite sides of cylindrical specimens of concrete. The elastic modulus is related to the energy supplied to the material by ultrasonic waves, which depends on how compact the composite is. Generally speaking, the dynamic elastic modulus of PP fiber-reinforced concrete is

$$E_d = \frac{V^2 \rho (1 + \nu)(1 + 2\nu)}{1 - \nu} \tag{50.1}$$

where V is the pulse velocity, ρ is the density of the reinforced concrete, and ν is the Poisson ratio.

50.4.2 TPO (Thermoplastic Olefin)

TPO-based compounds, as thermoplastic substrates, make inroads into automotive applications such as car cladding and rug backing for automotive flooring due to its compromising price/performance. Paint adhesion and friction-induced paint damage are directly related to the molecular weight of PP (polypropylene) and crystallinity of elastomer. Polyolefins are also used in pipe fittings, packaging films, surgical implants, wire insulation, beverage cases, trash-can liners, produce bags, and canteens. Thermoplastic silicone and olefin blends are used to extrude glass run and dynamic weather-stripping car profiles.

References

ACLOCK B, et al, 2007. The Effect of Temperature and Strain Rate on the Mechanical Properties of Highly Oriented Polypropylene Tapes and All-Polypropylene Composites[J]. Composites Science and Technology, 67(10): 2061-2070.

ARIVAMA T, 1994. Viscoelastic-plastic Deformation Behavior of Polypropylene after Cyclic Preloadings[J]. Polymer Engineering and Science, 34(17): 1319-1326.

ARRIAGA A, et al, 2010. Impact Testing and Simulation of a Polypropylene Component: Correlation with Strain Rate Sensitive Constitutive Models in ANSYS and LS-DYNA[J]. Polymer Testing, 29(2): 170-180.

BARRE S, BENZEGGAGH M, 1994. On the Use of Acoustic Emission to Investigate Damage Mechanics in Glass Fiber-Reinforced Polypropylene[J]. Composites Science and Technology, 52(3): 369-376.

BENZEGGAGH M, BENMEDAKHENE S, 1995. Residual Strength of a Glass/Polypropylene Composite Material Subject to Impact[J]. Composites Science and Technology, 55: 1-11.

BRACKET P, et al, 2008. Modification of Mechanical Properties of Recycled Polypropylene from Post-Consumer Containers[J]. Waste Management, 28(12): 2456-2464.

BRIAN C, et al, 2002. The Mechanical Properties and Thermal Performances of Polypropylene with a Novel Intumescent Flame Retardant[J]. Journal of Applied Polymer Science, 115(7): 1663-1666.

BROSTOW W, 2008. Polypropylene + Polystyrene Blends with a Compatibilizer. Part 2: Tribological and Mechanical Properties[J]. e-Polymers, 34: 1618-7229.

CASAVOLA C, et al, 2011. Experimental and Numerical Characterization of the Impact Response of Polyethylene Sandwich Panel: A Preliminary Study[J]. Applied Mechanics and Materials, 70: 195-200.

CHAN C, WU J, LI J, et al, 2002. Polypropylene/Calcium Carbonate Nanocomposites[J]. Polymer, 43(10): 2981-2992.

CONLE F, REHKOPF J, 2009. Analysis of the Results of Strain Controlled Fatigue Testing of Reinforced Polypropylene[J]. SAE 2009-01-0258.

DA C H, RAMOS V, DE O M, 2007. Degradation of Polypropylene (PP) during Multiple Extrusions: Thermal Analysis, Mechanical Properties and Analysis of Variance[J]. Polymer Testing, 26(5): 676-684.

DENAULT J, GUILLEMENET J, 1996. Continuous Carbon and Glass Fiber Reinforced Polypropylene: Optimization of the Compression Molding Process[J]. International SAMPE Symposium, SAMPE, (41): 1688-1700.

DHOBLE A, et al, 2005. Mechanical Properties of PP-LDPE Blends with Novel Morphologies Produced with a Continuous Chaotic Advection Blender[J]. Polymer, 46: 2244-2256.

DOMINGGUEZ C, et al, 2006. Izod Impact tests of Polypropylenes: The Clamping Pressure Influence[J]. Polymer Testing, 25(1): 49-55.

DRUBETSKI M, SIEGMANN A, NARKIS M, 2007. Electrical Properties of Hybrid Carbon Black/Carbon Fiber Polypropylene Composites[J]. Journal of Material Science, 42(1): 1-8.

FANEGAS N, et al, 2008. Optimizing the Balance between Impact Strength and Stiffness in Polypropylene/ Elastomer Blends by Incorporation of a Nucleating Agent[J]. Polymer Science and Engineering, 48(1): 80-87.

GROVE D, KIM H, 1995. Fatigue Behavior of Long and Short Glass Reinforced Thermoplastics[J]. SAE 950561.

GU R, KOKTA B, 2009. Mechanical Properties of PP Composites Reinforced with BCTMP Aspen Fiber[J]. Journal of Thermoplastic Composite Materials, 23(4): 513-542.

HE B, et al, 2011. Mechanical Properties of Long Glass Fiber-Reinforced Polypropylene Composites and Their Influence Factors[J]. Journal of Reinforced Plastics and Composites, 30(3): 222-228.

HILLMANSEN S, et al, 2000. The Effect of Strain Rate, Temperature, and Molecular Mass on the Tensile Deformation of Polyethylene[J]. Polymer Engineering and Science, 40(2): 481-489.

HOUSHYAR S, SHANKS R, 2006. Mechanical and Thermal Properties of Flexible Poly (propylene) Composites[J]. Macromolecular Materials and Engineering, 291(1): 59-67.

HOUSHTAR S, et al, 2005. The Effect of Fiber Concentration on Mechanical and Thermal Properties of Fiber-reinforced Polypropylene Composites[J]. Journal of Applied Polymer Science, 96(6): 2260-2272.

HUANG L, et al, 2006. Mechanical Properties and Crystallization Behavior of Polypropylene/Nano-SiO_2 Composites[J]. Journal of Reinforced Plastics and Composites, 25(9): 1001-1012.

KHONDKER O A, et al, 2006. Mechanical Properties of Textile-Inserted PP/PP Knitted Composites Using Inject-Compression Molding[J]. Composites, Part A, 37: 2285-2299.

KIM J S, et al, 2009. Evaluation of Dynamic Tensile Characteristics of Polypropylene Composites with Temperature Variation[J]. Journal of Composite Materials, 43(23): 28312853.

KONOU E, FARASOGLOU P, 1998. Determination of the True Stress-Strain Behavior of Polypropylene[J]. Journal of Materials Science, 33(1): 147-153.

KRISTIINA O, CLEMONS C,1998. Mechanical Properties and Morphology of Impact Modified Polypropylene-Wood Flour Composites,Journal of Applied Polymer Science, 67: 1503-1513.

LEE Y, PARK N, YOON H, 2010. Dynamic Mechanical Characteristics of Expanded Polypropylene Foams [J]. Journal of Cellular Plastics, 46(1): 143-155.

LIN Y, CHEN H, CHAN C, et al, 2008. High Impact Toughness Polypropylene/CaCO3 Nanocomposites and the Toughening Mechanism[J]. Macromolecules, 41(23): 9204-9213.

MA C, et al, 2007. Phase Structure and Mechanical Properties of Ternary Polypropylene /Elastomer/Nano-$CaCO_3$ Composites[J]. Composites Science and Technology, 67: 2997-3005.

MARTINEZ-BARRERA G, et al, 2011. Mechanical Properties of Polypropylene-Fiber Reinforced Concrete after Gamma Irradiation[J]. Composites, Part A, 42: 567-572.

MATSUDA K, 2002. Prediction of Stress-Strain Curves of Elastic-Plastic Materials Based on the Vickers Indentation[J]. Philosophical Magazine A, 82(10): 1941-1951.

MECHRAOULI A, et al, 2011. Mechanical Properties of Polypropylene Structural Foams with Fiber-Reinforced Skins[J]. Journal of Cellular Plastics, 47(2): 115-132.

MICHAELI W, JURSS D, 1995. Thermoplastic Pull-braiding: Pultrusion of Profiles with Braided Fiber Lay-up and Thermoplastic Matrix System (PP)[J]. Composites, 27A, 1: 3-7.

MIRJALILI F, et al, 2009. Mechanical Properties of α-Al_2O_3/PP Nano Composite[J]. Journal of Applied Sciences, 9: 3199-3201.

MOORE A L, et al, 2009. Thermal Conductivity Measurements of Nylon 11-Carbon Nanofiber Nanocomposites [J]. Journal of Heat Transfer, 131(9):091602/1-091602/5.

NAKAI S, et al, 2008. Numerical Simulation of a Polypropylene Foam Bead Expansion Process[J]. Polymer Science and Engineering, 48(1): 11-18.

NAKASON C, et al, 2006. Thermoplastic Vulcanizates Based on Maleated Natural Rubber/Polypropylene Blends: Effect of Blend Ratios on Rheological, Mechanical, and Morphological Properties[J]. Polymer Engineering and Science, 46(5): 594-600.

NEOGI S, et al, 2003. Role of PET in Improving Wear Properties of PP in Dry Sliding Condition[J]. Bulletin of Material Science, 26: 579-583

NOH W, NOH J, 2011. A Study on Scratch Resistance Improvement of Polypropylene Compounds[J]. SAE 2011-01-0461.

OTA W N, et al, 2005. Studies on the Combined Effect of Injection Temperature and Fiber Content on the Properties of the Polypropylene-Glass Fiber Composites[J]. Composites Science and Technology, 65: 873-881.

POON B. C, et al, 2007. Structure and Deformation of an Elastomeric Propylene-Ethylene Copolymer[J]. Journal of Applied Polymer Science, 104: 489-499.

RAHMAN R, et al, 2010. Physico-Mechanical Properties of Jute Fiber Reinforced Polypropylene Composites [J]. Journal of Reinforced Plastics and Composites, 29(3): 445-455.

RENNER K, et al, 2005. Analysis of the Debonding Process in Polypropylene Model Composites[J]. European Polymer Journal, 41(11): 2520-2529.

REZAEI F, YUNUS R, IBRAHIM N A, et al, 2007. "Effect of Fiber Loading and Fiber Length on Mechanical and Thermal Properties of Short Carbon Fiber Reinforced Polypropylene Composite[J]. Malaysian Journal of Analytical Sciences, 11 (1): 181-188.

SILVIS H C, et al, 1995. The Use of New Polyolefin Elastomers for Impact Modification of Polypropylene[J]. SAE 950559.

SMITH G D, et al, 2001, Non-isothermal Fusion Bonding of Polystyrene[J]. Polymer, 42: 6247-6257.

SOARES B G, 2008. A Novel Thermoplastic Elastomer Based on Dynamically Vulcanized Polypropylene/Acrylic Rubber Blends[J]. EXPRESS Polymer Letters, 2(8): 602-613.

SOPHER S, GRANTHEN G, 2011. Materials and Design Innovation Techniques for Expanded Polypropylene (EPP) Products Used in Automotive Interior Applications[J]. SAE 2011-01-0247.

TAKEDE H, HATA N, 1989. Estimation for Failure Life of a Radiator Fan Carrier under Cyclic Loading[J]. SAE 890443.

THIO Y, ARGON A, COHEN R, et al, 2002. Toughening of Isotactic Polypropylene with $CaCO_3$ Particles[J]. Polymer, 43(13): 3661-3674.

THITIHAMMAWONG A, et al, 2007. Effect of Different Types of Peroxides on Rheological, Mechanical and Morphological Properties of Thermoplastic Vulcanizates Based on Natural Rubber/Polypropylene Blends[J]. Polymer Testing, 26: 537-546.

THOMASON J L, VLUG M A, 1996. Influence of Fiber-length and Concentration on the Properties of Glass Fiber-reinforced Polypropylene: Part I. Tensile and Flexural Modulus[J]. Composites, A27: 477-484.

THOMASON J L, VLUG M A, 1996. Influence of Fiber-length and Concentration on the Properties of Glass Fiber-reinforced Polypropylene: Part II. Strength and Strain at Failure[J]. Composites, A27: 1075-1084.

UPINDER P.S, et al, 2009. Evaluation of Mechanical Properties of Polypropylene Filled with Wollastonite and Silicon Rubber[J]. Materials Science and Engineering, A 501: 94-98.

WAN W, YU D, XIE Y, et al, 2006. Effects of Nanoparticle Treatment and Mechanical Properties of Polypropylene/Calcium Carbonate Nanocomposites[J]. Journal of Applied Polymer Science, 102: 3480-3488.

WEISS R A, 1981. Mechanical Properties of Polypropylene Reinforced with Short Graphite Fibers[J]. Polymer Composites, 2(3): 95-101.

YANG H S, KIM H J, LEE B J, et al, 2007. Effect of Compatibilizing Agent on Rice Husk Flour Reinforced Polypropylene Composites[J]. Composite Structures, 77: 45-55.

YANG K, et al, 2007. Mechanical Properties and Morphologies of Polypropylene/Single-Filler or Hybrid-Filler Calcium Carbonate Composites[J]. Polymer Engineering and Science, 47(2): 95-102.

YUNUS R, et al, 2011. Mechanical Properties of Carbon Fiber-Reinforced Polypropylene Composites[J]. Key Engineering Materials, 471/472: 652-657.

ZHANG Q, et al, 2004. Crystallization and Impact Energy of Polypropylene/$CaCO_3$ Nanocomposites with Nonionic Modifier[J]. Polymer, 45(17): 5985-5994.

ZUIDERDUIN W, WESTZAAN C, HUÉTINK J, et al, 2003. Toughening of Polypropylene with Calcium Carbonate Particles[J]. Polymer, 44 (1): 261-275.

YANG Y, et al, 2011. Mechanical Property and Hydrothermal Aging of Injection Molded Jute/Polypropylene Composites[J]. Journal of Materials Science, 46(8): 2678-2684.

AUSTIN J R, KONTOPOULOU M, 2006. Effect of Organoclay Content on the Rheology, Morphology, and Physical Properties of Polyolefin Elastomers and Their Blends with Polypropylene[J]. Polymer Engineering and Science, 46: 1491-1501.

CORAN A Y, PATEL R, 1983. Rubber-Thermoplastic Compositions. VIII. Nitrile RubberPolyolefin Blends with Technological Compatibilization[J]. Rubber Chemistry and Technology, 56: 1045-1060.

HOTTEN R, 2011. Optimization of Scratch Resistance for Molded in Color Interior Thermoplastic Olefin Injection Molded Plastics[J]. SAE 2011-01-0464.

JESTER R, 2011. Film Co-extrusion-Cyclic Olefin Copolymer"Plastics Technology, 57(11): 39.

LEE H, et al, 2006. TPO Based Nano-composites. Part Ⅱ. Thermal Expansion Behavior[J]. Polymer, 47(10): 3528-3539.

LIU Y, KNOTOPOULOU M, 2006. The Structure and Physical Properties of Polypropylene and Thermoplastic Olefin Nanocomposites Containing Silica[J]. Polymer, 47(22): 7731-7739.

MILLS N J, GILCRIST A, 1997. Creep and Recovery of Polyolefin Foams-Deformation Mechanisms[J]. Journal of Cellular Plastics, 33(3): 264-292.

NAKASON C, et al, 2006. Thermoplastic Vulcanizates Based on Maleated Natural Rubber/Polypropylene Blends: Effect of Blend Ratios on Rheological, Mechanical, and Morphological Properties[J]. Polymer Engineering and Science, 46(5): 594-600.

NOMURA T, et al, 1993. Structure of Super Olefin Polymer[J]. Japanese Polymer Science and Technology, 50(1): 87-91.

RYNTZ R A, 2004. The Influence of Compositional variations in Compounded Thermoplastic Olefins (TPO) on the Physical and Mechanical Attributes of Injection Molded Plaques[J]. Journal of Vinyl and Additive Technology, 3(4): 295-300.

VAN HATTUM F W J, et al, 1998. A Study of the Thermomechanical Properties of Carbon Fiber-Polypropylene Composites[J].Polymer Composites, 20(5): 683-688.

WANG P Z, et al, 1999. Quantitative Characterization of Scratch Damage in Polypropylene (TPO) for Automotive Interior Applications[J]. SAE 1999-01-0243.

WANG Y, ARRUDA E M, 2006. Constitutive Modeling of a Thermoplastic Olefin Over a Broad Range of Strain Rates[J]. Journal of Engineering Materials and Technology, 128(4): 551-558.

WU J, et al, 2009. Reinforcement of Dynamically Vulcanized EPDM/PP Elastomers Using Organoclay Fillers: Dynamic Properties of Rubber Vibration Isolators and Anti-vibration Performance [J]. Journal of Thermoplastic Composite Materials, 22(5): 503-517.

ZHOU Y, MALLICK P K, 2005. Fatigue Performance of an Injection Molded Talc-Filled Polypropylene[J]. Polymer Engineering and Science, 45(4): 510-516.

Table 50.1　Mechanical Properties of PP（Polypropylene）and Related Composites

Material-DAM	$T/℃$	E_T	ρ	ν	(α, ε)	α	k	γ	β	K_{IC}
PP（Bulk; True stress-strain data）	23	1.1	0.91	0.43	（22,2%） （28,4%） （33,8%） （35,14%） （36,27%）	96	0.15	1925	—	1.9
	83.6(T_g)	—	—	—	—	—	—	—	—	—
	168(T_m)	—	—	—	—	—	—	—	—	—
PP/3CaCO$_3$（True stress-strain data: W_f=3%）	23	1.2	0.91	0.43	（26,2%） （32,4%） （37,8%） （38,14%） （40, 56%）	91	0.15	1925	—	1.8
PP/10CaCO$_3$	23	—	—	—	—	—	—	—	—	1.6
PP/20CaCO$_3$	23	—	—	—	—	—	—	—	—	1.3
PP/30CaCO$_3$	23	—	—	—	—	—	—	—	—	0.7
PP/1Clay	23	—	—	—	—	—	—	—	—	2.7
PP/3Clay	23	—	—	—	—	—	—	—	—	4.1
PP/5Clay	23	—	—	—	—	—	—	—	—	5.5
PP/15CF（PAN; V_f=15%）	23	4.7	—	—	$\sigma_{uts}=50$	18	0.7	—	—	—
PP/10GF	23	—	—	—	—	—	—	—	—	3.7
PP/20GF（L×209 mm×13 μm）	23	4	1.03	0.4	（59,5%）	43	0.25	1 622	—	5
	80	—	—	—	—	—	—	—	—	—
PP/30GF	23	6	1.15	0.4	（85,3%） （76,4.5%）	35	0.27	1470	—	—
	−40	—	—	—	—	—	—	—	—	—
PP/40GF	23	8.6	1.21	0.4	（90,4%）	27	0.36	1020	—	—
PP/45GF/15Mineral	23	12.3	1.52	—	（150,2%）	—	—	—	—	—
PP/27Gr（V_f=27%）	23	—	—	—	$\sigma_{uts}=47$	—	—	—	—	—
PP Yarn	23	1.7	0.91	—	（240,1.4%）	—	—	—	—	—

continued

Material-DAM	$T/℃$	E_T	ρ	ν	(α, ε)	α	k	γ	β	K_{IC}
All-PP(PP/PP) (Composites: Bidirectional weaves of PP/PP)	23	5	0.92	0.4	$\sigma_{uts}=180$	41	0.36	—	—	—
50PP/50NBR (TPV; Non-compatible Blends)	23	—	—	—	(17,23%)	—	—	—	—	—
PP/PP-g-MA/ NBR/NBR-COOH TETA (TPV; Compatibilized Blends)	23	—	—	—	(19, 50%)	—	—	—	—	—
55PO/45EO	23	0.45	—	—	(12.3, 29%) (17, 440%)	—	—	—	—	—
PP/40Talc (//)	23	7.7	—	—	(27.3,2.3%)	—	—	—	—	—
PP/40Talc (⊥)	23	7.4	—	—	(22.2,1.7%)	—	—	—	—	—
PP/40Talc(WL)	23	7.2	—	—	(17.6,0.8%)	—	—	—	—	—
PP/Wood flour ($V_f=40\%$; maleated PP/ Ponderosa)	23	4.1	—	—	(32.3,2%)	—	—	—	—	—
PP/Wood fiber ($V_f=40\%$; maleated PP/ Ponderosa)	23	4.23	—	—	(52.3,3.2%)	—	—	—	—	—

Notes: DAM = Dry as Molded;

GF (CF) = Reinforced with glass (carbon) fibers, by weight unless V_f given;

T_g(℃) & T_m(℃) = Glass transition point and melting point, respectively;

EO, Gr, Mineral, Talc, Wood Floor, Wood Fiber = Reinforcements, by weight;

WL = Wetline;

⊥ , // = Perpendicular and parallel to wetline as injection-molded.

Table 50.2 Fatigue ε-N Properties of PP (Polypropylene)-Based Composites

Material	$T/^\circ\text{C}$	$\mathrm{d}\varepsilon/\mathrm{d}t$	σ_{f}'	$\varepsilon_{\mathrm{f}}'$	b	c	K'	n'	$\sigma_{\mathrm{f}}@2N_{\mathrm{f}}$	R
PP	23	—	—	—	—	—	—	—	$13.8@5\times10^8$	—
PP/20%E-glass ($V_{\mathrm{f}}=20\%$; // flow direction)	23	10 Hz	—	—	—	—	—	—	$18@10^6$ $23@10^5$	0.25^+ 0.25^+
PP/20%E-glass ($V_{\mathrm{f}}=20\%$; $\perp$ flow direction)	23	10 Hz	—	—	—	—	—	—	$14@10^6$ $17@10^5$	0.25^+ 0.25^+

Notes: 0.25^+ = Both high and low stress levels are positive.

Table 50.3 Mechanical Properties of PP (Polypropylene)-Based Orthotropic Composites

Specification	$T/^\circ\text{C}$	ρ	E_{xx}	E_{yy}	E_{zz}	G_{xy}	G_{xz}	G_{yz}	ν_{xy}	ν_{xz}	ν_{yz}
All-PP (Continuous pp-taped fibers compacted at 140 ℃)	−40	—	—	—	—	—	—	—	—	—	—
	23	0.77	12.93	0.91	0.91	0.8	0.8	—	0.36	0.36	—
All-PP (Continuous pp-taped fibers compacted at 160 ℃)	−40	—	—	—	—	—	—	—	—	—	—
	23	0.77	12.95	1.52	1.52	0.8	0.8	—	0.38	0.38	—
PP/E-glass (Long E-glass fibers randomly oriented; X-// flow direction and Y-$\perp$ flow direction)	23	0.77	6.5	5.0	—	—	—	—	—	—	—

Table 50.4 Orthotropic Mechanical Strength of Unidirectional PP Composites

Material	$T/^\circ\text{C}$	$(\sigma_{11\mathrm{u}},\ \varepsilon_{11\mathrm{u}})$	$(\sigma_{22\mathrm{u}},\ \varepsilon_{22\mathrm{u}})$	$(\sigma_{33\mathrm{u}},\ \varepsilon_{33\mathrm{u}})$	$(\sigma_{12\mathrm{u}},\ \varepsilon_{12\mathrm{u}})/$ $(\sigma_{23\mathrm{u}},\ \varepsilon_{23\mathrm{u}})/$ $(\sigma_{13\mathrm{u}},\ \varepsilon_{13\mathrm{u}})$
PP/34%E-glass ($V_{\mathrm{f}}=34\%$; Continuous bi-directional woven fabrics)	23	$\sigma_{11}=438$	$\sigma_{22}=438$	—	—/—/—
PP/20%E-glass ($V_{\mathrm{f}}=20\%$; Long fibers randomly oriented; 1: // flow direction and 2 or 3: $\perp$ flow direction)	23	$\sigma_{11}=114$	$\sigma_{22}=68$	$\sigma_{33}=68$	—/—/—

Table 50.5   Mechanical Properties of TPO (Thermoplastic Olefin) and Related Composites

Material-DAM	$T/°C$	E_T	ρ	ν	(α, ε)	α	k	γ	β	K_{IC}
TPO	23	1.31	1.08	—	(20, 186%)	59/108	—	—	—	—
(Raw)	$120(T_m)$	—	—	—	—	—	—	—	—	—
TPO	23	—	—	—	(33, 1.5%) (43, 4.7%)	—	—	—	—	—
(Car Cladding)	$120(T_m)$	—	—	—	—	—	—	—	—	—

Notes: DAM = Dry as Molded;

      GF (CF) = Reinforced with glass (carbon) fibers, by weight unless V_f value is given;

      $T_g(°C)$ & $T_m(°C)$ = Glass transition point and melting point, respectively.

Table 50.6   Thermomechanical Creep Parameters of PP

Material	$T/°C$	Stress/MPa	Strain Rate/s^{-1}	$A/(MPa^{-n}\cdot s^{m-1})$	$Q/(J\cdot mol^{-1})$	n	m
PP	25	$E=1$	—	1.85	$Q/(RT_k)=8$	1.566	−0.826

Notes: Creep equation: $\dfrac{d\varepsilon_{creep}}{dt}=A\left(\dfrac{\sigma-\sigma_{th}}{E}\right)^n t^m \exp\left(\dfrac{-Q}{RT_k}\right)$, $\sigma>\sigma_{th}$;

      σ_{th}: Stress threshold and $\sigma_{th}=0$, if not specified;

      E: Young's modulus; If given that $E=1$, it means E is not specified.

Chapter 51

PPA (Polyphthalamide)

51.1 Introduction

PPA (**P**oly**p**hthal**a**mide) is a semi-crystalline polyamide-extended polymer with the addition of an aromatic ring structure to the polyamide. The aromatic ring structure imparts many advantages over aliphatic nylons, such as elevated glass transition temperatures and melting points, higher deflection temperatures, better chemical resistance, more robust dimensional stability, and lower absorption of moisture and solvents. Du Pont's Zytel HTN is a PPA family of different grades.

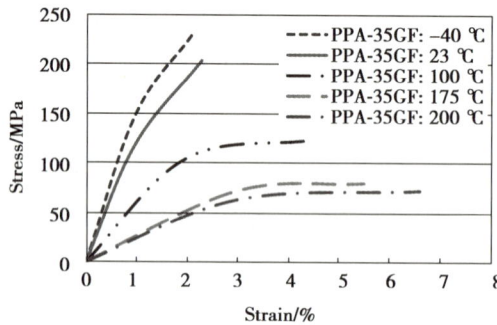

Fig. 51.1 Stress-Strain Curves of PPA/35GF Composites at Different Temperatures

Material properties of PPA (Polyphthalamide) reinforced with fibers are given in Table 51.1. Stress-strain curves of PPA/35GF and PPA/45GF composites reinforced randomly with short glass fibers (35% and 45% by weight, respectively) at different applicable temperatures are shown in Fig. 51.1 and Fig. 51.2, respectively.

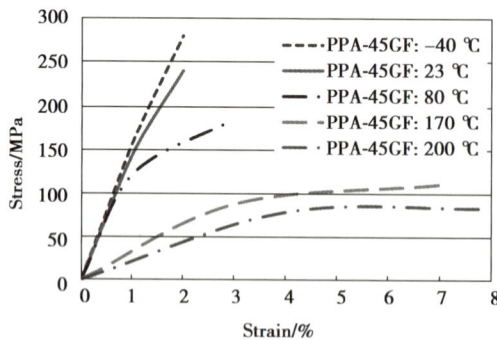

Fig. 51.2 Stress-Strain Curves of PPA/45GF Composites at Different Temperatures

51.2 Applications

PPA (Polyphthalamide) and its composites are used to replace metals (aluminum, zinc, and brass) in automotive applications at elevated temperatures such as automotive under hood components, including electric connectors, bushings, thermostat housings, water pumps, charge air coolers. It also has found a degree of favor in some components in transmissions and engine oil systems, such as position sensors. Tire pressure monitoring sensors, which have to be light due to the high centrifugal forces and vibrations as tires rotate, are another application for PPA.

References

GARRETT D, OWENS G, 1995. Polyphthalamide Resins for Use as Automotive Engine Coolant Components [J]. SAE 950192.

LYONS J, TINIO E, AND BERRY S, 1995. Creep, Stress Rupture, and Isothermal Aging of Reinforced Polyphthalamide[J]. Journal of Applied Polymer Science, 56(9): 1169-1177.

Table 51.1   Mechanical Properties of PPA（Polyphthalamide）and Related Composites

Material-DAM	$T/^\circ C$	E_T	ρ	ν	(α, ε)	α	k	γ	β	K_{IC}
PPA	23	2.2	1.13	0.39	(62, 28%)	93	—	—	—	—
	134(T_g)	—	—	—	—	—	—	—	—	—
	303(T_m)	—	—	—	—	—	—	—	—	—
PPA/30GF	23	11	—	0.39	(115,1%) (200,2.5%)	15/70	—	—	—	—
	149	—	—	—	(62,2%) (81, 5.6%)	—	—	—	—	—
	−40	—	—	—	(150,1%) (230,2.1%)	15/70	—	—	—	—
PPA/35GF	23	12.5	—	—	(120,1%) (204,2.3%)	15/70	—	—	—	—
	100	—	—	—	(105,2%) (124,4.5%)	15/70	—	—	—	—
	175	—	—	—	(72,3%) (80, 5.5%)	21/95	—	—	—	—
	200	—	—	—	(63,3%) (72.4,6.6%)	21/95	—	—	—	—
	−40	—	—	—	(155,1%) (280,1.6%)	—	—	—	—	—

continued

Material-DAM	$T/^\circ C$	E_T	ρ	ν	(α, ε)	α	k	γ	β	K_{IC}
PPA/45GF	23	16	—	—	(142,1%) (240,2%)	15/60	—	—	—	—
	80	—	—	—	(120,1%) (185,3%)	15/60	—	—	—	—
	170	—	—	—	(87,3%) (110,7%)	—	—	—	—	—
	200	—	—	—	(78,4%) (83,8%)	—	—	—	—	—
PPA/30CF	23	29.3	1.33	—	(301,1.7%)	—	—	—	—	—

Notes: DAM = Dry as Molded;

GF (CF) = Reinforced with glass (carbon) fibers, by weight unless V_f is given;

$T_g(^\circ C)$ & $T_m(^\circ C)$ = Glass transition point and melting point, respectively.

Chapter 52

PPE (Polyphenylene Ether)

52.1   Introduction

PPE (**P**oly**ph**enylene Ether), poly (2, 6-dimethyl-1, 4-phenylene ether), is a linear noncrystalline polyether obtained by the oxidative polycondensation of 2, 6-dimethylphenol in the presence of a copper-amine-complex catalyst. Mechanical properties of PPE and the related are listed in Table 52.1. It is an amorphous high-performance thermoplastic, with unusual resistance to acids and bases, outstanding dimensional stability, excellent mechanical and thermal properties, and excellent dielectric properties over a wide range of frequencies. Its physic characteristics are stable over a wide range of temperatures, with the glass transition temperature being around 215 ℃. Its water absorption is the lowest among all the engineering thermoplastics. The surface can be printed, hot-stamped, painted, or metalized. Welds and heat staking are possible through heating elements, friction, or ultrasonic welding. PPE is thermoformed at a temperature between 145 ℃ and 170 ℃. However, it has poor chemical resistance and color stability-coating required for some applications.

52.2   PPE-PA (Polyphenylene Ether-Polyamide ; also called Modified PPO) Blends

A modified PPO alloy combines the superior heat resistance, stiffness, and dimensional stability of amorphous PPO with the inherent chemical resistance, excellent flow, and paintability of semicrystalline polyamide (PA). With its excellent surface finish (Class A) straight from the mold, the high-performance engineering material is an excellent candidate for applications where plastics and metals are painted together at elevated temperatures, as in automotive exterior body panel applications. Besides its broad resistance to aggressive environments, the modified PPO resin also features lower water absorption, lower warpage, and lower specific weight. Due to its high inherent strength and rigidity, PPE-PA requires less glass reinforcement than straight PA to

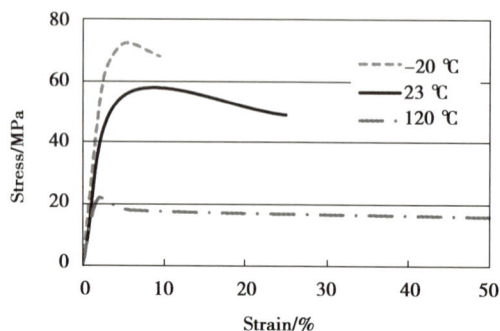

Fig. 52.1   Stress-Strain Curves of PPE-PA at Different Temperatures

reach the same composite strength. Stress-strain curves of PPE-PA at different temperatures are reconstructed using several discrete points taken from GE Noryl GTX914, as shown in Fig. 52.1. Their fatigue properties are given in Table 52.2.

52.3   PPE-PP (Polyphenylene Ether-polypropylene) Blends

A copolymer made of PPE (Polyphenylene Ether) and PP (polypropylene) is an engineering thermoplastic olefin that combines the flowability and chemical resistance of PP with PPE's high-temperature performance, surface hardness, and rigidity.

52.4   PPE-PS (Polyphenylene Ether-Polystyrene) Blends

PS-modified PPE has an amorphous molecular structure that provides excellent heat resistance, dimensional stability, and mechanical properties. It also exhibits outstanding superiority in flame retardance. Material properties of PPE, including its glass transition point, vary with the content of polystyrene. Flow characteristics of PPE-PS resin allow thin-walled molding, twinscrew extrusion, and injection molding [Gupta et al.]. It also helps reduce material usage and final part weight. Through modification and the incorporation of fillers, such as glass fibers, the properties can be extensively modified. PPE/PS had good paint/foam/foil adhesion without pretreatment. Stress-strain curves of PPE-PS at different temperatures are reconstructed using several discrete points taken from GE Noryl 731, as shown in Fig. 52.1.

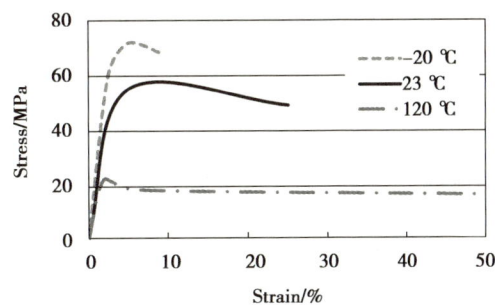

Fig. 52.2   Stress-Strain Curves of PPE-PS at Different Temperatures

52.5   Applications

PPE (Polyphenylene Ether) blends are used for structural parts, electronics, household, and automotive items that depend on high heat resistance, dimensional stability, and accuracy. PPE is an excellent insulation polymer for electric cables and wire harnesses working at elevated temperatures, at which the other two popular insulation polymers (PVC and XLPE) may experience thermal degradation.

PPE-PA resin is used in automobiles ranging from small parts such as automotive fuse-boxes and tank flaps to large body panels such as fenders and tail-gates.

PPE-PS resin is an excellent candidate for instrument panels. It is also used by major manufacturers of fluid engineering equipment in applications such as pumps, impellers, manifold blocks, and water meters.

References

GUPTA S, et al, 2008. Anomalous Mechanical Behavior on Recycling of Poly (phenyleneether)-Based Thermoplastic Elastomer[J]. Polymer Engineering and Science, 48(3): 496-504.

MORYE S S, 2005. A Comparison of the Thermoformability of a PPE/PP Blend with Thermoformable ABS. Part I: Small Deformation Methods[J]. Polymer Engineering and Science, 45(10): 1369-1376.

MORYE S S, 2005. A Comparison of the Thermoformability of a PPE/PP Blend with Thermoformable ABS. Part II: Large Deformation Methods[J]. Polymer Engineering and Science, 45(10): 1377-1384.

ROBERTSON J W, et al, 1966. Properties, Processing and Potential Automotive Applications of PPO Polyphenylene Oxide Resins[J]. SAE 660002.

WONG S, BANDARU S, 2008. Mechanical Properties and Strain Fatigue Lives of Insulation Materials[J]. Journal of Material Science, 44: 365-373.

WU S, LIN T, SHYU S, 2000. Cure Behavior, Morphology, and Mechanical Properties of the Melt Blends of Epoxy with Polyphenylene Oxide[J]. Journal of Applied Polymer Science, 75(1): 26-34.

TEKEDA K, et al, 1998. Effect of Distribution of PPE and Interface between two Phases on Fluidity, Mechanical and Thermal Properties of PS/PPE/AS Alloy[J]. Key Engineering Materials, 137: 100-106.

TIONG S K Y, 1996. Fracture Toughening Behavior and Mechanical Properties of Polyphenylene Oxide/High-Impact Polystyrene Blends[J]. Polymer Engineering and Science, 36(21): 2626-2633.

ZEMPEI M, 2001. Plastic Material Introduction for Machine Designers: Denatured Polyphenylene Ether (PPE) [J]. Machine Design, 45(6): 42-44.

Table 52.1   Mechanical Properties of PPE (Polyphenylene Ether) and Related Composites

Material-DAM	$T/℃$	E_T	ρ	ν	(α, ε)	α	k	γ	β	K_{IC}
PPE(Bulk)	23	2.6	1.08	0.38	(57, 25%)	64	0.22	—	—	15
	215(T_g)	—	—	—	—	—	—	—	—	—
PPE/PA6, 6 (Noryl GTX914)	23	5	1.07	0.38	(25,1%) (60,6%) (57, 35%)	41/74	—	—	—	—
	120	4.2	—	—	(26,5%) (28, 30%) (30, 100%) (37, 180%)	—	—	—	—	—
	125(T_g)	—	—	—	—	—	—	—	—	—
	150	4.0	—	—	(21,5%) (23, 20%) (22, 45%) (28, 205%)	—	—	—	—	—
	250(T_m)	—	—	—	—	—	—	—	—	—
PPE-PA6, 6/ 30GF (i.e. PPO/30 GF; True s-s)	23	5	1.07	0.38	(60,0.5%) (95,1%) (125,1.5%) (175,2.5%)	—	—	—	—	—
PPE-PP (Nory RF 1132)	23	1.34	0.97	0.38	(35, 6.5%) (32, 195%)	96	—	—	—	—
	−20	—	—	—	(60,2.5%) (72,5%) (68,9.5%)	—	—	—	—	—
PPE-PS (Noryl 731)	23	2.5	1.1	0.38	(55,5%) (49, 25%)	70/80	0.24	—	—	—
	120	—	—	—	(22,2%) (18,6%) (16, 50%)	—	—	—	—	—
	−20	—	—	—	(57,1%) (92,1.8%)	—	—	—	—	—
PPE-PS/20GF (Noryl GFN2)	23	—	—	—	(55,1%) (82,1.9%)	—	—	—	—	38
	120	—	—	—	(32,2.3%) (28, 54%)	—	—	—	—	—

continued

Material-DAM	$T/℃$	E_T	ρ	ν	(α, ε)	α	k	γ	β	K_{IC}
PPE-PS-PA	23	3	1.25	—	(59,7%)	52	—	—	—	—
PPE/30GF	23	7.33	1.28	—	(113, 4.6%)	31	0.16	—	—	31
	215(T_g)	—	—	—	—	—	—	—	—	—

Notes: DAM = Dry as Molded;

GF (CF) = Reinforced with glass (carbon) fibers, by weight unless V_f is given;

T_g(℃) & T_m(℃) = Glass transition point and melting point, respectively.

Table 52.2   Fatigue ε-N Properties of PPE (Polyphenylene Ether) and Related Composites

Material-DAM	$T/℃$	$d\varepsilon/dt$	σ_f'	ε_f'	b	c	K'	n'	$\sigma_f@2N_f$	R
PPE (Bulk)	23	—	—	—	—	—	—	—	15@ 10^6	—
PPE-PS/20GF	23	—	—	—	—	—	—	—	38@ 10^6	—
PPE/30GF	23	—	—	—	—	—	—	—	31@ 10^6	—

Chapter 53

PPS (Polyphenylene Sulfide)

53.1　Introduction

PPS (**P**oly**p**henylene **S**ulfide) consists of aromatic rings linked with sulfides (an organic polymer). It has the highest heat deflection temperature of melt-processable thermoplastics, yet no known solvent below 200 ℃. PPS is a crystalline (crystallinity 55%~65%) white powder polymer with high heat resistance (continuous service temperature up to 240 ℃), mechanical strength, stiffness, flame resistance, chemical resistance, dimensional stability, wear resistance, creep resistance, and flame resistance. Nevertheless, it can be electroplated. Mechanical and fatigue properties of PPS and its related composites are given in Tables 53.1 and 53.2, respectively. Orthotropic mechanical properties and strengths are given in Tables 53.3 and 53.4, respectively.

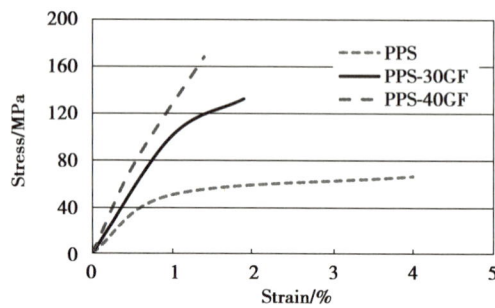

Fig. 53.1　Reinforcement of PPS by Short Glass Fibers (Percentage by Weight) in Radom

The tensile modulus of a glass-fiber reinforced PPS unidirectional lamina increases as crystallinity develops, while the tensile modulus of a random glass-fiber-reinforced PPS composite decreases with thermal cycling [Cao and Chen]. Typical stress-strain curves of PPS and its glass fiber-reinforced composites are depicted in Fig. 53.1, and the material softening with an increasing temperature is demonstrated in Fig. 53.2.

Thermal cycling at elevated temperatures increases the degree of crystallinity of carbon fiber-reinforced PPS composites, as evidenced by the increasing melting point [Cao et al.].

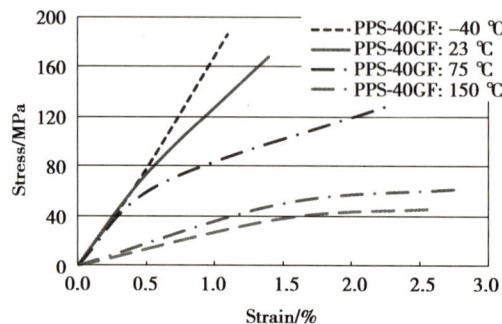

Fig. 53.2　Typical Stress-Strain Curves of PPS/40GF (40% by Weight) Composites at Different Temperatures

53.2   Applications

Carbon fiber-reinforced PPS (Polyphenylene sulfide) composites have been successfully used in components on the leading edge of Airbus A340 and A380 wings.

One interesting application is PPS-bonded Nd-Fe-B magnets. The bonded Nd-Fe-B magnets can be produced by mixing the magnetic Nd-Fe-B powder with polymer resins (e.g. PPS and PA) followed by a molding process such as injection molding, and compression molding, extrusion, or even calendaring. PPS has a higher melting point than PA and thus can be used for higher operating temperatures. The tensile strength of PPS bonded Nd-Fe-B is reduced significantly at an elevated temperature. Its tensile strength reduces to 17 MPa at 180 ℃ from 66 MPa at room temperature. Debonding in the interface area between Nd-Fe-B and PPS is the leading cause of failure at temperatures between 100 ℃ and 180 ℃.

One special application is PPS/15CF/15Kevlar/15PTFE composite, which may be used for components with high-speed relative sliding. Its static and dynamic coefficients of friction can go as low as 0.08 and 0.05, respectively. It may work fine for a heavy-duty environment, in which loading is too high for POM (acetal).

References

ARICI A, et al, 2006. Influence of Annealing on the Performance of Short Glass Fiber-Reinforced Polyphenylene Sulfide (PPS) Composites[J]. Journal of Composite Materials, 39(1): 21-33.

BAHADUR R, BAR-COHEN A, 2005. Thermal Design and Optimization of Natural Convection Polymer Pin Fin Heat Sinks[J]. IEEE Transactions on Components and Packaging Technologies, 28(2): 238-246.

BOEY F, et al, 1991. Annealing Effects on the Dynamic Mechanical Properties of Aromatic Polyphenylene Sulphide Fiber Reinforced Composite[J]. Polymer Testing, 10(3): 221-228.

BRADY D G, 1995. Polyphenylene Sulfide (PPS)[J]. Engineering Plastics, Engineered Materials Handbook, ASM International, 2: 186-191.

CAO J, CHEN L, 2005. Effect of Thermal Cycling on Carbon Fiber-Reinforced PPS Composites[J]. Polymer Composites, 26(5): 713-716.

GARRELL M G, et al, 2003. Mechanical Properties of Polyphenylene Sulfide (PPS) Bonded NdFe-B Permanent Magnets[J]. Materials and Engineering, A, 359(1-2): 375-383.

GOTAL R, KADAM A, 2010. Polyphenylene Sulphide/Graphite Composites for EMI Shielding Applications

[J]. Advanced Materials Letters, 1(2): 143-147.

JIANG Z, et al, 2011. Mechanical and Thermal Properties of Polyphenylene Sulfide/Multiwalled Carbon Nanotube Composites[J]. Journal of Applied Polymer Science, 123(5): 2676-2683.

MA C, et al, 1988. Studies on Thermogravimetric Properties of Polyphenylene Sulfide and Polyetherether Ketone Resins and Composites[J]. Thermoplastic Composite Materials, 1(1): 39-49.

MILLER A, WEI C, GIBSON A G, 1995. Manufacture of Polyphenylene Sulfide (PPS) Matrix Composites via the Powder Impregnation Route[J]. Composites, Part A, 27(1): 49-56.

ROMAN T, et al, 2004. PPS-metal adhesion: a Density Functional Theory-Based Study[J]. Solid State Communications, 132(6): 405-408.

SINMAZCELIK T, TASKIRAN I, 2007. Erosive Wear Behavior of Polyphenylene Sulfide (PPS) Composites [J]. Materials in Engineering, 28(9): 2471-2477.

STILL R, MADDEN D, 1991. Mechanical Design Considerations for the Use of Polyphenylene Sulfide (PPS) Compound in Underhood Applications[J]. SAE 912539.

TANTHAPANICHAKOON W, et al, 2006. Mechanical Degradation of Filter Polymer Materials: Polyphenylene Sulfide[J]. Polymer Degradation and Stability, 91(11): 2614-2621.

VIEILLE J, AUCHER J, TALEB L, 2011. Carbon Fiber Fabric Reinforced PPS Laminates: Influence of temperature on Mechanical Properties and Behavior[J]. Advances in Polymer Technology, 30(2): 80-95.

WU D, et al, 2009. Study on Physical Properties of Multiwalled Carbon Nanotube /Poly(phenylene sulfide) Composites[J]. Polymer Engineering and Science, 49(9): 1727-1735.

Table 53.1 Mechanical Properties of PPS (Polyphenylene Sulfide) and Related Composites

Material-DAM	$T/°C$	E_T	ρ	ν	(α, ε)	α	k	γ	β	K_{IC}
PPS	23	3.4	1.35	0.38	(50,1%) (66,4%)	50	0.30	1 830	—	2
	180	—	—	—	$\sigma_{uts}=17$	100	—	—	—	—
	288(T_m)	—	—	—	—	—	0.30	—	—	—
PPS/30GF	23	13	1.58	—	$\sigma_{uts}=-230$; (100,1%) (150,1.8%)	20/62	—	—	—	—
	120	—	—	—	(60,1%) (95,3%)	15/125	—	—	—	—
	150	—	—	—	(40,1%) (58, 3.4%)	—	—	—	—	—
	-40	—	—	—	(77,0.5%) (190,1.1%)	20/40	—	1000	—	—

continued

Material-DAM	$T/℃$	E_{T}	ρ	ν	(α, ε)	α	k	γ	β	K_{IC}
PPS/40GF	23	15	1.64	—	$\sigma_{\mathrm{uts}}=-250$; $(73, 0.5\%)$ $(175, 1.5\%)$	20/40	0.20	—	—	—
	75	—	—	—	$(65, 0.6\%)$ $(130, 2.3\%)$	20/40	0.20	—	—	—
	150	—	—	—	$(50, 1.5\%)$ $(62, 2.8\%)$	15/80	0.25	—	—	—
	200	—	—	—	$(38, 1.5\%)$ $(46, 2.6\%)$	15/80	0.25	—	—	—
	$288(T_{\mathrm{m}})$	—	—	—	—	—	0.25	1500	—	—
PPS/40GF /20Mineral	23	21	1.95	—	$(160, 1.2\%)$	—	0.61	—	—	—
PPS/50GF	23	15	1.72	—	$\sigma_{\mathrm{uts}}=-230$; $(75, 0.5\%)$ $(176, 1.0\%)$	—	—	—	—	—
PPS/15CF/15 Kevlar/15 PTFE	23	14.5	1.5	—	$(159, 1.5\%)$	—	—	—	—	—

Notes: DAM = Dry as Molded;

GF (CF) = Reinforced with glass (carbon) fibers, by weight unless V_{f} is given;

Kevlar, Mineral, PTFE = Reinforcements, by weight.

Table 53.2   Fatigue ε-N Properties of PPS (Polyphenylene Sulfide) and Related Composites

Material	$T/℃$	$\mathrm{d}\varepsilon/\mathrm{d}t$	σ_{f}'	$\varepsilon_{\mathrm{f}}'$	b	c	K'	n'	$\sigma_{\mathrm{f}}@2N_{\mathrm{f}}$	R
PPS	23	—	—	—	—	—	—	—	24	—
PPS/40GF	23	—	—	—	—	—	—	—	54	—

Table 53.3   Mechanical Properties of PPS Reinforced by Weave

Material-DAM	$T/℃$	ρ	E_{11}	E_{22}	E_{33}	G_{12}	G_{13}	G_{23}	ν_{12}	ν_{13}	ν_{23}
PPS/CF(5-harness stain-weave fabric $[0°, 90°]_{4s}$)	23	1.6	57	57	—	4.18	—	—	0.033	—	—

Table 53.4 Orthotropic Mechanical Strength of Fabric-Reinforced PPS Composites

Material	$T/\text{°C}$	$(\sigma_{11u}, \varepsilon_{11u})$	$(\sigma_{22u}, \varepsilon_{22u})$	$(\sigma_{33u}, \varepsilon_{33u})$	$(\sigma_{12u}, \varepsilon_{12u})/$ $(\sigma_{23u}, \varepsilon_{23u})/$ $(\sigma_{13u}, \varepsilon_{13u})$
PPS/CF(5-harness stain-weave fabric $[0°,90°]_{4s}$)	23	$(745, 1.1\%)$	$(745, 1.3\%)$	$(110, 2.8\%)$	—/—/—

Chapter 54

PS (Polystyrene) and SAN (Styrene-Acrylonitrile)

54.1　Introduction

PS (**P**olystyrene) is a polymer made from aromatic monomer styrene, and SAN (Styrene-Acrylonitrile) is a further-extended product from styrene. Typical stress-strain curves of PS, SAN, and SAN/35GF plastics are depicted in Fig. 54.1. Their mechanical and fatigue properties are listed in Tables 54.1 and 54.2, respectively.

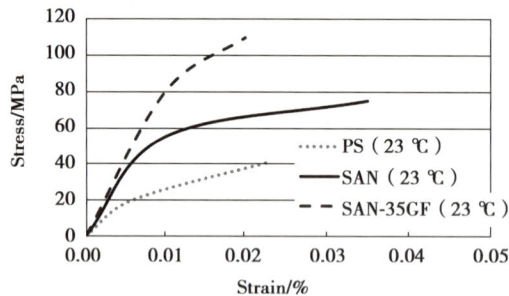

Fig. 54.1　Stress-strain Curves of PS (Bulk), SAN, and SAN/35GF Plastics

54.2　PS (Polystyrene) Solids

Pure polystyrene is transparent and can be easily colored. Due to its brittleness, the rubber may be added to improve the ductility with a slight loss of transparency.

54.3　PS Foams

EPS (Expanded Polystyrene) foam, with cellulose and starch, is rigid and tough closed-cell foams and has a specific weight ranging from 0.012 to 0.064. Both tensile and compressive strengths increase with the density. EPS geofoam consists of approximately 98% air and 2% polystyrene [BASF Corp., 1997]. The air entrapped within the foam makes EPS foam excellent for heat insulation.

XPS (Extruded Polystyrene) foam consists of closed cells, offering improved surface roughness higher stiffness and reduced thermal conductivity as compared with EPS. Its specific weight ranges from 0.028 to 0.045.

54.4   SAN (Styrene Acrylonitrile)

SAN (**S**tyrene **A**crylo**n**itrile) resin is a copolymer plastic consisting of styrene and acrylonitrile-a copolymer with alternating repeat units of styrene and acrylonitrile. Its chemical formula is $(C_8H_8)_n$—$(C_3H_3N)_m$. The relative composition is typically based on 70%~80% styrene and 20%~30% acrylonitrile. The copolymer has a glass transition temperature greater than 100 ℃ owing to the acrylonitrile units in the chain.

54.5   Applications

PS (Polystyrene) in solid is used to manufacture unbreakable glasses for gauges, windows, and lenses in light of its optical properties. Another application is its amenability to high-quality printing. Labels can be printed directly on the polystyrene part to produce attractive containers.

EPS (Expanded Polystyrene) foam beads can be molded into huge blocks that can be cut into sheets for thermal insulation. Some egg cartons and carryout food containers are thermoformed products of EPS foam.

XPS (Extruded Polystyrene) foam beads can be molded to produce hot drink cups, ice chests, or foam packaging. They are also used for packaging applications such as foam cartons for automotive trims as shipped, because they exhibit good damping properties.

SAN (Styrene acrylonitrile) is widely used in place of polystyrene if a better thermal resistance and higher strength are so in demand.

References

ANTONY P, PUSKAS J, 2003. Investigation of the Rheological and Mechanical Properties of a Polystyrene-Polyisobutylene-Polystyrene Triblock Copolymer and its Blends with Polystyrene[J]. Polymer Engineering and Science, 43(1): 243-253.

BANDYOPADHYAY A, CHANDRA B G, 2007. Studies on Photocatalytic Degradation of Polystyrene[J]. Materials Science and Technology, 23(3): 307-317.

BOURBIGOT S, et al, 2004. Solid-State NMR Characterization and Flammability of StyreneAcrylonitrile

Copolymer Montmorillonite Nanocomposite[J]. Polymer, 45: 7627-7638.

BUDTOV V P, GANDEL'SMAN M I, 1980. Mechanism of Strengthening of Polystyrene Plastics with Rubber [J]. Mechanics of Composite Materials, 15(5): 524-529.

CAI Y, et al, 2007. Morphology, Thermal and Mechanical Properties of Poly (StyreneAcrylonitrile)(SAN)/ Clay Nanocomposites from Organic-Modified Montmorillonite [J]. PolymerPlastics Technology and Engineering, 46: 541-548.

CHOI Y S, XU M Z, CHUNG I J, 2003. Synthesis of Exfoliated Poly(styrene-acrylonitrile) Copolymer-Silicate Nanocomposite by Emulsion Polymerization: Monomer Composition Effect on Morphology[J]. Polymer, 44: 6989-6994.

COHEN J T, et al, 2002. A Comprehensive Evaluation of the Potential Health Risks Associated with Occupational and Environmental Exposure to Styrene[J]. Journal of Toxicology and Environmental Health Part B: Critical Reviews, 5: 1.

DONALD A M, KRAMER E J, 1982. Craze Initiation and Growth in High Impact Polystyrene[J]. Journal of Polymer Science, 27(1): 3729-3741.

DOROUDIANI S, KORTSCHOT M T, 2004. Expanded Wood Fiber Polystyrene Composites: Processing-Structure-Mechanical Properties Relationships[J]. Journal of Thermoplastic Composite Materials, 17: 13-30.

ENOMOTO K, et al, 2003 Injection Molding of Polystyrene Matrix Composites Filled with Vapor Grown Carbon Fiber[J]. JSME Int Journal. Ser A. Solid Mech Mater Eng Soc Mech Engineers, 4693: 353-358.

HANEEFA A, et al, 2008. Studies on Tensile and Flexural Properties of Short Banana/Glass Hybrid Fiber Reinforced Polystyrene Composites[J]. Journal of Composite Materials, 41(15): 1471-1489.

IMAD A, 2001. A Visco-Elastic-Plastic Behavior Analysis of Expanded Polystyrene under Compressive Loading: Experiments and Modeling[J]. International Journal of Cellular Polymers, 20: 189-209.

JANSEN K, PANTANI R, TITOMANLIO T, 1998. As-molded Shrinkage Measurement of Polystyrene Injection Molded Products[J]. Polymer Engineering and Science, 38: 254-264.

JUTKOFSKY W S, TEH S J, NEGUSSEY D, 2000. "Stabilization of an Embankment Slope with Geofoam[J]. Transportation Research Board, 1736: 94-102.

KUMAR V, 2005. Phenomenology of Bubble Nucleation in the Solid-State Nitrogen-Polystyrene Microcellular Foams[J]. Colloids and Surfaces A: Physicochem. Eng. Aspect, 263: 336-340.

MIHAI M, HUNEAULT M A, FAVIS B D, 2007. Foaming of Polystyrene/Thermoplastic Starch Blends[J]. Journal of Cellular Plastics, 43(3): 215.

MOORE J D, 1971. Electron Microscope Study of Microstructure of Some Rubber Reinforced Polystyrenes[J]. Polymer, 12(8): 478-486.

OZKAN E, 1994. Thermal and Mechanical Properties of Cellular Polystyrene and Polyurethane Insulation Materials Aged on a Flat Roof in Hot-Dry Climate[J]. Journal of Testing and Evaluation, 22(2): 149-160.

PANWAR V, MEHRA R, 2009. Study of Electrical and Dielectric Properties of StyreneAcrylonitrile/Graphite Sheets Composites[J]. European Polymer Journal, 44(7): 2367-2375.

PARK C P, 2005. Methods of Expanding Polystyrene to Ultra Low-Density Foam[J]. Journal of Cellular Plastics, 41(4): 389-399.

PLAZEK D J, 1965. Temperature Dependence of Viscoelastic Behavior of Polystyrene[J]. Journal of Physical Chemistry, 69: 3480-3487.

PUCCI A, et al, 2012. Polymerizable Ionic Liquids for the Preparation of Polystyrene/Clay Composites[J]. Polymer International, 61: 426-433.

QIAN D, et al, 2000. Load Transfer and Deformation Mechanisms in Carbon NanotubePolystyrene Composites [J]. Applied Physics Letters, 76(20): 2868-2870.

RENJANADEVIM B, GEORGE K, 2009. Modification of Polystyrene using Nanosilica for Improvement in Mechanical Properties[J]. Progress in Rubber, Plastics and Recycling Technology, 25(2): 103-111.

SADABADI H, 2007. Effects of Some Injection Molding Process Parameters on Fiber Orientation Tensor of Short Glass Fiber Polystyrene Composites (SGF/PS)[J]. Journal of Reinforced Plastics and Composites, 26 (17): 1729-1741.

SINGH D, et al, 2007. Synthesis and Characterization of Nano alumina-Styrene Acrylonitrile High Impact Composite as a Plausible Civilian Armor Material[J]. Journal of Composite Materials, 41(23): 2785-2805.

SMITH R, et al, 2000. Predictive Modeling of the Properties and Toughness of Polymeric Materials: Part I: Why Is Polystyrene Brittle and Polycarbonate Tough? [J]. Journal of Materials Science, 35: 2855-2867.

SONG B, et al, 2005. Strain-Rate Effects on Elastic and Early Cell-Collapse Responses of a Polystyrene Foam [J]. International Journal of Impact Engineering, 31: 509-521.

ZHANG J G, et al, 2006. Fire Properties of Styrenic Polymer-Clay Nanocomposites Based on an Oligomerically-Modified Clay[J]. Polymer Degradation and Stability, 91: 358-366.

ZHI C, et al, 2006. Boron Nitride Nanotubes/Polystyrene Composites[J]. Journal of Materials Research, 21 (11): 2794-2800.

Table 54.1 Mechanical Properties of PS (Polystyrene), SAN (Styrene-Acrylonitrile), and Related Composites

Material-DAM	$T/°C$	E_T	ρ	ν	(α, ε)	α	k	γ	β	K_{IC}
PS (Solid; General Purpose; e.g. BASF 168N)	−40	3.7	—	—	(43,2%) (48,8%)	—	—	1450	—	—
	23	3.5	1.05	0.35	(20,0.6%) (58,2.3%)	70	0.12	1300	—	1.1
	50(High service temperature)					—	—	1400	—	—
	100(T_g)	—	—	—	—	—	1700	—	—	—
	270(T_m)	—	—	—	—	0.15	2270	—	—	—
PS (Solid; High Impact, Increasing Rubber; e.g. BASF 495F)	−40	2.7	—	—	(43,2%) (48,8%)	—	—	1450	—	—
	23	2.1	1.05	0.35	(26,4%) (25, 10%) (35, 47%); $\sigma_{crs,1\,000}=15.7$	70	0.12	1300	—	2
	60	1.6	—	—	(16,4%) (15,8%) (20, 50%) (21, 60%) (19, 68%)	—	—	1450	—	—
	80	1.3	—	—	(12.5,4%) (11.5,8%) (11.5, 50%) (9, 83%)	—	—	1500	—	—
	95(T_g)	—	—	—	—	—	1900	—	—	—
	270(T_m)	—	—	—	—	—	2270	—	—	—
PS/30GF	23	6	1.3	—	(85,1%)	25	0.18	—	—	—
EPS Foam, Expanded	23	0.003	0.012	0.1	(−0.07,−10%) (−0.025,1%); $\sigma_{uts}=0.25$	—	0.03	—	—	—
EPS Foam, Expanded	23	0.011	0.033	0.1	(−0.23,−10%) (−0.13,−1.5%); $\sigma_{uts}=0.5$	—	0.033	—	—	—
XPS Foam, Extruded	23	—	0.036	—	—	—	0.033	—	—	—
	100(T_g)	—	—	—	—	—	—	—	—	—

continued

Material-DAM	$T/°C$	E_T	ρ	ν	(α, ε)	α	k	γ	β	K_{IC}
SAN(70 styrene/30 acrylonitrile)	23	3	1.08	—	(70,3%) (70,4%)	80	0.17	1180	—	—
	85(High service temperature)									
	106(T_g)	—	—	—	—	—	—	—	—	—
SAN/10GF	23	4.1	1.14	—	(84,3%) (84,4%)	—	—	—	—	—
SAN/20GF	23	5	1.21	—	(91,3%) (91,4%)	—	—	—	—	—
SAN/30GF	23	6.4	1.28	—	(95,2%) (95,3%)	—	—	—	—	—
SAN/35GF	23	6.8	1.36	—	(110,2%)	25	0.19	—	—	—
SAN/40GF	23	6.9	1.36	—	(95,2%) (95,3%)	—	—	—	—	—

Notes: GF (CF)= Reinforced with glass (carbon) fibers by weight;

$T_g(°C)$ & $T_m(°C)$ = Glass transition point and melting point, respectively.

Table 54.2   Fatigue ε-N Properties of PS (Polystyrene), SAN (Styrene-Acrylonitrile), and Related Composites

Material	$T/°C$	$d\varepsilon/dt$	σ_f'	ε_f'	b	c	K'	n'	$\sigma_f@2N_f$	R
SAN	23	—		—	—	—	—	—	27	—

Chapter 55

PSU (Polysulfone)

55.1   Introduction

PSU (**Polysu**lfone) is rigid, transparent, amber-colored, retaining high strength properties between −100 ℃ and 150 ℃. It is known for its toughness and stability at elevated temperatures. It has high dimensional stability. Polysulfone membranes are easy to manufacture with reproducible properties and a controllable size of pores down to 40 nanometers. Mechanical and fatigue properties of PSU and its related composites are listed in Tables 55.1 and 55.2, respectively. Representative stress-strain curves of PSU (Polysulfone) and glass fiber-reinforced composites are reconstructed using some discrete data obtained from [Ultrason, BASF] and [Udel, Solvay] as shown in Fig. 55.1 and Fig. 55.2.

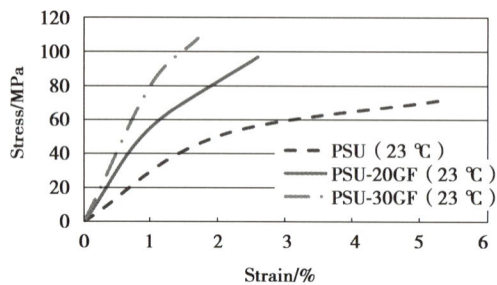

Fig. 55.1   Influence of GF Reinforcements on Stress-Strain Curves of PSU Composites at the Room Temperature

55.2   Applications

PSU (Polysulfone) is ideal for electric/electronic housing and connectors, with exceptional water steam resistance. It is also used as a dielectric in capacitors. PSU is a good candidate for medical devices as its high hydrolysis stability allows its use in medical applications requiring autoclave and steam sterilization.

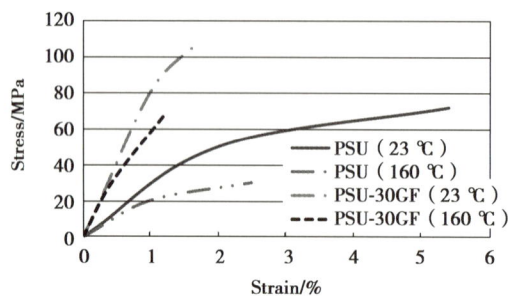

Fig. 55.2   Representative Stress-Strain Curves of PSU (Polysulfone) and PSU/30GF Composite at Different Temperatures

References

GAUDICHET-MAURIN E, THOMINETTE F, 2006. Ageing of Polysulfone Ultrafiltration Membranes in Contact with Bleach Solutions[J]. Journal of Membrane Science, 282(1-2): 198-204.

Linares A, Benavente R, 2009. Effect of Sulfonation on Thermal, Mechanical, and Electrical Properties of Blends Based on Polysulfones[J]. Polymer Journal, 41: 407-415.

ROUAIX S, et al, 2006. Experimental Study of the Effects of Hypochlorite on Polysulfone Membrane Properties [J]. Journal of Membrane Science, 2(1-2): 137-147.

SUN H, MARK J E, 2002. Preparation, Characterization and Mechanical Properties of Some Microcellular Polysulfone Foams[J]. Journal of Applied Polymer Science: 86(7): 1692-1701.

WATON R K, 1966. Polysulfone-A New Thermoplastic Resin for the Automotive Industry[J]. SAE 660003.

WOLFF S H, ZYDNEY A L, 2004. Effect of Bleach on the Transport Characteristics of Polysulfone Hemodialyzers[J]. Journal of Membrane Science, 243(1-2): 389-399.

WU C, et al, 2009. Ion Exchange Membranes from Sulfonated Polysulfone through Phase Inversion: Influence of Ion Exchange Capacity on Membrane Morphology[C]. AIChE 2008 Annual Meeting, Philadelphia, PA, USA.

Table 55.1　Mechanical Properties of PSU (Polysulfone) and Related Composites

Material-DAM	$T/°C$	E_T	ρ	ν	(α, ε)	α	k	γ	β	K_{IC}
PSU	−40	—	—	—	—	—	900	—	—	—
	23	2.6	1.25	0.37	(50,2%) (72, 5.4)	56	0.26	1100	—	12
	100	—	—	—	(60, 4.1%)	62	—	—	—	—
	150(High service temperature)				(35, 3.9%)	64	—	1600	—	—
	160	—	—	—	(20,1%) (33,2.5%)	—	—	—	—	—
	190(T_g)	—	—	—	—	70	—	—	—	—
PSU/20GF	23	6	1.4	0.41	(55,1%) (97,2.6%)	23/52	0.20	—	—	30
	90	—	—	—	$\sigma_{uts}=80$	—	—	—	—	—
	120	—	—	—	$\sigma_{uts}=67$	24/62	—	—	—	—

continued

Material-DAM	$T/℃$	E_T	ρ	ν	(α, ε)	α	k	γ	β	K_{IC}
PSU/30GF	23	8.8	1.49	0.42	$(80,1\%)$ $(108,1.7\%)$	19/49	0.22	—	—	>30
	100	—	—	—	$\sigma_{uts}=105$	18/59	—	—	—	—
	150	—	—	—	$\sigma_{uts}=80$	17/65	—	—	—	—
	160	8.0	—	—	$(29,0.4\%)$ $(67,1.2\%)$	—	—	—	—	—

Notes: DAM = Dry as Molded;

GF (CF) = Reinforced with glass (carbon) fibers, by weight unless V_f is given;

$T_g(℃)$ & $T_m(℃)$ = Glass transition point and melting point, respectively.

Table 55.2   Fatigue ε-N Properties of PSU (Polysulfone) and Related Composites

Material	$T/℃$	$d\varepsilon/dt$	σ'_f	ε'_f	b	c	K'	n'	$\sigma_f@2N_f$	R
PSU	23	—	—	—	—	—	—	—	$12@10^7$	—
PSU/20GF	23	—	—	—	—	—	—	—	$30@10^7$	—

Chapter 56

PTFE (Polytetrafluoroeth-ylene; Teflon)

56.1　Introduction

PTFE (**P**oly**t**e**t**ra**f**lu**or**o**e**thylene), also called Teflon after DuPont's brand name, has been famous for its low friction with a high melting temperature (327 ℃). PTFE is a completely fluorinated polymer manufactured when the monomer tetrafluoroethylene (TFE) undergoes free radical vinyl polymerization. When TFE polymerizes into PTFE, the carbon-to-carbon double bond becomes a single bond, forming a backbone (i. e. long chain of carbon atoms). PTFE has an interesting combined set of mechanical properties, including low shear strength, low surface tension, low coefficient of friction, low yield strength, high toughness. It has good environmental corrosion resistance, as being insoluble in all known solvents. Mechanical properties of PTFE are given in Table 56. 1. The specific weight is 2. 16 at 23 ℃, which is high compared to other thermoplastics. Representative stress-strain curves are demonstrated in Fig. 56.1.

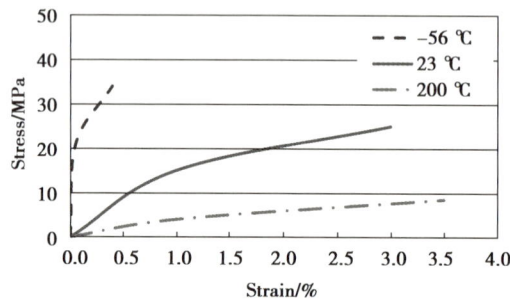

Fig. 56.1　Stress-Strain Curves of PTFE (Polytetrafluoroethylene) at Different Temperatures.

Fillers having high shear moduli are encapsulated and bound by PTFE with a lower shear modulus. Fillers for PTFE can be glass, carbon, graphite, PP (Polypropylene), PPS (polyphenylene sulfide), polyester, bronze, stainless steel, MoS_2 (molybdenum disulfide), Al_2O_3 (alumina), CaF_2 (calcium fluoride), and Wollastonite (calcium silicate):

(a) Glass: Enhanced wear resistance and good chemical resistance;
(b) Carbon: Increasing thermal resistance and resistance to deformation;
(c) Graphite: Extremely low friction and good compressive strength and wear resistance;
(d) Bronze: Improved compressive strength, wear resistance, and thermal conductivity;
(e) PEEK: High temperature and stress limits and resistance to most chemical reagents;
(f) MoS_2: Softening abrasiveness-reducing wear rate;
(g) Stainless steel: Improved thermal conductivity and reduced cold flow;
(h) PA/PPS: Reduced wear and abrasiveness for soft mating while keeping low friction.

PTFE has the lowest coefficient of friction against steel among all the known solid lubricants. As lubricants, PTFE resin can be dispersed into thermoplastic resins such as PA, PPS, and POM, significantly improving surface-wear characteristics. A chart of wear rate versus friction for some PTFE-based blends is given in Fig. 56.2. The friction coefficient of PA66/PPS filled with 20% of PTFE by volume is as low as that of pure TPFE under the same dry condition. Because TPFE has a static coefficient of friction lower than its dynamic coefficient of friction when it slides against steel, the slip-slick phenomenon occurs.

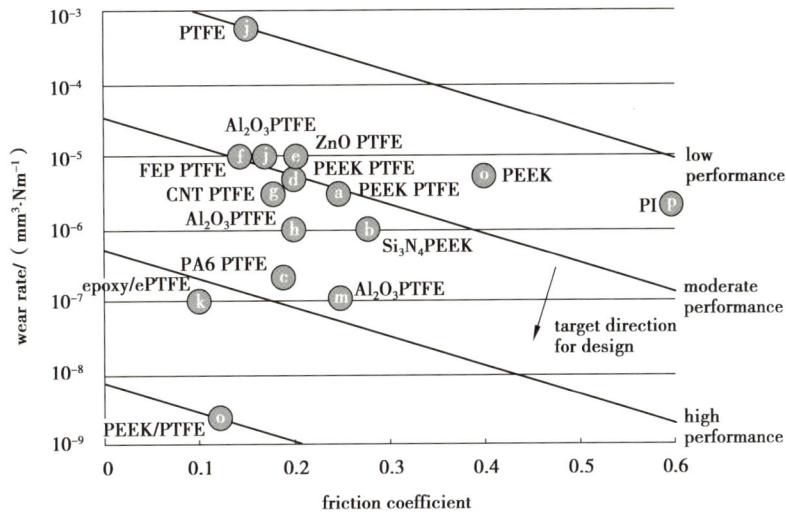

Fig. 56.2   Wear Rate versus Friction of PTFE (Polytetrafluoroethylene)-Based Blends

56.2   Applications

Applications of PTFE (Polytetrafluoroethylene) include seals for automotive fuel supply and fuel injection systems, exhaust gas sensor components, sealing and anti-friction elements for aircraft, coatings for pistons, heating elements, rolls, membranes, non-metallic gaskets, and insulation material for cable harness and other electrical applications.

One way to produce an ideal self-lubricating material is to form a solid lubrication film on the surface of a rigid substrate. Non-lubricating bearings based on PTFE are a typical application.

Non-sticking PTFE syringes are virtually immune to chemical attacks with a working temperature from cryogenic to 260 ℃. PTFE may be shaped by compression and sintering into bottles or beakers where its chemical stability and non-wettability make it suitable for use in extreme circumstances.

References

ADENA L, RINK M, POLASTRI F, 2004. Simulation of PTFE Sintering: Thermal Stresses and Deformation Behavior[J]. Polymer Science and Engineering, 44(7): 1368-1378.

BERGSTROM J S, HILBERT L B, 2005. A Constitutive Model A Constitutive Model for Predicting the Large Deformation Large Deformation Thermomechanical Thermomechanical Behavior of Behavior of Fluoropolymers Fluoropolymers[J]. Mechanics of Materials, 37: 899-913.

BIJWE J, et al, 2005. Influence of PTFE Content in PEEK-PTFE Blends on Mechanical Properties and Tribo-Performance in Various Wear Modes[J]. Wear, 8(10): 1536-1542.

BURRIS D, et al, 2007. Polymeric Nanocomposites for Tribological Applications[J]. Macromolecular Materials and Engineering, 292: 387-402.

CHEN Z B, et al, 2006. Mechanical and Tribological Properties of PA66/PPS Blend. Ⅱ. Filled with PTFE [J]. Journal of Applied Polymer Science, 101: 969-977.

HEINE S, et al, 1999. The Application of Engineering Thermoplastics for Sealing Automotive Engines[J]. SAE 1999-02-24.

KHEDKAR J, NAGULESCU J, MELETIS E I, 2004. Sliding Wear Behavior of PTFE Composites[J]. Wear, 252: 361-369.

KLETSCHKOWSKI T, et al, 2005. Computational Analysis of PTFE Shaft Seals[J]. Computational Material Science, 32(3-4): 392-399.

LAPPAN U, GEIBLER U, LUNKWITZ K, 2000. Changes in the Chemical Structure of Polytetrafluoroethylene Induced by Electron Beam Irradiation in the Molten State[J]. Radiation Physics and Chemistry, 59: 317-322.

LEHMANN D, et al, 2002. New PTFE-Polyamide Compounds[J]. Designed Monomers and Polymers, 5: 317-324.

LI J, 2009. Mechanical Properties of a Polyamide 6-Reinforced PTFE Composite[J]. Plastics, Rubber and Composites, 38(5): 201-205.

LUA X, et al, 2006. Surface Characterization of Polytetrafluoroetherlene Transfer Films during Rolling Sliding Tribology Tests Using X-ray Photoelectron Spectroscopy[J]. Wear, 261: 1155-1162.

MU L W, et al, 2010. Comparative Study of Tribological Properties of Different Fibers Reinforced PTFE/PEEK

Composites at Elevated Temperatures[J]. Tribo logy Transactions, 53: 189.

POMPE G, et al, 2005. Reactive Polytetrafluoroethylene/Polyamide Compounds. Ⅰ. Characterization of the Compound Morphology with respect to the Functionality of the Polytetrafluoroethylene Component by Microscopic and differential Scanning Calorimetry Studies[J]. Journal of Applied Polymer Science, 98: 1308-1316.

RAE P, DATTELBAUM D, 2004. The Properties of Poly(tetrafluoroethylene)(PTFE) in Compression[J]. Polymer, 45: 7615-7625.

SPEERSCHNEIDER C J, LI C H, 2007. A Correlation of Mechanical Properties and Microstructure of Polytetrafluoroethylene at Various Temperatures[J]. Journal of Applied Physics, 24(10): 3004-3007.

TANAKA K, KAWAKAMI S, 1982. Effect of Various Fillers on the Friction and Wear of PTFE-Based Composites[J]. Wear, 79: 221-234.

TEVRÜZ T, 1999. Tribological Behaviors of Bronze-filled Polytetrafluoroethylene Dry Journal Bearings[J]. Wear, 230: 61-69.

TEVRÜZ T, 1998. Tribological Behavior of Carbon Filled Polytetrafluoroethylene (PTFE) Dry Journal Bearings [J]. Wear, 221: 61-68.

VAN DER MEER D W, et al, 2005. Oriented Crystallization and Mechanical Properties of Polypropylene Nucleated on Fibrillated Polytetrafluoroethylene Scaffolds[J]. Polymer Engineering and Science, 45(4): 458-468.

WEIR C E, 1953. Transitions and Phases of Polytetrafluoroethylene (Teflon)[J]. J Res Natl Bureau Stand, 50 (2): 95-97.

XIN F, et al, 2006. A Study on the Wear Behavior of Polytetrafluoroethylene, Filled with Potassium Titanate Whiskers[J]. Wear, 261: 1208-1212.

YUICHI N, et al, 2003 Mechanical Properties of Polytetrafluoroethylene (PTFE) Thin Film Sputtered on the Metal Substrates[J]. Journal of the Vacuum Society of Japan, 46(12): 827-834.

ZHANG Z, 2008. A Simple Constitutive Model for Cyclic Ratcheting Deformation of TPFE with Stress Rate Effect[J]. Polymer Science and Engineering, 48(1): 29-36.

ZUBIR N, ISMAIL A, 2002. Effect of Sintering Temperature on the Morphology and Mechanical Properties of PTFE Membranes as a Base Substrate for Proton Exchange membrane[J]. Songklanakarin J. Sci. Technol, 24: 823-831.

Table 56.1　Mechanical Properties of PTFE（Polytetrafluoroethylene；Teflon）and Related Composites

Material-DAM	$T/℃$	E_T	ρ	ν	(α, ε)	α	k	γ	β	K_{IC}
PTFE（Bulk；True stress-strain）	73（Low service temperature）									
	−56	—	—	—	(21,5%) (34, 40%)	—	—	—	—	—
	−40	—	—	—	—	97	—	—	—	—
	23	0.56	2.16	0.46	(−27,−25%) (−14,−5%); (15, 100%) (25, 300%)	130	0.26	1050	—	—
	100(T_g)	—	—	—	—	—	—	—	—	—
	200	—	—	—	(−9,−26%) (−4,−5%); (4, 100%) (8.5, 350%)	200	—	—	—	—
	327(T_m)	—	—	—	—	—	—	—	—	—
PTFE（Sintered at 385 ℃）	23	14.2	2.16	0.46	(15, 100%) (19, 351%)	130	0.25	1050	—	—
PTFE Fiber	23	—	2.1	0.46	(362, 19%)	130	0.25	1050	—	—
PTFE/ 40Bronze	23	—	3.3	—	(16, 50%)	—	—	—	—	—
PTFE/ 55Bronze/ 5MoS$_2$	23	1.5	3.9	—	(13, 90%)	101	0.72	—	—	—
	−73（Low service temperature）									
	−55	—	—	—	(25,5%) (32, 10%) (36, 19%)	—	—	—	—	—
PTFE/15GF (V_f=15%)	23	1	2.2	—	(−28,−44%) (−20,−20%); (10,5%) (12, 10%) (15, 21%) (20, 60%)	120	0.43	—	—	—
	100	—	—	—	(3,5%) (6.5, 21%)	—	—	—	—	—
	200	—	—	—	(1.6,5%) (4.5, 24%)	—	—	—	—	—

continued

Material-DAM	$T/°C$	E_T	ρ	ν	(α, ε)	α	k	γ	β	K_{IC}
PTFE/25GF	23	—	2.22	—	(10, 150%)	110	0.38	—	—	—
PTFE/23GF/ 2MoS$_2$	23	—	2.25	—	(10, 100%)	—	—	—	—	—
PTFE/10Gr	23	—	2.13	—	(10, 150%)	—	—	—	—	—
PTFE/15Gr	23	1.4	2.12	—	(9.5, 230%)	125	0.45	—	—	—
PTFE/20CF/ 5Gr	23	1.2	2.1	—	(11.6, 70%)	84	0.44	—	—	—
PTFE/25CF	23	—	2.08	—	(13.1, 75%)	108	0.66	—	—	—

Notes: DAM = Dry as Molded;

GF (CF, Gr) = Reinforced with glass (carbon, graphite) fibers, by weight unless V_f is given;

$T_g(°C)$ & $T_m(°C)$ = Glass transition point and melting point, respectively;

Bronze, Gr, MoS$_2$ = Reinforcements by weight.

Chapter 57

PU (Polyurethane)-Thermoplastic, Thermoset, and Elastomeric

57.1   Introduction

PU (**Poly**urethane), abbreviated PUR, is a polymer consisting of a chain of organic units joined by urethane (carbonate) links. Its products are often called "urethanes". Depending on its chemistry, cross-linking, and processing, polyurethane can be

(a) Thermoplastic Polyurethane (TPU),
(b) Thermoset Polyurethane, or
(c) Elastomeric Polyurethane.

Material properties of PU and its related composites are given in Table 57.1. Polyurethane polymer is a combustible solid that ignites if exposed to an open flame. Its thermal conductivity is low, and it begins to break down at a temperature around 240 ℃.

Amine-cured urethane without filler has a stress-strain curve closely resembling filler-reinforced elastomers. Polyol-cured urethane does not behave like filler-reinforced elastomers.

Natural cotton, bamboo, and wool fibers may be used as reinforcements in a polyurethane-based matrix to improve sound absorption.

57.2   Polyurethane Foams

Polyurethane foams with rigid closed cells, called untransformed foams, possess excellent energy-absorbing properties and are used as impact limiters for various packaging applications. They can absorb large quantities of energy as they transmit stress equal to their crushing strength. Their mechanical properties are significantly anisotropic. The specific damping capacity as a function of pre-strain and cyclic strain for untransformed foams is given as follows [Friss et al.]:

ε_{mean}	$\varepsilon_{amplitude}$	tan δ-Transformed	tan δ-Untransformed
0%	±2%	0.168	0.161
0%	±10%	0.178	0.157
−50%	±2%	0.212	0.21
−50%	±10%	0.158	0.153

Transformed open-cell polyurethane foams have been previously made to be re-entrant in that their cell ribs are inwardly bent, which results in the foam exhibiting a negative Poisson's ratio. Otherwise, it is called untransformed.

Rigid polyurethane foams can endure a good temperature domain, varying from $-200\ ℃$ to $100\ ℃$. During the short period between mixing and final curing, rigid polyurethane foams are extremely adhesive, which allows the foam to bond effectively with a wide range of building facings. The adhesion is so strong that the bond strength is usually stronger than the tensile strength and shear strength of the foam. PU foams, made from aromatic isocyanates, discolors turning from off-white to yellow to reddish-brown as exposed to visible light.

57.3   Thermoplastic Polyurethane

The TPU (Thermoplastic Polyurethane) family or the thermoplastic polyurethane elastomers are classified into polyester and polyether types. TPU's as a family are noted for their inherent toughness providing outstanding abrasion resistance and tear resistance.

57.4   Applications

Solid PU's are embraced in the interior parts with steel inserts or other materials, such as steering wheels, gearshift knobs, brake handles, headrests, armrests, instrument panels, and door panels. They are also used in solid tires. Modern roller blades and skateboards are more cost-effective with the introduction of tough and abrasion-resistant polyurethane.

Polyurethane foams have been used to damp out vibrations. Polyurethanes are also widely used in flexible foam seating with high resiliency, rigid foam insulation panels, microcellular foam seals and gaskets, durable elastomeric wheels and tires, automotive suspension bushings, electrical potting compounds, high-performance adhesives, surface coatings and sealants, Spandex fibers, seals, gaskets, carpet underlay, and complex plastic parts (such as for electronic instruments).

TPU (Thermoplastic Polyurethane) has been successfully applied in automotive underhood components in addition to low-temperature applications (e.g. cable jackets).

References

AHN T, et al, 1993. Thermal and Mechanical Properties of Thermoplastic Polyurethane Elastomers from Different Polymerization Methods[J]. Polymer International, 31(4): 329-333.

AJILI S H, et al, 2003 Study on Thermoplastic Polyurethane/Polypropylene (TPU/PP) Blend as a Blood Bag Material[J]. Journal of Applied Polymer Science, 89(9): 2496-2501.

BUYUKAKINCI B Y, et al, 2011. Thermal Conductivity and Acoustic Properties of Natural Fiber-Mixed Polyurethane Composites[J]. Tekstil ve Konfeksiyon, 21(2): 124-132.

CHEN W, LU F, WINFREE N, 2002. Dynamic Compressive Response of Polyurethane Foams of Various Densities[J]. Experimental Mechanics, 42: 65-73.

CHOU C, et al, 1998. A Constitutive Model for Polyurethane Foams with Strain-Rate and Temperature Effects [J]. SAE 980967.

DARVISH K K, TAKHOUNTS E G, MATHEWS B T, et al, 1999. A Nonlinear Viscoelastic Model for Polyurethane Foams[J]. SAE 1999-01-0299.

FENG Ye, 2011. Morphologies and Mechanical Properties of Polylactide/Thermoplastic Polyurethane Elastomer Blends[J]. Journal of Applied Polymer Science, 119(5): 2778-2783.

FRIIS E A, LAKES R S, PARK J B, 1988. Negative Poisson's Ratio Polymeric and Metallic Foams[J]. Journal of Materials Science, 23: 4406-4414.

HU J L, et al, 2005. Dependency of the Shape Memory Properties of a Polyurethane upon Thermomechanical Cyclic Conditions[J]. Polymer International, 4(3): 600-604.

JACKVICH D, et al, 2008. Temperature and Mold Size Effects on Physical and Mechanical Properties of a Polyurethane Foam[J]. Journal of Cellular Plastics, 44: 327-345.

JOULAZADEH M, NAVARCHIAN A H, 2010. Effect of Process Variables on Mechanical Properties of Polyurethane/Clay Nanocomposites[J]. Polymers Advanced Technologies, 21: 263-271.

LU Q, MACOSKO C W, 2004. Comparing the Compatibility of Various Functionalized Polypropylenes with Thermoplastic Polyurethane (TPU)[J]. Polymer, 45: 1981-1991.

LUO H, et al, 2010. Characterization of the Compressive Behavior of Glass Fiber Reinforced Polyurethane Foam at Different Strain Rates[J]. Journal of Offshore Mechanics and Arct ic Engineering, 132(2): 021301.

MAJI A K, et al, 1995. Mechanical Properties of Polyurethane-Foam Impact Limiters [J]. Journal of

Engineering Mechanics, 121(4): 528-540.

MORIMOTO K, et al, 2004. Thermal Conductivity and Thermal Expansion Behavior of Glass Fiber-reinforced Rigid Polyurethane Foam[J]. Polymer Engineering and Science, 24(12): 943-949.

MOTT P, et al, 2002. Acoustic and Dynamic Mechanical Properties of a Polyurethane Rubber[J]. Journal of American Acoustic Society, 111(4): 1782-1790.

NEWMAN C R, FORCINITI D, 2001. Modeling the Ultraviolet Photodegradation of Rigid Polyurethane Foams [J]. Industrial and Engineering Chemistry Research, (40): 3336-3352.

NIKJE M, TEHRANI, 2010. Thermal and mechanical properties of polyurethane rigid foam/modified nanosilica composite[J]. Polymer Science and Engineering, 50(3): 468-473.

PARK Y, COLTON J, 2005. Fatigue of Reinforced-Polyurethane-Based, Sheet Metal Forming Dies [J]. International Journal of Fatigue, (28): 43-52.

RASSHOFER W, SCHOMER D, 2003. European and National ELV Regulations on Car Recovery, Their Impact on Polyurethane Applications in the Automotive Industry and a Proposal by the German Plastics Industry to Solve the Plastics Recovery Issue[J]. SAE 2003-01-0644.

ROBINSON G N, et al, 1994. High Performance Polyurethane Coating Systems Utilizing Oxazolidine-Based Reactive Diluents[J]. Journal of Coating Technology, 66(839): 69-74.

SONNENSCHEIN M, GUILLAUDEU S, LANDES B, et al, 2010. Comparison of Adipate and Succinate Polymers in Thermoplastic Polyurethanes[J]. Polymer, 51(16): 3685-3692.

VALENTINE C, CRAIG T A, HAGER S L, 1993. Inhibition of the Discoloration of Polyurethane Foam Caused by Ultraviolet Light[J]. Journal of Cellular Plastics, (29): 569-590.

WONGTIMNOI K, et al, 2011. Improvement of Electrostrictive Properties of a Polyether-Based Polyurethane Elastomer Filled with Conductive Carbon Black[J]. Composites Science and Technology, 71(6): 885-888.

XU B, et al, 2010. Thermal-Mechanical Properties of Polyurethane-Clay Shape Memory Polymer Nanocomposites [J]. Polymers, 2(2): 31-39.

XU B, et al, 2009. Mechanical Properties of Attapulgite Clay Reinforced Polyurethane Shape-Memory Nanocomposites[J]. European Polymer Journal, (45): 1904-1911.

ZHANG S C, et al, 2012. The Effects of Density on Thermal Conductivity of Al2O3 Fiber Composite Papers [J]. Key Engineering Materials, (512/515): 543-546.

ZHANG Z Z, et al, 2008. Effect of Carbon Fibers Surface Treatment on Tribological Performance of Polyurethane (PU) Composite Coating[J]. Wear, (264): 599.

ZHAO G, WANG T, WANG Q, 2011. Surface Modification of Carbon Fiber and Its Effects on the Mechanical and Tribological Properties of the Polyurethane Composites[J]. Polymer Composites, 32(11): 1726-1733.

ZHOU S, et al, 2004. Study on the Morphology and Tribological Properties of Acrylic Based Polyurethane/Fumed Silica Composite Coatings[J]. Journal of Material Science, 39(5): 1593-1600.

Table 57.1 Mechanical Properties of PU (Polyurethane) and Related Composites

Material-DAM	$T/℃$	E_T	ρ	ν	(α, ε)	α	k	γ	β	K_{IC}
PU (Solid; Thermoplastic)	23	0.8	1.2	0.4	(5, 200%) (8, 390%) (12, 1000%) (23, 2300%)	—	0.26	—	—	—
	30(T_g)	—	—	—	—	—	—	—	—	—
PU/40GF	23	10	—	—	(190, 2%)	—	—	—	—	—
	10	—	—	—	—	—	0.021	—	—	—
PU Foam (Cell size = 0.3 mm; Air in cells)	23	0.003 7	0.006	—	(0.5, 31%)	—	—	—	—	—
	30(T_g)	—	—	—	—	—	—	—	—	—
	50	—	—	—	—	—	0.026	—	—	—
PU Foam(Cell size = 0.3 mm; 33%Isopentane +64%CO_2+3% Air in cells)	23	0.003 7	0.006	—	(0.5, 31%)	—	—	—	—	—
	30(T_g)	—	—	—	—	—	—	—	—	—
	50	—	—	—	—	—	0.0182	—	—	—
PU Foam/1% Nanosilica	23	0.006 3	—	—	(0.54, 26%)	—	—	—	—	—
	30(T_g)	—	—	—	—	—	—	—	—	—
PU Foam/2% Nanosilica	23	0.0067	—	—	(0.66, 24%)	—	—	—	—	—
	30(T_g)	—	—	—	—	—	—	—	—	—
PU Foam/3% Nanosilica	23	0.0071	—	—	(0.68, 32%)	—	—	—	—	—
	30(T_g)	—	—	—	—	—	—	—	—	—
PU Foam/8% Cotton	23	0.014	—	—	—	—	0.041	—	—	—
	30(T_g)	—	—	—	—	—	—	—	—	—
PU Foam/12% Cotton	23	0.02	—	—	—	—	0.042	—	—	—
	30(T_g)	—	—	—	—	—	—	—	—	—
TPU (Generic; Soft)	23	—	—	0.5	(5, 25%) (7, 50%) (9.5, 75%) (14, 100%)	—	—	—	—	—

continued

Material-DAM	$T/^\circ C$	E_T	ρ	ν	(α, ε)	α	k	γ	β	K_{IC}
TPU (Ester-based; Shore 85A; New)	23	—	1.17	0.5	(25, 520%)	—	—	—	—	—
	$-34(T_g)$	—	—	—	—	—	—	—	—	—
TPU (Ester-based; Shore 85A; Aged)	23	—	1.17	0.5	(42, 600%)	—	—	—	—	—
	$-34(T_g)$	—	—	—	—	—	—	—	—	—
TPU (Ester-based; Shore 95A; New)	23	—	1.17	0.5	(35, 700%)	—	—	—	—	—
	$-34(T_g)$	—	—	—	—	—	—	—	—	—
TPU (Ester-based; Shore 95A; Aged)	23	—	1.17	0.5	(51, 460%)	—	—	—	—	—
	$-34(T_g)$	—	—	—	—	—	—	—	—	—

Notes: DAM = Dry as Molded;

GF (CF) = Reinforced with glass (carbon) fibers, by weight unless V_f is given;

$T_g(^\circ C)$ & $T_m(^\circ C)$ = Glass transition point and melting point, respectively;

Cotton, Nanosilica = Reinforcements, by weight.

Chapter 58

PVC (Polyvinyl Chloride)

58.1   Introduction

PVC (**P**oly**v**inyl **C**hloride) consists of repeating vinyl groups (ethenyl) having one of their hydrogens replaced with a chloride group. It can be rigid (with a low volume of plasticizers) or flexible (with a high volume of plasticizers). Stabilizers are required to reduce its sensitivity to heat and light. PVC is glueable and weldable. It can be machined, as well as bent nicely when heated up. Mechanical properties of PVC and its related composites are listed in Table 58.1. Representative stress-strain curves of flexible and more rigid PVC's are given in Fig. 58.1.

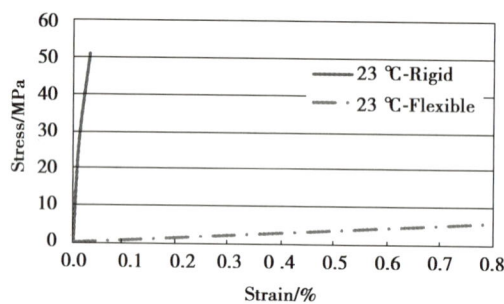

Fig. 58.1   Stress-Strain Curves of PVC (Polyvinyl Chloride) with Different Hardness

CPVC (Chlorinated polyvinyl chloride) is a thermoplastic produced by chlorination of polyvinyl chloride (PVC) resin. Chlorine gas is decomposed into free radical chlorine that reacts with PVC in a post-production step, replacing a portion of the hydrogen in the PVC with chlorine. CPVC shares most of the features and properties of PVC. CPVC has a significantly higher resilience and fracture toughness, allowing greater flexure and crush resistance. Reinforcement with natural fibers has become a research fashion recently.

58.2   Applications

PVC (Polyvinyl Chloride) shares 10% of automotive plastics (2001), including dash pads and trims. PVC is also an excellent insulation polymer for electric cables and wire harnesses, but not at elevated temperatures. Its continuous service temperature is suggested to be less than 60 ℃.

CPVC, mainly used as plumbing materials such as pipes, exhibits comparatively high impact and tensile strength and is non-toxic. CPVC can withstand corrosive water at a temperature up to 82 ℃.

References

ABU BAKAR A, HASSAN A, YUSOF A F M, 2005. Mechanical and Thermal Properties of Oil Palm Empty Fruit Bunch-Filled Unplasticized Poly (Vinyl Chloride) Composites[J]. Polymers and Polymer Composites, 13(6): 607-617.

ASHORI A, et al, 2011. Mechanical Properties of Reinforced Polyvinyl Chloride Composites: Effect of Filler Form and Content[J]. Journal of Applied Polymer Science, 120(3): 1788-1793.

CRESPO J E, 2008. Study of the Mechanical and Morphological Properties of Plasticized PVC Composites Containing Rice Husk Filters[J]. Journal of Reinforced Plastics and Composites, 27(3): 229-243.

DJIDJELLI H, et al, 2007. Preparation and Characterization of Poly (Vinyl Chloride)/Virgin and Treated Sisal Fiber Composites[J]. Journal of Applied Polymer Science, 103: 3630-3636.

EDWARDS D B, LEHMAN B, COHEN R, 1992. Fatigue Testing of PVC Pipe Fittings[J]. Journal of Vinyl Technology, 14(2): 69-73.

KAMEL S, 2004. Preparation and Properties of Composites Made from Rice Straw and Poly (Vinyl Chloride) (PVC)[J]. Polymers for Advanced Technologies, 15: 612-616.

KLEINER L W, PAZUR A S, 2004. Conductive PVC Composites: Part 1: Physical and Electric Properties [J]. Journal of Vinyl Technology, 4(4): 157-159.

LEBLANC J, et al, 2007. Effect of the Fiber Content and Plasticizer Type on the Rheological and Mechanical Properties of Poly (Vinyl Chloride)/Green Coconut Fiber Composites [J]. Journal of Applied Polymer Science, 106(6): 3653-3665.

NGUYEN P X, MOET A, 2004. Fatigue Fracture of Short-glass-fiber-reinforced Polyvinyl Chloride: A Crack Layer Approach[J]. Journal of Vinyl Technology, 7(4): 140-149.

REN Y, et al, 2010. Effect of Poly(epichlorohydrin) on the Thermal and Mechanical Properties of Poly(vinyl chloride)[J]. Journal of Applied Polymer Science, 118(6): 3416-3424.

SUMMERS J W, et al, 2004. Vinyl Composites-Fiber Glass Reinforced PVC[J]. Journal of Vinyl Technology, 12(2): 99-104.

SUN S, et al, 2006. Effects of Surface Modification of Fumed Silica on Interfacial Structures and Mechanical Properties of Poly (Vinyl Chloride) Composites[J]. European Polymer Journal, 42(7): 1643-1652.

TUNGJITPORNKULL S, SOMBATSOMPOP N, 2009. Processing Technique and Fiber Orientation Angle Affecting the Mechanical Properties of E-glass Fiber Reinforced Wood/PVC Composites [J]. Journal of Materials Processing Technology, 209(6): 3079-3088.

TUNGJITPORNKULL S, et al, 2007. Mechanical Properties of E-Chopped Strand Glass Fiber Reinforced

Wood/PVC Composites[J]. Journal of Thermoplastic Materials, 20(6): 535-550.

ZHENG Y, et al, 2007. Study on the Interface Modification of Bagasse Fiber and the Mechanical Properties of Its Composite with PVC[J]. Composites, Part A, 38: 20-25.

Table 58.1 Mechanical Properties of PVC（PolyVinylChloride）and Related Composites

Material-DAM	$T/℃$	E_T	ρ	ν	(α, ε)	α	k	γ	β	K_{IC}
PVC-U（Rigid）	23	2.8	1.37	0.38	(27,1%) (51,3%)	110	0.17	1250	—	3
	60（High service temperature）									
	77(T_g)	—	—	—	—	—	—	—	—	—
	172(T_m)	—	—	—	—	—	0.17	1800	—	—
f-PVC（Flexible）	23	—	1.4	0.38	(8, 100%) (12, 280%)	110	0.17	1250	—	—
PVC（Flexible Foam）	23	0.007	1.22	—	(10, 150%) (21, 400%)	—	0.15	1047	—	—
PVC/10GF（Rigid）	23	4.9	1.45	0.43	(62,3.5%)	38.4	—	—	—	—
	172(T_m)	—	—	—	—	—	—	—	—	—
CPVC	23	3.2	1.54	0.38	(65,30%)	80	0.16	1000	—	—
	82（High service temperature）									
	114(T_g)	—	—	—	—	—	—	—	—	—
	395(T_m)	—	—	—	—	—	—	—	—	—

Notes: DAM＝Dry as Molded;

GF（CF）＝Reinforced with glass（carbon）fibers, by weight unless V_f is given;

T_g（℃）& T_m（℃）＝Glass transition point and melting point, respectively.

Chapter 59

PVDF (Polyvinylidene Fluoride)

59.1　Introduction

PVDF (**P**oly**v**inyli**d**ene **f**luoride or **p**oly**v**inyli**d**ene di**f**luoride) is a family of highly non-reactive and pure thermoplastic fluoropolymers. Mechanical properties of PVDF (Polyvinylidene Fluoride) are given in Table 59.1. It is injection moldable at a melting temperature between 200 ℃ and 250 ℃.

After being poled in a high electric field PVDF becomes a ferroelectric polymer exhibiting pyroelectric and piezoelectric effects (Chapter 132) as transformed from phase α to phase β. PVDF experiences compression instead of expansion (or vice versa) when exposed to the same electric field because it has a negative d_{33} value in Eq. (132.3), unlike piezoelectric ceramics (e.g. PZT). Electric polarization (P_r) that occurs in a semi-crystalline polymer such as PVDF is nonlinear with hysteresis at high electric fields (E_c), Fig. 59.1 [Hassison and Ounailes].

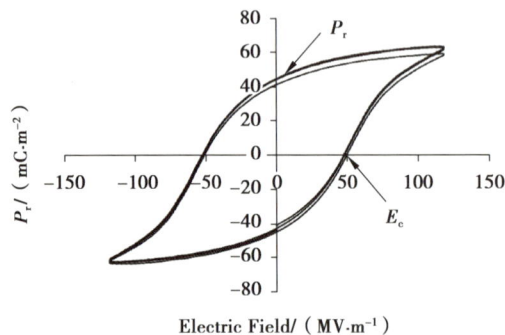

Fig. 59.1　Typical Polarization Hysteresis of Semi-crystalline PVDF

PVDF tends to demonstrate time-, temperature-, and frequency-dependent behaviors, such as viscoelastic creep, dielectric relaxation, and measurable energy losses under cyclic loading conditions.

59.2　Applications

PVDF-α (α phase) is commonly used as insulation on some electrical wires due to its low weight, low thermal conductivity, high chemical corrosion resistance, good heat resistance, low permeability, low moisture absorption, low flammability with low smoke emission, fair ductility at low temperatures, and high elastic modulus up to high temperatures. It can easily be welded with very outstanding line strength.

PVDF-β (β phase), due to its piezoelectric properties, has been used in batteries, tactile sensor arrays, inexpensive strain gauges, and lightweight audio transducers.

References

AMBROSY A, HOLDIK K, 1984. Piezoelectric PVDF Films as Ultrasonic Transducers[J]. Journal of Physics, E, 17(10): 856-859.

BYSTROV V, et al, 2007. First Principle Calculations of Molecular Polarization Switching in P(VDF-TrFE) Ferroelectric Thin Langmuir-Blodgett Films[J]. Journal of Physics: Condensed Matters, (19): 456210-456214.

CHANG W, et al, 2008. Phase Transformation and Thermomechanical Characteristics of Stretched Polyvinylidene Fluoride[J]. Materials Science and Engineering, A, (480): 477-482.

DILLON D, et al, 2006. On the Structure and Morphology of Polyvinylidene Fluoride-Nanoclay Nanocomposites [J]. Polymer, (47): 1678-1688.

HE X, et al, 2003. Phase Transition and Properties of a Ferroelectric Poly(vinylidene fluoridehexafluoropropylene) Copolymer[J]. Journal of Applied Physics, 97(8): 183.

HOU M, et al, 2012. Increase the Mechanical Performance of Polyvinylidene Fluoride (PVDF)[J]. Advanced Materials Research, 393-395: 144-148.

HUANG W, et al, 2010. Nanocomposites of Poly(vinylidene fluoride) with Multiwalled Carbon Nanotubes[J]. Journal of Applied Polymer Science, 115(6): 3238-3248.

JEONG J, et al, 2011. Influences of Intensity of Electric Field on Properties of Poly(vinylidene fluoride-tetrafluoroethylene) Thin Films during Annealing Process[J]. Japanese Journal of Applied Physics, (50), 04DK09.

KATAOKA H, et al, 2000. Conduction Mechanisms of PVDF-type Gel Polymer Electrolytes of Lithium Prepared by a Phase Inversion Process[J]. Journal of Physical Chemistry, B, 104(48): 11460-11464.

KAWAI H J, 1969. Piezoelectricity of Poly(vinylidene Fluoride)[J]. Japanese Journal of Applied Physics, 8 (7): 975-976.

KOCHERVINSKII V, 2003. Piezoelectricity in Crystallizing Ferroelectric Polymers [J]. Crystallography Reports, 48(4): 649-675.

MANO J, et al, 2004. Dynamic Mechanical Analysis and Creep Behavior of β-PVDF Films[J]. Materials Science and Engineering, A, (370): 336-340.

MENG Y, YI W, 2011. Application of a PVDF-based Stress Gauge in Determining Dynamic Stress-Strain Curves of Concrete under Impact Testing[J]. Smart Materials and Structures, 20(6): 065004.

NIX E L, WARD I M, 1986. The Measurement of the Shear Piezoelectric Coefficients of Polyvinylidene Fluoride[J]. Ferroelectrics, (67): 137.

OMOTE K, OHIGASHI H, KOGA K, 1997. Temperature Dependence of Elastic, Dielectric, and Piezoelectric Properties of Single Crystalline Films of Vinylidene Fluoride Trifluoroethylene Copolymer[J]. Journal of Applied Physics, 81(6): 2760.

SATHIYANARAYAN S, et al, 2011. Nonlinear and Time-dependent Electromechanical Behavior of Polyvinylidene Fluoride[J]. Smart Materials and Structures, 15(3): 767.

VINOGRADOV A, et al, 2004. Damping and Electromechanical Energy Losses in the Piezoelectric Polymer PVDF[J]. Mechanics of Materials, 36: 1007-1016.

ZHANG Q, et al, 2002. Poly(Vinylidene Fluoride)(PVDF) and its Copolymers[M]. Encyclopedia of Smart Materials, 1/2: 807-825.

Table 59.1 Mechanical Properties of PVDF (Polyvinylidene Fluoride)

Material-DAM	$T/℃$	E_T	ρ	ν	(α, ε)	α	k	γ	β	K_{IC}
PVDF	$-40(T_g)$	—	—	—	—	—	—	—	—	—
	23	1.1	1.78	0.34	(40, 100%) (43, 200%)	120	0.12	1120	—	—
	150(High service temperature)									
	$177(T_m)$	—	—	—	—	—	—	—	—	—

Notes: DAM = Dry as Molded;

$T_g(℃)$ & $T_m(℃)$ = Glass transition point and melting point, respectively.

Thermoset Plastics

Chapter 60

Amino-MF, UF, and PAE

60.1   Introduction

Hard and stain-resistant amino plastics appear in various translucent and opaque colors.

Aminos are moldable but do not burn even in the open flame. The three most used amino resins are MF (**M**elamine **F**ormaldehydes), UF (**U**rea **F**ormaldehydes), and PAE (**P**oly **A**mino **E**ster). They are resistant to solvents such as cleaning fluids, gasoline, and oils. Mechanical properties of different kinds of amino are listed in Table 60.1.

60.1.1   MF (Melamine Formaldehydes)

MF (Melamine Formaldehydes) is one of the hardest and stiffest isotropic polymeric systems. A fast-growing and essential application for MF resins is hard-wearing MF impregnated cellulose paper used to prepare flooring laminates. The formation of water-resistant covalent bonds is regarded to be the reason for the reduction of water sensitivity in MF-treated paper and cotton fabrics.

60.1.2   UF (Urea Formaldehydes)

UF (Urea Formaldehydes) is made from urea and formaldehyde, heated in a mild base such as ammonia or pyridine. Amino resins are considered a family of thermosetting resins, of which urea-formaldehyde resins make up 80% produced globally. It is rigid and brittle and comes along with a high modulus of elasticity, tensile strength and strain, and heat-distortional temperature. Low water absorption and low mold shrinkages are another two attributes.

60.2   Applications

Amino resins are extremely useful as adhesives, especially for gluing tire cords to rubber carcass and laminated lay-ups for kitchen counters. Molded products of amino plastics include switch cover plates, buttons, electric mixer housings, radio cabinets, coffee makers, and doorknobs Amino resins are also employed as surface coatings on paper and fabric, as well as used in molding powders.

References

AKYUZ K, et al, 2010. Physical and Mechanical Properties of Urea Formaldehyde-Bonded Particleboard Made from Bamboo Waste[J]. Internatio nal Journal of Adhesion and Adhesives, 30(3): 84-87.

BLIZNAKOV E, et al, 2000. Mechanical Properties of Blends of HDPE and Recycled UreaFormaldehyde Resin [J]. Journal of Applied Polymer Science, 77, 3220-3227.

BREY D M, ERICKSON I, BURDICK J A, 2008. Influence of Macromere Molecular Weight and Chemistry on Poly(beta-amino ester) Network Properties and Initial Cell Interactions[J]. Journal of Biomedical Materials Research, A, 85: 731-741.

BROSTOW W, et al, 2008. Tribology Properties of Blends of Melamine-Formaldehyde Resin with Low Density Polyethylene[J]. Polymer Engineering and Science, 48(2): 292-296.

DUNKY M, 1998. Urea-Formaldehyde (UF) Adhesive Resins for Wood[J]. International Journal of Adhesion and Adhesives, 18(2): 95-107.

GINDL W, JERONIMIDIS G, 2004. Wood Pulp Fiber Reinforced Melamine-Formaldehyde Composites[J]. Journal of Materials Science, 39(9): 3245-3247.

GRANADO A, et al, 2004. Phase Behavior and Mechanical Properties of Blends of Poly (butylene terephthalate) and P(amino-ether) Resin[J]. Journal of Applied Polymer Science, 91(1): 132-139.

HAGSTRAND P, OKSMAN K, 2001. Mechanical Properties and Morphology of Flax Fiber Reinforced Melamine-Formaldehyde Composites[J]. Polymer Composites, 22(4): 568-578.

HSAHIM R, et al, 2009. Physical and Mechanical Properties of Fire Retardant Urea-Formaldehyde (UF) Medium Density Fiberboard[J]. Journal of Materials Processing Technology, 209(2): 635-640.

HENRIKSSON M, BERGLAND L, 2007. Structure and Properties of Cellulose Nanocomposite Films Containing Melamine Formaldehyde[J]. Journal of Applied Polymer Science, 106(4): 2817-2824.

KIM S, et al, 2006. Thermal Analysis Study of Viscoelastic Properties and Activation Energy of Melamine-Modified Urea Formaldehyde Resin[J]. Journal of Adhesion Science and Technology, 20(8): 803-816.

OSEMEAHONE S A, BARMINAS J T, 2007. Study of Some Physical Properties of UF (Urea Formaldehydes) and UP (Urea Proparaldehyde) Copolymer Composite for Emulsion Paint Formulation[J]. International Journal of Physical Sciences, 2(7): 169-177.

SINGHA A S, et al, 2008. Mechanical Properties of Natural Fiber Reinforced Polymer Composites[J]. Bulletin of Materials Science, 31(5): 791-799,

SUN G, ZHANG Z, 2001. Mechanical Properties of Melamine-Formaldehyde Microcapsules[J]. Journal of Microencapsulation, 18(5): 593-602.

VOIGT B, et al, 2005. Electrical and Mechanical Properties of Melamine-Formaldehyde-Based Laminates with Shungite Filler[J]. Polymer Composites, 26(4): 552-562.

VOIGT B, et al, 2003 Carbon Fiber Reinforced Melamine-Formaldehyde[J]. Polymer Composites, 24(3): 380-390.

ZHONG J, WEI J, 2007. Mechanical Properties of Sisal Fibre Reinforced Ureaformaldehyde Resin Composites [J]. Express Polymer Letters, 1(10): 681-687.

Table 60.1   Mechanical Properties of Amino-MF (Melamine Formaldehydes), UF (Urea Formaldehydes), and PAE (Poly Amino Ester)

Material-DAM	$T/^\circ C$	E_T	ρ	ν	(α, ε)	α	k	γ	β	K_{IC}
MF	23	3.06	1.55	0.33	(62,2.4%)	63	0.4	1255	—	—
	$200(T_m)$	—	—	—	—	—	—	—	—	—
MF(Filled with Cellulose)	23	12	1.55	0.33	(65,0.6%)	29	0.4	1255	—	—
	150(High service temperature)									
UF	23	1.57	1.55	0.33	$\sigma_{uts}=-240$; (2,110%)	63	0.19	1200	—	—
	$119(T_m)$	—	—	—	—	—	—	—	—	—
UF (Filled with Cellulose)	23	9	1.55	0.33	$\sigma_{uts}=-240$; (65,0.8%)	29	0.19	1200	—	—
	80(High service temperature)									

Notes: DAM = Dry as Molded;

$T_g(^\circ C)$ & $T_m(^\circ C)$ = Glass transition point and melting point, respectively;

Cellulose = Reinforcement by weight.

Chapter 61

BMI (Bismaleimides)

61.1　Introduction

BMI (**Bism**ale**im**ides) is produced by the condensation reaction of a diamine with maleic anhydride. Material properties of BMI depend very much on its curing process and after treatments. It can be processed basically like epoxy, cured around 177 ℃. After an elevated temperature post-cure (e.g. 232 ℃), it exhibits superior mechanical properties such as a continuous use temperature at 200 ℃ and a glass transition temperature of 260 ℃ or above. Mechanical properties of BMI (Bismaleimides) are listed in Table 61.1. Orthotropic elastoplastic properties of fiber-reinforced BMI-composites and their corresponding failure values are given in Tables 61.2 and 61.3, respectively. Stress-strain curves of BMI-based adhesives at elevated temperatures are shown in Fig. 61.1. As an adhesive, BMI is recommended for elevated-temperature applications, while epoxy is more suitable for low-temperature applications.

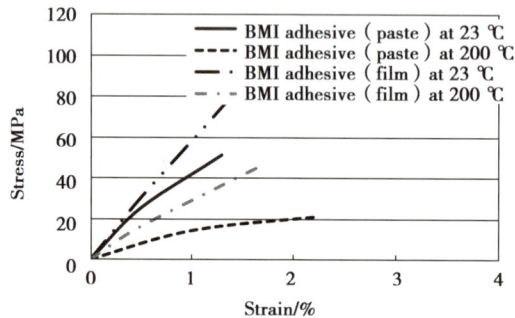

Fig. 61.1　BMI [(Bismaleimides)-based Adhesives: Net BMI Paste and BMI−3.7%GF Film (3.7% Glass Fiber by Volume] at Different Temperatures

BMI resin is suitable for RTM (resin transfer molding) like unsaturated polyesters, vinyl esters, and acrylates. However, BMI is the only one that meets the requirements of high-performance composites for strength, modulus, and thermo-oxidative stability.

BT (**B**is-maleimide **T**riazine) resins are heat-resistant thermosets made of bismaleimide triazine resin, co-reacted with epoxy, to give a resin system with some flexibility. The proportions in the blend are varied to produce different properties: a resin with 10% bismaleimide by weight is used for general-purpose circuit boards, as it has a similar curing temperature to epoxy resins. A special process for forming the chip-packaging composition includes add particulate fillers to BMI, achieve a coefficient of linear thermal expansion as low as 20 μm/m/℃ at room temperature.

BMI resins are extremely brittle. Morphological control is important in optimizing fracture toughness. Thermoplastics such as PEI (polyetherimide) may be used as a toughness modifier for the thermosetting networks of BMI.

Sheets of millimeter-long multi-walled CNTs (Carbon Nanotubes) with stretch alignment and epoxidation functionalization reinforce BMI so much that composites exhibit an unprecedentedly high tensile strength of 3080 MPa and tensile modulus of elasticity of 350 GPa [Chen et al.]

61.2   Applications

BMI (Bismaleimides) is merged into composites as a prepreg matrix used in electrical printed circuit boards. BT (bis-maleimide triazine) is a standard substrate material for BGA's (Ball Grid Arrays) to prepare PCB's (Printed Circuit Board) and PWB's (Printed Wire Board)-giving lower dielectric constant than FR-4. Their service life is several times that of conventional glass epoxy boards.

Carbon-fiber reinforced BMI composites are widely used for aircraft and aerospace composites such as wing leading edge structures and aft fuselage unit of Boeing 787. Adhesive joints used in supersonic aircraft need to withstand low temperatures such as -55 ℃ when traveling subsonically at high altitude and high temperatures such as 200 ℃ when traveling at Mach 2 or above.

BMI (Bismaleimides) is also used as a coating material and as the matrix of glass-reinforced pipes, particularly in high temperature and chemical environments.

References

AHN K J, SEFERIS J C, 2004. Prepreg Process Analysis[J]. Polymer Composites, 14(4): 349-360.

BOYD J D, CHANG, GLENN E C, 1993. Bismaleimide Composites for Advanced High Temperature Applications[J]. 38th International SAMPE Symposium, 10-13: 357-363.

CAIN K, GLINKA G, PLUMTREE A, 2003. Damage Evolution in an Off-Axis Unidirectional Graphite Bismaleimide Composite Loaded in Tension[J]. Composites, Part A, 34: 987-993.

CHEN Q, et al, 2010. Functionalized Carbon-Nanotube Sheet/Bismaleimide Nanocomposites: Mechanical and Electrical Performance beyond Carbon-Fiber Composites[J]. Small, 6(6): 763-766.

COSTA M, et al, 2005. Hygrothermal Effects on Dynamic Mechanical Analysis and Fracture Behavior of Polymeric Composites[J]. Materials Research, 8(3): 335-340.

CRISTEA M, et al, 2008. Dynamic Mechanical Analysis on Modified Bismaleimide Resins[J]. Journal of Thermal Analysis and Calorimetry, 93(1): 69-76.

DASILVA L, et al, 2005. Measurement of the Mechanical Properties of Structural Adhesives in Tension and

Shear over a Wide Range of Temperatures[J]. Journal of Adhesion Science and Technology, 19(2): 109-141.

FAN J, et al, 2002. Static and Dynamic Mechanical Properties of Modified Bismaleimide and Cyanate Ester Interpenetrating Polymer Networks[J]. Journal of Applied Polymer Science, 88(8): 2000-2006.

FAN S, et al, 2008. The Application of Thiol-ene Reaction on Preparing UV Curable Bismaleimide-Containing Liquid Formulation[J]. European Polymer Journal, 44: 2123-2129.

HU X, et al, 2010. Bismaleimide Matrix Composites with High Wear Resistance Modified by Potassium Titanate Whiskers[J]. Advanced Materials Researc h, 146-147: 1733-1736.

JIN J, et al, 2001. On Polyetherimide Modified Bismaleimide Resins, Ⅱ. Effect of the Chemical Backbone of Polyetherimide[J]. Journal of Applied Polymer Science, 81: 350-358.

JU J, MORGAN R J, 2004. Characterization of Microcrack Development in BMI-Carbon Fiber Composite under Stress and Thermal Cycling[J]. Journal of Composite Materials, 38(2): 2007-2023.

LIU Y L, CHEN Y J, 2004. Novel thermosetting resins based on 4-(N-maleimideophenyl) glycidylether: Ⅱ. Bismaleimides and Polybismaleimides[J]. Polymer, 45: 1797-1804.

LOWE A, et al, 2002. Interfacial Ageing of High Temperature Carbon/Bismaleimide Composites[J]. Composites, Part A, 33: 1289-1292.

LV X, et al, 2010. Effect of Thermal-Oxidative Aging on the Mechanical Properties of Carbon Fiber Reinforced Bis-Maleimide Composites[J]. Advanced Materials Research, 152-153: 829-833.

OGLIHARA S, et al, 2003. Nonlinear Stress-Strain Behavior in Carbon/Bismaleimide Laminates[J]. Proceedings of the JSASS/JSME Structures Conference, Japan, 45: 48-50.

VARMA I K, et al, 1987. Effect of Triallyl Cyanurate on the Properties of Bis-Maleimide Resins[J]. Journal of Applied Polymer Science, 33(1): 151-164.

XIONG Y, et al, 2004. Glass Transition Temperature in the Curing Process of BMI Modified with Diallylbisphenol-A[J]. Journal of Applied Polymer Science, 91(5): 3244-3247.

ZHANG, et al, 2009. Thermally Self-Healing Polymeric Materials: The Next Step to Recycling Thermoset Polymers[J]. Macromolecules, 42(6): 1906-1912.

ZHENG H, LI Z, ZHU Y, 2007. Bismaleimide Modified by Allyl Novolak for Super Abrasives[J]. Chinese Journal of Chemical Engineering, 15(2): 302-304.

Table 61.1　Mechanical Properties of BMI (Bismaleimides) and Related Composites

Material-DAM	$T/°C$	E_T	ρ	ν	(α, ε)	α	k	γ	β	K_{IC}
BMI (Bulk)	23	4.1	1.25	0.35	(41,1%) (72.4,2.2%)	45	0.6	—	—	—
	200	—	—	—	—	65	—	—	—	—
	219(T_g; As cured)			—	—	—	—	—	—	—
	285(T_g; After heat treatment)					—	—	—	—	—
BMI (Bulk; Hexcel F650)	23	4.6	1.21	0.35	(92,2%) (103, 4.8%)	49	0.6	—	—	—
	191	2.85	—	—	(28,1%) (55,2.2%)	—	—	—	—	—
	195(T_g; As cured)		—	—	—	—	—	—	—	—
	204	2.02	—	—	$\sigma_{uts}=40$	65	—	—	—	—
	273(T_g; After heat treatment)					—	—	—	—	—
	−55	5.5	—	—	(59,1.1%)	—	—	—	—	—
BMI Adhesive	23	4.4	1.28	0.35	(25,0.5%) (51,1.3%)	45	—	—	—	—
	100	3.6	—	—	(46,1.4%)	—	—	—	—	—
	200	1.43	—	—	(21, 2.24%)	65	—	—	—	—
	219(T_g; As cured)		—	—	—	—	—	—	—	—
	260(T_g; After heat treatment)			—	—	—	—	—	—	—
	−55	7.4	—	—	(69,1%)	—	—	—	—	—
BMI/3.7%GF (Adhesive Film; $V_f=3.7\%$)	23	6	1.33	0.35	(30,0.5%) (80,1.4%)	45	—	—	—	—
	100	5.2	—	—	(69,1.5%)	—	—	—	—	—
	200	3.1	—	—	(47, 1.74%)	65	—	—	—	—
	280(T_g; After heat treatment)					—	—	—	—	—

Notes: DAM = Dry as Molded;

　　　　GF (Gr) = Reinforced with glass (graphite) fibers, by weight unless V_f is given;

　　　　T_g(℃) & T_m(℃) = Glass transition point and melting point, respectively.

Table 61.2　Mechanical Properties of BMI Reinforced by Unidirectional Fibers

Material-DAM	$T/°C$	ρ	E_{11}	E_{22}	E_{33}	G_{12}	G_{13}	G_{23}	ν_{12}	ν_{13}	ν_{23}
BMI/60%Gr ($V_f=60\%$)	23	—	173.1	8.5	8.5	5.5	—	—	0.32	—	—

Table 61.3 Orthotropic Mechanical Strength of Continuous Unidirectional Fiber-Reinforced BMI (Bismaleimides) Composites

Material	$T/℃$	$(\sigma_{11u}, \varepsilon_{11u})$	$(\sigma_{22u}, \varepsilon_{22u})$	$(\sigma_{33u}, \varepsilon_{33u})$	$(\sigma_{12u}, \varepsilon_{12u})/(\sigma_{23u}, \varepsilon_{23u})/(\sigma_{13u}, \varepsilon_{13u})$
BMI/58%Gr($V_f = 58\%$)	23	(2610,1.5%)	(60,0.72%)	(60,0.72%)	(118,10%)/—/—

Chapter 62

EP (Epoxy; Peroxide)

62.1   Introduction

EP (**Ep**oxy) resin is a thermoset material with a low degree of polymerization before cure. It is prone to crystallization as being a super-cooled fluid. Its ultimate compressive strength is significantly higher than its ultimate tensile strength, so is its ultimate compressive strain much higher than its ultimate tensile strain. Material properties of epoxy depend very much on its curing process (temperature and time duration). In general, an epoxy of high glass transition point and good mechanical performance comes from well-controlled hot-curing resin (e.g. 180 ℃) with fillers. The glass transition temperature of epoxies may range from 90 ℃ to 250 ℃. The glass transition point of a specific epoxy decreases with increasing moisture content.

Mechanical properties of epoxies and related composites reinforced with random short fibers are listed in Table 62.1. Their fatigue and creep properties are given in Tables 62.2 and 62.3, respectively. Resin L135i, an epoxy with low viscosity cured at room temperature for 24 h and post-cured at 60 ℃ for another 24 h, has low strength at an elevated temperature [Fileder]. Resin 6376, cured at 180 ℃, has a good strength performance even at 150 ℃ [Fileder]. Representative stress-strain curves of EP (Epoxy) and its related random fiber-reinforced composites at different temperatures are shown in Fig. 62.1.

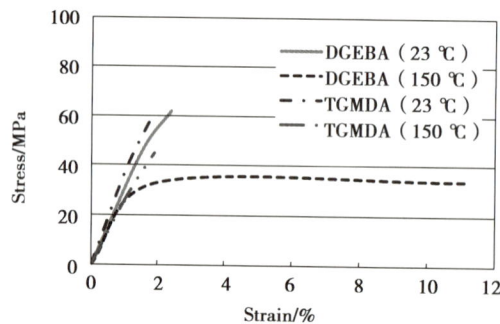

Fig. 62.1   Mechanical Properties of EP (Epoxy) at Different Temperatures

Epoxy resin is famous for its application to continuous fiber-reinforced composites as the matrix. Mechanical and thermal properties of epoxy-based composites are shown in Tables 62.4 and 62.5, respectively. Their fracture strengths are given in Table 62.6.

Most epoxies for use in automotive applications are nearly universally difunctional epoxies such as diglycidyl ether of bisphenol-A (DGEBA), while aerospace-grade materials typically use tetrafunctional epoxies like tetraglycidyl methylene dianiline (TGMDA). Tetrafunctional epoxies provide higher stiffness and strength than difunctional materials.

62.2   Applications

Glass fiber-reinforced epoxy has been used for automotive structural parts, while carbon fiber-reinforced epoxy for aircraft wings and fuselage.

Another popular structural application of epoxy is FR4 (Fire Retardant 4) for PCB (printed circuit board), which is a stack of layered epoxy matrices reinforced with woven glass fibers. Material properties of epoxy reinforced with continuous glass fibers for structural applications are given in Tables 62.3 and 62.4. Material properties of FR4 are discussed in detail in Chapter 129.

References

ABDEL-MAGID B, et al, 2003. Flexure Creep Properties of E-Glass Reinforced Polymers[J]. Composite Structures, 62: 247-253.

ABOT J L, et al, 2004. In-plane Mechanical, Thermal, and Viscoelastic Properties of a Satin Carbon/Epoxy Composite[J]. Composites Science and Technology, 64: 263-268.

ABDULLAH A, et al, 2012. Fatigue Behavior of Kenaf Fiber Reinforced Epoxy Composites[J]. Engineering Journal, 16(5): 105-113.

ARIKAN A, KAYNAK C, TINCER T, 2002. Influences of Liquid Elastomer Additives on the Behavior of Short Glass Fiber Reinforced Epoxy[J]. Journal of Polymeric Composites, 23(5): 792-795.

Aronhime M, et al, 1986. Effect of Time-temperature Path of Cure on the Water Absorption of High T_g Epoxy Resins[J]. Journal of Applied Polymer Science, 32: 3589-3626.

Bisanda E T N, Ansell M P, 1991. The Effect of Silane Treatment on the Mechanical and Physical Properties of Sisal-Epoxy Composites[J]. Composites Science and Technology, 41(2): 163-176.

BENZEGGAH M, KENANE M, 1996. Measurement of Mixed-mode Delamination Fracture Toughness of Unidirectional Glass/Epoxy Composites with Mixed-mode Bending Apparatus[J]. Composites Science and Technology, 56: 439.

BONHOMME J, et al, 2006. Fractography and Failure Mechanisms in Static Mode I and Mode II Delamination Testing of Unidirectional Carbon Reinforced Composites[J]. Polymer Testing, 28: 612-617.

BRITO Z, SANCHEZ G, 2000. Influence of Metallic Fillers on the Thermal and Mechanical Behavior in Composites of Epoxy Matrix[J]. Composite Structures, 48(1-3): 79-81.

CARTER J T, et al, 2003. The Development of a Low-Temperature Cure Modified Epoxy Resin System for Aerospace Composites[J]. Composites, Part A, 80: 83-91.

CHEN J K, SUN C T, 1985. Failure Analysis of Graphite/Epoxy Composite Subjected to Combined Thermal and Mechanical Loading[J]. Journal of Composite Materials, 19: 408-423.

CHEN W, ZHOU B, 1998. Constitutive Behavior of Epon 828/T-403 at Various Strain Rate[J]. Mechanics of Time-Dependent Materials, 2: 103-111.

D'ALMEIDA J R M, NUNES L M, PACIORNIK S, 2004. Evaluation of the Damaged Area of Glass Fiber-Reinforced Epoxy-Matrix Composite Materials Submitted to Ballistic Impacts[J]. Composites Science and Technology, 64: 945-954.

FIEDLER B, et al, 2001. Failure Behavior of Epoxy Matrix under Different Kinds of Static Loading[J]. Composites Science and Technology, 61(11): 1615-1624.

FLOR G, et al, 1989. A Thermal Study on Moisture Absorption by Epoxy Composites[J]. Journal of Thermal Analysis and Calorimetry, 35(7): 2255-2264.

GERSON A, et al, 2010. Curing Effects of SWNT Reinforcement on Mechanical Properties of Filled Epoxy Adhesive[J]. Composites, Part A, 41(6): 729-736.

GONO P, et al, 2001. Combined Effects of Humidity and Thermal Stress on the Dielectric Properties of Epoxy-Silica Composites[J]. Material Science and Engineering, B, 83(1-3): 158-164.

HASUR M V, et al, 2004. Performance of Stitched/Unstitched Woven Carbon/Epoxy Composites under High-Velocity Impact Loading[J]. Composite Structures, 64: 455-466.

JAIN P, et al, 2002. Flame Retarding Epoxies with Phosphorous[J]. Journal of Macromolecular Science-Polymer Review, 42(2): 139-182.

JEONG Y, et al, 2015. Modeling and Measurement of Sustained Loading and TemperatureDependent Deformation of Carbon Fiber-Reinforced Polymer Bonded to Concrete[J]. Materials, 8: 435-450.

KOYANAGI J, et al, 2010. Time and Temperature Dependence of Carbon/Epoxy Interface Strength[J]. Composites Science and Technology, 70: 1395-1400.

KUCZYNSKI J, SINHA A K, 2001. Strain Measurement and Numerical Analysis of an Epoxy Adhesive Subjected to Thermal Loads[J]. IBM Journal of Research and Development, 45(6): 783-788.

LI C, STRACHAN A, 2011. Molecular Dynamics Predictions of Thermal and Mechanical Properties of Thermoset Polymer EPON862/DETDA[J]. Polymer, 52(13): 2920-2928.

LITTELL J D, 2008. Measurement of Epoxy Resin Tension, Compression, and Shear Stressstrain Curves over a

Wide range of Strain Rates Using Small Test Specimens[J]. Journal of Aerospace Engineering, 21(3): 162-173.

LIU W, VARLEY R, SIMON G, 2007. Understanding the Decomposition of Fire Performance Process in Phosphorous and Nano-modified High Performance Epoxy Resins and Composites[J]. Polymer, 48(8): 2345-2354.

MCELROY D L, WEAVER F J, BRIDGMAN C, 1988. Thermal Expansion of EpoxyFiberglass Composite Specimens[J]. International Journal of Thermophysics, 9(2): 233-243.

MWAIKAMBO L Y, BISANDA E T N, 1999. The Performance of Cotton/kapok FabricPolyester Composites [J]. Polymer Testing, 18(3): 181-198.

NAIK N, et al, 2009. Stress-Strain Behavior of Composites under High Strain Rate Compression along Thickness Direction: Effect of Loading Condition[J]. Materials and Design, 31(1): 396-401.

OGASAWARA T, 2009. Torsion Fatigue Behavior of Unidirectional Carbon/Epoxy and Glass/Epoxy Composites [J]. Composite Structures, 90: 482-489.

PANDINI S, PEGORETTI A, 2008. Time, Temperature, and Strain Effects on Viscoelastic Poisson's Ratio of Epoxy Resins[J]. Polymer Engineering and Science, 48(7): 1434-1441.

PEREIRA A B, 2005. Interlaminar Fracture of Woven Glass/epoxy Multi-directional Laminates[J]. Composites, Part A: Applied Science and Manufacturing, 36: 1119-1127.

PORTER J H, et al, 1995. The Development of Epoxy Resin Composite Laminates That Are Thermoformable at a Temperature below 200 Degrees C and Using Vacuum Pressure[J]. SAE 950557.

PREGHENELLA M, PEGORETTI A, MIGLIARESI C, 2005. Thermo-mechanical Characterization of Fumed Silica-Epoxy Nanocomposites[J]. Polymer, 46(26): 12065-12072.

RATH S K, et al, 2004. Cationic Electron-Beam Curing of a High Functional Epoxy: Effect of Post Curing on Glass Transition and Conversion[J]. Polymer International, 53(7): 857-862.

REIS P N B, et al, 2009. Fatigue Life Evaluation for Carbon/Epoxy Laminated Composites under Constant and Variable Block Loading[J]. Composites Science and Technology, 69: 154-160.

RZEPKA S, et al, 2008. A Multilayer PCB Material Modeling Approach Based on Laminate Theory[J]. Proceedings of the 9th International Conference on Thermal, Mechanical and Multiphysics Simulation and Experiments in Micro-electronics and Micro-systems, Freiburg, Germany: 234-243.

SCHADLER L, GIANNARIS S, AJAYAN P, 1998. Load Transfer in Carbon Nanotube Epoxy Composites[J]. Applied Physics Letters, 73(26): 3842-3844.

SHAN Y, LIAO K, 2005. Environmental Fatigue Behavior and Life Prediction of Unidirectional Glass-Carbon/Epoxy Hybrid Composites[J]. International Journal of Fatigue, 24: 847-859.

SRIVASTAVA V, et al, 2007. Application of Probabilistic Neural Network for the Development of Wear mechanism Map of Glass Fiber Reinforced Plastics[J]. Journal of Reinforced Plastics and Composites, 26 (18): 1893-1906.

SRIVASTAVA V, KAWADA H, 2001. Fatigue Behavior of Alumina-fiber-reinforced Epoxy Resin Composite Pipes under Tension and Compressive Loading Conditions[J]. Composites Science and Technology, 61: 2393-2403.

TAO G, XIA Z H, 2007. An Experimental Study of Uniaxial Fatigue Behavior of an Epoxy Resin by a New Noncontact Real-time Strain Measurement and Control System[J]. Polymer Science and Engineering, June 1, 47(6): 780-788.

TSIAFIS I, et al, 2004. Mechanical Properties Determination of Various Epoxy Resin by Means of Nanoindentations[J]. Journal of the Balkan Tribology Association, 10(1): 73-80.

TUTTLE M E, GRAESSER D L, 1990. Compression Creep of Graphite/Epoxy Laminates Monitored Using Moire Interferometry[J]. Optics Lasers Engineering, 12(2): 151-171.

VALLIAPPAN M, ROUX J A, VAUGHAN J G, 1996. Die and Post-die Temperature Cure in Graphite/Epoxy Composites[J]. Composites, B, 27(1): 1-9.

VASSILEVA E, FRIEDRICH K, 2003. Epoxy/Alumina Nanoparticle Composites. I. Dynamic Mechanical Behavior[J]. Journal of Applied Polymer Science, 89(14): 3774-3785.

WAN Y Z, et al, 2005. Friction and Wear Behavior of Three-Dimensional Braided Carbon Fiber/Epoxy Composites under Lubricated Sliding Conditions[J]. Journal of Materials Science, 40(17): 4475-4481.

WANG B, et al, 2004. Theoretical Prediction and Experimental Study of Mechanical Properties for Random and Magnetically Aligned Single-Walled Carbon Nanotube/Epoxy Composites[J]. Materials Research Society Symposium Proceedings, 791: 331-339.

WU J, CHENG X H, 2006. The Tribological Properties of Kevlar Pulp Reinforced Epoxy Composites under Dry Sliding and Water Lubricated Condition[J]. Wear, 261: 1293-1297.

WU X, et al, 2008. Experimental Characterization of the Impact-Damage Tolerance of a Cross-Ply Graphite-Fiber/Epoxy Laminate[J]. Journal of Polymer Composites, 29(5): 534-543.

YANG N H, et al, 2007. Multi-Axial Failure Models for Fiber-Reinforced Composites[J]. Journal of ASTM International, 4(2), Paper ID JAI100533.

ZAKIAH A, ANSELL M P, SMEDLEY D, 2006. Influence of Nanofiller on Thermal and Mechanical Behavior of DGEBA-Based Adhesives for Bonded-in Timber Connections[J]. Mechanics of Composite Materials, 42 (5): 419-430.

ZHOU Y, et al, 2008. Improvement in Electrical, Thermal and Mechanical Properties of Epoxy by Filling Carbon Nanotube[J]. Express Polymer Letters, 12(1): 40-48.

ZHOU Y, PARVIN F, JEELANI S, et al, 2008. Improvement in Mechanical Properties of Carbon Fabric-Epoxy Composite Using Carbon Nanofibers[J]. Journal of Materials Processing Technology, 198 (1-3): 445-453.

Table 62.1   Mechanical Properties of EP (Epoxy) and Related Random Fiber-Reinforced Composites

Material-DAM	$T/°C$	E_T	ρ	ν	(α, ε)	α	k	γ	β	K_{IC}
DGEBA (Medium T_g)	−200	—	—	—	—	23	—	—	—	—
	−100	—	—	—	—	36	—	—	—	—
	23	3.06	1.3	0.33	(45,1.5%) (62,2.4%)	65	0.23	1255	—	0.5
	80	—	—	—	—	—	0.25	—	—	—
	100	—	—	—	—	—	0.256	—	—	—
	150	1.65	—	—	(33,2%) (34, 11.2%)	—	—	—	—	—
	155(T_g)	—	—	—	—	—	—	—	—	—
	270(T_m)	—	—	—	—	—	—	1884	—	—
TGMDA with DDS (High T_g)	23	3.72	1.3	0.33	(37,1%) (59,1.8%)	45	0.45	—	—	1
	150	2.62	—	—	(26,1%) (45,1.9%)	—	—	—	—	—
	250(T_g)	—	—	—	—	—	—	—	—	—
EP/25%SiC/ 3%CF (V_f = 25%; 3%)	23	—	—	—	—	—	1.23	—	—	—
EP/15% Kenaf (V_f=15%)	23	4.0	—	—	σ_{uts}=58	—	—	—	—	—
EP/45% Kenaf(V_f= 45%)	23	7.8	—	—	σ_{uts}=101	—	—	—	—	—
EP/40%Sisal (V_f=40%)	23	3.5	—	—	σ_{uts}=37	—	—	—	—	—

continued

Material-DAM	$T/℃$	E_T	ρ	ν	(α, ε)	α	k	γ	β	K_{IC}
EP for PCB (Low T_g)	23	8.3	1.91	0.33	$(-117,-9.5\%)$ $(-97,-0.2\%)$; $(31,0.2\%)$ $(48,0.8\%)$	30	1.0	1123	—	7
	41	4.0	—	—	—	—	—	—	—	—
	47	2.02	—	—	—	—	—	—	—	—
	88(T_g)	—	—	—	—	70	—	—	—	—
	150	—	—	—	—	124	—	—	—	—
	270(T_m)	—	—	—	—	—	—	1884	—	—
L135i	−40	—	—	—	$(-110,-8\%)$; $(80,2.3\%)$	—	—	—	—	—
	23	2.5	1.23	0.33	$(-103,-14\%)$; $(25,1\%)$ $(68,4\%)$	30	—	—	—	—
	80	—	—	—	$(2, 6.3\%)$	—	—	—	—	—
	90(T_g)	—	—	—	—	70	—	—	—	—
	150	—	—	—	—	124	—	—	—	—
EP 6376	−40	—	—	—	$\sigma_{uts}=-285$; $\sigma_{uts}=110$	—	—	—	—	—
	23	2.5	1.23	0.33	$\sigma_{uts}=-265$; $\sigma_{uts}=104$	—	—	—	—	—
	150	—	—	—	$\sigma_{uts}=-153$; $\sigma_{uts}=61$	—	—	—	—	—
	210(T_g)	—	—	—	—	—	—	—	—	—
EP/50%E-GF ($V_f=50\%$)	23	—	—	—	—	19.6	2.89	—	—	7
EP/50%E-GF/10%Al_2O_3($V_f=50\%$; 10%)	23	—	—	—	—	24	1.32	—	—	—
EP/50%E-GF/15%Al_2O_3($V_f=50\%$; 15%)	23	—	—	—	—	16.6	1.72	—	—	—

continued

Material-DAM	$T/°C$	E_T	ρ	ν	(α, ε)	α	k	γ	β	K_{IC}
EP/50%E-GF/10%FlyAsh (V_f=50%; 10%)	23	—	—	—	—	18.5	1.69	—	—	—
EP/50%E-GF/15%FlyAsh (V_f=50%; 15%)	23	—	—	—	—	14.8	1.23	—	—	—
EP/40%E-GF/10%SiC (V_f=40%; 10%)	23	—	—	—	—	7.4	3.51	—	—	—
EP/35E-Glass/15%SiC (V_f=35%; 15%)	23	—	—	—	—	3.7	2.76	—	—	—

Notes: DAM = Dry as Molded;

DGEBA = Diglycidyl ether of Bisphenol A (commercial epoxy);

TGMDA = Diglycidyl ether of Bisphenol A (epoxy for aerospace applications);

E-Glass = E-glass fibers;

EP for PCB = Epoxy for electric circuit boards, including flame retardance;

E_T(GPa) = Tensile modulus of elasticity;

GF (CF) = Reinforced with glass (carbon) fibers, by weight unless V_f is given;

T_g(°C) & T_m(°C) = Glass transition point and melting point, respectively;

Al_2O_3, Flyash, Kneal, SiC, Sisal = Reinforcements, by weight.

Table 62.2   Fatigue ε-N Properties of EP-Based Composites

Material	$T/°C$	$d\varepsilon/dt$	σ_f'	ε_f'	b	c	K'	n'	$\sigma_f @ 2N_f$	R
EP/15%Kenaf (V_f=15%)	23	—	—	—	—	—	—	—	29@ 5.5×10^5	—
									—	—
									41@ 1.2×10^3	—
									50@ 50	—
EP/45%Kenaf (V_f=45%)	23	—	—	—	—	—	—	—	50@ 7.6×10^5	—
									060@ 1.1×10^5	—
									80@ 4.3×10^3	—
									91@ 300	—

Table 62.3 Normalized Prony Parameters for Creep/Relaxation of Epoxy

Material-Dam	$T/℃$	E_0 or E_∞/MPa	N	$[p_i/MPa, T_i(h)], i=1,2,\cdots,N$
Epoxy-HT	23 40	$E_0=3.46$ $E_0=3.0$	3	$[0.43,0.1075][0.25,5.883][0.00065,58.33]$
Epoxy-RT	23 40	$E_0=3.46$ $E_0=3.0$	3	$[0.11,1.583][0.16,10.77][0.41,69.93]$

Table 62.4 Mechanical Properties of Epoxy Reinforced by Continuous Fibers

Material-DAM	$T/℃$	ρ	E_{11}	E_{22}	E_{33}	G_{12}	G_{13}	G_{23}	ν_{12}	ν_{13}	ν_{23}
EP/Boron Fiber ($V_f=45\%$; UD)	23	2	200	20.7	20.7	5.6	5.6	3.5	0.27	0.27	0.1
EP/Boron Fiber ($V_f=60\%$; UD)	23	2	200	18.5	18.5	5.6	5.6	3.5	0.27	0.27	0.1
	120(Cure temperature)										
EP/CF($V_f=60\%$; UD)	23	1.6	130	11	11	6	6	3.6	0.3	0.3	0.1
	120(Cure temperature)										
EP/57%CF($V_f=57\%$; UD)	23	1.6	131	6.4	6.4	4.2	4.2	—	0.32	0.32	0.1
	130(T_g)	—	—	—	—	—	—	—	—	—	—
EP/CF (IM7/8552)	23	1.6	171	9	9	5.3	5.3	3	0.32	0.32	0.1
EP/70%CF($V_f=70\%$; Fabric)	23	1.6	70	70	—	5	—	—	0.1	—	0.3
EP/HMCF($V_f=60\%$)	23	1.6	175	8	8	5	—	3	0.32	0.32	0.3
	120(Cure temperature)										
EP/HMCF($V_f=50\%$; Fabric)	23	1.6	85	85	—	5	—	—	0.1	—	0.3
EP/CF Weave (AGP370-5H/3501-6)	23	1.6	95	95	12.8	6	—	—	—	—	0.3
EP/GF(E-glass) ($V_f=60\%$; UD)	23	1.9	39	8.3	8.3	4.1	4.1	—	0.29	0.29	0.1
	120(Cure temperature)										
	−50	—	57.4	—	—	—	—	—	—	—	—

continued

Material-DAM	$T/°C$	ρ	E_{11}	E_{22}	E_{33}	G_{12}	G_{13}	G_{23}	ν_{12}	ν_{13}	ν_{23}
EP/60GF(V_f=60%; UD;S-2 Glass; RH=50%)	23	1.9	55.6	19	—	—	—	—	0.29	0.29	0.1
	80	—	56.1	—	—	—	—	—	—	—	—
EP/GF (E-glass) (V_f=50%; Fabric)	23	1.9	25	25	—	4	—	—	0.29	0.29	0.3
EP/GF(V_f=70%; Weave 1008)	23	1.9	12	12	—	—	—	—	0.29	0.29	0.3
	130(T_g)	—	—	—	—	—	—	—	—	—	—
EP/GF(V_f=66%; Weave 2116; 0.132 μm lamina)	23	—	14.8	14.8	—	—	—	—	0.29	0.29	0.3
	130(T_g)	—	—	—	—	—	—	—	—	—	—
	−20	—	12.8	12.8	—	—	—	—	—	—	—
EP/GF(V_f=66%; Weave 2116; 0.154 μm lamina)	23	1.9	12	12	—	—	—	—	0.29	0.29	0.3
	100	—	11.5	11.5	—	—	—	—	—	—	—
	130(T_g)	—	—	—	—	—	—	—	—	—	—
	150	—	4	4	—	—	—	—	—	—	—
EP/GF (Weave 7628)	23	1.9	24.5	19.8	—	—	—	—	0.29	0.29	0.3
	170(T_g)	—	—	—	—	—	—	—	—	—	—
EP/GF (L.Truck Leaf Spring)	23	2.6	34	6.53	6.53	2.43	2.43	1.7	0.29	0.29	0.3
	150										
EP/GF(V_f=48%; Knitted Leaf Spring; Fibers −97% long-itudinal;3% trans-verse)	23	—	38	13	13	1	0.2	—	—	—	0.3
	150										
EP/Gr (V_f=63%; AS04; UD)	23	1.6	138	9	9	6.9	6.9	—	0.26	0.26	0.1
	120(Cure temperature)										
EP/Gr(V_f=60%; T300; UD)	23	1.6	131	10.3	10.3	6.9	6.9	—	0.22	0.22	0.1
	120(Cure temperature)										
EP/Gr(UD Pitch Graphite)	23	1.6	169	6.2	6.2	5.6	5.6	2.6	0.31	0.31	0.4
EP/Kevlar(V_f=60%; UD; Kevlar 49/934)	23	1.4	76	5.5	5.5	2	2	—	0.34	0.34	0.3
EP/Kevlar(V_f=50%; Fabric)	23	1.4	30	30	—	5	—	—	0.2	0.2	0.3

continued

Material-DAM	$T/°C$	ρ	E_{11}	E_{22}	E_{33}	G_{12}	G_{13}	G_{23}	ν_{12}	ν_{13}	ν_{23}
EP/Spectra (EP826/Spectra 900)	23	—	30.7	3.52	3.52	0.21	0.21	—	0.32	0.32	0.1
EP/Zylon-HM(V_f = 59%)	23	1.6	140	—	—	—	—	—	0.3	0.3	0.1

Table 62.5 Orthotropic Thermal Properties of Epoxy-based Composites

Material-DAM	$T/°C$	α_1	α_2	α_3	k_1	k_2	k_3	γ	β_1	β_2	β_3
EP/Boron Fiber(V_f = 60%; UD)	23	18	40	40	—	—	—	—	0.01	0.3	0.3
EP/CF (Pitch)(V_f = 55%; UD)	23	—	—	—	270	1.17	1.17	—	—	—	—
EP/CF (Pitch)(V_f = 40%; UD)	23	—	—	—	190	0.73	0.73	—	—	—	—
EP/CF (Pitch)(V_f = 20%; UD)	23	—	—	—	92	0.36	0.36	—	—	—	—
EP/CF (PAN)(V_f = 60%; UD)	23	≈0	28	28	—	—	—	—	0.01	0.3	—
	−200	4	4	8	—	—	—	—	—	—	—
	−200	6	6	30	—	—	—	—	—	—	—
	−100	4	4	49	—	—	—	—	—	—	—
EP/CF (RTM)(V_f = 60%; Fabric)	23	2.1	2.1	57	—	—	—	—	0.03	0.03	—
EP/GF (E glass)(V_f = 60%; UD)	23	6	35	35	—	—	0.63	—	0.01	0.01	0.3
	100	—	—	—	—	—	0.74	—	—	—	—
EP/Gr(AS4)(V_f = 63%; UD)	23	−0.9	27	27	—	—	—	—	0.01	0.01	0.02
EP/HMCF(V_f = 60%; UD)	23	≈0	25	25	—	—	—	—	0.01	0.3	0.3
EP/HMCF(V_f = 50%; Fabric)	23	1.1	1.1	—	—	—	—	—	0.03	0.03	—

continued

Material-DAM	$T/°C$	α_1	α_2	α_3	k_1	k_2	k_3	γ	β_1	β_2	β_3
EP/Kevlar($V_f = 60\%$; UD)	23	4	40	40	—	—	—	—	0.04	0.3	0.3
EP/Kevlar($V_f = 50\%$; Fabric)	23	7.4	7.4	—	—	—	—	—	0.07	0.07	0.3

Notes: α_1, α_2, α_3(μm/m/°C) = Coefficients of linear thermal expansion of a unidirectional lamina;

k_1, k_2, k_3(W/m/°C) = Thermal conductivities of a unidirectional lamina;

β_1, β_2, β_3(μm/m/%) = Swelling coefficients of linear moisture expansion;

γ(J/kg/°C) = Specific heat capacity;

RTM = Resin transfer molding.

Table 62.6   Orthotropic Mechanical Strengths of Unidirectional Fiber-Reinforced Epoxy Composites

Material	$T/°C$	$(\sigma_{11u}, \varepsilon_{11u})$	$(\sigma_{22u}, \varepsilon_{22u})$	$(\sigma_{33u}, \varepsilon_{33u})$	$(\sigma_{12u}, \varepsilon_{12u})/(\sigma_{23u}, \varepsilon_{23u})/(\sigma_{13u}, \varepsilon_{13u})$
EP/Boron($V_f = 60\%$; UD)	23	$(-2800, -1.4\%)$ $(1400, 0.7\%)$	$(-280, -1.9\%)$ $(90, 0.6\%)$	$(-280, -19\%)$ $(90, 0.6\%)$	$(140, 2.8\%)/—/—$
EP/60%CF($V_f = 60\%$; UD)	23	$(-1200, -0.85\%)$ $(1500, 1\%)$	$(-250, -2.5\%)$ $(50, 0.5\%)$	$(-250, -2.5\%)$ $(50, 0.5\%)$	$(70, 1.4\%)/—/—$
EP/57%CF($V_f = 57\%$; UD)	23	$\sigma_{11c} = -1530$ $\sigma_{11c} = 1867$	$\sigma_{22c} = -214$ $\sigma_{22c} = 26$	$\sigma_{33c} = -214$ $\sigma_{33c} = 26$	$\sigma_{12u} = 100/—/—$
	130 (T_g)	—	—	—	—
EP/50%CF($V_f = 50\%$; Fabric)	23	$(-570, -0.8\%)$ $(600, 0.85\%)$	$(-570, -0.8\%)$ $(600, 0.85\%)$		$(90, 1.8\%)/—/—$
EP/CF(IM7/8552)	23	—	$\sigma_{22t} = 97$	—	$\sigma_{12u} = 113/—/—$
EP/HMCF($V_f = 60\%$; UD)	23	$(-850, -0.45\%)$ $(1000, 0.55\%)$	$(-200, -2.5\%)$ $(50, 0.45\%)$	$(-200, -2.5\%)$ $(50, 0.45\%)$	$(60, 1.2\%)/—/—$
EP/HMCF($V_f = 50\%$; Fabric)	23	$(-150, -0.15\%)$ $(350, 0.4\%)$	$(-150, -0.15\%)$ $(350, 0.4\%)$		$(35, 0.7\%)/—/—$
EP/GF (E glass)($V_f = 60\%$; UD)	23	$(-600, -1.5\%)$ $(1000, 2.5\%)$	$(-110, -1.35\%)$ $(30, 0.35\%)$	$(-110, -1.35\%)$ $(30, 0.35\%)$	$(40, 1\%)/—/—$
	-50	$\sigma_{uts} = -1910$ $\sigma_{uts} = 2500$	—	—	$—/—/—$

continued

Material	$T/℃$	$(\sigma_{11u}, \varepsilon_{11u})$	$(\sigma_{22u}, \varepsilon_{22u})$	$(\sigma_{33u}, \varepsilon_{33u})$	$(\sigma_{12u}, \varepsilon_{12u})/(\sigma_{23u}, \varepsilon_{23u})/(\sigma_{13u}, \varepsilon_{13u})$
EP/60S2-Glass($V_f=$ 60%;UD;RH= 50%)	23	$\sigma_{uts}=-1670$ $\sigma_{uts}=2300$	$\sigma_{uts}=-245$	—	—/—/—
	80	$\sigma_{uts}=-1227$ $\sigma_{uts}=1976$	—	—	—/—/—
EP/GF(E-Glass)($V_f=$ 50%;Fabric)	23	$(-420,-1.7\%)$ $(440, 1.75\%)$ $(440,1.75\%)$	$(-420,-1.7\%)$	— —	$(40,1\%)/—/—$
Ep/GF(Leaf Spring Design)	23	$\sigma_{11t}=610$	$\sigma_{22t}=118$	—	—
EP/Gr ($V_f=63\%$)	23	$(2280,1.5\%)$ $\sigma_{11t}=1725$	$(57,0.6\%)$ $\sigma_{22t}=228$	— —	$(76,1\%)/—/—$ —
EP/Kevlar ($V_f=60\%$)	23	$(-280,-0.35\%)$ $(1300,1.7\%)$	$(-140,-2.3\%)$ $(30,0.5\%)$	$(-140,-2.3\%)$ $(30,0.5\%)$	$(40,1\%)/—/—$
EP/Kevlar($V_f=$ 50%; Fabric)	23	$(-190,-0.6\%)$ $(480,1.6\%)$	$(-190,-0.6\%)$ $(480,1.6\%)$	— —	$(50,1\%)/—/—$
EP/Zylon-HM (UD; $V_f=59\%$)	23	$\sigma_{11t}=2700$	—	—	$\sigma_{12u}=70/—/—$

Chapter 63

PBA (Polybenzoxazine)

63.1　Introduction

PBA (**P**oly**b**enzox**a**zine) belongs to the family of addition-curable phenolic resins. PBA has been able to overcome many of the limitations on epoxies. PBA possesses some intriguing properties such as low cross-linking density, high glass transition point, high thermal stability, easy processing ability, low water absorption, near-zero shrinkage upon curing, good mechanical integrity, and good dielectric properties. A brittle-typed polybenzoxazine can be toughened by alloying with more flexible resins such as epoxy or polyurethane.

It was shown [Kumar] that the mechanical strength and modulus of chopped carbon fiber (CF) reinforced polybenzoxazine composites enhanced dramatically at approximately 17 mm carbon fiber length: 470% increase in tensile strength of the composites with respect to the neat PBA and 200% in tensile modulus. It was suggested that the maximum fiber content should not exceed 50% by weight. Mechanical properties of PBA (Polybenzoxazine) and its related composites are given in Table 63.1.

63.2　Applications

PBA-a (Polybenzoxazine) resins, a class of ring-opening phenolic resins that expand upon polymerization, are a new low-cost phenol-formaldehyde (phenolic) substitute for use in aircraft interior decorative panels. Dielectric properties of composites can be improved using high dielectric constant ceramic powders, e.g. barium titanate. $BaTiO_3$/PBA-a (Titanate/polybenzoxazine) composites are suitable materials for low-temperature fabrication of embedded capacitor technology.

References

AGAG T, JIN L, ISHIDA H, 2009. A New Synthetic Approach for Difficult Benzoxazines: Preparation and Polymerization of 4, 4'-Diaminodiphenyl Sulfone-Based Benzoxazine Monomer[J]. Polymer, 50: 5940-5944.

ALLEN, 2006. Physical and Mechanical Properties of Flexible Polybenzoxazine Resins: Effect of Aliphatic Diamine Chain Length[J]. J. of Applied Polymer Science, 101(5): 2798-2809.

ARDANUY M, et al, 2011. Foaming Behavior, Cellular Structure and Physical Properties of Polybenzoxazine Foams[J]. Polymers for Advanced Technologies, 23(5): 841-849.

COSTA L, et al, 1998. Flame-retardant Properties of Phenol-formaldehyde-type Resins and Triphenyl Phosphate in Styrene-Acry-lonitrile Copolymers[J]. Journal of Applied Polymer Science, 68: 1067-1076.

GHOSH N N, et al, 2007. Polybenzoxazines-New High-Performance Thermosetting Resins: Synthesis and Properties[J]. Progress in Polymer Science, 32: 1344-1391.

HUANG J, et al, 2011. Preparation and Thermal Properties of Multi-walled Carbon Nanotube/Polybenzoxazine Nanocomposites[J]. Journal of Applied Polymer Science, 122(3): 1898-1904.

ISHIDA H, CHAISUWAN T, 2003. Mechanical Property Improvement of Carbon Fiber Reinforced Polybenzoxazine by Rubber Interlayer[J]. Polymer Composites, 24(5): 597-607.

ISHIDA H, RIMDUSIT S, 1998. Very high thermal conductivity obtained by boron nitridefilled polybenzoxazine [J]. Thermochimica Acta, 320(1-2): 177-186.

ISHIDA H, ALLEN D, 1996. Physical and Mechanical Characterization of Near-Zero Shrinkage Polybenzoxazines[J]. Journal of Polymer Science, Pol. Phys, 34(6): 1019-1030.

JANG J, SEO D, 1997. Performance of Improvement of Rubber-Modified Polybenzoxazine[J]. Journal of Applied Polymer Science, 67: 1-10.

JUBSILP C, TAKEICHI T, RIMDUSIT S, 2011. Property Enhancement of Polybenzoxazine Modified with Dianhydride[J]. Polymer Degradation and Stability, 96(6): 1047-1053.

KIM S S, PARK D L, LEE D G, 2004. Characteristics of Carbon Fiber Phenolic Composites for Journal Bearing Materials, Composite Structures, 66: 359-366.

KUMAR K, et al, 2009. Synthesis and Properties of New Polybenzoxazines Containing (Substituted) Cyclohexyl Moieties[J]. Polymers for Advanced Technologies, 20(12): 1107-1113.

PAKKETHATI K, et al, 2011. Development of Polybenzoxazine Membranes for Ethanol-Water Separation via Pervaporation[J]. Desalination, 267: 73-81.

RIMDUSIT S, et al, 2011. Chemorheology and Thermomechanical Characteristics of Benzoxazine-Urethane Copolymers[J]. J. of Applied Polymer Science, 121(6): 3669-3678.

RIMDUSIT S, et al, 2010. Kevlar Fiber-Reinforced Polybenzoxazine Alloys for Ballistic Impact Applications [J]. Engineering Journal, 15(4): 23-40.

RIMDUSIT S, et al, 2005. Toughening of Polybenzoxazine by Alloying with Urethane Prepolymer and Flexible Epoxy: A Comparative Study[J]. Polymer Engineering and Science, 54(3): 288-296.

SU Y, CHANG F, 2003. Synthesis and Characterization of Fluorinated Polybenzoxazine Material with Low Dielectric Constant[J]. Polymer, 44: 7989-7996.

TAKEICHI T, KAWAUCHI T, AGAG T, 2008. High-Performance Polybenzoxazines as a Novel Type of Phenolic Resin[J]. Polymer Journal, 40(12): 1121-1131.

TIPTIPAKORN SUNAN, et al, 2010. Thermal Degradation Kinetics of Polyurethane /Polybenzoxazine Alloys [J]. Advanced Materials Research, 214: 439-443.

WIRASATE S, et al, 1998. Molecular Origin of Unusual Physical and Mechanical Properties in Novel Phenolic Materials Based on Benzoxazine Chemistry[J]. Journal of Applied Polymer Science, 70(7): 1209-1306.

YEGANEH H, et al, 2008. Synthesis and Properties of Polybenzoxazine Modified Polyurethanes as a New Type of Electrical Insulators with Improved Thermal Stability[J]. Polymer Engineering and Science, 48(7): 1329-1338.

Table 63.1　Mechanical Properties of PBA (Polybenzoxazine) and Related Composites

Material-DAM	$T/^{\circ}C$	E_T	ρ	ν	(α, ε)	α	k	γ	β	K_{IC}
PBA foam (Bisphenol-A)	23	0.75	0.4	—	$\sigma_{uts}=40$	0.09	—	—	—	—
	$166(T_g)$	—	—	—	—	—	—	—	—	—
PBA (Bisphenol-A)	23	3.3	1.2	0.2	(37,1.6%)	55	—	—	—	—
	$166(T_g)$	—	—	—	—	—	—	—	—	—
PBA membrane (Bisphenol-A-hda)	23	2.0	1.2	0.2	(65, 4.1%)	55	—	—	—	—
	$171(T_g)$	—	—	—	—	—	—	—	—	—
PBA/20PU (Bisphenol-A)	23	—	—	—	—	—	—	—	—	—
	$175(T_g)$	—	—	—	—	—	—	—	—	—
PBA/40PU	23	1.3	—	—		—	—	—	—	—
	$220(T_g)$	—	—	—		—	—	—	—	—

Notes: DAM = Dry as Molded;

　　　 GF (CF)= Reinforced with glass (carbon) fibers, by weight unless V_f is given;

　　　 $T_g(^{\circ}C)$ & $T_m(^{\circ}C)$= Glass transition point and melting point, respectively.

Chapter 64

PCN (Polycyanurate) and CE (Cyanate Ester)

64.1   Introduction

PCN (**Pol**y**cyan**urate) is a relatively new class of high-performance polymer with outstanding properties. Its dielectric properties are superior to all other known thermoset plastics. Mechanical properties of polyisocyanurateyanurates are given in Table 64.1.

Polycyanurates based on BPA (bisphenol-A), i.e.2, 20-bis(4-cyanatophenyl) isopropylidene, are among the first commercialized CE resins. Both the tensile strength and tensile strain of PCN increase with increasing content of PTMG (Polyoxytetramethylene Glycol) and reach the peak at 20% of PTMG by Weight [Kripotou et al.].

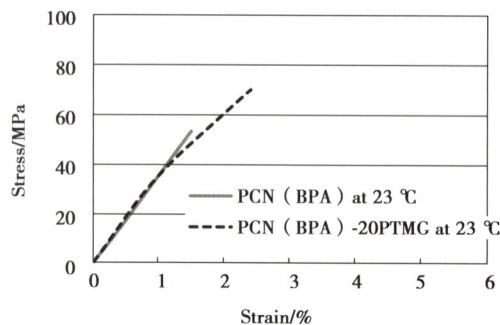

Fig. 64.1   Stress-Strain Curves of PCN (BPA) and PCN Composites Reinforced with 20% of PTMG (Polyoxytetramethylene Glycol) by Weight

Polycyanurates based on BPC (bisphenol-C), i.e.1, 1-dichloro-2, 2-bis(4-hydroxyphenyl) ethane, have mechanical, thermal, and processing characteristics similar to BPA (bisphenol-A) analogs, but they are more ignition resistant and have extremely low heat release rate in forced flaming combustion. Polyisocyanurate-based on BPC (bisphenol-C) has exceptional fire resistancetypically passing the Federal Aviation Administration heat release requirement for aircraft interior materials Title 14 Code of Federal Regulations 25.853(a-1).

Polycyanurates based on BPE (bisphenol-E), i.e. bis-(4-cyanatophenyl)-1, 1-ethane, have good processability with a very low viscosity (0.09~0.12 Pa · s in terms of absolute viscosity) at the room temperature and low damping before the onset of glass transition. Fumed silica and other fillers can be used to increase the storage modulus and lower its damping further [Goertzen & Kessler].

Mechanical properties and manufacturing processes of fiber-reinforced PCN composites are quite similar to those of fiber/epoxy composites. However, they offer additional benefits such as having lower moisture uptake, reduced outgassing, higher glass transition temperature, lower optical loss, lower dielectric constant, better adhesion, lower cure shrinkage, higher fracture toughness, and high thermal stability, including excellent resistance to thermally induced micro cracks. Stress-strain curves of PCN (BPA) and PCN composites are depicted in Fig. 64.1.

64.2   Cyanate Ester

CE (**C**yanate **E**ster) resins possess high thermal stability and moisture resistance, low ionic contaminant concentration, good dielectric properties, and benefit from being single component materials. CE resins have been touted as potential epoxy replacements for epoxies in high temperature encapsulation applications. Though developed during the 1980s, CE resins join epoxy resins and bismaleimide resins as the third major class of thermosetting resins.

Another remarkable aspect of CE resins is their polymerization via a cyclotrimerization reaction to form a polyisocyanurate (PCN) thermoset in a high yield.

64.3   Applications

Polycyanurates are used for electronic applications with high demands on dielectric properties, high glass temperature requirements in composites, and good dimensional stability at molten solder temperatures, usually between 220 ℃ and 270 ℃. Potential applications include highspeed electronic circuits, optical switches, optical attenuators, multiplexers, demultiplexers, splitters, combiners, and radomes.

Polycyanurates are a new class of thermosetting polymers having properties superior to epoxies for spacecraft applications. polyisocyanurate composites are currently used in satellite programs and expected to have increased applications in satellite and launch vehicles.

References

ANTHOULIS G I, et al, 2008. Synthesis and Characterization of Polycyanurate/Montmorillonite Nanocomposites [J]. Journal of Polymer Science, Part B: Polymer Physics, 46(11): 1036-1049.

BERSHTEIN V, et al, 2007. Structure and Dynamic/Compositional Heterogeneity in Amorphous Polycyanurate-Poly(tetramethylene glycol) Hybrid Networks[J]. Journal of Macromolecular Science, Part. B: Polym. Phys, 46(1): 207-230.

CHANG J, HONG J, 2000. Morphology and Fracture Toughness of Poly(Ether Sulfone) Blended Polycyanurates [J]. Polymer, (41): 4513-4521.

ESSLINGER J R J, FRUCHTNICHT O, 2004. Cyanate Ester Matrix Technology for Improved Thermal Performance of Filament Wound Missile Structures[J]. SAMPE J, 40(6): 9-15.

FANG Z, WANG J, GU A, 2006. Structure and Properties of Multiwalled Carbon Nanotubes/Cyanate Ester Composites[J]. Polymer Engineering and Science, 46: 670-679.

GEORJON O, GALY J, 1997. Effects of Crosslink Density on Mechanical Properties of High Glass Transition Temperature Polycyanurate Networks[J]. Journal of Applied Polymer Science, 65 (12): 2471-2479.

GOERTZEN W K, KESSLER M R, 2008. Dynamic Mechanical Analysis of Fumed Silica/Cyanate Ester Nanocomposites[J]. Composites, Part A, 39: 761-768.

GOERTZEN W, KESSLER M, 2007. Thermal and Mechanical Evaluation of Cyanate Ester Composites with Low-Temperature Processability[J]. Composites, Part A, 38(3): 779-784.

GRIGORYEVA O, et al, 2002. Effect of Hybrid Network Formation on Adhesion Properties of Polycyanurate/ Polyurethane Semi-Interpenetrating Polymer Networks [J]. Polymer Engineering and Science, 42 (12): 2440-2448.

GUO J, SIMON S, 2010. Pressure-Volume-Temperature Behavior of Two Polycyanurate Networks[J]. Journal of Polymer Science: Part B: Polymer Physics, 48(23): 2509-2517.

GUO J, SIMON S, 2009. Effect of Crosslink Density on the Pressure Relaxation Response of Polycyanurate Networks[J]. Journal of Polymer Science: Part B: Polymer Physics, 47(24): 2477-2486.

HAMERTON I, et al, 1996. Molecular Modeling of the Physical and Mechanical Properties of Two Polycyanurate Network Polymers[J]. Journal of Materials Chemistry, 6: 311-314.

HOPKINS R, LIPELES R, 2005. Preparation and Characterization of Single Wall Carbon Nanotube-Reinforced Polycyanurate Nanocomposites[J]. Polymer, 46: 787.

IKENO T, et al, 2011. A Molecular Dynamic Simulation of Crosslinking of Bisphenol and Triazine by United Atom Model: A Polycyanurate Model[J]. Chemistry Letters, 40 (3): 309-311.

KRIPOTOU S, et al, 2006. Structure-property Relationships in Brittle Polymer Networks Modified by Flexible Cross-links[J]. Materials Science- Poland, 24(2): 477-492.

LEE Q, SIMON S, 2008. Curing of Bisphenol M Dicyanate Ester under Nanoscale Constraint [J]. Macromolecules, 41(4): 1310-1317.

LIANG K, et al, 2006. Cyanate Ester/Polyhedral Oligomeric Silsesquioxane (POSS) Nanocomposites: Synthesis and Characterization[J]. Chem Mater, 18(2): 301-312.

LIU J, et al, 2011. Cyanate Ester Resin Modified by Hydroxyl-Terminated Polybutadiene: Morphology, Thermal, and Mechanical Properties[J]. Polymer Engineering and Science, 51(7): 1404-1408.

MAROULAS P, et al, 2009. Molecular Mobility in Polycyanurate/Clay Nanocomposites Studied by Dielectric Techniques[J]. Journal of Composite Materials, 43(9): 943-958.

MONDRAGON L, et al, 2006. Properties and Structure of Cyanate Ester/Polysulfone/Organoclay Nanocomposites [J]. Polymer, (47): 3401-3409.

SHIN D C, et al, 1999. Synthesis and Optical Characterization of Polycyanurates with Pendent Second-Order Nonlinear Optical Chromospheres[J]. Polymer Journal, 31(12): 1200-1204.

TANG Y, KONG J, GU J, LIANG G, 2009. Reinforced Cyanate Ester Resins with Carbon Nanotubes: Surface Modification, Reaction Activity and Mechanical Properties Analyses[J]. Polymer-Plastics Technology and Engineering, 48: 359-366.

YAMEEN B, et al, 2008. Polycyanurate Thermoset Networks with High Thermal, Mechanical, and Hydrolytic Stability Based on Liquid Multifunctional Cyanate Ester Monomers with Bisphenol A and AF Units[J]. Macromolecular Chemistry and Physics, (209): 1673-1685.

ZALDIVAR R J, NOKES J P, 2011. Identification and Evaluation of Progressive Thermal Degradation Caused by Carbamate Formation in Cyanate Ester Resin-Based Composites[J]. Polymer Engineering and Science, 51(1): 158-169.

Table 64.1　Mechanical Properties of PCN (Polycyanurate) and CE (Cyanate Ester) and Related Composites

Material-DAM	$T/℃$	E_T	ρ	ν	(α, ε)	α	k	γ	β	K_{IC}
CE	−20	—	—	—	—	42	—	900	—	—
	23	2.6	—	0.29	$\sigma_{uts}=86$	49	0.26	1100	—	—
	50	—	—	—	—	—	0.23	—	—	—
	100	—	—	—	—	52	0.27	1430	—	—
	120	—	—	—	—	—	—	1500	—	—
	247(T_g)	—	—	—	—	—	—	—	—	—
CE/15CNT	0	—	—	—	—	21	—	800	—	—
	23	—	—	—	—	24	0.295	850	—	—
	100	—	—	—	—	26	0.33	1120	—	—

continued

Material-DAM	$T/℃$	E_T	ρ	ν	(α, ε)	α	k	γ	β	K_{IC}
CE/25CNT	−20	—	—	—	—	14	—	800	—	—
	23	4.5	—	0.29	$\sigma_{uts}=50$	15	0.4	830	—	—
	50	—	—	—	—	—	0.42	—	—	—
	100	—	—	—	—	17	0.45	1100	—	—
PCN (BPA)	23	3.4	1.2	0.29	(17,0.5%) (53,1.5%)	65	—	—	—	—
	289(T_g)	—	—	—	—	—	—	—	—	—
PCN (BPA)/ 20 PTMG	23	3.5	1.3	0.29	(35,1%) (70,2.4%)	65	—	—	—	—
	270(T_g)	—	—	—	—	—	—	—	—	—
PCN (BPC)	23	3.5	1.3	0.29	(35,1%) (60,1.5%)	65	—	—	—	—
	275(T_g)	—	—	—	—	—	—	—	—	—
PCN (BPE)	23	2.7	1.3	—	—	65	—	—	—	—
	200	2.1	—	—	—	—	—	—	—	—
	295(T_g)	—	—	—	—	—	—	—	—	—

Notes：DAM = Dry as Molded；

GF (CF) = Reinforced with glass (carbon) fibers, by weight；

T_g(℃) & T_m(℃) = Glass transition point and melting point, respectively；

PTMG = Polyoxytetramethylene Glycol.

Chapter 65

PF (Phenolic)

65.1   Introduction

PF resins are synthesized by the reaction of phenol with formaldehyde. It is a brittle thermoset material with good thermal, chemical, and dimensional stability. Phenolic resin has been used as a matrix for composites mainly because of its flame-retardant behavior and high char yield after pyrolysis, resulting in a self-supporting structure. The thermo-oxidative stability in phenolic compounds can be enhanced by adding of ceramic powders such as silicon carbide and boron carbide. Because it is brittle and low in interlaminar shear strength, phenolic is not a popular matrix for composites compared with epoxy, polyester, and vinyl ester. Stressstrain curves of a typical PF and its composite reinforced with randomly oriented short glass fibers are given in Fig. 65.1.

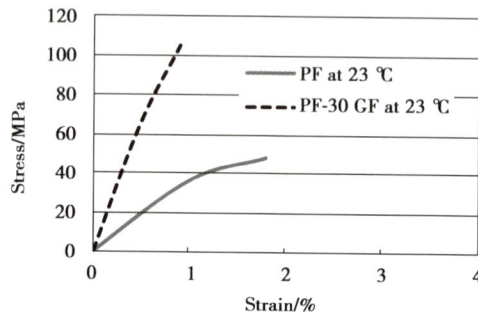

Fig. 65.1   Representative Stress-Strain Curves of PF (Phenolic) and Related Composite Reinforced with Randomly Oriented Short Glass Fibers

PF parts, as-molded, may be post baked (or called heat-treated) for several reasons: (a) dimensional stability of part, (b) out-gassing residual molded-in ammonia that can corrode electric contacts, (c) strength improvement, and (d) increase in a glass transition point. T_g (glass transition point) of a phenolic depends very much on post-bake conditions (temperature and time durations) and so that $T_g = 260$ ℃ can be achieved with proper heat treatment.

65.2   Applications

Phenolic molding compounds are found in a various of automotive items such as pump parts, lamp casing, and brake pistons. It is a popular bonding material for brake linings due to its outstanding fire safety properties like low smoke emission, low toxicity, and low heat release. Bakelite, a phenol-formaldehyde resin, is used in electrical insulators and plastic ware. PF has also been used in commutators and bobbins for electric motors.

With their excellent flame-retardant properties (Costa et al.), superior to PU, PE, PS foams, phenolic foams are suitable for use as building insulation and in other industrial applications.

References

BARRE S, et al, 1996. Comparative Study of Strain rate Effects on Mechanical Properties of Glass Fiber-reinforced Thermoset Matrix Composites[J]. Composites, A, 27: 1169-1181.

CHARALAMBIDES M N, WILLIAMS J G. 1995. Fracture Toughness Characterization of Phenolic Resin and Its Composites[J]. Polymer Composites, 16(1): 17-28.

CHIANG C, MA C, 2004. Synthesis, Characterization, Thermal Properties and Flame Retardance of Novel Phenolic Resin/Silica Nanocomposites[J]. Polymer Degradation and Stability, 83: 207-214.

GARDZIELLA A, PILATO L, KNOP A, 2000. Phenolic Resins[M]. 2nd edition, Springer, New York, NY, USA.

HEIMBS S, et al, 2007. Strain Rate Effects in Phenolic Composites and Phenolic-Impregnated Honeycomb Structures[J]. Composites Science and Technology, 67: 2827-2837.

HO S C, CHERN L, J H, et al, 2005. Effect of Fiber Addition on Mechanical and Tribological Properties of a Copper/Phenolic-Based Friction Material[J]. Wear, 258: 861-869.

HUNTER J, FORSDYKE K L, 1989. Phenolic GRP and Its Recent Applications[J]. Polymer Composites, 10 (2): 169-185.

LANDI V R, 1986. The Effect of Molding Time and Temperature on the Modulus and Glass Transition of Phenolics[J]. Polymer Composites, 7(3): 152-157.

MCMANUS H, SPRINGER G, 1992. High-temperature Thermomechanical Behavior of Carbon-Phenolic and Carbon-Carbon Composites. Ⅰ. Analysis[J]. Journal of Composite Materials, 26(2): 206-229.

MCMANUS H, SPRINGER G, 1992. High-temperature Thermomechanical Behavior of Carbon-Phenolic and Carbon-Carbon Composites. Ⅱ. Results[J]. Journal of Composite Materials, 26(2): 230-255.

MORII T, et al, 1999. Interfacial Effect on the Mechanical Properties of Glass/Phenolic Composite[J]. Advanced Composites Letters, 8(6): 295-301.

MOURITZ A P, MATHYS Z, 2000. Mechanical Properties of Fired-Damaged GlassReinforced Phenolic Composites[J]. Fire and Materials, 24: 67-75.

REDJEL B, 1995. Mechanical Properties and Fracture Toughness of Phenolic Resin[J]. Plastics, Rubber and Composites Processing and Applications, 24(4): 221-228.

SHEN H, LAVOIE A, NUTT S, 2003. Enhanced Peel Resistance of Fiber Reinforced Phenolic Foams[J].

Composites, Part A: Appl. Sci. Manufact., 34(10): 941-948.

ST JOHN N A, BROWN J R, 1998. Flexural and Interlaminar Shear Properties of GlassReinforced Phenolic Composites[J]. Polymer Composites, 29: 939-946.

STRAUSS E L, 2004. Strength of Polybenzimidazole and Phenolic Laminate-to-Metal Joints [J]. Polymer Engineering and Science, 6(1): 24-29.

TANI J, et al, 2007. Thermal Expansion and Mechanical Properties of Phenolic Resin/ZrW_2O_8Composites[J]. Journal of Applied Polymer Science, 106(5): 3343-3347.

YEH M, et al, 2007. Glass Transition Temperature of Phenolic-Based Nanocomposites Reinforced by MWNTs and Carbon Fibers[J]. Key Engineering Materials, 334-335: 713-716.

Table 65.1　Mechanical Properties of PF (Phenolic), PBA (Polybenzoxazine), and Related Composites

Material-DAM	$T/\degree C$	E_T	ρ	ν	(α, ε)	α	k	γ	β	K_{IC}
Phenolic (Injection grade)	23	3.6	1.45	0.24	(36,1%) (48,1.8%)	36	0.37	1170	—	—
	$260(T_g)$	—	—	—	—	—	—	—	—	—
Phenolic Foam	23	—	—	—	—	—	0.02	—	—	—
Phenolic/30GF (Random short)	23	13.2	—	—	(66,0.5%) (105,0.9%)	—	—	—	—	—
	200	—	—	—	$\sigma_{uts} = 55$	—	—	—	—	—
	$260(T_g)$	—	—	—	—	—	—	—	—	—

Notes: DAM = Dry as Molded;

　　　 GF (CF) = Reinforced with glass (carbon) fibers, by weight unless V_f is given;

　　　 $T_g(\degree C)$ & $T_m(\degree C)$ = Glass transition point and melting point, respectively.

Chapter 66

PI (Polyimide)

66.1　Introduction

PI (**P**oly**i**mide) is a polymer of imide monomers, with dimensional stability. It is lightweight, flexible, and resistant to heat and chemicals. It is a popular bonding material for high-temperature applications. If a polymeric adhesive is expected to resist extremely high temperatures, the polyimide adhesive is likely the best option. Otherwise, epoxy adhesives are generally compatible at moderate temperatures. Mechanical properties of PI (Polyimide) are given in Table 66.1.

Glass, carbon, and quartz fibers have been used to reinforce PI (Polyimide). A proper amount of fibers significantly slows down the viscoelastic behavior of PI at an elevated temperature. Viscoelastic deformation of carbon fibers-reinforced PI (Polyimide) composites is an Arrhenius linear type at an elevated temperature between 195 ℃ to 265 ℃ [Omiya]. Short fibers, randomly oriented or well-aligned, enhance not only the ultimate tensile strength but also the ultimate tensile strain. Graphite or PTFE (polytetrafluoroethylene) as a filler can significantly improve the wear resistance and decrease the friction coefficient of the PI composites reinforced with short carbon fibers [Zhang et al.] [Samyn et al.]. Representative stress-strain curves of PI (Polyimide) and its related composites are shown in Fig. 66.1.

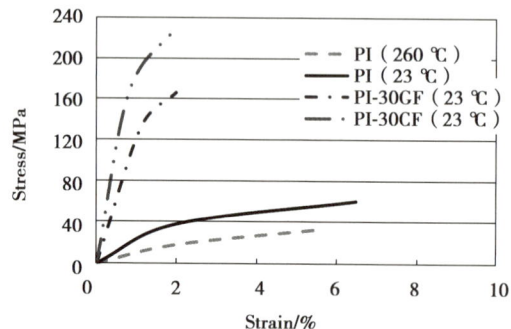

Fig. 66.1　Mechanical properties of PI (Polyimide) and Its Related Composites Reinforced with Randomly Oriented Short Fibers

66.2　TPI (Thermoplastic Polyimide)

Mechanical properties of TPI (Thermoplastic Polyimide) resemble those of PEI. It is heat and water-resistant. Mechanical properties of TPI reinforced with fibers are given in Table 66.2 and fatigue properties in Table 66.3.

The COPA family or polyether block amide elastomers are based on a block copolymer of nylon 12 (a polyamide) and a polyether. Through the proper combination of polyamide and polyether blocks, a wide range of grades offers a variety of performance characteristics such as durability and flexibility.

66.3   Applications

66.3.1   PI (Polyimide)

A variety of polyimide composites are cost-effective alternatives to cast-metal parts [Schmeckpeper], such as non-load bearing aircraft engine components such as vent tubes, nozzle flaps, and bushings. Polyimide bearings such as Dupont Vespel bearings (Polyimide−15% graphite) may outperform bronze bearings in the coefficient of friction, i.e. 0.07 versus 0.11. Polyimide is also used in the electronics industry for flexible cables, insulating films on magnet wires, and medical tubings.

Polyimide is also used as a high-temperature adhesive in the semiconductors for automotive electronics, as well as printed circuit boards and body parts of modern airplanes.

66.3.2   TPI (Thermoplastic Polyimide)

TPI (Thermoplastic Polyimide) has a niche market in military vehicles (especially marine vehicles), in addition to its accepted applications to blades of wind mills. TPI provides flexible and rigid tubing, sealing, mounting and transfer tapes, and adhesives. Thermoplastic polyimide film is the superior dielectric film for use in flexible printed circuits (FPC), wire and cable insulation.

COPA's have been limited to niche markets due to their cost, such as areas having been extensively used for the need of a long flex life, such as air hose coils for the air brake systems on trucks.

References

BROWNING C, MARSHALL J, 1970. Graphite Fiber Reinforced Polyimide Composites [J]. Journal of Composite Materials, 4(3): 390-403.

CHEN J, et al, 2006. Short Carbon Fiber-Reinforced PMR Polyimide Composites with Improved Thermo-oxidative and Hygrothermal Stabilities[J]. High-Performance Polymers, 18(3): 265-282.

DEAK T, CZIGANY T, 2008. Investigation of Basalt Fiber Reinforced Polyamide Composites[J]. Materials Science Forum, (589): 7-12.

DRUKKERA E, GREENA A, MAROMB G, 2003. Mechanical and Chemical Consequences of Through Thickness Thermal Gradients in Polyimide Matrix Composite Material[J]. Composites, Part A, (34): 125-133.

KUDAIKULOVA S K, 2006. The Structure and Properties of New Metalized Polyimide Films with High Electro-Optical Performances[C]. Advanced Optoelectronics and Lasers, (2): 93-96.

KUNG H, 2005. Effects of Surface Roughness on High-temperature Oxidation of Carbonfiber-reinforced Polyimide Composites[J]. Journal of Composite Materials, 39(18): 1677-1687.

LI J, CHENG X, 2008. The Effect of Carbon Fiber Content on the Friction and Wear Properties of Carbon Fiber Reinforced Polyimide Composites[J]. Journal of Applied Polymer Science, 107(3): 1737-1743.

ODEGARD G, CLANCY T, GATES T, 2005. Modeling of the Mechanical Properties of Nanoparticle/Polymer Composites[J]. Polymer, (46): 553-562.

OGASAWARA T, ISHIDA Y, ISHIKAWA T, et al, 2004. Characterization of Multi-Walled Carbon Nanotube/Phenylethynyl Terminated Polyimide Composites[J]. Composites, Part A: (35): 67-74.

PUTKONEN M, et al, 2007. Atomic Layer Deposition of Polyimide Thin Films[J]. Journal of Materials Chemistry, (17): 664-669.

SELBY J, PHILPOTT M, SHANNON M, 2001. Fabrication of Mesoscopic, Flexible, High Pressure, Micro-Channel Heat Exchanger (MHEX)[J]. Transactions of NAMRI, 29: 469-476.

SAMYN P, DE BAETS P, SCHOUKENS G, 2011. Role of Internal Additives in the Friction and Wear of Carbon-Fiber-Reinforced Polyimide[J]. Journal of Applied Polymer Science, 116(2): 1146-1156.

SOMIYA S, 1994. Creep Behavior of a Carbon-Fiber-Reinforced Thermoplastic Polyimide Resin[J]. Journal of Thermoplastic Composite Materials, 7(2): 91-99.

SUNG N, MCGARR F, 1976. The Mechanical and Thermal Properties of Graphite Fiber Reinforce Polyphenylquinoxaline and Polyimide Composites[J]. Journal of Applied Polymer Science, 16(6): 426-436.

YOKODA R, YAMAMOTO S, YANO S, et al, 2001. Molecular Design of Heat Resistant Polyimides Having Excellent Processability and High Glass Transition Temperature[J]. High Performance Polymers, 13: S61-S72.

YUDIN V, et al, 2008. Morphology and Mechanical Properties of Carbon Fiber Reinforced Composites Based on Semicrystalline Polyimides Modified by Carbon Nanofibers[J]. Composites, Part A, 39(1): 85-90.

ZHANG X, PEI X, WANG Q, 2011. Effect of Solid Lubricant on the Tribological Properties of Polyimide Composites Reinforced with Carbon Fibers[J]. Journal of Reinforced Plastics and Composites, 27(18): 2005-2012.

LI J, 2011. The Mechanical and Tribological Properties of Thermoplastic Polyimide Composites Filled With Carbon Nanotube[J]. Journal of Reinforced Plastics and Composites, 29(21): 3297.

MONTGOMERY S, LOWERY D, DONOVAN M, 2008. High Heat Amorphous Thermoplastic Polyimide[J]. ANTEC 2008(2): 1292-1295.

TAKEI S, et al, 1998. Electrical Properties of Thermoplastic Polyimide[C]. IEEE 6th International Conference on Conduction and Breakdown in Solid Dielectrics, 349-352.

Table 66.1   Mechanical Properties of PI (Polyimide) and Related Composites

Material-DAM	$T/℃$	E_T	ρ	ν	(α, ε)	α	k	γ	β	K_{IC}
PI [Vespel SP-1]	23	3.2	1.43	0.41	(38,2%) (61,6.5%)	45	0.35	1150	—	42
	260	—	—	—	(19,2%) (33, 5.5%)	54	—	—	—	16.5
	308(T_g)	—	—	—	—	—	—	—	—	—
	400(T_m)	—	—	—	—	—	—	—	—	—
PI/30CF	23	20.7	1.43	0.4	(166,0.8%) (230,2%)	6/45	0.49	—	—	—
PI/30GF	23	11.9	1.56	0.4	(131,1.1%) (166,3%)	17/45	0.37	—	—	—
PI/15Gr	23	—	1.5	0.4	$\sigma_{uts}=45$	—	—	—	—	—
PI/15MoS$_2$	23	—	1.59	0.4	$\sigma_{uts}=41$	—	—	—	—	—

Notes: DAM = Dry as Molded;

  GF (CF, Gr) = Reinforced with glass (carbon, graphite) fibers, by weight;

  T_g(℃) & T_m(℃) = Glass transition point and melting point, respectively;

  MoS$_2$ = Reinforcement by weight.

Table 66.2 Mechanical Properties of TPI（Thermoplastic Polyimide）and Related Composites

Material-DAM	$T/°C$	E_T	ρ	ν	(σ, ε)	α	k	γ	β	K_{IC}
TPI	23	2.76	1.33	0.41	$\sigma_{ucs}=-120$； （92,57.6%）	53	0.5	1130	—	—
	100	—	—	—	—	—	—	1130	—	—
	150	—	—	—	$\sigma_{ucs}=-76$； （58, 90%）	—	—	—	—	—
	$250(T_g)$	—	—	—	—	—	—	—	—	—
	300	—	—	—	—	—	—	1600	—	—
	$388(T_m)$	—	—	—	—	—	—	—	—	—
TPI/30CF	23	12.4	1.44	0.4	$\sigma_{ucs}=-207$； （229,2.34%）	6/47	—	—	—	—
	150	—	—	—	$\sigma_{ucs}=-102$ （144,4%）	—	—	—	—	—
	$250(T_g)$	—	—	—	—	—	—	—	—	—
	$388(T_m)$	—	—	—	—	—	—	—	—	—
TPI/20CF	23	10.1	1.44	0.4	$\sigma_{ucs}=-195$； （177, 2.14%）	—	—	—	—	—
TPI/10CF	23	7.3	1.44	0.4	$\sigma_{ucs}=-168$； （137, 3.4%）	—	—	—	—	—
TPI/30GF	−40	—	—	—	—	—	—	—	—	—
	23	10.5	1.56	0.4	$\sigma_{ucs}=-188$； （165,3%）	16/53	—	—	—	—
	150	—	—	—	$\sigma_{ucs}=-88$； （106,4%）	—	—	—	—	—
	230	—	—	—	$\sigma_{ucs}=63$	—	—	—	—	—
	$250(T_g)$	—	—	—	—	—	—	—	—	—
	$388(T_m)$	—	—	—	—	—	—	—	—	—

Notes：DAM＝Dry as molded；

GF（CF）＝Reinforced with glass（carbon）fibers, by weight；

T_g（°C）& T_m（°C）＝Glass transition point and melting point, respectively.

Table 66.3 Fatigue ε-N Properties of TPI（Thermoplastic Polyimide）and Related Composites

Material	$T/°C$	$d\varepsilon/dt$	σ_f'	ε_f'	b	c	K'	n'	σ_f@$2N_f$	R
TPI	23	—	—	—	—	—	—	—	24.5@5×10^5 31.5@3.8×10^5	— —

Chapter 67

UP (Unsaturated Polyester)

67.1   Introduction

Polyester is a category of polymers that contain the ester functional group in their main chain. It can be thermoplastic or thermosetting, as a function of the degree of cross-inking, while some polyester resins are thermoplastic such as PET (Polyethylene Terephthalate) and PBT (PolyButylene Terephthalate).

UP (**U**nsaturated **P**olyester) resins are thermoset plastics formed by the reaction of dibasic organic acids and polyhydric alcohols, cured exothermically. Liquid UP resins are stable for months at room temperature, but it can be triggered to cure by a peroxide catalyst. The glass transition temperature, melting temperature, thermal stability, and chemical stability increases with increasing the aromatic parts of polyesters.

Unsaturated polyesters have good dimensional stability and rigidity due to their low water absorption and low shrinkage. The properties of an unsaturated polyester change very much according to the applied additives and reinforcements. UP resins can be made very flame retardant and chemically resistant, and they also give excellent weatherability. Glass fiber-reinforced polyester composites may be derived through SMC (Sheet Molding Compounds) or BMC (Bulk Molding Compounds). Mechanical properties listed in Table 67.1 are for typical UP (unsaturated polyester). Representative stress-strain curves of UP are shown in Fig. 67.1. Short fibers, randomly oriented or well-aligned, enhance not only the ultimate tensile strength but also the ultimate tensile strain.

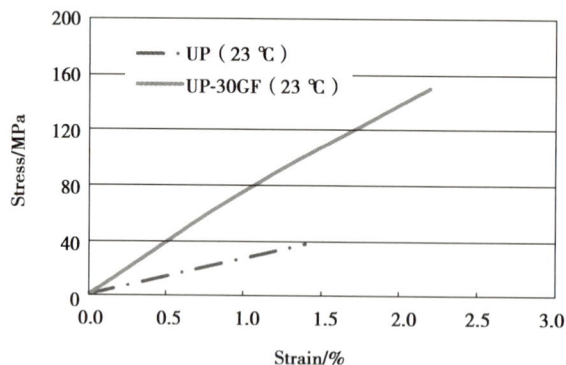

Fig. 67.1   Mechanical Properties of UP (Unsaturated Polyester) and Related Composites

Mechanical properties of typical TPE (thermoplastic copolymer elastomers) from different suppliers, e.g. Vyloshot GM-950-R02 from Toyobo as conductors for electric connectors via melt molding, are listed in Table 67.2.

Orthotropic mechanical and thermal properties of polyester reinforced with continuous fibers are given in Tables 67.3 and 67.4. Their orthotropic mechanical strengths are given in Table 67.5.

67.2　Applications

Established automotive markets for UP (Unsaturated Polyester) include bumper beams, body panels, sunroof frames, catalytic converter heat shields, dashboard carriers, seat structures, battery supports, and spring systems. Two other major applications of UP (Unsaturated Polyester) are sheet molding compounds (glass-fiber-reinforced polyester composites) and toners for laser printers. Glass fiber-reinforced UP composites were first used in aircraft ducting boat hulls.

References

CAO Y, FUKOMOTO I, 2007. Evaluation of Mechanical Properties of Injection Molding Composites Reinforced by Bagasse Fiber[J]. Journal of Solid Mechanics and Materials Engineering, 1(10): 1209-1218.

CHANG J, et al, 1996. The Thermal Degradation of Phosphorous-Containing Co-polyesters[J]. Polymer Degradation and Stability, 54(2-3): 365-371.

CHEN X, WU L, ZHOU S, YOU B, 2003. In Situ Polymerization and Characterization of Polyester-Based Polyurethane/Nano-Silica Composites[J]. Polymers International, 52: 993-998.

DHAKA H N, et al, 2009. Effect of Water Absorption on the Mechanical Properties of Hemp Fiber Reinforced Unsaturated Polyester Composites[J]. Composites Science and Technology, 417-418: 161-164.

DAVALLO M, PASDAR H, MOHSE M, 2010. Mechanical Properties of Unsaturated Polyester Resin[J]. International Journal of ChemTech Research, 2(4): 2113-2117.

DU Y, et al, 2010. Kenaf Bast Fiber Bundle-Reinforced Unsaturated Polyester Composites. II: Water Resistance and Composite Mechanical Properties Improvement[J]. Forest Products Journal, 60(4): 366-372.

HUGUET S, et al, 2002. Use of Acoustic Emission to Identify Damage Modes in Glass Fiber Polyester[J]. Composites Science and Technology, 62: 1433-1444.

IDICULA M, NEELAKANTAN N, OOMMEN Z, et al, 2005. A Study of the Mechanical Properties of Randomly Oriented Short Banana and Sisal Hybrid Fiber Reinforced Polyester Composites[J]. Journal of Applied Polymer Science, 96(5): 1699-1709.

ISHA M R, et al, 2009. Mechanical Properties of Kenaf Bast and Core Fiber Reinforced Unsaturated Polyester Composites[J]. 9th National Symposium on Polymeric Materials, 11: 012006.

LALY A P, SABU T, 2003. Polarity Parameters and Dynamic Mechanical Behavior of Chemically Modified Banana Fiber Reinforced Polyester Composites[J]. Composites Science and Technology, 63: 1231-1240.

MONTEIRO S, et al, 2005. Mechanical Strength of Polyester Matrix Composites Reinforced with Coconut Fiber Wastes[J]. Revista Matéria, 10(4): 571-576.

MOURITZ A P, MATHYS Z, 2001. Post-fire Mechanical Properties of Glass-Reinforced Polyester Composites [J]. Composites Science and Technology, 61(4): 475-490.

PAVLIDOU S, et al, 2004. Mechanical Properties of Glass Fabric/Polyester Composites: Effect of Silicone Coatings on the Fabrics[J]. Journal of Applied Polymer Science, 91(2): 1300-1308.

PETROVIC Z, JAVNI I, WADDON A, et al, 2000. Structure and Properties of Polyurethane-silica Nanocomposites[J]. Journal of Applied Polymer Science, 76: 133-151.

PIHTILI H, TOSUN N, 2002. Investigation of the Wear Behavior of a Glass-FiberReinforced Composite and Plain Polyester Resin[J]. Composites Science and Technology, 62: 367.

POTIYARAJ P, et al, 2007. Physical Properties of Unsaturated Polyester Resin from Glycolyzed Pet Fabrics [J]. Journal of Applied Polymer Science, 104(4): 2536-2541.

PUSATCIOGLU S, et al, 1979. Variation of Thermal Conductivity and Specific Heat during Cure of Thermoset Polyesters[J]. Journal of Applied Polymer Science, 24(4): 891-1141.

SPRING G S, 1984. Model for Predicting the Mechanical Properties of Composites at Elevated Temperatures [J]. Journal of Reinforced Plastics and Composites, 3(1): 85-95.

SREEKANTH M S, BAMBOLE V A, MHASKE S T, et al, 2009. Effect of Concentration of Mica on Properties of Polyester Thermoplastic Elastomer Composites[J]. Journal of Minerals & Materials Characterization and Engineering, 18(4): 271-282.

SRINIVASABABU N, et al, 2009. Effect of Environmental Conditions on Okra Fiber: Flexural and Impact Properties of Okra Fiber Reinforced Polyester Composites[J]. International Journal of Applied Engineering Research, 4(9): 1833-1849.

TANG Y, et al, 2008. Mechanical Properties of 3-D Glass/Polyester Resin Cellular Woven Composite under Impact Loading[J]. Pigment and Resin Technology, 37(6): 410-415.

VASQUEZ A, RICCIER J, CARVALHO L, 1999. Interfacial Properties and Initial Step of Water Absorption in Unidirectional Unsaturated Polyester/Vegetable Fiber Composites[J]. Polymer Composites, 20(1): 29-37.

VILAY V, MARIATTI M, TAIB R, TODO M, 2008. Effect of Fiber Surface Treatment and Fiber Loading on the Properties of Bagasse Fiber-Reinforced Unsaturated Polyester Composites[J]. Composites Science and Technology, 68: 633-638.

WANG J G, et al, 2011. Preparation and Characterization of Marble/Unsaturated Polyester Resin Composite Materials[J]. Advanced Materials Research, 152-153: 825-828.

Table 67.1   Mechanical Properties of UP（Unsaturated Polyester）and Related Composites

Material-DAM	$T/^\circ\mathrm{C}$	E_T	ρ	ν	(α, ε)	α	k	γ	β	K_IC
UP	23	3.4	1.28	0.38	$\sigma_\mathrm{uts}=-140$； （15，0.55%） （37，1.4%）	31	0.209	900	—	0.4
	80	—	—	—	—	—	0.218	1250	—	—
	100	—	—	—	—	—	0.222	1200	—	—
	$140(T_\mathrm{g})$	—	—	—	—	—	—	—	—	—
	$250(T_\mathrm{m})$	—	—	—	—	—	—	—	—	—
UP/25%GF （Random；short）	23	4.7	—	—	$\sigma_\mathrm{uts}=69$	—	—	—	—	—
	$250(T_\mathrm{m})$	—	—	—	—	—	—	—	—	—
UP/30%GF （Random；short； $V_\mathrm{f}=30\%$）	23	8	1.4	—	$\sigma_\mathrm{uts}=-150$； （75，1%） （120，2.2%）	—	—	—	—	—
UP/50%Sisal （$V_\mathrm{f}=50\%$）	23	13	—	—	（47，2.2%）	—	—	—	—	—
	90	—	—	—	—	—	—	1400	—	—

Notes：DAM＝Dry as Molded；

GF（CF）＝Reinforced with glass（carbon）fibers，by weight；

$T_\mathrm{g}(^\circ\mathrm{C})$ & $T_\mathrm{m}(^\circ\mathrm{C})$＝Glass transition point and melting point，respectively.

Table 67.2   Mechanical Properties of Polyester-Based TPEs

Material-DAM	$T/^\circ\mathrm{C}$	E_T	ρ	ν	(α, ε)	α	k	γ	β	K_IC
Hytrel（DuPont 7246；TPE-Polyester）	$-40(T_\mathrm{g})$	—	—	—	（−95，−25%） （−48，−10%）； （53，5%） （66, 13%）	—	—	—	—	—
	23	0.48	1.25	0.45	（−60，−25%） （−35, 10%）； （14，5%） （20, 10%） （25, 28%） （46, 360%）	—	—	—	—	—
	100	—	—	—	（−32，−25%） （−19，−10%）； （14, 25%） （38, 480%）	—	—	—	—	—
	120	—	—	—	（−23，−25%） （−13，−10%）； （9, 10%） （10, 25%） （35, 460%）	—	—	—	—	—
	$218(T_\mathrm{m})$	—	—	—	—	—	—	—	—	—

continued

Material-DAM	$T/^\circ\text{C}$	E_T	ρ	ν	(α, ε)	α	k	γ	β	K_IC
	$-65(T_\text{g})$	—	—	—	—	—	—	—	—	—
	23	0.05	1.14	0.45	(6.8, 50%) (9, 500%)	190	0.2	—	—	—
Vyloshot (GM− 950; TPE- Polyester; Shore A=94)	60	—	—	—	(4.5, 50%) (6.2, 280%)	—	—	—	—	—
	80	—	—	—	(2.8, 30%) (4.2, 115%)	—	—	—	—	—
	100	—	—	—	(1.9, 20%) (2.5, 47%)	—	—	—	—	—
	180	—	—	—	—	—	0.14	—	—	—
	$190(T_\text{m})$	—	—	—	—	—	—	—	—	—
Vyloshot (GM- 955; Shore A= 70)	$-77(T_\text{g})$	—	—	—	—	—	—	—	—	—
	23	—	1.05	0.45	(4.3, 1400%)	190	0.2	—	—	—

Table 67.3 Mechanical Properties of Polyester Reinforced by Continuous Fibers

Material-DAM	$T/^\circ\text{C}$	ρ	E_{11}	E_{22}	E_{33}	G_{12}	G_{13}	G_{23}	ν_{12}	ν_{13}	ν_{23}
UP/70%GF (V_f=70%; UD)	23	1.9	—	—	—	—	—	—	—	—	—
UP/45%GF (V_f=45%; Woven Roving)	23	1.6	—	—	—	—	—	—	—	—	—
	120(Cure temperature)										
UP/55%GF (V_f= 55%; Satin Weave)	23	1.7	—	—	—	—	—	—	—	—	—

Table 67.4 Orthotropic Thermal Properties of Polyester-Based Composites

Material-DAM	$T/^\circ\text{C}$	α_1	α_2	α_3	k_1	k_2	k_3	γ	β_1	β_2	β_3
UP/45%GF (V_f=45%; Woven Roving)	23	—	—	—	—	—	—	—	—	—	—
	120(Cure temperature)										

Notes: α_1, α_2, α_3($\mu\text{m/m}/^\circ\text{C}$) = Coefficients of linear thermal expansion of a unidirectional lamina;

k_1, k_2, k_3($\text{W/m}/^\circ\text{C}$) = Thermal conductivities of a unidirectional lamina;

β_1, β_2, β_3($\text{mm/m}/\%$) = Swelling coefficients of linear moisture expansion;

γ($\text{J/kg}/^\circ\text{C}$) = Specific heat capacity.

Table 67.5   Orthotropic Mechanical Strengths of Unidirectional Fiber-Reinforced Polyester Composites

Material	$T/{}^\circ\!C$	$(\sigma_{11u}, \varepsilon_{11u})$	$(\sigma_{22u}, \varepsilon_{22u})$	$(\sigma_{33u}, \varepsilon_{33u})$	$(\sigma_{12u}, \varepsilon_{12u})/$ $(\sigma_{23u}, \varepsilon_{23u})/$ $(\sigma_{13u}, \varepsilon_{13u})$
UP/70%GF ($V_f=70\%$; UD)	23	$\sigma_{11c}=-350$ $\sigma_{11t}=800$	—	—	—
UP/45%GF ($V_f=45\%$; Woven Roving)	23	$\sigma_{11c}=-150$ $\sigma_{11t}=250$	—	—	—
UP/55%GF ($V_f=55\%$; Satin Weave)	23	$\sigma_{11c}=-250$ $\sigma_{11t}=350$	—	—	—

Table 67.6   Fatigue ε-N Properties of UP（Unsaturated Polyester）and Related Composites

Material	$T/{}^\circ\!C$	$d\varepsilon/dt$	σ_f'	ε_f'	b	c	K'	n'	$\sigma_f@2N_f$	R
UP/50Hemp	23	—	—	—	—	—	—	—	$19@10^6$ $23@10^5$ $33@10^3$	— — —

Chapter 68

Silicone

68.1   Introduction

Silicones are polymers that combine silicon with carbon, hydrogen, oxygen, and other chemical elements. It has an outstanding heat resistance and good electric properties. Silicone polymers are a class of hybrid organic/inorganic polymers that show desirable surface properties such as low surface energy and high flexibility. Silicone adhesives enable even a very high molecular weight chain to achieve optimal orientation at the interface. The excellent resistance to oxygen, ozone, ultraviolet (UV) light, and sunlight has led to widespread use of silicones in the automotive industry. Some common forms include silicone oil, silicone grease, silicone resin, and silicone rubber. Silicone rubber is addressed in Chapter 24. Mechanical properties of silicone and its related composites reinforced with unidirectional fibers are given in Tables 68.1 and 68.2, respectively.

68.2   Applications of Silicone Solids

Typically rubber-like solid silicone is heat-resistant, and it is used in gaskets, sealants, adhesives, lubricants, insulators, electrical connectors, and external trims. Silicone functions well as adhesives (or glues) in a wide working temperature range, from −70 ℃ to 260 ℃.

Silicone has robust compatibility with body tissues, leading to its medical applications such as breast implants.

68.3   A Special Application of Silicone Oil

Silicone oil is used in a visco fan clutch that has the task of making the frictional connection to the fan wheel depending on the temperature and controlling its speed. Cooling fans are needed only during low-speed driving when air circulation is at a minimum or during prolonged load conditions when maximum engine cooling is needed. If no cooling air is required, the visco clutch switches off and continues to run at a lower speed.

A thermostatic fan clutch may be triggered by a bi-metal element, which is exposed to environmental temperature. A bore hole is released by a pressure pin, and silicone oil flows from the store into the working chamber. There, the drive torque is transferred to the fan wheel, the continuously variable speed of which is set automatically based on the operating conditions by means of wear-free viscous friction. More fluid is admitted into the coupling at higher temperatures, causing the fan rotation to increase. At lower temperatures, the spring closes the valve, decreasing fluid in the coupling, and the fan rotation decreases. A mechanical-controlled fan clutch can also fail in a stuck-on position where engine power is lost even when the fan is not necessary. A common symptom of such a fan clutch failure is overheating at idle or in heavy traffic.

In the case of the electrically driven EV (Electro-Viscous) clutch (Fig. 68.1), control takes place directly via sensors. A regulator processes the values, and a pulsed control current carries these to the integrated electromagnet. The defined guided magnetic field regulates the valve which controls the internal oil flow via a solenoid [Lee et al.], which is controlled by a solid-state device, operated by a pulse-width-modulated (PWM) signal from the PCM (Power Control Module). An additional sensor (e.g. Hall-effect sensors used in GM's trucks) for fan speed completes the feedback circuit. These electronically controlled clutches provide the potential to control the level of engagement depending on any number of inputs, including fan speed, vehicle speed, engine oil temperature, transmission oil temperature, coolant temperature, airconditioning system pressures, and ambient air temperature. Cooling to match requirements improves the level of coolant temperature. This offers several advantages:

(a) Reduced fan noise;
(b) Reduced parasitic losses, for improved fuel economy;
(c) Reduced false engagements at stop light idle;
(d) Improving A/C (air-conditioning system) idle and city traffic performance;
(e) Reduced A/C compressor warranty as it operates at a lower head pressure.

During engine startup, an EV fan clutch will engage and match the engine speed for up to 3 minutes.

Fig. 68.1   Engine Fan Clutch Operated Using Fluid Silicone

Bad fan clutches can also cause poor performance of the car's air conditioning system because the fan also cools the condenser, which is installed in front of the radiator. Another symptom is an extra (abnormal) grinding sound from the engine area, which may be caused by worn bearings in the fan clutch.

References

MEL T, 1995. Prevention of Oil Webpage in Silicone Automotive Gaskets[J]. SAE 950196.

WU Y, et al, 2005. Temperature Effect on Mechanical Properties of Toughened Silicone Resins[J]. Polymer Engineering and Science, 45(11): 1522-1531.

Table 68.1 Mechanical Properties of a Generic Silicone Polymer (See Chapter 24 for Mechanical Properties of Silicone Rubbers)

Material-DAM	$T/^{\circ}\mathrm{C}$	E_T	ρ	ν	(α, ε)	α	k	γ	β	K_IC
Silicone	23	0.007	1.4	0.48	(2.5,180%)	270	0.4	1280	—	—
	$250(T_\mathrm{m})$	—	—	—	—	—	—	—	—	—

Notes: DAM = Dry as Molded;

$T_\mathrm{g}(^{\circ}\mathrm{C})$ & $T_\mathrm{m}(^{\circ}\mathrm{C})$ = Glass transition point and melting point, respectively.

Table 68.2 Mechanical Properties of Silicone Reinforced by Straight Continuous Fibers

Material-DAM	$T/^{\circ}\mathrm{C}$	ρ	E_{11}	E_{22}	E_{33}	G_{12}	G_{13}	G_{23}	ν_{12}	ν_{13}	ν_{23}
Silicone/12.1%GF (V_f=12.1%)	23	—	8.76	1.94	1.94	1.95	1.95	—	0.47	0.47	0.48

Notes: $\nu_{ij}E_{jj}=\nu_{ji}E_{ii}(i=1, 2, 3; j=1, 2, 3; i \neq j)$.

Chapter 69

VE (Vinylester)

69.1   Introduction

VE (**Vinyl**ester) is a resin produced by the esterification of an epoxy resin with an unsaturated monocarboxylic acid. The reaction product is then dissolved in a reactive solvent (e.g. styrene) for after treatment. Almost all properties of vinylester are intermediate between polyester and epoxy. Vinylester provides thermal and mechanical properties similar to epoxy at a cost slightly higher than polyester. Mechanical properties of VE (Vinylester) are listed in Table 69.1. Orthotropic mechanical and thermal properties are given in Tables 69.2 and 69.3, respectively.

Vinylester, unsaturated polyester, and epoxy are the three main resins for structural fiber-reinforced composites. All three kinds of composites depend on the curing process and post-cure treatments. Stress-strain curves of vinylester reinforced with dog bone-shaped nanofibers of carbon at different temperatures are presented in Fig. 69.1.

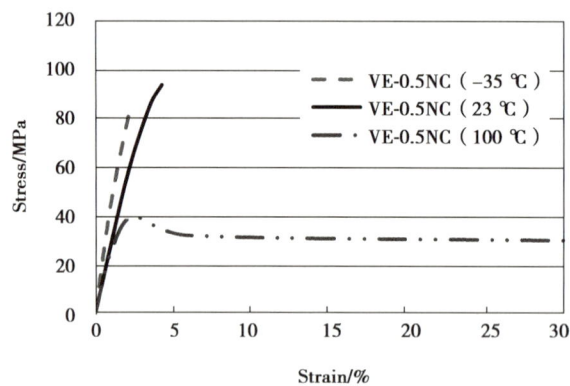

Fig. 69.1   Stress-Strain Curves of Vinylester Reinforced by 0.5% (by Weight) of Nano Carbon Dog Bone-Shaped Fibers

69.2   Applications

Structural vinylester-based sheet molded composites (SMC) for automotive applications exhibit reasonable heat resistance and fracture toughness. They are also popular for marine and spa applications.

References

BUCK S E, et al, 2001. Mechanical and Microstructural Properties of Notched E-Glass/Vinyl Ester Composite

Materials Subjected to the Environment and a Sustained Load[J]. Materials Science and Engineering, A, 317: 128-134.

CHANDRADASS I, 2008. Effect of Clay Dispersion on Mechanical, Thermal and Vibration Properties of Glass Fiber-Reinforced Vinyl Ester Composites[J]. Journal of Reinforced Plastics and Composites, 27(15): 1585-1601.

CHEN Y H, et al, 2011. Influence of Carbon Nanotubes on Mechanical and Thermal Properties of Glass Fiber Reinforced Vinyl Ester Resin Composites[J]. Materials Science Forum, 675/677: 419-422.

DAVEY S W, et al, 2005. Vinylester/Cenosphere Composite Materials for Civil and Structural Engineering[J]. FRP International, 2(2): 2-5.

DELA OSA O, et al, 2006. Loss of Mechanical Properties by Water Absorption of Vinyl-ester Reinforced with Glass Fiber[J]. Journal of Reinforced Plastics and Composites, 25(2): 215-221.

BOWTHMANN, et al, 2006. Mechanical Properties of Glass and T700 Carbon Vinylester Composites[J]. Journal of Advanced Materials, 38(2): 52-63.

KU H, et al, 2007. Mechanical Properties of Vinyl Ester Composites Cured by Microwave Irradiation: Pilot Study[J]. Key Engineering Materials, (334-335): 537-540.

KU H S, 2003. Vinyl Ester Particle Reinforced Composites Using Microwaves[J]. Journal of Composite Materials, 37(22): 2027-2042.

LEE S H, WAAS Y M, 1999. Compressive Response and Failure of Fiber Reinforced Unidirectional Composites [J]. International Journal of Fatigue, 100: 275-306.

NOURANIAN S, et al, 2009. Response Surface Predictions of the Viscoelastic Properties of Vapor-grown Carbon Nanofiber/Vinyl Ester Nanocomposites[J]. Journal of Applied Polymer Science, 130(1): 234-247.

PARK R, JANG J, 2004. Effect of Surface Treatment on the Mechanical Properties of Glass Fiber/Vinylester Composites[J]. Journal of Applied Polymer Science, 91(6): 3730-3736.

PLASEIED A, FATEMI A, 2009. Tensile Creep and Deformation Modeling of Vinyl Ester Polymer and Its Nanocomposite[J]. Journal of Reinforced Plastics and Composites, 28(14): 1775-1788.

PLASEIED A, FATEMI A, 2008. Deformation Response and Constitutive Modeling of Vinyl Ester Polymer Including Strain Rate and Temperature Effects[J]. Journal of Materials Science, 43(4): 1191-1199.

QI N, ZHAO L, 2011. The Mechanical Properties of Jute Fiber Mats Reinforced Vinyl Ester Resin Composites [J]. Advanced Materials Research, 284-286: 277-283.

RODRIGUEZ E, et al, 2006. Mechanical Properties Evaluation of a Recycled Flax Fiber-reinforced Vinyl Ester [J]. Journal of Composite Materials, 40(3): 245-256.

ROY R, et al, 2001. Impact Fatigue Behavior of Carbon-reinforced Vinylester Resin Composites[J]. Bulletin of Material Science, 24(1): 79-86.

SELMY A, EL-SONBATY I, KHASHABA U, et al, 2004. Dynamic Viscoelastic Behavior of GFR/Vinylester and GFR/Epoxy Composites[J]. Proceedings of the 4th International Engineering Conference, Mansoura University, Egypt, 1: 515-525.

SLIFKA A J, SMITH D R, 1997. Thermal Expansion of an E-glass/Vinylester Composites form 4K to 293K[J]. International Journal of Thermophysics, 18(5): 1249-1256.

WINKLER M, 1990. Automotive Under-the-Hood Applications in Vinylester Resin SMC/BMC [J]. SAE 900633.

Table 69.1   Mechanical Properties of VE (Vinylester) and Related Composites

Material-DAM	$T/℃$	E_T	ρ	ν	(α, ε)	α	k	γ	β	K_{IC}
Vinylester	23	3.2	1.1	0.3	(40,5%) (77,17%)	65	0.21	1800	—	—
	60	—	—	—	—	—	0.22	—	—	—
	100	—	—	—	—	—	0.23	—	—	—
	118(T_g)	—	—	—	—	—	—	—	—	—
Vinylester (RTM)	23	3.2	1.1	0.3	—	65	0.18	1800	—	—
	60	—	—	—	—	—	0.188	—	—	—
	100	—	—	—	—	—	0.201	—	—	—
VE/0.5NC (Room Moisture)	−35	—	—	—	(43,1%) (86,2.3%)	—	—	—	—	—
	23	3.8	1.1	0.3	(55,2%) (85,3.5%) (94,4.3%)	—	0.24	—	—	—
	100	—	—	—	(25,1%) (40,2.5%) (32,6%) (15.4,30%)	—	—	—	—	—
	118(T_g)	—	—	—	—	—	—	—	—	—
VE/10Gr (d_f=14 μm; W_f=10%)	60	—	—	—	—	—	0.404	—	—	—
	100	—	—	—	—	—	0.424	—	—	—
VE/10Gr (d_f=55 μm; W_f=10%)	60	—	—	—	—	—	0.404	—	—	—
	100	—	—	—	—	—	0.423	—	—	—

continued

Material-DAM	$T/°C$	E_T	ρ	ν	(α, ε)	α	k	γ	β	K_{IC}
VE/10Gr (d_f=75 μm; W_f=10%)	60	—	—	—	—	—	0.346	—	—	—
	100	—	—	—	—	—	0.377	—	—	—
VE/10Gr (d_f=150 μm; W_f=10%)	60	—	—	—	—	—	0.335	—	—	—
	100	—	—	—	—	—	0.357	—	—	—

Notes: GF (CF, Gr) = Reinforced with glass (carbon, graphite) fibers;

$T_g(°C)$ & $T_m(°C)$ = Glass transition point and melting point, respectively;

NC (Nano Carbon) = Reinforcement by weight.

Table 69.2   Mechanical Properties of VE Reinforced by Straight Continuous Fibers

Material-DAM	$T/°C$	ρ	E_{11}	E_{22}	E_{33}	G_{12}	G_{13}	G_{23}	ν_{12}	ν_{13}	ν_{23}
VE/Glass (E-glass/470-36)	23	—	24.4	6.9	6.9	2.9	2.9	—	0.32	—	—

Notes $= \nu_{ij}E_{jj} = \nu_{ji}E_{ii}$ (i=1, 2, 3; j=1, 2, 3; $i \neq j$).

Table 69.3   Orthotropic Thermal Properties of Unidirectional Fiber-Reinforced Vinylester Composites

Material-DAM	$T/°C$	α_1	α_2	α_3	k_1	k_2	k_3	γ	β_1	β_2	β_3
VE/54%GF (E-glass; V_f=54%)	23	—	—	—	—	—	—	—	—	—	—
	60	—	—	—	0.246	0.28	0.322	—	—	—	—
	80	—	—	—	0.268	0.3	0.343	—	—	—	—
	100	—	—	—	0.3	0.33	0.353	—	—	—	—
VE/60%CF (Composite Block; V_f=60%)	23	—	—	—	—	—	—	—	—	—	—
	60	—	—	—	0.876	0.464	0.239	—	—	—	—
	100	—	—	—	1.035	0.543	0.286	—	—	—	—
VE/75%CF (Composite Block; V_f=75%)	23	—	—	—	—	—	—	—	—	—	—
	60	—	—	—	1.636	0.426	0.305	—	—	—	—
	100	—	—	—	2.407	0.453	0.323	—	—	—	—

Notes: α_1, α_2, α_3(μm/m/°C) = Coefficients of linear thermal expansion of a unidirectional lamina;

k_1, k_2, k_3(W/m/°C) = Thermal conductivities of a unidirectional lamina;

β_1, β_2, β_3(μm/m/%) = Swelling coefficients of linear moisture expansion;

γ(J/kg/°C) = Specific heat capacity.

Chapter 70

Zylon (PBO)

70.1   Introduction

Zylon is the trademarked name of crystalline PBO (**P**oly**b**enz**o**xazole) or poly(**p**-phenylene-2, 6**b**enzobis**o**xazole), which is quite flexible and has a very soft hand in spite of its extremely high mechanical properties. As a bulk material, it is an isotropic thermoset plastic with the following special properties:

(a) Dimensionally stable against humidity, as its moisture regain is as low as 0.6%;

(b) Quite flexible in spite of its extremely high mechanical properties;

(c) Well resistant to creep and abrasion resistance, even at elevated temperatures;

(d) Very Stable with most organic mediums (methanol, gasoline, brake fluid, etc.).

Zylon can be degraded by visible light, UV light, moisture, and seawater. Its products are therefore usually protected by a synthetic coating or melted-on jacket.

PBO fiber is the strongest and stiffest of commercially available fibers. It is an orthotropic material with a negative coefficient of thermal expansion in the fiber direction, and therefore Zylon fiber-reinforced plastics (ZFRP) expand in the fiber direction during cooling down from room temperature to liquid helium temperature.

70.2   Applications

Zylon is used in a number of applications that require high strength with excellent thermal stability and high flame resistance. It can be processed into various product forms, such as continuous filament, staple fiber, spun yarn, woven and knitted fabrics, chopped fiber, and pulp.

References

CERVENKA A J, et al, 2005. Micromechanical Phenomena during Hygrothermal Ageing of Model Composites Investigated by Raman Spectroscopy. Part Ⅱ: Comparison of the Behavior of PBO and M5 Fibers Compared with Twaron[J]. Composites, Part A, 36(7): 1020-1026.

CHIN J, et al, 2007. Temperature and Humidity Aging of Poly(phenylene-2-6benzobisoxazole Fibers: Chemical and Physical Characterization[J]. Polymer Degradation & Stability, 92: 1234-1246.

COLOMBAN P, et al, 2007. Micro-Raman and IR Study of the Compressive Behavior of Poly(Paraphenylene Benzobisoxazole)(PBO) Fibers in a Diamond-anvil Cell[J]. J. Raman Spectroscopy, 38: 100.

DAVIES P, et al, 2010. Tensile Fatigue Behavior of PBO Fibers[J]. Journal of Materials Science, 45(23): 6395-6400.

KITAGAWA T, YABUKI K, YOUNG R J, 2001. An Investigation into the Relationship between Processing, Structure, and Properties for High-Modulus PBO Fibers. Part 1. Raman Band Shifts and Broadening in Tension and Compression[J]. Polymer, 42(5): 2101-2112.

KITAGAWA T, MURASE H, YABUKI K, 1998. Morphological Study on Poly-pphenylenebenzobisoxazole (PBO) Fiber[J]. Journal of Polymer Science, Part B, 36: 39-48.

KRAUSE S J, 1988. Morphology and Properties of Rigid-rod Poly(p-phenylene benzobisoxazole)(PBO) and Stiff-Chain Poly(2, 5(6)-benzoxazole)(ABPBO) Fibers[J]. Polymer, 29(8): 1354-1364.

SAID M A, et al, 2006. Investigation of Ultra Violet (UV) Resistance for High Strength Fibers[J]. Advances in Space Research, 37(11): 2052-2058.

Table 70.1　Mechanical Properties of Zylon (PBO or Polybenzoxazole)

Material-DAM	$T/\text{℃}$	E_T	ρ	ν	(σ, ε)	α	k	γ	β	K_{IC}
Zylon-HM (Bulk)	23	—	1.56	—	—	—	—	—	—	—
	650(Decomposition temperature)									
Zylon-HM (Fiber)	See Tables 3.1, 3.2, and 3.3 for its orthotropic material properties.									
	650(Decomposition temperature)									
Zylon-AS (Bulk)	23	—	1.54	—	—	—	—	—	—	—
	650(Decomposition temperature)									
Zylon-AS (Fiber)	See Tables 3.1, 3.2, and 3.3 for its orthotropic material properties.									
	650(Decomposition temperature)									

Notes: AS = As spun;
HM = High modulus.